CAREER GUIDANCE AND COUNSELING THROUGH THE LIFESPAN

Systematic Approaches

SIXTH EDITION

EDWIN L. HERR
The Pennsylvania State University—Emeritus

STANLEY H. CRAMER
State University of New York at Buffalo—Emeritus

SPENCER G. NILES
The Pennsylvania State University

Boston ▪ New York ▪ San Francisco
Mexico City ▪ Montreal ▪ Toronto ▪ London ▪ Madrid ▪ Munich ▪ Paris
Hong Kong ▪ Singapore ▪ Tokyo ▪ Cape Town ▪ Sydney

Executive Editor: Virginia Lanigan
Editorial Assistant: Robert Champagne
Production Supervisor: Joe Sweeney
Editorial–Production Service: Walsh & Associates, Inc.
Composition and Prepress Buyer: Linda Cox
Manufacturing Buyer: Andrew Turso
Cover Administrator: Linda Knowles
Electronic Composition: Omegatype Typography, Inc.

For related titles and support materials, visit our online catalog at www.ablongman.com.

Library of Congress Cataloging-in-Publication Data

Herr, Edwin, L.
Career guidance and counseling through the lifespan : systematic approaches / Edwin L. Herr, Stanley H. Cramer, Spencer G. Niles. — 6th ed.
p. cm.
Includes bibliographical references and index.
ISBN 0-321-08139-0
1. Vocational guidance—United States. I. Cramer, Stanley H. II. Niles, Spencer G. III. Title.

HF5382.5.U5H39 2004
331.7'02'0973—dc20

2003052322

Printed in the United States of America

10 9 8 7 6 5 4 3 2 1 09 08 07 06 05 04 03

Samuel L. Herr (August 23, 1903–September 7, 1968),
weaver, laborer, mechanic, school custodian,
whose respect for the dignity of work was exceeded
only by his respect for the dignity of people.

Amber, Christopher, and Alicia Herr,
whose grandfather would be proud that
they have incorporated his legacy and love.

Pat Herr, whose forty years of support, love,
and unconditional positive regard have made work,
in all its forms, possible and fulfilling.

Rosalind—talented, unflaggingly energetic, and creative.
With love through eons to eternity.

Hugh S. Niles, who taught about love and work
through example. Jennifer and Jonathan Niles,
who teach about love and family daily.

CONTENTS

PREFACE

Theory and practice in career development in the United States, and in much of the rest of the world, are in a dynamic state. Maturing theoretical perspectives; transitions to transnational and global economies; dramatic shifts in occupational structures; high unemployment rates among some groups of youths and adults; demands for higher levels of literacy, numeracy, flexibility, and teachability in the labor forces of industrialized nations; concerns about the quality of work life and worker productivity; and changes in the organization of work and in the composition of the labor force have combined to change the content, processes, and consumers of career interventions and services. These factors have increased the national and international significance of career development programs and interventions and made them more comprehensive in their application to settings and populations across the lifespan. They also have spawned the development of iterations in the language of career interventions, including, most recently, "the practice of career development."

In this book, we chronicle the evolution of career guidance, career counseling, and other interventions from the 1800s to the present. We place into contemporary perspective the social, political, and economic trends across the world that are elevating the sociopolitical roles of career guidance and career counseling in advancing human resource development in the twenty-first century. In addition to tracing the roots of professional counseling and counseling psychology in vocational guidance and vocational psychology, we examine the concepts and language systems on which current approaches to interventions in career behavior rest. We also discuss the applications of systematic approaches to the practice of career development for children, youths, and adults in various settings: schools, colleges and universities, business and industry, and community agencies.

Several major themes are stressed in this edition. First is the recognition of the effect of career services as instruments of human development and mental health. To understand this effect, it is necessary to probe the history of career guidance, career counseling, and counseling psychology; contemporary shifts in social values and in the meaning of work; international economic competition; dramatic changes in the nature of career patterns and occupational structures and the individual ability, flexibility, and adaptability required to cope with such changes; relationships between work and mental health; and the emphases of theoretical approaches that have shaped current views of the career development of persons across the life span. These topics are examined in Chapters 1 through 5.

The second primary theme emphasizes our belief that career development practices require developmental as well as remedial approaches. This belief mandates that career interventions be thought of as systematic programs or processes designed to effect certain preplanned or practitioner-client agreed-on behavioral outcomes. To aid in the tailoring of career guidance or career counseling programs to the special characteristics and needs of children, youths, and adults, we consider in Chapter 6 the stages and techniques of systematic planning appropriate to different settings: workplaces, schools and universities, and rehabilitation settings. In Chapters 7 through 11, we examine the rationale for and the developmental characteristics of career intervention techniques particularly important to elementary, middle school, and high school students and to adults in higher education, in the workplace, and in other community settings. Salient features of this sixth edition are the expanded treatment of career guidance and counseling in international contexts and the global economy, with regard to mental health and unemployment, among diverse adult populations, and in the workplace. Chapter 12 gives particular attention to special adult career problems of major concern in business and industrial settings.

The third major theme of the book is the identification of particular techniques, assessment devices, materials, and resources that can help career specialists implement theories, planning strategies, and program models with individuals and groups. Although much pertinent information is interspersed throughout the book, Chapters 13 through 15 focus directly on these applications.

The fourth theme accents the research and social issues that must be resolved as the systematic provision of career interventions moves to advanced levels of professional maturity across the life span. In Chapter 16, we address such issues, future research needs, and the growing trend to view quantitative and qualitative research methods as different but complementary ways of studying careers and career interventions.

This text reflects not only experience, ideas, and knowledge that we have gathered over many years, but also suggestions made by colleagues. We thank our reviewers who offered their helpful criticism and recommendations about needed revisions: Ernie Biller, University of Idaho; Grant Hayes, University of Central Florida; Cynthia L. Jew, University of Redlands; Jill C. Jurgens, Old Dominion University; John C. Lanshe, University of Akron; Paul E. Meacham, University of Nevada, Las Vegas; and Debra Osborn, University of South Florida.

We also wish to express our debt to the many persons cited in this book and to those in particular who gave us permission to quote their work. Just as concepts of career guidance and career counseling have evolved over time, our understanding of these processes have been shaped by many friends, colleagues, associates, and students who have shared their insights with us in person and in the professional literature. We are grateful to the long line of bright and talented people who have influenced our professional lives. We are also indebted to Peggy Tressler, Judy Kauffman, Darla Homan, Amy Seachrist, and Heather Homan, whose word processing, proofreading, and organizational excellence have been major factors in bringing the book to a successful conclusion.

Finally, we wish to express our personal respect and appreciation, as former students, to the late Donald E. Super, professor emeritus of Teachers College, Columbia University. Dr. Super served each of us as an intellectual guide, advisor, friend, and mentor. Professor Super, who died in June 1994, was a much respected and beloved role model for each of us in his continuing pursuit of excellence in his theoretical conceptions, research processes, intervention models, teaching, and professional leadership. His scholarly and personal legacy to professionals in career development and counseling throughout the world is comprehensive in its scope and enduring in its substance. Much of his work lives in this book—in content and in spirit.

Edwin L. Herr

Stanley H. Cramer

Spencer G. Niles

CHAPTER ONE

Perspectives on the Practice of Career Development

NEEDS, TRADITIONS, AND EMERGING CHALLENGES

KEY CONCEPTS

- The emerging phrase, the practice of career development, combines the perspectives of career development theory and those of career interventions.
- As the organization and availability of work is changing around the world so, too, are perspectives on how career paths are likely to be altered in the future: short-term, fragmented, managed by individuals rather than employers.
- Career counseling, career education, and career guidance are not interchangeable in meaning.
- Career interventions are evolving in response to economic, political, and social changes, and to changes in techniques and content.
- Career guidance encompasses a vocabulary of work, individual development, and interventions in career behavior.
- Career development is important to children, youth, and adults in the anticipation of planning for, preparation for, and implementation of work.
- Career guidance, career education, and career counseling can be systematically planned and required counselor competencies specified for each.
- Career counseling, career education, and career guidance are international phenomena. They are becoming major sociopolitical emphases in national development plans concerned with human resource development and the global economy.

In the 30 years since the first edition of this book was published, the world of work and the world of career interventions have changed dramatically. Nations across the world are now in the middle of comprehensive economic, political, and social transitions, in which career development will be a major sociopolitical instrument. As nations compete for economic viability in a global economy, the quality and purposefulness of their human resources become fundamental concerns in their policies and legislation. Whether a nation's purpose is to build human capital, match persons and occupations, help students choose educational options that prepare them for their career choices, develop work identity and career planning skills, serve as a labor exchange, or deal with persons who are unemployed or who suffer major work adjustment problems, models of career interventions tailored to such goals are being developed, refined, and implemented.

Within such contexts, in response to high unemployment rates, constant economic recession and stagnant job creation, some authors have proclaimed the end of work (Rifkin, 1995) in the forms in which it has been known during the past century or so. Other authors have suggested that jobs as a way of organizing work are social artifacts that have outlived their usefulness (Bridges, 1994). In this view:

> *There still is and always will be enormous amounts of work to do, but it is not going to be contained in the familiar envelopes we call jobs.... The job is an idea that emerged early in the nineteenth century to package the work that needed doing in the growing factories and bureaucracies of the industrialized nations. Before people had jobs, they worked just as hard but on shifting clusters of tasks, in a variety of locations, on a schedule set by the sun and the weather and the needs of the day."* (p. 64)

But jobs as fixed, clearly defined sets of tasks that have comprised our organizations of work are giving way to the effects of technology that reduce repetitive and manual tasks, to increasing expectations and multiple responsibilities for multitasking by individual workers, to using temporary and part-time employees to get certain types of work done, and to outsourcing particular tasks to firms who handle specialized types of work tasks.

Underlying such changes are many factors that will be discussed throughout this book. The effects of advanced technology have already been noted. But, in addition, the needs for particular kinds of work that is customized, rather than mass-produced in products that are exact duplicates of one another, that is constantly changing in form and substance, and in its acceptability in a global economy, are heightening the need for work organizations that are flexible and able to constantly reinvent themselves. The traditional view of a job is seen as too rigid, too inflexible, to represent the fundamental organization of work in the future.

Changes in the organization of work are also changing conceptions of individual career development. New career paths are being forecast that are much more dependent on individual career management rather than institutional management of the career of its employees. Increasingly, it is argued that workers of the future will have to assume responsibility to keep their competencies vibrant and relevant so that they will be employable, teachable, and flexible. Within such contexts, new terms are arising to capture the emerging changes in career development for many persons in many occupations. These will be discussed in subsequent sections of the chapter.

As changes ensue in the organization and language of work and in patterns of individual career development, changes in how career interventions are being seen are also occurring. In many ways these perspectives are subtle nuances but they carry interesting implications. For example, depending upon the historical period under consideration, the language of career interventions used by a particular nation, a specific agency within that nation, or policy and legislation related to career interventions, the traditional terms used have included career guidance, career counseling, career education, or career services. Sometimes these terms are used interchangeably within or across nations; sometimes they are quite specifically differentiated in meaning. However, the point here is that at the beginning of the twenty-first century a new phrase has emerged: *the practice of career development.* This phrase combines in one term both career development, the behavior to be sought, and career interventions, the techniques used to influence career behavior. Through at least the second half of the twentieth century, the term *career development* was used to describe the theories about the factors and influences that combine to shape individual career behavior over the life span. In essence, the influences on career behavior were seen as the targets of the techniques or processes known as *career interventions* used "to enhance a person's career development or to enable that person to make more effective career decisions" (Spokane, 1991, p. 22). Inherent, then, in the current use of the term the practice of career development "are two sets of theories or conceptual categories, one that explains the development of career behavior across the life span and the other that describes how career behavior is changed by particular interventions" (Herr, 2001, p. 196).

Thus, the organization, language, and availability of work; the ways that persons learn and express their career development; and the ways professions provide interventions designed to facilitate career development change and evolve. They are historical creations, always in process, the shape, substance, and labeling of which respond to social, political, and economic trends in the United States and, indeed, throughout the world.

CHALLENGES TO THE PRACTICE OF CAREER DEVELOPMENT

As thoughtful observers consider the challenges to the practice of career development (e.g., career guidance, career counseling, career education, and other career services and interventions), in the early decades of the twenty-first century, they face the overriding reality that as the structure of the world's economy is transformed from a collection of separate economies to an interdependent global economy, new demands are being placed on human resources. It has become axiomatic in national development plans, in international forums, and in the world's media that the key factor in a nation's ability to compete in the growing global economy is the quality of that nation's workforce as defined by the literacy, numeracy, flexibility, teachability, and employability that characterize it.

Nations in different parts of the world have for several decades understood the coming challenges to help their workforces become more productive, purposeful, and able to adapt to change. Some nations have made the development of human resources national priorities and they have created technological and organizational systems intended to help maximize the productivity of these human resources. A major component of these systems of human resource development is the range and deployment of career services and interventions.

Although the definitions of the various types of career services and the processes they use vary, they include activities, treatments, and other interventions designed to facilitate an individual's career development; to help persons to make more effective career decisions; to alter a specific vocational behavioral pattern or enhance their induction; and to smooth adjustment within a particular work organization or enterprise. Major questions concerning human resource development and, particularly, career services in any nation have to do with the accessibility of such services, their purposes, to whom they will be available, and who will deliver them. These are not simple issues. In a global economy, nations approach such matters differently and from different cultural traditions; answers to these questions also change as nations go through different phases in their own industrial or technological evolution, placing different demands on their human resources. Under such conditions, the content and processes of career guidance and counseling are being redefined and made more indigenous to the nations and the populations they serve and more comprehensive in the career concerns to which they are addressed.

The changing effects upon the expectations and processes of career interventions are reflections of the fact that such interventions do not arise in a vacuum. They are responses to the changing dynamics of the world of work and to shifting individual career concerns as the latter are affected by political, social, economic, and technological change. Consider briefly some of the changes of the last thirty years that are now affecting the world of work.

Obviously, one can note the dissolution of the Soviet Union (Skorikov & Vondracek, 1993), the major changes in political and economic systems as have occurred in Hungary (Ritook, 1993) and other European nations, and the end of apartheid in South Africa (Mathabe & Temane, 1993). In these nations and others, the democratization of opportunity, increases in individual freedom of job choices, and growing recognition of the need to provide formal support for *all* individuals to plan, prepare for, and be productive in their work life has led to efforts to train counselors and to provide new approaches to career counseling. As a result, the practice of career development and the interventions that comprise it (e.g., career counseling, career education, career guidance) have now become worldwide phenomena.

Beyond the political and social changes just cited, there are many other changes in the delivery and the contexts for work that affect individual behavior and aspirations. One of these is workplace technology and its demands. The pervasiveness of advanced technology and its effects on the language, qualifications for, processes, and organization of work is a central element in the preparation for and the implementation of work across industries, occupational levels, and nations. With regard to the influence of advanced technology in the workplace one can assert, for purposes of discussion, that, without the sophistication and worldwide availability of advanced technology, particularly computers and the Internet, there would be no global economy, no integrated international economic market structure. There would be no digital (technological) divide between rich and poor nations or populations in the United States. There would be no references in the popular press to the *old* economy and the *new* economy or to the *e-age* (the electronic age), *e-commerce* (electronic commerce), or the *information age,* no new classification of nations as *fast* or *slow* depending upon their ability to operate within world standards of technological adaptation in relation to the production of goods and currency transfers; no just-in-time distribution of goods and services, or other by-products of the comprehensive use of, indeed, dependence on, advanced technology, in financial services, transportation, manufacturing, distribution or other business and industrial processes. Within these contexts, one can argue that among the many impacts of advanced technology in the workplace are those related to modifying the importance of time (work can be done by robots and other forms of technology twenty-four hours a day with minimal human involvement), of knowledge and responsibility (increasing numbers of workers must become knowledge workers who know both when and why to do their job tasks), of geography (national political or physical boundaries do not inhibit the flow of electronic information, data, and instructions among work locations differing in time zones and space), of national economic and political sovereignty (it is difficult for nations to survive economically unless their markets are world markets and they are engaged in significant import-export trade) (Herr, 1999).

Advanced technology in the workplace can be described in many ways. Certainly, when one talks about information technology, it is possible to emphasize computers, software, and telecommunications. But the ultimate symbol of information technology is the Internet, which in comparison to many other forms of advanced technology can be applied across the entire economy, including both goods and services. It can be conceived as offering:

> *A new information system, a new marketplace, a new form of communication, and a new means of distribution...among its many attributes, it allows producers and consumers to seek the cheapest price in the global market...speeds up the diffusion of information and...lowers its costs. (*Economist, *April 21, 2000, pp. 65–66)*

CHANGES IN THE ORGANIZATION OF WORK AND CAREER PATHS

One can also cite the effects of the global economy and the regional free trade zones (e.g., the North American Free Trade Agreement, the European Union) as stimuli to the downsizing and the reorganization of work and to a changing work culture. Handy (1996) is among those who speaks of a vast reconfiguration of the world of work in which some 75 percent of the newly jobless are coming from the ranks of managers, professionals, and administrative and technical staff, rather than skilled or semi-skilled blue-collar workers. According to Handy, heightened competition in the global marketplace and, particularly, price wars and quality wars are forcing companies to downsize their personnel to only those who represent the core tasks of the company, not those who in previous decades might have been carried as part of a permanent work force but who are no longer considered necessary parts of such a permanent core—he cites cooks and lawyers, accountants and public relations people, art directors and security guards, economists and particular types of maintenance specialists. To explain this reconfiguration of the work world, Handy uses three rings that begin with an inner core or circle of permanent workers—these are the persons whose skills are necessary to manage, provide technical support to, and sell the products of the core functions of a business. These workers are paid well, have long-term identity with the company, and have well-paid health, educational, and retirement benefits. By decreasing this inner core of permanent employees, corporations decrease their overhead costs for the retirement, health, and other benefits for persons whose skills are not central to the mission of the organization or needed on a daily, year-round basis. The second ring of the work force is occupied by temporary, part-time, or contingent workers whose time and skills are purchased as needed or on a seasonal basis. Handy calls these workers a *portfolio* class, persons who will document and sell their skills in *episodes* to firms that need their services for specific projects or periods of time rather than in continuing relationships with the same organization. Such persons may have to work several part-time jobs simultaneously to have sufficient income or to purchase the health and other benefits that their temporary employers do not supply.

The third circle is comprised of persons who are employed by an outsourcing company that specializes in particular services, for example, custodial and maintenance, customized goods production, marketing, food service catering, advertising, accounting, law, data entry, outplacement counseling, or transportation.

The net effect of this three-ring configuration of the workforce just described is to remove what had been permanent jobs in a firm and reassign them to part-time status or to other firms that subcontract to do specific tasks. In this sense, companies are no longer holistic in the persons they permanently employ. They determine what types of skills are central parts of their core staff and then purchase whatever other skills they need on a temporary or subcontract basis.

Such a reconfiguration of work literally forces many workers, who would in earlier decades be employed in large organizations and would function in various support roles, to become essentially self-employed, managers of their own careers, people who must constantly adapt to change and develop new skills that companies are willing to purchase on a temporary basis or that outsourcing firms can purchase to subcontract to other organizations. Thus, earlier concepts of linear, long-term organizational careers are no longer valid for many workers. New types of "careers" and "career patterns" are forming for persons in each of the three rings of the work force Handy described but theories of work and theories of career adequate to describe such reconfigurations of the workforce have not yet been fully formed.

NEW CONCEPTS OF CAREER

Even so, scholars in Europe, in North America, and in other parts of the world have begun to speak to the issues and challenges related to the emergence of new concepts of career. These observers suggest that such new configurations of work and of career are qualitatively different than the way careers have been viewed for the last several decades. For example, in the view of Arnold and Jackson (1997), writing in the *British Journal of Guidance and Counseling,* several factors affect how the notion of a new career is conceived. In their view, in many nations:

> *The changes taking place in the structure of employment opportunities mean a widening diversity of career patterns and experiences.... More and different sorts of career transition will be taking place. One consequence may be that in the future more men will experience the kind of fragmented careers that many women have experienced.... More people will be working for small and medium-sized employers, and there will be more people who are self-employed.... They highlight the need for lifelong learning and an appropriate strategy for career guidance to support people especially during career transitions. (pp. 428–429)*

In the United States, Hall and his associates (1996), rather than use the term *new careers,* have described them as *protean careers* as follows:

> *People's careers increasingly will become a succession of "ministages" (or short cycle learning stages) of exploration-trial-mastery-exit, as they move in and out of various product areas, technologies, functions, organizations, and other work environments.... this protean form of career involves horizontal growth, expanding one's range of competencies and ways of connecting to work and other people, as opposed to the more traditional vertical growth of success (upward mobility). In the protean form of growth, the goal is learning, psychological success, and expansion of identity. In the more traditional form, the goal was advancement, success and esteem in the eyes of others, and power. (pp. 33, 35)*

The issue is not so much that such new conceptions of careers are not valid but rather for whom are they valid: for what occupations, what jobs, what segments of the workforce? How widespread across firms and industries is the current notion of *new careers* or *protean careers* a useful paradigm? How are these concepts related to the roles and processes of career counselors? How do these perspectives need to be incorporated in occupational and career information? New careers as they have been described obviously have important consequences for the preparation for work and for the attitudes and behaviors that persons seeking work or changing their work patterns need to acquire. At a minimum, emerging conceptions of new careers emphasize the importance of persons acquiring the skills that underlie personal flexibility and the ability to adapt to change. How do counselors help people to become more flexible in their vocational identities and to adapt readily to changing skill needs and to changes in workplaces? What we know about some of these questions will be addressed in other chapters of this book. For now, however, suffice it to say that the term *protean* comes from the myth of the Greek sea god Proteus, who was able to change form constantly. Clearly, in the future workers in many occupations and career paths will need to be able to learn to take on new work behaviors and work persona more frequently than has been traditional. They will be expected to engage in multitasking, being able to perform an array of processes rather than only narrow specialties. They will be expected to be engaged in learning to keep their skills timely and relevant. Facilitating such adaptations to changes in the workplace will be a significant challenge to career counselors.

As new metaphors (protean careers, the e-age) are being created to capture the reconfiguration of work, shifting career patterns, and required behavior of persons preparing for work and adjusting to it, one can argue that both counselors and their clients—youth or adults—must become increasingly appreciative of the trends that flow from the global economy. By way of context, as "new careers" unfold, neither nations nor professions (e.g., counseling) can afford to be concerned only about the intellectual or social elite of the society. Rather, in the global economy, workforces will be required that have the capability to be productive and purposeful at all levels of the occupational structure from the managerial and professional levels through the skilled and semiskilled levels. In highly competitive economic environments, workers must be able to function with quality and efficiency at the levels of creativity, invention, and innovation as well as at the implementation and application levels, in customer service, in quality control, in goods production, and in services delivery. Unless workers at all occupational levels of functioning have both technical skills and interpersonal, planning, and learning skills, the occupational structure can be fragmented into the haves and have nots, encumbered by an underclass of persons who have neither the skills nor the motivation to be trained and retrained for an occupational structure that is constantly being reconfigured.

TRENDS RELATED TO THE GLOBAL ECONOMY

In essence, as the effects of the implementation of advanced technology in the workplace change how workers and machines interact, change the social psychology and the flow of information in the workplace, eliminate more middle management as well as semiskilled jobs, and make more possible the decentralization of where work is done across the world, career development of individuals in a global economy is potentially impacted in multiple ways. Such trends as the following (adapted from Herr, 1999) become part of the context in which career guidance and counseling must function and individual choices made:

- A growing labor surplus, frequently including highly trained and skilled workers, now exists across the world. In this sense, U.S. youth and workers are no longer competing for jobs with their neighbor in the next classroom seat or the next town; they are competing for jobs with persons in other nations who are eager to do the work generated in the U.S. economy that can be done in their own country, by applying advanced technology in locations around the world, or by opportunities for immigration to the United States.
- Many nations in the world are experiencing major and continuing problems of unemployment. At the beginning of 1994, about 30 percent of the world's labor force—820 million people—were unemployed or underemployed (International Labour Organization, 1994). Various observers have suggested that the most important development in Europe in recent decades is the rise and persistence of unemployment. The European Commission (1998) indicated that in 1997 unemployed persons amounted to approximately 18 million, representing 10.7 percent of the civilian labor force across the European nations, including nearly 12 percent in Italy and Finland and almost 20 percent in Spain. These figures remained essentially the same in 2000 (*Economist,* April 21, 2000). More than half of the unemployed persons in many of these nations have been out of work for more than a year, suggesting that these persons may become permanently unemployed. Persons in these nations are seeking ways to attract work from the United States that can be done more cheaply and efficiently in their nation. In many instances, they have created facilities by which they can download information from satellites, analyze it, do data entry, and upload it or engage in other kinds of work that can be done through advanced technology.
- Organizational transformations, including mergers and downsizing, are reducing total corporate workforces and stimulating new models of personnel development, not just personnel management, for permanent core employees.
- The pervasive effects of advanced technology upon the economic climate and the occupational structures of the world have changed what types of work or production are done in particular nations, the organization and language of work, the content of work and role of workers, and the education and skill requirements for many traditional and emerging occupations.
- A contingent workforce has grown around the world, including large numbers of temporary employers who may not have long-term institutional identification or health and pension benefits and may become part of the *working poor.*
- The growing number of technologically intensive workplaces has given impetus to the importance of the knowledge worker and of literacy, numeracy, communication, and computer literacy skills as prerequisites for employability and lifelong training in many of the emerging occupations.
- Given the demand on competent, productive, and purposeful workforces, there is, in legislation and in the implications of career theory, advocacy for career-relevant schooling by which stu-

dents can be systematically prepared with the skills necessary in the occupational structure and in other life roles.

- As part of the international initiatives designed to reduce student floundering and drift following high school graduation, there are government policies in many countries concerned about the school-to-work transition, the seamless progression from school to employment, and effective induction into the workforce.
- Growing knowledge of the importance of work to the individual identity of many persons has clarified the linkages between positive or negative career experiences and mental health, self-esteem, purposefulness, physical well-being, and the practice of an internal locus of control.
- Overemphases on college education in many nations has resulted in an overeducated workforce but one that experiences significant skill shortages at the blue-collar and technician levels.
- Demographic trends across the world related to democratization of opportunity and other factors emphasize the importance of women, persons of color, and immigrants as comprising large proportions of the new entrants to the workplace. (Adapted from Herr, 1999, pp. 37–38)

In many ways each of these trends represent unique challenges to the practice of career development as counselors work with children and youth exploring work opportunities that occur behind fences, in skyscrapers, that are computer driven and not available to be observed except in videotapes and other vicarious information sources; with young adults trying to convert their expectations about work into the realities of particular workplaces, jobs, and supervisory practices; with mid-career adults whose original job choices are being refashioned and significantly modified by the need to learn new computer skills or who are experiencing involuntary unemployment; and with older adults who wish to continue employment but on a reduced basis or who need assistance to contemplate the personal implications of retirement. These sets of career concerns are confounded by issues of gender, age, race, educational level, geography, perceptions of the centrality of work in one's identity, socioeconomic background and cultural traditions, and one's acquired skills. They are also effected by the metaphors about work and one's relationship to it to which individuals are socialized in their particular historical cohorts as these are captured in such metaphors as the Generation Xer, the Baby Boomer, the Lonely Crowd, the Wired Loner, the Geek, the Organization Man, or the Status Seeker (Tolson, 2000). Such metaphors often combine social class, education, and history in relation to one's view of what work means, what it should provide, and how it should be organized in one's life.

Implicit in such perspectives is that an array of contextual factors are increasing the comprehensiveness and the importance of career guidance and career counseling in contemporary societies. As individuals become interdependent players in a global economy, the practice of career development as an instrument of national and of individual goals is becoming a major instrument of governmental policy in nations around the world. Although political, economic, and cultural differences differentiate the goals of individual nations, they tend to share several common needs in which career guidance and career counseling are prominent interventions. They include:

- Ways to develop functionally literate, personally flexible, purposeful, competent, and productive workforces
- Mechanisms to help youth make the transition from school to work and to facilitate the demographic shifts in access to work of emerging workforces—women, minority group members, and immigrants
- Theories and practices that focus on the career needs of the poor and minimally educated as well as the affluent and well educated, females as well as males, persons with disabilities as well as the abled
- Procedures to help persons adjust to work effectively and to obtain job satisfaction, workplace loyalty, and mobility
- Strategies to address high rates of youth unemployment or rapidly aging workforces
- Effective approaches to absorbing immigrant populations into the workforce
- Methods by which employers can become increasingly responsive to the needs of employees by viewing them in holistic rather than fragmented ways as assets to be nurtured rather than costs to be reduced, as objects of personnel development not just personnel management

- Approaches to addressing the psychological, physiological, and behavioral issues associated with unemployment and underemployment of specific populations
- Paradigms that allow career guidance and counseling to facilitate mental health as well as economic well-being

While there are many other specific issues that could be addressed here, those cited are sufficient to suggest the expanding range of problems to which career interventions are directed in schools, communities, and workplaces. In some instances, career counseling or other career interventions are the preferred method of responding to such problems; in many other instances, career counseling or career interventions are only one component of a program of activities designed to resolve the human resource, job, or career issue involved. In such situations, career counseling and other career services are seen as complementary components to transition mechanisms implemented to facilitate the movement from school or university to employment, job training or retraining, financial incentives, or support systems, including such state and federal policy initiatives as changing welfare to workfare, and the provision of apprenticeships or internships, on-the-job training, or other methods designed to address a particular job, or occupational or economic issue.

However these models of the deployment of career services differ in shape and substance across nations, they are assuming greater importance in both philosophical and practical terms. Such a reality is captured in the eloquent comments of Watts, Dartois, and Plant (1988a) in their report, *Educational and Vocational Guidance Services for the 14–25 Age Group in the European Community*. In this report, the authors suggest that "educational and vocational guidance services have a key role in any advanced society, both in fostering *efficiency* in the allocation and use of human resources, and in fostering *social equity* in access to educational and vocational opportunities" (p. 1). These dual notions of efficiency and social equity, however simple, are fundamental concepts underlying the rationale for as well as the utility of career services, however they are described or deployed. Indeed, nations vary in whether they employ career interventions to emphasize efficiency in the development of their workforce or social equity in providing equal access to education and work for all people regardless of their gender, age, or ethnicity. In either case or in both, the nature and freedom of individual choice are at issue. Some of the factors shaping such choices follow.

FACTORS AFFECTING THE CHOICE AND CONTENT OF WORK

Although many volumes could be written to summarize the major dynamic or contextual factors that will ultimately shape individual choices about work in the twenty-first century, for our purposes here, we will cite only selected major trends and some of their implications. Not only will these factors affect the nature of the occupational structure and the availability of work, they also will affect individual choice making; preparation for, transition to, and integration into the workforce; and adjustment to the workplace. Such effects will become the content of career guidance and career counseling as well as the shapers of human resource policies and practices and, particularly, of the form and substance of the practice of career development.

Of primary importance in affecting the content of the labor market is the comprehensive application in the workplace of advanced technologies, for example, computers, satellites, fiberoptics, microprocessors, genetic engineering, self-replicating robots, and synthetic materials and energy sources, as well as such processes as new decision and management strategies. However such technologies are defined, they change the organization and the language of work, its content, the role of workers, and the skill requirements to engage in work, particularly in those occupations that involve either high technology or technology-intensive processes.

In addition to its other dramatic influences on the nature of work, advanced technology, particularly computer technology and the Internet, has also changed the social psychology of work and of broader life roles. In both overt and subtle ways, technology defines our world; it both restricts and facilitates the choices we can make, providing great latitude in some instances and almost none in others; and it alters people's mental representation of their options and responsibility for processes and outcomes. The research of Kipnis (1997) indicates that technology can affect how people explain their own and others' behavior and the attributions they use to talk about their feelings of competence and satisfaction. In this context, Kipnis has argued:

> *Technology is altering day-to-day relations between people in dramatic ways. Robots, computers, audio and video entertainment centers... are freeing people from the need to depend on each other on a daily basis. With increasing frequency, we are using new technologies, rather than [other people], to do our work, to provide us with goods and services, to entertain us, and to give us emotional support and companionship. (p. 210)*

Thus, the implementation of computers and the Internet have redefined the social role of workers, changed the relationships among workers in organizations, and changed the flow of information within organizations.

From a global perspective, advanced technology becomes critical at every step of international trade, communication, production, and distribution as raw materials, labor forces, and ideas are integrated into world systems of commercial interaction. Technology now makes it possible to move ourselves or goods to anywhere on the surface of the earth within hours and to communicate worldwide in a fraction of a second (College Placement Council Foundation/Rand Corporation, 1994, p. 5). Thus, geographic and political boundaries no longer serve to contain or to centralize work. "Just as pollutants flow from nation to nation, so capital and technological knowledge flow across national borders altering economic sovereignty as they diffuse" (White, 1990, p. 10). As such, technology has given superordinate importance to work forces that are literate, flexible, adaptable, and teachable.

Although frequently not made explicit, the contemporary influence of advanced technology is a function of the intricate linkage of scientific discovery and technology. Under current conditions of international economic competition, the nations of the world, with the United States a dominant player, are devoted to the rapid translation of scientific ideas into different forms of technology that can yield commercial profit and, simultaneously, transform the home, the workplace, the healthcare system, and the entertainment systems rapidly and with increasing frequency. As new science creates new technology, new tools for research are created and these in turn initiate new questions, new problems to be solved, new roles for workers and work processes. In such circumstances, worker's knowledge of how to apply advanced technology to industrial, business, or other economic sectors is prized. In many instances, human skills and machine capabilities are becoming linked in new ways as systems of productivity, in which technology is the tool and the human operator is the troubleshooter, the planner, the creator using advanced technology to extend his or her research, to minimize boundaries of time and space, and to depict, model, and rehearse solutions to business, construction, engineering, health, or transportation problems without having to commit tangible assets in a trial-and-error process.

In addition to the new products and processes that have resulted from the merger of science and technology, new technologies focused on management, workplace practices, and the deployment of workers have led to new processes unknown a decade ago, for example, total quality management, worker teams, just-in-time inventories, and workplaces as learning communities.

Such realities emphasize the importance of knowledge as one of the major, if not *the* major, foundations of human resource development, economic development, and competitiveness. More and more work is knowledge based rather than physical or manual or based on experience without an understanding of why processes work. Knowledge work is not typically a series of repetitive actions, but rather a sequence of figurative dialogues between the worker and the data, whether the worker is monitoring and troubleshooting a computer-driven lathe or a robot, engaging in computer-aided design, or diagnosing what computer module is not functioning in an automobile (Bridges, 1994). The implications that follow suggest that the skills of schooling and learning and the skills of the workplace are increasingly complementary and overlapping. Educational abilities and achievements, and in particular occupational skills possessed, will become major elements of individual career development. Such a reality puts those with minimal training or capability of learning at the risk of being permanently dislocated or unemployed or constantly on the move to find jobs they can do. Frequently, racial or cultural minority group members or immigrants tend to experience the most difficulties in dealing with the educational and psychological ripple effects of advanced technology—often because they have been underserved in receiving the systematic information useful in planning for such occupational transitions or they have lived in locations where educational provisions are less good than that received by majority culture members, thereby placing them at a competitive disadvantage.

What is also suggested is that nations, including the United States, cannot solve their competitive problems by pouring billions of dollars into capital equipment or physical facilities and not into worker training, retraining, and other support systems. As the effects of the implementation of advanced technology in the workplace change how workers and machines interact, change the social psychology and the flow of information in the workplace, eliminate more middle management and unskilled and semiskilled jobs, and make more possible the decentralization of where work is done across the world, more work has become based on knowledge and learning activity, rather than on experience.

Alvin Toffler, the author of *The Third Wave* (1980) and *Future Shock* (1970), in the third book of his important trilogy, entitled *Powershift, Knowledge, Wealth, and Violence at the Edge of the 21st Century* (1990) has contended that knowledge has now become the world's prime commodity and its by-product is the use and acceleration of time—in terms of the speed of capital movements, transactions, and investments; the speed with which ideas are converted into products and processes; and the speed with which plans are translated into action. In his view, knowledge will rapidly replace cheap labor and raw materials as the primary requisite to effective international competition, to requiring workers to work smarter, and to improving the quality of life within communities and nations. He has suggested that the nations of the world are being characterized in new ways—not just into the nations of the North and the South, or into those communist and capitalist, but into the fast and slow nations of the world based on their level of technology and development and their ability to function within the quality controls and the accelerated delivery of goods and services expected by the global market. As a result, the economic aspirations of the nations whose technological capabilities are limited and their human resources uneducated and inflexible will suffer in international competition.

Peter Drucker (1993), the international scholar of work organization and management, has professed for some time that knowledge has replaced experience in most of the emerging occupations in the world as the primary requisite for employability. According to him, until quite recently there were few jobs requiring knowledge. That is no longer true. In the twenty-first century, knowledge has become the economy's foundation and its true capital.

While it is important to acknowledge that more than 50 percent of the contemporary U.S. labor force is composed of knowledge workers—executives, managers, engineers, scientists, analysts, programmers, teachers, designers, illustrators, sales representatives, copy writers, statistical and data entry clerks, secretaries—it is also important to note that not all knowledge workers require a college degree. Indeed, while college going is the dominant activity in which students participate in the United States after they leave high school, there is a mismatch between the number of students going to college and the number of occupations requiring a college degree. Only 23 percent of occupations now require a baccalaureate degree but there are upward of 70 percent of high school graduates attending college in many parts of the nation. In reality, however, only two in three college graduates will find college-level work, and no more than one in two will find a job in a profession (Gray & Herr, 2000).

As a result of the large proportions of high school students who enter college, few aspire to or enter the skilled trades or the ranks of technicians, areas in which there are skill shortages across the nation, shortages that, for the most part, college graduates will not be able to meet. Many of the occupations with skill shortages are also knowledge work, often requiring some postsecondary education but not a baccalaureate degree. There are examples of high skill/high wage occupations not requiring a baccalaureate degree in craft and construction, health care, manufacturing, customer service, technical service, repair, and installation occupations that in many parts of the nation are standing vacant because of a lack of applicants.

Gordon (2000) argues that "we are educating people for the wrong future" (p. 49). As suggested above, few young people imagine themselves working in service, craft, or technical industries, even though government predictions are that these sectors will be the leaders in creating new jobs over the next ten to fifteen years. Gordon notes that more than 190,000 technical jobs were vacant in the year 2000, as employers are unable to find qualified applicants. He argues that by 2005, more than one million new high-tech workers will be needed. While it is possible that the recession of 2001 and 2002 as well as the U.S. focus on warring against international terrorism may have changed the number of technical workers required for the foreseeable future, it is clear that the trends he identifies are likely to prevail. In line with other changing definitions of careers, Gordon has contended that a new definition of career is necessary—one that is less focused on individual "progression up a career ladder in a progression or organization and more on recognizing opportunities and adapting" (p. 49).

There are two further ways in which advanced technology and the worldwide dispersion of technological and scientific knowledge have made an impact on human development in a world economy. These are the globalization of the workforce and a world global labor surplus. First, because of the push for high productivity, the availability of high technology, the search for cheap and talented labor, and the location of manufacturing and sophisticated service ventures in areas of likely growth, often in the emerging or the developing nations, capable workforces are no longer confined to a limited number of nations in the world. There is a growing globalization of the workforce (Martin, 1992). As a result of rapidly emerging electronic infrastructures, increasingly sophisticated work is being decentralized, parceled out by Japan, Europe, and the United States to workforces in faraway nations that have become particularly skilled in specific processes. In an era of advanced technology and telecommunications, there is a growing supply of hypereducated workers in nations throughout the world who represent a pent-up pool of talent that can respond to the decentralization of the design, development, and implementation of work at remote geographic locations. Given the availability of such processes as faxes, satellites, computers, and other technologies, these members of the global workforce can directly compete with a nation's domestic workforce in virtually any information-based industrial or business process (Martin, 1992).

There is a further factor to be noted here: the growth of a global labor surplus. As foreign investments and mergers occur among corporations in Western and Eastern Europe or the United States and the newly industrializing nations, the facilities and processes created through the application of advanced technology make the resulting factories or other workplaces much less labor intensive. Consequently, the numbers of blue-collar workers, clerical staff, and managerial employees are reduced or kept limited with the use of contingency work forces, outsourcing, subcontracting, part-time work, and other processes used to keep the number of permanent employees at a minimum. The workers unemployed through such processes become part of the global labor surplus that stands ready to compete with domestic workforces.

Before leaving such matters, it is useful to note briefly two related phenomena that counselors will increasingly encounter as they work with young and older workers. The first of these is stress in the workplace.

Although stress in the workplace is an extremely complex subject, Landy (1992) has captured its essence effectively as it relates to many of the major factors we have just cited as shaping the context of work for the immediate future:

> *Part of the difficulty in dealing with the topic of stress in the workplace is that it will not stand still long enough to give us a good look. The nature of work is changing rapidly. No one can ignore the revolution in work that is represented by computer technology. Everyone from the teenager operating the french fry machine at McDonald's to the psychiatrist diagnosing affective disorders has been affected by the introduction of the computer into the workplace (Garson, 1988; Zuboff, 1988).... It has become abundantly clear that the introduction of a video display terminal at the work site is not simply placing a screen on a desk. The correlative changes in work methods, social interaction patterns, patterns of supervision, and productivity goals are extensive.... Coupled with such technological changes, there are also dramatic changes occurring in the work force (Greller, 1990). Work groups are becoming older. Additionally, new members of the working population are more demographically diverse and possess skill sets and value systems that are not identical to those possessed by earlier generations. These changing skills and values also have implications for understanding stress in the workplace. It is becoming increasingly clear that the gap between skills demanded in new technological environments and skills possessed by the work force is growing (Herold, 1990). This gap is bound to make itself felt in increased worker strain resulting from performance problems that represent increased demands coupled with diminished resources. This is likely to be just as true of existing workers whose*

skills are becoming obsolete as it is with new workers whose skills are deficient. (pp. 120–121)

Inherent in Landy's observations are many reasons for growing stress in the workplace. They include role conflict, inability to perform the tasks demanded effectively, uncertainty or inadequate knowledge about an event or events that require action or resolution, concern about the physical consequences of the work to be done and where it is done, participation in autonomous work groups and meeting the productivity expectations of co-workers, interpersonal relations with supervision, work overload, ambiguous roles, work control experienced or exercised, perceived task demands, rewards and punishments in work, and time urgency. These stressors, whether perceived or actual, are brought to the counselor as part of the worker's emotional response to the workplace. As such, they become the content of career counseling and part of the expanding range of *career issues* with which counselors are increasingly confronted.

A final factor that has stretched the traditional career role of the counselor is working with those who are unemployed. The issues of unemployment in the current world are complex and they are changing. By way of context, it is accurate to suggest that unemployment has been a concern in most of the industrialized nations for a hundred or more years. Through most of this period, however, unemployment was treated as an individual, not a state, problem and an economic issue, not a psychological or social one. Increasingly, nations have realized that not only is unemployment a complex and difficult problem for the individuals affected, but unemployment is also a major social and economic issue that is increasingly global in its impact. In the past several years, the U.S. unemployment rate of approximately 4 to 6 percent has been much better than many other nations. But it is useful to acknowledge that regardless of the rate of unemployment, one of the reasons the needs for expanded career counseling, career guidance, and other career services are getting reinforcement and support in national policies and legislation is because, in an aggregate sense, unemployment costs money: it reduces the productive capacity of nations, and it cuts the energy of its human capital resources to be competitive and purposeful. Unemployment increases the costs to governments of their social security and social service systems, the safety net that must be put in place to provide a financial floor for those who are out of work, discouraged, and without resources to sustain themselves or their family. In addition, as we will discuss more fully in Chapter 2 and elsewhere in this book, the costs for medical treatment and mental health and psychiatric services and responses to violence and abuse all increase with rises in unemployment. Increases in imprisonment, mortality rates, suicides, and other physiological, behavioral, emotional, and stress-related disorders have been found to correlate significantly with increases in the rate of unemployment (Herr, 1993). It is within such contexts that federal and state policies and the recommendations of national commissions advocate the increased provision of career guidance and career counseling, again as sociopolitical instruments, that help to increase what Watts, Dartois, and Plant called the efficiency and social equity of the distribution of human resources across occupational and training needs. This is not to suggest that federal or state policies are unconcerned with the plight of the individual person who is unemployed. They are not. But their concern is a macro-concern, an analysis of the national and international economic environment, that argues the collective, not the individual, effects of unemployment, the reduction of which becomes a national economic and social priority.

While these prefatory comments could continue to address the factors shaping current work environments, the demands on workers in a global economy, and the broadening of perspectives on the functioning of career services—career guidance, career counseling, career education, other career interventions—in promoting the efficient and equitable choice of, preparation for, transition to, and adjustment to the workplace, the remainder of the book will further examine and apply these concepts. Before doing so, it will be useful to place into historical context the evolution in the United States of the terms *vocational guidance* to *career guidance* and *vocational counseling* to *career counseling.* As one learns about contemporary challenges, it is also useful to understand the historical events that gave rise to the practice of career development.

THE PRACTICE OF CAREER DEVELOPMENT: TERMS IN TRANSITION

The major contemporary terms of importance—career guidance and career counseling—have for the past century been in evolution. At the beginning of the twentieth century, the terms of preference that were generally used were vocational guidance and vocational counseling. In the last half of the twentieth century, the terms that emerged and became the major nomenclature were career guidance and career counseling, although other terms were also important in certain settings and as used by particular authors. These included the frequent use of career services and career interventions as descriptive terms. At the end of the twentieth century, the phrase "the practice of career development" has been subtly inserted into the language of the field. This term is reflected, for example, in the revised name of the National Vocational Guidance Association, which became the National Career Development Association in 1985. A year later the *Vocational Guidance Quarterly* was renamed the *Career Development Quarterly.* Both of these changes occurred amid objections by some persons committed to retaining the historic names and concepts that had defined the professionals who had specialized in theories and practices related to career behavior for most of the century.

One of the concerns about the growing use of the phrase "the practice of career development" is that "career development" is used in this term to describe both the total constellation of psychological, sociological, educational, physical, economic, and chance factors that combine to shape individual behavior over the life span (Sears, 1982); the traditional meaning of the term; and the interventions or practices that are used "to enhance a person's career development or to enable that person to make more effective career decisions" (Spokane, 1991, p. 22). Thus, inherent in the current usage of the term career development are two sets of theories or conceptual categories: one that explains the development of career behavior across the life span, and the other that describes how career behavior is changed by particular interventions in it at particular points of individual transition (Herr, 2001). It is not clear that the persons who advocated for changes in the names of the National Career Development Association, the *Career Development Quarterly,* or the practice of career development did so on the basis of conceptual perspectives rather than political considerations, but it seems likely that terms like *the practice of career development* will grow in usage in the future.

This brief discourse is simply to affirm that terms, like professions, evolve and change across time. Such terms, like language in general, are historical, indeed social, creations that respond to social, political, and economic trends. So it is with such terms as career guidance and career counseling or, earlier in the century, vocational guidance and vocational counseling.

Thus *career guidance* and *career counseling* are both old and new terms. They are old in the sense that they rest on the heritage yielded by three-quarters of a century of what had been known as vocational guidance in the United States. They are old in the role they have played in the origins of counseling in this nation at the beginning of the twentieth century. They are also old in the part they have played in the shaping of counseling and of counseling psychology as areas of specialization distinct from clinical psychology in the early 1950s (Herr & Cramer, 1987). Career guidance, the broader of the two terms, and a term preferred in some other nations, is new because its emphases, conceptual models, and consumer populations tend to go beyond those typically associated with earlier models of vocational guidance and to embrace life-span career concerns. These concerns transcend initial choice of work and initial occupational adjustment to address questions of work and family roles, work and leisure, and work and mental health. Such questions, along with the transition points throughout life when decisions about such matters are implemented, constitute the content of career guidance and of career counseling. The evolution of both career guidance and career counseling has represented a series of *paradigm shifts* (Kuhn, 1962) in conceptual models and models of practice throughout the late nineteenth and the twentieth centuries.

Emerging theoretical perspectives, rapid changes in occupational content, economic realities, legislative mandates, problems of youth and adult unemployment, concerns about the quality of work life and worker productivity, questions about the school-to-work transition, and shifting labor force demographics (such as greater participation by women and minorities) have subtly but inexorably redefined the content, the time spectrum, the technologies, and the consumers of career service. Such pressures and forces have increased the comprehensive nature of career guidance, career counseling, and career services and made them processes of international importance. During the evolution of such change, it has become obvious to theorists, researchers, and practitioners that career interventions, however described, do not operate in a political, economic, and social vacuum. Rather, it is within these contexts that anxieties about achievement and other purposes, information deficits, indecisiveness and role confusion originate and become the content of career guidance and counseling.

The use of the terms *career guidance* and *career counseling* began tentatively in the 1960s, having burst into increasingly common usage only since the early 1970s. The present terms have been stimulated by many phenomena: rapid and diverse social and occupational change, maturation of theoretical perspectives about career behavior, and rising demand in many settings, by both youths and adults, for assistance in career planning, job search, and job adjustment skills. Career education, a major educational movement spawned in the 1970s, was also instrumental in reasserting the priority that career development needs to have in schools, colleges and universities, and workplaces. Increasingly, human resource systems, employee assistance programs, and the organization of career services in corporations and governmental agencies have extended the application of career guidance and career counseling to new settings and populations. In this chapter we will examine the evolution from vocational guidance to career guidance during the twentieth century; describe some of the language, issues, and trends associated with this evolution; discuss career counseling as separate from career guidance; and place the support for these processes into international perspective.

VOCATIONAL GUIDANCE: A HISTORICAL EVOLUTION TO THE LANGUAGE OF CAREER

Although it is possible to trace both the philosophies and the practices of vocational guidance far into antiquity (Capintero, 1994; Dumont & Carson, 1995), our concern here is confined to the rise of vocational guidance in the United States, beginning in the late 1800s. Table 1.1 provides a chronological listing of some of the most important milestones in the evolution of the practice of career development during the twentieth century.

The late nineteenth and early twentieth century was a time of intense change. In a relatively short fifty years, following the devastating costs of the war between the states, the Civil War, the United States made the transformation from a national economy that was agriculturally based to one that was—as part of the industrial revolution that was spilling over from Europe to the United States—increasingly based in manufacturing and industrial processes. The latter process required major inputs of people with physical strengths and industrial experience to fuel the industrial processes occurring in many of the cities on both coasts and in the Midwest of the United States. This ravenous need for human resources was fed by immigration to both coasts by persons from Europe and from Asia seeking improved economic opportunity and enhanced personal freedom and by the large movement of persons within the United States from the farms to the cities. As the latter occurred, urbanization, immigration, and occupational diversity came to describe the economic and social milieu in which the nation was forming its new character. These changes were accompanied by a rise in national concerns about the need to strengthen vocational education and to provide information and support by which persons seeking work could identify and gain access to available jobs. By the late 1800s, the information about jobs, occupations, and workplaces was becoming so complex that families or local neighborhoods could no longer serve as the primary sources of occupational information or of the allocation of jobs. Such circumstances gave rise to the need for more formal mechanisms, rudimentary forms of vocational guidance, that began to emerge in settlement houses, in Young Men's Christian Associations, in community centers, and in schools.

These societal changes spurred an array of concerns that began to shape the substance and processes of vocational guidance. These concerns took multiple forms and came from different elements of the social sector. Educators and industrialists were asking how to bridge the gap between school and the realities of the adult world; how to strengthen and expand vocational education; how to define the appropriate content of education in a society of social, economic, and political flux; how to address changing family structures, diminished extended kinship systems, child labor, and the shifts in child rearing practice that accompanied migration of families and the consuming force of the industrial revolution. Industrialists were concerned about how best to place adults into a rapidly growing and shifting occupational structure, how to reduce unnecessary disruptions and costs related to the large number of workers who moved from job to job because they were not

TABLE 1.1 Selected Milestones in the Evolution of Career Development Practices in the Twentieth Century

Many events and persons have shaped the practice of career development in the twentieth century. The following compilation of such influences is not exhaustive, but it does provide a decade-by-decade chronicle of the selected social, political, and economic events and responses to them that have affected the contemporary legacy on which career development practices will build during the twenty-first century.

1900–1920

Significant questions about the focus of education; World War I; expansion of vocational education; rising concerns for mental hygiene.

Frank Parsons founded the Breadwinner's College in 1905 to provide vocational training and guidance.

The Vocational Bureau, founded by Frank Parsons, opened in Boston and is recognized as the first organization to provide a systematic process for providing vocational guidance and counseling. Its services were subsequently incorporated in the public schools of Boston.

Frank Parson's book *Choosing a Vocation* was published posthumously in 1909. He provided the original conceptual and process elements of vocational guidance and vocational counseling.

Jessie B. Davis organized a program of vocational and moral guidance in the schools of Grand Rapids, Michigan. The program included counseling with respect to courses and extracurricular activities.

Binet introduced his intelligence scales in the United States in 1907.

In 1910, delegates from a variety of organizations and institutions attended the first national conference on vocational guidance held in Boston under the leadership of David Snedden, Frank Thompson, and Meyer Bloomfield.

Meyer Bloomfield succeeded Parsons as head of the Vocational Bureau in Boston; he taught the first vocational-guidance course at Harvard University in 1911.

In 1913 the American edition of Hugo Munsterberg's work in Germany, *Psychological and Industrial Efficiency,* was published in which experimental psychology was applied to vocational choice.

The National Vocational Guidance Association (NVGA) was formed in 1913 in Grand Rapids, Michigan. Its first publication, the *Vocational Guidance Bulletin,* was started in 1915.

The U.S. Bureau of Education published Bulletin No. 14, *Vocational Guidance,* which summarized the papers presented at the organizational meeting of the NVGA in 1913.

The Army Committee on Classification of Personnel, in developing and administering the Army Alpha and Beta tests for use in World War I, laid a base for occupational classification and selection in the civilian sector and stimulated concern about guidance and counseling's growing emphasis on classification and selection.

The Smith Hughes Act of 1917 provided reimbursement for vocational guidance services.

The U.S. government instituted programs in 1918 for World War I veterans with disabilities, marking the beginning of vocational rehabilitation counseling.

In 1918 the National Education Association caused deterioration in the early partnership between vocational education and vocational guidance because it accepted a craft rather than a technical training emphasis in vocational education and a guidance-for-education rather than for-jobs conception of vocational guidance.

The U.S. Bureau of Education (the forerunner of the U.S. Office of Education) published the *Cardinal Principles of Secondary Education* in 1918, in which were cited areas of student behavior to which many observers related guidance (e.g., vocation, citizenship, worthy use of leisure time, ethical character).

1920–1940

Concern about the dignity and rights of children; psychometrics flourished; economic depression caused concern about job placement and unemployment.

Technological unemployment and worldwide depression were major social issues.

George-Reed (1920), George-Elizy (1934), and George-Dean (1936) Acts provided direct support to guidance by providing reimbursement for vocational-guidance activities.

The U.S. Employment Service was created by the Wagner-Peyser Act (1933).

The Occupational Information and Guidance Service was established under George-Dean Act funds in the Division of Vocational Education, U.S. Office of Education (1938).

In 1939, the *Dictionary of Occupational Titles* was published by the Bureau of Labor Statistics, U.S. Department of Labor. In 1940 the Occupational Outlook Service was established in the Bureau of Labor Statistics.

(continued)

TABLE 1.1 Continued

A major view of the period was that guidance had two major functions: distribution (helping students to find educational-vocational opportunities effectively), and adjustment (helping students adjust to environmental requirements). A contrasting view emphasized that guidance was a clinical process that rested on the work of applied psychologists concerned with the measurement of individual differences.

The Depression emphasized a placement approach in vocational guidance.

1940–1950

World War II; women entered the workforce in unprecedented numbers; higher education expanded to absorb veterans; postwar economic and industrial expansion; Cold War began with the Soviet Union.

Carl Rogers published *Counseling and Psychotherapy* (1942), which conceived of counseling as concerned with other than traditional medical models and disease entities and of the counselor as a directive authority.

During World War II, women successfully worked in manual and technical jobs previously reserved for men.

Experimental use of the General Aptitude Test Battery by the U.S. Employment Service was initiated in 1945.

Return of veterans to society spurred the use of classification tests and the importance of career guidance and counseling at secondary and postsecondary levels.

George Barden Act authorized salaries and travel expenses of vocational counselors and supported counselor-training courses. As such, it spurred certification of counselors, the definition of and provision of suitable content for appropriate courses at the graduate level, and the profession of counselors.

The *Occupational Outlook Handbook* was first published in 1948.

1950–1960

Korean War; Sputnik launched, thus causing widespread debates about American education; education and guidance seen as instruments of national defense.

In 1951, the historic NVGA definition of vocational guidance is changed from an emphasis on what is to be chosen to the nature of the chooser.

Carl Rogers published *Client-Centered Therapy* (1951), which conceived the helping relationship in terms of the provision of specific ingredients of a therapeutic situation.

In 1951, the NVGA, the American College Personnel Association, the National Association of Guidance Supervisors and College Trainers, and the Student Personnel Association for Teacher Education merged to form the American Personnel and Guidance Association (APGA), the predecessor of the American Counseling Association (ACA).

In 1951, Donald Super launched the Career Pattern Study, introducing the concept of vocational development.

In 1952, the *Vocational Guidance Quarterly,* the predecessor to the *Career Guidance Quarterly,* began.

In 1956, for the first time a computer successfully completed a simulation of human problem solving.

Sputnik was launched (1957), thus initiating a reappraisal of the offerings and rigor of the American high school and of the need to identify and encourage students with potential to be scientists.

In 1957, Super published the *Psychology of Careers,* which laid out the rationale and the processes to view vocational guidance not only in terms of immediate choice but also in broader perspectives involving intermediate and future goals. The book applied the emerging perspectives of career development theory to choice behavior, presented a developmental-task concept of career development in different life stages, and emphasized the importance of the self-concept as the organizing mechanism of career behavior.

Titles V-A and V-B of the National Defense Education Act of 1958 required states to submit plans to test secondary school students so that academically talented students could be identified and encouraged to enter the hard sciences and other forms of higher education; funds were provided for extensive training of secondary school counselors. Title V-A provided funds for support and development of local school guidance and counseling programs. Title V-B appropriated funds for counseling and guidance institutes for the purpose of upgrading the qualifications of secondary school counselors. The act, which initiated an enormous increase in the number of school counselors across the nation in addition to the identification of academically talented students, also included provisions supporting the career development of students by counselors.

Career-development and vocational-development theories emerged in the works of Eli Ginzberg, Donald Super, Anne Roe, John Holand, and David Tiedeman.

1960–1970

Civil rights movement escalated; war in Vietnam caused major values upheavals and economic difficulties; major federal legislative outpouring to counteract unemployment, poverty, and other social ills; "Do your own thing" became a credo; rise in professionalism; computer-assisted career guidance systems begin to emerge as important complements to career guidance and career counseling.

Third edition of the *Dictionary of Occupational Titles* was published.

Major expansion of vocational education occurred under the Vocational Education Act of 1963 and the Amendments of 1968; the emerging notions of career development theory were apparent in the legislation.

The Vocational Education Act of 1963 specifically stated that vocational guidance and counseling were to be provided to students planning to enroll or enrolled in vocational-education courses.

Civil Rights Act passed in 1964. The civil rights movement accelerated the democratization of educational and occupational opportunities for those in minority groups.

In 1964, Henry Borow edited *Man in a World at Work,* the fiftieth anniversary volume of NVGA and the first NVGA decennial volume.

In 1966, John Holland authored *The Psychology of Vocational Choice,* the first book-length discussion of his theory.

The women's rights movement heightened concerns about the need for guidance efforts to reduce effects of sex stereotyping and sex bias in student choice making and in access to occupations.

Vocational and career development theories began to be used as organizing content for guidance programs.

Vocational Education Act Amendment of 1968 advocated a need for career programs, responses to the disadvantaged and physically handicapped, and the expansion of a broadened concept of guidance and counseling, including its extension into the elementary schools. These pieces of legislation stimulated a large number of national and state conferences on vocational guidance, innovative projects in career guidance, counseling, and placement.

Counselor education programs mushroomed.

1970–1980

International tensions rose; energy problems emerged; unemployment, particularly of youth, became a major issue; concerns about overeducation and a lack of technical education; concerns about survival skills.

In 1971 career education was introduced as a priority of the U.S. Office of Education. The Educational Amendments of 1974 made career education a law of the land and initiated the Office of Career Education in the U.S. Office of Education; Kenneth Hoyt became commissioner of career education.

In 1974, Herr edited *Vocational Guidance and Human Development,* the second NVGA decennial volume.

The Career Guidance and Counseling Act of 1975 was introduced into Congress under the leadership of APGA. Although it was not passed by the Congress, its language and concepts appeared in later pieces of legislation.

The Educational Amendments of 1976 included major support for guidance and counseling in Titles I, II, and III; Title II provided major support for vocational guidance.

Pressures for accountability in guidance and counseling mounted.

Fears of economic crisis and concerns about widespread unemployment among youth continued to spur career and vocational guidance emphases.

1980–2000

Many political changes swept the world: the Cold War ended; apartheid ended in South Africa; many nations formerly under Communism moved to market economies; the global economy became a reality; the practice of career development became a worldwide phenomenon; computer-assisted career guidance systems grew in number and capability; women and minorities became major sources of new entrants to the workforce.

In 1982, the Joint Training Partnership Act (JTPA) replaced the Community Employment Training Act (CETA), providing career guidance for disadvantaged youth and for workers needing retraining.

In 1982, Carol Gilligan published *In a Different Voice,* stimulating renewed attention to the differential career behavior of women and men. Other women theorists advanced these perspectives in important conceptual and empirical work.

Comparative studies of the effects of computer-assisted career guidance systems with and without counselor assistance to users began to appear in the professional literature.

In 1984, Norman Gysbers edited *Designing Careers: Counseling to Enhance Education, Work, and Leisure,* the third NVGA decennial volume.

In 1984, the Carl D. Perkins Vocational Education Act advocated programs designed to improve, extend, and expand career guidance and counseling programs to meet the needs of vocational education students and potential students. Subsequent Perkins Acts

(continued)

TABLE 1.1 Continued

in the 1990s (e.g., Carl D. Perkins Vocational Education and Applied Technology Acts) continued to provide major fiscal support for career guidance.

In 1984, the Report of the National Commission on Secondary Vocational Education, *The Unfinished Agenda,* advocated that comprehensive career guidance programs be available to all students and, in philosophy at least, reaffirmed the importance of strong career guidance programs to vocational education.

In 1984, the credentialing of nationally certified career counselors (NCCC) was initiated.

In 1985, the NVGA changed its name to the National Career Development Association.

In 1986, the *Vocational Guidance Quarterly* was renamed the *Career Development Quarterly.*

In 1992, the Americans with Disabilities Act (ADA) was passed, requiring employers to provide reasonable work accommodations to persons with disabilities.

The Internet grew rapidly throughout the 1990s, incorporating job search and career counseling web sites. New ethical questions emerged concerning the preparation for and use of the Internet by career counselors.

In 1994, the School-to-Work Opportunities Act provided funds for and advocated career exploration and counseling.

In 1998, the Workforce Investment Act provided career guidance and counseling for disadvantaged youth, adults, and dislocated workers.

From E. L. Herr and M. Shahnasarian, Selected Milestones in the Evolution of Career Development Practices in the Twentieth Century. *Career Development Quarterly, 49,* 225–231.

aware of their capabilities or the opportunities available to them, and how to alleviate general job dissatisfaction experienced by many workers. The social reformers of the time focused their attention on the poor physical and economic conditions in which many immigrants lived, the effects on children, often age 10 or less, working in factories and coal mines for 10–12 hours a day without access to schooling or opportunities for healthy development, and the fact that workers in many industries were treated as chattel of employers, not as persons of dignity with the right to determine their own destinies. Such a philosophy was evident in a document published by the U.S. Bureau of Education (predecessor of the U.S. Office of Education) in 1918, reflecting on the conditions from which vocational guidance was rising:

> *Education in a democracy, both within and without the school, should develop in each individual the knowledge, interests, ideals, habits and powers whereby he will find his place and use that place to shape both himself and society toward even nobler ends. (Rosengarten, 1936, p. xix)*

Third, vocational guidance was spawned in a milieu of social and economic change, human suffering, and a dawning recognition of the needs of individual differences and dignity. It was viewed as a significant component of the cries for educational reform as well as for social reform. The vocational guidance interventions that began to evolve were both practical and humane, designed to help students to learn about their characteristics and options and to help persons to be matched with the needs of the occupational structure, in ways that could preserve the order and the rationality of their choices and to make such choices in ways that were not coerced or forced.

Such ideas were radical at the beginning of the twentieth century but they were consistent with the historical movement—the political and social conditions of the time. It is within such circumstances that change becomes imperative and that it can take root and flourish. Brewer (1942), one of the important chroniclers of the rise of vocational guidance in the United States, cited four major influences that stimulated such processes: the division of labor, the growth of technology, the extension of vocational education, and the spread of modern forms of democracy. Cremin (1961), a historian of education, speaking to vocational guidance and vocational counseling as part of educational reform, and particularly the Progressive Education Movement of the late 1800s and the first fifty years of the twentieth century, indicated that social reformers of the time believed:

> *Vocational counseling would lead to greater individual fulfillment…that people suited to their job would tend to be active in the creation of more efficient and humane industrial systems…[therefore] the craft of vocational guidance would serve not only the youngsters who sought counsel, but the cause of social reform as well. (p. 12)*

But social reform in this context also meant educational reform and, particularly vocational education reform. Stephens (1970), also a historian, speaking to the origins of vocational guidance contended:

> *To many leaders of the vocational reform movement… it was apparent that vocational education was but the first part of a package of needed educational reforms. They argued that a school curriculum and educational goals that mirrored the occupational structure created merely a platform and impetus for launching youth into the world of work. What was clearly needed to consummate the launch were guidance mechanisms that would shape their safe and efficient arrival on the job. Without guidance experts it was argued, other efforts at reform would be aborted…. Therefore, in the name of social and economic efficiency, the argument continued, the youth who has been carefully trained would also have to be carefully counseled into a suitable occupational niche. (p. xiv)*

The rich heritage of support for vocational guidance as a philosophy and as a set of formal mechanisms occurred, however, without a scientific basis for vocational guidance as we know it today. There were not yet tests of aptitudes or interest inventories; Alfred Binet had not yet brought his intelligence scales from France. There was no *Dictionary of Occupational Titles* or *Occupational Outlook Handbook.* There were no comprehensive classification systems to describe the American occupational structure. Only an elementary understanding of individual differences and the crudest beginnings of aptitude or performance testing existed. Palmistry, phrenology, graphology, and physiognomy were methods still widely used to obtain insight into one's future (Rosengarten, 1936).

What was not in short supply was the conceptual genius to lay the bases for the formal development of vocational guidance. Many persons in the late nineteenth century made significant contributions to a climate and a primitive but growing knowledge base on which vocational guidance and vocational counseling could be built. Exemplary of such persons were Alfred Binet's work in France on intelligence testing; Spranger's work in Germany on types of personalities in relation to different types of jobs; Munsterberg's research in Germany on occupational choice and worker performance; and in the United States the work of Jesse B. Davis and Eli W. Weaver on the educational and career problems of students; William Rainey Harper on the scientific study of the student; G. Staney Hall on child study; and John Dewey on the restructuring of education.

Enter Frank Parsons

Clearly, the dominant visionary and architect of vocational guidance and counseling in the first decade of the twentieth century was Frank Parsons. An engineer and lawyer by training, Parsons had spent much of his life dealing with various reform movements. During the 1880s and 1890s, he had been highly involved with settlement house activities along the northeastern coast, especially in Boston. Under the general credo that "It is better to choose a vocation than merely to hunt a job," Parsons established the Vocations Bureau in Boston. Parsons worked to provide a scientific basis for assisting immigrants and others in effectively choosing work. He also became an outspoken critic of the Boston public school system and was a major advocate of educational reform. Parsons attacked the public schools for their specialization in book learning and he argued that "book work should be balanced with industrial education; and working children should spend part time in culture classes and industrial science" (Stephens, 1970, p. 39). He saw the process of adapting vocational guidance to the school as totally relevant to educational reform.

Parsons contended that in the early education of youth, "We must train our students to full powers of action…in the various lines of useful work so far as possible according to their aptitudes as brought out by scientific tests and varied experience" (Stephens, 1970, p. 40). Parsons's posthumously published book, *Choosing a Vocation* (1909), elaborated various techniques that he found useful in helping adolescents identify or diagnose their capabilities and choose jobs with reasonable expectations of success. To accomplish these goals, Parsons advocated a wide variety of means, including reading biographies, observing workers in their settings, and examining existing occupational descriptions. Parsons used extensive lists of questions for client self-study and sharing with the counselor. He developed techniques to assist counselees to be introspective about their own likes and dislikes, successes and limitations, and to talk with the counselor about how to engage in *true reasoning* (decision making) related to the information they had. Although it is rarely noted, Parsons was inclusive of and tailored approaches to both young men and young women. He assumed that many, but not all, of the vocational techniques he used were of equal value to boys and girls and men and women, and he provided special attention to information about industries open to women and how these positions could be accessed. He also provided statistics about occupations in which both men and women were employed as well as those that employed primarily men.

As a frame of reference for the *career interventions* he used, Parsons proposed a three-step set of concepts that defined his view of vocational counseling or, as he called the procedure, *true reasoning*. This process became the basis for perhaps the most venerable approach to career interventions in the twentieth century: the trait and factor or matching approach. His tripartide approach was stated as follows:

> *First, a clear understanding of yourself, aptitudes, abilities, interests, resources, limitations, and other qualities. Second, a knowledge of the requirements and conditions of success, advantages and disadvantages, compensation, opportunities, and prospects in different lines of work. Third, true reasoning on the relations of these two groups of facts. (Parsons, 1909, p. 5)*

This schema defined the elements of what is now known as an actuarial, matching or trait-and-factor approach to counseling. Such a position assumes that the individual can be described as possessing certain traits (interests, skills, aptitudes, and so on), that different occupations or educational alternatives can be described as requiring differing amounts and configurations of such traits, and that by matching individual traits and occupational requirements through a procedure such as *true reasoning* a choice would occur. More important, Parsons's three-step procedure stimulated research focused on better and fuller information about individual differences and methods of assessment (first step), occupations (second step), and the decision-making process itself (third step). Although many other approaches to vocational guidance and counseling have been presented in the ensuing nine decades, much of the history of vocational guidance in this century can be understood in terms of which of Parsons's three steps was most dominant in the theoretical positions and practices of a particular decade.

From 1909 until the present, the first two steps in particular of Parsons's formulation have spurred research and developmental efforts. The first step has stimulated psychometric efforts to identify and measure individual differences and determine their relationship to occupational satisfaction or success. The second step has stimulated attention to the acquisition and use of occupational information. Together, the use of tests and information with clients has had a continuing effect on vocational guidance and vocational counseling practices up to the present. More recently, the third step, true reasoning, has been given considerable research and theoretical attention under the general rubric of decision making.

It is important to note that what is usually described in the professional literature as guidance and counseling or counseling psychology began, in fact, as vocational guidance. The original intent of Parsons and his contemporaries was to provide direct assistance to persons needing to make occupational choices and was not oriented to the range of personal-social adjustments later incorporated into the provinces of counselors and psychologists. Indeed, vocational guidance and vocational education were seen as complementary parts of a comprehensive reform movement, focusing on the rational distribution of persons within a growing reservoir of occupational opportunity: the concept of efficiency as it was used earlier in this chapter.

The First Fifty Years of Vocational Guidance

Much of the twentieth century was dominated by efforts to develop content for each of the elements of Parson's model, add steps to it (Salomone, 1988), integrate it with other compatible concepts (e.g., Person-Environment Fix) (Chartrand, 1991), and provide scientific bases to each of the steps—identifying and measuring individual differences, documenting differences in occupational content and activity, and clarifying the elements of the decision-making process.

The work of Parsons created a framework within which both research and the evolution of career intervention occurred during the first fifty years of the twentieth century. Stemming from the one-to-one vocational counseling techniques described by Parsons (1909) in *Choosing a Vocation,* which were largely creative and conceptual and not scientifically based, vocational specialists in the United States began a quest for test and inventories that offered empirical information on which to base individual counseling. The focus of such vocational guidance interventions tended to be on the development of aptitude tests and interest inventories, on analyses of individual differences in performance, and on efforts to predict who would be successful in what occupational task. These foci emphasized the development of interventions related to the *content of choice,* what was available to be chosen, what traits these options required of the individual, and ways to reliably measure these individual differences. Both in the civilian and in the military sectors, the classification and selection of persons for jobs and for military assignments were major applications of vocational guidance as it was unfolding.

From 1900 to 1930, three trends prevailed: Vocational guidance emphasized the study of occupations rather than the study of individuals; vocational educators predominated as vocational guidance practitioners; and vocational guidance and vocational education were largely seen as complementary components of a total effort to distribute students and others across the proliferating occupational structure.

Two independent approaches to vocational guidance tended to arise in the 1920s and the 1930s: one provided by school counselors (guidance and counseling) and the other provided by vocational educators and specialists employed by the U.S. Department of Labor or by rehabilitation agencies. Except for a few major centers for vocational assistance during the Depression, efforts to rehabilitate the physically handicapped, and the incorporation of vocational guidance procedures into military classification during World War II, vocational guidance, when it existed, was aimed at adolescents and young workers seeking initial employment.

During the 1920s, 1930s, and 1940s, vocational guidance, as practiced by the relatively few school counselors then in existence, initially adopted Parsons's model as it was applied in the Boston Public Schools and then in other large cities; courses on occupational information and self-study were developed, and the vocational counseling that existed was essentially directive and advice giving in its delivery. But during this period, vocational guidance became responsive to other forces that modified its approaches. One force was the growing knowledge of individual differences, the awareness of personality dynamics in vocational choice and work adjustment, and the general influence of a psychological approach to vocational guidance. A second force, also psychological, was a growing developmental view of the individual. Reinforced by perspectives such as those of Dewey, Stratemeyer, and the so-called progressives, American education took on "the rhetoric of child-centered pedagogy" (Cremin, 1961). During this period, progressives applied Freudian concepts to child study. Their efforts in the schools focused principally on mental health rather than on skill preparation except for the occupational education sponsored by and largely confined to definitions promulgated by the Smith-Hughes Act of 1917. An even more developmentalist notion was espoused by the advocates of a life adjustment approach to education. This approach advocated that the student learn facts across fields of knowledge relating to specific problems that recur in life, that the artificial barriers between school life and the life of the world beyond the school be minimized, and that the elements of each life situation have a cumulative effect in subsequent life stages and educational experiences; for example, using leisure time wisely and earning a living were among the persistent life situations to the affective life of the child and to longitudinal processes rather than to the more narrow definition of acquiring task skills in specific occupations.

A third force that affected perspectives on vocational guidance and counseling challenged information giving as the primary technique and instead advocated therapeutic treatment or psychotherapy as alternatives.

Although the direct effects of the three forces just cited on vocational guidance and counseling practitioners, mainly school counselors, are not easy to document, it is fair to suggest that these forces tended collectively to tie guidance and counseling to an educational mission, to a diagnostic-clinical rather than vocational and information-giving approach to students, and to the psychological or affective rather than performance aspects of individuals. As a consequence, vocational guidance became less than a top priority of school counselors.

The type of vocational guidance practiced primarily by vocational educators and manpower specialists was receiving a somewhat different form of stimulus. The Great Depression of the 1930s had reaffirmed the importance of job training in the various federal programs (Civilian Conservation Corps and others) instituted during that time for the occupationally displaced. Vocational educators were active in developing such programs. More important, perhaps, was the U.S. Department of Labor publication of the *Dictionary of Occupational Titles* and initiation of the *Occupational Outlook Service,* which gave a level of comprehensiveness and credibility to occupational information unavailable before that time. The Minnesota Stabilization Research Institute, as well as other similar agencies, undertook studies of vocational choice and adjustment in efforts to identify and demonstrate methods of educational and industrial rehabilitation of workers uprooted by industrial changes. One outcome of this activity was the development of new tests of vocational capabilities. Upon the United States' entry into World War II, the application of psychometrics to the selection and classification of personnel assumed massive proportions, and the expertise of vocational educators was instrumental in the development of training programs for an increasingly technical military establishment.

These experiences caused vocational educators to change their perspectives on vocational guidance; they became strongly imbued with a market demand philosophy. Vocational educators viewed vocational guidance as a mechanism for matching individual and job or individual and education curriculum. Such an approach emphasized the importance of individual competency or aptitude for job training or available jobs. This was the criterion to which vocational guidance addressed itself rather than individual preferences, interests, or values—criteria seen as primary in more psychologically based viewpoints.

The Precursors of Career Guidance and Counseling

For most of its first fifty years, whether responding to a market demand philosophy or a more psychologically oriented one, vocational guidance was concerned with predicting occupational choice or occupational success from an individual's test scores before entry into the labor market. The primary emphasis was on matching the aptitude for performance from the results of test profiles of those seeking employment to the requirements of available options, always attempting to maximize the compatibility or congruence between the two. Vocational guidance was largely confined to one point in the life of the individual, that is, either entry into the labor market or readjustment with an immediate alternative after occupational dislocation. Further, its major reference point was the requirements of the occupational structure rather than individual preferences or values.

Since 1950, this traditional view of vocational guidance has been repeatedly challenged. In that year, Robert Hoppock, president of the National Vocational Guidance Association, announced that the traditional view of vocational guidance was "crumbling" (Hoppock, 1950). In 1951, Donald Super recommended revision of the official National Vocational Guidance Association definition of vocational guidance, one that had stood since 1937: "the process of assisting the individual to choose an occupation, prepare for it, enter upon it, and progress in it" (Super, 1951). The 1951 revision recommended by Super amended this perspective by defining vocational guidance as "the process of helping a person to develop and accept an integrated and adequate picture of himself and of his role in the world of work, to test this concept against reality, and to convert it into a reality, with satisfaction to himself and to society."

The definition offered by Super and adopted by the National Vocational Guidance Association did not emphasize the provision of occupational information at a particular time, nor did it emphasize a simple matching of individual to job. Rather, it emphasized the psychological nature of vocational choice. Indeed, Super's definition effectively blended the personal and vocational dimensions of guidance, which previously had been arbitrarily separated, into a unified whole. The resulting base for conceptions of vocational guidance was self-concept oriented. It focused primarily on self-understanding and self-acceptance, to which occupational and educational alternatives available to the individual can be related. It suggested that the earlier rationale for vocational guidance was too limited, its emphasis on occupation alone outmoded, and its techniques applied too mechanically.

The significant reconceptualization of the definition of vocational guidance in 1951 was consistent with several forces that were converging in the 1940s and 1950s. By 1951, the work of Carl Rogers (1942) on client-centered therapy had begun to cause significant shifts in how traditional views of counseling and psychotherapy were being seen. Rogers's writings questioned the validity of medical models of psychotherapy or, indeed, career counseling, in which the counselor was the expert and the client was the subordinate. In such a view, the counselor was typically seen as one who used batteries of aptitude or other tests to predict the individual's likely success in occupational training or job performance and, as the expert, to inform the client of the results. The reference point was how the individual's profile of traits matched with those required by available jobs, not necessarily with the client's values or preferences. Rogers's view of counseling was not based on psychometrics, testing, the occupational structure, or imposing external information on the client as fact. Rather, Rogers applied the postulates of existential or individual psychology to counseling, including career counseling, contending that rather than emphasizing tests and occupational information as principal tools of counselors, the emphasis should be on the internal perceptual field of the client. In this view, the client should be an active part of the counseling dyad, a collaborator in determining what types of external information, if any, would be relevant to the concerns they brought to the counselor rather than being an inactive recipient of information that may or may not be relevant to the client.

The second major force that made the redefinition of vocational guidance in 1951 viable was the beginning of a major rise in the construction of theories of career behavior in the 1940s, 1950s, and accelerating in the 1960s and through the rest of the twentieth century. Although by 1951 much had been learned about the importance of individual differences in career behavior, relatively little had yet been published about how individual differences developed, when, and by what influences. In the early 1950s, the vocational development theories of Ginzberg, Ginsburg, Axelrod, and Herman (1951) as well as the Career Pattern Study and the Psychology of Careers (Super, 1957; Super, 1969a) pioneered by Super and his colleagues began to construct an explanatory system of the tasks, factors, influences, and processes that influenced and mediated individual career development across the life span.

Treatment or Stimulus?

Perhaps the most important point made by Super's 1951 definition of vocational guidance is that vocational guidance can be construed in at least two different ways: (1) as a treatment condition or (2) as a stimulus variable (Crites, 1969, p. 22). These two conceptions are not mutually exclusive, but they do represent different perceptions of the needs of students, clients, or workers and of the time frame within which vocational guidance operates. These two types of vocational/career guidance may also be conceived as different ways of knowing. For example, as a vocational or career counselor one may use a diagnostic paradigm such as that advocated by Crites (1969), which includes three stages or elements: differential diagnosis, dynamic diagnosis, and decisional diagnosis. Differential diagnosis is really a normative approach. It rests on such information as those found in the taxonomies that follow. The differential diagnosis tries to find a way to classify and label the presenting career concern(s) brought to the counselor. For example, using the Williamson taxonomy that follows, is a particular client telling me that he or she has made no choice and does not know how to choose among available options, or is the person suggesting to me that he or she is experiencing an uncertain or an unwise choice? As the counselor discusses the client's career concerns, the examples of taxonomies given in the next pages represent different hypotheses about the client's concerns that can be explored and used as a gross classification of the issues to be dealt with and to which interventions can be addressed.

The second form of career diagnosis, the dynamic diagnosis, is focused on why the problem or career concern identified in the process of differential diagnosis has occurred. What have been the underlying factors, the etiology, that have shaped and caused the career concern?

The third form of diagnosis, the decisional diagnosis, essentially focuses on the client's ability to choose, to use the insights and interventions inherent in the first two forms of diagnosis—differential and dynamic—to create a plan of action.

It needs to be noted here that in career guidance and career counseling the term diagnosis is rarely, if ever, used. The term *diagnosis* stimulates thoughts of medical diagnosis, of counselor directiveness, of a major emphasis on the use of tests, inventories, and other forms of external criteria rather than collaboration between counselor and client, a psychological and internal view of career concerns and influences on them. The preferred terms in career counseling rather than diagnosis are *appraisal* or *assessment.* How one engages in that process will depend upon one's theoretical perspective, as examined in other parts of this book, but it will likely involve explicitly or implicitly the counselor raising three questions: What is the career concern or problem? What are the factors that have affected the evolution of this problem? Is the person able to choose and make a commitment to a plan of action? As the counselor addresses these three questions, a fourth one arises: Is this a situation in which a treatment or stimulus approach or both is appropriate?

Treatment: A Problem Orientation. If career vocational guidance or career counseling is seen as a treatment condition, it will be seen as problem oriented or, at least, as appropriate primarily at decision points or at other periods of transition when people are most vulnerable to career crises and discontinuity, and thus treatment will be restricted in time. In this sense, career vocational guidance and counseling will be viewed, either directly or indirectly, as responding to taxonomies of vocational problems or to difficulties in choice by applying certain techniques or knowledge to resolve them. In such a perspective, the career counselor is likely to define the difficulties experienced by persons with whom he or she works in ways similar to those proposed by Williamson, Bordin, Byrne, Robinson, Bordin and Kopplin; Crites, Campbell, and Cellini; or, more recently, by Lowman. These taxonomies of the career problems persons experience can be viewed chronologically.

Among the earliest of taxonomies, Williamson (1939) suggested that vocational problems can be described as:

1. No choice: Individuals cannot discriminate sufficiently among occupations to select one and commit themselves to it.
2. Uncertain choice: A choice has been made, but the person is uncertain about it.
3. Unwise choice: There is a disagreement between the individual's abilities or interests and the selected occupation.
4. Discrepancy between interests and aptitudes: There is disagreement in the type or amount of these two traits as they interact or should interact in defining choice. (p. 428)

Bordin (1946, p. 174), commenting on Williamson's problem categories, suggested that "the assignment of the individual's difficulties to one of these sets of classes of difficulties does not provide a basis for predictions of the relative success of different treatments." This observation led him to develop five other problem categories more psychologically oriented than those of Williamson:

1. Dependence
2. Lack of information
3. Self-conflict
4. Choice anxiety
5. No problem

Byrne (1958) expressed displeasure at the generalization to high school students from the college samples used by Williamson and Bordin. He suggested that the problems could more adequately be described as:

1. Immaturity in situation
2. Lack of problem-solving skill
3. Lack of insight
4. Lack of information
5. Lack of assurance
6. Domination by authority (p. 187)

Robinson (1963) suggested another modification of the Bordin diagnostic constructs into the following categories:

1. Personal maladjustment
2. Conflict with significant others
3. Discussing plans (instead of Bordin's no-problem category)
4. Lack of information about environment
5. Immaturity
6. Skill deficiency (p. 332)

In 1973, Bordin and Kopplin elaborated Bordin's early taxonomy to reflect motivational conflicts that bring clients, particularly college students, to vocational counseling. This scheme involves five basic categories, four of which are divided into subcategories of problem presentation. The categories are ordered to show an approximate structure of lesser to greater disturbance. Somewhat analogous to Tyler's (1961) paradigm of choice-versus-change counseling, discussed elsewhere in this book, Bordin and Kopplin suggest that categories A through C refer to persons who are primarily oriented to decision making, while categories D and E refer to persons who must first make changes in the self before engaging in decision making. The classification in paraphrased form is as follows:

A. Synthetic difficulties. The major problem is difficulty in synthesizing or achieving cognitive clarity for reasons reflected in the following subcategories:

    A_1 diverse interests
    A_2 restricted experience
    A_3 realistic obstacles

B. Identity problems. The major problem is associated with the formation of a viable self-concept or self-percept. Contributing factors might include the following:

    B_1 inappropriate sex model
    B_2 differentiation issues
    B_3 paralysis because of problems of integration of one's roots
    B_4 lack of identity
    B_5 unrealistic identity
    B_6 superimposed identity
    B_7 no model

C. Gratification conflicts. The client is blocked because of approach-avoidance conflicts in gratifications in available work identities.

D. Change orientation. The client is dissatisfied with personal characteristics that a vocational choice might help to change:

    D_1 developmental change with occupational representation
    D_2 therapeutic change in which person attempts to alter stable personality characteristics by adopting an occupational identity that represents desired characteristics

E. Overt pathology. The disturbance is so severe that a vocational focus is not feasible:

    E_1 choice possible
    E_2 choice impossible

F. Unclassifiable: Motivational conflict.

G. Unclassifiable: No motivational conflict.

In modifying Williamson's earlier classification structure, Crites (1981) identified eight vocational problem categories. He used measures of an individual's interests, aptitudes, and occupational choices as the bases for his classification. They include the following three categories and eight problem emphases:

- Adjustment
    - Adjusted
    - Maladjusted
- Indecision
    - Multipotential
    - Undecided
    - Uninterested
- Unrealism
    - Unrealistic
    - Unfulfilled
    - Coerced

Campbell and Cellini (1981) proposed a diagnostic classification of adult career problems that is related to developmental theories of career development and adult career problems. Although the full diagnostic taxonomy is provided in Chapter 2, for our purposes here, the four major problem categories and their major subcategories are identified without the presumed causal factors related to each. The major problem categories and subcategories are:

1.0 Problems in career decision making
    1.1 Getting started
    1.2 Information gathering
    1.3 Generating, evaluating, and selecting alternatives
    1.4 Formulating plans to implementing decisions
2.0 Problems in implementing career plans
    2.1 Characteristics of the individual
    2.2 Characteristics external to the individual
3.0 Problems in organization/institutional performance
    3.1 Deficiencies in skills, abilities, and knowledge

  - 3.2 Personal factors
  - 3.3 Conditions of the organizational/institutional environment
- 4.0 Problems in organizational/institutional adaptation
  - 4.1 Initial entry
  - 4.2 Change over time
  - 4.3 Interpersonal relationships

Finally, Lowman (1993) has proposed a first step toward a clinically useful taxonomy of work-related dysfunctions. This taxonomy is primarily directed toward the understanding of work problems of psychological origin: "psychological conditions in which there is a significant impairment in the capacity to work caused either by characteristics of the person or by an interaction between personal characteristics and working conditions" (p. 4). The taxonomy in abridged form includes three broad categories of concern:

- I. Determining the relation between psychopathology and work dysfunctions. Included here are determinations about whether such characteristics do or do not affect work performance and are or are not affected by work performance.
- II. Disturbance in the capacity to work.
  - A. Patterns of undercommitment
  - B. Patterns of overcommitment
  - C. Work-related anxiety and depression
  - D. Personality dysfunctions of work.
  - E. Life role conflicts
  - F. Transient, situational stress
  - G. Other psychologically relevant work difficulties
- III. Dysfunctional working conditions.

Lowman's book elaborates each of these categories and the subelements that compose the particular pattern. For example, under patterns of overcommitment are included obsessive-compulsive addiction to the work role (workaholism), Type A behavioral pattern, and job and occupational burnout. A further discussion of how these patterns and related perspectives can be used to consider mental health in the workplace and to counsel persons experiencing them is provided in Chapter 2.

While there are other taxonomies that can be cited, two recent approaches will suffice for our purposes here. One is by Peterson, Sampson, Reardon, and Lenz (undated) in the Career Center at Florida State University. These authors conceptualize individual differences in decision making in three groups: decided, undecided, or indecisive. Each of these categories have subsets of decision status by individual. For example, under the category of decided individuals, there are three different decision styles: Decided-Confirmation, Decided-Implementation, and Decided-Conflict Avoidance. Respectively, persons in the first group are able to specify a choice, but they want to confirm or clarify their choice and contrast it with other possible choices. In the second category are people able to specify a choice but who need assistance in executing the choice. In the third category are persons who have made a choice as a way of reducing their conflict and stress, although they tend to reflect characteristics of persons who are undecided or indecisive.

The second major category refers to persons described as undecided. Again there are three subcategories of persons seen as undecided: Undecided-Deferred Choice, Undecided Developmental, and Undecided-Multipotential. These are classes of decision making that, in turn, describe persons who are unable to specify a choice but they do not need to do so immediately. Therefore, they can defer the decision until a later point. The second class are persons who need to choose, are unable to commit to a choice, and who lack knowledge of self, occupations, or decision making. The final class in the undecided category are those who are undecided and multipotential. These are people with high levels of talents, multiple interests, and opportunities, who are essentially undecided because they have too many choices, too many things they can do, and thus find specifying one choice difficult.

The third category is indecisive persons. These are persons who typically have issues that prevent them from making a specific occupational choice because they have some form of maladaptive approach to problem solving, considerable anxiety, a lack of necessary information. These latter issues need to be addressed prior to focusing on commitment to a specific choice.

A second recent taxonomy of difficulties in career decision making is more empirically based than some of the other taxonomies described here. The latter tend to be descriptive or theoretical but not necessarily based on research findings. Gati, Krausz, and

Osipow (1996) have identified 44 difficulties in career decision-making, created the Career Decision Difficulties Questionnaire (CDDQ) to test the proposed taxonomy, and applied the questionnaire to two different cross-cultural samples: one Israeli and one American. The first sample consisted of 147 men and 112 women, ages 19 to 23, who were nearing the end of their military service. The second sample consisted of 186 men, 105 women, and 13 who did not identify gender, ages 17 to 23, at a large midwestern university in the United States. The resulting taxonomy included 10 scales representing subcategories of three major categories of career decision-making difficulties that occur prior to beginning the process of career decision making and during that process. The major category of career decision-making difficulties prior to beginning the process of career decision making is defined as *Lack of Readiness,* which is in turn divided into four subcategories of difficulties entitled *Lack of Motivation, Indecisiveness, Dysfunctional Myths,* and *Lack of Knowledge about Process (STEPS).* During the process of career decision making, two other broad categories of career decision-making difficulties are seen as occurring. The first category is *Lack of Information* about three subcategories: *self, occupations,* and *ways of obtaining information.* The second category is *Inconsistent Information* which is due to *unreliable information, internal conflicts,* and *external conflicts.* Each of the 10 scales underlying the three major categories of difficulties include items that relate to each subcategory of career decision-making difficulty. For example, under the subcategory Lack of Motivation, one of the four subscales subsumed by the major category, Lack of Readiness, three difficulties are identified: unwillingness to make a career decision, work is not perceived as the most important thing in life, and feeling that time will lead to the right career choice. Under the third category, *Inconsistent Information,* the subscale Internal Conflicts assesses examples of career decision-making difficulties including unwillingness to compromise, several equally attractive career alternatives, or dislike of accessible career alternatives.

As the content of the taxonomies presented here suggests, these classifications tend to vary according to their inclusion of decision theory, developmental, psychodynamic, or sociological descriptions of occupational or career problems. In most cases, an implied deficit of some type in the behavioral repertoire of the individual forms the basis on which the strategies for career counseling or career guidance or a specific treatment approach will be selected. In addition, each of these models assumes that the observed problem is likely to occur at a decision or transition point. Thus, it is further implied that career counseling or guidance will be effective as a post hoc response to a problem that is already present and that impedes the individual's progress to some new phase of life, that is, entry into the labor force, selection of a specific occupation, advancement in an occupation, and so forth.

The weaknesses of most of these classification systems lie in their descriptive rather than their predictive character. Typically, they tend not to be based on empirical findings about their validity but to evolve from theoretical and anecdotal explanations of career behavior as viewed through specific conceptual lenses. As such, the criteria they use frequently lack reliability from one rater to another, the cause or specific behavioral anchors lack precision as defining properties of the particular classifications, and the inclusiveness of the vocational problems represented or the populations described varies from one classification to another (Rounds & Tinsley, 1984). Nevertheless, such classifications of vocational or career problems have enriched the communications or language about the nature of and differences among such problem categories, created a pool of hypotheses useful to counselors in helping clients be more explicit about their concerns and dilemmas, and spurred the construction of psychometric instruments designed to measure the behaviors subsumed in those problem categories. However incomplete or primitive such classifications are, they are steps toward creating a science of vocational or career psychology and a matrix of presenting problem-treatment interactions.

Stimulus: A Developmental Orientation. Conceiving of career guidance or career counseling as a stimulus variable process requires a different set of assumptions from viewing it as treatment. As a stimulus variable, career guidance can be more effectively viewed longitudinally and developmentally. The time frame in which it operates depends partly on the setting of the program and partly on the characteristics of the students or adults progressing through the setting.

As a stimulus variable, career guidance or career counseling not only responds to existing problems but also aids in the acquisition of knowledge, attitudes, and skills through which one can develop the behaviors necessary to cope with decision points, to acquire an occupational identity, or to develop career maturity. In the diagnostic categories previously identified, career interventions were triggered by the presentation of the problem by the person to be assisted. Career interventions as stimulus, however, is more future oriented and developmental, facilitating through group processes, psychoeducational approaches, or systematic programs of activities, behaviors that anticipate choices and build career adaptability, maturity, and planning rather than reacting only to situations in which crises trigger action.

Career interventions conceived as a stimulus process fits well within any framework concerned with primary prevention. Indeed, the basic focus of career interventions as stimulus is educative, incorporating the philosophy and content of career models. The *raison d'être* of such an approach is the facilitation, indeed the maximization, of growth in career development rather than the repair of deficits or difficulties in career decision making.

Career Models Emerge

In addition to issues of treatment or stimulus, since Super's redefinition of vocational guidance in 1951, there has been a subtle but important shift from occupational to career models in the vocational guidance literature. The occupational model in which the primary focus was matching the characteristics of the individual to the requirements of jobs available was the primary emphasis before 1951. Obviously, its influence has been continually significant, but it has competed increasingly with a series of broader perspectives on choice spawned by the career model.

By definition, career embraces a longer time frame than does occupational choice. Indeed, the concept of career embraces prevocational activity such as the effects on students of educational programs and options as well as the post-vocational activity manifested by the retiree or the pensioner working part-time. Prime considerations in a career model are not the differences among occupations but rather the continuity or discontinuity in the individual's career development, the interactions of educational and occupational choices across time, and the sequence of occupations, jobs, and positions held.

Career models introduce several aspects into the concept of vocational guidance that are not apparent in the occupational model. One concerns developmental career guidance. In such an emphasis, the career development guidance practitioner is concerned not only with immediate choice of training or job, but also with intermediate and long-range goals and the relation of immediate choices to those goals. Thus, personal values, the clarity of the self-concept, personal planfulness, and exploratory behavior vis-à-vis choice options become important variables to be considered in career guidance. In addition, personal behaviors, attitudes, and different kinds of skills are seen as appropriately developed by career development practitioners if they are not present in the student's or adult's behavioral repertoire.

Such conceptions of vocational guidance, and subsequently career guidance, are concerned not only with an individual's potential performance on some set of occupational tasks but also with the attitudes and knowledge that facilitate or impede the choosing, learning, and using of such technical skills—what has been described elsewhere as general employability (Herr, 1984). More important, perhaps, a career model reinforces a view of vocational or career guidance as more than a set of services available at some specific decision point or for persons who, for some reason, are experiencing choice conflicts or work adjustment problems. Career models emphasize the role of career interventions in systematically educating students or adults to the knowledge, attitudes, and skills that will be required of them at future choice points, in planning their educational programs, in selecting and preparing them for work, and in helping them anticipate and prepare for career paths available to them within a workplace. This approach is in contrast to intervention only after it has been clearly established that particular persons have not acquired the necessary skills and behaviors and are now experiencing problems because of these deficits in their behavioral repertoire. (This is what has previously been described as a treatment approach.)

The use of career models in vocational guidance slowly began to elevate the concern for self-understanding to the same level of importance as occupational understanding or task mastery. In this view, the primary objectives of vocational guidance are seen as developing the individual's skills to make a free and informed choice of career and appropriately preparing for that career rather than for the needs of the labor market.

Wrenn (1964) summarized such a perspective well in this observation nearly four decades ago:

> *The planning for which the vocational counselor can be held responsible is planning for work satisfactions from both employed and nonemployed activity.... One way to suggest the new emphasis is to say the counselor helps the student to define goals, not merely to inventory capacities. And it is clear that these must be life goals, not occupational goals only. There must be a dovetailing of work in employed and nonemployed settings if life is to be meaningful to the majority of people.... It is imperative that vocational counselors accept responsibility for helping students see their work life whole. (p. 41)*

In the late 1950s and early 1960s, such perspectives were part of a significant period of growth in school counseling, spurred on by the National Defense Education Act and the constant need to reassess what goals and directions such services should include. This development also touched on the latter part of the dramatic period of change in counseling, spurred on by Carl Rogers's challenges to conventional clinical approaches, resulting in shifts to client-centered, nondirective techniques that deemphasized testing, prediction, and the use of information. Finally, this was the middle stage of the rise of career development theory and its major concern for the role of the person's self-concept as the stimulus for decision making and commitment to various occupational and life goals. Although each of these influences can be examined in great depth, suffice it to say that the interaction of these events and developments continued to be incorporated into the concepts of vocational guidance. With them came a continuing assimilation into perspectives on vocational guidance of those emphases previously seen as the concern only of educational or personal counseling.

Of major concern to the shape of vocational guidance and counseling during the 1960s were discussions of its relationship to the process of decision making and to the therapy process. Boy and Pine (1963) summarized many of the significant issues of the time as follows:

> *The proponents of "vocational guidance" state quite emphatically that the school counselor's first job is vocational counseling and that therapeutic counseling is purely secondary. Yet in the light of the Super, Roe, and Ginzberg theories of vocational development, with their stress on the significant role of the self-concept in the process of vocational development, how can vocational counseling be divorced from therapeutic counseling? If, as Super indicates, the process of vocational development is essentially that of developing and implementing a self-concept, can effective vocational counseling take place just through dispensing and discussing occupational information without considering the psychodynamics of the self-concept? If vocational counseling is a primary task, should not school counselors provide the student with the opportunity to reach new insights, to explore and see his self-concept, to develop and to implement it? (p. 225)*

Such broader and longer-term views of the purposes and content of vocational guidance affected not only perspectives on school counseling, but also perspectives on employment counseling as provided by the U.S. Employment Service. During the 1960s and 1970s, a number of observers contended that, whereas employment counseling is generally distinguished from other vocational counseling in that it is typically done with job applicants or employability program enrollees for limited purposes and for a limited time, a more comprehensive and professional role definition of employment counseling was needed in a bureaucratic government agency environment under frequent pressure for case closures, positive termination, and job placements (Darr, 1981). In response to the growing theoretical and process notions that were then moving vocational guidance and counseling toward career guidance and counseling, Sullivan (1970) suggested an enlarged and more developmental approach to employment counseling:

> *Through employment counseling, the client is assisted with self-exploration and vocational planning. The Employment Counselor assists the client to discover, evaluate, and synthesize his values, attitudes, and feelings, needs, and desires, motivation forces, self-concept, family and financial pressures, preferences for life style, physical capacities, aptitudes, school achievement, prior work history, skills, and interests. The client is assisted in formulating vocational questions, in exploring vocational alternatives, and in evaluating the possible consequences of various choices or decisions. The Employment Counselor furnishes personal, occupational, and environmental information to the client, as required, regarding his*

plans, choices, or problems. The client is encouraged to establish short-term reachable goals related to his interests and to develop concrete steps (supportive services, rehabilitation, education, training, stop-gap work try-outs, and employment) which would readily lead to such goals and result in fast concrete payoffs with respect to the goals. The Employment Counselor then helps the client to develop long-term vocational plans which are broken down into manageable goals, in a time scale that the client believes he can tolerate and at a level of difficulty which the client believes himself capable of accomplishing. (p. 127)

Such a perspective is more than a unidimensional approach to vocational guidance or counseling. It embodies a series of interventions and a developmental perspective consistent with what has come to be viewed as comprehensive career guidance.

COMPREHENSIVE CAREER GUIDANCE

By the late 1960s and early 1970s, the term *career guidance* was appearing in the professional literature almost as frequently as the term *vocational guidance.* The redefinitions and the paradigm shifts associated with the emerging term *career guidance* were creating new metaphors. Career guidance was being termed a lifestyle concept that embodied the need to combine work and leisure counseling (McDaniels, 1978), one that needed to address sex role differentiation and the reduction of sex bias (Hansen & Keierleber, 1978), and one devoted to the holistic development of a career-conscious individual (Gysbers & Moore, 1971, 1981). The implications for the goals of career guidance that emerged from such paradigm shifts were effectively summarized by Hansen (1981) as follows:

1. Career guidance needs to move from a focus strictly on jobs to a focus on life patterns.
2. Career guidance needs to help make clients aware of their own career socialization.
3. Career guidance needs to move from a focus on slotting individuals into what is (matching) to preparing them for the lifestyle choices and options of what might be.
4. Career guidance needs to move from a focus on occupational choice alone to the larger sphere of people's lives and the interface of the vocational and the personal.
5. Career guidance needs to help clients achieve role integration in rapidly changing societies.
6. Career guidance needs to help individuals move beyond the stereotypic choices women and men have made in the past to expanding the range of options they are willing to consider and choose. (p. 28)

Such shifts in goals and terminology were not simply semantic but implied shifts in the role and the purpose of the counselor. Career guidance, as a broadened interpretation of vocational guidance, began forcefully to communicate the importance of an emphasis on the following major organizing themes for career guidance:

1. Efforts to develop decision making: Career guidance is concerned with helping students and adults develop decision-making skills as well as define, get, and use information appropriate to different choices.
2. Concern for the self-concept: Decisions and plans express the self-concept of the chooser. It is necessary that career guidance help the student or adult achieve self-understanding before or as a part of occupational awareness. Thus, information about occupations needs to go beyond the facts of salaries or work content to include their possible relation to aspirations and values or their potential ability to provide satisfaction for psychosocial needs.
3. Concern for lifestyles, values, leisure: Education, leisure, occupation, or career all interact to create or influence a lifestyle. The way the student or adult comes to deal with such an issue is related to the clarity and characteristics of personal values. Career guidance, then, cannot attend to occupational choice without examining the educational or personal/social implications that it holds—its relation to personal values—in both the present and the future.
4. Free choice: Career guidance is directed not to specific subsets of choices (e.g., vocational education) alone within a larger category (e.g., educational curricula) but to the range of choices available, the personal characteristics and aspirations to which these choices need to relate, and the likely outcomes of specific choices. Their validity as choices lies in the comparative advances

each has over other possible choices in relation to specific personal criteria. Indeed, the safeguarding of individual integrity argues against any form of prescriptive guidance or counseling that coerces the person into pursuing specific careers or other life patterns.

5. Individual differences: Fundamental to a free society is an acknowledgement of differences in individual talents, opportunities by which the range of these talents can be identified and nurtured, and the freedom of each individual to develop and express these talents in a unique way.
6. Flexibility and the ability to cope with change: Career guidance must help persons consider contingency planning, multiple routes to goals, flexibility in goals, and other notions of tentativeness as methods of coping with rapid change in social and occupational conditions.

By the 1980s, these concepts had become almost commonplace attributions to the purposes of career guidance and to career counseling. As suggested previously, career guidance was in a dynamic state, adding new concepts, new populations, and new techniques. It was becoming increasingly *comprehensive.*

Comprehensive career guidance has come to mean many different things in the professional literature. *Comprehensive* has sometimes been used to mean programmed, preplanned, or systematic. At other times, it has meant longitudinal—articulated over an extended period of time, whether from kindergarten to grade twelve in the public schools; during the four years of college or university; over the six months spent in a halfway house or rehabilitation facility; or across the period of one's tenure within a particular firm, business, or government agency. At still other times, *comprehensive* has referred to a developmental content designed to equip consumers of career guidance with the attitudes, knowledge, and skills by which they can anticipate, plan, and act on a variety of career-related tasks. Finally, *comprehensive* has been used to connote the many ways intervention in career development can occur without confining counselors to a one-to-one framework.

But career guidance as comprehensive means something else, perhaps more important than any of its other meanings. Comprehensive career guidance can also mean inclusive, for all people regardless of gender, age, race, or other characteristics. To these ends, in the 1970s, 1980s, and through the end of the twentieth century, theory building has increasingly focused its attention on the career development of women and of minority populations, not only on men. The works of Astin (1984), Betz and Hackett (1986), Farmer (1985), Farmer and associates (1997), Gilligan (1982), Hansen (1981), Hansen and Minor (1989), and Leong (1995), among others, have been instrumental in describing the differential influences on the career development of and the need for career interventions tailored to the career patterns and the career behavior of women, men, and minority groups. The specifics of these perspectives will be discussed elsewhere in the book.

Needs for Career Guidance and Counseling: A Lifespan Perspective

A major implication of comprehensive career guidance is its applicability to many kinds of adult populations. As the evolution of vocational guidance to career guidance suggests, the traditional forms of vocational guidance have frequently been focused on adolescents and often been delivered within the school. Increasingly, the practice of career development—career guidance programs, career counseling, career services—is being addressed to the total spectrum of adult populations, including retirees. These programs are occurring in community centers, in institutions for postsecondary education, in government agencies, and in business and industry.

Under the impetus of an expanding knowledge of adult development, it has become obvious that in addition to the need to accommodate the special needs of women, racial and ethnic minorities, and handicapped populations, the special requirements of adults must also be responded to within the practice of career development. This perspective does not disparage the significant assistance provided by rehabilitation agencies, employment services, or college career development and placement centers. Rather, it suggests that however good these agencies are, they frequently deal only with visible or severe problems of occupational choice or adjustment. In many cases, their interactions with clients are short-lived and limited to points of crisis rather than to career planning and to helping an individual come to terms with the future. Such agencies often cannot deal with the person who is experiencing job alienation or dissatisfaction in subtle and quietly agonizing ways or the college student who views college as an end in itself rather than as an intermediate career decision. Neither can such agencies deal in depth with the woman who has been out of the labor force before her children were in school and now does not know where to seek information about starting a career. There are many such persons, but they are often invisible.

As people age, they reassess choices and plot the possibilities of still attaining certain idealized goals, sometimes with anxiety and despair. As opportunities for advancement decrease, persons in their forties and fifties frequently take stock of how their achievements measure up to the self-concepts around which they had organized their self-esteem. If what they believe they have achieved falls significantly below what they expected from life, they may seek to change career patterns if time and circumstances still permit. In other instances, such opportunities may no longer be available to them, and they will have to accept the notion that it is too late for them to accomplish those visions on which their view of personal success rested. In either situation, career guidance, career counseling, or other career interventions are needed. In addition to these persons, many other persons will be at a stage of career deceleration as a way of anticipating retirement. Until fairly recently, little attention has been given to the career needs of such persons for assistance in considering volunteer work, the management of free time, part-time work, continuing education, and self-concept adjustments in which full-time work is no longer a central focus of identity.

Some observers report that a great many members of the work force are dissatisfied with the work they perform, but they do not know how to extricate themselves from it. Such persons need emotional support while they consider acting on their mid-career crises, and they need help to sort out the costs and benefits of executing the changes they are considering. Often such persons have been out of the educational mainstream long enough to have virtually no knowledge of training or career options currently available.

Some studies have suggested that as many as 40 percent of the American adult population is coping inadequately with typical life problems (for example, getting work and holding a job, buying things, managing economic life, and parenting). Available evidence suggests that such persons need to experience skill-building approaches that are organized around the life crisis they are facing.

Some of the adults who need to be served by the practice of career development will have multiple problems of substance abuse, marital discord, child abuse, lack of transportation, or inadequate financial or nutrition management skills that need to be treated in multidimensional or "comprehensive" ways. To deal only with such persons' economic needs and to assume that all the other consequences of unemployment will take care of themselves is unrealistic and inappropriate. Therefore, programs of career intervention for such persons will need to interface more effectively with other agency programs in collaborative efforts to give the problems of work and social adaptation simultaneous attention.

Most contemporary adults had little opportunity as adolescents to assess their own characteristics or to plan ways by which their values and goals could be achieved via various alternatives available to them. In line with the rationale of early perspectives on vocational guidance, it was assumed that choosing an occupation or, indeed, a college to enter marked the end of the need for assistance by a counselor. As a result, many adults continue throughout life unaware of their potentialities or preferences, often experiencing a vague but gnawing disaffection with what they are now doing or what the future may hold. In many instances, the career choices they made were random and often shallow commitments to those occupations or educational experiences that were available or visible at a time when they had to choose. Having never experienced the use of available exploratory resources, many such persons now experience an information deficit. They simply do not know what options are available, how to access them, or how to identify them.

A variety of national and local surveys report that adults would like to have or to have had more opportunities for career guidance and career counseling than has been available to them. For example, in 1989 a telephone survey of adults was conducted by the Gallup Organization for the National Occupational Information Coordinating Committee and the National Career Development Association (National Occupational Information Coordinating Committee, 1990). The survey found that nearly two-thirds of American adults would seek more information about career options if they were starting their careers over again, with African Americans (79 percent) and Hispanics (75 percent) showing the greatest interest in additional career data, followed by a majority of whites (63 percent). Only four out of ten working adults followed a definite plan in mapping out their careers, with college graduates (62 percent) more likely than high school graduates (32 percent) to plan a career. Thirty percent got started through a series of chance circumstances (18 percent) or took the only job that was available (12 percent), and 23 percent were influenced by family and friends.

Twenty-seven percent of African Americans said they took the only jobs that were available to them, compared to 19 percent of Asians, 17 percent of Hispanics, and 10 percent of whites. Twenty-seven percent of all respondents said that they needed additional assistance in finding information about jobs, with African Americans reporting the highest need (44 percent) and whites the least (25 percent) among ethnic groups. Fifty-three percent of the respondents said public high schools are not providing the training in job-seeking skills for students who are not going to college, and 40 percent said high schools are not providing enough help to students to choose careers.

The survey further found that an estimated 12.5 million U.S. adults (7 percent of the adult population) needed help in 1989 in selecting, changing, or getting a job. Nineteen percent of Asians and 15 percent of African Americans reported that they needed assistance in the labor market. For whites, the figure was 6 percent, and for Hispanics 8 percent.

Equally important are the results involving relationships between career development and mental health (discussed later in this book). Twenty-five percent of the respondents said job stress or pressure had interfered with their off-the-job relationships; 20 percent said job stress had affected their ability to do their jobs.

The findings for the 1989 Gallup survey essentially parallel those of an earlier survey on career development by the Gallup Organization in 1987 (Gallup Organization, 1987). In the 1987 data, however, somewhat fewer (about 10.8 million employed workers) reported the need for help in selecting, changing, or obtaining a job. About one in three of the respondents (32.7 percent) reported that they had gone to no source for help or advice in career development. Those respondents who did seek help with their career development (41.2 percent) typically sought help through such self-directed activities as library visits, reading classified ads, taking interest inventories, or some combination of these options. Fewer than one in five (17.2 percent) respondents reported that they had sought assistance from school or college counselors, and fewer than 9 percent indicated that they had used publicly available job service counselors. About half of all respondents (51.1 percent) believe that most adult Americans do not know how to interpret and use information to make intelligent career decisions. Significantly more college graduates (66.7 percent) believe this than do high school graduates (46 percent).

In summarizing the broad implications of the 1987 Gallup poll data, Lester and Frugoli (1989) suggest that among the many findings important to career counselors four were particularly significant:

1. There is a strong need for and interest in career information on the part of both youth and adults.
2. Individuals are extremely interested in career planning.
3. There is a perception that individuals need help in getting career information, and many need help in using such information.
4. There is a need to target career information to the noncollege bound (p. 69).

Essentially the same pattern of findings from Gallup Poll data collected in 1980 reported by Lester and Frugoli were reaffirmed by the analysis of Hoyt and Lester of 1993 Gallup Poll data reported in 1995. Among the major findings reported by Hoyt and Lester (1995) are the following:

- "Racial differences continue to operate as a deterrent to equity of career development opportunities for Black as compared to White adults in the United States" (p. 74).
- "Significant differences in career development exist among adults with various kinds of educational experiences. Career development and type/level of education attained are definitely related for most persons" (p. 53).
- "Career development needs exist, to a significant degree, among adults in all age categories" (p. 88).
- "A high priority needs to be placed on meeting the career development needs of persons who drop out of four-year colleges/universities prior to receiving a degree" (p. 93).

- "Special attention must be provided to those youth who either (a) drop out of high school or (b) seek to enter the labor market with only a high school education" (p. 94).
- "The need for greater employer involvement in career development continues to be sizable" (p. 93).

In 1999, a fourth Gallup Poll was conducted in collaboration with the National Career Development Association. Many of its findings about work in America were remarkably consistent with those reported in 1993 and 1989. Two broad themes that were different in the 1999 survey were the effects of globalization and of workplace technology and its demands. Both of these factors are beginning to be significant in their influence on workers perspectives about their jobs. Selected 1999 findings included:

- Between 9 and 10 percent of all adults report that they annually need help in career planning and making a career change. The current civilian labor force in the United States as of 2000 was approximately 140 million persons, of whom 134,240,000 people were actually employed. Therefore, 10 percent of this number represents between 13 and 14 million persons each year who need career guidance or career counseling. This is especially true in the age groups up to age 40. Important questions are how many of these persons are actually being served? By whom?
- Seven in ten adults report that if they were starting over, they would try to get more information about the job and the career options open to them than they got the first time. These data tend to support other perceptions that suggest that many other people are swept into jobs, not because they have explored them on the basis of available information, but because the jobs are there and they enter them with relatively little planning or thought. Often people remain in the jobs they enter early in their careers because of many factors causing such inertia: family obligations; fear of change; a lack of information about what else might be available; a lack of information about their personal characteristics or of the elasticity, the relevance, of their competencies to other jobs.
- Some 42 percent of the adults reported that their most frequent source of career help were friends or relatives to help them select, change, or get a job. Some 47 percent of the respondents indicated that they would seek a counselor to help them with these issues.
- When asked about sources the respondents have ever used about jobs or careers, the most frequently cited sources were newspapers, magazines, and television (42 percent); friends, relatives, and associates (35 percent); about 16 percent used a career information center in a community college or university, and about 12 percent used a career site on the Internet or in a public library. The latter was more true of the 18-to-40 age groups.
- One in five adults (21 percent) reported visiting a counselor or other career specialist to learn about possible career choices. Most who report seeing a counselor do so either in high school or in college. One in eight (13 percent) saw a high school counselor and 31 percent saw a counselor at a community college. These data suggest that 80 percent of the adult respondents have never seen a counselor and 87 percent of high school graduates never saw a counselor. The question is why not? How can this situation be improved? These findings seem to suggest that there are serious needs to consider the evenness of the deployment and access to counselors.
- Some 41 percent of employed adults report that they started in their job or career through a conscious choice and plan; 59 percent did not. Deliberate planning was more characteristic of those with a college education than of those of fewer years of education. The primary influences on the plans made were friends and associates (18 percent) or parents and other relatives (10 percent). Only 2 percent said they were influenced by school, college, or career counselors and 3 percent by a counselor, job/career specialist, or placement office in a public service or job training program.

The presence of career education programs, comprehensive career guidance programs, and a broader range of career interventions and career services today may alleviate some of the problems cited in the Gallup reports among tomorrow's adult populations. But because such programs are not universally available and differ in quality, and because the population is mobile, they cannot totally eliminate such needs. Career counselors and other career guidance specialists in the future will need to provide a shifting blend of preplanned and spontaneous on-demand responses to the various consumer groups with whom they will deal.

The need for career guidance or career counseling is not confined to adults. Students in elementary and secondary schools as well as those in colleges give evidence of such needs.

National reports suggest that such needs for career guidance among secondary school students remain unmet. For example, the National Commission on Secondary Vocational Education (1985) states:

> *Inadequate student knowledge subtly but formidably constrains student access to vocational education. Students and parents need to be accurately informed about what vocational education is, how it relates to their personal and career goals, and how it can be used to help them achieve their goals. One does not choose what one knows little about or is constrained from choosing by unexamined social attitudes.... We need comprehensive career guidance programs that will provide this information and remove some of the subtle status distinctions involving vocational education. Comprehensive guidance means counseling that is available to all students, covering all subjects, leading to all occupations. (p. 10)*

The need for comprehensive career guidance among secondary school students is not confined to those enrolled in or choosing vocational education. This need spans the spectrum of student subgroups. For example, the College Entrance Examination Board (Commission on Pre-College Guidance and Counseling, 1986) has stressed the need for strengthened school career guidance programs for economically and socially disadvantaged students who are potentially college bound. The Business Advisory Committee of the Education Commission of the States (1985), in a national report dealing with the growing problem of alienated, disadvantaged, disconnected, and other at-risk youth, recommends "new structures and procedures for effecting the transition from school to work or other productive pursuits.... Young people today need more and better guidance than ever before" (p. 26). The report goes on to cite the need for coordinated programs, including career counseling, financial assistance, summer jobs, cooperative education options, and role models if such at-risk youth are to be reconnected to schooling and to work. The Research and Policy Committee of the Committee for Economic Development (1985), in a major report dealing with business and the public schools, strongly recommended that schools provide, among other emphases, exploratory programs to assist in career choice, job search, and general employability skills (for example, how to behave in an interview and get to work on time) and employment counseling (p. 31). The National Alliance of Business (1984), in a major analysis of the nation at work, particularly relationships between education and the private sector, has argued for more school-to-work transition programs including job placement assistance, career counseling, cooperative career information activities with business, and counseling about vocational-technical program alternatives to college degree programs (p. 8).

The Commission on Workforce Quality and Labor Market Efficiency supported by the U.S. Department of Labor (1989) was empowered to consider the challenges of what is considered a workforce crisis in the United States as demographic trends, technological change, and increased international competition create shortages of skilled workers and an excess of unskilled workers. Among its strong recommendations was that attention be paid to the dynamics of the school-to-work transition, with state employment security agencies and private industry councils establishing school-based employment services with direct connections to employers. The report encourages employers, both small and large, to provide information on job openings and to consider filling vacancies with recent high school graduates. The intent is that students be provided with evidence that the system works for those who have the necessary skills. Such a recommendation strongly argues that career guidance in schools must not only be active in educating students for choice, but also be directly involved with concrete steps to help place students in community jobs as an important aspect of their effective transitions from school to work.

The William T. Grant Foundation Commission on Work, Family and Citizenship (1988), in its report *The Forgotten Half,* has advocated fulfilling the needs of students not bound for college, for whom career guidance and other services are unevenly available throughout the United States. In particular, this report has given strong emphases to school, parent, and community cooperation in ensuring programs necessary for the effective transition of these students to work. Among the specific areas emphasized would be significantly expanded career information and counseling, career information centers, programs to train parents as career educators, and the involvement of community mentors and community-based organizations in supporting efforts to improve counseling and career orientation.

Together, these reports and polls continue to give evidence that certain needs for career guidance and counseling are yet unmet and that both panels of distinguished observers and the public at large want the schools to provide opportunities and services by which the career development of America's youth will be strengthened.

These important national reports of the 1980s laid a foundation for legislative, research, and conceptual responses to the need for more comprehensive career services for adolescents in high school and in the transition to work. For example, in the 1990s, there were several major pieces of federal legislation adopted by the U.S. Congress that were intended to address the career development needs of adolescents and adults and the impact of such legislation continues to make an impact in the first decade of the twenty-first century. Such legislative actions included the School to Work Opportunities Act in 1994, the Carl D. Perkins Vocational and Technology Education Amendments of 1998, and the Workforce Investment Act of 1998. Each of these acts addressed the importance of providing transitional services, including the stronger linkage of schools and employees, for students negotiating the passage from school to employment. Each of these acts has provided for career interventions available for youth and adults and for increasing the access of youth and adults to federal job training and education programs and to career services, regardless of income or employment status, whether disadvantaged youth, adults, or dislocated workers. Indeed, the Workforce Investment Act of 1998 created one-stop centers around the nation that included the provision of such core services as:

- Initial assessment of skills, aptitudes, abilities, interests, and needs for service
- Job search and placement assistance, including career counseling when appropriate
- Labor market and other information to support decision making, including job listings and the skills necessary to obtain these jobs, local occupation in demand and their skill requirements, the availability of support services, and information on the performance of authorized training providers
- Follow-up services, including counseling, for individuals placed in employment

These types of federal initiatives have been buttressed by a growing number of innovative uses of the Internet to disseminate national information about educational and occupational opportunities. A final observation is that these federal legislative initiatives have supported directly or indirectly comprehensive career guidance programs. In turn, they have spawned research about the impact of such programs. For example, Lapan, Gysbers, and Sun (1997) found that students in schools with more fully implemented guidance programs, including career guidance components, were more likely to report that they had earned higher grades, their education was better preparing them for their future, their school made more career and college information available to them, and their school had a more positive climate. Contemporary views of career guidance suggest that it is more than a set of activities and services; it is a systematic program aimed at specific outcomes (Gray & Herr, 2000).

Finally, there are major needs for career services in postsecondary education. Studies of graduate and undergraduate students continually indicate that a major problem, and perhaps the most prevalent problem, involves vocational choice and career planning. Research throughout the 1970s and 1980s systematically supports the view that at least one-half of America's college-going population feels a need for assistance with career planning, career choice or both (Kramer, Berger, & Miller, 1974; Snyder, Hill, & Derksen, 1974; Weissberg et al., 1982; Williams et al., 1973), and that these findings are also true of community college populations, international students (Walter-Samli & Samli, 1979), men and women in engineering and the sciences (Cooper & Robinson, 1987), and returning adult students (Griff, 1987).

The following two examples illustrate typical findings of these studies. In the first study, 1625 students at the University of Georgia were queried about their academic, career, and personal needs (Weissberg et al., 1982). A greater percentage of students expressed career development needs than either academic or personal needs. For example, more than 80 percent of the students wanted to explore job opportunities related to their majors and obtain work experience in a career area, 77 percent wanted to develop job-seeking skills, and 72 percent wanted to learn how to prepare for their careers. Over half said they would like to explore their career interests, values, and abilities; obtain information; talk to a career counselor about career plans; and learn how occupations can affect their future life.

The second study (Healy & Reilly, 1989) considered the career needs of 1540 women and 1386 men from ten community colleges in California. The researchers divided the student sample by age and gender and assessed their career needs across seven categories: (1) knowing more about interests and abilities; (2) understanding and deciding on career goals; (3) becoming more certain of career plans; (4) exploring careers related to interests and abilities; (5) selecting courses relevant to career goals; and (6) developing job-finding skills. They found that all age cohorts from 17–19 through 41–50 and both sexes reported at least minor needs in each category, with major needs in each category more likely among younger students. The lowest needs for the older students were in deciding on career goals, becoming more certain of plans, and obtaining jobs, whereas their highest needs were in exploring jobs related to talents and interests and selecting courses related to goals. Women of all ages reported more need to become certain about their career plans and men a greater need to obtain a job. Collectively, these studies and the many others available make clear the need for career guidance and counseling services in postsecondary institutions—technical, two-year, and four-year. They also affirm that such needs pertain to younger and older students, to traditional and reentry women, and to virtually every segment of the postsecondary population as well as the tendency of many of these populations to decide on careers earlier and more specifically than before (Keller, Piotrowski, & Rabold, 1990). An emerging trend for career counselors in higher education is to help college students understand the importance of and acquire skills related to globalism—cross-cultural competencies, a foreign language facility, internships in international agencies and corporations, and participation in study-abroad programs (College Placement Council/Rand Corporation, 1994).

Comprehensive career guidance programs have come to serve all elements of the population—children, youth, and adults—in formal educational settings, in a wide range of community agencies, and in business and industry. As the need for and the responses to career guidance have become more comprehensive, the need for clarity about the meanings of key concepts in career guidance and career counseling has grown. In the next sections some of these concepts are reviewed.

CAREER COUNSELING

Although the terms *vocational* or *career guidance* and *counseling* often have been used interchangeably, they do not mean the same thing to all authors. The term *guidance* tends to be used more broadly than *counseling* and is likely to embrace a larger range or series of activities than does the term *counseling.* Indeed, counseling is frequently seen as only one of the functions by which guidance objectives are met. *Guidance* is also a term that has historically been identified with schools rather than with community agencies, private practitioners, or workplaces. As the provision of career services has moved from a primary locus in the schools to noneducational settings with increasing frequency, the term *career counseling* has also been used more commonly than the term *guidance.*

Spokane (1991) has avoided the dichotomy of career guidance or career counseling by using the term *career intervention.* In his view, "Career interventions can be defined broadly as any direct assistance to an individual to promote more effective decision making, or more narrowly focused, intensive counseling to help resolve career difficulties" (p. 22).

As theory and research on career behavior have matured, they have acknowledged both the complexity of influences on and the psychological characteristics of career choice and adjustment throughout the life span. This development has given credence to career counseling as a therapeutic modality that goes beyond dispensing and discussing information and to the inseparability of career and personal counseling. Crites (1981) has suggested that as insights from client-centered and psychodynamic approaches have been applied to career counseling, choice problems are viewed as essentially personality problems. Therefore, the assumptions that guide the provision of career counseling need to be considered in relation to personal adjustment counseling or psychotherapy.

Crites uses the term *career counseling* to refer specifically to an *interpersonal* process focused on assisting an individual to make an appropriate career decision: "Ideally, it involves active participation in the decisional process, not simply passive-receptive input of information" (p. 11). For Crites, career counseling is both more and less than personal adjustment counseling or psychotherapy. "Vocational and personal problems are different, but they do interact. Thus, career counseling often embraces personal counseling but it goes beyond this to explore and replicate the client's role in the main area of life—the world of work" (p. 11).

Crites (1981) identifies five propositions to support his perspective that "comprehensive career counseling, synthesized from the best models and methods of career counseling, also incorporates the best from theories of counseling and psychotherapy and goes considerably beyond them" (p. 14). His five propositions are as follows:

1. The need for career counseling is greater than the need for psychotherapy.
2. Career counseling can be therapeutic.
3. Career counseling should follow psychotherapy.
4. Career counseling is more effective than psychotherapy.
5. Career counseling is more difficult than psychotherapy. (pp. 14–15)

Rounds and Tinsley (1984) support Crites's viewpoint in their assumption that:

> *Career intervention is simply a form of psychological intervention designed to affect vocationally related feelings, attitudes, cognitions, and behaviors. Thus, it is a form of psychotherapy and should be viewed as a method of behavior change and tied to psychotherapy theory.... We believe that a conceptual shift in which career interventions are understood as psychological interventions (and career counseling as psychotherapy) would foster advances in the understanding of vocational behavior change processes. (pp. 138–39)*

Although these propositions are supported by considerable empirical data as well as interesting conceptualizations, other theorists tend to view career counseling somewhat differently.

Brown (1985) pushes the interaction of career counseling and personal counseling even further than Crites. Brown, who defines career counseling "as the process of helping an individual select, prepare for, enter, and function effectively in an occupation" (p. 197), views career counseling "as a viable intervention with clients that have rather severe emotional problems." In particular, Brown distinguishes between clients who have intrapsychic (cognitive or emotional) problems and those who work in a nonsupportive, stress-producing environment that may cause symptoms that appear to be intrapsychic mental health disorders rather than functions of poor person-work environment fit. Obviously, how the counselor makes such distinctions will determine whether the therapeutic approach focuses on intrapsychic changes, as in personal counseling and psychotherapy, or on altering the work environment or choosing another work environment through career counseling. Such a view obviously extends both the range of problems likely to be addressed by career counseling and the settings in which career counseling should be offered.

In their 1991 book, Brown and Brooks offered the following definition of career counseling:

> *Career counseling is an interpersonal process designed to assist individuals with career development problems. Career development is that process of choosing, entering, adjusting to and advancing in an occupation. It is a lifelong process that interacts dynamically with other life roles. Career problems include, but are not limited to, career indecision and undecidedness, work performance, stress and adjustment, incongruence of the person and work environment, and inadequate or unsatisfactory integration of life roles with other life roles (e.g., parent, friend, citizen). (p. 5)*

Central to the view of Brown and Brooks is whether individuals possess cognitive clarity, which they define as "the ability to objectively assess one's own strengths and weaknesses and relate the assessment to environmental situations" (p. 5). If career counselors determine that clients are not simply undecided, but rather are experiencing indecisiveness, the equivalent of a deficit in cognitive clarity, Brown and Brooks suggest that "appropriate action may require postponement of consideration of career related matters until cognitive clarity is attained" (p. 6). Thus, moderate mental health problems may require interventions other than career counseling, and temporary crises *as well as* temporary or long-term stress require personal rather than career counseling. In some instances, cognitive clarity concerns can be handled while career development concerns are being addressed; in other cases, the counselor must first concentrate on the factors related to the lack of cognitive clarity or refer the client for personal counseling or what other theorists would define as psychotherapy.

In some contrast to those observers who contend that career counseling is a form of psychotherapy, Spokane (1991) views career counseling as a particular type of career intervention that should be distinguished from psychotherapy. He suggests that there have been misapplications of psychotherapy to career situations. He cites four critical characteristics that distinguish career problems from personal or interpersonal problems:

1. "The social environment forces adjustments in individual career aspirations and impedes sharp changes in choice patterns" (p. 7).
2. "The principle of congruence (person-environment fit) is considered in some way in nearly all theories of career development" (p. 7).
3. "The public has come to expect a special career intervention technology of interest inventories and computer interventions that is independent of most theory positions and results in a more structured and predictable course of intervention than is generally the case in psychotherapy" (pp. 7–8).
4. "Career development proceeds both continuously and discontinuously, and requires certain critical choices at a predictable number of transition points (e.g., high school graduation), as well as the continuous formation of a vocational identity through a series of small but serial choices (Osipow, 1983)" (p. 8).

The sum of Spokane's view suggests that although career counseling overlaps psychotherapy as a dyadic intervention, the extent of overlap is still an open question. Certainly, career counseling is not simply psychotherapy as traditionally practiced, nor are career problems simply personal or interpersonal problems. He further suggests that other career interventions bear little similarity to psychotherapy.

Zunker (1986a) tends to take a broader view of the processes included in career counseling than do Crites, Brown, and Brooks or Spokane. In his view, career counseling tends to embrace components or strategies that differ for diverse populations. For example, according to Zunker, career counseling for adults in career transition would include seven components or strategies: experience identification, interest identification, skills identification, value and needs identification, education/training planning, occupational planning, and finally the development of a life learning plan (pp. 236–248). Career counseling for women would include such components or strategies as job search skills, working climate, lifestyle skills, and support and follow-up (pp. 262–268). Within his conception of career counseling, Zunker uses broad terminology that others might define as more guidance than counseling. In fact, he is talking about the broader definition of career intervention as used by Spokane (1991). His attempt to wed the special characteristics of different populations to the treatments or strategies they receive offers a useful perspective.

Whether one argues that career counseling is a form of psychotherapy, is more important than psychotherapy, or is composed of processes that go beyond and are uniquely different from psychotherapy, there seems to be little evidence that career theorists and researchers are content to view career counseling as isolated from personal counseling or the content of career counseling as intellectual, rational, and unaffected by emotional crises of personal identity, family concerns, and related issues. Krumboltz (1993), for example, has stated emphatically that "career and personal counseling are inextricably intertwined. Career problems have strong emotional components... when we discover the complex circumstances that are interwoven into our clients' problems, it becomes almost impossible to categorize any given problem as either 'career' or 'personal'" (p. 143). Betz and Corning (1993) have argued that career and personal counseling should not be viewed as different types of counseling because: "(a) the holistic philosophy of counseling emphasizes helping 'whole' persons whose lives contain many important and meaningful roles and activities, including among others, work or career and love and friendship relationships; (b) recent research on the implications of gender and race for career development further demonstrates the inseparability of our 'career' and 'personal lives'; and (c) there are numerous commonalities in the 'career' and 'personal counseling process'" (pp. 137, 138).

Super (1993) has suggested that there are really "different kinds of counseling, situational and personal, and that these are not dichotomous but rather on a continuum" (p. 132). He further elaborates the point to suggest that situational counseling has "subspecialties that focus on differing types of situations (career, family, etc.), and personal counseling focuses on individuals whose problems are based primarily in their own approach to and coping with situations, not on factors in the situations they encounter." In this perspective, these two positions—situational and personal—are really extremes on a continuum (p. 135), and the best counselors are those who have sufficient training and flexibility to help a counselee deal with whatever combination of developmental and adjustment problems he or she confronts (p. 136).

In Figure 1.1 Herr has constructed a potential continuum of career counseling emphases by using the content of the National Career Development Association's (1985) statement "What do career counselors do?" as well as the enlarging view of career counseling discussed in this chapter and elsewhere in the book. Consistent with Super's notion that career counseling is on a continuum of intervention foci, the figure also acknowledges the growing perspective that career and personal counseling must fuse if selected work adjustment problems are to be dealt with effectively. As portrayed in Figure 1.1, this fusion occurs on a continuum from choice, indecision, and situational concerns to change, indecisiveness, and personal concerns. Such a view suggests that different career counseling emphases have relevance for different career problems.

Such views are buttressed by the perspectives of Gysbers, Heppner, and Johnson (1998), who state:

> *Contrary to the classic stereotype, we believe that career counseling belongs in the general class of counseling because it has the same intrinsic characteristics and qualities that all forms of counseling possess. It differs from the rest of the class, however, because presenting problems often focus on work and career issues, and quantitative and qualitative assessment procedures and information are used more frequently. (p. 3)*

As indicated in the diverse perspectives identified here and as will be elaborated more fully in Chapter 14, there is not a commonly accepted definition of career counseling. The content of career counseling, the subject or focus of the interaction between the counselor and the client, can range across issues of ability and aspiration, learning about or implementing a model of career planning and choice, evaluating and acting on available options integrating work and other life roles, reassessing choices made and considering alternative career paths, developing strategies by which one can more effectively deal with the characteristics of a particular work environment or specific barriers within it, and examining and formulating goals by which to change intrapsychic attitudes or overt behaviors that have negatively affected the client's adjustment and progress within a workplace. Whichever of these issues is present in the interaction of the counselor and the client, counseling can be seen as a verbal process not primarily designed to change the person but rather to help him or her to identify and effectively use the resources available for coping with, and hopefully mastering, the educational, vocational, or personal/social challenges with which they are currently confronted. In these senses, whatever the precise theoretical framework used, career counseling emphasizes maximum collaborative efforts between the counselor and the client(s) to assist the client to clarify the current situation of concern (e.g., needs for career planning, choice among options, an untenable work environment, work-family issues), clarify his or her personal role within the situation and action goals to be pursued, identify information of relevance to the situation, and engage in a process of the development of insight about options and of problem solving with regard to a plan of action. Thus, career counseling is a purposeful relationship between a professional counselor and a counselee or client in which the specific processes and information used vary with the latter's needs and in which the counselor and counselee collaborate to facilitate self-clarification, evaluation of opportunities available, decision making, planning, and action by the counselee.

In some contrast to career guidance, which tends to be used to describe a program of group activities or interventions, including career counseling, to meet specific developmental goals, career counseling is much more likely to be seen as a dyadic or small-group process in which the focus is on the implications of information, perceptions, or anxieties unique to a particular client or counselee. Such a view tends to accord with that approved by the Board of Directors of the National Career Development Association (1991) in which "career counseling is defined as counseling individuals or groups of individuals about occupations, careers, life/career roles and responsibilities,

FIGURE 1.1 Perspectives on a Continuum of Career Counseling Foci

Choice **Indecision** Career Counseling			**Change** **Indecisiveness**
Educational Supportive Problem solving Conscious awareness	Enable the individual to identify and use resources available to help cope with life.	Fusion of career and personal counseling	Reconstructive focus on reframing past experiences. Reinterpreting ego identity and meaning. Deciding and acting upon ways to replot career pathways.
• Conduct individual and group counseling sessions to help clarify life/career goals. • Administer and interpret tests and inventories to assess abilities interest, etc., and to identify career options. • Encourage exploration activities through assignments and planning experiences. • Utilize career planning systems and occupational information systems to help individuals better understand the world of work.	• Provide opportunities for improving decision-making skills. • Assist in developing individualized career plans. • Teach job-hunting strategies and skills and assist in the development of resumes. • Help identify available career paths in a firm and its requirements for advancement. • Clarify with workers their marketable, transferable, elastic work skills and where they might be applied. • Assist in the identification of work personality, work competencies, and work goals.	• Help resolve potential personal conflicts on the job through practice in human relations skills. • Teach stress reduction, anger management, assertiveness, communication skills. • Help clients develop emotion-focused coping strategies to manage the emotions aroused by stressors and therefore maintain affective equilibrium. • Teach clients how to monitor stressors and engage in positive problem solving. • Assist in understanding the integration of work and other life roles. • Provide retirement planning. • Teach advancement strategies. • Help individuals to improve their fit with their work role. • Clarify elements of personal job satisfaction in relation to the organizational culture, behavioral expectations, and job demands.	• Provide support for persons experiencing job stress, job loss, career transition. • Provide opportunities for displaced workers to vent their anger and their feelings about personal concerns. • Provide problem-focused coping by which to actively change the self and develop a more satisfying work situation. • Provide job-separation counseling. • Provide referral for substance-abuse treatment. • Provide family counseling. • Assist in modifying irrational career beliefs. • Address underlying issues which lead to work dysfunctions.
Situational			**Personal**

Source: From "Career Counseling: A Process in Process," by E. L. Herr, 1997, *British Journal of Guidance and Counseling, 25*(1), Figure 1, p. 91. Copyright © 1997 by British Journal of Guidance and Counseling. Reprinted with permission.

career decision making, career planning, leisure planning, career pathing, and other career development activities (e.g., resume preparation, interviewing and job search techniques), together with issues or conflicts that individuals confront regarding their careers" (p. 1).

A Vocabulary for Career Counseling and Guidance

As suggested in the previous section, every occupation and profession has its own language system, its own way of using symbols to identify boundaries of domain, time, and space within which its work activities and prerogatives occur. So it is with career counseling and guidance. Key definitions allow the philosophical themes that give career guidance and career counseling a sense of coherence and common cause to be translated to a more operational level. These definitions address both the processes involved and the content or focus of such processes; while some of these concepts are now a quarter century or more old, they are the roots of much of the language in the field.

Career: Various conceptions of career exist, and observers tend to emphasize different aspects of the term. For example, McDaniels (1978) has contended that a career is more than one's job or occupation. It is a *lifestyle* concept that also involves a sequence of work or leisure activities in which one engages throughout a lifetime. Hansen and Keierleber (1978) argued for an expanded concept of career that includes helping individuals make choices related to work, education, and family as interrelated phenomena affecting role integration. Gysbers and Moore (1981) proposed that the term *life career development* be substituted for the term *career* in order to reflect self-development over the life span through the integration of the roles, settings, and events in a person's life. The NCDA defines *career* as the totality of work and leisure one does in a lifetime (Sears, 1982). Raynor and Entin (1982) maintain that:

> *A career is both a phenomenological concept and a behavioral concept. It is the link between what a person does and how that person sees himself or herself. A career consists of time-linked senses of self that are defined by action and its outcomes. A career defines how one sees oneself in the context of one's social environment—in terms of one's future plans, one's past accomplishments or failures, and one's present competences and attributes. (p. 262)*

In perhaps the most classic concept of career, Super (1976) has defined it as:

> *the course of events which constitutes a life; the sequence of occupations and other life roles which combine to express one's commitment to work in his or her total pattern of self-development; the series of remunerated and nonremunerated positions occupied by a person from adolescence through retirement, of which occupation is only one; includes work-related roles such as those of student, employee, and pensioner together with complementary avocational, familial, and civic roles. Careers exist only as people pursue them; they are person-centered. It is this last notion of careers, "they exist only as people pursue them," which summarizes much of the rationale for career guidance. (p. 4)*

In sum, then, careers are unique to each person and created by what one chooses or does not choose. They are dynamic and unfold throughout life. They include not only occupations but prevocational and postvocational concerns as well as integration of work with other roles: family, community, leisure.

Career Adaptability: Readiness for career decision making in adulthood.

Career Counseling: A largely verbal process in which a professional counselor and counselee(s) are in a dynamic and collaborative relationship, focused on identifying and acting on the counselees' goals, in which the counselor employs a repertoire of diverse techniques or processes, to help bring about self-understanding, understanding of the career concerns involved and behavioral options available, as well as informed decision making in the counselee, who has the responsibility for his or her own actions.

Career Development: The total constellation of psychological, sociological, educational, physical, economic, and chance factors that combine to shape the career of any given individual over the life span (Sears, 1982); those aspects of an individual's experience that are relevant to personal choice, entry, and progress in educational, vocational, and avocational pursuits; the process by which one develops and refines such characteristics as self-identity and career identity, planfulness, and career maturity. The lifelong behavioral processes and the influences on them that lead to one's work values, choice of occupation(s), creation of a career pattern, decision-making style, role integration, self-identity and career identity, educational literacy, and related phenomena. Career development proceeds—smoothly, jaggedly, positively, negatively—whether or not career interventions exist. Career development can be seen as the object of an intervention.

Career Maturity: The repertoire of behaviors pertinent to identifying, choosing, planning, and executing career goals available to a specific individual as compared with those possessed by an appropriate peer group; being at an average level in career development for one's age (after Super, 1957). Attitudinal and cognitive readiness to cope with the developmental tasks of finding, preparing for, getting established in, pursuing, and retiring from an occupation (Super, 1984b, p. 39).

Career Intervention: "Any activity (treatment or effort) designed to enhance a person's career development or to enable that person to make more effective career decisions" (Spokane, 1991, p. 22).

Technique: "A time-limited application of career intervention principles designed to accomplish a focused goal or to alter a specific vocational behavior. A career life line and a vocational career sort are examples" (Spokane, 1991, p. 22).

Strategy: "A philosophy or plan of action, or a group of techniques intended to change the vocational behavior of an individual, group of individuals or an organization. Career counseling of an individual by a single counselor is an example" (Spokane, 1991, p. 22).

Program: "An organized compilation of techniques or strategies with specific and well-defined objectives that is designed to alter systematically the vocational behavior of a group of individuals in a specific behavior setting (e.g., school, work, or community) over time" (Spokane, 1991, p. 22).

Career Management: The personal state of actively and consciously participating in shaping one's career and accepting responsibility for the activities and choices made toward those ends (Hansen & Tennyson, 1975).

More recently, career management has been conceived of as interventions designed to shape careers in organizations, not only by the individuals concerned but also formally and informally by their managers (Doyle, 2000). In this view it is assumed that the workplace and its management uses various methods to orient and fit the individual's career development into that which is congruent with the organization's goals and that the individual worker plans his or her career paths in accordance with organizational signals and possibilities. As noted elsewhere in this chapter, however, organizational trends suggest that increasingly workplaces and managers are expecting employees to engage more fully in their own career planning and career management with the organizational or employer role in such processes decreasing. The latter process is at the root of terms like protean career or boundaryless careers. These terms suggest that work organizations are in intense competition for market share, for the inclusion of advanced technology to increase productivity, and in the effectiveness of the use of time to cope with shortened cycles of change. As a result, the new work environments being created are shifting from preordained and linear orderly structures, with clear guides for employee action and well-formed career paths, to perpetually changing career paths and possibilities where uncertainty and flexibility are the order of the day and in which employees have the responsibility to make sense of their environments and to plan their skill development and career paths accordingly (Littleton, Arthur, & Rousseau, 2000).

Career Education: Educational and work experiences used systematically to help students and adults acquire knowledge and attitudes about self, work, and the skills by which to identify, choose, plan, and prepare for work and other life options. Career education in schools and universities may infuse career-related concepts into the academic curriculum, provide occupational and educational information, foster work-based learning, and offer courses in career planning and decision making (Hoyt, 1978; Niles & Harris-Bowlsbey, 2002).

Career Guidance: A systematic program of counselor-coordinated information and experiences designed to facilitate individual career development and, more specifically, career management; a major component of career education integrating family, community, and school to facilitate self-direction; a set of multiple processes, techniques, or services designed to assist an individual to understand and to act on self-knowledge and knowledge of opportunities in work, education, and leisure and to develop the decision-making skills by which to create and manage his or her own career development. May include the development of job search, job interview, and job adjustment skills and placement into a chosen occupation.

Career Path: A term typically used in business and industry to describe a series of positions available in some occupational or specialized work area, ordinarily connoting possibilities for advancement.

Career Ladder: A term typically used in business and industry to describe opportunities for upward mobility in an occupational area or across occupational areas within a firm. Usually portrays increasing levels of experience and skill. "A succession of jobs available to an individual worker with each job successively offering increased responsibility and wages and more desirable working conditions" (Evans & Herr, 1978, p. 32).

Career Lattice: A term typically used in business and industry to portray all the opportunities in a firm or a subdivision of a firm including those available for upward and horizontal mobility (such as lateral transfer). As such it portrays the opportunities to shift from one career ladder to another.

Occupation: A group of similar jobs found in different industries or organizations. Occupations exist in the economy and have existed in history, even when no man, woman, or child is engaged in them. Occupations, trades, and professions exist independently of any person. Careers, on the other hand, exist only when people are pursuing them (Super, 1985b, p. 1).

Job: A group of similar paid positions requiring some similar attributes in a single organization.

Position: A group of tasks to be performed by one person; in industry, performed for pay. Positions exist whether vacant or occupied; they are task and outcome defined, not person centered (Super, 1976).

Leisure: Time free from required effort or for the free use of abilities and pursuit of interests (Super, 1976). Relatively self-determined activities and experiences that are available owing to discretionary income, time, and social behaviors; they may be physical, social, intellectual, volunteer, creative, or some combination of all five (Sears, 1982).

Avocation: An activity pursued systematically and consecutively for its own sake with an objective other than monetary gain, although it may incidentally result in gain (Super, 1976).

Career Awareness: The inventory of knowledge, values, preferences, and self-concepts that an individual draws on in the course of making career-related choices.

Work: The systematic pursuit of an objective valued by oneself (even if only for survival) and desired by others; directed and consecutive, it requires the expenditure of effort. It may be compensated (paid work) or uncompensated (volunteer work or an avocation). The objective may be intrinsic enjoyment of the work itself, the structure given to life by the work role, the economic support that work makes possible, or the type of leisure that it facilitates (Super, 1976). An activity performed for the purpose of providing goods and services to others and in some way making a social contribution (Hall, 1986).

PERSPECTIVES ON COUNSELOR ROLE IN CAREER GUIDANCE AND CAREER COUNSELING

The historical evolution of approaches and definitions pertinent to career guidance and career counseling has led to considerable speculation about the counselor's role. These perspectives have been captured in various role statements and in a number of articles throughout the twentieth century. These descriptions of counselor role have varied in their emphases in different historical periods, depending on what particular process or problem was evident at that time. For example, perspectives on the career counselor's roles with computer technology and the Internet are likely to vary from those expected when they work with persons with disabilities, or the unemployed, or persons making the transition from school to work or to career education.

Typical of such role statements is the 1985 position paper on the role of the school counselor in career guidance. In this paper, the American School Counselors Association recommended that counselors should concentrate on the delivery of a series of common, core experiences that should lead to the acquisition by students of career maturity. These core experiences include:

- Clarifying work values and developing coping and planning skills
- Assessing abilities, personality traits, and interests through formal and informal measures
- Providing occupational and career information, linking community resources with guidance
- Helping students learn interviewing and job-hunting skills, and increasing their awareness of

educational and training opportunities, including financial aid
- Encouraging training, goal setting, and decision-making related to a tentative career path
- Integrating academic and career skills in a school curriculum
- Reviewing and evaluating student action plans

That statement of counselor roles in career education could be augmented by the contemporary perspective of Niles and Harris-Bowlsbey (2002) suggesting the variety of roles career counselors play in the design and implementation of career development programs and services in their work settings. Niles and Harris-Bowlsbey argued that such roles would include *advocacy* with various stakeholders to improve career planning services; *coordination* of internal staff and persons in external settings (e.g., employers, agencies, or community organization personnel) to deliver parts of the program of services; *participation* in which counselors using group work, individual counseling, instruction, assessment, computer-based systems, and websites deliver all or parts of a career development program of services; *designers and developers or managers* of career development programs or services.

While the perspectives and position papers describing the counselor's role in career guidance or in career education offer comprehensive insights, few have addressed in a specific manner the counselor's role in career counseling. This situation was first rectified in 1981, when the Board of Directors of the National Vocational Guidance Association (now the National Career Development Association) approved a comprehensive set of counselor competencies essential to the practice of vocational/career counseling. They defined minimum competencies in six areas: general counseling, information, individual/group assessment, management/administration, implementation, and consultation.

In January 1991, the Board of Directors of the National Career Development Association revised the minimum career counseling competencies adopted by the Board of Directors of the National Vocational Guidance Association in 1981. Several new categories were added to the original six categories, and additional skills and knowledge emphases were included in some of the original categories. In addition to combining some of the original categories, new categories of minimum skills added in 1991 included those in career development theory, special populations, supervision, ethical/legal issues, and research/evaluation. In 1997, the career counseling competency statements were refined further, renamed, and an eleventh category, technology, was added. The eleven categories are:

- Career Development Theory
- Individual and Group Counseling Skills
- Individual/Group Assessment
- Information/Resources
- Program Promotion, Management, and Implementation
- Coaching, Consultation, Performance Improvement
- Diverse Populations
- Supervision
- Ethical/Legal Issues
- Research/Evaluation
- Technology

Each of the competency categories starts with a statement clarifying the competency category and then identifies the skills and knowledge undergirding each designated competency area. For example, under the category individual/group assessments, it is expected that some of the essential skills include the demonstration of ability to:

1. Assess personal characteristics such as aptitude, achievement, interests, values, and personality traits

...

3. Assess conditions of the work environment (such as tasks, expectations, norms, and qualities of the physical and social settings)

...

5. Use computer-delivered assessment measures effectively and appropriately

...

7. Administer, score, and report findings from career assessment instruments, appropriately

...

10. Write an accurate report of assessment results (National Career Development Association, 1997)

The competencies cited in each of the eleven career counseling competencies can serve as a guide for career counseling training programs or as a checklist for persons wanting to acquire or to enhance their skills in career counseling.

The competencies cited in each category reflect the changing demands on career counselors and the skills needed to maintain one's currency and competence to deal with emerging issues for clients or students.

The 1981 competency statements of the NVGA were placed into a new and popularized form in the 1985 *Consumer Guidelines for Selecting a Career Counselor,* set forth by the National Career Development Association (the newer name of the NVGA). Under the heading "What Do Career Counselors Do?" the following is stated:

> *The services of career counselors differ, depending on competence. A professional or Nationally Certified Career Counselor helps people make decisions and plans related to life/career directions. The strategies and techniques are tailored to the specific needs of the person seeking help. It is likely that the career counselor will do one or more of the following:*
>
> - *Conduct individual and group personal counseling sessions to help clarify life/career goals*
> - *Administer and interpret tests and inventories to assess abilities, interests, etc., and to identify career options*
> - *Encourage exploratory activities through assignments and planning experiences*
> - *Utilize career planning systems and occupational information systems to help individuals better understand the world of work*
> - *Provide opportunities for improving decisionmaking skills*
> - *Assist in developing individualized career plans*
> - *Teach job-hunting strategies and skills and assist in the development of resumes*
> - *Help resolve potential personal conflicts on the job through practice in human relations skills*
> - *Assist in understanding the integration of work and other life roles*
> - *Provide support for persons experiencing job stress, job loss, career transition (pp. 1–2)**

These career counseling functions are incorporated as part of the content of Figure 1.1.

*From "What Do Career Counselors Do?" 1985 *Consumer Guidelines for Selecting a Career Counselor.* Copyright © 1985 AACD. Reprinted with permission. No further reproduction authorized without written permission of American Association for Counseling and Development.

There are other excellent analyses of necessary skills for career counselors, but the statements identified here generally represent the perspectives of professional associations and scholars; they are both representative of thinking among practitioners and influential in shaping such thinking.

The position papers cited here share a generally common view about the roles for which the career counselor or other career specialist should be responsible. They each view the counselor as an activist involved in both group and individual activities designed to promote knowledge, attitudes, and skills that individuals need for self-definition and career planning. Rather than being confined to a one-to-one model of interaction in an office situation, the counselor is seen as a collaborator, a resource person, and a consultant. In general there is advocacy for the counselor to play a developmental role, providing experiences by which persons can acquire mastery behaviors appropriate to effective career development, rather than only a treatment or remedial role for youth or adults who have had difficulty making choices and found their job skills wanting.

Counselors are expected to understand career development, to be able to help educators or employers to realize career development implications for curriculum or training modifications, and to create learning opportunities relevant to the broad range of human talent. It is also expected that counselors will work with others in effecting placement of students and adults in educational and occupational opportunities in the community through which their career development can be enhanced.

A developmental approach to career counseling is not likely to mean that counselors will have no further responsibility for crisis counseling, for remediation in the traditional sense, or for assisting students or adults at particular decision points. In all likelihood, such needs will always be present, although it is assumed that the incidence of crises can be reduced if counselors use developmental techniques to equip individuals with self-understanding, career awareness, and decision-making skills. It is also assumed that emphasizing developmental approaches to career guidance allows the counselor to have a positive effect on the lives of more persons than can a counselor who relies exclusively on one-to-one, crisis-oriented approaches. It is not assumed that counselors' eclectic use of developmental career guidance approaches will eliminate the need for individual counseling. Rather, it is expected that such processes will continue to help students and adults personalize and test the insights they obtain from career guidance emphases in curriculum, work experience, simulations, and other approaches.

Trends in Counselor Role

Professional association position papers, proposed or actual legislation, articles on counseling literature, and the mapping of broad trends in student or client needs for assistance with career issues provide the conceptual fuel that triggers trends, including expanded counselor roles. Some of these trends are explicit; they typically extend processes that have been in evolution for a decade or more. Other trends are more vague and ill-defined.

Given the fact that career counseling and career guidance operate at the intersection between individuals and their environments, they represent switching mechanisms, guides, and therapeutic agents in such contexts. As such, counselors or other specialists implementing career services are, in the future, likely to serve as brokers or maximizers of opportunities; as interpreters of the relationships between training or retraining and new career paths; as classifiers and providers of information and collaborators in its use; as support systems by which persons can acquire insight into their own stereotypes and irrational beliefs that have hindered their risk taking and mobility; as stimuli through which individuals can increase their feelings of self-worth, power, and self-efficacy; as providers of psychoeducational mechanisms by which persons can learn certain skills—for example, assertiveness, anger management, decision making, conflict resolution, stress reduction, and job searching—necessary to exploring and mastering a successful and meaningful work life; as mentors offering feedback, coaching, and advice about career related tasks; as advocates for the culturally different and those at risk as therapeutic agents who signify hope and possibility in a confused and seemingly unsupportive work world.

Application of Systematic Approaches to Career Guidance. As new techniques of career guidance or career counseling emerged in the twentieth century, a growing emphasis on planned or structured programs arose. In the first edition of the book (Herr & Cramer, 1972), we advocated that vocational guidance be seen as a total system of interacting techniques and personnel that could facilitate the individual acquisition of knowledge, attitudes, and skills leading to effective career behavior. Although we continue to believe that counselors must apply systems thinking to the practice of career development, the term *systems* connotes to some a task so formidable that they reject it as a real solution to advancing the effectiveness of career services or programs.

As a compromise, then, in the second, third, fourth, and fifth editions, and now in the sixth, we have proposed that, if speaking of a systems approach to career services suggests too threatening or too overwhelming a task to be realistic, the term *systematic approach* might be better. Regardless of which term one uses, however, the trend for the counselor seems apparent. In the future, the goals for the practice of career development and the methods by which these goals will be met must be identified in each setting—educational institution, agency, or workplace—for both accountability and programming effectiveness.

If any criticism of career guidance and counseling has been enduring, it is that it is difficult to assess its outcomes or to know in any specific sense what it contributes to broad social or educational goals. Until recently, descriptions of career development programs have largely dealt with the processes to be expected rather than the products. However, in an era of accountability, legislators, administrators, and consumers are frequently heard to say, "We want to know what you intend. What are your goals? How do you distinguish your contributions from those of other educational or social processes?" Fortunately, in the last two decades there have been excellent analyses of the outcomes to be achieved through career guidance, career counseling, and career interventions. Several of these major syntheses have been discussed in this chapter. Others will be cited throughout the book. On balance, these analyses of research outcomes support the positive effects of career interventions on a wide range of career problems.

Systems thinking or a systematic approach endeavors to specify clearly the results sought and the specific methods by which such results will be obtained. In the process, a systematic approach to career services, would recognize that objectives must be stated explicitly, that the relationship of the counselor's contributions to these objectives must be stated clearly in relation to the contributions of other persons, and that ways of assessing whether or not career guidance, career education, or career counseling objectives are being met must be identified and carried through. The basic question for career development programming continues to be "Which resources or combination of resources (people, places, media) are appropriate for fostering what type of development in what type of client under what conditions (time, place, size of group, and so on) to achieve what purposes?" (Phillips, 1966). This requires a statement of program goals, behavioral objectives for students or clients, linkage of career interventions and resources to behavioral objectives, and an evaluative procedure (Chapter 6 addresses many of these procedures).

Such planned approaches to career guidance are outcome based (Johnson & Johnson, 1982) rather than function based. Planned programs are assumed to clarify what counselors can contribute to the school, college, or workplace in which they are employed; the differences they can make in the lives of students or adult workers; and the degree to which they can be held accountable for selected outcomes or domains.

Walz and Benjamin (1984) have summarized the advantages of systematic career guidance delivery in the following paraphrased form:

1. A developmental emphasis: The systematic approach gives program planners the opportunity to design a proactive delivery system that anticipates needs and problems and develops appropriate strategies for dealing with them.
2. Effective use of available resources: Program designers can tailor components of the delivery system (for example, counseling, media, information resources, computer-based guidance) to desired outcomes. This customizing avoids the shortcoming in traditional methods of overusing a particular intervention such as individual counseling.
3. Amenability to change and innovation: With clearly stated goals and objectives and specified modes of delivery, it becomes easier to locate difficulties and target areas needing change or improvement and then to provide the training and resources needed by the staff to accomplish the new or revised goals and objectives.
4. Relative ease of evaluation: Evaluation is an integral and necessary component of the systematic approach. Specific standards for judging behavioral change allow for more objective evaluation, and where there is a discrepancy between proposed and actual outcomes, new methods can be developed and implemented.
5. Avoidance of faddism: Clarity in objectives and in modes of delivery provides a source of insulation against faddism or opportunistic responses to "catchy" ideas that have not been tested systematically.
6. Promotion of community effort: Knowledge of what the program is about fosters a higher degree of articulation by community members and stimulates them to find ways that they can be involved. (pp. 28–29)

Flowing from such reasons for systematic approaches to the delivery of career guidance, career education, or career counseling, contemporary planned, or structured, programs related to specific career counseling content or to the dynamics of particular life career transitions have been developed in response to changing paradigms and metaphors about the counseling process itself; to the need to more efficiently and effectively deploy the counselors available in new configurations of direct and indirect services to students and clients; to growing knowledge of the information, attitudes, and skills that comprise concepts like career maturity or adaptability, personal flexibility, optimization of behavior, self-renewal; and certainly to a rising crescendo of calls for clarification of the outcomes of counseling, career guidance, or related interventions and counselor accountability for achieving such outcomes.

The Counselor as Applied Behavioral Scientist. To plan systematically for the delivery of any form of career intervention and to respond to individual differences, the counselor will likely become more eclectic in the future. Rather than being theory-bound or a practitioner of a single process (such as individual counseling), the counselor will need to use a range of techniques and processes both with groups and with individuals. The application of these techniques will need to be tailored to specific problems presented by individuals or to developmental purposes. In general, the application of these techniques will cause the counselor to have a broad acquaintance with a range of theories, concepts, and ideas bearing on career development and the empirical evidence of the effectiveness of these ideas. There seems to be no question that among the techniques to be employed in the practice of career development, there will be heavy reliance on psychoeducation techniques and structured group experiences to build skills required by particular clients.

As the career counselor increasingly becomes an applied behavioral scientist, the model of systematic eclecticism wedded to an ongoing concern for evaluation and research will incrementally expand the science and knowledge base on which career counseling and guidance rest. Fundamentally, such a model assumes that specific approaches to career guidance or counseling are effective for some purposes and not for others, and that students or adult clients come to counselors for a variety of reasons. In response, the career counselor practicing systematic eclecticism collaborates with the client to select those approaches that are most relevant to the problem presented or to other unique needs of the client. A further assumption is that the career counselor should be trained in a repertoire of approaches—individual, group, assessment, psychoeducation, self-monitored, and so forth—that would be based on scientific analysis of their effectiveness under certain conditions and for specific purposes.

The trend for the career counselor to be an applied behavioral scientist who practices systematic eclecticism suggests levels of analysis, goal setting with counselees, and perspectives that go beyond those historically emphasized in career counseling. For example, systematic eclecticism suggests that it is not now possible to view any single theory as having sufficient explanatory power to cover all of the needs for career services brought to counselors. Rather, it suggests that the future will require an increase in the conception of career guidance, career counseling, or career education and counselee outcomes as a matrix of possible interactions; that most counselees will have more than one problem that needs to be addressed; and that the counselor's role will be to help the counselee experience a combination of approaches, treatments, and experiences effectively matched to his or her needs. The treatments chosen will be evidence-based (Sexton, 2001).

Implicit, if not explicit, in the paradigm of the counselor as an applied behavioral scientist is the parallel concept of the scientist-practitioner, as advanced by the American Psychological Association's view of the Counseling Psychologist. Inherent in such notions is a respect for and a professional commitment to engaging in research and evaluation of career interventions used with different populations and for different reasons. Of relevance to the systematic planning for and the effective execution of career guidance and career counseling are familiarity with and contributions to the research findings of relevance to one's professional domain. Many of these research findings have been consistently supported by research studies and they have become part of the scientific base on which the field rests. Although this book contains many such findings, it is also useful to be knowledgeable about summaries thereof; one such summary is that of Campbell et al. (1983). These researchers classified empirical studies of positive effects of career guidance into five broad categories:

1. *Improved school involvement and performance* (41 studies). These researchers conclude that the majority of the studies reported gains in student career development outcomes that they attribute primarily to interventions involving individualized career development learning experience (for example, experience-based career education, special guidance classroom activities, career exploration, and counseling).
2. *Personal and interpersonal work skills* (31 studies). Nineteen studies used as a dependent variable self-awareness; 5, interpersonal and life skills; and 6, work values. The majority of the studies that examined the effect of career interventions on these outcomes reported positive effects (26 of the 31).
3. *Preparation for careers* (14 studies). Twelve of the 14 studies examined showed positive gains in career preparation among people exposed to each of four types of intervention: counseling, classroom career guidance instruction, employer-based career education, and hands-on career exploration activities.
4. *Career planning skills* (34 studies). Twenty-seven of these studies demonstrated positive outcomes. Although the researchers who performed these studies tended to employ a variety of types of intervention to increase career planning skills in students and adults, they identified career or vocational counseling as the major process in over half the studies.
5. *Career awareness and exploration* (44 studies). Thirty-one of these studies showed positive

results. Career and vocational exploration, experience-based career education, counseling, and career education classroom activities gave the best results.

Based on their review of empirical studies, Campbell et al. (1983) came to the following conclusions:

- Vocational guidance interventions achieve their intended outcomes primarily if guidance personnel provide structured interventions in a systematic developmental sequence.
- Vocational guidance has demonstrated its effectiveness in influencing career development and adjustment of individuals in the five broad outcome areas.
- Vocational guidance has been successful in assisting individuals representing a wide range of subpopulations and settings, including those in correctional institutions, vocational training centers, community colleges, and those susceptible to academic, economic, and psychological problems.

Other reviews of empirical studies of the outcomes of career interventions, including those of Holland, Magoon, and Spokane (1981); Oliver and Spokane (1988); Rounds and Tinsley (1984); Sexton, Whiston, Bleur, and Walz (1997); and Spokane and Oliver (1983), have found positive and important findings to guide the work of the counselor engaged in career work. These reviews indicate that career education, career counseling, and career guidance do yield positive results and the general effectiveness of such interventions is no longer at issue. More specifically, however, such reviews have provided important insights into the elements of effective interventions. For example, according to Holland, Magoon, and Spokane (1981), these would include:

1. Occupational information organized by a comprehensive method and easily accessible to a client
2. Assessment materials and devices that clarify a client's self-picture and vocational potentials
3. Individual or group activities that require the rehearsal of career plans or problems
4. Counselors, groups, or peers that provide support
5. A comprehensive cognitive structure for organizing information about self and occupational alternatives

Oliver and Spokane's (1988) reviews of the effectiveness of career interventions have indicated that individual counseling, although much more costly than other approaches, is the most efficient intervention in terms of amount of gain per hour of effort. They have also reported that longer (at least 10 sessions) and more comprehensive sessions, although they require much more time from the client and from the counselor, yield roughly twice the beneficial effects of briefer interventions. Reviews that have extended the findings of Oliver and Spokane have indicated that career counseling is effective for a variety of concerns including indecision and facilitating career maturity (Whiston, Sexton, & Lasoff, 1998).

The Counselor as Change Agent. In providing a comprehensive program of career guidance, the counselor will probably depart from the one-to-one mode of interaction with clients as the principal strategy. Counselors will be increasingly involved in collaborative efforts with teachers, parents, administrators, community agency personnel, and employers to modify the environments that shape their clients' lives. Examples of the activities in which counselors are likely to become engaged include creating positive climates for learning; modifying curriculum content; working with employers to provide work-study experiences, exploratory opportunities, realistic employment requirements, and more mentally healthful work environments; and actively seeking job placement for clients. There seems to be little question that counselors will need to persist in giving their skills to educators, parents, and management or supervisory personnel in industry to sensitize these individuals to the needs of all persons for self-esteem, achievement, and opportunities to share in decision making and governance. In such circumstances, the counselor will likely serve as a consultant or a resource person to these "significant others" who influence the lives of various groups in different educational settings or in workplaces.

Career Development and Leisure. Comprehensive career guidance programs of the future will need to concern themselves with the range of roles affected by whether work is seen as a central commitment of individuals. As suggested at several places in this book, one of those roles is leisure. In some types of work, it may not be possible to find personal fulfillment, satisfying human relationships, or a sense of achievement. In such instances, persons need to look elsewhere for outlets for such needs. The leisure world of volunteer activity, hobbies, and nontechnical learning may serve such needs for self-fulfillment. Some people may be forced into extended periods of leisure because of a lack of jobs or work opportunity, work dislocation, reduced work time, or early retirement. Some may seek leisure opportunities because they are not committed to work as a central concept in their lives. Regardless of what reason motivates persons to engage in leisure activity, how they choose and conceptualize the use of leisure in their lives will be a legitimate and growing emphasis in career counseling.

McDaniels (1989) has persuasively argued that career counseling must embody both leisure counseling and work counseling. He suggests that counselees may increasingly seek help in leisure or work or both. In his view, "A skilled career counselor of the future should be able to provide assistance in both areas separately or in a combined holistic approach.... Individuals need a holistic, not a compartmentalized approach in order to find satisfaction in the changing world of work and leisure in the 1990s and beyond" (p. 182). McDaniels is not alone in his advocacy of more attention to leisure within the concept of career counseling; Bloland and Edwards (1981) have argued for a career counseling conceptualization that blends work and leisure. They recognize work and leisure as playing complementary roles in the lives of people but also hold that leisure can play two roles when it seeks to make up for dissatisfaction felt in work. They build their theoretical structure on the work of Kando and Summers (1971), who suggest that leisure can respond in two ways to dissatisfaction at work: (1) supplemental compensation (positive feelings through leisure are also adequately experienced through work), and (2) reactive compensation (avocational activities are used to recover from unpleasant work experiences).

Some evidence suggests that leisure time is a mixed blessing for many people (Herr & Watts, 1981). For some persons, leisure time is unstructured or idle time that leads to substance or alcohol abuse or even antisocial and criminal activity. Obviously the availability of leisure time varies among people, and their ability to use it without additional stress or conflict also varies widely. Clearly, such ambivalence and ambiguity about how leisure fits into life priorities, how decisions about effective uses of leisure can be made, and the competencies to use leisure time effectively are important elements of future models of career interventions and the frequent content of career counseling.

Career Guidance as Content or Curriculum. One of the major outcomes of developmental career guidance during the past twenty years has been the rise of workshops, group approaches, self-directed modules, and other programs. Most of these are planned or structured programs described earlier. Some of these are designed to facilitate individual decision making by "educating persons to choose." Others are built around specific clusters of career development tasks found to be most significant at different chronological life periods or at particular transition points. They may include attempts to influence the development or acquisition of a positive self-concept, interpersonal skills, control over one's life, the discipline of work, presenting oneself objectively, knowledge of resources, preferred lifestyles, and other career management tasks.

There are many examples of career guidance content available. Some are delivered by computer-assisted career guidance systems. Many local and state departments of education as well as some corporations have created career development materials for use by counselors and others to implement systematic career development programs in different settings with different populations. In 1988, the National Occupational Information Coordinating Committee published *The National Career Counseling and Development Guidelines,* which give examples of how to plan career guidance programs for adults in human service agencies, for students in postsecondary institutions, and for students in elementary, middle/junior, and high schools. The guidelines suggest relevant content at each of these levels. Whatever the source of content, it must be tailored to the special needs of different youth or adult subpopulations. As integral parts of comprehensive career guidance programs, content can be expanded to focus on whatever type of self-development, skill acquisition, or exploratory behavior is necessary in different work environments or educational settings.

Herr and Johnson (1989) have suggested that, depending on the population and the purpose to be served, career guidance content in group programs tends to deal with three categories of skills: work context skills, career management (including career planning and job search and access skills), and decision-making skills.

Work context skills are related to the psychological aspects of the situation in which work activity is carried on but can be viewed separately from the technical skills of work performance.

In some nations, observers would suggest that these are the elements of industrial discipline; in others, they would be called affective work competencies. In any case, they include knowledge and skills associated with employer-employee relations and supervisor-worker relations, interpersonal skills with coworkers, willingness to follow rules, adaptability, punctuality and regularity in attendance, pride in work, self-discipline, and efficiency. Such work context skills tend to be those that research studies and surveys of employer preference have shown repeatedly to be at the heart of work adjustment, job satisfaction, and work satisfactoriness. Their lack is at the core of reasons for workers being discharged. Although more subtle and psychological than work performance skills or numeracy and literacy, they can nevertheless be analyzed and taught.

In many ways, however, the teaching of work context skills is incomplete without attention to a second category of individual learning described as *career management*. Indeed, it is conceivable that many of the problems now associated with work context (such as worker alienation and mid-career crisis) are really problems of self-learning or deficits in career planning or job search and access skills. These skills, like work context skills, are more psychological than technical, and they can be taught. They are typically now described under the rubric of career development, concentrating on helping people to become aware of their self-characteristics (such as aptitudes, values, and interests), their career opportunities (such as occupational alternatives, educational options, and the relationship between subject matter and jobs), and the bringing together of self-opportunities and career opportunities into a plan of action. Such learning is designed to help individuals become more purposeful, goal directed, and capable of self-management. It emphasizes individual ability to deal with change, become more flexible, and be able to take responsibility for one's own career. It includes attention to decision-making skills, job search and interview strategies, and general planfulness. It also includes concern for such emphases as the ability to use exploratory resources to reality-test choices, constructive use of leisure, personal economics skills, and other pertinent areas of behavior by which one is helped to get and keep a job. In general, they reflect that forging a career requires at least two types of knowledge: self-knowledge and job knowledge.

With respect to self-knowledge, individuals need to come to terms with who they are; what kinds of commitments they are willing to make; what their aptitudes, interests, values, and goals are; and how competent or confident they feel. In essence, self-information is a base for anything else; that is, knowing one's strengths and weaknesses, preferences, and goals defines an evaluative foundation to which any option or action can be referred to determine its relevance. This base of information also helps one determine what information one has, what one needs, and what should be secured.

Job knowledge includes the range of work options available and the ways in which these might be accessed as well as how one might create one's own job through self-employment. This requires having knowledge about and considering the personal relevance of such matters as the characteristics of curricular majors available, their prerequisites and content; the relationship between subject matter and occupations in which that subject matter is required; the outcomes of pursuing various curricula (What is the placement record? Into what kinds of jobs are people placed?); the matching of personal characteristics with those required in preferred curricula or occupations; entrepreneural skills; and so forth.

In addition, considerations of occupational and other opportunities will probably require information about methods of access and about how to market oneself. Are the preferred occupations available locally? If not, where are they available? How are potential employers identified? What is the best procedure for contacting an employer? What information or procedure is pertinent to the completion of letters of inquiry, resumes, applications? What types of questions or other conditions are likely to prevail in an interview situation? How does one follow up a contact with an employer?

A third area of emphasis beyond that of work context or career management skills is that dealing with the *decision-making* process itself. One could argue that such a distinction is overly pedantic and that this learning is typically incorporated into the knowledge previously described. That may be true, but decision-making skills are, nevertheless, a type of content that has integrity in its own right as a systematic method that can be applied repeatedly to process information, weigh alternatives, and project consequences of actions. Perhaps most important, decision making is the way people can establish relations between actions in the present and the future expectations about the consequences of those decisions. Thus, decision making becomes an important way of establishing an internal locus of control.

Career Counseling and Mental and Behavioral Health

Although career counseling has been historically portrayed as primarily oriented to economic health, choice of an occupation, the development of prevocational skills, and the preparation for work, that perspective is too restrictive. As suggested by the expanding definitions of career counseling discussed earlier in this chapter, career counseling is being increasingly seen as a therapeutic modality, a specific application of personal adjustment counseling, or even psychotherapy when it is applied to specific problems related to work. In this context, Herr (1989) has addressed the growing research base that links career development, work, and behavioral and mental health. This research, which will be more fully explored in Chapter 2, suggests that among other roles career counseling is critical to giving unemployed and underemployed youths and adults a sense of purposefulness and positive self-efficacy, thus to reduce the stress-related side effects of hopelessness and despair. Such outcomes are not benign. The past decade has seen a growing number of research findings that demonstrate the variety of life difficulties and physical and mental health problems that ensue when work life is unsatisfactory or when job dislocation or unemployment occurs. Distress about work and particularly about unemployment is associated with a range of personal and social problems—for example, depression, anxiety, physiological effects (cardiovascular disease, early death), suicide, spousal or child abuse, abuse of alcohol and other drugs, anger, violence, impaired interpersonal relationships, grief and mourning, and feelings of victimization. As Spokane (1989) has observed, "it is reasonable to assume that there is more to career development than has met the eye for the past 75 years, and that it is no longer possible to avoid the overlap between career development and psychopathology" (p. 23).

The stress reactions and stress-related physical and psychological diseases that accompany problems of work adjustment, work choice, and the exit from work bring career counseling directly into the realm of the emerging movement in behavioral health and more broadly into the realm of behavioral medicine and mental health. Such career counseling approaches in business and industry can provide dislocated workers, unhappy workers, maladjusted workers, and unemployed or underemployed workers information, support, encouragement, skill building, or some combination of these to facilitate hope and reduce feelings of being an unworthy social isolate. Skill-building approaches can deal directly with such matters as anger management, assertiveness, planning, interpersonal competencies, and openness to constructive supervision. Such approaches are not just matters of occupational choice and adjustment; they also help people create reality and meaning for themselves within the context of work and career. The latter is directly related to behavioral and mental health.

Basic Academic Skills and Career Development

Just as there are rapidly emerging relationships between career development and mental health, there are also relationships between basic academic skills and career development that will significantly affect what career counselors will do and how they will do it. Given the changes in the global economy and the fact that work forces that are literate, flexible, and teachable are necessary to successful engagement in international competition, the possession or lack of basic academic skills is now a major element of individual career development. The assessment and analysis of individuals' basic academic skills are prime ingredients in what occupations they are likely to be able to consider, for what training they are likely to be eligible, and whether they can find employment in technological occupations or are relegated to occupations in which the career ladders are much shorter. In a society in which knowledge has replaced experience as the primary requisite for employment in an occupational structure in which more than half of the workers are now engaged in "knowledge work" (Drucker, 1989), basic academic skills—computation skills, literacy, communication skills—become primary employability skills. As projected in many reports, given the ability of the United States to automate many of its unskilled and semiskilled jobs and to export other low-skill jobs to other nations where wage rates are low and desire for such jobs is high, few new jobs will be created in the future for persons who cannot read, take and act on instructions, do basic mathematics, and communicate effectively. Such requisites will be seen as fundamental employability skills in order to avoid reductions in economic development of individual firms and other enterprises caused by employees who are unable or unwilling to learn new production systems or new management strategies. Such basic academic skill development will also need to include the development of the other general employability skills discussed at length elsewhere in this book. As a reflection of the need to combine both types of skills, one national study has suggested that "today's new mathematically-based technologies require better computational and literacy skills, and the structures require employees with more interpersonal and organizational skills. The increased importance of the working team suggests the need for better communications and teamwork skills" (Carnevale & Gainer, 1989). These combinations of basic academic skills, general employability skills, and technical skills will maximize the personal flexibility and the life options of the workers entering the labor market, those retraining to remain within it, and those entering "new or protean careers" that maximize the individual's management of their own career. Career counselors must attend to each of these three skill sets as interdependent elements of individual career development.

The Counselor as Technologist

Many counselors have been trained to believe that the primary, if not total, explanation for behavioral change in their clients is counselor personality (for example, the provision of empathy, unconditional positive regard, and so on). Assuming that such a premise is too limited a concept of the counselor's role with diverse client needs, the counselor's professional repertoire typically now includes several forms of technology that extend the counselor's potential to effect behavioral change. Games, work samples, films, problem-solving kits, self-assessments, computer interactive systems, the Internet, and various methods of depicting virtual reality are but a few of the means developed to provide learning and simulated experience designed to increase client exploration and planning.

Computer-assisted career guidance (CACG) systems have become a core element in the delivery of career and educational guidance services in the United States and in many other nations. Trends in CACG system development include increased diversity of systems, increased availability of information within the systems, greater potential for integrating CACG systems with existing career guidance services and programs in different types of organizational settings, closer collaboration among system developers, and interest in international and non-English-language versions of CACG systems.

Perhaps the most rapidly developing tool available to career counselors and the technology most likely to have a dramatic influence on what career counselors of the future do and how they do it is the Internet. The Internet in its simplest description is the linking of computers at individual sites through existing computer networks around the world to create an international network of information sources and processes that can be used to deliver career counseling (e.g., chat rooms, e-mail, online counseling, group conferences, bulletin boards of information, job postings, direct applications for jobs and resume submission to employers, opportunities for self-help sites, two-way videoconferencing). Bolles (1997) has suggested that the Internet can be helpful to job hunters or career changers as a place to:

1. Search for job vacancies or job listings provided by employers
2. Post your resume so potential employers can review it
3. Get some job-hunting help or career counseling
4. Make contacts with people who can help you find information, or help you get an interview, at a particular place
5. Find information or do research on fields, occupations, companies, cities (p. 7)

Obviously, the potential contributions of the Internet to the practice of career development are enormous and complex. Because of the magnitude of the information on the Internet (in 1998, there were more than 11,000 sites reporting job vacancies on the Internet; it was estimated that more than 60,000 pages of information were being added to the Internet each day), even with the use of some excellent search engines, it is very difficult to sort out particular jobs or to find appropriate websites to review. Embedded in the rapid growth, lack of quality controls, and enormity of possible career information, the need for the intervention of career counselors will take on new forms and there will be ethical issues, client access issues, confidentiality, and information relevance issues that will need to continue to be examined and dealt with (Sampson, Kolodinsky, & Greeno, 1997).

Technology applied to career development will expand rather than recede, and thus the career counselor of the future will need, in addition to expertise already cited, to have a conceptual framework and personal competencies by which to use such resources effectively. To these ends, Peterson, Sampson, and Reardon (1991) have placed the counselors' role in using various forms of technology within a cognitive information-processing paradigm. Their approach provides a theoretical approach to how students or clients process information about themselves and career options and become effective decision makers. Such views are clearly in accord with the need for counselors as technologists also to be applied behavioral scientists and planners as they select career interventions, design a career service center, or use career information and media.

Although computers, the Internet, and other technologies have redefined the repertoire of skills and resources counselors can bring to bear on career related concerns, computers and technology are valuable only to the degree that the outcomes they facilitate are appropriate to the program planning or counseling outcomes to be achieved. Such a reality affirms again that counselors as applied behavioral scientists and planners must be proficient in the selection and implementation of multiple interventions. Career counselors must learn to view the use of computer-assisted or Internet approaches to individual career development as part of a plan—as one of the treatment options—not the only, or even the preferred, approach for all counseling problems. Thus, counselors must see technology of any kind as a tool by which to extend their skills and potentially to meet certain counselee needs, not as a separate and autonomous system.

Special Needs Populations

The United States is a nation of immigrants who have carried with them from Europe, Africa, Asia, and South America the traditional values with which they were imbued in their land of origin. Nations do differ in the psychological character they embrace (Peabody, 1985), and such models are perpetuated in the lives of persons across generations through family traditions, ethnic churches, community groupings, and other media. A continuing challenge to career counselors is how to attend to the cultural diversity inherent in the widening portions of the population to be served. What does this diversity mean for career counseling, the counselor as technologist, the content and curriculum of career guidance, or other topical categories?

But suggesting that all persons have special needs derived from their cultural history does not suggest that such a condition eliminates the need to attend to more restricted and focused definitions of special needs populations. Although the specific group characteristics may change, there will continue to be groups of persons who have special needs for career guidance. Ordinarily, these are groups who have been denied equity in their access to educational and occupational opportunities because of racial and sexual bias or discrimination because of age or disability. Bias or discrimination of any kind is a waste of human resources, and it is a matter that career counselors and related specialists can help reduce or eliminate.

As the pressures and demands on citizens intensify and additional at-risk groups come into public visibility, the constituent groups who have experienced bias and discrimination and need career counseling become more comprehensive.

Counselors have many possibilities for action both at the client level and at the institutional level. In the former, it is a matter of helping youths and adults free themselves from the psychological limits on choice that they experience because they have incorporated other people's beliefs that women (or men, for that matter) or persons of particular racial, age, or physical disability characteristics should not consider certain educational or job options. Frequently, they have also internalized the implied reasons for restricting such choices; for example, they may believe that if one has a specific set of group characteristics (such as race or gender), one is ipso facto inferior or less able than others. In the second place, the institutional level, it is a matter of trying to keep employers, parents, teachers, and other gatekeepers of the opportunity structure from restricting free access to jobs and education based on such stereotypes. The reduction of bias will include the whole repertoire of counselor and career guidance strategies, including those of cognitive restructuring and support groups as well as resource, collaborative, and consultative roles. The requirements for such emphases are basic to any rationale for a planning model for the practice of career development.

Techniques useful in dealing with special career problems experienced by different special needs populations are discussed elsewhere in this book. Of particular note is the growing recognition in the literature and in legislation that special needs populations comprise not only persons denied equality because of historical social discrimination based on race, gender, or age. In addition, research and theory of the last decade have also demonstrated that persons at significant points of transition in their lives (for example, divorce, loss of a loved one, sudden unemployment) become vulnerable, and thus, at least temporarily, people with special needs. Although such a condition may be dynamic, not fixed as are race and gender, it can nevertheless cause problems for the person at work and in other parts of life; career counseling can be helpful in such situations.

Cost-Benefit Analysis

One of the trends related to career services that has not yet made a major impact on the field but continues to promise to do so is that of the cost-benefit ratios associated with the provision of career interventions to various populations for different purposes. The actual conceptual and empirical literature on this subject, relevant to career counseling or to career services, is limited. Frequently, the literature that does discuss this issue typically does not speak to the specific dollars saved or stimulated by effective career interventions although it is clear that the authors believe that such cost-benefit ratios do exist and that they favor the efficacy and benefits of career interventions. Although hypothetical, for example, one can consider the amount of state aid that a school receives for every student, who as a result of counseling or education and training has decided not to drop out of school prematurely, as a benefit that accrues to counseling. Thus, the thousands of dollars of school aid based on average daily membership of students who remain in school after being at risk of early school leaving is a tangible benefit of the efforts of sensitive and effective counselors. Similarly, effective counselor intervention in the early identification and the treatment of an at-risk child who does not subsequently become a juvenile delinquent or become incarcerated is a substantial cost saving to the society. So, too, is the unemployed person, the person on welfare, or the person with a disability who finds appropriate training and work because of the efforts of an effective career counselor. Each of these persons becomes a taxpayer, an economic contributor to the society, rather than a drain on the society's resources.

Although not typically expressed in this manner, a positive correlation between a career intervention and an important career outcome tends to mask the fact that there are costs and benefits implicit in such statistics that are not typically tallied and considered. Increasingly, those relationships need to be made more explicit so that the field can develop a cost-benefit mentality that does not now exist.

In general terms it is fair to argue that researchers in the United States have not typically cast the outcomes of career guidance and career counseling in economic terms. Nevertheless the significant effects of career interventions for different populations and different purposes reported in this chapter and in this book do have economic values that may in the future become more important to articulate. As limited financial resources are to be distributed across a growing range of individual and social needs, it seems inevitable that the accountability mentality now pervasive in the United States and in many other nations of the world will grow. The practice of career development, similar to psychotherapy, medical care, and other therapeutic processes, will be increasingly placed under the scrutiny of public policymakers as evidence of their contributions to national priorities are considered. In many instances, these contributions will be seen in both their economic costs and in their economic benefits.

In large measure, there has been more attention to the economic value of career guidance in the United Kingdom than has been true in the United States. For example, Kileen, White, and Watts (1992) have examined in some depth the potential economic effects of career guidance, the evidence available about such effects, and the future of the evaluation of career guidance in terms of the economic benefits that such activities yield. These authors have observed that while researchers in career guidance and counseling have typically been concerned about the value of these interventions for the individual, in fact the potential economic benefits of effective career guidance and counseling extend to education and training providers, to employers, and to governments. In this context, they state, "In policy terms, guidance services serve a number of different constituencies. In addition to individuals, they offer benefits to *education and training providers,* in increasing the effectiveness of their provision by helping learners to be linked to programmes which meet their needs. They also offer benefits to employers, in helping potential employees to come forward whose talents and motivations are matched to the employer's requirements. Finally, they offer benefits to *governments,* in making maximum use of the society's human resources" (p. i).

In subsequent analyses, Kileen (1996) has described how career guidance can lead to economic benefits at the individual, corporate, and national level. At the individual level, Kileen argues that economic benefits accrue from the effects of career guidance on *labor-supply decisions,* that is, individual decisions to participate and at full- or part-time levels in the labor market. The decision to participate and the magnitude of that participation relates to economic benefits (e.g., wages) acquired. A second area of the effect of career guidance is on *human capital decisions*—decisions about the amount and kinds of competence (education, training, other experience increasing one's competence) to acquire with both the cost (e.g., investment in education or training and wages foregone during that period) and the increased income, the benefit that accrues. A third area of career guidance effects are *job search decisions:* "decisions about the kinds of jobs and wage levels to aim at, how long to search before changing one's goals, and so forth" (p. 80). In this context, it is expected that if search costs are reduced and the amount of information processed in a given amount of time is increased, people will *match* themselves more quickly and efficiently, helping them to be less inclined to accept jobs below their skills and abilities, to obtain employment or reemployment and/or wage benefits more rapidly, and to be less inclined to enter occupations where they are likely to be rapidly unemployed.

One can make related analyses of the effects of career interventions at the corporate or organizational level. For example, if the supply of labor, persons who have invested in relevant training, is increased and available to the employer to select from the costs of recruitment will be reduced, training will be less likely to be wasted, and turnover costs will be diminished. At the national level, effective career interventions may help to reduce unemployment and the costs thereof. It may also stimulate persons who are unemployed, or performing jobs below their skill levels to reenter the labor market and thereby increase their productivity and positively influence the Gross Domestic Product (GDP).

Such perspectives need to pervade more completely the thinking of career counselors and the research designs related to career programs and services in order to capture more comprehensively the importance of what the practice of career development contributes to society and the various forms of evidence necessary to document that contribution in both psychological and economic terms.

INTERNATIONAL APPROACHES TO CAREER GUIDANCE AND CAREER COUNSELING

As suggested earlier in this chapter, career guidance, career education, and career counseling have become international phenomena. They are not exclusive inventions or provisions of the United States. Many nations have implemented or refined mechanisms designed to facilitate individual decision making, reduce underemployment, and aid job adjustment. Different nations arrange their career counseling or career guidance systems in ways reflective of the placement of their career specialists in ministries of labor, ministries of education, school districts, regional catchment areas, or local job service bureaus. The growth of career guidance specialists and programs across the world are now major content emphases in annual or biennial conferences of specialists under the auspices of such associations as the International Association for Educational and Vocational Guidance, the International Association of Applied Psychology, and the International Round Table for the Advancement of Counseling, as well as the

Canadian Career Development Foundation and the American Counseling Association, which has a large international membership and has been engaged in a number of bilateral conferences in recent years in locations outside the United States.

Obviously the approaches taken to the practice of career development—career guidance, career education, or career counseling—by other nations are colored by their own political belief systems, economic conditions, cultural traditions, and conceptions of free and informed choice of educational and occupational opportunity. Indeed, across the world the particular approaches being taken to the delivery of career services are no longer dependent on Eurocentric models or theories but are becoming increasingly indigenous and customized to cultural and political conditions. Thus, they differ in the degree to which the career guidance specialists or career counselors are trained in a formal, academic setting yielding a baccalaureate or master's level or doctorate or by a series of brief workshops; whether the practice of career development is primarily a function of government policies and centralized provisions of career services or decentralized to many private entrepreneurs who deliver such services; whether there are differentiated delivery services for different target groups of consumers or essentially the same for all; whether career services are focused in the schools, the universities, or government agencies, primarily for adolescents, adults, or populations across the lifespan; whether the provision of career guidance and counseling utilizes advanced technology, and the purposes to be served; and whether the outcomes for which career guidance and counseling are implemented are guided by particular theoretical models or cultural traditions. As a result, such approaches are not necessarily interchangeable across national boundaries. As nations experience particular levels of industrialization, technology, occupational specialization, and diversity, and as available information about the possibility structure existing in that nation expands, needs for career interventions grow and change in ways defined by political and economic factors in that nation.

Inherent in the growth and in the change in the provision of career services and in the forms of career interventions that occur in different nations, there are fresh visions of what is possible to address problems facing certain nations that may not have the psychological or economic freedom to view as do other nations. Although, again, these possibilities may not be fully transportable across national systems, they nevertheless open up new possibilities of addressing problems shared across nations. For example, in Australia, because fewer employment counselors are available to assist a larger number of adolescents and adults seeking work, advocacy has grown to provide client self-help resources that may achieve many of the outcomes usually done in individual counseling. The intent is to use audio, video, and computer technologies more extensively for "the development of user-friendly, self-contained, client self-help packages focusing on specifically defined areas of employment counseling need." In addition, there are efforts to use the telephone more effectively as a medium for providing employment information to clients. There is also a nationwide telephone information service for career decision making that provides fifteen three- to five-minute information messages on aspects of career planning, implementation, and adjustment. Other telephone services are being planned or established, covering job information, employment trends, job variances, and other relevant information (Pryor, Hammond, & Hawkins, 1990).

More recent labor market policies in Australia have created Job Network, a national network for more than 300 private, community, and government organizations, with which the Australian government contracts to provide flexible and tailored assistance to job seekers. The need for such services by individual users is defined by five categories ranging from job matching to intensive assistance. The access to the services offered by Job Network is through one of 290 Centrelink customer service centers across Australia that provides a uniform national service for registering job seekers, administering unemployment benefits, assessing job seekers' eligibility for labor market assistance, referring clients to Job Network assistance, administering tests, and enforcing compliance with conditions of income support (McCowan & Mountain, 2000). Like other nations whose approaches to career guidance and career counseling will be cited in this section and elsewhere in the book, the Australian approach to Centrelink centers is similar to one-stop career centers in the United States and other nations and the tailored assistance defined by category of need is similar to that offered by the multi-tiered approach taken by the Public Employment Security Offices in Japan.

In Britain, government policy now requires each secondary student and, therefore, school leaver to have records of achievement (ROAs) and individual action plans (IAPs). These documents are drawn up by students and their teachers or counselors, listing achievements, as a basis for future planning and to facilitate self-awareness and awareness of potential career outcomes to be sought. In addition, these activities are now incorporated into the government's Technical and Vocational Education Initiative and Extension policy that provides cash-value instruments to school-leavers to "buy" vocational training contingent on individual action planning using a National Record of Achievement, which includes a personal record, an action plan, an assessment record, and certificates. The British approach has stimulated the use of career portfolios in the United States to document individual career competencies and experiences for employment purposes.

Finland has used a similar approach to individual action plans as has Britain. However, in Finland they are called a personal study program (PSP) and are developed by employment offices, in combination with individual or group counseling, with each adult student before beginning vocational education and training. The PSP includes information on previous studies and relevant work experiences and leisure activities. The PSP then becomes part of an assessment process of the client's skills, professional and general qualifications, special abilities and personal goals. As a decision about a particular form of vocational education is chosen by the adult student, the PSP becomes the starting point for an educator to design a program of studies. In the context, the PSP is seen as a way of thinking, as an instrument for creating a learning environment and organizational culture, and as a way of promoting student self-assessment, career planning, and general life planning as important components of one's technical studies. In this sense, a PSP is seen as a way of promoting the contextualization of vocational education (e.g., understanding what one is doing, why one is doing it) and thereby personalizing study experiences (Kurhila & Onnismaa, 2000).

There are many other important national approaches to the school-to-work transition or to career counseling that should be cited. Often these approaches offer new constructs, terms, processes that can spur innovation in other nations. Among these is the development and use of group employment counseling in Canada (Amundson, Borgen, & Westwood, 1990), as well as peer career counseling and distance education (Cahill & Martland, 1995) in facilitating career planning; psychosocial counseling for the unemployed with the collaboration of trade unions in the state of Bremen in Germany (Kieselbach & Lunser, 1990); the assignment in Finland of an employment services counselor to a vocational school to co-coordinate with the school guidance counselor the schools career services including individual guidance, counseling and planning services; employment exchange and cooperation with employers; access to the Internet and information material; placement of students in further education or in work, and follow-up on these placements; and teaching entrepreneurial skills and advising how to set up a business (Kurhila & Onnismaa, 2000); the nationwide network of Public Employment Security Offices (PESO) in Japan, their three-tier system of interventions for job applicants, with varying needs for assistance and the national computer assisted information system by which labor supply and demand information can be made available (Watanabe, Masaki, & Kamiichi, 1990), a new course of study to help students acquire knowledge of career decision-making processes (Senzaki, 1993) and specialized services for women, older workers and school drop-outs (Watanabe & Herr, 199[illegible] [illegible]g Kong, the extensive use of career info[illegible]hing services, workshops, and lectures [illegible]nning and various support service are p[illegible] youth and adults. In secondary schools, career teams are established to promote career services that are carried out primarily by career teachers (Li, 2000) and the attempt to create transnational linkages among the members of the European Community in order to make more available the provision of career guidance resources and to facilitate mobility through improving people's access to the help and information they require as they consider opportunities and requirements for jobs in the current twelve member states.

Many of these nations and others around the world have shown leadership and creativity in advancing theory and practice in career development. Canada has been one of those nations that has used creative national approaches to promoting research, innovative approaches, and the dissemination of career development practices and materials. The Canadian concept of "career" has changed over the past decades and given rise to important new conceptions of career development services for children, youth, and adults. Career, rather than a traditional view focused on full-time work in a single field of endeavor, is increasingly seen in relation to the need for multiple job changes across a career, incorporating the need for an emphasis in career development on work tasks rather than jobs. Within such contexts career development services in Canada have increasingly used technology—the computer and the Internet—as major tools to prepare persons for choices about education, training, and employment; placed major emphasis on individual responsibility—providing people with the tools to manage their own career development and to view personal career development as an ongoing learning process, not only an emphasis of importance when one is at a career crisis; implemented efforts across local, provincial, and federal levels to implement standards for the delivery of career services; and fostered governmental efforts to motivate a business and industry focus on the connection between school and work, and the participation of employers in work experience, cooperative education programs, career fairs, and other youth employment programs (Team Canada, cited in Plant, 2000).

Denmark, too, while engaged in the professionalization of its career services, has raised many important conceptualization and implementation issues in career development concepts and practices. The practice of career development is coordinated at the national level by the National Council on Educational and Vocational Guidance and at local and regional levels by career development committees. Careers education in schools takes place beginning in grade one and continues to the end of compulsory schooling at grade nine or ten. The development and execution of individual action plans are important aspects of careers education at each grade level. The end of compulsory education is a key decision point with students able to choose among work options, upper secondary schools (gymnasium), vocational education, higher education, or other forms of further education. Adults, too, have multiple opportunities for education and training, including second and third choice options, for persons who have dropped out of, not been successful, or need to initiate new career paths. Career development services are extensive and essentially provided on a lifelong basis. The practitioners of career services in different settings tend to be primarily teachers, with limited training in career counseling frequently delivered in short in-service training courses while the practitioner is engaged in daily counseling work. There is one master's degree and one doctoral program available in Denmark with career specialization.

Even though the available academic training for career development is limited, Denmark through national legislation has been committed to the importance of such services. Educational institutions at all levels have integrated careers education into their curriculum. For five million inhabitants of Denmark, there are estimated to be some 15,000 professionals, paraprofessionals, and nonprofessionals working in career development work. Most of these persons work in career development on a part-time basis, combining teaching and counseling/career development work. National legislation views career development as a continuous process, and one which emphasizes the importance of individual choice. But, perspectives on career development have changed overtime from a focus on the relationship between the individual and the society to "human resources" where human capital and the economic value of career development are assessed in more rigorous terms (Plant, 2000, p. 134). In the latter context, career guidance and career counseling have been submitted to various quality assurance evaluations using such quality indicators as client-centeredness; accessibility, transparency, and coherence of the services; well-trained counseling staff; valid, precise, and comprehensive career information; referral to other counseling specialists; follow-up; user satisfaction; and linkage to ethical considerations (Plant, 2000, p. 135).

Like several other nations, Denmark has recently instituted one-stop centers, known as counseling houses, in which career counselors offer different types of career development activities for different types of users, including information and counseling for training, educational options, and alternative job opportunities; training and improvement of job-search skills; and information on the labor market and on different wage-subsidy and training schemes.

Among the future issues related to career development raised in Denmark that have important implications for other countries are:

- The need to raise the level of professionalism in Danish career development services.

- The need to establish joint multidisciplinary bases of career counseling. Counseling services that are intended to cooperate should be designed, from the outset, to take part in a coordinated effort. The point is that linkages, including referrals and other forms of cooperation, among counseling services are sometimes negatively affected because counselors in different settings work under different conditions, have different goals and differing degrees of professionalization.
- The need to reflect the reality of the informal economy in career counseling. The informal economy—bartering goods and services, do-it-yourself projects and assistance to friends, construction and domestic assistance or professional services like law and accounting for unofficial or unrecorded payments—is a way of avoiding taxes. Swapping skills for skills rather than money represents the equivalent of 100,000 jobs in Denmark (Plant, 2000, p. 140) and hundreds of thousands, if not millions, more in other nations. How ought career counseling, whose content has typically been jobs in the formal economy, relate to such phenomena as the informal economy? How can the informal economy be seen as another option for some clients and under what assumptions? How can it be seen as a potential form of career counseling engaging in job creation?

In speaking about issues facing career development services in Denmark, Plant (2000) raises another ethical issue that has not yet received much discussion in the professional literature: what he calls *green career development* (Plant, 2000). Within this context Plant has raised questions about the role of career development services in helping persons make sustainable career choices that consider environmental problems such as pollution, the toxicity of industrial processes, and conservation rather than exploitation of natural resources. Thus, he raises issues about the clash of economic development and environmental and human concerns and how career counselors should address such concerns with clients as they consider their career choices.

The Netherlands has been engaged for several years in developing a new approach to career development in which lifelong learning and employability are the major targets of a process-oriented, longitudinal, and coherent approach. In sum, a major issue has been the development of career services "that support the individual in becoming more employable in a changing situation" (Oomen & de Vos, 2000). Thus, the intent of career development services is to:

> *Enable the individual to establish a meaningful relationship between education and training, work and life development. In this way, the individual can decide on a work orientation and develop a working identity connected to the dynamic of the work order. If this is successful, the uncertainty over role and livelihood can be transformed into a new perspective of the future and new opportunities. (p. 222)*

To accomplish such goals, career development in the Netherlands assumes that individuals must not only acquire specific career skills but must be able to answer three questions:

> *What sort of person am I, with respect to motivation, interests, strengths and weaknesses? Given my qualities, in what area of work can I make a meaningful contribution to society? In what type of vocational role can I establish a meaningful exchange with others? The first question relates to personal identity. The second relates to the capacity to determine a course at school or the course of work. The third question is about developing a working identity. (p. 222)*

In a major sense, these questions and their theoretical implications drive the perspectives in the Netherlands on how career development practices should be implemented in schools and with adults in employment services. These approaches focus, among other emphases, on helping individuals seek a pattern in experiences that have attracted them in the past, the life themes that have given continuity to their self-concepts, and answering "What sort of work suits the sort of person I am?" These perspectives have led to the classification of work and of work types, the identification of *core dilemmas* in a specific career field, and to the conception of a career development service as a *powerful learning environment.* Related to such perspectives, national action programs have been developed to focus on young people from ethnic groups in major cities, to combat unemployment, and to prevent and combat prejudice, discrimination, and racism. Careers education and guidance have been made mandatory in all secondary schools with specific career development goals for student to achieve specified. At the adult level, a *chain* of *strategic alliances* has been developed between public employment offices, private providers of career development services, employers, and other related agencies. The intent is that this chain of career development services will provide prevention, care for sick workers, reintegrate unemployed workers, provide welfare intervention, and payments to persons with disabilities or out of work (Oomen & de Vos, 2000).

These brief synopses of how selected nations have developed policies related to career development; have created new conceptions of the meaning of career; have developed the necessary infrastructure of career information and career guidance practitioners for schools, tertiary institutions, adults, and marginalized groups; and have used technology does not do justice to the whole complex of career activities in which these nations are engaged. Nor does it include many other nations that are also engaged in important contributions to the theory and practice of career guidance, career counseling, or other forms of career development services. Nevertheless, these brief examples of how the nations referenced are approaching the career needs of their citizens illustrates the richness of the models of theory and practice that are now arising around the world in small and large nations and in nations at different levels of economic development. As U.S. professionals read these accounts of how other nations are responding to the career needs of their citizens, such perspectives represent a mirror by which we can reflect on our own assumptions, coherence, theory and practice, and career development infrastructure in the United States. In some cases, the approaches of other nations validate our own; in other instances, the creativity and implementation of unique approaches to career development services in other nations give models of excellence to learn from and aspire to emulate.

In some of these nations, the career development responses are shaped by and take forms that are indigenous to the particular nation's resources and policies; in other nations and transnational groups, career guidance services tend to converge with philosophies and practices that are present in North America.

For example, in a study of educational and vocational guidance services for the 14 to 25 age group in the European community, Watts, Dartois, and Plant (1988a) have contended that there are three key strands in guidance in schools that can be identified. These trends are similar to those in North America or, more specifically, in the United States as reported elsewhere in this book. They suggest some convergence in how career guidance is viewed among industrialized nations and, in particular, how Europe is viewing career guidance in schools.

According to Watts and colleagues (1988a):

The first [trend] is that educational and vocational guidance is increasingly being seen as a continuous process, *which:*

Should start early in schools.
Should continue through the now often extended period of transition to adult and working life.
Should then be accessible throughout adult and working life.

So far as schools are concerned:

Guidance is more and more being seen not as an adjunct to schools but as an integral part of the educational process.
This is resulting in the growth of specialist guidance roles within the schools.
It is also producing a recognition of the need to involve all *teachers in guidance to some extent, and to develop ways of supporting them in their guidance roles.*
Guidance elements are increasingly being built into the curriculum, in the form of careers education programmes, work-experience programmes, etc.
Where external agencies work into schools, their role is now more and more viewed as that of a partner or consultant to the guidance services within the school itself.

The second key trend is the move towards what Watts, et. al. have termed a more open professional model, *in which the concept of an expert guidance specialist working with individual clients in what sometimes appears to be a psychological vacuum is replaced, or at least supplemented, by a more diffuse approach in which:*

A more varied range of interventions is used. These may include:

- *Guidance elements within the curriculum of education and training programmes.*
- *Group-work alongside one-to-one work.*
- *Use of computers and other media.*

More attention is given to working with and through networks of other individuals and agencies. This may involve:

Supporting "first-in-line" teachers, supervisors, etc. in their guidance roles.

Involving parents and other members of the community as resources in the guidance process.
Working with "opportunity providers" to improve the opportunities available to young people.

Such a model offers the prospect of being a more cost-effective approach to guidance, as well as being based more closely on the ways in which choices actually tend to be made in practice.

The third and final trend, closely linked to the other two, is towards a greater emphasis on the individual as an active agent, *rather than as a passive recipient, within the guidance process. This can be seen in, for example:*

The growth of programmes of careers education, work experience, etc. designed to provide young people with a range of skills, attitudes, knowledge and experiences which will help them in making their own career decisions.
The growth of interest in counselling as opposed to advice-giving.
The reduced emphasis on psychometric testing, and the increased interest in encouraging self-assessment rather than "expert" assessment.
The development of self-help approaches in occupational information centres and in computer-aided guidance systems.
The interest in "education for enterprise" as a way of developing young people's self-reliance and initiative.
The participation of young people in the preparation of information booklets and in running youth information centres.
*The individual young person is thus now increasingly seen as the active centre of the guidance process, with the guidance specialist being available partly as a specialist referral point and partly as a means of activating other resources for young people to draw upon (pp. 93–95).**

What is evident in the growth and the diversity of the provision of career programs and intervisions in different nations is that societies throughout the world are in transition. In some, the changes are revolutionary; in others, evolutionary. It is a rare nation, if it exists, that is not influenced by turmoil surrounding its economic climate, achievement images, value structure, employment or unemployment rates, educational structure, male/female relationships, quality of life, and other matters that bear on the kind of work available, who does it, and how people get access to it and advance within it. Obviously, career development in each nation is a function of the prevailing political, economic, educational, and industrial systems of that nation and of the resources devoted to career counseling, career guidance, or career education and the forms they take.

Historically, societies have varied on at least two dimensions in their approaches to helping youth and adults with career development (Watts & Herr, 1976). The two dimensions can be distinguished by (1) whether the primary locus is the needs of society or on the needs of the individual, and (2) whether the approach basically accepts the status quo or is concerned with changing it in prescribed directions. Figure 1.2 graphically illustrates this point. Each of the four cells in the figure carry different implications for the nature and content of career development. Basically, each asks whether the purpose of career interventions is human development, facilitating individual free choice and purposeful action, or developing human capital and deciding how it will be used for the good of the state. Career services can be and are developed in various nations from each or a combination of the answers possible.

In an important sense, career guidance and career counseling, the practice of career counseling, does not occur independent of the political, economic, and social structure of the nation in which

	Needs of Society	Needs of the Individual
Change	Social Change Approach	Individual Change Approach
Status Quo	Social Control Approach	Non-Directive Approach

FIGURE 1.2 International Approaches to Helping Youth and Adults with Career Development (Reprinted form 1981 comprehensive set of counselor competencies of National Vocational Guidance Association. © AACD. Reprinted with permission. No further reproduction authorized without written permission of American Association for Counseling and Development.

*From A. G. Watts, in association with Colette Dartois and Peter Plant, *Educational and Vocational Guidance Services for the 14–25 Age Group in the European Community.* Copyright © 1988 Commission of the European Communities. Reprinted with permission.

they are implemented. They must be understood and appreciated as sociopolitical processes shaped by the legislation and policies of a specific country and by the prevailing aspects of culture. Of particular importance in the latter regard are such elements of culture as "the nature and rigidity of the class and caste structure, the value system, the relationship of the individual to the group, and the nature of the enterprise system" (Super, 1985a, pp. 12–13). These elements vary in their interaction from nation to nation. Whatever the combination, they are the mediators of the opportunity structure; of which career paths and mobility factors are available; of the social metaphors that translate into sanctioned or supported behavioral models; of contingencies or reinforcements that result in cognitive structures, habits, and information processing; of the in-groups and the out-groups of the society; of the images of individual achievement possible; and of expectations for person-institutional loyalties or identification. They dictate whether the state's goals or those of the individual will be preeminent. These elements define which groups are at risk (or marginalized) or considered to be societal problems. They create the context within which career guidance and counseling inadvertently or systematically respond to the ethnocentrisms that differentiate societies, political belief systems, and individual choice.

Such cultural artifacts differentiate how people will conceive and play out the self-concept: as a bundle of roles subjugated to the family or other group, as in a collectivist society, or as a system of self-pictures available to discriminate behavior in ways unique to the individual (Triandis, 1985). Cultural diversity also is manifested in the type of career counseling problems experienced by persons in different nations and in the varieties of psychopathology that are apparent, how they are understood and interpreted by persons experiencing them and the broader society, and the course from onset to cure they are likely to describe (Draguns, 1985).

Within this broad context of national differences, Super (1974) suggested that in examining career guidance practices among the developed nations, four conflicting trends are apparent. The current authors have adapted the language and provided commentary about each to accent their viability in contemporary terms. As suggested in the examples of national approaches to career development previously discussed, these four sets of factors, while more than twenty-five years old, still describe the differences in professionalization and availability of career guidance, career counseling, and other career interventions across the world. Some of these differences are apparent in the overview of national approaches and issues previously discussed in this section.

1. *Personpower utilization versus human development.* In the first situation, career guidance or career counseling can be viewed as an instrument of national policy by which persons can be directed and trained in educational and occupational areas reflecting economic and social needs. Or, in the latter instance, career services can be seen as reflecting a national policy that emphasizes self-fulfillment, social welfare, and personal happiness. These are not necessarily mutually exclusive views, but it is likely that in most nations one of the two possibilities predominates as the basis for career guidance and counseling.
2. *Occupational choice versus vocational development.* The basic conflict here has to do with whether one views career interventions as leading to an immediate job or occupational choice or as a process of helping individuals clarify and act on intermediate and future goals. In the second perspective, even when immediate choice is under consideration, is it considered in relation to such matters as the place of work in the preferred lifestyle, preferences for leisure, life goals broadly conceived, or the relationship of this job or position to those one hopes to achieve in the future?
3. *Information dissemination versus counseling.* The fundamental issue in this dichotomy is whether the provision of accurate information about educational and occupational information is adequate in itself or whether people need the assistance of specially trained individuals to sort out the implications of such information in relation to personal interests, values, needs, and abilities.
4. *Professional guidance versus lay guidance.* This conflict has to do primarily with the form and intensity of the training people need to do effective "career guidance" and whether a nation can afford to commit the resources and the training necessary to professionalize its career specialists. This is reflected in the fact that some nations train people with less than a baccalaureate degree

in brief workshops to become *career counselors;* other nations believe that such professional work requires a master's degree or more.

The prevailing professional rhetoric, if not always the practice, of career development favors those elements of the four conflicts that emphasize human development, vocational (career) development, counseling, and professional guidance. Saying this, however, does not preclude the fact that in the United States, as in other nations, theories, techniques, and programs of career guidance, career education, or career counseling are never value free.

Under any model of implementation, career interventions represent some form of environmental modification that in turn carries a set of assumptions with political overtones. In any transactional view of individual-environmental interaction, it is societal factors—political, religious, economic, historical—that largely determine the types of problems that are appropriate for counselors or career guidance practitioners to deal with. This perspective is played out in the legislative entitlements or definitions of service that can be provided, in the policy focus, in the resources committed to career guidance and counseling, and whether career development mechanisms are carried out by individual practitioners or in collaboration among practitioners and among organizations (Borgen, 2000).

Although the global economy and international economic competition suggest that many career problems can be classified and labeled in similar ways across nations, it does not follow that definitions and provisions of career guidance, career counseling, or the practice of career development are either the same or at the same level of development from nation to nation. As political and economic systems vary and change so do the priorities for, the openness to, and the resources available to institute and extend systems of career services.

In a major sense, the openness to career services in any nation depends upon how the macroeconomic trends emanating from the global economy, that have been identified earlier in this chapter as shared across nations, are actually viewed by policy makers at national, regional, and local levels. Frequently, nations choose which economic or human resources trends are, in fact, likely to be of most impact on them and what resources can be made available to respond.

At an individual level, it is possible to argue that the types of questions that youths and adults bring to career guidance specialists or counselors are less directly labeled products of the global economy and more directly related to how individuals view the current societal belief systems about such matters as personal choice, achievement, social interaction, self-initiative, marriage, prestige, occupational or educational status, and many other aspects of life. The resulting anxieties, deficits, or indecisiveness that people experience as they compare themselves with what society in the form of parents, teachers, peers, spouses, employers, self-improvement books, or the mass media say they should believe or do represent a large part of the content with which career guidance specialists or counselors deal.

Flowing from such a point of view is the notion that the questions different societies "permit" or encourage their citizens to ask about themselves and their future and the resources placed at the disposal of the individual to sort out answers to these questions vary cross-culturally in fairly dramatic ways. Herr (1974, 1978a) has attempted to analyze the types of work-related questions populations are likely to ask whose nations differ on an industrial, postindustrial, or information-based occupational continuum. In particular he distinguishes among the types of work, information systems, work-related questions, and guidance processes likely to exist in the least developed societies, developing nations, and developed or postindustrial nations.

As one moves across these three categories of economic development, the roles of families change as information disseminators and reinforcers of certain socially stratified occupational or educational choices; "have nots" change from a majority to a minority position in the society; occupational diversity and service roles increase; work becomes less visible and increasingly "walled off" from those who must choose it; information about opportunities becomes more sophisticated, more abundant, and more likely to be delivered by electronic or telecommunications methods; personal questions shift from those primarily addressed to physical survival and increasingly become more existential ("Who am I?" "What do I want to be?" "What sort of person can I be?); and career guidance and career counseling tend to become more conceptually based and seen as specialized occupations (professions) in their own right. Although such perspectives are overly simplified, and, indeed, caricatures of reality, they do cast into bold relief the fact that career development mechanisms do not exist in a political, social, or economic vacuum. They are interactive, if not symbiotic, with the characteristics of the societies in which they exist.

The speed and the comprehensiveness with which the provision of career development programs and practices have expanded across the nations of the world has accelerated rapidly. As the relationships previously suggested between industrialism, information, economic development, the diversity of roles available, education and work, the need to provide information about work, and encouragement of achievement in systematic rather than random ways have become valid, then the practice of career development in some form is inevitable in virtually every nation. Perhaps the more salient point is that in an increasingly technological world, both international organizations and governments have become more aware that the major questions regarding technology are not technical but human questions (Herr, 1994b). Among these questions are not only those of how to develop workers able to discharge the occupational task-specific skills required to design, operate, and maintain the various forms of technology, but also, more importantly, how to help people come to terms with such matters as their work values, work commitments, work productivity, and the personal discipline associated with these matters; in short, their general employability skills.

Acknowledgment of the effects of cultural diversity on such outcomes will continue to stimulate a search for those elements that are common and effective across national models of career guidance and counseling and those elements that must be considered indigenous to a particular nation or culture.

THE LEGACY OF THE TWENTIETH CENTURY—THE CONCEPTUAL BASE FOR THE TWENTY-FIRST

It is appropriate to conclude this first chapter with a brief overview of some of the elements of the historical conceptual legacy that is available to career counselors and other career development specialists. In essence this brief synopsis is a summary of some of the major elements of what is known about career development that can be used as a basis for planning about theory and practice in the twenty-first century. Such information helps professionals—whether theorists or practitioners—consider what voids exist in our knowledge and in what we can do. It allows for analysis of the challenges likely to arise in the decades ahead, and, ultimately, the implications of these for the roles of counselors engaged in the theory and practice of career development.

As the previous sections of this chapter have suggested, career guidance and career counseling are being challenged to find new terms for these forms of intervention, new conceptual paradigms, and new scientific bases to respond to the new questions that continuously emerge from a world economic and occupational structure that is in major flux. The changes contemplated and the uncertainty experienced by individual users of career services across the world become the content with which counselors deal.

Against such a context, however, the authors of this book would argue that counselors, wherever they are located, have a legacy of concepts and practices on which to build, refine, and make innovations in their professional theory and practice in the future. They include the following (Herr, 1995, 1999):

- Career guidance and counseling have become worldwide phenomena. They are no longer the creature of a particular culture or society but have become incorporated in diverse forms across national and cultural boundaries. While the implementation of career guidance and counseling is not even across the world in its availability, in trained personnel, in resources, there are professionals on every continent and in most nations who are providing leadership to the advancement of career guidance and counseling, to the preparation of practitioners, to the development of indigenous theory and research and culturally relevant practices (e.g., Herr, 1999).
- Theories of career behavior and, less so, of career practice have been developed and have gained in credibility across national and social and economic contexts. These have combined insight into the cognitive and emotional aspects of individual career development with how such behavior can be changed, learned, and relearned, through individual counseling, group work, tests and assessments, and technological interventions (computer-aided processes and the Internet) (Savickas & Walsh, 1996).

- A body of knowledge has evolved that affirms that persons differ in how they view the meaning of work and its value or salience in their lives. These differences arise in gender, and in cultural, educational, and economic variations. It also has been generally accepted that work roles and work adjustments are interactive with family roles and other life style issues and that as choices are to be made, individuals need to consider the balances of such roles in their lives and the potential role conflicts that may occur in the multiple roles they play (Super & Sverko, 1995; Super, 1990).
- Researchers have generally established that neither individual behavior nor the shape and substance of career guidance and counseling occurs in a vacuum. Rather events external to individuals (e.g., economic trends, shifts in occupational structures and job availability, changing educational and performance requirements for jobs) shape the types of content and concerns clients bring to counselors (Vondracek, Lerner, & Schulenberg, 1986) and they also shape the policies and legislation that often define what is expected of career guidance and counseling and how and where they are to be implemented and by whom (Herr, 1998). As a result, in some nations, career development theories are primarily sociological, not psychological, in origin. The former accent the overriding importance of contextual factors—demands of the workplace, limits on individual choice by socioeconomic class and characteristics of the family unit—that constrain decision-making freedom. The latter accent the importance of individual action, knowledge, and skills that can overcome contextual factors (Herr, 1999).
- Regardless of context, theorists and researchers construe individual career behavior as oriented to meaning-making and constructing one's reality by decisions one makes or avoids, rather than simply being passive receptors of information or knowledge from external sources. This is the essence of constructivism (Peavey, 1994; Rosen & Kuehlwein, 1996), as well as narrative analysis and related approaches to intervention (Cochran, 1997; Watkins & Savickas, 1990).
- Researchers and theorists have demonstrated that virtually all persons experiencing transition points in their lives can profit from career guidance and counseling and that the career questions and concerns of the child, the adolescent, and the young, mid-career, and older adult may have common elements but are developmentally and experientially different and require career guidance and counseling programs that differ in emphases and interventions (Herr, 1986; Sexton, Whiston, Bleuer, & Walz, 1997).
- A growing scientific knowledge base demonstrates that a wide range of career counseling interventions have positive effects on career information deficits, client needs for support, and help with identifying and selecting options available to them (Campbell, Connel, Boyle, & Bhaerman, 1983; Spokane & Oliver, 1983; Spokane, 1991). Observers increasingly contend that schools, colleges and universities, and workplaces can be made more career relevant by including career guidance and counseling objectives and practices as central to their missions (Herr, 1995).
- Researchers have shown that effective career intervention consists of specific elements. Among others, they include: (1) occupational information organized by a comprehensive method and easily accessible to a client; (2) assessment materials and devices that clarify a client's self picture and vocational potentials; (3) individual or group activities that require a rehearsal of career plans or problems; (4) counselors, groups, or peers that provide support; and (5) a comprehensive cognitive structure for organizing information about self and occupational alternatives (Holland, Magoon, & Spokane, 1981).
- Technology, such as computer-assisted career guidance systems, can provide an important extension of the counselor's skills, help clients retrieve information about their options in an accurate and timely fashion, and rehearse the effects of their options and counseling programs, not as interventions independent of counselors, but as important adjunctive strategies (Sampson, Shahnasarian, & Reardon, 1987).
- Individual career development and how it unfolds is not simply an issue of economic livelihood or even of self-concept. Rather how the search for and the acquisition of work occurs and how the individual is inducted into and adjusts to work is also a mental health issue. Job stress and the loss of work, particularly involuntary unemployment, has been found to manifest itself in

physiological, psychological, emotional and behavioral problems and the effects of these are not confined to the person who has lost his or her job but ripples in effects through families, spouses, children, friends, and others (Borgen & Amundson, 1984; Kleinman, 1988).

- Most theorists and practitioners have come to view career guidance and career counseling as primarily focused on decision making and on taking action and implementing plans. But career guidance and career counseling are not just about helping clients gain insight into their difficulties; rather their intent is to help persons identify and learn behaviors and plan and execute actions that are likely to change the conditions, personal or external, that brought them to career guidance and counseling originally. Increasingly it has become recognized that for persons who have experienced major work adjustment problems, unusual job stress, involuntary unemployment, and underemployment, career counseling cannot be separated from personal counseling. Indeed, such approaches fuse into a comprehensive or multidimensional set of perspectives and techniques that help the individual reframe who he or she is and who they want to be and to reconstruct their irrational career beliefs, emphasize how to evaluate options available, prepare for them, and act to achieve them (Herr, 1997; Krumboltz, 1993).

With some overlap with the set of concepts just addressed, Savickas (2000, pp. 58–64) has identified, from an extensive review of the professional literature and longitudinal studies, fourteen facts that career specialists know for sure. They are presented here without the comprehensive and articulate commentary supporting each of these facts that Savickas has provided to validate them. They are:

1. Childhood socialization influences adult work performance and job satisfaction.
2. Part-time work affects the socialization and development of adolescents.
3. Knowing how the world of work is organized eases vocational decision making and job transition.
4. Vocational exploration and information lead to better career decisions.
5. Career interventions effectively ease occupational choice and enhance work adjustment.
6. Interests shape occupational preferences and enhance learning during training.
7. Personality and ability determine job performance more than interests.
8. Congruence between the workers and the job improves performance.
9. The transition from school to work can be smoothed.
10. Organizational socialization of new employees promotes satisfaction and performance.
11. Work can be structured to foster emotional well-being.
12. Workers can learn to cope more effectively with occupational stress.
13. Work-family connections can be made less conflictual and more integrative.
14. Individual differences among aging workers can be used to retain and retrain productive workers.

These brief syntheses of key concepts that comprise the legacy of career development and constitute major elements of the knowledge base underlying career practices suggest the status of career theory and career practice at the end of the twentieth century. This conceptual legacy will undoubtedly expand and become more culturally sensitive in the twenty-first century. So will the evenness with which career guidance, career counseling, and other career interventions will become available across the world. Many of the voids now present in the theory, research, and practice of career development will be systematically closed in the decades ahead while new questions and challenges will unfold.

At a minimum Herr (2001) has contended that the trends for the immediate future will include:

- *Growth in the practice of career development as a world-wide phenomenon.* In the next century, the practice of career development is likely to be more comprehensive in scope, more evenly distributed and accessible, and more indigenous as nations increasingly tailor the practice of career development to their needs.
- *The practice of career development increasingly will be seen as an instrument to strengthen individual human dignity.* In a world that continues to struggle with conflicting desires either to degrade or enhance human dignity, assaults on human dignity continue to occur as a function of economic and workplace issues and persistent

high unemployment rates among some populations. In such conditions, the practice of career development, among its other functions, serves as a mechanism by which to provide persons hope, the affirmation of their individual dignity and worth, and the support to establish new career directions.

- *The practice of career development increasingly will be seen as an instrument of personal flexibility.* As new concepts of "career" continue to emerge that are qualitatively different from traditional views of this process, at the least, many persons in the twenty-first century will need to learn:

  How to change with change, accept ambiguity and uncertainty, negotiate job or career changes multiple times in their working lifetimes, be able to plan and act on shifting career opportunities,...and have the motivation to be career resilient—to persist in the face of change and unplanned for problems and difficulties. (Herr, 2001, p. 208)

- *Career counselors will take on expanded roles.* Career counselors will increasingly take on new roles including those as planners, applied behavioral scientists, and technologists as they tailor their career practices to settings and populations whom they serve.
- *The science underlying career counseling, career guidance, and other interventions making up the practice of career development will expand dramatically.* Emphases on identifying and using evidence-based or results-based interventions (Sexton, Whiston, Bleuer, & Walz, 1997) will lead to a comprehensive matrix of presenting problems and the interventions found to be most effective in resolving career issues under different conditions, by gender, at specific developmental ages. In addition, such career counseling interventions and programs will be seen in cost-benefit terms to help facilitate the deployment of career counseling resources in the most effective manner.

SUMMARY

In this chapter, we have examined the international and historical evolution of the contexts, content, and concepts of what is coming to be called the practice of career development, although in the United States and in other nations the terms career guidance, career counseling, career education, and career interventions remain in standard usage. We have continued to use the term comprehensive career guidance to reflect its importance to all segments of the population—children, youths, and adults—as well as its growing availability, albeit with different terminology in community agencies, business and industry, and educational settings. We have discussed the importance of approaching such programs of interventions in structured, planned, and systematic ways. We have identified the growing vocabulary associated with the practice of career development and the trends in the roles of career counselors that continue to emerge. We have expanded our coverage of international approaches to career development to reflect the important work in designing career interventions that are customized to the career issues and the policies of a growing number of nations around the world. And we have concluded Chapter 1 with a synopsis of what we have learned about the theory and practice of career development in the twentieth century and the challenges likely to unfold during the twenty-first century.

In Chapter 2, we will examine contemporary meanings of work, job stress, and related issues dealing with the content and organization of work. In Chapter 3, we will discuss the occupational structure, its changing nature, and its classification. In Chapter 4, we will consider the variety of current theoretical and research models essential to understanding career behavior. In Chapter 5, we will explore the career problems of specific population groups (e.g., women, persons with disabilities, minority group members).

Chapters 1 through 5 describe much of the content of career guidance and career counseling: differences in occupational and life alternatives, influences on work values; career identity; choice-making strategies; and the special circumstances relating to access and adjustment to work associated with gender, social circumstances, disability, and other factors. The remaining chapters of the book tend to describe the multiple interventions subsumed under the terms career counseling, career education, career guidance, and career services.

CHAPTER TWO

Work: Meaning, Access, Adjustment

KEY CONCEPTS

- The term *work* has multiple definitions, its own vocabulary, and different meanings across cultures, groups, and time.
- When one chooses a job, an occupation, or a career, one also makes decisions, purposefully or inadvertently, about leisure, continuing needs for education, status, prescriptive or discretionary use of time, and the work culture in which job tasks will be performed.
- Job satisfaction is a complex term incorporating matters of job context and job content, overall satisfaction, and facet satisfaction.
- Many research studies link work and mental health, unemployment, stress-related physical problems, work pathology, family disorder, substance abuse, and other forms of interaction.
- The transition to work is comprised of at least three stages and multiple sets of barriers that young workers and adults must negotiate and master if such transitions are to be successful. Educational institutions, transition mechanisms, and employers each have specific contributions to make to the movement into and adjustment to work.
- A central organizing goal of the practice of career development is the choice of and effective implementation of work in one's life.
- The global economy will likely require new forms of organizational flexibility. But flexibility in the work place is not possible without personal competence and flexibility. Such behaviors will serve as stimuli to more comprehensive models of career counseling and other career interventions.

Work is the term of central concern in this chapter. A central organizing goal of career education, career guidance, and career counseling is the facilitation of the choice and implementation of work in one's life. When one chooses a job, one chooses a whole series of things in addition to the work content or tasks to be performed. One also chooses the persons with whom one will work, the role expectations of others, the social status ascribed to the job, the likely types of leisure in which one will engage and with whom one will likely experience leisure, how much vacation time will be taken and when vocations will occur, the types of continuing education or training required, the style of supervision, whether one's use of time is rigidly prescribed or discretionary, and the *work culture* in which the job tasks will be performed. Put somewhat differently, Landy (1989) has suggested:

> *Work is something that happens to an individual. It is a treatment of sorts. People go to a work setting and are exposed to various elements. These elements include things such as heat and light and noise. In addition, there are such elements as pay and supervisory style and coworkers. Even the duties and responsibilities that make up the "job" are treatments. Workers are exposed to a work pace, a certain demand for productivity, and accountability. (p. 600)*

The term *work culture* and the notion of work as a treatment that happens to a person in a work setting is also captured by the term *corporate culture.* Schein (1999) suggests that "organizations develop powerful cultures that guide the thinking and behavior of their employees" (p. xiv) and these cultures make a difference to corporate performance, to how work is organized, and to organizational identity. Depending upon how they are implemented and whether they change in response to shifting external environmental conditions, organizational cultures can be dysfunctional; a serious constraint on learning, change, and strategic planning; a spur to individual employee fit with its goals; and a reinforcement of its values with regard to the importance of the individual worker role within the organization's structure.

Just as nations, societies, geographic regions, and specific groups of people can be described in terms of their culture—their shared histories of language, ethnicity, and experience—so, too, can industries (e.g., construction, financial services, health care), corporations, or particular workplaces. At each of these organizational levels, the work or corporate culture embodies a strong and often unconscious set of forces that define the individual and collective behavior, ways of perceiving, thought patterns, values, vocabulary, patterns of dress and other behaviors. Think for a moment about the setting, the equipment used, the necessary knowledge required, and the problems to be solved by persons who work on highway construction, in a bank, or in a hospital. It is not difficult to visualize the differences that occur in the tasks performed, the language used, the clothing worn, the assumptions about their work that workers experience in each of these types of work cultures. It is likely that workers in each of these industries will incorporate different organizational assumptions and identities—the building of highways for purposes of safety and efficient travel, the processing of financial transactions accurately and honestly, the prevention and treatment of human disease or injury. It is also likely that workers in each of these settings will take on subidentities associated with the actual work they perform within that setting: construction equipment operation, clerical, technical, direct customer service, financial services, surgery, and so on. The elements of organizational culture, however, go beyond effects on individual behavior and, in a larger sense, determine the strategy, goals, and modes of functioning in particular industry, a corporation, or a specific workplace.

Implicit in what has been described is the reality that work or corporate culture is comprised of levels of organizational culture that vary in their visibility. On balance, organizational cultures are comprised of a continuum of factors from those that are visible (e.g., the type of clothing worn on the job, the level of formality between workers and managers, the equipment or tools used to do the work) to the explicit commitments (e.g., strategies, goals, philosophies) and the basic underlying assumptions (the beliefs and values) that are shared and taken for granted as the organization goes about its work. These latter elements of the corporate or work culture are essentially the accumulated learnings within an organization that buttress the methods used and the actions taken.

Within these contexts, corporate cultures vary in the typologies that describe their emphases on how people relate to each other and how they do their job, such as the degree of sociability expected among workers, teamwork versus individual accountability, the internal or the external focus of the firm, whether flexibility or stability and control guide managerial decisions, the kinds of information and control procedures needed to operate effectively, how rewards and status are allocated, communication processes used, and authority relationships vis-à-vis workers and management. Since organizations, even multinational organizations, ultimately operate within a national culture, the assumptions of that culture tend to become reflected in the organizational culture as it relates to individual rights, collectivist or group goals, loyalty and commitment to one's job, employment security, and male/female relationships.

While much more can be said about the elements of work or corporate culture and the national or international effects on some of its assumptions, several points need to be made. One is that when a person chooses a job, one also chooses the culture, the behavioral expectations, and the beliefs about human relationships, group boundaries, and work performance that characterize the work place in which the job chosen will be carried out. Second, elements or emphases of the work culture tend to be firm specific; while they may speak to technical issues, their effects tend to be more psychological as they describe, give meaning and predictability to the work place. Three, not all elements of the work culture are visible; some elements function at deeper levels of shared beliefs and learning, which to be successful workers need to learn and adapt to. Four, workplaces are comprised of systems of performance and networks of relationships that guide decisions about the flow of information and material, processes, and policies as well as the organization of the work to be done.

Given such diverse and interactive outcomes from a choice of work, it is paradoxical that the multiple meanings of work are rarely discussed in the career guidance literature. Indeed, work is frequently treated as a monolithic abstraction, almost as though all work is the same or as if the word *work* has a single meaning.

To treat work as though it has the same meaning for all people in all occupations and workplaces is to restrict the vision of how career counseling or career guidance should be tailored to the needs of people who experience work differently. Counseling is a verbal profession. It has, as a major part of its content, words and other symbols by which people communicate their perceptions of themselves and the work world. How a counselor responds to clients' problems and concerns depends on the labels and the definitions by which these questions, problems, or concerns are classified and the success of the counselor's efforts is related to how congruent these classifications are to what the counselee is actually experiencing.

Chapter 1 identified some of the terms of major significance to the understanding and practice of career guidance and career counseling. It was suggested there that the career counselor will function differently if the client's immediate concern is choosing a specific job, considering a choice of occupation and the training required, or deliberating about how such matters might fit with lifestyle, family roles, availability and use of leisure, or personal aspirations as these combine to shape a career. Terms such as *employment and employability, job, occupation,* and *career* are not interchangeable. They represent different choices for the client and for the career counselor. They also embody different meanings, levels of abstraction, time frames, and complexities that need to be reflected in counselor behavior.

THE LANGUAGE OF AND PREPARATION FOR WORK

Although work can be defined in a variety of ways, some definitions summarize several major concepts. Shertzer (1981) has combined many of these as he talks about work as the activity by which humans exercise control over their lives; as the channel through which we act on and change our environment, a way we produce ourselves, as we work to produce the society that defines us; physical or mental effort directed toward producing something; economic employment by which to earn a living; activity that is required and for which, typically, payment is made.

Other authors take a more direct approach to the definition of work. For example, in Tolbert's view (1980), work is defined as "purposeful mental, physical, or combined mental-physical activity that produces a service to others as well as a material product" (p. 32).

With yet another emphasis, Super (1976) defines work as:

> *The systematic pursuit of an objective valued by oneself (even if only for survival) and desired by others; directed and consecutive, it requires the expenditure of effort. It may be compensated (paid work) or uncompensated (volunteer work or an avocation). The objective may be intrinsic enjoyment of the work itself, the structure given to life by the work role, the economic support which work makes possible, or the type of leisure which it facilitates. (p. 20)*

This definition does not equate work and occupation, as is often the case. Rather, it allows for work to be nonpaid, to be outside the formal job structure identified as occupation, to include homemakers, members of alternative communities, and those self-employed in the invisible and illegal economy as workers (G. Miller, 1980).

The National Vocational Guidance Association (NVGA) in its glossary of terms defines work as a conscious effort, other than having as its primary purposes either coping or relaxation, aimed at producing benefits for oneself or others (Sears, 1982).

Super also proposes definitions for other words appropriate to a language of work. They include the following:

Labor: Productive work for survival or support, requiring physical or mental effort.

Employment: Time spent in paid work or in indirectly paid work such as homemaking.

Leisure: Time free of required paid or unpaid work, in rest, play, or avocations.

The NVGA glossary defines leisure as relatively self-determined activities and experiences that are available owing to having discretionary income, time, and social behavior; the activities may be physical, intellectual, volunteer, creative, or some combination of all four (Sears, 1982).

Play: Activity that is primarily recreational and relaxing; engaged in for its own sake; it may be systematic or unsystematic, without objective or with a temporary and personal objective; it may involve the expenditure of effort, but that effort is voluntary and easily avoided by the player (p. 22).

Super's definitions of work and related terms are basically psychological; they tend to place the perceptions, definitions, and motivations relative to work within the individual's actions. Another way to define work is from a sociological perspective. In this connection, Braude (1975) contends:

> *The sociologist argues that the human being is not an economic animal and that only, nor is he a psychological mechanism and that only, nor is he wholly political or exclusively cultural. If man is human at all, the sociologist says, this humanity stems from the necessary inclusion in groups and in the web of groups that make up society. (p. 4)*

Flowing from this perspective, Braude goes on to argue:

> *Narrowly conceived, work is simply the way in which a person earns a living. From a broad perspective, a person works in order to maintain or enhance any of the statuses that are his by virtue of his membership in a multiplicity of groups.... As long as the person defines, or has defined for him, the activities in which he is engaged as in some manner related to his survival, either physical or social, then we can say that person is working.... The work that any individual performs is articulated with that of others who work and with the containing social structure by its location within the division of labor. (pp. 12–13)*

These definitions of work and related terms suggest that such concepts are complex. They deal with both individual perceptions and actions as well as the social interactions and roles through which individual behavior is played out. Indeed, Braude (1975) maintains that work needs to be understood within a context of people, position, and purpose.

Definitions of work change across time and across societies. Super (1984b), with respect to changed perspectives on work, contends:

> *The approach of recent years has shifted from a focus on work alone as* the *central life concern to an interest in the quality of life, life in which work is* one *central concern in a constellation of roles such as homemaking, citizenship, and leisure that interact to make for life satisfaction. The terms* work motivation *and* job satisfaction *are now perhaps not displaced by, certainly incorporated into, the terms* quality of life *and* life satisfactions. *(p. 29)*

Even where definitions of work or the structure of values implicit in such definitions are similar from country to country, the hierarchical order or relative importance of work differs within and across societies. Super's multinational Work Importance Study (Super, 1984b, p. 36) has found, for example, that risk taking as a work value is more highly valued in the United States than in Yugoslavia and more by English-speaking Canadians than by French-speaking Canadians. Ronen's research in Japan (1979) has indicated that in contrast to most Western countries, where economic rewards are a material value, in Japan they are a prestige value, signifying the esteem in which the worker is held by the employer. In a study of 540 employees of a large industrial corporation in Hungary, Elizur and Shye (1990) found that the quality of work life (QWL) was strongly related to the employees' perceptions of their quality of life (QOL) in more general terms, and that employees' quality of work performance is affected by both their QOL and their QWL. England (1990) has also demonstrated that patterns of work meanings and related work outcomes are differently distributed among the work forces of Japan, Germany, and the United States.

Kabanoff and Daly (2000) have reported findings about the differences in values espoused by Australian and U.S. organizations matched by industry. The Australian organizations were seen as more bureaucratic than the U.S. organizations and to value authority, performance, and reward. In contrast, U.S. organizations were more likely to value teamwork, participation, commitment, performance, reward, and normative and affiliative values. The labels of the two primary organizations were, for the Australian, elite, and for the U.S., meritocratic. In the first instance, this organizational form is seen as "top-down" and inflexible in style, with command and control values common; in the U.S. value set, there was a greater emphasis on performance within a strong relational emphasis, in which effort, excellence, and achievement along with a concern for employees were values.

In a study of the person-organization fit of 581 volunteers from two matched organizations (hospitals and management consultancies) in Australia and in Southeast Asia, the researchers examined two types of fit: (1) individual orientation to individual-collectiveness and national cultures, and (2) individual orientation to individual-collectivism and organizational collectivism and organizational culture. On average, employees in organizations located in Southeast Asia endorsed more collectivistic and less individualistic values than employees in Australia. In particular, these national culture groups differed on vertical collectivism, the importance of subordinating one's own interests and goals to group interests and goals. Employees who were collectivistic in their values reported greater commitment and tenure in the Asian organizations. Although positive relationships were also found in Australia, the relationships between organizational commitment and tenure were much weaker in Australia. In sum, the authors concluded that employees' orientations on individualism versus collectivism did not affect commitment and tenure in individualistic cultures, but only in collectivistic cultures, which have strong norms supporting such attitudes and behaviors.

However it is viewed, work is a term having multiple definitions, meanings that shift across time, and hierarchical elements that differ within and between societies.

Work can be viewed as an *economic* process that represents market value for effort expended and thus represents an exchange process between the worker and the employer that is defined by wages, tasks involved, and productivity. Work is also a *psychological* process by which individual needs for affiliation, competency, identification, structure, purpose, and community can be met. Lastly, work is a *sociological* process that tends to occur within a network of other roles, relationships, role demands and expectations: worker–coworker, server–customer, supervisee–supervisor, manager–subordinate. "Work is, in most cases, a social activity, requiring interactions with patients, customers, students, superiors, colleagues, and so on. Just to survive, it is necessary to depend on the work of others. This is particularly true in a specialized economy, where few people produce supplies for their own food and shelter" (Sharf, 1992, p. 235). As such, the specific content and context of work needs to be a central concept in the counselor's interpretation of the importance of work and the practice of career development.

Despite the conceptual complexity associated with work, frequently in career development and career counseling we talk of choices, options, and decisions without using the word *work*. We act as though everyone understood that work is implied and as though the meaning of work were similarly understood by everyone using it. We also act as though the place of work in the lives of men and women is static, unchanging with age. In doing so, however, we corrupt the richness, diversity, and dynamism that the word *work* stands for. For example, if we confine our use of *work* only to task performance or work content, we are likely to emphasize a counselee's aptitudes, achievement, and work performance potential. In doing so, we may overlook the fact that, in either choice of or adjustment to work, the issue for a particular client may not be task performance but rather how one understands the workplace and its expectations, one's ability to get along with coworkers or to share values and interests with them, one's preferences for the intensity and style of supervision, or one's ambivalence about shifting attachments to work as one ages. As one focuses on each of these emphases, possible assessments, questions, and reality-testing experiences emerge that are different from those appropriate to thinking only about whether one can learn or do work tasks per se.

There are several other words that are also related to work as a context, as a process, and in relation to preparation before we leave this emphasis. With regard to the preparation for work, it has become increasingly obvious that skills training alone is inadequate unless such training also focuses on improved self-confidence, valuing what one is being trained to do, possessing general employability skills (e.g., punctuality, honesty, reliability), learning job search skills, developing techniques of career management, and clarifying a sense of purpose in work. While more needs to be said about how these ingredients of training vary across occupations or workplaces, from the standpoint of the language of work these ideas have enlarged the meaning of the term *employability*. In general usage, employability refers to the composite set of traits and skills that permits an individual to meet the demands of the workplace. *Employability*, then, is the expected end result of the preparation for work. It is the learned capacity of an individual to function in a particular work context. It involves both specific employability skills and general employability skills. *Specific employability skills* relate to the work tasks, the technical tasks, performed in a particular job. *General employability skills* encompass the affective cognitions and behaviors that relate to personal willingness to learn new tasks, accept new roles, and perform in a cooperative and productive manner. They involve basic academic skills, work habits and attitudes, interpersonal skills, ability to accept supervision and follow work rules, understanding the work culture, engaging in career planning, job search and access, ability to use exploratory resources, and self-knowledge of strengths and weaknesses. The amount and type of specific or general employability skills that will be included in the preparation for work will differ across jobs, occupations, and workplaces, and will depend on whether the preparation programs are *preemployment* or *on-the-job training*. The former typically includes secondary school and higher educational curriculum and government-sponsored training in vocational or technical schools, apprenticeships, cooperative education, and so forth. The latter is training that takes place in a workplace to focus on skills specific to a job or process that is specifically related to the job tasks in a particular firm.

Within such contexts, it is necessary to compare the terms *employability* and *employment.* These are not the same. *Employability* is the intended outcome of preparation for work; it signifies that an individual has the *potential* to perform in the workplace. However, because the person is employable does not mean that he or she will be employed. *Employment* means that the person has secured a job and is working in a paid capacity for a specified number of hours per week. Employment depends on the availability of jobs for which the person has the desired skills. If jobs are not available or, if available, they require skills that the person does not have, someone may have employability skills but be unemployed because of a mismatch between the skills offered by the person and the skills demanded by the workplace. This is the condition in many parts of the world today as occupational structures and work organizations are undergoing restructuring and other transformations which accompany political and economic change. Included in such transformations are the transitions from the *old economy to the new economy,* or the differences in job requirements available in either sector of the occupational structure. While precise definitions of these two terms are yet to be established, in general the term *old economy* refers to older, more established companies in industries such as transportation, manufacturing, agriculture, metal extraction, chemical production, and construction. The term *new economy* usually refers to the growth-oriented sectors of technology and the Internet. The new economy includes technology-intensive occupations that are information driven and frequently focus on the provision of knowledge and services.

The work available in both the old economy and the new economy is changing in performance requirements and in magnitude. Some of the forces operating in both sectors of the economy are captured in the research findings of Moskowitz and Warwick (1996):

> *Occupations that once offered solid careers are in decline, while positions once unheard of are now among the fastest growing.... The number of workers employed in any occupation depends in large part on the demand for the good or services provided by those workers. Over the last decade or so, for example, increased use of computers by businesses, schools, scientific organizations, and government agencies has contributed to large increases in the number of systems analysts, programmers, and computer repairers. However, even if the demand rises for goods and services provided by a group of workers, employment may not increase at all or may increase more slowly than demand because of changes in the way goods are produced and services are provided. In fact, some changes in technology and business practices cause employment to decline. For example, while the volume of paperwork is expected to increase dramatically, the employment of typists and work processors will probably fall. This reflects the growing use of word-processing equipment that increases productivity and permits other office workers to do more of their own typing. (p. 3)*

Certainly such changes have modified career paths and expectations for workers in many industries and workplaces. And, it has increased the proportion of the workforce who are considered *knowledge workers,* persons who know why as well as how to do their jobs. Currently, almost 60 percent of the American workforce are white collar, information workers, or knowledge workers. These terms reflect the growing need for employees to "work smarter, to manage the quality of what they do, and to become able to use various forms of technology in the problem-solving and information analysis inherent in their work" (Helgesen, 1996). The growing need for knowledge workers in an increasing number of occupations and knowledge organizations leads to the need for such workers to be subjected to continual upgrading—just like the tools they use, which are primarily technological in nature. As the proportions of knowledge workers grow, so do workplaces as *learning organizations.* The notion of the workplace or the corporate organization as a learning organization is a relatively new concept but one that is consistent with the reality that more work is being done by knowledge workers, who function not only on the basis of experience but on the bases of theory and information that explain why and how they do what they do. Directly and indirectly, how knowledge work is done and to what it is applied is a function of the wedding of science and technology, in which industrial and post-industrial processes reflect scientific discovery and its translation into forms of technology that can be applied and exploited commercially, in the home, in the health-care system, in the workplace.

Thus, in more and more occupations, workers must *know* as well as be able to *do*. In an increasing number of jobs, humans and machines seem to be entering into new partnerships, becoming linked as systems of productivity, in which technology becomes the tool and the human operator is the troubleshooter, the planner, the creator, the problem solver. Such jobs require workers who can deal with ideas in the workplace. As new science creates new knowledge and, in turn, new technology, it also shortens the time in which knowledge is useful before it is replaced with new knowledge and the need for new learning. This is the genesis of the call for *lifelong learning* for workers in many occupations in the old and new economies. But it also relocates where much of that learning should take place. Historically, the knowledge necessary to work was acquired through *institutional learning:* in high schools, vocational schools, community colleges, and universities. But if workplaces are increasingly technology-intensive, places where ideas must quickly be translated into work processes and products, then workplaces must be places in which learning is prized and fostered as a major tool of economic competition. Thus in contrast to or, perhaps more precisely, as a supplement to institutional learning, *organizational learning* goes on inside a workplace, at the level of individual workers or teams of people. Therefore:

> *The organizational learning movement is occupied with questions of the nature of learning in organizational environments and with what managerial leaders can do to enhance learning processes within organizations. The great contribution of this movement is to see the managerial leader as affecting the kind of learning that goes on in an organization and to define one of his or her role responsibilities as enhancing the learning of others. (Vaill, 1996, p. 52)*

Within this context, then:

> *The learning organization is a different kind of social system.... It is constituted to learn and grow and change—as opposed to traditional bureaucratic models constituted to be stable and predictable in their operation, to hold the line and not to change. (Vaill, 1996, p. 53)*

It is important to acknowledge here that the use of knowledge workers and learning organizations also affects how workers are managed. Indeed, just as "knowledge workers" is a new term in the lexicon of the workplace, so is the term "knowledge managers" (Wagner, 2002). Basically, traditional models of managers viewed them as overseers of workers, as persons who served as a link between the workers and executives, as persons who were in control of specific types of information, as persons who stood aloof from the workers and the work they were managing. In an environment populated by large proportions of knowledge workers, knowledge managers must make decisions and do work themselves. They need to become more like a player/coach, knowledge workers themselves who facilitate learning communities of workers who share what they know and learn with each other and engage in joint problem solving, who encourage knowledge workers to continuously upgrade their skills and engage in knowledge transfer, who engage in recruiting and retaining high achievement and productive knowledge workers.

As the full import of the language system of work is considered, as exemplified in this brief section and in other chapters of the book, it is easier to understand why observers are expecting "*new careers*" (Arnold & Jackson, 1997) and "*protean careers*" (Hall & Mirvis, 1996) to characterize the future. These terms suggest diverse career paths, discontinuous and sometimes fragmented, in which the individual worker in many occupations will need to be a learner throughout his or her working life, a person who can take on many roles, change with change, be able to adapt and be flexible, and manage his or her own career.

Human Capital and Returns on Investment

The major changes taking place in the workplace will require new combinations of technical skills, human relations skills, and cognitive skills (Handy, 1996) and they will require new content and processes of career guidance and career counseling across the life span. At issue will be a new language of *human capital investment* and *returns on investment.* The term *human capital* is now about forty years old and can be considered from various vantage points. At a national level, or indeed an organizational level, one can think of human capital as skilled, educated people. But from an individual standpoint, and from the viewpoint of career guidance and career counseling, human capital is possessed by the individual worker and invested when he or she takes a position. Davenport (1999) has defined human capital and its components by breaking it into its elements: ability, behavior, effort, and time. An abridged and paraphrased version of components of Davenport's model can be defined as follows.

Ability means "proficiency in a set of activities or forms of work" (p. 19). Ability is comprised of three subcomponents: *knowledge*—"command of a body of facts required to do a job...the intellectual context within which a person performs" (p. 19); *skill*—"facility with the means and methods of accomplishing a particular task" (p. 19); and *talent*—inborn faculty for performing a specific task, roughly synonymous with aptitude (p. 20). *Behavior* means "observable ways of acting that contribute to the accomplishment of a task" (p. 20). *Effort* "is the conscious application of mental and physical resources toward a particular end.... Effort activates skill, knowledge, and talent and harnesses behavior.... By applying or withholding it, we control the when, where, and how of human capital contribution" (p. 21). *Time* "is the most fundamental resource under individual control. The most talented, skilled, knowledgeable, and dedicated worker will produce nothing without investing time in the job...jobs have become more autonomous. Consequently, time allocation strategies make an increasingly important difference in how much a worker invests in the job" (p. 21).

In summary of human capital investment, Davenport suggests that that how a worker performs a task depends on ability and behavior. The choice of one task over another at a given moment requires a time allocation decision. "The combination of ability, behavior, effort, and time investment produces performance, the result (from the organization's perspective) of personal investment" (p. 22).

From a career counseling perspective each of the elements of human capital investment is a target of intervention, whether it be individual counseling, exploration, assessment, reframing or some other technique designed to help the person clarify and act on his or her ability, behavior, effort and time allocation as well as his or her desire to invest discretionary human capital in a specific organization or a specific job. The latter, according to Davenport, is also a function of the return on investment provided by an organization. *Return on investment* is comprised of the rewards required to elicit or maintain the individual's investment of human capital. Davenport indicates that there are four categories of factors that motivate individual workers to invest their discretionary human capital:

1. Intrinsic job fulfillment, which includes factors related to the job itself: interest, challenge, opportunities for creativity and social interaction, which at its heart reflects the gratification that comes from doing a challenging job well.
2. Opportunity for growth, which includes opportunities to increase one's abilities, personal growth, and advancement within the organization.
3. Recognition for accomplishments by peers, supervisors, and friends, including respect, esteem, and inclusion in important organizational initiatives.
4. Financial rewards, including compensation and benefits based on the worker's performance and productivity.

Different persons want different types and amounts of return on their discretionary human capital investments just as different jobs require different investments of ability, behavior, effort, and time. In essence, however, these elements underlie individual motivation and tie together individual commitment, human capital investment, and performance within a work environment context.

In the remaining sections of this chapter, we will consider more fully several emphases that derive from work and that are of particular importance in the practice of career development. They include work values and the meaning of work to different groups of people; job satisfaction; work and mental health; employment and unemployment; the transition to work; work and leisure; affective work components; occupational survival skills; and an emerging concern for personal flexibility in a global economy. We will briefly deal with such notions as the division of labor, specialization, work tasks, work roles, and good and bad work. In short, in this chapter we hope to increase the reader's sensitivity to the language of work and its meaning for the practice of career development. Because other chapters speak directly to dealing with specific career problems, we will concentrate here on linking various categories and concepts of career intervention to differences in the meanings and concepts of work.

THE CONCEPT OF WORK

From the earliest days of recorded history, work has been the subject of controversy. It has been seen as punishment or as the way to eternal salvation. It has been viewed as fit only for slaves to do so that their masters would have unfettered leisure or as the context in which humankind can achieve its most creative and influential purposes. Anthropologists and historians have argued that work has been instrumental in creating civilizations by causing people to engage in mutual effort to survive and to advance their quality of life. The division of labor that differentiates people into classes of functional activity has been seen by some sociologists as the basis for social stratification, classes, castes, and other types of social systems.

The issues surrounding work are so pervasive and so central to human existence that Pope John Paul II devoted a papal encyclical to the subject in 1981: "Laborem Exercens" (On Human Work). This was the first such statement the Roman Catholic Church had delivered on work in nearly ninety years. Selected statements from the encyclical strike directly at the meaning of work and its dynamics:

> *Because fresh questions and problems are always arising, there are always fresh hopes, but also fresh fears and threats connected with the basic dimension of human existence: man's life is built up every day from work, from work it derives its specific dignity, but at the same time work contains the unceasing measure of human toil and suffering and also of the harm and injustice which penetrate deeply into social life within individual nations and on the international level.*

Former U.S. Secretary of Education Bell (Riegle, 1982) has conveyed a sense of the meaning of work somewhat differently from Pope John Paul II, but no less dramatically:

> *Work in America is the means whereby a person is tested as well as identified. It is the way a youngster becomes an adult. Work shapes the thoughts and life of the worker. A change in atmosphere and lifestyle can be effected by an individual by simply changing the way he or she makes a living. For most of us in adult life, being without work is not living. (p. 1114)*

Whether viewed through a secular or a spiritual lens, such a powerful medium obviously carries diverse meanings for individuals choosing or engaging in work. Although virtually all paid work has the potential to meet the economic needs of humans, all work, paid and nonpaid, has the additional potential to meet broad social and psychological needs: effective interaction with others, personal dignity, a sense of competency or mastery, identification with some purpose or mission larger than oneself, and human relationships.

Table 2.1 suggests the range of needs or purposes that work can provide. Such purposes or needs are not necessarily mutually exclusive. The same person may attempt to achieve several different types of economic, social, and psychological purposes from work simultaneously, even though one category may be emphasized in shaping work motivation.

Perhaps more importantly, the different purposes work can serve (as shown in Table 2.1) present another way of viewing the return on investment that individual workers seek. Many employers assume that workers place "the greatest value on high wages and job security. In reality, employees typically rank these two factors below such factors as having interesting work and feeling appreciated for the jobs they do" (Davenport, 1999, p. 34). The perspectives in Table 2.1 indicate that work or the investment by an individual of his or her discretionary human capital is far more than an economic exchange between the worker and the organization. It is also one that emphasizes psychological, recognition, and affiliation needs.

At the least, the meanings of work to individual as forms of return on investment are heterogeneous, not homogeneous. They can be classified in many different ways, as suggested by Table 2.1. But they can also be used to classify workers. Moses (1999), for example, has suggested a typology of workers in which the meaning of and the motivation for work varies although the economic, social, and psychological purposes of work pervade the typology. Her six profiles of the new worker styles in abridged and paraphrased form are:

1. *Independent thinkers or entrepreneurers.* These are persons who seek autonomy, who want to

TABLE 2.1 Different Purposes Work Can Serve

ECONOMIC	SOCIAL	PSYCHOLOGICAL
Gratification of wants or needs	Place to meet people	Self-esteem
Acquisition of physical assets	Potential friendships	Identity
Security against future contingencies	Human relationships	Sense of order
Liquid assets to be used for investment or deferred gratifications	Social status for the worker and family	Dependability, reliability
Purchase of goods and services	Feeling of being valued by others for what one can produce	Feeling of mastery or competence
Evidence of success	Sense of being needed by others to get the job done or to achieve mutual goals	Self-efficacy
Assets to purchase leisure or free time	Responsibility	Commitment Personal evaluation

shape their work, to be in charge, to be responsible for their successes and failures.

2. *Lifestylers.* Motivated by flexibility, these persons want to enjoy their work but see it as a means to an end, not an end in itself. They want work that allows them to pursue their personal passions and external interests or obligations (e.g., balancing work and family life, eldercare responsibilities, participation in sports, outdoor activities, other leisure interests).
3. *Personal developers.* Such persons seek learning and growth in work and in life and they evaluate their work opportunities against such goals. They want to be stretched, to acquire new skills, to be exposed to new experiences and learning; they may have strong commitment to their profession but not to a particular employer.
4. *Careerists.* Rather more like traditional views of persons who seek increasing responsibility, promotion, and getting ahead, these workers are ambitious and motivated by advancement, prestige, and status. They are likely to take a long view of their career, but unlike traditional workers committed to advancement, they are not committed to predictable advancement in a particular organization. They are willing to look across work settings and move to where increased responsibility and advancement are available.
5. *Authenticity seekers.* Motivated by opportunities for self-expression, these persons are not conformists to corporate expectations or norms. They are less committed to "what's good for the company" and more committed to personal values, personal styles of behavior, and independent thinking.
6. *Collegiality-seekers.* These persons are motivated by belonging to and identifying with a group; they are persons who have strong needs for affiliation, team-building, group membership, and working with people they like rather than working independently. (Moses, 1999, pp. 45–51)

Cultural and Organizational Perceptions of Work

The different purposes that work can serve are related to how central work is—to the degree of general importance that working has in the life of an individual—at any given time. Such purposes are also related to the work outcomes sought or the levels of such values as family, leisure, duty, obligation, and so on. These purposes tend to vary across cultures and national boundaries.

Among a growing number of cross-cultural efforts to understand the importance of or the needs from work in different nations, Hofstede (1980) developed a *motivational map of the world* that does not support a universal order of work needs. Hofstede's research suggests that similar personnel policies designed to motivate the work behavior of employees will have different effects in different countries. Such findings are supported in cross-cultural research done by Silverthorne (1992), who compared work motivation in the United States, Russia, and the Republic of China (Taiwan). The samples used in the study consisted of both managers and employees. One question had to do with whether managers in each of these three nations accurately perceived the factors that motivated their employees as these were reported by the workers themselves. It was found that managers in the United States perceived quite accurately the work factors important to their workers. Russian managers' perceptions, in contrast, were negatively correlated with those of Russian workers, suggesting either a lack of clarity or a total misinterpretation of what was important to workers they supervised. In Taiwan, the managers were more likely than Russian managers to report with relative accuracy what motivates their workers, but their perceptions did not appear to be as accurate as those of American managers. The assumption of these findings is that supervisory behavior, responses to workers' needs and work environments, would be different in these cultures and would produce different levels of work motivation in workers.

Beyond the issue of managers' perceptions of workers' motivational factors, there is the question of how these differ in the three cultures. Among the more than 1200 workers in the sample from the United States, the top five work motivational factors in rank order were: "full appreciation of work done," "work that keeps you interested," "job security," "promotion and growth in organization," and "good wages." In Russia, a different set of motivators emerged in rank order from one to five: "promotion and growth in organization," "feeling in on things," "work that keeps you interested," "personal loyalty to workers," and "tactful disciplining." In Taiwan, the content and rank order of the motivational factors were different still. Included from rank one to five were: "job security," "good wages," "promotion and growth in organization," "full appreciation of work done," and "work that keeps you interested." In essence, these rank orders of work motivation factors across cultures reflect the opportunity structure available, working conditions, economic security, presence of social safety nets, and workers' perceptions of management styles. They also suggest that if certain factors can be taken for granted in a particular society (e.g., job security or feeling in on things), these are not perceived as major motivators; in such cases, other extrinsic or intrinsic motivators may be more important.

The research of Aycan, Kanungo, Mendonca, Yu, Deller, Stahl, and Kurshid (2000) examined a different and interesting aspect of the impact of culture on human resource management practices as measured by a ten-country comparison. Using a Model of Culture Fit to potentially explain the way in which sociocultural factors influence internal work culture and human resources management practices, a 57-item questionnaire was responded to by 1,954 employees from business organizations in ten countries. Cross-cultural differences were found among four sociocultural dimensions: power distance, paternalism, loyalty toward community, and fatalism. The first dimension, *power distance,* was defined as the extent to which status hierarchy and power inequality exist and are accepted in society and its institutions. The second, *paternalism,* means a dyadic and hierarchical relationship between a superior and his or her associates and a role differentiation in this relationship. The third, *loyalty toward community,* has to do with the extent to which individuals feel loyal to their communities and compelled to fulfill their obligations toward in-group members (relatives, clans, organizations) even if in-group members' demands inconvenience them. The fourth dimension, *fatalism,* has to do with the belief that whatever happens must happen.

In addition to the four sociocultural dimensions, five managerial assumptions about employees in their organizations were seen as representing the internal work culture. These were:

- *Malleability* refers to managerial assumptions that employees, by nature, can change and improve their skills given the appropriate training and development opportunities
- *Proactivity* is concerned with whether employees take personal initiative to achieve their job objectives or simply react to external demands
- *Responsibility-seeking* has to do with whether or not employees accept and seek responsibility in their job
- *Participation* involves managerial assumptions about whether or not employees prefer delegation at all levels and like to be consulted in matters that concern them
- *Obligation toward others,* related to whether employees feel obliged to fulfill their responsibilities towards others in the workplace

Finally, the sociocultural dimensions and the internal work culture assumptions about employees were examined in regard to whether managerial assumptions and sociocultural dimensions were related to the use of three human resource management practices: job enrichment, empowering supervision, and performance-reward contingency.

The results were that these were culture-specific patterns of relationship among the three sets of variables. The nations in the sample did differ in terms of sociocultural dimensions (e.g., paternalism, power distance) and managerial assumptions about employees attitudes and behavior (e.g., malleability, responsibility seeking). Further, these variables were reflected in managerial use of human resource management practices. For example, managers who characterized their sociocultural environment as fatalistic also assumed that employees, by nature, were not malleable. Since they did not believe their employees could change, they did not administer job enrichment, empowering supervision, and performance-reward contingency. Managers who valued high loyalty assumed that employees should fulfill obligations to one another, engaged in empowering human resource practices. Managers who perceived paternalism and high power distance in their sociocultural environment assumed employee reactivity and did not provide job enrichment and empowerment practices.

In a major analysis of the findings of the Work Importance Study (Super & Sverko, 1995), it was found that there are similarities and differences across nations in both the importance of values and in the salience of work. Similarities suggested by comparing the national samples of the fourteen nations included in the Work Importance Study indicated that three intrinsic values tended to be strong everywhere: personal development, ability utilization, and achievement. In contrast, values that tended to be of little importance across the nations surveyed were willingness to risk, ambition for authority, and prestige. In the interpretation of such international findings, one can argue that people in many nations of the world define fulfillment of one's potential as a major value whatever that means in a specific, individual sense.

With regard to the salience of work within and across nations, it was found that work values tend to differ between adolescence and adult samples. In relative terms, youth identify leisure as the most important activity of their life; adults identify work as the most important activity, with homemaking a close second. One can suggest from such findings that youth experience a "crisis of commitment to work" or that the change from leisure as the most important activity in adolescence to work and homemaking as far more important than leisure to the adult is the result of a process of maturation. The latter seems to be the more plausible explanation.

But, again in terms of differences in values and role importance across nations, not simply in terms of youths versus adults, Super and Sverko found that nations did cluster differently (for example, across the three major clusters identified, it was found that in one cluster—which included the Canadian, U.S., South African, and one Australian sample—the predominant value pattern suggested a drive for upward mobility, material success and prestige). In a second cluster—including Belgian (Flemish), Croatian, Italian, Polish, Portuguese, and two Australian samples—the dominant value pattern incorporated positive relationships and understanding among people, a tendency toward a dominant lifestyle, and a rejection of authority. In a third cluster—comprising three Japanese samples—the high values were those of creativity and aesthetics, and low ratings of values related to upward mobility and material success.

England's (1990) research on the meaning of work across advanced industrialized and technological nations has indicated that eight patterns of the meanings of work could be identified in which work was more or less central to the pattern but in which different perceptions of the meaning of work were expressed. In adapted form, the eight patterns are identified as follows:

- *Pattern A—nonwork centered, nonduty-oriented workers.* Lowest work centrality of the eight persons. These persons do not value working highly and they do not have an orientation toward duty to employers and society through working. Highly leisure-oriented and comfort-oriented in work goals. Value interpersonal relations highly. Characterize working by saying it is work "if you must do it" (p. 36).
- *Pattern B—nonwork-centered, high duty-oriented workers.* Low work centrality score. Relatively high family, religious, and leisure orientations. Comprise the highest number of workers in the eight patterns who defined working as an activity that "is not pleasant" (p. 36).

- *Pattern C—economic worker pattern.* Average work centrality scores. High economic values and low expressive values. Contained highest number of all eight groups who defined workers in terms of "being told what to do" and as "being physically strenuous" (p. 37). Strong economic orientation to work.
- *Pattern D—high rights and duties economic workers.* Average work centrality, high economic work values, and very high levels of obligation and entitlement. Contained highest number of all eight groups who defined working in terms of "obtaining a feeling of belonging" (p. 37).
- *Pattern E—low rights and duties noneconomic workers.* Average work centrality scores, low economic values, low obligation norms, and low entitlement norms. Most status and prestige-oriented of all eight groups. Contained lowest number of all eight groups who defined working in terms of "if it contributes to society" (p. 37). High number who described working as "mentally strenuous" and "not pleasant" (p. 37).
- *Pattern F—moderately work-centered, noneconomic, duty-oriented workers.* Moderately high work centrality, low level of economic values. They show a strong company orientation and are highly concerned with the products and services they produce or provide. Of all the groups, they most strongly define working in terms of "contributing to society" (p. 38).
- *Pattern G—work-centered and balanced work values workers.* High work centrality, relatively high economic and expressive values. Second highest group to define working in terms of "something which adds value" and "being accountable for their work" (p. 38).
- *Pattern H—work-centered expressive workers.* High work centrality scores, low economic values, and high expressive work values. Highly concerned about the types of tasks they do, the type of occupation in which they work, and the types of products or services they produce or provide. "They give the highest endorsement of all eight groups to the statement, 'Working itself is basically interesting and satisfying.'" They are highly concerned with "contributing to society" through their work and contain the highest number of all groups who defined working "as something which adds value and in terms of 'being accountable'" (p. 38).*

England's research showed that the labor forces of the United States, Japan, and Germany were represented differently by the proportions of workers who could be described by each of these eight patterns. From his database, England estimated that in these countries, the percentage of workers in each pattern was as follows:

Pattern	United States	Germany	Japan
A	7.0	13.8	8.8
B	2.33	19.7	12.0
C	14.50	20.6	10.4
D	5.4	15.3	4.9
E	12.8	4.0	4.6
F	14.0	6.3	1.1
G	16.8	14.7	32.4
H	6.2	5.6	15.8

Notice the contrast between the labor forces of Germany and Japan and the labor forces of the United States.

In addition to suggesting how work meaning or the centrality of work and related values vary in the labor force of each of these countries, England's research also describes relationships between each of the patterns of work meanings and values for work outcomes: (1) income; (2) quality of work; (3) occupational satisfaction; and (4) job satisfaction. In general, the values of the last relationship increase across patterns A to H, with the outcome values for each occupation for patterns E, F, G, and H generally higher than the outcome value patterns for groups A, B, C, and D.

Although the meaning of work is individually defined and a major mediator of work adjustment, not only are individual purposes for working important, but also what organizations require of workers. Perspectives on what individuals expect to gain from work and what organizations expect to receive from

*Adapted from George W. England (1990, January), The patterning of work meanings which are coterminous with work outcome levels for individuals in Japan, Germany, and the USA. *Applied Psychology: An International Review, 39*(1), 36–39.

individuals function in complex ways. Morgan (1980, p. 65) has identified these two sets of dimensions:

Dimensions that individuals have expectations of receiving and organizations have expectations of giving:

- A sense of meaning or purpose in the job
- Personal development opportunities
- The amount of interesting work that stimulates curiosity and induces excitement
- The challenge in the work
- The power and responsibility in the job
- Recognition and approval for good work
- The status and prestige in the job
- The friendliness of the people, the congeniality of the work group
- Salary
- The amount of structure in the environment (general practices, disciplines, regimentation)
- The amount of security in the job
- Advancement opportunities
- The amount and frequency of feedback and evaluation

Dimensions that organizations have expectations of receiving and individuals of giving:

- Performing nonsocial job-related tasks requiring some degree of technical knowledge and skill
- Learning the various aspects of a position while on the job
- Discovering new methods of performing tasks; solving novel problems
- Presenting a point of view effectively and convincingly
- Working productively with groups of people
- Making well-organized, clear presentations both orally and in writing
- Supervising and directing the work of others
- Making responsible decisions well and without assistance from others
- Planning and organizing work efforts for oneself or others
- Utilizing time and energy for the benefit of the company
- Accepting company demands that conflict with personal prerogatives
- Maintaining social relationships with other members of the company outside of work
- Conforming to the pathways of the organization or work group on the job in areas not directly related to job performance
- Pursuing further education on personal time
- Maintaining a good public image of the company
- Taking on company values and goals as one's own
- Seeing what should or must be done and initiating appropriate activity*

The reciprocity noted by Morgan between what workers want and give to the organizations by which they are employed and what employers expect and give to employees, is related to the concepts of the Theory of Work Adjustment advanced by Dawis and Loftquist (1984), or Dawis (1994). In essence, this theory proposes that work adjustment occurs when job satisfaction by the employee and job satisfactoriness by the employer is achieved. This theory suggests, as the work of Morgan cited previously implies, that both the employee and the employer have their own goals and if these come into adequate levels of correspondence, job satisfaction and work adjustment are likely to occur for the employee, and the employer will find the employee satisfactory. Said another way, the goal for the employee is correspondence between individual needs and the rewards (or reinforcers) found in the work environment. The goal for the employer (who creates the work environment) is congruence between the individual worker's abilities and the demands of the work which they do. In this context, then, there is a kind of ongoing tension to achieve equilibrium between the employee's job satisfaction and the employer's judgment of the employee's satisfactoriness. The disruptions to such equilibrium are the employee's job dissatisfaction or the employer's concern that the employee is unsatisfactory. In order to adjust this work disequilibrium for the worker or the employer, targets of career intervention that might be addressed to reestablish equilibrium between worker and employer are work demands, work capacities, work rewards, and individual needs. How each of these possible sources of disruption of equilibrium

*Reprinted from Carole W. Minor (1990), Career development: Theories and issues. *Adult Career Development: Concepts, Issues and Practices,* edited by Zandy B. Leibowitz and H. Daniel Lea (pp. 34–35). Copyright © AACD. Reprinted with permission.

in the work place are dealt with depends on worker personality style (e.g., flexible, active, reactive persevering) as well as the styles of the work environment (e.g., the kinds of behavioral reinforcer patterns or employer-employee interaction patterns that exist). In either case, these issues are at the core of much career counseling content.

It suffices to say here that such individual/organizational purposes may be congruent or in opposition. As such, they may define good work–bad work or job satisfaction–dissatisfaction for any given individual.

The perspectives of Dawis and Loftquist, Aycan and associates, Super and Sverko, England, and Morgan are affirmations that cultural traditions and histories give their members particular *world views* or *perceptual windows* on events, including acceptable behavior at work, the meaning of work, and interactions with work organizations. Cultural constructions of achievement images and belief systems are likely to be incorporated into the individual citizen's psyche and information-processing mechanisms as well as into the economic organizational systems that prevail in a given nation (Herr, 1990). At least two points can be made in such a context. One is that people moving from one nation to another are likely to bring with them the perceptions of work and their role in it that predominate in their nation of origin. Thus, in a pluralistic society such as the United States, there will be a profusion of culturally defined meanings of work and work behavior that must be accommodated in the workplaces of the society. The second point is that institutions, policies, and social technologies in a given nation are likely to be organized and applied in ways that reflect the values and perspectives about human resources or individual behavior that predominate in that society.

These cultural constructions about the meaning of work are also major factors in the formation and playing out of personal identity. "Identity is more than the sum of a person's immediate interests. It involves the way people think about themselves, what they care about, the kinds of commitments they make, and the point of view they take. Identity also involves what we can take for granted and what requires explanation" (Feinberg, 1993, p. 18). In essence, individual identity is affected by whether the traits and values of selfhood in a particular society are ambiguous or clear. As an increasing number of observers have pointed out, American values are ambiguous; Japan and some other nations offer clarity about the core values of the society. At its worst, societies like that of the United States, where values are ambiguous or in transition, where the place and family of birth does not carry predictable consequences in what choices one can make or implement, and where the choice process is predicated on individual action and is therefore highly psychological, can lead to a fragmented sense of identity. It can also lead to confusion about work goals, ambivalence about whether one can incorporate the dominant values of the society, and how one should deal with persons of different cultural backgrounds whose values about work and work behavior are different from one's own. In this context, one of the underlying problems that seems to be affecting national policies, mental health issues, and individual perspectives is whether it is possible to have either a strong coherent national or individual identity and at the same time porous, open, fluid relationships with people whose cultural identities, national aspirations, or individual aspirations are different than one's own. However such questions are answered, the effects are apparent in the structures and mechanisms created by any given society.

To carry the analogy of work meaning, performance, and organizational interaction further, it is useful to contrast the United States and Japan on some of these dimensions. In the United States, unfettered individual achievement, freedom, justice, and liberty are dominant social values, and the burden of achievement in the workplace rests with individual action. Given such a set of assumptions, work and other organizations can be and are structured to reflect expectations for individual behavior and responsibility. Japan views such social values differently; dominant social values include loyalty, conformity, hierarchy, duty, and obedience. As a result, organizational forms are created that are different from those created in the United States. For example, Japan's economic and political system has been called a *developmental model* rather than a *regulatory model*—a term used to describe the United States and the United Kingdom (Dore, 1987). Developmental models set clearly defined strategic economic goals, attempt to ensure that workers are constantly prepared to manage and implement the processes required to meet such goals, and to identify with the economic targets as well as to identify their personal contributions necessary to achieve such outcomes.

The Japanese notion of a *developmentally* oriented work organization includes a major emphasis on harnessing the tacit skills and latent talents of workers from the factory floor to the management office. At each of these levels, workers are put to the task of diagnosing problems and organizing information that will improve productivity and corporate knowledge. In this model, the management objective is to *figuratively* make every worker an industrial engineer designed to help the organization collectively seek continuous improvement and to look beyond a narrowly focused view of immediate job completion. Within such a concept, training of workers is concerned with teamwork, multifunctional approaches, interpersonal skills, and problem-solving capabilities. Thus, the intent of the Japanese system of labor management is to create conditions under which workers will be encouraged to cooperate and develop collective awareness and diagnostic skills (Wood, 1990).

A developmental model contrasts with that of a *regulatory* model, which is more concerned with the processes and rules of competition, not the substance. In the view of some observers, the regulatory model assumes that individuals or organizations will constantly try to "beat the system," that they have a natural tendency to slack off or to abuse power, and that they must be regulated in order to promote equity, access, and fairness in competition (Fallows, 1989). The main point is that the meaning of work and the shape of work organizations will be differently defined in political, cultural, or organizational terms, depending on whether one's model is regulatory or developmental. In the former view, each person in the corporation or workplace is expected to maximize his or her short-term gains and to be autonomous and unconstrained by anything but one's personal ability to cope with market forces and competition. In such a perspective, both success and failure are individual matters. In a developmental view, each person is believed to be part of the whole, to deserve fair treatment and the support necessary to do his or her job, to be respected and consulted, and to be assured of an adequate income and security. The latter view is much more likely to promote personnel development within work organizations than personnel management. It is also more likely to promote cooperation, compromise, identity, and loyalty to the organization rather than aggressiveness, entrepreneurship, risk taking, and individual achievement.

The intent here is not to set up a dichotomy of economic organizations or cultures; clearly, these emphases on regulation or development are on a continuum, not simply one or the other. The important point is that individual perspectives on the meaning of work, or on what work values and behaviors should be manifested, do not occur in a vacuum. They are shaped by and reinforced within cultures and in the work organizations and policies that reflect such cultural differences.

Brislin (1993), in discussing culture's effects on the world of work, has observed that the workplace is the most important setting in which intercultural interactions take place. One can argue for this view in terms of the interdependence of institutions, persons, and products that is occurring across nations as the dynamics of the global economy begins to erode national economic sovereignty and as these dynamics blur the impact of political boundaries as persons from diverse cultural traditions are increasingly required to work together for common economic goals. Similarly the workplace in a highly pluralistic and culturally diverse nation such as the United States is a place, because of legal requirements and the changing demographics of the workplace, that has expanded the intercultural interactions that take place among workers. As Brislin has analyzed cultural differences across nations in the way work is seen and implemented, and that result in cultural differences that can shape problems between workers, he cites five issues: (1) the relative emphasis in a society on individualism, attaining goals through individual action and effort, versus collectivism, attaining goals through group effort; (2) power distance between bosses and subordinates, in essence the amount of distinctiveness among various categories of workers in their access to power and in their relative status levels; (3) uncertainty avoidance, the degree to which rules, laws, norms, and informal guidelines reduce unpredictability and uncertainty about one's employment, security, retirement and other matters; (4) masculinity-femininity goals in the workplace as these relate to whether the dominant values are assertiveness, competitiveness, and a tough approach to decision making that sometimes downplays the feelings of people affected, compared to greater valuing of cooperativeness, pleasant coworkers, positive social relationships, "good" working conditions; and (5) the influence of Confucianism or other perspectives on people's values in the work place. Confucian thought has been seen as highly influential in stimulating the current rise in economic development in the major Asian nations. In these contexts, Confucian thought may suggest such guidelines for work behavior as the following: that persons of unequal status relationships do have mutual obligations to each other—for example, respect, obedience in return for protection and consideration; that the family is typical of all social organizations, thus the person is not socialized to look on himself or herself as an individual but to find identity and maintain harmony within the group; and that virtue in life consists of working hard, acquiring useful skills, obtaining as much education as possible, not spending excessively, and persevering in the face of difficult tasks. In societies and in individuals that embrace such principles there is a respect for tradition and for other values that provide a context in which some behaviors are sanctioned and others are constrained. In societies or in individuals who do not subscribe to Confucian principles but emphasize other values, the organization of work, the context and climate of work, and the relationships and behavior of workers are likely to be different.

Although much more deserves to be said about cultural differences in the worldviews of workers and work organizations, the points made are sufficient to indicate the range of and potential conflicts among work values and the resulting behaviors that can occur between nations or within a single, pluralistic workplace. As such, these issues, however vague or well defined, can be at the base of economic difficulties between nations, between supervisors and supervisees, and among coworkers or workers and customers.

Meanings of Work Vary across Time

The meanings attached to work differ not only across groups and cultures, but also across time. As suggested previously, work has been seen differently through history. Toffler (1980) has described such shifts in terms of three waves of change across the world: agricultural, industrial, and advanced technological. Each of these brings with it different forms of work and meaning. Maccoby and Terzi (1981) suggest that there have been four major work ethics throughout American history and that elements or residuals of each of these coexist today: the Protestant ethic, the craft ethic, the entrepreneurial ethic, and the career ethic. In addition, they contend that a fifth ethic, that of self-fulfillment, is rapidly emerging as a major motivation to work. The point of such observations is that "each work ethic implies a different social character, different satisfaction and dissatisfaction at work, and a different critique of society" (p. 165).

The changes in the meaning of work described by Maccoby and Terzi and by Toffler have not ended. As the application of advanced technology to the content and structure of the workplace has accelerated, it has been instrumental in changing the power relations, the hierarchical characteristics of authority in the workforce, the flow of information among workers, and other factors that have in many contexts changed perspectives of individuals and of organizations on the meaning of work. Contemporary management authorities are, for example, suggesting that as new forms of work and requirements for workers' skills are emerging, new expectations of workers are also emerging:

1. To invent or own our work (rather than as owned and created by the employer)
2. To be self-initiating, self-correcting, self-evaluating (rather than dependent on others to frame the problems, initiate adjustments, or determine whether things are going acceptably well)
3. To be guided by our visions at work (rather than be without a vision or be captive of the authority's agenda)
4. To take responsibility for what happens to us at work externally and internally (rather than see our present internal circumstances and future external possibilities as caused by someone else)
5. To be accomplished masters of our particular work roles, jobs, or careers (rather than have an apprenticing or imitating relationship to what we do)
6. To conceive of the organization from the 'outside in,' as a whole; to see our relation to the whole; to see the relation of the parts to the whole (rather than see the rest of the organization and its parts only from the perspective of our own part, from the'inside out')" (Kegan, 1994, pp. 152–153)

It would be inaccurate to contend that all organizations or management consultants expect all workers to function in the ways described here or to find meaning in the autonomy, self-responsibility, analysis, and planning that are inherent in these expectations. Some organizations, however, will expect such behavior, and some workers will expect to find opportunities to express themselves in ways so described. Although such perspectives may be at the cutting edge of how new technologies are affecting the new organizations and contexts of work, they add to the complexity of the meanings of work that are present in some form in the workplaces of the nation.

Such multiplicity of work values or meanings complicates the practice of career development significantly. Similarly, it complicates the seeking of answers to such general or popular questions as "Has the motivation to work declined?" The probable answer to such a question is more questions: "What kind of work are you talking about? Which group of workers holding what type of work ethic are you considering?" Beyond such questions, however, it appears that despite certain popular rhetoric to the contrary, Americans' motivation to work is still quite high, although certain jobs and styles of supervision are not looked on with much favor.

JOB SATISFACTION

From the meanings of work just discussed, it is obvious that in most of the work in which people engage we find a confrontation of the individual with the organization. The ingredients of this confrontation yield satisfaction or dissatisfaction, feelings of competence or inferiority, and motivation to be productive or to experience work alienation.

Among the more controversial issues facing the American business, industrial, and labor complex and, indeed, government policy is that of job satisfaction or job alienation. Sometimes the professional literature, the popular press, and certain research findings leave one with the impression that processes of self-understanding, finding meaning in achievement, or choice are important only during the exploration or anticipation phases of youth. Such a perspective belies the reality that adults must continue to cope with trying to implement a self-concept in their lifestyles, in their work, in their choices, and in their planning. Efforts to grapple with skills in interpersonal relationships and in learning or relearning continue, for most people, as long as they live. As E. Gross (1975) has observed, "Socialization is far from complete in childhood; it goes on throughout persons' lives, involving adjustment to and becoming members of schools, universities, occupations and becoming socialized to appropriate roles in old age."

Perspectives on Job Satisfaction

Job satisfaction is a complex term as well as a significant one for the practice of career development. The importance of the concept is evident in Palamore's (1969) often-quoted fifteen-year follow-up study that indicated that job satisfaction is the best predictor of longevity, better than physicians' ratings of physical functioning, use of tobacco, or even genetic inheritance.

But *job satisfaction* is not a singular term. As efforts to measure it have shown, at issue is both overall satisfaction and *facet* satisfaction. The latter assesses satisfaction with particular facets or elements of work—for example, pay, coworkers, supervision, working conditions, and types of work. It is possible for a worker to be dissatisfied with specific facets of his or her work but still report an overall sense of job satisfaction (Dawis, 1984).

Inherent in the notions of overall satisfaction and facet satisfaction are the distinctions of job content and job context. Research approaches to job satisfaction have typically treated these as separable and having different implications for job satisfaction. For example, Herzberg, Mausner, and Snyderman (1959) proposed a classic two-factor theory of job satisfaction (also sometimes called dual-factor or motivation hygiene theory), which suggested that satisfaction and dissatisfaction are really two distinct sets of processes. The factors associated with *job content*—achievement, recognition, advancement, responsibility, the work tasks—are the *satisfiers* or *motivators* that lead to job satisfaction. The factors associated with the *job context*—compensation, supervision, coworkers, working conditions, company policies and practices—are the *dissatisfiers* or *hygiene* factors that cause dissatisfaction, but they cannot cause satisfaction. Only the factors associated with job content, the satisfiers or motivators, can lead to satisfaction. Although controversial, the Herzberg and associates theory did lead to a large amount of research on job satisfaction that, while mixed in result, has helped to clarify the importance of facet satisfaction and, particularly, the separateness of external variables into the categories of satisfiers and dissatisfiers.

Another theoretical approach to job satisfaction, equity theory (Pritchard, 1969), added other factors to those of Herzberg's that were also considered relevant to job satisfaction. Of principal interest is the notion that satisfaction depends on personal feelings of fairness, justice, or equity when what is obtained is compared to what is desired and how this ratio compares to that obtained by other reference persons. Thus, equity theory not only adds to the conception of factors affecting job satisfaction those related to reference outcomes, but it also shifts the focus of attention from a major or exclusive emphasis on what the environment provides or does to the individual to the individual's cognitions about such events. As one of the four psychological concepts underlying the *Theory of Work Adjustment* (Lofquist & Dawis, 1969), satisfaction is defined as affect—or feeling or emotion—resulting from one's evaluation of the situation. Thus, the generic concept satisfaction includes both positive affect (satisfaction) and negative affect (disaffection) (Dawis, 1994, p. 35).

The theory of work adjustment, formulated by Lofquist and Dawis (1969), is a classic approach to job satisfaction. Basically, in this original model the fit among individual needs, skills and abilities, and technical organizational requirements is the seedbed for satisfaction, and if such satisfaction is attained, high performance will ensue.

The Lofquist and Dawis model emphasizes that work is more than the accomplishment of some set of tasks. It is also a place of human interaction and psychological reinforcement, which may be far more significant in creating job satisfaction than merely performing tasks.

Lofquist and Dawis (1969; Dawis, 1994) contend that job satisfaction and work adjustment result from correspondence between individual and environment. The major assumptions that underlie this theory are:

- Each individual seeks to achieve and maintain correspondence with his or her environment.
- Work represents a major environment to which most individuals must relate.
- In the case of work, then, correspondence can be described in terms of the individual fulfilling the requirements of the work environment, and the work environment fulfilling the requirements of the individual.
- The continuous and dynamic process by which one seeks to achieve and maintain correspondence with one's work environment is called *work adjustment.*
- This stability of the correspondence between the individual and the work environment is manifested as tenure in the job.
- *Satisfactoriness and satisfaction* indicate the correspondence between the individual and the work environment. Satisfactoriness is an external indicator of correspondence derived from sources other than the worker's own self-appraisal. Satisfaction is an internal indicator of correspondence; it represents the individual worker's appraisal of the extent to which the work environment fulfills his or her requirements.
- The levels of satisfactoriness and satisfaction observed for a group of individuals with substantial tenure in a specific work environment establish the limits of satisfactoriness and satisfaction from which tenure can be predicted for other individuals.
- The work personalities of individuals who fall within the limits of satisfactoriness and satisfaction for which substantial tenure can be predicted may be inferred to be correspondent with the specific work environment.

An important aspect of this theory and the program of related research is the correspondence between the individual's needs and the reinforcer system that characterizes the work setting. Such a view is similar to the early work of Henry A. Murray (1938) and the work of Holland (1973a) in assessing the importance and the degrees of tolerance associated with person-situation congruence. Lofquist, Dawis, and their various colleagues have distinguished work settings and occupations based on their profile of reinforcers of individual behavior: twenty different reinforcers are seen as potentially composing a work setting (see Table 2.2); implicit in these categories are six emphases—safety, comfort, status, altruism, achievement, and autonomy (Rounds et al., 1981); different persons will have needs profiles that accord with or are incompatible with the reinforcer profile of any given occupation or setting.

TABLE 2.2

OCCUPATIONAL	REINFORCERS
Ability utilization	Recognition
Achievement	Responsibility
Activity	Security
Advancement	Social service
Authority	Social status
Company policies and practices	Supervision-human relations
Compensation	Supervision-technical
Coworkers	Variety
Creativity	Work conditions
Independence	Autonomy
Moral values	

Their job *satisfaction* and tenure in that setting will vary accordingly.

To assess an individual's job *satisfactoriness* one can compare the individual's scores on ability tests, such as the General Aptitude Test Battery, with Occupational Aptitude Patterns, published by the U.S. Department of Labor for different occupations. Together these two assessments—of individual satisfaction (correspondence of needs and occupational reinforcers) and satisfactoriness (correspondence of individual abilities with occupational requirements)—were integrated into the Minnesota Occupational Classification System in 1975 and coordinated with the *Dictionary of Occupational Titles* and the Holland Codes cited elsewhere in this book. Other research suggests that occupations can be classified in terms of their provision of different classes of reinforcers, including whether reinforcement is largely predictable or nonpredictable, social reinforcers and interaction with people on the job is high or at a minimum, or self-generated or internal reinforcement mechanisms (e.g., feelings of accomplishment) are prominent compared to external reinforcers (Dawis, Dohm, & Jackson, 1993). In general, such data have not been systematically included in the information routinely used for job exploration by counselors and clients, although there are some related sources of information in which this information is included that could be helpful for such purposes. One major example is the *Minnesota Occupational Classification System III: A Psychological Taxonomy of Work* (Dawis et al., 1987).

Findings about Job Satisfaction

In a major review of the job satisfaction literature, Dawis (1984) has suggested that "from a cognitive standpoint, job satisfaction is a cognition, with affective components, that results from certain perceptions and results in certain future behaviors. As a cognition, it is linked to other cognitions, or cognitive constructs, such as self-esteem, job involvement, work alienation, organizational commitment, morale, and life satisfaction. To understand job satisfaction, we must examine its relationship to these other constructs" (p. 286).

In considering the consequences of job satisfaction, Dawis goes on to contend that "from a behavioral standpoint, job satisfaction is a response (a verbal operant) that has behavioral consequences. On the positive side are tenure, longevity, physical health, mental health, and productivity; on the negative side, turnover, absenteeism, accidents, and mental health problems" (p. 289). "The turnover literature documents a negative relationship between job satisfaction and turnover.... Quitting the job is the means by which the individual avoids the aversive condition that is job dissatisfaction.... The absenteeism literature has likewise documented a negative relationship between job satisfaction and absenteeism; like turnover, absenteeism is a form of avoidance adjustment" (p. 289). "Negative but low correlations have been reported between job satisfaction and accidents" (p. 289). Dawis also reports that job dissatisfaction is related to mental and physical health problems, including psychosomatic illnesses, depression, anxiety, worry, tension, impaired interpersonal relationships, coronary heart disease, alcoholism, drug abuse, and suicide.

Dawis concludes his analysis by contending that "it would seem best to think of job satisfaction as an outcome of job behavior. As an outcome, or consequence of job behavior, job satisfaction can be seen as a *reinforcer* that has consequences for future job performance and other work behavior (absences, turnover). Future satisfactory job performance can be maintained by present job satisfaction. Future absence or turnover behavior can be made more likely by present job dissatisfaction, acting as a negative reinforcer" (p. 291).

These views of job satisfaction or dissatisfaction are not inconsistent with the recent conceptual propositions of Davenport (1999) about human capital investment by individuals and their expectations of return on investment as reflected in their needs for some combination of financial rewards, recognition, intrinsic fulfillment, and growth opportunities. Davenport, in discussing job satisfaction, suggests that the relationship between job satisfaction and work performance is a function of rewards and can be described as "strong performance brings rewards, which in turn increase satisfaction." In other words, satisfaction does not engender performance; rather, performance through the mechanism of rewards produces satisfaction (p. 31).

Person-Job Fit: Work and Personality

Fundamental to the issues inherent in the job satisfaction literature is the matter of person-job fit and its implications for individual commitment to work. Many national reports published during the 1980s and 1990s generated public debate about the quality of work life. Embedded in such debate are experimentation with new approaches to designing work organizations, employee health and well-being, workplace participation and democratic management, productivity and the quality of work life, the relationship of satisfaction to performance, and work-related stress and dissatisfaction. The core of such concerns is the *fit* between person and job, and in a larger sense the fit between person and organization. As noted by Van Vianen (2001), "Person-environment fit theory originates in two basic assumptions: (1) that human behavior is a function of the person and the environment, and (2) that the person and the environment need to be compatible" (p. 1).

Hackman and Oldham (1981) have picked up this theme in their research. In contrast to many other theorists about job satisfaction and productivity, they link these directly to the fit of person to job. They state:

> *One of the major influences on organizational productivity is the quality of the relationship between people who do the work and the jobs they perform. If there is a good "fit" between people and their jobs, such that productive work is a personally satisfying experience, then there may be little for management to do to foster high motivation and satisfaction—other than support the healthy person-job relationship that exists. But if that fit is faulty, such that hard and productive work leads mainly to personal discomfort and distress, then there may be little that management can do to engender high productivity and satisfying work experience (p. 173).*

They further maintain:

> *Even as work organizations have continued to get bigger, more mechanical, more controlling of individual behavior, and more task specialized, the people who work in these organizations have become more highly educated, more desirous of "intrinsic" work satisfaction, and perhaps less willing to accept routine and monotonous work as their legitimate lot in life.... Ways of structuring jobs and managing organizations that worked in this century, it is argued, cannot work now because the people who populate contemporary organizations simply will not put up with them (p. 175).*

Another way of saying this is that the descriptions of workers as passive, confused, irrational, and nonresistant to manipulation by management, which were promulgated by the Hawthorne studies, are now being viewed as more mythology than fact (Bramel & Friend, 1981).

Various social psychological and sociological studies of work have documented the importance of numerous aspects of work experience for adult self-esteem. Schwalbe's (1988) research, for example, has suggested that self-perceived competence in the workplace is the most important source of self-esteem, with reflected appraisal (for example, having coworkers think of you as a good person) next, and their social comparisons with the skills and abilities of other persons as third most important. Schwalbe has suggested that one can think of person-environment fit as self-esteem centered. If persons attach various degrees of importance to different sources of self-esteem, the issue of fit in the workplace becomes a complex one for a career counselor or an employer. Apparently, trying to maximize the fit between an individual and a work environment is not only related to sources of self-esteem that people seek, but also how these differ by age. For example, Mortimer and Finch (1986) found that the experience of autonomy at work and related conditions of work are consequential for the self-image at different age periods.

Such perspectives argue that an extremely important role for career counseling in business and industry is that of worker classification and assessment as well as job redesign, based on models of management that allow for greater worker participation in decisions about work processes, flex-time, quality circles, worker ownership of product quality, worker autonomy, perceived self-competence, and so forth.

Inherent in much of the literature on job satisfaction and on person-job or organization fit, is the question of work and personality. The study of personality as a construct in psychology, and more specifically in the workplace, has ebbed and flowed during the twentieth century. But currently, as the nature of work and its organizational changes are accelerating around the world, there is a renewed appreciation for individual differences and personality styles as factors in the implementation and success of work processes and organization.

Issues of character, temperament, flexibility, and teachability each appear in the professional and the popular literature describing the requirements of the evolving workplace. So, too, do such psychological constructs as locus of control, self-efficacy, and self-monitoring, or what have been called the Big Five Factor Model of Personality: Neuroticism, Extraversion, Openness to Experience, Agreeableness, and Conscientiousness (Costa, 1996). Among the issues raised as one looks at the relationships between personality and work are: Is personality a fixed trait or a learned disposition? Can different organizational styles alter one's personality dispositions? Can personality dispositions change from prolonged exposure to jobs of particular kinds? Do high discretion and complex roles enhance intellectual flexibility, self-directedness, and similar attributes, in essence constituting an efficiency enhancement model (Nicholson, 1996)? In what kinds of work roles do personality variables have greater or lesser behavioral relevance? Can personality profiles be matched to organizational cultural profiles? Can persons of particular personality profiles serve effectively in team-oriented cultures or in other more autonomous and self-directed work roles? As many work roles in so-called protean careers are becoming weak in structure and ambiguous in specific role expectations, is the scope for personality to have an impact on behavior increased? What are the behaviors associated with different personality traits and how are they related to different types of work performance (Schneider, 1996)?

While answers, at least partially formed, exist for many of these questions related to personality effects in the workplace, the fundamental point is that personality is related to behavior and to actions taken in work organizations and, as such, to organizational fit. But the question remains, which personality factors in which jobs or organizations and what is the relationship of the importance of personality constructs vis-à-vis other individual factors such as abilities and so on? How are personality constructs and other constructs or traits linked in particular jobs, organizations or other settings (Adlar, 1996). These are both research questions and career counseling questions, as counselors work with adults engaged in issues of organizational fit and work adjustment.

Career Counseling, Job Satisfaction, and Person-Organization Fit

The models of job satisfaction, motivation, and work performance discussed here and in Chapter 4 provide both conceptual stimuli and a potential blueprint for the variety of activities in which career counselors can engage effectively in business and industry. These will be detailed more fully in Chapters 11 and 13. What is known about job satisfaction, work and personality, and person-organization fit supports such counselor roles in the workplace as the following:

- Educating first-line supervisors and managers about current perspectives on job satisfaction, work motivation, and work performance
- Providing information to workers about career paths, career ladders, and the avenues and requirements for mobility within the organization
- Classifying workers by technical skills and psychological needs to maximize person-job fit with regard to content, supervisory style, and related factors
- Conducting workshops and seminars to increase workers' understanding of their educational opportunities, their employability skills, and their understanding of the organizational characteristics with which they interact
- Consulting with managers about job redesign and work enrichment schemes
- Providing support groups for workers in various types of transitions (such as new jobs, geographical relocations, overseas transfers, shifting family structures)
- Providing individual counseling about personality style, work behavior, and career development

- Conducting assessments of job satisfactions and worker aspirations
- Intervening in the workplace environment to help shape policies that improve quality of work life or that modify jobs to allow workers with particular handicaps to perform effectively
- Identifying effective reinforcers in the work setting and translating them into person-job fit
- Brokering in-plant and formal training and retraining opportunities to increase worker competencies
- Helping employers understand the motivational elements of workers' discretion and human capital investment and the various elements included in the concept of workers' expected Return on Investment

WORK AND MENTAL HEALTH

One of the major themes that emphasizes both the important meaning work has for many and the difficulties that ensue when one's work life is unsatisfactory is that of work and mental health. In the previous section, we discussed some of the mental and physical problems that are corollaries of job dissatisfaction. Such corollaries have also been found in an historical line of data that has become increasingly visible, particularly in the psychological literature of the past two decades.

In 1985, McLean traced the previous one hundred years of occupational mental health efforts. In the United States, such emphases took root in the second decade of this century as industrial psychiatry, and questions about the mental hygiene of industry and about unemployment and personality began to emerge. In the 1920s, behavioral scientists from a broad range of disciplines began to address studies of worker turnover, employee morale, working conditions, work productivity, and individual worker needs and characteristics. In 1924, Mayo (quoted in McLean, 1985) conducted the classic but flawed studies of the working conditions at the Hawthorne plant of the Western Electric Company near Chicago. More than 20,000 employees were interviewed, and several small experimental groups were intensively observed as changes were made in their work situation. As McLean observed:

> *The Hawthorne studies concluded that a work organization has both economic and social functions. The output of a product may be considered a form of social behavior and all the activity of a plant may be viewed as an interaction of structure, personality, and culture. If any of these variables is altered, Mayo noted, change must occur in each of the other two variables. Further, reactions to stress on the part of the individual employees arise when there is resistance to change, when there are faulty control and communication systems, and when the individual worker must make adjustments to his structure at work. (pp. 33–34)*

As the decades since the 1920s have intensified the interest of mental health professionals in occupational mental health, it has become an accepted axiom that business and industry, the workplaces of the nation, turn out two main commodities: material goods and human satisfactions. Analyses of the implications of such an axiom as it is mediated by organizational characteristics; the presence of satisfiers and dissatisfiers; the application of psychiatric insights to attempts to understand the outcomes of persons under the stress of war, in or out of combat; the problems of defense workers under intense production pressure; the post-traumatic stress following violence in the workplace; and workers performing in less-than-optimal working conditions have all laid the base for the current understandings of the work-stress connection and the diverse workplace responses known as human resource development (HRD), employee assistance programs (EAPs), and related programs. These programs deal with a broad range of issues from alcoholism to family mediation to educational counseling to financial planning, outplacement, or preretirement planning. Major conferences and the professional literature deal increasingly with issues of worker absenteeism, stress management, drug abuse in industry, the changing meaning of work, the emotionally troubled employee, or mental health and work organizations. Specific attention seems to ebb and flow between focusing on the mentally ill worker and the prevention of work stress, the creation of an occupational setting that is mentally healthy, the delivery of mental health services directly to workers, and considering the work organization to be the patient. However the issue is conceived, it accents the relationships that exist between work and mental health.

As the ripple effects of corporate downsizing of work forces, increasingly automated or technologically oriented industrial or business processes, growing diversity in the demographic characteristics of the workforce, and the multiple pressures on work organizations and individual workers that accompany intense international economic competition combine to produce new expectations on workers and managers to perform efficiently and in a cost-effective manner, new stresses and strains arise. Growing awareness of how the content and organization of work affects the psychological health of workers has led to major international conferences and publications about these matters. In one such international conference, the American Psychological Association and the National Institute for Occupational Safety and Health brought together in 1990 some three hundred experts from the United States and abroad from the fields of psychology, occupational medicine, epidemiology, public health, and business to consider the topic *Work and Well-being: An Agenda for the 1990s* (Keita & Sauter, 1992). The stimulus for the conference topic was the international recognition that "psychological strain is quickly becoming one of the most prevalent, costly and debilitating forms of occupational ill-health" (p. viii). Among the objectives of this conference were finalization of an action plan to protect the psychological health of workers by improving working conditions, improving education and health service delivery pertinent to work-related psychological disorders, and improving the surveillance of work-related psychological disorders and risk factors.

The content of this interdisciplinary conference, as is true in the broader studies and discussions of work and mental health, suggested that there were many problems deserving special consideration. One of these is the special burden of stress placed on minorities, women, and older workers in the workplace and in society in general. In this context, Koop (1992) suggested, "Issues of race, gender, and aging continue to impact health and well-being disproportionately across the nation. I hope you will remember the link between work stress and family stress, the added burden of difficult economic times, the looming threat for many of unemployment, and the stressful necessity of working multiple jobs for the economic survival of so many of our families" (p. 3).

Koop, who at the time of the conference served as surgeon general of the United States, went on to suggest, "Finally, let me say that our nation needs a much larger sustained cadre of professionals who have a focused expertise on health in the workplace, who can serve the corporate business world, who can consult effectively with labor, who can teach with excellence, and carry out practical research in our academies" (p. 4). Such a view tends to validate this book's suggested broadening of the definition of the content of career counseling and of the roles of career counselors and counseling psychologists in working not only with persons choosing jobs and occupations, but also with those for whom work adjustment, family-related and work-related stress, and underemployment or unemployment have become major personal crises.

As Millar (1992), director of the National Institute of Occupational Safety and Health, has reported, "Today mental disorders are the leading cause for social security disability claims in the United States. In the 1980s, they surpassed awards for musculoskeletal disorders." There is no doubt that job-related stress and other psychological disorders are rapidly becoming one of the most pressing occupational safety and health concerns in the country today (p. 5). Millar cited a number of findings from studies by government and corporate researchers that indicated, in paraphrased form:

- The number of workers' compensation claims resulting from mental disorders has increased from 1980 to 1990.
- Approximately one in ten workers are suffering from depression, and the cost to society and business is nearly $27 billion annually.
- Electronic monitoring of workers exacerbates job stress.
- The issue of greatest prominence to the workplace in the 1990s would be stress and if some major corporations had one thing to do to improve production, it would be to institute a marriage maintenance program, since divorce is "killing" many workers.
- What the worker brings to the job may be as important as what the job brings to the worker. Stress off the job can play an important role in stress on the job (p. 6).

Sauter (1992) has reported Social Security Administration data that show social security awards for mental disorders are now more common than for any other type of disability. This effect is far more dramatic in the prime working years. Workers below age 50 experience as much as two to four times the disability for mental disorders as for musculoskeletal or circulatory problems. All this translates to the fact that nearly 600,000 workers are disabled for reasons of psychological disorders. The fiscal, let alone emotional, burden is dramatic. Annual payments to these individuals can be estimated at about $5 billion, with another $5 billion in payments to their families and dependents. Lost wages can be estimated at nearly $10 billion. Although the effects of job stress per se have not been isolated, some sources place the annual cost of stress-related disorders in the $100 billion range (Sauter, 1992, p. 12).

The findings of the international conference held in 1990 combining the expertise of the American Psychological Association and the National Institute for Occupational Safety and Health were updated in 1999. The findings on work, stress, and health were at least as bleak in 1999 as they were in 1990. According to a summary of the findings by McGuire (1999), there were several themes. They included that American workers are working harder and longer than they have in the past two decades just to maintain their standard of living. The result is a workforce more at risk than ever for psychological, physical, and behavior health problems, leading to social and family disruptions. At the conference, discussions ensued about the increasing workload experienced by men and women and resulting concerns about such new terms as time poverty and time famine. For those at work, absences due to stress-related illness are of growing concern. Indeed, the perspective continues that psychological disorders are one of the ten leading occupational diseases and injuries in the United States. Estimates at the conference were that a quarter to a third of workers have high job stress and are drained and used up at the end of the day. This perspective is associated with the rapid and remarkable increase in the number of workers working longer hours. The average hours Americans work each week is 47, with some 20 percent of the workforce averaging 49 hours per week. The number of hours Americans work per week has risen by 8 percent in the last 20 years. But, even as they work longer and harder, more American workers are concerned about losing their jobs. The rise in stress-related problems in the workplace translates in increased health-care costs, with billions of dollars of economic loss associated with problems of low morale and decreased productivity of the workforce.

Increasingly, U.S. workers in comparison to workers in other nations are being seen as obsessed with work and as workaholics. According to the findings of the International Labour Organization, in 1999, American workers had exceeded the work week of the Japanese to become the longest-working nation per week and per year in the advanced industrial world. In comparison with Western Europeans, Americans worked the equivalent of eight weeks longer per year. In Norway and Sweden, ordinary workers get four to six weeks of vacation and up to a year of parental leave. In France, a 35-hour work week has now become government policy, as a way of cutting unemployment.

The validity of these perspectives is enhanced by other relevant data. For example, Shilling and Brackbill (1987) report that the results of the 1985 National Health Interview Survey indicated that a projected 11 million workers report "health endangering" levels of mental stress at work. Such surveys indicate that mental health problems are pervasive in the workplace. Annually, approximately 550 million working days are lost to U.S. industry due to absenteeism; it is estimated that approximately 54 percent of these absences are in some way stress related (Elkin & Rosch, 1990). Similar findings are reported in Britain, and in all likelihood other industrialized nations, where the Confederation of British Industry (Sigman, 1992) has estimated that, in the United Kingdom, 360 million working days are lost annually through sickness, at a cost of £8 billion or roughly $12 billion, and that at least half of these days are lost to stress-related absence. Although there are direct costs in the loss of productivity, workers' compensation, labor turnover, and other expenses, there are less clear-cut indirect costs of treatment for stress-related illnesses and job dissatisfaction (Cooper & Cartwright, 1994).

Certainly, since 1999, job-related stress and psychological disorders continue to grow in their physical and financial costs to individuals and to the nation's economic productivity. There are increasingly well-defined relationships between anxiety, stress, rage, and physical and mental disorders. Stress of all types lowers the threshold for what provokes anger and often the anger is displaced from the environment, which causes stress to other environments—from having a bad day at work to driving an automobile in traffic and experiencing anger at the carelessness of other drivers. Coming home from work after a day of considerable stress makes the person especially vulnerable to becoming enraged at home by some event (the children being too noisy, meals not being on time) that under other circumstances would not create powerful emotions. In such cases anger can build on anger and stress can lead to anxiety out of proportion and out of place (Goleman, 1995). Anxiety, which tends to be evoked by high levels of stress including pressures in the workplace, has been linked to a variety of physical effects, including compromising the immune system, which accelerates the development of a range of diseases and illnesses—cancer, diabetes, atherosclerosis, asthma, gastrointestinal problems, problems with the nervous system, colds, flu, herpes. Such research findings seem most clearly associated with mental stress and anxiety, high-pressure jobs, jobs high in strain (high-pressure performance demands while having little or no control over how to get the job done), and high pressure in daily lives such as that of a single mother trying to juggle day care and a job (Goleman, 1995). Growing evidence suggests that men and women are vulnerable to the same stressors at work (Barrett & Hyde, 2001).

Some research studies are examining the role of dispositional variables—stable and consistent ways of thinking, feeling, and acting—as they are associated with job stress, family stress, or work-family conflict. For example, Stoeva, Chiu, and Greenhaus (2002) studied the role of negative affectivity as a factor that may contribute to high levels of work-family conflict. Such dispositional variables represent a "frame" through which appraisals or evaluations of specific situations are made. Earlier research has shown that persons with high negative affectivity are likely to experience high levels of subjective distress, depression, nervousness, and anxiety, as well as feelings of anger, contempt, disgust, and fear. Negative affectivity has often been studied as a confounding variable between stress and its outcome. In this sense, whether the individual is assessed as being characterized by positive affectivity or negative affectivity, such dispositions frame perceptions of the environment and vulnerability to the effects of stressors in his or her life. Thus, these researchers studied their hypothesis that persons with a trait or disposition of negative affectivity will experience more work-family conflict through the effect of this trait on the individuals' perceptions of the stressfulness of their work and family environments. The researchers also hypothesized that work-family conflict is more likely to occur when individuals are engaged in multiple roles—worker, spouse, parent—since each of these roles place demands on time, energy, and commitment. As the reader is well aware, in a world of dual earners in families, such multiple roles are becoming the average situation for most mothers and fathers. In such circumstances the pressures of each of these roles may interfere with the ability to perform effectively in one or more of the other roles, presenting effects on the work role by pressures emanating from the family role or vice versa. The results of this study demonstrated that persons with high negative affectivity experience more stress in the workplace and in the family than do persons with low negative affectivity and, in turn, these perceptions of high job and family stress are related to extensive work-family and family-work conflict: work interference with family roles or family interference with work roles.

The importance of such research affirms that not all persons experience stress in the same way from the same stressors. It also illustrates that career counseling devoted to work-family conflicts needs to address the dispositions or personality traits of the persons involved and their interpretations of the stress they are experiencing in the job or family context. Indeed, this type of stress research suggests that dispositions, such as negative affectivity, help to explain why people make appraisals of their job or family contexts as stressful. Finally, these research findings indicate that negative affectivity and other factors related to stress may be embedded in the context in which they occur and related to sociocultural processes of learning and interpretation.

Beyond the issue of personal appraisal and subjectivity of evaluations of stress in the work place is another theoretical approach to stress that is increasing in attention. Conservation of Resources (COR) theory predicts that resource loss is the principal ingredient in stress (Hobfoll, 2001). This theory relies more centrally on the objective and culturally constructed determination of the stress process rather than on the individual's subjective appraisal of the situation. According to Hobfoll, "The basic tenet of COR theory is that individuals strive to obtain, retain, protect, and foster those things they value." "They do so in a world that they see as innately threatening, requiring a constellation of their personal strengths, social attachments, and cultural belonging in order to survive. These valued entities are termed resources" (p. 341). In such a view, stress is produced by the threat of loss of resources, the actual loss of resources, or when individuals fail to gain sufficient resources following significant resource investment. Decisions about the ranking of the importance of resources is both an individual issue and a product of culture. As resource losses occur or are threatened, individuals may engage in resource replacement as well as resource substitution to offset resource loss. For example, "loss through interpersonal conflict at home can be partially compensated for, at least, by greater investment in work-related resources" (p. 350). When resource losses occur and compensatory efforts are not yielding utility to the person, *accommodative coping* may result in downgrading goals, reframing outcomes, no longer fighting old battles. However, while cognitive reframing is typically considered a stress-reduction process, when stressors and stressful events are experienced in areas central to identity or other highly valued life domains more stress may result and some persons may reject cognitive reframing as appropriate for them. What COR theory would advocate is that in stress reduction the first issue is not cognitive reframing, but changes in objective circumstances, cultural interpretations of environmental difficulties that lead to stress, and the practice of active coping behavior by which to build resource systems.

Career Development and Mental Health

As the statistics cited previously indicate, distress about work is associated with a range of social and personal problems. Counseling psychology, and counseling theory in general, is just beginning to make the link between career development and mental health (Herr, 1989). Until now, for the most part, the focus of attention has been on the structure of career development and its changes over time (Chapter 4 focuses on such content), not on the relationships between career patterns and mental health. But there is a growing and compelling body of evidence suggesting that such relationships do exist; that the characteristics of work (e.g., Lewin-Epstein, 1989), absence of work, or underemployment are reflected in behaviors that suggest various problems in living or, indeed, mental illness; and that there may, in fact, be psychological and mental health consequences of difficult career decisions (Spokane, 1989).

Until the past decade, with few exceptions, career counseling and career guidance have been historically portrayed as significantly more oriented to economic health, to choice of an occupation, and to the development of prevocational skills and the preparation for work than to the reduction of stress and other factors that put people at risk of experiencing physical and mental disorders. As suggested in Chapter 1, however, traditional and restrictive views of the purpose and potential of career counseling are slowly changing in the face of growing evidence that career development and human development are connected; satisfaction or dissatisfaction in one of these affects the other. Thus, in national policies, commission reports, and a growing segment of professional literature, career counseling and guidance are being seen as critical ingredients in giving underemployed, unemployed, vocationally dissatisfied, or indecisive youth and adults a sense of purpose and self-efficacy; in so doing, career guidance or counseling is expected to be helpful in diminishing the stress-related side effects of hopelessness and despair associated with a work life that is seen as unsatisfying or mismatched to the individual's aspirations and abilities.

Implicit in such perspectives is the reality that problems with work may be intrapsychic, environmental, or interactive. Work problems that are intrapsychic may involve individual preoccupations with self-esteem, irrational beliefs, deficits in interpersonal skills, inability to appropriately tolerate constructive supervisory relationships appropriately, or involvement in addictive processes or substances. Work problems that are environmental in origin include exposure to a management or supervisory style that is negative for that person and creates a pathological work situation, a work setting that provides no opportunity for advancement or for the levels or kinds of rewards to which a person aspires, or a work context that is racially or sexually biased and stifles individual mobility or security. An interactive work environment is one in which there is a mismatch between the individual's skills and environmental expectations—a lack of person-job fit. In each of these situations, the workplace becomes an environment in which both positive and negative, healthy and unhealthy, good and bad outcomes are stimulated; a context in which conflicts, thwarted ambitions, and emotional distress from one's life outside that workplace can be brought into the workplace to shape one's life as a worker. As such, the workplace becomes a crucible for mental health issues that revolve around work and become the content of career counseling and career guidance.

As recognition of the effects of stress and of the related disorders becomes more widely assimilated in the literature of counseling psychology and counselor education, the definition of counselor roles and competencies required to provide assistance to adults dealing with work adjustment problems broadens the views of interventions necessary and stimulates new paradigms of function. For example, although most interventions concerned with mental health, psychological disorders, or stress in the workplace are targeted at the individual level, there are also pressures for counselors to provide interventions at the interface of the individual and the organization or at the organizational level. The first of these may mean the provision of workshops on stress management for workers and managers as well as training of supervisors and middle managers on the career needs of workers and ways to provide workers with information, support, and decision-making opportunities likely to reduce stress or dissatisfaction. In the latter case, the counselor may work with the management of the firm to do *stress audits,* which assess the levels of stress in different parts of an organization, the particular stressors at issue, and ways to create a more mentally healthy environment. Such multilevel assessment and intervention by the counselor requires clarity about who is one's client and the purposes of the intervention. It also requires the counselor to have competencies in many domains: cognitive-behavioral and rational-emotive behavioral techniques; counseling skills; group-facilitation skills; teaching about occupational mental health and related topics, problem-solving skills; knowledge of relevant research about lifestyle options of concern to stress management (e.g., diet, exercise); and understanding of occupational, organizational, family, social, and cultural issues related to mental health, career development, and the workplace (Palmer & Dryden, 1994).

UNEMPLOYMENT AND MENTAL AND EMOTIONAL DISTRESS

Probably the most dramatic example of the connection between mental and emotional distress and work is that of unemployment. By way of context, it is accurate to suggest that unemployment has been a concern in most of the industrialized nations for a hundred or more years (Garraty, 1978). Throughout most of this period, unemployment was treated as an individual, not a state, problem and an economic issue, not a psychological or sociological one. Increasingly, nations have realized that while unemployment is complex and difficult for the individuals affected, unemployment is also a major social and economic issue that is increasingly global in its impact. Unemployment, then, is a process that carries societal and individual costs. The reality of the growing interdependence of the world's economies means that the effects of high unemployment rates in a particular nation or region of the world will be reflected indirectly, if not directly, in the economic well-being and employment rates of nations whose export-import trade balances will be lowered and ultimately reflected in job losses far from the original point of economic and employment downturn. We see this wavelike effect of unemployment washing across nations throughout the world as the effects of economic difficulties in one nation radiate slowly but surely among economic or trading partners in other parts of the world.

Job Insecurity and Underemployment

Often accompanying unemployment are two other phenomena that are less well known or documented. Job uncertainty is one; underemployment is another.

Before being unemployed, voluntarily or involuntarily, many persons go through a long or a short period of uncertainty and insecurity about whether or not they will leave or lose their current job. It is not surprising that such job insecurity is detrimental to employee attitudes and well-being.

As discussed in this chapter, the preceding chapter, and elsewhere in the book, the organization, content, and availability of work has changed dramatically in the last several decades. As noted by Sverke and Hellgren (2002), "intensified global competition has forced organizations to cut production costs and become more flexible; periods of economic recession have led to widespread organizational closure with unemployment and growing insecurity in its wake; new technologies have paved the way for less labor intensive production and also restricted the employment alternatives of less skilled workers; the rapid restructuring from manufacturing to service production has called into question employees' views of the stability of their employers; and a belief in the market-driven economy has changed government policies and in many countries resulted in relaxations of employment legislation" (p. 25).

One of the results of such widespread change in the availability and nature of work is job insecurity. As applied primarily to involuntary changes in their job, the construct of job insecurity often manifests negative reactions as workers contemplate the future existence of their job and their powerlessness to do anything about a threatened job situation. Thus, job insecurity is a subjective phenomenon related to how a worker perceives the immediate work environment and its effects on placing his or her job at risk.

Individual workers differ in their experiences of job insecurity and in their feelings about their job being at risk. Factors like marital status, age, industry, attachment to a particular job or location are likely to affect the intensity of job insecurity. Indeed, sometimes job insecurity is focused on losing aspects of a valued job—being demoted, working with certain coworkers, having to change work locations, deterioration of job conditions—rather than being unemployed per se.

As we will discuss at some length in the next section on the psychological and physiological consequences of unemployment, feelings of job insecurity have a psychological impact on the employee's overall life satisfaction. Similar to our previous discussion of job stress, anticipation of a stressful event can be as important a source of anxiety as the actual loss of a job. Among other consequences that frequently accompany job insecurity are physical problems, mental distress, reduced job satisfaction, negative work attitudes and behavior, attempts to find other employment, and deterioration in the viability of the work organization itself.

In short, job insecurity, in a changing work environment, has become both a growing career counseling problem and a problem for employers. Within such contexts, career counseling has got to help the worker deal with both the objective and the subjective characteristics of the current job situation. This requires analysis of the current labor market, potential organizational changes, and other factors affecting the likelihood of job changes as well as the worker's perceptions of their employability, social support, and control in the situation. From an organizational perspective, job insecurity can be addressed by acknowledging individual concerns about job security, providing advanced knowledge of job changes anticipated, fair treatment to all employees related to such changes, and providing for support groups, outplacement counseling, and related processes to help workers with their employment transitions.

One of the processes that also needs consideration when counselors address job loss or unemployment is underemployment (Prause & Dooley, 2001). Sometimes seen as a step from unemployment to reemployment, underemployment also can be seen as less satisfactory or economically less desirable than the original job one had. Underemployment is frequently characterized by part-time rather than full-time work or work which only partially provides an outlet for the range of talents an individual can bring to the workplace or provides very low pay. Some research has suggested that as people are required to change jobs, moving from adequate employment to underemployment, they are likely to experience decreases in self-esteem. They also may experience alcohol abuse. Interestingly, in the study by Prause and Dooley, underemployed workers experienced more elevated depression than those who were fully and adequately employed, but less depression than those who were unemployed. Thus, underemployment, while certainly less desirable than adequate, full employment, is better than no job. Persons in underemployment are a target group for career counseling designed to help them gain skills and actions by which to gain full employment, greater self-esteem, and reduced psychological distress.

Unemployment: A Worldwide Phenomenon

The issues of job insecurity, underemployment, and unemployment in the current world context are complex and they are changing. One can begin with numbers. The August 28, 1993, issue of the *Economist* proclaimed, "Unemployment is Europe's most pressing domestic problem; that industry within the European community must become more competitive and thus put some of Europe's 17 million unemployed back to work." By the end of 1993, the average unemployment rate within the nations of the European community was over 11 percent of the workforce (*Economist,* August 28, 1993, p. 43). By the end of 1994, the number of unemployed people in Europe was expected to be nearing 20 million people, roughly equal to the populations of Greece and Portugal combined.

At the beginning of 1994, about 30 percent of the world's labor force of 820 million people were unemployed or underemployed (International Labour Organization, 1994). The European Commission (1998) indicated that in 1997 unemployed persons amounted to approximately 18 million, representing 10.7 percent of the of the civilian labor force with over 12 percent unemployment in Italy and Finland and almost 20 percent in Spain. Given the economic recession in Europe and in Asia that has continued into 2003, the number of unemployed persons around the world continue to be major policy and humanitarian issues. Indeed, the recessionary effects as they ebb and flow in different nations cause unemployment rates to change accordingly. For example, as Europe has begun to increase its general economic health, the average unemployment rate of countries in the European Union has fallen from over 10 percent to 8.5 percent in 2002. However, within such an average, there continue to be large disparities in unemployment rates among individual nations. For example, in 2002, Spain's unemployment rate remained at 13 percent, Belgium 11 percent, and Germany nearly 10 percent. In contrast, the Netherlands unemployment rate was about 2 percent. In other parts of the world, economic difficulties have also given rise to unemployment rates. For example, Japan, a nation that since the 1960s has had very low unemployment rates, often less than 2 percent, but which has now experienced a stagnant economy for twelve years, is now experiencing rates of 5 percent and rising at the same time as its vaunted system of life long employment is being dismantled (*Economist,* March 2, 2002, p. 98).

In addition to Japan, these figures are essentially descriptive of the status of the nations constituting the twelve nations in the European Community. These nations have experienced economic cooperation, reduced tariff barriers, mobility of workers, and work opportunities within the EFTA trading block that nations outside of its boundaries do not have. Thus, many of the nations of Eastern and Central Europe that are not now included in such free trade agreements experience even more difficult economic situations and higher unemployment rates than those just reported. The nations of Eastern and Central Europe, particularly Bulgaria, Czechoslovakia, Hungary, Poland, and Romania, have been labeled transition countries (Sorrentino, 1992, p. 43), primarily because they are each in the throes of moving from centrally planned economies to market economies; from high ratios of state sector employment to private sector economies; from large institutional employment to a rapid rise in private entrepreneurs with fewer than twenty-five employees, and often in self-employment enterprises of one or two persons part-time and concentrated in basic services, such as retailing or catering and craft industries; from the stability of price controls to the uncertainty and indeed inflationary surge that at least initially accompanies a free market economy.

It is important to acknowledge that whatever unemployment rate is used to summarize unemployment in a nation, that rate masks a variety of dynamics and averages a range of unemployment that actually differs among subpopulations. Within the European Community figures, which cited an average of 11 percent unemployment, the range was actually 1.3 percent in Luxembourg to nearly 17 percent in Ireland (Rappoport, 1992). In a related example, Ritook (1993) has reported, "In March 1993, the rate of unemployment [in Hungary] was 11–12 percent. This percentage is far higher in East Hungary than in Budapest, much higher among the untrained than among the trained, and much higher among those just starting their careers than among those thirty years of age or older" (p. 34). The point is well taken not only in Hungary but in other nations. In the United States, unemployment rates among African American inner-city youth have historically been significantly higher than for white youth; adolescent unemployment rates have been higher than those of adults; minority higher than majority persons; women returning to the labor force higher than men; and immigrants higher than nonimmigrants.

Although much more could be said about the rates of unemployment in nations around the world, the dynamics of the global economy have created new pressures on unemployment and have changed it from a national or subnational phenomenon to an international phenomenon that affects virtually all of the nations of Europe, many in the Far East, in South and North America, and in Africa. The interdependence of nations engaged in the emerging global economy not only share in world-wide recessions, as have gripped industrialized nations for the past ten and more years, but also they share in the mismatch between changing job requirements and the skills of the existing national labor forces and, ultimately, the ripple effects on employment spawned by the transformation of economic conditions in nations around the world.

The Social and Fiscal Costs of Unemployment

One of these ripple effects, a major factor in understanding the importance of unemployment, is the fact that unemployment costs money: It reduces the productive capacity of nations; it cuts the energy of its human capital resources to be competitive and purposeful. Unemployment increases the costs to governments of their social security and social service systems, the safety nets that must be put in place to provide a financial floor for those who are out of work, discouraged, and without resources to sustain themselves or their family; the costs for medical treatment, mental health and psychiatric services; and responses to violence and abuse all increase with rises in unemployment. Increases in imprisonment, mortality rates, suicides, and other physiological, behavioral, emotional, and stress-related disorders have been found to correlate significantly with increases in the rate of unemployment. In one estimate of such costs in the United States in 1985, it was calculated that as a result of high unemployment rates at that time, the costs of the lost productivity of workers was $19 billion annually, unemployment benefits cost $9 billion, and other financial assistance to unemployed persons cost another $6 billion per year, adding up to a staggering $34 billion cost per year for the effects of unemployment (Shelton, 1985). But these figures, now nearly twenty years old, however large, are conservative in their estimation of lost revenue that would have accrued if these workers were secure and able to purchase goods and services in ways that they desired.

There are also costs not included in the estimates cited that are more directly attributable to stopping the rise of unemployment by youth training, adult retraining, and other labor market schemes. At present, the European countries spend between 1 and 3 percent of their Gross Domestic Products on these benefits. Reducing unemployment would help governments ease the burdens on already strained economies and allow them to divert funds into more productive ventures. One of the corollary costs supportive of a view of unemployment as a crisis in many nations relates to the fact that to an increasing degree in many nations, unemployment is not a temporary situation but one likely to be long-term for many persons. "Many of those who leave the job market will find it hard to get back in: nearly half of Europe's unemployed have been out of work for a year or more, compared with just 6% of Americans." (*Economist,* August 28, 1993, p. 43). A study of long-term unemployment reported in July 1993 (*Economist,* July 24, 1993, p. 101) indicated that almost 7 of every 10 unemployed Italians and more than 6 out of 10 Belgians had been jobless for more than a year. Thus, long-term unemployment symbolizes the potential rise of a permanent underclass; further disparities between the haves and the have nots; the permanent reduction of productivity, revenues, and taxes that might otherwise be available to a nation; and the growing realization that a person out of work for over a year is less likely to get a job or keep it than one unemployed for a brief time.

Individual Reactions to Unemployment

Talking about the factors related to unemployment in a macro or an abstract and academic way masks the reality that, regardless of national unemployment rates, whether 2.5, 7, 12, or 40 percent, for the individual who is unemployed, the rate is 100 percent. Unemployment is not simply a social or national crisis; it is virtually always a personal crisis for the person experiencing it. And, although unemployment is likely to be an economic crisis, its meaning is typically much more fully found in the psychological, behavioral, and emotional corollaries of disrupted or confused meaning, identity, affiliation, and negative feelings of self-esteem that for the individual accompany this crisis. For these reasons, at several points in this book it is contended that career counseling is a mental health modality when it is put at the service of the unemployed, the underemployed and those with major work adjustment problems.

But unemployment, underemployment, and problems in the workplace spill over into other parts of one's life as well. Kieselbach and Lunser (1990), reporting on their research in the state of Bremen and elsewhere in Germany, have suggested that the major psychosocial problems experienced by the unemployed sample they studied and the percentage who experienced the problem include:

1. Problems with partner (47 percent)
2. Accusations leveled by family (47 percent)

3. Excessive alcohol consumption (44 percent)
4. Difficulties contacting others (39 percent)
5. Problems looking for work (36 percent)
6. Trouble with the government's labor office (33 percent)
7. Loss of status (33 percent)
8. Crisis of self-esteem (25 percent) (p. 192)

Kieselbach and Lunser go on to suggest that for many people affected, unemployment represents a stressful life event that massively changes many everyday routines, relationships, social roles, and central aspects of the perception of self and others. Furthermore, unemployment leads to forms of psychosocial distress often unanticipated by the individual concerned, which can intensify through the accumulation of daily hassles. In many cases, such a crisis cannot be overcome by the person affected using his or her own coping resources but can be resolved by seeking professional help.

Ritook (1993), in her analysis of five types of unemployment in Hungary, indicates that persons of different ages, work experiences, characteristics, and attachments to work deal with unemployment differently. Similar findings have been reported by England (1990) and Neff (1985) in relation to worker-organization interaction and attachment. Ritook has suggested the following classification structure.

The first type includes people over 40 who have spent their entire lives in a large enterprise and become suddenly unemployed; they feel they have lost their foothold. Theirs is not a simple financial problem but the loss of the purpose of their existence. Loss of self-confidence, feelings of shame and self-blame are characteristic features, usually accompanied by extreme short temper, dissatisfaction with society, and the feeling of having been cheated. The majority of these people hesitate to accept the training offered in some other skill. They pass through a period of severe depression. They have the feeling that everything on which they have built their lives has collapsed.

Another group of unemployed—mostly under 40—easily get used to a free life. Some of them enjoy this new way of life for months. From time to time, they undertake occasional work without committing themselves, and begin to look for more serious work after the subsidized period ends. Within this second type, there is a similar group that after some weeks of an emotionally active mood become depressed like those in the first group. It is not so much a crisis of work values, to which they are not bound as deeply as the other group, but their way of life passing through a true crisis. They ask and wait for help, not only financially but also for a change in their way of life.

Young people starting their careers—the third type—are in the most dangerous situation. They have the best possibility of support and of obtaining work. But, in their case, the rhythm of life linked to work has not yet developed, and they are content for quite a long time not to be bound to anything. This lack of a disciplined way of life and of suitable career socialization might lead to a greater danger of drifting in the direction of deviance.

Those who, even before the period of mass unemployment, were often without work, form the fourth type. People with low qualifications, struggling with the problems of socialization, almost unable to solve the conflicts arising in their places of work, belong to this group. The fifth type comprises refugees who often live under similar conditions to those described in the fourth type. It is difficult to find jobs for them, particularly if they do not speak the majority language.

Indicators of Links between Career Development and Mental Health

In addition to the studies cited earlier, the past quarter century has seen a growing literature in economics, industrial psychology, organizational theory, and psychiatry as well as in counseling which demonstrates that personal adjustment and work adjustment exist in a symbiotic relationship; and that a variety of life difficulties and mental problems ensue when work life is seen by individuals as unsatisfactory or unavailable.

Among the specific problems found in the research literature to be associated with unemployment and economic decline are first admissions to psychiatric hospitals, rises in rates of infant mortality, increased deaths from cardiovascular and alcohol-related diseases, imprisonments, sharp increases in suicide rates, chemical dependency and violence, and greater demand for mental health services owing to increased psychological impairment of the population (Brenner, 1973, 1979; Prause & Dooley, 2001; Pryor & Ward, 1985); threats to the structural interdependence between the family and the workplace (Kantor, 1977); stress in the children of unemployed parents—such as moodiness at home, new problems in school, strained relationship with peers (Liem & Rayman, 1982); digestive problems, irritability, and retarded physical and mental development (Riegle, 1982); increased reports of depression, anxiety, and interpersonal problems by spouses as the period of unemployment continues (Herr, 1989; Labich, 1993; Shelton, 1985); short-term unemployment degenerating into long-term exclusion unemployment (European Commission, 1998); and the risk of social exclusion that leads to alienation of the individual from society at large.

Thus, effects of unemployment touch not only the individual who is unemployed but all parts of the system of which he or she is a part. For each of the persons involved, it is common to have manifested a wide range of physical, emotional, and social stresses and strains. There are other vantage points on how unemployment affects career development and mental health as well.

Mangum (1988) and others have shown that assumptions that early unemployment is a transient matter that simply "ages out" is not correct. Unless young people attain some early success in the labor market, they are likely to be doomed to a life of jagged unemployment because of problems of a lack of credibility with employers, lack of information relevant to effective job access and adjustment, and a lack of identity as a worker. These deficits put them at risk compared with their age cohorts unless they benefit from dramatic and systematic intervention both in terms of economic programs and in terms of counseling programs. A related Australian study (Feather & O'Brien, 1986) that followed a relatively large sample of school-leaving students from high school to employment or unemployment found that unemployment led to decreases in perceived competence, activity, and life satisfaction and an increase in depressive effect. Other studies have reported similar findings (Winefield & Tiggemann, 1989).

Other research supports the finding that unemployment, problematic work relationships, and stressful work conditions play significant roles in the development of physical and mental health problems (e.g., Brenner, 1987; Frese & Mohr, 1987; Levi, 1984; Joelson & Wahlquist, 1987; Rose, Hurst, & Herd, 1979). Levine (1979) has reported on both the reactions to unemployment and the emotional consequences of unemployment. He reports that reactions to unemployment tend to unfold in three stages: (1) optimism, (2) ambiguity, and (3) despair. Life event changes perceived as stressful—job loss or major career changes are typically so identified—have been repeatedly shown to precede the onset of mental illness. Thus, demoralization and despair associated with severe work or economic or family problems trigger distress, which has biological and physiological as well as psychological correlates (Kleinman, 1988).

In the language of stress, difficulties at work are not only stressful life events, but also stressors that may cause the individual to keep attempting to cope with or adapt to the resulting stress and strain until he or she runs out of physical and mental resources or gets beyond the capability of existing support systems to buffer the person from such feelings of uncontrollable threat. Depending on the cultural or social meanings attributed by the person, his or her family, or the community to work conflict or to unemployment, the person may consciously or unconsciously seek ways to express the problem. Sometimes the expression is a physical one (e.g., backache); sometimes it is mental (e.g., depression, anxiety, or other symptoms); sometimes it is behavioral (e.g., spouse or child abuse, violence). Which of these *symptoms* of work problems is likely to occur is probably a function of the particular cultural symbols of such distress which that person has been conditioned to believe is appropriate (Helman, 1985). This does not mean that all cases of backache are somatic expressions of mental distress but rather it says that in some cultures or social groups, work conflicts or other aspects of career distress may be somatocized, symbolized by backache, chronic pain, or other physical symptoms rather than depression or anxiety or other more clearly psychological disorders. The data seem consistent, that distress about work and, particularly, unemployment are associated with a range of personal and social problems. According to research in Australia (Feather & Davenport, 1981), the more an individual is motivated to work, the more likely he or she is to experience depressive affect as a result of unemployment. Shamir (1986a) found somewhat similar results among several samples of unemployed workers in Israel. In addition, Levine (1979) has reported that while there are individual differences in coping with unemployment, the virtually predictable emotional and cognitive consequences include boredom, identity diffusion, lowered self-esteem, guilt and shame, anxiety and fear, anger, and depression. Prolonged unemployment frequently is characterized by periods of apathy, alternating with anger, sadness, sporadic optimism, few habits of regular structured activities, few meaningful personal contacts, and ominous feelings of victimization, lack of personal power, and low self-worth (Schlossberg & Leibowitz, 1980; Herr, 1989). These are not benign reactions. They are typically accompanied by psychological, cognitive, and behavioral outcomes.

One of the most recent groups to be studied is male and female managers. The organizational downsizing and effects of advanced technology available to workers at all levels of organizations have altered the roles of middle and senior managers and, in some situations, have caused them to bear the brunt of job cutbacks. In one study of unemployed female managers (Fielden & Davidson, 1996), it was found that these persons experienced significant decreases in self-esteem, self-confidence, and self-worth and that the most significant sources of stress experienced by unemployed female managers occurred during the job search with discrimination being encountered at all stages of the process. Duffield's research (1994, quoted in Fielden & Davidson, 2001) indicated that managers, in general, in situations of continued unemployment lose confidence in their managerial abilities, which in turn inhibits their job search and reduces the likelihood of their obtaining suitable employment. Fielden and Davidson (2001) undertook to identify both gender differences and similarities in the experiences of unemployed male and female managers. The quantitative segment of the study, which involved responses to an extensive questionnaire, included 115 females and 169 males, all unemployed managers, recruited throughout England. Prior to the development of the questionnaire, the qualitative segment of the study included semi-structured interviews with 20 male and 20 female unemployed managers randomly selected from executive job clubs throughout England. The results indicated that the experiences of unemployment are not always the same for male and female managers, with women experiencing additional sources of stress. Further, the impact of unemployment in the psychological well-being of male managers is significant but, in comparison, the impact on the psychological and physical well-being of unemployed female managers is substantially greater. The main sources of stress reported by unemployed male managers arose from the financial impact of unemployment, the extensive amount of ageism they faced during job search, and the loss of the creativity outlet as a result of job loss. These losses were compounded by a lack of control over job loss and the lack of notice that their employment was going to be terminated. The inability of male managers to fill time was a significant source of stress, which was frequently linked to feelings of isolation and boredom.

The unemployed female managers were faced with a greater number of stressors than their male counterparts. These included stigma, prejudice, discrimination, financial deprivation, and loss of social life. The reactions of others were a direct source of stress. The families and friends of unemployed female managers were frequently "unsupportive." An overall decrease in social contacts resulted in high levels of loneliness and isolation. The inability to relax was the main behavior outcome of unemployment experienced by female managers. It impacted on mental and physical well-being and the ability of female managers to cope with their situation. Sleeping patterns were also affected. In general, unemployed female managers experienced poorer mental health than women in the general adult population, including increased levels of anxiety and negative emotion, loss of self concept, decreased self-efficacy and a loss of self-confidence. Unemployed female managers also reported increased sickness and an increased likelihood of significant illness.

The results of this study "indicate that unemployed female managers experience significantly greater sources of stress than their male counterparts, have less access to effective moderators of the stress process, and suffer significantly poorer mental and physical well-being as a result of their experience during unemployment" (Fielden & Davidson, 2001).

Borgen and Amundson (1984), in a major study of the experiences of unemployed persons from a variety of educational, cultural, and work backgrounds in Canada, extend the findings of Levine. Borgen and Amundson contend that the experience of unemployment depicts an emotional "roller coaster" that is comparable in its impact and stages to those found by Kübler-Ross (1969) as describing the grief process associated with loss of a loved one: denial, anger, bargaining, depression, and acceptance. In regard to Maslow's (1954) model of preponent needs, which suggests that as needs at the bottom of a hierarchy are satisfied, other needs emerge, Borgen and Amundson suggest that unemployment brings with it a needs shift, involving tumbling down the hierarchy from need levels attained under previous employment to more primitive need levels that are dominant under unemployment. According to Maslow, the categories of needs that emerge as lower levels of needs are routinely met or taken for granted, begin with the most basic, the physiological needs, and proceed next to the safety needs (security, stability) to the love and belonging needs (relatedness), to the esteem needs (prestige, self-worth, recognition), and, finally, to the self-actualization needs (creative self-expression). Although it is rare that persons actually attain the highest level of self-actualization in their work, it can be assumed that most persons successfully employed will be able to attain needs beyond the most primitive physiological necessities and to meet needs for safety, love, belonging, and esteem. The research of Borgen and Amundson further suggests that whatever needs are gratified in employment shift downward significantly under unemployment. The psychological reactions under such circumstances are not only those of loss as defined by the Kübler-Ross paradigm previously identified, but also feelings of victimization similar to those experienced by persons who find themselves in the role of victim as a result of rape, incest, disease, and crime. Such feelings include shock, confusion, helplessness, anxiety, fear, and depression (Janoff-Bulman & Frese, 1983).

Borgen and Amundson's research is important for at least two other reasons. One is that unemployment is experienced differently by different groups of males and females who did or did not anticipate job loss and by immigrant populations. The second is that the factors that vary among these groups and mediate the emotional reactions to unemployment include attachment to the job, social status, individual personality variables, financial situation, social support system, and future expectations, each of which may be a target of career intervention.

In applying Amundson and Borgen's model to the situation that occurs when a long-established plant closes, Hurst and Sheperd (1986) found similar emotional stages to occur among workers anticipating job loss. In such instances, the emotional roller coaster is likely to be prolonged as older workers remain while younger workers are laid off to pare down the work force of the plant to be closed. In this research, that of Lopez (1983), and that of Amundson and Borgen, groups varied in their reaction to job loss. Hurst and Sheperd found in their sample that those employees most likely to experience prolonged depression are the few who are handicapped by physical, skill, and age barriers, and those with very low self-esteem. Even for those workers who do not experience clinical depression, there tend to be "feelings of loss, sadness, resentment, and anger because of the end of the company, close collegial relationships and a way of life for most employees" (Hurst & Sheperd, 1986, p. 404). In a related study, Burke (1986) reported that employees working in poorer jobs in Canada after a plant closing reported less life satisfaction, more psychosomatic symptoms, and greater alcohol consumption.

Borgen and Amundson's research highlights what other theorists and researchers have also observed in relation to the interaction of mental health, state of the economy, and unemployment or related phenomena. One is that such relations are likely to include multiple variables, not simply unidimensional relationships. Different people experience economic downturns and unemployment differently, and mental health outcomes can be precipitated by factors in the environment (sociogenic) as well as factors within individuals (eugenic) (Berg & Hughes, 1979). Brenner (1979) has attempted to clarify the differences among some of these concepts. For example, physical and mental health are not unitary concepts. Some people react to stress in physical terms (e.g., cardiovascular disease, cirrhosis, hypertension, chemical dependency, early death); others in behavioral terms (e.g., aggressiveness, violence, spouse abuse, child abuse); others in psychological terms (e.g., depression, anxiety). Thus, precipitating factors in the environment (e.g., a plant closing, losing a job) can cause different reactions among people (e.g., physical, behavioral, psychological) depending on individual predisposing factors to stress. Other research suggests that persons show unique and consistent patterns of response to stress, which underlie the possibility of developing diagnostic profiles of persons likely to develop stress-related disorders (Robinson & Kaplan, 1985).

Interventions in Unemployment

Throughout this analysis of unemployment, career counseling has been alluded to as the principal intervention strategy. In these instances, the term has been used as a generic term encompassing a variety of intervention emphases (e.g., social skills training, psychoeducation, computer-assisted career guidance, individual and group career/personal counseling). Also implied in the discussion is a matrix of problem-treatment interactions that can be identified. Inherent in such a matrix is the reality that different social institutions and mechanisms prominent at different life stages have a role to play in addressing the knowledge, attitudes, and behaviors related to unemployment.

While other parts of this book will address the interventions used by counselors on behalf of the unemployed, let it be noted here that in whichever model of career counseling one accepts, it is clear that the transitions in the occupational structure described in this chapter and others in the book will cause the psychological and transitional consequences for the unemployed to be a continuing concern for counselors in many settings, whether they work directly with the unemployed, or with their children or other family members. At the least, counselors will need to be more knowledgeable about the different types of unemployment, the factors that cause it, who is likely to be affected and why, and how the victims of unemployment can be helped to extricate themselves from such circumstances.

Although the unemployed are not homogeneous in their characteristics or reasons for unemployment, several broad principles can be articulated in working with them. First, counselors will need to help the unemployed understand and anticipate the psychological facets of unemployment, particularly the relationships between jobs, joblessness, and mental health. A growing literature is now available about the physiological and psychological problems associated with unemployment and economic uncertainty. Also highlighted is the relationship between unemployment and low self-esteem, mental illness, family discord, and spouse and child abuse. Various observers have noted an irrational willingness—perhaps even a need—for people to blame themselves for social processes for which they are not responsible. Counselors need to help people develop a transactional understanding of mental health that explores the fact that some problems come from personal, internal dysfunctions, but that many, if not most, are provoked and maintained by external factors, such as unemployment, which overwhelm some people but not others. Those who are overwhelmed tend to blame themselves for circumstances they could confront and cope with, although not necessarily control. Clients must be assisted to gain perspective on unemployment but not to accept it as personally inevitable or as a condition from which they cannot escape.

Second, counselors must help people examine the range of community resources available in the event of unemployment or in order to avoid it. They need to help people see themselves as part of a system—not as social isolates. This requires being aware of services provided by church, education, or social welfare groups as well as those offered by governmental units or the private sector. It is in this context that counselors can help the unemployed to see themselves as social beings operating within a system of social institutions designed to provide experience, skill development, livelihood, and well-being. As the unemployed understand these perspectives, their ability to be active rather than reactive and socially conscious rather than individually isolated is likely to be enhanced. The importance of social support to the unemployed has been found to be of major importance in several studies (Kinicki & Latack, 1990; Lichtman, 1978; Mallinckrodt & Fretz, 1988).

Third, counselors need to recognize that those who experience unemployment are likely to need more than support. They are people who may have multiple problems to deal with: transportation, racial discrimination, lack of basic skills, poor industrial discipline, family discord, and drug or alcohol problems. Thus, people need to be helped to understand the interactive effects of such problems with the condition of unemployment. Counselors can encourage basic skill training in many of these areas and provide information about others. Counselors also can serve as advocates for job needs to employers, community groups, and governmental bodies. In this role, counselors can aspire to be catalysts to stimulate the development of programs designed to create jobs, stimulate self-employment, and otherwise reduce unemployment.

As these three principles suggest, counselors have many roles to play with the unemployed. Among specific examples, Hayes and Nutman (1981) have suggested five ways in which the unemployed person can be helped by the counselor:

1. Enhancing or maintaining the individual's self-esteem by helping him or her manage anxiety and develop more effective problem-solving skills

2. Improving the fit between the individual and his or her life space
3. Promoting job-seeking skills
4. Developing new work-related skills
5. Developing positive attitudes toward work and acceptable work habits (p. 112)

Lopez's research (1983) has suggested that counseling approaches designed to assist employees because of business failures might include such paraphrased possibilities as the following:

1. Clarifying with workers their marketable, transferable, and work skills and helping them to develop short-term plans by which such skills might be realistically applied in other situations
2. Creating opportunities for displaced workers to vent their feelings about vocational and personal concerns
3. Helping workers to identify and assess their sources of financial, family, marital, and other types of personal support
4. Helping clients to obtain and use timely information on referral services, employment outlook, and available placement service
5. Reinforcing with workers the ideas that they are skilled and mature and that the job losses they experience are not because of their personal incompetence or negligence, but rather that this experience is not something that they caused

Frequently the effects of unemployment radiate through the family system and put its structure at risk. Nelson (1983, p. 19) has suggested that a family crisis intervention model may be an appropriate framework to use with many unemployed families. In addition to the specific interventions used, this model would include such emphases as the following:

1. Identify stresses induced by alterations in the individual, family, and environment
2. Assess the coping mechanisms of each family member
3. Identify family system characteristics that may influence alternative coping patterns
4. Assess resources available in the family's environment.

Steinweg (1990) provided six strategies of working with displaced employees that tend to summarize several other perspectives just cited; (1) helping clients to develop a broad sense of self-esteem; (2) aiding clients to maintain a sense of structure in their lives and to keep their activity level high; (3) assisting clients in developing and utilizing a system of social support; (4) encouraging clients to accept external causal attributions for their unemployment; (5) referring clients to community agencies as necessary; and (6) referring clients to vocational rehabilitation agencies as appropriate.

Pryor and Ward (1985) have recommended that in discharging such roles, the following techniques be used: relaxation training, systematic desensitization, assertiveness training, modeling, using video play to increase self-presentation skills at job interviews and in other situations, psychological assessment, job search skills, and coping with living on unemployment benefits (pp. 4–14). Borgen and Amundson (1984) emphasized additional techniques: effective listening, job search support groups, retraining, reassessment of self and values, early notification of job loss, and early and coordinated intervention for those about to be unemployed. Many other theorists suggest stress reduction as well as self-actualization activities.

PSYCHOLOGICAL AND WORK PATHOLOGY DISORDERS

Beyond the general relationships between work and mental health just cited, there are also more serious matters. For example, there are problem employees whose work pathology and psychopathology often merge. These are persons for whom corporations have long provided units dedicated to occupational mental health (McLean, 1973). Staffed by psychiatrists or clinical psychologists, such units are frequently augmented by the referral of problem employees to outside consultants through employee assistance plans or through various health care or insurance plans. As counseling psychologists and other career counselors specialists are increasingly employed by corporations and government agencies, treatment of such problems in the workplace may become more common.

In considering serious problems of mental illness in the workplace, it is sometimes difficult to know whether work induces mental illness or people bring mental illness to work. Huffine and Clausen (1979) have engaged in one of the few long-term studies of the effects of mental illness on careers. They intensively studied 36 married white men after they had entered a Washington, D.C., area mental hospital between 1952 and 1958 as first-admission patients with diagnoses of functional psychosis, affective disorder, severe psychoneurosis, or character disorder. Their data revealed that, in itself, being labeled mentally ill does not determine the course of a man's career even though he may be confined for months in a public mental hospital. They found that men whose symptoms subsided—either at the end of the initial episode or within a few years thereafter—did not suffer gross occupational setbacks. Indeed, it was found that the career of a man who was able to establish his competence before the initial onset of mental illness stands a good chance of surviving prolonged, even severe, symptoms.

However, about one-third experienced lower occupational status and more repeated failure than before admission. Success despite mental illness tends to depend on success of previous socialization into a work role and competence developed before becoming mentally ill. In situations in which these two conditions exist, the result seems to be a resilient work role, making it unnecessary to sacrifice a career to mental illness. Although this study did not pursue them, factors in the character and structure of the workplace may also facilitate or impede reestablishment of a career after an episode of mental illness.

The interaction of the dynamics of the workplace with the individual's needs and characteristics is not confined to how such environments respond to or support people who are recovering from mental illness. Earlier in this chapter, we also spoke about how organizational forms were reflections of cultural images about expected work behavior in terms of individual achievement or collective identity and teamwork, and in organizational terms such as regulatory or developmental models. In the last decade, there have been many books addressed to how organizations stimulate excellence in worker performance, and how some leading corporations organize their environments to enhance worker productivity, innovation, and personal growth.

But there are also books and articles that attempt to describe and explain how some work organizations reinforce or create conditions of worker pathology. For example, Schaef and Fassel (1988) have addressed what they have described as *addictive organizations,* organizations that reflect the characteristics of individual addicts: denial, distrust, anger, manipulation, and coercion. At one level, they suggest that, given the large number of employees who are addicts to processes or substances:

> *scores of nonrecovering addictive and codependent employees are inevitably replicating their dysfunctional family in the workplace. Family systems theory has long recognized that problems not solved at one level always occur elsewhere; this is also true of addicts and codependents in corporations. They do what they know best, and that is to operate addictively wherever they are. (p. 7)*

At a second level, they address the effect on organizational pathology that occurs when dysfunctional managers, active addicts themselves, negatively affect the climate of the system they are administering and the employees with whom they relate. A third level of perspective is how organizations can and do function as the addictive substance in its mission, its products, its centrality as an organization in employees' lives, and in the loyalty it expects. Depending on how those characteristics are arranged, organizations can both stimulate and reward workaholism while denying its negative meaning to the person's family life and mental health. They further argue that addictive organizations tend to perpetuate and patch up problems instead of facing and solving them.

According to such perspectives, addictive organizations are likely to be characterized by problems of communication, gossip, fear, isolation, dishonesty, suppressed feelings, sabotage, projection, disrespect, confusion, control, denial, forgetfulness, self-centeredness, grandiosity, and planning as a form of control. These negative organizational dynamics and their support or stimulation of worker pathology are seen as in contrast to those organizations that are moving out of or avoiding an addictive system. The latter manifests such positive organizational dynamics as the following: supporting the mission of the organization by a structure that is congruent with the mission; promoting self-responsibility in employees; providing permeable rather than rigid boundaries between levels and elements of the organization; multivaried-multidirectional communication throughout the organization; integrated work teams and situational leadership; a sense of morality in the way of working and in product development; congruence in formal and informal goals;

and a commitment to a process model of change (Schaef & Fassel, 1988, p. 9).

> *Although they do not define the issue in terms of an addictive model of organizations, London and More (1987), specialists in employee development and organization effectiveness at AT&T, also contend that individual, environmental and organizational factors interact to affect how people make career decisions and transitions. The environment, in the form of the company, boss, job, and larger socioeconomic conditions, affects the decisions and transitions people are likely to face, as well as strengthens or weakens their career motivation (p. xvi)....*
>
> *Organizations have considerable influence over how their employees feel. Organizations can create stress, but they also have the potential for reducing and preventing it. (p. 195)*

The sources of career stress in organizations take many forms. They include role conflict, role or task overload or underload, role ambiguity, discrimination and stereotyping, marriage/work conflicts, interpersonal stress, feelings of inadequacy, discordant values, and progress toward career goals.

Depending on the structure of organizations and how closed or open they may be, threats and psychological injuries to workers are a part of work life (Hirschhorn, 1988). How stressful or problematic they become depends on personality characteristics of the workers, previous experience, the nature of the psychological boundaries that exist in a work setting, and other factors. Frequently, workers perceive that work entails risk, and "risks are experienced psychologically as threats that must be aggressively met, contained, and ultimately transformed into challenges and opportunities" (p. 33). Many people who experience role conflict, role overload, or lack of confidence, or whose understanding of the work organization's expectations or dynamics is inadequate, however, experience anxiety that, in turn, can become a precursor of a more serious problem as it progresses or persists. Hirschhorn has suggested:

> *Feelings of anxiety are the fundamental roots of distorted or alienated relationships at work.... A work group manages its anxiety by developing and deploying a set of social defenses. By using these social defenses, people retreat from role, task, and organizational boundaries. They may try to manage their anxiety by projection of blame or scapegoating others, by bureaucratizing their work, resorting to excessive paperwork to reduce face-to-face communications, or engaging in excessive checking and monitoring of their work to reduce the anxiety of making difficult decisions. Such social defenses may depersonalize relationships at work and distort the worker's capacities to accomplish his or her primary work task. As a result potential individual-organizational pathologies can arise and spiral in complexity toward more difficult physical and mental reactions to distortions with the meaning of work or, indeed, to various forms of mental stress or illness.*

The factors associated with work pathology and worker-organizational structure are only now being more fully probed, but insights arising from research in such areas are likely to have important implications for the supportive role that can be played by the career guidance specialist or counseling psychologist in industry. It is likely that such professionals will at least need to assist managerial and supervisory personnel as well as the afflicted person's coworkers in understanding what behaviors might be expected in different forms of mental distress or illness and, indeed, that it is likely that no symptoms will be observable at all because of the control exerted by medication or other treatment, or a combination thereof. They will also probably actively attempt to improve person-job fit or, indeed, efforts to make organizations more developmental, supportive, and reparative environments in which workers can grow and be productive.

Work pathology per se is not one of the 18 classes or groups of conditions described by the American Psychiatric Association (1981) in the third edition of its *Diagnostic and Statistical Manual of Mental Disorders* (DSM-III) or in the 1987 revision, the DSM-III-R. Rather, any of the 18 categories of mental, social, and behavioral disorders included in this manual can appear in the workplace as a function of workers' distress or upset. Beyond that, however, the DSM-III-R does identify occupations, job changes, and related work processes as psychosocial stressors that can produce aberrant behavior as one copes with or adapts to the stress related to such processes. Occupational functioning is also one of three areas of adaptive functioning by which mental illness can be diagnosed; the other two are social relations and leisure time. Furthermore, occupational and social impairment constitutes one of the 15 symptom groups included in the DSM-III-R.

In DSM-IV (American Psychiatric Association, 1994) mental disorders are grouped in 16 major diagnostic classes (e.g., Substance Related Disorders, Mood Disorders, Anxiety Disorders) and one additional section, "Other Conditions That May be a Focus of Clinical Attention." It is in the latter category and on Axis IV: Psychosocial and Environmental Problems that one finds attention to "Occupational Problems." Axis IV is for reporting psychosocial and environmental problems that may affect the diagnosis, treatment, and prognosis of mental disorders (as described on Axes I and II, Clinical Disorders and Personality Disorders, respectively). Thus, it is possible to assume, as was the case in earlier versions of the DSM, that the clinical and personality disorders described in the categories of behavior, attitudes, emotions subsumed under Axis I and Axis II could certainly manifest themselves in any setting or situation in which human behavior takes place, including the workplace. The placement of occupational problems within Axis IV suggests that "many such problems arise from psychosocial or environmental difficulty or deficiency, a familial or other interpersonal stress, an inadequacy of social support or personal resources or other problems relating to the context in which a person's difficulties have developed" (American Psychiatric Association, 1994, p. 29). In this context, occupational problems would include examples such as unemployment; threat of job loss; stressful work schedule; difficult work conditions; job dissatisfaction; job change; discord with boss or co-workers. The latter emphases are each discussed throughout this chapter and elsewhere in the book.

Rather than *work pathology,* or mental disorder, one frequently finds the term *psychological disorders* (Sauter, Murphy, & Hurrell, 1992) used in relation to occupational health issues. Psychological disorders "connotes a category of problems encompassing a wide array of social, behavioral and biomedical conditions with diverse and often unknown etiologies" (p. 18). These disorders are of general concern in the occupational health arena, often investigated under the general rubric of job stress, and believed to be amenable to workplace interventions. Although similar to work pathology, psychological disorders in the workplace are not always identified in such recognized systems of medical classifications such as the DSM-III-R or DSM-IV of the American Psychiatric Association. However psychological disorders are seen by personnel representing such groups as the National Institute for Occupational Safety and Health as significant functional disturbances or risks for development of clinical disorders (Sauter, Murphy, & Hurrell, 1992). These conditions include: (1) affective disturbances such as anxiety, depression, and job dissatisfaction; (2) maladaptive behavioral and lifestyle patterns; and (3) chemical dependencies and alcohol abuse. Obviously, some of these conditions are quite clearly identified in the psychiatric literature and, as Sauter, Murphy, and Hurrell (1992) indicate, "The occupational involvement in psychological disorders is not a matter of dispute in the mental health community. 'Psychological stressors', specifying'occupational stress' as a major diagnostic axis is listed in the DSM-III" (p. 19).

According to Sauter, Murphy, and Hurrell (1992), epidemiologic and health care data on cost and causes are providing a clearer picture of the occupational relevance of psychological disorders. For example, they report studies that show mental disturbances are most heavily concentrated among workers with lower income, lower educational level, fewer skills, and less prestigious jobs. They also report on studies indicating that specific occupations and job factors present particular risks. For example, physicians, dentists, nurses, and health technologists have higher than expected rates of suicide and of alcohol and drug abuse. Nurses and other health care workers have increased rates of hospital admissions for mental disorders and elevated admission rates to mental health centers. They also report studies of a wide range of working conditions (e.g., role stressors, job demands in excess of control) that are related to job-risk factors, adverse affective states, and job dissatisfaction. They suggest that "most current approaches to job stress embodies an unfavorable interaction between worker attributes and job conditions that leads to psychological disturbances and unhealthy behaviors and ultimately to physiological ill health" (p. 23). By category, the major psychosocial risk factors that relate to psychological well-being in the workplace include work load and work pace, work schedule, role stressors (e.g., role ambiguity and role conflict), career security factors, interpersonal relations, and job content. There are also intervening factors, situational and personal variables that originate outside the job, that can and do interact with the psychosocial job factors cited and may compound their potency. These include such factors as

Type A behavior patterns, family problems, financial difficulties, and major life changes (Sauter, Murphy, & Hurrell, 1992). In broad terms, the responses to these categories of psychosocial risk factors include job design to improve working conditions; surveillance and sensitivity to the pressure of psychological disorders and risk factors; information dissemination, education, and training; and enrichment of psychological health services for workers.

Within such a context, then, work is both a condition of mental health and a condition of mental disorder (W. S. Neff, 1985, p. 7). W. S. Neff (1985), in an insightful and useful perspective, indicates that it is important to distinguish between the necessary and the sufficient conditions of work:

> *By the former set of conditions, we are referring to the fact that most work situations present us with an irreducible aggregate of requirements, which we must meet in order to be able to work at all. Some degree of moticity, a measure of manual dexterity, the ability to comprehend and follow instructions, the ability to perform a task—all of these can be described as the necessary requirements of work. On the other hand, the ability to meet these requirements may not be* sufficient *to make us workers. We cannot be so fearful of authority, for example, that the mere presence of a supervisor reduces us to a state of apparent paralysis. We cannot (usually) decide for ourselves how long we shall work, when we shall begin, or at what pace we shall proceed. Work situations are* social *situations, characterized by very complex sets of norms, rituals, customs, and social demands. It is thus possible for an individual to be able to meet the necessary conditions of work without being able to meet the sufficient conditions. (p. 13)*

As a function of cause, of content, and of manifestation, some norms of mental or social pathology may require specific types of differential treatment in the workplace. Neff (1977, 1985) has suggested several broad patterns of what might be considered work psychopathology. The underlying theme of such problems may be difficulty with authority figures, with interpersonal relations, with the meanings of work, or related conflicts. In particular, he reports five patterns of behavior that lead to failure at work. The patterns, in paraphrased form, are:

Type 1. These are people who appear to have major deficiencies in work motivation and a negative conception of the role of worker. Such people have not been socialized to value work for themselves, or they attribute negative stereotypes to the work role (such as "work is for squares"). They may view work as societal pressure for them to conform to a regimentation they prefer to avoid or resist. They pursue impulse gratification now, rather than deferred gratification and planning for the future. Persons so characterized, particularly in the extreme cases, may be made to work under powerful social coercion but will likely meet only minimum standards of productivity and will require continuous, close supervision. From a counseling view, such people need to be assisted in developing an internal locus of control and to be placed in work settings that provide graduated incentives for productivity.

Type 2. These are individuals who experience fear and anxiety as the predominant responses to demands to be productive. A fairly common type, such persons may be fearful of inability to perform effectively or have little positive self-regard. Their previous life is likely to have been a series of failures. They may interpret constructive criticism as personal threat; be acutely uncomfortable, perhaps immobilized by anxiety, in a competitive situation; and treat opportunities for cooperative work with others as situations likely to expose personal vulnerability. Such people are likely to respond favorably to conditions arranged to offer them success experiences. These individuals probably require supervisory support and encouragement while discovering that there are work roles that can be performed without constant personal deprecation. They may sometimes require a constantly sheltered work role that does not demand new and rapid challenges or expectations. Therapeutically, such persons could likely profit from cognitive restructuring or rational-emotive approaches that focus on their self-labeling and its behavioral consequences.

Type 3. This type includes people whose basic behavioral style is open hostility and aggression. They perceive supervision and criticism as attacks to which to respond with anger or violence. In such people the work expectations of society are internalized as restrictive and hostile demands on them. Such people are frequently energetic and able if placed in work they can do independently of others. They frequently do not have difficulty in finding employment, but rather in maintaining it. The typical reason for dismissal or quitting is inability to get along with others because of, in the extreme circumstances, manifestations of paranoid psychosis or, in other situations, intense irritability, physical aggression to others, or constant anger. This type of behavioral problem is very difficult to deal with in a work setting, although it may respond to long-term therapy or newer approaches to anger management and reduction.

Type 4. Included here are people whose behavior is characterized by marked dependency. Because of socialization problems in early childhood, the individual internalizes precepts that personal welfare depends on pleasing authority figures; that independent behavior by the worker can threaten such a relationship; and that childlike compliance is the chief defensive strategy to be used in any circumstance (home, school, work) in which others are perceived as all-powerful authority figures. Such people may work effectively to please a supervisor as long as close and continuous management is present. They typically require constant emotional support from the supervisor, whose patience is likely to be sorely tried in attempting to respond to the constant personal irresponsibility and emotional immaturity displayed by the worker.

These people are likely to require selective placement in situations in which they receive considerable personal approval and support. Therapeutically, they need assistance in examining their view of authority relationships and the types of trade-offs they are consciously or unconsciously engaging in through their dependency behaviors.

Type 5. These people display a marked degree of social naïveté. They simply lack knowledge about themselves as workers, about work content, and about the realities and demands of the work environment. In such cases, the focus of the counselor is not on the individual's rejection of work or resistance to components of the workplace but on ignorance. The procedure is to provide the worker with social learning or a specific educational experience in which information about the organization and expectations of work is primary.

The five types of inadequate work patterns suggested by Neff are hypothetical but represent some of the potential interactions between work and the mental health of some workers. Without some type of intervention, people characterized by such work behaviors will likely fail, quit, or be dismissed. Career counselors, counseling psychologists, or other human resource development specialists will need to provide differential treatment to cope with the variety of problems.

Lowman (1993), has provided a taxonomy of work dysfunctions that both complements and updates the typology of Neff. Lowman's use of the term *work dysfunctions* refers to psychological conditions in which there is "a significant impairment in the capacity to work caused either by characteristics of the person or by an interaction between personal characteristics and working conditions" (p. 4). In this regard, Lowman's focus is on the clinical treatment of psychological problems in which the major conflicts to be addressed by counseling or psychotherapy are work related. In Chapter 1, the outline of Lowman's taxonomy of psychological work-related dysfunctions was presented. These included, under disturbances in the capacity to work, patterns of undercommitment, patterns of overcommitment, work-related anxiety and depression, personality dysfunctions, work-life role conflicts, transient situational stress, and other psychologically relevant work difficulties such as perceptual inaccuracies. Lowman has essentially described the content of each category, which in abridged form is as follows:

Patterns of undercommitment have "in common the tendency to be underinvolved in a way that makes the individual less effective than his or her ability structure or career profile would otherwise suggest" (p. 52). Included within such a pattern are persons who exhibit such behaviors as underachievement, temporary production impediments, procrastination, occupational misfit, organizational misfit, fear of success, and fear of future (pp. 51–55).

Patterns of overcommitment refer to those work dysfunctions in which there is "too intense identification with and involvement in the work rate such that personal psychological (and sometimes) physical health is potentially impaired" (p. 55). Included are such symptom groupings as obsessive-compulsive addiction to the work role (e.g., workaholism), Type A behavior, and job and occupational burnout (pp. 55–56).

Work-related anxiety and depression can be associated with any work dysfunction, although because of its pervasiveness can be considered a separate category. Work-related anxiety can be either situational (a result of a poor interpersonal relationship in a job to which one otherwise is well suited) or a generalized condition. Work-related depression is a common condition in situations in which work dysfunctions occur; such situations require careful evaluation to determine whether one should treat the depression before or after work problems (p. 56).

Personality dysfunctions and work are among the most emotionally volatile and difficult to manage workplace problems. "They may reflect long-standing characterological problems of the individual, dysfunctional authority patterns or disordered peer relationships among other psychological dynamics" (pp. 56–57). Included in this category are authority problems or conflicts with supervision, often as functions of unresolved conflicts with parental figures.

Life role conflicts may involve the effects of stress off the job, of stress on the job and vice versa. These situations involve the impact of the emotional issues and conflicts that the worker brings from his or her nonwork life to the workplace as well as how problems with one's work role can be carried into and affect one's nonwork life (pp. 57–58).

Transient, situational stress is usually short-lived and arises from reactions to changes in work roles, new jobs, new supervisor, and so on, and is ordinarily amenable to crisis or short-term intervention (p. 56).

Lowman cites other classes of work dysfunction, including such matters as perceptual inaccuracies or perceptual discrepancies in how a worker and a supervisor view a given situation as well as dysfunctional working conditions, including defective job design, defective supervision, and dysfunctional interpersonal employee relationships, in which changing the nature of the job rather than the person is the primary therapeutic strategy.

The taxonomy of work dysfunctions of Lowman, the perceptions of Neff of broad patterns of work psychopathology, and the diagnostic taxonomy of adult career problems proposed by Campbell and Cellini (1981) and introduced later in this chapter, as well as the examples of taxonomies of career problems that were introduced in Chapter 1 indicate that the relationship between work and mental health is complex. These examples also show that the needs for career interventions in response to the various categories of career problems are on a continuum from assistance with deciding on what information is needed, how to get it, and how to evaluate it; through a variety of career-planning and decision-making steps; to problems of work entry; adaptation and adjustment; and, in the more difficult situation, the interactions of family-career conflicts, work dysfunctions, or work psychopathology that are triggered and fueled by particular relationship or contextual issues in the workplace.

Persons who are having mental health problems in the workplace may not display psychiatric symptoms—paranoia, character disorders, severe psychoneurosis—although they may be depressed, preoccupied with family problems, abusing alcohol, or otherwise behaving ineffectively. In short, they may have become problem employees.

Peace (1973) suggests that problem employees can be seen first as simply employees with problems. If sufficient help is not received, they may become problems to themselves. If self-understanding and other forms of assistance do not occur at this point, the employee may then become a problem for management. In this view, employees never become a problem for management until they have first become problems to themselves. The problem employee is a person who has an emotional problem that he or she has neither solved nor escaped. Becoming a problem employee is not a voluntary process but one that evolves as the worker acts in ways that make sense in the tangled emotions being experienced but that alienate or anger coworkers, supervisors, and others.

From a somewhat different perspective, Nolan (1973) defines a problem employee as "one who does not conform to the social vocational role expected of him at his place of employment" (p. xi). From this standpoint, physical disability, psychological maladjustment, neurosis, and so forth are not in themselves characteristics of problem employees. Nor is a person in good physical and psychological health necessarily a nonproblem employee. The actual definition of a problem employee depends on the standards set by the work organization. Many factors affect such definitions and thus preclude a simple listing of personality traits or deficits as problematic in themselves. The possibilities across a spectrum of worker types have been identified by Nolan (1973, p. xiii) as follows:

1. Some job applicants have psychological problems at the time of hiring; they may get worse, improve, or stay the same on employment.
2. Some employees who may or may not have been maladjusted at the time of employment develop

problems at a later date. These problems may or may not be influenced by the job setting.

3. Some employees show average or superior job performance despite—or because of—their problem.
4. Some employees who are not technically regarded as psychologically handicapped still cannot function effectively under certain work conditions or leadership types.

Obviously, counseling psychologists, career counselors, and other career guidance practitioners involved with industry will have many opportunities to engage in counseling, skillbuilding, classification, consultation, education, and referral as the relationships between work and mental health attract increasing attention in the future.

WORK AND LEISURE

The effective use of leisure may be a mediating factor in relation to work and mental health. Leisure may also be seen as an alternative to work if insufficient work is available to meet the needs of all people or if changes in the nature of work make growing amounts of leisure accessible to more people. Certainly the debate about the nature and importance of leisure has escalated in the past three decades as the onset of automation, robotics, and other machine-machine systems has altered the character of many forms of work. Supposedly, technological advances have freed people to engage in more leisure activities. For some, leisure seems synonymous with idleness or fewer hours of work. To other observers, the effective use of leisure is in itself a serious matter because idleness and the inadequate use of leisure can bring with them anxiety, frustration, crime, and other social problems.

In the most obvious counterpoint, the type of work one engages in affects how much time one has for leisure pursuits, what these pursuits are likely to be, and with whom and when they will occur. But leisure and how it is used also have to do with quality of life. For example, some observers describe retirement and aging as representing for many a transition from a work role to leisure role. Others suggest that persons must balance work and leisure as sources of need satisfaction. The questions in such cases are "Can leisure also provide the self-esteem potentially available from work? Can leisure be growth-producing just as work can be? Does leisure deserve the same sort of attention and resources as does planning for work or other aspects of career?"

The answers to such questions are debatable. In recent decades, leisure has rarely been seen as having merit in itself either as a lifestyle or in excessive portions as a complement to work. As the meanings of work and work ethics in this society change toward greater emphasis on holistic approaches to well-being and self-actualization, the part that leisure plays in such circumstances is being reexamined by many observers.

Concepts of Leisure

One of the concepts useful in thinking about leisure is that time is a commodity to be rationally used (Wilson, 1981). Therefore, the planning of a career involves considering how one will use the time available. It has been suggested that the only thing all humankind shares is twenty-four hours a day. The way we use these hours differentiates us. Obviously, the partitioning of time available into work, leisure, family and community roles, idleness, and learning is a matter of values as well as of resources and information.

The use of time interacts with the use of language. As has been said both here and in the first chapter, language shapes how we view people and problems and what we do about them. Language sets limits on perception; we can see only that which we have been linguistically trained to see. As Wilson (1981) has so effectively articulated:

> *Our language is beautifully adapted to the world of organized work, but ill-adapted to the world of unorganized leisure. We have many words and many perceptual frames to describe the product of goods or the rules of bureaucratic behavior. But one's tongue twists or falls silent when we try to tell of contemplation or love, of writing a poem, or pondering a philosophy. (p. 283)*

Wilson reminds us, "One of our great hazards in considering leisure is that it is so commonly thought of as a residue, an empty category of experience that is 'left over' when other life sustaining activities have been accomplished" (p. 284). Instead, in his view, leisure requires alertness, involvement, and immersion. It is an active rather than passive process, in which one is not compelled to engage but is frequently the condition in which "peak experience," growth, and self-actualization can occur. Kelly (1981) goes beyond this position in his wedding of leisure sociology and existential theory to contend that the essential variety of leisure offers "an especially apt environment for trying out identities not fully established and the non-serious consequences of play affording opportunity for risk in self-presentation" (p. 312).

E. L. Jackson (1988) acknowledges that leisure provides psychological as well as practical benefits for persons of all ages but indicates that such benefits can be realized only if one is aware of the role of leisure and how to use it to receive these benefits. In particular, Jackson suggests that individuals experience many constraints or obstacles that prevent them from obtaining the potential benefits of leisure. Included as constraints are work commitments, family commitments, lack of awareness of opportunities, shyness, and low motivation. Pertinent to such obstacles to the life satisfactions afforded by leisure are counseling models intended to be useful for different populations and purposes.

Tinsley and Tinsley (1982), for example, have suggested four categories of leisure counseling or guidance: *leisure guidance,* dealing with such foci as values clarification and self-knowledge related to leisure issues; *leisure decision making,* focusing on affective and cognitive dimensions, self-awareness, and self-exploration of potential leisure impediments; *leisure education,* dealing with didactic instruction about types of leisure, potential benefits, and assessment of potential difficulties in leisure and how these might be overcome; and *leisure counseling,* in which leisure is seen as a state of being and counseling is viewed as a process by which people are helped to attain a *state of leisure.* Such an approach is a holistic model, which focuses on how the individual may make leisure a meaningful component in personal development. Burlew (1989) has reported on the use of the Life-Long Leisure Graph, a tool to help counselors investigate client leisure needs, as a method of helping clients implement the concept that psychological needs are satisfied through both work and leisure activities. His research with graduate students using the graph suggests that it can be helpful in identifying patterns of needs and values, defining how needs and values are being met, planning to meet needs and values, and examining developmental patterns, as these provide a visual framework for a comprehensive career guidance or counseling approach to individual clients that includes leisure as a major component.

McDaniels (1984b), one of the few counseling leaders to write prolifically about the work/leisure connection, contends that an adequate conceptualization of career must include both work and leisure in a holistic framework. He uses the formula $C = W + L$ to advance the notion that career equals work plus leisure. He also proposes the formula $CC = LC + WC$ (p. 574) to reinforce the point that career counseling should include both leisure counseling and work counseling. He strongly asserts that "a skilled career counselor of the future should be able to provide assistance in both areas separately or in a combined holistic approach" (pp. 574–575). He advocates a life-span approach to work and leisure that clearly articulates the role of leisure in career development.

McDaniels identifies unresolved issues in dealing with work and leisure in career development and career counseling as well as changes in work and workers that make imperative more serious attention to the work/leisure connection. In his view, unresolved issues include: Do we live in a work or a leisure society? Is *leisure* a dirty word? Do schools prepare students for leisure? Can leisure satisfaction replace job satisfaction?

In 1989, McDaniels elaborated the concepts he articulated in 1984. He emphasized that work and leisure counseling should be incorporated into a life-span approach. Within such a context, he argued that counselors should engage in a variety of actions that enhance institutional and individual responses to the changing role of leisure and work in the United States. Among the examples of such action he supports are the following:

- Encourage parents to promote leisure in the home.
- Help schools and youth groups become involved in leisure activities.
- Emphasize leisure in the workplace.
- Encourage community agencies to assist in leisure development. (pp. 188–191)

McDaniels has also given examples of how counselors can help people discover what they are good at. One of these examples is to help people see leisure in the broadest possible way by examining specific possibilities within such dimensions as the following: creative, physical, intellectual, social, volunteer, and combined dimensions. Beyond such analyses, he advocated the use of courses, clubs, inventories, leisure-work models, and community resources by which persons can be encouraged to explore, participate in, or put their leisure to work.

Leisure Counseling

McDaniels's views of leisure counseling suggests different roles counselors might play in helping clients come to grips with leisure issues. In some cases, the question is one of identifying the leisure opportunities that exist. In others, the question is one of values clarification toward work and leisure. In still other cases, the individual needs to be helped to consider in depth the lack of leisure they are experiencing and their unhappiness about such a situation. Counselors need to help some persons find leisure *moments* during their daily activity or consider leisure to try on personal roles that may not yet be fully formed. It seems obvious that the constructive choice and control of leisure in one's life are extremely important to self-esteem, holistic health, and other positive characteristics. A lack of such conditions is conducive to stress, *burnout,* possible antisocial acts of vandalism, crime, and so on.

McDowell (1976) has defined leisure counseling as "a helping process which facilitates interpretive, affective, and/or behavioral changes in others toward the attainment of their leisure well-being" (p. 9). Edwards (1980) maintains, "Leisure counseling is a process that occurs when a trained leisure counselor helps one person or a group of persons, of any age, to determine their present leisure interests, attitudes, and needs—then assists them in choosing and following leisure pursuits that are practical, satisfying, available, and unharmful" (p. 1). Leclair (1982) suggests that leisure counseling is "a process using contemporary counseling techniques to facilitate the awareness of client's thoughts, feelings, and values toward leisure as well as to develop the client's decision-making skills involved in leisure participation" (p. 294). Just as in other areas of controversy and possible stereotyping, counselors must consider their own values about leisure and the different models of leisure in which clients might engage so that they can provide resources and effective planning assistance.

THE TRANSITION AND ADJUSTMENT TO WORK

Although perspectives on the meaning of work to different persons and different cultures, the role of leisure in individual patterns of career development, or the interaction of work and mental health are interesting topics that can be treated separately, they are, in fact, important elements of the transition to and adjustment to work. The transition to work brings the individual's employability into conjunction with opportunities for employment. As indicated earlier in this chapter, employability and employment are not synonymous terms. *Employability* refers to one's potential for gaining access to, adjusting to, and being productive in the workplace. Therefore, employability refers to a composite set of traits and skills that permit the individual to meet the demands of the workplace. Employability relates to the ability to hold a job even if no jobs exist. Most observers now believe that employability can be broken into subsets of skills. Usually these are divided into such emphases as general employability skills, occupational-specific skills, and firm-specific skills. The latter two sets of skills usually refer to those that are technical and focused on the content of work. General employability skills usually refer to the emotional, affective self-management, and decision-making or planning aspects of choosing, preparing for, and adjusting to the demands of the workplace. In a society in which teamwork, changing organizations of work, shifting expectations of workers, cultural diversity in one's co-workers, and adjusting to different management styles and organizational entities become major issues in both choosing and adjusting to work, the quality and scope of an individual's general employability skills become extremely important aspects of career development.

The term *employment*—in contrast to the term *employability*—refers to holding a job. One can have highly developed employability skills but be unemployed. *Employment* means that the occupational structure has opportunities in which one's employability potential can be realized. Obviously, the smaller the gap between one's employability skills and the requirements of available jobs, the more likely it is that an individual will be employed. But these relationships are complex. At different stages of the transition to work, mobility through work structures, or changes in one's career paths, different types or combinations of general employability skills are required. Similarly, as the job market, the occupational structure, or the organization of work moves through various transformations, the general employability skills they require are likely to change as well. Later in this chapter, the changing demands on workers' *personal flexibility* as a function of the emerging global economy will illustrate the reality, discussed earlier in the chapter, that employability skills are not absolute but are likely to change across time, cultures, political systems, and nations.

Counselors need a thorough understanding of the skills and perspectives embodied in the term *general employability.* They also need to understand the challenges and employability skills for workers at the beginning of their work life and at various points along a continuum of consolidation and advancement at work.

Human Resource Development for the Twenty-First Century

Before turning to specific aspects of the initial transition to work or to work adjustment, it is useful to consider the larger context for such a discussion. That context can be found in the ongoing concern about the facilitation of human resource or work-force development in the United States and in other nations that was described in Chapter 1. Given the demands on human resources that international economic competition is creating, the skills and knowledge that individual workers will need to be able to function effectively in the rapidly changing information and technologically rich work environments that are emerging are changing. Therefore, the types of career services that will be needed to facilitate such human development, the planning for addressing such matters becomes complex. These kinds of issues are driving educational reform efforts in the United States and elsewhere as changes in the structure and content of schools are being recommended in national reports, government policies, and legislation. As nations attempt to develop or refine their particular model of how schooling should be related to workforce development, they engage in a search for the types of career relevant knowledge, attitudes, and skills that enable adolescents and young adults to emerge from the secondary school with elements of personal flexibility by which they can compete in an occupational structure that is in constant flux.

The outcomes that result from such analyses are described in somewhat different ways but they also exhibit considerable commonality across the industrialized countries. For example, in the United States, one such model has been described by the Secretary of Labor's Commission on Achieving Necessary Skills (U.S. Department of Labor, 1991) in the report *What Work Requires of Schools,* which contends that schools should provide five categories of competencies or workplace *know how* and a three-part foundation of skills and personal qualities that are needed for solid performance in the workplace. The five competencies are the abilities to (1) identify, organize, plan, and allocate resources, such as time; (2) work with others; (3) acquire and use information; (4) understand complex interrelationships; and (5) work with a variety of technologies.

These five competencies were described in the U.S. Department of Labor's SCANS report (1991) as spanning the chasm between the worlds of the school and of the workplace. Equally important is the declaration in the SCANS report that these five competencies involve a complex interplay with the three elements of the foundation on which they rest, that is, what schools must teach: the basic academic skills; higher-order thinking skills; and the application of selected personal qualities, such as responsibility, self-esteem, sociability, self-management, and integrity and honesty (pp. 4–5).

The recommendations of the SCANS report bear some overlap with what U.S. Secretary of Labor Reich (1991) has argued is required in the current transformation of work and the need for new qualities of learning in the emerging workplace. In his view, the current global system as it is evolving and being refined is made possible not only by technology, but also by four key human skills that underlie symbolic-analytic services, defined as problem solving, problem identifying, and strategic brokering using symbols, data, words, and oral and visual representations as work media that are now important in so many jobs. Such skills are:

- *Abstraction:* Ability to work with, bring order to, and make meaning out of large amounts of information; to shape raw data into patterns that can be dealt with

- *Systems thinking:* Being able to see the whole, to see how parts are linked, and to determine how problems arise and their connection to other problems
- *Experimentation:* Having the capacity and perspective to set up procedures to test and evaluate alternative ideas, ability to systematically explore a range of possibilities and outcomes
- *Collaboration:* Ability to work in teams, to collaborate, to engage in the communication of abstract concepts, to maintain a dialogue, to share perspectives, and to create consensus as necessary

It can be argued that there are different skills needed by adolescents and adults pursuing different levels of education or different levels of technical performance. But there seem to be basic skills that need to be available to students who are not intending to go to college or to be in professional or managerial roles. The skills required of less-educated workers are, in a sense, also those that more educated workers perform but with greater intensity and greater frequency. They include the ability to deal with customers in person or on the telephone, read paragraphs, write paragraphs, do arithmetic, use computers (Holzer, 1996). Such findings are not surprising given earlier statistics reported that indicate that some 58 percent of American workers are now considered knowledge workers, people who deal with information and apply it in their job. Nor are such findings surprising in an economy in which service to customers is a growing emphasis in the emerging information-based occupational structure.

In a study in which human resources specialists and employers in a variety of industries were interviewed about the characteristics being sought in prospective employees, the top two characteristics identified were communication skills and positive attitude. The other important attributes identified as important by employers were a strong work ethic, confidence, intelligence, and a high energy level. Also mentioned were integrity, motivation, leadership, and the ability to fit into the company and be a team player (Gill & Lewis, 1996)

Although these perspectives on what students should learn in school and those reported in other chapters are extremely useful in their articulation of the substance of both general and technical employability skills important in preparing young people for the transition to work, they are insufficient. As Herr (1994b) has pointed out, human resource development or workforce development needs to be conceived of in three phases, not one. The first phase is what the schools and postsecondary educational institutions do or should do in preparing adolescents and young adults with the career-relevant knowledge, skills, and attitudes necessary for success in the workplace. The second phase is what takes place in the transition process from school to work. The third phase has to do with the responsibilities of employers in the induction of young workers into the employment enterprise.

Transition Services

With respect to the transition to employment, one can argue that it makes little sense to provide for human resource development, for career planning and preparation in the schools or in higher education, if at the end of these educational processes, school or university graduates are literally cut adrift with no assistance to make the transition from school to employment.

In particular, the school-to-work transition phase, the bridging period between secondary school and employment, has not been treated in the United States as a unique period in the career development process, when youth experiencing the job search, the move from part-time to full-time work, and the dynamics of interviewing and negotiating for a job have special needs that require the availability of sensitive, competent support services and processes. Unfortunately, in the United States, the responsibility for assisting a youth to get a job has been poorly defined. The schools have been vague about their responsibility in this process after the former student graduates or leaves the school as a dropout. Community agencies have not had clearly specified assignments to assume major responsibilities for youth in the school-to-work transition; or when, for example, the U.S. Employment Service has been given a role in collaborating with schools or providing specific services to place youth in jobs, the national resources to provide such support have been jagged in their availability, or they have been available only for selected groups of persons with special needs, if at all.

In one set of observations pertinent to school-to-work transition services in the United States (Educational Testing Service, 1990), the question has been posed:

> *Who links school and work? The answer is that the young themselves are largely left to their own devices (p. 3).... In the United States the institutions of school and those of work are separate and almost far apart. There are quite limited arrangements to facilitate this transition [to work], (p. 4).... Most developed countries have highly structured institutional arrangements to help young people make this transition; it is not a matter left to choice, Germany does it through the apprenticeship system, combining work and on-the-job instruction. In Japan, the schools themselves select students for referrals to employers, under agreements with employers. In other countries, there is either a strong employment counseling and job placement function within the school system or this function is carried out for the student by a labor market authority of some type, working cooperatively with schools. ...To be sure there are some school systems [in the United States] that have good linkages to the work world, often found in the guidance offices of vocational [education] schools, or as the natural operation of cooperative education programs. But the general pattern has been one of doing a whole lot more to link high school students to college than to work. (p. 22)*

In this regard, Barton (1991) has contended that school counselors spend disproportionate amounts of time in counseling college-bound students; he argues that only 6 percent of high school counselors spend more than 30 percent of their time helping students find jobs, so job placement assistance for work-bound youth is almost nonexistent.

Clearly, one of the major corollaries of the rise of the global economy and the growing attention in the United States to the characteristics and the intensity of international economic competition is the awareness that other nations are dealing with workforce development and the transition from school to work in ways that are different and often more effective than is true in the United States.

In examining what is occurring in workforce preparation, it is frequently necessary to include both the first phase (what is taking place in schools), and the second phase (what types of transition services are available), to understand the existing mechanisms and their purposes in other nations. It is probably fair to suggest that the first phase of a national priority on human resource development rests on seeing schools as mediums for *social engineering,* in the most positive sense, of all the attitudes and skills of significance to the workforce.

Although the school may be the primary institution in providing the basic knowledge and skills important to work force development, other agencies in the community, in government, and in the workplace must provide the transition services, independent of or in collaboration with schools, that will insure smooth and systematic progress in the movement from school to employment. Some of the specific mechanisms that other nations use in this process are discussed in the international section of Chapter 1 and in Chapter 9 and the roles of counselors in facilitating such processes are identified, particularly in Chapter 9. Perhaps most important, as U.S. awareness of the need to improve its preparation of youth for workforce entrance and for effective transition to employment has grown, after many years of scattered and noncomprehensive approaches to these problems by a patchwork of local, state, and federal efforts, there has been a renewed effort at the federal level to revisit the importance of work-based learning—for example, cooperative education, tech-prep programs, youth apprenticeships (which will be discussed in depth in Chapter 9), new approaches to the expansion and utility of such approaches, the transition of youth from school to employment, and the roles of employers in this process.

This national effort to have employers and educators join forces to prepare students for the workplace has been called by some observers as "the school to work revolution" (Olson, 1997). The context in which such initiatives have been instituted has been described as follows:

> *The disconnect between educators and employers has contributed to a severe motivation problem in schools. Students see no connection between what they are learning—or how well they learn it—and their future career goals. So they have little incentive to work hard in school.... Today, the connection between work and learning is more important than ever. The skills required for well-paid employment are rising. Repetitive jobs on the assembly line are being replaced with new jobs that require workers who can think mathematically, read well, solve problems, and use computers. Such workers must be able to communicate orally and*

in writing, work in groups, and monitor their own performance. Constant change means that most jobs now require continued learning even after formal education ends. An increasingly fluid labor market requires individuals to keep learning so they can move from one job to the next. Many of tomorrow's jobs have not even been created yet. (pp. 2–3)

As persons in the United States have studied what other nations are doing in making schooling more career relevant for students and increasing the mechanisms by which to insure a successful passage through the school-to-work transition, it has become clear that these processes are complex combinations of experiences and events that need to be planned and provided resources for their accomplishment. Career education in the 1970s and early 1980s tried to address the structural dichotomies between academic and vocational knowledge by arguing that both are important and that no student, whatever their ultimate goal, should be locked into only a limited set of courses which do not allow for exploration or for keeping one's options open. Although there are many school districts still implementing career education principles and processes, the number of such school districts has decreased, and the language of their programs has taken new forms.

Indeed, the 1983 National Commission on Excellence in Education, and its highly publicized report *The Nation at Risk,* swung the balance in education toward greater emphases on requiring a larger number of academic courses for high school graduates and, because of its elective status, toward an erosion of vocational education programs throughout the United States. As an antidote to such trends, the Carl D. Perkins Vocational Education Act (U.S. Congress, 1984) and, more recently, the Carl D. Perkins Vocational Education and Applied Technology Act (U.S. Congress, 1998) have tried to influence national and state educational policies by a range of initiatives, including funding curriculum development that integrates academic and vocational skills for vocational education and for academic students, advances the articulation of vocational/technical programs from the secondary school into the community college and beyond, advocates comprehensive career guidance programs for all students, and promotes equity and excellence for minorities in relation to their opportunities in vocational education and in the occupational structure.

In particular, federal initiatives in the areas of work-based learning and the school-to-work transition accelerated when, in 1993, President Clinton proposed the School-to-Work Opportunities Act, which was subsequently passed by the U.S. Congress in 1994. The School-to-Work Opportunities Act has provisions designed to spur the development of local partnerships between schools and employers to develop school-to-work programs and make them available to all students. Such programs combine classroom learning with real-world work experience. They train students in general job-readiness skills as well as in industrial-specific occupational skills or career clusters. The School-to-Work Opportunities Act helps high schools and community colleges create programs in cooperation with employers, to develop the academic skills and attitudes toward work that too many adolescents lack today and that both educational and community agencies have neglected, abandoned, or diminished in importance. Thus, the School-to-Work Opportunities Act rests on many concepts and recommendations that have been available for some time in the United States and in other nations, but not fully implemented—for example, "Skill Certificates," a portable, industry-recognized credential issued by a School-to-Work Opportunities Program under an approved plan, which certifies that the student has mastered specific skills at particular levels of competency.

The School-to-Work Opportunities Act designates the needs for both a work-based learning component and a school-based learning component as well as a connecting activities component. The former includes a planned program of job training and experiences, including skills to be mastered at progressively higher levels that are relevant to a student's career major (a coherent sequence of courses or a major field that leads to a first job) and that result in the award of a skill certificate; job shadowing, on-the-job training for academic credit; paid work experience; workplace mentoring; instruction in general workplace competencies; and broad instruction in a variety of elements of an industry.

The school-based component includes career exploration and counseling; initial selection by interested students of a career major by the beginning of the eleventh grade; a program of study designed to meet the challenging academic standards for all students established under the GOALS 2000: Educate America Act and the requirements necessary for a student to earn a skill certificate; and regular scheduled evaluations to identify student academic strength and weaknesses and the need for learning opportunities necessary to master core academic and vocational skills.

The connecting activities component includes a number of possibilities, such as matching students with the work-based learning opportunities of employers; serving as a liaison between the school and the employer, or the student and parent or community agency; providing technical assistance and services to employers relative to the design of work-based learning components, training teachers, workplace mentors, and counselors; and integrating school-based and work-based learning components and related matters.

The potential of legislation such as the School-to-Work Opportunities Act to affect positively the first and second phases of workforce development in the United States—that which occurs in schools and transition services by which students are supported through the transition and matched with job opportunities—is vast. Although not emphasized here as fully as it could be, much of the success of this and related legislation will depend on the models and the quality of career counseling and other interventions implemented. More information about specific counselor roles in support of such efforts will be identified in other parts of the book.

The Role of the Workplace in Human Resource Development

A potential outcome of the legislative emphases just discussed is the possible impact on the third phase of workforce development, that which is the responsibility of the employers. In such a context, we talk not only about employer collaboration with schools in providing work-based learning and transition components, but also about the services and the support systems that occur in workplaces and in advocacy by employers. Workforce development in these terms has to do with how new employees are oriented to their jobs, to the culture and expectations of the workplace, to their contributions to the mission of the enterprise as well as the degree to which new or older workers receive employer-provided training and the nature of that training. This third phase, employer responsibility for workforce development of individual workers, has to do with how human resource development processes and systems are provided by an enterprise, the mentoring and information they provide to employees, the encouragement and training provided to have workers develop loyalty and commitment to long-term mobility within the firm, incentives to improve their competencies, and the ability to find ways to do their job better and to relate as a team player and as a person of service to his or her customers, however they are defined. It has to do with whether or not individual enterprises make a connection between their human resource policies and business strategy.

One of the human resource dimensions of particular importance to enterprises is the degree to which they are involved in job training. In one report to the U.S. Congress (Hilton, 1991), the U.S. Office of Technology Assessment concluded that only a few U.S. firms use training as part of a successful competitive strategy in contrast to firms in Germany and Japan. Indeed, it has been shown that many U.S. firms do not pick up the development of new workers where schools leave off: Younger workers, ages 16 to 24, receive a disproportionately small share of employer training. These estimates suggest that German firms invest more than twice as much each year in worker training as their U.S. counterparts and nearly seventeen times as much in training per apprentice as U.S. employers invest in training per average worker.

One of the tasks of the workplace in inducting or orienting new workers and of career counseling at the point of entry into a job is to help youth and other workers recognize both their own reasons for working and the reasons why employers would hire them and the expectations they have for the worker's contribution to the productivity and climate of the workplace. That such reconciliation of worker and workplace needs does not always occur is seen in the dismissal of workers, in jagged early labor market experiences, and in other problems of work stability or adjustment.

These are areas about which training, induction, career counseling, and career guidance can make a difference. What is not clear is the degree to which employers actually provide direct training and supervision of the entry-level skills of new workers. Employer responsibilities on behalf of their role in the school-to-work transition and in the induction of young workers to the context and the content of their jobs are particularly critical, based on studies which show that the quality and availability of supervision of work experience has an important impact on the school-to-work transition and on work adjustment (Silberman, 1994; Stern, McMillan, Hopkins, & Stone, 1990).

The problem is that while undoubtedly becoming more responsive to workers as people who do not leave their family and personal problems at the door when they enter the workplace or leave problems on the job when they go home, employers and workplaces are quite uneven across the United States in the induction and adjustment services or supervision provided to workers, including young workers. Also, the degree to which employers are cognizant of and build on what schools or available transition services do to prepare young workers for the transition to employment is unclear.

In an idealized sense, if the role of schools or universities or transition services is fully successful, at the end of the transition from school to work, young workers will be responsive and mature, prepared to relinquish some adolescent roles and take on new roles, attributes, habits, and values expected in the adult work culture. In short, they are expected to be ready to perform as competent workers, understand the firm for which they will work, be able to manage interpersonal affairs on the job, accept responsibility, and function responsibly. Some work-bound youth can fit such an idealized model; some cannot.

Within such perspectives, there are many individual patterns of dealing with labor market entry and adjustments. The explanations for these patterns are wide-ranging. Some young people have not acquired the self-understanding, knowledge of educational or occupational opportunities or planning skills advocated here. In essence, they have not acquired the planfulness, undergone the exploration, acquired the information, developed the reality orientation, or accepted the responsibility for choice that would characterize them as career mature in late adolescence (Super, 1985b). Some young persons enter the school-to-work transition with little knowledge of their personal values, preferences, and skills and they have inaccurate stereotypes of jobs and work contexts. They have not developed good work habits (e.g., punctuality, dependability, honesty, social skills) that elicit patience and training from their work supervisor. Many young persons experience difficulties in the school-to-work transition because of barriers imposed on their job search as a function of racism or sexism or, indeed, reverse ageism (employers assuming they are too young to handle a job independently and effectively.)

Whether the behavior of youth moving through the school-to-work transition is stable or unstable undoubtedly varies from individual to individual. What seems not to vary in gross terms are the complexities that compose the transition environment through which adolescents and other young workers pass. Mangum (1988) has stated, "There are cultural norms, labor market realities and human development processes which compose the transition environment. No program to improve a transition can expect success which does not take into account these constraints. Employers control and dispense jobs and any successful program must ultimately help youth to meet employer expectations" (p. i). Thus, adjustment to work has to do with attitudes, task-specific skills, knowledge and feelings. New workers must learn what is expected of them and how to do new job tasks; they need to learn the informal rules that operate in the workplace, the procedures required, and the hierarchies of policies and persons; how they fit into the total organization of the company; the ways to adapt to coworkers and to their supervisor's styles; how to prove oneself and use training opportunities; and how to maintain a good work attitude and willingness to work hard. When such adjustments are not made, particularly those which are affective or emotional in content, high school graduates or school-leavers lose their jobs.

The point is that if the school-to-work transition is to culminate in the successful induction into work, employers, managers and supervisors, and career counselors in work organizations will need increasingly to view young workers new to a workplace as a constituency needing special support as these youths go through the dynamics associated with induction and work adjustment. Indeed, youths, young adults, and adults entering or reentering the work force will need to be seen in the throes of both the uncertainty and the promise that characterizes *transitions* at any point in life, and their needs should be seen and planned for within the expanding understanding of career development as a subset of human resource development.

One of the growing complications in the previous paragraphs is the implication that workplaces and employers manage the employee's career development. But, as has been discussed previously in this book, concepts of new careers or protean careers really reflect the expectation that employees will manage their own careers and insure their personal employability. The implications of calling new forms of careers protean careers come from the symbolization of Proteus, the mythical Greek sea god of many forms, suggesting that workers of the future will need to be more resilient, many sided, flexible, and fluid in their interactions with their career opportunities. In the view of Hall and Mirvis (1996), the concept of the protean career provides a different way of thinking about the relationship between the organization and the employee. They suggest that the historical assumptions about one's relationship to an organization have changed, as has the social contract between the employer and the employee. Thus, the essence of the protean career is that of a process that the person, not the organization, must manage. According to them, "The Protean person's own personal career choices and search for self-fulfillment are the unifying or integrating elements in his or her life" (p. 20).

The Initial Transition to Work

As such concepts are implemented in school-to-work processes, one outcome may be a change in how the initial transition to work by persons leaving high school or postsecondary education occurs in the future. Much of the contemporary vagueness and inconsistency in transition services or employer induction of new workers may give way to the initiation of a virtual career ladder of steps and services that facilitate the movement of the young worker from career-relevant and work-based programs in schools, through the systematic implementation of school-to-employment transition services, and then into the induction and adjustment to a job. If such goals do occur as policy makers and counselors would hope, it will be useful to compare the initial transition to work in the future with that which has been observed in the past and in the present.

Contemporary research studies show that, as a group, young workers in the United States enter the labor force gradually rather than abruptly on the completion of school and that their career attitudes are substantially formed before the first job itself. Then a trial-and-error period typically precedes complete assimilation into the labor force. Large numbers of teenagers and young adults combine school and work before completing the transition. This process is made possible largely through opportunities for part-time employment in the secondary labor market (including fast-food restaurants, service stations, agriculture, odd jobs, and retail stores).

Super's paradigms of career development from the early 1950s through the late 1980s have tended to label the period overlapping the school-to-work transition as that of *trial-little commitment.* It is seen as a point where a first job is located and is tried out as a potential life work. Commitment, however, is seen as still provisional, and if the job is not appropriate, the person may reinstitute the process of crystallizing, specifying, and implementing a preference.

Within such perspectives, there are many patterns of dealing with the school-to-work transition. Some people flounder from one opportunity to another; some people convert a previously part-time job into a full-time one; some people approach jobs quite cautiously and hold back their commitment while they test their fit with the job tasks, coworkers, and organizations; some people take work in which they are essentially underemployed, their talents and abilities are only partially challenged by the job; and some young people are unable to find work and are unemployed.

Frequent unemployment and other poor labor market experiences during the early years have a deleterious effect later, in part because periods of unemployment represent loss of work experience, information, and skills that may put the person at a competitive disadvantage in the eyes of an employer and may also have an injurious effect on attitudes toward work.

Mangum (1988) has stated, "There is a substantial minority, primarily from culturally and economically deprived backgrounds, who are permanently scarred by their unsuccessful experiences [in attempting to secure and be successful in work]" (p. 1).

Youth whose adolescence and young adulthood are characterized by unsuccessful labor market experiences are likely to be cast into marginal roles in adolescence and to have these reflected in their later life in economic marginality in adulthood. There are many reasons for these early labor market problems—families with low economic resources, a lack of significant role models, a lack of relevant information about jobs, disintegrating family support systems, poor educational preparation, early school leaving, teenage pregnancy, crime, substance abuse, discrimination (Herr, 1994b).

The demoralizing effects of prolonged unemployment have been documented in many reports in the United States and elsewhere. As discussed at length earlier in this chapter unemployment has been characterized as a global phenomenon and one that is unequally distributed among the nations of the Third World and the industrialized societies. Such studies have shown that unemployment is destructive enough for adults, who have already achieved a work identity, and who because of their life experience and knowledge may find it possible to see unemployment as a social rather than a personal problem. Young persons or women entering the labor force for the first time have no such identity or experience to sustain them, and their resulting sense of rejection and worthlessness may well reinforce negative self-images that have already been established at school or in the family. Borow (1989) has indicated:

> *The net effect of youth's limited contact with and uncertainty about the working world has not been so much to engender anti-work attitudes, as is often claimed, as to create persistent anxieties about the nebulous vocational future. Attending these anxieties, in any case, is an insidious form of avoidance behavior, a reluctance to plan and to explore, and a resultant slowing of the process of career development (p. 9).*

The most serious problem in this regard is found among those youths who are both out of school prematurely and out of work. In addition, major transition problems are frequently experienced by certain groups of disadvantaged youth, particularly but not exclusively black males and females, Hispanic youth, Native Americans, and inner-city and rural poor. According to Borow (1989):

> *A disproportionate number of youths among socioeconomically disadvantaged populations appear to exhibit depressed levels of achievement motivation, self-efficacy expectations, and other important indicators of competitive coping behaviors. (p. 9)*

Many disadvantaged youth are likely to experience disordered career patterns and be characterized by the following:

- Negative self-image and feelings of inadequacy as workers-to-be
- Fatalistic attitude and distrust in the efficacy of rational planning
- Unrealistic picture of the world of work
- Poor understanding of the sequence of preparatory steps leading to a stated vocational goal (Borow, 1989, p. 10)

Such problems continue to plague many children of low socioeconomic background or who have other characteristics that have led to poor educational preparation or discrimination.

Employment Transition Problems

Persons entering the labor force without a substantial base of experience are likely to experience a variety of transition problems to which career guidance programs and career counselors must be prepared to respond. The sophistication and the organization of contemporary work frequently walls off young people from jobs they might choose and how information about available work might be obtained. Many counselors and teachers suffer from the same lack of knowledge. In some cases, students find that what they studied in school is unrelated to available jobs or to new processes, materials, or technological developments. Many young people, high school or university, influenced by their parents' experiences of seeking long-time employment in a company and having their career development managed by their employer, are not aware that such conditions are not likely in the future. These entrants to the workforce will need to acquire the skills of personal career management, the ability to change with change, and personal flexibility as we describe it at the end of the chapter. In this sense, it has become evident that many of the problems experienced by the workforce are not simply technical, but psychological and sociological.

As much as many persons need to acquire occupational task skills, they also need assistance to clarify or strengthen their self-attitudes and to assess and sometimes change their personal habits, emotional responses to life situations, attitudes toward work, planning skills, and methods of adjusting to new jobs.

In one study of functional competencies for adapting to the world of work, Selz, Jones, and Ashley (1980) asked four national respondent groups (general adult population, high school seniors, public school teachers, and employers) to establish the priority of competencies important to occupational adaptability. Fifty percent or more of all samples thought one would have a great deal of difficulty at work if one did not have the following abilities:

- Use reading, writing, and math skills the job calls for
- Use tools and equipment the job calls for
- Get along with others
- Deal with pressures to get the job done
- Follow rules and policies
- Have a good work attitude

A further example of employee perceptions of skills and attitudes needed by students in the transition to work is available from a project funded by the Parker Pen Company in cooperation with the Wisconsin Department of Public Instruction (Oinonen, 1984). This study was concerned with both the skills that students need for job entry and the degree to which schools are preparing students for the transition. In the project, some 7400 surveys were sent to some 2500 businesses employing 50 or more workers. As in similar studies, high schools are seen as preparing students for the world of work only adequately and only in some areas. For example, in the Wisconsin study, 34 percent to 42 percent of the employers reported that high schools were preparing students at a good to excellent level in these competencies:

- Works with others and improves job skills
- Accepts advice and supervision
- Speaks well enough to be understood
- Maintains personal health
- Follows through on assignments

At the other end of the spectrum, only 3 to 10 percent of the employers thought that high schools were preparing students at a "good" or "excellent" level in the following:

- Understands U.S. economic system
- Has general knowledge of business operations
- Recognizes and solves problems by self
- Understands career ladders and advancement
- Writes well
- Demonstrates spelling and grammar skills
- Applying and interviewing for a job

Put in a somewhat different way, employers in this survey believed that it will be increasingly necessary to emphasize the following skills for high school students engaging in the transition to work:

- Writing, spelling, grammar
- Arithmetic
- Flexibility, learning new skills
- Oral communication, speech
- Applied computer literacy
- Reading/interpretation of blueprints and instructions
- Business economics
- Technology (applied science)
- Human relations
- Decision making

Looked at from the perspective of interview behavior, Gill and Lewis (1996) asked employers to identify things that job seekers have done that made them stand out as strong candidates. The answers included:

- Communicated well and engaged early in conversation
- Had lots of confidence in themselves
- Enthusiastic, eager to do the work, and willing to give 100 percent rather than displaying a nine-to-five attitude
- Proud of who they are and what they can contribute to the organization
- Innovative with new ideas for the company
- Explored all avenues for landing the job, including networking, friends, and the like
- Gave honest responses during the interview
- Knew a great deal about the company and the position
- Genuine willingness to try anything
- Professional-looking and creative resume
- Really packaged and sold themselves
- Strong letters of recommendation
- Had background and skills for the job
- Good internship or were involved in a mentor program

The interview skills reported here look more fully like the attitudes important in new or protean careers where the employee feels in control of and able to manage his or her personal career.

The types of transitional, entry-level, or interview skills reported here permit counselors to alert students and new workers to the types of preparations, skills, and attitudes they will encounter as they enter the workplace. For some persons, these competency sets will serve as diagnostic tools to help identify why some persons are having difficulty in these transitions. Finally, much of what career counselors will be concerned about is helping students and others develop the attitudes and general employability skills that are of primary significance in choosing, implementing, and adjusting to work.

Affective Work Competencies

In the studies reported here of either transition to work or work adjustment, what seems to be repeated is that, although job skills and *task teachability* are important, so, too, is what some nations call *industrial discipline,* and what Kazanas's (1978) described twenty-five years ago as *affective work competencies.* Many observers have long contended that people typically do not lose their jobs because they cannot perform them but rather because of *personality.* That term has been used in a vague, almost glib, way to represent some complex of behaviors that do not fit the expectations of the work setting, and so persons with such deficiencies have been dismissed. Kazanas's research confirmed that what has so often been characterized as personality factors in unemployment can really be defined in terms of the characteristics, habits, values, or attitudes comprising affective work competencies. He contends that within management theory and behavioral research in industry, there has been a shift in emphasis from cognitive and psychomotor behavior to the social and psychological components of affective behavior.

A review of the research on why employers discharge or fail to promote employees identified fifteen behaviors, the first seven of which were common across studies (Kazanas, 1978, p. 32):

1. Carelessness
2. Laziness
3. Absence/tardiness
4. Disloyalty
5. Distraction
6. Too little or too much ambition
7. Lack of initiative
8. Dishonesty
9. Noncooperativeness
10. Lack of courtesy
11. Unwillingness to follow rules
12. Troublemaking
13. Irresponsibility
14. Lack of adaptability
15. Misrepresentation

The opposite of the reasons for being dismissed are the affective work competencies identified by employers as important to work adjustment (Kazanas, 1978, p. 34):

1. Punctuality
2. Honesty
3. Reliability
4. Dependability
5. Initiative
6. Helpfulness
7. Cooperation
   a. Willingness to cooperate
   b. Ability to get along with others
   c. Character skills—performance as a coworker
8. Willingness to learn
9. Sense of humor

Also now classic in their origin, affective work competencies, can be taught and must be seen as part of the content of career guidance programs. Such skills reflect a worker's understanding of the sociology and psychology of the *work culture.* With such an understanding of the organizational structure and expectations that mediate the performance of work, school counselors or other career guidance specialists can encourage the development of affective work competencies not simply as arbitrary or capricious value sets but as *occupational survival skills* (R. C. Nelson, 1979).

Although worker deficits in employability skills reported here have been studied primarily in young workers as they enter the labor force, a growing research base has shown similar deficits in information, planning, and job-seeking skills among older workers experiencing occupational dislocation. As the occupational structure changes, the inadequacies in skills of the adult population as identified here are exacerbated. For example, according to a joint publication of the U.S. Department of Education and the U.S. Department of Labor (1988), "New technology has changed the nature of work—created new jobs and altered others—and, in many cases, has revealed basic skills problems where none were known to exist" (p. 3). Such findings have stimulated the need for *literacy audits* among workers and the necessity of introducing basic skills training directly into the work place where such audits show that it is needed. In such processes, it has become clear that many workers requiring retraining do not have the basic academic skills that permit them to learn new tasks and procedures. Such persons are, in fact, often functionally illiterate.

Other studies also speak to such problems. One national study of employers found that 30 percent of those surveyed reported that secretaries have difficulty reading at the level required by the job; 50 percent reported managers and supervisors unable to write a paragraph free of grammatical error; 50 percent reported skilled and unskilled employees, including bookkeepers, unable to use decimals and fractions in math problems; 65 percent reported that basic skills deficiencies limit the job advancement of their high school graduates (Berlin & Sum, 1988). In another example, the New York Telephone Company, in a major recruitment effort, found that from January to July 1987, only 3,619 of 22,888 applicants passed the examination intended to test vocabulary, number relationships, and problem-solving skills for jobs ranging from telephone operator to service representative (U.S. Department of Education & U.S. Department of Labor, 1988). More recent analyses have suggested that, in general, firms report that only about 50 percent of recent high school graduates are qualified for entry-level positions. Inadequate computational and problem-solving skills are among the most serious deficiencies, with the lack of verbal and writing skills also reported as problems. In addition, workers, particularly young workers, exhibit deficiencies in interpersonal skills, a poor attitude toward work, and an inability "to fit in" (Bassi, 1996, p. 16). Such issues affect the economic security of the United States in a global economy and, indeed, the job access and mobility of many adults. They will increasingly become formidable concerns in career counseling and career guidance as the press for knowledge workers continue.

Multidimensional Barriers to Work

For many adults, transition to work and work adjustment are multidimensional problems. Often when people are provided job training or occupational information or encouragement or career counseling and they still do not get work and adjust to it, we assume that they do not really want to work, they prefer welfare, or they are lazy. It is more likely that we have provided help in only one of the dimensions of life that is affecting their transition to and effective induction into work. Barriers to work can include child care, health, transportation, social and interpersonal conflicts, financial problems, legal problems, emotional-personal problems, drug and alcohol abuse problems, job qualifications, discrimination, and language and communication problems. In such perspectives, we again see the need for career guidance approaches to take a multidimensional view of individual problems with work and a differential treatment approach to the resolution of the various problems experienced by any given individual.

It is useful to reaffirm that the transition to work and the adjustment to work are not single events but dynamic ones likely to recur throughout the life of adults. Clearly, the nature of work in the United States is interwoven with the need to learn as one moves into a new job, adapts to a changing job, and advances in a career. Therefore, as work in the U.S. society increasingly replaces experience with knowledge as a major criterion of admission and success, career guidance programs and practitioners must also respond to such conditions. We will need to provide clients with assistance in sorting out alternative and often nontraditional forms of learning and their implications for personal time commitments, travel, residency, and occupational preparation. Such assistance must be provided with an awareness of the fact that adults deciding to return to school also have many personal responsibilities and emotional demands on their time and energy. Also at issue may be adult problems with learning, such as lack of self-confidence in one's ability to learn, unrealistic expectations of progress, theoretical or irrelevant learning tasks, seeking help too late or from the wrong sources, lack of efficient reading and study habits, press of time, and related matters.

Papalia and Kaminski (1981) have discussed various counseling skills required in an industrial environment. They indicate that career counselors should advise and counsel on programs offered by local and regional institutions of higher education. They should help employees prepare and process material related to tuition reimbursement, matriculation, admission, or assessment of prior learning. Of particular importance in some work settings is the career counselor's role in negotiating the offering of special credit and noncredit courses, either in-house or at a campus location, locating special resource personnel needed to offer special programs and renting space and equipment from area educational facilities so that industry can conduct its own programs in these locations.

In another classic approach that continues to have contemporary utility, Campbell and Cellini (1981) have developed a diagnostic taxonomy of adult career problems. In doing so, they have indicated that across the stages of adult career behavior, four common tasks tend to recur: (1) decision-making; (2) implementing plans; (3) achieving organizational/institutional performance at an acceptable level; and (4) accomplishing organizational/institutional adaptation so that the individual can effectively take part in the work environment. They then developed a diagnostic taxonomy of problems in each of these areas that can be used to classify client problems (Table 2.3).

In broad terms, this taxonomy represents an array of adult career problems to which differential treatments can be related. It also provides a structure from which groups of persons needing similar assistance could be inferred and relevant skill-building efforts constructed. It suggests needs for content and process in career counseling or career services for adults. Subsequent chapters will address many of these issues in depth.

COUNSELING FOR PERSONAL FLEXIBILITY

As discussed in Chapter 1 and briefly noted in this chapter, the structure of the world's economy is changing rapidly. National economies are eroding and being integrated into an interdependent global economy. This process is setting new standards for the quality of a nation's work force and for the creation of educational and counseling processes that will imbue students, citizens, and workers with the knowledge, attitudes, habits, and skills that are necessary in the societies they hope to create for the twenty-first century. As the occupational structure of a nation changes owing to the pervasive influence of advanced technology, transnational commercial interaction, or a pool of jobs to choose from that are more international in scope, it is likely that the meaning of work, as well as the skills necessary to work, also change. The behaviors, skills, and attitudes the industrialized societies are seeking for their work force can be summarized under the term *personal flexibility* (Herr, 1990).

As noted by Piero, Garcia-Montalvo, and Gracia (2002), flexibility is a pervasive concept considered to be a necessary response to global competition and it clearly has an impact on both labor markets and organizations and on individuals. In the workplace, flexibility has taken on several forms: temporary and fixed term contracts, outsourcing, flexible time, part-time working, overtime, job rotation, multitasking. However, organizational or workplace flexibility is unlikely to be possible in any setting or nation without personal flexibility at the individual level.

Personal flexibility, as used in this text, means in its most simplest form, the ability of an individual to change with change, to be comfortable with change and be able to adapt to it, to be able to take on new roles required, and to relinquish roles that are no longer relevant. As has been suggested in Chapter 1 and now in Chapter 2, negotiating one's career in the future will be done within different work organizations, work structures, work tools, work content, and work requirements than was true for most Americans fifteen or twenty years ago. The concepts one reads about or sees on television daily—downsizing in the workplace, knowledge workers, doing more with less, decentralization, just-in-time inventories, telecommuting, self-governing work units, the new economy, the global economy—are each symptoms of change although it may be hard to grasp the totality of these implications when one is exposed only to small fragments of the changes to come in choosing, preparing for and implementing one's work roles.

A variety of international scholars have described the emerging contexts and their implications for individual workers that are now pressing upon us as a result of international economic competition. For example, Arnold and Jackson (1997), speaking from a European perspective, have argued that changes in the way work is organized result in new concepts about careers that are qualitatively different from their predecessors. According to their analyses, there will be a widening diversity of career patterns and experiences, more and different sorts of career transition will take place, many men will experience the fragmented types of careers that many women have

TABLE 2.3

1. Diagnostic Taxonomy Outline: Problem Categories and Subcategories

1.0 Problems in career decision making
- 1.1 Getting started
  - A. Lack of awareness of the need for a decision
  - B. Lack of knowledge of the decision-making process
  - C. Awareness of the need to make a decision, but avoidance of assuming personal responsibility for decision making
- 1.2 Information gathering
  - A. Inadequate, contradictory, and/or insufficient information
  - B. Information overload, i.e., excessive information which confuses the decision maker
  - C. Lack of knowledge as to how to gather information, i.e., where to obtain information, how to organize it and how to evaluate it
  - D. Unwillingness to accept the validity of the information because it does not agree with the person's self-concept
- 1.3 Generating, evaluating, and selecting alternatives
  - A. Difficulty deciding owing to multiple career options, i.e., too many equally attractive career choices
  - B. Failure to generate sufficient career options owing to personal limitations such as health, resources, ability, and education
  - C. The inability to decide owing to the thwarting effects of anxiety such as fear of failure in attempting to fulfill the choice, fear of social disapproval, and/or fear of commitment to a course of action
  - D. Unrealistic choice, i.e., aspiring either too low or too high, based on criteria such as aptitudes, interests, values, resources, and personal circumstances
  - E. Interfering personal constraints which impede a choice such as interpersonal influences and conflicts, situational circumstances, resources, and health
  - F. The inability to evaluate alternatives owing to lack of knowledge of the evaluation criteria—the criteria could include values, interests, aptitudes, skills, resources, health, age, and personal circumstances
- 1.4 Formulating plans to implement decisions
  - A. Lack of knowledge of the necessary steps to formulate a plan
  - B. Inability to use a future time perspective in planning
  - C. Unwillingness and/or inability to acquire the necessary information to formulate a plan

2.0 Problems in implementing career plans
- 2.1 Characteristics of the individual
  - A. Failure of the individual to undertake the steps necessary to implement his or her plan
  - B. Failure or inability to successfully complete the steps necessary for goal attainment
  - C. Adverse changes in the individual's physical or emotional condition
- 2.2 Characteristics external to the individual
  - A. Unfavorable economic, social, and cultural conditions
  - B. Unfavorable conditions in the organization or institution central to the implementation of one's plans
  - C. Adverse conditions of or changes in the individual's family situation

3.0 Problems in organization/institutional performance
- 3.1 Deficiencies in skills, abilities, and knowledge
  - A. Insufficient skills, abilities, and/or knowledge on position entry, i.e., underqualified to perform satisfactorily
  - B. The deterioration of skills, abilities, and/or knowledge over time in the position due to temporary assignment to another position, leave, and/or lack of continual practice of the skill
  - C. The failure to modify or update skills, abilities, and/or knowledge to stay abreast of job changes, i.e., job obsolescences due to new technology, tools, and knowledge
- 3.2 Personal factors
  - A. Personality characteristics discrepant with the job, e.g., values, interests, and work habits
  - B. Debilitating physical and/or emotional disorders
  - C. Adverse off-the-job personal circumstances and/or stressors, e.g., family pressures, financial problems, and personal conflicts

D. The occurrence of interpersonal conflicts on the job which are specific to performance requirements, e.g., getting along with the boss, co-workers, customers, and clients

3.3 Conditions of the organization/institutional environment

A. Ambiguous or inappropriate job requirements, e.g., lack of clarity of assignments, work overload, and conflicting assignments

B. Deficiencies in the operational structure of the organization/institution

C. Inadequate support facilities, supplies, and resources, e.g., insufficient lighting, ventilation, tools, support personnel, and materials

D. Insufficient reward system, e.g., compensation, fringe benefits, status, recognition, and opportunities for advancement

4.0 Problems in organizational/institutional adaptation

4.1 Initial entry

A. Lack of knowledge of organizational rules and procedures

B. Failure to accept or adhere to organizational rules and procedures

C. Inability to assimilate large quantities of new information, i.e., information overload

D. Discomfort in a new geographic location

E. Discrepancies between the individual's expectations and the realities of the institutional/organizational environment

4.2 Changes over time

A. Changes over the life span in one's attitudes, values, life style, career plans, or commitment to the organization which lead to incongruence between the individual and the environment

B. Changes in the organizational/institutional environment which lead to incongruence between the individual and the environment, e.g., physical and administrative structure, policies, and procedures

4.3 Interpersonal relationships

A. Interpersonal conflicts arising from differences of opinion, style, values, mannerisms, etc.

B. The occurrence of verbal or physical abuse or sexual harassment

Source: Reprinted from "A Diagnostic Category of Adult Career Problems" by R. E. Campbell and J. V. Cellini from *Journal of Vocational Behavior, 19,* pp. 175–190. Copyright © 1981, with permission from Elsevier.

long experienced, and more people will be working for small and medium-sized employers or in self-employment. All of these demands strengthen the needs for lifelong learning and for the availability of career counseling and other career services to support people during what is expected to be many more career transitions and employment in perhaps nine or ten jobs during one's working life in the future.

Hall and Mirvis (1996) have suggested that because of the dramatic changes in work in which organizational and social cultures have changed so much, many people no longer expect—or, in many cases, want—a long-term career within a particular organization. Thus, in their view we see the beginning of what they call *protean career,* a career that is driven more by the individual than by the organization. As we learned earlier, the term *protean* derives from the mythical Greek sea god Proteus (Lifton, 1993). Proteus was able to take many forms in response to crisis, just as students and workers of the future will need to be resilient, many sided, flexible, and fluid in their interactions with their career opportunities. Hall and Mirvis proffer this view:

> *The Protean Career is not what happens to the person in one organization. The Protean person's own personal career choices and search for self-fulfillment are the unifying or integrative elements in his or her life. The criteria of success is internal (psychological success), not external. (p. 20)*

The concepts advanced by Arnold and Jackson and by Hall and Mirvis suggests that while persons in the workplace increasingly need to change and adapt, they need personal anchors and a sense of personal constancy as they are remaining flexible and adaptable to the changing external environments which they must engage. Such challenges have led Lifton (1993), a psychiatrist, to examine the notion of the protean self as a psychological phenomenon integral to our times. He observes that while many of our lives seem unpredictable with few absolutes, people turn out to be surprisingly resilient. In his positive view, human possibilities, as incorporated in the protean self, must be predicted on openness and change, on a many-sided self in constant motion. Lifton has suggested:

> *Without quite realizing it, we have been evolving a sense of self appropriate to the restlessness and flux of our time. This mode of being differs radically from that of the past, and enables us to engage in continuous exploration and personal experimentation...the self turns out to be surprisingly resilient. It makes uses of bits and pieces here and there and somehow keeps going. (p. 1)*
>
> *If the self is a symbol of one's organism, the protean self-process is the continuous psychic recreation of that symbol. Although the process is by no means without confusion and danger, it allows...for a self of many possibilities. (p. 5)*
>
> *Proteanism involves a quest for authenticity and meaning, a form seeking assertion of self. The recognition of complexity and ambiguity may well represent a certain maturation in our concept of self.... Proteanism, then, is a balancing act between responsive shape shifting, on the one hand, and efforts to consolidate and cohere, on the other. (p. 9)*

The very important observations of Lifton about the characteristics of a protean self—resilience, malleability in an uncertain and ambiguous present—provides an affirmation that individuals can and do achieve personal flexibility and that career counseling will increasingly need to address both the elements of importance to achieving personal flexibility and the reality that many persons do not possess such elements or they resist the concepts of change and flexibility (Piero, Garcia-Montalvo, & Gracia, 2002). They prefer to close off or constrict the self-process, to engage in psychic numbing so as to avoid the challenges of change, to try to make their world stand still, or to engage in a search for absolute dogma and perceptions of the world they live in as unalterable and certain. In a sense, both proteanism and resistance to proteanism involves choice and are likely to be encountered by the career counselor attempting to help persons with needs for personal flexibility, rather than diffusion in the midst of a turbulent and changing world as well as for feelings of authenticity, spirituality and empathy.

Personal flexibility also can be considered through other lenses. One of these is that of emotional intelligence. Goleman (1995) has suggested that emotional intelligence is more important than IQ and is comprised of such attributes as self-awareness and impulse control, persistence, zeal and self-motivation, empathy and social deftness (p. xi). According to Goleman, these are the qualities that mark people who excel in real life: whose intimate relationships flourish, who are stars in the workplace. These are also the hallmarks of character and self-discipline, of altruism and compassion—basic capacities needed if our society is to thrive. From a different perspective, these individual attributes are antidotes to emotions out of control, to mindless aggression, to despair, and the disintegration of civility and concern for other people. Thus, these attributes that can be taught and reinforced by career counselors are additional perspectives on how persons can be both grounded and flexible, able to bring intelligence to emotion, and capable of acknowledging that "the market forces that are reshaping our worklife are putting an unprecedented premium on emotional intelligence for on-the-job success" (p. xiii). Emotional intelligence also includes the basic skills of teamwork, cooperation, helping people to learn how to work together more effectively. Goleman has suggested:

> *As knowledge-based services and intellectual capital become more central to corporations, improving the way people work together will be a major way to leverage intellectual capital.... To thrive, if not survive, corporations would do well to boost their collective emotional intelligence. (p. 163)*

A further look at the ingredients of personal flexibility in the emerging workplace comes from a monograph entitled *The Employee Handbook of New Work Habits for a Radically Changing World* published by Price Pritchett and Associates, an international consulting firm (Pritchett, 1994). Intended not as a theoretical treatise but as a set of thirteen ground rules for job success in the information age, there are many important examples of behaviors related to the need for personal flexibility. They include, in abridged and paraphrased form:

1. *Become a quick-change artist.* Taking care of your career these days means managing perpetual motion. Your organization will keep reshaping itself, shifting and flexing to fit our rapidly

changing world.... Take personal responsibility for adapting to change.

...

3. *Speed up.* Organizations cannot go fast if their employees go slow.... Develop a reputation as one who pushes the change process along.
4. *Accept ambiguity and uncertainty.* Careers won't be cut and dried as they used to be...perpetual change will be crucial if the organization is to survive in the years to come.... Develop your ability to improvise and to go on guess work to some extent.
5. *Behave like you're in business for yourself.* Organizations are reshaping themselves to become more entrepreneurial.... You have to operate as though you are self-employed and carry responsibility for your own career mobility.
6. *Stay in school.* We must constantly refuel ourselves, become perpetual students, or we risk becoming obsolete.
7. *Hold yourself accountable for outcome.*
8. *Add value.* Make sure you contribute more than you cost.

...

11. *Practice kaizen*—continuous improvement. Think of it as the daily practice of perfection.

...

13. *Alter your expectations.* Embrace change and develop the work habit you need for job success in the Information Age.

Personal flexibility as the target of career guidance and counseling in a global economy is not likely to have an absolute meaning across the world. Nevertheless, as the perspectives just cited suggests there tend to be clusters of knowledge and skills that will be important for those workers in the industrialized and in the Information Age societies who will be either directly or indirectly affected by the changes in the meaning or content of work or the shifts in work organizations necessitated by the global economy. Since the concept of a global economy is still young and growing, the notion of *personal flexibility* is itself a term in the very early stages of development. What is described here is undoubtedly a primitive treatment of how models of personal flexibility are likely to be mediated by political, cultural, and organizational structures across the world and what the behavioral elements of such models are. Nevertheless, there are categories of skills subsumed under the broad rubric of personal flexibility that, at this early stage of conceptualization, seem relevant to working within the context of global economic transformations, intense psychological change, shifts in the organization of work, and career opportunities that are not confined to one community, culture, or nation. Such emerging concepts will inexorably broaden the rolls of career counselors in the future.

The Elements of Personal Flexibility in a Global Economy

Basic Academic Skills. Given the characteristics of the emerging technologies that are increasingly critical to international competition, basic academic skills—literacy, numeracy, communications—are perhaps the ultimate employability skills. Within the industrialized, technological, information-based nations, few new jobs will be created for those who cannot read, follow directions, and use mathematics. In an information-based economy, knowledge has replaced experience as the requisite for a growing proportion of the jobs being relocated or created around the world. Without basic academic skills, it is difficult to comprehend how individuals can possess personal flexibility and teach-ability or be capable of engaging in lifelong learning, a condition that increasingly will be required to maintain personal flexibility. Personal possession of these skills will certainly depend on the quality and nature of schooling and training one receives in one's life and in the personal understanding that, in many of the emerging jobs across the world, working and learning have become blurred and essentially interchangeable concepts.

Although it is not accurate to argue that the only skills of value in the future will be high-level intellectual skills, it is certainly accurate to suggest that basic academic skills and the ability to acquire the knowledge bases necessary in the occupational structure as it is emerging will be minimal requirements for many workers in the global economy. Not every worker is or will be directly involved in a high-technology occupation or one that is technology intensive, but the pervasive application of advanced technology throughout the occupational structure is causing the educational skills required in the workplaces of the world to rise. This phenomenon is related to the fact that the automation of work is easiest in the lower-skilled jobs; by eliminating many unskilled and semiskilled jobs through technology, the average education or training required in the remaining jobs or in the emerging occupations is increased. Undoubtedly, there will continue to be a large number of jobs with medium to low-skilled requirements, but jobs that are currently in the middle of the skill distribution will be the least skilled occupations of the future, and there will be very few *net* new jobs created for unskilled workers. The future of occupational structures in the industrialized world is to eliminate more and more unskilled jobs and to put an increasing premium on higher levels of reading, computation, communication, and problem-solving or reasoning skills. In essence, the skills learned in school and the skills learned on the jobs will be increasingly seen as complementary and interactive.

Given such realities, career counseling for personal flexibility will need to acknowledge, perhaps for the first time in history, that educational skills and choices must be clearly seen as major components of career development and, therefore, that career counselors must be seen as integral to learning systems for youth and for adults, cognizant of the likely outcomes of different education and training options, and brokers of such opportunities tailored to the needs of different individuals.

Adaptive Skills. But personal flexibility will not be confined to intellectual skills. As technological adaptation of a variety of forms continues to be implemented in the occupational structures and work places of the world, the economic development of individual firms and other enterprises will suffer if its employees are not able or willing to learn new production systems or new management strategies. Although academic skills in reading, mathematics, and science are important to such processes, there are other qualitative skills likely to be critical in such employment environments as well. One set of such overarching skills has been defined by the U.S. Congress's Office of Technology Assessment (U.S. Congress, 1988) as including the following:

- Skills of problem recognition and definition:
  Recognizing a problem that is not clearly presented
  Defining the problem in a way that permits clear analysis and action
  Tolerating ambiguity
- Handling evidence:
  Collecting and evaluating evidence
  Working with insufficient information
  Working with excessive information
- Analytical skills:
  Brainstorming
  Hypothesizing counter arguments
  Using analogies
- Skills of implementation:
  Recognizing the limitation of available resources
  Recognizing the feedback of a proposed solution to the system
  The ability to recover from mistakes
- Human relations:
  Negotiation and conflict resolution
  Collaboration in problem solving
- Learning skills
  The ability to identify the limits of your own knowledge
  The ability to ask pertinent questions
  The ability to penetrate poor documentation
  The ability to identify sources of information (documents and people)

These skills are important not only to manufacturing, but also to service industries. They represent the survival skills necessary in an environment of rapid change and one that is information-rich.

In addition to the skills cited previously, an increasing number of employers are extending their conception of basic skills to include self-discipline, reliability, perseverance, accepting responsibility, and respect for the rights of others. Other observers are discussing the needs for adaptive skills and for transferable skills. Adaptive skills are also referred to as coping skills, occupational employability skills, work survival skills, or, sometimes, career employment skills. They frequently involve skills necessary in positive worker-to-worker interaction or worker-work organization interaction. Thus, they frequently include work context skills, self- and career management skills, and decision-making skills. In large measure, included here are many of the skills discussed under emotional intelligence in the previous section. *Transfer skills* "enable a person to draw on prior learning and previous experience for application to new and different situations" (Pratzner & Ashley, 1985, p. 19). Such skills include those involving learning to learn, dealing with change, being a self-initiator, coping, and self-assessment skills. Mobility skills are those related to making a career or job change and include job-seeking and job getting, interviewing skills, resume preparation, and carrying out alternative job search strategies. Each of these skill sets is increasingly subsumed under the notion of general employability skills discussed earlier in the chapter. Such general employability skills are important across the spectrum of work and are, in that sense, elastic in their application and less likely to become quickly obsolescent than are technical or work performance skills. Like technical skills, general employability skills must be learned through some complex of modeling, reinforcement, and incentives. These general employability skills do not substitute for the basic academic skills or job performance skills, but they are clearly mediators of how such academic or job performance skills will be practiced, and they are important dimensions of personal flexibility.

There is another set of skills, only dimly perceived, in a societal trend that is only vaguely understood. In addition to the shift from manufacturing to service in the United States, there has also been a shift from Fortune 500 companies, large multinational organizations, to companies that employ fewer than 100 workers as the sources of new jobs in this economy. In part because of the adaptation of advanced technologies to their work processes and in part because of the effects of international competition, the Fortune 500 companies in the United States have essentially created no new jobs since 1978. They have rearranged jobs and career ladders, but they have not added significant numbers of new jobs for more than a decade. Thus, the United States is experiencing a major rise in self-employment and in small businesses, which require sets of skills embodied in such terms as *entrepreneurial behavior* and *innovation.* It has also been contended that, as the larger corporations require down-scaling in size and *deinstitutionalizing,* there are needs for entrepreneurs within such organizations. As the workplace, the organization of work, or the content of work undergoes transformation, there are needs for persons who have the skills and desires to manage innovation and change, to be entrepreneurs and futurists helping corporations to anticipate possible market niches they could effectively occupy, consider ways to have corporate divisions compete with each other to provide new products or services, or to identify possible mergers with other companies that would insure more competitive market positions.

Some of the skills associated with entrepreneurial behavior are taught in courses that stress the pragmatics of owning and running a business: accounting, marketing, deploying resources, sources of risk capital, and time and resource management for example. In a large sense, the skills associated with entrepreneurial behavior involve acquiring understanding of systems, risks, and change. These are combined behaviors, strategies, and traits. They are essential to systematic innovation, whether in creating a new, small business or modifying an existing one to take advantage of new market forces and potentiality. By definition, "systematic innovation therefore consists of the purposeful and organized search for changes, and in the systematic analysis of the opportunities such changes might offer for economic or social innovation" (Drucker, 1986, p. 35). Systematic innovation requires the entrepreneur to be able to monitor the unexpected, the incongruities between reality as it actually is and as it could be or ought to be; innovation based on process needs, filling missing links, redesign of old processes around new knowledge; and changes in industry structure or market structure that catch everyone unaware. Systematic innovation also requires the entrepreneur to monitor demographic changes; changes in perception, mood, and meaning; and new knowledge, both scientific and nonscientific.

One might argue that being an entrepreneur is to be a manager of information and, in turn, of innovation. It is to be a futurist. It is to be one who views needs in systems terms. It is to be cross-disciplinary in one's reading and analysis. It is to be a professional learner, if you will, frequently a generalist, not a specialist in a restricted sense.

Entrepreneurial behavior is an essential ingredient in many aspects of the global economy, in government, in service industries, in manufacturing, and in education. The skills needed are directly related to working and learning, although our perceptions of these skills are yet to be fully understood and addressed in most of our learning environments. It is likely that, whether such behaviors are manifested in self-employment, in small venture industries, or in transforming older industries into new economic structures, entrepreneurial behavior will be critical to many nations in both domestic and international economic development.

Career Motivation

Given the world of uncertainty and complexity that characterizes the global economy, there are other competencies that need to be embodied in personal flexibility. Many of these have been described under the concept of protean careers and the associated skills of career self-management. Another such model is that of London and Stumpf (1986), which is directed to the ingredients of career motivation. There are three parts of career motivation that fit well within a concept of personal flexibility, as we have been shaping it. These are "being resilient in the face of change, having insight into one's self and the environment, and identifying with one's job, organization, and/or profession as career goals" (p. 25). Each of these dimensions includes subelements. For example, career resilience is comprised of belief in oneself, need for achievement, and willingness to take risks; career insight means having clear career goals and knowing one's strengths and weaknesses; and career identity is comprised of job, organization, and professional involvement, need for advancement and recognition, and wanting to lead. By definition, *career resilience* has to do with "the extent to which we keep our spirits up when things do not work out as we would have liked. This includes how resistant we are to career barriers or disruptions affecting our work" (p. 26). Such a perspective suggests that individuals need to feel that they are competent to control their responses to what happens to them, that one can effectively discriminate how to act in cooperation with others or independently. In some sense, this interpretation of career resilience is not unlike concepts such as an internal versus an external locus of control. *Career insight* refers to the extent to which people are realistic about themselves and their careers and how accurately they relate these perceptions to their career goals, set specific career goals, and formulate how they can achieve these goals. *Career identity* is the extent to which they are involved in their jobs, careers, and professions.

The concept of *personal flexibility* is not unlike that of *personal competence* or *life development skills.* In each of these perspectives, personal flexibility or competence can be defined as a series of skills or forms of knowledge that an individual acquires either through processes of socialization or training. More subtle, perhaps, is this assumption:

> *All human beings are capable of a far greater repertoire of behaviors than any single person ever exhibits. Each of us, because of the accident of birth, begins life in a particular social context, within which we learn to make certain responses and not others. (Segall, Dasen, Berry, & Poortinga, 1990, p. 23)*

Thus, it is possible to suggest that personal flexibility represents not a substitute for culturally defined perceptions of necessary life development skills, but another repertoire of skills, an alternative set of cultural competencies, that people need to learn about and possess as these relate to their ability to master change, cross-cultural migration, and other career dimensions influenced by the global economy.

In such a view, the targets of intervention for counseling for personal flexibility may be one or more of the following skill sets for particular individuals: *cognitive or physical skills,* that is, alternative models of conceiving problems, problem solving, or reasoning about self or others or ways of performing or doing certain tasks; *interpersonal skills,* such as initiating, developing, and maintaining relationships (for instance, self-disclosing, communicating feelings accurately and unambiguously, being supportive, and being empathetic, being able to resolve conflicts and relationship problems constructively); and *intrapersonal skills,* such as developing self-control, tension management and relaxation, setting goals, taking risks, and so on (Danish, Galambos, & Laquatra, 1983).

Amundson, a Canadian counseling psychologist (1989), has approached the concept of personal flexibility as we are describing it from the perspective of competence. In his perspective, "competence refers to a state of being as well as to a state of doing. A competent person is one who has the capacity (or power) to adequately deal with emerging situations" (p. 1). Amundson suggests that there are eight components required to define his model of competence and that to be competent in almost any job demands some capability in each of these eight areas: (1) sense of purpose; (2) self/other/and organizational understanding; (3) communication and problem-solving skills; (4) theoretical knowledge and understanding of facts and procedures; (5) practical experience; (6) a supportive organizational context, which, at minimum, has elements that allow people to achieve without wasting time and resources; (7) a support network that allows competent people to give and to receive help as part of maintaining their competency; and (8) self-confidence, including acceptance of oneself, the strength to learn from mistakes, and perseverance.

It is likely that, as research into the requirements for human behavior within information-rich environments, in which advanced technology, knowledge, cultural diversity and global economies evolve, conceptions of the elements of life coping skills, of competence, or of personal flexibility will gain credibility as organizing themes for career guidance and career counseling in many settings. Such research will serve to demystify the problems of living, which require different combinations of the skills integral to personal flexibility in interpersonal relations; coping with cultural identity confusion; work adjustment in a culturally different environment; geographic rootlessness, uprooting and reestablishing family and other social support systems; anticipating and handling change; managing anxiety and stress more consciously and with more control; assuming personal responsibility for one's life; gaining an internal locus of control; and increasing feelings of power or reducing feelings of powerlessness. Among others, these involve developing skills of interpersonal communications, anger management, assertiveness training, decision-making values clarification, intercultural sensitivity, and stress reduction as major foci for career counselors' work with clients. Such emphases will require counselors to concentrate on prevention rather than only on remediation, to give increased attention to helping people develop self-control and the skills they need to regulate their behavior, and to adopt a more integrated approach to the interactive effects of how people think, feel, and act. The promotion of personal flexibility in workers of the future will necessitate at least these emphases.

CONCLUSIONS

This chapter has emphasized that the knowledge, skills, and attitudes important to the transitions to work and to work adjustment are dynamic. As the national and, indeed, global economies are transformed and create new possibilities for choice, new forms of knowledge and new skill patterns emerge. A contemporary metaphor for the new combinations of information and skill that an increasing number of workers across the world will need to possess is *personal flexibility.* This term represents a summary of the perspectives held in parallel with such terms as *protean careers, emotional intelligence, personal competence,* and *life development skills.* As such, the term *personal flexibility* creates a focus toward the likely interaction of person, occupational opportunities, and the dynamics of the workplaces in the twenty-first century.

Since 1945, our society has largely replaced the words *stability* and *scarcity* as characteristics of our economy with the words *change* and *abundance* even though all groups in the population do not share such conditions equally. This reversal has occurred largely because of science and technology's fantastic abilities to harness energy and to translate this energy into person-machine systems. No occupational group is unaffected by the explosion of knowledge, changing social values, transformations in corporate hierarchies, occupational and geographic mobility, new housing patterns, and similar phenomena that attend the fundamental realignment of our occupational structure and our economic base. These processes are now escalating under the influence of international competition and the economic interdependence of nations.

To assume, however, that work is disappearing or that a society with leisure as its principal characteristic has emerged, is still premature. It appears more accurate to suggest that many new types of work and career patterns are appearing and that much of the work to be done requires new levels of personal commitment and capability.

However, there is no evidence that work will cease to be a central force in defining individual lifestyles in the foreseeable future. Therefore, a broad understanding of work and its potential meaning to different clients is crucial to the effective practice of career development, career guidance, career counseling, and counseling psychology.

SUMMARY

We have talked in this chapter about the terms that are associated with work and its differences in meaning across groups and across time. We have examined current perspectives on job satisfaction and the relationships between work and mental health. We have considered the transition to work including multidimensional barriers to work, adult career problems, and the affective work competencies important to work. We have talked about the ingredients of change in work places and the growing need for persons to be able to adapt to change and to engage in such paradigms as that of Protean careers or emotional intelligence. Finally, we have introduced the term *personal flexibility* as an emerging target of career counseling and guidance for persons prepared for work in a world in rapid change. These topics have been discussed in terms of their implications for the practice of career development, their critical importance in the developing and the technologically advanced, information-rich nations, and their significance for new paradigms of purpose and function.

CHAPTER THREE

The American Occupational Structure

KEY CONCEPTS

- Career counseling is future-oriented and requires some reasonably accurate ideas about the occupational contours that are likely to exist when an individual is ready to enter the labor market. Although current forecasting methods are relatively crude and imprecise, they are broadly useful in career counseling.
- The information society requires that those who have the best jobs have the most education, but education will not guarantee the best jobs.
- By whatever system jobs and occupations are classified, the aim is to achieve order and to reduce the potential chaos of information overload. Getting the occupational structure reduced to manageable proportions facilitates decision making.
- The occupational structure is the centerpiece of a matrix of work options, educational avenues, tasks and contexts, personal investments, and outcomes that combine to compose the American "possibility structure" that counselees must conceptualize, explore, anticipate, and choose from, and to which they must gain access.
- The occupational structure can be conceived of in terms of subsystems of requirements and rewards that when classified reflect such factors as interests, aptitudes, competencies, educational requirements, points of entry, tasks, settings, supervisory structures, enterprises, income, and prestige. These factors provide ways to tailor exploration and analysis of the occupational structure to individual needs.
- The occupational structure is in constant flux, as are the characteristics of those in the labor force.

It is important for counselors to understand the characteristics of the occupational structure because individuals must know what is possible—what opportunities exist now and will exist in the future—if they are to make effective decisions. In one sense, career decision making is the process of relating relevant characteristics of self to appropriate aspects of the worlds of work, education, and training. Intimate knowledge of that external world is necessary if counselors are to help counselees reduce that huge universe to manageable proportions. When career counseling is directed toward immediate placement, only an understanding of the current occupational structure is required. However, when career counseling has its more common emphasis on some future point of choice and entry, counselors and counselees must operate on the basis of informed speculations about the changing occupational structure.

THE CHANGING SCENE

Futurism is popular today, and a great many futurists are attempting to predict what the United States will be like ten, twenty, fifty, or one hundred years from now (McDaniels, 1989; Rifkin, 2000; Stenberg, 1994; Wegmann, Chapman, & Johnson, 1989). All agree on only one point: The future will bring change. Beyond this simplistic conclusion, however, futurists agree on very little. Whether predictions emanate from historical and qualitative analyses or from more empirical and quantitative bases, conclusions suggest that the occupational structure of the United States is one of those societal elements that will undergo the greatest upheaval. What precise form this flux will take, however, is arguable. We may view this problem in terms of the difficulty of making occupational projections and in terms of scenarios for the future.

Occupational Projections

The relative accuracy of occupational forecasts is moot. Virtually everyone, including labor forecasters and their critics, agrees that forecasts are not completely accurate; they never can be. Consequently, the Bureau of Labor Statistics generates numbers that such publications as the *Occupational Outlook Handbook* translate into broader employment growth phrases such as "much faster than the average for all occupations" (an increase of 36 percent or more), "faster than average" (an increase between 21 and 35 percent), and "more slowly than the average for all occupations" (an increase of between 0 and 9 percent), and "decline" (a decrease of 1 percent or more). Errors in prediction are caused by a number of factors, including recession or boom periods, inaccurate estimates of the rate and type of technological change, devastating diseases of unprecedented impact such as AIDS, events such as September 11th, obsolescent data on projections of employment by industry, changes in the demand for products or services, composition of the population, work attitudes in flux, changes in training opportunities, and alterations in retirement patterns. The clear message is that caution must be applied in using occupational projection data in career counseling.

To improve occupational projections, the Bureau of Labor Statistics provides forecasts based on alternative assumptions about the future in terms of economic growth. In addition, it has created an industry-occupation matrix that describes industry employment by occupation. These changes in forecasting help to gainsay the arguments of critics who maintain that the two major errors of past prognosticators have been in assuming that the future is a simple extrapolation of the present and in basing forecasts on a singular view of coming events rather than on the interactive effects of several simultaneous forces.

Although propensity for errors will persist and although our forecasts are likely never to be elegant, the data on labor forecasting are accurate enough to be useful to counselors and to individuals in career planning. Indeed, we have no choice; we *must* use future-oriented data. The lag between preparation for an occupation and entry into that occupation is frequently protracted over years. One needs some idea, however imperfect, of what the occupational demand is likely to be at the time of entry as well as at the time of choice.

Future Scenarios

Futurists present their visions as *scenarios,* potential slices of future history. As we read the work of various futurists, we are struck with the great number who are akin to the biblical Jeremiah. The future, they maintain, will be terrible unless we repent our ways. Unfortunately, even downside futurists do not seem to agree on what it is that we have to repent. Contrasted to this outlook are the Pollyanna futurists. Everything will be all right, they claim, smiling brightly. "We have survived and flourished until now; we shall prevail in the future." Sandwiched between the doom-and-gloom crowd and the head-in-the-sand bunch are the realists, many of whom offer fascinating predictions that have implications for career guidance and counseling.

The U.S. labor force is now largely occupied with information handling. In fact, more people are engaged in manipulating information than in mining, agriculture, manufacturing, and personal services combined. This change is largely the result of advances in microelectric technology, wherein data can be handled in a few picoseconds (one second contains as many picoseconds as there are seconds in 31,700 years). The shift has moved the United States from an agricultural society to an industrial society, and now to a service-based, information-oriented society. The term *compunications* is sometimes given to this phenomenon of the marriage of microelectronics and information processing. In this age of high technology, we are talking about a society that is service-oriented rather than goods-oriented and that is dominated by a professional-technical class (rather than the business people who dominated the industrial society).

The increase in technology brings new occupations and different work modes. The incipient field of robotics is one consequence. Robotics takes us one step further along the automation-cybernetics continuum. We are witnessing ever more complex machines under the control of people. This, in turn, will lead to greater needs for training as individuals do more intellectual, higher-level work. We are also witnessing machine-machine systems that monitor, control, initiate, and terminate work with only a little supervision, done by a few skilled technicians. In the early 1800s approximately 70 percent of the U.S. population was engaged in agriculture; now about 3 percent are in agriculture, and approximately 70 percent are in service. Goods are produced with fewer operatives as our machines get bigger and better. Even in a very large goods-producing company, fewer than one-half of the employees are typically involved in production. Workerless factories now exist. The obvious consequence of the new technologies and machines is job displacement. Bridges (1994) describes it as the " organizational de-jobbing."

Care should be taken not to overemphasize the types of employment created by the technological revolution. For every computer and data processing specialist added to the workplace in the next ten years, there will be a concurrent 15 percent increase in administrative support workers, a 15.5 percent increase in salesworkers, and a 10 percent increase in unskilled laborers (U.S. Department of Labor Bureau of Labor Statistics, 1997). Among the occupations with the largest job growth over the next ten years are cashier, salespersons (retail), truck drivers, receptionists, and teacher aides.

An increasing number of workers will also become members of the "contingent workforce" (Rifkin, 1995). Contingent workers are employed to complete a project; once the project is done, so is their employment. This development led Bridges to conclude that "the much aligned social entity, the job, is vanishing like a species that has outlived its evolutionary time" (Bridges, 1994, p. 62). The rise of contingent workers (and the disappearance of the traditional way of organizing work) also encompasses a rise in anxiety, insecurity, and ambiguity about the future. Many workers are struggling to cope with the lack of certainty they experience in their work lives. Insecurity about the future leads some to feel compelled to work longer and harder, minimizing time available for other life roles. For some, this creates additional conflicts and feelings of guilt related to reduced participation in life domains other than work.

It is clear that the advance of our scientific technology has not been accompanied by similar progress in our social technology. We have made relatively little progress in the development of social policies to encourage the career development of women while protecting the welfare of the family. Although men and women share the workplace, they often do not share the household responsibilities (Niles & Goodnough, 1996). Many women "report a lack of time together with their family as their greatest family concern" (Levey & Levey, 1998, p. 231). The issue will not disappear in the next ten years. The labor force participation of women in nearly all age groups is projected to increase in the next decade. Men's labor force participation rates are projected to continue to decline for all age groups under 45 years of age. Thus, women's share of the labor force will increase from 46 to 47 percent (U.S. Department of Labor Bureau of Labor Statistics, 1997). Issues such as maternity benefits, childcare, and part-time or flextime work are still not resolved. Currently, childcare is available to only a small percentage of working mothers. Occupational stress and the quality of work life also await the development of effective social technologies.

Some are predicting that family-supportive company policies will increase because the baby-boomers are reaching upper-management levels and are more sympathetic to family concerns than were their predecessors. Hence, for example, they foresee an increase in on-site childcare opportunities, flexible working hours, and sick leave for children's illnesses. Others envision a time when employees will select their own supervisors, leading to increased morale and productivity. All of these social changes are predicated on the assumption that job satisfaction is at least as important to U.S. workers as are traditional incentives such as job security and wages. Thus, employers must offer more quality-of-work life benefits to attract the best workers.

Current occupations will, of course, serve as the foundation for new occupations in the future. Whether they stem from technological progress or from social concerns, new occupations are invariably related to old. A gene splicer is still likely to be a biologist. A fiberoptics technician probably will be a physicist. Environmental engineers can be air pollution control engineers, radiological health engineers, solid-waste engineers, industrial hygiene engineers, sanitary engineers, water pollution control engineers, and environmental compliance engineers, but they are still engineers. New occupations tend to spring from existing ones. They do, however, tend to merge disciplines (biochemists, geophysicists, bionicists).

One of the major problems generated by a movement toward a knowledge society is overeducation. Several commentators have indicated an oversupply of college graduates. The U.S. Department of Labor suggests that only approximately 23 percent of all job openings will require four or more years of college (only 3.1 percent will require a master's, doctoral, or first professional degree). Given current rates of college attendance and economic growth, that figure translates into an annual surplus of approximately 140,000 graduates. This situation is seen as one of inflated credentialism and has led some observers to maintain that problems of job satisfaction, underemployment, and unfulfilled ambitions will be exacerbated. In fact, in the near future, there will be no profession for which supply does not exceed demand (unless, of course, *demand* is redefined). Various solutions to this potentially dangerous situation have been proffered: educational upgrading; equalizing access to higher education; ending credentialism; equalizing income distribution; job redesign or profit sharing; total employment; concentration on school-to-work transitions; reducing college enrollments; upgrading job requirements; a national person-power policy; and career education, among others. There is obviously no easy solution. For years, we have known that too little education is a career handicap; now we must cope with what was once unthinkable—that too much education may be equally constricting. Smith (1986) neatly summarizes the situation by stating: "A college education was once sufficient for the attainment of a good job. It is clearly no longer sufficient, but, at the same time, it is all the more necessary" (p. 95). Employment in occupations that do not require a postsecondary education are projected to grow by about 12 percent and occupations that require at least a bachelor's degree are projected to grow by 22 percent through the year 2008 (U.S. Department of Labor Bureau of Labor Statistics, 2000b).

This relatively new development should in no way obscure the fact that undereducated and unskilled workers are still the major problem in the labor force. The less people are educated, the more likely it is that they will be unemployed and the less money they are likely to earn over the course of their working lives. Education is essential to acquiring a high-paying job. In fact, all but a few of the 50 highest-paying occupations require a college degree. However, a number of occupations (e.g., blue-collar supervisors, electricians, and police officers) do not require a college degree but offer higher than average earnings (U.S. Department of Labor Bureau of Labor Statistics, 2000a). There are, to coin a phrase, "other ways to win" (Gray & Herr, 1998).

Labor force entrants—particularly those entering the labor force for the first time—account for the majority of unemployed teenagers. At the other end of the spectrum, men aged 55 to 65 without a high school diploma, leave the labor force in significantly greater proportion than high school and college graduates of comparable ages. The undereducated are also the unskilled and the poor. Of this group, many have latent ability, and, if motivated and trained, could contribute meaningfully to the labor force. Unemployment is typically low in the professional and skilled occupations and is generally high for the less skilled segments of the labor force.

Although the general educational attainment of the U.S. worker is rising, a substantial proportion of the population remains undertrained for specific skilled jobs and undereducated for general adult competency. As we have observed, people do not need just more education. There is ample evidence to suggest that individuals can be retrained and gain entrance to an occupational level previously unavailable to them. Hence, *undereducation* may not be as much of a problem as is *inappropriate* education.

With regard to job growth within occupational specialties, the professional specialty occupations are projected to have the fastest rate of growth among occupational groups over the 1998–2008 time period. Technical and managerial occupations are also expected to experience significant growth during the 1998–2008 time period. Administrative support, precision production, craft, and repair, and agricultural occupations are projected to experience slow growth. These projections have implications especially for workers who are African Americans and Hispanics because members of these groups are currently overrepresented in occupations with the projected slowest rates of growth and underrepresented in the occupations projected to have the higher growth rates. One should keep in mind, however, that occupations with the fastest growth do not necessarily provide the most *new* jobs—just the *better* ones.

Later in this chapter, we shall investigate further some likely changes in the occupational structure in the United States. For now, it is sufficient to remind ourselves that a few decades ago there was no aerospace industry, no computer industry, no airport security guards, and no television industry.

THE PAST, PRESENT, AND FUTURE OF THE LABOR FORCE

The Past

Several striking changes have occurred in the American occupational structure during the last 50 years:

- The number of employees in goods-producing industries has remained relatively constant, while the number of employees in industries providing services has increased dramatically. Consequently, more than twice the number of workers are now involved in the provision of services as are employed in the production of goods.
- The number of employees in blue-collar occupations has increased relatively little, while the number of employees in the white-collar occupations increased markedly. Currently, approximately 60 percent of workers are classified as white collar.
- The average educational attainment of the labor force has risen appreciably. More than 87 percent of workers now have at least a high school education.

About 36 percent of all workers age 18 and over have completed at least one year of college. Currently, three out of four jobs require some education or technical training beyond high school. At the same time, one of every four ninth-grade students will not graduate high school and a higher percentage of minority and poor students will drop out (National Alliance of Business, 1986). In some states the dropout rate is mind-boggling (e.g., 42 percent in Florida; 39 percent in Georgia, Arizona, and Louisiana; 38 percent in New York; 35 percent in Texas and South Carolina; and 34 percent in California).

In an insightful analysis of data in occupational projections, Hoyt (1988) argued that the large number of college graduates offers a challenge to career development professionals to assist those who will *not* graduate from college. Citing the huge projected increase in the number of salespersons, paralegals, and nurses aides, for example, and arguing that about one-third of the jobs in the year 2000 will require less than a high school education, he states, "Career guidance professionals have clear responsibility for heeding such figures. We cannot, in effect, afford to continue concentrating our career guidance efforts on those who least need help (the bright college-bound students) while essentially ignoring those whose career development needs are greatest" (p. 34). Although this does not imply that the college-bound have less need for career assistance, it is certainly accurate to assert that both groups have career needs that must be met and that neither can be ignored.

- The proportion of women in the labor force has increased significantly. About one-quarter of all managers are now women, and more than 50 percent of American women now work outside the home. In fact, of a workforce in the United States of approximately 125 million, about 67 million (over one-half) are women. The percentage of women in the labor force who have children under age 18 has increased markedly and steadily since 1946, whereas the percentage of women in the labor force without children under 18 has remained relatively constant (DaVanzo & Rahman, 1993).
- The number of people of color in the professions has increased. Occupational mobility for persons of color is not now nearly so formidable a barrier to be overcome as it once was. At the start of the twenty-first century over one-third of the U.S. population was nonwhite.
- Part-time work has increased considerably. More than one in every five workers is a part-time employee.
- Job turnover has increased; that is, the average number of jobs held over a work lifetime has gone up (for men).
- The number of self-employed workers decreased strongly until the 1970s. It has, however, increased steadily since 1972.
- The elderly who dropped out of the labor force to retire are predicted to reenter; some nearing the age of retirement may decide not to retire because of labor shortages in some areas or due to financial need.

The Present

The current civilian labor force (all persons working and looking for work) in the United States is probably most accurately portrayed in Table 3.1. This table was

TABLE 3.1 Occupation of Employed Persons 16 Years Old and Over, by Years of School Completed and Sex: 1990

SEX AND OCCUPATION	TOTAL EMPLOYED IN THOUSANDS	TOTAL	*Percentage distribution by years of school completed*							MEDIAN SCHOOL YEARS COMPLETED
			Elementary school		*High school*		*College*			
			LESS THAN 5 YEARS	5 TO 8 YEARS	1 TO 3 YEARS	4 YEARS	1 TO 3 YEARS	4 YEARS	5 YEARS OR MORE	
1	2	3	4	5	6	7	8	9	10	11
All occupational groups	99,032	100.0	1.0	4.2	7.9	39.1	20.8	15.5	11.5	12.4
Managerial and professional specialty	28,693	100.0	0.1	0.6	1.7	16.8	19.1	30.0	31.7	15.9
Executive, administrative, and managerial	13,934	100.0	0.2	1.0	2.7	26.3	23.4	28.7	17.7	15.0
Professional specialty occupations	14,759	100.0	0.0	0.3	0.7	7.8	15.1	31.3	44.8	16.3
Teachers, except college and university	3,718	100.0	0.0	0.1	0.4	5.8	7.5	36.7	49.5	16.5
Teachers, college and university	706	100.0	0.0	0.3	0.3	2.3	4.1	10.6	82.4	17.1
Technical, sales, and administrative support	29,713	100.0	0.2	1.2	4.4	44.4	28.2	16.1	5.6	12.5
Technicians and related support	3,373	100.0	0.1	0.4	1.8	28.2	35.5	22.5	11.5	14.1
Sales occupations	11,019	100.0	0.2	1.9	5.8	39.1	24.3	21.5	7.2	12.9
Administrative support, including clerical	15,321	100.0	0.1	0.9	3.9	51.8	29.4	10.8	3.1	12.4
Service occupations	11,684	100.0	2.3	8.9	14.6	48.4	18.2	5.7	1.9	12.0
Precision production, craft, and repair	11,988	100.0	1.1	6.3	13.2	52.7	20.1	5.1	1.6	12.1
Operators, fabricators, and laborers	14,232	100.0	2.8	10.1	17.1	53.2	12.8	3.2	0.9	11.9
Farming, forestry, and fishing	2,722	100.0	6.1	14.7	13.0	42.5	13.7	7.4	2.5	11.9
Men										
All occupational groups	54,571	100.0	1.3	5.0	8.5	36.8	19.7	15.8	12.9	12.5
Managerial and professional specialty	15,793	100.0	0.1	0.8	1.8	15.1	17.3	29.6	35.3	16.0
Executive, administrative, and managerial	8,489	100.0	0.2	1.3	2.9	22.2	21.3	31.4	20.7	15.6
Professional specialty occupations	7,304	100.0	0.1	0.3	0.6	6.8	12.6	27.4	52.3	16.6
Teachers, except college and university	995	100.1	0.0	0.2	0.3	5.1	7.1	29.8	57.2	16.7
Teachers, college and university	450	100.0	0.0	0.2	0.4	2.2	3.3	7.8	86.0	17.1
Technical, sales, and administrative support	10,777	100.0	0.3	1.5	3.9	33.2	28.5	23.4	9.1	13.7
Technicians and related support	1,703	100.0	0.1	0.5	1.8	26.3	34.6	23.3	13.4	14.3
Sales occupations	6,099	100.0	0.3	1.7	3.8	31.6	26.2	27.0	9.5	13.9
Administrative support, including clerical	2,975	100.0	0.4	1.8	5.4	40.4	29.7	16.3	6.0	12.7
Service occupations	4,414	100.0	2.9	9.2	11.0	43.5	22.4	8.0	3.0	12.1
Precision product, craft, and repair	10,959	100.0	1.0	6.3	13.1	52.5	20.4	5.1	1.6	12.1
Operators, fabricators, and laborers	10,359	100.0	2.5	9.7	16.3	53.0	14.0	3.6	0.9	11.9
Farming, forestry, and fishing	2,270	100.0	6.7	15.6	13.5	41.5	13.3	7.0	2.5	11.8

Women										
All occupational groups	44,458	100.0	0.7	3.2	7.3	41.9	22.1	15.1	9.7	12.4
Managerial and professional specialty	12,899	100.0	0.0	0.3	1.4	18.9	21.4	30.6	27.3	15.8
Executive, administrative, and managerial	5,445	100.0	0.1	0.5	2.4	32.7	26.7	24.5	13.2	14.1
Professional specialty occupations	7,455	100.0	0.0	0.2	0.8	8.8	17.6	35.1	37.6	16.1
Teachers, except college and university	2,723	100.0	0.0	0.1	0.5	6.0	7.6	39.1	46.7	16.4
Teachers, college and university	256	100.0	0.0	0.4	0.0	2.3	5.1	16.0	76.2	17.0
Technical, sales, and administrative support	18,936	100.0	0.1	1.0	4.6	50.8	28.0	11.9	3.5	12.4
Technicians and related support	1,671	100.0	0.1	0.2	2.0	30.0	36.5	21.7	9.5	14.0
Sales occupations	4,919	100.0	0.2	2.1	8.3	48.4	21.9	14.7	4.4	12.3
Administrative support, including clerical	12,346	100.0	0.1	0.6	3.5	54.6	29.3	9.5	2.4	12.3
Service occupations	7,270	100.0	1.9	8.7	16.9	51.4	15.7	4.3	1.2	11.9
Precision production, craft, and repair	1,028	100.0	1.4	6.2	14.2	54.6	16.6	5.4	1.6	12.0
Operators, fabricators, and laborers	3,873	100.0	3.4	11.2	19.4	53.6	9.6	2.1	0.7	11.8
Farming, forestry, and fishing	451	100.0	3.5	10.4	10.6	47.7	16.0	9.3	2.7	12.0

Note: Because of rounding, details may not add to totals.

Source: U.S. Department of Labor, Bureau of Labor Statistics, Office of Employment and Unemployed Statistics, Industry and Occupation tables, unpublished. (This table was prepared March 1991.)

chosen for presentation because it displays the labor force not only in terms of its current demographic distribution, but also in terms of the past and projections for the future, thus making demographic shift in the labor force more readily apparent. The accuracy of these data in describing the current labor force will vary; the national unemployment rate changes, and consequently, this affects the proportion of workers in various categories.

The median age in the United States rose from 28.1 in 1965 to about 33 in 1990, to 35.3 in 2000. Geographically, the Northeast and north central states continued to lose population, while the South gained and the West gained somewhat less.

It is apparent that in the 1990s, the extraordinarily large proportion of so-called *prime age* workers (75 percent) led to greatly increased competition for higher level jobs and necessitated more lateral job moves to increase job satisfaction. Drucker (1982) addresses this situation, indicating that, in fact, jobs for the young will have to be restructured. No longer will fast promotions prevail, for even capable individuals will have to spend many years not far removed from the entrance level. Consequently, he makes an eloquent plea for career assistance in the workplace:

> *But, above all, there is need to counsel the young. There is need to make sure they have someone to whom they can talk in the organization, if only to unburden themselves. There is need of someone who is concerned with the problem of the young getting to the place in the organization—or outside the organization, for that matter—where their strengths are most likely to be productive and recognized. (pp. 170–171)*

The occupational structure is a constantly changing phenomenon. Szafran (1992) has demonstrated that over a forty-year period (1950–1990), the great preponderance of occupations have experienced growth but that virtually all experienced short-term periods of growth and decline. Over these decades, there was a total shift of 10 to 15 percent of the labor force into different occupational categories.

The Future

Now let us look at the more difficult task. Given the flaws in forecasting discussed earlier, what will the occupational structure be in ten or fifteen years? The $7.6 trillion economy of 1998 is expected to reach $9.5 trillion by 2008 (U.S. Bureau of the Census, 2002). Employment is expected to reach 160.8 million (an increase of 20.3 million or 14 percent over 1998 levels). Because of the pig-in-the-python phenomenon of the baby-boom generation aging, the age distribution of the labor force has changed, reflecting a smaller proportion of young workers and an increasing proportion of middle-aged workers. The labor force age of 45–64 will grow faster than any other age group over the next ten years (U.S. Department of Labor Bureau of Labor Statistics, 1997). In fact, the percentage of workers age 25–34 is expected to decline by almost three million, reflecting the decrease in births in the 1960s and 1970s. As noted earlier, women will continue to increase their labor force participation in the next decade. The Asian-and-other labor force and Hispanic labor force are projected to increase faster than other groups (44 percent and 36 percent, respectively, between 2000 and 2010) as a result of high immigration rates and higher than average fertility rates. In the 2000–2010 time period, the black labor force is expected to grow by 21 percent, more than twice as fast as the 9 percent growth rate projected for the white labor force. White, non-Hispanic workers accounted for 73 percent of the labor force in the year 2000 but will account for 69 percent of the labor force in the year 2010. By the year 2006, the black and Hispanic labor forces will be nearly equal in size (ftp://146.142.4.23/pub/news.release/ecopro.txt.)

Professional and related occupations and service occupations are projected to increase the fastest and to add the most jobs—an additional 7.0 million and 5.1 million, respectively—in the 2000–2010 time period. These two groups—on opposite ends of the educational attainment and earnings spectrum—are expected to provide more than half of total job growth over the 2000–2010 period. As employment in the service-producing sector increases by 19 percent, manufacturing employment is expected to increase by only 3 percent over the 2000–2010 period. Manufacturing will return to its 1990 employment level of 19.1 million, but its share of total jobs is expected to decline from 13 percent in 2000 to 11 percent in 2010.

Health services, business services, social services, and engineering, management, and related services are expected to account for almost one of every two nonfarm wage and salary jobs added to the economy during the 2000–2010 period. These sectors account for a large share of the fastest-growing industries.

Occupations with fast growth and high pay that are also projected to have the largest numerical growth between 1998 and 2008 include computer systems analysts, registered nurses, computer support specialists, computer engineers, teachers (secondary school), social workers, college and university faculty, and computer programmers (U.S. Department of Labor Department of Labor, 2000b).

Occupations with the largest numerical decreases in employment between 1998 and 2008 are projected to be farmers, sewing machine operators (garment), child-care workers (private household), word processors and typists, bookkeeping, accounting and auditing clerks, cleaners, and servants (private household).

In 2010, the baby-boom cohort will be ages 46 to 64, and this age group will account for a substantial share of the labor force. The median age of the labor force will continue to rise, even though the youth labor force (aged 16 to 24) is expected to grow more rapidly than the overall labor force for the first time in twenty-five years. The relative shortage of youth and the great increase in prime age workers—those with expectations of promotions—will inevitably lead to increased competition for desirable jobs. Therefore, the labor force will probably have to be more mobile in seeking employment and advancement. From the late 1960s through the 1970s, the labor force increased by more than 2 percent annually. It currently increases less than 1 percent per year.

Even though the growth rate of the workforce will decrease, people of color will be represented at a higher rate: 25 percent of new entrants (U.S. Department of Labor Bureau of Labor Statistics, 2000b). Such increase will be attributable to higher immigration rates, the increasing number of illegal aliens entering the labor force, and the relatively higher birthrate of persons of color. Hence, although there will be fewer youth entering the labor force, there will be a greater percentage of persons of color. In fact, well into the twenty-first century, there are predicted to be relatively fewer children and youth and a growing proportion of middle-aged and older individuals.

The point that all these changes emphasize is that trends in occupational and industrial growth necessitate continual adjustments in career decisions. Using the best information now available, counselors and counselees can plan for the future insofar as supply-and-demand factors affect career decisions. For example, we have already witnessed the fact that reduced openings for teachers caused many college students to major in other fields and caused those who majored in education to enter other occupations. In the past, two out of every three women college graduates entered teaching. Obviously, even with upturns in the employment of teachers at the elementary school level, in certain specialty areas, and with existing shortages in several secondary school subject areas, women who previously chose to major in education have broadened their outlook on career opportunities.

One ominous demographic factor is the fact that the less-educated proportion of the population is growing faster than any other segment. It is estimated that 23 million adults are functionally illiterate. (National Alliance of Business, 1986) Typically, they are the least prepared for work; their dropout rates are high and will continue to grow as will the incidence of teenage pregnancies. Simultaneously, entry-level jobs are requiring more and more basic skills, analytical skills, and interpersonal skills. In addition, millions of manufacturing jobs will be restructured and millions of service jobs will become obsolete. Therefore, continuing and increased dislocation and disruption in people's career patterns are likely. Current efforts at improving education and training to respond to these needs (such as requiring competency tests, more schooling, specifically mandated subjects, restructuring the schools, school-to-work transition programs, at-risk efforts, and so forth) may or may not be successful. Life-long education will obviously need to be expanded. In the information age, those with education are the rulers, those without education, both preparatory and continuing, are the peasants.

As technology creates new hardware and techniques, new jobs are created. Consider the case, for example, of some relatively recent inventions in the medical field. Computerized axial tomography (CAT) scanners, ultrasound, nuclear scans, gene splicing, and fiber-optic instruments all require technical and support personnel. The microcomputer explosion has obviously led to the creation of a great number of jobs, ranging from software and hardware design to entrepreneurial ventures to retailing. The majority of jobs will soon require computer skills. Relatively recent developments, such as superconductors and ceramic engines, will likely have equally stunning impact on the configuration of and the skills required in the world of work. Some countries are more geared than others to respond to the challenge of technology. In the United States, fewer than 10 percent of the baccalaureate degrees are awarded in engineering; but in Japan, engineering degrees account for 21 percent; in the former USSR, 35 percent.

There are many predictions about changes in the *nature* of work as well as in the *type* of work. It is difficult to know which, if any, of the incipient efforts to change the nature of work are likely to become popular. A simple cataloging of some of these predictions should illustrate the potential effect on career counseling:

- *Job redesign,* to use the particular talents of individual workers and accommodate higher levels of education
- *Job sharing,* in which two or more individuals share a full-time position on a less than full-time, full-pay basis
- *Flexible scheduling,* or flextime, whereby individuals put in an eight-hour day but are able to choose (within prescribed parameters) when these daily eight hours are worked. Or they may work four ten-hour days or some similar variation.
- *Quality control circles,* whereby workers negotiate and are responsible for quality standards of both work and materials
- *More part-time jobs* and temporary work to allow homemakers and retirees to earn supplementary income
- *Sabbaticals,* much as in academia, for personal and organizational development
- *Job rotation* to relieve monotony and to increase breadth of worker understanding
- *Flexibility of rewards,* wherein workers may choose from a menu of possibilities the combination of pay and benefits that best fits their needs
- *Power sharing,* or democratization, leading to greater cooperative group governance
- *Flexible retirement,* including time of retirement (earlier or later than usual) and type of retirement (phase out, as in a four-, three- or two-day week, or all at once)
- *Nontraditional rewards,* such as time off for high-quality work, bonuses for safe work
- *Improved career ladders* so that individuals may perceive an escape from plateauing at a terminal level
- *Home-based work,* whereby individuals produce goods or perform services in their own homes
- *Educational benefits,* both through the formal educational system and at the work site, paid for by the organization (including opportunities for retraining and retooling)
- *Copreneurs,* married entrepreneurial couples that give new meaning to the "mom and pop" business.

The shape of the future with regard to the quantity and quality of work in the United States is not sharply focused. Counselors and counselees who are willing to try to form some sense of what those contours will be, however, are likely to be rewarded.

RELATION OF THE OCCUPATIONAL STRUCTURE TO CAREER GUIDANCE AND COUNSELING

Several parts of this text have and will identify the antecedents and the processes of career decision making. Weaving throughout this discussion are the factors that produce individual differences shaping personal styles of approach to choice and implementation of choice. In this chapter, perhaps the important point to be made is that such considerations are valid only if many choices exist and if any given individual has the political and social freedom to choose among opportunities. The fact that these two conditions do exist in the United States has historically impelled the provision of career guidance to foster not only freedom of choice, but also informed choice as well.

Individuals must choose something; in terms of this book, they must choose an occupation and, indeed, a career pattern, and a lifestyle from among the thousands of existing possibilities. The *Dictionary of Occupational Titles* (DOT), for example, lists 12,741 jobs. New jobs are created each day, and obsolescent jobs are phased out of existence.

If, however, as we have contended several times, personal identity is acquired through such behaviors as exploring, committing, planning, and seeing oneself and what one does in the present as affecting the future, then career guidance should aid the choice of an occupation within the broad context of "career." This context connotes not only a choice at a point in time, but also a series of immediate and intermediate choices made to achieve one's goals at a future time.

For individuals to relate themselves to the educational and occupational alternatives available to them, they need some "handles" to help them see how these alternatives differ. Later in this book (Chapter 15), we will detail many types of occupational information, both regionally and nationally based and directed toward current vacancies and likely future developments. Helping young people and adults make informed choices about their educational and occupational decisions includes helping them understand how occupational choices interact with lifestyle opportunities, training requirements, future career options.

To bring some order into what can well be a chaotic situation, various schemes have been devised to classify, in logical ways, the thousands of individual jobs and the variety of educational and training programs. Each scheme emphasizes at least one characteristic for differentiating occupations. As will be indicated in Chapter 6 (career guidance objectives), in Chapters 7 through 12 (the application of career guidance practices at different developmental levels), and in Chapter 15 (information systems), these occupational differences can be used to give substance to efforts at assisting career development and choice; to reality-test one's characteristics against job requirements; and to create filing systems or person-machine interaction systems to provide better access to information.

One of the prime differences between occupational alternatives relates to levels and kinds of education or training. A system of classifying differences in educational and training opportunities by overt and covert criteria will not be elaborated on here—except as it is included in the variables for classifying occupational characteristics in the DOT. However, it is important, when considering the range of opportunities in the American occupational structure, to recognize the relationship between level and kind of education or training and level and kind of work.

OCCUPATIONAL CLASSIFICATION SYSTEMS

People have made attempts to classify occupations from ancient times. Hopke (1979) points out that primitive societies classified workers into two categories: physical laborers and nonlaborers (such as priests, chiefs, and medicine men). Others talked of the three-class system: peasants, nomads, and the priestly or educated classes. As society became more complex, so did work and its classifications. Some of the classifications were indeed fanciful and curious. For example, there have been classifications by physical characteristics, such as brain weight and head size (Sorokin, 1927). The brains of physicians and university teachers averaged 1500 grams; the brain weight of unskilled laborers averaged only 1410 grams. The head size of full professors was 35.79 centimeters; of associate and assistant professors, 35.72; of instructors, 35.64; and of students, 34.58.

As we have become more sophisticated, classifications of occupations have been formulated for various purposes on both a priori and post hoc bases and with their roots in economics, psychology, and sociology. Some are careful attempts at empirical derivation; others are slightly better than incense burning. Among the major classification systems are the following:

- By *industry,* as in the Census Classification below.
- By *socioeconomic group,* for example, bourgeoisie, proletariat; blue collar, white collar; lower, middle, upper classes.
- By *ability and/or aptitudes.* Ghiselli (1966) has demonstrated, as indicated in Chapter 4, that "in terms of their requirements, jobs are not organized into clear cut and separate groups. Rather there is a continuous variation among jobs, and they form clusters that do not have distinct boundaries. Second, jobs which superficially appear to be similar in terms of nature of work may have quite different ability requirements, and jobs which appear to be quite different may have very similar requirements" (p. 111). This finding that, despite mean occupational differences on ability dimensions, the heterogeneity of ability within occupational groups is substantial has been verified over the decades.
- By *occupation.* An obviously cumbersome method if one uses single occupations, since there are over 12,700 titles listed in the DOT; by groupings of occupations according to the Census Classification or the DOT, the system is sensible.
- By *interests.* Most interest inventories classify occupations by interest patterns of those in the occupations. Jackson and Williams (1975) contend that they have isolated twenty-three distinct occupational clusters based on interest. The U.S. Employment Service (USES) operationalizes the worker trait by occupational group concept in terms of eleven basic

occupational interest factors, which are now used in the U.S. Department of Labor's *Guide to Occupational Exploration* and for which an interest inventory is available. Thus, one can combine the General Aptitude Test Battery (GATB) and the Interest Inventory for a broader assessment than was previously possible with USES materials. The USES Occupational Interest areas are artistic, scientific, plants and animals, protective, mechanical, industrial, business detail, selling, accommodating, humanitarian, leading-influencing, and physical performing. Holland's classification, although based on personality types, may also be considered an attempt at classification by interests. Holland himself, however, has indicated that different occupations include a variety of types and subtypes (Holland & Holland, 1977).

• By *field and level.* Roe's two-dimensional classification by eight fields of interest and six levels of occupations, described in detail later in this chapter, has proven to be a useful taxonomy.

• By *field, level and enterprise.* Super (1957) suggested adding a third dimension to Roe's scheme to indicate the enterprise or the general setting where work is performed

• By *income.* The range of income within occupational groups is so wide as to make classification on this basis almost meaningless. As with ability classification, there are mean differences among occupations, but the within-occupation variability is substantial.

• By *type of work.* This type of classification can take many forms, ranging from dichotomies such as physical-nonphysical to the more sophisticated descriptions of people-data-things activities outlined later in this chapter and contained in the discussion of the DOT. The Minnesota Occupational Classification System attempts to classify occupations by a combination of ability requirements, work reinforcers (need satisfiers), and environmental style dimensions (Dawis, Lofquist, Henly, & Rounds, 1979). The ACT World-of-Work Map is also an extension of the DOT.

• By *educational or occupational prerequisites.* Again the DOT system of classifying occupations according to educational level is a good example of this type of taxonomy. Classifications such as these are easily implemented in practice by means of occupational materials such as the Bureau of Labor Statistics' "Jobs for Which You Can Qualify If You're a High School Graduate," "Jobs for Which You Can Train through Apprenticeship," or "Jobs for Which You Will Probably Need a College Education."

• By *occupational duties performed.* Part of the DOT presents occupational descriptors—the tasks performed by people in the occupation. Although such information is basic to anyone considering an occupation, it is so narrow that classification solely on this basis is rather unwieldy.

• By *life span.* It is possible to classify occupations according to such dimensions as early entry–early leaving, early entry–late leaving, or late entry–late leaving. A professional athlete, for example, would have an early entry–early leaving occupation, whereas a physician would have a late entry–late leaving occupation.

• By *rewards.* Rewards can comprise financial or honorific benefits, improvement in working conditions, or a combination of these factors. In one sense, the status classifications of occupations described later are examples of this type of taxonomy.

• By *age.* Kaufman and Spilerman (1982) have demonstrated that the majority of detailed census occupations conform to one of five basic age profiles: (1) occupations in which young workers are overrepresented (such as entry-level occupations); (2) occupations in which middle-aged workers are concentrated (such as supervisors, foremen, and managers); (3) occupations in which the elderly are overrepresented (such as contracting occupations); (4) occupations with a uniform age distribution (such as crafts); and (5) occupations with a U-shaped age distribution (such as undesirable jobs).

• By *worker attributes and job characteristics.* O*NET, the Occupational Information Network, is a comprehensive database of worker attributes and job characteristics. Developed as the replacement for the *Dictionary of Occupational Titles* (DOT), the Department of Labor seeks to make O*NET the nation's primary source of occupational information. The database contains information about knowledges, skills, abilities (KSAs), interests, general work activities (GWAs), and work context. O*NET data and structure will also link related occupational, educational, and labor market information databases to the system

The USOE Clusters

The career education movement stimulated the development of a new occupational cluster system by the U.S. Office of Education (USOE). Because of the prestige of that office and because of the funds for career education that emanated from that source, the 15-cluster taxonomy quickly became a highly used classification system. Commercial materials, especially, were rushed to market, packaged within the USOE cluster framework. Similar to many other clustering models, the USOE clusters begin with the assumption that all work can be classified, involving either the production of goods or the provision of services. These two activities are then organized into 15 occupational clusters. Within each cluster there is a hierarchy of occupations ranging from professional to unskilled:

1. *Business and office* (e.g., data processor, bookkeeper, accountant, file clerk)
2. *Marketing and distribution* (e.g., salesperson, marketing researcher, economist, systems analyst)
3. *Communications and media* (e.g., reporter, photoengraver, script writer, electronic technician)
4. *Construction* (e.g., architect, paperhanger, bricklayer, roofer, plasterer)
5. *Manufacturing* (e.g., machine operator, chemist, welder, tool and die maker)
6. *Transportation* (e.g., pilot, truck driver, auto mechanic, aerospace engineer)
7. *Agri-business and natural resources* (e.g., farmer, miner, farm agent, wildlife manager)
8. *Marine science* (e.g., sailor, diver, fisher, marine biologist)
9. *Environment* (e.g., forest ranger, meteorologist, geologist, tree surgeon)
10. *Public services* (e.g., counselor, fire fighter, police officer, probation officer)
11. *Health* (e.g., psychologist, veterinarian, dentist, speech pathologist, chiropractor)
12. *Recreation and hospitality* (e.g., waitperson, chef, golf pro, cashier)
13. *Personal services* (e.g., beautician, priest, mortician, TV repairperson)
14. *Fine arts and humanities* (e.g., dancer, author, jeweler, piano tuner)
15. *Consumer and homemaking education* (e.g., interior decorator, seamstress or tailor, home economist, model)

The USOE cluster classification system is not without its critics. Some of the criticisms revolve around issues of cost and other practical considerations of implementation. Some center on challenging the theoretical assumptions underlying the categories. The most obvious perceived disadvantage of the USOE clusters, however, is the problem of overlap. A number of occupations can be located in more than one cluster; the categories are thus not mutually exclusive. Although this criticism is not unique to the USOE clusters (it applies equally to several other category systems), it does point out potential weaknesses in the system that must be overcome if it is to be more effective than other systems. In general, the USOE clusters have been used less as the career education movement has lost its momentum.

Census Classifications

Since 1970, the U.S. Bureau of the Census has conducted a decennial accounting of the demographics of the United States. Legislation has increased the frequency of that nationwide census of population. To provide a framework within which to classify the work world, the Bureau of the Census has devised two distinct classification systems: one that is descriptive of the industries in which people work and another that is related to occupational categories. Each of these is briefly discussed.

Industrial Classification. A commonly used classification model is the federal government's Standard Industrial Classification System (SICS). It offers a comprehensive listing of types of industry within 11 major categories (note similarities to USOE clusters):

1. Agriculture, forestry, fishing, and mining
2. Construction
3. Manufacturing
4. Transportation
5. Communications and other public utilities
6. Wholesale trade
7. Retail trade
8. Finance, insurance, and real estate
9. Business and repair services
10. Personal, entertainment, and recreation services
11. Public administration

These categories, in turn, are divided into 84 less broad industrial classifications. For example, retail trade is composed of eight subcategories:

1. Building materials, hardware, garden supply, and mobile home dealers
2. General merchandise stores
3. Food stores

4. Automotive dealers and gasoline service stations
5. Apparel and accessory stores
6. Furniture, home furnishings, and equipment stores
7. Eating and drinking places
8. Miscellaneous retail

Finally, these 84 categories are further delineated by specific industries within them. Basically, the SICS describes *where* people work; it gives little or no indication of what people do. It is a classification system that is useful in gathering statistics and sometimes in filing occupational information. Otherwise, it has little utility for direct career guidance and counseling.

Occupational Group Classification. The 2000 Census of Population Occupational Classification is as follows:

- *Managerial and professional specialty occupations*
  - Executive, administrative, and managerial occupations
  - Professional specialty occupations
- *Technical sales and administrative support occupations*
  - Technicians and related support occupations
  - Sales occupations
  - Administrative support occupations, including clerical
- *Service occupations*
  - Private household occupations
  - Protective service occupations
  - Service occupations, except protective and household
- *Farming, forestry, and fishing occupations*
- *Precision production, craft, and repair occupations*
- *Operators, fabricators, and laborers*
  - Machine operators, assemblers, and inspectors
  - Transportation and material moving occupations
  - Handlers, equipment cleaners, helpers, and laborers

These census classifications are valuable because the U.S. Bureau of the Census periodically updates the distribution of workers into occupational categories and by industry. Thus, they provide data to a variety of consumers in terms of an accepted classification system.

Status Classifications

Another classification system is based on the status of occupations. Status level is usually determined by the perceived prestige of an occupation, which, in turn, is based on such factors as the amount of money earned, power, the type of work involved, the degree of responsibility for social welfare, the amount of education necessary, and other prerequisites. Some people mistakenly believe that earning power is the primary criterion of status. That this is not so is evident by examining the various prestige scales. For example, one scale ranked 100 occupations according to prestige (Smith, 1943); ranked highest was U.S. Supreme Court Justice; and ranked lowest was the occupation of professional prostitute. Available data suggest that a "successful" prostitute makes considerably more money annually than does a jurist sitting on the highest court.

The classic prestige scale is the one established by the National Opinion Research Center of the University of Chicago. It is generally referred to as the NORC Scale of Occupational Prestige and presents the following prestige hierarchy of occupations (National Opinion Research Center, 1947):

- Government officials
- Professional and semiprofessional workers
- Proprietors, managers, and officials (except farm)
- Clerical, sales, and kindred workers
- Crafts and kindred workers
- Farmers and farm managers
- Protective service workers
- Operatives and kindred workers
- Farm laborers
- Service workers (except domestic and protective)
- Laborers (except farm)

The NORC Scale closely parallels another prestige ranking system, Duncan's Sociometric Status Index of 1950. The average status score for all occupations is 30. In relation to that average, the following occupational group scores prevail:

- Professional, technical, and kindred workers, 75
- Managers, officials, and proprietors (except farm), 57
- Sales workers, 49
- Clerical and kindred workers, 45
- Craftsmen, foremen, and kindred workers, 31
- Operatives and kindred workers, 18

- Service workers (except private household), 17
- Farmers and farm managers, 14
- Farm laborers and foremen, 9
- Private household workers, 8
- Laborers (except farm and mine), 7

These occupational status rankings as well as others have remained relatively stable for the past half-century. The results may be somewhat suspect, because perceptions of the status of newer occupations cannot be compared with earlier perceptions since the occupations did not exist. Also, most respondents used to establish prestige hierarchies are college students. This fact could prejudice the results. Hence, it may be dangerous to generalize the results of occupational status studies.

Usually, only a relatively few occupations are included in these types of ranking hierarchies. More recently, however, researchers (Chartrand, Dohm, Dawis, & Lofquist, 1987) drawing on data from the Minnesota Occupational Classification System have developed a regression equation that allowed them to assign prestige rating estimates to about 2000 occupations.

The relative constancy of occupational prestige over time is not to say that the occupational structure is unresponsive to generational changes. A classic example was the great upsurge of scientific and engineering careers stimulated by Sputnik and the resulting reactions all the way through the space program. Then, because of federal deemphasis of the space program and subsequent massive technical and scientific unemployment, the United States found itself with a surplus of scientists and engineers. Thus, fewer students opted for training in these areas. Now, however, scientists and engineers are again in demand. Also in the late 1960s and early 1970s, we witnessed a reluctance of college graduates to enter large corporate business and industrial structures because of the perceived depersonalization of such organizations, because of a movement away from material goals on the part of many students of that generation, or because of some other factor. Now, one of the "hot tickets" in colleges and universities is the management major, and corporate recruiters on campus are inundated with interviewees.

The point is that, to some extent, the way in which occupations are perceived and consequent interest in entering them are contingent on supply and demand. Supply and demand, in turn, are shaped by priorities in the society and by the prevailing work ethic of each generation. To an equal extent, some occupational areas seem to endure, as is the case with the health sciences.

In any case, occupational status classification systems are useful in that they permit individuals in the process of career development and choice to project into the future to discern probable changes in occupational status levels. If young people are to appreciate the dignity that they can bring to all work, they must understand the bases on which some occupations are perceived as prestigious and on which others are not. If occupational prestige is a consideration in career decision making, it is important that individuals understand the factors that determine prestige.

The obverse of prestige or status is a relatively new concept—*occupationism*—devised by Krumboltz (1991). He defines occupationism as discrimination against individuals based solely on their occupation. Thus, a person's place in the perceived prestige hierarchy may be positive or negative and does not take into account how well or poorly a person might perform the duties of the occupation. Although Krumboltz emphasizes the undesirable consequences of occupationism, Carson (1992) points out that there can be desirable forms of occupationism.

Holland's Classification System

Many classification schemes are based on the psychological characteristics of workers. One example is the system developed by Holland and his associates. In Chapter 4, Holland's theory of career development is described; one should note that it is based on a theory of personality types. Evolving out of this theory are six classes of occupations: realistic, investigative, artistic, social, enterprising, and conventional. Each of these has 5 to 16 subclasses; within each subclass, occupations are arranged by the years of general education required. In all, 1156 common occupations are included. All occupations are arranged in a system that uses the six Holland code letters:

- Realistic occupations (R) include skilled trades and many technical and some service occupations.
- Investigative occupations (I) include scientific and some technical occupations.
- Artistic occupations (A) include artistic, musical, and literary occupations.

- Social occupations (S) include educational and social welfare occupations.
- Enterprising occupations (E) include managerial and sales occupations.
- Conventional occupations (C) include office and clerical occupations.

The two or three classes that people in a specific occupation most resemble are designated in order by the code letter for those classes. Thus, counselors, for example, are designated SEA, meaning that they most of all resemble people in social occupations, that they next most resemble people in enterprising occupations, and that they still less resemble people in artistic occupations. If one takes the six categories and looks for possible combinations, more than 100 emerge. One of the difficulties with the Holland system is that for some combinations, few occupations have as yet been identified. One form of the Holland system, therefore, uses only a two-letter designation, thus, counselors are SE.

To relate his classification scheme to a more familiar system and one that provides occupational information, Holland further identifies occupations by their fourth edition DOT code numbers. These numbers provide a description of the occupation and estimates of interests and aptitudes associated with it. Thus, the occupation of counselor is described in DOT designation 045.107–010, and by the three occupational classes or types that counselors most resemble, SEA.

Finally, a 1 through 6 designation describes the level of educational development demanded by an occupation. Levels 5 and 6 refer to college training; levels 3 and 4 mean high school and some college, technical, or business training; and levels 1 and 2 mean only elementary school or no special training. We now have the complete Holland classification for the occupation of counselor.

DOT	Ed	Code
0.45–107010	5	SEA

The Holland classification system has been applied to interest measurement and to a variety of other aids in career planning. Many of these are described in later chapters. There has been a great deal of research that attempts to validate Holland's occupational groupings and to establish their effectiveness in career research, career guidance, vocational education, and social science. Thus far, the Holland taxonomy has generally withstood the rigors of close empirical scrutiny and stands as an excellent example of an attempt to classify occupations psychologically. As shall be seen in Chapter 16, the Holland system has been converted into a career guidance delivery system, through the *Self-Directed Search,* and it provides one of the reporting frameworks for the Strong Interest Inventory. Moreover, the SDS has lately been used by the Department of Defense as a career guidance aid to be used with the results of the Armed Services Vocational Aptitude Battery (ASVAB), an instrument administered more than a million times a year. There remain some questions regarding aspects of the translation of Holland's theoretical model to an operational model (such as the validity of self-estimates of aptitudes and the relationships of the six categories to each other in terms of their hexagonal arrangement), but the system has value in that it does what any good occupational classification scheme should do—it breaks down the complex and confusing occupational world into manageable categories to which individuals can then relate important self-characteristics. Prediger, Swaney, and Wei-Chang (1993) have combined elements of the Holland Hexagon, DOT classification, and the ACT World-of-Work Map into a more detailed hexagonal structure.

Field and Level

Most occupational classification systems are unidimensional—that is, they classify occupations based on a single factor or variable. As previously noted, it is possible (and desirable) to classify occupations by combining two or more variables into a multidimensional scheme. One of the first attempts of this sort was made by Roe (1954) and later modified by Moser, Dubin, and Shelsky (1956) (Table 3.2). Roe's classification system combines eight fields and six levels. The eight fields, which are based on the work of interest measurement researchers, are outdoor-physical, social-personal, business contact, administration-control, math-physical sciences, biological sciences, humanistic, and arts. Her levels are based on the responsibility, education, and prestige involved in an occupation. These levels are professional and managerial (higher), professional and managerial (regular), semiprofessional and low managerial, skilled support and maintenance, semiskilled support and maintenance, and unskilled support and maintenance.

The field-level classification system is another attempt to bring order into the potential chaos of our awareness of the thousands of existing jobs. The assumption is that no single dimension is adequate to do this job; therefore, dimensions must be combined. If counselors understand such a multidimensional structure and understand their counselees, they can help individuals relate their self-characteristics to the occupational structure.

Standard Occupational Classification Manual

Development of a Standard Occupational Classification (SOC) Manual started in 1966; it is basically an attempt to bridge the Census Classification and the DOT. It includes the best features of the International Standard Classification of Occupations (ISCO), the Canadian Classification and Dictionary of Occupations, and the British Classification of Occupations and Directory of Occupational Titles. The classification covers all occupations in which work is performed for pay or profit but does not include volunteer work. The SOC tries to reflect the current U.S. occupational structure based on work performed and place of work. It is structured on a four-level system: division, major group, minor group, and unit group. It runs from gross description to finer detail as one goes from division to unit; and it includes DOT numbers and census occupation codes.

The Standard Occupational Classification (SOC) system is used by all Federal statistical agencies to classify workers into occupational categories for the purpose of collecting, calculating, or disseminating data. All workers are classified into one of over 820 occupations according to their occupational definition. To facilitate classification, occupations are combined to form 23 major groups, 96 minor groups, and 449 broad occupations. Each broad occupation includes detailed occupation(s) requiring similar job duties, skills, education, or experience. There are 821 detailed occupations. The 23 major groups in the SOC system are designated by a two-digit number as follows:

11-0000 Management Occupations
13-0000 Business and Financial Operations Occupations
15-0000 Computer and Mathematical Occupations
17-0000 Architecture and Engineering Occupations
19-0000 Life, Physical, and Social Science Occupations
21-0000 Community and Social Services Occupations
23-0000 Legal Occupations
25-0000 Education, Training, and Library Occupations
27-0000 Arts, Design, Entertainment, Sports, and Media Occupations
29-0000 Healthcare Practitioners and Technical Occupations
31-0000 Healthcare Support Occupations
33-0000 Protective Service Occupations
35-0000 Food Preparation and Serving Related Occupations
37-0000 Building and Grounds Cleaning and Maintenance Occupations
39-0000 Personal Care and Service Occupations
41-0000 Sales and Related Occupations
43-0000 Office and Administrative Support Occupations
45-0000 Farming, Fishing, and Forestry Occupations
47-0000 Construction and Extraction Occupations
49-0000 Installation, Maintenance, and Repair Occupations
51-0000 Production Occupations
53-0000 Transportation and Material Moving Occupations
55-0000 Military Specific Occupations

Each two-digit major group is further classified into minor groups (designated by the first three digits). The fourth and fifth digits in the system indicate the broad occupation. For example, teachers are classified within the Education, Training, and Library Occupations as follows:

25-1000 Postsecondary Teachers
- 25-1010 Business Teachers, Postsecondary
- 25-1011 Business Teachers, Postsecondary

25-1020 Math and Computer Teachers, Postsecondary
- 25-1021 Computer Science Teachers, Postsecondary
- 25-1022 Mathematical Science Teachers, Postsecondary

TABLE 3.2 A Classification of Occupations (Revised from Roe)

LEVEL	I SERVICE	II BUSINESS CONTACT	III BUSINESS ORGANIZATION	IV TECHNOLOGY
1. Professional and managerial, (higher)	Research scientist (social)	Sales manager (large corporation)	Cabinet member President (large corporation)	Inventor (industrial research) Research scientist (engineering)
2. Professional and managerial, (regular)	Administrator (social welfare) Manager (penal institution) Probation officer Social worker	Personnel manager Sales engineer	Banker Broker CPA Hotel manager	Air Force (pilot) Engineer Flight analyst Superintendent (factory)
3. Semi-professional and managerial	Employment interviewer Nurse (registered) Physical director (YMCA) Recreation therapist	Confidenceman Freight traffic agent Salesman, auto, insurance bond, real estate Wholesaler	Accountant Owner (small grocery) Postmaster Private secretary	Aviator Brine foreman (DOT Foreman II) Contractor (general, carpentry, etc.) Engineer (locomotive)
4. Skilled	Army Sergeant Barber Chef Headwaiter Policeman Practical nurse	Auctioneer Canvasser Survey worker Salesman (house to house)	Compiler Morse operator Statistical clerk Stenographer	Blacksmith Carpenter Dressmaker Paperhanger Plasterer foreman (DOT Foremen I) Shiprigger
5. Semiskilled	Chauffeur Cook Elevator operator Firemen (city) Fortuneteller Navy, Seaman	Peddler Salesclerk Ticket agent	Cashier Clerk (file) Mail carrier Telephone operator Typist	Carpenter (apprentice) Crane operator (portable) Meat curer Railroad switchman Truck driver
6. Unskilled	Bellhop Janitor Streetsweeper Watchman	Newspaper boy	Messenger	Carpenter's helper Deckhand Laborer, foundry

Source: From *Journal of Counseling Psychology,* Vol. 3, pp. 27–31. Published by the American Psychological Association.

V OUTDOOR	VI SCIENCE	VII GENERAL CULTURAL	VIII ARTS AND ENTERTAINMENT
Research engineer, mining	Dentist Doctor Research scientist (physics, chemistry)	Judge Professor (history, math, etc.)	Orchestra conductor TV director
Conservation officer Fish and wildlife specialist Petroleum engineer	Chemist Geneticist Pharmacist Veterinarian Physicist	Clergyman Editor News commentator Teacher (high school, primary)	Architect Baseball player (major league) Critic Sculptor
Apiarist County agent Farmer (small independent owner) Forest ranger	Chiropodist Embalmer Physical therapist	Justice of the Peace Law clerk Librarian Reporter	Ad artist Athletic coach Interior decorator Photographer
Landscape gardener Miner Rotary driller (oil well)	Medical technician		Chorine Illustrator (greeting cards) Window decorator
Farm tenant Fisherman Gardener Hostler Nursery worker Trapper		Library attendant	Clothes model Lead pony boy
Animal tender Ditcher Farm laborer Nursery laborer		Copy boy	Stagehand

25-1030 Engineering and Architecture Teachers, Postsecondary
- 25-1031 Architecture Teachers, Postsecondary
- 25-1032 Engineering Teachers, Postsecondary

25-1040 Life Sciences Teachers, Postsecondary
- 25-1041 Agricultural Sciences Teachers, Postsecondary
- 25-1042 Biological Science Teachers, Postsecondary
- 25-1043 Forestry and Conservation Science Teachers, Postsecondary

25-1050 Physical Sciences Teachers, Postsecondary
- 25-1051 Atmospheric, Earth, Marine, and Space Sciences Teachers, Postsecondary
- 25-1052 Chemistry Teachers, Postsecondary
- 25-1053 Environmental Science Teachers, Postsecondary
- 25-1054 Physics Teachers, Postsecondary

25-1060 Social Sciences Teachers, Postsecondary
- 25-1061 Anthropology and Archeology Teachers, Postsecondary
- 25-1062 Area, Ethnic, and Cultural Studies Teachers, Postsecondary
- 25-1063 Economics Teachers, Postsecondary
- 25-1064 Geography Teachers, Postsecondary
- 25-1065 Political Science Teachers, Postsecondary
- 25-1066 Psychology Teachers, Postsecondary
- 25-1067 Sociology Teachers, Postsecondary
- 25-1069 Social Sciences Teachers, Postsecondary, All Other

25-1070 Health Teachers, Postsecondary
- 25-1071 Health Specialties Teachers, Postsecondary
- 25-1072 Nursing Instructors and Teachers, Postsecondary

25-1080 Education and Library Science Teachers, Postsecondary
- 25-1081 Education Teachers, Postsecondary
- 25-1082 Library Science Teachers, Postsecondary

25-1110 Law, Criminal Justice, and Social Work Teachers, Postsecondary
- 25-1111 Criminal Justice and Law Enforcement Teachers, Postsecondary
- 25-1112 Law Teachers, Postsecondary
- 25-1113 Social Work Teachers, Postsecondary

25-1120 Arts, Communications, and Humanities Teachers, Postsecondary
- 25-1121 Art, Drama, and Music Teachers, Postsecondary
- 25-1122 Communications Teachers, Postsecondary
- 25-1123 English Language and Literature Teachers, Postsecondary
- 25-1124 Foreign Language and Literature Teachers, Postsecondary
- 25-1125 History Teachers, Postsecondary
- 25-1126 Philosophy and Religion Teachers, Postsecondary

25-1190 Miscellaneous Postsecondary Teachers
- 25-1191 Graduate Teaching Assistants
- 25-1192 Home Economics Teachers, Postsecondary
- 25-1193 Recreation and Fitness Studies Teachers, Postsecondary
- 25-1194 Vocational Education Teachers, Postsecondary
- 25-1199 Postsecondary Teachers, All Other

This system is obviously useful for research and classification purposes. It remains to be seen how utilitarian it will be for the development of career-related materials and for other practical applications.

The Dictionary of Occupational Titles

Perhaps the most widely used occupational classification system is that employed in the *Dictionary of Occupational Titles.* The DOT was first issued in 1939 to meet the needs of the public employment service system to standardize occupational information to facilitate job placement, employment counseling, career guidance, labor market projections, and personpower accounting. Subsequent editions of the DOT appeared in 1949, 1965 and 1978, and a brief supplement appeared in 1982. The edition was somewhat revised and updated in 1991.

The fourth edition of the DOT contains information relating to approximately 12,700 jobs. This figure is a consequence of the addition of some 844 new jobs and the addition of approximately 1609 new occupational definitions.

All jobs in the fourth edition of the DOT are designated by a nine-digit number. Previously, a six-digit number had been used; however, three additional digits have been added to provide each occupation with its own code in order to expedite computerized analyses. The first of the nine digits refers to an occupational category, of which there are nine:

0/1. Professional, technical, and managerial occupations
2. Clerical and sales occupations
3. Service occupations
4. Agricultural, fishery, forestry, and related occupations
5. Processing occupations
6. Machine trades occupations
7. Benchwork occupations
8. Structural work occupations
9. Miscellaneous occupations

These nine occupational categories are divided into 82 two-digit occupational divisions, which are then subdivided into 549 three-digit occupational groups. For purposes of illustration, the two-digit occupational divisions and the three-digit occupation groups relating to the 0/1 occupational category and the 00/01 division are presented:

Example of two-digit division
0/1 professional, technical, and managerial occupations

00/01 Occupations in architecture, engineering, and surveying
02 Occupations in mathematics and physical sciences
04 Occupations in life sciences
05 Occupations in social sciences
07 Occupations in medicine and health
09 Occupations in education
10 Occupations in museum, library, and archival sciences
11 Occupations in law and jurisprudence
12 Occupations in religion and theology
13 Occupations in writing
14 Occupations in art
15 Occupations in entertainment and recreation
16 Occupations in administrative specializations
18 Managers and officials, n.e.c. [not elsewhere classified]
19 Miscellaneous professional, technical, and managerial occupations

Example of three-digit group
00/01 occupations in architecture, engineering, and surveying

001 Architectural occupations
002 Aeronautical engineering occupations
003 Electrical/electronics engineering occupations
005 Civil engineering occupations
006 Ceramic engineering corporation
007 Mechanical engineering occupations
008 Chemical engineering occupations
010 Mining and petroleum engineering occupations
011 Metallurgy and metallurgical engineering occupations
012 Industrial engineering occupations
013 Agricultural engineering occupations
014 Marine engineering occupations
015 Nuclear engineering occupations
017 Drafters, n.e.c.
018 Surveying/cartographic occupations
019 Occupations in architecture, engineering, and surveying, n.e.c.

The middle three digits of the nine-digit code number refer to worker traits. Jobs require that people function in relation to data, people, and things. Each of these three items has a hierarchy of relationship levels, and the code digit refers to the highest level within the hierarchy at which a worker is required to function. Following are the hierarchies for each digit.

Data (fourth digit)
0 Synthesizing
1 Coordinating
2 Analyzing
3 Compiling
4 Computing
5 Copying
6 Comparing

People (fifth digit)
0 Mentoring
1 Negotiating
2 Instructing
3 Supervising
4 Diverting
5 Persuading
6 Speaking-signaling

7 Serving
8 Taking instructions—helping

Things (sixth digit)
0 Setting up
1 Precision working
2 Operating—controlling
3 Driving—operating
4 Manipulating
5 Tending
6 Feeding—offbearing
7 Handling

Hence, the more a worker functions with complex responsibility and judgment, the lower the number on each list; the less complicated the function in relation to data, people, and things, the higher the number. Compiling data is a more complex task than copying data; instructing people is more complicated than serving them; and precision work with things is more intricate than manipulating them.

The final three digits of the nine-digit code indicate the alphabetical order of titles within the six-digit code groups. Many occupations may have the same first six digits. Therefore, the last three digits serve to differentiate a particular occupation from all others. If a six-digit code is applicable to only one occupational title, the last three digits will be 010.

To illustrate, let us "read" the nine-digit codes for a sample occupation: marine architect.

Marine Architect (001.061–014)
0 = A professional, technical, and managerial occupation
0 = An occupation in architecture, engineering, and surveying
1 = An architectural occupation
0 = Synthesizes data
6 = Speaks to people
1 = Precision work with things
014 = Alphabetically distinguishes from other 001.061 occupations (e.g., landscape architect)

Each entry in the DOT contains the following information: (1) the occupational code number; (2) the occupational title; (3) the industry designation; (4) alternate titles (if any); (5) the head statement (summary of occupation); (6) task element statements (specific tasks worker performs); (7) "may" items (duties performed by worker in some establishments but not in others); (8) undefined related titles (if applicable). To illustrate, the entry for marine architect follows:

> *001.061–014 Architect, Marine (profess. & kin.) architect, naval; naval designer.*
>
> *Designs and oversees construction and repair of marine and craft and floating structures, such as ships, barges, tugs, dredges, submarines, torpedoes, floats, and buoys. Studies design proposals and specifications to establish basic characteristics of craft, such as size, weight, speed, propulsion, armament, cargo, displacement, draft, crew and passenger complements, and fresh or salt water service. Overseas construction and testing of prototype in model basin and develops sectional and waterline curves of hull to establish center of gravity, ideal hull form, and buoyancy and stability data. Designs complete hull and superstructure according to specifications and test data. In conformity with standards of safety, efficiency, and economy. Designs layout of craft interior including cargo space, passenger compartments, ladder wells, and elevators. Confers with MARINE ENGINEERS (profess. & kin.) to establish arrangement of boiler room equipment and propulsion machinery, heating and ventilating systems, refrigeration equipment, piping, and other functional equipment. Evaluates performance of craft during dock and sea trials to determine design changes and conformance with national and international standards.*

The fourth edition of the DOT is a single volume of 1371 pages and provides essentially the same data that were packaged in the two volumes of the third edition. The DOT user will find it separated into nine sections: an introduction and summary listings; master titles and definitions; term titles and definitions; occupational group arrangement; glossary; alphabetical index of titles; occupational titles arranged by industry designation, an industry index; and an appendix that explains the data, people, and things system.

There are three basic arrangements of occupational titles. The *occupational group arrangement* is appropriate if the user has sufficient information about the job tasks, wants to know about other closely related occupations, or wants to be sure he or she has chosen the most appropriate classification using the other arrangements. *Occupational titles arranged by industry designation* is appropriate if the user knows only the industry in which the job is located, wants to know about other jobs in an industry, or wants to know about work in a specific industry.

The *alphabetical index of occupational titles* is appropriate if the user knows only the occupational title and cannot obtain better information. A shortened, easier-to-use version of the DOT is the Guide for Occupational Exploration.

The fourth edition of the DOT presents few problems of usage for the counselor. Besides its direct value as a comprehensive reservoir of information on approximately twenty thousand separate jobs, the DOT provides a framework for use in a variety of other career-related resources (such as Holland's SDS, CIS, and so on). Unfortunately, the DOT may not be published in the future—a victim of budget cuts.

O*NET

O*NET, the Occupational Information Network, is the Department of Labor's comprehensive database of worker attributes and job characteristics that was developed to replace the *DOT.* Unlike the *DOT,* O*NET is not meant to be used in print form. Rather O*NET was developed for on-line (http://www.doleta.gov/programs/onet/) or CD-ROM use.

The O*NET database contains information about knowledges, skills, abilities (KSAs), interests, general work activities (GWAs), and work context related to 1172 occupations. Each occupational title and code is based on the most current version (1999) of the Standard Occupational Classification system. O*NET data, and its structure, also link related occupational, educational, and labor market information databases to the system (e.g., America's Job Bank, America's Career InfoNet).

According to the Department of Labor, O*NET can be used by career counselors, State Occupational Information Coordinating Committees, and employers to:

- Align educational and job training curricula with current workplace needs
- Create occupational clusters based on KSA information
- Develop job descriptions or specifications, job orders, and resumes
- Facilitate employee training and development initiatives
- Develop and supplement assessment tools to identify worker attributes
- Structure compensation and reward systems
- Evaluate and forecast human resource requirements
- Design and implement organizational development initiatives
- Identify criteria to establish performance appraisal and management systems
- Identify criteria to guide selection and placement decisions
- Create skills-match profiles
- Explore career options that capitalize on individual KSA profiles
- Target recruitment efforts to maximize person-job-organizational fit
- Improve career counseling

Career explorers can use O*NET to:

- Explore career options
- Search for occupations that use your skills
- Examine related occupations
- View occupational snapshots, including the most important characteristics of the worker and requirements of the work
- View details of occupations, such as skills, knowledges, interests, and activities
- Use crosswalks to find corresponding occupations in other classification systems
- Connect to other on-line career information resources

Of course, these claims have yet to be validated via research studies so they must be offered with a dose of caution. Nevertheless, the objectives established by the Department of Labor for O*NET seem realistic given its structure and the data it comprises. The Department of Labor's three objectives for O*NET are: (1) to provide a common language to describe workers and the jobs they perform; (2) to develop a job database that is relational; and (3) to provide information about the transferability of skills and the ability to the time requires to retrain for related jobs (http://online.onetcenter.org/).

Elements of Content Model used in O*NET. The content model for O*NET (http://www.onetcenter.org/content.html) is organized into six major domains: (1) Worker Characteristics, (2) Worker Requirements, (3) Experience Requirements, (4) Occupation Characteristics, (5) Occupational Requirements, and (6) Occupation-Specific Information. The structure enables the user to focus on areas of information that specify the key attributes and characteristics of workers and occupations. The following sections briefly describe the information included within each section.

Worker Characteristics. Enduring characteristics that might influence both performance and the capacities to acquire knowledge and skills required for effective work performance.

Traditionally, abilities have been the most common technique for comparing jobs in terms of these characteristics. However, recent research supports the inclusion of other types of worker characteristics. In particular, interests, values, and work styles have received support in the organizational literature. Interests and values reflect preferences for work environments and outcomes. Work style variables represent typical procedural/process differences in the way work is performed. Thus, all of these characteristics (i.e., abilities, interests, values, and work styles) are included in this domain.

Worker Requirements. Category of descriptors referring to work-related attributes acquired and/or developed through experience and education.

Worker requirements represent developed attributes of an individual that may be related to work performance. Knowledge represents the acquisition of facts and principles about a domain of information. Experience lays the foundation for establishing procedures to work with given knowledges. This set of procedures is more commonly known as skills. Skills may be further divided into basic skills (skills, such as reading, that facilitate the acquisition of new knowledge) and cross-functional skills (skills, such as problem solving, that extend across several domains of activities).

Experience Requirements. Requirements related to previous activities; explicitly linked to certain types of work activities.

This domain includes information about the typical experiential backgrounds of workers in an occupation or group of occupations. Information about the professional or organizational certifications required for entry and advancement, preferred education or training, and required apprenticeships are identified in this section.

Occupational Characteristics. Variables that define and describe the general characteristics of occupations that may influence occupational requirements.

Organizations do not exist in isolation. They must operate within a broader social and economic structure. To be useful, an occupational classification system must incorporate these global contextual characteristics. O*NET provides this information by linking descriptive occupational information to statistical labor market information. This includes compensation and wage data, employment outlook, and industry size information.

Occupational Requirements. A comprehensive set of variables or detailed elements that describe what various occupations require.

This domain includes information about typical activities required across occupations. Task information is often too specific to describe an occupation or occupational group. The O*NET approach is to identify generalized work activities (GWAs) or dimensions that summarize the kinds of tasks that may be performed within multiple occupations. Using this framework it is possible to use a single set of descriptors to describe many occupations. Contextual variables (e.g., the physical, social, or structural context of work) that may impose specific demands on the worker or activities are also included in this section.

Occupation-Specific Information. Reflects variables or other Content Model elements in terms of selected or specific occupations.

Occupation-specific information details a comprehensive set of elements that apply to a single occupation or a narrowly defined job family. This domain parallels other Content Model domains in that it includes requirements such as knowledges, skills, tasks, and machines, tools, and equipment. Similarly, labor market information defined by industry or occupation is also provided here. This domain is particularly important for specifying training, developing position descriptions, or redesigning jobs.

Using comprehensive terms such as the one's listed above to describe the KSAs, interests, content, and context of work, O*NET provides a common frame of reference for understanding what is involved in effective job performance. The goal of O*NET's common language is straightforward: "improve the

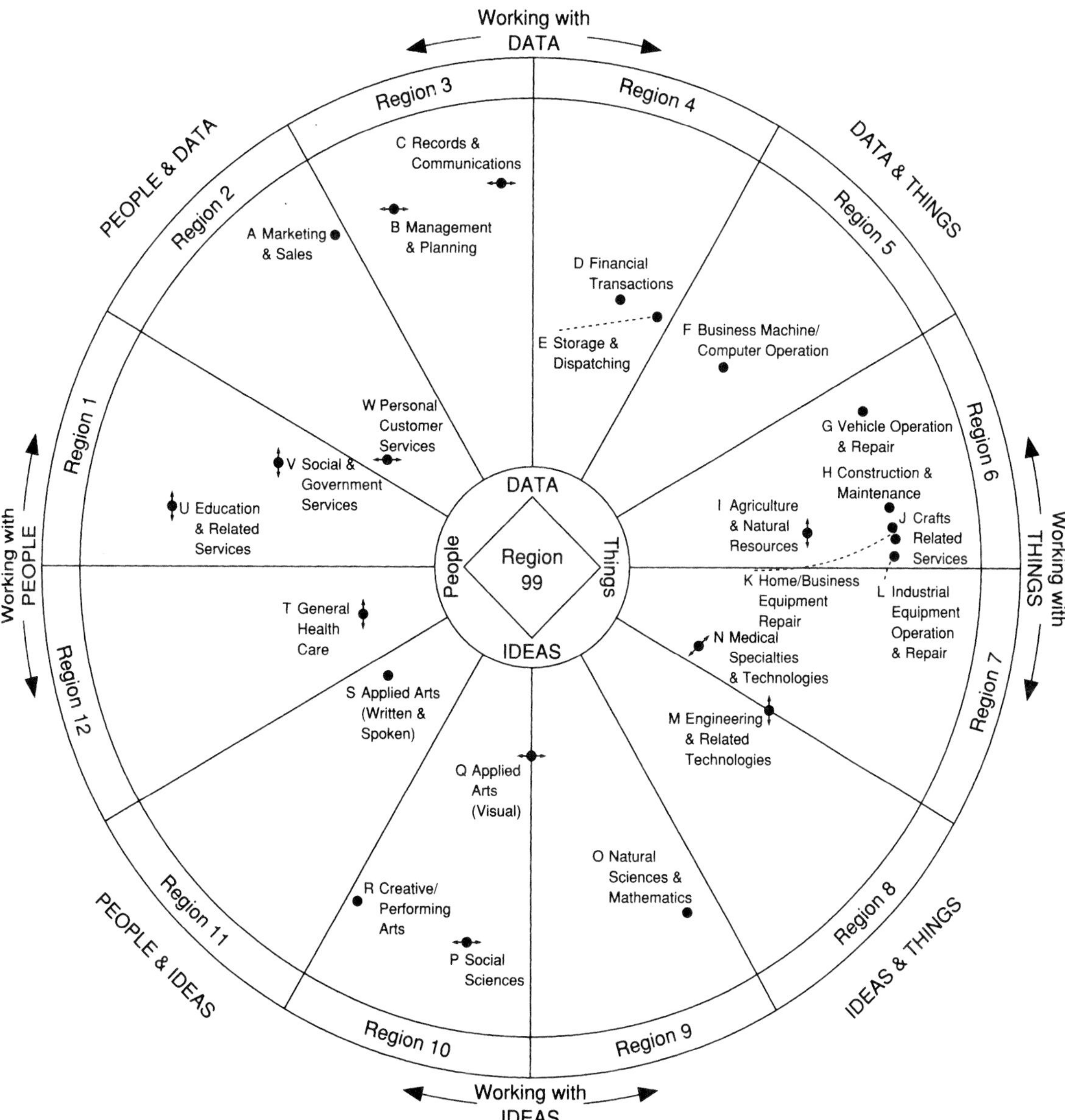

The location of a Job Family on the map shows how much it involves working with DATA, IDEAS, PEOPLE, and THINGS. Arrows by a job Family show that work tasks often heavily involve both PEOPLE and THINGS (←→) or DATA and IDEAS (↕). Although each Job Family is shown as a single point, the jobs in a family vary in their locations. Most jobs, however, are located near the point shown for the Job Family.

FIGURE 3.1 World-of-Work Map (2nd Edition)

Source: From *Interim Psychometric Handbook for the Third Edition ACT Career Planning Program,* Levels 1 and 2. 1985.

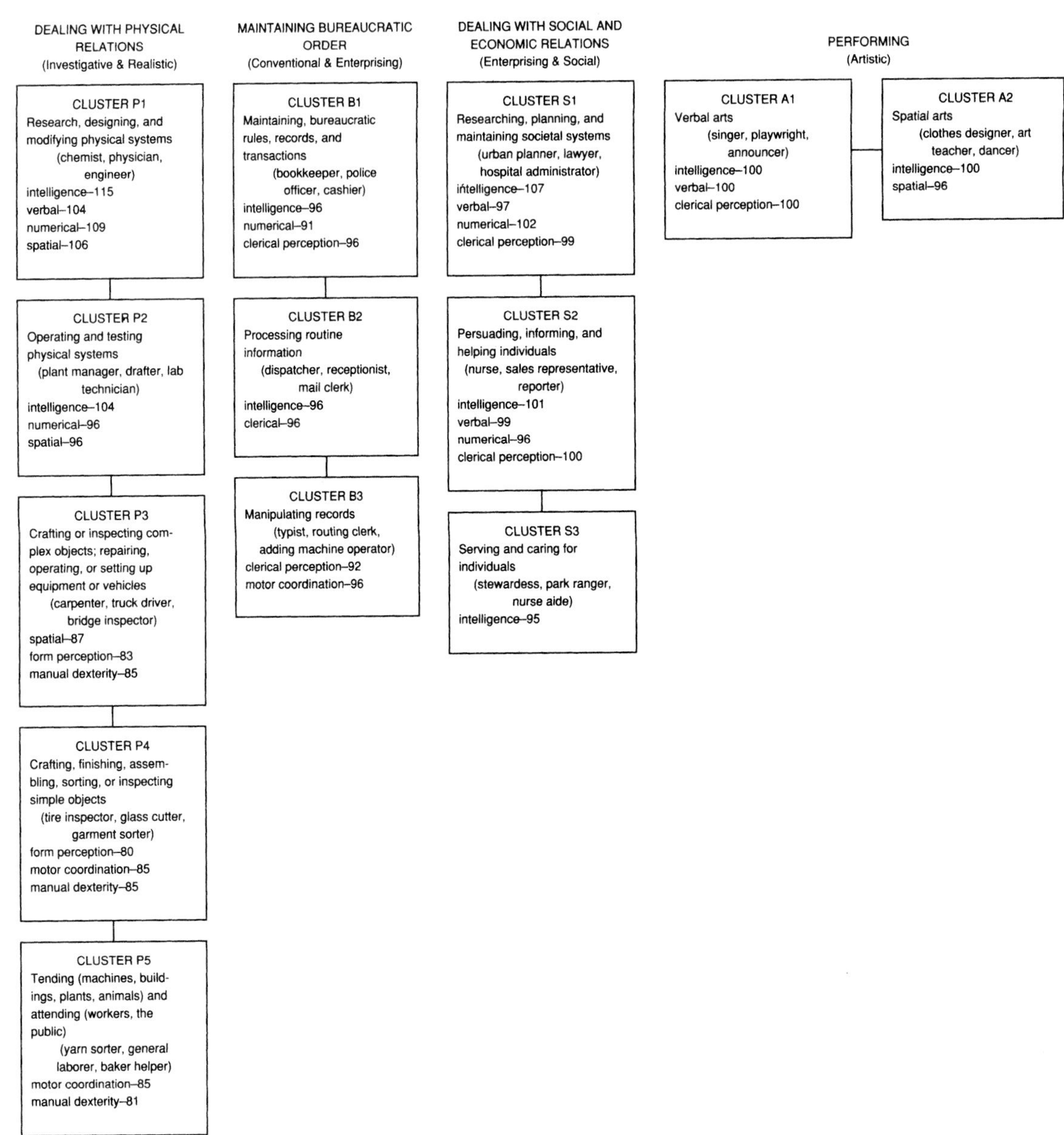

FIGURE 3.2 Occupational Aptitudes Pattern (OAP) Map

Source: Reprinted from "Development and implications for a theory of job aptitude requirements" by L. S. Gottfredson from *Journal of Vocational Behavior, 29,* pp. 254–291. Copyright © 1986, with permission from Elsevier.

quality of dialogue among people who communicate about jobs in the economy, generate employment statistics, and develop education and training programs." Employer hiring requirements will have the same meaning for human resource practitioners, workers, education and training developers, program planners, and students.

O*NET represents the most recent generation of occupational information resources. The number of elements contained in O*NET establishes it as the most comprehensive resource available. Not only does the fact that it is on-line result in easy access for those with computers, this format also allows for continuous updating of occupational information. Arguably, O*NET is the wave of the future for occupational information resources.

Maps

A number of classification schemes designate themselves as "maps"—representations of the world of work based on various criteria. Two examples of such maps are the ACT World-of-Work Map (ACT, 1985) and the Occupational Aptitude Patterns (OAP) Map (Gottfredson, 1986b).

World-of-Work Map. The World-of-Work Map was devised by the American College Testing Program (ACT) and is used as an aid in their Career Planning Program (CPP). The World-of-Work Map begins with an addition to the DOT people-data-things dimension: ideas. According to ACT, data/ideas form one similar set of work task dimensions, whereas people/things constitute another. In a circular arrangement (see Figure 3.1), things lead into data and things on one side and ideas and things on the other; similarly, the remaining three dimensions flow into neighboring realms. Six job clusters can be located within the eight work task combinations: business contact, business operations, technical, science, arts, and social service. Each of these, in turn, can be further refined. The social service job cluster, for example, consists of general health care, education and related services, social and government services, and personal/customer services. All of these are located in Regions 1, 2, and 12 of the World-of-Work Map.

It is arguable whether such a system is an improvement over other systems. Initially the World-of-Work Map presents the information seeker with a seemingly complex task that may discourage its use. It does, however, offer some refinement of the accepted and respected DOT.

Occupational Aptitude Patterns Map. The Occupational Aptitude Patterns (OAP) Map is based on an analysis of Occupational Aptitude Pattern scores derived from the General Aptitude Test Battery of the U.S. Employment Service. It further categorizes aptitude clusters according to their relationship to the Holland typology of work environments. Inspection of Figure 3.2 reveals that the map contains four major categories dealing with physical relations, maintaining bureaucratic order, dealing with social and economic relations, and performing. In turn, these four categories are comprised of thirteen clusters, each of which displays a general intellective or psychomotor aptitude characteristic.

This map is relatively new, and the practical applications have yet to be thoroughly investigated. One observation with which one is immediately struck is that the map seems to confirm empirically what Roe suggested intuitively in her scheme: within fields, higher levels of task demand higher levels of general intelligence. Requirements for interests and temperaments within fields may account for additional differences.

SUMMARY

Occupational classification schemes provide ways of examining the occupational structure in the United States, an understanding of which is essential to career guidance and counseling. Such classification systems are valuable in that they provide a framework for the delivery of career guidance services. The occupational system helps us to understand the total social system of our society, because it is a society's primary structuring element. We have described several unidimensional and multidimensional systems. Each, in its own way, provides a means of bringing manageable form and order into the potential chaos of occupational investigation.

CHAPTER FOUR

The Development of Career Behavior and Choice

KEY CONCEPTS

- Career development approaches encompass perspectives from multiple disciplines that provide windows into both the structure of and the longitudinal changes in career behavior. In general, the major career theories deal with different but overlapping problems.
- The influences on and outcomes of career development are one aspect of socialization as part of a broader process of human development.
- For purposes of classification, theoretical and research approaches to career development can be divided in many ways. In this chapter, five major emphases are described: trait-and-factor, actuarial, or matching approaches; decision theory; situational, sociological, or contextual approaches; psychological approaches; and developmental approaches.
- A major emphasis within most career development theories is the creation of choice-making paradigms: ways to understand the interdependence of decisions, risk-taking behavior, time perspectives, and the interaction of personal self-referents and choice strategies.
- Theories and research describing career behavior provide the conceptual glue for as well as describe where, when, and for what purpose career counseling, career education, career guidance and other career interventions should be implemented. The conceptual perspectives reviewed in this chapter deal with several interacting emphases: (1) the flow of understandings, experiences, commitments, values, and skills by which one forges the many facets of personal identity—self, educational, occupational, and career; (2) the process of decision making as the way one expresses personal identity in a choice; and (3) the functional relationships between time, social structures, and personal attributes. Each of these emphases deserves much more attention than space permits in this chapter. Therefore, the intent here is to highlight major families of conceptual approaches that attempt to explain the acquisition of work-related behavior, the anticipation of career options, and adjustments to the settings in which that behavior will be implemented.

As studies pertinent to career development have ensued, the concepts involved have tended to broaden and become more interdisciplinary. Super (1990) has contended:

> *The pioneers of career development are people from four disciplines. They are differential psychologists interested in work and occupations, developmental psychologists concerned with "the life course," sociologists focusing on occupational mobility as a function of social class, and personality theorists who view individuals as organizers of experience. (p. 197)*

To these representatives of core disciplines in career development, one can also add the growing perspectives of political scientists, economists, and organizational development theorists as people concerned about the development and allocation of human resources in national and global economies and the interactive effects of persons and environments as new forms of work organizations emerge in service-based and information-based economies.

As a function of the diversity of disciplinary lenses applied to career behavior, some research is more pertinent to occupational choice at a specific point in time or to adjustment within a work setting than to career development across time. Some research is concerned with the structure of choice, work behavior, or "career adaptability" within a particular life stage, whereas other research is concerned with how such structures change over time, the role of chance in career choice, and the continuities and discontinuities in career patterns throughout life. Increasingly, research and speculation in career development have shifted from almost a total concentration on adolescence and young adulthood to greater attention to career behavior in middle and late adulthood. As a result, it can be argued that career development theory and life-span developmental psychology are growing more congruent in their perspectives and methodology, if not deliberately, then certainly inadvertently.

Life-span developmental psychology is an empirical, multidisciplinary science that is concerned with the description and explication of ontogenetic (age-related) influences, normative history-graded (evolutional) influences, and nonnormative life events as they influence behavioral change from birth to death (Goulet & Baltes, 1970) as well as with the relationship between intervention and life-span development (Blustein, 1997; Danish, 1981; Fuchs, 1978; Vondracek, Lerner, & Schulenberg, 1986; Vondracek & Porfeli, 2002). In their idealized sense, both life-span psychology and career development, as a special instance of life-span psychology, are more than the additive result of different age-related studies with different groups of subjects in different educational or work settings. The intent in both cases is more holistic and longitudinal in understanding the influences on and the life histories of persons as they engage in the various roles available to them across time. In fact, existing career development theory and research do not meet the idealized criteria just suggested, but derive for the most part from less systematic, segmental theories and more disparate sources.

Given such a reality, one of the major reasons for studying the various approaches to career theory rather than concentrating on only one emphasis, whatever that may be, is the fact that no one theory is sufficient to explain the totality of individual or group career behavior. Thus, as Super (1992) observed, the question of "which theory is better" is specious because the theories complement each other in addressing various facets of the complexity of career behavior. In this sense, each theory has its own measure of quality in adding to the comprehensiveness of insight about career behavior that now exists.

One of the growing issues in the professional literature is whether career theories are actually converging, becoming more similar in their constructs and thus more susceptible to being brought together into a unified science (Savickas, 2000;Savickas & Lent, 1994). Many observers have called for efforts directed to such an outcome. Osipow (1990), for example, has analyzed how four major sets of career theory—trait and factor, social learning, developmental, and work adjustment—have come to resemble each other in important ways. Hackett, Lent, and Greenhaus (1991) have argued the need to work toward integrating career theories to:

1. Bring together conceptually related constructs (e.g., self-concept, self-efficacy)
2. Explain more fully outcomes that are common to a number of career theories (e.g., satisfaction, stability)
3. Account for the relations among seemingly diverse constructs (e.g., interests, needs, ability, self-efficacy)
4. Identify the major variables crucial to an overarching theory of career development (p. 28)

This plan of action outlined by Hackett and colleagues is both reasonable and valuable but unlikely to be fully consummated in the near future given the magnitude of the task and the constant infusion into the literature of new concepts and research findings. Such theory unification is also a daunting task because of the current lack of coverage of the career behavior of selected subpopulations: persons with disabilities, women, persons of color, immigrants, nonprofessional/nonskilled workers, and persons who are gay, lesbian, or bisexual. Research deficits in knowledge about the career behavior of such populations leaves significant voids in the ability to be comprehensive and unified in explanations of career behavior. This knowledge gap has led researchers to point to the need to more fully understand contextual factors influencing career development of individuals from diverse backgrounds (Subich, 2001).

In addressing such issues, Richardson (1993), states that "the fact that the theoretical and research literature in vocational psychology-career development is notably oriented toward the White middle class…a subtext of recent major reviews acknowledges that racial and ethnic minorities are underrepresented

decreased during the 1980s.... Moreover, there is almost no acknowledgment that poor and lower class populations, regardless of race or ethnicity are almost totally absent from this literature" (p. 426). Tinsley (1994), in response, differs in his views of some of the issues raised by Richardson. For example, he believes that there have been studies of theories, such as the Theory of Work Adjustment (Loftquist & Dawis, 1969), for years and no sex or economic level differences have been observed. In his view, however, "there is a tendency to dismiss general models that have applicability to both sexes and all economic class levels as limited in applicability [only] to White, middle-class men" (p. 109).

Whichever side of this debate one takes, given the complexity of the issues of gender, race, and economic status, we must conclude that career development theory is, as yet, relatively fragmented and incomplete, particularly when addressing women, the socially disadvantaged, and the economically disadvantaged members of society. In speaking to the particular problems of gender, Osipow (1983), for example, has observed:

> *Few special explanations or concepts have been devised to deal with the special problems of the career development of women.... Most of the masculine-based tests and theories fail to really provide a useful vehicle for the understanding of the career development of women. (p. 187)*

Although true, it is also useful to observe, as do Fitzgerald and Crites (1980):

> *Existing theories of career choice, although developed on men, have much to offer...unless [one] assumes that males and females are somehow fundamentally different in their needs and aspirations. It seems reasonable to assume that all individuals, regardless of sex, share the basic human need for self-fulfillment through meaningful work. (p. 46)*

Despite the large amount of research now attempting to identify factors related to how male and female career behaviors differ, the unique influences on each, and particularly the effects of stereotyping, organizational discrimination, and socialization on gender differences in psychological development (Gilligan, 1982a), it is fair to contend that what is known about women's career development has not resulted in a "relevant theoretical conceptualization...which is capable of integrating existing knowledge and guiding future research and intervention" (Hackett, 1985, p. 48).

The perspective of this book, however, is that, with due respect for the voids in necessary knowledge about women, minorities, and other groups in the society whose career behavior has been particularly affected by the magnitude of social change in the last quarter century, what is currently known provides a basis for programmatic efforts to spur the development of effective career behavior. Such efforts can, in turn, result in important information that can advance career theory and research in a more inclusive manner. If one views the confluence of approaches, theory, and research with objectivity and boldness, one finds tentative sets of constructs and propositions to explain differential career behavior and decision making, as well as to provide guidelines for aiding such processes. In a related view, other observers (e.g., Tinsley, 1994) would suggest that it is important that counseling psychologists and counselors not lose interest in theories before their usefulness has been exhausted. Tinsley suggests that even in theories that have been available for thirty or forty years, there are needs for systematic programs of research to test many of their postulates.

Speaking to several of the theories discussed in this chapter, Bell, Super, and Dunn (1988) suggest that when taken together they can form "a composite picture of career and personality theory and practice, yielding a dynamic and diagnostic anagram to both widen and deepen our understanding to personal adjustment and career development. When these perspectives are integrated, they embrace both personal and career counseling" (p. 3). These observers further suggest how these theories contribute to the career counselor's pool of diagnostic and conceptual insights. For example, the psychodynamic approaches of Bordin and Roe focus on *why* clients behave as they do, Roe going beyond Bordin in dealing with later interpersonal as well as intrapsychic forces.... Both Super and Ginzberg supply a time perspective, looking ahead and asking *when* important decision points are likely to occur.... Occupational information gathered according to Holland's hexagon or Roe's occupational descriptions can be used to acquaint clients with occupational options that fit their career goals and show them *how* to discover more satisfying work environments (pp. 3–4).

Although this is not the whole of the chapter's content, the observations of Bell, Super, and Dunn indicate both the rationale for and the integrative nature of the theoretical perspectives about career behavior explored in this chapter as the conceptual frame of reference from which career interventions can emerge and to which interventions can be addressed.

In this sense, each of the major theoretical perspectives explored here serves as a seedbed of hypotheses that counselors can use to help explain and test with individual clients possible factors, deficits, and influences related to their clients' presenting career problems, dilemmas, and anxieties. Because of the multidimensional nature of the problems that most clients face, it is likely, as Bell, Super, and Dunn (1988) suggest, that relevant hypotheses about or explanations of client behavior will reside in more than one theoretical approach as these differ in their emphases on intrapsychic, developmental, person-job matching, exploration, or situational factors. Put another way, "Each theory is an attempt to depict some part of reality and does so by deliberately ignoring other complexities.... [A theory is] a picture, an image, a description, a representation of reality. It is not reality itself. It is a way we can think about some part of reality so that we can comprehend it" (Krumboltz, 1994, p. 12).

CAREER DEVELOPMENT IN PERSPECTIVE

M. Katz (1973, p. 89) has stated, "The content of vocational guidance is defined as the opportunities for choice that society permits among educational and occupational options." Placing that idea in a broader view suggests that the content of career guidance or career counseling includes not only choices among educational and occupational options but also those of lifestyle—the degree to which work will be a central way of fulfillment for a particular individual and the ways the person will cope with the possibility of free and informed choice in pursuing personal direction and planning.

As suggested in Chapter 1, an overriding goal in any form of career intervention is the facilitation of free and informed choice in the individual. The assumption is that choice cannot be free unless it is informed. A further assumption is that the types of information available to an individual depend on how free the person is to consider different options or lifestyles. The latter, of course, can be diminished or strengthened by political conditions, historical events, family circumstances, the rigidity of social class constraints on mobility, and many other contextual phenomena. Given that reality, however, for one to choose freely, one needs knowledge, not only about what is available from which to choose, but also about the personal characteristics that might be emphasized in evaluating and acting on available choices. This latter goal requires, in addition to knowledge, clarification of personal values, interests, and attitudes as these are related to self-characteristics; environmental alternatives (occupational, educational, personal, and social options); and the decision-making process itself.

Career development, as the term is used in this chapter, refers to the body of speculation and research that focuses on understanding the factors underlying free and informed choice; the initial evolution of personal identity in regard to work; the transition, induction, and adjustment to work; and the ongoing adjustments adults must make as they incorporate new learning about themselves and the world of work into their career behavior. Borow (1961) has summarized the matter well in his statement that theories and research examining career development are in reality "a search for the psychological meaning of vocationally relevant acts (including the exploratory vocational behavior of youth) and of work itself in the human experience." Super (1980, p. 283) has observed that "careers have been viewed variously as a sequence of positions occupied by a person during the course of a lifetime" (Super, 1957), as a decision tree portraying the decision points encountered by a person going through school and into the world of work (Flanagan & Cooley, 1966), and as a series of life stages in which differing constellations of developmental tasks are encountered and dealt with (Buehler, 1933; Super, 1957).

The latter view has been significantly advanced by Vondracek, Lerner, and Schulenberg (1986) and Vondracek and Porfeli (2002), who contend that career development is a life-span phenomenon, properly studied from a multidisciplinary viewpoint in which a contextual perspective to understanding career behavior is essential as is a *dynamic interactional* view that emphasizes that the individual and the context change interdependently over time, thereby making choice and adjustment a continuous process.

Osipow (1983) has summarized many of the emerging attempts to integrate a wide range of perspectives in his discussion of a "systems view of career behavior." He states that such a view explicitly recognizes that various situational and individual factors operate to influence career behavior in a broad way. With a highly sophisticated systems approach to career development questions about the role of the biological, social, and situational factors in occupational behavior would become more explicit and... understandings of the interactions between these views would be more likely to emerge (p. 314). Osipow's notion of a systems view of career behavior is important not only because it acknowledges that such behavior is interactive and complex, but also because it is congruent with a systems view of career guidance and counseling that is responsive to the complexities found in career behavior. Thus, the position taken by Osipow and the position of this book and its previous editions is that a systems approach that recognizes the multidimensional influences on and character of career behavior needs to be responded to by an intervention system that reflects the multidimensional ways that can alter such behavior. The intentions of such analyses are to help counselors both with problem identification and with intervention design (Jepsen, 1984b, p. 136).

Although career development is a part of and interactive with the broader range of human development, it also emphasizes one aspect of socialization, what Crites has called "vocationalization" (1969, p. 88) and Borow has called "occupational socialization" (1984, p. 161). In Borow's terms, "Socialization then, is the intricate birth-to-death process by which one acquires one's view of the human world and its institutions, one's beliefs, loyalties, convictions of right and wrong, and habitual response modes. The learning is both formal and informal, deliberate and incidental, conscious and unconscious" (p. 161). "The socialization process, then, speaks to the articulation of the motivational system of the personality with the structure of the social system" (Parsons, 1951, p. 32). As E. Gross has observed (1975), "although traditional studies of socialization have focused on infancy and childhood, recent research has turned to adult socialization. Such research suggests that socialization is far from complete in childhood; it goes on throughout persons' lives" (p. 141). The importance of Gross's observations has been amplified in the virtual explosion of perspectives on adult career development that have become available in the recent past (Niles, 2002).

The processes of vocationalization or occupational socialization, as a part of career development, as it is described throughout this book, speaks to the various factors—psychological, sociological, cultural, political, economic—which, across time, result in self-career identity, decision-making ability, and career maturity. Such socialization processes, as we see it, have to do with those processes and factors that aid or impede one's acquisition of the values, knowledge, and skills leading to effective career behavior.

Most importantly, however, our contention is that the individual processes of occupational socialization or vocationalism, as described by career development concepts, can be understood, anticipated, and influenced by systematic programs of career counseling, career guidance, or career education. Career development concepts, then, are not descriptions of the inevitable; rather, they describe the possible and sometimes the probable behavioral results, if no intervention occurs to help the individual cope consciously with such possible or probable outcomes as they relate to his or her goals.

APPROACHES TO CAREER DEVELOPMENT AND CHOICE

Career development is concerned with broader phenomena than those represented by the terms jobs or *occupations.* The emphasis on the psychological or sociological study of careers (career development in this context) is on the continuities and discontinuities in the lives of groups (Super, 1954). The psychology and sociology of occupations stress characteristics of single or categorized occupations (Super, 1969b). The occupational model is primarily concerned with prediction from one point in time to another. "It takes prediction data at an early stage of the career and uses regression methods to predict success to one occupation, or uses discriminant analyses as a means of assessing the likelihood of being found, later, in each of the several possible occupations." The career model "is one in which the individual is conceived of moving along one of a number of possible pathways through the educational system and on into and through the work system" (Super, 1969a, p. 3). Both of these models are important for different reasons.

To make an arbitrary distinction, the occupational model, which stresses matching or actuarial relationships of person and job, is central in career counseling applied to an *immediate* job or occupational choice; the career model undergirds career guidance or counseling as a stimulus to *intermediate* and *long-range* career planning. Put another way, the major unit of concern in an occupational model is the differences in work content across occupations and their relationship to the individual's characteristics (e.g., aptitudes and interests). The major unit of concern in a career model is the clarity and accuracy of the self-concept as the evaluative base by which to judge, and plan for, potential options.

The approaches describing career development or some aspect of it have been classified in several ways. Hilton (1962) originally labeled them as models of attribute matching, need reduction, economic man, social man, and complex information processing. Osipow (1968, pp. 10–11) classified such approaches as trait-factor approaches, sociology and career choice, self-concept theory, and vocational choice and personality theories. Crites (1969) discusses them as nonpsychological theories (such as accident, economic, cultural, and sociological) and the psychological theories (such as trait-and-factor, psychodynamic, developmental and decision). Holland and Gottfredson (1976) have described the two main traditions for understanding careers as the developmental view and the differential view. Jepsen (1984a) has divided career theories into those that are structural or developmental. Savickas (2001) uses objective and subjective categories to classify theories with person-environment theories in the former category and development and postmodern theories in the latter group.

In a manner similar to Savickas, Young (1988) divides career theories into those that describe behavior as either empowering or enabling. Empowering behavior is seen in this perspective as deterministic and predictable. Enabling behavior is seen as more flexible; it is that which takes advantage of contextual events, such as those due to happenstance or chance, and uses them for purposes of self-development. Holland's theory (1985) of personality typologies and personality-environment matching is an example of an empowering theory. Mitchell and Krumboltz (1990) and Krumboltz (1994) whose research emphasizes influences on change and development, are examples of enabling theory.

Other observers classify career development perspectives with somewhat different systems. Super (1981) has contended, "The approaches and theories of the past 75 years fall into three main categories: those that match people and occupations, those that describe development leading to matching, and those that focus on decision making" (p. 8). As shown in Table 4.1, several types of approaches are included under each of the three main categories.

These attempts at classification highlight the factors, emphases, or disciplinary bases that distinguish one theory or research effort from another. In general, the categories depicted are not mutually exclusive or independent, but they attempt to explain differential

TABLE 4.1 Types of Approaches to Occupational Choice and Career Development

MATCHING	DEVELOPMENTAL	DECISION MAKING
Differential	Life-stage and identification	Process
Aptitudes		
Personality		
Situational	Life-span, life-space, and personal constructs	Style
Structure		
Context		
Socialization		
Phenomenological	Stage and determinants	Process-style-situation
Self-concept	Path models	
Congruence	Regression models	

Source: From *Career Development in Britain,* edited by A. G. Watts, Donald E. Super, and Jennifer M. Kidd. Copyright © 1981. Reprinted by permission of Hobsons Publishing.

career behavior and choice from somewhat varied vantage points.

For our purposes in this chapter, career development approaches and their proponents will be considered in the following sequence: trait and factor, actuarial, or matching; decision; situational or sociological; psychological; and developmental. Where possible, the disciplinary antecedents or roots of each approach will be identified.

Trait-and-Factor, Actuarial, or Matching Approaches

Trait-and-factor or matching approaches, coupled with actuarial methods, constitute a venerable theme in career counseling and other career interventions. Rooted in the psychology of individual differences, applied psychology, and differential psychology, these approaches conceive of the person as an organization of capacities and other properties that can be measured and related to the requirements of training programs or occupations. Based on empirically derived information on differences among people occupying various occupations or correlates of choice or satisfaction, trait-and-factor approaches are more descriptive of influences on choice than they are explanatory of career development.

In the trait-and-factor approach, the individual is conceived of as possessing a pattern of traits—such as interests, aptitudes, achievements, personality characteristics—that can be identified through objective means, usually psychological tests or inventories, and then profiled to represent the individual's potential. Trait-and-factor approaches consider occupations similarly, that is, as composed of factors required in successful job performance that can be profiled according to the "amounts" of individual traits they require. When one profile is overlaid on the other, the probable degree of fit between person and job can be identified. Practitioners using this approach seek to present an objective picture of their client's occupational options. Thus, this approach is based on a "psychology of possession" (Savickas, 1993). That is, most times, the goal is to inform the client as to the degree to which he or she possesses particular attributes (e.g., aptitudes, interests). To place their feedback into a larger perspective for their clients, counselors using a trait-and-factor approach compare their client's results to the distribution of scores emanating from normative samples of individuals whom have taken the same assessment.

Such an approach represents the essence of the *occupational model* previously identified in this chapter and in Chapter 1. As Super (1969b) has noted, vocational psychology, from its beginnings until shortly after 1950, was essentially a psychology of occupations. The occupation was the subject, and the persons in it were the sources of data on the occupation. Thus, from an actuarial standpoint, predictions can be made using individual traits as predictors and the degree to which these traits are possessed by successful persons in different occupations as the criteria. Further, the techniques and results of the numerous studies combining different traits and different occupational requirements also provide a means of appraising an individual's possibilities.

C. H. Miller (1974, p. 238) has suggested that the assumptions underlying the trait-and-factor approach include:

1. Vocational development is largely a cognitive process; decisions are to be reached by reasoning.
2. Occupational choice is a single event. In the spirit of Parsons, choice is stressed greatly and development little.
3. There is a single "right" goal for everyone in the choice of vocation. There is little or no recognition that a worker might fit well into a number of occupations.
4. A single type of person works in each job. This is the other side of the coin of the third assumption. Taken together, these two notions amount to a one-person, one-job relationship—a concept congenial to the trait-factor approach.
5. There is an occupational choice available to each individual.

D. Brown (1984, p. 12), paraphrasing a review of trait-and-factor theory by Klein and Wiener (1977), suggested that current thinking includes these premises:

1. Each individual has a unique set of traits that can be measured reliably and validly.
2. Occupations require that workers possess certain traits for success, although a worker with a rather wide range of characteristics can be successful in a given job.

3. The choice of an occupation is a rather straightforward process, and matching is possible.
4. The closer the match between personal characteristics and job requirements, the greater the likelihood for success (productivity and satisfaction).

Historically, trait-and-factor studies have provided the technical foundation for elaborating the three-step process of vocational guidance as laid down by F. Parsons (1909) and described in Chapter 1. As psychological instruments have been developed to assess individual traits and as knowledge has been accumulated about differences in occupational and educational requirements, including aptitudes, interests, and personality factors, career guidance processes, under the influence of trait-and-factor approaches, have become an increasingly scientific aid to choice. This approach stands in contrast to pre-Parsonian assumptions that subjective descriptions of occupational or training requirements are a sufficient basis for choice.

The assumptions on which trait-and-factor approaches rest, while contributing historically to the current practice of career guidance and career counseling can lead to a narrow perspective on career development. Trait-and-factor approaches have been primarily oriented to specific occupations or tasks as the criteria toward which predictor variables, such as aptitudes, mental ability, socioeconomic characteristics, interests, values, personality manifestations, and other variables, are directed. Career development, however, is not concerned solely with the choice of an occupation; it is also concerned with the process by which such choices can be purposefully integrated within a patterning of decisions, thereby maximizing freedom of choice and implementing the personal meaning of the way one conceives his or her traits.

The trait-and-factor problem today is not simply the task of relating a predictor, such as a test score, to some final occupation, but the consideration of patterns of attributes and their relationship to the sequence of decisions young persons or adults must make in establishing themselves in the world of work. As these procedures are used, they diminish a major weakness of trait-and-factor approaches—the view of individual traits and environmental requirements as relatively static rather than dynamic.

Clearly, if used with insight into the predictive limitations of trait-and-factor procedures, such information can be valuable in providing a person with a sense of the "odds" one faces in pursuing specific choices or the incremental differences that exist between where one is now and where one hopes to be in terms of various educational or occupational options. Meeting such goals requires the counselor to be able to identify relevant tests and select those appropriate in collaboration with a specific client. As will be explored further in other chapters, there are many types of tests, derived using different processes, purposes, and reference groups, and yielding different types of scores. Thus, a counselor functioning within a trait-and-factor context will need to possess a strong background in measurement, in testing, and in occupational classification systems in order to accurately represent what test scores mean and to present them in a way which is relevant to other sources of information available to a particular client. A persistent finding limiting the overall usefulness of trait-and-factor, or actuarial, approaches has been that the typical measures used predict training success more effectively than job success. For example, based on various traits, one can predict with reasonable accuracy whether an individual will successfully complete a carpenter's apprenticeship or some type of formal education (such as medical school). However, those trait patterns are less likely to predict whether the person will be a successful carpenter or physician after completion of training because of the complexity of other emotional and background variables involved in such success in each given work situation.

An additional concern related to the measures often used in trait-and-factor approaches is that the normative samples used in developing measures typically are not representative of society at-large. Often, samples are restricted to university and high school students comprised of primarily White, middle-class individuals. Using such measures with individuals not represented in normative creates serious concern about the validity of the assessment results and is a practice that should be avoided (Fouad, 1994).

Even though there are limitations to predictions from traits, D. Brown (1984) has asserted that "Generally, trait measures have been positively related to job success and job satisfaction. When our best available (not our average) validity coefficients are considered, these measures have not only been positive but relatively strong" (p. 14).

Brown's enthusiasm for trait-oriented thinking and results is not shared by all observers. Some observers believe that trait-and-factor ideas have been absorbed into other theoretical approaches (Osipow, 1983), that the rigidity of trait-oriented notions of matching individuals and occupations led to a decline in the adherents of trait-oriented thinking (Weinrach, 1979), or that practitioners are not current with trait techniques and the procedure is in incipient decline (Crites, 1981), and that trait-oriented thinking has less relevance in the postmodern era (Savickas, 1993).

Regardless of which of these positions one takes, the fact remains that even though the trait-and-factor approach has much to commend it—statistical sophistication, testing refinement, and technological application—the resulting predictions of individuals' success in specific occupations have been less precise than one would like. This limitation becomes problematic when counselors do not make this limitation known to their clients. Because assessment results often are presented in the form of computerized printouts, clients can mistakenly conclude that these results are precise and error-free. The common manifestation of this is the client who states, "I took a test and it told me I should be a..." Brown (1984) has acknowledged this situation when he stated, "As the situation stands, trait measures do not account for any more than 36 percent of the variance associated with various criteria and usually the portion is less" (p. 14).

The point is that aptitudes and other predictors of occupational success are important but so are other manifestations of personality, such as values, energy levels, motivation, perseverance, person-situation fit, and so on. The latter are likely to explain the variance not predicted by trait measures. In a related view, Krumboltz (1994) has suggested that among the shortcomings of trait-and-factor theories are that they "do not help us understand the emotional and skill acquisition tasks required for a job search, they do not inform us about overcoming job-related phobias, they do not address problems associated with handling sexual harassment, job burnout, the constantly changing employment environment, dual career families, or retirement planning. All of this, plus much more, is involved in career counseling" (p. 16).

If one were to subscribe to the trait-and-factor approach as the sole description of career development and decision making, one would have to assume that people have a much greater degree of self-insight than most seem to have—self-insight not simply of the measurable aspects of the self but of the self as a wholly functioning organism and the relationships between self and the personally important components of the options among which one can choose. In addition, if one considers the counselor as the major source of information about self-characteristics and occupational factors, one must face the possibility that the counselee is accepting such information based on faith in an authority figure. Consequently, choices made are not affirmations of identity developed from insights into self-characteristics and a personal view of the world. Rather, they are made because it is expedient to assume that the person will find success in an occupation based on statistical findings indicating that he or she fits into certain occupation populations. As indicated previously, trait-and-factor approaches maintain that choice is primarily conscious and cognitive. Such a premise seems more hopeful than valid as succeeding approaches to career development in this chapter will demonstrate. Choice occurs not only as a function of relating an individual's traits to the characteristics of alternatives, but also as a function of complex interaction between the person's developmental history and environment. In fact, the richness or impoverishment of the reservoir of experience, the accuracy and relevance of the information possessed, the distortion in appraisal of self-characteristics or possibilities of reaching aspirations, the scope and nature of the self-concept system, and many other combinations of factors also enter into choice, frequently making it more psychological than logical.

It is also important to acknowledge that some of the criticisms of trait-and-factor models are time-bound, oriented to historical models of trait-and-factor approaches, not contemporary ones (Chartrand, 1991). Thus, trait-and-factor models are not only those that have taken a limited and superficial approach to implementing Parsons's three-step (self-knowledge, occupational knowledge, true reasoning) model of *Choosing a Vocation* (1909), or the early conceptions of Williamson (1939), which emphasized the gathering of actuarial and clinical information, diagnosing and drawing inferences about the client's strengths and weaknesses and the nature and cause of their presenting problems. Trait-and-factor approaches also include such classic research on occupational classification and test development as occurred in the Minnesota Employment Stabilization Research Institute, particularly during the 1930s and 1940s the outcomes of which were used in World War II and later in classifying and assigning huge numbers of military personnel to training and to technical positions. Depending on how one conceptualizes trait-and-factor approaches to career behavior and to career decision making, one could include the psychodynamic model of Bordin, Nachman, and Segal (1963), the personality typology model of Holland (1973a, 1985), or the Theory of Work Adjustment of Dawis and Loftquist (1984), among other possibilities, as approaches that are in the tradition of differential psychology and of the study of the relationships between individual traits and occupational or workplace factors. If these well-researched and classic models were routinely classified in books such as this one within the trait-and-factor tradition, as they could legitimately be, they would significantly add to the contemporary importance and validity of trait-and-factor models. We have classified the Bordin and colleagues, Holland, and Dawis and Loftquist work under different emphases in this chapter, and in previous ones, to accent their conceptual emphases and the focus on specific career problems that they represent. It would be equally appropriate to discuss them here or to acknowledge as we are doing that such approaches have a dual designation as a matching approach and as an approach that emphasizes different types of content (psychodynamic needs, personality types, needs, and reinforcers).

Chartrand (1991) would contend that contemporary models of trait-and-factor approaches have evolved into "person × environment" approaches (P × E) that include such models as those exemplified by the counseling process developed by Rounds and Tracey (1990). This four-step model emphasizes the primary goals in counseling of facilitating career decision making, planning, and adjusting through the acquisition of problem solving. In this model, as in others reviewed in the next section: "Ideally, a client moves from acquiring and compiling information to integrating that information in a systematic fashion" (Chartrand, 1991, p. 522). The four steps involved in the Rounds and Tracey model are, in abridged form: encoding—perceiving information and appraising its meaning; goal setting—establishing concrete, realistic goals and organizing them into a coherent sequence; developing plans and pattern matching—problem solving that takes into account alternate solutions, multiple avenues for reaching those solutions, and consideration of different consequences of any action; and acting—the implementation of a solution.

The observations cited here suggest that contemporary trait-and-factor approaches blend assumptions in the historical models of this approach with those that are evolving from such roots into new models of person-environment fit. As Chartrand (1991) has summarized them:

> *First, people are viewed as capable of making rational decisions. This does not mean that affective processes can be ignored.... Second, people and work environments differ in reliable, meaningful, and consistent ways. This does not mean that "a single type of person works in each job." ...Third, the greater the congruence between personal characteristics and job requirements, the greater the likelihood of success.... This means that knowledge of person and environment patterns can be used to inform people about the probability of satisfaction and adjustment in different educational and work settings. (Chartrand, 1991, p. 520)*

Perhaps within the explanation of the latter assumption, is the bridge to emerging views of career behavior that are discussed elsewhere. As Chartrand states, "The P × E fit approach moves beyond the assumption of congruence, to include the notion of dynamic reciprocity.... That is, P × E fit is a reciprocal process with individuals shaping the environment and the environment influencing individuals.... These latter assumptions acknowledge the dynamic nature of P × E interactions and the agency of human behavior" (p. 520).

However trait-and-factor approaches are conceived, they have stimulated important research studies about individual differences in the predictor variables that play major roles in the choice of preparation for, and success in education, training, and employment. Because of space limitations, no attempt will be made here to discuss the voluminous literature pertaining to each of the prediction-criterion interactions that a full treatment of this topic deserves. Instead, the presentation that follows will identify and highlight major predictor variables used in the tests and predictive processes that are encompassed by trait-and-factor approaches.

Primary Predictors Used in Trait-and-Factor Approaches. The decades of research studies exploring individual traits and their significance in different settings and in various forms of career-related behavior have yielded a large number of significant variables. Each of the following has shown a significant relationship to educational achievement, to success in particular types of training, to choice of particular occupations or curricula, to realistic decision making, or to job satisfaction: abilities (scholastic achievement, spatial relations, abstract reasoning, clerical speed and accuracy, eye-hand coordination, fine or gross manual dexterity); needs and interests; stereotypes and expectations; work values; influences of significant others; size of community in which one is reared; childrearing patterns; socioeconomic background; general psychological adjustment; risk taking; levels of aspirations; level and type of occupational information possessed; career maturity (vocational choice attitudes and competencies); sex differences; racial differences; personality characteristics (acceptance of responsibility, honesty, and so forth); and curriculum pursued in school.

The large number of these variables suggests the validity of a rather simple point: Given sufficient ability to perform a particular work activity, the choice of, satisfaction with, or advancement in that work activity depends on a complex range of psychological, personality, and possibility factors. Within such perspectives there are variables or combinations of variables that set ceilings on likely choices or performances and other variables that mediate the satisfactoriness of possible choices or whether specific options are acceptable or desirable. Among the most important of these are aptitudes and abilities, needs and interests, values, stereotypes and expectations, adjustment, risk taking, and aspirations.

Aptitudes. A person's intelligence and other aptitudes play a significant part in the occupation-al level he or she is likely to attain, the training the person is likely to be admitted to or succeed in, and the work he or she is able to perform. Intelligence and aptitudes do not relate in the same fashion to each of these possibilities. Intelligence or specific aptitudes typically correlate more highly with success in training than with success in work performance—principally because the latter is based on a wider range of expectations and criteria than the former. There are differences between learning to do something and applying one's knowledge in a work setting in which one's work skills must be integrated with those of others, performed under rigid deadlines, or conditioned by other dimensions eliciting personality traits.

Research studies also tend to support the relationship between ability and the levels attained within career fields. Thus, although personality, values, or interests may lead to the selection of a particular job family or occupation, ability influences the particular career role attained within that field. In one of the most comprehensive studies on aptitudes and jobs, L. Gottfredson (1986b) has studied the occupational aptitude patterns used by the U.S. Department of Labor and their implications for a theory of job aptitude requirements. In constructing an Occupational Aptitude Pattern (OAP) Map, comparing it with other skill-based and aptitude-based classifications as well as with the Holland (1985) typology of work environments, and with ratings for complexity of involvement with data, people, and things, Gottfredson concluded the following:

1. General intelligence is the major gradient by which aptitude demands have become organized across jobs in the U.S. economy.
2. Within broad levels of work, the aptitude demands of different fields of work differ primarily in the shape of their cognitive profiles.
3. Different aptitude demand patterns arise in large part from broad differences in the tasks workers actually perform on the job.

Gottfredson elaborated her first conclusion by further stating, "Differences in the general intelligence demands among jobs not only constitute the single most important aptitude distinction among jobs, but also influence or constrain all other aptitude demands in some way.... Intelligence is more useful than any other aptitude factor, whether group or general, for predicting job performance across the full spectrum of jobs and job families." She also goes on to conclude that the higher the job level, the more important intelligence is; the lower the job level, the more useful motor aptitudes are, relative to cognitive ones, in predicting job performance.

Gottfredson's (1986a) research conclusions are essentially validated in other research. For example, Baeher and Orban (1989) have indicated that research demonstrates that general cognitive ability is important at all levels of the occupational structure. In addition, higher-level positions require higher levels of general cognitive ability. This research, however, also suggests that, although cognitive ability is of importance in all the higher-level occupations, predictive validity in these occupations would be increased by adding a personality measure. The best prediction is increased by a combination of these measures. In addition, both sets of predictors are differentially important for different occupational specialties and levels of organizational functioning. At the lower level of occupational complexity, although general cognitive ability continues to be important, general psychomotor ability becomes important, and such measures add substantially to the prediction of performance in less complex jobs. Thus, regardless of which general cognitive ability is the most significant single predictor of job training success or job performance, the point is that in less complex jobs, cognitive ability has an analog in personality measures such as drive, self-reliance, and potential for creative and innovative behavior. In stressful jobs, such as police work, the additional predictor of major consequence beyond general cognitive ability is likely to be measures of emotional health, and in some technical jobs, measures of spatial relations ability.

Needs and Interests. Needs and interests typically have been found to be closely related. The relationship among needs, occupational interests, and personality identification has been demonstrated in the extensive research related to Holland's theory, described later. It also has been found that inner-directed and other-directed personalities differ in their occupational interests, as do persons who are decided and undecided.

The relative importance of interests to vocational decisions has been studied by Bordin, Nachmann, and Segal (1963). Certain occupations evidently satisfy specific needs, and these needs are related to interests (Kohlan, 1968). In response to these relationships, there has been a significant merger between the work of Strong and that of Holland, perhaps most clearly seen in the format and scoring of the Strong Interest Inventory. Although the rationale and empirical base of each differ, they do identify differences in occupations similarly in regard to the interests held by people who occupy them (Campbell & Holland, 1972). With respect to career maturity, Wigington (1982) has demonstrated that high scores on the Kuder Occupational Interest Surveys are significantly correlated with scores on the Career Maturity Inventory. Spokane (1998) highlighted the convergent validity among interest inventories using score profiles from a client who took the Kuder Occupational Interest Scales, the Campbell Interest and Skill Survey, the Strong Interest Inventory, and the Unisex Edition of the ACT Interest Inventory. Spokane's article demonstrates how interest inventory results can be used by skilled career counselors to help clients uncover underlying dimensions of their career decision dilemmas.

Melamed and Meir (1981) have also demonstrated relationships between interests, job congruity, and selection of avocational activity. Using employed persons from 21 to 65 years of age in Australia and in Israel, they found that (1) people tend to select leisure activities congruent with their personality patterns; (2) people in congruent occupations (as measured by personality pattern and occupational code) were vocationally satisfied and conceived their preferred activities as an extension of the type of activities they do at work; and (3) people in incongruent occupations are vocationally dissatisfied and compensate for this by selecting compensatory leisure activities, and they tend to show higher salience (importance) for their avocational activities than for their work activities. Finally, researchers have also found a relatively weak relationship between interests and abilities with correlations between them generally being in the .20 range (Ackerman & Heggestad, 1997; Harmon, Barton, & Carson, 1999). The process of interpreting interest inventories, a topic that has received relatively little attention in the research literature, was the focus of a special issue of the *Career Development Quarterly* (Savickas, 1998). This special issue provides valuable information as to how results from various interest inventories can be incorporated into the career counseling process.

Values. There is considerable evidence that what an individual values both in work itself and in the rewards that work is perceived as offering affects vocational decisions and is internalized fairly early in development. Values, however, cannot be viewed in isolation. The values a person holds are the products of upbringing, environment, cultural tradition, education, and a host of other variables. Super, Savickas, and Super (1996) contend that there is an important relationship between values and interests:

> *Values provide a sense of a purpose. They serve as stars to steer by in guiding individuals to specific places within life spaces, places that can be the center of meaning, locales for need satisfaction, and venues for the expression of interests. Values are more fundamental than interests because values indicate qualities or goals sought, whereas interests denote activities or objects in which values are sought. (p. 138)*

Brown contends that as values emerge, they "influence all aspects of functioning, including processing of data, and thus what may be clear to one person who holds one value may be unclear or irrational to a person who does not hold that value" (Brown, 1996, p. 341). Brown and Crace (1996, pp. 211–219) go on to offer seven propositions outlining the function of values in career decision-making and life role satisfaction:

1. Values with high priorities are the most important determinants of choices made, providing that the individuals have more than one alternative available that will satisfy their values.
2. The values included in the values system are acquired from society, and each person develops a small number of values.
3. Culture, sex, and socioeconomic status influence opportunities and social interaction and thus considerable variation in the values of subgroups in our U.S. society can be expected.
4. Making choices that coincide with values is essential to satisfaction.
5. The result of role interaction is life satisfaction, which differs from the sum of the marital, job, leisure, and other roles satisfaction indices taken separately.
6. High functioning people will have well-developed and prioritized values.
7. Success in any role depends on the abilities and the aptitudes required to perform the functions in that role.

Available data are clear that occupational groups can be differentiated by discriminant analysis in terms of the values and personalities of their membership. Vocational maturation for both men and women involves the development of differentiated work values (C. H. Miller, 1974). Jurgensen (1978) over a thirty-year period ranked the importance of ten factors that make a job good or bad as perceived by some 57,000 applicants for jobs in a public utility. He found the order for men to be security, advancement, type of work, company, pay, coworkers, supervisors, benefits, hours, and working conditions. Women considered types of work more important then any other factor, followed by company, security, coworkers, advancement, supervisor, pay, working conditions, hours, and benefits. The interesting finding was that changes in these rankings overtime were almost inconsequential.

An important variation on this theme is research on the effects of organizational work values on job choice. Judge and Bretz (1992), for example, reported research findings with a sample of professional degree students that show that organizational work values—levels of a-achievement, concern for others, fairness, honesty—significantly affected job choice decisions, at least as much as pay and promotion opportunities. Indeed, individuals were likely to choose jobs whose value content was similar to their own value orientation. Other research suggests work values are independent of job knowledge. Therefore, it cannot be assumed that being clear about one's work values also means having enough job knowledge to make realistic choices. It would seem then that work values and job knowledge need to be addressed separately in the career counseling process (Sampson & Loesch, 1981).

Stereotypes and Expectations. Expectations and stereotypes also appear to influence vocational decision-making. Information that people have regarding occupations is often indirect and stereotypic. Such stereotypes have been found to develop by the beginning of elementary school or earlier (Rosenthal & Chapman, 1980; White & Brinkerhoff, 1981) and are frequently sex-linked (Garland & Smith, 1981; Trusty, Ng, & Plata, 2000). As they go about making a vocational choice, persons may search for environments that they perceive will meet their needs and expectations (Holland, 1963), and it seems likely that stereotypes of occupations are held by such searchers and that these are part of a foundation for vocational choice (Hollander & Parker, 1969, 1972). Research shows that persons have well-developed stereotypes about the personalities and persons in different occupations particularly as these relate to achievement orientation versus helping orientation (Levy, Kaler, & Schall, 1988).

Adjustment. General psychological adjustment also affects vocational choice. Schaffer (1976) studied the work histories of male psychiatric patients. The results indicate that the more severe the maladjustment, the less likely the men were to have been employed above the semiskilled level and that there was a direct relationship between severity of disorder and unemployment time. In addition, job satisfaction and success were found to vary as a function of the personality characteristics of the different diagnostic groups. Heath's research (1976) has shown that psychological maturity, whether measured in adolescence or adulthood, consistently predicts vocational adaptation.

Risk Taking. Another personality variable that seems to be related to vocational choice is risk taking. Early work by Ziller (1957) found that there was a significant relationship between vocational choice and a propensity for risk taking. Subsequent studies (Burnstein, 1963; Mahone, 1960; Morris, 1966) also found evidence that risk taking plays a part in vocational decisions making. However, a large-scale study by Slakter and Cramer (1969) has demonstrated that although there is some evidence that risk taking is related to vocational choice, the current measures of risk taking are too crude to capitalize on this relationship. Witmer and Stewart (1972) have reported findings showing that a preference for taking risks reflects a general lifestyle. Thus, the high-risk person's openness to new experiences and that person's rejection of tradition may indicate self-confidence in dealing adequately with life contingencies.

Aspirations. Level of aspiration appears to contribute to vocational choice. At least in men, level of aspiration seems relatively constant during secondary schooling (Flores & Olsen, 1967). In a study of 2,743 college freshmen, Perrone, Sedlacek, and Alexander (2001) reported that career aspirations for men were related to intrinsic interests and high-anticipated earnings, whereas women based career goals on intrinsic interest and prestige of the occupation. Level of aspiration is also frequently related to level of self-esteem, with persons of higher aspiration also persons of higher self-esteem (Prager & Freeman, 1979). Level of aspiration relates to educational experiences, curriculum choice and hence vocational choice. For example, Ma and Wang (2001) found that positive peer support, high motivation, and good instruction can help high school students success in their schoolwork, which in turn builds their confidence and results in students developing more ambitious career aspirations. Wang and Staver (2001) also reported that instructional quantity and home environment were significantly related to adolescents' career aspirations.

Helwig (1998) used Gottfredson's (1981) stage development approach to examine career aspirations in elementary school children. In this study, Helwig reported: (a) that occupational aspirations develop among second- to sixth-grade students, and (b) that children in his study chose more socially valued occupations as they matured.

Research regarding the importance of aspirations and career development has also been extended in a national sample of young men and women between the ages of 14 and 24, showing that the category of a person's earlier job (using Holland's classification) forecasts the category of later jobs, and that there is significant agreement between a person's current occupation and vocational aspiration (Nafziger, Holland, Helms, & McPartland, 1974). It also has been found that aspirations, expectations, and vocational maturity are related in graduate students and rehabilitation clients. Thus, whether one's expectations are similar to one's aspirations appears to depend on past success-failure experiences, education, and consequent vocational maturity (Walls & Gulkus, 1974). When vocational aspirations and job opportunities as determinants of later jobs held are studied, it is found that men more often achieve congruence between their aspirations and their field of employment by changing aspirations to match the job field rather than the other way around, and that early jobs are more predictive of later field of work than are early aspirations (Gottfredson & Becker, 1981).

Summary of Traits and Factors. Although the above analysis is not exhaustive, it is clear that a great many variables enter into career decision making: abilities, work values, occupational stereotypes and expectations, residence, family socioeconomic status and childrearing practices, general adjustment, personality factors including needs and propensity for risk taking, educational achievement, level of aspiration, and gender. Each of these is influenced by and overlaps with the others. They are in dynamic interrelationship. The preponderance of one or more variables in vocational decision-making depends heavily on the individual making the choice. Some individuals are more influenced by certain factors than others. A major characteristic of trait-and-factor approaches is that they describe relationships between variables and choices, but they do not explain how such variables develop. We must turn elsewhere for such insights.

Decision Theory

Decisions are not simply benign, independent behaviors that persons emit impulsively. Rather, decisions are the conjunctions between self and environment. Decisions are the public testimonies people make about how they view themselves, and how they view their opportunities and the relationships between them. Decisions are like tips of icebergs; they symbolize but do not describe all of the hidden meanings of a choice, the factors that shape it, or the hope or despair that attended the particular decision taken. As Alfred North Whitehead has reminded us, "People create their realities by the decisions they make." Until the act of choice occurs, possible choices remain potentialities. Once the choice is made, what was a possibility now becomes a reality, an entity that forever remains a part of one's life as a chemical trace or in some other form.

The importance of the decision process has made it a central construct in career guidance and career counseling as well as a major focus of inquiry in theory and research. Increasingly apparent in the professional literature are attempts to theorize about educational and occupational choice through the use of decision models. The major factor that differentiates these models from others reviewed in this chapter is their primary emphasis on the *process of decision making*. For purposes of this section, a variety of approaches with diverse conceptual roots are reviewed, such as cognitive, economic, mathematical, and social learning.

In historical terms, decision-making models are economic in origin. A fundamental assumption in many of these approaches, based on Keynesian economic theory, is that one chooses a career goal or an occupation that will maximize gain and minimize loss. The gain or loss is not necessarily money but can be anything of value to the individual. A given occupation or career pathway might be considered as a means of achieving certain possibilities—for example, greater prestige, security, social mobility, or a spouse—when compared to another course of action. Implicit in such an approach is the expectation that the individual can be assisted to predict the outcomes of each alternative and the probability of such outcomes. The assumption is that the person will then choose the one that promises the most reward for his or her investment (such as time, tuition, union dues, delayed gratification) with the least probability of failure.

A major notion in decision theory is that an individual has several alternatives or courses of action. In each of them, certain events can occur. Each event has a value for the individual, a value that can be estimated through some method of psychological scaling. Also, for each event, a probability of its occurrence can be estimated through actuarial prediction. If, for each course of action, the value of each event is multiplied by its probability and these products are summed, the sound choice from this point of view would be the alternative in which the sum of the expected "values" is the greatest. Such a perspective has led to the use of decision trees, flow charts, and game trees to describe the decision-making processes. The different paradigms explaining decision theory provide counselors with models, graphs, and concepts that help them to discuss the process of decision making directly with their clients. As such, the paradigms provide cognitive maps of the decision-making process itself as well as how different variables or behaviors affect the process.

Expectancy Theory. Decision theory is frequently expressed in mathematical terms as an expectancy times value theory of motivation (Raynor & Entin, 1982) or as expectancy/valence theory (Vroom, 1964; Lawler, 1973). For more than fifty years, many investigators have used the concepts embedded in these approaches to understand relationships among variables in a dynamic state as they affect individual behavior or as they have attempted to understand the relationship among inputs to choice or work motivation more generally. In a cognitive theory of motivation, individuals are viewed as rational persons who have beliefs and anticipations about future events in their lives. Steers and Porter (1975) summarize the theory in the following way: "It argues that motivational force to perform—or effort—is a multiplicative function of the expectancies, or beliefs, that individuals have concerning future outcomes times the value they place on those outcomes." Vroom (1964) uses the term *valence* to refer to affective orientations, positive or negative, toward outcomes but distinguishes these preferences (valences) from the actual satisfaction they offer (their value). In general, it is assumed that means acquire valence as a consequence of their expected relationship to ends. In this view, positive valence, particularly in the face of uncertain outcomes, is not sufficient to motivate choice or action. It must be combined with expectancy, the degree to which the individual believes that preferred outcomes can be attained (are probable). Finally, it is assumed that people choose from among alternative acts the one that has the strongest positive or weakest negative force (value) and the most likelihood of occurring.

Lawler (1973), in a similar approach to that of Vroom, also uses the terms *valence* and *expectancy* to explain individual action. He suggests that all of the theorists using such a framework maintain that the tendency to act in a certain way depends on the expectancy that the act will be followed by a given consequence (or outcome) and on the value or attractiveness of that consequence (or outcome) to the actor. Lawler (1973) continues this line of thinking by distinguishing two types of expectancies about which people are concerned; (*E* » *P*) and (*P* » *O*). The first, Effort » Performance, has to do with the person's estimate of the probability that he or she can accomplish the intended performance (such as perform the tasks required, meet a deadline) in the particular situation. The second, Performance » Outcomes, has to do with subjective probability estimates that if a particular performance is achieved it will lead to certain outcomes (a pay raise, promotion, or some other reward). In extending Vroom's position, Lawler argues that motivation or choice is a function of the attractiveness of outcomes, the valence, and the two expectancies cited: that one can do what needs to be doe and if one is able to do so, the probability that a desired outcome will result. An additionally useful characteristic of Lawler's view is his analysis of how people achieve perceptions of *E* » *P*, their ability to perform. Among others, he cites communications from other people, learning, personality factors, self-esteem, and past experiences in similar situations as influencing one's perceptions about the ability to perform as required in a particular situation.

An extension of expectancy × valence notions has been used by Raynor and Entin (1982) as the basis for a general theory of personality, motivation, and action. The basic hypothesis of the theory is as follows:

> *When doing well* now *is seen by the person as a necessary prerequisite for earning the opportunity to try for later success (termed a contingent path), individual differences in achievement-related motives (the motives to achieve success and to avoid failure,* M_S *and* M_{AF}, *respectively) are accentuated and become apparent in action, so that success-oriented individuals* ($M_S > M_{AF}$) *are more motivated to do well but failure-threatened individuals* ($M_{AF} > M_S$) *are more inhibited by the prospect of failure, as compared to when immediate activity has no such future implications (termed a noncontingent path) (p. 3)*

Raynor and Entin integrate these concepts and others with theory concerning self-identify, self-image, self-evaluation, and self-esteem. In oversimplified form, they found that earning the opportunity to continue along a contingent path was important for self-evaluation because attainment of the future goal that was contingent on immediate success is anticipated to provide feelings of self-worth.

Wheeler and Mahoney (1981), in applying an expectancy model to occupational preference and occupational choice, reinforce the fact that economic and psychological models have not tended to distinguish between occupational preference (occupations to which people are attracted), and occupational choice (occupations persons actually choose to enter). The former is a function of valence as it was discussed in the previous section; the latter is a function of the attraction to an occupation, an expectancy of entering an occupation, and the costs of preparing for an occupation. Applying such a model to the preferences and choices of 98 business and 30 psychology students, they found strong support for the distinction between the two concepts. Occupational preference was a function of pure attraction. Choice involved a compromise a-among attraction, expectancy of attaining an occupation, and expected costs. They also found that this process is likely to differ for various groups since different groups are more strongly influenced by economic cost-benefit analysis and other groups are primarily influenced by the attractiveness of the occupation regardless of how much it costs to attain that occupation.

Brooks and Betz (1990) applied Vroom's model of expectancy and valence to predicting occupational choices in college students. Their results, as a sophisticated test of Vroom's concepts, were important. For example, they found that the expectancy × valence interaction for an occupation accounted for from 12 percent to 41 percent of the variance in tendency to choose that occupation, and that expectancy alone was essentially as good a predictor as was the product of expectancy × valence. Gender differences in occupations chosen were marked and consistent with the traditional domination of occupations by gender. The gender differences were reflected in and consistent across expectancy, valence, and likelihood of choosing an occupation. Finally, it was found that the concept and measurement of expectancy are similar to those of career-related self-efficacy expectations as earlier reported by Betz and Hackett (1981) in their adaptation of Bandura's model.

Self-Efficacy Theory. Bandura (1977) has proposed a view of behavior change that he has called self-efficacy. Bandura contends that behavior change and therefore decisions made are mediated by expectations of self-efficacy: expectations of beliefs that one can perform a given behavior. The theory states that the level and strength of self-efficacy will determine (1) whether a coping behavior will be initiated, (2) how much effort will result, and (3) how long the effort will be sustained in the face of obstacles. This model proposes four principal sources from which expectations of self-efficacy are derived: performance accomplishments, vicarious experience, verbal persuasion, and emotional arousal. As does Lawler, previously cited in expectancy theory, Bandura also distinguishes between an outcome expectancy and an efficacy expectancy. An outcome expectancy refers to the person's estimate that a given behavior will lead to particular outcomes. An efficacy expectation is an estimate that one can successfully execute the behavior required to produce the outcomes sought. Efficacy expectations vary on such dimensions as magnitude, generality, and strength.

According to Bandura (1977), self-efficacy appears to be able to be increased and strengthened as a result of various types of treatments, but several general concepts are important to the understanding of the theory. First, people cognitively process information differently. Depending on how they judge the many factors bearing on their performance, they vary in their perceptions of self-efficacy. Second, people have many different types and amounts of efficacy-relevant experiences. Providing one new source of efficacy information will not necessarily affect the overall level of self-efficacy. Research data (Bandura, 1977; Bandura, Adams, & Meyer, 1977), however, suggest that with understanding of the concept of self-efficacy, the sources from which it is derived, and its potential effect on vocational behavior, intervention procedures can be devised to increase individual levels of self-efficacy.

Self-efficacy theory has become an important explanatory system relative to many different forms of behavior: social skills, stress reactions, phobias, coping behaviors, achievement, sports performance, decision-making style, and so on (Bandura, 1982b). For example, Mau (2000) conducted a cross-cultural study using samples of college students from the United States and Taiwan and reported that career decision-making self-efficacy was significantly associated with career decision-making style for the students in his study. Specifically, students who described themselves as "rational" in career decision making tended to perceive themselves as more competent in career decision making when compared to students who described themselves as "dependent" in their decision making. However, the dependent approach to decision making was less robust in predicting self-efficacy for the Taiwanese students. Mau noted that the Taiwanese cultural orientation toward collective decision-making styles may place a higher value on dependent decision making than the individualistic orientation more evident in the United States. The Mau study highlights the importance of considering cultural values in research and practice related to self-efficacy and career development.

In several important studies, self-efficacy has been found to relate to mathematics performance, to career entry behaviors such as choice of college major and academic performance, ethnic identity status, and to gender differences pertinent to a variety of career behaviors (Betz & Hackett, 1981; Betz & Hackett, 1983; Betz & Hackett, 1986; Campbell & Hackett, 1986; Gloria & Hird, 1999; Hackett, 1985; Hackett & Betz, 1981; Lent & Hackett, 1987). In general, these studies have found significant gender differences in self-efficacy relevant to perceived career options and in male and female mathematics performance. Because mathematics is so critical as a foundational skill or knowledge set for scientific and technical occupations, avoidance of such skills also likely eliminates women or men who have low self-efficacy in mathematics from such occupations. Although these studies of self-efficacy suggest that such behavior is complex and that tests of the concept do not always yield the expected results, in general it is found that success experiences produce increases in self-efficacy, in task interest, and in ability ratings, but failure depresses these ratings. Although not all studies have shown gender differences in self-efficacy vis-à-vis career options or mathematics performance, where such is not observed there do tend to be differences in strength and direction of self-efficacy for men and women in either failure or success groups, with women in failure groups typically rating themselves lower on evaluation of performance and on potential ability than men. Women in success conditions are more likely to rate luck as a significant influence on their performance than men.

Lent, Brown, and Hackett (1994, 1996) have proposed a social cognitive theory of career and academic interest, choice, and performance that is not confined only to the effects of self-efficacy beliefs, but also adds concerns about the effects of expected outcome and goal mechanisms and how these may interrelated with gender, contextual, experiential, and learning factors.

Specifically, the social cognitive career theory (SCCT) (Brown & Lent, 1996; Lent & Brown, 1996; Lent, Brown, & Hackett, 1994) builds upon the assumption that cognitive factors play an important role in career development and career decision-making behavior. SCCT "is concerned with the specific cognitive mediators through which learning experiences guide career behavior; with the manner in which variables such as interests, abilities, and values interrelate; and with the specific paths by which person and contextual factors influence career outcomes. It also emphasizes the means by which individuals emphasize personal agency" (Lent & Brown, 1996, p. 320).

SCCT draws heavily from Albert Bandura's (1986) social cognitive theory. Specifically, SCCT incorporates Bandura's (1986) triadic reciprocal model of causality that assumes that personal attributes, the environment, and overt behaviors "operate as interlocking mechanisms that affect one another bidirectionally" (Lent, Brown, & Hackett, 1996, p. 379). Within this triadic reciprocal model, SCCT highlights self-efficacy beliefs, outcome expectations, and personal goals. Thus, SCCT incorporates research applying self-efficacy theory to the career domain (Hackett & Betz, 1981; Lent & Hackett, 1987).

Bandura (1986) defines self-efficacy beliefs as "people's judgments of their capabilities to organize and execute courses of action required to attain designated types of performances" (p. 391). Self-efficacy beliefs are dynamic self-beliefs and are domain specific. Self-efficacy beliefs provide answers to questions pertaining to whether specific tasks can be performed. Self-beliefs about abilities play a central role in the career decision-making process. People move toward those occupations requiring capabilities they think they either have or can develop. People move away from those occupations requiring capabilities they think they do not possess or that they cannot develop.

Four sources shape self-efficacy beliefs: (1) personal performance accomplishments, (2) vicarious learning, (3) social persuasion, and (4) physiological states and reactions (Bandura, 1986). The most influential of these sources is the first (personal performance accomplishments). Successful accomplishments result in more positive or stronger domain specific self-efficacy beliefs and failures lead to more negative or weaker domain specific beliefs. Outcome expectations are beliefs about the outcomes of performing specific behaviors. Outcome expectations include beliefs about "extrinsic reinforcement (receiving tangible rewards for successful performance), self-directed consequences (such as pride in oneself for mastering a challenging task), and outcomes derived from the process of performing a given activity (for instance, absorption in the task itself)" (Lent, Brown, & Hackett, 1996, p. 381). Outcome expectations influence behavior to a lesser degree than self-efficacy beliefs. Thus, outcome expectations are what people imagine will happen if they perform specific behaviors.

Personal goals also influence career behaviors in important ways. Personal goals relate to one's determination to engage in certain activities to produce a particular outcome (Bandura, 1986). Goals help to organize and guide behavior over long periods of time.

The relationship among goals, self-efficacy, and outcome expectations is complex and occurs within the framework of Bandura's (1986) triadic reciprocal model of causality (i.e., personal attributes, external environmental factors, and overt behavior). In essence, person inputs (e.g., predisposition, gender, and race) interact with contextual factors (e.g., culture, geography, family, gender role socialization) and learning experiences to influence self-efficacy beliefs and outcome expectations. Self-efficacy beliefs and outcome expectations in turn shape people's interests, goals, actions, and eventually their attainments. However, these are also influenced by contextual factors (e.g., job opportunities, access to training opportunities, financial resources).

Self-efficacy beliefs can be modified in several ways. When ability is sufficient, but self-efficacy beliefs are low due factors such as racism and sex-role stereotyping, clients can be exposed to personally relevant vicarious learning opportunities (Luzzo, Funk, & Strang, 1996). Clients with sufficient ability but low self-efficacy beliefs can also be encouraged to gather ability-related data from friends, teachers, and others to counteract faulty self-efficacy beliefs. Counselors can also work collaboratively with these clients to construct success experiences (e.g., by taking specific academic courses, participating in volunteer experiences) to strengthen weak self-efficacy beliefs. In processing these success experiences, counselors can challenge clients when they identify external attributions for their successes and disregard internal stable causes (i.e., ability) for their successes.

In direct and indirect ways, the concepts and the language of both expectancy theory, self-efficacy, and social cognitive career theory permeate many of the career interventions designed to facilitate the decision-making process. The observant reader will note such relationships in many of the approaches that follow.

Decision-Making Paradigms. Many paradigms describing the decision-making process have evolved from earlier conceptions of problem solving or scientific analysis. Pitz and Harren (1980, pp. 321–322), for example, have indicated that any decision problem can be described in terms of four elements:

1. The set of *objectives* that the decision maker seeks to achieve
2. The set of *choices,* or alternative courses of action, among which the decision maker must choose
3. A set of possible *outcomes* that is associated with each choice
4. The ways each outcome might be assessed with respect to how well it meets the decision maker's objectives, the *attributes* of each outcome

Or instead, as Krumboltz and Baker (1973) identified as task approach skills important in career decision making, the following steps:

1. Recognizing an important decision situation
2. Defining the decision or task manageably and realistically
3. Examining and accurately assessing self-observations and worldview generalizations
4. Generalizing a wide variety of alternatives
5. Gathering needed information about the alternatives
6. Determining which information sources are most reliable, accurate, and relevant
7. Planning and carrying out the above sequence of decision-making behaviors

As Gati, Shenhav, and Givon (1993, p. 53) have observed, the characterization of the stages of decision-making is theory dependent. In an effort to define stages of decision making that are compatible with several theoretical approaches, they offered the following sequence of stages:

- Defining or structuring the decision problem (e.g., selecting a major or choosing a career)
- Selecting a set of aspects or criteria relevant to the decision (e.g., yearly income, prestige, indoor-outdoor)
- Ranking or rating by importance the various aspects identified as relevant to the specific decision
- Explicating the individual's preferences regarding the various levels of those aspects identified as the more important ones
- Identifying occupational alternatives the characteristics of which are compatible with the career decision maker's preferences
- Testing the feasibility of these alternatives
- Collecting relevant information on the few alternatives identified not only as compatible with preferences but also as feasible

- Ranking alternatives from most to least preferred based on all the information
- Implementing the most preferred alternative

Gati and his coworkers (Gati, Fassa, & Houiner, 1995) provided additional information pertaining to their views of the career decision-making process contending that due to "individuals' limited mental, material, and time resources, it is impractical for them to acquire comprehensive knowledge about all possible options" (p. 212). Thus, the best course of action is to identify a limited number of options that can be focused on for in-depth exploration.

Based on the complexity related to sorting through the information involved in career decision-making (e.g., a broad array of self-characteristics and promising occupational alternatives), Gati, Fassa, and Houiner outline a six-step framework for career decision making. Each step involves three phases. First, the career counselor presents the goal and the expected role of the client. Second, the client becomes actively engaged in the process by providing answers to a series of questions posed by the counselor. Third, the counselor provides feedback to the client related to the client's responses. During the third phase, the counselor and client also process discrepancies between the counselor's perceptions of the client and the client's responses. The counselor and client apply these three phases to each of the six steps.

In the first step of the framework, the counselor and client define and structure the decision problem. For example, the specific decision needing to be made is clarified is identified The counselor and client also clarify the goal of the decision and specify the potential options from which the choice may be made.

The second step requires the identification of relevant aspects of the decision problem (e.g., specific values, abilities the client desires to use in work, preferred working conditions). The third step requires the ranking of these aspects by importance. Step four has two parts. The first part of step four requires the identification of the optimal level (i.e., the most desirable variation or level in that aspect) and the second part requires identifying the less desirable, but still acceptable, level(s) on which the client is willing to compromise.

Step five involves sequentially eliminating occupations incompatible with the preferences identified by the client. Specifically, the counselor and client consider each option in light of identified aspects beginning with the aspect selected as most important by the client. For example, the counselor might note that several occupations being considered by the client are incompatible with the client's preference to not attend college. Once the number of options being considered has reached a manageable level, the elimination process is concluded.

Step six requires the counselor and client to review the previous steps taken and reexamine whether the client is satisfied with previous answers he or she provided. Also during this step participants clarify why certain alternatives previously considered were eliminated in the process. Those alternatives that were deleted because of a relatively minor discrepancy are also reviewed and the client is encouraged to consider whether compromising a specific aspect is a possibility (e.g., eliminating the option of teaching solely due to a desire for high income).

Clarke, Gelatt, and Levine (1965) suggested nearly four decades ago a somewhat different labeling of the decision-making paradigm that still has implications for the information required by the person doing the choosing. In paraphrased form, the stages are as follows:

- *Information about alternative actions:* Before deciding what to do, a person needs to know what alternative courses of action are possible.
- *Information about possible outcomes:* The person needs to know to what results the alternative actions available are likely to lead.
- *Information about probabilities linking actions to outcomes:* How likely are alternative actions to lead to different outcomes? What are the probabilities—high, medium, low—of certain results occurring from different actions?
- *Information about preferences for the various outcomes:* The person needs to consider the values he or she wishes to apply to different outcomes.

Together these emphases in decision making suggest that the individual needs both a prediction system and a value system to make decisions among preferences and expectancies for action within a climate of uncertainty. Gelatt (1962) proposed a decision-making framework in which information is the "fuel" of the decision maker and actions taken may be terminal (final) or investigatory (that is, instrumental in both acquiring and requiring more information). Within this framework, Gelatt contended that there are essentially three elements of the decision-making process, each of which requires different information. Figure 4.1 summarizes this point.

In 1989, Gelatt amended his 1962 model to respond to new knowledge about the conditions under which decision making occurs. Gelatt has argued for *positive uncertainty* as the new decision-making framework for counseling. He suggests that, "the new view of the decision-making world does not mean destroying the old approach and erecting a new one. It means discovering new connections between the old view and new insight.... What is appropriate now is a decision and counseling framework that helps clients deal with change and ambiguity, accept uncertainty and inconsistency, and utilize the nonrational and intuitive side of thinking and choosing" (p. 252). In this view, Gelatt is not proposing a new decision strategy as much as he is accenting the decision maker's legitimate use of nonobjectivity or subjectivity in the choices he or she makes in the constant presence of uncertainty. Thus, in the information society with its ambiguity and paradoxes, Gelatt has suggested a new definition of decision making as "the process of arranging and rearranging information into a choice or actions" (p. 253).

Gelatt specifically contends that in his amended model, reflections, flexibility, and both rational and intuitive thinking must occur in a holistic way. "In his current view, the future does not exist and cannot be predicted. It must be imagined and invented.... Rational strategy is not obsolete, it is just no longer sufficient" (p. 255). Therefore, "helping someone decide how to decide must move from promoting only rational, linear, systematic strategies to recommending, even teaching, intuitive situations and sometimes inconsistent methods for solving personal problems or making decisions" (p. 253).

FIGURE 4.1 A Graphic Concept of the Gelatt Model

INFORMATION NECESSARY	
Predictive System	Alternative actions Possible outcomes of actions Probabilities of outcomes of actions
Value System	Relative preferences among probable outcomes
Decision System	Evaluation of priorities or rules

Gelatt's views about positive uncertainty are consistent with a theoretical perspective that is rapidly emerging in career theory and in psychology more generally. This perspective is interpretive and social constructionist in its main premises (Walsh, Craik, & Price, 1992). As such, this approach emphasizes how individuals interpret their current and past circumstances and how they construct or create meaning for themselves. Such a view diminishes the role of assessment and prediction and expands the idiosyncratic nature of the individual as an active participant and shaper of "meaning-making" (Walsh & Chartrand, 1994). McAuliffe (1993), applying the developmental theories of Kegan (1982) to career transitions, has argued that the individual's meaning-making framework, or constructive developmental stage, contributes significantly to his or her adaptiveness when faced with career challenges.

From this frame of reference, McAuliffe (1993) contends that career counseling "can be construed as a development-enhancing activity—one that helps individuals to achieve greater flexibility, renew their self-definition, and to live in a transformational, dialectical relationship to themselves and the environment. The principles of constructive-developmental theory may serve as a foundation for a career counseling paradigm in which career is treated as a quest, an unfolding that requires participation by the meaning-making individual" (p. 27).

Peavy (1994) has talked about the nature of meaning making and constructivist thought as applied to career counseling. In his view, "meaning is created through interaction between participants in the interactive process and through the mental processes of the individual. Meaning-making and constructing-processes which are rooted in minds and interactions replace, at least in part, the concepts of information-processing and behavior.... Humans are viewed as active organizers of their own experience-worlds. The individual 'creates' a self through organized patterns of meaning.... The fact that we construe a way of acting as meaningful increases our propensity for 'doing' the activity" (p. 32). Against this kind of context, Peavy (p. 34) has suggested an approach to decision making by the counselor that involves four steps in what he calls constructivist career counseling. These are framed as four questions:

1. How can I form a cooperative alliance with this client? (Relationship factor)
2. How can I encourage the empowerment of this client? (Agency factor)
3. How can I help this client to elaborate and evaluate his or her constructions and meanings germane to this decision? (Meaning-making factor)
4. How can I help this client to reconstruct and negotiate personally meaningful and socially supportable realities? (Negotiation factor)

The perspectives of Walsh and Chartrand, McAuliffe, and Peavy are essentially captured in Cochran's view that "agency in career, the willingness to act, to bring something about, to achieve life goals, should be the prime topic in career theory. Career theory should provide a systematic account of how persons become agents rather that patients, a victim of circumstances regarding career. The aim of career counseling is to enhance agency regarding career" (Cochran, 1997, p. 209).

Although Gelatt's insights into "positive uncertainty" related to the concepts of the person as meaning maker and agent are important in a world of increasing decision ambiguity and unpredictability, it is useful to return to his original concepts of risks in decision making. This perspective remains a useful one to the career counselor.

The Gelatt perspective emphasizes the need for accurate and complete information in each of the systems necessary to a choice of and values about a particular situation, and it implies that risks vary among outcomes of possible actions. In one sense, the better the information a decision maker has, the clearer are the risks that the person takes in implementing different actions. The risks are not necessarily reduced, but it is assumed that knowing them provides the chooser a more rational basis for deciding what magnitude of risk is worth taking or whether the probabilities of a pay-off occurring for the risk involved are too low. Obviously, the degree of risk one is willing to take varies among persons and leads to different choice-making styles—some people are highly aggressive, others quite cautious, still others are in between these bipolar reference points.

Jepsen (1974) has reported research showing that individual differences in decision making can be classified in terms of strategy types in adolescents. He clustered groups of adolescent decision makers into twelve types based on how they organized data about themselves and career options. These clusters reflect differences in planning activity. Examples of three of the twelve types will illustrate Jepsen's view of individual differences in this area:

Strategy-type 3: Sought little career information and viewed current actions as relevant to planning. Considered only a few occupational alternatives and few reasons for considering either occupations or post-high school actions. Few outcomes were anticipated for preferred post-high school activity.

Strategy-type 6: Named many alternative occupations and post-high school activities and reasons for each. Many possible outcomes were anticipated, many intrinsic and self-appraised reasons were given. Planning activity was very high.

Strategy-type 9: Few actions were taken on plans, and little information was sought. Vaguely stated and low-level occupational alternatives were reported, and a single class of reasons was given for considering them.

Subsequent research by Jepsen and Prediger (1981) demonstrates that career decision styles are unique components of vocational behavior and development. Factor analytic studies by Phillips, Friedlander, Pazienza, and Kost (1985) lend support to that view.

Arroba (1977) has also studied styles of decision making and suggested several categories: for example, the compliant, no-thought, emotional, intuitive, logical, and hesitant. Arroba contends that any one individual may use a number of styles at different times and in different situations. Thus, a person may be logical in important new situations, compliant in unimportant familiar situations, and hesitant in important situations that contain unfamiliar elements and for which relevant data are lacking.

Other investigators have followed from Jepsen's research to seek additional insight into decision styles and the mechanisms that differentiate them. For example, Nevill, Neimeyer, Probert, and Fukuyama

(1986) have examined aspects of cognitive structure in relation to vocational information processing and decision making. In particular, they have focused on individual differentiation—the number of different dimensions of judgment contained in a vocational schema—and integration—the level of organization or interrelationship among these dimensions. They did find differences among persons who were high and low on these variables. One finding was, for example, that under conditions of high differentiation, greater self-confidence was associated with high levels of integration.

In an elaboration of his earlier work on decision styles, Jepsen (1989) has more recently combined several concepts related to the process of adolescent decision making with the antecedent conditions that prompt decisions and to which they are responses. He discusses the developing ability to cope successfully during important career decision points. He suggests that adolescent career development includes mastering decision-making *processes* as well as finding satisfying *content:*

> *It involves learning effective ways to decide in addition to finding actions that lead to pleasing outcomes.... successful decision making provides the maturing person with a heightened sense of potency, competency, and identity that form the basis for continued growth in the adult years. Failure to master the challenges of career decision points during this age may leave the person with dampened hopes, self-doubts, regrets, and confusion about his/her identity. (p. 78)*

Jepsen (1989), in this model, identifies the factors in the social context that prompt the adolescent to deal with a career decision point and the internal mechanisms by which such messages are received and processed. He suggests that the adolescent's social environment is composed of several primary reference groups that are principal agents of socialization as well as the purveyors of messages about expectations for action by the adolescent. These social groups may include the family of origin, classes and activities in school, peer friend groups, the extended family, the coworker group on a job, a religious group, or the group of families constituting a neighborhood. In turn, these groups send intermittent powerful messages, not delivered to all adolescents in the same way or with the same power, but nevertheless with content conveying aspects of a general expectation for the adolescent to take actions necessary to enter productive work roles. Adolescents, then, respond overtly and covertly to these messages. Overt responses typically include statements or actions and covert responses involve private thoughts and feelings. The two forms of response may not be consistent with each other. As Jepsen indicates, "adolescents may say things publicly that are not consistent with what they are thinking privately" (p. 85). The expectations for such inconsistency may lie elsewhere in this chapter as described by expectancy-valence or self-efficacy conflicts or the presence of vocational beliefs concerning oneself or other processes of doubt, lack of confidence, defensiveness, or feelings of vulnerability shaping their internal or covert self-talk.

Depending on how the messages are appraised by the adolescent, overtly or covertly, the adolescent's emerging goals and anticipated means (a plan) for reaching such goals will likely be revised or strengthened within the limits of his or her available strategies, rules or criteria, risk-taking style, cognitive resources, and emotional states.

Although this brief summary does not fully describe all of the elements and dynamics of Jepsen's model, it does connect adolescent decision making to the social context that stimulates and shapes the content and strategies likely to be employed. It also suggests counselor actions of relevance, including:

> *First, counselors can help adolescents to distinguish and clarify the powerful messages communicated by the particular groups in their social environment.... Second, counselors can help adolescents to focus on their covert responses and thus reveal what they are telling themselves.... Third, counselors help adolescents to appraise the content of powerful messages.... Fourth, counselors help adolescents to inventory their resources for meeting the demands of the decision.... Fifth, counselors help to orchestrate the delivery of powerful messages through organizing and facilitating discussions between adolescents and representatives of the reference groups identified earlier. (pp. 88–89)*

In Jepsen's analysis of possible counselor roles in relation to a linking of several psychological and sociological explanations of the social context and the processes of adolescent decision making, he also distinguishes two general categories of theory and practice in the decision-making literature. One line of research and inquiry has dealt with *prescriptions* about the elements and the processes that comprise rational behavior. The thrust of such approaches is the assumed need to derive a set of recommended steps for reducing errors in decision making. The second approach is to develop *descriptions* of behavioral patterns. According to Jepsen:

> *The prescription of external, rational principles, while important, is secondary to the identification of internal perceptions and conceptions about past and anticipated future experiences. The decision-making model provides a conceptual framework for organizing and assessing the adolescent's critical experiences. Rather than using the framework as a more-or-less fixed ideal from which to prescribe next steps, counselors use the framework to organize inductively the decision maker's thought and feelings into a general strategy and, then, to assess the strategy for desirable attributes of the decision-making process such as thoroughness, detail, consistency, and continuity. The decision-making concepts serve as categories into which the decision maker's reflections or experiences—past, present, and future—are sorted. (p. 82)*

Another important line of inquiry relative to decision-making style has to do with career indecision. Researchers (for example, Osipow, Carney, Winer, Yanico, & Koscher, 1976a) have focused on developing measures of indecision and taxonomy systems in the elements of indecision. One important outcome of this line of research has been the construction of the Career Decision Scale (Osipow, 1980), described more fully elsewhere in the book. Basically the 19 items of the CDS were designed to examine different dimensions of career indecision. Slaney (1988), in a review of the literature of career decision making, suggested that career indecision research has shown inconsistent or contradictory findings because researchers have been unable to differentiate between persons who are undecided about their career and those who are generally indecisive. He proposed that the former may be a normal developmental state, which career information or career interventions can modify. In contrast, indecisiveness may be more a characteristic trait of the individual and require more intensive and lengthy treatment. Other researchers have arrived at similar distinctions between problems of indecision and indecisiveness (for instance, Salomone, 1982). In response to Slaney's perspective, Vondracek et al. (1990) used four factor-based CDS scales to describe career decision behavior among 266 junior high and 199 senior high students, consisting of 222 boys and 243 girls. Among these students, the researchers were able to differentiate between different types of undecided clients as well as between undecided and decided clients. Using CDS factor scales described as diffusion, support, approach-approach, and external barriers, they were able to identify students who were undecided because they are confused and lack information about occupations (high score on diffusion); those who are undecided because several occupations have great appeal for them (high score on approach-approach); students who need support and reassurance for a tentative decision (high score on support); and those who cannot reach a decision because they perceive either internal or external barriers to decision making (high score on external barriers). Obviously, each of these types of indecision suggests interventions that differ by type.

Undecidedness has also been studied among university students. Lucas and Epperson (1988, 1990) conceive such a phenomenon as involving multiple variables. In their 1990 study, 196 students undecided on career options completed a battery of personality questionnaires that included emphases on state and trait anxiety; self-esteem; work salience; relationship or leisure orientation; locus of control; vocational identity; perception of barriers; need for information; and planful, intuitive, or dependent decision-making style. The results from these variables were submitted to cluster analyses to determine subtypes. The results confirmed the view that different forms of career indecision exist and that in this study five clusters or types of such undecidedness could be identified. The types identified varied, for example, from high anxiety to little or no anxiety; from low self-esteem to high self-esteem; from external to internal locus of control; from dependent to non-dependent decision styles and across the other variables examined. Although such variables may not be inclusive of all relevant variables, they do support the differences in factors producing career undecidedness in clients and in the need for different forms of career guidance intervention to be considered by type.

Phillips, Pazienza, and Walsh (1984) studied the effectiveness of different decision-making styles on career decision making and found that although the evidence did not show that a rational style was the most effective, a style that included dependence on others could be damaging early in the decision process.

Osipow and Reed (1985) applied the Johnson (1978) model of decision-making styles to a measure of decision/indecision among college students. The Johnson model includes four characteristics on two bipolar scales of decision making: spontaneous-systematic and internal-external. Spontaneous decision makers make decisions holistically and quickly; systematic decision makers collect information carefully and proceed logically in making a decision. Internal individuals process information privately and quietly; external deciders think out loud and talk to others about decisions. Osipow and Reed's research suggested a continuum of most to least undecided among these types including the most undecided (spontaneous-external) followed by spontaneous-internal, systematic-external, and systematic-internal, who are the least undecided.

Niles, Erford, Hunt, and Watts (1997) examined the relations among decision-making styles and career development in college students. Using cluster analysis, Niles and his colleagues identified 5 subgroups among 199 female and 133 male college students based on their decision-making styles, career decision-making self-efficacy, and career development task accomplishment. The results provide support for the positive relationship between a systematic (rather than spontaneous) decision-making style and adaptive vocational behavior. Those using a systematic decision-making style approach decisions in a rational and logical fashion. They actively seek all relevant information and accept personal responsibility for their decision-making. Systematic decision-makers can be contrasted to spontaneous decision makers who make decisions holistically and quickly (Johnson, 1978).

Graef, Wells, Hyland, and Muchinsky (1985) constructed measures of vocational indecision from a variety of biographical indicators used with college students. They were able to predict typologies of student characteristics that did or did not relate to vocational decidedness, vocational identity, and vocational maturity. Their results indicated that the overall construct of vocational decidedness differs for males and females, both with regard to the specific parts of the construct and the life history factors that are antecedents to each criterion element of the decidedness construct.

Building from much of the research described previously and other work that has focused largely on variations in career decidedness, Blustein, Ellis, and DeVennis (1989) are among researchers dealing with the steps that take place beyond making a choice. These researchers are concerned about commitment to an occupational choice; the sense of attachment to a choice made. In their preliminary findings, they have demonstrated that commitment is a developmental process that begins with an uncommitted, exploratory phase and progresses to a highly committed phase. In addition, persons can be described in terms of their openness or closedness to the exploratory and developmental experiences of the commitment process.

Some researchers have begun to link problem-solving self-appraisal to career decision and indecision. Holland and Holland (1977) suggested that career decision making could be viewed as a specific instance of problem solving with the latter defined as the complex chain of goal-directed events, including both cognitive and overt responses, that are intended to reduce some unsatisfying element of a problematic situation (for example, marital conflict, indecision about educational or occupational choices, or depression). Larson and Heppner (1985) studied differences between those who appraised their problem-solving skills as positive or negative in relation to their scores on two measures of career decision-indecision. They found that persons who perceived themselves as positive problem solvers were more confident about their decision-making ability and occupational potential, less likely to view the source of indecision outside themselves, and more likely to have related their abilities to an occupational field, and they endorsed fewer antecedents of career indecision than did the self-perceived negative problem-solvers.

Zakay and Barak (1984) have proposed a model of decision making that accents the meaning of the values involved in the decision. More specifically, the investigators suggest that in such a meaning model, an *ideal alternative* (IA) is formed in a decision situation. Such an IA has meaning values and importance weights assigned by the chooser to each meaning dimension. The psychological distances between the meaning vectors of IA and each alternative that offers the smallest difference or distance between its dimensions and those of the IA is chosen. Such a view suggests further that the greater the distance between the closest alternative to the ideal alternative and the ideal alternative itself, the higher the level of the individual's indecisiveness; the smaller the distance, the higher the chooser's choice confidence. The meaning viewpoint of the model proposes that any variable is possible and important. They also emphasize the attention that personal preferences, beliefs, perceptions, interests, habits, and needs should receive in such a model, as these represent elements of the individual's personal "decision-space." In two tests of the model, the investigators demonstrated that their data supported the validity of the model, its utility in understanding cognitive and behavioral indecisiveness, and its potential use in modifying the decision-making process.

A similar point can be made relative to the valuing of outcomes likely from different actions. Each person clearly or vaguely applies a scale of values important to him or her to each available alternative in a decision. The strength of the values in relation to the probability of the outcome actually occurring is seen by some observers as the crux of the decision process (Katz, 1963, 1969). Katz (1963) has suggested, in a model of guidance for career decision making, that an index of "investment" be developed to represent the substance of what an individual risks or loses in preparing for or electing any career option. This assumes that the person can be helped to determine the "odds," the chances of success in entering or attaining some alternative. More importantly, however, it means that knowing the odds is insufficient for decision making. As Katz has indicated, persons must also assess the importance of success to themselves in each option or the seriousness of failure. To make such assessments immediately places one's decisions in a value domain. Thus, decision making includes the identifying and the defining of one's values: what they are and what they are not, where they appear and where they do not appear.

Another way of conceiving the application of decision theory to choice is seen in the approach of Kalder and Zytowski (1969). In this model, the elements consist of inputs (such as personal resources, intellectual and physical characteristics, time, capital), alternatives (possible actions at a choice point), and outputs (the probable consequences of various actions). Again one undergoes a process of scaling what one has to give up to get various outcomes and how probable such occurrences are. The chosen alternative is assumed to be the one that offers the highest net value—the best value available when input costs and output costs are balanced. Implicit in such a model is the assumption that the decision maker has sufficient information about personal characteristics and the alternatives available to rank the values, utilities, and sacrifices associated with each possible action.

Brayfield and Crites (1964) have stressed the importance of considering choice as occurring under conditions of uncertainty or risk. According to Brayfield and Crites, the individual assigns a reward value (utility) to alternative choices and appraises the chances of being able to realize each of them (subjective probability). As a result, the person will attempt to maximize the expected value in making a decision. Thoreson and Mehrens (1967) have also addressed this point. They state, "Objective probabilities are not directly involved in the decision-making process, but are only involved insofar as they are related to subjective probabilities. The question that arises is the extent to which certain information (objective probability data) actually influences what the person thinks are his chances (subjective probability) of an outcome occurring" (p. 167). Although formal decision theory conceives of decision making as (1) a process, (2) having an essentially rational base, and (3) involving the selection of a single alternative at a particular point in time (Costello & Zalkind, 1963), the influence of individual subjectivity in interpreting information about oneself and about various options gives substantial credence to Hansen's (1964–1965) position that decisions are frequently more psychological than logical. Every counselor must keep the possibility of personally introduced bias in information constantly in mind, as clients are assisted to determine what sorts of information they need and what the acquired information means. Rather than assuming that the client will process information rationally and comprehend its full implications instead of filtering it through a personal set of incomplete or stereotyped images, the counselor must be directly involved in ensuring that the client considers pertinent information with as much objectivity as is possible.

A Social Learning Approach to Decision Making. Krumboltz, Mitchell, and Gelatt (1975); Mitchell and Krumboltz (1984b, 1990, 1996); and Krumboltz (1994) proposed and subsequently refined a social learning theory of career selection. In their view, the social learning theory of career decision making is an outgrowth of the general social learning of behavior, proposed by Albert Bandura, with its roots in reinforcement theory and classical behaviorism. "It assumes that the individual personalities and behavioral repertoires that persons possess arise primarily from their unique learning experiences rather than from innate developmental or psychic processes. These learning experiences consist of contact with and cognitive analysis of positively and negatively reinforcing events" (Mitchell & Krumboltz, 1984b, p. 235). Such an approach does not imply that humans are "passive organisms that are controlled by environmental conditioning events. Social learning theory recognizes that humans are intelligent, problem-solving individuals who strive at all times to understand the reinforcement that surrounds them and who in turn control their environments to suit their own purposes and needs" (p. 236).

More recently, Mitchell and Krumboltz (1996) have focused their work on developing the learning theory of career counseling that "integrates the practical ideas, research, and procedures of many counselors to extend Krumboltz's social learning theory of career decision making" (p. 233). The social learning theory of career decision making explains the origins of career choice and the learning theory of career choice and counseling describes what counselors can do to help their clients resolve their career dilemmas. Because they view the social learning theory of career decision making as being subsumed under the learning theory of career counseling, Mitchell and Krumboltz recommend that the entire theory be labeled as a "learning theory of career counseling" (p. 234).

Krumboltz and associates have indicated that "real life is always more complicated than our theories" but that it is possible to call attention to the events most influential in determining career selections. In this regard, it is believed that "People learn their preferences by interacting with their environment in a long and complex series of experiences" (Krumboltz, 1994, p. 17). In particular, in their learning theory of career counseling they point to the following four categories of factors as being the primary influencers of career development:

1. Genetic endowment and special abilities (such as race, sex, physical appearance and characteristics, intelligence, musical ability, artistic ability, muscular coordination).
2. Environmental conditions and events (such as number and nature of job and training opportunities, social policies and procedures for selecting trainees and workers, neighborhood and community influences, rate of return for various occupations, technological developments, labor laws and union rules, changes in social organizations, physical events like earthquakes or floods, family characteristics, community and neighborhood emphases).
3. Learning experiences such as *instrumental learning experiences* (ILEs), in which antecedents, covert and overt behavioral responses and consequences are present. (Skills necessary for career planning and other occupational and educational performances are learned through successive ILEs). *Associative learning experiences* (ALEs) in which the learner pairs a previously neutral situation with some emotionally positive or negative reaction (observational learning, and classical conditioning are examples).
4. Task approach skills (such as problem-solving skills, work habits, mental set, emotional responses, cognitive processes that both influence outcomes and are outcomes themselves).

These four types of influences and their interactions lead to several types of outcomes. The outcomes of these learning experiences are not automatic and they are interpreted by individuals differently. Such learning and related observations ultimately become part of the beliefs that individuals develop about themselves, their choices, and the world around them. These are classified as:

1. *Self-observation generalizations* (SOGs): overt or covert statements evaluating one's own actual or vicarious performance in relation to learned standards
2. *Worldview generalizations:* overt or covert statements about one's beliefs regarding how the world functions.
3. *Task approach skills* (TASs): cognitive and performance abilities and emotional predispositions for coping with the environment, interpreting it in relation to self-observation generalizations, and making covert or overt predictions about future events. With relation to career decision making specifically, TASs might include such skills as value-clarifying, goal-setting, alternative-generating, information-seeking, estimating, planning.
4. *Actions:* entry behaviors that indicate overt steps in career progression (such as applying for a spe-

cific job or training opportunity, changing a college major)

The Krumboltz and associates model accents the instrumentality of learning experiences in producing preferences for activities as well as task approach skills. Krumboltz, Mitchell, and Gelatt (1975) state, "It is the sequential cumulative effects of numerous learning experiences affected by various environmental circumstances and the individual's cognitive and emotional reactions to these learning experiences and circumstances that cause a person to make decisions to enroll in a certain educational program or become employed in a particular occupation" (p. 75). Within a decision theory frame of reference, then, this model suggests that becoming a particular kind of worker or student is not a simple function of preference or choice but "is influenced by complex environmental (e.g., economic) factors, many of which are beyond the control of any single individual." These factors can be learned by the individual, and career decision-making skills can be systematically acquired.

Mitchell and Krumboltz (1984b, 1990, 1996) have discussed a comprehensive inventory of empirical studies over the past two decades that provide considerable evidence to support the processes of the social learning theory of career decision making. It is apparent that the systematic research work of Krumboltz and colleagues has provided significant evidence to support many of the hypotheses that can be generated by the theory and has also provided insight into possible career counseling interventions.

In 1994, Krumboltz identified the testable propositions that derive from the theory as it has evolved. Included are the following:

People will prefer an occupation if:

- They have succeeded at tasks they believe are like tasks performed by members of that occupation.
- They have observed a valued model being reinforced for activities like those performed by members of that occupation.
- A valued friend or relative stressed its advantages to them and/or they observed positive words and images being associated with it.

A converse set of propositions can be stated as follows:

People will tend to avoid an occupation if:

- They have failed at tasks they believe are similar to tasks performed by people in that occupation.
- They have observed a valued model being punished or ignored for performing activities like those performed by members of that occupation.
- A valued friend or relative stressed its disadvantages to them and/or they have observed negative words and images being associated with it." (p. 19)

Among the many practical applications of Krumboltz's (1983) work is that which deals with the private rules of decision making and how these can be influenced by irrational beliefs. For example, Krumboltz has identified several types of problems that can arise from faulty self-observation, generalizations, or inaccurate interpretation of environmental conditions. The problems he identifies include the following:

1. Persons may fail to recognize that a remediable problem exists.
2. Persons may fail to exert the effort needed to make a decision or solve a problem.
3. Persons may eliminate a potentially satisfying alternative for inappropriate reasons.
4. Persons may choose poor alternatives for inappropriate reasons.
5. Persons may suffer anguish and anxiety over perceived inability to achieve goals.

Accordingly, Krumboltz suggests that beliefs that can potentially cause distress in career decision making are based on faulty generalizations, self-comparison with a single standard, exaggerated estimates of the emotional impact of an outcome, drawing false causal relationships, ignorance of relevant facts, and giving undue weight to low-probability events. Krumboltz contends that some of these beliefs and private rules in career decision making are related to the fact that making decisions is a painful process that involves at least four causes of stress: threat to self-esteem, surprise, deadlines, and absence of allocated time for decision making. These stresses, in turn, lead to such reactions as impaired attention, increased cognitive rigidity, narrowed perspectives, and displaced blame.

Finally, Krumboltz contends that there are methods for identifying and acting on the private beliefs and stresses identified. They include: assessment of the content of the client's self-observation and world view generalizations and the processes by which they arose; structured interviews; thought listing; *in vivo* self-monitoring; imagery; career decision-making simulations; reconstruction of prior events; behavioral inferences and feedback; use of psychometric instruments; use of cognitive restructuring techniques to help alter dysfunctional or inaccurate beliefs and generalizations; use of simple positive reinforcement; providing appropriate role models; use of films including problem-solving tasks for viewers; use of computerized guidance systems to provide and reinforce problem-solving tasks; teaching belief-testing processes; analyzing task-approach skills and teaching those in deficit (Krumboltz, 1983; Mitchell & Krumboltz, 1984); the use of the Career Beliefs Inventory (Krumboltz, 1988a) to identify presuppositions that may block people from achieving their career goals.

The comprehensive conceptualizations by Krumboltz and colleagues about decision making and interventions in it have made extensive contributions to the professional literature in terms that have been summarized previously but for, perhaps, a more important reason. In contrast to many other theories, which tend to emphasize either environmental factors, particularly social and economic influences on decision making, or intrapsychic individual processing of psychological events, the social learning approach as articulated by Krumboltz has attempted to provide insight into each of these sets of factors and their interactions.

For these reasons and others, the social learning theory of Krumboltz is seen as having considerable compatibility with major aspects of Super's self-concept theory, with the development of interests as depicted by Holland's hexagon, and with Gottfredson's theory of occupational aspirations (Krumboltz, 1994). Indeed, some observers (Subich & Taylor, 1994) have suggested that the learning principles that form the basis for the social learning theory may be fundamental to processes embedded within other career development theories and may provide an accounting of the mechanisms that underlie other theories (p. 167).

Cognitive Information Processing. A second recent cognitively oriented career intervention model is the cognitive information processing (CIP) approach developed by Peterson, Sampson, Reardon, and Lenz (1996). The CIP model includes several dimensions. First, the approach uses a pyramid to describe the important domains of cognition involved in a career choice. These first three of these domains are those traditionally included in career theories: self-knowledge (values, interests, skills), occupational knowledge (understanding specific occupations and educational/training opportunities) and decision-making skills (understanding how one typically makes decisions). The fourth domain is metacognitions and includes self-talk, self-awareness, and the monitoring and control of cognitions (Sampson, Peterson, Lenz, & Reardon, 1992a).

Knowledge of self and occupations form the foundation of the pyramid and then decision-making skills and metacognitions build upon this foundation. The second dimension of the CIP approach is labeled the CASVE cycle. The CASVE cycle represents a generic model of information processing skills related to solving career problems and making career decisions. These skills are: (1) communication, (2) analysis, (3) synthesis, (4) valuing, and (5) execution (CASVE).

The use of these skills is cyclical beginning with the realization that a gap exists between a real state and an ideal state (e.g., an existing state of career indecision and a more desired state of career decidedness). Becoming aware of such gaps can occur internally through the existence of ego dystonic emotional states (e.g., depression, anxiety), the occurrence of behaviors such as excessive tardiness, absenteeism, or drug use, or the existence of somatic symptoms (e.g., headaches, loss of appetite). Or people can become aware of such gaps through external demands (e.g., the need to make a decision to accept or reject a job offer). Career problems, therefore, involve cognitive, affective, behavioral, and physiological components. Interpreting these internal and external cues involves *communication.*

Once a career problem is recognized, it must be *analyzed* as to what is required for problem resolution. For example, if more self-information is required, then the type of information needed must be clarified (e.g., values, interests, abilities). If environmental information is required, then the nature of the information required must also be identified (e.g., information pertaining to job requirements). The next step within analysis is to identify the specific steps that can be taken to acquire the information needed.

Synthesis involves two-phases: (1) elaboration and (2) crystallization. During elaboration, solutions to career problems are identified via brainstorming.

During crystallization, solutions that are consistent with one's abilities, interests, and/or values are identified. The outcome of these two phases comprising synthesis is a manageable list of alternatives that are acceptable to the client.

Valuing involves first examining and prioritizing each of the alternatives generated in light of one's value system, the benefits to be gained and the costs incurred with each alternative, each alternatives' impact on significant others and society, and the probability that the alternative will result in a successful outcome (i.e., removing the gap). Once the alternatives have been prioritized, the optimal alternative is identified.

The *execution* phase involves converting the optimal alternative into action. A plan of action is developed to implement the alternative and achieve its goal. Thus, the execution phase involves identifying the specific steps necessary to operationalize the solution chosen in the valuing phase.

Once the plan has been enacted, one returns to the communication phase to determine whether the alternative was successful in resolving the career problem. Once again, cognitive, affective, behavioral, and physiological states are assessed in evaluating the success of the alternative (e.g., Do I feel less anxious? Am I more content with my career situation?). If the evaluation is negative, then recycling through the CASVE phases occurs with the new information acquired from enacting the first alternative.

A third dimension of the CIP approach is the *executive processing domain*. The function of the executive processing domain is to initiate, coordinate, and monitor the storage of and retrieval of information (Peterson, Sampson, & Reardon, 1991). This domain involves metacognitive skills (Meichenbaum, 1977) such as self-talk, self-awareness, and control. Positive self-talk is required for effective career problem solving. Negative self-talk leads to career indecisiveness. Self-awareness is necessary in monitoring and controlling internal and external influences on career decisions. Effective problem solvers and decision makers are aware of their values, beliefs, biases, and feelings. They use this awareness in generating and selecting problem solutions. Control and monitoring are essential for deciphering the information needed to resolve a career problem and for knowing when one is ready to move to the next phase in the CASVE cycle. The "control and monitoring of lower-order functions insures that an optimal balance is met between impulsivity and compulsivity" (Peterson, Sampson, & Reardon, 1991, p. 39) thereby providing a "quality control mechanism to ensure a complete, orderly, and timely progression through the CASVE cycle" (Peterson, Sampson, Reardon, & Lenz, 1996, p. 439).

The pyramid model can be used as a framework for providing career development interventions (Sampson, Lenz, Reardon, & Peterson, 1999). For example, the self-knowledge domain can be addressed through standardized and non-standardized assessments. The occupational knowledge domain can be addressed by engaging in job shadowing exercises and by reading about occupational biographies (as when Ronald was encouraged to conduct occupational information interviews). The five steps of the CASVE cycle can be used to teach decision-making skills. And, the executing processing domain provides a framework for exploring and challenging clients' dysfunctional metacognitions.

Peterson, Sampson, and Reardon (1991) have outlined a seven step sequence for delivering individual, group, and classroom career development interventions. Step 1 involves conducting an initial interview with the client. During this step, the counselor attempts to understand the context and nature of the client's career problem. The counselor develops an effective working relationship with the client by responding empathically to client statements and by using basic counseling skills (e.g., clarification, summarization, reflection of affect, immediacy, self-disclosure).

Counselors introduce clients to the pyramid model and the CASVE cycle to clarify client concerns and to provide clients with a model for understanding the career decision making and problem solving processes (Sampson, Peterson, Lenz, & Reardon, 1992a). During Step 1, counselors focus on questions such as "What are the client's perceptions of the extent of their development in each of the domains? How does the client typically make career decisions? Which metacognitions, if any, are dysfunctional and need changing? At which phase is the client currently focused? (Sampson et al., 1992a, p. 73).

Step 2 involves conducting a preliminary assessment to determine the client's readiness for career decision making. The CIP approach, uses the Career Thoughts Inventory (CTI) (Sampson, Peterson, Lenz, Reardon, & Saunders, 1996) to identify clients with dysfunctional career thoughts and, thereby, provide an indication of career development interventions that may be required to address the client's executive processing domain.

In Step 3, counselors and clients work collaboratively to define the career problem(s) and to analyze potential causes of the problem. Here, counselors communicate nonjudgmentally their perceptions of clients' gaps between a real state of career indecision and the desired or ideal state of career decidedness (Cochran, 1997). Clients respond by agreeing with counselors' perceptions or by clarifying and restating the gap they are experiencing.

In Step 4, counselors and clients continue collaborating by formulating achievable career problem solving and decision making goals. The formulation of goals leads to developing an individual learning plan (ILP) in Step 5. ILP's provide clients with a guide concerning what activities they need to engage in and what resources they need to use to achieve their goals. Although ILP's provide a mechanism for monitoring and evaluating client progress, they may also be revised as clients acquire more information about themselves and their career concerns.

Step 6 in the CIP approach requires clients to execute their individual learning plans. Counselors can provide support, feedback, and assistance to clients as they complete their ILP. Counselors can challenge clients with dysfunctional career thoughts to revise their thinking and then take action to complete their ILP. Finally, during Step 7, counselors and clients conduct a summative review of client progress and then generalize new learning to other current and future career problems.

The learning theory of career counseling and the cognitive information processing approach, with their emphases on both internal mechanisms and the effects of the social context on decision-making opportunities and reinforcements, are also theoretical bridges to what in the next section is described as situational, sociological, and contextual approaches.

Situational, Sociological, and Contextual Approaches

The social structure, as it is organized in a particular nation, is entwined with the characteristics of the majority and minority cultures that compose it. But regardless of whether a particular society is culturally pluralistic or homogeneous, it will create roles and achievement images for individuals to follow that serve as mechanisms to match individual self-interest to the collective good, whether such "good" be economic development, political stability, or some other goal. Such societal definitions of roles, who occupies them, how they are played out, and to what end are reflected in the information people receive and the behaviors or skills that are rewarded. Segall and coworkers (1990) suggest that more sophisticated cross-cultural research underscores the plausibility of expecting that people in different cultural settings would vary in the way they learn to solve problems and in the patterns of skills they acquire. Now it is understood that cultures vary in the salience attached to certain skills, in the combination of basic cognitive processes that are called upon in any given context, or in the order in which specific skills are acquired (p. 94). "In any society, there is likely to be a meaningful relationship between child training emphases and adult behavior.... Children are likely to be induced to behave in ways compatible with adult roles that they will have to assume, with these roles in turn reflective of socioeconomic complexity and social organization" (p. 236).

Such cultural constructions of achievement images, appropriate behavior, and belief systems are likely to be incorporated into the individual citizen's psyche through family, school, and religious institutions as well as embodied into the economic and organizational systems that prevail in a given nation. Thus, cultures represent templates or guides that encourage children, youth, and adults to embrace some values, information, behaviors, and personal goals, and not others. For reasons of history, tradition, religious influence, and other factors, the occupations, knowledge, and skills valued are likely to differ from those of other societies or cultures.

In pluralistic societies, such as the United States, environments that people occupy are not unidimensional. They are physical, social, political, economic, and cultural. The interactions among these aspects of one's "life space" influence how gender and family roles are conceived, the achievement images likely to be nurtured, the resources available, and the accuracy and form of knowledge provided about opportunities.

In some contrast to more psychologically oriented theories of career development, which accent the effects of individual action in creating one's own reality and in forging careers through choices made, sociological perspectives tend to accent the environmental factors that facilitate or constrain individual action. As Hotchkiss and Borow (1990) suggest:

> *Psychologists are interested in how constellations of personal attributes, including aspirations, aptitudes, interests, and personality traits, shape subsequent job performance and satisfaction. Sociologists, by contrast, generally are more interested than psychologists are in how such institutional factors as formal rules, informal norms, and supply-and-demand forces shape the settings in which individuals work.... Sociologists have generally viewed paid employment and occupational choice as embedded in a broad system of social stratification. (p. 263)*

Thus, sociologists are primarily concerned about the structural factors that condition or limit individual choices and their consequences. Sociological or situational emphases portray change from place to place and from time to time. In other words, the context in which career behavior unfolds is different across nations, communities, and families. It is different from one socioeconomic group to another. The career context is also different across time. As social, economic, and technological conditions change at a national or global level, they reflect the decrease of some types of work opportunities and lifestyles and the emergence of others. Similarly, one's place in a birth order of siblings in a family modifies the career context available. Thus, the course of one's development is dependent on when one is born, how many others are growing up at the same time and competing for opportunities available, how sex roles are defined in one's historical time, and other phenomena. People are in dynamic interaction with their environment. Vondracek, Lerner, and Schulenberg (1986) portray such interaction as follows: "Dynamic interaction means that the context and organism are inextricably embedded in each other, that the context consists of multiple levels changing inter-dependently across time, and that because organisms influence the contexts that influence them, they are able to play an active role in their own developments" (p. 37).

There are several notions in the professional literature about the multidimensionality of environments as they affect career development. Gibson (1979), for example, has discussed the idea that environments offer "affordances"—objects, events, people—that can provide information, stimulation, and possibilities to people who can perceive such "affordances." Indeed, it is possible to think of formulating taxonomies of the affordances provided by different environments and their possible responses to different individual needs or perceptual systems.

In another view, Bronfenbrenner (1979) has also emphasized the importance of the interaction between the developing person, the environment, and the interaction between the two. His concern is that although the behavioral sciences tend to acknowledge such interaction between the person and the environment, the major theoretical and research attention has been focused on the properties of the person rather than on the characterization of environments and their implications for the person. Bronfenbrenner introduces a number of concepts that are of importance within the present section, but that are also important to the last part of this chapter, when we discuss developmental approaches more directly and, in particular, perspectives on adult transitions. For example, Bronfenbrenner describes such events as finding a job, losing a job, and retiring as *ecological transitions* that occur throughout the life span when "a person's position in the ecological environment is altered as the result of a change in role, setting, or both" (p. 26). These transitions reflect the consequences of both changes in the person and in the environment across time.

Another concept important to a sociological, situational, or contextual view of career development is Bronfenbrenner's *principle of interconnectedness.* This principle envisions the environment as being composed of several interrelated systems that affect each other and individual psychological development. He offers four ecological structures to define the environment:

1. In the *microsystem,* the more intimate aspects of the individual's development in the family, in the school, or in the workplace occur; it is composed of the interpersonal relationships, goal-directed molar activities, and system-defined roles and expectations a person experiences in a given setting such as a family or school.
2. The *mesosystem* links together the major microsystems, the child's family and school, the family and workplace expectations at a particular point in the parent's life.

3. The *exosystem* includes indirect effects on a person from a spouse's or parent's microsystems, for example, the workplace.
4. The *macrosystem* includes the major cultural-level, national-level, societal-level belief systems, ideologies, and morés about sex roles, personality models to be emulated, and similar social metaphors (Vaizey & Clark, 1976) that organize majority or dominant visions of appropriate behavior and sanctions on it.

Each of these systems has its own impact as a career context, as a generator of environmental circumstances and situations, that both affects and is affected by individual psychological development.

One's social class membership is, for example, a function of family heritage, resources, and status. This is a microsystem issue. How the family or child interacts with the school is a mesosystem issue but obviously is affected by the social class membership of the child and how that is interpreted in intellectual, power, or behavioral terms by the school. The child's social class membership is also an exosystem issue in the sense that a child, or a spouse in many instances, inherits from the parent (or spouse) a level of financial or social status that derives from the occupation of that parent or spouse. The child does not generate the social class membership but is characterized by such status as an indirect effect of the parent's role in a particular exosystem. Finally, at the most generalizable level, the macrosystem may be the generator of images that suggest that certain family structures (microsystems) or social classes are better than others or are problematic. In turn, such reinforcement and interactions ripple through the four ecological systems defined by Bronfenbrenner and affect the child's or the family's conceptions of self, opportunities, values, or other cognitive structures.

This description grossly oversimplifies the interaction of person and context. It does not begin to address the many intricacies and subtleties that compose the psychological processes by which individuals accommodate the physical, social, and cultural aspects of their environment, or, indeed, how the four ecological systems defined by Bronfenbrenner vary for individuals or for nations. Nevertheless, such differences do prevail.

Without using the term *macrosystem,* Watts, Super, and Kidd (1981) have illustrated the variance of that structure in a comparison of the evolution of career development theory in Britain with that of the United States:

> *It is intriguing that theories of career development in the USA have been so heavily dominated by psychologists whereas in Britain the contributions of sociologists have been much more prominent. The dominant focus in the USA has been on the actions of individuals, while in Britain indigenous theoretical work has been more preoccupied with the constraints of social structures.... The failure of the American social-structural evidence to have much influence on career development theory seems to be due basically to cultural and historical factors. From the beginning of its independent existence, the USA has been formally committed to the proposition that all men are created equal.... As a result, there is belief that the individual controls his own destiny; that if he has appropriate abilities, and if these can be appropriately developed, his fate lies in his own hands. (p. 3)*

The observations of Watts are helpful in capturing the essence of situational or sociological perspectives on career development. Watts reminds us that perspectives on career development contain are situated in specific contexts that have political, sociological, psychological, historical, and economic determinants. More recently, Hansen (1997, 2002) has proposed a model of career development that seeks to describe some of this situational factors influencing the career development process.

Hansen's integrative life planning model (ILP) (Hansen, 1997) is unique in that Hansen contends that ILP is a new worldview for addressing career development. The "integrative" aspect of ILP relates to the emphasis on integrating the mind, body, and spirit. The "life planning" concept acknowledges, in a fashion similar to Super's (1980) life-space theory, that multiple aspects of life are interrelated. The ILP framework also draws upon psychology, sociology, economics, multiculturalism, and constructivism and takes a holistic approach by encouraging people to connect various aspects of life as they engage in the career decision making process. Rather than a life-span model, ILP focuses on adult career development and is based on the following assumptions:

1. Changes in the nature of knowledge support the addition of new ways of knowing to career development theory, research, and practice.

2. Career professionals need to help students, clients, and employees develop skills of integrative thinking- seeing connections in their lives and in their local and global communities.
3. Broader kinds of self-knowledge (beyond interests, abilities, and values) and societal knowledge (beyond occupational and educational information) are critical to an expanded view of career, including multiple roles, identities, and critical life tasks in diverse cultures.
4. Career counseling needs to focus on career professionals as change agents, helping clients to achieve more holistic lives and become advocates and agents for positive societal change through the choices and decisions they make. (Hansen, 2002)

Hansen (1997) uses these four broad assumptions to identify six career development tasks confronting adults today. The six tasks reflect Hansen's emphasis on social justice, social change, connectedness, diversity, and spirituality. For example, the first task is labeled as "finding work that needs doing in changing global contexts." Here Hansen suggests that adults consider focusing on work that will result in a more socially just world (e.g., preserving the environment, understanding and celebrating diversity, advocating for human rights, and exploring spirituality). Hansen encourages people to identify what they can do to contribute to positive change for social and environmental justice.

The second task Hansen identifies is "weaving our lives into a meaningful whole." This task emphasizes the point that few things are more personal than a career choice (Niles & Pate, 1989). Occupational choices are intertwined with other life role choices and must be considered holistically and within the greater context of one's life. These task also suggests that persons must draw upon their subjective experiences in clarifying and articulating their career choices.

Hansen's third task is an extension of the second and is labeled as "connecting family and work" and emphasizes life role integration. This task also highlights the need to examine gender-role expectations and stereotypes. ILP advocates for gender equity in life role participation. Hansen also advocates for valuing self-sufficiency and connectedness within men and women.

"Valuing pluralism and inclusivity" represents the fourth task confronting adults. Hansen notes the importance of celebrating diversity and developing multicultural competencies as critical for work and non-work activities.

Hansen's fifth task relates to "managing personal transitions and organizational change." Given the constancy of change in everyday experience, developing skills to cope effectively with transition is an essential task of adult development. Tolerating ambiguity, developing personal flexibility (Herr & Cramer, 1996), and being able to draw upon a reservoir of self-awareness and social support all help to negotiate life changes successfully.

The sixth task in ILP is that of "exploring spirituality and life purpose." Spirituality embraces purpose, meaning, connectedness, and a sense of community. People engage in spiritually-based career decision making when they examine the degree to which career options foster positive treatment of others, the environment, and themselves.

Person-Environment Interactions: The Family. During most of the twentieth century, observers from many disciplines reported on the effects of social or socioeconomic class on occupations chosen, educational goals, and on other aspects of work identity and career (Borow, 1989; Hotchkiss & Borow, 1990). Underlying those observations are the attainments of parents and the effects of different family constellations of values and information as important predictors of occupational choice and of work adjustment. Although not the only important mediator of social class or social status in children, family characteristics are conduits for their particular culture, history, and meaning systems and, as such, they represent the seedbed for differences across classes in the socialization, or vocationalization, of the young (Stewart & Healy, 1989). The research of Chusid and Cochran (1989) found that work is pervaded by the reenactment of family themes, and that the meaning of a career change can be understood as a significant development of dramas from the family of origin that were restaged in work.

Hotchkiss and Borow (1984), speaking to the major sociological work on family effects on status attainment, contend that the basic premise in such a model is that career statuses, such as education, occupation, and income are passed from generation to generation by a sequence of interpersonal processes. Parental status in particular influences the status achieved by their children indirectly through a chain of effects. Attitudes characteristic of different status levels are passed from parent to child, both immediately by parent contact with the child and less directly through the youth's contact with adults other than parents and with peers who come from similar backgrounds. This process is termed *significant-other* influence. Interpersonal relations with significant others help to shape the career plans of youth, and those plans affect career attainments (p. 139).

Family influences, including childrearing patterns and socioeconomic level, also appear to have an effect on occupational choice and on career maturity. Indeed, Levine (1976) has suggested that the influence of social and economic origins on later life is so well documented that it could almost be considered axiomatic. Some representative studies of such phenomena follow. Basow and Howe (1979) examined the influences of various models on the careers of 300 randomly chosen college seniors. They found that parents were the most influential models, and nonparent, nonteacher adults were the least influential. They also found that females were significantly more affected by female models than were males.

Hollender's (1972) studies of male high school and college students found that maternal influences on vocational interests are stronger in high school and paternal influences stronger in college years. Oliver's research (1975) indicated that a girl's father is more important than her mother in determining the degree of her career commitment as a collegiate undergraduate. Oliver concluded that antecedent family variables influence the development of motivational patterns that are associated with career and homemaking orientation in college women. Smith's findings (1980) showed that whether the mother worked was a major influence on high school girls' orientation toward the role of housewife versus paid employee. Anderson (1980) found that high school seniors used the educational achievement of their same-sexed parent as a primary factor in setting their educational goals. In general, such a process served to lower the educational goals of the girls in the sample.

Roe's theory of vocational choice, described later in this chapter, rests on the hypothesis that childrearing processes partly determine subsequent vocational choices. Medvene (1973) found that the long-term developmental effects of parental avoidance, concentration, and acceptance of their children are important to both emotional-social and educational-vocational clients who come to college counseling centers.

Available evidence suggests that family socioeconomic status is comprehensively related to career choice. Socioeconomic differences are associated with differences in information about work, work experience, and occupational stereotypes, which, in turn, affect vocational interests. Dillard's study (1976) of black youth concludes that socialization or vocationalization processes, significantly influenced by the family, rather than ability differences in reading achievement, account for career maturity differences in this sample. McKay and Miller (1982) found that elementary school children from middle and upper socioeconomic backgrounds choose white-collar and professional occupations as goals more often than children from lower socioeconomic backgrounds; that these attitudes are firmly established by the time a child is in grade three; and that there is a positive relationship between socioeconomic level and complexity of data manipulation in occupational choices.

Friesen (1986) has contended that in trying to understand the positive effects between socioeconomic status in families and the vocational attainment of children, it is necessary to comprehend both opportunity and process. In the first instance, the higher the socioeconomic status (SES) of the family, the more likely parents are to have the resources to finance educational opportunities that lead to higher-status occupations. With regard to process, there are other matters involved. For example, different socialization patterns exist among SES groups. As illustrative, the research of Kohn (1977) has shown that middle-class parents tend to value self-direction in their children, and lower SES parents tend to value conformity. These findings also suggest that the values at the job may be transmitted to the home, which, in turn, are translated into childrearing practices. Schulenberg, Vondracek, and Crouter (1984) contend that the childrearing practices employed by parents with their sons as compared to their daughters lead to differences in their vocational development. Block (1983) and Hoffman (1977) have also reported studies that indicate that parents tend to reinforce certain behaviors in boys that they do not reinforce in girls. In such research, it tends to be found that parents expect their sons, more frequently than their daughters, to be independent, self-reliant, highly educated, hard-working, ambitious, career-oriented, intelligent, and strong-willed. In contrast, the daughters are expected to be kind, unselfish, attractive, loving, well-mannered, have a good marriage, and be a good parent.

In addition to the important elements of SES that families pass on to children, from a contextual standpoint they are also locations in which children learn about and meet or not meet their needs for relationships and connectedness. Blustein (1994) has synthesized much of the pertinent literature in this area. For example, he has suggested that how families provide relational models in early and later child-parent relationships has much to do with the growth of identity exploration and commitment, how adolescents separate and individuate from their families, and the adaptive degree of such individuation. These processes in a family system facilitate or impede career development; both connectedness to a secure base, and autonomy from the family are important ingredients in the career decision-making process. With regard to such processes, Blustein notes that, "for example, the novel and complex activities of career exploration are likely to be more comfortable for a person if one is able to experience support, nurturance, and instrumental assistance from family members and friends." Also of importance, according to him, is the notion of mirroring, which may be exemplified by parents encouraging their children to demonstrate newly developed computer skills and then responding with sincere interest in and admiration of their children's emerging talents. Clearly, the research and the analysis of pertinent literature suggests the extremely important role of the family as a mediator of children's ego identity and in creating the psychological environment within which their career development unfolds.

In applying family systems theory to the effects of families in the decision-making process, research by Kinnier, Brigman, and Noble (1990) indicates that familial dynamics and the process of career decision making are intertwined. Indeed, family enmeshment, in which family members are undifferentiated from or overly dependent on each other, was found to be related to difficulty in making decisions about their careers, and to career indecision. In a somewhat different approach using sophisticated sociometric processes, Rockwell's (1987) research has demonstrated that occupational preference is socially constructed and is highly influenced by the career decision maker's expectations of approval from significant others for making certain occupational choices.

Given the rapid growth of the application of systems theory to the understanding of and therapy with families in psychology, several perspectives seem to be related to this context. As is reflected in the situational and sociological views reported in this section, psychology in general has become aware that understanding of the individual requires an understanding of his or her social setting, a primary aspect of which is the family. In addition, it has become clear that to understand the family, a counselor needs to understand its position in the larger social setting and in relation to other social institutions. As reported elsewhere in this book, work choice and adjustment are not simply individual matters. They are also affected by and affect family harmony, resources, emotional conditions, and other matters. Hoffman (1986, pp. 179–188) has identified some of the processes by which research shows that work affects families:

1. Work provides material resources that affect the families' economic well-being.
2. Being employed or not employed and the particular occupation confer status that affects the family's status in the community, the worker's status in the family, and the worker's self-concept.
3. Behaviors at work are repeated in the home.
4. Work experiences affect ideas about what qualities are important in adulthood and thus influence childrearing patterns.
5. Work affects the worker's personality and intellectual functioning and thus influences his or her behavior in the family. The child is affected through parental childrearing practices and identification with the parent.
6. Authority structures at work are repeated in the family and are reflected in childrearing patterns.
7. Moods generated at work are carried over to the family.
8. The family may be used as a complementary source of need satisfaction: the worker may seek to satisfy in the family needs unsatisfied or engendered at work.

9. Work takes time, energy, and involvement from the family. In addition to the loss itself, this can lead to stress from overload or guilt.
10. Work can be a source of stress either because of the above processes or because it is intrinsically dangerous or insecure.

Although each of these processes deserves to be discussed at length, the simple statement of them suggests the types of situational effects on families and on children that different combinations of these processes might produce. As the reader examines other theoretical approaches in this chapter, certain of these processes will be reflected in many of them. In a collective sense, the processes identified here show both the power and the complexity of the family in inducting children into work roles and providing a source of security and satisfaction for the working parent whose needs at work may not be fully satisfied.

Whether from a contextual, sociological, or a situational perspective, the family is a facilitator of experiences that expand or limit family members' knowledge of occupations, a reinforcement system of contingencies and expectations that subtly or directly shape work behavior, and a purveyor of socioeconomic status. The home is itself a workplace and a center in which social and occupational roles are modeled either by the members of the nuclear family or the network of friends and acquaintances with which this unit interacts (Herr & Best, 1984).

Accident Theories. In addition to the family as a major instrument of contextual, sociological, or situational effects on career development, some authors have advanced an accident theory of occupational choice or career development. Some observers suggest that the term accident theory refers to the "accident of birth." In broader terms, the perspectives usually encompassed by accident theory gives primary visibility to the role of chance or unforeseen events as major determinants of personal opportunities for choice. Such perspectives recognize that most of the major career theories attempt to describe normative and, in that sense, predictable patterns of behavior that are typical and frequent in different populations. But accident or chance theories are also acknowledgments that career development occurs in social and economic contexts in which unforeseen events may deflect or disrupt patterns of choice and development that were rationally planned. These views suggest that chance encounters, influential people, fortuitous or other events are likely to occur and shape or change individual career behavior.

Chance Encounters. In one exposition of such a view, Bandura's (1982a) central theses is that chance encounters play a prominent role in shaping the course of human lives. For his purposes, "A chance encounter is defined as an unintended meeting of persons unfamiliar to each other.... Human encounters involve degrees of fortuitiveness. People often intentionally seek certain types of experiences, but the persons who thereby enter their lives are determined by a large element of chance" (p. 748). Bandura also describes how fortuitous symbolic encounters mediated through another's actions profoundly affect life paths. Symbolic encounters might include hearing a particular lecture, reading a particular book, unexpectedly witnessing a particular event on television or in reality, which has such an effect on an individual that it stimulates the pursuit of a new life path. According to Bandura, some chance encounters "touch people only lightly, others leave more lasting effects, and still others branch people into new trajectories of life" (p. 749). He suggests that psychology is not able to predict fortuitous occurrences, nor does it have much to say about their occurrence except that personal bents and social structures and affiliations make some types of encounters more probable than others. Here we find the particular importance of social class, family background, geographic residence, and similar contexts increasing the likelihood of some encounters and decreasing the likelihood of others.

Bandura further suggests that if psychology cannot predict the likelihood of chance encounters, it can provide the basis for predicting the nature, scope, and strength of the effects they are likely to have on human lives. He suggests that "neither personal proclivities nor situational imperatives" operate as independent shapers of the course of lives. Chance encounters affect life paths through the reciprocal influence of personal and social factors that are likely to determine the effect of chance encounters. Table 4.2 shows these factors in paraphrased chart form from his narrative of the process.

Bandura's work to date rests primarily on observation and biographical data. It is an attempt to de-

TABLE 4.2 A Synthesis of Bandura's Perspectives on Factors Influencing Chance Encounters

PERSONAL DETERMINANTS OF THE EFFECT OF CHANCE ENCOUNTERS	SOCIAL DETERMINANTS OF THE EFFECT OF CHANCE ENCOUNTERS
Entry Skills Interest, skills, personal knowledge likely to gain acceptance or sustain contact with another path	***Milieu Rewards*** The types of rewards and sanctions an individual or group provides if a chance encounter alters a life
Emotional Ties Interpersonal attractiveness tending to sustain chance encounters so that certain social determinants operate	***Symbolic Environment and Information*** Images of reality provided by other than direct experience; different individuals or groups furnish different symbolic environments
Values and Personal Standards Unintended influences more likely to be important if persons involved share similar standards and value systems	***Milieu Reach and Closedness*** Chance encounters with a relatively closed milieu—e.g., cults, communal groups—have the greatest potential for abruptly reordering life paths
	Psychological Closedness Belief systems provide structure, directions, and purpose in life. Once persons, through a chance encounter, get caught up in the belief system of a particular group, it can exert selective influence on the course of development and erect a psychological closedness to outside influence. Beliefs channel social interactions in ways that create their own validating realities.

velop into an effective conceptual framework the psychological processes that are subsumed or activated by what is more popularly called chance or accident. In this sense, he makes the following point: "Fortuitous influences may be unforeseen, but having occurred, they enter as evident factors in causal chains in the same way as prearranged ones do" (p. 749). Bandura has not attempted to speculate about the number of people whose career development is a function of chance encounters or how such a view applies across occupational groups. There are other findings, however, that bear on such matters.

Preparation and Planning. Hart, Rayner, and Christensen (1971) studied the degree of preparation, planning, and chance in occupational entry among 60 men representing professional, skilled, and semiskilled occupational levels. They found that most men at the professional level entered their occupation primarily through planning and preparation. At the skilled level, some men entered their occupations through planning, whereas many others were primarily influenced by chance events. Those who entered occupations at the semiskilled level were primarily influenced by chance events. Partially based on the earlier work of Hart and colleagues, Salomone and Slaney (1981) studied the perceived influence of chance and contingency factors on the career choices of 447 female and 470 male nonprofessional workers. In some contrast to the findings of Hart and colleagues, Salomone and Slaney found that chance factors were much less important than were personal qualities in influencing vocational decisions. The authors conclude as follows:

Perhaps the "chance theory" was seen as a reasonable alternative by sociologists writing in the 1940s and 1950s but clearly, the workers of the 1970s—including nonprofessional skilled and unskilled workers—appear to assess their personal inclinations (interests and needs), their skills and abilities, and their personal and family responsibilities before making vocational choices. In large measure, they perceive themselves as using rational processes to arrive at their occupational decisions (p. 34).

Not agreeing fully with the findings of either Hart or Salomone and Slaney, Scott and Hatalla (1990) examined the perceptions of women college graduates regarding the influence of selected chance and contingency factors upon their career patterns twenty-five years after graduation. Their findings indicated that a significant proportion of the sample perceived eight contingency factors as influential in their career pattern and that the chance factor "unexpected personal events" was also perceived as influential by a significant proportion of the women in the sample. Although contingency factors were more likely to be perceived as having influence on career patterns than chance factors, "unexpected personal events" was a consistent and influential factor across the various career patterns of women observed in the study. Consistent with other studies, the contingency factors perceived as most influential by the highest percentage of respondents were awareness of skills and abilities, perception of interests, educational level, and awareness of intelligence. These were primarily internal determinants of identity and in comparison with chance factors are predictable and available to the person's awareness as they engage in career planning and choice.

Cabral and Salomone (1990) have synthesized the literature on choice factors, particularly as they relate to adult career development. They offer a number of concepts that extend the role of chance in career behavior, individual ability to control or cope with chance, and the relationship between chance and personality. With regard to the control of chance, they contend that there are two conclusions to be drawn. One is that "chance operates on a continuum from events or encounters that are totally unforeseen (a natural disaster, the sudden death of a spouse, or a conversation on an airplane, for instance), to those that are at least in part under the control of the individual (overhearing information concerning a job opportunity during a meeting of a professional organization, or deciding to enter graduate school in a newly-emerging field after learning of that field through one's mentor)" (p. 10). A second conclusion is that persons respond differently to unforeseen encounters or events.

Cabral and Salomone explain the latter in terms of two possible personality dimensions: *locus of control* and *self-concept*. They argue that persons "with external locuses of control, as well as those who offer empowering-deterministic explanations for the behavior, will be more susceptible to the influence of chance events or encounters. More importantly, these individuals will be less likely to be proactive when chance events or encounters do occur" (p. 11). In contrast, it would be assumed that persons with an internal locus of control would be somewhat less affected by unforeseen events and encounters, would attempt to control of diminish the uncertainty they represent, or would instead embrace these encounters and events as opportunities to seize and act on. How individuals function in terms of chance, according to Cabral and Salomone, is also a function of the individual's self-concept or self-conceptions, which act as filters through which the individual perceives events and people in his or her contexts, guides and edits information received in memory, serves as cognitive schemata that aid in the definition of people and events, and provides a basis for choice and evaluation. Individuals are likely to behave in ways that reinforce and implement their self-concept.

Cabral and Salomone (1990, p. 14) conclude their discussion of chance and its effects on career decisions with the following key points:

- Chance, defined as foreseen and uncontrollable events and encounters, is inevitable and plays an important role in shaping career decisions.
- Career decisions in the lives of individuals are not purely rational, nor are they in most instances based purely on chance. Some combination of planfulness and happenstance seems to drive the decisions and development of an individual's career.
- The critical dimensions of chance encounters or events are their timing in relation to the individual's development and the contexts within which they occur.
- "Chance" actually encompasses a range of events or encounters that vary greatly in the degree of control that the individual has over them. It is possible to affect the potential for certain types of chance events or encounters by entering or avoiding different contexts.
- Individuals are most vulnerable to the effects of chance during life transitions, particularly those that occur early in the career and those that have not been anticipated.

Mitchell, Levin, and Krumboltz (2000) contend that the potential for benefiting from chance depends on two principles: (1) exploration generates opportunities to experience unplanned events which may potentially increase the quality of one's life, and (2) timely and skilled action empowers people to capitalize on the opportunities presented by the unplanned events. Thus, career counselors must seek to motivate their clients to participate in exploratory behavior and assist their clients in recognizing and acting on the opportunities presented to them (Krumboltz & Henderson, 2002). Five skills, in particular, are useful in helping clients take advantage of serendipitous events: (1) curiosity, (2) persistence, (3) flexibility, (4) optimism, and (5) risk taking (Mitchell, Levin, & Krumboltz, 2000).

Culture and Social Class Boundaries. The factors bearing on choice or development are not restricted to chance or intervening variables. The breadth of the individual's culture or social class boundaries has much to do with the choices that can be considered, made, and implemented. No more vivid an example exists than that of people raised in poverty. Poor people are not just rich people without money. Their life space, possibility structures, level and types of reinforcement, models, and social resources all differ as a function of their social status. Therefore, an important factor in the career development of an individual is the effect of the culture and society on the goals one is conditioned to value. Within this context are found such elements as family income levels, social expectations, levels of social mobility, and psychological support for patterns of educational and occupational motivation.

Lipsett (1962) argued over forty years ago that counselors must understand the implications of the following social factors for a particular individual as they interact with career development:

1. Social class membership—for example, occupation and income of parents, education of parents, place and type of residence, ethnic background
2. Home influences—for example, parental goals for the individual, influence of siblings, family values, and counselee's acceptance of them
3. School—for example, scholastic achievement, relationships with peers and faculty, values of the school
4. Community—the "thing to do in the community," group goals and values, special opportunities or influences
5. Pressure groups—the degree to which an individual or his or her parents have come under any particular influence that leads him or her to value one occupation over another
6. Role perception—the individual's perception of self as a leader, follower, isolate, and so forth; the degree to which one's perception of self is in accord with the way others perceive one

The important concern here is that the factors identified by Lipsett operate directly or indirectly in every individual's life. The degree to which they operate as determinants or constraints in development and choice, however, can be assessed only in the individual case. Counselors must be alert to how much clients have accepted the attitudes and values held by the various aspects of their environments, have personally tested such perspectives, and whether those perspectives facilitate or restrain choice-making.

Feck (1971), in a major study of urban disadvantaged youth, identified 15 basic needs, including those that are career-related. These needs are:

1. Security and stability in one's environment
2. Successful education experience
3. Recognition for achievement
4. Love and respect
5. Legal sources of finance
6. Financial management
7. Proper housing
8. Good health
9. Development of basic communication skills
10. Salable work skills
11. An appreciation of the meaning and importance of work
12. Successfully employed or adult peer-group models
13. Positive self-concept
14. Job opportunities and qualifications
15. Socially acceptable attitudes and behaviors

In a land that prides itself on its freedom and opportunity, such needs should be comprehensively met for all citizens. But, again, when context, situational, and sociological perspectives are invoked, it becomes evident that social class factors create barriers or complications that thwart such need fulfillment. For example, Kessler and Clary (1978), in their research on social class, found that lower social classes experienced more undesirable life events that require extensive readjustment than did middle or upper classes. Thoits (1982) also found that disadvantaged persons are more vulnerable and reactive than their more advantaged contemporaries to life stressors, particularly to the impacts of health-related events. To meet the needs specified by Feck, the disadvantaged need an open system of opportunity (Griffith, 1980), information on world of work and available resources (Williams & Whitney, 1978), relevant and appropriate education, training, and counseling, (Smith, 1980) and, perhaps, as much as anything else, a strong sense of control. Without a strong sense of personal control, a feeling that one's personal action makes a difference, life comes to be viewed as a big crap game in which the individual simply does not count.

A major study of youth unemployment has clearly shown that social class and racial differences exist in the amount of unemployment experienced by various subpopulations of youth (Adams & Mangum, 1978). Indeed, such social class differences are also apparent in the use of resources and other types of mechanisms to aid in the transition from school to work. Similarly findings have been reported in another major work on the youth labor market (Osterman, 1980).

Trusty, Ng, and Plata (2000) investigated the relationship among gender, socioeconomic status, and race-ethnicity using a sample from the National Education Longitudinal Study of 1988. Trusty and his colleagues found a relationship between Holland types and social class. For example, the higher the SES of male study participants, the less likely they were to select college majors that could be classified as being primarily Realistic. For women in their study, increases in SES were significantly related to decreases in selecting college majors in the Conventional and Realistic categories.

Perhaps the most important point gleaned from sociological studies of career development and choice is that although the preferences of individuals across various social or economic classes are essentially the same, however, those who experience less opportunity have lower expectancies of being able to achieve their preferences than people who are economically advantaged. In other words, what they would prefer to do is not what they expect to be able to do. Thus, it is likely that occupational preferences will reflect the family's occupational level and, therefore, the child's socioeconomic milieu.

Some sociologists even argue that developmental notions of career guidance based on individual choice are unrealistic. Roberts (1977), a British sociologist, is one of the foremost proponents of such a view. In essence, he does not believe that most people choose, in any precise sense of that term. Instead, they are chosen or act as opportunities arise rather than in some longitudinal preplanned way. He summarizes the point as follows: "The notion that young people possess freedom of choice and that they can select careers for themselves upon the basis of their own preferences is pure myth. It is not choice but opportunity that governs the manner in which many young people make their entry into employment" (p. 145). As factors affecting such a circumstance, he identifies the mechanisms of educational selection, the patterns of recruitment into different types of employment, home background, and other social structure factors.

Whether or not one is as adamant about social structure factors in career development as is Roberts, situational approaches to career development suggest that the socioeconomic structure of a society operates as a percolator and a filter of information. In essence, one's position among the social strata making up a nation has much to do with the kind of information one gets, the alternative actions one can take, and the kind of encouragement one receives. Persons are often selectively rewarded or reinforced in certain kinds of behavior depending on the group to which they belong. Women's Liberation, Black and Brown Pride Movements, Gay Liberation, and the Grey Panthers are examples of reactions against the constraints in opportunity imposed because of the stereotyped images held by various segments of society.

In a pluralistic culture such as the United States, persons of different ethnic or racial backgrounds are likely to differ in the types of role models available to them. Perhaps more important, different cultures allocate values differently and these values have consequences for behavior. Unfortunately, these value differences are rarely responded to by school or by helping professionals (Harrington, 1975).

Although the mass media, and television in particular, may convey general achievement images that all of us are encouraged to emulate, information about how such images are accomplished or planned and prepared for is not as accessible. Thus, counselors and counseling psychologists have a major responsibility to reduce the correlations between membership in certain groups and success. Individual competence and desire, not group membership, must become the criterion by which relevant information and encouragement are provided to people regardless of their sex, race, or other situational determinants. Having a pluralistic population does not mean having a caste system in which some persons remain at low status levels, because they are denied information or opportunity to seek other levels in the society.

Psychological Approaches

Psychological approaches to career development stress intrinsic individual motivation more than the other approaches discussed thus far do. Tying the psychoanalytic, need, and self-emphases into a single body of psychological approaches, Crites (1969, p. 91) observes, "each of them proposes that the most significant factor in the making of a vocational choice is a motivational or process variable. For this reason, they contrast sharply with the trait-and-factor theories, which emphasize the observable characteristics of the individual and not the inferred states or conditions which prompt him to behave as he does."

The major assumption of the psychological approaches is that because of differences in personality structure, individuals develop certain needs or drives and seek satisfaction of these needs or drives through occupational choices. Thus, it is contended that different occupational or, indeed, curricular areas are populated by persons of different need types or personality types. These approaches rather consistently develop a classification of personality or need, and then relate it to gratifications available in different environments—occupational or educational (Silver & Spilerman, 1990). In one sense, the distinguishing characteristics of these approaches are the disciplinary lenses through which career-related phenomena are viewed and the emphasis on the antecedents of vocational behavior as a function of some form of self-classification, conscious or unconscious.

Bordin's Psychodynamic View. At the core of any psychodynamic view of work or other aspects of life is the "depth psychology" of Sigmund Freud. As is well known, Freud devoted much of his life to creating a theory of personality encompassing both its conscious and unconscious aspects and the notions of how childhood personality development profoundly influences adult life, including one's work life. However, the most comprehensive application of classic psychoanalytic concepts to occupational choice or career development has been made by Bordin, Nachmann, and Segal (1963), called the Michigan Group. Although preceded by Brill's (1948) psychoanalytic concepts of guilt and exhibitionism and of the pleasure and reality principles to explain the choice attraction of various vocations, Bordin, Nachmann, and Segal have extended the emphasis on the gratification that various types of work offer to meet certain individual impulses. Much like Brill, they consider "work as sublimation—but in the broad sense of all activity other than direct gratification, rather than in the narrower sense of pregenital impulses turned into artistic activities" (p. 110). For the more commonly described traits such as interests and abilities, they substitute individual modes of impulse gratification, the status of one's psychosexual development, and levels of anxiety. More specifically, they maintain that connections exist between the early development of coping mechanisms and the later development of more complex behaviors. They assert that adult occupations are sought for their instinctual gratifications, as need for these is developed in early childhood, and that in terms of personality formation and the needs inherent in the individual structure, the first six years of life are crucial.

From analyses of such roles as accountants, creative writers, lawyers, dentists, social workers, clinical psychologists, plumbers, physicists, and engineers, Bordin and colleagues conceived an elaborate matrix of the basic need-gratifying activities found in different occupations. They divided psychic and body-part classifications into those activities important to psychoanalytic thinking. They then related these to the potential gratification, the objects from which gratification is available, and the sexual mode of gratification that exists in each of the occupations indicated. According to Bordin and associates, the psychic dimensions by which occupations can be described include the ability of the occupation to satisfy anal, exhibiting, exploratory, flowing-quenching, genital, manipulative, nurturing, oral, aggressive, rhythmic, and sensual needs. The means by which occupations potentially respond to these needs are their instrumental modes (such as tools, techniques, or behaviors used) and the objects dealt with (such as needs of clients, pipes and plumbing fixtures, and money).

To illustrate the Bordin, Nachmann, and Segal position, it might be useful to consider the antecedents relating to a person whose occupation is a lathe operator. The hypotheses would be that such a person's primary instinctual gratifications during the first six years of life came from oral aggressive activities—biting, chewing, and devouring. The theory would hold that these activities are converted from teeth to the fingers to knives, saws, and drills and, possibly, to biting and cutting words and ideas. In the case of the lathe operator, the assumption would be that the gratification found in oral aggressiveness tends to become fixation manifested in personality, and now finds its adult counterparts in such activities as the use of tools for cutting, grinding, and drilling.

Bordin (1984, 1990) reformulated the theory as it was originally conceived with Nachmann and Segal. As he suggested in 1989, "the present point of view retains much of the earlier emphasis on the fate and transformation of basic motivations (libidinal and others) but gives prominence to ego development... including, of course, ego identity" (p. 96). In particular, he defines seven propositions that emanate from the basic proposition that "the participation of personality in work and career is rooted in the role of play in human life" (p. 96). "The spirit of play is caught in the term spontaneity, which is used to refer to the elements of self-expression and self-realization in our responses to situations. Spontaneity is a major key to differentiating work from play. What marks the essence of play is its intrinsically satisfying nature" (p. 97). He then proposes several propositions that fuse his concern with spontaneity and play, his earlier psychoanalytic perspectives, and his current linkage to ego development and ego identity. His propositions as they appear in his 1990 formulation include the following:

1. This sense of wholeness is sought by all persons, preferably in all aspects of life, including work (p. 105).
2. The degree of fusion of work and play is a function of an individual's developmental history regarding compulsion and effort (p. 108).
3. A person's life can be seen as a string of career decisions reflecting the individual's groping for an ideal fit between self and work (p. 109).
4. The most useful system of mapping occupations for intrinsic motives will be one that captures lifestyles or character styles and stimulates or is receptive to developmental conceptions (p. 115).
5. The roots of the personal aspects of career development are to be found throughout the early development of the individual, sometimes in the earliest years (p. 116).
6. Each individual seeks to build a personal identity that incorporates aspects of father and mother, yet retains elements unique to oneself (p. 116).
7. One source of perplexity and paralysis at career decision points will be found in doubts and dissatisfactions with current resolutions of self (p. 117).

In extending these propositions that flow from Bordin's unique view of the interaction of work and play, or its equivalents found in spontaneity, effort, and compulsion, and in the distinctions between intrinsic and extrinsic rewards, satisfactions, and motives, it has been suggested that "it is natural for individuals to seek a maximum fusion of work and play, the fusion of inner and outer pressures, and the maximum coincidence of inner and outer motives" (Bordin, 1994, p. 55). In converting such possibilities into occupational choice, there are developmental experiences, external pressures, and other events that inhibit self-expression in choice, that argue for responding to and accepting external pressures to implement specific career choices, the compulsions to behave within certain boundaries established by such phenomena as institutional racism and sexual stereotyping. In this context, Bordin has observed that, "We must be sensitive, whether in research or in counseling, to the inhibitions and freedoms the person feels in self-expression, how much this person feels able to expend great effort, and how much he or she feels vulnerable or dependent on outside pressures, whether they be personal or impersonal" (Bordin, 1994, p. 56).

Bordin further contends that "the degree to which a person succeeds in fusing work and play is an important determinant of the degree to which career choice is determined and expressed by personality" (p. 56). Thus, he suggests that we need a new kind of occupational analysis, one that helps individuals to examine job performance as a way of life, one that is geared to personality, lifestyles, and intrinsic motives. To advance his view of occupations as containing opportunities for various mixes of satisfactions, more or less malleable fitting either diverse or more limited mixes of intrinsic motives, Bordin has suggested identifying sets of intrinsic motives that can be found somewhere in the range of productive work and include the following as major sets of motives: precision, nurturance, curiosity, power, aesthetic expression, and ethics and concern with right or wrong. Such a view represents more than a statistical match of person-job fit dimensions; it is seen by Bordin as a potential taxonomy of intrinsic motivations to appreciate more fully and implement how career choice is determined and expressed by personality.

Adler's View. Although Freud's work has been acknowledged repeatedly as a dominant conception of psychology, and particularly of personality theory, future historical writings may give a larger share of that prominence to Alfred Adler. Many current emphases in holistic psychology, the importance of the self-concept as a stimulus to behavior, the individual's ability to hold goals consciously and to plan in accordance with them, the transactional nature of individual personality as a product of social forces, and many concepts of normality have their roots in Adlerian perspectives. Certainly the concepts of Bordin articulated previously are not antithetical to those of Adler.

In strong opposition to Freud's major premise that human behavior is essentially determined by inborn instincts, Adler believed that such behavior was motivated by social urges. He fashioned a humanistic theory of personality that was the antithesis of Freud's view (Hall & Lindzey, 1957).

Adler stressed a subjective, creative system of behavior through which persons search for experiences that aid in fulfilling their unique style of life. The self is an important cause of behavior and, indeed, the focus of individual uniqueness. The individual is conscious of inferiorities and of goals held. According to Adler (1927), the major goal of individuals is to overcome inferiority and to obtain superiority within some notions of social interest. There are innumerable ways to strive for superiority, and how this is accomplished fits into a unique style of life. In a sense, persons perceive, learn, and retain what fits their style of life and ignore everything else. In doing so, however, Adler believes that humankind possesses a creative self by which personality is built out of the combined material of heredity and experience. The creative self gives meaning to life and formulates both goals and the means to goals (Adler, 1935).

Although Adler did not make a work a central concern of his theory, there is no question that his concepts of personality describe work motivation and the work setting as a place to implement social interest, unique lifestyles, and superiority.

Adler's theory forms the structural framework for Savickas's career style assessment model. Note that many of Adler's concepts will appear in different guises in more recent theories described in this chapter.

Jung's View. A contemporary of Adler and Freud, and a competitor of Adler for being considered one of the world's great thinkers in psychology overshadowed only by Freud's impact on psychology's view of human behavior, Carl Gustav Jung developed what came to be termed *analytical psychology* (Jung, 1916). Both his theory of psychoanalysis and his method of psychotherapy, analytical psychology, rejected Freud's emphases on sexual gratification, the repetition of instinctual themes, and the influences on a form of childhood personality development as predictive of adult life. Jung wedded "causality" (the conditioning of one's individual and racial history) with teleology (one's aims and aspirations) to explain behavior. Thus, Jung argued that both "the past as actuality and the future as potentiality guide one's present beha-vior.... For Jung, there is constant and often creative development, the search for wholeness and completion, and the yearning for rebirth" (Hall & Lindzey, 1957, p. 78). Jung viewed personality as a complex of interacting systems, and he introduced a rich vocabulary of terms and ideas to the psychological literature to provide explanations for the concepts he advanced. Many of the notions now prominent in present-day psychology and in theories of career development originated with Jung's voluminous writings. In some cases he borrowed terms from other psychologists; in other cases he borrowed terms and concepts from mythology, religion, archeology, and other disciplines; in other instances, he created his own terms. Among the systems about which he was concerned were the ego, the personal unconscious and its complexes, the collective unconscious and its archetypes, the persona, the anima and animus, and the shadow. He talked of psychic energy and psychic values. Although few contemporary writers acknowledge it, Jung introduced the term *self-actualization* as the goal of individual development, the ultimate end to which humankind strives, the progression of development from a global to a differentiated to an integrated state.

With respect to the principal connection of Jung's theory to contemporary manifestations in career counseling and career assessment, the conceptual origins on which the Myers-Briggs Type Indicator rests would probably be the most recognizable to readers. Jung distinguished two major attitudes or orientations of personality, the attitude of extraversion and the attitude of introversion. An extraverted attitude orients the person toward the external, objective world; an introverted attitude orients the person toward the inner, subjective world (Jung, 1933). In addition, Jung described four fundamental psychological functions: thinking, feeling, sensing, and intuiting. It is these functions in combination with extraverted-introverted orientations that create the base for the Myers-Briggs assessment of types and its attempt to measure the basic differences in the way individuals prefer to use their perception and judgment. The Myers-Briggs Type Indicator measures 16 MBTI types, which are reflected in different combinations of the four separate indices that emanate from Jung's work: attitudes related to Extraversion (E) or Introversion (I); processes of perception assessed by Sensing (S) or Intuition (N); processes of judgment as reflected in Thinking (T) and Feeling (F); and the style of dealing with the outside world as shown by Judgment (J) or Perception (P) (Myers & McCaulley, 1985, p. 3). Thus, the type that is identified from the four basic preferences reflects the dominant process by which people are likely to habitually direct their transactions with their environment, education, work, and social interactions.

The psychoanalytic view of occupational choice or career development has less research to validate its assumptions than most of the other emphases discussed in this chapter. In addition, criticisms have been leveled at the theory's inadequacy to consider the effects of external forces on choice, such as economic, cultural, or geographic limitations, although such criticisms are not often focused on such persons as Adler or Jung. Finally, the psychoanalytic position of Freud, in particular, suggests that career guidance or career education could do little after early childhood to alter individual career development. The role of the counselor would be limited to helping persons identify the pertinent mode of gratification they seek and the occupations that might satisfy those needs. Bordin's view would not accept such a perspective but would argue for increased attention in contemporary career counseling approaches to career choice, as an expression of personality, occupations as a way of life, and techniques that help clients deal with conflicts in career between intrinsic and extrinsic motivation, spontaneity, and compulsion.

Roe's Approach. The theoretical and research efforts of Anne Roe (1956) also apply personality theory to career development. Roe marries two major personality theories to vocational behavior: (1) the earlier work of Gardner Murphy (1947)—in particular, Murphy's canalization of psychic energy and emphasis on the relationship between early childhood experiences and later vocational choices; and (2) Maslow's (1954) theory of prepotent needs. Roe also accents genetic factors as these interact with need hierarchies to determine vocational behavior and choice. "In other words, given 'equal' endowments genetically, differences in occupational achievement between two individuals may be inferred to be the result of motivational differences which theoretically are likely to be the outcomes of different childhood experiences" (Osipow, 1968, p. 18).

In a retrospective view of her work (Roe & Lunneborg, 1984), Roe has stated:

> *My theoretical concerns have focused on two apparently disparate areas and their subsequent integration—personality theory and occupational classification. My purpose has been to view the whole range of occupations in terms of their relationship to individual differences in backgrounds, physical and psychological variables, and experiences. (p. 31)*

Roe's (1953) early conceptualizations derived from her studies of different types of scientists. From such research she concluded that some personality differences evolve from childrearing practices (such as rejecting, overprotecting, democratic) and that these differences are related to the kinds of interaction that such persons ultimately establish with other people—

toward or not toward them—and with things. Affected strongly by the psychoanalytic notion that the first few years of life encompass the primary experiences shaping adult behavior, she identified the substance of three primary childrearing practices.

She describes the first as *emotional concentration on the child,* which includes the opposite extremes of overprotective and overdemanding behavior. Children who have been intensely conditioned to receive need gratification from their parents if certain contingencies were met might choose occupations that would give them a high level of feedback and reward—such as the performing arts. The second childrearing pattern is that of *avoidance of the child.* The continuum of parental responses in this pattern might include emotional rejection of the child as well as physical neglect. The hypotheses here would be that the child would look to nonpersons and things, and would have limited contacts with others as bases for gratification. In such instances, scientific and mechanical interests are likely to develop as ways of finding gratification without reliance on others. The third childrearing practice is *acceptance of the child,* which might involve either casual acceptance or loving acceptance, incorporating the child into the family unit as one among equals in a democratic process. In this third childrearing practice, it is assumed that a child's independence is encouraged, and that he or she may seek occupations that balance personal and nonpersonal interests without the need for isolation from others or intense approval from them.

Roe suggests then that there are relationships between the psychic energy, genetic propensities, and childhood experiences that shape individual styles of behavior, and that the impulse to acquire opportunities to express these individual styles is inherent in the choices made and the ensuing career behavior. Thus, the strength of a particular need, the delay between the arousal of the need and its satisfaction, and the value that the satisfaction has in the individual's environment are the conditions—shaped by early childhood experiences—that influence career development. These inputs to Roe's thinking can be summarized into two perspectives on the origin of vocational interests, that (1) career directions are first determined by "the patterning of early satisfactions and frustrations," and that (2) "the modes and degrees of need satisfaction will determine which needs will become the strongest motivations" (Roe & Siegelman, 1964, p. 5). Roe's 1984 summary of her research findings shows that there is no direct link between parent-child relations and occupational choice. She concludes, however, that this finding does not invalidate her propositions concerning needs and interests as determinants of motivation and accomplishment (Roe & Lunneborg, 1984).

As Roe's work was taking shape after World War II, so was that of Maslow, whose theory has probably been the most influential yet developed in shaping the concepts of needs. To elaborate her need constructs, Roe applied Maslow's theory of prepotent needs to career behavior. Maslow (1954) arranged human needs in a hierarchy in which he conceived the emergence of higher-order needs as contingent on the relative satisfaction of lower-order, more primitive needs. The needs in ascending order are as follows:

1. Physiological needs
2. Safety needs
3. Needs for belongingness and love
4. Needs for importance, self-esteem, respect, and independence
5. Need for information
6. Need for understanding
7. Need for beauty
8. Need for self-actualization

One or two simple illustrations of the meaning of Maslow's hierarchy will be useful here. For example, one might cite the instance of a child doing poorly in school who comes from a home where food is scarce and the parents are considering divorce. A teacher might chastise the child for not doing his or her homework and not caring about school. The more accurate view is that the child is preoccupied with satisfying physiological and safety needs. Until these can be relatively taken for granted, the child is unlikely to be motivated by needs for information or understanding. A similar translation can be made in seeking certain kinds of work. The person who has lived through a Depression where work is limited and large numbers of people have no money or little food is likely to view the security aspects of work more positively than the person who has not been exposed to such poverty and is freer to seek high-order needs in work.

Roe's concerns with specific childrearing practices, the manner in which the parents interact with the child, the resulting need structure, and the ensuing orientation toward or away from persons were measured by the Parent-Child Relations Questionnaire, constructed by Roe and Siegelman in 1963 (Roe & Lunneborg, 1990). The results were translated into a useful field and level classification of occupations, including the following (Roe, 1956, pp. 143–152; Roe & Lunneborg, 1984, 1990):

Fields	Levels
I. Service	1. Professional and managerial (1)
II. Business contact	2. Professional and managerial (2)
III. Organizations	3. Semiprofessional, small business
IV. Technology	4. Skilled
V. Outdoor	5. Semiskilled
VI. Science	6. Unskilled
VII. General culture	
VIII. Arts and entertainment	

This conceptualization of the occupational structure has been variously represented as a two-dimensional matrix, a circular array, and as a cone. The original notion was that this was a two-dimensional classification of fields or job families that were primarily defined by their content expressed by a things-versus-person orientation. The second dimension, levels, deals with the work complexity or responsibility involved in a particular job. The choice of fields is considered to be a function of interests; the level attained depends on genetic factors manifested in intelligence as well as the style of environmental manipulation.

This field and level classification, which also has been described as a circular array (Roe, 1956) of occupational groups contiguous in their emphasis on people (groups I, II, III, VII, VIII) or on things (groups IV, V, VI), has been supported by Perrone (1964). He found that high school boys with similar scores on cognitive measures tend to prefer similar occupational groups as defined by Roe's eight groups. Indeed, when job changes are examined, they are found to be nonrandom. That is, people typically move from one job in one group to another in the same group as defined by Roe's classification scheme. They do not typically move to a group in which the orientation or activity is in direct opposition to the initial group (Hutchinson & Roe, 1968). The research of Knapp and Knapp (1977), among others, has also supported such findings.

While studies of Roe's model of the occupational classification structure have been supportive, although less so for women than for men, as Roe suggested herself, the research on the effects of parent-child relations and occupational choice has not shown direct links or has yielded negative results, even though there exists some evidence that adult attitudes toward or not toward persons are affected by early childhood experiences (Roe & Lunneborg, 1984, 1990)

The personality approach of Bordin, Nachmann, and Segal earlier discussed (and that of Roe) implies that occupational choices are made as aspects of self-classification, whether the central focus is impulse gratification or need satisfaction. Thus, occupational choices and career patterns are affirmations of personal behavioral styles.

In sum, Roe's pioneering work in career development has had an important impact on interest assessment and on career development research. Although more difficult to trace, it is also likely that her work on early family determinants of vocational choice and needs satisfaction has been incorporated into the practice of career counseling as a stimulus to hypotheses that might be tested with individual clients and that might be related to analyses of occupational classifications that could be personally relevant (Roe & Lunneborg, 1990).

Holland's Theory. Holland's (1966, 1973a, 1985, 1997) approach gives explicit attention to behavioral style or personality type as the major influence in career choice and development. In this sense, Holland's work is part of a long tradition of conceptualizations of individual differences in personality type encompassing the work of such persons as Spranger (1928) and Murray (1938). Spranger described six basic types of individuality: theoretic, economic, aesthetic, social, political, and religious. Murray proposed a series of needs and press (environmental characteristics, reinforcers, rewards) that he combined into a need-press paradigm designed to explain differential behavior in organizations.

Holland's theory has been described as structural-interactive: "Because it provides an explicit link between various personality characteristics and corresponding job titles and because it organizes the massive data about people and jobs" (Weinrach, 1984, p. 63).

Holland has suggested that structural-interactive approaches share several common themes:

1. The choice of an occupation is an expression of personality and not a random event, although chance plays a role.

2. The members of an occupational group have similar personalities and similar histories of personal development.
3. Because people in an occupational group have similar personalities, they will respond to many situations and problems in similar ways.
4. Occupational achievement, stability, and satisfaction depend on congruence between one's personality and the job environment. (Holland, 1982, p. 2)

As might be expected from the content of such propositions, Holland (1997) has indicated that the intellectual roots for his theory are in differential psychology—primarily interest measurement—and in typologies of personality (p. x).

Indeed, Holland's contributions are equally prominent in the area of environmental assessment and in understanding person-situation interactions as they are in understanding individual behavior. Much of his effort has been devoted to developing structures for understanding and predicting the behavior of persons in different types of environments. Holland and his associates have also made extremely important contributions to the understanding of vocational interests in relation to personality characteristics; to the importance of both academic and nonacademic accomplishments to life; and to the development of instruments useful both in testing his theoretical propositions and in translating his theory into career guidance tools. The most notable of the latter are the Vocational Preference Inventory, My Vocational Situation, the Self-Directed-Search, and the Holland themes used in the Strong-Campbell Interest Inventory. Finally, Holland's theory has generated hundreds of studies in the past two decades that have tested, refined, and extended his propositions with diverse populations, in different settings, and in many nations of the world (Holland & Gottfredson, 1990). We will identify a few studies to suggest some of the lines of ongoing inquiry after we identify the primary assumptions of the theory.

Holland assumes that the individual is a product of heredity and environment. As a result of early and continuing influences of genetic potentialities and the interaction of the individual with his or her environment, there develops a hierarchy of habitual or preferred methods for dealing with social and environmental tasks. The most typical way in which an individual responds to the environment is described as *modal personal orientation.*

Four assumptions constitute the heart of Holland's theory:

1. In our culture, most persons can be categorized as one of six types: realistic, investigative, artistic, social, enterprising, or conventional.
2. There are six kinds of environments: realistic, investigative, artistic, social enterprising, and conventional.
3. People search for environments that will let them exercise their skills and abilities, express their attitudes and values, and take on agreeable problems and roles.
4. A person's behavior is determined by an interaction between his personality and the characteristics of his environment. (Holland, 1973a, pp. 2–4; 1985)

To emphasize the interactive character of his theory, found in person-situation correspondence, Holland has classified work environments into six categories analogous to the six personal orientations. In other words, he describes the person and the working environment in the same terms. Accordingly, Holland makes explicit, more than do most of his contemporaries, that occupations are ways of life, environments that manifest the characteristics of those inhabiting them as opposed to being simply sets of isolated work functions or skills. In addition, Holland has extended his examination of types of occupational environments to educational environments, particularly collegiate.

In condensed and paraphrased form, the major emphases of the six personality types and their relationships to pertinent occupations are as follows:

1. The *realistic (R)* type has a preference for activities that require the explicit, ordered, or systematic manipulation of objects, tools, machines, animals; this type has an aversion to educational or therapeutic activities. Examples of occupations that meet the needs of realistic types are surveyor and mechanic.
2. The *investigative (I)* type has a preference for activities that entail the observational, symbolic, systematic, and creative investigation of physical, biological, and cultural phenomena to understand and control such phenomena; this type has aversion to persuasive, social, and repetitive activities. Examples

of occupations that meet the needs of investigative types are chemist and physicist.

3. The *artistic (A)* type prefers ambiguous, free, unsystematized activities that entail the manipulation of physical, verbal, or human materials to create art forms or products; this type has an aversion to explicit, systematic, and ordered activities. Examples of occupations that meet the needs of artistic types are artist and writer.

4. The *social (S)* type prefers activities that entail the manipulation of others to inform, train, develop, cure, or enlighten; this type has an aversion to explicit, ordered, systematic activities involving materials, tools, or machines. Examples of occupations that meet the needs of social types are social science teacher and vocational counselor.

5. The *enterprising (E)* type prefers activities that require the manipulation of others to attain organizational goals or economic gain; this type has an aversion to observational, symbolic, and systematic activities. Examples of occupations that meet the needs of enterprising types are political scientist, salesman, and executive.

6. The *conventional (C)* type prefers activities that entail the explicit, ordered, systematic manipulation of data, such as keeping records, filing materials, reproducing materials, organizing written and numerical data according to a prescribed plan, operating business machines and data processing machines to attain organizational or economic goals; this type has an aversion to ambiguous, free, exploratory, or unsystematized activities. Examples of occupations that meet the needs of conventional types are accountant and clerk. (Holland, 1973, pp. 14–18)

Obviously, it is unlikely that persons fall solely into one of the major personality types described. Therefore a coding system has been devised to indicate the person's primary and secondary types (Holland, Vierstein, Kuo, Karweit, & Blum, 1970). These codes are reflected in three-letter combinations—each letter corresponding to the first letter of one of the six types. For instance, a code of RIA would indicate that the person is most like the Realistic type, next most like Investigative, and third most like artistic. Holland and colleagues have also classified hundreds of occupations according to the same three-letter code system. For example, for the code RIA, two occupations are listed—architectural draftsman and dental technician. It is assumed that a person obtaining the code RIA should begin to explore these two occupations and then examine related areas through the use of the *Dictionary of Occupational Titles* and other pertinent references. Holland and his colleagues have also devised a *Dictionary of Holland Codes,* which list occupations alphabetically that are related to the various major permutations of Holland codes (Gottfredson, Holland, & Ogawa, 1982).

Holland, like Roe, addresses level hierarchies within occupational environments. The level hierarchy, or the particular responsibility or skill level within an occupational field that one gravitates to, is dependent on the person's intelligence and self-knowledge. Self-knowledge refers to the amount of accuracy of self-information as contrasted with self-evaluation, which refers to the worth the personal attributes to him or herself.

Holland's theory (1973a, 1985, 1997) contends that individual behavior is a function of the interaction between one's personality and environment, and that choice behavior is an expression of personality. Thus, people seek those educational and occupational settings that permit expression of their personality styles. Since persons inhabiting particular environments, occupational or educational, have similar personality characteristics, their responses to problems and interpersonal situations are likely to be similar. For these reasons, interest inventories are personality inventories, and vocational stereotypes held by individuals have important psychological and sociological implications. Put another way, it is possible to suggest that, as persons explore occupational possibilities, they use stereotypes of themselves and stereotypes of occupations to guide their search. If their preferences are clear and their information about self or occupations accurate, they will likely make effective choices. If their understanding of their personality type or appropriate occupations is unclear, they are likely to be indecisive and vacillate among possible choices. In Holland's view, the adequacy of information about the self and various occupational possibilities is crucial.

Finally, Holland (1997) hypothesizes that congruent interactions of people and environments belonging to the same type or model, in contrast to incongruent interactions, are conducive to more stable vocational choice, higher vocational achievement, higher academic achievement, better maintenance of personal stability, and greater satisfaction.

In 1976, Holland and Gottfredson extended and clarified some of the earlier theoretical propositions. They did so by exploring four major questions.

1. How do personal development, initial vocational choice, work involvement, and satisfaction come about?

> *People grow up to resemble one type or another because parents, schools, and neighborhoods serve as environments which reinforce some behaviors more than others and provide different models of suitable behavior. The reinforcement consists of the encouragement of selected activities, interests, self-estimates, and competencies.... Different cultural influences as well as other aspects of the interpersonal milieu, such as sex-role socialization, race, religion, and class promote the development of some types more than others by differential encouragement of the experiences (activities, interests, competencies, etc.) that lead to different types. (p. 21)*

2. Why do most people have orderly careers when the individual jobs in their work histories are categorized using an occupational classification scheme?

> *The majority of people manage to find work that is congruent with their type. More explicitly, the average person searches for or gravitates toward work environments in which his/her typological predilections and talents (activities, competencies, perceptions of self and world, values, traits) are allowed expression and rewarded.... By definition, well-defined types know what activities and competencies bring them satisfaction and congruency.... Orderly careers are also encouraged by the stereotyped ways in which employers perceive a person's credentials. (p. 21)*

3. Why do people change jobs? What influences their search for new jobs?

> *People change jobs because they are dissatisfied, because they are incompetent, because other workers wish them to leave, and for other personal and environmental reasons: better climate, physical disability, dissatisfied relatives, more money, and other influences. In theoretical terms, people leave because of excessive person-environment incongruency, or because of an opportunity to increase their congruency. (p. 21)*

4. Why do some people make vocational choices that are congruent with assessment data, others do not, and still others are undecided?

> *People with consistent and well-defined personality patterns are expected to be "good decision makers because of the implications of differentiation and consistency; integration of preferred activities, competencies, occupational preferences and self-estimates; and compatibility of primary dispositions.... [Some personality] types may be better decision makers than others.... The making of decisions at appropriate times (end of high school, end of sophomore year, when to change jobs, when to marry, etc.) may reflect only different rates of development and different environmental contingencies. (p. 22)*

In the 1985 refinement of his theory, Holland discussed the secondary assumptions that augment the four key assumptions addressed previously. These secondary assumptions—which can be applied to both persons and environments—include the following:

Consistency: Some types of persons or environments have more relationship to each other than do others. Thus, "degrees of consistency or relatedness are assumed to affect vocational preference" (p. 4).

Differentiation: "The degree to which a person or an environment is well-defined is its degree of differentiation.... Personal identity is defined as the possession of a clear and stable picture of one's goals, interests, and talents. Environmental identity is preset when an environment or organization has clear, integrated goals, tasks, and rewards that are stable over long time intervals" (p. 5).

Congruence: Different personality types require different environments. "Incongruence occurs when a type lives in an environment that provides opportunities and rewards foreign to the person's preferences and abilities—for instance, a realistic type in a social environment" (p. 5).

Calculus: "The relationships within and between types or environments can be ordered according to a hexagonal model in which the distances between the types or environments are inversely proportional to the theoretical relationship between them" (p. 5).

Following the emphases on the four key assumptions identified earlier, Holland, added a fifth assumption (Holland, 1984), that of identity. In essence, identity has to do with the possession of a clear and stable picture of one's goals, interests, and talents. With regard to identity in organization, the focus is on the organization's clarity, stability, and integration of goals, tasks, and rewards.

As indicated at the beginning of this section, Holland himself and his associates have been extremely productive in both generating and testing his theoretical propositions. As one might expect with a theory that is both comprehensive in the questions it stimulates and dynamic, the findings reported as somewhat mixed, although they typically support the theoretical propositions. To illustrate the range of research engendered by Holland's theory, a few selected studies will be described.

Personality type and values: Laudeman and Griffith (1978) studied the relationship among personality typology, environmental orientation, and values of six different groups of male seniors at a midwestern university. Each group represented one of Holland's primary personality types through the following majors: mechanical engineering, electrical engineering, elementary education, accounting, marketing, and art of music education. Holland's Vocational Preference Inventory (VPI) was used to assess personality types and the Allport-Vernon-Lindsey Study of Values was used to measure six basic values or motives in personality. Although there were some inconsistencies among engineering and education majors with regard to their highest mean scores on the VPI personality scales, the researchers concluded that male college seniors in this sample did generally reflect personality types and value dimensions that correspond with their major field of study in accordance with what would be predicted by Holland's theory.

Consistency: Holland's notion of consistency has also been tested in different ways. This concept, advanced in 1973, is related to his six major personality types, which are arranged in a model that corresponds to their intercorrelations (see Figure 4.2).

In looking at the hexagons for men and women, one can see that those personality types with the highest positive correlations are arranged together on the outside of the hexagon, whereas those types with the smallest correlation are the farthest apart on the diagram. The intermediate distances have correlations of intermediate size.

Consistency, according to Holland, is the degree to which the dominant and subdominant interest types (the first two expressed vocational choices) of a person or an environment are similar to each other as demonstrated by their adjacent position or closeness on the hexagonal model. The assumption is that persons whose dominant personality (interest) types are essentially consistent would be more integrated in their characteristics (traits, values, perceptions) than persons whose interest types are much more disparate. Such consistent persons would likely be more predictable and higher achievers than inconsistent persons. Erwin (1982) examined changes in college majors, course withdrawals, and other indices of academic performance in relation to Holland's construct of consistency but found only weak support for the construct as it was measured in this study. Wiley and Magoon (1982), however, studied the construct of consistency in social personality types (222 college

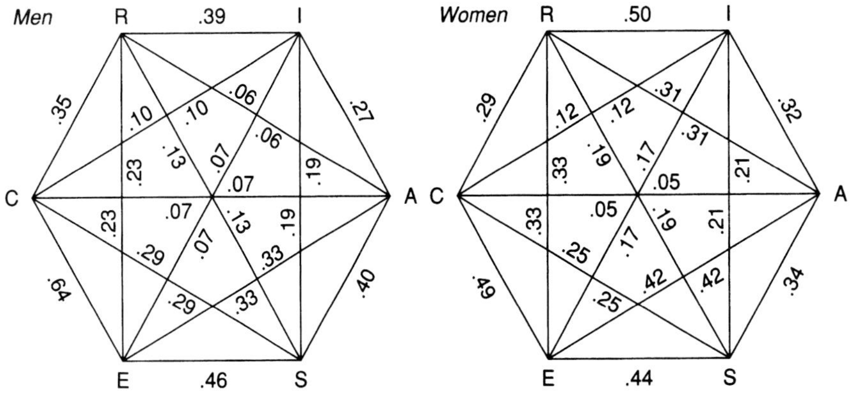

FIGURE 4.2 Holland's Hexagons for Men and Women

Source: Reprinted from *Perspectives on Vocational Development,* edited by John M. Whitely and Arthur Resnikoff. APGA Press, 1972. © AACD. Reprinted with permission. No further reproduction authorized without written permission of American Association for Counseling and Development.

freshmen) in relation to persistence in college and academic achievement. They found significant results in favor of the construct. For example, high- and medium-consistency subjects persisted in college at a higher rate than low-consistency subjects and the relationship between consistency and college grade-point averages was also significant.

Congruency: Related to the studies of Erwin and Wiley and Magoon of the usefulness of Holland's typology for predicting persistence and performance in college, Bruch and Krieshok (1981) studied Holland's notion of congruence and person-situation compatibility among theoretically oriented engineering majors. The researchers hypothesized that high congruence (an investigative student in an investigative major) compared to moderately high congruence (a realistic student in an investigative major) would result in greater persistence and better academic performance. The hypotheses were confirmed in that high student-curriculum congruence (I-type student in I-type major) demonstrated greater academic achievement and persistence in the initial engineering major over a two-year period than did student-curriculum congruence that was moderate.

Spokane (1979) followed up 232 women and 386 men in their senior year who had taken the Strong-Campbell Interest Inventory in their freshman year. He found that congruent students were more satisfied and differentiated than incongruent students and that they perceived themselves to be more congruent. Barak and Rabbi (1982), in a study of 293 undergraduate students randomly stratified across majors representing different Holland categories, found that consistent students tend to persist in college, do not change majors, and achieve more than inconsistent students. Consistency in this study related to people who possess a consistent personality pattern and an integration of similar interests, competencies, values, traits, and perceptions and was reflected here in the degree to which students at registration made the first two choices of major in the same or adjacent Holland category (investigative-investigative, investigative-realistic, and so on).

Meir (1989) and other researchers have expanded the concept of congruence and its demonstrated relationship to satisfaction and well-being in several ways. In particular, they have tested the cumulative effect of three kinds of congruence: (1) occupational congruence as originally proposed in the Holland theory; (2) avocational congruence—the degree to which one's avocational choice suits one's interests; and (3) skill congruence—the extent to which the individual feels that opportunities exist by which one can express one's skills in the occupational role. In two studies of male and female teachers, it was found that the different types of congruence had a cumulative effect on well-being. Those with one congruence were higher on the well-being scale than those with no congruences. Those with either two or three congruences were higher than those with only one.

Gottfredson and Holland (1990), in a longitudinal and statistically complex study of 345 newly hired tellers (75 percent female, 74 percent between 18 and 26 years of age) over a four-month interval, found that person-job congruence did have substantial correlations with job satisfaction in a well-defined, homogeneous sample. Such results support the hypothesis that congruent work environments allow the expression of a person's interests and competencies. In some contrast to expectations from other research, however, the study did *not* find that person-job incongruence resulted in counterproductive work behavior, role ambiguity, or role conflict.

Spokane (1985) conducted a comprehensive and insightful review of the major studies of person-environment congruence in Holland's theory of careers. He divided the studies into two basic categories of research design. The first category incorporated those studies that typically take place at one point in time, employ correlational techniques, and compare subject classified as congruent or incongruent on some set of criterion variables. The second design category contains time series or experimental designs that study change in congruence over time. Spokane included in his analysis 40 correlational and 23 change studies. His summary of the conclusions from the correlational studies supports Holland's predictions that congruence is associated with performance, satisfaction, and stability. More specifically, within the set of 40 studies, positive relationships were found in 3 or more studies between congruence and (a) academic performance and persistence, (b) job satisfaction, (c) stability of choice, (d) perceived congruency, and (e) personality (ego strength). Nonsignificant correlations were found in three or more studies between congruence and (a) self-concept and (b) sociability-based measures of personality.

The conclusions from the change studies suggest that adjustments or shifts from science to nonscience occupations are largely complete by age 30 and that personality modifications accompany such changes and are geared in the direction of the shifts. People who remain in an environment become and perceive themselves to be more similar to the modal personality type found in that setting. When placed in a congruent environment, individuals feel a better fit.

In summarizing his review of congruence research, Spokane indicates that such research "reveals a consistent relationship between congruence and a number of measures of vocational satisfaction and adjustment. We also conclude that incongruence can be resolved by a change in the person, a change in job, or both" (p. 336). He also cites some important implications of congruence for counseling; for example, the concept of congruence is a useful organizer for a client as long as it is not used to suggest that the client is likely to find a perfect job. Citing the perspectives of Gottfredson (Gottfredson, 1981), his review suggests that counselors should help clients "to outline ranges or zones of congruent occupations that are delimited by (a) field, (b) level, (c) sex type, and (d) amount of effort and education required" (p. 336). Two other important counseling implications that flow from this review are that (a) frequently, incongruence may more likely be resolved by a change within the client or a change in personal aspiration than by a change in job, and (b) individuals whose measured interests are incongruent with the job or college major they have chosen can be identified early in their careers and helped to examine their situation through counseling or other means.

More recently, Spokane, Meir, and Catalano (2000) reviewed 66 studies published between 1985 and 1999 that evaluated Holland's congruence hypothesis. Spokane and his colleagues pointed to the need for researchers to work to continually improve their design and methodology in conducting congruence research.

Occupational classification: In 1973, Helms suggested that the Holland Occupational Classification system could be used to organize occupational information, analyze work histories, and develop occupational exploration plans for clients. These possible uses exist at least partially because Holland's system organizes occupations "into homogeneous groups based on their psychological similarities" (Helms, 1973, p. 69).

Scanlan (1980) has applied Holland's occupational classification system to self-employed men and found it useful in differentiating what he described as craft entrepreneurs and opportunistic entrepreneurs. He also found that, in accordance with the theory, the educational interests of respondents, the types of occupations they held before self-employment, and the types of work on which craft and opportunistic entrepreneurs spend their time in the course of operating their businesses all reflect the three-letter Holland codes by which they were differentiated. Jones (1980a), for example, has shown how the Holland typology can be useful with the *Guide for Occupational Exploration* published by the U.S. Department of Labor in 1979. Rounds, Davison, and Dawis (1979) used a multidimensional scaling procedure to examine the fit of Holland's hexagonal model to the General Occupational Theme scales of the Strong-Campbell Interest Inventory, which are based on the Holland model. The fit for men was good. For women, the relationship was less good, suggesting caution in the use and interpretation of the SCII occupational themes for women.

In a related study Elan (1994) applied the RIASEC theory to graduating medical students to explain their secondary career choices. The findings indicate that specific medical careers tended to attract particular personality types. For example, orthopedic surgery attracted students characterized by an RSI typology; psychiatry those with an ISA. In addition, it was found that, when comparing the undergraduate majors of medical school graduates, investigative students are more likely to apply and to gain entrance to medical schools.

Holland, Gottfredson, and Baker (1990) have extended earlier research on the predictive validity of vocational aspirations—categorized according to an occupational classification system based on the Holland theory—which suggests the efficiency of such an approach as compared to the use of an interest inventory. This study of Navy recruits (467 men and 250 women) was designed to examine the coherence and validity of vocational aspirations (concurrent, retrospective, and predictive) and to provide a more explicit psychological interpretation of such phenomena. The main findings were that expressed vocational preferences—singly or in combination—were superior to the interest inventory (in this case, the Vocational Preference Inventory) in tests of predictive, concurrent, or retrospective validity. The conclusions of the authors were that these results, as tests of relationships to their retrospective preferences about civilian occupations and preferences for Naval occupations early and late in basic training, were "consistent with the literature showing the substantial predictive validity of categorized self-expressed aspirations or preferences" (p. 340).

Gottfredson (1980) compared six schemes for describing occupations to examine the construct validity of Holland's typology of work environments and to estimate the amount of information shared by these commonly used classification systems. The five occupational classification systems studied, in addition to the Holland system, included occupational prestige, activities and requirements presented in the DOT, self-direction, the twelve major census categories, and the occupational reinforcer patterns formulated in the Minnesota Theory of Work Adjustment (Lofquist & Dawis, 1969). Acknowledging limitations in both the data available for the occupations examined and the differing or uncertain validity of the classification schemes used, Gottfredson's evidence does support the construct validity of Holland's occupational scheme. She finds that it is superior to the census classification scheme in its potential flexibility and interpretation. She does recommend, however, that the Holland work typology be supplemented by a measure of occupational prestige so that the resulting information would include a paradigm of work type by level. Gottfredson also contends that a greater specificity is needed in the domains of job characteristics to which Holland's constructs apply than has been true in the past. For example, Holland's characterizations are more applicable to some types for occupational differences (for example, worker traits required and job activities performed) than to others (for example, work products or job context).

Rounds, Shubsachs, Dawis, and Lofquist (1978) classified 181 occupations, for which reinforcer rating data were available, into the six Holland environmental models. The Minnesota Job Description Questionnaire provides ratings of 21 reinforcers (such as ability utilization, achievement, activity, advancement, and authority) in different occupations (see Chapter 16). The authors concluded that the results provided only modest support for Holland's environmental formulations, particularly that of consistency. They also reported finding a different order of intercorrelations among the Holland Scale that has been used to construct the hexagon (RCSIAE or REAISC rather than RIASEC as proposed by Holland). Finally, they suggested that descriptions of occupational environments based on vocational interests and vocational preferences, as is Holland's, differ from those based on environmental characteristics (occupational reinforcers and behavioral requirements) such as the Minnesota Theory of Work Adjustment. Gottfredson (1980) has suggested that the data of Rounds et al. be reevaluated to account for the effects of prestige level. Super (1981), however, would likely be somewhat more supportive of the findings of Rounds et al. because he contends that the one fundamental methodological flaw in most of Holland's work "is the fact that both Holland's predictors and his criteria have been preferences.... The predictor has usually been either the score on an interest inventory consisting of occupational titles or expressed vocational preferences classified according to Holland's preference (another occupational title) expressed at some later date" (p. 20).

Validity by sex and by race/ethnicity: Another line of research dealing with Holland's theory has to do with its validity for men and women and across racial groups. Doty and Betz (1979) studied the concurrent validity of Holland's theory for men and women employed in an enterprising occupation. In general, the findings suggested that, at least within an employed sample, Holland's theory is valid for both men and women as defined by equally high scores on the E-theme in the Strong-Campbell Interest Inventory and the Self-Directed Search and by relationships between enterprising scale scores and job satisfaction. Walsh, Bingham, Horton, and Spokane (1979) studied the differences between 155 college-degreed black and white women employed in three traditional male occupations (engineering, medicine, and law). They found that white and black women in the same occupation tended to obtain similar mean scores on the VPI and the SDS. Ward and Walsh (1981) also studied the concurrent validity of Holland's theory for employed noncollege-degreed black women. The subjects were 102 black women working in occupations representing each of the six vocational environments described by Holland. Four scales of the VPI and four scales of the SDS successfully differentiated the work environments of the women consistent with Holland's theoretical propositions.

Trusty, Ng, and Ray (2000) used national data to study the longitudinal effects of several variables (e.g., eighth-grade reading and mathematics achievement scores, self-esteem, and locus of control) on choice of Holland (1997) social type college majors versus other majors. More specifically, they examined these effects for four of the five major racial/ethnic groups in the United States (Asian/Pacific Islanders, Hispanics, African Americans, and Whites). Effects of mathematics scores and gender on choice of social majors were fairly consistent across racial/ethnic groups, whereas effects of reading scores and SES differed across racial/ethnic groups. Results for Whites were most consistent with Holland's theoretical formulations regarding the effects of variables on choice of social type educational environments.

How people acquire their characteristics: One line of research inquiry that has not been fully explored deals with how people become various types. Perhaps the central assumptions about the matter lie in Holland's perception that "a person becomes oriented toward some occupations as opposed to others because of a special life history of activities, competencies, self-perceptions, values, and so forth. Consequently, if we desire to change the vocational aspirations of a person or a special group, we must change the experience of people before they arrive at the age when they must go to work" (Holland, 1973b, pp. 5–6). Holland's theory has been characterized by its comprehensive attention to the structure of career behavior and the determinants of career choice; it has not professed to be a process or developmentally oriented approach to change in such factors over time. Indeed, as Holland (1994) has indicated in speaking of the strengths and weaknesses of his theory: "In general, the strengths of typologies lie in their ability to provide information. In contrast, the weaknesses of typologies lie in their neglect of the processes entailed in change and development" (p. 50). The latter emphases lie more clearly in the theories described in the next section of this chapter, developmental approaches.

In sum, then, Holland's theory continues to stimulate other lines of inquiry, raise new questions, and find new applications. Although much research remains to be done on the hypotheses generated by the theory, it continues to be a major conceptual structure for considering choice, persistence, and performance in educational and occupational settings. Weinrach and Srebalus (1990) have summarized the most important changes in Holland's theory over the course of its history presented here in abridged form:

> 1. The theory has expanded its constructs, becoming more comprehensive and explicit.
> 2. Throughout its evolution, new concepts (for example, identity) have been added to prop up others. The theory's limitations are more explicit.
> 3. The theory remains in the tradition of differential psychology.
> 4. It has moved away from all-or-none distinctions among environmental and personality types and toward statements of degree and patterning.
> 5. All major constructs have operational definitions, and these enable careful empirical verification of the theory.
> 6. A two-dimensional scientific model (the hexagon) has been added.
> 7. Empirical evidence, pro and con, has been generated in more than 450 studies across populations of diverse characteristics.
> 8. Application of the theory to career planning and counseling has been encouraged through the development and refinement of practitioner and self-help tools.
> 9. Procedures have been developed to teach the theory and evaluate mastery of it.
> 10. Although continually open to revision based on empirical evidence, Holland's theory has successfully resisted modifications intended to satisfy prescriptive cultural and political pressures. (Weinrach & Srebalus, 1990, pp. 47–48)

Developmental Approaches

Developmental emphases on career behavior and decision making differ from the approaches previously discussed, not because they reject the latter but rather because they are typically more inclusive in their constructs, more concerned with longitudinal expressions of career behavior, and more inclined to highlight the importance of the self-concept. They tend to be process-oriented in their conceptions of how career behavior develops and changes over time.

Ginzberg, Ginsburg, Axelrad, and Herma. Ginzberg, Ginsburg, Axelrad, and Herma (1951)—a team composed of an economist, a psychiatrist, a sociologist, and a psychologist—were early leaders in speculating about career development as a process that culminates in an occupational choice in one's early twenties. In particular, they asserted that "occupational choice is a developmental process: it is not a single decision, but a series of decisions made over a period of years. Each step in the process has a meaningful relation to those which precede and follow it" (p. 185). Ginzberg and colleagues identified four sets of factors, the interplay of which influences the ultimate vocational choice: individual values, emotional factors, the amount and kind of education, and the effect of reality through environmental pressures. These factors undergird the formation of attitudes, which converge to shape occupational choice. More particularly, Ginzberg and colleagues saw choice as a process delimited by life stages, in which certain tasks are faced by preadolescents and adolescents. Within the interaction that occurs as these tasks are confronted, compromises between wishes and possibilities contribute to an irreversibility as the process unfolds.

Ginzberg and associates have labeled the gross phases of the vocational choice process—the period of development—as fantasy (from birth to age 11), tentative (11 to 17), and realistic age (age 17 to early twenties). Except for fantasy, each of these periods has subaspects. Thus, the tentative period is divided into stages of interest, capacity, value, and transition. Following this period, there emerges the realistic period, which is broken into exploration, crystallization, and specification.

Ginzberg and colleagues have given credence to the notion that vocational behavior finds its roots in the early life of the child and develops over time. They have indicated that vocational behavior and career choice become increasingly reality-oriented and specific as one moves toward the choice itself.

In the reformulation of his theory 20 years after the first statement, Ginzberg (1972) suggested some modifications. First, he contended that the process of occupational choice-making does not end at young adulthood. Rather, it is likely to occur throughout the individual's working life with changes in goals or work situations requiring decision making and remaking. Second, Ginzberg has dampened his emphasis on the irreversibility of occupational choice. Finally, he has substituted the term *optimization* for the earlier term *compromise*. The point here is that individuals constantly try to improve the occupational fit between their changing selves and circumstances. As shifts continue to occur in work and other aspects of life, the person must deal with new decisions designed to balance possible gains against economic and psychological costs. Ginzberg's reformulated theory now includes the following elements (paraphrased):

1. Occupational choice is a process that remains open as long as one makes and expects to make decisions about work and career. Often occupational choice and working life are coterminous.
2. The decisions made during the preparatory period (principally schooling through adolescence) will help shape later career, but changes occurring in work and life will also influence career.
3. Decisions about jobs and careers are individual attempts to optimize the fit between personal priority needs and desires and the work opportunities and constraints that occur.

In 1984, Ginzberg again reviewed his 1951 and 1972 theoretical constructs and suggested their modification. By the time of his most recent reformulation, Ginzberg's three original colleagues had died, and, therefore, the 1984 formulation was his own summary of the research he had engaged in for three-and-a-half decades in the Institute for the Conservation of Human Resources, which he headed at Columbia University.

In the 1951 formulation of their theory, Ginzberg and colleagues had focused on three concepts: process, irreversibility, and compromise. Originally, they gave little attention to the possibility of reopening decisions and their effects on career development after the age of 20 or so. By 1984, however, Ginzberg had modified the early perspectives to suggest that "what happens to a person before he reaches twenty will affect his career, but he retains considerable scope for later decision making" (1984, p. 179).

In 1972, and again in 1984, Ginzberg suggested a reformulation of the factors involved in a lifelong choice process, including the original choice (essentially what the 1951 formulation addressed), the feedback between the original choice and later work experience, and economic and family circumstances. Ginzberg contends, then, that "if the original choice did not lead to the anticipated satisfactions, the individual was likely to reopen the choice process, which in turn would be conditioned and influenced by the degrees of freedom permitted by his family circumstances and the economy" (1984, p. 179). Such a perspective led to a third and current restatement of the core concepts of his theory: "Occupational choice is a lifelong process of decision making for those who seek major satisfactions from their work. This leads them to reassess repeatedly how they can improve the fit between their changing career goals and the realities of the world of work" (1984, p. 180). Ginzberg goes on to say: "these emendations, improvements, and corrections of our original theory, first developed in 1951, still conceive of occupational choice as a process in which the early decisions an individual makes will restrict his or her later scope of action. Our theory predicts that the individual will make a career choice that will balance competing interests and values and take into account the opportunities available and the costs of pursuing them" (1984, p. 180).

Super's Developmental Approach. The developmental approach that has received the most continuous attention, stimulated the most research, influenced the field of vocational psychology most pervasively, and is the most comprehensive is that promulgated by Super and his many colleagues in the longitudinal Career Pattern Study, which provided much of the data to test his theoretical perspectives (Super et al., 1957; Super, Starishevsky, Matlin, & Jordaan, 1963; Super, 1969a, 1969b; Jordaan & Heyde, 1979). This approach is an integrative one, stressing the interaction of personal and environmental variables in career development.

Super provided early input into the original Ginzberg et. al statement but believed that it was deficient in several respects (Super, 1953). According to his view, the Ginzberg position did not take into account previous pertinent research (such as the nature of interests in vocational choice); it failed to describe "choice" in an operationally acceptable way; it made a sharp distinction between choice and "adjustment" when, in fact, the two were blended in adolescence and virtually indistinguishable in adulthood; and it failed to delineate the process of compromise.

In response to these conditions, Super formulated his own theory consisting of ten major propositions, each of which was testable and, indeed, could provide the framework for a longitudinal research study. The original ten propositions were put forward in 1953, expanded to twelve in 1957 (Super & Backrach, 1957), and expanded again in the 1970s and 1980s. In 1990, they included the fourteen that follow:

1. People differ in their abilities and personalities, needs, values, interests, traits, and self-concepts.

2. People are qualified, by virtue of these characteristics, each for a number of occupations.

3. Each occupation requires a characteristic pattern of abilities and personality traits, with tolerance wide enough to allow both some variety of occupations for each individual and some variety of individuals in each occupation.

4. Vocational preferences and competencies, the situations in which people live and work, and, hence, their self-concepts change with time and experience, although self-concepts, as products of social learning, are increasingly stable from late adolescence until late maturity, providing some continuity in choice and adjustment.

5. This process of change may be summed up in a series of life stages (a "maxi-cycle") characterized as a sequence of growth, exploration, establishment, maintenance, and decline, and these stages may in turn be subdivided into (a) the fantasy, tentative, and realistic phase of the exploratory stage and (b) the trial and stable phases of the establishment stage. A small (mini) cycle takes place in transitions from one stage to the next or each time an individual is destabilized by a reduction in force, changes in type of manpower needs, illness or injury, or other socioeconomic or personal events. Such unstable or multiple-trial careers involve new growth, reexplorations, and reestablishment (recycling).

6. The nature of the career pattern—that is, the occupational level attained and the sequence, frequency, and duration of trial and stable jobs—is determined by the individual's parental socioeconomic level, mental ability, education, skills, personality characteristics (needs, values, interests traits, and self-concepts), and career maturity and by the opportunities to which he or she is exposed.

7. Success in coping with the demands of the environment and of the organism in that context at any given life-career stage depends on the readiness of the individual to cope with these demands (that is, on his or her career maturity). *Career maturity* is a constellation of physical, psychological, and social characteristics; psychologically, it is both cognitive and affective.

It includes the degree of success in coping with the demands of earlier stages and substages of career development, and especially with the most recent.

8. Career maturity is a hypothetical construct. Its operational definition is perhaps as difficult to formulate as is that of intelligence, but its history is much briefer and its achievements even less definitive. Contrary to the impressions created by some writers, it does not increase monotonically, and it is not a unitary trait.

9. Development through the life stages can be guided, partly by facilitating the maturing of abilities and interests and partly by aiding in reality testing and in the development of self-concepts.

10. The process of career development is essentially that of development and implementing occupational self-concepts. It is a synthesizing and compromising process in which the self-concept is a product of the interaction of inherited aptitudes, physical makeup, opportunity to observe and play various roles, and evaluations of the extent to which the results of role playing meet with the approval of superiors and fellows (interactive learning).

11. The process of synthesis of or compromise between individual and social factors, between self-concepts and reality, is one of role playing and of learning from feedback, whether the role is played in fantasy, in the counseling interview, or in such real-life activities as classes, clubs, part-time work, and entry jobs.

12. Work satisfactions and life satisfactions depend on the extent to which the individual finds adequate outlets for abilities, needs, values, interests, personality traits, and self-concepts. They depend on establishment in a type of work, a work situation, and a way of life in which one can play the kind of role that growth and exploratory experiences have led one to consider congenial and appropriate.

13. The degree of satisfaction people attain from work is proportional to the degree to which they have been able to implement self-concepts.

14. Work and occupation provide a focus for personality organization for most men and women, although for some persons this focus is peripheral, incidental, or even nonexistent. Then other foci, such as leisure activities and homemaking, may be central. (Social traditions, such as sex-role stereotyping and modeling, racial and ethnic biases, and the opportunity structure, as well as individual differences, are important determinants of preferences for such roles as worker, student, leisurite, homemaker, and citizen (Super, 1990, pp. 206–208).

In a major sense, Super made explicit the intimacy of career development and personal development. He synthesized much of the early work of Buehler (1933), Hoppock (1935), and Ginzberg, Ginsburg, Axelrad, and Herma (1951) in his longitudinal attempt to focus developmental principles on the staging and the determination of career patterns. He characterized the career development process as ongoing, continuous, and generally irreversible; as a process of compromise and synthesis within which his primary construct—the development and implementation of the self-concept—operates. The basic theme is that the individual as a socialized organizer of personal experience chooses occupations that will allow him to function in a role consistent with his self-concept and that the latter conception is a function of his development history. (The male pronoun is used precisely here, because Super's research and theory have primarily dealt with men, not women, although others have extended his work to women. In his later theoretical work and empirical studies, he addressed the applicability of his theory to both genders [Super, 1990]. Further, because of the range of individual capabilities and the latitude within occupations for different combinations of traits, he indicated that most people have multipotentiality.)

Although Super's approach has been labeled typically as a developmental self-concept theory (Osipow, 1968, p. 117), Super himself labeled it differential-developmental-social-phenomenological psychology (Super, 1969b). Such a label indicates the confluence of knowledge bases to explain career development that this approach has attempted to synthesize and order. Super (1984a, 1990) suggested that what he has contributed is not an integrative, comprehensive, and testable theory but rather a "segmental theory, a loosely unified set of theories dealing with specific aspects of career development taken from developmental, differential, social, and phenomenological psychology and held together by self-concept or personal-construct theory" (p. 194) and by learning theory (1990, p. 199).

In his conception of a career model, as contrasted with an occupational model, Super intended "to denote a longitudinal, developmental approach rather than a single-choice, matching approach such as that of differential psychology and of congruence theory as used by Holland" (Super, 1984, p. 198). Super suggested:

> *[S]elf-concept theory, as I have used it, is both very similar to and very different from congruence theory as Holland has used it. It is similar, in that occupational choice is viewed as the choice by the individual of a role and a setting in which the person will fit comfortably and find satisfaction, as the implementation of a self-concept. It is different in that Holland's interest has been primarily in the single choice and in the assessment of people and occupations for more effective matching, whereas mine has been in the nature, sequence, and determinants of the choices that constitute a career over the life span (1984, p. 205).*

In 1990, Super suggested that self-concept theory and the term *self-concept,* as he has used these terms during the course of his research, might have been better called *personal construct theory* and *personal constructs* (Kelly, 1955) to show the individual's dual focus on self and on situation. In addition, the use of personal constructs by Super may have, in his view, given greater emphasis to individuals' perceptions of and construction of their environment within the social, economic, and political determinants of careers, as well as the psychological and sociological perspectives in the family context. Such notions of the individual's dynamic organization of and action about conceptions of self and society is implicit through many of the central elements of the theory. For example, Super depicted "a career as the life course of a person encountering a series of developmental tasks and attempting to handle them in such a way as to become the kind of person he or she wants to become. With a changing self and changing situations, the matching process is never really completed" (Super, 1990, pp. 225–226). Similarly, "career maturity is defined as the individual's readiness to cope with the developmental tasks with which he or she is confronted because of his or her biological and social development and because of society's expectations of people who have reached that stage of development. This readiness is both affective and cognitive" (Super, 1990, p. 213). It involves affective variables such as career planning, or planfulness, and career exploration, or curiosity. It also involves, among others, such cognitive characteristics as knowledge of the principles of career decision making and ability to apply them to actual choices; knowledge of the nature of careers, occupations, and the world of work; and knowledge of the field of work in which one's occupational preference falls.

Super gave prominence to individuals' mastery of increasingly complex tasks at different stages of career development. Here he attempted to synthesize the work of Miller and Form (1951) and of Havighurst (1953) by integrating these two perceptions of life-stage phenomena into a more elaborate set of constructs. Miller and Form, after extensive analysis of the work histories of a sample of men, conceived the following work periods as descriptive of a total life perspective: initial (while in school), trial (early, short-lived, full-time work), stable (normally mature adult), and retirement (after giving up employment). These work periods, in concert with those of Buehler (1933)—growth (childhood), exploration (adolescence), establishment (young adulthood), maintenance (maturity), and decline (old age)—provided the outline of Super's thesis, although he originally focused on the exploratory and establishment stages.

These two stages are divided into substages. The exploratory stage breaks down into the tentative, transition, and trial (with little commitment) substages; the establishment stage, into the trial (with more commitment), stabilization, and advancement substages (Super, 1969b). He further formulated gross developmental tasks—crystallization, specification, implementation, stabilization, and consolidation—which rest on substages and metadimensions contributing to increasing vocational maturity (Super et al., 1963). Within these stages are factors, internal as well as external to the individual, that influence the choices made. These factors continue to narrow the array of options the individual considers. There is an emphasis on vocational convergence and greater specificity in behavior.

For more than a quarter of a century, Super, his colleagues, and a great number of doctoral students carried on the Career Pattern Study to attempt to validate and refine this theory. This longitudinal effort has studied the lives of more than 100 men from the time they were in ninth grade until they were well into adulthood, 35 years of age and beyond, as they have gone about occupational choice, preparation, and participation in work.

In the course of the Career Pattern Study, insights into life stages and the developmental tasks that comprise them have become refined. These are portrayed graphically in Figure 4.3. (Also see Table 6.3 in Chapter 6, which synthesizes from writings by Super and Jordaan a broad view of Super's perspectives on the life stages and their composition.)

Each of the career development tasks identified in Figure 4.3 can be further subdivided into the specific behaviors required to complete the task. For example, Table 4.3 reports a factor analytic model of vocational maturity in ninth grade that provides an outline of elements to which either instruction or guidance processes might be related. This level of specificity has provided much of the content for career education models as well as systematic planning for career guidance and counseling.

In his analysis of vocational maturity in adulthood, Super (1977, 1985b) postulated that the same five factors are important in mid-career as are important in adolescence: planfulness or time perspective, exploration, information, decision making, and reality orientation. He contended, however, that the tasks, the topics to be explored, and the kinds of information needed by 40-year-old adults are different from those important to adolescents. He further contended, "Although the content of decisions differs, decision-making principles are the same at any age and in dealing with any life stage" (p. 9). However, because career development in adulthood is substantially more heterogeneous as compared to adolescence, Super (1977) suggested

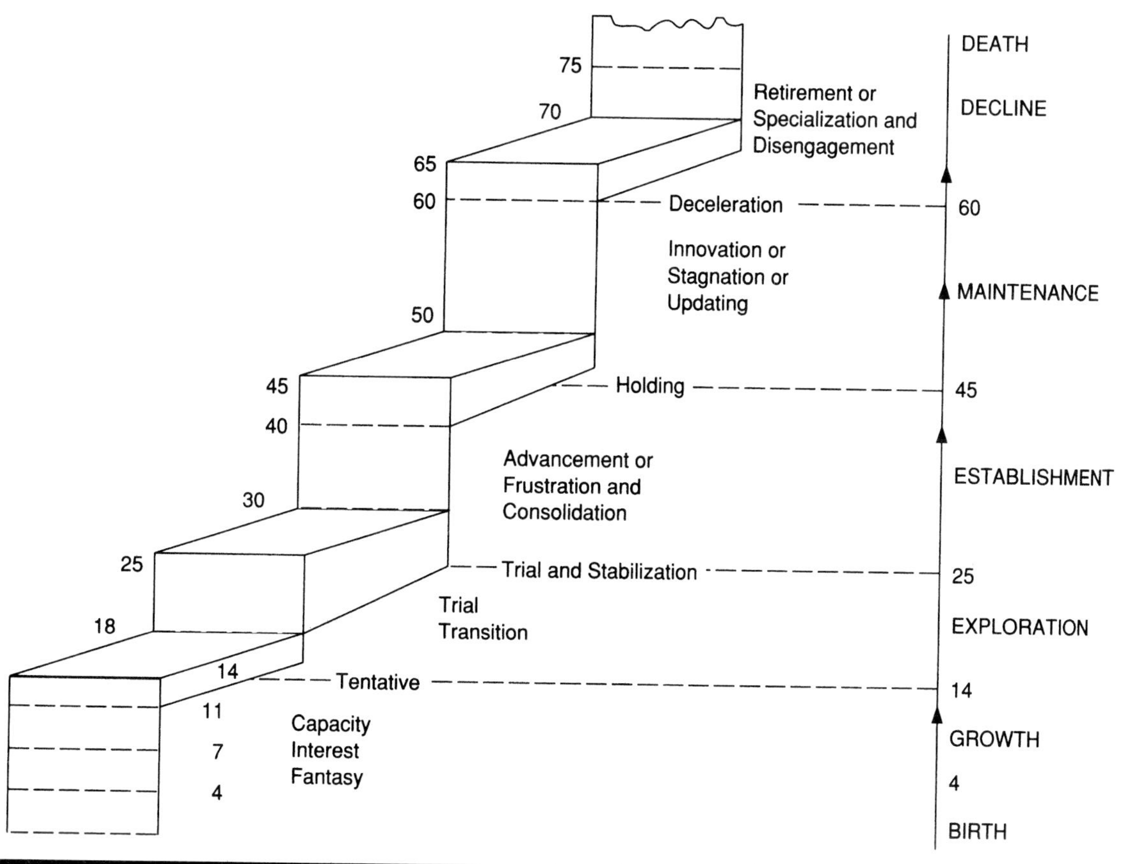

FIGURE 4.3 Life Stages and Substages: Super's 1957, 1963, 1981 Formulation
Source: From Donald E. Super, *New Dimensions in Adult Vocational and Career Counseling,* Columbus, OH: Center on Education and Training for Employment (formerly NCRVE, Ohio State University). Copyright 1985. Used with permission.

TABLE 4.3 A Factor Analytic Model of Vocational Maturity in Ninth Grade

FACTOR I	**PLANNING ORIENTATION**
A.	Acceptance of responsibility
B.	Specificity of information (more immediate types)
C.	Specificity of planning
D.	Steps taken to obtain information
E.	Awareness of the need for choices
FACTOR II	**THE LONG VIEW AHEAD**
A.	Awareness of the need for ultimate choice
B.	Specificity of information (remoter types)
C.	Entry planning
D.	Awareness of factors in choice
E.	Awareness of contingency factors
F.	Acceptance of responsibility
FACTOR III	**THE SHORT VIEW AHEAD**
A.	Specificity of planning
B.	Awareness of the need for immediate choices
C.	Acceptance of responsibility for choice
D.	Steps taken to obtain information for high school
FACTOR IV	**THE INTERMEDIATE VIEW**
A.	Awareness of factors in choice
B.	Awareness of need for intermediate choices
C.	Specificity of post—high school plans
D.	Awareness of contingency factors

Source: Reprinted from *Measuring Vocational Maturity for Counseling and Evaluation,* National Vocational Guidance Association, pp. 13 and 14. Copyright © 1974 American Association for Counseling and Development. Reprinted with permission.

that readiness for career decision making in adulthood should be called *career adaptability* rather than *career maturity.* This view, in turn, is related to his use of the terms *maxicycle,* to describe the five major life stages explored by this theory, and *minicycle,* to describe the growth, exploration, establishment, maintenance, and decline that occur within a maxicycle at points of transition from one stage to the next (or whenever careers become unstabilized, leading to new growth, reexploration, and reestablishment). Within such contexts, he reaffirmed (1984a, 1990) that in his life-stage model, the terms *trial* and *transition* have been intended to denote recycling of tasks through minicycles. These continuing processes of reexploration and reestablishment are analogous to what other theorists describe as transitions.

The term "career adaptability" reflects this dynamic interaction between the person and the environment. Savickas (1997) noted that the "construct of adaptation offers a potential bridge across the individual differences, developmental, self, and contextual segments in life-span, life-space theory" (p. 253). To measure the career concerns confronting adults (i.e., the tasks with which the person must with cope successfully to adapt to his/her career context) Super and his colleagues developed the Adult Career Concerns Inventory (Super, Thompson, Lindeman, Myers, & Jordaan, 1986).

To date, empirical evidence supporting some of these propositions has been mixed. For example, Blustein (1988) studied the relationship between career choice crystallization (CCC) and the behaviors considered to be part of Vocational Maturity (VM): career planning, career exploration, decision-making skills, world of work information. In a study of 158 community college male and female students, Blustein found that the career planning component of the Career Development Inventory, the scales used to measure vocational maturity, was related to career decidedness as career commitment but not to the other components of VM career exploration, decision-making skills, and world of work information. These clusters of developmental tasks and VM components seem not to be as clearly related to career choice commitment and decidedness as the theory would support, at least for this sample. Some other studies have suggested similar low to moderate correlations between VM and career decidedness (for instance, Fretz & Leong, 1982a; Jepsen & Prediger, 1981).

Niles, Lewis, and Hartung (1997) examined the construct validity of the Adult Career Concerns Inventory and a behavioral version of the Adult Career Concerns Inventory (ACCI-B) with initial career explorers. The ACCI-B related as expected to vocational identity, need for occupational information, career choice certainty, and career indecision. Niles and his colleagues recommended using both the ACCI and ACCI-B when working with client's making an initial career choice. In 1998, Niles, Anderson, and Goodnough used responses to the Adult Career Concerns Inventory to identify different ways adults use exploratory behavior to cope with career development tasks. Cluster analysis results identified seven ways in which adult career counseling clients use exploratory behavior to manage their career development (e.g., to maintain until retirement, to innovate and establish in their chosen occupation, to recycle to a new occupation, to innovate to move ahead in their occupations). The results of the study help to operationalize aspects of Super's career adaptability construct. The results also support Super and Knasel's (1981) contention that career adaptation parallels Piaget's model of adaptation based on the two processes of assimilation and accommodation. That is, as adults cope with their changing work and working conditions, adults make an impact on their environments and their environments make an impact on them.

From 1976 to 1979, Super lived and worked in England and began to test his theoretical propositions there. While doing so, he also elaborated aspects of his conceptual models. One aspect of his conceptual formulations was the Life-Career Rainbow (1980, 1981, 1984, 1990, 1994) to depict how various roles emerge and interact across the life span. He labeled the figure the Life Career Rainbow to emphasize the fact that it deals with both the life span and the life space, with the course of life, and with the major life roles. It also can be made to show for any given person the timing of the entry into and exit from each of the roles (Super, 1994; Super, Savickas, & Super, 1996) the possible conflicts among concurrent roles, and those of most contemporary participation and value to the individual. Figure 4.4 depicts the Life-Career Rainbow.

Super (1980, 1990) suggested that most people play nine major roles in their life, which emerge in approximate chronological order as follows: (1) child (son or daughter), (2) student, (3) leisurite, (4) citizen, (5) worker (including unemployed worker and nonworker as ways of playing the role), (6) spouse,

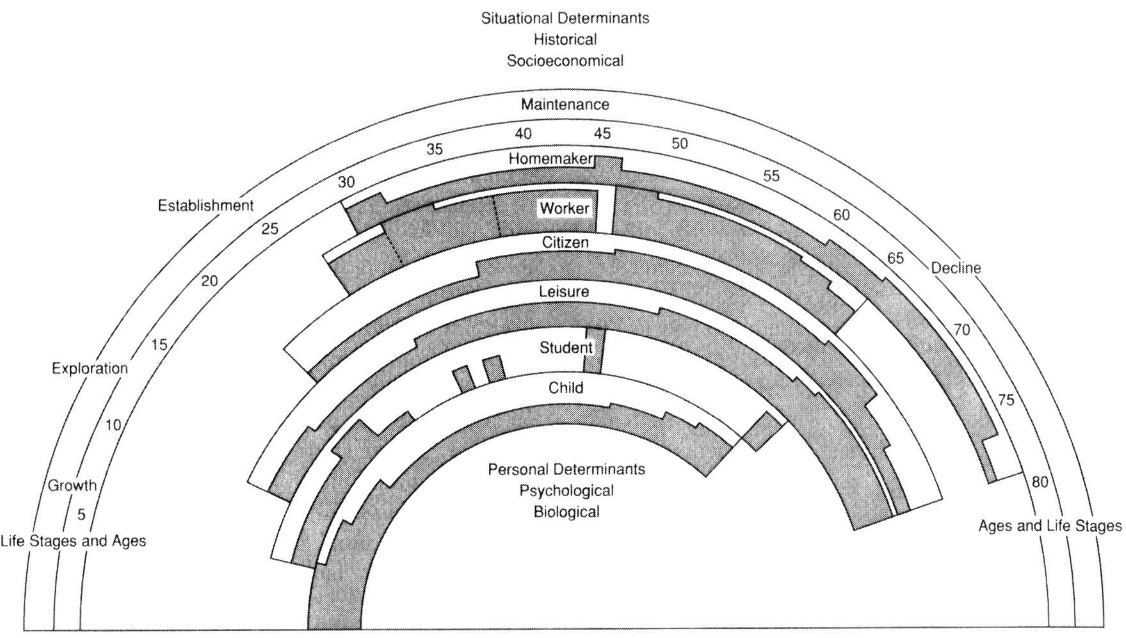

FIGURE 4.4 The Life-Career Rainbow: Six Life Roles in Schematic Life Space
Source: From "A Life-Span, Life-Space Approach" by Donald E. Super from *Career Choice and Development: Applying Contemporary Theories to Practice*, 2e, edited by D. Brown & L. Brooks. Copyright © 1990 by Jossey-Bass, Inc., Publishers. Reprinted with permission of John Wiley & Sons, Inc.

(7) homemaker, (8) parent, and (9) pensioner. The constellation of interacting, varying roles constitutes the career (1980, p. 284). The principal theaters in which these roles are played include (1) the home, (2) the community, (3) the school (including college and university), and (4) the workplace. Although there are other roles and other theaters, the ones identified tend to be the most common.

Each role tends to be played primarily in one theater, although some roles, such as worker, may spill over, for example, from the workplace to the home, and cause conflict and confusion; nowadays the boundaries between life roles are becoming blurred due to technology and changing working conditions (e.g., many people now work at home). It is in role shaping, redefining the expectations of others and of the role itself with one's conception of it, as well as in the choice of positions and roles, that the individual synthesizes personal and situational role determinants.

With respect to the relationship between earlier performance and later positions and roles, Super maintained, "The nonoccupational positions occupied before the adult career begins influence both the adult positions which may be occupied and the way in which their role expectations are met. Thus the amount and type of schooling is one determinant of occupation entered, and the first occupational position, both its type and job performance, is one determinant of later occupational positions open to the individual" (1980, p. 286). Similarly, relationships occur between earlier and later performance throughout life and, indeed, between preretirement and satisfaction with one's life in retirement.

Super went on to suggest that the fact that people play several roles simultaneously in several theaters means that occupation, family, community, and leisure roles affect each other. "Success in one facilitates success in others, and difficulties in one role are likely to lead to difficulties in another" (1980, p. 287).

Super indicated, "The simultaneous combination of life roles constitutes the *life style;* their sequential combination structures the *life space* and constitutes the *life cycle.* The total structure is the *career pattern*" (1980, p. 288). Accordingly, roles increase and decrease in importance with the life stage and according to the developmental tasks that are encountered with advancing age.

Decision points occur before and at the time of taking on a new role, of giving up an old role, and of making significant changes in the nature of an existing role (1980, p. 291). Super identified a graphic model of career decision making that involves cycling and recycling and is rational, prescriptive, developmental, and emergent. It is shown in Figure 4.5. What this model does not portray is that the time intervals at any one step may vary greatly. Depending on the circumstances that surround the career decision point, the total model may emerge over years, days, or weeks.

Super (1980) contended:

> *The decision points of a life career reflect encounters with a variety of personal and situational determinants. The former consist of the genetic constitution of the individual modified by his or her experiences (the environment and its situational determinants) in the womb, the home, and the community. The latter are the geographic, historic, social, and economic conditions in which the individual functions from infancy through adulthood and old age. (p. 294)*

These determinants affect *preference, choices, entry* into the labor force and assumption of the worker role, and role *changes.*

Throughout the 1980s and the early 1990s, Super redefined and clarified the intention of the Life-Career Rainbow: to bring into one model the maturing and playing of a changing diversity of roles by individuals as these occur across the life span and as they structure the life space, as continuously influenced by biological, psychological, and socioeconomic determinants. The result has been a model, called the Archway Model, "designed to bring out the segmental but unified and developmental nature of career development, to high-light the segments, and to make their origin clear.... It tells the same story as the Rainbow but tells it in a different way" (Super, 1990, p. 199, 201). Figure 4.6 depicts the Archway Model.

Using a Norman arch as the graphic representation of the Archway Model, now called the Archway of Career Determinants (Super, 1994), the doorstep portrays the biographical-geographical foundations of human development. The large stone on the left supports the person (psychological characteristics), and the large stone on the right supports the society (economic resources, economic structure, social institutions). These societal factors act on the person, and the person acts on them as he or she grows and functions as a unit in society—the context in which the individual pursues his or her educational, familial,

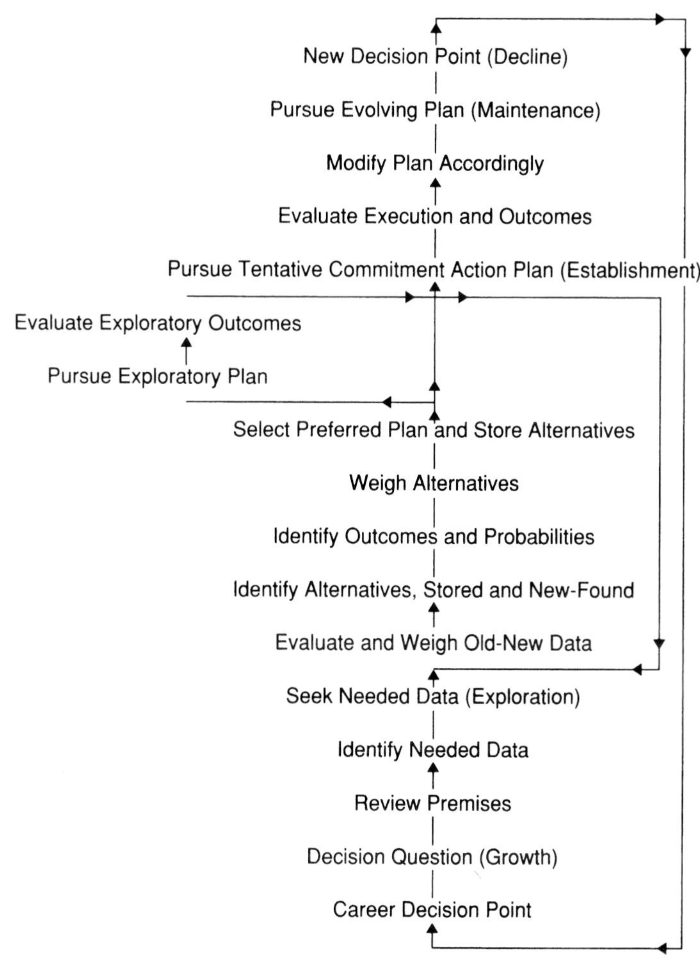

FIGURE 4.5 A Developmental Model of Emergent Career Decision Making
Source: Reprinted from "A Life-Span, Life-Space Approach to Career Development" by Donald E. Super from *Journal of Vocational Behavior, 16*(30), p. 295. Copyright © 1980, with permission from Elsevier.

occupational, civic, and leisure careers. Each stone in the composite columns depicts a determinant, with those that are more basic nearer the base of the structure. Those that are the outcomes of these determinants form the arch (Super, 1994, p. 67).

The left-hand column of the archway depicts the qualities of personality that constitute a person: the *biological base,* the *needs* and *intelligence* that develop from it in interaction with the environment, and the *values* that derive from needs as objectives that are sought in activities though likely to lead to the attainment of those values; activities are synthesized as *interests.* Also parallel to these personality traits on the left-hand column are aptitudes as derivatives of general intelligence and special aptitudes. The top of the left-hand column is denoted as *achievements* that result from "the use, misuse, or disuse of personal resources."

Although the vectors and arrows reflecting the reciprocity of influences between the left-hand column, personality, and the right-hand column, society, are not shown in the model, Super clearly intended to

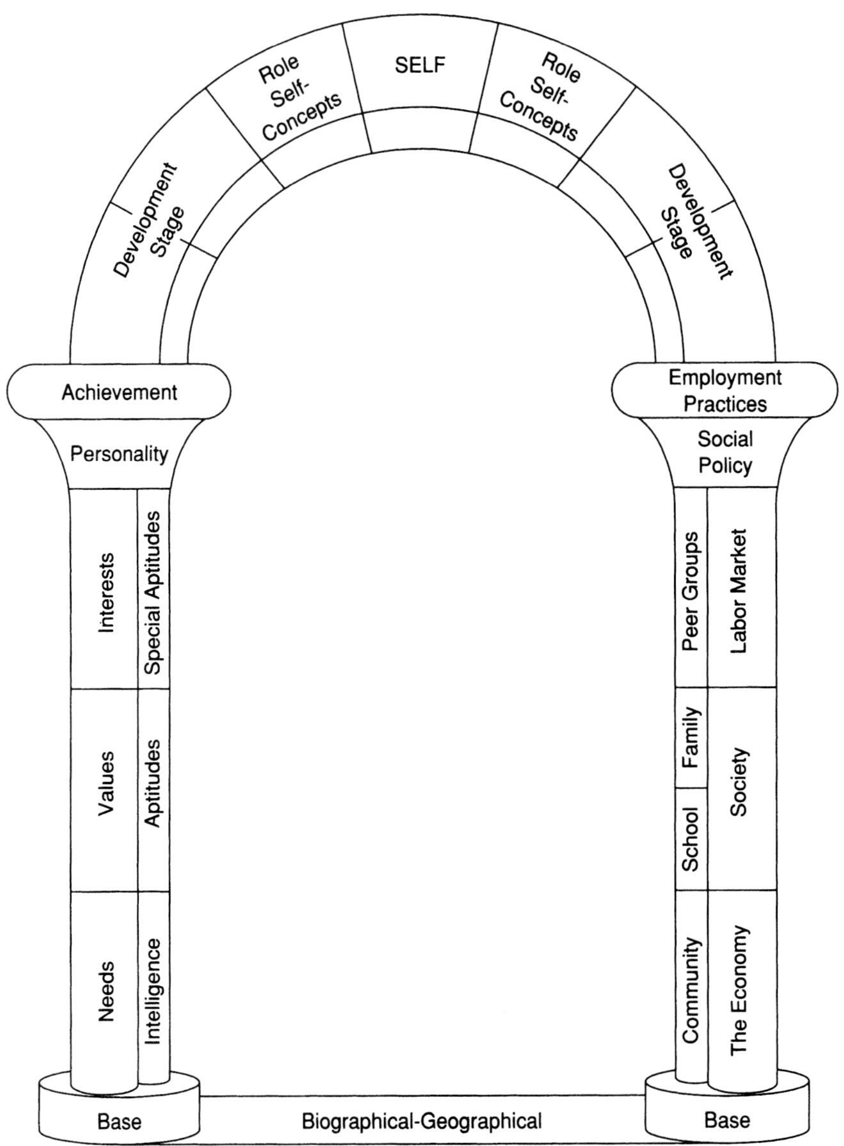

FIGURE 4.6 A Segmental Model of Career Development
Source: From "A Life-Span, Life-Space Approach to Career Development" by D. E. Super from *Career Choice and Development: Applying Contemporary Theories to Practice,* 2e, edited by D. Brown and L. Brooks. Copyright © 1990 by Jossey-Bass, Inc., Publishers. Reprinted by permission of John Wiley & Sons, Inc.

stress the interaction between the factors depicted in these two columns. He stated:

> *Natural resources, the economy, and the family influence the development of aptitude, values, and interest, as does their use in school and work. The individual, using his or her abilities and seeking outlets for interests, acts on society in visible ways (for example, as a leader, as a protagonist in enacting equal rights legislation) and in ways that escape notice (for example, by quietly fitting into and helping a new and innovative organization to function). (Super, 1990, p. 203)*

The right-hand column culminates in societal factors producing such outcomes as social policy and employment practices, whereas the left-hand column's emphasis on personality factors is manifested in achievements.

Joining the columns is the arch, which depicts the career. It, too, is composed of stones, representing conceptual components or segments. These components include the developmental stages of childhood and adolescence, young adulthood, and maturity, as well as the positions (child, worker, spouse, and so on) that one occupies in moving through these developmental stages. The *keystone* of the archway is the person who, through decision making, reflects the bringing together of personal and social forces as these are organized into self-concepts and roles in society. According to Super, the cement that holds all of these stones or segmented theories about the person and society together is learning theory:

> *Today we would say that interactive learning is the theory that explains the relationships of the segments of the Career Archway; social learning…but also learning in encounters with objects, facts, and ideas.… Interactive experiential learning, self-concept, and occupations-concept formation takes place through the interaction of the individual and the environment. This is what the Career Archway is designed to bring out. (Super, 1990, p. 204)*

Super (1994) further contended, "the archway is important in illustrating the ways in which the qualities of the individual and his or her society contribute in systematic rather than chaotic ways to career development. It emphasizes, too, that it is the individual who in his or her own way, synthesizes the effects of these determinants: it is the person, the self—the keystone of the arch—who is the decision maker (Super, 1994, p. 67).

Just as Holland and some other theorists noted in this chapter have done, Super tried to operationalize his theoretical propositions by creating instruments to assess them. Major examples of these instruments include the Career Development Inventory, the Adult Career Concerns Inventory, the Work Values Inventory, and more recently the Values Inventory, the Salience Inventory, and the Life Career Rainbow. Each of these instruments attempts to describe or to measure individual career behavior in ways that are useful in defining goals for counseling, in explicating a clients' career maturity, adaptability, or levels of career planfulness, knowledge and attitudes about choice, intrinsic and extrinsic life career values, and the relative importance to the client of five major life roles: student, worker, leisurite, citizen, and homemaker. Super's propositions have also provided the underlying theoretical foundations for such instruments as the Career Maturity Inventory (Crites, 1973).

Finally, in deference to his own early work as a counselor and to his continuing efforts to make his concepts accessible both to researchers and practitioners, Super frequently focused on the relationship of his career theory and career counseling as a process. Specifically, Super and his associates (Super, Osborne, Walsh, Brown, & Niles, 1992; Osborne, Brown, Niles, & Miner, 1997) developed the Career Development Assessment and Counseling Model (C-DAC) to translate Super's theory into practice. Additional examples of his perspectives on career counseling approaches are discussed in Chapter 14.

Donald E. Super passed away in June 1994. Following his death, a special issue of the *Career Development Quarterly* (September 1994) reviewed his contributions to career development theory and career counseling. Although it is not possible to review the total contents of that volume here, it is useful to reaffirm some of the major constructs and themes identified there as among his many major contributions. They include his conceptualization and measurement of work values cross-culturally; the central place of the self-concept in his theory; his view of the content of developmental tasks and the extrapolation of how the individual coped with these at certain life periods is likely to affect future behavior; his perspectives on the life stages that define career, career choice readiness, and career adaptability; his measurement of the centrality of work as defined by the concept of salience; the interaction between life and work roles captured by the Life Career Rainbow; and his attention to the cultural context in which the self-concept and the life roles that follow are played out. Although there are other emphases that could be cited in his major shaping of the theory of career development and his reframing of the practice of career counseling, his was a remarkable and enduring contribution.

Tiedeman's Paradigms. The work of Tiedeman and his associates, particularly O'Hara, added perspective to some elements of Super's original propositions. In regard to Tiedeman particularly, Super (1969a) stated:

> *Some men continue to change occupations throughout life, while others have stable periods followed by new periods of trial, which in turn lead to stabilization for a second or third time. Thus, there are stable (direct entry into the lifework), conventional (trial leading to stability), unstable, and multiple-trial careers. The life stage processes continue more or less throughout life, repeating themselves in the sequence: INITIAL—TRIAL—STABLE—DECLINE. Tiedeman's (1958) use of this concept in theorizing about position choice, each decision concerning the occupancy of a position involving exploration, establishment, and maintenance, is a useful refinement. (p. 4)*

Tiedeman, alone and with O'Hara, views career development as part of a continuing process of differentiating ego identity. In these terms, how a person's identity evolves depends on early childhood experiences within the family unit, the psychological crises—as defined in terms of Erikson's constructs (1963)—encountered at various developmental stages, and the agreement between society's meaning system and the individual's meaning system, as well as the emotional constants of each.

In essence, Tiedeman has emphasized an occupational decision-making paradigm within the staging phenomena (à la Erikson) making up career development. Tiedeman has maintained that Super's developmental perspective is probably an accurate way of viewing the process of career choice, but he further believes that an explicit statement about the characteristics of individual decisions needs to be made. To this end, Tiedeman has offered the following model of decision making (Tiedeman, 1961):

- I. The period of anticipation
  - A. Exploration (random and acquisitive activity)
  - B. Crystallization (emerging of patterns in the form of alternatives and their consequences leading to clarification and comment)
  - C. Choice (organizing in preparation for implementations)
  - D. Specification (clarification)
- II. The period of implementation and adjustment
  - A. Induction (person largely responsive)
  - B. Reformation (person largely assertive)
  - C. Integration (satisfaction)

Each of these stages is intended to represent a change in the dominant condition of the decision process. Indeed, each decision-making stage is represented by a qualitatively different psychological state.

Tiedeman's model is not limited to the formulation of a choice (anticipation), but also considers what happens when one attempts to implement that choice (induction). Basically, this process indicates that there is constant reciprocity between the person's self-concept and the environmental expectations as decisions are made and implemented. If the individual's ability to take on role expectations as defined by the environment is not stretched beyond tolerance, the person will stay in the position and integrate these expectations into the ego concept. If this does not happen, however, the person will likely reinstitute the process of anticipation. Tiedeman and O'Hara also suggest that individual personality is shaped by perceptions of career choices and also somewhat by the individual's conformance to the norms and values of those persons already established within the occupational setting. They stress the intimacy of self-concept and career concept as a person gradually matures through many small decisions.

Tiedeman's later work has become increasingly independent and critical of Super's developmental perspectives. For example, in 1977, Dudley and Tiedeman observed, "In brief, Super did not provide any conceptualization of the personality as an active force with complex inner organizations; he did not provide an adequate notion of the person as an agent in formation of a career pattern" (p. 6). In his evolving collaboration with others (Dudley & Tiedeman, 1977; Peatling & Tiedeman, 1977; Tiedeman &

Miller-Tiedeman, 1977), Tiedeman has been increasingly instrumental in emphasizing the power of the individual to create a career and in advancing notions of autonomy, competence, and agency as major ingredients of such processes. He and his colleagues are pursuing ways to facilitate conceptions of the human career as a holistic concept, in which career and the process of career development are one. In so doing, Tiedeman is continuing to add substance to his self-constructionist concept of the ability of individuals to exercise control over the development of their own career and over the career decision-making process.

Tiedeman and colleagues have viewed career development as a "within to without" phenomenon rather than the reverse, which is more typical in conceptions of career development. In this view, anticipation of choice, the first major category of behavior in the original Tiedeman paradigm (1961), is seen as a creative process of hierarchical restructuring in which the individual continues to transform self and environmental subsystems as movement toward accommodation or implementation occur. The conceptualizations have been aided by the evolution from a cubistic model to a pyramidal one. The cubistic model (Miller & Tiedeman, 1972) suggests that three dimensions are involved in leading a decision-guided life that is proactive (from within to without) rather than reactive (from without to within). Each of the basic conditions is comprised of three steps along the way to greater maturity, sophistication, or consciousness in action:

1. *Problem condition.* Steps: problem forming (vicarious), problem solving (acting out), solution using (autonomous use)
2. *Psychological states.* Steps: exploration, clarification, accommodation
3. *Self-comprehension.* Steps: learning about, doing, doing with awareness. (Miller & Tiedeman, 1972)

This schematic provides a language system by which one can help the individual with self-comprehension and movement toward greater control of personal decision making and the recycling of it. Miller and Tiedeman (1977) subsequently simplified the cubistic model into a pyramid containing many of the same concepts and others particularly important to her efforts to facilitate decision making with adolescents. The pyramidal model of decision-making comprehension consists of four levels—learning about, problem solving, solution using, and solution reviewing—which are each elaborated and coupled with a hierarchy of decision strategies.

As Tiedeman and Miller-Tiedeman's work unfolds (1984), it continues to build on the early work of Tiedeman and O'Hara, to which have been added more recent conceptions of ego development, decision-making strategies, and values. The latter are incorporated into the counseling and education processes designed to help persons become more consciously and proactively engaged in career decision making.

In summarizing their perspectives, Tiedeman and Miller-Tiedeman characterize them as follows:

> *Ours is not a theory that allows another to predict the behavior of a subject (common reality). Rather, ours is a value-laden model that allows a person to put his or her own decision-making activity into perspective for him- or herself (personal reality). The model is therefore merely a description of what may be internally experienced during decision-making. However, as the individual comes to understand what occurs as he or she thinks, while acting on information from the common reality, she or he will have the capacity to be proactive. With this kind of awareness and confidence, the personal reality will then reign over the common reality. (Tiedeman & Miller-Tiedeman, 1984)*

Tiedeman and, in particular, Miller-Tiedeman are evolving a conceptual, linguistic, and process structure designed to accept the power of the person to create and to be in a human career. Although other approaches to career development do not oppose such notions of individual power to create a career, Tiedeman and Miller-Tiedeman seem dedicated to self-empowerment as the central proposition in such a process. As such, their work predates and is congruent with many of the concepts described under constructivist theory earlier in this chapter and in Chapter 17.

Recently, Miller-Tiedeman (1999) proposed a career development model that views life as career and incorporates process philosophy as well as narrative and constructivist notions into the career intervention process (Cochran, 1997; Savickas, 1993). Miller-Tiedeman's "new careering" model is based on three assumptions: (1) differentiation: each moment differs from every other moment; (2) subjectivity: everything in the universe has an interior reality; and (3) communion: everything relates to everything else (1999, p. 56). Eleven principles emerge from these assumptions: (1) life self-organizes, (2) each individual has a career theory that matters most, (3) complementarity, (4) the whole is more than the sum of its parts, (5) the observer cannot separate himself or herself from what he or she observes, (6) interrlationships, interconnection, and interpenetration are the rules not the exception, (7) guiding by inner wisdom using intentions, (8) lifecareer values both right and left decisions, (9) no one of us has all it takes to make our dreams come true, (10) reality continually creates itself in our mind; therefore, each person lives his or her own mythology, and (11) support and relatedness exist in all of life (pp. 61–75).

These principles provide direction for exploring logical, emotional, and spiritual aspects of development. Miller-Tiedeman's "new careering" model provides useful conceptualizing for helping career theorists and practitioners think and act creatively in addressing career concerns. Such approaches remind us that decision making, the development of self-identity, and life changes do not occur in a vacuum. They occur within political, economic, historical, and social conditions that influence the achievement images and belief systems on which individuals base their actions. They occur as dynamic and reciprocal processes between person-environment interactions.

Savickas's Model of Time in Career Development. Savickas's conceptualization and research link how people experience and structure time to their conceptualization of their career and to how they enact vocational behavior. He contends that optimal career success and satisfaction follow from an experience of time that is characterized by an orientation to a future that is densely populated with events clearly connected to present behavior.

Savickas contends that persons require a sense of subjective career that allows them to experience self-conscious thoughts about the vocational past, present, and future. Its essence, a subjective career emerges from beliefs about and attitudes toward time. In his view, unless individuals envision a subjective career that extends into the future, they rarely seek career counseling. In contrast, he views the modal career counseling clients as those who seek to reduce anxiety about the future; who want the counselor to help them take responsibility for their lives and to design their occupational futures. In Savickas's view, some persons have not learned how the culture, particularly the middle-class culture, in the United States conceptualizes and uses time to structure life roles. Thus, they may orient themselves to the past or present, not the future, and lack a sense of the future as the major emphasis of subjective career, or they may view time so differently from the dominant occupational culture that they experience vocational failure and dissatisfaction.

Although, as described in the previous section of this chapter and in Chapter 6, Super's theoretical perspectives on career development have emphasized time perspective as one of the five major factors in career maturity in adolescence and in career adaptability in adulthood, few career interventions have been designed to incorporate this concept. In contrast, Savickas has built his concept of career interventions on three organizing constructs as they relate to time: (1) time perspective, (2) time differentiation, and (3) time integration.

According to Savickas (1990b), *time perspective* refers to how individuals "view and orient themselves to time.... time imagery related to achievement motivation" (p. 5). An individual's time perspective also includes an orientation to time zones: past, present, and future.

The career culture considers future orientation as the prime precursor of mental health and career achievement. A future orientation enables one to deal with gratification and work for tomorrow. A future orientation increases anxiety and, in turn, occupational commitment because work is an outgrowth of anxiety about survival in the future. Career interventions typically work to create or reinforce a future orientation by making the future seem important and by creating anxiety about what one will do in the future (p. 7).

In this view, *time differentiation* is seen as making the future real. The density and extension of events within time zones tends to define which time zone is the more real for the client. "An individual who densely populates the future with anticipated events which extend far into the horizon has a schema ready for career planning. A differentiated future provides a meaningful context for setting personal goals.... While a future orientation may create anxiety, future differentiation alleviates anxiety by envisioning the future and one's place in it" (Savickas, 1990b, p. 8). Teaching persons about anticipated events, and how to think about and label them may be important interventions. In this context, career counseling involves "helping people create, articulate, and enact their dreams" (p. 10).

In the third dimension of this approach, *time integration* enables planning. "Temporal integrations refers to the sense of connectedness among events across time zones.... Continuity among them, how, and when provides the cognitive schema for realistic planning.... Discontinuity reduces predictability and makes planning illusive. When life is viewed as an unbroken thread, individuals can become aware of enduring themes and patterns in life, strengthen their sense of identity, and choose activities that require a perseverance.... Optimism that presents behavior can be organized to achieve future goals moves enactment of plans" (Savickas, 1990b, p. 11). Career interventions used to deal with time integration combine attention to planning attitudes, competencies, contingent planning, and purposeful action.

Much more deserves to be said about Savickas's model of career interventions appropriate to dealing with each of the three time constructs—perspective, differentiation, integration—as fundamental to a conception of a personal subjective career. These constructs and interventions are fundamental to a conception of career development as movement across life stages and time. Research directed to such views can be found in the following references: Savickas, Silling, and Schwartz (1984), and Ringle and Savickas (1983).

The Gottfredson Model of Occupational Aspirations. Among her other research and theoretical writings, Gottfredson (1981) has proposed a developmental theory of occupational aspirations in which she has sought to integrate, in a broader approach, a variety of principles from psychological theories as well as type theories of vocational choice. According to Gottfredson, her theory "accepts the fundamental importance of self-concept in vocational development, that people seek jobs compatible with their images of themselves. Social class, intelligence, and sex are seen as important determinants of both self-concept and the types of compromises people must make, thus the theory integrates a social systems perspective with the more psychological approaches" (1981, p. 546).

Gottfredson's theory is a stage theory that, similar to Ginzberg and colleagues and Super, conceives of the self-concept becoming increasingly differentiated and complex as a child grows. Thus, as the child and adolescent ages, refining occupational aspirations, one of the major processes involved is the continuous adding of self-concept characteristics. Similar to self-concepts, occupational images held by people can be characterized by their complexity and differentiation and their comprehensiveness and specificity. Gottfredson suggests that persons construct cognitive maps of occupations in which the similarities and differences among such occupations tend to include only a few major dimensions: sex-type (masculinity/femininity), level of work (prestige), and field of work. Although persons across gender and socioeconomic classes tend to agree on how occupations can be placed in hierarchies within these categories, Gottfredson also suggests that persons create their own cognitive maps of acceptable alternatives based on one's conception of one's social space—the person's view of where he or she fits into society. Within the construction of such individualized cognitive maps of job-self compatibility, children and adolescents create boundaries of acceptable jobs based on tolerable sex-type images, tolerable levels of prestige, and tolerable levels of effort to attain them.

Gottfredson (1981) portrays the developmental stages and their effects on occupational aspirations by describing four major stages with assorted substages or elements. In paraphrased outline form, they appear as follows:

Stage 1. Orientation to size and power (ages 3–5 years)
Stage 2. Orientation of sex roles (ages 6–8)
Stage 3. Orientation to social valuation (ages 9–13 years)
- Awareness of social class
- The development of preferences for level of work
- Differences in preferences by social class and ability level
- Circumscription of range of preferences

Stage 4. Orientation to the internal, unique self (ages 14+)
- Perception of self and others
- Specification of vocational aspirations (1981, p. 555)

Gottfredson provides many interesting concepts to describe boundaries and motivational dimensions related to the development of occupational aspirations. For example, she states:

> *Some aspects of self-concept are more central than others and will take priority when compromising occupational goals. One's occupation constitutes a very public and continuing presentation of self, and some people have priorities for what aspects of self they want to emphasize or present unambiguously.... Gender self-concept will be the most strongly protected aspect of self, followed by the maintenance of one's social standing or worth, that is one's social class and ability self-concepts.... Thus, people will tend to sacrifice interest in field of work to maintain sextype and prestige, and to some extent will sacrifice prestige level for sextype if that is also necessary. (p. 572)*

Within this context, she also suggests two other manifestations of compromise: "Exploration of job options ends with the implementation of a satisfactory choice, not necessarily the optimal potential choice," and "People accommodate psychologically to the compromises they make."

Gottfredson's concepts have begun to initiate research by others to test her perspectives. In particular, Gottfredson's theory suggests that elements internalized at an earlier age (for instance, sex type) will be more resistant to change then elements internalized later in development. Thus, "vocational interests are sacrificed first, job level second, and sex type last" (1981, p. 549). The findings of Hesketh, Elmslie, and Kaldor (1990), who studied the Gottfredson theory of compromise with 73 career-dissatisfied adults and 90 high school students, suggested an alternative model of compromise that indicated that interests were more important in career choices than either sex type or prestige, because interests are of a compound nature, incorporating the latter. Such a view also suggests that counselors may be able to help clients who have rejected occupations based on one attribute (for example, sex type or prestige) to understand the basis of their rejection and to reconsider such choices on the basis of more complex attributions (for example, interests).

ADULT DEVELOPMENT

Although adult career development is a major focus of the work of Super, Tiedeman, and Ginzberg and, certainly, Holland's work on the structural aspects of career behavior, there is also a group of persons who have targeted their theorizing and research on adult development exclusive of concerns about the total life span or about the early stages, childhood or adolescent, of career development (e.g., Hansen, 2002). As suggested elsewhere in this chapter, much of the early work in career development theory and research was focused on adolescent exploration, anticipation, and the formulation of preferences, although major theorists have speculated about adult development as well as adolescent development (e.g., Krumboltz & Henderson, 2002; Peterson, Lumsden, Sampson, Reardon, & Lenz, 2002; Vondracek & Porfeli, 2002). Research of the last two decades or so has made clear that exploration and change do not end with adolescence but continue throughout life. Adulthood is also dynamic; it is a time of changes of self-concept and aspirations, a time of transitions, crises and reformulations, a time of minicycles and personal redefinitions.

Just as it is true in the range of theories described earlier in this chapter, adult development theorists view adult career behavior and the adult experience from different perspectives. Schlossberg (1986) has suggested that there are four such perspectives: one that explains adult behavior within the cultural context, a second that focuses on the psychological developmental stages of the individual, a third view that discusses the adult experience in terms of transitions, and a fourth perspective that examines continuity and change over the life span. Schlossberg has classified that major theorists in each of these four categories by the major concepts they espouse and by the counseling or institutional practices that such concepts support. Table 4.4 represents her analysis of such perspectives, concepts, and practices.

Schlossberg's Work

Nancy Schlossberg is among the major theorists of adult development and adult career development. In addition to her own important concepts, Schlossberg has synthesized the work of other adult theorists into perspectives that are pertinent to career guidance and counseling. Summarizing the work of major theorists in adult development, Schlossberg (1978) has advanced five propositions about adult development that reflect some of the change that occurs. These propositions follow in paraphrased form:

1. *Behavior in adulthood in determined by social rather than by biological clocks.* In childhood and

TABLE 4.4 The Adult Experience: Perspectives, Concepts, and Practices

PERSPECTIVES	CONCEPTS	PRACTICES
Cultural	*Bertaux* Life Stories depend on work structure *Rosenbaum* Career mobility results from organizational structure *Kanter* Individual progress is determined by opportunity structure	Change or modify system Hire and promote older individuals Gear admissions and financial aid to older part-time individuals
Developmental Age/Stage	*Levinson et al.* Invariant sequence of developmental methods Life structure Dream, mentor Polarities *Erikson* Unfolding of life and restoring of inner issues Hierarchical stages *Gould* Release from childhood assumptions Tinkering with inadequacies *Perry, Loevinger, Kohlberg* Hierarchical sequence Sequence in ego development and moral development *Fiske, Gutman* Men and women express the dormant part of themselves at midlife *Gilligan* Critique of models based on men and applied to women Hierarchical models obscure other voices	Design programs for people at different stages Programs for returning students, preretirees Design programs for people who process work differently Differential teaching, advising, and counseling Assess congruence of supervisor, supervisee along dimensions of personality, learning style, achievement Sensitize faculty, counselors, and others to age, social class bias
Transitions: Life Course/ Life Span/ Life Events	*Neugarten, Moore, & Lowe* Socially created rather than biologically determined transitions *Lowenthal (Fiske), Chiriboga, Thurnher* Life span Stage not age Coping with transitions; balance of resources to deficits Sex differences *Schlossberg* Types of transitions: anticipated, unanticipated, nonevents Coping moderators: transition, environment, self Transition process: over time, for better or worse *Pearlin* Coping, no life events, is central issue Classification of life strains and coping responses	Design programs for people in similar transitions Support from others who have successfully negotiated the same transition Provide cognitive map Offer programs at several times: before, during, after transition Teach individual coping skills To change situation To modify meaning of situation To relax

(continued)

TABLE 4.4 Continued

PERSPECTIVES	CONCEPTS	PRACTICES
Life Span: Continuity and Change	*Neugarten* Capacity of individual to select, ignore, or modify socializing influence Fanning out and variations Fluid life span *Vaillant* Early trauma not predictive of later behavior *Pearlin* Variability Differential distribution of strains by sex, age, different patterns of coping *Brim, Kagan* Orientation (not yet theory) toward constancy and change Discontinuities rather than sequencing are studied Importance of variability based on cohort, sex, age, social class	Multiple programs for larger population Individual and group programs Media Other

Source: N. K. Schlossberg, Adult development theories: Ways to illuminate the adult experience. *Adult Career Development: Concepts, Issues, and Practices,* edited by Zandy B. Leibowitz and H. Daniel Lea. (Alexandria, VA: National Career Development Association, 1986.) Copyright © American Association for Counseling and Development. Reprinted with permission.

adolescence, biological development or deterioration is a greater factor than in adulthood. Beyond the changes occasioned by menopause or the possible rapid physical change of late, late adulthood, most of the effects on behavior in adulthood are social, not biological. Social norms about when and how certain behavior should occur—when one should marry, settle down in a job, or retire—tend to affect perceptions of and stimulate action regarding major life events. To be out of synchronization with such events may cause feelings of uncertainty, anxiety, or inadequacy. Although these age-related norms may be changing under the influence of the increasing numbers of adults returning to school, changing careers in midlife, entering new careers after retirement, and trying out new marital styles and lifestyles, socially defined age-appropriate behavior remains a powerful influence on life-career behavior.

2. *Behavior is at times a function of life stage, at others of age.* Many theorists have identified distinct chronological periods in which specific tasks, problems, structures, and states of mind are likely to occur. Levinson and colleagues (1978), to be discussed in the next section, advocates such a view. Other theorists (such as Lowenthal, Thurnher, Chiriboga, et al., 1976) attribute less importance to age per se and much more importance to what types of events or tasks the person is actually dealing with. This is a "stage approach."

3. *Sex differences are greater than either age or stage differences.* In the various adult life stages, men and women differ dramatically, partly because of early socialization and partly because their identities tend to be defined differently. The identities of men tend to be defined primarily in terms of direct achievement. Women define their identities more in terms of vicarious achievement, not through their own activities and accomplishments but through those of the dominant people in their lives (usually men) (Lipman-Blumen & Leavitt, 1977).

4. *Adults continually experience transitions requiring adaptations and reassessment of the self.* In opposition to notions that adulthood is one of stability and certainty, the concept of transitions suggests that adults are constantly experiencing change either deliberately, because it is chosen, or inadvertently, because of forces external to the self. Such changes can engender growth, new concepts of self, or crisis and deterioration. In either case, stress frequently accompanies the transition and requires adaptation.

5. *The recurrent themes of adulthood are identity, intimacy, and generativity.* Identity, intimacy, and generativity, as defined by Erikson (1950), recur throughout the individual's life. Identity may become an issue whenever the individual faces a transition. This, in turn, raises questions of generativity: What meaning does my life have? What have I contributed to the world? What have I created? Intimacy refers to free, open, spontaneous, affectionate, trusting responses with all of those with whom we have close human ties. These relationships tend to sustain energy and motivation to develop identity and to cope with matters of generativity. They are apparently crucial successful adaptation to transitions.

Schlossberg (1984) has explored many of the perspectives that underlie a framework for helping adults in transition. In particular, she suggests that adults must be looked at as individuals who relate differently to transitions. The transition itself must be examined in terms of its type, context, and impact, with the transition process considered in relation to how the person reacts to it over time. In addition, the individual's coping resources need to be examined to determine if they are assets or liabilities, resources or deficits, either intrapsychically or environmentally. Certainly, a major ingredient of understanding adult variability in transitions is an understanding of some of the major views of adult development.

The Importance of Adult Transitions

As the propositions of adult development provided by Schlossberg suggest, transitions are the central focus of much current theoretical attention. Indeed, Perry (1982) has contended that "special needs populations" can be conceived of in two ways: (1) as those who are experiencing equity difficulty in gaining access to education and work because of bias, discrimination, quotas, prejudice, and other forms of social gate-keeping; and (2) those who are at risk because of transitions—changing families, midcareer job dislocation, retirement. In much of the literature, transitions are portrayed as frightening or traumatic. Indeed, as Schlossberg (1981) has asserted, the current definitions of transition have actually grown out of crisis theory. Some theorists, however (such as Parkes, 1971) prefer the term *psychosocial transition* to play down the notion of crisis. It is in this perspective that Levinson, Darrow, Klein, Levinson, and McKee (1978) talk of *developmental transition* to represent "a turning point or boundary between two periods of greater stability" (p. 57).

Levinson and colleagues (1978) have extended the models of Havighurst, Ginzberg, and colleagues, and Super and colleagues by adding the notion of transition to each of the life stages portrayed in those models. In other words, one does not abruptly change life or career stages (exploration to establishment, establishment to maintenance), but instead engages in a period of activity over time that represents a transition to the next life stage. Levinson and associates use the term *era,* much as other theorists use the term *stage* or *phase* (p. 18). According to Levinson and associates, there are four such eras in life: childhood and adolescence, ages 0–22; early adulthood, 17–45; middle adulthood, 40–65; and late adulthood, 60 on. The transition between eras consistently takes four or five years—not less than three and rarely more than six. Transitions are developmental periods that link the eras and provide some continuity between them, a boundary zone. "The nature of each era is reflected in the evolution of a man's careers in work, family, and other settings, his involvement in solitary and social enterprises, and his broader life plans and goals" (p. 30). The masculine pronoun is used precisely here because Levinson's work, like that of Super, was based on research with men. He and his colleagues studied forty men in considerable depth over several years as the empirical base for his theoretical perspective. They split the subjects into four groups of ten men each from one of four occupational subgroups: hourly workers in industry, business executives, university biologists, and novelists.

In addition to eras and transitions, Levinson and colleagues use several other terms to describe career development as they see it. Primary among these is *individual life structure.* The life structure refers to the patterning of one's life at a given time and to the engagement of the individual in society. Levinson (1977) contends that a life structure has three aspects:

1. The nature of the man's *sociocultural world,* including class, religion, ethnicity, race, family, political systems, occupational structure, and

particular conditions and events, such as economic depression or prosperity, war, and liberation movements of all kinds.

2. His *participation in his world*—his evolving relationships and roles as citizen, worker, boss, lover, friend, husband, father, member of diverse groups and organizations.
3. The *aspects of his self* that are expressed and lived out in the various components of his life and the aspect of the self that must be inhibited or neglected within the life structure (1977, p. 100).

This aspect is expanded (Levinson et al., 1978) to reflect the idea that a man selectively uses and is used by his world, through his evolving relationships and roles as citizen, lover, worker, boss, friend, husband, father, and member of diverse groups and enterprises. Participation involves transactions between self and world. (p. 42)

In this view (Levinson, 1977; Levinson et al., 1978), adult development is the evolution of a life structure through alternating stable periods and transitional periods. The primary developmental task of a stable period "is to make certain crucial choices; build a life structure around them and seek to attain particular goals and values within this structure" (1977, p. 100). Each stable period has its distinctive tasks that reflect the requirements of that time in the life cycle. The primary developmental task of a *transitional period* is "to terminate the existing structure and to work toward the imitation of a new structure" (1977, p. 100). In this process, a man reappraises the existing life structure, explores possibilities for change in the world and in the self, and moves toward the crucial choices that will form the basis for a new life structure in the next stable period. Each transitional period also has its own distinctive tasks reflecting its place in the life cycle.

Levinson and colleagues (1978) describe choices as the primary components of the life structure. To describe and analyze the life structure is to consider the choices a person makes and how the person deals with the consequences. "Every choice is saturated by both self and world. To choose something means to have a relationship with it. The relationship becomes a vehicle for living out certain aspects of the self and for engaging in certain modes of participation in the world" (p. 44). (See Chapter 6 for specific development tasks in adulthood according to Levinson et al., 1978.)

Kanchier and Unruh (1988) conducted a study of 464 managers and former managers (298 nonchangers, 166 changers) who were employed in middle and senior executive positions by one large Canadian organization. The purpose of the study was to attempt to clarify the process of occupational change by identifying, exploring, and describing the transition periods of the life cycle and the disengagement stages of the occupational cycle to determine if they are interrelated and to ascertain if changers and nonchangers differ on the variable used to assess these transitions.

Using the Job Descriptive Index and the Self and Work Perception Questionnaire, as well as two-hour semistructured interviews, they found that changers were significantly more dissatisfied than nonchangers with their corporate positions. A significantly larger percentage of changers than nonchangers (in the Age 30 and Mid-Life Transition categories) underwent critical self-evaluation with respect to personality traits and career values and goals. Significantly more changers than nonchangers experienced traumatic events other than job dissatisfaction, such as marital break-up, death of a parent, illness, extensive travel, or birth of a child. Many changers said that these experiences precipitated and encouraged self-appraisal and were related to the changes they noted in personality traits and career values and goals. The researchers suggested, as would be described by Levinson and colleagues (1978) and by other transition theorists that career life cycles seemed to be interrelated; that the transition periods of changers' life cycles seemed to be integrated with the disengagement stages of their occupational cycles. During the disengagement stages of their occupational cycles, changers were also questioning their career and life goals. These self-appraisals were often intensified by traumatic events and associated with shifts in values. Changers felt they were growing and developing in their careers and indicated that they would probably enter, master, and disengage themselves from several occupations or job tasks throughout their lives to enhance their career and personal growth. For changers, career development seemed to be a continuing search for a better fit between their occupations and their developing personalities.

The researchers, in addition to linking career change to transitions at different age periods and with regard to different events, suggested that counselors should give positive recognition to job changes as real opportunities for personal and professional growth and enhanced career marketability. "Adults, including those in their fifties or older, should be encouraged to view transitions as suitable times to (a) describe, explore, and evaluate the nature of the conflicts they are experiencing; (b) challenge, revise, or modify their career and life goals; and thereby (c) acquire a sense of mastery over their lives" (p. 136).

The importance of adult transitions as the focus of counselor behavior has also been addressed by Watts (1980), who has suggested three roles that derive from theory about adult career development. One addresses *developmental stages* in the life cycle, as these are related to various periods of chronological age. In such a perspective, the role of the career counselor with adults would be to help persons understand, adapt to, and master the requirements of the developmental tasks characteristic of each stage. A second model focuses on *roles*. This model views aging as a process of learning new roles and relinquishing old ones. The career counseling response here would involve periodic stock taking about roles and about the interactions and transitions between them, learning to let some roles go and developing the skills and insights to take on new roles. The third model focuses on *life events,* which involve significant transitions. Here the career counseling role is one concerned with coping with crises and realizing the growth potential that may be innate with such crises. Each of these approaches has relevance to where particular adults are in their career development and in their transitions.

Career Stages in Organizations

Although there are many adult developmental theories that might be cited, it will suffice here to report only one other perspective, that is, that different settings are comprised of or trigger different types of career transitions or organizational career stages. Additional perspectives on such matters are discussed in Chapter 6 and 11 as well as in other parts of this book. For example, Dalton, Thompson, and Price (1977) have suggested four progressive career stages in organizations: apprentice, colleague, mentor, and sponsor. Schein (1978) divides the career life cycle into four stages: entry, socialization, mid career, and later career. Hall (1976, 1986) discuss early career, middle career, and later career stages. As examples of his later career stages, spanning ages 45 to 60, Hall has identified the following tasks and levels:

- Awareness of advancing age
- Awareness of body changes related to aging
- Knowing how many career goals have been or will be attained
- Search for new life goals
- Marked change in family relationships
- Change in work relationships
- Sense of work obsolescence
- Feeling of decreased job mobility and increased concerns for job security

Inkson and Arthur (2002) recommend that to manage their career development effectively, adult workers can focus on "core competencies" that are generalizable among organizations. They draw upon the work of Hall (1992) to categorize core competences in three arenas: a company's culture: its mission, values, beliefs, and strategic purpose; a company's know-how: its accumulated skills, expertise, and areas of special competence; and a company's networks: its relationships with suppliers, customers, other companies, and others. Inkson and Arthur note that workers can align their career investments with the organization's competencies but should emphasize transferable rather than company-specific investments. "This thinking provides a framework that seems helpful to understand career dynamics beyond rather than within single organizational settings" (Inkson & Arthur, p. 297). DeFillippi and Arthur (1996) developed individual competencies to correspond to the core organizational competencies. Individual competencies are: Knowing-why (corresponding to company culture): the ever-changing energies, values, interests, motivations and personal circumstances and goals that an individual brings to work; Knowing-how (corresponding to company know-how): the individual abilities, qualifications, skills, and expertise, accumulated as a result of career and life experience; and Knowing-whom (corresponding to company networks): the reputation and networks that an individual develops within and beyond the employing company. In the Inkson and Arthur model, workers are encouraged to proactively assess the degree to which their individual competencies mesh with a particular organization's competencies and the time-limited work projects that serve as learning episodes for workers and organizations.

Regardless of which model is used to explain career transitions within organizations or the more global models of adult career development, each stage portrayed involves different activities, relationships, and developmental tasks. They, in turn, require different emphases in the delivery of career guidance and counseling.

Although many of the adult development models described in this section—and earlier theoretical perspectives described in other sections of this chapter—have validity for or have been related to women, such is not always true. The next chapter and Chapter 16 will portray some of the theoretical dimensions unique to women and minority groups and some of the ongoing questions about male and female differences in career development; however, it is useful here to cite Gilligan's perspectives about women's career development: (1) There are qualitative differences in how men and women process and interpret the world, and (2) there are sex differences in adult development not reflected in many of the current models. Gilligan (1982a) asserts that "women define themselves in a context of human relationships," whereas men tend to devalue such relationships. She further contends, "attachment and separation anchor the cycle of human life...the concepts of attachment and separation that depict the nature and sequence of infant development appear in adolescence as identity and intimacy and then in adulthood as love and work" (p. 151). "This reiterative counterpoint...tends to disappear" in many developmental models. Gilligan's view of Levinson's concept of the dream is tied to achievement. Gilligan contends, "In all these accounts the women are silent...thus there seems to be a line of development missing from current depictions of adult development, a failure to describe the progression of relationships toward a maturity of interdependence" (p. 155). Gilligan (1982b) rightly contends that even where sex differences are identified and examined, they are not effectively incorporated in most adult development models:

> *Male and female voices typically speak of the importance of different truths, the former of the role of separation as it defines and empowers the self, the latter of the ongoing process of attachment that creates and sustains the human community.... Since this dialogue contains the dialogue that creates the tension of human development, the silence of women in the narrative of adult development distorts the conception of its stages and sequences. (Gilligan, 1982a, p. 155)*

IMPLICATIONS FOR CAREER GUIDANCE, COUNSELING, AND CAREER EDUCATION

In the several approaches covered in this chapter, career development is described as a process shaped by an interplay of self-references, self-knowledge, knowledge about training, educational and occupational opportunities, genetic and early childhood influences, evolving personality styles, and patterns of traits that individuals express cognitively and psychologically in their choice behavior and career identity. The collective finding of these descriptions of career development is that like all human behavior, it is complex and is part of the total fabric of personality development.

Osipow (1986) has captured much of the complexity of career development as it has been explored in this chapter when he compares his views of 1969 and 1986 on how careers unfold by stating:

> *There is nothing that I said in 1969 that I would not say now. Career development still seems essentially socially bound. Careers are still subject to considerable change over the life span. Career choice and implementation, as well as adjustment, expose individuals to a great many stresses. Abilities still significantly affect how people's careers unfold and their levels of attainment, and the environment appears to provide an important context in which career development takes places. (p. 161)*

The development of career-related behavior is characterized by progressive growth and learning operating from infancy through adulthood within a network of impinging forces internal and external to the individual. Within this context, choice behavior involves a series of interdependent decisions that are to some extent irreversible but are efforts to optimize the individual's situation and are intimately tied to the individual's personal history, to personal perceptions of the future, and to both antecedent experiences and future alternatives.

Many of the existing approaches to career development are based on limited samples of rather privileged persons; most often these samples are of men rather than women. They are, in general, addressed to those in the middle range of socioeconomic characteristics rather than to those who veer from this classification in either direction. Consequently, these approaches tend to emphasize the continuous, uninterrupted, and progressive aspects of career development that seem possible primarily in those whose choice barriers are minimal, for whom both psychological and economic resources are available to aid purposeful development, and in whom a high correspondence between self-concept and vocational concept is most probable. Such criteria do not fit all the persons about whom career counselors, career guidance practitioners, or educators must be concerned.

Another characteristic of these current approaches to career development is that although they predict that individuals with particular need hierarchies or self-concepts will reject occupations and career patterns that do not seem compatible with their personal characteristics, little attention is given to the possibility that work itself it not central to the lifestyles or aspirations of some persons, or that it has connotations that repel rather than attract. For many persons, choices are based not on what they want to do but on what they do not want to do. For these people, choice seems to be more nearly a matter of moving toward an ideal. For other persons, work is not the central commitment for investment of identification or energy that many theories assume.

Another point of concern in present descriptions of career development is the age or level of maturity required to make choices. "Most would feel that a certain maturing process must take place before youth (ages 14 to 18) can sensibly make choices—especially vocational ones" (McDaniels, 1968). McDaniels rebuts this assumption by stating that youth "are not too young to choose, only too poorly prepared to make choices." Thus, in much of the thinking about career development, there is insufficient attention to the heterogeneity in maturity in every group within the population whether classified by age, sex, race, social class, or any other basis.

Perhaps the most important point of all in analyzing current approaches to career development is that theories of career behavior largely describe what happens if nothing is done to influence the process. Other chapters in this book discuss theories of intervention in such behavior. Thus, theories of career development describe the targets of intervention: which behaviors should be developed; what influences should be diminished in effect; what cognitive or psychological structures should be strengthened. Although several longitudinal approaches have emerged—for example, Super's Career Pattern Study (1957, 1990, 1994), Crites's Vocational Development Project (1969), Gribbons and Lohnes's Readiness for Vocational Development (1968)—their purpose has not been to influence career development systematically, but only to describe it at different stages of life.

Other theories have been focused on the structural properties of career behavior (Holland, 1966, 1973a, 1985, 1992, 1997) or on the specifics of decision making. Although each of these has been important to understanding the evolutionary complexities of career identity and choice, they have focused only on selected interventions in such processes. Taking due cognizance of the caveats expressed, the following career development implications would seem to provide a conceptual base for planning career guidance or career education activities and for implementing career counseling:

1. The concept that people are only economic animals and that work is chosen only for the livelihood it offers is too simplistic. Work also provides a means for meeting needs of social interaction, dignity, self-esteem, self-identification, and other forms of psychological gratification.

2. Individual differences ultimately characterize the style, preference, and performance of people occupying various occupational and educational roles. Although these are between group differences in the personality types and abilities of people in different occupations, there are also significant within-group differences that-vary across occupations.

3. Personal, educational, occupational, or career maturation is composed of complex learning processes that begin in early childhood and continue throughout life.

4. Choice occurs not as a single point in time but in relation to antecedent experiences and future alternatives. Such choices are frequently social and time limited in perspective. Decisions interact and are interdependent as they shape choices.

5. Decision making is continuous, tentative, and often more psychological than logical. Specific choices are triggered by messages, directly or subtly expressing expectations for action from reference groups, the mass media, or institutions that constitute the social context in which decisions are made.

6. Because of the importance to adult behavior of early childhood experiences in the family, the school, and the community, intervention to facilitate positive career development needs to begin during the first decade of life. This is the nursery of human nature, when attitudes are formed that are ultimately reflected in career commitment or rejection.

7. Career development is composed of tasks with which persons must cope in each life stage. Many of these tasks are culturally defined; some are age related; some are stimulated by transitions.

8. Value systems, both individual and cultural, are important in shaping career development.

9. Career information must include not only objective factors such as earning possibilities, training requirements, and numbers of positions available, but also the social and psychological aspects of careers.

10. To be effective, career information should be provided in contexts, actual or simulated—for example, gaming, field trips, career-sensitive curricula, work study, role playing, computer-mediated information retrieval—by which individuals can project themselves into possible career roles, act them out, and test their meaning.

11. Because occupational and career choices are methods of implementing an individual's self-concept or expressing their personality style or type, information about self-characteristics—attitudes, aptitudes, values—is as necessary as career or occupational information. Unless the person knows what personal resources he or she has to commit to choice and the outcomes sought, the person has no guidelines by which to evaluate whether anything is of value to him or her.

12. Career development concepts provide the substance for program goals for career guidance and career education that can be translated into behavioral expectations for students or adults and pertinent experiences created to facilitate such behaviors for persons in different life stages. Such concepts represent hypotheses to be tested with individuals in career counseling.

13. Career development theory indicates that decision making involves action. Therefore, ways need to be found to help persons take responsibility for their own learning and for their own direction. Persons need to be helped to develop planning skills and the courage to execute their plans.

14. Persons need to be helped to develop an awareness that they do have choices, to determine at any given time what kind of decision is involved and the factors inherent in the decision that make a personal difference.

15. An individual's career development is not isolated from development in physical, emotional, and mental areas.

16. Choice opportunities for most persons are so complex that career guidance provided solely in the family or neighborhood is likely to be inadequate for today's realities.

17. Occupational choices and career patterns are basic to one's lifestyle and reflect developmental experiences, personality, goals, and so forth.

18. Career choice can be an essentially rational process if the person knows how to select and obtain appropriate information and then is able to apply a comprehensive and appropriate decision-making process to it. All choices, however, have elements of uncertainty about them.

19. Career choice is frequently a compromise between the attractiveness of an alternative, the likelihood of attaining it, and the costs of attaining it. Major elements of choice making are one's feelings of self-efficacy about performing the tasks required in a choice alternative and the likelihood that it will lead to the outcomes sought.

SUMMARY

In this chapter, the concept of career development has been defined and described, and the possibility of influencing such development rather than leaving it to random events has been discussed. Five major approaches to describing career development—trait-and-factor, decision, situational, psychological, and developmental emphases—have been discussed and some of their implications identified.

Whatever the process of occupational or career decision making, it is clear that choice involves a series of minidecisions made over a relatively long period of time. If systematic assistance in making these decisions can be provided, there is an increasing likelihood that the decisions will be "good"—appropriate for the chooser. The factors that enter into a job, occupation, or career decision and the process by which that decision is made are highly complex. Content and process are intricately related. What a systematic approach to career guidance or an effective application of career counseling accomplishes is to bring some order into what is typically a chaotic, haphazard choice.

Finally, it is important to reassert that the present perspectives on career development are incomplete in describing the behavioral development at issue. They have not been formulated as a result of or in conjunction with repeated or longitudinal studies as much as one would hope. Neither do they use enough samples from female, disadvantaged, or culturally different populations so that one can feel confident of the similarities or dissimilarities across subcultures that are implied in some of the theoretical speculation. The particular career problems and the ways theoretical approaches fit various special populations will be discussed in Chapter 5.

CHAPTER FIVE

Career Development and Counseling of Diverse Populations

KEY CONCEPTS

- Although career development theory and research, as described in Chapter 4, applies in general to diverse populations, diverse populations also have unique concerns or problems that need specific attention.
- Career interventions with diverse populations emphasize techniques somewhat different from those used with the general population or call for different emphases in the use of common techniques.
- Of particular importance to the provision of career services to diverse populations is the reduction of stereotypes, discrimination, environmental barriers, and other forms of bias that may impede the career development of such groups.
- No particular population is homogeneous in its characteristics, problems, or treatment by the larger society. There is as much variability within groups as there is between populations and majority groups. Therefore, counselors must guard against unconscious stereotyping, leading to bias, in their personal interactions with members of diverse populations—whether women, people of color, immigrants, gay men and lesbians, or persons with disabilities.

Chapter 4 presented a summary of what we know about so-called majority groups. Several other populations are thought to be sufficiently distinct from these groups on whom career development normative data have been gathered that they should be treated differently. We agree that these other populations have some unique concerns; we also believe that much of what we have learned about career development can, in fact, be applied to them. Differences between their career development and that of those who are members of majority groups may, in fact, be more a matter of degree than of kind.

There are many diverse populations that could legitimately be discussed in a book addressing career development. For example, workers on late shifts represent one of every six full-time employees. It is assumed that these workers have unique problems that cause them to suffer from sleep disturbances, digestive and nervous disorders, and disruptions of family life, all of which negatively affect marriages. Hence, we might well treat this population separately. Because of space limitations, however, we must limit the populations we will discuss. The populations we have chosen are women, persons of color, immigrants, persons who are gay, lesbian, or bisexual, and persons with disabilities. The career development literature of the last twenty-five years is voluminous in most of these areas. Although we have learned a great deal from this research, there is more to be learned about career development processes and career interventions related to diverse populations (Sue, 1999).

In each case, we will present an overview of research relating to the population and offer suggestions for career counseling. In some of these areas, the research findings conflict. We have tried to make as much sense as possible out of these inconsistencies and to be temperate in our conclusions. With each group, we encourage counselors to draw on a great deal of conventional career development theory. This chapter should provide information to supplement that knowledge.

WOMEN

Throughout this book, we look specifically at the unique career development needs of women. We emphasize women because of their large-scale entry into the labor market and because we are learning more about their career development each day. That knowledge guides practice and instructs us how to apply differential interventions to enhance the career development of women.

During the 1970s, 1980s, and 1990s, the number and percentage of women in the labor force rose continually. Although the curve of female participation in the labor force has begun to flatten, the proportion of women in the U.S. workforce is expected to continue to increase modestly. Unfortunately, women tend to be concentrated in poorly paid occupations and they also remain the primary person responsible for home and family (Niles & Goodnough, 1996). Most women work because of economic necessity, whether they are single, divorced, separated, widowed, or part of a dual-worker household in which their partner's wages are less than is necessary to exist beyond the poverty level. Yet similiar to men, most women (women of color and white) report that they participate in the labor force for reasons in addition to economic necessity (Cook, Heppner, & O'Brien, 2002; Herring & Wilson-Sadberry, 1993). Women account for a bit less than half of all workers, although a relatively large proportion of women (about one-quarter) hold part-time jobs. The average woman can expect to spend about three decades of her adult life in the labor force; and the more she is educated, the greater the probability that she will be employed.

In the United States, about 65 percent of women between the ages of 15 and 65 work, placing the United States second to Sweden (78 percent) and just above Canada (63.5 percent). At the lower extreme of female labor force participation in developed countries are Italy (43 percent) and Ireland (38 percent). Although gender pay disparities continue to exist, women made huge gains in the past two decades (going from earning 61 percent as much as men to 72 percent). This decrease in the disparity was primarily a result of the increase in women's education and work experience (Sorensen, 1991). Women still constitute more than 98 percent of secretaries and typists, about 85 percent of nursery school and kindergarten teachers, 97 percent of child-care workers, 93 percent of registered nurses and dieticians, and 91 percent of bank tellers—to cite a few examples of the continued concentration of women in traditional, relatively low-paying occupations. More than half of all children under 18 have working mothers. All these data reflect a relatively recent phenomenon. The number of working mothers has increased tenfold since the period immediately preceding World War II, and the number of women workers has more than tripled.

These data clearly indicate the effect of women in the work force. They do not emphasize, however, the increased female participation in many professional and managerial occupations.

Apparently, *tokenism,* or the low proportion of one sex in a workplace dominated by the opposite sex, has different consequences for men and women (Zimmer, 1988). For instance, studying policewomen and male nurses, Ott (1989) concluded that being a minority had opposite effects on men and women. Male-majority police teams resist women when they have large enough numbers to constitute a "critical mass," but female nurses exhibit no similar resistance to men when their numbers increase. Jolly, Grimm, and Wozniak (1990) probed sex desegregation patterns in professional and managerial occupations and determined that desegregation is present and increasing in these higher-status fields. The desegregation rates are highest, however, in occupations in which men are paid less and the number of workers is declining. Fields that pay the most to their professional and managerial workers are the most resistant to sex desegregation. Despite gains, Farmer, Rotella, Anderson, and Wardrop (1998) reported that men were 18.7 times more likely than women to be in higher-prestige occupations in science, math, or technology.

Understanding gender differences in career decision-making behavior provides useful information for understanding the career development process for women and men. Gati and Saka (2001) found that males in a study of Israeli adolescents reported more difficulty than girls regarding external decisional conflicts and dysfunctional career beliefs. Morgan, Isaac, and Sansone (2001) examined gender differences in the career choices of college students. The results of their study indicate that women reported more interpersonal work goals, more interest and competence in education and social service careers, and more perceived opportunities for involvement with others in work than men. Men reported more extrinsic reward goals and more interest and perceived competence in math/science careers.

Mau and Bikos (2000) examined the relative importance of school, family, person/psychological, race, and sex variables in predicting educational and vocational aspirations in a national longitudinal sample that followed men and women from tenth grade to two years beyond high school. Mau and Bikos found that females in their study had higher educational and vocational aspirations than did the men. One wonders whether the pressure women experience not to pursue lucrative and prestigious occupations to allow for the possibility of assuming major responsibility for home and family moderates the aspirations of many women (Cook, Heppner, & O'Brien, 2002). Research results related to this questions have been mixed (Phillips & Imhoff, 1997).

Meinster and Rose (2001) investigated the influence of romantic relationships and educational aspirations on the vocational interests of adolescent women attending all-female schools. Although they found that romantic relationships and educational aspirations were not related, they did find that aspiration level was related to investment in the work role with girls with high aspirations expressing more investment in work than family roles and women with low aspirations expressing equal investment in work and family. All in all, then, the great strides made by women in the recent past may still leave them short of occupational equity (Huffman & Torres, 2001) and, clearly, there is much more to understand especially in the area of multiple role involvement and career behavior. It seems obvious, however, that family and career issues are more interdependent for women than for men.

Two factors have combined to cause the significant change in the gender composition of the work force. Antidiscrimination laws and executive orders have been enacted or enforced more rigorously. Simultaneously, the consciousness raising of women in regard to careers has been a target of women's rights groups and professional helpers (counselors and other human relations workers). Both of these endeavors have attempted to alter the composition of the labor force. In large measure, they have succeeded. The still obvious imbalance in the labor force has resulted from discriminatory practices in employment and in entry to advanced training for certain occupations and from a low level of aspiration among women. The career "undershooting" of women, in turn, has been ascribed to occupational stereotyping, early childhood conditioning, fear of failure, fear of success, problems of self-efficacy, and a variety of other childrearing and socialization practices. For example, the American Association of University Women (AAUW) conducted a national study of all available research on the subject of girls in school (AAUW Report, 1992). One conclusion was that girls are systematically discouraged from taking courses of study essential to their future employment and economic well-being. Although this indictment is indeed harsh, it is probably more accurate than not. One recommendation is that schools should evaluate teachers, administrators, and counselors on the degree to which they promote and encourage gender-equitable and multicultural education (Tang & Cook, 2001).

Hence, attempts at changing the sexual composition of the labor force have centered on legally removing discrimination barriers on the one hand, and on changing the career aspirations of women on the other. It is clear from the preceding data that the strategy has been successful (although still too slow in the opinions of many). Research on the career development and behavior of women is one of the most popular areas of investigation in vocational psychology (Fitzgerald & Harmon, 2001).

In the following sections, we will summarize the research on various aspects of the career development of women. Specifically, we will investigate stereotypes, time parameters, traditional versus pioneer versus homemaker career studies, role models, male-female differences, self-efficacy and discontinuities in female career development. We will then present implications for the counseling of women.

Stereotypes

As we shall see in Chapter 7, the sexual stereotyping of occupations begins at a young age. For many individuals, this stereotyping remains endemic to careers throughout life.

Some argue that stereotyping begins at birth (if not sooner). One study (Bridges, 1993) seriously scanned birth congratulations cards. Images of physical activity were more prominent on boy cards. Verbal messages of expressiveness (sweetness and sharing) were more apparent on girl cards. Pierce (1993) investigated fiction in teen magazines and concluded that female teens are portrayed as dependent rather than independent and that occupations are typically segregated by gender. Further illustration of this early establishment of stereotypical gender roles is provided in research by Adler, Kless, and Adler (1992). Using qualitative, ethnographic research methods, they studied preadolescent children in and out of the elementary school setting. They concluded that young boys achieved popularity based on their athletic ability, "coolness," toughness, social skills, and success in cross-gender relationships. Girls achieved high status based on parents' socioeconomic status and their own physical appearance, social skills, and academic success. The differential socialization of boys and girls may be intertwined with sports. For example, there is some evidence that boys' sports play is dominated by team (as opposed to individual) activity across development, whereas girls gradually turn to individual and dyadic sports. Thus, socialization in team play may produce a differential moral reasoning in males and females (Vaughter, Sadh, & Vozzola, 1994). In an age of Title IX, this argument is tenuous.

By high school, the sexual stereotyping of interests and mathematical ability has become well ingrained (Morgan, Isaac, & Sanson, 2001). One study (Robinson-Awana, Kehle, & Jenson, 1986) asked seventh-grade boys and girls to respond to a self-esteem inventory as themselves and again as they thought a person of the opposite sex would respond. Results showed that both boys and girls believed girls had lower self-esteem, thus concurring with a stereotypical belief (an exception was that the more academically talented females rated boys significantly below themselves). This study serves as yet another example of the negative consequences of stereotyping.

Women in adolescence and young adulthood also demonstrate that they select from only a few occupational possibilities and too often on a sex-typed basis. Results of research with adolescents consistently show that females have lower occupational expectations than males, largely as a consequence of traditional sex-role socialization. For adolescent females, there is reason to believe that domestic and work-role expectations are related to both generalized sex-role attitudes and specific plans for adult domestic roles. In short, too many females see the sexes in stereotypical ways and believe that women and men should enact different domestic and occupational roles. The fact that many occupations are sex-traditional simply perpetuates sex-role stereotypes, sustaining the division of labor as a self-fulfilling prophecy (Yount, 1986).

Of course, the degree of support women and men receive in their career behavior undoubtedly influences career choices and career persistence. Phillips-Miller, Campbell, and Morrison (2000) investigated the relationships between work satisfaction, work-related stress, marital-family stress, and spousal support for career activity among 242 veterinarians (110 women and 132 men). All participants in this study were married and employed full-time. Phillips-Miller and associates found that the women in their study reported significantly greater marital-family stress and less perceived spousal support for their career behavior than did the men in the study. The lack of support and greater marital-family stress women experience obviously presents substantial (and unequal) challenges to women trying to cope with work and family roles.

Stereotypes insinuate themselves into career decision making in various insidious ways, most of which are inimical to both males and females. Coltrane and Adams (1997) found that television commercials in the 1990s contained gender stereotyping and occupational segregation. Women were more likely than men in the commercials to be portrayed as unemployed or employed in service or clerical occupations and as behaving in more gender-stereotyped ways. Coltrane and Adams concluded that the media clearly perpetuate work-family segregation and gender inequality.

Women erroneously think that they know more about traditional fields and less about nontraditional ones, reflecting the way they may think about themselves and impinging on self-efficacy expectations. Further, some decision-making penalty is apparently associated with being nonstereotypical. Those who are nontraditionally sex-typed seem to be more vocationally undecided than men or women who are traditionally sex-typed (Gianakos & Subich, 1986).

Related to the concept of stereotypes is the idea of expectations. Do the work expectations of men and women differ in terms of a variety of parameters, such as income, performance, and so on? The research data available to us suggest that there are indeed significant differences in gender expectations. Hartman and colleagues (1988) and Bridges (1988) both conducted studies that demonstrate these differences in perception. In the former study, both male and female part-time college students viewed high job performance as more masculine and poor performance as more feminine. In the latter study, women proved much more likely than men to base their career choice on stereotypical considerations. Bridges states, "Thus women may tend to select their careers on the basis of either the perceived sex-related skills or the sex-appropriateness associated with the occupation, whereas males may be more likely to consider less stereotypical characteristics, such as salary, personal interest, and value on achievement in the field" (p. 88). In terms of differences in income expectations, H. L. Smith and Powell (1990) asked male and female college seniors to reveal their expectations for income after graduation. Although both male and female respondents were equally informed and relatively accurate about the earnings of other college graduates, they differed in the estimates of their own incomes. Men were more likely than women to *self-enhance*—that is, to see themselves competent enough to earn "top dollar."

Stereotypes, of course, also apply to men entering female-dominated occupations. We are just now beginning to see some work on the psychology of men in terms of gender differences in career development (Gati & Saka, 2001). Research such as that of Lemkau (1984) indicates that the same stereotyping factors that operate for women also work for men in nontraditional occupations: lower adherence to traditional sex roles, behavior less sex-stereotyped, and more tendermindedness (as measured by the Catell 16 PF). Nozik (1986) supported these results and also found that men who enter nontraditional occupations (both professional and skilled) generally came from families in lower socioeconomic strata. Fitzgerald and Cherpas (1985) conducted a study that determined male and female counselors could be equally guilty of sexism.

An instructive study of female marines and male nurses (Williams, 1989) suggests that whereas women marines are segregated and harassed, male nurses are welcomed and encouraged, receiving far less overt stereotypical treatment. The psychoanalytic interpretation that the investigator provides for the results may or may not be accurate; if it is accurate, however, it suggests deeply ingrained, not necessarily conscious reactions that will not be changed in the short run. In addition, some work argues that not only are men and women treated differently at work because of stereotypes, but also they actually work differently; that is, in male-dominated work women tend to be more service-oriented to clients, have a more nurturing attitude toward colleagues, and use power differently from men (Lunneborg, 1990). This focus of inquiry may help to establish whether men and women in comparable positions indeed have different work styles or work personalities attributable to gender.

Chusmir's (1990) review of the relatively scant research on men who make nontraditional career choices (i.e., occupations that have less than 30 percent of same-sex workers) revealed that these men can be described modally as follows:

> *They likely possess many of the same traits and characteristics often attributed to women. Contrary to stereotypes, nontraditional men generally are comfortable with themselves and their masculine sexuality. They have a well-balanced gender role identity.... Their background as well as their personality is nontraditional. Nontraditional women tend to come from a background of family stability and close contact with both a supportive father and mother, whereas nontraditional men likely grow up in a family environment of instability—children whose parents were divorced or in which one of the parents was deceased. Their greatest influence came from women (mothers and important other females), and they often had a distant relationship with their father. (p. 14)*

In Chapter 13, we shall discuss the effects of stereotyping and the psychology of attractiveness on decisions relating to job-seeking behaviors, such as interviewing for employment. Clearly, in some cases, gender stereotyping has an effect when applicants are assertively feminine (e.g., too much makeup, too strong a perfume scent) or excessively masculine (e.g., unshaven, slovenly, overly aggressive). There is some encouraging research, however, suggesting that sex effects, in general, are minimal or absent in performance appraisals by supervisors (Hartung & Rogers, 2000; Kinicki & Griffeth, 1985; Morrow & McElroy, 1984; Thompson & Thompson, 1985), and that sex stereotypes are decreasing among college students (Beutell & Brenner, 1986). If such is indeed the case, the outlook is improving. Unfortunately, most such studies are analogue in nature (that is, simulated rather than real-life), and there may be differences between laboratory-type results and those found in the actual workplace.

The sad fact is that U.S. youth still cling to traditional stereotypes regarding division of labor in the home and occupational attainment of men and women. Male perceptions of life roles, on average, are far from egalitarian, and although there certainly is movement toward more equity, it is not likely to come in the majority of relationships for some time. It is more likely to come occupationally than domestically, in our judgment. The more females can be encouraged by teachers and counselors to expand their career aspirations and view of life roles and the more both males and females can be helped to examine their own restrictive and restricting attitudes, the more likely it is that a genderless egalitarianism will exist in the future. The primary point of attack is, logically, at the earliest age possible; intervention becomes increasingly difficult as stereotypes become more ingrained. Further, gender stereotyping is so ingrained at so early an age that intensive and protracted interventions are probably necessary to alter attitudes. Van Buren, Kelly, and Hall (1993) attempted to promote nontraditional career choices in eighth-grade and eleventh-grade girls and boys by means of showing a brief videotape of men and women in nontraditional occupations. The intervention had virtually no effect. Clearly, early and deep interventions are required.

Time Parameters

The career needs, aspirations, and life plans of women need to be continually evaluated and upgraded. Research quickly becomes obsolete, and the findings of the recent past do not necessarily apply to the present or the future.

Spitze and Huker (1980) looked at data on sex-role status from 1938 and 1978 and concluded that there were strong historical effects; that is, trends in attitudes over time may be explained more by the general climate during a given period than by changes in specific individual experiences and attributes.

In addition, Harmon (1989) has examined the extent to which changes over time in women's career aspirations can be attributed to developmental causes, historical influences, or both. She studied college female cohorts from 1968 and 1983 and determined that both developmental and historical influences were operative. Among her conclusions: "Overall, there are several differences which suggest that historical effects have produced a group of young women who are more aware of the need for women to be employed and are considering less traditional careers for women than their older counterparts at the same age" (p. 60).

In another longitudinal study of women's career development, S. R. Jenkins (1989) studied a group of 111 college women as seniors in 1967 and followed them up in 1981. Among other findings, she discovered little sex difference in factors that predict occupational attainment in teaching and entrepreneurial business; what was predictive for men was also predictive for women. Another remarkable finding, among many, was the migration of these women out of planned teaching careers and into other fields, probably because these other opportunities opened to them at this period in history.

Of course, sometimes the more things change, the more they remain the same. At the college level, Frank (1988) researched male and female students' acceptance of women managers. Demonstrating that perceptual stereotypes have not radically changed from those reported in the 1970s, she determined that men "perceived women managers as being less knowledgeable and possessing poorer managerial skills than male managers.... Female students showed a greater preference for a male boss" (p. 107).

Fiorentine (1988), in a time series analysis of college freshman from 1969 to 1984, determined that the value women placed on status-attainment goals increased substantially. Simultaneously, however, the value they placed on domestic-nurturant goals did not greatly decrease. Thus, while the sexes are apparently becoming more alike in career values and goals, women are experiencing more conflict regarding homemaking versus career values.

In 1983, Pirnot and Dustin (1986) administered the Study of Values to 93 women categorized as career-oriented or homemakers. The results were compared to those of a group of women who responded to the instrument in 1966. The researchers discovered substantial differences in both groups from 1966 to 1983: Religious values decreased, and economic and aesthetic values increased. Other intergenerational differences gleaned from cross-sectional research have been observed by Faver (1984), who found the relationship between career orientation and achievement orientation is stronger in younger women (22–44) than in older women (45–64). A clear illustration of how women have adapted to revolutionary changes in life patterns over the past eight decades is provided by Hullbert and Schuster (1993). They document the change from traditional roles to roles that combined work and family and show how historical conditions and changing life conditions have interacted and continue to do so.

The implication of these studies is clear: counselors must remain in touch with the literature and developments of the times. We are all aware of counselors who appear to be caught in a time warp, assuming that everything is as it was. When dealing with the changing status and needs of women, especially, such ingenuousness can be harmful.

Traditional versus Pioneer versus Homemaker

Studies of the factors that distinguish career-oriented women from non-career-oriented women or women in traditional occupations from women in "pioneer" occupations offer few guidelines for practice. Their results are frequently conflicting and their conclusions simplistic. Among the more instructive studies, however, are those that hint at factors distinguishing one group of women from another in terms of career orientation. These studies make the following suggestions:

- A girl exposed to a maternal model of work competence tends to be more career-oriented.
- Those who are career-oriented or who are planning nontraditional careers achieve higher grades, make a career choice later, come from more advantaged homes, and experience more personal identity and acceptance conflicts.
- They have fathers with higher educational levels and are more likely themselves to be childless.
- They tend to receive more encouragement from teachers, counselors, friends, and significant others.
- They exhibit higher esteem needs.
- They may have a greater propensity for risk taking in the sense that women who score higher on the Strong Interest Inventory Adventure scale tend to enter more nontraditional occupations than do lower-scoring women. (Douce & Hansen, 1990)
- They manifest stronger career-centeredness and career salience.

An exception to the finding of stronger commitment to work in nontraditional women is demonstrated in a study by Ellermann and Johnston (1988), who found that college women in both traditional and nontraditional majors were highly committed to their future careers (although women in nontraditional majors were significantly less committed to a home and family). None of these studies, however, provides truly definitive answers.

Holms and Esses (1988) reached general conclusions in their study of the motivation of Canadian high school girls for a traditional or nontraditional type of career. They state:

> *Girls who obtained higher marks in school, identified with either masculine or androgynous trait dispositions, had more liberal attitudes toward women, and were from higher socioeconomic backgrounds aspired to higher levels of education, were more highly committed to a career, and aspired to more highly prestigious occupations. (p. 313)*

Examining the career choices of adolescent women, O'Brien and Fassinger (1993) determined that those who selected nontraditional and prestigious careers tended to possess high ability and strong agentic characteristics (e.g., math self-efficacy, liberal gender role attitudes).

Mazen and Lemkau (1990) compared women in traditional and nontraditional occupations in terms of their scores on the California Psychological Inventory (CPI). Their analysis revealed a high number of similarities, but five of the CPI scales did differentiate (in rational directions) traditional and nontraditional women: femininity, communality, self-control, capacity for status, and dominance.

Jome and Tokar (1998) investigated dimensions of masculinity and choice of traditional college majors. They reported that career-traditional men in their study endorsed antifemininity and toughness norms and reported difficulties concerning restrictive emotionality and affectionate behavior between men. However, career-traditional and career-nontraditional men did not report different endorsements of status norms, difficulties concerning success, power and competition, and conflicts between work and family relationships. Career-traditional men did manifest higher homophobic attitudes than career-nontraditional men.

Comparing women in traditional occupations to pioneers to homemakers is, in the final analysis, highly complex. It has been repeatedly demonstrated that female career patterns are much more complex than those of males. Add this finding to the fact that there is extreme overlap among these three groups of women on almost all variables—within-group variation is almost as large as between-group variation—

and it is easy to understand why no clear and consistent findings have emerged.

One of the difficulties in research relating to differences among so-called traditional and nontraditional occupations is that of definition: What constitutes an atypical or nontraditional occupation? Hayes (1986) catalogued ten different terms in studies used to describe the sexual segregation of labor: nonsextypical, gender-concentrated, gender-dominant, gender traditional and gender nontraditional, sex-congruent and sex-incongruent, sex-labeling, sex-linked, sex-segregated, sex-typed, and sexual separation of labor. Depending on definition and source, percentages of males and females in an occupation can vary considerably.

All in all, we can say little with certainty about differences among women who choose pioneer careers compared with those who select traditional careers and compared with those who elect to be full-time homemakers. Although we can speak of some modal characteristics, there is great variance in each of these three groups.

Role Models

Earlier literature suggested that career models, especially female models, appeared to exert a strong influence on the career aspirations of women. Whether the model is a working mother, an occupational model—who is also enacting simultaneous roles of wife, mother, and worker—or a professor, career-oriented women have reported that such a model has been influential in the formulation of their career goals. Although it is clear that role model influences are predictive of women's career-related aspirations and choices, Hackett, Esposito, and O'Halloran (1989) confirmed that these models are not necessarily female.

The popular media have played up the idea of "mentor" in the work progress of successful career women. The notion here is that of an established powerful figure in an occupational field (usually male) who takes a woman under his aegis and guides and, in a sense, manipulates her rise in that field. Subsequently the idea of mentor (also termed, occasionally, "patron" or "rabbi") in the career development of women has proved useful. We know that mentors beget mentors in that those who had a mentor become mentors for others; we know that mentor relationships are most often established in the first five years of one's career; we know that more women are becoming mentors as their numbers increase in top management positions; we know that women experience a mentor relationship much less seldom than men; we know that as workers, in general, get older, they generally get more interested in mentoring; and we know that most women are now advised that the route to upper-level jobs is through a mentor. Cesari (1985) advocates intrapersonal mentoring, that is, teaching women to take control of their own job socialization. Ryan (1985) would see this teaching role as appropriate for counselors. F. A. Kaufman and colleagues (1986) maintain that counselors are in a good position to help in the development of mentor relationships:

> *First, they can provide information to potential mentors and protégés about the advantages of mentorships. Second, they can assist in identifying and matching individuals on the basis of teaching and learning styles, values, and interests. Third, they can establish and monitor mentorship programs in schools and professional organizations. Fourth, they can provide ongoing training in the mentorship process. (p. 577)*

Several studies have confirmed the importance of role models in the career development of women. Lunneborg and Lunneborg's (1985) research has demonstrated that both male and female role models influence the careers of women who hold a nontraditional work orientation. These models (in high school, college, and graduate school) were positive influences and included parents, siblings, teachers, friends, and other adults. In terms of parents, the encouragement and support of *both* a mother and a father is most important in fostering nontraditional careers. Shepard and Marshall (2000) conducted a qualitative study of young women living in rural areas and found that the women in their study expressed the need for role models especially with regard to resolving conflicting values concerning work and family. The suggestion is strong that for both men and women the developmental support and encouragement of important adult figures is an essential variable in career development.

Aspects of Sex Differences

Presently, no clear theory exists relating to the career development and choice of women. Rose and Elton (1973), among others, have argued for a separate theory of career choice for males and females. Barnett (1971) has offered some interesting thoughts that might lead to such a theory, but her effort illustrates the confounding of sex with other personal variables in decision making. For example, she states:

> *For a college woman, her decision to pursue a career is intimately related to her femininity, her need for independence, her self-concept, and her plans for marriage. It is influenced also by the expectations of her social group, family, and college peers and her responses to these groups. For each woman, the planning process and the feeling accompanying it reflect her position with respect to these four factors. (p. 31)*

That statement seems sensible. It would appear equally sensible, however, if one substituted male adjectives and pronouns. Perhaps male-female distinctions in career development and career choice are not so much a matter of kind as a matter of degree. Notions of masculinity and femininity are certainly important in career choice. Are they more important for women? Probably. Plans for marriage are important in the general life planning of both men and women. Are they more important for women? Probably. Perhaps what is needed is a theory of career development and career choice that applies to both sexes, but that might weight various factors according to gender and weight other factors according to such variables as age, race, socioeconomic class, and so on.

Astin (1984) provides one of the most thoughtful attempts to move toward a theory of career development that more adequately encompasses the possibility of differences in degree—rather than kind—by gender. This model (alluded to in Chapter 4) attempts to describe the career-related behavior of both men and women, albeit in a first-step, rudimentary form that requires testing. Astin proposes four constructs in her need-based sociopsychological model of career choice and work behavior:

1. *Motivation* in the form of three primary needs (for survival, pleasure, and contribution), which are the same for both sexes. Work—defined as activity intended to produce or accomplish something, and which can take the form of paid employment, volunteer work, or family work—has the capacity to satisfy these needs.
2. *Sex-role socialization,* whereby social norms and values are inculcated, through play, family, school, and early work experiences. In the process of satisfying the three needs through these childhood activities, the individual develops certain experiences that directly influence career choice and work behavior.
3. *The structure of opportunity,* which includes economic conditions, the family structure, the job market, the occupational structure, and other environmental factors that are influenced by scientific discoveries, technological advances, historical events, and social and intellectual movements.
4. *Work expectations,* including perceptions of one's capabilities and strengths, the options available, and the kinds of work that can best satisfy one's needs. The individual's expectations are initially set by the socialization process and by early perceptions of the structure of opportunity. They can be modified, however, as the structure of opportunity, changes. (pp. 124–125)

Astin's ideas certainly merit research to determine their usefulness in explaining and predicting career choice and behavior. Although there has been initial enthusiasm for her constructs, she is not without her critics who, perhaps unfairly, harshly attack her work not as an early piece designed to elicit research but as though it were a fully developed theory. Fitzgerald and Betz (1984), for instance, take issue with Astin's work for not being integrated with extant knowledge of career choice and behavior, for offering poorly defined constructs, for failing to give suggestions for measurement, for not generating predictions, and for not giving credit to the women's movement, among other perceived shortcomings.

Farmer (1985) also attempts to provide a theoretical perspective that applies to both males and females. She investigated possible differential effects of background, personal, and environmental influences on aspiration, mastery, and career commitment. Her multidimensional model warrants continued research and development. So too does a model developed by Fassinger (1990).

King (1989a) offers an additional causal model for career maturity as a result of her investigation of sex differences among high school students. She found a basically similar causal pattern for these male and female adolescents, but also found sex differences, with a higher level of career maturity in girls largely related to their sense of control over events in their lives and a cohesive family that provided cultural opportunities.

Gilligan (1982a) is another theorist whose work excites a number of researchers. Hotelling and Forrest (1985) have considered the implications of Gilligan's theory of sex-role development for counseling in general, but it remains for someone to test her constructs specifically in terms of career development. Gilligan argues that dependence-independence and relationships are experienced differently by the sexes, leading to differences in intimacy and empathy. She challenges Erickson's classic ordering of identity and intimacy, suggesting that although it may hold true for men, it is insufficiently descriptive of women. The result is extreme responses by women. As Hotelling and Forrest described the condition:

> *From Gilligan's perspective, a woman's development is restricted because she fails to realize that she must incorporate both self-care and care for others into her identity. Many women may view this as an overwhelming task. Two responses, both of which can be maladaptive, are the "superwoman" phenomenon (an attempt to uphold extremely high standards both at work and home) and the "male" model (which requires one to excel at work only). The consequence of the first model are emotional and physical strain and overload; often the woman feels not only exhausted and confused but guilty if she does not perform all tasks perfectly. The second model, which defines self through separation, may result in a woman progressing in her career but ignoring her need for connection with others. The expectation to maintain autonomy and independence in a vacuum of human intimacy at work can be painful, confusing, and lonely to a woman who has learned that connection with others is essential. (p. 184)*

The dichotomous thinking expressed by Gilligan and her supporters has been criticized by those who deny that men have any less need for intimacy than women and who see Gilligan's different voices as a dangerous perpetuation of stereotypes. Critics should take note, however, that much here is potentially useful to explore.

There are studies on a variety of sex differences in career development and career choice. For example, investigating reactions to work of more than 3500 men and women factory workers, Loscocco (1990) found that male and female workers were similarly influenced by specific personal and job characteristics and that both were most affected by the intrinsic and financial rewards of their jobs. In a ten-year longitudinal study of rural, low-income adolescent females, Wilson, Peterson, and Wilson (1993) found that family-of-origin variables (e.g., father's education and parental socialization experiences that encourage attainment) were much more influential in career attainment of this population than is the case with women from more advantaged households.

Studying 204 female managers, Ornstein and Isabella (1990) questioned whether Levinson's age stages or Super's psychological stages (see Chapter 4) were descriptive of changes in career attitudes. Their conclusion was that Super's career development model was *not* supported and that Levinson's stages were closer, but offered far from robust support. These results are interpreted to mean that there are major differences between men and women in terms of career development, largely because women's careers are less continuous, their career development is less heterogeneous than men's, and employing organizations may exert more influence on their career development than do career stages. In any case, a woman's age was more predictive of her career experiences than was her career stage.

Another study of sex differences, using Project Talent data (Card, Steel, & Abeles, 1980), determined that although women had higher grades and higher test scores than men in high school, eleven years after high school the men had acquired more education and were earning more money. The authors attributed these sex differences primarily to greater conflict for women between the roles of spouse/parent and the roles of student/worker. Variables that measured the onset, duration, and extent of family-related commitments were more strongly related to female than to male realization of potential.

Occasionally the mass media promulgate the findings of writing that appears in the professional literature and tag it with a "cute" descriptor. Such was the case in 1989 when F. N. Schwartz published her notions about a dual-track managerial career for women and promptly found it labeled the "mommy track."

Briefly, this argument states that women managers cost companies more than men managers because of career interruptions, greater turnover and plateauing, and so on. Schwartz suggests that there are two types of women managers. One type resembles men (career-primary women) and are career-first people. The majority of women, however, are what she terms career-and-family women, those who want to pursue serious careers while also rearing children. Schwartz maintains that corporate America can bring the costs of women managers in line with those of men by allowing women certain accommodations, among which are family supports (e.g., maternity leave, flexibility of work hours, child care). This would, in effect, create two tracks—a fast track for men and a slower track for women—but both would eventually end up in the same place: at the top rungs of the corporate management ladder.

There are those who maintain that women face a "glass ceiling" that limits their advancement in top management (a phenomenon also allegedly present in minority career development). This "glass ceiling" implies an invisible barrier put up by white men to deter the upward mobility of women beyond middle management. Whatever the reason—conscious or unconscious discrimination, systemic barriers, or the like—it is clear that substantial gender and racial differences exist within corporate management (Morrison & Von Glinow, 1990) and that equity is not a realistic short-term prospect.

The meaning of leisure is apparently different for women than for men. Although relatively little research has emerged regarding women and leisure, Henderson (1990) did review the sparse collection of extant scholarship and determined that women experience leisure in a different context from men and give it less time and a lower priority. Further, women tend to perceive their leisure as a family activity, in that they use the home as a "container" for leisure. Strikingly, many women apparently feel that they are not entitled to leisure; they feel that they are undeserving because of the way they perceive their role obligations in life. A special issue of the *Journal of Leisure Research* has been devoted to leisure in the lives of women (Henderson, 1994). Especially germane is the discussion of constraints in examining women's leisure. A constraint to leisure is any factor that mitigates between some possible activity and preference for or participation in that experience (e.g., childrearing, work, marriage demands).

Men and women also evidently experience divorce differently with respect to work. R. R. Peterson (1989), for example, investigated the issue using a cohort of almost 4000 women, aged 30–44, about whom data were available from 1967 to 1977. In general, these women responded to divorce and consequent economic hardship by work adjustment, achieving at least partial economic recovery, but their predivorce work history determined the degree of economic resiliency.

With television situation comedies and stand-up comedians focusing on premenstrual syndrome (PMS) and with all the other media attention given to the topic, it is not surprising that PMS has been addressed with regard to work. Although no specific research exists in relation to work, Phillips and Bedeian (1989) have reviewed the general PMS literature and concluded that there is currently no scientific proof that PMS affects behavior (including work behavior). Both men and women, however, believe that it does. Therefore, they view wellness programs within employee assistance programs as appropriate sites in which to address attitudes toward PMS. They cite corporations that hold PMS awareness days to inform women about the cause of PMS and about palliative measures. Employer education is also necessary, they feel, so that PMS will not be used as an artificial barrier to higher-paying, more responsible jobs for women.

Two final observations related to sex differences are as follows. In general, the higher the occupational level, the more gender differences in work values blur; the lower the occupational level, the greater the differences between men and women (Mason, 1994), although a few differences persist despite occupational level (Elizur, 1994). Career aspirations, according to some research, may be more gender related than racially or ethnically influenced (Arbona & Novy, 1991).

Self-Efficacy

One of the most researched constructs of the past decade, especially as applied to women's career development, is that of self-efficacy. Although the studies have been effected almost entirely with college student populations and the occupational definition of career self-efficacy is not precise across studies, the results have been fairly consistent in exposing a relationship between self-efficacy and career considerations, career exploration activities, school achievement, and actual choice of a career.

This theory suggests that because of differential socialization, women lack strong expectations of personal efficacy for a variety of career-related behaviors. Hence, they fail to realize their capabilities and talents in work. Self-efficacy expectations, it is assumed, are lower among women than men. If one performs a task successfully, expectations of efficacy for the task are increased. It is hypothesized that women have fewer opportunities to demonstrate successful task accomplishments. They may also have fewer chances to watch other people succeed, to experience success vicariously. It is thus thought that they may lack same-sex models. Anxiety frequently prevents the development of facilitative efficacy expectations, and females are considered more likely to have anxiety responses. Finally, information about personal efficacy comes from the verbal encouragement and persuasion of others. It is thought that women receive less encouragement from counselors and others. So expectations of personal efficacy tend to be weakened for women.

Nevill and Schlecker (1988) conducted a study that demonstrated a relationship between perceived career options and self-efficacy expectations and consequently suggested that counselors should reinforce the behaviors of their female counselees that lead to enhanced exposure to and experience of nontraditional occupations (e.g., modifying females' mathematics self-efficacy beliefs).

Even at the university level, there is some tentative evidence that women may shy away from mathematics and science careers based on their beliefs or concerns about combining career and family responsibilities (Lips, 1992).

A continuing debate relates to the merits of women attending a same-sex or a coeducational institution and the subsequent effects on their career self-efficacy. Scheye and Gilroy (1994) found no primary effects in this regard, indicating that the type of educational environment, in and of itself, has no influence on the development of a woman's self-efficacy. Novi and Meinster (2000) examined friends' influence on the achievement-related choices of 88 female high school students attending a private school. Results indicated that the study participants reacted more positively to achievement-oriented situations as compared to affiliation situations that were presented to them during the course of the study. The influence of peer groups on achievement orientation was weaker for those participants who were in groups with lower levels of cohesion. Bergeron and Romano (1994) found that although degree of self-efficacy affected career decision making, the relationship was independent of gender. Multon, Brown, and Lent (1991), in a meta-analysis, concluded that self-efficacy beliefs were indeed related to academic performance, but equally for males and females. Stickel and Bonett (1991) did find gender differences in the sense that women may not enter into nontraditional careers both because they doubt their ability to perform the tasks and because they question their ability to combine the work tasks with home and family responsibilities. Church, Teresa, Rosebrook, and Szendre (1992), studying minority high school equivalency students, determined that "both men and women reported greater self-efficacy and willingness to consider occupations dominated by their own gender, with women showing a greater tendency to reject occupations dominated by the opposite gender" (p. 498). One study (Matsui & Onglatco, 1992) discovered that for female office workers in Japan, self-efficacy moderated the stress-strain relationship.

Self-efficacy has been suggested as a reason for the proportionately few women pursuing mathematics and science careers. Research by Lopez and Lent (1992) and by Lent, Lopez, and Bieschke (1991), however, found that with high school mathematics students (while it certainly seemed valid that self-efficacy perceptions affected performance), no such gender barrier existed; in fact, the self-efficacy scores, math grades, and academic self-concepts of the girls in the study were higher than those of the boys. Self-efficacy is one of a number of possible self-referent cognitive processes (what we tell ourselves about ourselves) that may affect behavior. With self-efficacy, the idea is that when people think that they will perform well, they expect a positive result (self-evaluation), and their performance is improved; when they anticipate that they will do poorly, they give themselves a negative self-evaluation, and their performance is thus impaired (Sanna & Pusecker, 1994). A contrary finding comes from the research of Chartrand, Camp, and McFadden (1992), who discovered no relationship between self-efficacy and academic performance or persistence in female undergraduates.

Self-efficacy with regard to careers is usually measured by Taylor and Betz's (1983) Career Decision-Making Self-Efficacy Scale. Psychometric properties appear to be acceptable (Luzzo, 1993b). There are about a dozen other measures, including most notably Rooney and Osipow's (1992) and a shorter form of the same instrument (Osipow, Temple, & Rooney, 1993).

Betz (1992) offers a number of suggestions regarding how self-efficacy theory can be used in career counseling, specifically in terms of how society may alter the career choices of women. These generally revolve around the counselor's intervening to increase a women's expectations of efficacy. Perhaps the most effective of such interventions would be to give women the opportunity to perform successfully, to expose them to successful role models, to help them control anxiety, to express belief in the person's ability to perform the tasks, and to reinforce meeting goals. Further implications for counseling come from Niles and Sowa (1992), who suggest that counselors need to encourage clients to become active participants in the career development process, to help clients manage the stress of career uncertainty, and to use a client's self-efficacy level in the counseling process (e.g., clients with low self-efficacy may need more support and encouragement).

All in all, the construct of self-efficacy offers a promising area for research and possible interventions to enhance the career development and behavior of women.

Discontinuities in Female Career Development

Although more and more women are displaying uninterrupted career patterns, discontinuities obviously abound. The major source of male discontinuity was formerly the military draft. This discontinuity has not been a problem for several years. For women, the primary source of discontinuity is children. The discontinuity of career development in women is seen as a paramount barrier to occupational upward mobility.

Lassalle and Spokane (1987) identified seventeen women's career patterns, based on degree of participation (full time, part time, or out) and occupational level, at four different age points (18, 22, 25 to 26, and 29 to 30). They found evidence to suggest that "the more consistent and extensive the labor force participation, the greater the respondent's occupational advancement. The data also indicated that a woman's attachment to the labor force tends to be bimodal: either strong or almost nonexistent. Very few women were in patterns in which labor force participation was primarily part-time or sporadic" (pp. 63–64).

Some see a chicken-egg argument in relation to women's fertility and employment. Which causes which? Does childbearing constrain labor force participation, or can we use labor force activity to predict a woman's expected fertility? The dominant effects are probably from fertility to employment in the short run and from employment to fertility in the long run.

One study of about 500 midwestern female college students (K. L. Peterson, 1985) suggests that discontinuity is not foreign to women in higher education. Although anticipated levels of work involvement were important, women in the study experienced considerable doubt and confusion about working throughout their lifetime; that is, they anticipated that they would not be continuously employed. Such an attitude would obviously affect career choice. Lifelong career commitment may be related to the particular major a woman chooses; for example, Katz (1986) found no differences in the relative career commitment of men and women in baccalaureate-level management majors and MBAs. Hock, Morgan, and Hock (1985) report that women generally adhere to these earlier-determined plans to work continuously or not. Using a longitudinal approach, they found that of 172 new mothers, 75 percent of those planning to stay home did so, and only 25 percent of the mothers who planned to stay home worked instead. They concluded that "married women of low career orientation appear to meet their needs through home, family, and non-work roles" (p. 399).

In any case, career interventions with women should include assurance that women understand the nature of continuous and discontinuous career patterns and the effect of fertility on those phenomena. In Chapter 12, we will further discuss these consequences for women who seek to return to the labor force or who seek to enter it for the first time after a protracted period of childbearing and childrearing. Such women have rarely considered the consequences of discontinuity before the fact and frequently, therefore, experience trauma after the fact.

Career Counseling of Women

Given differences in the career development of women, what are the implications for the career counseling of women in contemporary society? One must assume that at all levels, but especially at the higher occupational levels or in nontraditional careers, women will exhibit more conflict than men, will experience differences in job-seeking patterns, and will have to overcome more obstacles to career advancement. The techniques applicable to the career counseling of women are the same as those used for men, but they differ in the intensity with which they must be pursued.

Such techniques as networking, peer counseling, and professional support are especially useful with women clients. Networking is a process of identifying existing social networks, enhancing connecting networks along new lines, and channeling information through these created guidance networks. These networks are made up of contact persons for educational and employment advice and placement. It is ironic, in contemporary society, that while old-boy networks are being vilified and legislated against as a job-finding technique, networking can be valuable for women in job-finding and promotion. Not the least important network is that of the family, which, in addition to providing social support, also helps members get jobs, especially blue-collar jobs (Grieco, 1987). Employees serve as sources of information and sponsors for family members in the job market. Peer counseling can range from simple support groups to more action-oriented endeavors. Professional support and counseling can assume a variety of forms.

A number of techniques are appropriate in counseling women. Various stress-reduction programs have proved successful in decreasing emotional exhaustion and personal strain. Higgins (1986), for example, reports that both a progressive relaxation and systematic desensitization program and one emphasizing instruction in time management, rational-emotive therapy, and assertiveness training were equally effective in reducing stress among working women. In fact, the reduction of stress for women who are experiencing conflict because of multiple role demands is the focus of much writing and research (e.g., Ashurst & Hale, 1989; Mowbray, Lanir, & Hulce, 1984; G. Nelson, 1990; Swanson-Kauffman, 1987). Specific techniques, ranging from mutual-support self-help groups to professional interventions, are discussed in Chapter 11 in the section dealing with occupational stress.

Foss and Slaney (1986) conducted a videotaped career intervention with eighty college women to determine its effect on the woman's traditionality of choice and that of a hypothetical daughter. Results indicated that although the use of the videotape was effective, subjects were generally "aware of the advantages of less traditional careers but were not reflecting this awareness in their own career choices as clearly as in the choices for their daughters" (p. 199).

The idea of counselor stereotyping and sex bias is, of course, not new. Male counselors seem to ascribe different motivations (such as success avoidance) to male and female undergraduates, and even female counselors do not accurately perceive sex differences in motivating factors (Karpicke, 1980). Mercado and Atkinson (1982) offer evidence that male counselors encourage male and female high school students to explore occupations along sex-stereotypical lines. Further, a physical-attractiveness bias may enter vocational counseling. Indeed, given what we know about the psychology of attractiveness—that attractive individuals are ascribed all sorts of positive characteristics and nonattractive people are not—it would be surprising to discover that it did not. Such biases are difficult to counteract.

Gaming and simulation are other techniques that have been applied to the career counseling of women. For example, Hammer-Higgens and Atwood (1989) describe *The Management Game,* a psychoeducational intervention for both counselors and clients that gives them some forewarning and enables them to experience vicariously some of the hostile elements that women will face within the corporate structure. It also suggests ways of overcoming these barriers.

To help women cope effectively with managing the time demands associated with multiple role involvement, Cook, Heppner, and O'Brien (2002) recommend that career counselors work to assist women in learning negotiation skills to empower them to ask for what they need (e.g., more flexible work hours) from their employers. Cook and her colleagues point out that some women are disinclined to negotiate with their employers due to fear that they will be perceived as not being team players or hard workers. Some women of color may experience pressure to be role models for others and, therefore, reluctant to negotiate for fear of being viewed as having special needs. Learning negotiation skills may also empower some women to ask their partners for assistance with home and family responsibilities.

A special section of the *Career Development Quarterly* (June 2002) addresses the career development of women of color and white women. The section contains six career counseling cases that address various concerns women confront in their career development. The authors of the career cases provide excellent examples of career interventions that help women advance in their career development.

Finally, Sundal-Hansen (1984) suggests a career future scenario in which sex equity produces a future society with 10 characteristics. The first three of these ideal characteristics provide a resounding finish for this section:

1. Women and men will be able to make choices and decisions more according to their authentic interests, talents, values, and preferences and to explore a wide variety of fields, subjects, and activities not labeled by sex. These changes will allow for the development of the multipotentialities of both women and men. Children will be exposed to and will be free to explore a wider variety and range of options in activities, hobbies, interests, roles, and behaviors. They will experience sex-fair childrearing at home and sex-fair education, counseling, and curriculum at school.

2. There will be more equitable distribution of men and women in education and work. Movement will be away from occupational and educational segregation toward more equal distribution of the sexes in all kinds and levels of education and occupation. Business and industry will pay more attention to human needs in the workplace, with flextime and flexplace, parental leave, child care services available to employees, multiple benefit options, and other kinds of employee assistance programs reflecting a new corporate perspective on, responsibility for, and commitment to the personal and family needs of workers.

3. Women and men will have more solid relationships because they will be able to relate to each other as equals, instead of women being "less than" men and men "more than." They will learn to respect each other at home and in the workplace, to resolve conflicts constructively, to negotiate roles, and to share tasks. They will find creative new patterns for working out work/family relationships in dual careers, in blended families, and in single-parent and other family types. (pp. 24–41)

PEOPLE OF COLOR

There are many groups on which we might possibly focus. We will limit our attention to only four: African Americans, Hispanics, Asian Americans, and Native Americans. In the not-too-distant future, half of all Americans will be from these four groups (U.S. Bureau of the Census, 1998). The amount of space devoted to each is probably representative of the amount of research that appears in the professional literature.

Two major problems are complicating factors in studying race and ethnicity in relation to career development. One is the confounding of race and ethnicity. If there are other social or behavioral sciences that agree on the use of the terms, psychology is not among them. Considerable disagreement exists regarding what is meant by *race* and whether the concept is useful even if an agreed-on meaning can evolve (Yee, Fairchild, Weizmann, & Wyatt, 1993). The second problem is the overlap between being economically disadvantaged and being culturally disadvantaged, because poverty tends to cross racial and ethnic boundaries. Poverty tends to define culturally diverse groups in greater proportion than the majority (even though Whites represent the largest number—rather than percentage—of people living in poverty). Using national samples, Trusty and Harris (1999) found that socioeconomic status (SES) had the strongest effects on lowered educational expectations and unrealized expectations. Additional research summarized by Trusty (2002) supports the powerful influences of SES on postsecondary educational expectations and attainment. Thus, the key element is not culture, race or ethnicity so much as poverty. This is not to say that discrimination is not real; it obviously exists. Brown (1995) notes the discrimination that exists toward African Americans based on colorism (i.e., skin tone), Leong and Serafica (1995) discuss the negative consequences of Asian Americans being labeled as the "model minority group." Although the percentage varies, currently about 14.5 percent of the U.S. population is classified as poor (family of four about $15,141), and about 40 percent of the poor are children under 18.

The United States is still a white majority country (71.6 percent). African Americans constitute 12.8 percent of the population; Hispanics, 11.3 percent; Asian Americans 4.4 percent; and Native Americans .9 percent. Multicultural populations, however, are growing at a much higher rate than whites. From 1990 to 2000, while the white population grew about 9.4 percent, the African American population increased by approximately 20.8 percent, Hispanics by almost 43.4 percent, and Asian Americans by almost 43.7 percent (U.S. Bureau of the Census, Bureau of Labor Statistics, 2002). Hispanics are expected to surpass African Americans to become the largest multicultural group in the United States sometime within the next two decades. It is predicted that by the middle of the next century, the United States will no longer be a predominantly white society. All counselors are being challenged to become culturally aware and to understand their own cultural heritage and worldview as well as those of their clients. The term "culture" represents a complex concept that many are challenged to define. Matsumoto (1996) defines culture as "the set of attitudes, values beliefs, and behaviors shared by a group of people, but different for each individual, communicated from one generation to the next" (p. 16). Matsumoto's definition identifies the challenge for counselors—understanding how cultural influences manifest themselves in the life of the individual.

African Americans

The data indicate that the plight of African Americans, especially inner-city men, is horrific. According to one study (Glaberson, 1990), nearly one of every four young African American men (20 to 29 years of age) in New York State is in a state prison or a local jail, on probation, or on parole. The number of young African American men in custody on any given day (45,000 out of 193,000 in New York State) is double the number of African American men enrolled in all the colleges in the state. This pattern is mirrored across the country. Over 50 percent of young urban African American men were unemployed in the 1980s, worked part-time jobs involuntarily, or earned poverty-level wages (Lichter, 1988). Forty-eight percent of African American families are headed by women, and more than half of all African American children are born out of wedlock (Staples, 1986).

In the past two decades, the situation has worsened. R. L. Taylor (1990) argues that "industrial decentralization, combined with structural shifts in city economies from centers of goods-producing or manufacturing activities to higher order service-providing industries, has severely affected the employment opportunities of inner-city African Americans, especially the job prospects of poorly educated African American youths.... Such structural changes have substantially reduced the number of unskilled and semiskilled jobs in those industries that have traditionally attracted and economically upgraded previous generations of African Americans" (p. 7). The consequences to African American families are obvious, as are the effects on crime rates.

Lest one automatically blame the African American family structure for so many ills, it is instructive to read the work of Lewis and Looney (1988). Their research looked into eighteen inner-city, poor African American families and compared them with middle- or upper-middle-class white families that they had previously studied. They concluded that the white and African American families were much more alike than different and what appeared to "work best" in fact worked best for both African American and white families. L. E. Jenkins (1989) points out that the family is embedded within a larger-scale social system that sometimes does not act in a manner designed to enhance the psychological health of that family. The inner-city African American family is thus frequently regarded in terms of its negative aspects rather than its strengths. If African American parents (including female heads of households) have good parenting skills, achievement in children emerges much as it does with whites. Obviously, the more compatible the cultures of the home and the school, the greater the probability of successful academic achievement. There are those who maintain that being a single, poor African American mother can be a viable alternative family pattern (Jarrett, 1994).

Simultaneously, however, the number of culturally diverse group members who are middle-class is growing. It is true about 30 percent of African Americans live in poverty, but about one-third can be considered middle class. Nearly half of all African Americans own their own homes, and about 1.5 million work as managers, business executives, and professionals. In terms of education, the high school completion rate of African Americans is essentially the same as that of white, European Americans (Brown, 1995). Unfortunately, however, the discrepancies emerge in postsecondary educational attainment. For white Americans between the ages of 25 and 29, 34 percent hold a bachelor's degree compared to 18 percent of African Americans in the same age category (U.S. Bureau of the Census, 2002). The negative economic consequences of not having a postsecondary degree have been well documents (Snyder & Shafer, 1996).

An examination of some of the research related to the career development of African Americans reveals that although there has been a recent increase in research on career development and behavior of precollege African Americans, there has been relatively little on higher education and adulthood. Most research on post-secondary subjects has concentrated on access: Do African American students in compensatory programs achieve as well as regularly admitted students? Are admissions tests as predictive for African Americans as for whites? Much less research has been devoted to process and exit-related concerns: What effect does the collegiate experience have on the values and attitudes of African Americans? Why do African Americans tends to gravitate toward certain occupations? What are unique African American career-related problems?

Nevertheless, there are some useful findings. First, one should not assume that African American students come to higher education with anything but ambition, an appreciation for work, and high career expectations. At the same time, however, the career development of African Americans is more likely than advantaged populations to be delayed or impaired. This lag can manifest itself at the college level in such problems as a discrepancy between a desire for a college education and a career choice that does not require that level of education, a general lack of knowledge of alternatives, possible skills deficits, and an unclear picture of self in relation to the world of work. These problems are hardly unique to African Americans, but they may be more characteristic of African American students as a group than of whites.

The school obviously has a role to play in the development of African American youth, and according to many observers, it has failed to exercise that role with vigor and skill. Grant and Sleeter (1988) longitudinally (over a seven-year period) studied 24 lower-middle-class junior high school students who were of different racial backgrounds. They found a gradual narrowing of dreams as the students went through secondary school. In junior high, these youngsters projected themselves into a wide band of future career roles, with no anticipation of racial, social, class, or gender barriers. The concept of institutional racism was alien to them; they valued education, visualizing it as a way to achieve their dreams. Because of the school's low demands on them, however, they put forth minimal effort. Their dreams were largely abandoned as the students progressed through school, and the school itself assumed an important role in that abandonment. "In spite of students' interest in further education, in spite of their good behavior in school, and in spite of the fact that the majority had normal learning ability, both the junior and senior high school faculty (with the exception of a very few individuals) accepted students' failure to empower themselves through education, and in doing so, ensured that they would fail" (p. 38). It is moot whether the increased number of African American children in private schools (Slaughter & Johnson, 1988) will change this conclusion.

Within-group differences among African Americans are probably as broad as between-group differences between African Americans and whites. Once again, social class is the confounding variable. There is no doubt that in the aggregate African Americans are disadvantaged, not only compared to the white majority but also compared other minorities. To be sure, strides have been made. Since World War II, the earnings of African American men have increased faster than those of white men. Since 1975, however, these gains have stabilized. Up to 1975, the gains were usually attributed to the declining proportion of African Americans in the South, increased education, and a period of relatively full employment. In general, additional education translates into additional earnings for African Americans at about the same rate as for whites.

Similarities are as much present between and among cultures as are differences. Gifted African American students experience similar social-cultural and psychological difficulties as do gifted students in the dominant culture (Ford, Harris, & Schuerger, 1993). African American college students, similiar to white students, experience increasing educational realism across the college years (Bowman & Tinsley, 1991). In general, return to work following a first birth is little different for African American and white women (Yoon & Waite, 1994). High-achieving African American women and white women tend to prefer an intrinsic-direct achieving style most strongly, which suggests that personal standards for excellence were the most salient for these women (Fassinger, 1995).

In the late 1980s, the National Career Development Association commissioned the Gallup Organization to determine the needs of adults for career assistance. African American adults expressed the strongest needs of any racial or ethnic group. Further, occupational information was perceived as terribly insensitive to the needs of minorities. Finally, according to reports, discrimination in the workplace persists (Brown, Minor, & Jepsen, 1991).

With so many African Americans unemployed, it is natural that many would see discrimination as a major cause (along with skills deficits and lack of work readiness). Indeed, how a worker perceives the possibility of employment discrimination affects several attitudes, including locus of control. Becker and Krzystojiak (1982) studied labor market discrimination and concluded that beyond racial identity, African Americans' perceptions of employment discrimination influenced their tendency to blame external forces for their plight (African Americans who feel they are discriminated against experience twice as much externality as African Americans who report no awareness of discrimination). Clearly, those African Americans who perceive discrimination in employment are affected in terms of their subsequent work attitudes, values, and behaviors.

Interestingly, however, one study (G. J. Johnson, 1990) has reported that being underemployed or underpaid (or both) did *not* seem to lower the self-esteem of African American men. The explanation given was that "perhaps African American men compensate for underemployment and underpayment by developing coping strategies whereby they assess their self-worth by personal and familial achievements which actually enhance their self-esteem" (p. 37).

What is bias and what is not bias in employment? Research has not yet provided definitive answers. Several studies have investigated aptitude measurement, for example, as a source of bias. Many assessment instruments, from the General Aptitude Test Battery (GATB) to work samples, have been carefully examined for ethnic differences that might lead to a conclusion of bias. Findings suggest that the use of a separate set of norms, for ethnic, sex, and disability groups may be appropriate. Although differences are apparently real, for whatever reason, it is also possible to exaggerate African American–white differences.

Other studies have investigated the validity of interest inventories with African Americans. Carter and Swanson (1990) reviewed eight studies of the Strong and concluded that there was "little evidence of the Strong's psychometric validity with African American samples" (p. 195). The instrument under examination was the old Strong Vocational Interest Blank (SVIB), not its later refinements; further, there was also no evidence that it is *not* valid. Hansen's (1987) research suggests that at least some Westernized interest inventories can be successfully used in other cultures. If African Americans can indeed be said to represent a different culture, cross-ethnic use is appropriate. The bulk of evidence although scanty, points toward the judicious use of inventories with African Americans.

What factors influence the career aspirations of African Americans? It is *not* the development of a positive racial identity (Evans & Herr, 1994) or perceptions of discrimination. With whites, racial identity is significantly related to work values (Carter, Gushue, & Weitzman, 1994), specifically, values of status and power.

Trusty (2002) used longitudinal data (eighth grade to two years beyond high school) to examine educational expectations of African American men and women. Results of Trusty's study indicate that parents' expectations, home-based parental involvement, and eighth-grade reading scores for women and eighth-grade mathematics scores for men had positive effects on the study participants' educational expectations two years beyond high school. Trusty suggests that the results of this study provide support for a growth model of career development for African American young people rather than a "blocked opportunities model."

The occupations that African Americans choose (or that are available to them) are relatively constricted. It is well known that in terms of the Holland classification, African Americans are underrepresented in the Enterprising and Investigative categories and overrepresented in the Realistic and Social categories. Enterprising occupations (such as sales and management) usually provide high income with less education than do other job families. African American youth, it is thought, should be exposed to more information about and experience in enterprising occupations. Why African Americans are not more highly represented in enterprising occupations is difficult to know. Past discrimination may have been directed more to managers, administrators, and salespersons than to educators, health personnel, ministers, and other social service workers. Whatever the reason, African Americans should become more involved in types of work that offer higher income differentials. Entrepreneurial business activities represent one such occupational category.

Similarly restrictive choices are made by African Americans in their tendency not to opt for science and engineering curricula in higher education. In 1988, African Americans constituted 1.3 percent of the total graduate enrollment in the physical sciences at doctorate-granting institutions, 1.4 percent in the mathematical sciences, and 1.7 percent in both computer science and life sciences (National Science Foundation, 1989). From 1975 to 1989, the number of doctoral degrees awarded to African Americans in the physical sciences, life sciences, and engineering remained stable, fluctuating narrowly between a low of 101 in 1980 and a high of 133 in 1978 (Vetter, 1989). African Americans tends to choose majors predominantly in the fields of social science, education, and health. Again, highlighting the influence of SES, however, Trusty, Ng, and Plata (2000) found that at middle and high SES, African Americans differed little from other racial-ethnic groups in choice of college major. Clearly African Americans, especially those from lower SES levels, need to be encouraged to explore careers that have been nontraditional for them. Malcolm (1990) suggests one way of getting African Americans attracted to such occupations:

> *Only by increasing the amount of time black children are engaged in meaningful educational activity in mathematics and science; by reaffirming the historical, contemporary and future role of blacks in science and engineering; and by valuing and recognizing participation in these fields within our communities and families can we ever expect to change the trickle of talent which currently flows from the pipeline into a flood. (p. 257)*

African American women in nontraditional occupations (e.g., law, medicine, engineering) report more barriers in their careers than do African American women in traditional occupations (e.g., social work, teaching, counseling). These barriers include perceived lack of support, marital discord, and race and gender discrimination. Woody (1992) points out that while African American women have more diversified employment than at any other time in history, they nevertheless remain concentrated in low-status positions in most workplaces.

Racial identity models generally suggest that individuals move from low to high racial salience as they meet challenges. They are often pulled by the duality in some sort of transition stage, and frequently there is a rapproachement with aspects of the dominant culture. This development of racial identity in African Americans is termed *nigrescence* (Cross, 1994; Parham & Austin, 1994).

There has been relatively little research to determine the difference between the expressed needs of African Americans for career planning and those of the majority population. One may hypothesize that African Americans express the same basic needs as their white counterparts in college: résumé-writing skills, job-interviewing skills, career-planning workshops, and so forth.

Among the solutions proposed, but lacking in empirical support, is that of Cheatham (1990), who proposes that the emphasis of interventions be *Africentric* for African American students. He argues that counselors must pay heed to a group's cultural uniqueness; specifically, the African American's values, truths, and meanings. Cheatham alleges that the dominant U.S. culture is Eurocentric and therefore clashes with values, attitudes, and beliefs that are strongly influenced by African origins. Consequently, Cheatham suggests different career interventions with African Americans. He proposes "the use of culture-specific information that enables the helper to distinguish between an African American client's psychosocial dynamics and behaviors, and those behaviors that are products of obligatory, grudging accommodation to normative majority culture (i.e., Eurocentric) structures" (p. 336). Included in such interventions would be a recognition of structural or racial discrimination, culturally influenced perceptions of the meaning of work, differential availability of career information and guidance, and economics and labor market forces that affect African Americans differentially. It remains for someone to operationalize this idea.

Hackett and Byars (1996) suggest that one of the more promising models for accounting for race and ethnicity in career development is the social cognitive career theory (Lent, Brown, & Hackett, 1994). More specifically, Hackett and Byars view social cognitive career theory as being particularly relevant for African American women. Concerning career counseling interventions with African American clients, Hackett and Byars note that "given the possible connections between ethnic identity, efficacy, and outcome expectations, it is important for counselors to assess and explore clients' ethnic identity development in addition to attending to skills, efficacy beliefs, outcome expectations, interests and goal setting" (p. 336). Walsh, Bingham, Brown, and Ward (2001) served as editors for a book entitled *Career Counseling for African Americans.* This book provides useful suggestions for a broad spectrum of career concerns (e.g., career counseling process, assessment, nontraditional careers, racial discrimination). For example, Phelps and Constantine (2001) offer an expanded definition of the glass ceiling to include race and ethnicity and discuss the obstacles African American professionals encounter in their career advancement. One must resist a temptation, however, to throw out the more universal, Eurocentric aspects of career interventions, for they indeed work with African Americans as well as the majority culture. Once again, we are talking of differences in degree rather than kind and the necessity to combine what is catholic to every person's career development with what is parochial to a unique subgroup's needs. The lack of either focus in an intervention diminishes the treatment.

Hispanics

As indicated previously, current predictions are that Hispanics will soon be the majority minority group in the United States. Even now, the Hispanic population outnumbers African Americans in four of the largest cities in the United States (Los Angeles, Houston, Phoenix, and San Antonio). The geographic concentration of these cities is one reason that almost nine of ten Hispanics live in ten of our fifty states. Their heritage may be from Mexico, Cuba, Puerto Rico, Central America, South America, or Spain itself. The largest Hispanic ethnic group is the Mexicans, followed, in order, by Puerto Ricans and Cubans. Clearly, they are a heterogeneous group.

Each of these major Hispanic groups has different unemployment rates and sex differences in workforce participation, although all groups are basically less well off than the general population. Among the Puerto Ricans and Mexicans there is a great deal of movement between the country of origin and the United States. Cubans have little or no movement back to Cuba. Cubans and Mexicans tend to be unemployed for shorter durations than do Puerto Ricans. These figures emphasize the heterogeneous character of Hispanics.

Hispanic workers are concentrated more in the lower-paid, lesser-skilled occupations of the total workforce. More than half of the employed Hispanic women are either clerical workers or nontransport operatives (dressmakers, assemblers, machine operators, and so on), both low-paid occupations. Hispanic men are disproportionately employed as operatives, service workers, and craft workers. Although a great percentage of Hispanics are not employed in agriculture, contrary to popular stereotype, about 7 percent work in that area compared with 1 percent of the white population. Although these data present a picture of Hispanic ethnic groups as generally underrepresented in the more remunerative occupations of society, some progress is being made. The children of first-generation and second-generation immigrants expect higher-status and better-paying jobs in the economy. The major task facing these groups is to acquire the education and occupational skills necessary to realize these aspirations.

As with any socioeconomically disadvantaged minority, young Hispanics generally have a constricted knowledge of and exposure to occupations. Consequently, they choose from a relatively limited array of alternatives. They may not have basic job-seeking skills (such as filling out applications), and they may need encouragement, motivation, and reinforcement to pursue occupations and opportunities not traditionally considered reachable by Hispanics.

Of course, the major difference between Hispanics and some other major U.S. minorities is language. The United States is the fifth largest Spanish-speaking country in the Western Hemisphere (after Mexico, Argentina, Columbia, and Peru). Those whose native language is not English tend to complete fewer years of schooling. Because more than half of the American Hispanic population are children or adolescents, this lack of language facility translates into high dropout rates. From this dilemma springs the controversy of bilingual education. Some want Spanish to be the first language of instruction and bilingualism the goal. Add to this strong family ties and cultural traditions (for example, Hispanics tend to have a deeply engrained sense of fatalism and destiny), and the career counselor has more than the "normal" problems with which to contend. There is not only heterogeneity among ethnic groups of Hispanics; there are also clear individual differences. Treating people as individuals while recognizing the cultural context from which they come is a fine-line activity.

The importance of attaining a true biculturalism in an English-speaking country (or of becoming completely acculturated and assimilated) cannot be overstressed. Gomez and Fassinger (1994) have demonstrated a clear relationship between degree of biculturalism in college-going Hispanics and their repertoire of achieving styles (greater flexibility and skills to adapt to new achievement situations).

Several organizations are dedicated to providing services especially for Hispanics. These organizations provide college financial assistance (for example, National Hispanic Scholarship Fund), special career and academic counseling (Aspira), and vocational training and job placement (the Puerto Rican Forum). In addition, Hispanics are a targeted and preferred group for various federal programs because of their lower levels of educational attainment, occupational and employment status, and income compared to the general population.

As with African Americans, Hispanics have been the focus of a number of studies that seek to determine occupationally relevant differences between them and the white majority. For example, McWhirter (1997) found that Mexican American students anticipated more career barriers than did Anglo-Americans. Lundberg, Osborne, and Miner (1997) reported that Mexican American adolescents displayed much less knowledge about occupations and career decision-making principles and much less career awareness than did Anglo-American adolescents. A fascinating study of the school achievement of white, Asian American, African American, and Hispanic students in relation to both parenting (familial values) and peer support suggest that when parents are warm, firm, and democratic, results are best, but that peers exert enormous influence. There are considerable racial and ethnic differences in beliefs about the rewards of academic success (Steinberg, Dornbusch, & Brown, 1992). For instance, students who think that they can succeed outside of school without doing well in school tend not to work at schooling. Students who believe that academic failure will be terrible tend to take a more active role in their education. The investigators found that "on average, African American and Hispanic youth devote less time to homework, perceive their parents as having lower performance standards, and are less likely to believe that academic success comes from working hard" (p. 726). In the case of Hispanics, with the largest dropout rate by far of any ethnic group, both parenting styles and the peer culture values and beliefs evidently combine to work against successful schooling. Ultimately, however, study of in-group differences may provide a more fertile area for research than does the study of between-group differences.

The attribution research with Chicana women produces similar results to that reported for African Americans in the previous section. Romero and Garza (1986) had a group of whites, African American, and Chicana women make causal attributions and rate occupational outcomes for women of all three ethnic groups in terms of task difficulty, competence, effort, luck, personal connections, gender, and ethnicity. The attributions for occupational outcome differed not only with the ethnicity of the rater but also with that of the person being rated. White women are relatively color-blind in that ethnicity does not seem to affect attributions of occupational success or failure. Chicana women attributed the occupational success of white women and the occupational failure of minority women to ethnic origin. Thus, ethnic factors do appear to affect attributions made for occupational success or failure.

Hernandez and Morales (1999) conducted exploratory research to understand the career development experiences of Latinas employed in counseling and faculty positions in higher education. Results of this qualitative study suggest that Latinas find higher education to be an inhospitable and nonsupportive place to work and that Latinas are inhibited from achieving the same levels of success as men or other women in higher education. Hernandez and Morales suggest that formalized mentoring programs would be useful to Latinas in helping them connect more strongly with the organizational structures of which they are a part.

Hispanic students are as open to career interventions as any other subpopulation. Rodriquez and Blocher (1988) demonstrated that diverse career interventions with academically and economically disadvantaged Puerto Rican college women in a special admissions program in a large urban college were effective in raising their career maturity and in changing their locus of control (moving them further toward a belief that they can control their environments and their futures).

The symbiotic relationship between work and mental health is certainly no more evident than with Hispanics (Knouse, Rosenfeld, & Culbertson, 1992). The effects of job discrimination, unemployment, underemployment, and other work-related factors have a significant impact on the general mental health of Hispanics. In terms of counseling mode, Hispanics, in general, prefer a direct, concrete counseling style and one that is clearly culture sensitive. Roles and expectations within the counseling dyad must be clear and explicit. Any assessments should be interpreted within a cultural and language context. Any community involvement is a plus.

Fouad (1994) agrees with these career counseling recommendations and reminds career counselors that counseling occurs within a cultural context that must be sensitive to familial and group-related variables that tend to be prominent with Hispanic clients. Fouad also cautions career counselors to evaluate the appropriateness of assessment tools for Hispanics. Finally, Fouad points to the urgent need for Hispanic high school and college students to receive culturally sensitive career interventions that invite parental involvement and help foster academic and career self-efficacy.

Reviewing the relatively sparse literature on career counseling with Hispanics, Arbona (1990) reached several conclusions:

> *Occupational aspirations and interest measurement among Hispanics are the two areas that have been examined most extensively by research. From the findings, it may be concluded that, in general, Hispanics want to educate themselves and enter demanding occupations. However, very little is known regarding their career decision-making process or the difficulties they face in pursuing their aspirations. The research reviewed also supports the notion that the Holland model may be used to assess the career interests of Hispanics and to help them explore the world of work. Research related to career progression behaviors, job satisfaction, and work values among Hispanics is very limited and does not allow for any firm conclusions.*
>
> *In terms of content, the career counseling research related to Hispanics is very limited and, for the most part, lacks a theoretical base. This research has not yet addressed the application of career development theories to Hispanics, nor has it examined the nature of career-related problems confronted by this group. With the notable exception of the research on vocational interests, we know very little about the applicability of career counseling instruments and the effectiveness of career interventions in working with this ethnic group.*
>
> *This review of the literature, however, underscores important issues. The findings of this body of research contradict traditional views that assume that Hispanics lack high educational and occupational aspirations. Instead, it suggests that the lack of occupational mobility among Hispanics is related to structural factors, such as socioeconomic status and lack of opportunities, and not to cultural traits. The literature reviewed also shows that Hispanics are not a homogeneous group and suggests that there are important differences between the various Hispanic sub-groups as well as between Hispanics from different socioeconomic backgrounds. Also, it is important to be sensitive to regional differences among Hispanics of the same ethnic group. (pp. 313–314)*

Asian Americans

In the 1980s, the Asian population of the United States grew by 70 percent. Between the years 2000 and 2010, the percentage of Asian Americans in the labor force will increase 44 percent. The Asian American student has received a great deal of press in the last few decades. Much of this publicity has promulgated the notion of a sort of "superstudent" who is able to leap curricula in a single bound and, faster than a speeding bullet, master all sorts of difficult tasks. The attractiveness of this image is further enhanced by the fact that the student is likely to be the son or daughter of first-generation immigrants.

In fact, Asian Americans do seem as an ethnic group to have, on average, achieved educationally at a high level, especially when compared to African Americans, Hispanics, and Native Americans. This ethnic group—like any other—is diverse; it has members of such origins as Japanese, Chinese, Cambodian, Vietnamese, Indian, Pakistani, Filipino, and Thai, among others, and they tend to achieve differentially (Isaacson & Brown, 2000; Sue & Abe, 1988). There is, of course, the unpublicized aspect of Asian Americans; that is, a large percentage of them have little or no education (Leong & Serafica, 1995; Sue & Padilla, 1986), they have sociopathic groups within their communities, and they tend to be underemployed. Hurk and Kim (1989) have traced the image of Asian Americans over a century in which they moved from being regarded as "unassimilable immoral heathens" to a successful model minority. They determined, however, that if success is equated with the principle of earnings equity, the image is primarily a myth, for underemployment is prevalent among Asian Americans. The fact remains, however, that more than eight in ten Asian American high school graduates are in college two years after high school graduation. The search for the cause of this phenomenal achievement has not produced definitive answers.

Sue and Okazaki (1990), for example, systematically reviewed the research relating to Asian American achievement, including the evidence for both hereditary differences in intelligence and family cultural values that foster educational achievement. They found no compelling evidence to support either hypothesis. Rather, they propose that these results were produced by Asian American culture interacting with the larger society. Specifically, they argue that Asian Americans perceived education as a vehicle for mobility, without which, because of discrimination and other restrictions to occupational mobility, their vertical movement is severely limited. This argument does not, of course, explain why Asian Americans would be thus motivated and other ethnic minorities, which experience similar barriers to occupational attainment, would not. There are those who make a persuasive case for the influence of the family on the achievement of Asian American students. Caplan, Whitmore, and Choy (1989) studied "boat people," Indochinese refugees who came to the United States, and concluded that "it is the family's ability to translate cultural values into a life style…that helps its members to confront adversity and prepares them for future success" (p. 148). Education begins in the home and is always tied to the values of the home. One could speculate from this conclusion that if assimilation leads to denial of cultural values in subsequent generations, achievement will be adversely affected.

Predictable stereotyping evidently exists in terms of college students' perceptions of "appropriate" occupations for Asian Americans. In a study conducted by Leong and Hayes (1990), for example, male Asian Americans were seen as successful engineers, computer scientists, and mathematicians, but not as successful insurance salespersons. Female Asian Americans were as sex-typed as the white population. Likewise, Asian American students are more likely to have considered investigative occupations than whites and less likely to consider enterprising or conventional occupations (Leung, Ivey, & Suzuki, 1994).

Leung's (1993) research hints at the fact that Asian American adolescents, more than is the case with whites, may prematurely constrict their career choices based on perceived prestige or sex type factors. In short, they may ignore variables such as their personal interests and aptitudes in deference to the prestige of an occupation. Leong and Serafica (1995) contend that educational attainment leads to fewer economic rewards for Asian Americans than it does for European Americans.

As with other ethnic groups, the career counseling of Asian Americans requires the application of some specific knowledge and skills, sometimes in addition to traditional approaches and sometimes in place of more generic interventions. Much of what we assume about counseling Asian Americans is based on cross-cultural research that emanates from studies of samples in foreign countries rather than Asian Americans themselves. For example, Khan, Alvi, Shaukat, Hussain, and Beig (1990) demonstrated the utility of Holland's Self Directed Search with college and university students in Pakistan. Should we assume that the findings pertain to Pakistani Americans?

Mau (2000) investigated the relationship between decision-making style decision-making self-efficacy for American and Taiwanese college students. Mau found a significant difference between these two groups of students with 66 percent of American students adhering to a rational (as opposed to intuitive) decision-making style and 56 percent of the Taiwanese students endorsing a rational style of decision-making. Exum and Lau (1988) researched fifty students from Hong Kong who were studying at a midwestern American university regarding their preferences for directive versus nondirective counseling. They concluded that a directive counseling approach was preferable, because these students require a counselor who is authoritative without being authoritarian. What these students apparently wanted was a counselor who projects self-confidence and provides structure, interpretation, and a solution to a problem. Again, can we transfer these findings to the counseling of Chinese American students? Fernandez

(1988) also addresses the counseling of Southeast Asian students, who compose more than 40 percent of the total foreign enrollment in U.S. colleges and universities. Considering the problem of culture shock, she argues that it is inappropriate to counsel these students in modes that require introspection, reflection, and extreme client verbalization. Behavioral approaches seem more appropriate. Also, individuals are not likely to make decisions without the advice and consent of their families, so working toward family cooperation would be useful. A special issue of the *Career Development Quarterly* (Leong & Pope, 2002) was devoted to challenges for conducting career counseling with Asian clients. Articles addressed career counseling in Japan (Tatsuno, 2002), Taiwan (Chang, 2002), China (Zhang, Hu, & Pope, 2002), Hong Kong (Leung, 2002), the Philippines (Salazar-Clemena, 2002), and Singapore (Tan, 2002). Many of these articles emphasize the need to understand a collectivistic orientation to career decision making, the need to incorporate family members in the career counseling process, and the need to work collaboratively to help clients resolve their career concerns. Can we hypothesize the same for Asian Americans? For all generations?

It is likely that when compared with whites, Asian Americans put more emphasis on extrinsic and security occupational values (i.e., making more money, having a stable, secure future) (Leong, 1991) and tend to emphasize a collectivistic orientation to career decision making (Leong & Serafica, 1995). Therefore, Leong (1993) suggests that career counselors be wary of any direct confrontations or challenges with Asian American clients. Sue (1994) agrees with Leong and advises counselors to be indirect and to do most of the initial verbalization and to use a formal interactive approach, especially when discussing personal issues, with Asian American clients.

Applying the family emphasis with an American sample of Chinese and Korean American parents, Evanoski and Tse (1989) provided culture-specific, bilingual career awareness workshops. Using bilingual role models and bilingual materials, these workshops were held in community settings and enhanced the career awareness of thousands of Chinese American and Korean American parents who—presumably—have enormous influence on the career choices of their children. These workshops were three hours long and emphasized exposure to various occupations and the role of the community college in facilitating access to those occupations.

To provide culturally sensitive career counseling to Asian American clients, Leong and Gim-Chung (1995) offer several suggestions. First, they recommend that career counselors encourage their Asian American clients to engage in broad career exploration to expand the range of career options they are considering. Second, they suggest that career counselors use structured and didactic approaches with Asian Americans. Such approaches reduce the threat and emotional risk associated with less directive therapies. When career counseling approaches are viewed as educational interventions, they also tend to reduce the stigma often associated with seeking counseling. However, career counselors are cautioned that group interventions could be risky due to discomfort with self-disclosure and the need to not lose face. Finally, Leong and Gim-Chung recommend involving parents in career interventions so parents can become aware of various career options and the career development process.

Native Americans

No other group in the United States has experienced deeper prejudice or is in a less-advantaged posture than Native Americans. Many Native Americans in the United States are concentrated on reservations (nearly 50 percent of all Native Americans live on Native American lands and some 275 reservations). Of those living outside the reservations, the largest concentrations of Native Americans are in Los Angeles, San Francisco, and Chicago. They are composed of many nations and over 450 recognized tribes, each with a rich heritage and unique character. The latest census data indicate a marked increase in the number of people declaring themselves to be Native Americans, perhaps signaling a heightened pride. Currently, more than 2.3 million Native American Indians live in the United States.

Native American cultures reflect values that differ substantially from the mainstream. Native Americans value sharing, cooperation, the group, a present-time orientation, harmony with nature, and a respect for elders (Herring, 1996). Isaacson and Brown (2000) note that poverty, lack of career information, geographic isolation, geographic relocation, a history of experiencing significant discrimination, and a lack of adherence to the mechanical monitoring of time each present substantial career challenges to Native Americans.

Despite the poverty that they have experienced and continue to experience, Native Americans have both reasonable career aspirations and formidable barriers to overcome in achieving these career goals. Herring (1990) believes that certain "career myths" exacerbate the already imposing roadblocks to the career development of Native American youth and lead to irrational beliefs. These are, in fact, the same myths that affect every minority; they include limited research findings about their career development and behavior, stereotypes, and lack of awareness and opportunities. As a result, Native Americans have extremely high unemployment rates and tend to enter a restricted number of occupations (one-third of Native Americans, of the relatively few who attend college, earned their degrees in education or social sciences). Herring suggests that use of Native American occupational role models from nontraditional occupations would be beneficial in expanding their career horizons.

The most common traditional occupational stereotype of the Native American is that of the skilled structural steel worker, daringly risking his life as he adroitly maneuvers thousands of feet above the ground. Although Native Americans do account for a disproportionately large percentage of structural steel workers, the total number so employed is a very small percentage of the Native American workforce. In one study, nontraditional, gender-based occupations were clearly considered by Navajo students on reservations, but the researchers attributed the findings of acceptance of nontraditional occupations to "limited contacts with the institutions and materials that transmit the biases of the majority culture" (p. 270). Thus, the students were less aware of the sex types associated with particular jobs (Beyard-Tyler & Haring, 1984). It would be interesting to replicate this study with Native Americans living off-reservation.

Thus far, the career needs of Native American students do not seem a great deal different from those of any other minority. To investigate the possibility of differential career attitudes of African American, white, and Native American high school students, C. C. Lee (1984) surveyed more than 500 tenth-grade rural students in the Southeast. Included in the sample were 70 Native American boys and 75 Native American girls, 92 African American boys and 114 African American girls, and 87 white boys and 82 white girls. Participants took both the Career Maturity Inventory and the Tennessee Self Concept Scale and responded to questions designed to elicit demographic and other data. Multiple regression analysis demonstrated that "different equations would be required to predict career choice attitudes, one each for African Americans, Whites, and Native Americans" (p. 181). Further, it was discovered that minority parents apparently had a greater impact on the career choices of their children than did white parents. Replication of this study with a nonrural sample would be useful. This study is cited because it demonstrates that there do indeed appear to be differences between the career development needs of Native Americans and the majority culture, and, in fact, there may be differences between Native American career needs and those of other minorities. Currently, however, we are unable to delineate those needs without further research. Some research, however, is instructive.

Steward (1993) has demonstrated through case studies that a Native American college student who is outgoing, active, and grateful is likely to have an advantage in both mentoring and hiring over an equally competent Native American student who does not exhibit these characteristics. Hence, counselors need to be sure that the latter type student is not neglected.

The self-efficacy of rural Native American adolescents has been measured as lower than that of Whites and Hispanics (Lauver & Jones, 1991). Such lack of confidence in one's ability to perform career-related tasks has clear implications for the type of intervention necessary to raise aspiration levels. Thomason (1991) urges the initial use of an active problem-solving approach. Further, LaFromboise, Trimble, and Mohatt (1990) suggest that counselors working with Native Americans understand the concept of *community* in Native American culture and of choice and religion. More than most counselees, Native Americans appear to prefer a counselor with similar ethnicity (Bennett & BigFoot-Sipes, 1991). Finally, Native American clients who live on reservations will likely differ from those who are assimilated in terms of their knowledge of the world of work and external pressures (Martin, 1991). Of those living on the ten largest reservations, less than half have earned a high school diploma (Carter & Wilson,

1992). Johnson, Swartz, and Martin (1995) note that the educational level of Native Americans is a "gatekeeper" that very often keeps Native Americans locked in poverty and having access to few occupational options.

As is the case with every culturally diverse group, the use of standard assessment instrumentation with Native Americans has received some research attention. Results have been mixed. Some studies have reported that differences in the results of interest measurement are so slight between Native American and white populations that routine use of existing instrumentation would be appropriate; other studies have found differences of sufficient magnitude to call for separate tribal norms (Epperson & Hammond, 1981; Gade, Fuqua, & Hurlburt, 1984). A study of the Strong (Haviland & Hansen, 1987) found no differences between female white and Native American college students but substantial differences between male white and Native American students. Clearly, a great deal more research is necessary before any definitive conclusions can be reached. At this time, the best guidelines for a counselor to use in interpreting tests and inventories with any minority would apparently be to exercise caution and always interpret in light of a counselee's sociocultural history. Johnson, Swartz, and Martin (1995) recommend using an eclectic career counseling approach that incorporates person-environment, social learning, and ecological models. But, they also go on to note that given the diversity among Native Americans it is difficult, at best, to prescribe one method for career counseling with Native American clients. Martin (1995) advises career counselors to consider the extent to which Native American clients use their native language versus English. Obviously, this informs the counselors as to which career assessments may be appropriate, which occupational information resources may be useful, and the style of communication within the career counseling process that may be required (e.g., it may be necessary for the career counselor to involve a native language proficient consultant during the course of career counseling). Understanding the client's cultural orientation, environmental context (e.g., the client's home community), and family structure are also important considerations when providing career counseling to Native American clients (Martin, 1995).

Counseling Culturally Diverse Clients

Several books are available that are useful to the counselor who is assisting culturally diverse clients with career development and choice issues (Atkinson & Hackett, 1995; Lee, 1995; Leong, 1995; McWhirton, 1994; Pedersen, 1994; Vacc, Wittmer, & DeVaney, 1988). In fact, however, guidelines are little different from those used in counseling people in general. Perhaps, as we maintain is the case with women, differences are more in degree than in kind. The counselor should know the cultural milieu of culturally different clientele, just as he or she should understand the cultural context of any client. Professional helpers should possess certain characteristics for performing culturally skilled work with various ethnic groups (or a representative of any cultural context, for that matter). Incorporating a contextual perspective is essential to providing culturally sensitive career counseling. However, Betz and Fitzgerald (1987) note that counselors must avoid the cultural uniformity myth. Because within group differences can be just as substantial as between group difference, career counselors must be mindful of, and sensitive to, each client's uniqueness.

Virtually every professional organization at almost every level (national, state, local) has devised and disseminated guidelines and codes for providing services to people of color and other diverse populations. The American Psychological Association has also promulgated guidelines for providing services to ethnic, linguistic, and culturally diverse populations (APA Office of Ethnic Minority Affairs, 1993). Among the nine major points (general principles) are the following (each general principle has several detailed subprinciples that are here omitted):

1. Psychologists educate their clients to the processes of psychological intervention, such as goals and expectations; the scope and, when appropriate, legal limits of confidentiality; and the psychologists' orientations.
2. Psychologists are cognizant of relevant research and practice issues as related to the population being served.
3. Psychologists recognize ethnicity and culture as significant parameters in understanding psychological processes.
4. Psychologists respect the roles of family members and community structures, hierarchies, values, and beliefs within the client's culture.

5. Psychologists respect clients' religious or spiritual beliefs and values, including attributions and taboos, because they affect worldview, psychological functioning, and expressions of distress.
6. Psychologists interact in the language requested by the client and, if this is not feasible, make an appropriate referral.
7. Psychologists consider the impact of adverse social, environmental, and political factors in assessing problems and designing interventions.
8. Psychologists attend to as well as work to eliminate biases, prejudices, and discriminatory practices.
9. Psychologists working with culturally diverse populations should document culturally and sociopolitically relevant factors in the records. (pp. 46–47)

These suggestions for desirable characteristics are certainly beyond contention, but they also apply to *any* clientele, not simply the culturally different. There is surely no doubt about the counselor's need to understand the characteristics of the counselee's ethnic or racial group and to have all the attending and responding skills characteristic of a good counseling relationship.

These guidelines are interesting, however, because they suggest that culturally different counselors may sometimes need to refer clients to others who may be more skilled with problems that center on membership in that group. This strategy is quite different from recommending that only a given ethnic, racial, or sexual counselor counsel individuals in that group. We reject the implication that in the long run only like-ethnics should counsel ethnics; by extension, only substance abusers should counsel substance abusers, only gays counsel gays, only divorced counsel divorced, only unemployed counsel unemployed, only schizophrenics counsel schizophrenics, and so on, *ad absurdum.*

As will be indicated in Chapter 15, AERA, APA, NCME, ACA, and ASHA have combined to produce a *Code of Fair Testing Practices in Education* (Joint Committee on Testing Practices, 1988). This document presents suggestions for both test developers and test users in terms of selecting tests, interpreting scores, striving for fairness, and informing test takers. The Association for Assessment in Counseling has published *Multicultural Assessment Standards: A Compilation for Counselors* (Prediger, 1993). Collating a number of other guidelines, it offers suggestions for the selection, administration, scoring, and use and interpretation of assessment instruments.

Ridley, Mendoza, Kanitz, Angermeier, and Zenk (1994) propose a curriculum for multicultural training that includes ten learning objectives:

1. Displaying culturally responsive behaviors
2. Ethical knowledge and practice pertaining to cultural issues
3. Cultural empathy
4. Ability to critique existing counseling theories for cultural relevance
5. Development on an individual theoretical orientation that is culturally relevant
6. Obtaining knowledge of normative characteristics of cultural groups
7. Cultural self-awareness
8. Obtaining knowledge of within-groups cultural differences
9. Learning about multicultural concepts and issues
10. Respecting cultural differences (p. 250)

Expanding on "cultural sensitivity" in a later article, Ridley and colleagues (1994) suggest that it is the "ability of counselors to acquire, develop, and actually use an accurate cultural perceptual schema in the course of multicultural counseling" (p. 130).

Hawks and Muha (1991) suggest four areas in which counselors can more effectively provide career assistance to minority students (with which the reader may or may not agree): (1) foster intrinsic motivation in students by emphasizing student-generated versus counselor-generated or teacher-generated transmitted knowledge (discover the relationship between current educational experiences and future job possibilities); (2) incorporate the student's language and culture in educational programs; (3) involve the minority community, especially parents, in the program; (4) advocate for students by viewing problems primarily as a result of the system versus a flaw in the student.

A thoughtful model of Minority Identity Development (MID) has been offered by Atkinson, Morten, and Sue (1983). Although this model has not been tested to any appreciable extent, it does offer a framework for intervention with minorities at various development stages. In summary form, the model appears in Table 5.1.

This model suggests that in stage 1, minority individuals prefer the cultural values of the majority cul-

TABLE 5.1 Summary of Minority Identity Development Model

STAGES OF MINORITY DEVELOPMENT MODEL	ATTITUDE TOWARD SELF	ATTITUDE TOWARD OTHERS OF THE SAME MINORITY	ATTITUDE TOWARD OTHERS OF DIFFERENT GROUP	ATTITUDE TOWARD DOMINANT GROUP
Stage 1—Conformity	Self-deprecation	Group deprecation	Discrimination	Group appreciation
Stage 2—Dissonance	Conflict between self-deprecation and apprecition	Conflict between group deprecation and group appreciation	Conflict between dominant views of minority and feelings of shared experience	Conflict between group appreciation and group depreciation
Stage 3—Resistance and Immersion	Self-appreciation	Group appreciation	Conflict between feelings of empathy for other minority experiences and feelings of culturocentrism	Group depreciation
Stage 4—Introspection	Concern with basis of self-appreciation	Concern with nature of unequivocal appreciation	Concern with ethnocentric basis for judging others	Concern with the basis of group depreciation
Stage 5—Synergetic Articulation and Awareness	Self-appreciation	Group appreciation	Group appreciation	Selective appreciation

Source: From D. R. Atkinson, et al., *Counseling American Minorities.* Copyright © 1983 Wm. C. Brown Publishers, Dubuque, Iowa. Reprinted by permission.

ture over their own. In stage 2, dissonance sets in and results in confusion and conflict. The dominant culture no longer seems clearly superior to the minority member's own culture. In stage 3, the minority individual rejects the dominant culture in a sort of reaction formation and totally endorses the minority views. In stage 4, the person begins to think less in terms of minority group dogma and more in terms of forming individual reactions. Finally, in stage 5, conflicts are resolved and individuals become comfortable with themselves and with their heritage. The recurrent theme throughout each of these stages is oppression, first as an individual experiences it and later as he or she strives to eliminate it both in his or her own life and in society. We have previously referred to the great heterogeneity on all variables that exists within any minority group. The MID model is another example. Within any given culturally different ethnic or racial group, identity issues may be resolved to a greater or less degree by individual members. The task of counselors is to determine at which stage an individual is functioning and how facilitating or self-defeating that stage might be in terms of career development.

Helms and Piper (1994) also point up the potential of the construct of racial identity (and, one infers by extension, sexual identity) to explain aspects of vocational development. They see research into racial identity as a more viable alternative to explaining career behaviors of minorities than the current preponderance of comparison studies. They believe that differences have blurred in the last decade. Some researchers suggest that racial identity models and ethnic identity and acculturation models can be combined into an integrated model for research purposes (Leong & Chou, 1994).

LaFromboise, Coleman, and Gerton (1993) have advocated the alternation model of biculturalism. In this model, persons become competent in two cultures without losing their cultural identity or having to choose one culture over the other. This competence can be developed by the person's achieving: "(a) knowledge of cultural beliefs and values, (b) positive attitudes toward both majority and minority group, (c) bicultural efficacy, (d) communication ability, (e) role repertoire, (f) a sense of being grounded" (p. 403). All of these are self-explanatory except *role repertoire,* which is defined as the range of culturally or situationally appropriate behaviors or roles possessed by an individual; and a *sense of being grounded,* which refers to a person's having established social networks in both cultures.

Pedersen (1990) argues that multicultural counseling should be organized around the construct of *balance,* by which he means "the identification of different or even conflicting culturally learned perspectives without necessarily resolving that difference or dissonance in favor of either viewpoint" (p. 552). In other words, what is advocated is a "walk-in-his-moccasins," nonjudgmental, sensitive approach to multicultural counseling in which there are no assumptions of "better" in terms of conflicting cultures. Similarly, writing from a framework of *nigrescence* (the process of becoming African American), Parham (1996) also urges that counselors help African Americans (and, by extension, any minority) to confront the question of how much to compromise their ethnicity or race to assimilate into the larger culture. Specifically, he identifies three issues: (1) self-differentiation versus preoccupation with assimilation (a feeling of being personally worthwhile without needing the validation of the majority culture); (2) body transcedence versus preoccupation with body image (coming to grips with self-image in relation to the "European" majority look); and (3) ego transcendence versus self-absorption (the development of ego strength by contributing to one's people as well as to oneself alone). All these compromises entail feelings of worth. The attitudes addressed by both Pederson and Parham would be especially important in career counseling. Coming from a different direction, Campbell and Hadley (1992) argue that because there are relatively few minorities in career planning and placement programs, active proselytizing and training must occur to attract minorities to become career counseling practitioners.

Trusty (2002) contends that one basic framework for conducting career counseling with persons of color comes from research related to occupational interests and choices (Day & Rounds, 1997). Specifically, Trusty notes that differences in interests, preferences, and choices among racial-ethnic or cultural groups arise from three variables: (1) differences in real and perceived social and economic opportunity structure, often referred to as barriers to career development, (2) awareness of occupational options, and (3) values differences. Differences in the opportunity structure relate to prejudicial treatment by employers, geographical constraints, and linguistic limitations. Awareness of occupational options relates to limited life experiences, perhaps due to poverty, lack of access to sources of occupational information and sources of support for career development. There is considerable empirical support for the importance of values in the career development of persons of color. For example, Trusty notes the importance of family values for Hispanic Americans and the valuing of occupational security and extrinsic rewards for Asian Americans. Trusty contends that these three variables offer a useful focal point for career counseling with persons of color.

All these research findings and suggestions for practice distill to the following guidelines for career counseling of culturally diverse clients:

1. Counselors should, above all, possess all the generic counseling knowledge, skill, understanding, ability, and behavior thought to be appropriate in any helping relationship.
2. Counselors should recognize their own attitudes and values as these impinge on counseling specific ethnic and racial groups; they must work to ensure that these internal frames of reference do not form road blocks to successful counseling. Obviously, white, majority counselors should uncover any possible biases toward African Americans, Hispanics, or other groups; professionals who are themselves culturally different should undergo similar self-scrutiny regarding the majority.
3. Counselors should be aware of the cultural context from which individuals come, but they should not assume that individuals are bounded by that culture. They are first and foremost *individuals* and only secondarily representatives of a specific racial or ethnic group.
4. Counselors should understand what aspects of career helping may need special attention with specific culturally different groups. All groups, minority or majority, will need the same career skills, attitudes, knowledge, and so forth; some

groups may need emphasis on a particular aspect of career development.

5. Counselors must help minorities to understand and internalize the fact that they *do* have a choice in career development, that given certain decisions and behaviors, certain consequences are likely to occur.
6. Counselors should help culturally different individuals understand that although they may encounter discrimination, they cannot be discouraged by it or consider themselves perpetual victims of it. They can be taught to deal with it and to use the vehicles available to surmount it. Counselors themselves can identify opportunities to take social action to counteract discriminatory practices in the workplace and the community.
7. Counselors must be sure that they understand which deficits and discontinuities in the career development of the culturally different are consequences of socioeconomic class and which are the result of membership in some specific racial or ethnic group.

IMMIGRANTS

The United States, of course, is a land of immigrants as are, most notably, Canada and Australia. Massive occupational assimilation has challenged U.S. social service agencies for more than a century. Today, the percentage of immigrants in the United States is the largest in more than fifty years—9.3 percent, or almost one of every ten Americans. That figure is short of the record 14.7 percent recorded in 1910 during a wave of mass European immigration. There are both legal and illegal immigrants to the United States, and immigration laws have confounded the two. Both types present opportunities for career counseling and guidance.

Legal and Illegal Immigrants

The legal immigrants in recent years have emigrated primarily from Southeast Asia (most notably the Indochinese, Laotians, Cambodians, Taiwanese, and Filipinos); Cuba, Haiti, and other West Indian islands; Colombia, Honduras, and other Central American countries; and Russia (specifically, Russian Jews). In addition, immigration quotas have been maintained for other countries that have traditionally supplied the United States with new citizens.

In 1990, the percentage of foreign-born residents in the United States was 7.9 percent (about 19.8 million), up from 6.2 percent in 1980, and 4.7 percent of the population in 1970.

Current estimates by the often criticized Immigration and Naturalization Service are that 3.2 million illegal aliens are in the United States.

In general, the last few decades have witnessed decreased immigration from northeastern and southeastern Europe, while evidencing dramatic increases from the Western Hemisphere and Asia. The U.S. Census Bureau estimates huge influxes of refugees are both a threat and a promise to the United States. The promise is one of enhanced human resources and the richness of cultural pluralism. Immigration has become an increasingly important source of population and labor force growth, moderating to some degree the slowing of population and labor force growth. The Census Bureau predicts that 820,000 to 1.2 million immigrants per year will enter the United States between 1996 and 2006. The perceived threat is to indigenous minorities.

Some say that the large number of immigrants creates jobs and stimulates demand; others argue that immigrants take jobs away from natives—an assertion for which little evidence has been found. Some view immigrants as a drain on welfare and a peril to unilingualism; others perceive them as adding a richness that moves us closer to the reality of a truly multiracial society. Although a fairly large number of natives may hold attitudes of resentment and hostility toward immigrants, there is relatively little overt antagonism, with the exception of a few pockets of protest. For example, Middle Eastern immigrants have experienced great incidents of hostility since September 11.

The basic challenge for these refugees is to find adequate employment to ensure economic self-sufficiency. This task is not so easy, considering that refugees, especially those whose emigration was largely unanticipated, frequently are not fluent in English. Others who are admitted for humanitarian reasons come with severe health problems. They have adjustment difficulties, but after a while the labor force participation of most immigrant groups tends to match that of the general population. Those who leave a country under considerable stress, however, tend to work a longer workweek, to represent a smaller proportion of white-collar workers, and to have a greater proportion of service workers. Many immigrants experience substantial pressure to conform to the majority U.S. culture and to abandon their cultural identities. The community to which an immigrant migrates often determines the degree to which they experience this pressure.

Refugees are likely to settle in geographical enclaves, probably since the majority is prone to have friends or relatives already there. It is well known that Southeast Asians have gravitated to California and Texas in large numbers, both initially and through secondary migration (movement from one state to another, once in the United States). Louisiana and Virginia are also states with large Southeast Asian populations. Cubans and West Indians have settled heavily in Florida, and Russian Jews and Colombians in New York City.

Some come to the United States in hard economic times, and the assistance available to them is, therefore, minimal. Add that fact to the language problem, exploitation by employers, union barriers, nonrecognition of skills, licensing restrictions, lack of information about the job market, and the normal anxiety of being a stranger in a strange land, and it is easy to comprehend some of the difficulties faced by immigrants. Most regard refugees as an at-risk population that requires primary prevention programs to reduce the stress of acculturation (Williams & Berry, 1991). One of the primary stressors, of course, is unemployment or underemployment.

The experience of the Cuban refugees is instructive. They came in two waves: early, beginning in 1959, and late, in 1980, when Castro loosened restrictions on emigration. In some respects, these immigrants were more fortunate than most Third World immigrants who settle in U.S. cities, for most had some urban industrial work experience. Most Cuban immigrants, similar to most immigrants of whatever country of origin, soon became members of an ethnic working class—in this case, the Cuban American working class. The jobs they got were likely to be as craftsworkers, machine operatives, or unskilled laborers. Few (especially in the latest wave) were professionals or managers. Many earlier immigrants had to take positions at a lower status than they had held in Cuba. All in all, occupational adjustment, especially in hard times, is not easy for immigrants, but they eventually assimilate. Obviously, the more help they get, the easier the task.

The Cuban experience is less painful than that undergone by some other immigrant groups. Disparate vocational experiences of Cuban and Haitian refugees in South Florida show that Cubans have access to an enclave employment option providing the same financial (and other) returns for work that are provided by employment in the primary labor market. Haitians lack an employment enclave; consequently, they tend to cluster into secondary and informal employment—if they work at all (Portes & Stepick, 1985). Thus, enclaves provide a buffer between the immigrants and the new country (Cobas, 1986).

A disproportionately large number of immigrants in certain groups (for example, Koreans, Greeks) seem to gravitate toward self-employment, which may be necessitated by disadvantages in the job market, possession of a business background in the country of origin, participation in the ethnic subeconomy, or some other reason (Cobas, 1986). In some immigrant groups, self-sacrifice and almost around-the-clock labor are prices willingly paid for self-employment in order that ensuing generations can lead the proverbial better life.

Illegal immigrants have an even more difficult task, because they are in constant danger of deportation and thus subject to exploitation. Estimates of total numbers of illegal immigrants range from 2.9 to 5.7 million. Some slip illegally into the United States; others enter legally and later violate the terms of their visas. The illegals and visiting labor force participants, it is assumed, are a source of cheap labor to exploiters who do not have to pay much attention to working conditions. It is argued that illegals thus displace native workers. It is more likely, however, that they replace legal immigrants. Unfortunately, the problem is such that counselors are not typically involved.

Once immigrant groups are in the country for a time, both generational changes and occupational advancement tend to lead to greater exogamy (marrying outside the immigrant group) and thus greater assimilation into U.S. culture. Assimilation usually takes place as people start at the bottom occupationally and gradually move up. Some people, however, remain in an all-enclave economy, working within immigrant-owned firms.

Legal immigrants, especially those whose emigration has been sudden, unanticipated, externally induced, and stressful, face many adjustments. Occupational adjustment may be the greatest of these.

There is a difference also in the adjustment of white as opposed to African American immigrants.

DeFreitas (1981), for example, discovered through his research that African American immigrants in New York City experience significant downward occupational mobility during their first few years after arrival. Downward mobility is especially severe among those with high-level occupational backgrounds in the country of origin. These results are consistent with hypotheses derived from previous research on the adjustment difficulties experienced by white immigrants. In contrast to most white immigrants who are able to subsequently recover much of their lost occupational status through upward mobility, however, foreign-born African American professionals, managers, and craftsmen appear less likely to regain their former occupational levels. Despite certain employment advantages when compared with indigenous African Americans, foreign-born African Americans are subsequently underrepresented in high-pay, high-status occupations relative to white men.

Studying Latin American refugees, Gonsalves (1992) identified five stages through which refugees pass. These stages are outlined in Table 5.2. Career counseling can be effected during any stage but obviously varies according to the specific stage. This description of acculturative stress and its impairment of occupational development and functioning is echoed by Smart and Smart (1995).

Counseling Immigrants

How can immigrants best be counseled about career concerns? To answer this question intelligently, we need to know more about the vocational development of immigrants than we do now. In most cases, immigration represents a discontinuity in career development for an individual. The nature and effect of that discontinuity have not been studied in depth.

One exception is the excellent work accomplished in Israel by Krau (1981, 1982). Although the findings from the Israeli experience are not completely applicable to the American scene, they have enough face validity to be worth further exploration and testing here. For example, Krau investigated how individuals cope with basically unanticipated emigration and whether cognitive dissonance might be a motivator explaining immigrants' behavioral strategy. Using eighty-nine new, educated immigrants to Israel (mainly from Russia and Romania), who were provided an accountancy

TABLE 5.2 Resettlement Stages, Professional Roles, Refugee Tasks, and Treatment Issues

STAGE	PROFESSIONAL ROLE	REFUGEE TASKS	TREATMENT ISSUES
Early arrival (1 week to 6 months)	Teacher, tour guide, resource specialist	Learning surroundings, remain involved with homeland, meet fellow refugees	Disorientation, sadness, anger, guilt
Destabilization (6 months to 3 years)	Teacher, psychotherapist	Acquire survival tools, learn the language, learn dating customs or more flexible gender roles, develop support group	Hostility, resistance to new culture, denial
Experimentation and stabilization (3–5 years)	Resource specialist, psychotherapist	Develop flexible culture learning, continue marital adjustment, remain linked to other refugees	Fear of failure, isolation, premature culture or identity foreclosure
Return to normal life (5–7 years)	Counselor, psychotherapist	Maintain flexible cultural accommodation, develop realistic expectations of new generations, develop a positive identity, expect lasting personality changes	Rigidity, intergenerational conflict
Decompensation (1 week to 7 years)	Crisis intervention	Meet survival needs; modify identity; re-entry into new culture; continue commitments; connect past, present, and future	Psychosis, identity disorders, depression, continuity of family, existential crisis

training program by the Ministry of Absorption, Krau discovered that any preparation for a career change took place basically *after* arrival in the new country. To cope successfully after the fact of immigration, some people reduce their self-image to become congruent with the lower status of their new career. For example, they tend to become less self-assertive. Some people, however, deny that their status has been lowered. Such denial results in less expressed satisfaction. In short, one can accept a lowered status and adopt a self-image that is congruent with that lowered status and, eventually, over time, work back to a higher level. Or one can deny the reality of lowered status and risk a poorer adjustment. Counseling such individuals thus involves helping them to minimize denial efforts.

Krau (1984) also found that immigrants, when compared with indigenous white-collar workers and executives, scored higher on measures of work centrality and job involvement and held more positive attitudes toward authority figures. Apparently, one method of coping for immigrants is to focus on work. The workplace may be regarded as a smaller societal unit, an environment that is a more hospitable surrounding with which to identify than is the larger society.

Krau has built a model of the career development of immigrants. The stages of model include crystallization, vocational retraining, job entry and trial, establishment, and maintenance. Although immigrants experience discontinuity because of emigration, Krau's model suggests that once they reach a new country, the process of career reconstruction is one of continuity. In his model, he matches coping behaviors with specific career development tasks of immigrants. His paradigm is partially presented in Table 5.3.

Preliminary research on the validity of the model is encouraging. From these early findings, it appears that the model of career stages accurately represents what most immigrants go through as they become in-

TABLE 5.3 A Career Development Model of Immigrants

CAREER STAGE	PROBLEM-CREATING CONDITION	COPING BEHAVIOR
Crystallization	Language difficulties	Learning
	Lack of information on labor market and job requirements	Help-seeking behavior
	Cognitive dissonance over status incongruence	Reduction of cognitive dissonance
Vocational retraining	Cognitive dissonance over status incongruence	Reduction of cognitive dissonance
	Need to accept unfamiliar occupation	Emotional acceptance of new occupation
	Lack of skill in new occupation	Acquisition of occupational knowledge and skills
Job entry and trial and tests	Competition on the labor market	Competitive behavior
	Short employment interviews	Efficiency in test situations and display of vocational knowledge and skills
Establishment	Job requirements	Conformity to requirements
	New work community	Openness to social contacts and new values
	Need for enculturation	
	Need for economic security	Effort to achieve a permanent income
Maintenance	Job requirements	Conformity to job requirements
	Need to heighten living standard and position in community	Effort to catch up economic community standards
		Effort to assert oneself in the community

Source: Reprinted from "The vocational side of a new start in life: A career model of immigrants" by E. Krau from *Journal of Vocational Behavior, 20,* 313–330. Copyright © 1982, with permission from Elsevier.

tegrated into the work world and culture of their new nation. Further, "skills critically defining the adjustment to one career stage are success predictors for the acquisition of adjust to the greater complexity needed to adjust to the requirements of the following period" (Krau, 1982, p. 328). Some highly educated, skilled immigrants who are fluent in the language of their new country may pass directly from the crystallization stage to job entry and trial, skipping the retraining stage. If the model holds, the counselor must determine where the individual is likely to experience the greatest difficulty in coping behavior and work preventively to ensure a smoother transition.

Most refugees, with time, appear to adapt to a changed occupational structure and their place in it. Anh and Healy (1985) studied 210 Vietnamese refugees in Los Angeles and Orange counties and determined that "refugees in the United States 3 or more years were more satisfied than were those present 1 or 2 years, and those in the United States 2 years were more satisfied than were those 1 year or less" (p. 81). Hence, those in the United States the longest were more fully employed and more satisfied with their jobs.

Finally, a caveat: simply because immigrants are grouped for census purposes does not mean that they are alike. Southeast Asians are a good example. Not only are the cultures different among the countries, but also within nations immigrants represent divergent cultures. Long-standing regional and national antipathies may make emigrants from one country loathe to be in a group with others from another nation or even their own. Great care should be exercised in setting up any career intervention to be certain that the group is not so heterogeneous that it is unworkable.

Most attempts to intervene in the career development of immigrants have focused on language training and vocational skills training. Lobadzinska (1986) urges that acculturation—formal learning about the American way of life—also be a focus of effort. One vocational training program for Indochinese adolescents has typical objectives (Vertiz & Fortune, 1984);

1. Identification of personal values, interests, aptitudes, and abilities
2. Communication of personal qualities to others
3. Identification of at least two types of preentry-level jobs that would provide viable experience toward tentative career options
4. Location of possible employment sites
5. Establishment of personal contact with potential employers to inquire about part-time jobs
6. Completion of job application
7. Interviews in small groups with personnel specialists from business and industry and a one-to-one situation with videotape (p. 231)

There is a tremendous need for research in the United States on the vocational development and behavior of immigrants. No comprehensive study exists, and the few small studies that we have are inadequate to provide a truly sound foundation upon which to construct either a theory or a repertoire of interventions. The work of Borgen and Amundsen (1985) in Canada offers a good example of the type of attention to immigrant career development that is needed in the United States.

In general, immigrants have strong needs for information (job market, skills required, and so on) and want a structured counseling procedure. Counselors need to assess their immigrant client's level of acculturation to understand the degree to which client has adopted the customs and culture of their new country. Language deficits must be addressed, and there must be a systematic effort to translate their skills to the American culture while also providing support for maintaining their culture-of-origin identity. Career counselors must also confront issues of alienation and disorientation in immigrants. Refugees pose additional problems that require attention. Gold (1988), for example, points out that compared to immigrants, refugees would most likely not leave their homes voluntarily, would not typically have as strong a support network, would not have planned their new life as thoroughly, would have brought fewer resources, and would probably have greater mental health problems.

PERSONS WHO ARE GAY, LESBIAN, OR BISEXUAL

The data—probably flawed—suggest that 2.8 percent of men and 1.4 percent of women identify themselves as gay or lesbian (Dunlap, 1994). These percentages are considerably higher in larger cities and lower in rural areas. Although the percentage of people who are gay, lesbian, and bisexual persons is estimated to be between 10 to 15 percent of the population, the percentage is likely higher among clients given the level of oppression gay, lesbian, and bisexual persons experience. Despite these substantial numbers, career development researchers have historically tended to ignore this population. For example, Croteau (1996) conducted a literature review focusing on empirical research published in the 1980s and 1990s that addressed vocational behavior of lesbian, gay, or bisexual workers. Croteau identified eleven studies that fit these criteria. Despite the lack of attention from researchers, clearly, there is the need to understand the career development experiences of this population and to identify relevant and efficacious career interventions.

That sexual orientation should have an impact on career development and choice is, in many ways, repugnant. Nevertheless, gays and lesbians are, in fact, barred from certain occupations (e.g., the armed services) and find vertical mobility blocked in other occupations simply because of their sexual orientation. This result of homophobia is one of the major reasons that gays and lesbians often hide their sexual orientation, living in fear of being "discovered," because their livelihoods are sometimes tied in with appearing "straight."

The negative bias against gay or lesbian persons is often more intense than that directed at any other minority group (Goleman, 1990). Whether homophobics doubt their own sexuality and seek reassurance in "gay bashing," whether some combination of fear and self-righteousness impels them to "save the morals of the world," whether they follow religious dicta (e.g., homosexuality is equated with evil), or whether some other reason prevails, gays, lesbians, and bisexuals are indeed targets of institutional and individual bias. There are those, for example, who feel they should not be teachers because of the alleged temptation to molest children, despite the fact that child molesters are overwhelmingly heterosexual.

Given the deliberate, systematic exclusion of gays from many occupations and the de facto segregation of gays and lesbians in many others, it is surprising that comparatively little scholarly attention has been paid to their career development issues. Moreover, most of the literature addressing the career development of gay and lesbian persons has been published in the last decade.

Hetherington, Hillerbrand, and Etringer (1989) addressed the career issues of gay men, who are reputed to have more uncertainty about their career choices and less job satisfaction than either heterosexual men or women or lesbians. Knowledgeable and sensitive career counselors should be aware of several of the issues they identify. One issue is *negative stereotyping,* for example, equating homosexuality with mental disturbance or assuming that certain occupations are dominated by gay men (e.g., photographer, interior decorator, flight attendant, nurse, and so on). A second issue is *employment discrimination,* because the legal status of those who have a different affectional preference from the majority appears to be moot and still evolving. Employment ads that include a declaration of no prejudice based on of sexual orientation are a good start. A third issue is that of *limited role models,* because gay men in the workforce are more or less an invisible minority. Limited role models may be presumed to have the same effect on gay men as the absence of competent occupational role models has on any minority.

A special section of *Career Development Quarterly* (December 1995) addressed the topic of career development interventions with gay and lesbian clients. In this special section, Fassinger (1995) discusses a vocational psychology for lesbian clients highlighting identity development processes and their interaction with the career development process. Prince (1995) takes a similar approach and discusses the interaction between sexual identity development and career development for gay men. Prince also identifies strategies (e.g., assimilation, confrontation, ghettoization, and specialization) that gay men often use to cope with the discrimination that exists in the workplace. Chung (1995) emphasizes the need for career counselors to consider personal and environmental factors when providing career counseling to gay, lesbian, or bisexual clients. Specifically, Chung notes that counselors need to be sensitive to their clients' possible nontraditional career interests and skills as well as their work values that may be related to their sexual orientation. Finally, Pope (1995) conducted a review of the literature related to career counseling with gay, lesbian, or bisexual clients. His review revealed nine widely recommended career interventions. These included the need for counselors to understand models of gay and lesbian identity development, to examine their own biases, to openly discuss employment discrimination, to openly discuss coming out in the workplace, to use special assessment procedures, and to support and encourage gay and lesbian professionals as role models.

More recently, Fassinger (1995) proposed a model of lesbian sexual identity development. Their model contains four phases. Phase 1 involves *awareness* and relates to the growing recognition of being different from the heterosexual norm. Phase 2 is labeled *exploration* and involves the active examination of questions arising in the first phase. Phase 3 is labeled *deepening/commitment* and involves a deeper understanding of one's sexuality and a commitment to one's group identity (i.e., lesbian). Phase 4 is *internalization/synthesis.* In this phase a woman experiences fuller self-acceptance of love for women as part of her overall identity. Understanding what phase of identity development a client is experiencing is important to being able to work effectively with that client.

Pope (2002) identified seven points that are important for career counselors to be aware of in providing assistance to gay and lesbian clients: (1) multicultural counseling skills are important for counseling with sexual minorities, (2) identity formation tasks that racial and ethnic minorities must accomplish are the same for sexual minorities, (3) there is a lesbian and gay culture, (4) families for sexual minorities are functional and not biological, (5) visible and hidden minorities are both included in multicultural counseling, (6) the results of oppression are very real and have an impact on the lives and careers of sexual minorities, and (7) there are specific cultural counseling competencies for gays and lesbians. Pope also noted the need for career counselors to engage in social action (Herr & Niles, 1998) by "lobbying for the inclusion of sexual orientation in the nondiscrimination policies of local employers, picketing a speech made by an ex-gay who claims to have become a happy, fully functioning heterosexual...and working toward changing the laws which criminalize certain sexual acts between two consenting adults as well as working to stop police entrapment" (p. 222). Concerning the latter, Pope contends that these laws are often used to deny gay men and lesbian women employment as teachers, counselors, police officers, and so on.

In terms of implications for career counseling, it is advocated that specialized programming be provided to address the needs of gay men and lesbian women. In addition to the traditional career interventions, gay men and lesbian women may need counseling to help them negotiate lifestyle and relationship issues, job interviews, and the choice of whether to divulge sexual orientation. For instance, should activities in gay organizations be listed on the résumé? Help in planning the transition from school to work is another focus area, because, in general, academic institutions provide a less hostile environment for gays and lesbians than does the world of work. Other career areas to confront are geographical concerns (e.g., whether to look for work where there is a substantial population of gays) and concerns of dual-career couples (much as with heterosexual couples—see Chapter 13). In the gay culture, there is talk of *discordant couples,* wherein one partner is "out" and the other is closeted. As Pope (2002) noted, using gay occupational role models would appear to be an effective strategy.

Lesbian women also have special needs, some of which overlap with those of gay men and some of which are unique (Hetherington & Orzek, 1989). Lesbian women are apparently relatively certain about and satisfied with their career choices when compared with gay men and heterosexual men and women. Which aspects of lesbian career development can be ascribed to gender and which to sexual orientation is arguable (e.g., the influence of sex-role attitudes). Standard career development issues such as self-concept formation and exposure to role models may be more complex phenomena for lesbian women than for heterosexuals. Occupational harassment and negative stereotypes are as real for lesbians as they are for homosexual men. Finally, lesbians grapple with unique dual-career and lifestyle issues. In addition to the usual career needs complicated by gender, lesbians must also determine what occupations are accessible and offer advancement and how to negotiate the job search.

Croteau and von Destinon (1994) surveyed gays, lesbians, and bisexuals seeking employment in student affairs. Even in this relatively liberal milieu, only about one-third chose to disclose their sexual orientation before being hired. A full quarter of the respondents believed that they had been discriminated against during the job search process (42 percent of the disclosers; 6 percent of the nondisclosers). Sussal (1994) advocates that once hired, homosexuals need special support from employee assistance programs.

Diamant's (1993) book on gay and lesbian issues in the workplace discusses concerns in such occupational areas as the military, the church, the helping professions, education, and athletics. Orzek (1992) views identity as a central factor affecting the career counseling of gays and lesbians. In her view, it is important for the counselor to discover the client's unique meaning attached to being gay or lesbian and to work from that frame of reference, tailoring career counseling to stage of sexual identity formation. In fact, most of the recent literature related to counseling gays and lesbians focuses on identity development models (Croteau & Thiel, 1993; Fassinger, 1995; McFarland, 1993; Prince, 1995; Walters & Simoni, 1993).

Clearly, a great deal of research needs to be conducted to determine how best to meet the identified career needs of gays and lesbians and to discover what other needs exist. Do gay men and lesbian women, for example, experience more stress at work than do "straights"? What career development decisions are influenced by gender, by affectional preference, and by sex-role attitudes? What are the effects of the interaction of these dimensions? How can gay men and lesbian women best negotiate work systems? How can they best change restrictive systems? Do gay men and lesbian women fall into different configurations from the general population in terms of Holland categories? Despite the recent increase in research addressing the career development needs of gay men and lesbian women, all these questions and many more await the results of research.

PERSONS WITH DISABILITIES

This section is intended to consider career-relevant aspects of a final special population, persons with disabilities.

Career Development of Persons with Disabilities

A person with disabilities is one who is usually considered to be different from a "normal" person—physically, physiologically, neurologically, or psychologically—because of accident, disease, birth, or developmental problems. Persons with disabilities, including physical and mental, typically feel less adequate than others, either situationally or generally. A disability, then, need not be a handicap. Physicians try to cure or palliate a disability; counselors try to remove or reduce a handicap, whether or not the disability can be helped, including looking at handicapping conditions within the individual's environment. Some, in fact, believe that persons with disabilities should be viewed as a minority group; as such, their problems are considered not so much physical as social and psychological (Fine & Asch, 1988), and problems are caused not so much by the disability itself as by the environment. Conyers (2002) notes that "the emergence of disability culture as a distinctive cultural phenomenon that is germane to the practice of multicultural counseling has been largely unrecognized by mainstream counselors" (p. 173). Conyers contends that this lack of attention to disability culture reflects a lack of awareness concerning disability and the disability rights movement. Gibson and Depoy (2000) suggest that conceptualizing disability as a culture has the advantage of placing disability within the human experience and drawing parallels among persons with disabilities and all other persons.

Hence, by *disabled* we mean a population that has a disability or several disabilities that may or may not be a vocational handicap. The disability may be *physical* (such as amputations, birth defects, cancer, heart problems, burns, deafness, blindness, multiple sclerosis, muscular dystrophy, orthopedic involvement, spinal injury), *intellectual* (mental retardation, learning disability, brain damage, speech and language disorders), *emotional* (mental illness, substance abuse, alcoholism, obesity and other eating disorders), or *sociocultural* (as discussed earlier in this chapter). In any case, best estimates are that in the United States more than 10 percent of the population have chronic physical, mental, or emotional conditions that limit their activity sufficiently to make a substantial career difference.

It is important to manifest sensitivity to terminology with regard to disability. *Disabled people* and *people with disabilities* are the current preferred terms. Preference is also for terminology that avoids *the* followed by an adjective—*the disabled, the blind, the mentally retarded,* and so on. Parking for disabled people, not handicapped parking, is appropriate. Extremes, such as *physically challenged* or *differently abled* should be eschewed. A little common sense will go a long way.

It may be reasonably expected that severe disability, either congenital or adventitious, will have a profound influence on an individual's career development. To a great extent this is true, but the effect is largely unpredictable by type of disability. In fact, for persons with disabilities, the within-group variability in terms of personality patterns and general adjustment is as great as the variability between them and the rest of the population. To be sure, those with disabilities may have certain functional limitations that restrict their freedom in choosing from among the vast array of occupations, and if the disability is not congenital, there is bound to be some discontinuity in career development.

These exceptional individuals are presumed also to be the victims of considerable prejudice by potential employers and possible bias by counselors. It is no doubt true that attitudes rooted in the concept of stigma affect behavior toward the disabled, just as sexism, ageism, and racism exist; some research suggests, however, that attitudes toward disabled people vary by type of disability. In the past, for example, employers appeared to be more willing to hire physically disabled people, than to hire functionally disabled (such as psychiatrically disabled) people.

These attitudes may be softening. For example, Conyers (2002) points out that many more advertisements include people with disabilities and focus on their positive contributions to society. As is the case with many stereotypical attitudes, they can frequently be altered by providing experiences permitting the development of greater empathy with the subject of the stereotype. With disabled people, for instance, Ibrahim and Herr (1983) used a role-playing situation in which individuals assumed a disability, and the experience had a significant effect in building positive attitudes toward those who actually had that disability.

Curnow (1989) contends that certain misconceptions of disability have limited the application of vocational development theory to persons with disability. The umbrella rationale for these misconceptions is the idea that compared with the nondisabled population, persons with disabilities have special needs that preclude the use of extant theories. In actuality, current vocational development theory may indeed by appropriate for the disabled population if, in addition, counselors consider the parochial or unique needs that disabled people bring to rehabilitation. The reader will recognize that this argument has been advanced earlier in this chapter in relation to several of the special populations discussed (e.g., women, minorities). In the case of disabled persons, these considerations would include (1) limitations in early experiences (e.g., less opportunity for exploration, restrictive view of vocational options, etc.), (2) decision-making ability (e.g., persons with disabilities have fewer opportunities to rehearse decision making), and (3) self-concept and disability (e.g., negative social attitudes and stereotypes contributing to less than positive self-image).

Goldberg (1992), however, maintains that no current theory is acceptable; consequently, he has drawn on the work of Super and Roe and has devised the Goldberg Scale to measure the vocational development of people with disabilities in terms of the effects of functional, psychological, and social limitations on vocational plans and rehabilitation. Among his propositions are the following:

> *People with acquired disabilities choose occupations that are consistent with previous vocational goals, interests, and values.... Individuals rarely choose a vocational objective that is in an entirely different occupational group or that is markedly different from an objective established in adolescence. Vocational plans, interests, and work values held prior to onset of disability are maintained after onset. When a vocational plan must be altered or redirected to accommodate the disability, the individual tends to remain within the same occupational group. Individuals tend to affirm their predisability identities, indicating that the severity of disability is not as important as predisability personality and vocational plans....*
>
> *People with congenital disabilities or developmental disorders of childhood tend to choose occupations that are consistent with parental aspirations and social class. Since persons with congenital disabilities have had a longer period to adjust to disabilities during their formative years, the impact of disability on vocational choice may be less than the impact of an acquired disability.... People with congenital disability are exposed to social stigma at an early age, and they must incorporate their disability into their image of themselves accordingly.*
>
> *After a vocational choice has been made, the maintenance of individuals at works depends on many factors. These factors include motivation to work, ability to cope realistically with disabilities, previous work history, and numbers of hospitalizations and outpatient therapies that interrupt normal work patterns. (pp. 169–170)*

One of the most significant recent developments relating to work and people with disabilities is the passage of the Americans with Disabilities Act (ADA) of 1990 and subsequent state laws. Under this Act, there is a distinction made between essential and nonessential job functions, and an employer may consider only the former when hiring or promoting. An employer may ask applicants to demonstrate how they will perform a job function, but they need not provide an accommodation unless the employee requests it. An employer cannot inquire about past compensation until after making a conditional job offer and may not refuse employment to a person with a disability with the rationale that such hiring might cause an increase in insurance costs. Both a Disabled Tax Credit and Targeted Jobs Tax Credit are available to employers. Access of people with disabilities to businesses, transportation, the workplace (15 employees or more), and telephone services is required. Interestingly, since the passage of the ADA, there appears to be no increase or decrease in the employment rates of people with disabilities.

Supported employment is the current "hot" method of integrating disabled persons into the workforce. Supported employment opportunities range from sheltered workshops or other modus operandi for people with developmental disabilities to total integration within a "normal" workplace. Supported employment refers to any paid employment for people with severe disabilities in an integrated (community-based) setting and requires on-site support by professional staff.

It is obviously impossible to deal with every disability within the confines of this book. Each disability is, in fact, the focus of a large body of literature related specifically to career development within that disability. Further, the reason rehabilitation counselors are available is to assist in the vocational rehabilitation of those with disabilities. In fact, a current emphasis in vocational rehabilitation is *transitioning,* a term used to indicate the importance of helping the disabled person to function vocationally and educationally within the larger society. All we are attempting to do in this chapter is to make the "generalist" career counselor aware of the possible functional limitations and the possible delayed, discontinuous, or impaired career development of those with disabilities.

Career Counseling of Persons with Disabilities

In a classic 1963 article, McDaniels argued that in cases of traumatic disability, the individual was required to regress to the tentative and realistic phases of the exploratory stage. In these substages, the task of the disabled person is to define and accept a modified self-concept with certain new limitations, to test these formulations in reality, and to find new ways to satisfy aspirations. Ultimately, according to McDaniels, the process of vocational redevelopment will be affected by pretrauma experiences in career, personal, and social circumstances; the types of concepts and decisions requiring modification; the specific type of disabling factors; and the availability of assistance and information. In the three decades since McDaniel's original theoretical conceptualization of vocational redevelopment for persons with disabilities, little has changed. We have more sophisticated tools, but the basic idea of career redevelopment and what it entails has not appreciably changed, even though different theoreticians may offer different contexts for redevelopment. Two examples are presented here, both of which deal with needs: One is based on Maslow's need hierarchy, and a second is based on a trait-and-factor orientation applied to the theory of work adjustment.

Maslow's need theory has been operationalized by Lassiter (1981) to apply to persons with disabilities and their vocational redevelopment. Within this context, he describes needs and their applications to work and work adjustment in competitive work settings:

1. Physiological needs
   - **a.** Need to learn to work in a wheelchair (for example, using the bathroom, traveling from home to job, taking a coffee break, meeting with fellow workers, dealing with different job performance tasks)
   - **b.** Need to learn new ways of being productive (for example, coping with a work schedule different from others; using specially structured pieces, instruments, or machines to meet job demands; receiving an individualized instructional program in mobility)
   - **c.** Need to accept responsibility for personal hygiene (for example, attend to toilet and other personal needs, learn to care well for his or her body and avoid medical complications and illnesses in order to avoid absenteeism, loss of productive activity, and more severe disablement)
2. Safety needs
   - **a.** Strong desire to remain in work similar to previous job and a preference for association with familiar people in the job

   - **b.** Need for a job that appear to offer tenure and stability with decent health and retirement plans, and so on
   - **c.** Need for a smoothly functioning, orderly position
3. Belongingness and love needs
   - **a.** Need to find new ways of developing feelings of belongingness
   - **b.** Need to analyze the potential for caring and being cared for that might be provided in the job setting if certain job modifications or support groups were developed
4. Esteem needs
   - **a.** Need to experience new feelings of competence and self-confidence that come from a person's exposure to new interpersonal skills and new tasks
5. Self-actualization needs
   - **a.** Need for self-awareness and self-actualization
   - **b.** Need to develop one's inner space (thoughts and feelings)
   - **c.** Acceptance and optimization of a life of severe disability

A different needs perspective is provided by those who advocate the use of the theory of work adjustment with disabled people (Dawis & Lofquist, 1978; Lynch & Maki, 1981). The theory of work adjustment is discussed at several points throughout this book, and many are enthusiastic about its application to disabled people. The theory suggests, in part, that individuals have work needs; occupations provide work reinforcers; if reinforcers equal or exceed needs, people will be satisfied at work. In other words, individuals adjust to work through the interaction between work personality and work environment. Melding this theory with a trait-and-factor approach, Lynch and Maki suggest that the counselor working with a disabled client use the traditional trait-and-factor steps: (1) *analysis*—getting information about the client; (2) *synthesis*—interpreting information about the client; (3) *diagnosis*—using interpretation of the data, combined with consideration of the functional limitations of the client, to identify assets of the individual; (4) *prognosis*—determining future options and developing a plan of action; (5) *counseling*—helping clients to know themselves and to use available resources to achieve their potential; and (6) *follow-up*—monitoring adjustment in the placement situation.

Cummings, Maddux, and Casey (2000) note that transition planning for students with disabilities is often ineffective because plans are developed too late in the student's education. Drawing on the work of Levinson (1998), they recommend a three-level planning process that begins in elementary school (with a focus on identifying needs, interests, abilities, etc.), continues in middle school (with an emphasis on career guidance activities as young adolescents focus on crystallizing their sense of self), and is followed by assessment in high school that includes experience-based measures such as work samples and situational assessment. There are many examples of such curricula, and they are easily found in journals with a focus on one or another disabled population.

In vocational rehabilitation, counselors will engage in some or all of the following activities: vocational testing, vocational assessment (work sampling, vocational evaluation), counseling, work adjustment training, prevocational activities, skills training, employment preparation, job development, job referral and placement, and postplacement counseling. Skills training is especially important with certain disabled populations, such as substance abusers (Deren & Randell, 1990), because "therapeutic counseling, psychotherapy, and/or chemotherapy intervention alone are not likely to ameliorate many of these clients' social, educational, and vocational deficits, and when clients complete treatment, many of the pressures that initially contributed to anti-social and substance abuse behavior may again become prominent" (p. 4).

In the vocational counseling of persons with disabilities, assessment is problematic. The Education of All Handicapped Children Act (PL 94-142), together with the Carl D. Perkins Vocational Education Act (PL 98-524), requires that school districts conduct vocational assessments for students with handicapping conditions in occupational education programs. These assessments must include the identification of vocational interests, abilities, and special needs in relation to each student's specific handicapping condition. No later than ninth grade, schools must provide students and their parents with information about occupational education opportunities for students with handicapping conditions. To effect a vocational assessment, counselors may simply have to conduct an interview with the student, parents, and teachers; use specialized vocational evaluation instruments (e.g., AP-TICOM, McCarron-Dial, MICRO-TOWER, MESA, TAP, and so on); or in some relatively few cases, engage in a comprehensive vocational evaluation that employs work itself (real, simulated, or situational) as an assessment tool. A comprehensive assessment usually results in a report that includes an evaluation of occupational interests, vocational strengths and weaknesses, learning style, language proficiency, recommendations for occupational program placement and/or exploration, modification or support services required (e.g., adaptive equipment), and some prognosis regarding rehabilitation success. Caston and Watson (1990) studied 185 cases in a state Bureau of Vocational Rehabilitation (BVR) office and discovered that only about one-quarter were provided a vocational evaluation. Although relatively few of these reports made specific job recommendations, about two-thirds of the clients ignored specific job recommendations and chose to work at different jobs. In other words, based on this sample at least, vocational evaluations were sparsely used and of modest impact. Other rehabilitation specialists believe that vocational evaluations have enormous importance for counseling persons with disabilities.

In any case, we must exercise caution in the use of tests with the disabled. Willingham (1988) investigated the use of tests to predict academic performance with hearing-impaired, learning-disabled, physically handicapped, and visually impaired examinees to determine the appropriateness of "flagging," (i.e., identifying scores that may not be comparable to those in standard tests because they were earned under nonstandard conditions). Willingham determined that academic performance is somewhat less predictive from the test scores of students with disabilities than from those without, but if time limits could be established for both those with disabling conditions and those without, admissions tests would be technically comparable.

In reaction to the limited usefulness of some of the traditional methods of career assessment, counseling and placement, Krieshok, Hastings, Ebberwein, Wettersten, and Owen (1999) used a narrative approach in providing career assistance to veterans in a Veteran's Administration medical center. They begin their narrative approach with clients by asking them to describe where they think they want to be one year from now. They then instruct clients to tell a story about their future assuming things will go well but also being as realistic as possible. As a stimulus to constructing the story, the counselor provides a list of topics that the client might want to address (e.g., skills, field of work, living situation, working conditions, pay, and so forth). If clients provide only general information as they tell their story, counselors ask for specific examples. After the story is finished, the counselor asks the client to identify what they will need to be doing six months from now to be moving toward their story. The client is then asked to describe what they need to be doing in the next three weeks to be moving toward the six-month point. Finally, the client is asked to describe what they need to be doing tomorrow to be moving toward the three-week point of their story. Clients are then asked to rate from 1 to 10 how satisfied they would be with their life if they achieved most of their story in one year. They are also asked to rate from 1 to 10 how likely it is that they will achieve most of their story in one year. The counselor then explores the client's doubts about achieving the story and encourages the client to identify resources that might be helpful in making the story a reality. Qualitative data provided by Krieshok and his associates indicate that their narrative approach is very useful for moving persons with disabilities forward in their career development. Creative approaches such as the one used by Krieshok and his colleagues appear to have substantial potential for providing career assistance to a wide variety of client populations.

Omizo and Omizo (1992), while recognizing the cautions in assessing those with disabilities, nevertheless highlight the importance of gathering appropriate data on career interests, aptitudes, and work-related adaptive behaviors and of combining them with medical, psychological, educational, and other data in order to create individual educational plans that are most effective.

Nester (1993) speaks to the issues of providing accommodation in assessment for specific disabilities, and she concludes that for those with visual impairments, appropriate media must be used (braille, large print, audiotape, or the like), and time should be extended. If test takers have physical or motor impairments, timed or speeded tests are inappropriate. Deaf people (but not typically hearing impaired people) also need accommodation, especially with regard to verbal tests. Finally, those with learning disabilities are so diverse a group that no generalizations are possible. Rather, their needs for and types of accommodation should be addressed on a case-by-case basis.

Another area of importance in counseling persons with disabilities is job readiness. To help disabled clients become job ready, the counselor provides training in such job-relevant aspects as increasing their motivation and willingness to work, getting them medically stabilized and ensuring their ability to function well interpersonally and emotionally, to follow orders, to have specific work skills, and to demonstrate good work habits. These attempts to mold work personalities extend to all disabled populations—physically impaired, sensorily impaired, alcoholics, and so on.

Another major consideration in the career counseling of disabled people is placement, which receives much more emphasis in the rehabilitation literature than in the more general career literature. Studies of the effectiveness of placement in vocational rehabilitation have consistently demonstrated that the time spent in this activity has a high "payoff," in the sense that total rehabilitation increases, and the number of cases regarded as failures decreases.

Career education and similar experiences also are frequently used in the vocational development or redevelopment of persons with disabilities. For instance, counselors may use community jobs, just as with nondisabled students, to provide a direct, independent career education experience for disabled students. In such a situation, students can reinforce social skills and put to use work behaviors learned in the classroom. In colleges, PL 93-112 requires career offices to provide without discrimination services to persons with disabilities. Many career centers have adapted their services to assist persons with disabilities. Visually impaired people, for example, are provided specially designed materials in braille and specific programs directed toward meeting their unique needs.

Herr (1982a) has collated a list of the knowledge and skills necessary for counselors who work frequently with persons with disabilities (pp. 21–22).

Knowledge

1. Federal and state legislation, guidelines, and policies dealing with exceptional persons
2. Rigors of exceptional persons
3. Types of classification, diagnostic tools, or processes and their limitations vis-à-vis work potential or skill
4. Informal assessment procedures for assessing interests, values, goals
5. Characteristics of different types of exceptionality, their causes, and their likely effects upon work behavior
6. Opportunities available in the local labor market for persons with different types of skills and different types of difficulties
7. The meaning of functional limitation and its use in counseling
8. Models of career development applicable to congenitally or adventitiously disabled people
9. The effects of social stigma, labeling, and stereotyping on the self-concept of exceptional persons
10. Characteristics of handicapped people related to employment skills, training programs, and potential occupational and educational opportunities
11. Ways of working with other specialists to facilitate a comprehensive approach to career exploration, career preparation, and career placement of exceptional persons
12. Examples of job redesign by which employers can accommodate the capabilities and/or functional limitations of various types of exceptionality
13. Methods of developing individual educational programs or individual employment plans
14. Fears, concerns, and needs of parents or spouses of exceptional persons and ways to work with total family unit
15. Models of developing daily living, mobility, job search, and work skills
16. Reference materials and directories pertinent to different categories of exceptionality

Skills

1. Ability to interpret and advise about legislation, policy, guidelines, and rights that affect exceptional persons and their family members
2. Ability to use diagnostic and informal assessment procedures with exceptional persons
3. Ability to assess functional limitations and use them in helping clients engage in occupational exploration and career planning
4. Ability to apply knowledge of career development theory to assist in the analysis of self-concept portrayal or developmental task deficits of individual clients
5. Ability to provide effective individual and group counseling of persons of different types of exceptionality and their families

6. Ability to work with other specialists in team approaches to clients for educational or employment planning and placement
7. Ability to work with employers in developing jobs restructuring for different types of exceptional persons
8. Ability to plan and implement different types of skill-building workshops or experiences necessary for employability and work adjustment*

For those people who have some type of disability, various rehabilitation agencies in the community can provide invaluable career help. To qualify for the career services of an agency of this type, an individual must be handicapped in seeking or keeping employment because of some mental or physical disability. Further, there must be some reasonable probability that the services will indeed bring employment benefit to the individual.

The generally accepted goal of vocational rehabilitation is to assist the individual with a disability to gain the ability to work and thus be self-sufficient. The major community agencies for helping to achieve this goal are the local offices of the Division of Vocational Rehabilitation (DVR). Speciality agencies (for the blind, cerebral palsied, and so on) also provide career services to disabled people. Besides providing guidance and counseling, such agencies help clients by providing physical and mental restoration services, training, maintenance and transportation, family services, interpreters for the deaf, readers for the blind, and placement, to cite just a few types of assistance.

We have observed that there is employer discrimination and prejudice toward persons with disabilities. These employers attitudes largely reflect those of the public in general. Hence, vocational rehabilitation counselors must not only work with clients to get them ready for employment, but also educate employers to get them to hire the disabled persons. Work readiness for clients may entail providing work at a rehabilitation center or in a sheltered workshop—"a work-oriented rehabilitation facility with a controlled working environment and individual vocational goals, which utilizes work experience and related services for assisting the handicapped person to progress toward normal living and a productive vocational status" (Association of Rehabilitation Facilities). Such a workshop may be transitional or long-term. About one-half million individuals per year are in such workshops. It may further involve providing clients with job-seeking skills or using vocational exploration groups to offer information and feedback. In general, vocational rehabilitation consists of intake, work tryout, work conditioning and training, job placement, and follow-up. Evaluation is usually by means of traditional psychometric instruments as well as by work samples.

There is ample documentation that for mental patients work is a needed form of activity; community-based settings lead to more successful vocational rehabilitation than hospital-based settings; and employer-hiring bias toward the psychiatrically disabled continues to exist.

The process of career helping for such individuals is really no different from that for other populations (although some of the substance obviously changes). As Anthony (1980) describes the process, it involves (1) determining client needs, (2) developing a rehabilitation plan, (3) providing work adjustment training, and (4) engaging in placement.

Several guidelines pertain not only to psychiatrically disabled people, but also to other populations with disabilities:

1. Past general history and prior work history are good predictors of future work adjustment.
2. Continual support, at least for the short term, is necessary.
3. A step-by-step, systematic career-helping program is best.
4. Vocational skill building (rather than a concern with diagnosis or symptomatology) is extremely important.
5. Tests of self-concept or ego strength are probably more useful predictors of work adjustment than are more traditional psychological tests.
6. Langer (1994) urges that counselors who work with disabled people be aware of the possible presence of depression (as a natural concomitant of loss). Accompanying depression in loss is often denial, and this denial can have obvious implications for work.

*Source: From E. L. Herr, Counselor education programs: Training for career development with exceptional people. *Careers, Computers and the Handicapped,* edited by Michael Bender, Lee J. Richmond, and Nancy Pinson-Milburn. (Austin, TX: PRO-ED, 1985). Reprinted by permission.

Whether the service is provided in a rehabilitation center, a rehabilitation workshop, or a rehabilitation residence, the goal is still to remove both internal and external barriers to a client's working. These barriers, as defined by G. N. Wright (1980), consist of an *occupational handicap* (the inability to perform at a satisfactory level all the essential requirements of an occupation), an *employment handicap* (difficulty in getting a suitable job because of discrimination), a *placement handicap* (difficulty in adjusting or readjusting to the world of work). The rehabilitation literature is replete with references to the concept of *vocational adjustment* or *work adjustment.* This concept is actually nothing more than the confluence of the worker's job satisfaction with the employer's idea of job satisfactoriness.

Since the 1973 Rehabilitation Act, counselors are responsible for providing each client with an Individualized Written Rehabilitation Program (IWRP). This movement toward systematic delivery and accountability requires a written statement of counselor and client responsibilities in the rehabilitation process, services to be provided, intermediate and long-range vocational goals, criteria for evaluation, review process, and postemployment services.

Toward the end of the phase in which barriers to seeking and keeping employment are removed, the rehabilitation career helper assesses, counsels, or engages in job development and placement. Job development usually involves securing job opportunities for those disabled clients who are not easily placed. As counselors actually place the clients, they must attend to such considerations as work tolerance (capacity for protracted effort), work readiness, job-seeking skills (including employment interviewing, job orientation, and possible job modification to accommodate a disability).

Roessler (1987) has provided an agenda for vocational rehabilitation intervention. He suggests ten needed initiatives in the provision of services and in public policy:

1. On a national level, vocational training policies should stress development of two tracks: (a) basic literacy and employability preparation for general service jobs, and (b) training in computer programming and information processing for high-technology positions.
2. Employers must have significant involvement in the development of curricula and employment transition mechanisms in vocational preparation programs.
3. The Social Security program needs to decrease disincentives to employment, such as loss of medical coverage, for persons with disabilities earning above a certain wage level.
4. Tax incentives to employers to hire "targeted groups" and to make necessary job accommodations must continue.
5. Deregulation efforts that affect worker safety and affirmative action should be resisted.
6. Vocational rehabilitation counselors must be informed about national economic projections, shifts in their local economies, vocational preparation opportunities, and entry requirements of new employment areas.
7. Evaluation of rehabilitation outcomes should expand to include both quantity and quality (primary market placement of case closures).
8. Rehabilitation services for many clients must include employability preparation (i.e., teaching clients how to complete job applications, respond in the job interview, and meet the interpersonal and task performance demands of work).
9. Counselors need to promote the supported employment movement and to clarify the ways in which they can contribute to its success.
10. Employers should expand employee assistance benefit programs to realize the cost savings possible through attracting and retaining a qualified workforce. (p. 19)

In total, rehabilitation agencies provide excellent career services for persons with physical, emotional, intellectual, or sensory disabilities. Although they are relatively new organizations (in existence largely since 1920), they have established a fine record of helping individuals with disabilities become useful workers.

SUMMARY

In this chapter, we have considered five populations, which are not necessarily mutually exclusive: women, people of color, immigrants, gay men and lesbian women, and persons with disabilities. For each, we have pointed out unique aspects of career development or redevelopment that require counselor interventions. These interventions emphasize techniques somewhat different from those used with the general population or call for different emphases in the use of common techniques. Also, we suggested that unconscious stereotyping, leading to bias, may be present in counselors and employers; and we offered information to gainsay such stereotyping. Finally, we are persuaded that when we learn more about the career development of these special populations, we shall ultimately conclude that the career differences between each of these groups and the majority are differences more of degree than of kind.

CHAPTER SIX

Systematic Planning for Career Guidance and Counseling

KEY CONCEPTS

- Systematic planning for career guidance and counseling can be defined in terms of five stages.
- Different purposes for planned programs of career development require different types of content.
- Theory and research findings represent the conceptual bases on which program planning rests.
- Selection of career development program goals and objectives should precede the selection of the activities or content of the program.
- There are multiple methods of evaluating career programs.
- Evaluation of career development programs and of the interventions that comprise them needs to include evaluation of costs and benefits.

Throughout this book, we discuss a large number of career interventions (e.g. individual counseling, group work, mentoring, engaging in self-directed exercises, reading directories of career or education information, participating in computer-assisted instruction) used by counselors and the trends and expectations within which they work. The latter include growing calls to more efficiently and effectively deploy the counselors available in new configurations of direct and indirect services to students and adult clients; to more effectively bridge the gap between theory, research, and practice by applying what is known about concepts like career maturity, career adaptability, career management to the career interventions used; and certainly there has been a rising crescendo of questions by persons in and out of the counseling profession attempting to clarify the outcomes of career counseling, career guidance, and related interventions and to hold counselors accountable for facilitating the knowledge, attributes, and behaviors that give substance to such concepts.

In broad terms these trends chronicle a movement away from a random deployment of counselors, and of the skills they possess, to an increasingly planned approach to defining the roles of these persons and to identifying their responsibility for achieving selected personal, academic, and career outcomes. One of the major mechanisms by which to accomplish these goals is involvement by career counselors and other human services professionals in designing planned programs of career counseling and career guidance or specifically designed interventions to achieve selected attitudinal or behavioral changes in students or other clients. Thus, planned approaches to intervening in the career development of students and adult clients occurs both on a preventive and a remedial basis, at the level of totally planned programs or in terms of individual workshops, group processes, or other interventions.

Basic notions underlying planned approaches to career counseling and career guidance programs is that such programs need to be compatible with the missions of the organizations (e.g. individual schools, colleges, workplaces, government agencies, correctional facilities) within which career programs are located. Such planning needs to insure that career counselors and other career specialists are coordinating their roles and using interventions that insure that the goals of the programs are being met, that the professional personnel involved are using the "best practices" identified by research evidence, tailoring their approaches to the unique needs of different demographic groups being served, and constantly evaluating what they are doing to improve its relevance to and impact on the consumers of the program.

Within the context of planned programs, there are other assumptions related to specific program emphases or interventions. For example, if one considers elements of career programs to have preventive uses, then one can argue that rather than waiting until a student or a client arrives in a counselor's office with a full-blown and difficult problem, planned preventive programs empower the career counselor to reach out, to be productive, in delivering information and skills to potential counselees before they have career problems in efforts to prevent their occurrence or reduce their severity. Examples of such planned approaches designed to prevent career problems, might include workshops in stress management, developing problem-solving skills, or assertiveness, values clarification, job search, or interview behavior. Planned programs might involve helping people reframe or re-script the narratives by which they act out their self-images and choices.

Such workshops may incorporate developmental content from a particular theorists' or researcher's work that is planned to meet the needs of a particular target group of counselees for attitudes, knowledge; and skills related to specific personal or psychological tasks of importance to the particular target group. The content of such programs may be age-related, tailored to the expected emphases of particular developmental periods (e.g., exploration, specificity of choice, induction into the work force, adjustment, mid-career change, preretirement, unemployment). Or the content of such planned programs may be more focused on what is known about how to alleviate particular career problems (e.g., occupational stress, indecision or indecisiveness about jobs, working in a nontraditional occupation or environment). Often, the content of planned programs serves as a support mechanism for persons engaged in significant transitions in their lives (e.g., from school to work, from line to supervisory jobs, preretirement). In such situations, planned programs help persons to normalize potential transitions in which they are currently engaged or anticipating. When such planned programs also include other clients or counselees who are concerned about the same types of transitions, and who bring their own unique experiences, anxieties, and solutions to the program content, counselees are both empowered and supported by such experiences to find self-renewal and new life directions as well as a reduction of tension and anxiety.

Planned career programs can be designed specifically to modify risk factors that predispose certain individuals or groups to particular types of problems in living. Such approaches may emphasize the elements of effective career planning and management, the transition to work, dealing with unemployment or underemployment, retirement or other concerns. In such cases, these approaches essentially involve a body of content that is psychological in nature, is designed to address some set of life skills, embodies various techniques of learning, frequently those of psychoeducational models (e.g., identifying the target behavior, modeling appropriate behavioral strategies, giving homework, providing practice and feedback), and provides support to the participants as they reframe and try to incorporate new life skills into their daily life.

Psychoeducational models are frequently a major treatment of choice in implementing planned programs dealing with a range of career concerns. Often the conceptual models for psychoeducational approaches are linked to cognitive-behavioral or behavioral theories but that relationship is not absolute. Psychoeducational approaches tend to combine educational procedures such as planned or structured curricula, didactic teaching, and specific content exercises and homework with a range of psychological techniques such as simulations, role playing, behavioral rehearsal, modeling, feedback and reinforcement. As suggested above, psychoeducational models and planned interventions can be used for preventive or for remedial purposes. In the latter case, psychoeducational models may be used to help clients learn skills that analysis of their particular career problem indicates they do not possess and need to acquire. For example, persons who have suffered career problems because they do not handle anger well may have such a problem because they have not acquired a sufficiently comprehensive repertoire of behaviors from which to select those that are most interpersonally sound or acceptable in the workplace. Therefore, when angry, they may immediately resort to verbal aggression or physical violence as their automatic response that, in turn, leads to education, job, or social maladjustment. The solution to their problem may be coping skills training by which to better understand what precipitates their anger, how to exert more self-control in dealing with anger-producing situations, and to learn communications, positive assertiveness, or other skills that allow them to express anger in a constructive fashion. As suggested earlier, such planned approaches can be used for a large variety of purposes by which to facilitate career development, career adaptability, employment readiness or specific types of career skills.

Such planned approaches are not static. As new conceptual and empirical knowledge about career relevant issues becomes available, such information frequently alters the content and processes of planned programs. As changes occur in the larger society—whether at the global political, economic, or social level or in a local industry—they tend to stimulate needs for new behavioral patterns and skills that either had not been expected or sanctioned or needed. Concepts like personal flexibility, positive uncertainty, Protean careers, personal career management are examples of terms that are relatively new in the career literature. As such, they argue that the behavioral norms that have been the traditional descriptions of career development—linear, age-related, long term employment, hierarchical promotion, career management by employer—are giving way in some occupations and some workplaces to much more focus on the individual as his or her own career strategist or manager, who is likely to change jobs and workplaces frequently, become involved in lateral or horizontal job movement rather than hierarchical, engage in multiple tasks and projects rather than narrowly focused skills, and participate in constant upgrading of one's skills and knowledge. Such different conceptions of how career development is likely to unfold in the future suggests that for some people planned programs that use linear developmental life stage tasks and the setting of long-term goals achieved in gradual and predictable ways are appropriate content; for other persons, helping them to gain self-confidence, personal flexibility, anticipation of the need for self-marketing, networking, cyclic short-term employment, and short-term goals, and to identify with certain skill performances (e.g., I am a computer specialist) rather than with a particular corporation (e.g., I work for XYZ Corporation) requires different program outcomes and skills. For example, as compared to traditional career planning—which assumes stable fixed career paths, goals that are largely age-dependent and equated with tangible rewards, external career markers, and that the organization they work for will chart their career direction—the emerging career models are much more attuned to change, career paths that are fragmented, multiple short-term objectives, related to personal satisfaction, flexible, and based upon the assumption that individuals will have to take "ownership" of their career and manage it themselves (Barner, 1994).

Given these evolving and essentially dichotomous views of career development and the changing perspectives on career skills needed by individuals, the planning of career programs and of the content of career interventions is increasingly complex. But certainly the role of career counselors as program planners is here to stay. As such, career counselors must weave together the technology of planning, the trends in the organization and performance of work as content, knowledge of theory and research in career counseling and career guidance, and identification of the needs of clients to be served as the elements that produce planned programs.

PLANNING: SOME PERSPECTIVES

Before returning to systematic planning for career guidance and counseling, it is useful to think briefly about planning itself. First, it is useful to note that there are many types of planning. They include, for example, strategic planning, comprehensive planning, long-range planning, program planning, and project planning (Cook, 2001). It is primarily the latter two types of planning on which we will concentrate in this chapter. But first some definitions.

Strategic planning tends to occur at the organizational level: a school or school district, college or university, a rehabilitation facility, a correctional institution, etc. These are considered strategic organizations. As such, these kinds of organizations have the responsibility for "creating and nurturing their own *culture*—the values and vision that lead, guide, and sustain everyone who is a part of the organization" (Cook, p. 48). Strategic organizations use their strategic plan to acquire and to allocate resources and create goals that are expansive in range and scope, often covering a period of five years or so. Strategic plans typically articulate the beliefs; mission statement; parameters (the boundaries in which the organization will operate); the internal analysis (strengths, weaknesses, internal organizational design, responsibility, decision making, and information flow) of the organization; the external analysis (predictions of the influence on the organization of such trends and influences as those social, demographic, economic, political, technological, scientific, and educational); competition (identification of other organizations providing the same goods, products and services to the same clients); critical issues (those issues that the organization must deal with if it is to survive or recreate itself); objectives (the organization's commitment to achieve specific, measurable end results); strategies (the commitments to deploy the organization's resources—people, facilities, equipment, money—toward the stated objectives; and action plans (detailed description of the specific actions required to achieve each strategy).

Action plans typically include specific reference to the strategy it supports, the objective to be met by the action plan, a detailed description of each step required to accomplish the plan, a description of assignments and responsibilities, a time line for the plan, and a cost-benefit analysis (Cook, p. 74).

While other approaches to strategic planning may use different language or components of the plan, strategic planning is a wide-ranging analysis of a strategic organization's values, aspirations, and means of getting to its goals. Since career guidance or career programs are not typically autonomous or strategic organizations, they do not usually do strategic planning per se. Rather, they are more likely to use action plans or program plans which are linked to the strategies and objectives of the organization's strategic plan of which they are a part.

Another type of planning has been described as *comprehensive planning,* which tends to focus on improving existing aspects of the organization by identifying and assessing each component of the organization in terms of its performance, needs, and future projections. Accreditation studies are frequently of this nature.

A further approach is *long-range planning.* This type of planning tends to be less comprehensive than strategic planning and less concerned about context. By practice, this type of planning is likely to look at individual aspects of an organization's current activities and judge them against criteria of what is or might be, but doing so in relative isolation from other aspects or components of the larger organization.

Program planning is more akin to what we describe in the following sections of this chapter. This form of planning, as suggested above, is usually conducted within the purview of the larger organization of which it is a part. Program planning may focus on initiating a new program of career services in a particular organization or planning modifications to an existing program to bring it into better alignment with an organization's strategic plan, or to renovate an existing program because of new research knowledge or policy mandates, or to address changing client demographics or other trends. Program planning is the process of creating a design by which to make a concept like a career counseling or career guidance or career services program operational, or it may be directed to a subset of such a program (e.g., development of a course in career decision making, a series of workshops on job search techniques for students in university dormitories).

Program planning usually consists of stages or phases, much as depicted later in this chapter in Table 6.1, that takes an idea—for example, the creation of a program of career services for a particular setting—tests the idea against what exists and what is desired, justifies it by identifying the intended outcomes, and describes how to make it work. Often this process uses the creation of hypotheses to guide the implementation and testing of different elements of a proposed program, carries out assessments or evaluations of need for the proposed program; establishes goals and objectives for the program using relevant research, theory, or policy mandates as the conceptual framework; details the relationships between goals or objectives and counselor roles and interventions to be used to meet the objectives; and describes how the program will be monitored and evaluated, using specific standards or processes.

A subset of program planning is sometimes called *project planning, intervention design,* or some similar title. Basically, this process typically focuses on a specific task to accomplish a specific purpose. For example, in order to insure that all students know how to manage their anxiety about test-taking, the career counseling program might propose a series of brief workshops designed to teach students to understand the symptoms of anxiety, the triggering mechanisms, and the techniques by which to manage anxiety. In this context it would be necessary to identify the task proposed in specific terms, to analyze the current status of such training, develop the objectives to be achieved by the proposed workshops, consider other possible ways to achieve the outcomes sought, specify the obstacles to be overcome in each possible course of action, and then make a decision about the specific action to be taken. Once such a decision is made, then many of the same processes used in program planning are implemented (e.g. describing intended outcomes, evaluating need for specific outcomes, identifying the relationships between goals or objectives, counselor roles, and the specific interventions used, and describing how the program will be monitored and evaluated).

Program Planning

As suggested in the previous section, planned programs can serve as a bridge to translate conceptual models, theory, and research into practice. Planned programs not only emphasize important content, but are useful in describing the likely results of counseling, group work, or other therapeutic approaches. Rather than arguing in the abstract that if a school, or community agency, or independent practitioner offers a specific, defined set of career processes or services, the outcomes for counselees will *probably* be positive, planned approaches define the outcomes or results, including competencies and other indicators, that translate the program content into behavior to be achieved and indicate the evaluative methods that will affirm that such outcomes have been achieved. The intervention strategies used in such planned programs can vary in relation to the intended outcomes and these can be evaluated in terms of their impact on the outcomes to be achieved. Such a process yields different, and more important, evaluative data than data which simply indicates that certain interventions are in place, but not whether these interventions make specific contributions to achieving the outcomes sought. When a planned program has a clear set of outcomes to be achieved, there are likely to be many processes or interventions that can be implemented to achieve selected individual outcomes. Focusing on the content of specific program outcomes and then determining what intervention (or interventions) is likely to be effective in achieving the intended outcomes is different than providing every counselee the same intervention (e.g., individual counseling) or set of interventions, whether they are relevant to the specific needs to be served or to the outcomes sought.

It is important to note here that planned programs of career services need to include time for unplanned activities. While such a notion sounds contradictory, it simply means that in any program there will be "walk-ins," counselees in crisis or experiencing dilemmas that do not lend themselves to immediately existing groups, workshops, or other planned activities. Opportunities must be available for these counselees to be seen and their needs assessed. Making time available to see such clients is part of a planned program of services and certainly addresses such outcomes as "meeting the individual needs of all students or workers or members of a particular group or setting." After intake and a period of individual counseling, many of these counselees will be able to be matched to selected planned interventions, whether self-directed, group, workshop, computer mediated, or other processes. Thus, while not all interventions with counselees are able to be planned in a specific sense, they still can be incorporated into a planned program of services.

Planning Skills

According to Katz (1974), managers at all levels need three distinct types of skills: (1) *technical* skill—the ability to produce the organization's goals or services; (2) *human* skill—the ability to work in groups as a leader or member; and (3) *conceptual* skill—the ability to see how organizational units and functions are integrated.

Fitz-enz (1990) extends these points in this way:

> *To be good managers, we must use both strategy and tactics. We use tactics for short-term problem solving and day-to-day administration. Strategy provides us with a frame of reference for operating and administrative systems, as well as for employee behavior. Strategic thinking requires a vision of what might be, creativity, risk taking, flexibility, and ambition. Effective strategists work with their staffs to set objectives and define priorities. They approach their function from a systems perspective. They acknowledge the inevitability of change as an antecedent of growth. Finally, they track progress and feed the data back into the system to optimize both efficiency and effectiveness. (p. 99)*

Yates (1996) has argued that a new role has emerged in the field of social service: "a highly educated professional who already has dual training as a practitioner and as a social scientist but who is asked to develop a third area of expertise—the management of social service systems. This three-in-one role demands a new conceptualization of human services—one that formally recognizes elements of the service system that are the foci of managerial and clinical and scientific efforts" (p. 1).

The views of Katz, Fitz-enz, and Yates apply to the role of the career counselor or career guidance professional as a planner and manager of career development programs regardless of setting: business and industry, education, community agency. The language of these authors may depart somewhat from that often used by career counselors, but the perspectives provided are in concert with the intent and content of this chapter. The primary purposes here are to consider the conceptual skills of counselors and career guidance specialists as they apply to systematic planning for career guidance and career counseling, to acknowledge that different settings and populations require modifications in the application of such systematic planning processes to accommodate their unique characteristics and needs, and to be conscious that change of any kind must proceed within the *institutional culture,* the interactive pattern of norms, beliefs, values, and behavior present in any level of organizational setting and its strategic plan.

If career counseling, career guidance, or career interventions are to be more than a series of random events or activities and limited encounters between counselors and counselees, they must be built on systematic planning, or a systems approach. Such planning requires the completion, in a logical order, of a set of steps that seek to answer several general questions: (1) Why have a career counseling or career guidance program? (2) What will be the goals of the program? (3) How will the goals of the program be achieved? (4) How will the achievement of career counseling or guidance goals be determined?

Systematic planning for career counseling or guidance is consistent with a national climate of support for program accountability and for efforts to implement evidence-based, results-based, skills-based, or outcomes-based human services, career guidance, or counseling programs rather than rely only on traditional models of process-based or services-based programs (Gysbers, 1990; Sears, 1993; Sexton, 2001). Implicit in evidence-based or results-based approaches to program planning and implementation is the assumption that planned programs can explain what counselors could or, indeed, should contribute to the mission of the school, university, corporation or other facility in which they are located; can identify what differences counselors can make in the lives of children, youth, or adults in such settings; clarify the degree to which they can be held accountable for selected outcomes, knowledge bases, or behavioral domains; and focus on incorporating interventions that have been shown by research evidence to be effective in reducing or eliminating particular types of career problems.

In some contrast to evidence-based or outcomes-based approaches, process-based or services-based programs tend to advocate making specific functions or roles to be performed by each counselor available in each setting. The assumption is that if the designated functions or processes are in place, the outcomes of the service or program will be positive. One criticism of process-based or services-based approaches is that because counselors are invariably busy people, if they do not have clearly specified outcomes and plans to achieve them, it is not clear what results may accrue from their efforts. A further criticism is that simply having traditional processes of career guidance and counseling in place does not ensure the flexibility or creativity in a program to cope with the changing needs of client populations in the United States today.

Johnson and Johnson (1982), leading advocates and practitioners of results-based approaches to guidance and counseling, suggest that when a program has a clear set of outcomes to be achieved, there are likely to be many processes that can be implemented to achieve individual outcomes. Focusing on the content of a specific program outcome and then determining what process (or processes) is likely to be effective in achieving it are different from focusing on putting in place a traditional process that may not be relevant to the needs to be served or the outcomes sought. In addition, outcome-based programs typically assume that clients in a setting—whether children, youth, or adults—learn differently and deserve to have access to more than one process or activity to help them achieve the desired results. Further, unless outcomes for a career guidance or counseling program are specified and defined, it is virtually impossible to hold such programs to accountability criteria or determine their effectiveness.

It is important to acknowledge that evidence-based, results-based, or outcomes-based programs and process-based or services-based programs are not mutually exclusive. Aspects of both can and do exist within a programmatic framework. The overriding issue is the systematic and planned effort to put into place those activities or services that are relevant to the needs of the client populations and the mission of the setting within which they are implemented.

Given the context just described, the planning for career guidance, career interventions, career counseling, or employee counseling programs does not occur in a vacuum. Such programs must be designed to achieve the purposes of the organization within which they are located as well as to facilitate the career development of those who are directly served. For example, "employee counseling programs are meant to provide effective means of dealing with problems in the workplace" (Lewis & Lewis, 1986, p. 209). Career development programs in corporate organizations "are comprised of two separate but interrelated functions: career planning, which is an individual process, and career management, which is an institutional process" (Gutteridge, 1986, p. 55). Each needs systematic planning. As schools are increasingly the target of national concern about their role in elevating the quality of the future workforce, career education and counseling programs have come to be seen as important to student needs for career exploration and planning as well as to the school's responsibilities to provide graduating students with the personal habits, knowledge, and skills to make an effective transition into the workplace. As suggested in subsequent chapters, career guidance and counseling in schools are concerned with facilitating students' exploration of the educational and career alternatives available to them; sharpening their understanding of their own abilities, interests, and values as bases for career choice; teaching them how to implement career planning; and helping them acquire the skills necessary for the transition to work or to postsecondary education. These wide-ranging goals are unlikely to occur without planned interventions.

Each of the institutional goals identified is interactive with the provision of direct services to students or to employees. Therefore, they represent the administrative and mission-oriented context against which programmatic planning must proceed.

Gutteridge speaks to such a point, using the language of industry, when he states that "human resource management is comprised of four distinct yet interrelated job systems: organizational design, human resource (manpower) planning, career development, and control and evaluation.... All of these subprocesses are influenced by a variety of internal and external environmental pressures" (1986, p. 53). Together, regardless of setting, such approaches are designed to create value through and for people (Fitz-enz, 1990). Such value is reflected in the knowledge, attitudes, skills, and behaviors for which career services or career counseling becomes responsible in a specific setting.

PROCESS OF SYSTEMATIC PROGRAM PLANNING

A systematic approach to program planning rests on the concept of systems analysis, which, in turn, is concerned with the examination of the interrelationships among the parts of a system to formulate goals and objectives. Science, the defense establishment, and industry have used systems analysis and related methods for several decades to make complex, interactive units manageable and more amenable to monitoring and evaluation. Depending on its relationship to other components within an organization, career counseling, career services, or career guidance may be seen as a system in its own right or as a subsystem of a larger whole.

Program planning, whether for career guidance or other purposes, is required to ensure that the goals for which career intervention is implemented are clearly understood, that the techniques or processes constituting the program are related to the goals, and that the criteria on which the program will be judged are explicit. These elements underlie the program's accountability and are the steps that lead to its evaluation.

Systematic planning, as we use the term, is not inconsistent with what others describe as strategic planning or strategic management. Although strategic planning can be done in various ways, as suggested earlier in this chapter, it is fundamentally a process of answering such basic questions of organizational management as the following:

1. Who are we?
2. What is our purpose?
3. On what will we focus?
4. What are we able to do?
5. What is absolutely necessary?

6. How will we operate?
7. What have we achieved? (Fitz-Enz, 1990, p. 81)

Or, said another way:

- What are our most important organizational issues?
- How are things different today from what they were three or five years ago?
- How are things likely to be different three to five years from now?
- What types of external changes can we expect in the near future?
- What types of internal changes can we expect in the near future?
- How do we compare to our competition in critical areas?
- Is our technology state-of-the-art?
- What can we do to close the gap between what we are and what we must become? (Fitz-enz, 1990, p. 84)

Kurpius, Burrello, and Rozecki (1990) have proposed a strategic planning model for practitioners in human service organizations that summarizes many elements common to comprehensive planning models. The steps in their plan are as follows:

1. Articulating the foundation
   a. Beliefs
   b. Creating a vision
   c. Defining a mission
2. Assessing the forces
   a. Analyzing external and internal factors
   b. Generating and assessing essential policies
3. Formulating the plan
   a. Specifying objectives
   b. Generating strategies
   c. Implementing action plans
   d. Recycling (p. 5)

Each of these recommended planning processes reflect elements similar to our earlier discussion of the components of a strategic plan. Such components include beliefs; mission; parameters; internal and external analyses of strengths, weaknesses, opportunities and challenges; objectives; strategies; action plans. As any of the possible planning processes are implemented, it is important to acknowledge that they are not only a series of steps to be conducted, they are also a state of mind, a commitment to visualizing the "big picture," an effort to understand how several discrete actions can be brought together into a cohesive program of career services that are effective in providing best practices to the consumers of the program, whether they are students, adults, special needs populations or other target populations.

In essence, whether you follow the steps of a strategic planning model or a systematic approach to career guidance or career intervention, the intent is the same: If you wish a program or an intervention to result in a particular type of employee, student, or client knowledge, skills, or behavior (for example, career maturity, self-understanding, decision-making skills), you build toward that goal by comprehensively taking into consideration the functional relations between the elements and people who affect such a goal. In conceiving such a system, the counselor or career administrator needs to take into account the interdependent effects of such variables as:

1. Learner, worker, or client characteristics
2. Resource characteristics available in a school, employment, or community setting (such as budget, materials available, referral sources, exploratory sites, personnel who can be involved)
3. Counselor characteristics
4. Effectiveness of various counselor techniques or career interventions for different purposes (e.g. evidence-based best practices)
5. Administrative or management requirements, policies, and mission goals.
6. Community or institutional expectations

This perspective is similar to such evaluation models as that described by Hughey, Gysbers, and Starr (1993) to assess the impact of the Missouri Comprehensive Guidance Program, which provides answers to the following questions:

- Are the program elements in place?
- Are counselors supervised and evaluated based on their job descriptions?
- Are procedures used to measure students' mastery of guidance competencies?
- Are procedures used to measure the impact of the program and the climate and goals of the school?
- Are the individuals served by the program and the patrons in the community satisfied with the program? (p. 31)

In systematic planning, one must begin with a statement of what is to be achieved in career guidance and counseling; what goals are to be accomplished; and what student, employee, or client development is to be facilitated. A basic premise of this book is that an understanding of the various approaches to career development provides the *content* for these considerations. (Chapter 4 identified the major emphases in career development theory and research, and this chapter extends the application of career development approaches to program planning more specifically. The theories of career development described elsewhere in this book should be reviewed as appropriate here.) This emphasis on beginning with goals for the program, the mission, is in contrast to beginning with counselor techniques that can be performed. In too many instances, counselors do what they know how to do without questioning what they are attempting to achieve. In the process, they lose sight of answers to such questions as: Why career guidance? How will students, employees, or clients be different as a result of exposure to career counseling? Without answers to such questions, however, career interventions lack direction and may be applied in areas for which counselors are not prepared, in which their skills are ineffective, or for which more effective interventions are available than are known or used.

Systems Approach to Career Education

Ryan (1974) identified six functions necessary to a systems approach to career education. In modified form, they are:

1. *Establish a conceptual framework:* Determine the rationale, define the basic concepts, specify the basic assumptions on which the program will be based.
2. *Possess information:* Gather, evaluate, and store data about the community, available resources, facilities, the population to be served. Determine what other information is necessary.
3. *Assess needs:* Compare the ideal program as built from the rationale, assumptions, and concepts of step 1 with the existing situation in the setting where this program is to be installed. Determine the discrepancies between what the program should be and what it now is. Assess the perceptions of parents, employers, managers, employees, teachers, students, or other consumers, administrators, and community representatives about what priorities the program should meet; these could be described as the assessed needs to which the program will be directed. Which of these groups you query depends on whether you are implementing a career guidance program in business and industry, a community agency, or an educational setting.
4. *Formulate the management plan:* Specify program goals and performance objectives for students, employees, or clients. Identify the processes that will be related to program goals. Specify the resources and constraints that need to be considered in putting the plan together.
5. *Implement the program:* Put the program plan into action. Provide in-service training to staff involved, order materials or resources necessary, offer the experience or processes related to program goals.
6. *Evaluate the system:* Monitor ongoing operations as well as the changes in knowledge, skills, and attitudes of the participants. Determine whether the program is meeting its goals and whether individual elements are effective.

While now a quarter of a century old, these steps are still valid for planning career development programs across settings, and they are consistent with the six steps that Wiggins (1985) proposed as necessary in achieving counselor program accountability: (1) setting goals, (2) assessing needs, (3) setting priorities, (4) planning interventions, (5) evaluating outcomes, and (6) reporting results. Again, such core components are consistent with newer elaborations of planning approaches discussed in earlier sections of the chapter.

FIVE-STAGE PLANNING MODEL

As a synthesis of many possible planning models, the broad aspects of the various stages of planning for a career counseling or career services program are described in Table 6.1. Each of the stages of planning portrayed in Table 6.1 has unique requirements and characteristics. In the rest of this chapter we will discuss the stages. Before we do so, however, we should remember that regardless of which planning paradigm one accepts, a systems approach is fundamentally a decision-making process. Indeed, a planning system involves the generation of a system of hypotheses. In

TABLE 6.1 Stages in Planning for and Implementing a Career Guidance Program

STAGE 1	STAGE 2	STAGE 3	STAGE 4	STAGE 5
1. Develop a mission statement, including a program philosophy 1.1 Review research and theory pertinent to career guidance and career development 1.2 Identify and review any pertinent federal, state or local legislation or regulations requiring career services, the outcomes expected, and for whom 2. Collect comprehensive data on what consumers (students, employees, adults) and others (parents, employers, teachers, administrators, community representa- tives) believe should be program priorities 3. Collect data on the current program—goals, resources 4. Identify where the target population—students, workers, other adults—currently stand on their career development 5. Determine discrepancies between what current program is and what it should be 6.0 Specify program rationale or vision 6.1 Describe theoretical and philosophical bases for the program 6.2 State assumptions 6.3 Define concepts	1. Specify program goals 2. Specify individual behavioral objectives to be achieved	1. Select alternative program processes 2. Relate program processes to problem goals or specific behavioral objectives 3. Identify resources necessary to implement various program processes 4. Identify personnel (teachers, counselors, human resource specialists, administrators, community representatives, first-line supervisors, parents, employers) who have contributions to make to various program processes	1. Describe evaluation procedures 1.1 Perform summative evaluation to assess whether total program goals are being met 1.2 Perform formative evaluation to assess whether program elements are contributing effectively to program goals 1.3 Identify evaluative data to be secured, from whom, and by whom 1.4 Build or secure data collection instruments 1.5 Decide on the form of data analysis and who will be responsible 1.6 Identify persons or groups to whom evaluative data will be provided and in what form	1. Identify milestones (crucial events) that must occur for program implementation 1.1 When staff in-service will occur 1.2 When information about the program must be prepared and sent to consumers 1.3 When materials and resources for the program must be ordered 1.4 When base-line data on participants will be collected 1.5 When program will be introduced

stage 1, program goals are hypotheses; they imply that if specified program goals are met, the conditions existing before the program is implemented will be eliminated or improved. Similarly, behavioral objectives are hypotheses that if persons obtain the behaviors specified, the program goals will be achieved. In stage 3, the selection of alternative program processes can be conceived of as a series of hypotheses that one process is more likely than another to result in the desired behavior for which it is accountable. The evaluation, summative or formative, designed to monitor the program is a series of tests of the hypotheses implicit in stages 1 through 3. Indeed, the evaluation scheme that evolves can be conceptualized almost as a pretest/posttest with the program elements considered to be treatments, the original conditions considered as baseline data, and the output or behavioral outcomes that result from the program as posttest data. Obviously, most career guidance programs cannot or will not be evaluated using pure experimental designs, but it can be helpful to think of much of program planning as analogous to such conceptualizations.

Stage 1: Developing a Program Rationale and Philosophy; Specifying the Mission

Stage 1 includes all the thinking and data collection that relates to developing a program philosophy and rationale. In the parlance of strategic planning these are the elements that describe the mission of the career program. It includes securing information about the characteristics of the setting in which the career development program is to operate and the resources to be committed to that effort. Such planning also includes developing needs surveys (questionnaires or structured interviews) to determine what consumers (students, employees, or other adults) and others believe the focus of the career counseling or guidance program should be. Together, these data will help determine what the current status of career development in the particular setting is and what different groups believe it should be. At the conclusion of stage 1, counselors and directors of counseling and guidance should have formulated a statement that clearly answers such questions as: Why career guidance? Why career counseling? Why a career development system? What are the discrepancies between what now exists and what other stakeholders (e.g., students, parents, teachers, employers) would like to have available?

In essence, the early stages of such a planning model need to accommodate the conceptual frames of reference on which the proposed program will be developed. For example, in the case of constructing a career guidance model for a school district with students at all grade levels and in multiple school buildings, it is necessary in the planning model to provide a philosophical base (what does developmental mean in this model?) and a comprehensive structure that can encompass the various guidance and counseling services that will be included. In addition, such a model calls for well-defined goals and objectives "that are specific enough to provide focus on student needs yet allow the actual nature of the program at each school to vary according to the developmental needs of the students" (Snyder & Daly, 1993, p. 38). Much of the content on which to plan such a model will be derived from locally collected needs assessment data.

Needs Assessment. As a device by which to clarify the difference between the current status and the desired state of career services and interventions, the process of needs assessment has become frequently used. As Cook (1989) contends:

> *All human service programs are developed based on the... implicit assumption of need in the population at risk. Programs will eventually fail or succeed depending on how well they address those needs. Consequently, need assessment is the first step in the program planning cycle and is essential for the effective delivery of services and the efficient allocation of resources.... Need is a relative concept that can be viewed as a discrepancy from some recognized standard or as the gap between an individual's desired and actual situation.... Need assessment usually seeks to define and prioritize an individual's expressed needs and then link these needs to service provision such as providing vocational counseling to a person who is disabled. (p. 462)*

Needs assessments can be used for many planning purposes; for example, demands for accountability, ways to clarify evidence of widespread criticism for unsolved problems in a program, and methods to respond to the increasing competition for scarce resources. Needs assessments go beyond such reasons to allow significant others of relevance in particular settings—consumers, employers, administrators, parents, the public at large—to participate in identifying appropriate program rationales, goals, directions, or even interventions.

Needs assessments are basically processes to document the difference between a current state of affairs and some target or desired state of affairs. As such, a needs assessment is a technique by which to identify the discrepancies between what is and what ought to be and determine how these discrepancies might be reduced. Similar to most other planning processes, needs assessments are exercises in logic and include a process of implementation that involves appropriate persons, minimizes time and personnel costs, and yields the documented needs and the planning priorities that are of concern to stage 1 expectations as they are described here.

Although there are many models of needs assessment, the Counseling and Personnel Services Clearinghouse at the University of Michigan has suggested the following classic four-phased structure (ERIC/CAPS, 1982, pp. 1–2):

Phase I. Planning and Designing the Needs Assessment

Step 1. Carry out preliminary activities.

- Set up needs assessment committee.
- Identify external priorities or limiting factors.
- Determine scope of assessment.
- Establish needs assessment schedule.
- Review committee resources and obtain commitment.

Step 2. Make specific plans and design needs assessment.

- Specify process and product goals (e.g., process goals refer to the intervention process itself, and product goals refer to student or employee outcomes as a result of the intervention process).
- Develop statements of program objectives with clarity, precision, measurability, feasibility, appropriateness, relevance, and logic.
- Set standards for all objectives.
- Discuss and agree on kinds of data to be gathered (performance, description, opinion, attitude, perception).
- Determine sources of data.
- Determine sample for data gathering (groups, sizes, strategies/methods).
- Select, modify, and develop data collection methods and instruments (quantitative and qualitative).
- Design analysis of existing variables.

Phase II. Conducting the Needs Assessment

Step 3. Obtain, organize, and summarize needs assessment data.

- Categorize all data to be collected (program, clients, resources, stakeholding groups).
- Collect and summarize data (existing and new) in each category.

Step 4. Analyze and interpret data to derive meanings.

- Employ arithmetic/statistical analysis.
- Identify specific qualitative elements.

Step 5. Conduct analysis of apparent relationships.

- Determine factors for each documented need according to standards and to category.
- Designate needs related to factors that can be addressed immediately, later or over extended periods of time, and not at all.

Phase III. Using the Needs Assessment Results*

Step 6. Select priorities.

- Assign priorities to each need(s) set.
- Assign priorities on basis of criticality over time (in consideration of currently available resources, limits of action authority, and so on).

Step 7. Plan program.

- Identify new program elements or modifications.
- Establish performance objectives.
- Allocate resources by priority and relative cost.
- Provide for coordination of resources.
- Assign tasks to individuals, teams, and groups, with timelines and milestones for accomplishment.

Step 8. Implement program.

- Provide resources for program change according to documented needs and priority assignments.
- Identify measures and means of data collection for each objective.

Phase IV. Review of Meta-Assessment

Step 9. Determine impact of change process.

- Decide on indicators to be accepted as evidence of improvement.

*A prior review of the anticipated utilization of results and an evaluation of the appropriateness of such utilization may be advisable. The early identification of possible barriers to the consecutive use of results prevents inefficient use of resources.

- Gather data to determine actual occurrence of improvement.
- Identify relationships between observed improvements and program changes.
- Relate observed improvements to originally documented needs.

The purpose of Phase IV is to look back at the process as a whole, relate the results to the objectives, determine the extent to which the process has succeeded, and modify the process for greater or further success during the next needs assessment cycle. Although such a process appears to encompass the whole of planning for career guidance, it does not. Needs assessments are only stage 1 techniques and must be coupled with other considerations as the development of a program rationale and philosophy is undertaken.

Another aspect of stage 1 is to review current research and theory on what the program's directions might be, what knowledge or behaviors might be affected by the program, and what basic concepts and assumptions should be considered. In Chapters 1 through 5, possible contributions have been made to such an analysis and should be reviewed. Chapter 4, in particular, speaks to the theoretical influences on career development at different ages for males and females and under different circumstances of socioeconomic, educational, or other status. Such conceptual elements define targets for career interventions and, in many ways, give career programs a rationale for existence. Many of these insights could be translated into program philosophy for a particular setting. In addition, it is important to identify pertinent federal, state, and local legislative initiatives or regulations that require or recommend the provision of career services, for whom and for what purpose. Such initiatives tend to reinforce the importance of planning, provide a frame by which to identify specific elements of a program, and serve as a source of funding for such efforts.

Basically, programs in career guidance and career counseling will have one of three emphases or a combination of these three. (1) In a *stimulus or developmental approach,* consumers are assisted in anticipating and exploring opportunities and how these relate to their personal abilities, preferences, and circumstances. In essence, the intent is to facilitate career development, to provide the tools the student or client needs for career planning, and to stimulate exploration and goal setting. (2) In *induction and adjustment* to a setting, the intent of the career program is to assist persons in translating their preferences or choices into action, consolidating these choices, and advancing within the settings in which they are implemented. (3) In a *treatment approach,* individuals may anticipate and explore but also are likely to undergo remediation or reconstruction of their attitudes, knowledge, and skills often to facilitate their work adjustment.

However a program emphasis is conceived, planning for it needs to include insights into the behaviors that the program intends to affect. These insights need to be translated into a program philosophy and rationale. For example, if the career program is to emphasize a stimulus approach, career maturity and the elements comprising it may be helpful input to conceptualizing a program philosophy and rationale. Although the usefulness of insights into the behavioral structure of career maturity is not confined to the stimulus approach to career guidance, the other two career guidance program emphases are likely to require other bodies of theory and research that are useful in conceptualizing and planning their particular intent.

Basically, stage 1, as suggested in Table 6.1, needs to accomplish several things. If the plan focuses on improving a program that has been in place for several years, a major question is what is the discrepancy between what is and what should be the content and process of the program? If the task is to plan a new program, the emphasis is on the latter, what should be the content and process of this program. The specification of such a task requires planning that considers the fit of the career program to the strategic goals of the organization in which it is located, any policies or legislation which are relevant to career development in such a setting, needs assessment data indicating preferences and expectations from different constituent groups, and certainly the body of research and theory that describes potential program content and best intervention practices.

Perhaps the major outcome to be achieved from Stage 1 planning is a mission statement which is a clear and concise expression of the career program's identity, purpose, and uniqueness. Conceptually, the mission of the career program is the lynchpin, the fundamental rock, on which the plan depends and by which the other planning stages are shaped and the results of the program judged.

Perspectives on Developmental Program Content. In a major sense, each of the three emphases of a career development program cited above, have available possible theoretical or research content that can be used to determine what a career program should address. Such content helps to translate global goals into performance objectives for students or adults which are relevant to the mission of the career program and to the needs of the particular populations (e.g., high school students, college students, midcareer adults, persons with disabilities, and so on) served by the career program. Thus, historically, in the first emphasis identified above as pertinent to career programs—a stimulus or developmental approach—goals that frequently appear in the professional literature are terms like career maturity, career planfulness, or career adaptability. Such global terms have acquired a substantial body of research that can be useful in helping career program planners to identify the specific elements that underlie career maturity, planning or adaptability and that can be the foci of specific interventions.

Thus, for example, it is necessary to convert the elements of career maturity into unifying themes and behavioral descriptions and place these along a developmental line leading to career maturity at some point in life, such as high school graduation, tenth grade, sophomore year in college, release from a rehabilitation facility, or at specific career transition points, such as when an employee is ready to be promoted to a new role.

When attempting such a task, however, one must realize that, just as in other developmental processes, individuals will differ in their readiness for various elements or aspects of career development and in the ways they develop this readiness. Not everyone will reach the same point at the same time, nor will all proceed through the elements of career development at the same pace. As previously indicated, the speed of such movement and the readiness for it will depend on the individual's personal history and many extrinsic and intrinsic factors.

The objectives of career development, then, rest on statements of expectations for specific target groups, which necessitate judgments of what individuals ought to be able to achieve and behavioral descriptions of these activities. But one must also realize that for optimum effect, career development should be personalized. Although the literal realization of such a goal may be too much to expect, any systematic attempt to aid career development requires an emphasis both on diagnosis and on the provision of diverse learning experiences. It is simply not enough to say to a person, "Be career mature." One needs to understand what being career mature means, what the consequences of career maturity are, how one acquires career maturity, and what opportunities are available to aid such an effort.

In essence, a systems approach to career maturity at its best would represent a planned continuum of experiences for individual students, employees, or clients. The individual should be exposed to the program based on assessed readiness and move progressively toward the goal of career maturity, planfulness, or career adaptability.

Fostering career maturity, planfulness, and adaptability requires both individualizing and personalizing. There are certain elements of effective behavior that all persons need to acquire individually. But there are also times when, as individual goals become clearer, the person needs the opportunity and the assistance to "create himself or herself"; that is, to develop ways of creating goals and a life-style independent of others.

It is important to realize that if career maturity or career adaptability or another goal is to be used as the goal of career development, and if a systems approach to achieving it is to be mounted, relevant measures are needed: (1) to assess personal readiness to make educational-vocational decisions or to participate in particular types of career development experiences, (2) to serve as diagnostic instruments for determining treatment, and (3) to evaluate the effectiveness of program strategies for facilitating career development. Many such assessment devices are described in Chapter 16.

Mastery of Development Tasks as a Function of Career Guidance. Several theorists have either directly or indirectly wedded particular developmental tasks with stages of increasingly mature career behavior. Thus, we can assume that the developmental task concept is useful, both as a description of the changing demands on individuals as they move through life and as a means of organizing those demands—

whether knowledge, attitudes, or skills—into a systems approach to career development.

If one accepts developmental tasks as an organizing structure for conceptualizing career development or facilitating career adaptability or maturity, one must then determine what the developmental tasks are that move one along a continuum to such goals. Chapter 4 presents many conceptualizations from which to draw. Table 6.2 presents major emphases in selected approaches that illustrate the point.

Table 6.3 summarizes such developmental tasks from Super's perspectives. While not parallel per se, these tables do agree that career development occurs in crucial steps with each systematically related to those preceding and succeeding it. These steps also relate to turning points in each developmental stage, where individuals either progress or fall back as a function of their success in grappling with the central issues of the stage. As such, they become useful in diagnostic terms and as planning content for career guidance programs or for career counseling protocols.

Although the illustrations in Table 6.2 and 6.3 are too gross to be directly translated into goals for career development programs, other pertinent points are discernible. For example, what does Havighurst's first stage (identification with a worker) suggest for a student who comes from a home and a culture in which there are no productive workers? If the achievement of later tasks depends on such identification, career interventions must respond to that lack. In accordance with the general rationale of developmental tasks, that missed stages leave a deficit in dealing with later tasks, the question becomes what resources, what role models, what experiences can the school, the corporation, or agency provide to help this particular person acquire a concept of work as a part of his or her orientation for the future? Or suppose we are talking about a man who has, in Super's terms, never been able to advance in an occupation. Do we simply consider this person a "loser" and try to dismiss him from the workplace or instead allow him to drift along at a mediocre level of productivity, assuming he can do no better? Or do we attempt to determine what prevents him from advancing? Is it his fear of responsibility? His preoccupation with family problems? His lack of clarity about the requirements of particular career paths in the work setting? Each of these and other hypotheses is reasonable and can be pursued in a career conference with the worker. Both Chapters 1 and 2 provide taxonomies of career problems that may suggest other hypotheses to be explored at an individual level. Once the problem is defined, a career guidance or career counseling approach can be instituted to help the person become more purposeful and productive.

Table 6.2 provides a frame of reference for formulating specific program goals and individual objectives. The themes presented are more global than objectives should be. For example, it does not provide behavioral descriptions that permit evaluation of an individual's accomplishment of the goals set for him or her.

Although some of the models of developmental tasks and behaviors pertinent to career development are old in historical terms, their concepts continue to be useful as input to program planning for career development, to the conceptualizing of behavioral substages, and to research. For example, the Career Pattern Study of Donald Super has focused principally on the exploratory and establishment steps of career development. It has been assumed that these are the stages crucial to education and, in particular, to curriculum development and to career guidance and career interventions. As Table 6.3 illustrates, the developmental tasks of Super that span these two life stages (from approximately age 14 to 25 plus) are as follows (you might wish to review the appropriate sections discussed in Chapter 4):

- Crystallizing a vocational preference
- Specifying it
- Implementing it
- Stabilizing in the chosen vocation
- Consolidating one's status
- Advancing in the occupation

Crystallizing a vocational preference has to do with the individual's "formulating ideas as to fields, and levels of work which are appropriate, self and occupational concepts which will enable him [or her], if necessary, to make tentative choices, that is, to commit oneself to a type of education or training which will lead the person toward some partially specified occupation" (Super, Starishevsky, Matlin, & Jordaan, 1963, p. 82). Specifying a vocational preference is the "singling out of a specific occupation and the attitude (not the act) of commitment to it" (p. 82). Implementing the preference is converting it into a reality. Thus, these separate stages are divided between all the factors in formulating a preference, on the one hand, and

TABLE 6.2 Selected Examples of Theoretical Conceptions of the Developmental Tasks and Competencies Related to Career Behaviors at Different Educational or Age Levels

HAVIGHURST (1964, P. 216)

Age 5–10

I. Identification with a worker—father, mother, other significant persons. The concept of working becomes an essential part of the ego-ideal. Selected developmental tasks of middle childhood include
   - Developing fundamental skills in reading, writing, and calculating
   - Learning physical skills necessary for ordinary games
   - Learning to get along with age mates
   - Developing conscience, morality, and a scale of values
   - Achieving personal identity

Age 10–15

II. Acquiring the basic habits of industry: Learning to organize time and energy to get a piece of work done (school, work, chores). Learning to put work ahead of play in appropriate situations

Age 15–25

III. Acquiring identity as a worker in the occupational structure; choosing and preparing for an occupation. Getting work experience as a basis for occupational choice and for assurance of economic independence. Selected developmental tasks of adolescence include:
   - Achieving new, more mature relations with agemates of both sexes
   - Achieving emotional independence of parents and other adults
   - Achieving assurance of economic independence
   - Selecting and preparing for an occupation
   - Acquiring a set of values and an ethical system as a guide to behavior
   - Getting started in an occupation

Age 25–45

IV. Becoming a productive person; mastering the skills of an occupation; moving up the ladder within the occupation

V. Maintaining a productive society
   - Achieving adult civic and social responsibility
   - Assisting teenage children to become responsible and happy adults
   - Developing adult leisure-time activities
   - Adjusting to aging parents
   - Accepting and adjusting to the physiological changes of middle age
   - Reaching and maintaining a satisfactory performance in one's occupational career

Age 45–65

VI. Contemplating a productive life
   - Adjusting to decreasing strength and health
   - Adjusting to retirement and reduced income
   - Adjusting to the death of a spouse
   - Establishing an explicit affiliation with members of one's age group
   - Establishing satisfactory physical living arrangements
   - Adapting to social roles in a flexible way

ERIKSON (1963, 2ND ED.)

Birth to approximately age 25

Basic trust (basic mistrust)
Autonomy (shame and doubt)
Initiative (guilt)
Industry (inferiority)
Fundamentals of technology
First sense of division of labor and of differential opportunity
Outer and inner hindrance
Identity (role confusion)
Ego identity and the tangible promise of career

Age 25 and beyond

Occupational identity
Sexual identity
Intimacy (isolation):
The capacity to commit oneself to concrete affiliations and partnerships and to develop the ethical strength to abide by such commitments
Ethical sense
True genitality

Age 45–60

Generativity (stagnation), productivity, creativity
Ego integrity (despair)

After Age 60

Integrity vs. Despair (disgust)

LEVINSON (1977)

Early Adult Transition (17–22)

1. Terminate pre-adulthood
   - Start moving out of the preadult world
   - Question the nature of the world and one's place in it
   - Modify or terminate existing relationships with important persons, groups, and institutions
   - Reappraise and modify the self that formed it
2. Begin early adulthood
   - Explore its possibilities
   - Imagine oneself a participant in it

- Consolidate an initial adult identity
- Make and test some preliminary choices for adult living

Four major tasks from 17 to approximately 30

1. Forming a dream and giving it a place in the life structure
2. Forming mentor relationships
3. Forming an occupation
4. Forming love relationships and family

Entering the Adult World (22–28)

1. Fashion a provisional structure that provides a workable link between the valued self and the adult society
2. Explore possibilities for adult living; keep options open; avoid strong commitments; maximize the alternatives
3. Create a stable life structure

- Become more responsible and make something of my life

Age 30

Transition (23–33)

- Make important new choices or reaffirm old ones

Settling Down (33–40)

1. Tries to establish a niche in society
    - Anchor life more firmly
    - Develop competence in a chosen craft
    - Become a valued member of a valued world

Age 25–45

- Define a personal enterprise, a direction in which to strive

2. Work at advancement
    - Strive to advance, to progress on a timetable
3. Becoming one's own person
    - Accomplish the goals of the settling down enterprise
    - Become a senior member in one's world
    - Speak more strongly with one's voice
    - Have a greater measure of authority

Mid-Life Transition (40–45)

1. A period of questioning of the life structure

HALL (1976, PP. 81–84)

Start at 45–60

- Awareness of advancing age
- Awareness of body changes related to aging
- Knowing how many career goals have been or will be attained
- Search for new life goals
- Marked change in family relationships
- Change in work relationships
- Sense of work obsolescence
- Feeling of decreased job mobility and increased concerns for job security

HERR (1991, P. 10)

Formation of basic attitudes and information about self and life opportunities

Subtasks (examples)

- Developing a sense of personal competence, self-worth, self-acceptance
- Developing a sense of life opportunities, their breadth, and their characteristics
- Developing the rudiments of a sense of academic readiness, self efficacy, and college consciousness
- Developing a sense of personal identity, uniqueness, a self-concept system
- Developing social relationships with peers and adults
- Beginning to understand and take responsibility for actions, understand the role of choices and decisions
- Understanding preferences and their linkages to opportunities

YOUNG ADOLESCENTS MIDDLE SCHOOL/JUNIOR SCHOOL MAJOR GUIDANCE TASKS

Exploring and reality testing attitudes and information about self, others, and opportunities

Subtasks (examples)

- Testing and refining aspirations
- Sustaining motivation
- Organizing and testing one's knowledge of social and physical reality
- Learning to work well in the peer group
- Engaging in a wide variety of experiences and opportunities in academic, career, and personal domains.
- Using and testing their skills and to reflecting upon their meaning
- Acquiring the life skills related to planning and choice of curriculum and career
- Learning about the connections between academic choices and future choices of education and work; learning how to keep options open
- Sharpening self-identity, feelings of self-efficacy
- Exploring and reality testing subject-matter and occupational skills and preferences

LATER ADOLESCENTS SENIOR HIGH SCHOOL MAJOR GUIDANCE TASKS

Specific planning related to imminence of making the transition from school to work or college

Sub-tasks (examples)

- Preparing for the transition from school to young adulthood
- Becoming self-reliant and achieving psychological independence from parents

(continued)

TABLE 6.2 Continued

- Expanding peer relationships and achieving the capacity for intimate relationships
- Learning to handle heterosexual relationships, dating, and sexuality
- Making plans to pay for college or other postsecondary education
- Learning how to manage one's personal health
- Learning to manage time
- Formulating a personal value system
- Differentiating career expectations and planning in accordance with such views
- Assuming responsibility for career planning and its consequences
- Keeping one's options open as fully as possible by taking courses to qualify for post-secondary education
- Developing skills important to life as a consumer and to effective use of leisure time

TABLE 6.3 A Synthesis of Super's Conception of Life Stages and Developmental Tasks

GROWTH	EXPLORATION
Birth	*14 years*
Self-concept develops through identification with key figures in family and school needs and fantasy are dominant early in this stage; interest and capacity become more important with increasing social participation and reality testing; learn behaviors associated with self-help, social interaction, self-direction, industrialness, goal setting, persistence. Substages: *Fantasy* (4–10 years) Needs are dominant; role-playing in fantasy is important *Interest* (11–12 years) Likes are the major determinant of aspirations and activities *Capacity* (13–14 years) Abilities are given more weight and job requirements (including training) are considered Tasks: Developing a picture of the kind of person one is Developing an orientation to the world of work and an understanding of the meaning of work	Self-examination, role try-outs and occupational exploration take place in school, leisure activities, and part-time work. Substages: *Tentative* (15–17) Needs, interests, capacities, values, and opportunities are all considered, tentative choices are made and tried out in fantasy, discussion, courses, work, and so on. Possible appropriate fields and levels of work are identified. Task Crystallizing a vocational preference *Transition* (18–21) Reality considerations are given more weight as the person enters the labor market or professional training and attempts to implement a self-concept. Generalized choice is converted to specific choice. Task Specifying a vocational preference *Trial-Little Commitment* (22–24) A seemingly appropriate occupation having been found, a first job is located and is tried out as a potential life work. Commitment is still provisional and if the job is not appropriate, the person may reinstitute the process of crystallizing, specifying, and implementing a preference. Tasks: Implementing a vocational preference Developing a realistic self-concept Learning more about more opportunities

those in formulating an actual choice on the other. In this context, choice can be represented by entering a postsecondary educational program designed to prepare one for a preferred goal or in entering employment and receiving on-the-job training in a particular area of work performance.

The implication of this line of reasoning is that the major emphasis in career development to the twelfth-grade level is on enabling the individual to crystallize and specify preferences or to anticipate the act of choice. It is also obvious, however, that many adolescents or high school graduates have not attained such maturity. Thus, college student personnel programs, industrial relations efforts, and rehabilitation programs or other community-based programs will need to provide opportunities for clients and workers to develop these same insights and skills in an abbreviated, accelerated time frame. Indeed, as other parts of this book indicate, many adults served by community agencies or by career services in business and industry are as ignorant about themselves and their opportunities as are children and youth. Therefore, the same type of planning content will be useful in developing programs focused on a stimulus approach.

What, then, are the behaviors or attitudes that foster the crystallization or specification of a vocational preference? What sub-elements could be set forth in a chart similar to Table 6.3? One such list is as

ESTABLISHMENT	MAINTENANCE	DECLINE
24 years	*44 years*	*64 years*
Having found an appropriate field, an effort is made to establish a permanent place in it. Thereafter changes that occur are changes of position, job, or employer, not of occupation. Substages: *Trial-Commitment and Stabilization* (25–30) Settling down. Securing a permanent place in the chosen occupation. May prove unsatisfactory resulting in one or two changes before the life work is found or before it becomes clear that the life work will be a succession of unrelated jobs. *Advancement* (31–44) Effort is put forth to stabilize, to make a secure place in the world of work. For most persons these are the creative years. Seniority is acquired; clientele are developed; superior performance is demonstrated; qualifications are improved. Tasks: Finding opportunity to do desired work Learning to relate to others Consolidation and advancement Making occupational position secure Settling down in a permanent position	Having made a place in the world of work, the concern is how to hold on to it. Little new ground is broken, continuation of established pattern. Concerned about maintaining present status while being forced by competition from younger workers in the advancement stage. Tasks: Accepting one's limitations Identifying new problems to work on Developing new skills Focusing on essential activities Preservation of achieved status and gains	As physical and mental powers decline, work activity changes and in due course ceases. New roles must be developed: first, selective participant and then observer. Individual must find other sources of satisfaction to replace those lost through retirement. Substages: *Deceleration* (65–70) The pace of work slackens, duties are shifted, or the nature of the work is changed to suit declining capacities. Many men find part-time jobs to replace their full-time occupations. *Retirement* (71 on) Variation on complete cessation of work or shift to part-time, volunteer, or leisure activities. Tasks: Developing nonoccupational roles Finding a good retirement spot Doing things one has always wanted to do Reducing working hours

follows, paraphrased from the work of Super, Starishevsky, Matlin, and Jordaan (1963, pp. 84–87):

1. *Awareness of the need to crystallize:* Fundamentally, this attitude acts as a precursor of those that follow. It has to do with developing an attitude of readiness to involve oneself in the succeeding elements, becoming oriented to the need to explore.

2. *Use of resources:* This element is principally a set of instrumental behaviors by which one copes with exploration, whether it is focused on self-understanding or occupational description; it is present in relation to many persons or objects: parents, counselors, teachers, materials, part-time jobs, employers.

3. *Awareness of factors to consider in formulating a vocational preference:* This involves knowledge of the possible bases for preferences—whether intellectual requirements, relationship between interests and appropriate outlets, need for alternatives, or availability of outlets for different self-characteristics, that is, security, prestige.

4. *Awareness of contingencies that may affect vocational goals:* The existing evidence suggests that this element and items 2 and 3 collectively contribute to narrowing preferences and adding stability to those preferences that remain. Fundamentally, this element concerns the factors that may impede implementation of a particular preference, and the alternatives that can be actualized if necessary.

5. *Differentiation of interests and values:* This element refers to the ability of the individual to differentiate the personally important from the unimportant and to concentrate attention on certain objectives and activities rather than others as a basis for decision making and for action.

6. *Awareness of present-future relationships:* This factor is concerned with coming to terms with the interrelationship between present activities and intermediate or ultimate vocational activities: for example, understanding educational avenues and their requirements as these provide access to different fields or levels of occupational activity.

7. *Formulation of a generalized preference:* All the factors described to this point should culminate in the formulation of a generalized preference, or crystallization. This level of preference is less a specific occupation than a general one out of which further specification will ensue. In such cases, the preference represented by a particular occupational title is likely to symbolize related activities that are liked rather than a specific occupation.

8. *Consistency of preference:* Consistency may be primarily verbal, or it may be manifested instrumentally in course selection and in such areas as extracurricular or part-time occupational activities.

9. *Possession of information on the preferred occupation:* This element represents possession of more specific information about the generalized preference. It is characterized by greater variety and accuracy of information and by better understanding than is represented by the formulation of a generalized preference.

10. *Planning for the preferred occupation:* The focus here is on deciding what to do and when and how to do it. As Super and Overstreet demonstrated in their work in 1960, specificity both of planning and of information are measurable characteristics of vocational maturity in early adolescence.

11. *Wisdom of the vocational preference:* This is in large measure a criterion of the previous elements. Although certain external criteria can be applied, it is generally assumed that wisdom is really more a function of the process by which a preference is developed than the preference itself.

12. *Specification:* This level of vocationalization represents elaboration of the preference, that is, more specific information and planning, a greater commitment to the preference, and a refinement of the steps already described, with a sharper focus on the particular preference and the steps preceding implementation.

As indicated in Chapter 4, throughout the history of the Career Pattern Study, the self-concept has been seen by Super as the synthesizing agent which translates personal self-perceptions into occupational preferences. To that end, Super (1951, 1953) proposed that "in expressing a vocational preference, a person puts into occupational terminology his ideas of the kind of person he is, in entering an occupation, he seeks to implement his self-concept, and in stabilizing in an occupation he attempts to achieve self-actualization. In a chronological sense, three phases of self-concept evolution occur: formation, translation, and implementation. Through growth and learning as well as the constant interaction of the individual with external influences the self-concept is modified and adjusted until a synthesis is finally evolved (Super, 1969b, p. 185).

Each of these crucial phases of the evolving self-concept has certain emphases and processes integral to it (Super, 1969b):

1. The formation process includes exploration of the self and of the environment, the differentiation of the self from others, identification with others who can serve as models, and the playing of these selected roles with more or less conscious evaluation of the result (reality testing).
2. The translation of self-concepts into occupational terms may take place through identification with an adult role model ("I am like him" or "I want to be like him"), experience in a role in which one has been cast, or learning that some of one's attributes should make one fit well into a certain occupation.
3. The implementation process involves action as in obtaining the specialized education or training needed for the preferred occupation or finding employment in it. (p. 19)

The discerning reader may ask why are we lingering on Super's theoretical concepts, which appear to be old, as input to the planning process. Several answers are relevant. One is that Super's work is the most comprehensive, research-based perspective on the elements of career maturity, career planfulness, and career adaptability available. Savickas (2001) summarizes this point eloquently:

> *Donald E. Super's signal contribution to the science of vocational psychology and the practice of career counseling arose from his taking a developmental perspective on occupational choice and work adjustment. He asserted that the individual differences view of occupations and workers ignored the longitudinal vantage point from which one can observe how individuals expand their vocational coping repertoires and move into more congruent positions. From this seminal insight, he elaborated important hypotheses about career maturity, salience, stages, patterns, and themes. Super's models and measures of these constructs remain as valuable today as when he introduced them in the 1950s. (p. 49)*

A second answer that reinforces Savickas's points is that Super's concepts have been adapted as the substance on which career programs have been built in nations around the world. Examples include Japan (Watanabe-Muraoka, Senzaki, & Herr, 2001), Spain (Repetto, 2001), and Britain (Watts, 2001), among others. In Japan, Super's developmental model, his concepts of life stages and career developmental tasks became the theoretical frame of reference for the recently created, competency-based model for a career guidance program through elementary to high schools (Watanabe-Muraoka, 1999). In Spain, a major career developmental program entitled Your Future Career has been created using Super's career development tasks and other concepts. The Spanish program is comprised of four subprograms: self-awareness, decision making, career exploration, and career planning and management. The program purposes are to provide middle and high school students (seventh to twelfth graders) competencies in self-awareness, awareness of other people, knowledge of the decision-making process, positive attitudes toward career exploration, and planning and management, as well as the skills needed to develop them (Repetto, 1994). In Britain, the evolution of career education in the schools was, in part, directly related to Super's concepts of self-awareness and career development.

Suggested Input to Program Goals of Stimulus or Exploration. The theory and research emanating from Super's Career Pattern Study, and the perspectives of Havighurst, Erikson, Levinson, and Hall, among others (see Table 6.2), have been treated as examples of appropriate input in formulating career guidance program rationale, program goals, and, indeed, performance objectives that are concerned with facilitating exploration, choice, anticipation, and adaptability. Before turning to the specific matter of formulating program goals and objectives per se, however, some synthesis of the aforementioned data is necessary.

To attain different aspects of career maturity, students, employees, or other adult clients need a comprehensive body of information that links what they are doing educationally at a particular time to future options in both education and work. They need to know what curricula or training opportunities will be available to them, what factors distinguish one curriculum or training opportunity from another, what components make up separate curricular pathways, or relate to specific steps on career ladders, what personal factors are relevant to success in different curricula, and how the various curricula are linked to different field and level responsibilities in the occupational world.

Students and adult clients also need self-knowledge. They need to be able to differentiate personal values and personal interests as these relate to personal strengths and weaknesses in abilities—verbal, quantitative, and scholastic. They need to be able to assess these elements of the self, to incorporate their meaning into the self-concept, and to relate this self-information to the choices with which they will be confronted.

Students and adults also need to understand the characteristics of the organizations in which they work or are likely to work as these determine role relationships, social relations, flexibility of coping behavior, level and kind of consumption, and changes probable throughout their occupational history.

Transcending this necessary base of knowledge is the motivation to use it in purposeful ways. In the making of decisions, there are skills that can be learned. Once a person has made a plan for some segment of life with which he or she is content to live, that person can make the next plan more intelligently and with less hesitation or conflict. But it must be remembered that one cannot make occupational or career decisions without educational implications and vice versa. Nor can effective planning and choice making occur without one's recognizing and assessing the psychological and emotional implications of various decisions.

The studies of Super and colleagues emphasize attitudes of planfulness, recognition of possible alternative actions, and ways to assess the desirability of outcomes based on personal preferences and values. Students and adults can be helped to evaluate the sequence of outcomes of immediate choice—proximate, intermediate, ultimate—as well as the factors that are personally relevant at experiential branch points, the probabilities associated with these factors, and the personal desirability of the three outcomes in the sequence. The fostering of planfulness and of career development involves providing the person not only with knowledge, but also with opportunities to apply the knowledge to his or her personal characteristics. Efforts to facilitate career development must, among other things, help individuals bring to work a sense of value, ego involvement, personal endeavor, and achievement motivation.

Input for Programs of Induction or Orientation. Before leaving stage 1, it is important to note that conceptualizations of input to the ingredients of career maturity are basic to planning for career programs that have stimulus, career exploration, or the facilitation of anticipation or choice as their major goals. To date, most planning concepts have been devoted to such purposes rather than to induction or orientation. The lack of conceptualization appropriate to these areas is fertile soil for both the application of theory and research. Nevertheless, there are career programs in which the major goals are induction or orientation. Such programs have various settings. They are particularly prevalent in colleges and universities and in business and industry. They are concerned with the behaviors of persons as they attempt to implement their preferences in the realities of a curriculum or a work setting and as they advance beyond exploration and anticipation to actual implementation of their preferences, induction into the realities of the work environment, and advancement in the occupation or the corporation they have chosen for themselves.

Schein (1971), for example, has described induction into an organizational career as a series of stages and transitions that also provides input to the planning of a career guidance or career development program. This is portrayed in Table 6.4. Hall's (1986, 1990) research has merged findings from vocational psychology and organizational theory into his model of psychological success, which centers on issues of identity and psychological success and how they are related over time in a career. Among many other important outcomes is Hall's research finding that the first year in an organization is a critical period for learning and, particularly, that the more challenging the person's initial assignment is, the more successful (in terms of salary and promotions) the person will be five to eight years later (1990, p. 429). Further, Hall's psychological success model indicates how task success can promote self-esteem, which promotes involvement, which, in turn, promotes higher goals and greater task success. Hall's work has also suggested that learning in an organization involves both short-term and long-term task and personal learning, which can be facilitated by career interventions. Short-term task learning has to do with improving performance, knowledge, skills and abilities. Long-term task learning has to do with improving adaptability. Short-term personal learning has to do with resolving issues regarding attitudes toward career and personal life. Long-term personal learning has to do with developing and extending identity (Hall, 1990, p. 43).

TABLE 6.4 Interaction of Worker and Organization in Career

BASIC STAGES AND TRANSITIONS	STATUSES OR POSITIONS	PSYCHOLOGICAL AND ORGANIZATIONAL PROCESSES; TRANSACTIONS BETWEEN INDIVIDUAL AND ORGANIZATION
1. Preentry	Aspirant, applicant, rushee	Preparation, education, anticipatory socialization
Entry (trans.)	Entrant, postulant, recruit	Recruitment, rushing, testing, screening, selection acceptance ("hiding"); passage through external inclusion boundary; rites of entry; induction and orientation
2. Basic training novitiate	Trainee, novice, pledge	Training, indoctrination, socialization, testing of the person by the organization, tentative acceptance into group
Initiation, first vows (trans.)	Initiate, graduate	Passage through first inner inclusion boundary, acceptance as member and conferring of organizational status, rite of passage and acceptance
3. First regular assignment	New member	First testing by the person of his or her own capacity to function; granting of real responsibility (playing for keeps); passage through functional boundary with assignment to specific job or department
Substages 3a. Learning the job 3b. Maximum performance 3c. Becoming obsolete 3d. Learning new skills, etc.		Indoctrination and testing of person by immediate work group leading to acceptance or rejection; if accepted, further education and socialization (learning the ropes); preparation for higher status through coaching, seeking visibility, finding sponsors, etc.
Promotions or leveling off (trans.)		Preparation, testing, passage through hierarchical boundary, rite of passage; may involve passage through functional boundary as well (rotation)
4. Second assignment Substages	Legitimate member (fully acceptable)	Process under No. 3 repeats
5. Granting of tenure	Permanent member	Passage through another inclusion boundary
Termination and exit (trans.)	Old-tmer, senior citizen	Preparation for exit, cooling the rites of exit (testimonial dinners, etc.)
6. Postexit	Alumnus, emeritus, retired	Granting of peripheral status

The work of Hall and of Schein connects the stages of one's career in an organization with the processes that might be put in place in a career guidance program to facilitate that stage. The latter reflects what will be discussed in stage 3 of this chapter. Additional input to induction or orientation goals is also found in the research of Campbell and Cellini (1981), discussed in the latter parts of Chapter 2.

What Schein's concepts and those of Campbell and Cellini, among others, illustrate is that it is not only the maxi-cycles and minicycles of individual career development that are important in career programs, but also that such career development is affected by organizational structures and expectations. Thus, different settings consist of or trigger different types of career transitions or organizational career stages. As reported elsewhere in the book, Dalton, Thompson, and Price (1977) have identified four progressive professional career stages in organizations: apprentice, colleague, mentor, and sponsor.

Hall (1976) speaks of early career, middle career, and later career stages within organizations. Schein (1978) divides the career life cycle for organizations into four stages: entry, socialization, midcareer, and later career. London and Stumpf (1986) speak of career motivation in the workplace as consisting of career resilience, career insight, and career identity. Regardless of which model one uses to explain career transition within organizations, each stage involves different activities, relationships, and psychologically related developmental tasks for different types of workers. As such, these stage requirements must lead to career guidance and counseling programs that are tailored to the characteristics of the different industrial and corporate settings in which they are to be implemented.

Super's model of Adult Career Adaptability is less concerned with the organizational context in which such adaptability unfolds and much more with the behavioral elements that need to be addressed in facilitating such adaptability. In this model, planfulness, exploration, information, decision making, and reality orientation represent the major factors or themes to which either individual career counseling or career programs might be addressed as essential elements of orientation or induction or, possibly, treatment.

Linear versus Nonlinear Career Development. One of the major issues in planning programs of career guidance, career services or career counseling is reflected in the major changes in the organization of work and in the nature of career development itself. We have used a variety of terms in this book to discuss such changes. Terms like *protean career, new career, personal flexibility,* and so on each suggest different conceptions of how persons will engage in work and how they will be required to assume responsibility for their own career development rather than expecting the organizations for whom they work to guide or manage their career paths over long-term relationships in one workplace.

One of the major changes in the relationship of individual career development and how work processes are unfolding is in the notion of linear versus nonlinear career development. During much of the last century, when the major career theories, including Super's concepts of career development, were created, the assumption was that the induction, adjustment, and implementation of work was essentially linear. Employees entered a particular job and incrementally evolved through different positions of growing responsibility until they peaked, plateaued, and finally declined and retired. That pattern assumes stable, fixed career paths and in the future it may still be descriptive of selected occupations, but for many persons the more likely scenario is that career paths will be fragmented and subject to change, career paths and mobility in the workplace will be horizontal rather than vertical, and rather than fixed long-term goals, many workers will focus on multiple, short-term objectives. Therefore, individual career development will shift from preparing persons to be career planners to preparing persons to be career strategists. However, there is not yet coherent theory to provide the specific goals or subgoals necessary for career services or career counseling to facilitate; rather there are glimpses of what is necessary.

Various observers have provided assumptions about career development in the future that are different from those that guide contemporary career theories. For example, as one considers Super's concepts of career development tasks, in large measure the life stages that are described in Super's theory are seen as age related. While Super has contended that such ages are permeable and that some persons will need to redo earlier choices by returning to exploratory behavior and reinitiating mini-stages of exploration and establishment if one loses one's job at age 40 or 50. Thus, Super would argue that while life stages can be described in an age-related set of linear, unfolding developmental tasks for many workers, such goals are not so precise and linear for all persons. Contemporary observers (e.g., Barner, 1994) would argue that workers in the future will likely need to create career plans that are flexible, with goals that are continually reassessed and contingency planning regarded as an essential component of such plans. In addition, career plans will emphasize multi-dimensionality and be clustered around several objectives that fulfill career needs at a particular point in one's life. Further, since work organizations are less likely to chart individual career directions, or promise long-term employment, individual workers will have to chart their own directions, and in this sense manage their own careers. They will need to constantly upgrade their skills to be sure they are always salable and constantly create and act on career strategies that meet their personal needs.

In such a scenario, personal flexibility will be essential and each worker, in order to be his or her own career strategist, will also need to be his or her own "futurist," constantly attending to trends in the areas of work in which they want to work, assessing changing skill needs, and constantly engaging in life-long learning activities to keep their competencies fresh and marketable. In such a changing career environment, Barner (1994) would argue that students or adults need to learn skills basic to preparing for the unfolding challenges. These include in abbreviated and paraphrased terms, the ability to carefully track the broader trends in one's field that are likely to provide growth opportunities or potential career roadblocks; develop a clear picture of one's underlying "career and lifestyle needs" and be aware of fundamental shifts in these personal needs and values"; be able to accurately benchmark one's skills against the best in one's field; monitor what one is worth in the market and how one can improve that worth; form contingency plans to cover the widest range of potential career changes including such possibilities as one's current job will be reasonably secure and offer solid promotional opportunities to such worst case scenarios as one's likelihood of being caught in a major organizational downsizing or a stock-market crash; and developing one's portable skills so that one is attractive and marketable across organizations (pp. 13–14). In such contexts, Barner suggests the need for four key survival skills: (1) *environmental scanning,* the ability to have and use professional and computer networks to identify potential employers and fact-breaking employment opportunities; (2) *portable skills,* the possessing of elastic skills, skills that are easily transferred to other workplaces, rather than skills the utility of which are narrowly confined to a particular workplace; (3) *self-management,* the ability to own one's career and manage it; and (4) *communication skills,* the ability to communicate clearly and effectively, across cultures and geographic locations, within high-stress and time-limited situations.

The concepts of Barner are echoed by other observers who have also identified the types of knowledge, attitudes, and skills needed by the worker of the future.

In Chapter 2, we addressed the elements of personal flexibility, many of which are relevant in our discussions here. It would be useful for the reader to review these elements as potential content of career programs designed to develop goals of stimulus, exploration, induction, or orientation.

There are other perspectives on content of importance to career counseling or career guidance programs as well. Such perspectives are typically for purposes other than developing career theory or the content of career counseling. Nevertheless, their insights suggest important topical areas for discussion and exploration related to a rapidly changing workplace. As we have said often in this book, anticipating and coping with change will require new sets of personal skills, personal competencies, and personal flexibilities which will be identified and absorbed into both the professional and popular literature on career counseling. Some examples follow.

Stephen R. Covey in his best-seller *The 7 Habits of Highly Effective People: Restoring the Character Ethic* (1989) includes a number of principles of human effectiveness. He sees the habits he espouses as a basic, primary internalization of correct principles upon which enduring happiness and success are based. He argues that these habits constitute a continuing process of renewal that helps one to consider their mental maps, perception of problems, character, and motives. In essence, these are also critical elements by which to navigate one's career. In abbreviated and paraphrased form, the habits of effectiveness are:

1. *Be proactive.* According to Covey, as human beings we are responsible for our own lives, our behavior is a function of our decisions, not our conditions. We can subordinate feelings to values. We have the initiative and the responsibility to make things happen.
2. *Begin with the end in mind.* Know what are your values, your aspirations, your center. Know what are your goals and priorities in life.
3. *Put things first.* Self-discipline. "The successful person has the habit of doing things failures don't like to do.... [Successful persons] don't like doing them either necessarily. But their disliking is subordinated to the strengths of their purpose" (p. 65).
4. *Think win-win.* Develop a frame of mind and heart that constantly seeks mutual benefits in all human interactions, based on the paradigm that there is plenty for everybody, that one person's success does not have to be achieved at the expense or exclusion of the success of others.

5. *Seek first to understand, then to be understood.* Diagnose what you are experiencing in your work setting before you prescribe or react impulsively.
6. *Synergize.* The whole is greater than the sum of its parts. The essence of synergy is to value differences—in others and in yourself—to respect them, to build on strengths, to compensate for weaknesses.
7. *Sharpen the Saw.* This is the essence of renewal, so that the other six habits can be possible. It means living a balanced life and expressing all four dimensions of our nature regularly and consistently in wise and balanced ways: *physical* (exercise, nutrition, stress management); *spiritual* (value clarification and commitment, study and meditation; *mental* (reading, visualizing, planning, writing; and *socio/emotional* (service, empathy, synergy, intrinsic security).

In another best-selling book of the past decade, whose dimensions somewhat overlap those espoused by Covey, Daniel Goleman (1995) has explored the notion of *Emotional Intelligence: Why It Can Matter More than IQ.* In this view, Emotional Intelligence comprises *self-awareness and impulse control, persistence, zeal and self-motivation, empathy and social deftness.* According to Goleman, these are the qualities that mark people who excel in real life: whose intimate relationships flourish, who are stars in the workplace. These are also the hallmarks of character and self-discipline, of altruism and compassion—basic capacities needed if our society is to thrive. Lack of emotional intelligence can sabotage the intellect and ruin careers. Emotional intelligence is not fixed at birth but can be nurtured and strengthened in all of us (frontispiece).

Perspectives like those of Covey and Goleman and others we cite in the book help to accent the tensions that persons experience as they try to maintain their integrity, core values, cognitive clarity, sense of security and being anchored at the same time that they are besieged by turbulent external forces, change, and challenges to their personal flexibility, their "protean self" (Lifton, 1993). Given such conflicting pressures for self awareness, environmental awareness, and the need to constantly consider alternatives or contingent strategies, we end this section with behavioral factors that have been found across Super's theoretical, research, and instrument development to describe career maturity in adolescence and career adaptability in adulthood. When combined with the perspectives of Covey, Goleman, and others, these behavioral factors constitute a frame of reference for planning for "new careers" (see Table 6.5).

Input to Treatment Program Goals. In the third emphasis in planning a career guidance or counseling program, one must often anticipate the need for treatment for some group of counselees. These are persons whose career development has been arrested or impaired or who have undergone trauma or disease sufficient to make their ability to choose or to experience work adjustment problematic. Many paradigms exist to explain such phenomena. A classic one is that of Tyler (1969), who has differentiated counseling into choice and change. The assumption is that persons who need to accomplish personality change, independence from others, and similar psychological maturity cannot deal with choice dilemmas until they resolve the more fundamental personality issues with which they are currently preoccupied. D'Alonzo and Fleming (1973) have suggested that the main psychiatric factors among employees and therefore the problems encountered in mental health programs in industry (as well as career development programs in business and industry) are as follows:

1. Improper discipline during childhood and youth
2. Job adjustment and responsibility; the need of all people to face reality with its attendant successes and failures; learning to accept criticism and to compensate for defects
3. Family problems
4. Health worries
5. Miscellaneous fears, phobias, anxieties, and so on. (p. 164)

Together these types of behavior are manifested in absenteeism, excessive turnover, alcoholism, industrial accidents, lowered productivity, and labor strikes (Dawis, 1984).

As discussed in Chapter 2, Neff (1977, 1985) and Lowman (1993) have identified several types of problem employees and the characteristics of their work psychopathology. For example, according to Neff (1985):

> Type I includes people who appear to have major lacks in work motivation; they have a negative conception of the role.

TABLE 6.5 Selected Behavioral Factors Descriptive of Career Maturity in Adolescence and Career Adaptability in Adulthood

PLANFULNESS OR TIME PERSPECTIVE

- Developing an attitude of readiness for planning a choice
- Developing an attitude of independence of choice
- Awareness of the need for choices
- Awareness of the need to crystallize a career choice
- Awareness of present-future relationships
- Awareness of immediate choices
- Awareness of intermediate choices
- Awareness of ultimate choices
- Specificity of planning

EXPLORATION

- Formation of self-concept
- Translation of self-concept into occupational terms
- Taking steps necessary to obtaining information relevant to possible next steps
- Identifying needed data
- Seeking needed data
- Identifying and using resources
- Reality-testing information obtained formulating a generalized preference
- Differentiation of aptitudes, values, and interests
- Evaluating exploratory outcomes
- Implementation of self-concept into actions related to obtaining the education or training for the preferred occupation or in finding employment in balancing life roles

INFORMATION

- Possession of information related to options available
- Acquisition of information on the world of information on the world of work, education and training, preferred occupational roles, other life-career roles
- Specificity of information of immediate and more remote concern
- Possession of information on the preferred occupation

DECISION-MAKING SKILLS

- Awareness of factors in choice and in formulating an occupational preference
- Awareness of contingency factors which affect career goals
- Identifying alternatives
- Identify outcomes and probabilities associated with options
- Evaluate and weigh old and new data
- Specification of preference
- Select preferred plan

REALITY ORIENTATION

- Acceptance of responsibility for choice and its consequences
- Reality testing of self-concept
- Ability to compromise and synthesize among available options and self-concept, social factors and aspirations
- Ability to learn from role playing and feedback
- Ego-involvement
- Personal endeavor
- Achievement motivation

These important notions that are emerging as we try to understand the rapidity and scale of change in workplaces around the world are likely to foster the creation of new taxonomies of career problems as we have discussed them in Chapters 1 and 2. Therefore, the type of content we have discussed here as planning content for career programs is also input to treatment program goals.

Type II includes individuals whose predominating response to the demand to be productive is manifest fear and anxiety.

Type III includes people who are predominantly characterized by open hostility and aggression.

Type IV includes people who are characterized by marked dependency.

Type V includes people who display a marked degree of social naivete. (pp. 238–243)

Each of these types of persons requires differential treatment typically of significant intensity as well as differences in level of supervision, information, and personality change.

On balance, neither career guidance programs nor career counseling emphasizes treatment of severe psychological problems, however they are defined. But persons with severe problems of motivation or adjustment do come to career programs and to career counselors for many reasons, including denial of the severity of their problems, because the career guidance program or counselor is the only mental health provider available or because these persons believe philosophies and activities of career counseling will be helpful to them. Therefore, the career counseling practitioner must be prepared to deal with such treatment issues or to include, in program planning, procedures by which such persons will be referred or therapists will be placed on a consultative retainer to deal with such cases as they arise.

Program Rationale for Planning. In summarizing stage 1 (developing a program rationale and philosophy), a particular school or college, corporation, or agency may synthesize from the foregoing steps a program rationale that includes such assumptions as the following:

1. Individuals can be equipped with accurate and relevant information translated into terms of personal development level and state of readiness.
2. Individuals can be assisted to formulate hypotheses about themselves, the choice points that will be in their future, and the options available to them.
3. Individuals can be helped to develop appropriate ways of testing these hypotheses against old and new experiences.
4. Individuals can be helped to come to terms with the educational and occupational relevance of what they already know or will learn about themselves and their futures.
5. Individuals can be helped to see themselves in process and to acquire the knowledge and skills that will allow them to exploit this process in positive, constructive ways.
6. Individuals acquire feelings of personal competence or power from self-understanding and the ability to choose effectively.
7. Increasingly, individuals must accept responsibility to manage their own career and to be a career strategist to meet their personal needs.

In addition, analysis of community, administrative, and consumer groups will have offered support or rejection of these assumptions and their priority in a career guidance or counseling program. Information will be acquired about whether or not the students or adults to be served by the program already possess such knowledge, skills, and behaviors or whether such outcomes need to be facilitated. As these judgments are made, they need to be translated into actual program goals and behavioral specifications for the students or adults who will be involved with the program.

Preceding the statement of program goals and behavioral objectives, most programs would typically have an introductory statement dealing in broad terms with several topics explaining "Why career guidance or career counseling?" These topics might include the following:

- Current social and occupational conditions faced by youth and adults
- Needs for career planning and other career development elements as perceived by students (adults) and community groups
- The present career guidance program
- Assumptions that guide new program thrusts
- Basic concepts of program directions

The particular content of such preliminary statements will vary from one setting to another. What is important in one setting with one type of population may not be important in another. In addition, the resources available (personnel, materials, money) to support the program as well as the amount of time the program will be in contact with the student or adult population to be served (twelve years, three years, four years, six months, three sessions) will need to be considered as the actual program goals to be adopted are decided on.

Stage 2: Stating Program Goals and Behavioral Objectives

Following the formulation of a rationale and philosophy for the career program that answers why career guidance or career counseling, or other career interventions, it is necessary to decide on what will actually constitute the program. As we have suggested in the previous section, a review of career development theory and selected popular literature will suggest many behaviors, types of knowledge, or skills that a career program might facilitate. Conducting needs assessments, analyzing resources available, and deliberating on the characteristics of the target groups to be served in a particular setting will likely reduce the many possibilities to those that constitute the most important goals for a particular program.

In stage 2 of systematic planning, the primary purpose is to translate the needs of career intervention in a particular setting, as identified in stage 1, into program goals and behavioral expectations. Such program goals and behavioral objectives are actually hypotheses saying that, if these goals are accomplished, the needs to which the career program responds in this setting will be met or reduced, consistent with individual differences manifested by persons served by the program.

Program Goals. Program goals and behavioral expectations for students or clients differ in their specificity and in their purpose. Program goals are general statements of program purposes or outcomes. Program goals should not deal with the processes by which they will be accomplished but concentrate instead on the outcomes to be achieved. Program goals should reflect the philosophy, theory, and assumptions underlying a program, as defined in stage 1 of systematic planning.

Examples of program goals in a particular setting might be as follows. As a result of the career program, all clients will be able to do the following:

1. Develop vocabulary for distinguishing self-characteristics, such as interests, aptitudes, values, roles, and self-concept.
2. Understand their unique pattern of personal characteristics (such as abilities, interests, values, attitudes, and so on).
3. Attain a positive self-concept (that is, a sense of self-respect, personal worth, and respect for one's own uniqueness).
4. Understand the variety and complexity of occupations and career opportunities available locally and within the state.
5. Understand the relationships between educational opportunities and occupational or career requirements.
6. Determine the basic characteristics and qualifications related to preparation for and performance of various occupational roles.
7. Understand the concept *lifestyle* and its relationship to career development.
8. Learn how to use a range of exploratory resources effectively.
9. Develop effective decision-making strategies and the skills necessary in carrying them out.

These goals are client-centered or student-centered. In general terms, they make explicit the career program's purposes, and they imply criteria by which their accomplishment might be judged. These are the global statements of outcomes around which the program will be structured. Decisions about behavioral expectations, processes, resource needs, and evaluative strategies will each flow from the statement of program goals.

Again, depending on the particular setting, there are many such outcome statements or goals. For example, LaVan, Mathys, and Drehmer (1983) have identified some of the outcomes expected from counseling practices provided by major American corporations. They include the following:

Career Counseling

- The retention of middle and upper levels of managers compared to some base year
- Preparation of candidates for various positions selected from within versus hired externally
- Attitude survey results indicating such dimensions as the degree of satisfaction with promotional opportunities, or the degree to which personal interest or preferences are used in selection
- The degree to which the organization's counseling activity compares to known successful systems

Although LaVan, Mathys, and Drehmer also talk about outcome indicators for outplacement counseling, personal problem counseling, retirement counseling, and alcoholism and drug counseling, those cited for career counseling within the corporate environment accent the importance of program goals being seen in terms of the expectations and outcome indicators indigenous to particular settings.

Another way to consider the development of program goals and their associated competencies and indicators is through use of the resources provided by the National Occupational Information Coordinating Committee (NOICC, 1988). In particular, the multivolume work *National Career Counseling and Development Guidelines* provides recommended competencies and indicators for each competency for elementary schools, middle/junior high schools, high schools, postsecondary institutions, and human service agencies. The competencies represent general goals, and the indicators represent specific knowledge, skills, and attitudes that individuals should master to deal effectively with lifelong career development tasks. The competencies at each level are consistent with the general developmental capabilities of individuals at that level, and studies (Freeman, 1994) have indicated that counselors view this content as important to very important, particularly at the elementary through the secondary level.

Program goals, as we describe them, could be extrapolated from competencies as described by the National Occupational Information Coordinating Committee before it was disbanded in 2000. To illustrate how such goals might appear for young adults across the three areas of emphasis included in the Guidelines referenced previously, the following goals could be cited:

- Career planning and exploration
  Skills in making decisions about educational and career goals
  Understanding of the impact of careers on individual and family life
  Skills in developing career plans
- Self-knowledge
  Maintenance of a positive view of self in terms of potential and preferences and assessment of their transferability to the world of work
  Ability to assess self-defeating behaviors and reduce their impact on career decision
- Educational/vocational development
  Ability to relate educational and occupational preparation to career opportunities
  Skills for locating, evaluating and interpreting information about career opportunities
  Skills for seeking, obtaining, keeping, and advancing on a job

Program goals might also be written to address the challenges of preparing persons to be career strategists. They might include:

- *Environmental Scanning.* Locate on the Internet a minimum of 10 web sites that focus on building professional and computer networks by which to identify changing employment trends in specific occupations of relevance to you.
- *Portable Skills.* Inventory your performance and context skills and identify which are elastic or portable across at least five occupations, career paths, or position descriptions.
- *Self-Management Skills.* Develop a portfolio of experiences or roles in which you have taken responsibility for the management of your career, anticipating and acquiring new skills, and formulating contingency plans related to short-term goals.
- Cite at least five short-term career objectives to be achieved in less than five years, suggest the cluster of activities by which they could be achieved, and a contingency plan to follow if your preferred activities are not possible.

Behavioral Objectives. Behavioral objectives, as compared to program goals, are more specific expressions of behavior. The specifying of statements of behavioral expectations for students or clients that underlie program goals is one of the most difficult aspects of systematic planning. It necessitates making value judgments of what people ought to be able to achieve, and it requires describing these in behavioral terms. Further, it frequently requires a range of behavioral expectations underlying each program goal so that individual differences in readiness or experience can be recognized.

As compared with program goals, behavioral statements for clients or students should describe observable performance or behaviors—outcomes that describe what individuals will be able to do, not what will be done to them (Mager, 1997). Program goals are usually stated so broadly that it is difficult to know when an employee or student has reached them, but behavioral objectives are measurable. Writing objectives require you to think of the performances that indicate that the program goal has been reached. In addition to writing objectives that are likely to be important to all consumers of the career intervention program, it is always important to remain flexible enough to accommodate individual objectives of a crisis nature or those that do not fit directly within the planned program emphases.

Approaches to Writing Objectives. The current emphases in objective development stress the important of defining the outcomes of career guidance in terms of observable human performance, citing the conditions under which they should be demonstrated, and determining the standard or criterion of success. Within this context, there are several ways of stating objectives based on different purposes. A major approach is that provided by the NOICC.

The frame of reference used by the NOICC's *National Career Counseling and Development Guidelines,* cited under the section on program goals, proceeds from competencies (program goals) to indicators (behavioral objectives). For example, one might use as an illustration the second competency under the area of self-knowledge, "Ability to assess self-defeating behaviors and reduce their impact on career decisions." According to the NOICC Guidelines, the indicators (behavioral objectives) important for a young adult to reach such a competency are as follows:

1. Identify symptoms of stress, fear, anxiety, avoidance, and ambivalence and apply coping strategies to deal with these.
2. Identify strategies for reducing discriminating attitudes and behaviors.
3. Recognize the symptoms of depression in self and others and identify sources of assistance.
4. Identify disadvantages of sex-role stereotyping and assess his or her behavior in relation to both women and men.
5. Develop behaviors, attitudes, and skills that contribute to the elimination of stereotyping and bias in education, family, and work environment.
6. Develop skills to manage resources.

The reader will note that the indicators (or behavioral objectives) used as examples do not describe broad, general career development goals as do program goals. Rather, these indicators describe specific attitudes, knowledge, and skills that students or adults need to develop the competencies or program goals to which the indicators are related. As such, they describe the outcomes sought and can be wedded to standards that identify the conditions under which they will take place. For example, when merged with a standard, the first indicator cited might be rewritten in this way:

1. Identify ten symptoms of stress, fear, anxiety avoidance, and ambivalence and present a fifteen-minute lecturette on coping strategies to deal with these symptoms.

This form of writing behavioral objectives is consistent with the history of writing behavioral objectives in its emphasis on the skill or behavior involved, the domain of concern, and some standard by which to judge whether the intended behavior has been achieved.

Obviously, each career program needs to develop independently a set of operationally stated objectives to guide its program's effort in fostering career development in the students or clients for whom it is responsible. The particular objectives developed will reflect the clients' characteristics as well as the available resources. Measures of individual performance of these objects will also be necessary. In schools, agencies, business or industrial settings, or other settings in which career interventions are implemented, in which there is great variability in the personal histories of the students or the clients, it will also be necessary to assess the degree to which individuals or groups can already perform the behavior. Finally, as such a system is implemented, it will be necessary to evaluate continuously whether the career guidance activities designed to accomplish the objectives are actually bringing about changes in the behavior of the persons exposed to them.

With the rise of career education in 1971, many efforts were undertaken to formulate models of tasks that persons need to perform to master the many elements constituting career-mature behavior.

For example, in 1990 the Florida Department of Education's *Blueprint for Career Preparation* described a six-year action plan that began in 1988. That "blueprint" included the following six steps:

1. Begin in kindergarten through fifth grade by developing in students an awareness of self, the value of work, and exposure to careers and technology.
2. By grade six, students—with the help of their teachers and parents—should assess personal aptitudes, abilities and interests, and relate them to careers. They should also learn the role of technology in the world of work.
3. In grades seven and eight, students should set career-oriented goals and develop four-year career plans for grades nine through twelve. These plans may change as they are reviewed annually, but it sets students on a course and provides a basis for curriculum selection. It also gets parents involved.

4. During high school, a new "applied curriculum" will make academic concepts relevant to the workplace, especially in communications, math, and science. Vocational courses are coordinated with academic instruction.
5. Students choosing postsecondary education programs should be able to gain employment successfully, advance within their fields, or change occupations. These programs include vocational technical centers, community colleges, and universities.
6. Educators should intensify efforts to share information and to involve parents, business, and the entire community in this process. Partnerships and the involvement of people beyond educators are critically important. (p. 4)

To monitor the progress of the state and the schools involved toward such goals, these six steps or program goals have sample competencies associated with them. For example, under Step 1, self-awareness and career awareness for grades kindergarten through five, the sample competencies include the following:

- Acquiring knowledge of the importance of a positive self-concept to career development.
- Developing skills for interacting with others
- Becoming aware of the importance of emotional and physical development in career decision making
- Acquiring an awareness of the interrelationship of lifestyles and careers
- Becoming aware of changing occupational roles for males and females (p. 9)

Given the goals of personal assessment and technological literacy in grade six, the sample competencies encompass the following:

- Developing and using a positive self-concept for career development
- Understanding the emotional and physical development required for proactive career decision making
- Understanding the value of personal responsibility, good work habits, and planning for career opportunities
- Comprehending the significance of technology in the world of work
- Identifying career opportunities in the field of technology
- Demonstrating technological literacy (p. 10)

Similar sample competencies are identified for each of the other steps in the career preparation blueprint. These, in turn, are wedded to activities and processes that meet the overarching or ultimate goal for the plan, that "students graduating from Florida's public schools shall be prepared to begin a career and continue their education at a postsecondary technical school, community college or university" (p. 9).

Business and industry as well as various government agencies have begun to introduce career development systems that use the types of program goal statements and behavioral objectives cited in the previous examples. Specificity of the goals and behavioral statements is frequently less elaborate, but the general models are similar. For example, Leibowitz and Schlossberg (1981) have identified a framework from which career planning skills can be identified, defined, and operationalized. These skills are arranged in stages of importance to both employees and managers. As such, they can serve as the planning framework for training workshops or for the development of career guidance programs in which managers have a major role. For each of the cells of this model, specific behavioral objectives can be defined and specific strategies identified to accomplish such goals. Table 6.6 presents the planning model proposed by Leibowitz and Schlossberg for industry.

Many other models of systematic planning could be identified here. Virtually all states and many industries and government agencies have now developed such approaches to career education and career guidance. These many examples offer a pool of goals and objectives from which one might select those appropriate to a given setting and, most importantly, to the conceptual framework for career guidance that one develops in stage 1 of one's planning.

In summary of stage 2 in systematic planning, a few points need reinforcement:

1. The specification of program goals and behavioral objectives for students or clients should not occur in a vacuum. These program directions should flow from a conceptual framework and a needs assessment pertinent to the local educational or agency setting.

TABLE 6.6 Career Planning Process Model

	STAGE 1	STAGE 2	STAGE 3
Employee responsibility	Explore	Understand	Take action
Manager responsibility	Listen Support	Identify Clarify	Select strategy Communicator Counselor Appraiser
Manager roles required	Communicator Counselor	Communicator Appraiser	Coach Mentor Advisor Referral Agent Advocate

2. Behavioral objectives provide an inventory of possible emphases that can help a counselor and counselee define what problems or skill deficits should be worked on.
3. Depending on the form in which behavioral objectives are written, both the career interventions to facilitate them and the criteria on which they might be evaluated can be specified.

Stage 3: Selecting Alternative Program Processes

The major problems in systematic planning for career programs occur in stages 1 and 2—deciding what needs exist, developing a conceptual framework for the program, and translating such insights into program and performance goals. Once the directions for the program are specified, it is then necessary to identify those processes that can facilitate the identified goals.

A major question in selecting program processes in relation to either program goals or performance objectives is what behavior is intended. The second question is what processes might facilitate these behaviors: individual counseling? group career development? work-study? behavior modification? values clarification? role-playing? the use of computer-assisted career guidance programs or the internet? It is conceivable that any one of these processes or many other acceptable techniques might be useful. It is necessary, however, to decide which available technique or process is likely to be the best. Viewed in this context, any career intervention or process must be considered a means to an end. It must also be evaluated in terms of the time available, resources required, competencies of personnel available, costs involved, and other such criteria as are appropriate in a particular setting. Table 6.7 suggests examples of the broad range of techniques or processes that could be used to facilitate career development and from which decisions can be made in relation to different program goals or behavioral objectives.

Hypothetical examples of how program goals, performance objectives, and activities or techniques can be presented for planning purposes follow (Table 6.8). A longitudinal program would include goals, behavioral objectives, activities, and evaluation methods arranged at different educational levels or within sequences appropriate to a particular agency or corporate constituency. Obviously a total program would include more goals than are identified here, but the essence of their formulation is reflected in the examples given. Again, it should be noted that any format may be used in a systematic approach to programming, as long as it is structurally sound and contains objectives consistent with the experiences required by those served by the program.

Table 6.9 is a further example of how expected student competencies developed as part of a comprehensive set of program goals can be tied to expected

TABLE 6.7 Examples of Techniques to Facilitate Career Development

Films	Career support groups for women or minorities
Discussions	Pre-retirement counseling
Developing bulletin boards	Role play
Making occupational role books	Job analyses
Creating listings of characteristics of self in relation to educational and occupational alternatives	Debate
Analyzing expectations of work	Interview: workers, employers, employment service counselors, college admissions people, postsecondary AVTS personnel
Collecting newspaper articles or magazine stories	Gaming
Writing short themes	Test interpretations
Developing games about interests	Making posters
Self-ratings	Contrast or compare characteristics of work or education
Field trips	Career library research
Resource people	Keep personal records for purpose of analysis
Examination of want ads	Publishing newspaper about career development concerns
Work samples	Doing follow-up study
Work study	Shadowing workers
Part-time work	Mentoring
Panels of recent graduates in different work or educational settings	Apprenticeships
Profile census data	Work study
Individual counseling	Internships
Testing	Computer-assisted career guidance programs
Group career counseling	Career guidance curriculum
Social modeling	Career awareness programs
Desensitization	Work simulations
Seminars on career paths/career ladders	Job search training
Peer discussion groups for women and minorities	Relaxation tapes
Career path publications	Job training clubs
In-house career counselors	Behavioral rehearsal
Reading biographies	Interview skills training
Formulating a written career development plan	Career resource center
Completing genograms of occupations held by extended family members or ancestors	Skills inventory—job matching system
Defining terms	On-the-job training
Committees	Job rotation
Assessment centers	School-to-work transition services
Selected Internet sites	Outplacement
Workshops on selected career topics	

counselor functions to facilitate these competencies. This model includes how counselors might function individually to facilitate the specific student competency at issue or how they may work with other staff or with staff and other resources to accomplish a particular outcome. One example each from many provided in the program model is drawn from the elementary, the middle school/junior high school, and the high school level to demonstrate the approach.

Stage 4: Developing an Evaluation Design

Although stages 1 and 2 of systematic planning require the most deliberation and compromise among

TABLE 6.8 Examples of Presenting Program Goals, Performance Objectives, and Activities/Techniques

NINTH-GRADE PROGRAM IN SELF-AWARENESS AND CAREER AWARENESS

PROGRAM GOAL	SUBGOAL	PERFORMANCE OBJECTIVES	CAREER INTERVENTIONS
1. To increase individual self-awareness	1.A. Reinforce awareness of one's strengths	1.A.1. The student will be able to give, in front of a group, a 5–10 minute oral description of himself or herself as if his or her best friend were describing him or her for membership in a club	1.A.1. The counselor will introduce a group discussion on the various components of a person (e.g., physical, emotional) and how these form a self-concept
		1.A.2. The student is able to write a two-page report for the counselor describing how his or her three greatest strengths have helped in situations with people within the previous two weeks	1.A.2. The counselor will explain the concept of a personal journal and its place during the entire course. The students will begin theirs with a one-page reaction of their feelings about the assignment

VOCATIONAL REHABILITATION IN A REGIONAL CORRECTIONAL FACILITY

PROGRAM GOAL	BEHAVIORAL OBJECTIVES	CAREER INTERVENTIONS
1. To help the client use available educational and occupational information for formulation of tentative vocational goals	1.A.1. The client can verbalize a basic understanding of the personal and situational factors and decisions that shaped her work history	1.A.1.1. Group sessions with a counselor
	1.A.2. From the "help wanted" columns in regional newspapers the client can identify jobs that (1) she or he is prepared for now, (2) could probably do with some remedial education and/or vocational training, and (3) are probably out of reach	1.A.2.1. Test and interest inventory results interpreted and discussed in individual counseling sessions 1.A.2.2. Use of career information kits and occupational briefs adapted to client's reading level 1.A.2.3. Use of tape recording of job descriptions, films, and displays to reach those clients with low reading levels
	1.A.3. In a gaming situation, the client can identify future decisions that must be made to reach the tentative goal he has set	1.A.3. Department-made adult game adapted from the life-career game

A COLLEGE PROGRAM FOR RETURNING WOMEN STUDENTS

PROGRAM GOAL	BEHAVIORAL OBJECTIVES	CAREER INTERVENTIONS
1. To help student develop decision-making skills	1.A.1. The student will identify and assess specific reasons for selecting a particular course of study or career choice	1.A.1.1. Role play the decision-making paradigm in regard to an interview with a department head about reasons for choosing a course of study

(continued)

TABLE 6.8 Continued

A COLLEGE PROGRAM FOR RETURNING WOMEN STUDENTS		
PROGRAM GOAL	**BEHAVIORAL OBJECTIVES**	**CAREER INTERVENTIONS**
		1.A.1.2. Discussion groups to provide support for decisions being made and carried out. Groups will challenge, suggest, foster, and support decisions 1.A.1.3. Taped interviews with representatives of various curricula will be considered in terms of placement record, role expectations, content in various courses of study

BUSINESS AND INDUSTRY		
PROGRAM GOAL	**BEHAVIORAL OBJECTIVES**	**CAREER INTERVENTIONS**
1. To help employee achieve desired job or career change	1.A. The employee will be able to identify the career change resources available in the Counseling/Career Planning, Education/Training and Job Opportunities units of the corporation	1.A.1. Provide the employee with a copy of organizational chart of major career change mechanisms available in the company. Discuss the functions of each component and what services are available in each unit 1.A.2. Have the employee identify intermediate career goals and identify the company provisions for job information and job transfer, programs of education and training provided, and career planning workshops available on topics of personal interest
2. To increase employee's awareness of career paths and placement of information	2.A. The employee will understand the use of career paths for personnel classification steps, placement, and mobility within the company	2.A.1. Lunchtime discussions will be held with all employees to acquaint them with use of career path charts in their department as well as open job listing, personnel networks, and replacement planning Representatives of the training section will identify the various training opportunities available to support different career path moves

the different directions a career development program might take, stage 4, the evaluation stage, seems to be the most threatening to many counselors. Apparently, some counselors equate evaluation with some highly sophisticated and esoteric skills beyond their ability to comprehend. Such a perspective is incorrect but widely held.

Gysbers and Henderson (1988) have stated in a direct and simple manner: "The purpose of evaluation is to provide data to make decisions about the structure and impact of the program and the professional personnel involved" (p. 263). In other observations Henderson and Gysbers (1998) contend that "planning involves assessing the needs of students

TABLE 6.9 Wisconsin Developmental Guidance Program

COMPETENCIES	LEVEL I COUNSELOR	LEVEL II COUNSELOR AND STAFF	LEVEL III COUNSELOR, STAFF, AND OTHER RESOURCES
Elementary School			
Acquire knowledge about different occupations and changing male/female roles	Provide occupational information to be used by all teachers as a classroom resource	Coordinate efforts to have a variety of people speak to classes about their nontraditional occupations	Provide mentorships for students who are interested in specific occupations
Middle/Junior High			
Understand decision-making skills	Work with students who exhibit an inability to make decisions	Carry out decision-making and problem-solving activities for groups and classes	Provide staff development on how decision making can be incorporated into all curricular areas
High School			
Develop the interpersonal skills necessary for harmony in the workplace	Counsel students displaying a lack of interpersonal skills	Do group work or team teaching to discuss how inter-personal skills are required for harmony in the workplace	Do staff development on how interpersonal skills are essential for all students as they enter the world of work

Source: Wisconsin Department of Public Instruction, 1986.

and other program clients against the vision and mission established for the program.... Evaluation is conducted in the context of the assessed needs, the program design, and the implementation plans" (p. 59). Obviously, then, evaluation cannot occur unless it is effectively planned. Nor can it occur if we are not clear about the goals we wish to accomplish or the ways these will be measured. If we have completed the stages of the systematic planning process outlined earlier in this chapter, the goals and the behavioral objectives the program seeks to accomplish should be clear. The question we need to raise now is, what evidence will we accept that the goals or objectives have been met? Some possibilities might include the following:

- Ratings of student, employee, or client performance by teachers, parents, counselors, or employers
- Judgments by experts of whether program goals have been met
- Follow-up studies of how students, employees, or clients plan, apply decision-making skills, and make accurate self-estimates after exposure to career guidance
- Scales of student or client attitude about themselves or career exploration or work
- Staff reaction sheets about changes in student or client behavior during or after a career guidance program
- Student or client opinion of how their behavior has been changed or improved as a result of career counseling or other career interventions
- Observations of student or client understandings and skills in role playing or actual situations
- Changes in school attendance, work punctuality, or other quantitative indices related to career program goals
- Scores on published standardized instruments:
  Assessment of Career Development
  Career Maturity Inventory
  Career Decision Scale
  Career Development Inventory
  Readiness for Vocational Planning
  Adult Career Concerns Survey
  My Vocational Situation

These instruments measure different aspects of personal knowledge about career development behaviors with regard to (1) what the person *knows about* personal attributes, occupational information, job selection, course and curriculum selection, school and career problem solving; (2) what the person *has done* in regard to involvement in career planning activities, involvement in a wide range of worker activities, involvement in activities related to preferred occupation(s); and (3) one's attitudes, preferences, and perceptions with regard to self, work, and information resources. For a comprehensive analysis of the specific content of each of these instruments, with regard to the emphases cited, see Kapes and Whitfield (2001) or the most recent *Mental Measurements Yearbook.* There are also other published instruments dealing with work values, interests, and planning that are pertinent to evaluation and that will be discussed in Chapter 15.

The basic point to be made here is that the type of evaluation and the resulting data will differ in accordance with the setting and the type of behavior being assessed. It depends on what the program goals are, what types of energy and personnel time can be committed to evaluation, what fiscal support is available for evaluation, and what evaluative competencies exist in the career counseling staff or can be obtained from outside experts.

A system of evaluation is concerned with whether the total program is meeting its goals, typically referred to as summative or product evaluation; and whether the individual processes or activities designed to accomplish particular goals or behavioral objectives are doing so effectively or more effectively than other possible processes or activities, typically referred to as formative or process evaluation.

Put in a simplistic way, summative or product evaluation requires that you have data about student, employee, or client performances in areas related to program goals before the career development program or procedure was implemented and similar data about the students or clients after the career intervention effort. This is necessary so that you can judge what changes took place, whether they were sufficient to justify the program, and what they mean for future program efforts. Summative or product evaluation is essentially concerned with the aggregate effects of the program in terms of its goals, rather than how well specific techniques or activities contributed to such outcomes.

Process evaluation is usually concerned with more experimentally oriented questions than is product evaluation. It seeks answers to whether individual behavioral objectives are met effectively by the techniques related to them, whether particular activities are more effective with some subgroups rather than others, and which program techniques or activities are most effective for what purposes with what groups.

The NOICC (1988) depicts the evaluation process and its inclusion of process or product evaluation, as well as the uses of evaluation results in programs related to students, as shown in Figure 6.1.

Lombana (1985) has extended the viewpoint expressed previously by discussing empirical and perceptual evaluation procedures. In doing so, she has created a two-by-two figure that has four quadrants contrasting client objectives with program objectives and empirical evaluation with perceptual evaluation. In her perspective, empirical measures assess whether or not a given objective was accomplished, whereas perceptual measures allow one to determine how the counselors' efforts were viewed by others. Program or client objectives can be measured through either empirical or perceptual evaluation, depending on what information is being sought for whom and for what purpose. Such a conceptual model is useful in sharpening the questions that need to be addressed in stage 4, developing an evaluation design, in the systematic planning model. Figure 6.2 portrays the quadrants and questions included in each as proposed by Lombana.

Regardless of whether the intent is to evaluate the products or the processes of career guidance, there is a logical sequence of steps that should be undertaken:

1. *Identifying goals and stating objectives.* This step has been covered sufficiently in this chapter so it will not be discussed further here.

2. *Choosing criterion measurements.* This is a crucial step. After evaluation criteria have been identified—goals for the program and objectives for the processes—ways of measuring them must be identified or devised. Criteria differ in the precision with which they can be measured. Commercially published instruments are available that can be used to evaluate some career program goals; for other goals, locally devised rating scales, self-reports, ob-

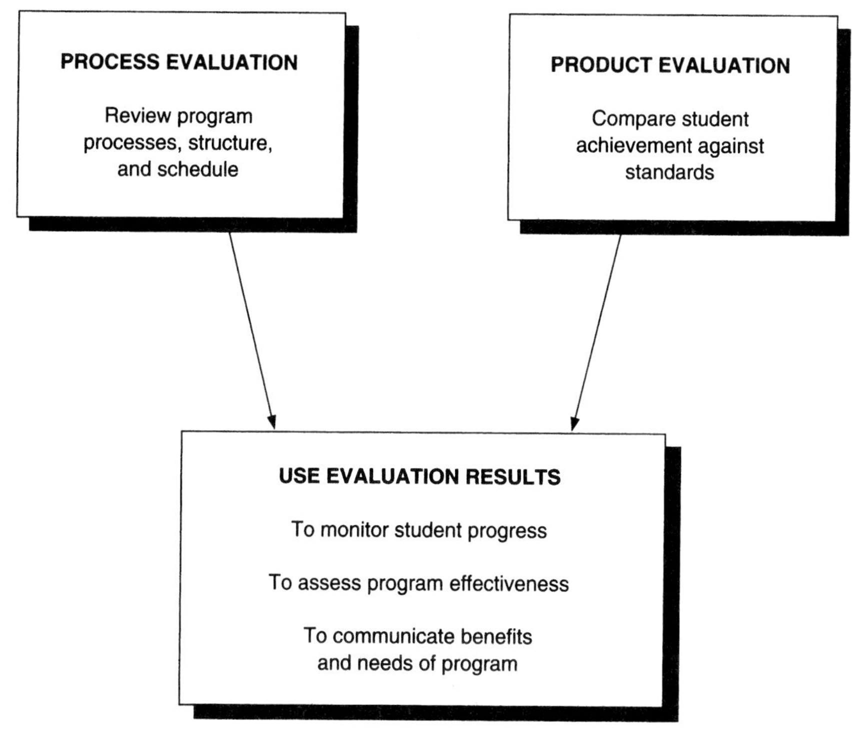

FIGURE 6.1 NOICC Evaluation Process

servations, and questionnaires will have to suffice. The point of overriding importance is ensuring that whatever information is gathered is clearly relevant to what the program goals and objectives are, not something else.

3. *Establishing levels of performance or standards.* It is necessary to decide at an individual or a group level of performance what is acceptable. From an individual standpoint, this may mean deciding, for each program goal, how many behaviors (1, 3, 5) must be successfully demonstrated or how many examples (1, 5, 10) must be listed, labeled, or otherwise shown within a particular behavior. From a group standpoint, it may be necessary to decide that some percentage of persons meet some portions of objectives (at least 70 percent of the group will complete 75 percent of the required objectives) for the project to be considered successful. There is no magical formula here. The judgment will likely be a judgment of what might be a reasonable improvement over baseline data.

4. *Specifying program elements.* In summative evaluation, the boundaries of the career development program need to be identified. The question is what specific elements in an agency, a school, a corporation, or a college are considered to comprise the career development program effort. By considering this question carefully, we can reassess the validity of the career program goals and reinforce their distinctiveness from those being carried on by other parts of the agency or institution in which the career guidance program is located.

In process evaluation, the critical issue is identifying the behavioral objectives or goals for which a particular intervention or technique is being done. How do these differ for different program processes? Do all the techniques or activities implemented have clear purposes in client or student behavior or are they being done for their own sake?

5. *Designing the evaluation.* This step is analogous to planning the preparations for a trip. It involves laying

Four Types of Accountability Procedures

	EMPIRICAL EVALUATION		
	I Primary Question: Did the counselor accomplish the task identified in the objective?	III Primary Question: Did the students (or other clients) change their behavior as a result of the counselor's efforts?	
PROGRAM OBJECTIVES	II Primary Question: How effective was the counselor's accomplishment, as perceived by others?	IV Primary Question: How effective were student (or other client) behavior changes as perceived by others?	CLIENT OBJECTIVES

FIGURE 6.2 Four Types of Accountability Procedures
Source: From Judy H. Lombana, Guidance accountability: A new look at an old problem. *School Counselor, 82*(5), 340–346. Copyright © 1980 AACD. Reprinted with permission.

out the data collection format and identifying the persons who will participate. The specific questions to be considered include the following:

a. Who will be involved? Will the career counseling staff conduct the evaluation alone? Will outside experts, state agency personnel, or some other group be involved in collecting or analyzing information? What amount of staff time is available for evaluative efforts, and how will other responsibilities be covered?

b. Sampling: From whom and about whom should information be obtained? What size groups will be involved? How can we ensure that the data we collect are representative of the persons about whose behavior we are most concerned?

c. Timing: When will information about the products or processes of career interventions be collected? Continuously? Immediately when a student or client completes an encounter with a career guidance activity? Six months after a person finishes his career guidance experience? At random times? Such decisions obviously affect the amount of effort which the evaluation process will require, what kinds of questions can be raised, how comprehensive the design will be.

6. *Collecting data.* How will the desired information be obtained? Questionnaires? Interviews? Observations? Commercial instruments? Will these instruments be purchased or developed locally? How much lead-time will be required to get these things accomplished before evaluation can begin? Can the information be machine scored or coded to protect confidentially? Does the content of the data collection instruments clearly relate to the goals and objectives (criteria) to be evaluated?

7. *Analyzing data.* How you analyze the information you collect depends on the kind of information you collect. Are the data ranked or on an interval scale? Do you have baseline data about students or clients for comparison purposes with post-career program information about these persons? Do you need between-group or within-group comparisons? The form of the information collected, the purpose of the evaluation, the research skill of the evaluator, and the time and money devoted to the evaluation will each affect the kind of information analysis that needs to be undertaken. Some people equate evaluation with statistics. Different statistical methods do help you summarize numerical information and, to be used appropriately, these methods each require particular types of information. For many purposes, simple comparisons by frequency count, percentages, or graphic representation (pie chart, bar graph) will be adequate to answer the evaluation questions. In other situations, correlation, analysis of variance or covariance, or path analysis may be more appropriate.

8. *Interpreting data.* Although statistical treatment of data can provide answers to many kinds of questions, the meaning of these answers becomes a matter of value judgment by someone or some group. The findings may be that 70 percent of the program goals were met for 60 percent of the persons involved. That is a statistical fact, but is it an acceptable indicator of program quality? Does it point to areas of needed program improvement? How does it compare with the characteristics of persons before the program began? The meanings of these questions are not matters of statistics but matters of counselor or administrative judgment—the ultimate substance of evaluation. As a part of systematic planning, it is important to know who will make such judgments and for what purposes.

9. *Reporting and using data.* Evaluating a career development program or a specific intervention always implies that the results may signal the need for change or a clearer indication of the status of the counselor's or the program's accountability. In either case, it is likely that administrators, boards of education, corporate boards of directors, trustees, and legislators will need to be apprised of the outcomes of the evaluation process. Although these persons may be influential in deciding on personnel, facilities, resources, or program directions, they may have little understanding of either career development or research. Therefore, the information collected and its analyses, no matter how complex, must be put into terms that these decision-makers can understand. Pictures, graphs, slides, and a clearly presented verbal report are typically preferred over statistics to convey essential information about career guidance to those who need to know. If handled effectively, such approaches represent major methods of communication, public relations, and accountability to the counselor's various publics. The major focus of evaluation here is on assessing a program's impact in such a way that decision makers can consider how much support to provide it in the future and what changes need to be made. Nevertheless, it is important to note that the basic data on which evaluative judgments are based are also important as feedback to the individual, so that insights pertinent to career maturation can be gained.

The evaluation stage constitutes a feedback loop in systematic planning of career guidance programs. It both provides insight into whether the program is meeting its goals and provides the base for action to improve the program. Although frequently treated as a step apart from program development, as suggested in this chapter and by a growing number of other observers, evaluation is integral to and a pervasive part of program development (Neukrug, Barr, Hoffman, & Kaplan, 1993).

Cost-Benefit Issues. To an increasing degree, administrators and other policy-makers are asking about the cost-benefit ratios or the cost-effectiveness of career development programs or specific interventions. These questions introduce new issues: Not only how well does the program work but at what cost? Are the outcomes worth the cost? What is the most effective treatment for a given career problem? What is the least expensive way to deliver this most effective intervention, treatment, or program? While cost-benefit analysis in career development programs are relatively rare, directors of career programs should consider collecting data on the time and resources interventions require, their costs, and their outcomes. Such information not only will enrich evaluations but is likely to become a required part of human services program evaluations, including career services, in the future (Yates, 1996).

In many ways, cost-benefit analyses are awaiting specific models of how to measure the various costs associated with delivery of career interventions (e.g., direct expenditures, capital costs, opportunity costs) and the benefits that accrue to implementation of these career interventions (e.g., short-term, long-term). At this point, in the development of cost-benefit analysis, it is much easier to identify the costs of delivering a career development program or career interventions than to identify the benefits likely to have been achieved as a direct and immediate result of the program and, particularly, later in the future. While, as stated above, the application of cost-benefit analyses of career services is still rare, it is not rare to see such expectations voiced in public policy supporting the prevision of career services. After reviewing the public policies and legislation of seventeen nations, Herr (2001) reported that the national papers reflect policy concerns for cost effectiveness in the implementation of career interventions to address a variety of sociopolitical purposes: facilitate human capital development, reduce unemployment, provide for the transition to work of special populations. But, in general, the national papers also suggested that the implementation of cost-benefit analyses as a national strategy has not become an *empirical* process, but rather a *presumptive* process; presumptive in the sense that economic and social benefits are expected to flow from the implementation of career services, although such hypotheses have not been tested. Thus, at this stage in the evaluation of career services most national policy papers tend to place their accent on *maximizing* the cost-effectiveness of career services rather than *demonstrating* the cost-effectiveness of career services. In this sense, national policies *presume* benefits to clients as defined in a wide range of expressed reasons for offering career services and for the development of practitioners to function across settings, population types, age levels, etc. However, again there are few reported efforts to empirically validate these presumptions. In an age of accountability and increased concern about most effective use of limited resources, it is likely that national policies and other types of support for career interventions across the life span will find it increasingly important to move from the assumption of important benefits from career services to their demonstrated results in cost-benefit terms. Although space limitations preclude a comprehensive review of cost-benefit analytic procedures, the reader may find it useful to review Swisher (2001).

Stage 5: Milestones

The last stage of systematic planning is really an adjunct to the other four stages. It is the specifying of critical times when major events must take place if the career guidance program is to become functional, or different, or evaluated at some specified time. In simple terms, milestones can be considered the time frame for the implementation of the planned program.

Let us assume that a school district, college, or corporation has totally reconstructed its career guidance priorities and developed a planned program that is due to begin in September. It is now the previous December and the four stages of systematic planning have been accomplished. We are now beginning stage 5, the specification of the things that must happen if the career program is going to become operational in September. What schedule of events should we consider? Some examples might include the following:

Milestones

February 15—Develop an inventory of all equipment and resources that need to be ordered for the career guidance program.

March 1—Complete all purchase orders for resource and equipment needs. Begin assembling an in-service package to be presented to all staff involved in the career guidance program.

March 15—Schedule presentations on program progress for administrative group and board of directors in May.

March 20—Identify evaluation instruments that need to be purchased and order them.

April 15—Complete in-service package. Schedule in-service presentations in early June.

May 15—Present orientation to program progress for administrators and directors.

June 15—Complete in-service of career guidance staff, community representatives, and instructional staff or first-line managers to goals, objectives, processes, and evaluative design for the career guidance program.

July 1—Check on the status of resources and equipment purchases. Follow-up on missing items.

July 15—Check on the availability of evaluative instruments. Meet with consultant personnel to finalize rating scale satisfaction inventory, or other such services.

August 1—Assemble a public information package for news media and institutional publication. Describe the needs for the program, its goals and objectives, and when it will be implemented.

September 1–10—Collect baseline data on how students, clients, and employees currently stand on behavioral expectations (knowledge, attitudes, skills) underlying program goals.

September 15—Implement program.

These are possible milestones that need to be met before a program is implemented. In many instances, these milestones would be more detailed or there would be more milestones to accomplish. On implementation, another set of milestones pertaining to data collection, analysis, and interpretation would need to be followed for the first year of operation. Both the milestones and the events described are changeable. Nevertheless, systematic planning is aided by using milestones. In the last analysis, that is the central point of this chapter—to demonstrate the need for systematic planning and the incorporation of the techniques that will facilitate it.

SUMMARY

In this chapter, we have proposed that the systematic or strategic planning of a career development or career counseling program occurs in five stages: (1) developing a program philosophy, (2) specifying program goals and behavioral objectives, (3) selecting alternative program processes, (4) describing evaluation procedures, and (5) identifying milestones. In each of these stages, a number of questions and decisions must be dealt with. We have discussed examples of each of these stages and the types of content appropriate to them. We have also suggested the emerging importance of cost-benefit analyses of career development programs as part of program evaluation.

CHAPTER SEVEN

Career Development in the Elementary School

KEY CONCEPTS

- Career-related learning in the elementary school involves systematic provision of knowledge and skills throughout the curriculum and extensive cooperation of teachers and counselors.
- Career guidance in the elementary school is not intended to force children to make premature choices but to avoid premature closure of future options.
- Major emphases of career development in the elementary school are on positive attitudes toward self and opportunities, feelings of competence, and ways in which school experiences can be used to explore and prepare for the future.
- There are relationships between work habits and attitudes developed in the elementary school and work habits in adulthood.
- Parental influence on children's career development is a major variable in the provision of career guidance in the elementary school.
- Career guidance programs in the elementary school can be planned and sequenced to respond to the changing developmental characteristics of elementary school children.

Career-related learning in the elementary school is not a new addition to the elementary school curriculum. In an important sense, such learning, whether identified as career guidance or by another term, makes explicit what has been implicit in elementary schools in the United States and in other parts of the world. Self-knowledge, knowledge of future educational and occupational alternatives, and development of rudiments of decision making by students generally have been considered as important ingredients of both elementary school philosophy and practice. So have other elements of awareness and knowledge that are increasingly being identified as significantly related to positive career development in adolescence and adulthood, including such contemporary topics as emotional intelligence (Goleman, 1995), self-efficacy outcome expectations and goals (Lent, Hackett, & Brown, 1999), and the reconceptualization of the elements of vocational exploration (Flum & Blustein, 2000).

Elementary teachers have for decades been instinctively aware of the need for children to deal with self-awareness and awareness of their community and its opportunities. For example, most readers will remember the efforts of kindergarten or first-grade teachers to have their students role play different workers in the school or community—fire fighters, teachers, police officers, store clerks, medical personnel, postal workers—by wearing hats or other clothing, and possibly displaying tools, that represented the work these people did. The intent of such exercises was and is to help students begin to appreciate the multitude of different jobs that make a school or a community function, the variety of ways work is performed, to stimulate students' interests in the types of opportunities from which they will select in the future, the different subject matter that is important in different jobs, and how people choose what they want to do.

These kinds of exercises occur frequently in elementary schools, but they are often the initiative of a particular teacher rather than identified as career guidance or related systemically to other career learning occurring in a particular elementary school. According to McGowan and Law (2000) career-related learning in primary schools is widespread in England, although not necessarily referred to by teachers in career terms. McGowan and Law identify a variety of examples of learning in British primary schools that have career relevance. They include in abridged and paraphrased form:

- In primary schools considerable attention is paid by teachers to life-relevant learning, elements of this learning are career relevant.
- Primary schools provide programs that seek to build student self-confidence and self-esteem, and include activities related to work roles in the community.
- Career learning is frequently conveyed by story telling and role playing.
- Primary schools often appoint a teacher to coordinate life-relevant aspects of learning; in some cases a coordinator for careers work is appointed.
- Most primary schools "map" themes to be reinforced across the curriculum; typically career-related learning is one of these themes.
- There is a direct relationship between the scope and the effectiveness of career-related work, and the emphasis placed on developing working partnerships with career community and with parents.
- There is little evidence of coherent, planned progression in career-related work, although primary schools are increasingly developing such plans and beginning to execute them.

Most readers will recognize the parallels between what McGowan and Law report as true in England with what might be said of elementary schools in the United States. In essence, current approaches to career-related learning or career guidance in the United States would make explicit what is now implicit career-related learning in the elementary school; reinforce the need for systematic career activities and information to occur throughout the elementary school curricula and to involve parents, teachers, and counselors in many forms of cooperative effort; and help elementary schools view themselves as career relevant schools with a major emphasis on student self and career awareness.

Within such contexts, researchers (e.g., McGowan & Law, 2000; Staley & Mangiesi, 1984) have observed that children's impressions of the working world, sex-typing of occupations, roles their parents or others play in different work settings and their personal abilities are formed at an early age, in some cases prior to school entrance. Out of such impressions, children begin to formulate and refine potential career aspirations at a relatively young age as their self-concept unfolds in relation to their evaluations of dimensions like gender, prestige, interest (Gottfredson, 1981). Elementary children through their experiences in the school, the family, and the community acquire impressions of the work people do, the kinds of people employed in different jobs, the overt impressions of the compensation they receive or the lifestyles people in various jobs experience, and the types of abilities required to do these jobs. While these impressions are often overgeneralized, inaccurate, or narrow and restricted, young children enthusiastically embrace some occupations as possible careers for themselves and essentially remove others from either present or future consideration.

Helwig (1998) has conducted a longitudinal study of the occupational aspirations and expectations of children at three points in time (second, fourth, and sixth grade). In an effort to test concepts derived from Gottfredson's theoretical perspective (1981) and that of Lent, Brown, and Hackett (1994), Helwig proposed the following hypotheses:

1. Children will identify fewer opposite-gender occupational aspirations from the second to the sixth grade.
2. Children will identify occupational aspirations with increasing social value between the second and sixth grades.
3. Consistent with increasing self-efficacy, children will identify more realistic (fewer fantasy) occupational aspirations from the second to the sixth grades.
4. Children will identify goals (occupational aspirations) consistent with perceptions of those in their environment (parents).

Based upon data collected through surveys and interviews from 208 students from four public elementary schools in second grade and their parents and subsequently collected in fourth (W = 160) and in sixth grade (N = 130), the following results were obtained.

For hypothesis one, the assumption that children will increasingly aspire to gender-appropriate jobs received support from boys but not for girls. Indeed, in this study, by sixth grade one-half of the girls in the sample aspired to male occupations. The speculation about this result by the researcher is that in general, male occupations carry more status and prestige and almost guarantee higher income than many traditional female occupations; girls are heeding the messages from schools and parents that they should consider nontraditional (meaning male) occupations. For hypothesis two, the assumption is that as children grow older they become more conscious of the social values attached to different occupations. This assumption and the related hypothesis were supported unambiguously. By the sixth grade, 89 percent of the sample aspired to professional, technical, and managerial occupations, occupations on which society tends to focus the highest social value and for which college preparation tends to be required. With regard to the latter, however, there are far more aspirants for college and for jobs that require a college degree than can be accommodated in the occupational structure (Gray & Herr, 2000), while there are shortages in persons interested in technical jobs that pay as much or more as the professional, technical, and managerial jobs but do not require a baccalaureate degree. For hypothesis three, if professional athletics are included among the fantasy occupations, the assumption underlying hypothesis three was not supported because it was found that boys through the sixth grade never gave up their fantasy occupations as did some 16 percent of the girls in the sample. For hypothesis four, the data suggested that from second grade to grade six, children's aspirations increasingly matched their perceptions of parents' expectations that their children would select aspirations that included entering professional, technical or managerial occupations. In essence, these children have internalized parental wishes and made them their own as they evolved their occupational aspirations.

Within such contexts, career learning or career guidance has the potential to provide children with accurate and relevant information, to challenge restrictive, negative, and stereotypical notions about themselves, and to keep their options open. It is clear that children are fascinated by work and workers and that they are influenced by the wishes and expectations of parents and other adults. Therefore, they will develop conceptions of careers and their interest in them even if inaccurate. There are possibilities that the student with accurate information may suffer harmful consequences and unintegrated concepts. In contrast, systematic career instruction and leaning is more likely to build organized knowledge structures and adaptive problem solving. "Potentially, there is a large difference between what students gain on their own with no systematic instruction and what is acquired with the aid of good instruction" (Walls, 2000, p. 143).

Thus, career-related learning in the elementary school is not intended to force or, even to encourage, children to make premature career choices but instead to prevent premature foreclosure of choices. Rather, career guidance focuses on student awareness of educational, occupational and other choices that will be available as they proceed through school and into the adult world, ways to anticipate and plan for them, and their relation of work habits, abilities and interests, and related personal characteristics. Many, perhaps most, students need to know that they will have opportunities to choose and the competence to do so. These students also need to know how to become aware of themselves, how they are changing, and how they can use school experiences to explore and prepare for the future

The importance of the attitudes formed by children in the elementary school about themselves, about others, and about their options has gotten increasing scrutiny recently. For example, Lent, Hackett, and Brown (1999) have applied their Social Cognitive Career Theory (SCCT) to the career development of elementary children. Essentially, these authors argue that if one of the goals of the senior high school period is successful transition from school to work, then it is necessary to view the school to work transition as a process, not an event. Therefore, successful transition to work, and, one might add, to post-secondary education and other life roles, depends upon how well students cope with earlier career tasks (e.g., the crystallization interests, career exploration, the cultivation of decisional skills). Such career tasks find their origins in the early life of the child, including the experiences of the elementary school.

Lent, Hackett, and Brown emphasize the importance of the interplay between three variables: self-efficacy, outcome expectations, and goals:

> *Self-efficacy, or confidence in one's ability to successfully perform a given task or set of tasks, helps to determine whether an individual will initiate, persevere, and succeed at particular endeavors.... The most robust source of self-efficacy beliefs is personal mastery experience; successful experience enhances self-efficacy*

> *which, in turn, raises the probability of future effective performance; failure experiences tend to diminish self-efficacy. (p. 299)*

Thus, if students are to develop accurate and positive self-efficacy, the elementary school and the career related learning that takes place must reinforce successful experiences, observations of persons who have succeeded in challenging roles, and emotional reactions that are positive rather than depressed and anxious.

The second set of variables of importance, according to Lent, Hackett, and Brown, is comprised of outcome expectations. These refer to one's beliefs that if they successfully perform these behaviors the result will be positive and valued outcomes. Outcome expectations have to do with helping students clarify the values they hope to achieve through work, their beliefs that they can perform work roles successfully, and that preferred outcomes will result. The third set of variables has to do with goals. Goal setting refers to:

> *One's determination to engage in a given activity or to effect a particular outcome such as completing a difficult high school course, graduating, entering post-secondary training, or getting a particular job. Goal setting is a critical mechanism through which people exercise personal control or agency. (p. 300)*

In the elementary school helping children link their interests and career-related goals, strengthen their self-efficacy, and clarify outcome expectations which they value are central to what needs to be reinforced in career-related learning in curriculum, in career guidance, in the activities to which parents expose children, and in the community resources made available to them.

Flum and Blustein (2000) add further insights into the goals of career-related learning in the elementary school, particularly in relation to the vocational exploration process. Again, with roots in the early life of the child, this process involves the appraisal of internal attributes (e.g., values, personality characteristics, interests and abilities) and exploration of external options and constraints that are relevant to various educational, vocational and relational contexts. Flum and Blustein view vocational exploration as more than a stage in one's career development, they see it as a process that is lifelong and adaptive. In their view, the process of vocational exploration includes activities directed toward "enhancing self-knowledge and knowledge of one's relevant environment...an attitudinal component, which refers to one's motivation for engaging in and sustaining exploration...and exploratory skills (p. 381). The process of vocational exploration yields two types of feedback: cognitive and affective. Essentially, in the first instance, the student obtains information from exploratory activities in which they are engaged and feelings about the information obtained.

Flum and Blustein contend that a core outcome of vocational exploration is self-construction, "the process of developing a coherent and meaningful identity and implementing that identity in a life plan" (p. 382). They further suggest, "When a person takes an active role in the process of self-definition and explores the different identity elements in order to author one's becoming, identity is self-constructed" (pp. 386–387). The kinds of exploration suggested here are seen as more likely if the student has a secure attachment to his or her parents and that others are involved who are significant to the student, offering psychological resources, and providing support likely to have a positive effect on the student's exploratory experiences.

A further perspective related to the behavioral elements of importance to career-related learning in the elementary school is that of "emotional intelligence." According to Goleman (1995), emotional intelligence includes self-awareness and impulse control, persistence, zeal and self-motivation, empathy and social deftness. These attributes are seen as qualities possessed by people who excel in real life in their interpersonal relationships and in the workplace. These are also the qualities that underlie character and self-discipline, altruism, and compassion. They begin to form early in life and can be taught to children, "giving them a better chance to use whatever intellectual potential the genetic lottery may have given them" (p. xii). This model, then, argues that emotions are at the center of aptitudes for living. We have until now, left the emotional education of our children to chance. But with the burgeoning evidence that there are more children in the present generation than ever before, who are troubled emotionally, lonely and depressed, angry and unruly, nervous and prone to worry, impulsive and aggressive and violent, we must find ways in education, including in the elementary schools, to help them learn the necessary human "competencies of self-awareness, self-control and empathy, and the arts of listening, resolving conflicts, and cooperation" (p. xiv).

Although there are other contemporary models of theory and research that reinforce the critical role of career-related learning in the elementary school, the perspectives of Lent and colleagues, Flum and Blustein, and Goleman reassert the importance of and extend the concepts that for the last several decades have given shape and substance to career guidance in the elementary school.

M. J. Miller (1989), among other authors, has stated emphatically that in the elementary school the initial stage of career development is self-awareness. Without self-awareness, other stages of career development, such as career awareness or decision-making, become meaningless. Thus, central to career guidance activities in the elementary school are those that address a child's awareness of self, feelings of autonomy and control, need for planful behavior, and desire for exploration.

It is not simply the formulation of career decisions and a sense of opportunity that is at issue in the elementary school. Social competence in children is considered to be a predictor of positive adult adjustment, and social skills deficits may indicate future problems. Children who are rejected and lack social skills are likely to continue having difficulties with relationships. If no effective intervention occurs through social skills training or other methods, such problems will likely appear later in the adult workplace in relation to behavior toward coworkers or supervisors (Cole & Dodge, 1983; Mehaffey & Sandberg, 1992).

Some researchers suggest that early classroom learning strategies may help predict the individual's tendencies to engage, dissemble, or evade in difficult workplace situations, particularly in early employment (D. A. Hansen & Johnson, 1989). Using an expectancy-valence model similar to that described in Chapter 4, Hansen and Johnson have described how learning strategies observed in the classroom as early as the elementary school and reinforced in the junior and senior high schools can lead to productive or nonproductive work strategies in early adulthood. To simplify the matter, a taxonomy of four classroom learning strategies is used by these researchers to describe the interaction of learning related to high or low task confidence or task value. These, in turn, lead to engaging, dissembling, evading, or rejecting tasks in the classroom or in the workplace.

To be more specific, *task engaging* means that the individual sees relative value in the required performance and is relatively confident of his or her ability to meet its demands. In a state of situational challenge, "the individual strives for an accurate understanding of the task and of the means to accomplish it, and enters into the required effort with intentionality. Ambiguity of assignment is met with efforts to clarify, interpret, and resolve" (p. 82). In *task dissembling,* "the individual sees a relative value in the required performance, but lacks confidence in his or her ability to meet its demands. In a situational quandary, the individual wants to perform, but is uncertain of what to do or how to do it, or whether it can be done. In the desire to succeed, to appear successful, not to fail, or at least not to appear to fail, the individual dissembles, pretending to understand, making excuses, denying, distorting, or engaging in undifferentiated thinking that includes elements that may not appear to be part of the situation. New situations and unfamiliar assignments are seen as threatening, rather than challenging, and are met with further dissembling" (p. 83).

In a third learning (workplace) strategy, *task evading,* the individual feels relatively confident of his or her ability to meet the demands of the assignment but sees relatively little value in it. He or she is in a situational dilemma, feeling ready and able to take on a challenge, but being unable in this particular situation to identify a task of sufficient value. The individual may go through the motions of task performance in an automatic fashion, usually accomplishing at least an acceptable minimum of output. But the task is neither actively engaged nor rejected: It is simply evaded. The individual is removed from the task, his or her attention is scattered, "given only partially to the performance and perhaps in more important part to other competing interests, such as daydreaming, distracting a neighbor, worrying about lacking money, planning a party, recalling a television drama, or even mentally rehearsing another more compelling performance in an area that is found challenging" (p. 83).

The final learning/work strategy is *task rejecting.* In this situation, "the individual lacks confidence in his or her ability and sees little value in the assigned task. In a situational state of psychological withdrawal, the individual neither actively engages assignments nor defends against them. He or she is in situational malaise, neither having a clear goal or valued task nor feeling able to secure one in this situation. He or she may appear passive, working within a system of understandings that are unresponsive to the present demands and restrictions of the situation (p. 84).

This taxonomy of learning or work strategies is not only present in the elementary schools but also can be found in junior high or senior high schools. Its use makes several points. One, the roots of work strategies that lead to productive or nonproductive results take hold in the early years of schooling, as do the sense of self-confidence and valuing of different tasks that underlie the different forms of individual behavior reflected. Two, everyone uses the dissembling, evading, or rejecting of tasks in some situations. The problem is that for some people they can become habitual strategies that may be employed with increasing frequency in response to decreasing levels of situational distress or discomfort. Third, preliminary research suggests that, whatever their genesis, nonproductive learning strategies can be reversed by situational and interactional interventions. With particular application to career guidance and career counseling, efforts to help individuals learn to recognize and control their tendencies to evade, dissemble, or reject tasks may be accomplished through individual and group work. Certainly, efforts to increase student self-efficacy and self-confidence to take on a wider range of tasks, with less feeling of threat, and efforts to help students gain assertive skills by which to clarify assignments or to indicate their lack of understanding when faced with ambiguity represent the types of behaviors that can be identified and reinforced in career counseling strategies in the elementary school and at other educational levels. In doing so, such interventions acknowledge that the effectiveness with which students can deal with challenge and threat within the learning environment is likely to be related to personal experiences of self-efficacy with particular situations or tasks, and that these experiences, in turn, are likely to be reflected in career decisions made.

The importance of the behaviors and attitudes that students incorporate in the elementary school can be seen from another perspective. Analyses of research addressing school dropouts suggest that the antecedents to the withdrawal from school at age 16 or so likely occur over a long period of time, probably beginning in the elementary school. As Finn (1989) has suggested, there are currently two major models that attempt to explain the underlying variables that lead to early school leaving. One of these is a *frustration—self-esteem model* that contends that poor school performance is hypothesized to lead to an impaired self-view (low self-esteem) and, in turn, to the child's opposing the context (the school) that is seen as responsible. This oppositional behavior may take different forms: disrupting the instructional process, skipping class, or even committing delinquent acts. There are many reasons for a child to evidence frustration at the instructional process—for example, poor psychological support from the home, a lack of continual evidence of adequacy through school-related success experiences, poor interaction with teachers, or a growth of acute distress and alienation from the world of school and adults in general.

These observations are not intended to suggest that oppositional behavior is entirely or even primarily the student's fault. Such behaviors can arise because schools have not provided programs or created environments that challenge students to feel competent and valued by teachers or peers. Indeed, alienation of students from the expectations of the school is often a self-protecting way of responding when one has been hurt, bored, or made to feel inferior by the climate or the activities of the school. *The fundamental point is that what happens in the life of the child in the elementary school does create patterns of behavior, positive or negative, that are likely to persist into the secondary school and adulthood.* Thus, they need to be the focus of the counselor's sensitivity and intervention, either to assist children in developing positive attitudes of self-esteem and ability or to help teachers and administrators create climates and classrooms that motivate such characteristics.

The second model is described as a *participation-identification model.* This model manifests two major variables: one behavioral, *participation,* and the other psychological, *identification.* Participation requires that the student have curricular experiences available that both retain his or her interest and engagement and result in learning and development. The second variable, identification, connotes a form of bonding, a sense of belonging, shared value, a feeling of being able to deal with and be congruent with the social group (other students, teachers, institutional norms). Identification and self-esteem have been found to be correlated—not independent.

The fundamental point to be made here is that the research reported by Hansen and Johnson and by Finn is illustrative of the power of the early developmental experiences of children in the elementary school to be precursors of persistence at later educational levels and in acquiring behaviors that are antecedents of work performance in adulthood. Thus, they are both challenges to and opportunities for career guidance and counseling in the elementary school.

Against such contexts, the assumptions that give career guidance credibility in the elementary school are as follows:

1. Awareness that styles of choice behavior in adolescence and adulthood are affected by the types of developmental experiences that occur in childhood
2. Acknowledgment that feelings of personal competence to cope with the future grow with knowledge of one's strengths, ways to modify weaknesses, skills in planning and using available exploratory resources, and understanding of relationships between schooling and its application in work and other community roles
3. Recognition that much career-related learning in elementary schools occurs, but is implicit rather than explicit in its goals, is fragmented rather than systematic in its presentation, and is in need of coordination across teachers, parents and community resources

A consideration of the characteristics of elementary school children will help to place some of these assumptions into perspective.

THE ELEMENTARY SCHOOL CHILD

Children of elementary school age are fundamentally generalists, in the sense that they are typically open to and they interact with a broad range of stimuli and modes of behavior. In their unbridled enthusiasm and curiosity, they have not yet been constrained by many of the social realities and stereotypes that plague and distort the perceptions of their older brothers and sisters and many adults with whom they identify. Yet they are vulnerable in the sense that attitudes and perceptions about life and their place in it are formative and are readily influenced by the environmental circumstances surrounding them, including accurate or inaccurate information about their competence, their options, and sex stereotyping. They also change in their capabilities, characteristics, and reactions to different experiences at different ages (Johnson & Kottman, 1992).

Environmental Influences

Environmental circumstances take many forms and have varied relationships to the growth and development of elementary school children. For example, Rich (1979) has demonstrated that children are most knowledgeable about occupations located in their own community. Therefore, if they come from a predominantly rural community, for example, with few occupations and these mostly of low socioeconomic status, it is such options to which they will likely aspire. Rich argues that such circumstances put rural students at a comparative disadvantage to their urban counterparts. She further contends that acquiring knowledge "about nonlocal occupations or more specifically about middle- and high-status occupations, could provide rural students with an equal opportunity to make more varied and more optimal occupational choices" (p. 325).

Environmental circumstances go beyond geography. A particularly powerful one is socioeconomic status. M. Holland (1981) found, in a study of 300 randomly selected sixth-grade students enrolled in 22 public schools in Georgia, that socioeconomic status was more useful in predicting the maturity of career attitudes than self-concept, race, sex, place of residence, or age. The data indicated that the higher the student's socioeconomic status, the higher the score obtained on the Attitude Scale of the Career Maturity Inventory (CMI).

Gender and socioeconomic characteristics can be either separate or interactive influences on career exploration. Hageman and Gladding (1983) studied children's willingness to accept men and women in various occupations and their own willingness to aspire to nontraditional occupations. The participants were 90 sixth graders (47 girls and 43 boys) and 84 third graders (39 girls and 45 boys) in two elementary schools that differed in the socioeconomic composition of their students. Although both schools were in suburban areas, a majority of the children in one school came from upper-middle-class and lower-upper-class families, whereas the other school's children were from upper-lower-class and lower-middle-class backgrounds.

The results of the Hageman and Gladding study indicated that a number of differences in perceptions of occupations prevailed among the groups. Sixth-grade girls were willing to accept both men and women in 16 traditionally male occupations; sixth-grade boys differed significantly from girls in this regard. The boys thought that only men should be employed as auto mechanics, architects, electricians, carpenters, doctors, school principals, astronauts, pilots, pharmacists, professional athletes, lawyers, dentists, truck drivers, police officers, radio announcers, and reporters. These sixth-grade boys also differed from girls in their belief that dental assistants and cleaner/servants should be women only.

When the perceptions of third-grade girls were compared to sixth-grade girls, they differed in their view of only one occupation, that of lawyer. The older girls were more willing to accept both men and women as lawyers. The study also found that sixth-grade girls chose nontraditional jobs as occupations they would like to have considerably more often than did third-grade girls (that is, 40 versus 25 percent). Although the research suggested that a large number of the girls were considering nontraditional occupations, it was also evident that, in line with other research on sex-stereotyping, most of the girls did not feel free to pursue a nontraditional career. A final finding of the study was that children from lower socioeconomic backgrounds were more conservative in their perceptions of appropriate occupations for men or women or for themselves than were children of higher socioeconomic background. Part of the explanation for such differences undoubtedly relates to role models available as well as to the children's perception of their own freedom of action in exploring or participating in career options.

Such findings apparently are also a function of the accuracy and comprehensiveness of the occupational information possessed by students in different grades. Walls (2000) assessed the accuracy of occupational knowledge possessed by 189 students in grades three, six, nine, and twelve (males and females were essentially equal in each grade). His findings indicated that on the six dimensions used in the study to assess student knowledge of 20 occupations (e.g., training time, availability, earnings, physical and mental requirements, and status), students were significantly less accurate on each of the six dimensions than students in the other grade levels. He also found that students generally improved across the grades in accuracy on each of the six dimensions.

Selected research studies also show that the formation of occupational aspirations and expectations is a function of where one lives and the socioeconomic conditions that prevail. Cook and colleagues (1996) studied the occupational aspirations and expectations of two contrasting populations (inner-city minority males from poor neighborhoods and white males living in more advantaged circumstances) in grades two, four, six, and eight. While both populations tended to be more realistic about their occupational aspirations and expectations the older they were, from the second grade on the occupational expectations of inner-city males mirrored existing race and class in adult job holdings. The gap between occupational aspirations and expectations was greater for the inner-city minority males and remained so across the grades than for the white males. The lower occupational expectations of the inner-city males were strongly related to their lower educational expectations, which were in turn related to fewer poor males having a biological father at home and more of these males seeing obstacles to success in the local social setting.

Research findings also suggest that there is a connection between childhood play activities and later career choices. For example, the research of Cooper and Robinson (1989) of retrospective descriptions of childhood games, activities, preferences, and aspirations by 214 men and 51 women enrolled in a variety of science, mathematics, and engineering courses at a midwestern technical university corroborate earlier studies that masculine and androgynous childhood activities may play a role in the development of skills necessary for later achievement in math and physical sciences. Implications of these findings by the researchers suggest that elementary school counselors who are concerned about eliminating or reducing gender limitations should promote a greater level of masculine and androgynous experiences for girls. In addition, counselors could work with students individually and in groups to modify attitudes that negatively influence girls' participation in these activities. Greater exposure to childhood activities found to be related to women's subsequent participation in nontraditional curricula or occupations could be coupled with the use of selected female role models to strengthen self-efficacy and interest in previously male-dominated roles in the technical and scientific fields.

It is interesting to note in more recent research that racial and gender differences in career choices may be changing in comprehensiveness. Bobo, Hildreth, and Durodoye (1998) have examined changing patterns in career choices among African American, Hispanic, and Anglo children in elementary schools. They discovered that in comparison with earlier studies, there were not major differences in the career choices of Anglo, African American, or Hispanic boys when compared across these groups nor were there major differences in the career choices of Anglo, African American, and Hispanic girls when compared to girls in the other groups. Boys across the racial groups listed 51 career choices and girls across the racial groups listed 56 career choices. While the career choices were not the same for girls and boys, it was clear in this study that girls are increasing the variety of career choices they consider and some of the gender bias in career choice identified in earlier studies is being overcome. Even so, boys were less likely then girls to select nontraditional careers.

To further the broadening of student career choices and the reduction in gender or racial bias that mediates such choice-making, Bobo and colleagues recommend several emphases to be included in elementary career guidance programs. They include, in paraphrased form, in the primary grades:

- Provide career information as early as preschool and adding detail to such information as students progress through the elementary school
- Help students from ethnically diverse and lower socioeconomic backgrounds explore career opportunities that go beyond ethnic or economic constraints
- Provide information that depicts males and females and persons from a range of cultural and linguistic backgrounds in nontraditional occupations
- Help parents to recognize their importance in their child's career development process and provide them information that can help broaden their occupational knowledge

In the intermediate grades:

- Provide opportunities for students to assess their career interests and to find information pertinent to their interests
- Provide opportunities for students to visit local businesses and industries to observe people working in diverse jobs and use employers and workers as resource persons to speak about different jobs and how to prepare for them
- Match students and mentors who have similar career interests
- Use newspaper ads and other material to explore the qualifications necessary to obtain and perform the jobs
- Create career days in which parents, local employers and employees, school alumni, and other persons can participate as mentors and as persons who can discuss their careers, the preparation and processes involved, and the positive and negative characteristics

In a different but related line of inquiry, Hughes, Martinek, and Fitzgerald (1985) have examined the role of self-esteem among boys and girls in relation to nontraditional career choices. The sample studied consisted of 66 students (35 girls and 31 boys) in a private laboratory school. The result of the study strongly supports the notion that for girls the relationship between self-esteem and nontraditional attitudes is reliably established as early as the primary years in school. In addition, the study showed that boys with high self-esteem persisted in maintaining stereotyped attitudes toward sex roles, whereas girls with high self-esteem made less traditional career choices. This study was not able to project how such sex-role stereotypes or, in contrast, freedom to consider nontraditional sex roles will translate into actual work choices in the future. It does, however, affirm that attitudes likely to undergird adult role behavior have antecedents in the early life of children.

A further major environmental circumstance affecting the career attitudes of children is their relationships with their parents and the attitudes of the latter toward school and work.

As Peeks (1993) has reported, "Decades of research document that families are critically important to the academic success of students.... For most students, the schools they attend make less difference to academic success than the families from which they come" (p. 248). This point has been reinforced by research that indicates that parental occupations are particularly influential in the career aspirations of elementary school students (Trice, Hughes, Odom, Woods, & McClellan, 1995).

Liontos (1992) has made the interesting observation that before school entrance many children in the United States lack the human and social capital needed to be ready to learn. In this instance, *human capital* was defined as those resources possessed by parents represented by educational, economic, and social status; *social capital* includes the networks or the communications that are available between parents and children. Given such perspectives and the view expressed throughout this book that the skills provided by schooling and those required by the workplace are increasingly complementary, it is clear that families are important both in attitudes toward school and toward career.

M. F. Miller (1978) has examined the childhood antecedents to career maturity attitudes in young adulthood and found some support for the hypothesis that parental attitudes and behavior reported as having occurred during childhood are positively associated with career maturity attitudes among community college students. Parental attitudes and behavior that impede general development and well being were found to be associated with attitudes indicative of career immaturity. As discussed elsewhere in this book, prolonged unemployment also tends to be associated with increases in child abuse, substance abuse, marital discord, intense anxiety, and insecurity. Such circumstances are likely to influence the views of work held by children in families significantly affected by unemployment.

Berry (1979) has reported that research indicates that many problems of older children, youth, and adults are a result of unresolved communication problems stemming from childhood (p. 515). She argues the importance of this matter for communication theory, which she contends "explains human growth and development itself because it is the social matrix from which the self-concept emerges and takes shape and it is the self-concept that gives direction to human life.... It is communication that (1) puts the individuals in touch with their own thoughts and feelings and (2) ties person to person and every person to a group" (p. 516). In this view, social interference with communication development takes place when the pattern of communication between the parent and child is unsatisfactory, at least from the child's point of view. Obviously, such disturbed communication patterns will affect not only the child's view of self, but also interactions with others in the school and, subsequently, in the workplace.

Seligman, Weinstock, and Owings (1988) studied the role of family dynamics in the career development of 5-year-olds. They found that children with a positive family orientation are likely to obtain information about their parents' activities and to receive more encouragement. These factors contribute to the child's career development. The researchers also found that the children's perceptions of their fathers as powerful, important, attractive, approachable, and warm were related to the development of articulated future goals in the children. Part of the explanation for this finding may be the fact that children at this age are attracted to power and mastery. Thus, the father, by his size and his accomplishment of having both a career and a family, can serve as a role model for the integration and the value of both endeavors. Such circumstances probably permit these children to identify with both aspects of their father's life and imagine themselves in similar roles.

These findings do not denigrate the role of the mother in determining the general climate of the family. Rather, they suggest that career guidance practitioners need to pay considerable attention to the role of the father and to the father-child relationship in shaping and promoting the career development of the young child.

Subsequently, Seligman, Weinstock, and Owings (1991) studied the career development of twenty-four 10-year-olds. They found that most of the students were knowledgeable about their parents' careers and about the nature and requirements related to their own career aspirations. Career goals were increasingly determined by interest as the children matured.

As a function of such environmental circumstances and others, levels of aspiration, achievement motivation, and self-perceptions have their genesis in the early years of the family and of schooling. Here are the roots of the behavior that will manifest itself many years later under the labels of career identity and commitment, or conversely, juvenile delinquency, early school leaving, and under employability. If Luchins's (1960) primacy effect is a valid premise—that the information obtained first carries the most weight in ultimate decisions—then in the case of elementary school age children, education and career guidance must focus considerable attention on attitude development, decision processing, and self-awareness as well as on knowledge of the broad characteristics and expectations of work. These are the ingredients of career development that underlie growing career maturity.

Children's Values toward Work

Many people believe that the elementary years are too early to give attention to children's career development. They believe that concerns about self-understanding and planning for the future are better saved for junior high school and beyond. Although adults might feel more comfortable if they did not need to plan career guidance responses to children's developmental needs in the elementary school, children do have such needs.

As elementary school children move through the elements of fantasy so characteristic of growth and learning at that life period, work is an important concern to them. By the time they have completed the first six grades of school, many of them have made tentative commitments to fields of work and to self-perceptions. The point here is not that the choices are irreversible or that this phenomenon is good or bad, but, rather, that it occurs. Parker (1970), for example, found that fewer than 10 percent of 29,000 students in the seventh grade in Oklahoma described themselves as not having vocational goals. Simmons (1962) discovered that the elementary school children in his study were very much aware of occupational prestige. Creason and Schilson (1970) found that of a sample of 121 sixth graders who were asked about their vocational plans, none indicated that they had no vocational plans, none indicated that they had no vocational preferences, and only eight indicated that they did not know why they chose their particular preference. In a related study, Davis, Hagen, and Strouf (1962) found that out of a sample of 116 12-year-olds, 60 percent had already made tentative choices. Nelson (1963) has demonstrated that as early as the third grade, children have well-developed attitudes regarding occupations and levels of education and that as early as ages 8 and 9, children tend to reject some occupations as holding no interest for them.

Rosenthal and Chapman (1982) have shown that children are aware of the sex stereotypes of certain occupations, and that, from an early age, children employ "linguistic markers" (for example, "lady doctor" or "male nurse") to denote those in nontraditional occupations. Using Krefting and Berger's (1979) findings that indicated that interacting with things is perceived as masculine, interacting with people is perceived as feminine, and interacting with data is perceived as both masculine and feminine, McKay and Miller (1982) studied third-grade and fifth-grade students. They found that boys had more complex interactions with things in their choices of occupational environments than did girls.

In somewhat similar findings, Bailey and Nihlen (1989) exposed 104 female and 122 male white and Hispanic kindergartners through fifth graders to ten nontraditional workers (e.g., female firefighter, male nurse) and allowed these children to ask questions of the workers. The most questions were asked by second and third graders and by females. When the questions were classified by content, it was found that females placed a higher priority on the feelings the workers had about their careers than males did, while males emphasized what the job entailed and how much it paid.

In studying subjects of several different ages, Shepelak, Ogden, and Robin-Bennett (1984) asked college, high school, and students in third and fifth grades to evaluate whether fictitious occupations arbitrarily assigned a gender label were positions appropriate for women, men, or both sexes. The use of imaginary occupations allowed the authors to circumvent the students' prior knowledge of the normative work world. There were few differences in the way students from the four age groups responded. Third- and fifth-grade students were likely initially to classify more occupations as open only to men. In general, however, all students were more likely to perceive those occupations with masculine labels as appropriate for men and not for both men and women.

Fitzgerald and Betz (1983) found in a review of the literature that female self-esteem correlates highly with nontraditional career choices. In their own study with boys and girls in grades three through six, they found for girls that the relationship between self-esteem and nontraditional attitudes is established as early as the primary school year. In addition, they found that girls but not boys with high self-esteem made less traditional choices concerning their future occupations than did girls with low self-esteem.

Gottfredson's (1981) research in occupational circumscription, reported in some depth in Chapter 4, suggests that as children grow older, the occupations acceptable to them are progressively reduced in number. This process of circumscription or reduction begins as early as age 6. According to Gottfredson's perspective, the occupations children first eliminate from consideration are those they perceive to be inappropriate for their sex. Between ages 9 and 13, children enter into a second phase of circumscription in which they begin to rule out occupations of insufficient prestige for their social class self-concept as well as occupations requiring effort beyond their view of their general ability level. Such research has indicated that by the time children are in the fourth grade, they have constructed a job-prestige hierarchy similar to that constructed by adults (Gottfredson, 1981). R. R. Miller (1986) has suggested that career education in the upper elementary grades should focus on counteracting the effects of occupational elimination based on social class inappropriateness or sex stereotyping. Thus, career education or career guidance in the elementary grades should include nontraditional role models, guest speakers, photographs and films, presentations, discussions, books, and field trips that focus on offsetting the premature foreclosure of options that tend to operate on sex and social class criteria unless interventions are planned and comprehensively provided.

Hales and Fenner (1972, 1973) have reported research findings indicating that values related to work begin to form in childhood and that these values enter into preadolescent vocational behavior. In particular, their research has shown that "although sixth-grade pupils differ in the work values which they hold, the work values of different groups (male-female, social classes) are more alike than they are dissimilar" (1973, p. 31). They further contend that an exploration of work values by elementary pupils may be useful in initiating analysis of the world of work from a perspective that is less dominated by sex and social class roles than is true of interests and aspirations. Borow (1970), too, has proposed that career development in the elementary school can be better understood if it is presented within the context of values and the valuing process. Cooker's research findings (1973) are similar to those of Hales and Fenner (1973), although he suggests somewhat sharper sex differences in values, with boys who value such things as money and control more than girls and girls who place more importance on altruism and helping others than boys; this finding suggests that the valuing process does begin in the preschool period. In other words, whether or not education and career guidance respond to this fact, the evidence shows that elementary school students have already begun to assimilate perceptions and preferences that may be wholesome and meaningful or distorted and ultimately harmful to aspirations and achievement.

Importance of the Early School Years

The first ten years of life have been called, correctly, the "nursery of human nature." This is the period of life when a child's goals, achievement motivation, and perceptions of self as worthy or inferior begin to be formulated. The concepts children acquire during this life stage directly influence later school success, career identity, adult interests, and general perspectives on life as their attitudes about success and failure develop early.

Elementary school children, in their play and school groups, are concerned with individual differences, work, adult life patterns, and personal feelings of competence, which they translate into self-perspectives and preferences for some work or educational activities to the exclusion of others. Whether based on accurate information or not, such perspectives direct the child's behavior unless subsequent experiences change such directions.

One can speculate that not all the information and influences from which these preferences and perceptions are derived are appropriate or accurate. Frequently, unrealistic career plans are made at this level because of the emphasis in parent and community attitudes as well as in textbooks on prestige fields, frequently defined as those requiring college preparation. Such an emphasis obscures consideration of other occupations that employ large proportions of workers, offer equally potent gratifications, and are growing in demand (Gray & Herr, 2000). Various studies have shown that only a small fraction of the many existing types of work are presented to children in elementary school texts and in basal readers. Frequently the occupations presented reinforce sex-typing or other unfortunate distortions.

This phenomenon is but one evidence of the increasingly rigid walls between the preadolescent (and the adolescent) and the occupational niches and educational options to which they must relate. Far too often, large segments of the student population—those from the culture of poverty and those from homes in which the children are economically favored but psychologically disadvantaged—have no systematic models of effective behavior or of enthusiasm to which to relate and no environmental support for developing personally and socially fulfilling behavior. Although all children have some adult models, they probably do not all have models who display a range of adequate behavior and a consistent career identity that provides a stable base for the child's self and occupational explorations.

The effects of a stagnated or unresponsive home or school life can be inferred from Hunt (1961). He points out that, according to Piaget:

> *The rate of development is in substantial part, but certainly not wholly, a function of environmental circumstances.... The greater the variety of situations to which the child must accommodate his behavioral structures, the more differentiated and mobile they become. Thus, the more new things a child has seen and the more he has heard, the more things he is interested in seeing and hearing. Moreover, the more variation in reality with which he has coped, the greater is his capacity for coping. (pp. 258–259)*

The danger exists that when the educational process does not create flexibility of behavior and awareness of ways to obtain goals, the seeds of an anomic situation are inadvertently planted. If we hold a carrot up to children, a culturally valued goal, whether a prestige occupation or a certain level of educational attainment, without expending equal energy in developing command of the means whereby children can obtain these goals, we have negated our concepts of individual differences and education as a process of development. Further, we are operating from a narrow view of ability and reinforcing a restrictive definition of individual talent.

Research indicates that many youngsters who drop out of school physically at age 16 have already dropped out of school psychologically as early as grade three. Frequently, this occurs because they fail to sense relationships between what they study in school and life as they experience it outside of school. Many children claim that there is nothing in the school experience that is of relevance to there needs or interests. According to McWhirter, McWhirter, McWhirter, and McWhirter (1994), limited life purpose, a sense of being without a viable future, is a characteristic of youth who are at high risk for dropping out. Some generalize school failures or feelings of incompetence to all academic experiences. They acquire a psychological set that generates resistance to schooling and to the possibility of working toward a self-fulfilling future. Such children probably do not comprise the majority of elementary school children. Many children do develop awareness of their personal uniqueness, possible life options, methods of planning, and ways of becoming responsible for their futures. Unless opportunities for the latter behavior to occur are systematically planned and the elementary school curriculum is augmented with career guidance activities, many other children may learn inadequate behaviors or incorrect information about themselves or their opportunities.

Many of the career guidance goals and career education emphases identified in this chapter or earlier ones have long been a part of the elementary school's philosophy. Dewey (1931), for example, believed that the child's knowledge began by doing and that industrially oriented themes, problems, and activities provided the potential to satisfy native tendencies to explore, to manipulate tools and materials, and to construct and create. Indeed, Dewey (1931) saw that industrial themes or problems could serve as a correlating medium for other subjects and as opportunities to acquire knowledge of the industrial world, the fundamental processes of economic life, and the sociocultural backgrounds of vocations. Unfortunately, restricted or incomplete information and a lack of systematic planning have reduced the power of many schools to achieve these goals. By implementing the stages of planning identified in Chapter 6 and incorporating many of the activities identified later in this chapter into a school's offerings, however, one should be able to make such goals accessible to more students.

COUNSELORS AND CAREER GUIDANCE

The elementary school counselor has many responsibilities and techniques for discharging this professional role. Historically the processes used by elementary school counselors have been defined as the three C's: counseling, coordinating, and consulting. How much each of these is used depends on the needs and resources that characterize a local setting. The American School Counselors Association (ASCA, 1977a) has stated, "Consistent with the philosophy of education, elementary school counseling concerns itself with children in the developmental process of maximizing their potential. The elementary counselor works within the educational framework and the child's total environment to enable each child to arrive at an identity and learn to make choices and decisions that lead to effective functioning as a worthwhile being" (p. 1).

In 1997, the American School Counselors Association reasserted its view of the role of the elementary school counselor and why it is important (Campbell & Dahir, 1997). In broad terms, this view argued, as has been suggested throughout this chapter that the "elementary school years set the tone for developing the skills, knowledge, and attitudes necessary for our children to become healthy, productive adults" (p. 68). To support such an outcome, ASCA endorsed the provision by elementary school counselors of a comprehensive developmental counseling program, with counselors working as a team with "School, parents and community to create a caring atmosphere whereby children's needs are met through prevention, early identification, and intervention" (p. 69).

Within this professional statement are a variety of functions which elementary school counselors implement; in an abridged manner, several of the functions most connected to career guidance or career-related learning would include the following roles:

Elementary school counselors:

- Implement effective classroom guidance focusing on understanding of self and others; coping strategies, peer relationships, and effective social skills; communication, problem solving, decision making, conflict resolution, and study skills; career awareness and the world of work; substance education and multicultural awareness
- Provide individual and small group counseling dealing with self-image, self-esteem, personal adjustment, family issues, interpersonal concerns, academic development, and behavior modification
- Provide assessment by helping students identify their skills, abilities, achievements, and interests through counseling and guidance activities, and interpretation of standardized tests
- Develop students' career awareness as a lifelong process of forming basic values, attitudes, and interests regarding their future world of work
- Coordinate school, community, and business resources, schoolwide guidance-related activities, and extracurricular programs that promote students' personal growth and skill development (p. 69)

It is within such a context that planning for career guidance becomes important for elementary school counselors. There are many ways to conceive the planning process. For example, with particular relevance to planning for career development interventions in the elementary school, Magnuson and Starr (2000) offer the following suggestions:

1. Become a constant observer of children.
   Notice how children approach tasks.
   Notice the activities in which children choose to participate.
   Observe and encourage the child's initiative-taking.
   Notice the thematic patterns emerging in each child's activities.
2. Consider the processing of an activity as important as the activity itself.
   To help children develop a sense of industry rather than inferiority, focus feedback on the specifics of children's efforts.
   Accompany career awareness and career exploration activities with opportunities for students to express their beliefs about themselves in relation to various occupations. (p. 100)

GOALS FOR CAREER GUIDANCE IN THE ELEMENTARY SCHOOL

In view of the multiple vantage points we have used to examine career related learning in the elementary school, there are many possible perspectives on appropriate goals of career guidance at this educational level. For example, to return to the theoretical model of career development proposed by Lent, Hackett, and Brown (1999) and discussed previously in this chapter, a Social Cognitive Career Theory would highlight six interrelated processes that need to be emphasized at various developmental levels leading to the school-to-work transition. The first three are particularly salient in the elementary school. These six processes are:

1. Acquisition of positive yet realistic self-efficacy and outcome expectations
2. Development of academic and career interests
3. The formation of linkages between interests and career-related goals
4. Translation of goals into actions
5. Development of academic and work skills and remediation of performance-related problems
6. Negotiation of social supports and barriers that affect the development of self and occupational beliefs and the pursuit of preferred academic/career options (p. 300)

There are other views directly related to the outcomes which students should demonstrate as a result of career guidance or career-related learning. They include the comprehensive set of developmental goals created by the Pennsylvania Department of Education (1994) that includes, among other emphases, career development goals for early childhood from 11 to 14 (grades six to eight). Although there are too many goals to reproduce here, selected examples will indicate the types of content identified.

Early Childhood

- Develop a positive attitude toward work
- Understand the importance of personal responsibility, dependability, and other good work habits
- Develop an awareness of the relationship between learning and work
- Be aware of a variety of careers and the student's view toward them
- Develop an awareness that persons who work in their communities are a source of information about careers

8–11 years

- Learn how to relate personal interests, leisure-time activities, and abilities to possible occupational choices without prejudice bias or stereotying
- Understand that effective work habits in school transfer to occupational settings
- Understand how decision making is related to career planning
- Understand the relationship between the needs of the community and the work performed by community members
- Learn the importance of working cooperatively with others at home and at school

Many of these goals are reflected in the more recent ASCA National Standards for School Counseling programs (Campbell & Dahir, 1997). These Standards are cast in three broad areas: Academic Development, Career Development, and Personal/Social Development. Each of these broad areas is comprised of three standards and the student competencies that undergird the achievement of the standards. While neither the standards nor the competencies are classified by elementary, middle or high school, one can identify those competencies that would be relevant at each level. For example, for career development, the three standards are:

Standard A: Students will acquire the skills to investigate the world of work in relation to knowledge of self and to make informed career decisions.

Standard B: Students will employ strategies to achieve future career goals with success and satisfaction.

Standard C: Students will understand the relationship between personal qualities, education, training, and the world of work.

Examples of student competencies for Standard A that would be appropriately pursued at the elementary level include:

- Develop skills to locate, evaluate, and interpret career information
- Learn about the variety of traditional and nontraditional occupations
- Develop an awareness of personal abilities, skills, interests and motivations
- Learn how to interact and work cooperatively in teams
- Learn how to set goals
- Understand the importance of planning

For Standard B, student competencies in the elementary school might include:

- Identify personal skills, interests, and abilities and relate them to current career choices

- Use research and information resources including the Internet, to obtain career information
- Demonstrate awareness of the education and training needed to achieve career goals
- Begin to develop a career portfolio

For Standard C:

- Understand the relationship between educational achievement and career success
- Learn how to use conflict-management skills with peers and adults
- Learn to work cooperatively with others as a team member

In another important example, the Wisconsin Developmental Guidance Model (Wisconsin Department of Public Instruction, 1986) recommends developmental competencies to guide the work of school counselors in the elementary, middle/junior, and senior high school. The K–12 competencies at each of these levels are divided into three major developmental areas: learning, personal/social, and career and vocational competencies. Under each of these major developmental categories are specific competencies that students at different educational levels should either learn about, understand, or apply. At the elementary school level, it is expected that the competencies (goals in our terms) in the career and vocational developmental area that should be the focus of the career guidance program are:

- Acquire knowledge about different occupations and changing male/female roles
- Become aware of personal interests and preferences
- Learn how to cooperate and coexist with others in work and play
- Understand what it means to work and how school work relates to future plans
- Become aware of worlds beyond the immediate experience

At the local level, the Upper Arlington City School District in Ohio (1992) has identified nine student outcomes to which the school counselors direct their K–12 group activities and counseling curriculum. These nine student outcomes are, in turn, broken into specific developmental tasks that the students at the different educational levels (K–5, 6–8, and 9–12) need to acquire if they are ultimately to achieve the student outcomes that all children should possess when they graduate from high school. At least three of these outcomes are directly related to career guidance. These outcomes and the tasks that are identified for students to achieve at grades kindergarten to five include:

Student Outcome #2—Students will set educational and career goals.
Tasks K–5
Students will:
- Identify their personal strengths and areas needing improvement
- Know their personal likes and dislikes
- Become aware of people different from themselves
- Know who to go to for help with their learning
- Learn about a variety of careers in different work settings

Student Outcome #3—Students will make effective decisions.
Tasks K–5
Students will:
- Describe choices and decisions they make
- Recognize that decisions have consequences
- Recognize that they are responsible for the consequences of their decisions
- Demonstrate steps in making decisions

Student Outcome #4—Students will analyze their personal skills, interests, and strengths.
Tasks K–5
Students will:
- Describe what they like to do
- Describe their own specific traits
- Identify and appreciate skills they possess
- Recognize that new skills will, and can, be acquired
- Understand self-esteem and factors that enhance or hinder self-esteem

The National Occupational Information Coordinating Committee (NOICC, 1988) has identified 11 competencies as well as the behavioral indicators for each that the committee views as representative of "the basic skills and attitudes that children should acquire to deal effectively with daily life, to make the transition into the middle/junior high school and to start developing an educational plan to insure their academic growth and continuing career development" (p. 12). As such, they also provide the bases for developing goals for career guidance in the elementary schools. The NOICC competencies (goals) for the elementary school are listed here:

1. Knowledge of the importance of a positive self-concept to career development
2. Skills for interacting with others
3. Awareness of the importance of emotional and physical development on career decision making
4. Awareness of the importance of educational achievement to career opportunities
5. Awareness of the interrelationship of work and learning
6. Skills for understanding and using career information
7. Awareness of the interrelationship of personal responsibility, good work habits, and career opportunities
8. Awareness of how careers relate to needs and functions of society
9. Understanding of how to make decisions and choose alternatives related to tentative educational and career goals
10. Awareness of the interrelationship of life roles and careers
11. Awareness of different occupations and changing male/female roles

Freeman (1994) developed a survey using the most recent competencies that NOICC now recommends for elementary school children and requested that practicing school counselors rate their importance on a 7-point Likert scale (e.g., 1, not important, to 7, very important). Those considered to be the most important for elementary school children and for which there was the most agreement by counselors included self-concept, interpersonal skills, awareness of growth and change, education awareness, personal responsibility, and understanding decision making. For purposes of planning, these would be important competencies with which to begin, although it is also clear from Freeman's data that the other competencies are not unimportant and probably become increasingly important as children move through the elementary school and approach the increasingly complex decisions required in the junior high school.

Depending on the setting and the characteristics of the children being served, many other goals specified in different forms, might be developed for a local program of career guidance. Others have been suggested in Chapter 6, and a careful reading of this text will suggest still others. Indeed, it may be more important for "significant others" to understand the developmental needs of children than for the children to understand their own needs. Such goals for career guidance in the elementary school can be useful in parenting classes or in efforts to stimulate community volunteers of PTAs to help give children work-relevant exploratory experience. Regardless of which goals are finally chosen, however, several thoughts need to be kept in mind.

The goals and the characteristics of elementary school children discussed earlier in this chapter should make one point clear: If career guidance in the elementary schools is to make a difference, simply providing periodic occupational units in which students are told about work is not sufficient. To be useful in the elementary school, information must be available in a wide range of reading levels and other sensory modes. In addition, activities will have to meet the diverse needs of students in their initial forays into career development. Parents need to be involved, and when this is not possible, some children need to be provided with adult occupational models. Counselors will have to be activists, initiating and coordinating experiences for different children both within and outside of the educational process. Educational materials and the attitudes of teachers need to contribute to career-related learning.

Parental Influences

The involvement of parents in this process is not limited to their role as the prime source of influence on their child's occupational perceptions at the time he or she begins school. Rather, at the elementary school level in particular, counselors can develop strategies to help parents answer these questions:

> *Why career guidance? When does career development begin? Is home environment related to career development? When should my child begin to explore occupations? What are schools and employment agencies doing in this field? How much education will my child need to succeed in different careers? Should a parent ever choose an occupation for his or her child? Should a parent encourage a child to work part-time while in high school? Do young people give*

sufficient thought to the choice of an occupation? (Knapp & Bedford, 1967)

By using such a strategy, counselors are making parents collaborators rather than isolates in the guidance process and in the education of their children.

Because parents have direct control over the environment in which their children are raised, they have the unique opportunity to expose them to experiences designed to enhance their self-fulfillment. As their children enter education, parents share but do not give up the responsibility for their development. Unfortunately, the complexity and dynamic quality of the current occupational structure make it difficult for most parents to serve as the chief career guidance agents for their children. Indeed, parents are frequently worried about their own occupational future, unsure of how their work contributes to a final product or fits into a total institutional pattern, or confused about the multitude of jobs they see around them.

Such circumstances are exacerbated when economic turmoil and major occupational restructuring are occurring, as in the present American environment. For many elementary school children, however, the problem of stable, informed parental support has been made more difficult because of the changing family structures within which so many children live. Owing partially to economic circumstances and partially to shifting social values, the single-parent household is becoming the new norm for childhood experience.

In such situations, many parents feel incapable of providing career guidance or other support to their children—some, because of economic and personal stresses, do not have the psychic energy to do so. Other parents are simply unclear about how they can be an effective part of their children's development. Often they need reassurance from counselors that they can make such a contribution as well as an understanding of what form it might take. Although not confined to the elementary school, specific ways that parents can contribute to the career guidance program include these:

1. Parents can encourage and help their children to analyze their interests, capabilities, and limitations.
2. In the work areas with which they are most familiar, they can help their children relate worker traits, conditions of work, lifestyles of workers, and potential opportunities for work.
3. They can discuss work values that they have experienced in themselves and others and relate some of the consequences.
4. Parents can discuss the economic condition of the family and help the youth to plan what education and training will help him or her break out of the constraints of these conditions.
5. Parents can provide encouragement and information as to how their child can use the knowledge, experience, and services of relatives, friends, fellow workers, and community or state agencies in exploring, planning, and preparing for their work role.
6. Parents can provide the necessary example and counsel to their children during crucial developmental periods to help them establish and maintain a positive self-concept.
7. They should display the attitude that *all* persons have dignity and worth no matter what occupational position they hold.
8. They can provide situations in which their children can experience decision making and carry responsibility for the consequences of their decisions.
9. They should provide open communication between home and school so that the experiences and the consultation possibilities in both environments can be used to meet the children's needs.
10. Parents should encourage their children to explore a wide spectrum of alternatives, both educational and occupational, without stereotyping or labeling any alternatives to discourage the child's consideration of them.
11. They should be sensitive to and acceptant of the ambivalence or tentativeness that children frequently exhibit about self-images or images of future career alternatives.
12. Without defensiveness about their lack of specific information, parents can help their children contact specialists or find information relevant to their concerns.
13. They can learn about the relationships between specific educational patterns and occupations to help their children to plan their educational experiences effectively.
14. Parents can provide opportunities for work within the home and the community with the opportunity to accept responsibility.

In a study of 382 parents of children in kindergarten, third, and fifth grade in five Maryland public schools, Birk and Blimline (1984) focused on both the importance of parental influence on elementary school children and parental perspectives of their role in their children's career development. They found that, although parents are for the majority of children the most influential agents of occupational exploration, many parents also convey biases and stereotypes about occupational goals and, particularly, sex-appropriate goals. Thus, these researchers recommend that school counselors help parents develop attitudes to do the following:

1. Accept the challenge to collaborate actively with counselors and teachers in the career development process.
2. Acknowledge and accept the importance of the parental role in career development.
3. Maintain a belief in the importance of a child's self-concept in career decision making.
4. Acknowledge the presence and value of work within the home family structure.
5. Advocate increased career opportunities for all without regard to social or sexual stereotypes. (p. 316)

In addition, Birk and Blimline suggest that counselors need to help parents to acquire accurate information about:

> *(a) [T]he role of parents in children's career decisions, (b) changing career choices and broadened options for males and females, (c) educational opportunities, (d) wage and salary statistics, (e) the importance and stages of career planning, (f) barriers to the career development process, (g) career resources in the school and community, (h) myths involved in sex-role stereotyping, (i) sex equity laws, and (j) ways to improve communication skills between the parent and the child." (p. 316)*

Gray and Herr (2001) would argue that while postsecondary options for their children may be quite remote for the parents of elementary school children, even at this level parental biases may cause children to foreclose options and to pursue particular options quite rigidly without considering what may be better options for them. Speaking to the particular social bias of parents toward college rather than technical skills that can be acquired with less than a baccalaureate degree, Gray and Herr have outlined five points for counselors to discuss with parents in order to help them keep their children's options open as long as possible and as thoughtfully as such decisions can be made. These basic points for parents that should be included in an elementary school program, or in a middle school, include in paraphrased and amended form, the following:

Point 1: Because more colleges are practicing a form of open admissions, with fewer colleges considered selective, getting into college is relatively easy, whereas graduating is not. Only about half who matriculate ever graduate in six years. Whether or not they graduate, most college students and/or their parents accrue sizable debt from loans that must be repaid after college matriculation.

Point 2: In the immediate decade or two, the number of four-year college graduates will far exceed the job opportunities requiring a baccalaureate degree. Current projections during this period are that no more than 23 percent of occupations in the United States will require a baccalaureate degree even though in some communities 70, 80, or 90 percent of graduating seniors in high school are entering college.

Point 3: Technical workers are the fastest growing and economically most promising segment of the labor force.

Point 4: The largest number and fastest growing group of jobs among technical workers can be trained for at the two-year associate degree level.

Point 5: On average, technical workers without a four-year college degree will earn higher salaries than all four-year college graduates, except those who obtain jobs in the professional ranks.

While these facts are not necessarily what parents want to hear, they are nevertheless potential counterpoints to some parental biases that can, even in the elementary school, begin to create expectations and plans for children that are neither realistic nor facilitative of career exploration.

RELATIONSHIP OF GOALS TO PROGRAM FUNCTIONS

As indicated in Chapter 6, program goals and behavioral statements of career guidance objectives should precede functions. Program goals should be cast as behavioral descriptions so that the counselor or teacher can evaluate whether the student has met the objectives specified for a grade or other educational level. Assuming for the moment that one has selected from Chapter 6 or has developed locally objectives pertinent to one's school setting and students, one must determine which functional options are available to accomplish the objectives. Several suggestions have already been offered in this chapter. The strategies should be concrete rather than abstract, at least in grades one through three; they should involve action rather than simply verbalization; and they should use multimedia approaches as much as possible. As stated previously, children are doers. They need to explore and try on different work roles.

Concrete Strategies for Implementing Goals

Other observations can be used to guide the selection and use of functions for fostering career development. One is that the characteristics of career development discussed in this book are largely acquired needs pertinent to students in the United States and other developed nations of the world but are not necessarily part of the developmental needs of children in all cultures. Therefore, one must decide for whom and for what purposes children must be prepared for career guidance or career related learning. One way to do this is to reinforce positively, through social approval from teachers, counselors, and parents, behaviors of children that are oriented to consideration of choices, information seeking, and participation in exploratory activities. If some teachers provide these experiences and encourage children to participate in or exhibit career development, but other teachers convey by attitude or behavior that these things are unimportant, many students are not likely to persist in the behavior. For example, if an elementary school child is trying to raise questions about work or choice making but is constantly patted on the head and told not to worry about those things now, the child is not likely to continue to consider them important. If they were, from the child's perspective, this teacher, who is a significant influence in the child's life, would deal with them.

Second, because many of the problems to which early efforts at career development are directed are remote, real or simulated experiences must be provided in which children can make decisions and experience the consequences of those decisions. This may be done by permitting children to plan a particular project and then analyzing the results or by working through illustrative case materials or games, identifying decision factors and alternative outcomes. From such immediate experiences, bridges are built from the world of the school to the world of work. Furthermore, ways must be found to convert daily intellectual problems into occupational problems, thus allowing children to learn a variety of responses to problem-solving circumstances.

The child must also be helped to develop cues by which personally important concepts and ideas can be distinguished from unimportant ones. The child needs to have translated into his or her terms such concepts as relative importance, compromise, irreversibility, synthesis, and developmental process.

To differentiate or integrate self-characteristics and characteristics of the occupational world, the child must be assisted in developing a broad repertoire of pertinent words—the language of occupations. Without them, students lack the tools for manipulating and symbolizing the world as it pertains to them.

Hunt (1970) has stressed the importance of symbolization to the student's ability to deal with the physical, social, and inner worlds as they relate to career development. She sees each of these three abilities as competencies that children must acquire as foundations for career development. In extending this line of reasoning, she recommends that children study workers primarily as problem solvers. Regardless of whether the medium used to help students develop an understanding of different occupations is a field trip, demonstration, film, or reading, students should be encouraged to ask these questions:

1. What is the nature of the problem of living that this person routinely solves?
2. What is the nature of this person's competencies?
3. What special tools does this person use for solving problems?
4. What special facilities does this person need?
5. Could I do what this person is doing?

In addition, Hunt has argued that from kindergarten through the third grade, the emphasis should be more on manipulative direct experience than on vicarious experience. The emphasis at these grade levels is on "Who am I?" rather than "What do others do for me or tell me about?" This also means that the tools or the media that are made available in these experiences must be physically manageable. Besides gaining an understanding about work, children must gain perceptions of themselves as successful with these tools or media. At the fourth-grade to sixth-grade levels, Hunt suggests that although concrete direct experiences are still vital, the array of tools and media needs to be expanded to provide more and more problem-solving challenges requiring exploration of information and acquisition of basic skills.

What is implicit in the position of Hunt is that people and work are irrevocably related. Thus, occupational information is valuable to the degree that it can diminish an outside-the-person focus and stimulate the child's learning and exploration as a part of seeing himself or herself in process and as having and exhibiting freedom of choice. This emphasis on people as workers and as problem solvers also reinforces for the elementary school child the importance of "me" and "my characteristics" as primary influences on "my future."

There are many excellent ways to achieve the learning for elementary children described by Hunt. Two of them include using mentors and using resource persons from the community to provide a career fair.

Terry (1999) has described a community/school mentoring program for elementary school students at the Windermere Boulevard School in Amherst, New York. After carefully defining the goals of the mentoring program and the characteristics of the mentors to be sought, the program was presented to a local Rotary Club. As a result of the school counselor's presentation, fourteen men and one woman agreed to participate. The counselor interviewed each of the prospective mentors in order to orient them and to learn enough about them to make a match with children who wanted to have a mentor.

Mentoring sessions occurred in the school, once a week for 45 minutes. Sometimes the mentor and the child read stories together and discussed them; sometimes the mentor and mentee played a game while discussing a child's school project. In still other cases, the child and mentor talked in depth about the mentor's work, why it was chosen, and so forth. Mentors also met with the child's parents and they sometimes took field trips together to the mentor's work place or to other sites.

Mentors and the participating students completed evaluations which indicated that the students learned new information about careers, the steps to higher education, and problem-solving techniques to deal with personal issues.

A second example by which one can present occupational information to elementary school children appropriate to their age is through the use of a multicultural career fair (Murrow-Taylor, Foltz, Ellis, & Culbertson, 1999). As a function of planning by an elementary school counselor, counselor educator, principal, and university staff, it was decided to have the resource persons visit the classrooms, rather than have a large display of many careers in a gymnasium or other venue. Thus, for the six grades, 24 resource persons were recruited, to provide four speakers for each classroom who would rotate among the classrooms for each grade level. Speakers for each grade level were recruited and assigned by grade level to represent diversity in occupational type, race, and gender. The speakers brought props, and used audiovisual and other equipment, and were interactive with children in their classrooms in order to maximize the details of the careers they represented as well as information about cooperation, good work habits, and so on. The sessions in each classroom were 45 minutes long.

The evaluations of the career fair and the resource persons by students and faculty were very positive. The results indicated that students learned new information about careers, and many children who did not have a male role model in their family enjoyed how male speakers came to class and paid attention to them.

Sequencing Career Guidance Experiences

The previous observations about how elementary school children learn and grow reinforce the importance of sequencing career development experiences from concrete to abstract. First-grade activities should differ from sixth-grade ones, even though the themes or the attitudes to be developed remain constant. In considering sequencing, one must also consider gender differences, as these affect knowledge about or realistic attitudes toward career development.

Bank (1969, p. 235) has suggested an approach by which to focus on the use of occupational role models across grade levels to emphasize particular categories by which jobs can be classified. The examples given have been modified to use contemporary gender-neutral language.

Kindergarten	School role models	Principal Teacher School secretary University professor
First grade	Community role models who help feed us	Grocer Milk deliverer Restaurant server
Second grade	Community role models who protect our health	Dentist Nurse's aide Doctor
Third grade	Models who protect our health and personal hygiene	Barber Beauty operator
	Models who provide shelter	Plumber Building cleaner
	Models who protect us	Lawyer Firefighter Police officer
Fourth grade	Models who provide transportation	Gas station manager Bus driver Airline attendant
Fifth grade	Models who provide communication	Postal worker Printer Photojournalist
Sixth grade	Models who provide for business	Banker Office secretary Salesclerk

Beyond the examples of using occupational role models to sequence career guidance experiences for elementary school children, many career education projects have identified specific concepts appropriate to each grade or educational level by which to organize activities or experiences for children. These approaches are similar to those suggested in Chapter 6. Although there are many examples available, two will illustrate the point here.

The Concepts of Awareness and Accommodation

Bailey and Stadt (1973, pp. 351–359) have suggested that kindergarten through sixth grade can be divided into two stages: awareness (kindergarten through grade three) and accommodation (grades four through six). These, in turn, can be broken into subgoals as follows:

Awareness (K–3)

1. Awareness of self
2. Awareness of different types of occupational roles
3. Awareness of individual responsibility for own actions
4. Development of the rudiments of classification and decision-making skills
5. Learning cooperative social behavior
6. Development of respect for others and the work that they do

Accommodation (4–6)

1. Development of concepts related to self
2. Developments of concepts related to the world of work
3. Assuming increased responsibility for planning one's time
4. Application of decision-making and classification skills
5. Development of desirable social relationships
6. Development of work attitudes and values

Each of these concepts stimulates the development of career guidance experiences that will facilitate the behaviors, attitudes, or knowledge involved. Somewhat similar is the sequence of concepts that guides the career development exemplary project in the District of Columbia Schools (1976). There are many subconcepts distributed across kindergarten through grade six, but the subconcepts and career development activities at each grade level are derived from five:

1. There is dignity in all work.
2. The life of a culture depends on its workers who produce goods and services.
3. There are many different kinds of work
4. Mankind uses tools for work.
5. Work has rewards.

In addition to such concepts, children would likely benefit from the realization that school is a child's work and that its rules, expectations, and content are organized in many ways parallel to the adult world of work.

EXAMPLES OF PROGRAM CONTENT

Approaches to sequencing of program content show awareness of the developing radius of the interests of elementary school students and their increasing capacity for abstractions. They do not, however, directly suggest what content to include or what emphases would lead to the outcomes suggested. There are many possibilities.

In Chapter 6, the Florida Blueprint for Career Preparation was cited as an example of the development of programs of career guidance at various state levels. As part of the follow-up to the Blueprint, the Florida State Department has identified what it describes as "best practices." Some of these follow for the elementary school (Florida Department of Education, 1990, p. 4).

Grades K–5

At the elementary school level, the Blueprint *calls for a career development program that infuses self-, career-, and technology-awareness activities into the curriculum.*

Schoolwide. *Dream Lake Elementary, in Apopka, offers an annual event called "Careers on the Move." On this day, community members bring the vehicles they use in their work to school and give brief presentations about their careers and how the vehicles are used in them. These presentations also include information about how math, reading, computer, or other skills are used; what specialized education the careers require; and the importance of timeliness and dependability. Students who view the vehicles also get to talk with the drivers and learn about such wide-ranging occupations as furniture delivery, tire service, telephone installation and repair, vehicle towing, cement mixing, carpentry, garbage collection, street sweeping, insurance investigation, and undertaking.*

Grade K–1. *Some methods are developing career resource centers—collections of puzzles, games, toys, tools, and other information that can be used for activities to help students understand what goes on in various careers. To increase parental involvement and interest, instruct students to ask their parents to donate something representative of their careers to the resource center. For instance, a carpenter might donate a measuring tape; a practice session on using the measuring tape would teach both a valuable skill and awareness of what a carpenter does.*

Grades 1–2. *A simply drawn map of the local neighborhood can be used to teach students at this level about their local streets as well as various careers. By following an imaginary bus driver or mail deliverer through these streets, children get practice in reading maps, counting turns, reading street signs, and experiencing what these people do when they work.*

Grade 3. *In a dark room, pour hot water into a wide-mouthed jar, then place ice cubes on top of the jar. Shining a flashlight through the middle of the jar will reveal the formation of a cloud. A discussion of how weather affects our lives can lead to lists of careers directly influenced by or dependent on weather—meteorologist, air-conditioning and heating mechanics, clothing manufacturers, builders, and health care workers.*

Grade 4. *After a class discussion of career clusters and the life-styles associated with various careers, students can complete a brief written self-appraisal which determines some of their likes and dislikes. When they share the results of this interest inventory with others in the class, other students can suggest careers that might satisfy their preferences.*

Grade 5. *By videotaping interviews with workers at various job sites around town about their jobs, students can develop map-reading skills, interviewing techniques, technological (VCR) expertise, and awareness of the careers they observe. While on the job sites, they can collect information about the location, type of environment, tools used, noise and/or comfort level, risks involved, attitudes of the people they observe, and a multitude of other factors.*

Another way of sequencing content has been advocated by Ridener (1973). Based on 23 concepts that are to provide the kindergarten through sixth-grade curricula, this approach emphasizes careers of the month, in which instructional guides tie occupations and careers to specific subject matter at each grade level. Thus, each month careers associated with different subjects are highlighted, but no one curriculum reinforces the career concepts throughout the year. The suggested sequence is used to introduce career concepts in a variety of ways throughout the school in September; in October, language arts careers are highlighted; November, math careers; December, science careers; January, social science careers; February, fine arts careers; March, vocational educational careers; and April, health and physical education careers. Finally, in May, activities occur by which the concepts focused on throughout the year can be reviewed and reinforced.

Schmidt (1976), working with a team of elementary school teachers and counselors in the Colorado Springs School District, designed a career guidance program built around two components. The first was concerned with increasing self-concepts of elementary children, and the second built on the first to help students explore careers. The self-concept component was divided into four basic areas: strength-building, in which students were taught how to identify strength in others; values identification, by which students could be helped to clarify their own value systems; goal-setting, in which students established minigoals important to larger aspirations and monitored their progress in achieving these; and life management, in which they discussed obstacles to their self-made goals and developed strategies for overcoming them.

The second component, career awareness, involved the use of several types of commercial resources. One, *Career Kits for Kids,* was used at the kindergarten through second-grade level and allowed students to role-play different types of workers and wear hats and uniforms that fit each particular role. Real workers in the selected areas were invited in to provide actual work process examples for the children and show them the tools used in the occupations. In addition, puppet shows and songs were made up by the children about different forms of work. The second commercial resource used in this component was a series of six filmstrip units (*Career Discoveries*—Guidance Associates) that dealt with broad career areas such as "people who influence others" and "people who make things." The emphases here were on the types of persons in different jobs; their lifestyles; and the strengths, values, and goals they brought to their job. Again, guest speakers were brought in and students compared their personal profiles developed in the self-concept component to those appropriate to different work options.

Related to the content and method suggested by Schmidt, it was implied by Sander, Westerberg, and Hedstrom (1978) that the world of children's literature offers a wide variety of ways to explore decision making or other career guidance objectives. They summarize ten stories from children's literature that could be useful. Included are stories dealing with decision making and the consequences of making unwise choices, self-awareness and economic awareness, and other topics.

Somewhat similarly, Nelson (1979) has described the CREST program, which, through three storybooks for children and related materials and activities, translates the concepts of choice awareness in a way that is intended to be understandable and engrossing for children. It helps them see the many ways in which they are in charge of themselves and the many alternatives they have as they choose their ways. Research on the project indicated that children in the experimental condition were able to produce more choices, and those choices were judged to be more positive, than were those of children in the control condition. Teacher responses were also found to be quite positive about the value of the CREST program.

Wircenski, Fales, and Wircenski (1978) reported on a project for a combined second-grade and third-grade class in the Lafayette, Indiana, schools. The specific objectives were to help the children learn the following concepts:

1. That the world of work is composed of many interrelated jobs to plan, design, advertise, manufacture, distribute, and service goods
2. That all jobs are important
3. That cooperation among all workers is important

These objectives were met by engaging the class in constructing a small wooden wagon and by carrying out activities related to the manufacture of the wagon in various subject areas. Students were assigned to various manufacturing tasks after job specialization required to assemble the wagon was studied. Examples of the uses of related subject areas included the following: music—a promotional song was written and sung by the students; art—a company logo was designed and advertising materials produced; English—various writing assignments dealing with the history of work, the importance of manufacturing, and career opportunities available were produced; math—material and supply needs were calculated and related production times and likely salaries were computed; social studies and science—the principles of manufacturing were studied. As part of the project, each student was interviewed, hired, and trained for his or her job. In engaging in the project, students were also exposed to the importance of work ethics, leadership, cooperation, and respect for others.

Fifield and Petersen (1978) have described the use of job simulation to enhance vocational exploration in the elementary schools. At the time of the report, more than 30 units based on the 15 USOE career clusters, discussed in Chapter 3 and in other places in this book, were being rotated through classrooms in Logan, Utah. The units were either located in classrooms or in mobile units moved among elementary schools. According to the authors, the following steps were taken to develop each simulation unit:

1. A mock-up site was prepared (for example, for the auto brake repair unit, a car fender appropriately mounted with backing plate and brake parts was provided; for the plumbing unit, the section of a wall in which a wash basin and pipe fixtures were installed was provided). In most cases, the mock-up used a workbench or work area where materials and tools were organized.
2. Appropriate materials and tools were assembled and made available for each unit. The student was required to perform only the essential tasks in completing each simulated unit. Real tools associated with the respective jobs were used, and the mock-up for the job was designed as realistically as possible.
3. Instructions and directions were narrated on a cassette tape that was accompanied by a set of written directions and appropriate pictures.
4. Supportive career materials, such as videotapes, catalogues, career brochure, and other literature pertaining to the occupations, were used as the principal source of illustrative materials. (p. 329)

Each unit was designed to be completely self-contained so that the teacher could serve strictly as a monitor.

Handel (1973) has suggested three techniques found to be useful as career guidance activities: career corner, seminar special, and brainstorming. Found to be useful with fifth and sixth graders, career corner comprises a large pegboard with manila packets containing information about various careers placed in an activity area. Pertinent film loops, filmstrips, and tapes can also be placed in the activity area and keyed to the information on the pegboard. Students can develop their own synopses of information in which they are interested and place them into a personal job bank folder for future use. The seminar special consists of devoting periodic morning meetings to visits from people in the community who bring objects they use in their work for the children to handle. These objects provide a focal point to discuss the career area each adult visitor represents. With some cross-class scheduling, several adults can be involved in adjacent rooms each morning, and students can move between them. Brainstorming in this situation was confined primarily to counselor-teacher discussions of the range of possibilities by which teachers could reinforce career development concepts in their subject matter. Although ultimately providing career guidance input to classrooms, this technique was found to increase rapport between the counselor and teachers and promote a team effort in career guidance.

Enhancing career awareness in the elementary school does not necessarily require expensive and sophisticated devices or processes. In line with the intent of the career education movement that was prominent and influential in schools in the 1970s and 1980s, it is important to meld diverse instructional materials and teaching strategies into a sequential program of career awareness, exploration, and preparation from kindergarten through grade twelve and beyond. Within that context, Staley and Mangiesi (1984) have described the use of books to enhance career awareness and to help elementary school students learn about career options.

Use of a wide assortment of informational, fictional, and biographical material provides children with vicarious experiences and the necessary background for dreaming and fantasizing about career options. In some instances, different types of books can be used as a supplement to discussions, field trips, and specific units about work. In other situations, books will form the nucleus for achieving particular career objectives such as providing positive role models, illustrating men and women in nontraditional occupations or with equal opportunities and commitments to work, and reinforcing opportunities for sexual and racial balance in the workplace.

Laramore and Thompson (1970) have suggested encouraging students to fantasize about what they would like to do as adults and then pantomime those jobs, letting other students guess who they are and what they are doing. Other suggestions they provide include the following:

1. Have students discuss their hobbies and attempt to relate them to occupations.

2. Have upper-grade, elementary school children discuss any part-time jobs that they hold around the home or in the community with regard to what they like, the satisfactions they get, or how they spend the money obtained.
3. Have students write a résumé of their own skills (weeding, cutting grass, baby-sitting, ironing) and have them discuss how they might sell these skills to prospective employers in their neighborhood. (pp. 263–264)

Johnson (1980) has described an elementary school career education program for kindergarten through sixth grades that was designed to help students learn about the free enterprise system and to develop an awareness of various jobs and job responsibilities within such a system. All students participated in a six-week course that highlighted job information through team teaching, lectures, group discussions, filmstrips, field trips, and guest speakers. After the six-week overview of the free enterprise economy, students moved into the specific teams dealing with one of four areas: banking, farming, manufacturing, or retailing. After learning about jobs in these specific categories, the children selected the jobs they could best perform and, in doing so, actually made managerial decisions. For example, the bankers set up the Loaning Ranger's Bank, which provided procedures whereby students could deposit from one to five dollars per week or borrow from established funds. In the process of this activity, the children served in such positions as tellers, posters, filers, bookkeepers, and couriers. Similar environments for hands-on experiences were created by the farmers who developed a cultivatable plot of land into the Green Acres Farm and participated in the decisions and actual tasks involved with land preparation, seed planting, fertilizing and watering plants, harvesting, and selling crops to local retailers. The retailing group organized an emporium in which students served as managers, supply clerks, bookkeeping staff, and salespeople. They took a loan with interest from the Loaning Ranger's Bank to purchase stocks of school supplies, paper, pencils, and so on, sold vegetables on consignment from the Green Acres Farm, and brokered craft items produced by the last group, the manufacturers, in their factory. Students in the Purple Polka-Dot Factory sold stock certificates for 25 cents each to obtain initial operating capital, elected a board of directors to supervise factory operations, and manufactured such products as purple polka-dot necklaces, fuzzy wuzzy pencils, big-nose bookmarkers, and faculty favorite cookbooks.

Activities for the four teams were integrated with school curricula—math, science, spelling, social studies, and language arts—necessary to perform the various functions in the clusters. Pretest and posttest data indicated that student participants gained knowledge about the vocabulary and processes of the free enterprise system. Informal reactions solicited from students, teachers, parents, and the community were overwhelmingly positive.

Obviously, either of the projects reported by Leonard or Johnson, or those previously described, represent major career guidance thrusts of importance to counselors. They constitute both the substance and the planned sequence of activity that can yield important insights and skills to empower elementary school children to grow in career consciousness, self-awareness, and optimism about future opportunities.

CAREER GUIDANCE TECHNIQUES IN THE ELEMENTARY SCHOOL

Throughout this chapter we have suggested many career development techniques appropriately used in the elementary school. Many others however, can be used to achieve particular program goals and behavioral objectives. Even the extensive list of techniques that follows is not exhaustive because creative elementary school counselors and teachers will find additional ways to achieve selected career guidance goals. These may be used with individual students or groups of students, by the counselor or by a teacher. Many can also be used by the counselor in serving as a resource to teachers.

As suggested by the NOICC (1988), career guidance and counseling programs in schools are based on seven processes: classroom instruction, counseling, assessment, career information, placement, consultation, and referral. The issue is what kind of content will they include. The following techniques represent examples that might be integrated with one of these seven processes.

Curriculum Infusion—Career Units

Provide reference books or biographies that portray personal decision making.

Show guidance films on selected topics.

Read poems such as Robert Frost's "The Road Not Taken" and have students compare them to decision making in their own lives.

Have students create and then discuss "I wish" poems.

Analyze short stories based on characters portraying different interests or values.

Select a career cluster requiring competence in particular subject matter (such as math, science, language) and identify occupations related to it.

Have students research some aspect of change—such as a means of transportation—compile pictures depicting changes and occupations affected, and arrange a bulletin board display related to the project.

Do oral reports on different occupations with the student pretending to be the worker in the report.

Have students write a paper on "The kind of person I am," "The kind of person I want to be," or "How I have changed in the past year."

Make a movie with students serving as plot writers, camerapersons, and graphic artists to illustrate communication careers.

Introduce a course on self science to focus on children's emotions. Use the tensions and traumas of the child's day as the content to explore feelings and problem solving. (Goleman, 1995, p. 268)

Use the ingredients of Emotional Intelligence as described by Goleman (1995) as the focus of discussions with students.

Have students prepare an autobiography and address at least three ways in which their life is influenced by family, school, and peers.

Display words in a prominent place that refer to leisure-time occupations such as lapidary, numismatist, spelunker, philatelist, bibliophile. Have students look up the meaning of these words and consider how they relate to the use of leisure time.

Build interest centers around different career clusters or ways to assess self-characteristics.

Provide listening centers that include individual earphones, recording devices, record players, tapes and cassettes dealing with worker interviews, study skills, and topics related to self-understanding.

Build into the curriculum one of the projects on social and emotional learning for elementary schools described in Goleman (1995), *Emotional Intelligence.*

Group Activities

Play "Let's Pretend" or "What's My Line" using occupations or careers as the content.

Role-play photo problems for children in grades one through three. Mount photographs depicting various problems or situations pertinent to self-understanding or occupational differences on display board, and have children role-play their interpretation of the photos.

Have students discuss unfinished stories available in the *NEA Journal* and in other sources that cause them to consider alternative solutions to various problems.

Have students design posters depicting the steps or conditions important to responsible decision making.

Have students probe a problem-solving situation by making up the behavior of puppets.

Engage students in values clarification exercises and then discuss how interests and values are different.

Discuss the concepts of self-efficacy, outcomes, and goals.

Have each student write a brief paper on what these three concepts mean to him or her personally.

Have students design table games to play different approaches to decision making, career options, or other life situations.

Write a skit using terms from the world of work.

Develop crossword puzzles using terms from the world of work.

Use the help-wanted section of a newspaper to identify words from the world of work.

Have students compose questions and take part in a class "quiz show" based on occupations and educational alternatives.

Have students compose a help-wanted advertisement for a particular job.

Bring in a tool or material, or a uniform or a picture of one, and use these as the basis for a creative writing lesson about the objects or workers who use them.

Have students write about a fantasy or daydream about doing a certain job, draw pictures of themselves doing it, and identify the tools necessary. Discuss in class.

Using local job-related events, have students develop career pyramids to illustrate the interdependence of jobs required to accomplish the goal (such as build a new apartment house, airport, supermarket).

Have students produce a short cartoon strip about some aspect of the world of work that went wrong.

Have students collect pictures of workers whose occupations are clearly a means of self-expression, such as writer, musician, artist, and generate class discussion on the way in which other occupations are a means of self-expression; pictures may be used for bulletin board.

Have students participate in everyday decisions such as what to do in free time, which homework assignment to do first, where to eat lunch.

Have students interview workers about the various purposes work serves for them (e.g. economic, psychological, social).

Have students learn the ingredients of conflict resolution and practice it in role-plays and in actual classroom situations.

Have students plan a class party or field trip, identify the compromises that must be made, and list the risks or consequences.

Have students design creative drama skits that deal with self-concept, values, making choices, and other pertinent topics.

Have students compare lists of interests, abilities, and achievements with occupations in which these are important.

Have students identify feelings from pictures (sad, happy, and so on) and relate them to past situations in which they experienced these feelings.

Have students identify different roles they play, list them on the board, and have discussions on how these roles are learned or why they are important.

Have students maintain a diary in which they note things that make them feel unique, worthwhile, and deserving of respect.

Have students construct a career pyramid that illustrates the different types of jobs in a career area at different levels of education and responsibility. For example, in health careers, discuss the range of opportunities from the ambulance driver or sanitary inspector to the most sophisticated specialist, physician, or researcher.

Have students compose a brief job profile for a worker in each of the career clusters.

Given a series of pictures illustrating various community workers (police officer, truck driver, salesperson, teacher, construction worker), have the students give a job title for each, discuss the work activities involved and the problems they solve.

Have students describe ten different workers who built, maintain, or operate the school.

Have students list major problems facing society and then identify an occupation or career cluster that they think will have greatest effect on solving the problems.

Using a list of twenty to fifty occupations, have students give an example of a need or function of the community that is met by each occupation.

Have students review selected sites on the Internet that discuss career opportunities and use the information obtained as content for classes or group sessions.

Have students keep a log of the examples of occupational stereotyping they discover while watching television and discuss in a class or group.

Using a list of ten to fifteen common occupations, have students describe those that are (1) mostly outside work, (2) mostly inside work, (3) both inside and outside work.

Using pictures of people at work, have students distinguish between those involving the production of goods or services.

Have students match pictures of tools and what they are used for (for example, rake-leaves, hammer-nails, saw-boards, screwdriver-screws). Discuss the use of tools for different purposes in school and in work.

Have students identify two commonly used tools in each career cluster.

Have dress-up clothes available for children to try on and pretend to be the workers. Discuss how they feel when they act out a particular worker's role and what would they like to know about such a worker.

Provide social skills training to help students understand the importance of getting along with others in a world where cultural diversity and teamwork are major emphases for the workplace of the twenty-first century.

Have students select an occupation of their choice and through a variety of media (resource books, filmstrips, interviews), develop an accurate description of a typical lifestyle for the worker in a chosen occupation.

Using a supply of magazines, have students locate one picture that breaks down the traditional male-female occupational role typing (male nurse, female physician, male secretary, female truck driver). Discuss.

Have students keep a log of all the examples of occupational stereotyping that they discovered while watching TV.

Using a list of leisure-time activities (baseball, art, photography, rock collecting), have each student identify at least one occupation that could result from an interest in each activity.

Have students pantomime a leisure activity in which they engage. Other students try to guess the activity. Play "Twenty Questions" based on leisure-time activities of the students.

Have students plan and carry out a Hobby Fair in which each student is invited to bring an example of his or her hobby and demonstrate or describe the hobby to the class.

Have students make a class display of various famous people engaging in their leisure field career.

In a role-playing situation, have students break into pairs and role-play an employer who is interviewing an applicant for a job. The interviewer wants to know why the person wants the job—besides the money.

Have children engage in comparison shopping while visiting a shopping center. Have children compare the costs of a box of eight crayons. Discuss.

Community Involvement

Create a job club to discuss jobs and job finding with adult resource persons.

Take field trips to sites that allow students to see how subject matter is applied to solve work problems or is necessary to facilitating work activity.

Invite resource persons to discuss how personal characteristics contribute to daily functioning or ask them to discuss their vocational history in relation to what they now do.

Have students "shadow" selected workers on the job to view the work activity in which they engage and the other types of workers with whom they interact.

Invite the director of the local adult education class to visit the school, discuss the program with students, and explain why adults take courses.

Develop and organize lists of resource speakers and field trips to observe the workers' roles in various occupations.

Visit a local factory and observe the entire production process. Assign small groups to study one aspect of the process thoroughly, make a display of it, and present it to the total class.

After an opportunity to interview a worker, have the student orally describe the career exploration of the worker, and the way in which the worker applied career exploration to the process of deciding to enter the career in which he or she is presently employed.

After talking with two adults in different occupational roles, have students list four ways in which their occupation influences the lifestyle of each (amount of spare time available, money to buy various items, travel versus staying in one location, hobbies, friends).

Interview a parent or relative to discover the personal satisfactions obtained from working and leisure activities.

Have students visit a local sports equipment store and discuss with the manager the growing demand for sporting equipment for leisure time.

Have the class visit a local craftsperson or invite the person to visit the class. Have that person discuss his or her work in terms of speed, efficiency, economy, and quality. If possible, have the students compare the handcrafted product with its mass-produced counterpart. Stress that society needs both types of products.

The career guidance techniques identified here are of little use unless they are planned for and integrated into a systematic effort. For example, a field trip is often merely a reward for students or teachers and has little intrinsic value. Its value can be significantly enhanced if students are prepared to look for certain things while at the field site and if they have an opportunity to discuss their observations on return from the site. The same is true of most of the other items mentioned in the foregoing list. In isolation, these techniques are of little value. When tied to specific program goals and behavioral expectations for children, introduced in a planned and meaningful way, and opportunities made available to reinforce the learning they present, such techniques have a powerful cumulative effect in moving elementary students toward progressive career maturity.

To achieve such goals in career guidance, the elementary school counselor, in cooperation with teachers, needs to consider the following:

1. How to individualize those career guidance techniques that will be used
2. How to increase teacher, parent, and student knowledge of career development and the ways career guidance techniques facilitate it
3. How to coordinate career guidance activities
4. How to develop or acquire special materials
5. How to implement cooperation, planning, and evaluation.

Obviously, some students will not achieve the behaviors identified throughout this chapter as necessary to career development by means of curricular or other group modes. Problems involving personal relationships, decision making and problem solving, adjustment to one's failures and successes, and meeting the demands of everyday living are best handled in an individually tailored counseling mode. The stimulus modes identified in most of the chapter examples lay an information base from which self-understanding, career awareness, and related coping or mastery tasks can arise. Individual and group tasks supplement each other depending on individual readiness and the tasks to be achieved.

SUMMARY

In this chapter, we have described an array of themes and practices that can be used in elementary school career guidance efforts to stimulate career development in children. Attention has been given to the characteristics of development manifested by elementary age children, and these characteristics have been set forth as the criteria to which career guidance efforts must be attuned. The major themes discussed were the importance of the elementary school as a shaper of attitudes toward the self and toward different aspects of the environment, the relationships between work habits developed in the elementary school and work behavior in adulthood, and the need of individual students to develop a vocabulary for distinguishing environmental characteristics and important aspects of their evolving selves. Relationship of goals to program function and the sequencing of career guidance program content and techniques have also been discussed.

CHAPTER EIGHT

Career Development in the Junior High/Middle School

KEY CONCEPTS

- Planning for career guidance and counseling in the junior high school/middle school must acknowledge the transitional character of this period and the importance of student exploration and planning.
- An important emphasis in career guidance and counseling in the junior high school is to help students understand the consequences of curricular and course choices made now—and planned for the senior high school—so that later options will not be prematurely closed.
- Students cannot explore or choose educational or occupational goals if they do not know about them. Timely, relevant, and accurate information is important to quality career development programs.
- Gender differences in information, models available, self-efficacy, and bias toward or away from particular choices become major factors in planning and delivering career guidance and career counseling in the middle school and the junior high school.

When examining the career development needs and characteristics of students at separate educational levels—elementary school, junior high school/middle school, and senior high school—it is tempting to declare that one of these is more important than another. Yet the essence of career development is that each of these life stages demands mastery of different emphases within an evolving consciousness of self-characteristics and of the life options to which these characteristics relate. In other words, career development, as mediated through the educational process, must be responsive to the developmental tasks that surface as children grow as well as to the characteristics of the institutions that influence their mastery of these developmental tasks. If the practice of career development is going to be a developmental process, the career guidance program must be continuous and cumulative. The outcomes obtained by students at one educational level must serve as the foundation for the next educational level.

In most career guidance models, programs for grades seven through nine emphasize exploration and planning. This does not imply that the elementary school emphases of self-awareness and career awareness have been completed, but rather that as children grow, they face new demands. Thus, they must develop increasingly complex behaviors. Indeed, it is likely that, for most students, self-awareness and career awareness will continue to be refined as self-exploration, career exploration, and planning proceed in the junior high or middle school and beyond. In this process of refinement, many students will continue to adjust both their aspirations and their expectations that they will achieve their aspirations or not, and, in the process, be required to compromise their aspirations (Armstrong & Crombie, 2000).

The need for preadolescents and early adolescents to acquire knowledge and skills important to exploration and planning comes from their opportunities to engage in activities farther from home and independent from the family as well as from the nature of the school itself.

The increasing needs of middle school and junior high school students to reflect their growing independence occurs in work itself. About half of all 12- and 13-year-olds engage in some form of work (Huang, Pergamit, & Shkolnik, 2001). While "the Fair Labor Standards Act prohibits employment of those younger than age 14, and restricts the hours and jobs allowed for those younger than 16...many youths have 'jobs' before these ages. These jobs, while not always like those of adults, frequently involve learning work behavior (for example, showing up at a particular time every week), personal responsibility (for example, caring for someone's child), remuneration, and other characteristics that teach young adolescents the basic structure of working for someone else" (p. 18). In their study of a national sample of 12- and 13-year-olds, Huang and colleagues report on the interviews conducted by the National Longitudinal Survey of Youth, 1997 Cohort, which asked the 12- and 13-year-old respondents about their job experiences since their twelfth birthday. Such experiences could include working for someone else (e.g., delivering newspapers) or doing tasks for several people—freelance jobs (e.g., baby-sitting or mowing lawns). Most of the jobs reported were freelance jobs.

According to Huang and colleagues, of the almost 3,000 12- and 13-year-olds surveyed, 52.5 percent had held a job, the average number of jobs held was 1.6, and the average age of initiation was 11.6 years. Thus, there is a major upturn in job initiation around 12 years of age, the time when many adolescents first get exposure to the working world. Too young to work legally at restaurants, stores, and other businesses, 75 percent of the jobs held by 12- and 13-year-olds include baby-sitting, yard work, or lawn mowing. These students spend an average of seven hours per week working and they receive an average of $23 a week. Girls are somewhat more likely than boys to have a job (54 percent to 51 percent); 59 percent of white youth had jobs compared to about 40 percent of African American and Hispanic youth. The higher the parents' earnings and the higher the parents' educational level, the higher the likelihood that their child would have a job. However, working 12- and 13-year-olds who are minority, poorer, and have less-educated parents tend to work longer hours per week.

While there continues to be controversy about whether or not children of 12 or 13 years should work, Huang and colleagues found in their study that the respondents who indicated that they spend time on homework, extra classes, watching television, reading for pleasure were more likely to hold a job.

The research of Rothstein (2001), again using the National Longitudinal Survey of Youth, 1997 Cohort, shows a similar work pattern to occur among 14- and 15-year-old youth. Some 57 percent of youth held a job at sometime at age 14; most of these were freelance jobs. Some 64 percent had worked during age 15. But during age 15, there was a shift away from primarily freelance jobs to employee jobs. For 14- and 15-year-olds, employee jobs were concentrated in a relatively small number of industries and jobs: eating and drinking places, grocery stores, construction, janitors and cleaners, farm workers, newspaper delivery, cooks and cashiers and general office clerks, waiters and waitresses. These jobs tended to be divided between male and female youth in traditional ways. With respect to freelance jobs, babysitting for females and yard work for males continued to be the most common jobs.

In either employee or freelance work, employment is much higher among white youth at ages 14 and 15 than among African American and Hispanic youth. For example, at age 15, 72 percent of whites, 48 percent of Hispanics, and 44 percent of African American youths had worked at some time. The differences in these numbers suggest that minority youth may live in areas with less economic opportunity and may have less access to transportation to where available jobs are located.

Aside from the increasing involvement in work by 12- to 15-year-old youth, the eighth and ninth grades are the first instances in the typical student's life of formal choice points; times when the individual is faced with external pressures to make a public decision and a potentially long-range commitment among competing alternatives. Such decisions are reflected in expectations of choice among specific courses, high school curricula, a particular high school or area vocational technical school to attend, or, in some instances, whether to remain in school at all.

The junior high/middle school is a transition period between childhood and adolescence as well as between general and specialized education. As such, its processes and goals reflect either solutions or further exacerbations of what Coleman (1974) perceives as the gap between "youth and adulthood" or what other observers see as the gap between "education and work" (Herr, 1994b).

It is a period that observers are increasingly citing as a time of particular vulnerability, a time when young adolescents may adopt self-damaging behavior patterns that can sometimes shorten their lives or diminish their prospects for the future. "Young adolescents experience biological, cognitive, and psychological changes that lead them to reappraise themselves and their relationships to their families and communities. These changes are often accompanied by disengagement from school, the onset of experimentation with alcohol and other drugs, and sexual activity. Research shows that problem behaviors manifested early tend to persist into later life" (Hamburg & Takaniski, 1989, p. 826). Many of the potential behavioral problems that begin to be visible among this age group are interrelated and are accompanied by poor school achievement. "Thus, early adolescence is a period when young people are choosing life-styles rather than among specific behaviors, life-styles that become progressively integrated and consolidated as the adolescent grows older" (Jackson & Hornbeck, 1989, p. 834).

Gibson and associates (1991) reported a study of what 13- to 15-year-old adolescents in disparate cultural and socioeconomic environments in 17 nations, including the United States, perceive to be their most pressing problems and what they do to cope. Using a questionnaire translated into the language of the countries in which the research was conducted by researchers in that nation, it was found that *family, schooling,* and *personal identity/self-concept* were the three most frequently cited classes of problems for all groups of adolescents, in disadvantaged and advantaged populations, across the nations surveyed. These three classes of problems, from the 13 possible classes divided into 100 categories on the questionnaire, accounted for 69.1 percent of the responses. Within the category of *schooling,* the categories of *academic failure* and *academic achievement* accounted for 18.6 percent of all responses, and within the *personal identity/self-concept* category, *growing up* and *self-confidence* consistently ranked first or second when all groups were considered.

Within the nine classes of coping strategies, divided into 37 categories of action, *individual problem solving* was the most frequently reported class of coping strategy, regardless of Socioeconomic status grouping; the categories of *trying harder* and *planning a solution* ranked first or second in all groups. In general, gender differences in these rankings were not found.

The findings of the study led Gibson and associates to conclude: (1) "Adolescent concerns are age-related and remarkably similar regardless of national background, socioeconomic grouping, or gender." (2) "Although adolescent concerns are more similar than different, the Disadvantaged/Poverty populations have a greater variety of problems than their more advantaged peers and at a higher percentage of some problems" (p. 214).

Factors such as present-future relationships, values, delayed gratification, personal responsibility, and choice consequences have real implications for individual students. How and to what degree the attitudes, knowledge, and skills making up these factors are acquired has implications beyond immediate adjustment at the junior high or middle school level. Such development is also predictive of success and satisfaction in the senior high school years and beyond.

In addition to these factors of importance to individual student development, the middle/junior high school experience also contributes to the knowledge and attitudes leading to informed entry into the occupational world. As has been noted throughout this book, students vary in the degree to which they obtain learning and instruction about occupations and employment; particularly important questions are whether such learning is implemented systematically from kindergarten to twelfth grade, and whether it is coordinated and integrated with curriculum. Walls (2000) has observed:

> *Although career planning increases with age… evidence is lacking that this planning, even in 12th grade, has a foundation in accurate and extensive knowledge concerning employment. Knowledge of occupations, particularly blue-collar careers, is neither stressed in school curricula nor assessed in the research. Rather than developing a mature cognitive architecture, the student may suffer potentially harmful consequences of superficial consideration and inaccurate integration of occupational knowledge. (p. 138)*

Walls research with 189 male and female students in third, sixth, ninth, and twelfth grades assessed the accuracy of their information on particular dimensions across the period covered from third to twelfth grades. The specific dimensions of occupations assessed were (a) time (training, preparation, (b) availability (positions, jobs), (c) earnings (pay, dollars), (d) physical (strength, stamina), (e) mental (thinking, knowledge), (f) status (respect, prestige), and (g) preference (like, enjoy). These dimensions were assessed across a matrix of 20 occupations well known and representing the spectrum of occupations. Walls found that students' knowledge and accuracy on these dimensions and occupations varied substantially across the grade levels studied. With regard to the ninth grade particularly, while generally more accurate than third or sixth grades, these students were more accurate on earnings, mental requirements, and status, than on time to prepare, physical requirements or availability of the jobs considered. In general, participants tended to favor those occupations they believed had high status, mental requirements, earning, and preparation time. Most frequent occupations cited by ninth graders were computer-related, doctor, lawyer, and teacher. Such findings allow counselors to identify informational linkages that students have not yet developed or about which their views are inaccurate and incorporate these into their career guidance initiatives. As Walls concludes:

> *Potentially, there is a large difference between what students gain on their own with no systematic instruction and what is acquired with the aid of good instruction.... How much a student values a particular occupation is integrally dependent or what the student knows or has constructed about that occupation. Impoverished occupational knowledge structures and inaccurate expectations can have undesirable consequences. (p. 143)*

Before turning to specific aspects of career guidance and career counseling in the junior high school/middle school, it is useful to think about the developmental characteristics of students at this age. Unless these matters are taken into consideration, much career guidance activity or career counseling is likely to be irrelevant. For ease of writing, *junior high school* is used subsequently in this chapter to include both middle school and junior high school students.

CHARACTERISTICS OF JUNIOR HIGH SCHOOL YOUTH

Junior high school students are not the same creatures who inhabited the elementary schools a year or two earlier. As a result of experience and growth, their horizons have widened. With pubertal changes near, either in themselves or in their peers, their perceptions of life have changed. Junior high students are more able than elementary-age children to comprehend relationships and to use abstract terms and symbols. They are preoccupied with belonging and conformity, being highly influenced by their like-sexed peers and less so by their opposites; they are also taking tentative steps toward independence from their families, although parents still play an active and influential role in their child's career development (Young, 1994). They are making more definitive strides in sorting themselves from the mass of students with whom they interact as they try on the multiple social roles that accompany school and community experience.

However, it is important to note, as the research of Schmitt-Rodermund and Vondracek (1999) with German youth under grade ten, indicate:

> *The roots of exploratory behaviors are put down in children rather than in adolescents. Parents seem to play an important role here. Their behavioral modeling as well as their activities together with their children, teach about how one can spend time and how one can find out one's likes and dislikes. This way of parenting very often is accompanied by a warm, and at the same time directive, parenting style that contributes to an atmosphere of receptiveness and openness to many interests. (p. 314)*

These researchers further found:

> *Strongest predictors for adolescent exploration were creative, technical, and cultural childhood activities, indicating that adolescents who as children explored more, that is, they engaged in a broad range of activities, had more interests and pursued more activities in their second decade of life as well. In addition, goal directedness was relevant for adolescent exploration. Adolescents, who were very achievement oriented and had high goals for the future reported a broader range of interests and more activities than those who were not very ambitious....*
>
> *Furthermore, results showed that exploratory activities were indeed related to identity status (Marcia, 1980). Identity achievers reported a broad range of interests and exploratory activities. Adolescents in identity diffusion had only few interests and did not engage in extensive exploratory activities. (p. 312)*
>
> *The level of exploration was related to occupational choice. Independently of their age, adolescents who had already made up their minds about what occupation they wanted to pursue in the future had explored more than those who did not yet have an idea of what to do. (p. 313)*

As a validation of many of the research findings reported here, Lefstein and Lipsitz (1986) have summarized the needs of this age group as follows:

- Diversity
- Self-exploration
- Meaningful participation
- Positive interaction with peers and adults
- Physical activity
- Competence and achievement

This list of needs reflects both the characteristics of the young adolescent and a template of emphases to which career guidance programs must be structured if they are to meet the developmental needs of this age group effectively. The needs of the typical junior high school child suggest that career guidance programs must offer them a wide variety of experiences and opportunities so that children at various rates of development can find something that fits their present stage of development and the issues with which they are preoccupied. Such programs must provide opportunities for these children to receive feedback about whom they are becoming, the opportunities opening to them, and their relationships with others. They need time and space to gain new experiences and to contemplate the meaning of these experiences for their lives. Young adolescents want to be active and to demonstrate their ability to be responsible for themselves and others. They seek opportunities to use their skills and to participate meaningfully. Within such contexts, young adolescents want positive experiences with adults and peers as they seek affection, support, information, and criticism.

Clearly, junior high school students are immersed in the continued development, refinement, and strengthening of basic skills begun in the elementary school, and they are beginning to converge on the more specialized experience of the senior high school. Their time focus is shifting, however subtly, from the immediate present to the future. Because choices of curricula and of the specific high school or vocational school they will attend a year or two hence are rapidly approaching, their sensitivity to work and its relevance to them as persons in the process of becoming is accentuated.

Indeed, it is possible to consider the ninth grade (in some schools, the eighth grade) deserving of special treatment compared to the earlier grades in the junior high school. While students are encouraged to explore comprehensively and to keep one's options open, students by the ninth grade are frequently encouraged to think seriously about their life and their future. This is a time when students are expected to begin to choose more systematically in terms of their preferences and abilities and a time when developmental theories of career development (see Chapter 4) would predict that students at approximately the ninth grade would move from general, undifferentiated, fantasy choices to those which begin to take on tentativeness about possible career choices.

Among other important career issues, problems of selecting a high school to attend and choosing courses in high school are matters of significance in the junior high school. Frequently this is true because junior high school students or their parents are unaware that when one chooses an educational course of action, he or she reduces, or at best alters, the alternatives available in the future.

Educational decisions made in the junior high school are obviously not benign, although they may be reversible. The fundamental point is that the problem of committing oneself to an educational plan, advertently or inadvertently, in the junior high school as one prepares for the transition to high school is one with ramifications that ripple throughout one's life. One can keep open or foreclose future opportunities by the course content and the course patterns that one chooses in the junior high school and in the transition to the intermediate or senior high school. When one makes such choices, one essentially limits or establishes an interactive network of future alternatives. For example, if one chooses to avoid courses in advanced mathematics, the likelihood of entering scientific, technological, or engineering curricula or occupations beyond high school is minimal to nonexistent. It is within such a context that Perry (quoted in Lozada, 1999) has argued:

> *When working with a ninth grader, the most important thing a school counselor must do is make sure the student is taking the most challenging classes possible.... Students should not get to their senior year and regret that they did not take the right high-level math or science courses to pursue a particular postsecondary program. (p. 31)*

Jordaan and Heyde (1979) observe:

> *Although they may not realize it, these curricular choices are also for many students' prevocational*

choices. The commercial curriculum is in effect pre-business; the industrial arts curriculum, preparation for a skilled trade; the college curriculum, preprofessional; and the general curriculum, a sort of no man's land with no clear-cut prevocational implications.... In pursuing a given curriculum they are, whether they know it or not, increasing the probability of being admitted to or excluded from certain fields of work and training programs. (p. 2)

As suggested previously, these perspectives are particularly true in the election of those courses that permit the student maximum freedom to qualify for educational opportunities beyond the secondary school while the student is reality-testing whether or not such further education is necessary for goal achievement. Because at the junior high school level in particular, school *is* work, the opportunity to use personal encounters with the different content and context of courses to explore present and future alternatives is important; it is also manageable.

Although the alternatives from which a junior high school student can choose are limited, they nevertheless represent the opportunity to practice collecting and analyzing information about alternatives, to anticipate outcomes, and to develop decision plans. Because such dimensions are crucial to successful career development, curricular decisions made in the junior high school provide the opportunity to help students consider how to maximize freedom of choice and assume responsibility for choices made while there is still time for reversing a choice and charting new educational routes if necessary.

Evidence from the national data base *High School and Beyond* reported in a 1986 publication of the College Board, *Keeping the Options Open: An Overview* (College Board Commission on Precollege Guidance and Counseling, 1986) indicates that junior high school students frequently do not understand and act on the consequences of their early academic choices. For example, data revealed that only 46 percent of students who expected in grade nine that they would enter college reported being enrolled in the academic (as opposed to the general or vocational) curriculum in grade ten. By their senior year, only about half the students reported being on a path that was congruent with their college expectations. Part of this phenomenon can be explained by the lack of assurance many students feel about being able to achieve the goals they set for themselves. Thus, if one uses the decision to go to or prepare for college as an example, when crucial choices about courses are made, it is important for students to believe that college is a real possibility for them, financially as well as academically. If younger adolescents and their families do not get timely and effective financial aid information, they are likely to make educational choices that limit rather than advance their academic aspirations (National Student Aid Coalition, 1985).

A similar situation arises when junior high school students and their families are at a crucial point of decision about choosing a vocational education curriculum. Unless they have timely and accurate information about access, work opportunities, and future postsecondary educational possibilities associated with attending a vocational education curriculum, they are likely to exclude such choice options from their deliberations (National Commission on Secondary Vocational Education, 1985).

The years of junior high school are, by design, transition years. Intensive, almost frenzied, exploration can be expected whether the school aids it or simply allows it to proceed. It is a period when such career development concepts as compromise and the congruence or incongruence between aspirations and expectations become operational as realities and when idealistic fervor or naïveté get their initial temperings in the reality testing of curricular, athletic, and part-time work experiences. It is also a time when values emerge with enough continuity to be measurable. Indeed, research shows that the development of work values is well underway by the fifth grade and that eighth graders display value profiles similar to those of fifth graders (Hales & Fenner, 1972). Unless the educational experiences provided students at this level are timely and appropriate to the questions that students are asking themselves, it is unlikely that they will have a significant influence on student behavior or choice making. This is a time, then, when change in the self and the world can be used as a focal point for planning and when student responsibilities through participation in planning can be related to the consequences of decisions. Various research studies have shown that the majority of junior high students exhibit a readiness for career planning. The question is, are schools and counselors prepared to help in this process?

Readiness of middle or junior high schools to systematically help students with their readiness for career planning can take many forms. Wahl and Blackhurst (2000) have argued:

> *An effective career guidance curriculum can lead students to realistic ideation about the various postsecondary options, the necessity of specific secondary and postsecondary training for certain careers, and how to prepare successfully for careers in a variety of fields...because minority students may turn to peers rather than professionals for career information (Mau, 1995), middle school counselors should routinely include the small group work [as a career development strategy]...[in which] counselors must be alert to—and ready to intervene in—group discussion that reinforces...cultural norms or societal expectations [that limit student exploration or career aspirations]. (p. 372)*

As the rest of this chapter suggests, there are many ways to assist students with their career readiness. They include information about jobs and hiring trends, training requirements for specific job families or career clusters and their implications for participating in postsecondary education; career days in which employers and professionals in the community discuss different occupations, their primary duties, what persons in these occupations do on a daily basis, and how to prepare for these occupations; and providing students with information about their measured aptitudes and interests and the relationships of these to various postsecondary training and career options.

Many states, encouraged by federal legislation related to the transition from school to work, now require or strongly encourage that no later than the middle or junior high school each student in collaboration with the school counselor create an individual career plan (ICP) and review it annually. Such a plan includes the career goals and preferences students begin to identify that can be related to each student's career interests, aspirations for postsecondary education, and individual aptitudes and achievements. Creating an ICP is a process the specific objective of which is to make a plan of action that the student will follow through high school and after graduation.

> *The plan provides concrete postsecondary plans and tentative career goals, identifies the steps (e.g., courses to be taken in high school) that are required, and reinforces the commitment and responsibility of each child to take charge of his or her career. (Gray & Herr, 2000, p. 119)*

In this sense, the process and responsibility inherent in the constructing and managing of individual career development lays the base for the types of behavior expected in adulthood as discussed in Chapter 2 in relation to protean careers and personal flexibility. The ICP is a written document developed jointly by students, their parents, and school personnel. It is typically included in the student's permanent record field and reviewed periodically as new and relevant data about the student are provided by the school that may help to clarify the validity of particular plans of action.

There are many different forms that an Individual Career Plan (ICP) can take. Increasingly such plans encourage students to document their progress in what has come to be called a career portfolio. Such portfolios can be done on paper or by electronic means, but whichever form they take, they chronicle the student's academic achievements, career-related experiences and competencies, career interests, part-time work and its nature, and other processes that depict a graphic record of the student's career development journey and acquisition of interests, experiences, skills, and aspirations across the elementary, middle school, and high school years.

One frequently used model is the "Get a...Life" Personal Planning Portfolio, developed by the American School Counselors Association with a grant from the National Occupational Information Coordinating Committee. The portfolio is developed systematically, recommends certain career activities at specific points from K to 12, and the resultant document follows the student throughout his or her school life. This Personal Planning Portfolio is divided into two parts. The first part, the personal file, contains individual reflections about tentative career plans as they evolve from year to year in response to the career guidance activities to which students are exposed. The second part, the competency file, contains objective data that the school system provides about a student's academic achievements and measured abilities. It also contains copies of certificates identifying student competencies that have career relevance (e.g., proficiency in keyboarding) or documentation of successful experiences in job shadowing, cooperative education, tech prep, and so on.

Again, the goal of this model and others like it is to move students from a state of career immaturity or naiveté about career planning to a state of evolving career maturity, job readiness, and tentative certainty.

Certainly, a by-product of this process is feedback to students and parents about the objective data on student achievement and about career interests, experiences, and patterns on which tentative future planning can be based and upon which individual readiness for the associated decisions can be reinforced.

Gender Differences

The junior high school years are also a time when gender differences exert important influences in curriculum choice and when choice considerations often become different in kind for males and females.

In the previous chapter, little emphasis was placed on differences in career development strategies based on gender. The intent was not to gainsay the influence of gender-typing on occupational stereotypes or on appropriate choices to be considered. Rather the assumption was that boys and girls both need a language of vocations, an orientation to preference, and the rudiments of how to differentiate interests and aptitudes and relate them to future educational options and the occupational clusters available. These experiences should be gained within a context that is not gender-biased. In the junior high school, sex effects become far more pronounced and perhaps make different guidance emphases necessary. As indicated in the conclusions of Chapter 4, career development theories give less than comprehensive attention to differences between males and females, but it is obvious—if for no other reason than the advanced biological maturity of girls—that differences will occur in the ways young men and young women approach occupational and career choices.

Gassin, Kelly, and Feldhousen (1993) have summarized studies suggesting that within the gifted population, girls and young women face problems that may lead them to devalue their talents and ultimately underachieve in school and in the workplace. These researchers also followed up some 605 former and current students from a Saturday enrichment program for gifted students sponsored by a large midwestern university. These students were enrolled in grades four through twelve during the 1989–90 academic years and either had an IQ of 130 and above or scored at the 95th percentile or above on two sections of a standardized achievement test. Other measures included eight items from the Vocational Identity Scale, ten items from the Career Planning Section of the My Vocational Situation instrument, and a single item measuring level of academic aspiration.

The results of the study showed that the gifted girls showed significantly greater career certainty at grades four through six than boys but seemed less certain than boys at grades seven through twelve, although the differences were not statistically significant. This study suggested that sex differences in the career development of gifted girls and boys are age specific, and they are not uniform for all career development variables: career certainty, career planning, and level of aspirations. As a result, the researchers suggested that gifted boys and girls may need different types of career education at different points in their educational careers. These perspectives also extend to the findings of research studies of other subpopulations of junior high school youth.

Kammer's (1985) study of rural, eighth-grade boys and girls indicated that many girls do not expect to attain their career goals and that boys and girls differ in their occupational choices according to traditional gender-role expectations as early as eighth grade. Haring and Beyard-Tyler (1984) suggest that such differences occur and are likely to keep women from pursuing nontraditional occupations because of three, if not four, factors: (1) sex-role socialization, (2) poor self-efficacy, (3) negative attitudes held by women and their peers, and possibly (4) counselor bias. The reader might wish to review Chapters 4 and 5 to further these perspectives.

Although it might be readily assumed that findings about gender differences in self-concept or in choice of work would be significantly different today as compared to findings of twenty or so years ago, that is not necessarily true. As research by the Search Institute (1988) reports, "some things remain puzzlingly the same" (p. 1). Some excerpts from these findings follow:

> *Test scores continue to reveal persistent differences between boys and girls on crucial matters of self-concept and self-esteem. There are also differences between boys' and girls' self-descriptions. In many instances, the girls' self-descriptions are unflattering even when the objective data contradict them. Young adolescent boys, for example, are more likely to rate themselves as "smart" than are girls, even though in the aggregate girls' school grades at that age are higher than boys'. Boys also tend more readily to*

> *attribute mistakes and failures to bad luck while girls tend to attribute them to their own inadequacies.... As compared with boys their own age, young adolescent girls give overall evidence of a lower self-image.... As compared with boys, girls are more afraid of success. And they are less pleased about being female than boys are about being males. (p. 1)*
>
> *...One of the questions young adolescents consciously put to themselves is, What am I good at? What can I do? Boys tend to answer with a list of their skills and abilities. Girls tend to answer with a self-deprecating, "Not much!"*

However:

> *Girls like school better than boys do throughout the middle school or junior high years. They also have higher educational aspirations. In our study, 81 percent of girls said they intended to go on to college or to graduate school, as compared with 68 percent of boys with plans for higher education.... In general, girls are more socially competent in early adolescence, finding it easier to make friends and share their feelings than boys do. Yet those abilities don't appear to change their suspicion that they are basically losers. (p. 1)*
>
> *We find that some young adolescent girls develop fear of success.... It is likely that a number of the differences between boys and girls discussed here contribute to this fear of success.... One of them is the need to have friends.... Another of the causes may be an increasing desire to be attractive to boys.... She is probably convinced...that you can't get a guy interested in you if you're smarter than he is. (p. 2)*
>
> *It is natural for both boys and girls, at about sixth or seventh grade, to begin to feel an increased compulsion to conform to traditional gender-role images. Boys want to conform to whatever they believe to be the masculine role and girls want to conform to the feminine.... Girls are also aware of what the traditional occupations are for women. Even though there are more women in traditionally male occupations, girls know which are expected and which are exceptions. They know that there is, for many of the traditional roles for women, no history of vocational training—for being a housewife, for instance, or being a waitress. They know that the pay in virtually all of the traditionally female occupations is low.*
>
> *In spite of some positive social changes, girls are still bombarded with messages that being female is not as good as being male.... Look at the premium our country still puts on competition and achievement—qualities more frequently displayed by males—versus the value accorded to the more frequently female qualities of comparison and human connection.... Growing up female in the U.S. is still a hazardous business (p. 3).**

The findings of the Search Institute's research on junior high school students is echoed in other research. As suggested, but not pursued, in the elementary school chapter, ideas and beliefs that reinforce the notion that most occupations are more appropriate for one gender than the other develop early in children's lives and persist throughout the process of schooling. Post-Kammer and Smith (1985) replicated Betz and Hackett's (1981) study of college women using a self-efficacy model of women's career development that suggests that many career-related problems faced by women may be due to low or weak self-efficacy expectations. Because efficacy expectations result from experience, traditional sex-role socialization of females, which includes occupation sex-role stereotypes, works against women developing high efficacy expectations in terms of specific career-related behaviors and skills. Self-efficacy expectations, when low or weak, constitute an internal barrier to women's career behavior and choices. In addition, external barriers to women, such as discrimination or lack of support systems, require strong self-efficacy expectations if they are to be overcome.

Post-Kammer and Smith (1985) used a population of eighth-grade and ninth-grade college-bound students to determine whether self-efficacy differences were present in this population. They were! Each gender had greater self-efficacy expectations about occupations traditional for their gender than for nontraditional ones.

A related issue for gender differences is that of work values in the junior high school. Post-Kammer (1987) examined the relationships between work values and career maturity between both sexes in the ninth and eleventh grades. Sex differences were reported for half of the work values, as measured by Super's Work Values Inventory, and three out of five for Crites Career Maturity Inventory subscales. There were no significant differences in the career maturity scores of the ninth-graders and eleventh-graders. Different work values, however, predicted the career maturity of boys and girls. It was found that "fewer

*Source: From Search Institute (1988), The risky business of growing up female. *Source, 4*(1), 1–4. Reprinted by permission.

values emerged as a result of the regression analysis for boys than for girls indicating that understanding the career maturity of girls may be more complex than understanding that of boys" (p. 65).

With respect to vocational maturity attitude, Herr and Enderlein (1976) found, in a study of 1553 students from ninth to twelfth grades in three school systems and across sex and curricular classifications, that girls displayed a higher mean Vocational Development Inventory—Attitude Scale score at all grade levels than did boys. Crites (1978) reported:

> *Longitudinal research…indicates…that sex differences do emerge during the high school years.… At each succeeding grade level (above the seventh grade) females had statistically reliable higher mean scores on the attitude scale than males. In other words, their attitudes toward the process of career choice matured at a faster rate than that of males. (p. 5)*

Addressing an issue that continues to be of concern in the United States, the research of Pedro, Wolleat, and Fennema (1980) indicate that, for whatever reason, there is evidence that women's educational and occupational options are limited by the preparation in mathematics they receive while in high school. In this study, they compared plans to study mathematics in high school among 400 female and 322 male ninth-grade and tenth-grade students from nine high schools in midwestern communities. Even though this sample was skewed toward higher-than-average enrollment in mathematics, they found the girls planned to study less mathematics than their male classmates, both during and after high school, even though they were achieving as well as their male counterparts. In addition, when career plans were studied, they found that the ninth-grade and tenth-grade girls in this sample tended to select the stereotypical female career areas that generally require little mathematics. As the authors note, with only the minimal preparation in mathematics, the female students will not be able to choose from the full range of options should they change their occupational plans later. This is particularly true in a society in which the emerging occupations are those of high technology. As discussed in other chapters, Hackett and her various co-researchers have been targeting mathematics self-efficacy as a crucial variable—one they are testing interventions by which to strengthen. To this end, Hackett (1985) has indicated that counselors must work not only with the interests, values, and abilities of each client, but also with their perceptions of the gender appropriateness of the options available. Specifically, counselors must actively bolster women's career-related and math-related self-efficacy expectations if more informed and nonstereotyped career choices are to occur.

Research by Westbrook, Sanford, and Donnelly (1990) in which 112 rural ninth-grade public school pupils were administered the goal selection scale of the CMI Competence Test and the ACT Career Planning Program found no significant ethnic or gender differences in career maturity of ninth-grade students. This study, and earlier studies by Westbrook and colleagues (1988), found that goal selection and appropriateness of career choices have more in common with scholastic aptitude than they have with each other. Viewed from this perspective, the career choice process, at least at this developmental level, is, to a great extent, a cognitive process. High-ability students in grade nine are likely to make more appropriate career choices than low-ability students. According to Westbrook, Sanford, and Donnelly (1990), such a finding is understandable, "because high-ability students qualify for more jobs and are not as likely to choose a job that is incongruent with their attributes" (p. 30).

The work patterns and the proportions of women in the labor force have changed significantly during the past several decades. It is expected that for the foreseeable future, women will enter the labor force in greater percentages than will men. Indeed, the U.S. Department of Labor Bureau of Labor Statistics (1994) indicated, "The percentage increase of women in the labor force between 1992 and 2005 will be larger than the percentage increase in the total labor force" (p. 11). By 2005, they are expected to constitute 48 percent of the labor force. Thus, as cultural constraints about what is acceptable work or schooling for women continue to fall away, it is expected that women will continue to seek more schooling and more employment than ever before.

Attitudes toward women working—and toward the job of homemaking—have undergone profound changes. The proportion of women in the work force, particularly wives and mothers, has increased dramatically. In 1994, 61 percent of married couples had wives in the paid labor force compared to only 30 percent of married couples in the 1960s (Farley, 1996).

The most common American family is now one in which both spouses work. The number of married couples who postpone having children to extend their careers has risen. More than half of all women with children under 18 are in the labor force. Fewer than 3 out of 10 women are full-time homemakers. Lone parents living with their children represent more than one in five households. Most such single parent households are headed by women. Estimates suggest that some 60 percent of children will live with only one parent before reaching 18 (Herr, 1999).

As a result of changing economic conditions and family forms, young women's relationship to the world of work is dramatically different from that of their mothers. Many more enter the labor force now, doing so at an earlier age, and most intend to work indefinitely. The primary activity of nonstudent young women in the late 1950s was more likely to be keeping house and caring for a family. Today's youth enter the labor market earlier, and most combine school with work. Many more are from single-parent families and a significant minority are single parents themselves (Herr, 1999).

Government projections indicate that increasing participation of young women and stable or declining participation for teenage boys in the workforce will continue in the twenty-first century. By the year 2000, the labor force had a larger share of young women and a smaller share of young men; indeed, by the turn of the twenty-first century, four out of every five women, ages 25 to 54, were employed.

Although such processes of women's involvement in work are accelerating, the pathways and the continuity with which these pathways can be pursued are still different for boys and girls. Homemaking is still a major role for women even though it may be as a part of a two-earner family or as a single parent. In either case, homemaking and work outside the home are likely to be combined for many women. Bearing at least one child continues to be pervasive among married women. These factors of homemaking and childbearing often cause either temporary or long-term discontinuities in the career development of women. As daycare centers, financial subsidies for home care of children, and other supports to working mothers are expanded, women will become more significant in their leadership and in their distribution throughout the occupational structure. These possibilities need to be considered in multiple role planning.

The other reality factor remains. Even though social reinforcement for working women is increasing and legislation bars overt obstacles, psychological barriers still tend to cause girls to have fewer job choices than do boys. Reasons for this phenomenon can be found in curriculum content selected by girls as well as in factors in the larger society.

Nieva and Gutek (1981) suggest that the continuing tendencies to consider jobs as male or female encourages the development of two labor markets—a male labor market and a female labor market (p. 5). Although efforts to reduce gender typing of occupations and the encouragement of women to enter nontraditional occupations has continued, with some exceptions there remain many occupations that are dominated by men or women. Indeed, many women and girls still plan to enter occupations that are traditionally dominated by women.

Similar to the discrimination that prohibits access to some occupations because of racial criteria, sex-typing can be expected to restrict women's access to some occupations in the foreseeable future even though women jockeys, coal miners, baseball umpires, commercial airline pilots, and long-haul truckers are no longer without precedent. Counselors continue to have a major job in helping to reduce high correlations between sex and occupation.

Girls tend to be "set" in a career earlier than boys (by about age 15), even though they may enter a career pattern with less thought than boys because of the residual effects of stereotyping of choices they are encouraged to pursue. Research continues to suggest that significantly more girls than boys report a definite vocational choice during this period. For these reasons, some observers advocate that counseling for girls should be different from that for boys. Whether counseling should be different in fact or should emphasize different things earlier is debatable, but it is not debatable that because the male's identity has been more historically cloaked in a career fabric than has the female's, girls have a different problem of identity achievement from that of boys. Cultural influences have historically assigned to boys in the United States a primary role as the breadwinner, and thus have reinforced in many ways that career development of boys is more important—not necessarily because of the benefits to the boy himself but because of the importance of the choices he makes to the well-being of his future family. Although this notion is changing, many of the historical effects remain in the attitudes of various persons.

Research also indicates that the occupational preferences of boys and girls at the junior high level and beyond are not the same, and this is true for both whites and African Americans. Although it is not clear why these differences occur—perhaps the incorporation of early sex stereotyping, maybe a lack of information across occupations—counselors need to help the student be clear that such differences are consciously held and are not simply a result of information or experiential deficits. Thus, if career guidance strategies are to respond to the needs of girls and to help them come to terms with career development—career maturity and identity—these strategies must be mounted no later than the junior high school period. To wait diminishes the likelihood that career development can be influenced for girls in optimum ways.

Approaches to Gender Differences in the Junior High School

Bartholomew and Schnorr (1994) have contended that broadening career options for young women through career counseling programs requires: (1) enhanced counselor awareness of gender role stereotyping, (2) breaking down women's gender role and occupational stereotypes, (3) helping women overcome math and science stereotypes, (4) improving young women's self-concepts, (5) enhancing young women's self-esteem and self-confidence, (6) addressing fear of success issues, (7) helping female students formulate realistic family and life-planning goals, (8) examining their peer influences, and (9) developing support systems (p. 246). Each of these elements of a career program can be manifested by particular activities, including mentoring: the use of selected videotapes and other media about gender role possibilities and stereotypes; the provision of female role models in mathematics and science occupations; the use of processes that encourage self-awareness, confidence, risk taking, perseverance; the reading of biographies and autobiographies about notable women and then discussing the kinds of choices the women made and the consequences and obstacles that were involved; helping young women to consider ways to balance and integrate various career and family life roles; promoting parental involvement with their child's career planning and exploration of opportunities; and creating ways to reinforce the importance for young women of planning their own life rather than allowing others to define it for them.

A basic strategy by which counselors can attempt to facilitate realistic exploration of career motivations in junior high school girls is by exposing them to nontraditional role models. Cramer, Wise, and Colburn (1977) examined the use of *stereotype debunking* as a method of combating sex stereotyping. It was found by Piost (1974) that showing a female computer programmer in a career film significantly increased the career motivation of eighth-grade girls for that career compared with their considerably lessened preference for the career when a male model was used in the same film.

Wilson and Daniel (1981) used a role clarification and decision-making workshop to help seventh-grade and eighth-grade students overcome sex-role stereotypes. Using a variety of activities—such as considering the lives of famous women, songs illustrating social norms and social change in men's and women's roles, discussion of characteristics required for different occupations, interest inventories, analysis of nontraditional jobs—they found in comparing an experimental with a control group that a relatively brief workshop (five sessions) is effective in influencing traditional sex-role attitudes.

Vincenzi (1977) has examined a related approach to minimizing occupational stereotypes that, although it used sixth graders as subjects, could be adapted to the junior high school. In this instance, 80 girls and 97 boys from nine sixth-grade classes were chosen randomly and assigned to experimental and control groups. The experimental group students were exposed to two 30-minute sessions a week for 10 weeks. During these sessions, the experimental group did the following:

1. Reviewed and discussed magazine articles concerning women working at jobs traditionally sex-typed as masculine and men at jobs traditionally sex-typed as feminine.
2. Examined and discussed the definitions of a stereotype and identified stereotypes other than occupations.
3. Met seven women who work in traditionally masculine occupations. Each woman spoke for 30 minutes, gave a short demonstration, and explained her job and why she chose it. Occupations

discussed were doctor, lawyer, chemist, television reporter, architect, telephone linesperson, and auto mechanic.

The research findings of this approach indicated that the number of occupations viewed as sex-typed by the experimental group was significantly reduced and that the experimental group improved significantly over the control group in the incidence of occupational stereotyping.

Another method of dealing with such concerns is to use women in nontraditional careers as guest speakers or as persons for students to shadow on the job. Such persons can also demonstrate the efficacy of multiple role planning. Beyond these types of recognition of sex differences at the junior high school level, counselors also need to help teachers and parents recognize sex-stereotyped activities and reinforcement in teaching materials, in educational policies about course options segregated by sex (such as home economics and shop), and in reading materials of various kinds. Counselors obviously have responsibilities to advance gender-fair notions about work. Put more positively, counselors can help teachers and parents to support enthusiastically career exploration that is unfettered by traditional sex biases. Such efforts, once begun, must continue in the senior high school, in higher education, and among adult populations.

Differences in Maturity

Of the entire educational span, the junior high school years have the widest range of maturity levels in the student population. The effects of pubertal changes; differences in the rates of male and female growth; and the general unevenness of physical, emotional, and intellectual development within and between the population of girls and boys contribute to this spectrum of maturational differences. Differences in readiness, questions of general academic progress, preoccupations with bodily change, peer conflicts, boy-girl relationships, and rebellion against family restrictions—each coexists with and often confounds the continuing process of career development.

As suggested by Johnson and Kottman (1992), in applying the behavioral and attitudinal components expected at each age level by the Gesell Institute of Child Development, "Counselors need to remember that each person has his or her own individual developmental timetable.... A typical sixth-grade class, therefore, may contain a variety of developmental stages. This is due not merely to the different birth rates of the students, but also to the different rates of development of the individual members of this class.... Guidance activities and counselor expectations and strategies should be formulated based on the maturational stages of students" (p. 13). Obviously, such a view extends beyond grade six to students throughout the junior high school.

A Time for Early School-Leaving

The junior high school years are a period when many students permanently absent themselves from formal education. Some of these students will have begun to drop out of school psychologically in the elementary grades. Others will do so in grades seven, eight, or nine. Still others who have found no meaning in school will not only terminate their psychological interaction with the education process, but also they will remove themselves physically. What the future holds for those without a high school diploma or marketable skills is discussed in several other places in this book. Career guidance and the broader educational process, then, must respond to potential dropouts not only by encouraging these students to remain in school or by lecturing them about the monetary value of a high school diploma, but also by altering the educational structure to make it more meaningful.

The reality is that many students who drop out are not getting anything in school that helps them get a better job, and they know it! In many instances, ways have not been found to move concrete, task-oriented instruction into the junior high school, where these students can get hands-on experiences that relate to real work as they see it. Nor is there opportunity to combine general education and work-study opportunities at the junior high school level.

The point is that for some youngsters at this level, purely academic content holds no appeal at all unless it has immediate relevance to salable skills and this relevance is made obvious. These students in the junior high school need access to a skill-centered curriculum similar to that contained in career and technical education or tech-prep as found in the senior high school. If they do not receive this opportunity, the chances are that they will leave the school as unemployable. Some of these young people do not have the tolerance or the ego-strength to wade through a morass of personally meaningless experiences until the ninth, tenth, or eleventh grades, when they can get more meaningful educational experiences. These students, however, should still be provided with experiences other than occupational task-specific skills to foster career development. Indeed, within the context of skill development, not only can they be helped to see where they might go, but also prescriptions of the specific ways of implementing their goals can be developed. For those for whom skill-centered training is most relevant and is the prime source of success experiences, training in decision making and planning that transcends job layouts can facilitate self-understanding and recognition of alternative ways of using evolving skills. Within this context, the concept of continuing education as a way of refining one's skills and becoming a more effective problem solver at work can be wedded to a knowledge of available apprenticeships, on-the-job training, postsecondary vocational technical schools, military service schools, and other pertinent experiences. It is clear that such task-centered, skill-oriented, and concrete experiences would be helpful to all students if used to relate self-characteristics to the alternatives available, but it is even clearer that such experiences are critical to preventing dropouts.

In a national report, the Hispanic Policy Development Project singles out the junior high school years as a crucial time to work on student motivation and aspiration. Research reported in this document revealed that 43 percent of Hispanic students who drop out leave school before grade ten, and 25 percent of all Hispanic students enter high school overage. The study ties Hispanic students' lack of motivation to continue their education to the anonymity many of them feel in the junior high schools and the lack of recognition of or respect for their cultural values (National Commission on Secondary Education for Hispanics, 1985).

PLANNING CONSIDERATIONS

In addition to the general planning considerations for career guidance discussed in Chapter 6, the introductory sections of this chapter suggest several specific characteristics of junior high school students that must be considered.

1. Because the junior high school is a transitional experience from the structured and general education of the elementary school to the less structured but more specialized education of the secondary school, students must be provided broad opportunity to explore their personal characteristics as well as those of the educational options from which they must choose. Opportunities to relate curricular options to the possible and subsequent educational and occupational outcomes seem highly desirable.

2. Because wide ranges in career maturity, interests, values, and abilities characterize junior high school students, a wide variety of methods are needed to accommodate the range of individual differences. Minority students and students whose parents have not completed high school frequently have not had the developmental experience or occupational knowledge enjoyed by whites or students from homes in which parents are well educated. These students may need special programs to facilitate their understanding of opportunities available to them, their requirements, and how to access them.

3. Because girls are more likely than boys to have made definitive vocational choices, career guidance programs must ensure that such choices were made deliberately and based on accurate, pertinent information.

4. Although students in the junior high school are capable of verbal and abstract behavior, exploration is enhanced if they are given concrete, hands-on, direct experiences as well.

5. Fundamental to the rapid changes that students experience in the junior high school is a search for personal identity. Therefore, career guidance programs must encourage students to explore their feelings, needs, and uncertainties as a base for evaluating educational and occupational options. Values clarification and other similar processes are helpful in this regard.

6. Research suggests that students in grades eight through ten do go through processes of compromise in their occupational aspirations and expectations that supports the perspectives of Gottfredson (1981, 1996) who outlines two processes in the development of occupational aspirations: circumscription and compromise. This theory is discussed more fully in Chapter 4, but, for the purpose here, circumscription can be considered as the process through which individual occupational aspirations are limited to a zone of acceptable alternatives; compromise is the process in which individual aspirations are converted to more realistic choices. Against such a context, the research of Armstrong and Crombie (2000) in a three-year longitudinal study of 601 students (290 male, 311 female) in three school districts in a midsized Canadian city, suggests that students can be classified into groups whose aspirations and expectations are either nondiscrepant or discrepant. Discrepant individuals are those for whom their preferred occupational aspirations are different from the jobs they actually expect to have. As a result, based on such factors as gender traditionality and SES/prestige expectations, they are likely to undergo a process of compromise overtime. The results of this study suggest that discrepant adolescents do change their aspirations in the direction of their expectations overtime, although they may adjust both their aspirations and their expectations. In either case:

> *The pattern of changes displayed by adolescents who reported discrepancies suggests that these individuals are at a developmental point where change is likely to occur. Adolescents who are at this point will undoubtedly benefit from information designed to connect their personal interests and abilities with actual occupational characteristics and requirements while attempting to reconcile their discrepant aspirations and expectations. (p. 97)*

GOALS FOR CAREER GUIDANCE IN THE JUNIOR HIGH SCHOOL

There are many statements of career guidance goals for middle school or junior high school youth. *The National Standards for School Counseling Programs* (Campbell & Dahir, 1997), published under the auspices of the American School Counselor Association, have specified that developmental guidance programs in schools should focus interventions on three domains: academic development, career development, and personal development. Under career development, the standards specify that middle/junior high school students should: (a) "acquire the skills to investigate the world of work in relation to knowledge of self and to make informal career decision," (b) "employ strategies to achieve future success and satisfaction," and (c) "understand the relationship between personal qualities, education and training, and the world of work" (p. 17).

Another example of goals for career guidance in the junior high school is that developed by the Wisconsin Department of Public Instruction (Wilson, 1986), which has recommended the following objectives:

- Understand decision-making skills
- Learn to cope with transition in school, home, and community lives
- Become informed about alternative educational and vocational choices and preparation for them
- Relate personal interests to broad occupational areas
- Understand and use communication skills
- Learn human conflict management with adults and peers
- Learn that sex-role stereotyping, bias, and discrimination limit choices, opportunity, and achievement (p. 7)

A further example of career guidance objectives in the junior high school is that proposed by the Pennsylvania Department of Education in its Program of Developmental Guidance and Counseling, which suggests that students should learn to do the following:

- Understand that achievement of one's goals in life are related to a positive attitude toward work and learning
- Learn how to use a career planning process by preparing an individual education/career plan for middle school and anticipate changes as a result of personal maturation and social needs
- Develop an awareness of the level of competency in academic areas needed to achieve career goals
- Understand how interests, work values, achievements, and abilities affect the career choice
- Learn that nontraditional occupations offer expanded career opportunities; understand what employers expect of applicants and employees
- Learn about leisure and recreational activities that best fit personal needs and interests and contribute to personal satisfaction
- Understand the personal qualities (e.g., dependability, punctuality, getting along with others) that are needed to secure and keep a job

- Know about the sources of information about available jobs and how to complete a job application
- Know about training opportunities in the community that will enhance employment potential
- Develop knowledge of the relationship between school subjects and future educational and occupational choices without regard for prejudice, bias, or stereotyping
- Be aware of alternative educational and vocational choices and the corresponding preparation for them
- Understand the challenges, adjustments, and advantages of nontraditional occupations
- Be aware of employment trends as they relate to training programs and employment opportunities in the local community
- Be aware of the factors that impede performance and productivity in the workplace

Such objectives, similar to those proposed by the Wisconsin Department of Public Instruction cited earlier, are excellent structures from which to build career guidance and counseling programs in the junior high school. Such sets of objectives tend to summarize for program development purposes many of the theoretical assumptions and research findings reported in Chapter 4, and they are congruent with the content of other relevant sets of objectives for junior high school students, such as those found in the National Occupational Information Coordinating Council *Career Development Guidelines,* found in Chapter 6 and elsewhere in this book.

EXAMPLES OF PROGRAM CONTENT

Career guidance programs or activities designed to incorporate many of the goals we have cited are now available in many junior high schools. Both the substance and the format of these approaches vary widely. Some examples follow.

The concepts of change—change in characteristics of the self and in environmental options—and personal flexibility has been mentioned elsewhere in this book as a possible unifying thread in career development and decision making. At the junior high school, such a theme can be related to the accelerating application of new technological discoveries to the occupational structure; it can reinforce the validity of preparing oneself to be versatile, personally flexible, and yet firmly grounded in the fundamental processes that undergird all occupations. The concept can be related to work habits, mechanical principles, structural design and architectural evolution, chemical and biological principles, numerical operations and measurements, or verbal communication as this relates to different role relationships. Therefore, students can be increasingly encouraged to ask of occupational and educational areas: Do I like it? What does it take? Do I have what it takes? Such questions can be tested in various courses as well as in the simulated or work experiences that will be discussed later in this chapter. Students can be encouraged to ask: Why am I taking biology or algebra or English? and How can I use it? Teachers must be encouraged to respond to these questions as meaningful, with fairly specific answers. This is the sort of climate that supports career development and connects what students are being exposed to educationally with the occupational world. It can expand students' awareness of possibilities.

When teachers are asked to consider how the subject they teach is related to occupations or careers at different levels of education or in different interest categories, a basic difficulty often is that their formal backgrounds have not prepared them to respond to such questions. One important type of resource to offset this condition was prepared by the Minnesota Department of Education. The Bureau of Pupil Personnel Services of this agency developed a series of charts describing the relationship between subject-matter courses and selected careers. An example of these is available in Table 8.1, presenting information on careers related to social studies.

Obviously, this table does not exhaust all the possibilities, but it does represent a method of connecting what one studies with how it might be used. At any point in the educational process, discussions, role playing, field trips, or other activities could be conducted to point up how social studies or other academic course content might be used in that particular occupation. One could relate academic subject matter to a people-data-things conception of the occupational structure or to other emphases, always trying to extend student perceptions or possibilities and the ways of access to them.

TABLE 8.1 Selected Careers Related to Social Studies

LEVEL	SERVICE	BUSINESS, CLERICAL, AND SALES	SCIENCE AND TECHNOLOGY	GENERAL CULTURAL	ARTS AND ENTERTAINMENT
B.A. or above	Social worker Psychologist FBI agent Counselor YMCA Secretary Clergy	Government official Industrial executive Market analyst Economist Buyer Arbitrator	Archaeologist Paleontologist Anthropologist	Judge Lawyer Philologist Editor News commentator Reporter Librarian	Museum curator Historian (Dramatic arts)
High school plus technical	Police sergeant Detective Sheriff Employment interviewer	Union official Bank teller Salesperson Wholesaler Retailer		Justice of the peace Radio announcer Law clerk	Tour conductor Travel bureau director Cartoonist
High school graduate	Police officer Religious worker Bus driver	Floor walker Interview (poll) House canvassers and agents		Library assistant	Museum guide
Less than high school graduate	Train porter Taxi driver Bellhop Elevator operator Usher	Peddler Newspaper carrier		Library page Copy person	

To offset the limited experience of some teachers in involvement with work-related material on their subject matter, various school districts have taken different approaches to this circumstance. Some districts pay groups of teachers to work during the summer, developing short units in the major subject areas on specific career topics. In this fashion, the regular curriculum can continue but with a change in emphasis that accommodates more career-oriented content. For example, in one Utah school district, as a result of such a summer workshop, sample units were developed by teacher teams and then distributed to all teachers in that subject area within the school district for testing and refining in the school curriculum. One such unit was newspaper reporting as a career in ninth-grade English classes. Many other school districts have developed learning activity packages that can be integrated into the full range of academic subject matter at various educational levels. Coordinators of Career Education in State Departments of Education are prime resources to identify examples of these in each state.

Hill and Rojewski (1999) have argued that career guidance programs in the junior high school and, indeed, later in the senior high school should focus on *how* work is done as well as *whether* it is done. The latter emphasis is particularly important for at-risk students who need assistance with their work ethic. Work ethic in this case includes interpersonal skills, initiative, and being dependable. These three personal characteristics and related characteristics such as individual responsibility, self-esteem, sociability, self-management, and integrity are often missing in the behavioral repertoire of at-risk students who exhibit poor attendance habits, lack of interest, discipline problems, and, sometimes, problems with the law within the community. Lacking the characteristics described above as elements of the work ethic, limit student opportunities at school and at work.

Hill and Rojewski studied the work ethic of 152 ninth-grade students in a midwestern metropolitan high school. Three questions guided the study: (1) Are there significant differences in work ethic among students classified as at risk, moderately at risk, and not at risk? (2) Are there gender differences in work ethic for the study participants? (3) Are differences in work ethic related to interpersonal skills, initiative, or being dependable? The Occupational Work Ethic Inventory (OWEI) and a Risk Behavior Scale were used as the primary measures. The results indicated that the mean scores on the OWEI subscales were higher (more positive) for not-at-risk students compared to moderately at risk or at risk students. The primary difference among the three groups was on being dependable, rather than interpersonal skills or initiative. The mean scores on the OEWI subscales were consistently higher for girls than for boys.

These data on the work ethic of at risk students, particularly as related to being dependable, suggested that among this sample, at-risk students cannot be relied on to be in the right place at the right time or to be doing what they should be doing. From a career development standpoint, these students need to be exposed to strong role models from the community, social influences to encourage dependability, and problem-solving activities based on real life circumstances that are designed to address the importance of being dependable. Within the instructional program of the school, expectations for student dependability should be high and encouragement of dependability prolific. Counselors can be involved in helping students find a mentor in the community, involvement in extra curricular activities that encourage positive affective behaviors, and participation in programmatic efforts to help at risk students develop in systematic and conscious ways self-efficacy, outcome expectations, and personal goals and to understand the importance of work ethic, work attitudes, and the issue of being dependable as major elements of achieving their career goals.

Career Clusters

One method of helping students relate their characteristics to occupational alternatives through exploration as well as develop increasingly sophisticated skills important to a family of occupations is career clustering. Career clustering has been integrated into many school-based career education models or projects. Often, broad groups of industry-related jobs—occupational or career clusters or career majors—are how some high schools organize their career exploration activities or in other cases their vocational education or tech prep programs.

In junior high school, the objective of career clustering has been to expose students to the full range of occupational choices that will be available later and to the notion of the relationships among occupations constituting a particular career family, to knowledge of the relative advantages and the requirements of each, and to provision of entry skills appropriate to a broad family of related occupations (such as construction or health care).

In most models, education for careers has strongly emphasized career awareness and career exploration before career preparation. It has further advocated that career preparation makes the student occupationally flexible. In this context, occupational or career clusters can be used to organize curriculum directed toward the preparation of students with skills, knowledge, and attitudes required for job entry into a family or cluster of occupations. This means that instructional teams can be developed to integrate mathematics, science, communications, and social studies around typical problems found in career clusters. Techniques such as flexible or modular scheduling, team teaching, independent study, and individualized instruction can be used to address differences in content or learning styles. Career clusters are also career guidance devices in that they provide students with awareness, comparative analyses of work performed and preparation required, and exploratory opportunities across several clusters of occupations.

Each occupational cluster can be divided into subclusters, which are further divided into discrete occupational functions at increasing levels of specificity requiring various types of education, from unskilled levels to graduate or professional education. Some states have developed modifications on the 15 or 16 career clusters developed by the U.S. Office of Education. Some cities have developed curriculum guides that can be used in exploratory or group guidance programs at grades seven and eight. Many commercial materials and audiovisual products have also been developed to deal with one or more career clusters to stimulate student exploration and career awareness.

Winter and Schmidt (1974) reported on how they used a cluster approach to integrate career education into the eighth-grade language arts curriculum at Scott Carpenter Junior High School in Westminster, Colorado. In particular, they developed seven modules, including an introduction to careers, self-awareness, decision making, occupational clusters, economic awareness, investigating an occupational cluster, and planning for the future.

The first module caused students to define the word *career,* to identify typical career patterns for men and women, and to identify reasons for working. A filmstrip entitled "Why Work at All?" was shown to stimulate student discussion on reasons for working.

In the self-awareness module, students were expected to identify their strengths and weaknesses as related to their abilities and interests and to match these with at least two potential careers. The relationships between school subjects and possible jobs were also examined. Workbooks, personal checklists, interpretations of results of the Ohio Vocational Interest Survey, and the writing of personal character sketches were activities used to support this module.

The major content of the decision-making module was a curriculum on decision making, entitled *Deciding,* developed by the College Entrance Examination Board. There are currently many other curriculum or decision-making materials available from the National Occupational Information Coordinating Committee, State Departments of Education, or commercial sources.

The occupational clusters module was presented through the "Popeye" comic books published by King Features Syndicate, which use cartoon characters to present information about jobs in each cluster. Students also constructed people pyramids showing how people from different clusters work together to produce different products.

The economic awareness module focused on how economics affects each student's life. Such concepts as economic systems, supply and demand, inflation, depression, and elements of production were discussed.

A variety of approaches was used in the module on investigating an occupational cluster. The Widening Occupational Roles Kit (WORK), *Job Family* booklets, and *Job Experience* Kits (all from Science Research Associates) were used as major resources for students in identifying a specific preferred cluster or area within a cluster to study. In addition, students wrote to at least one firm that offered jobs in the preferred cluster asking for information about the job and the firm. Students also took field trips to pertinent sites and had resource speakers from different occupations come to class to discuss their jobs.

In the planning module, students compiled lists of skills they would need to meet the requirements of jobs in the occupational cluster most related to their interests and aptitudes. Students also planned a tentative high school program of studies that would provide the necessary skills. During this module, the relevance of flexibility and tentativeness in planning as well as employment trends and the rapidity of change were considered.

While dated in its content, the model reported by Winter and Schmidt is an excellent application of clustering and related concerns now developed in the junior high school. The possibilities for expanding or modifying and updating such modular approaches to serve career guidance objectives in a local school are restricted only by the initiative and ingenuity of the local staff.

Using Self-Directed Career Interest Inventories

An important method of helping students to consider their career development, in combination with other career guidance interventions, is the use of self-directed career interest inventories. Three such inventories, studied by Jones, Sheffield, and Joyner (2000), include the Career Keys (Jones, 1987, 1993), the Self-Directed Career Explorer (Holland & Powell, 1994), the Job-O Enhanced (Cutler, Ferry, Kauk, & Robinett, 1995). Each of these instruments was used as the center of career interventions incorporated into eighth-grade social studies classes in a middle school in metropolitan North Carolina. The classes were randomly assigned to one of the interventions or to a control group. Some 159 students were distributed across the three intervention groups and another 42 were in the control group.

After the students completed their interest inventory and inventory designed to assess student satisfaction with the particular career interest inventory, students were then led by the counselor through career guidance activities using state government publications (e.g., *Career Choices in North Carolina, the University of North Carolina System*). These publications facilitated the further self-assessment of students about career choices, and discussed the characteristics of occupations organized by the Holland personality typology, work descriptions, salary, educational requirements, types of work setting, job outlook, training after high school, earnings and levels of education, colleges and schools, and some of the popular majors offered in the 16 universities in the state system.

The findings were that the students reported that taking each of the three instruments was a positive learning experience; it was a good use of their time; it gave them helpful career guidance; and they would recommend it to a friend. When specific variables potentially associated with each of the three instruments were examined, additional findings were obtained: the Career Keys initially suggested a greater number of occupations for students to consider than did the other two instruments; however, after three weeks the students who had taken the Self-Directed Search Career Explorer were still considering more occupations than the Career Keys or Job-O Enhanced; with respect to the variety of information-making by students stimulated by the three instruments, the Self-Directed Search Career Explorer was the most effective; while the instruments varied in effect among themselves, they typically did not yield statistically different results from those that occurred in the control group. The lack of significant differences between the use of the three self-directed career guidance and the control group across some of the instruments studied suggests that in some instances there may have been a lack of career readiness for such exploration or that the instruments did provide important stimulation to students that was not measured (e.g., introduction to new occupations, ones better suited to their abilities and needs, and the elimination of less-suited ones).

On balance, it does appear that self-directed career interest instruments can be useful in stimulating career exploration, particularly when the student results are followed by specific opportunities to research career possibilities suggested by results. The latter might include career fairs, the use of such directories as the *Guides for Occupational Exploration* or the *Occupational Outlook Handbook,* exploring careers on appropriate sites on the Internet, job shadowing, interviewing workers in specific career areas, and discussing careers with parents.

Other Sequential or Comprehensive Approaches

There are many other forms of comprehensive or sequential approaches to career guidance in the junior high school. One such program, entitled Project Career Reach, was developed at West High School, District 129, Aurora, Illinois (Bollendorf, Howrey, & Stephenson, 1990). Combining a career development model of junior high school career needs, a model of guidance objectives for program planning, a generic individualized career plan, and a marketing scheme to stimulate students to make use of the program offered by the guidance department, the six high school counselors designed Project Career Reach. They used five steps to develop the program: mission analysis, market analysis, resource analysis, strategic planning, and measures of program outcomes. The result was a multifaceted program intended to be systematically delivered. Included in Project Career Reach were the following:

- College night
- Achievement testing
- Peer counseling
- Registration
- School-business partnership
- Mini-workshops (such as financial aid seminars)
- Career speaker service
- Grade boosters
- College representatives
- Career center
- Practical composition (career English)
- Guidance Information System (GIS) searches of career-related information

After putting such program components in place, the counselors used all forms of media to reach students with different learning modalities and to encourage them to use the career programs. The school newspaper interviewed staff members and publicized activities for student readers. Signs were used as visual stimuli to publicize the career speaker series, the School-Work-Connection, the regional Career Fest, and other program emphases. Community newspapers and local radio and television announcements were also used to create visibility for the career guidance program.

As a result of the program, career information searches increased by 149 percent in the year following implementation of Project Career Reach. Nearly half of the students surveyed at the end of the program indicated their intent to be involved in other career development activities during the next school year. Students surveyed who were involved in the program indicated that they better understood careers and career information resources.

Other junior high schools use various types of courses to teach students about career development, For example, in Salem High School in New Hampshire, all ninth graders take a course called "Research, Career, and Study Skills" which is based on the school's career development competencies to be achieved by each student. This course begins with interest assessments and values inventories, based primarily in the computer-assisted career guidance program choices that allow students to relate their interests and values to postsecondary education opportunities, information on financial aid opportunities, and descriptions of more than 3,000 occupations.

The Cedar Rapid high schools offer a course for freshmen called Careers 101. In addition to interest and ability assessments, students learn job interviewing skills, visit the local job service office, explore occupations and engage in mock interviews for real jobs (Lozada, 1999).

Another type of comprehensive career guidance program for junior high school students is likely to be found in many state manuals on career education or career guidance. For example, the State Education Department of New York State has created a Home and Career Skills curriculum for implementation in grades seven and eight. This program is intended to develop skills that lead to effective decision making, problem solving, and management in the home, school/community, and workplace; develop concepts and skills basic to home and family responsibilities; and develop personal skills that will enhance employment potential. These objectives are intended to be met by applying the principles and process skills of decision making, problem solving, and management to all areas of daily living. The program or curriculum is comprised of a series of interrelated modules that can be combined in one unit or taught in sequence within other relevant courses.

Without dealing with the content, specific objectives, or activities in each module, the topical outline of the three modules directly related to career content includes the following:

- Process skills
  How do I decide? (decision making)
  How do I solve problems? (problem solving)
  How do I manage? (management)
- Personal development
  What makes me, me? (self)
  How do I relate to others? (others)
- Career planning
  What does working mean to me? (introduction to work)
  What kind of work can I do? (tentative plans)
  Can I make working work for me? (entrepreneurship)

The Broadening Horizons Project, a joint venture of the Arizona Department of Education and the Arizona State University, is designed to expand the career aspirations of eighth-grade girls, minority students, and handicapped students to include careers involving mathematics and science (Okey, Snyder, & Hackett, 1993). This project is based on the premise that any career guidance curriculum that attempts to increase the career aspirations of students must do more than provide career and self-assessment information. "It must also provide a means for students to increase their confidence in relation to the various goals explored" (p. 219). Because it has been determined from previous research studies that career self-efficacy can be strengthened by past performance accomplishments or success experiences, the Broadening Horizons Project uses experiential learning to increase the self-confidence of students participating in the project. About 50 percent of the career guidance curriculum is involved with direct work by the students with educational computer programs in mathematics and science. To make connections between the skills used in the computer programs in mathematics and science and the skills required in careers in which these skills are used, the other 50 percent of the career curriculum employs group counseling and various didactic presentations. The group counseling activities include assessment of skills and interests, brainstorming the identification of skills, and the integration of materials identifying potential careers. The didactic presentations include discussion about the range of differences in careers in mathematics and sciences, the skills required by these careers, and the educational and experiential prerequisites for entering these careers.

The Broadening Horizons program is implemented over the course of four 80-minute periods with a counselor and a mathematics or science teacher serving as a co-facilitator. Students are paired in their work on computers. During this experiential learning, the students are assigned specific computer tasks on specific software packages after which group discussion is conducted to discuss the skills required by the computer tasks and career applications of these skills and to provide specific didactic information about careers.

Both data-based and anecdotal information were used to evaluate the effectiveness of the project. According to the researchers, students completing pre- and post-surveys showed a marked increase in both career and academic self-efficacy, and anecdotal data from administrators, faculty, and students showed enthusiasm for the project and for creating school environments by which it could be accommodated.

As was stated earlier in this chapter, a major issue for students in the middle/junior high school is educational choice. In particular students must make critical choices of the high school they will attend or the four-year plan of studies they hope to pursue. If a developmental approach to career development has been taken from the elementary school forward, the decisions about a four year program of study should be the result of all of the career guidance that has occurred in the previous seven or eight years focused on one's considered interests, abilities, values and aspirations. Peterson, Long, and Billups (1999) have observed that to make important transitional educational choices, students must possess two fundamental competencies, "First, they should possess an accurate estimate of their interests, abilities, values, and talents combined with a vision of their future with accompanying aspirations that will enable them to realize their full potential as productive citizens in a global economy.... Second, students must become familiar with the high school curriculum in terms of: (a) its breadth of subject matter offered throughout the four years, (b) specific knowledge of courses within the domains of the curriculum, (c) appropriateness of courses relative to meeting their career aspirations, and (d) sequence of prerequisites for certain courses, particularly those in the mathematics and science areas" (p. 35).

To that end, Peterson and colleagues designed three career interventions at different levels of treatment intensity to help students with their high school educational choices. The first intervention, considered to be a minimal effort, consisted of a member of the middle school guidance staff making a general announcement in a social studies class that high school registration would be held in one week, that a high school counselor would come to the middle school to conduct the registration, and that students should prepare for the event by completing a trial high school program of study form in advance.

The second intervention, representing more involvement, added to the first intervention printed self-directed study material, containing state and school graduation requirements, a description of elective courses offered at the high school, and examples of a college preparatory curriculum and a vocational curriculum.

The third intervention was considerably more involved (four sessions) than the first two interventions. It consisted of a computer-assisted classroom intervention designed to foster career problem-solving and decision-making skills, using a cognitive information processing paradigm developed earlier by Peterson and his colleagues. This intervention was designed to enhance student information processing in four domains: self-knowledge, occupational knowledge, decision-making skills, and metacognitions that guide lower-order thought processes. Also, at focus, was the completion by each student, with the assistance of the school counselor, of a complete four-year plan for a high school program of study related to each student's interests and aspirations. Learning in groups was the counseling method used.

The criteria by which the outcomes of the three interventions were evaluated included the content of the four-year plan related to its completeness, specificity, appropriateness for career aspirations, and the sequencing of the courses planned. "The hypothesis tested was that the degree of mastery of educational decision-making capabilities as reflected in the listing of courses on the four-year plan of study would be directly related to the three levels of career interventions; that is, the higher the level of intervention, the higher the ratings on the respective four performance criteria" (p. 36).

A three-level, pretest-posttest design was employed which yielded the finding that both the Level 2 intervention, an announcement and handouts of printed material, and Level 3, with computer-assisted-classroom career guidance, were helpful in assisting students to prepare trial high school programs of study, particularly in mathematics and science. At the time of the post-tests, the percentages of the students meeting the criteria were as follows: Level 1, 25 to 54 percent; Level 2, 48 to 83 percent; Level 3, 100 percent. Additional findings were that students' apparently lack familiarity with mathematics and science requirements in the high school and they are often unaware of the consequences of their educational choices. Thus, students need the assistance of counselors and others to help compensate for their lack of knowledge about educational choices. According to the authors, schools should, at minimum, adopt the Level 2 intervention but they believe that, while more costly in time and resources, Level 3 can be seen as a prototype for schools and their guidance program in their role to assist students in educational decision making.

Using Community Resources in Career Guidance

One approach to facilitating career development among junior high school students is to involve systematically the use of community resources. Pinson (1980) has made the helpful observation: "Community in the abstract can be simplified if one views it through a student's eyes as three sets of establishment adults: school staffs, parents, and employers (less clear to the students is a fourth set of adults...organized labor)." Throughout Chapters 6, 7, 8, and 9, a variety of suggestions have been made about how school staff can facilitate the career development of students within subject matter areas. In Chapter 7, the role of parents in facilitating the career development of their children was discussed. Those observations about parents, like those about the characteristics of school staff, are relevant here as well.

During the 1970s, some school districts began to deal with the lack of career awareness among elementary, junior high, and senior high school students by developing community-based career education programs. Although the organization of such programs can become quite complex, they do permit the community to be used as a classroom. Links between the school and the business community frequently result in multiple outcomes. For example, students learn more about occupations and about themselves—their skills, interests, personality characteristics, and values. In addition, the school system gains cost-free expertise from community resources, and frequently schools receive for instructional purposes equipment and materials that businesses are replacing.

Hartman (1993), a teacher of ninth-grade students who have been out of the mainstream and placed into a special classroom with block scheduling of English, math, world history, and physical science because they failed the ninth grade, has argued persuasively that what is needed by these students is a redefinition of the work that they do in school so that its value is immediately obvious. In her view, rather than augmenting the regular curriculum, internships in the community should form the center of a student's experience for at least two years, until at age 16 these students would return to high school with "a better sense of what lies ahead and where they might want to focus their studies" (p. 406). Further, Hartman contends that, "These internships could cut across the business world and include community and state agencies. Student interns would provide free labor to places that need it and gain job contacts for the future. More important, students would be making a contribution to their communities and discovering the kinds of knowledge and skills required to function in the adult world" (p. 406).

In any community-based career education effort, there are major needs to locate resources; find community sites; recruit and schedule students for programs; orient students to expected behaviors at sites and to the information potential that should be sought; provide information about the program to school officials, parents, and community members; and carry out follow-up procedures.

Pinson (1980) has extrapolated from various documents and statements recommendations from business and industry about how they can be useful in career guidance. Selected recommendations and priorities include the following:

1. Using the business and industry community to validate civic and social outcome measures as well as the work competency indices developed by schools as exit requirements
2. Using community work stations as frequently for observation and exploration by elementary and

middle-school youth as for actual work experience at the secondary school level

3. Involving business and industry in ways that further curriculum objectives in all subject areas (i.e., assisting students to conduct a job search in the yellow pages could indirectly increase their reading achievement levels) (p. 138)

With respect to the contributions of organized labor to career guidance, Pinson recommends such ideas as the following:

1. Ongoing career development programs should more closely reflect the interests and needs of today's adult workers, as opposed to "the child as an adult."
2. Reconsider and revise the framework of work experience to take into account labor's views of economic realities: for example, more nonpaid work experience during school tenure.
3. Encourage the infusion of labor studies as part of a comprehensive thrust at all school levels. Involve union representation at the curriculum design level.

Pinson's advocacy of community resources in career guidance has many virtues. One of them is its systematic integration of learning and observation. Another is its purposeful use of the community as a learning laboratory. Third, such a program brings adults into contact with the concerns and interests of young persons and provides a natural method for the two groups to interact. Fourth, perhaps less directly, the program helps students develop reasons for a sense of pride and accomplishment in their schoolwork, beyond that of academic achievement.

There are some specific programs oriented to the use of community resources that are worthy of note. For example, the St. Louis public schools have extensive collaboration between the schools and resource persons from business and the community (Katzman, 1989). These include the following:

- *Traveling career panels,* in which seventh graders learn the importance of basic skills within the world of work and how these skills are applied by individuals on the job. A panel of two persons from business or industry visits a seventh-grade classroom, bringing tools and a classroom activity that typifies their job. A math panel, for example, might include a chef who brings a chili recipe for 20 people that needs to be converted to serve 100 and a corporate budget director who brings ledger sheets and teaches the students to form a personal budget. The class follows up with career-related field experiences to view the panelists in their work environment.
- *College planning conferences,* in which eighth-graders spend the day on a college campus as a way of helping students who never felt that they could have opportunities to envision such directions and to reinforce an incentive to enter high school, graduate, and plan for the future.
- *Career awareness fair,* in which eighth graders have an opportunity to watch career role models demonstrating their jobs. The fair is a way for more than 780 (in 1989) business persons and community members to reinforce how important it is to master the basic school subjects, remain motivated about learning, stay in school, and explore the diversified world of work. The 1989 fair had some 7000 eighth graders in attendance. Activities included building inspectors demonstrating blueprint reading; flight attendants showing students how to prepare for a flight; and chefs demonstrating the use of their utensils and the preparation of recipes. Students complete a number of prefair and post-fair activities and conduct career interviews while at the fair.
- *Business/school mentoring,* in which a business or community agency pairs with a middle or an elementary school to communicate with, provide career and motivational information for, and guide students over an extended period of time.*

When considering community involvement in career guidance at the junior high school levels, parents are frequently a neglected resource. However, parents can volunteer to take students to work with them, and they can have students work with them as interns if they own a business. They can drive students to field trips, serve as career center aides, or serve as resource speakers in classes on career guidance seminars. Retired grandparents can come into career guidance classes and show students how hobbies can be related

*Source: Abridged from Susan Katzman, A response to the challenges of the year 2000. *Career Development: Preparing for the 21st Century* by the Comprehensive Career Development Project for Secondary Schools in Tennessee. Copyright © 1989 University of Tennessee, Knoxville, Department of Technological & Adult Education. Reprinted by permission.

to careers. Within this context, it is useful to develop a resource file of parents' careers for various uses in career guidance. Such a file could classify these occupations by the U.S. Office of Education career clusters described in Chapter 3 and earlier in this chapter. Finally, parents often feel left out of career planning because they do not understand the relationship of class work to future careers. Helping them through PTAs or other methods to understand these relationships is likely to stimulate their positive involvement in the career development of their own children and to provide a powerful resource bank to supplement the career guidance efforts of the counselor or teacher.

A school/community-based project that combines many of the previously described examples in a comprehensive approach to career exploration for middle school youth has been reported by Rubinton (1985). A joint effort of the schools, a community college, the community, and the family, this federally funded project, Career Exploration for Youth (CEY), served children in public and parochial middle and junior high schools and their teachers, counselors, administrators, and parents in Brooklyn, New York.

The program contained four components emphasizing experiential learning. The first component was composed of hands-on career courses presented to students. These courses were activities-oriented and emphasized exploration in four career clusters: business and office, marketing and distribution, communications and media, and public service. The intent of the activities in each cluster included examination of myths about careers, examination of biases against and for careers familiar to children, motivation to explore unfamiliar and nontraditional careers, generation of career-related options in cluster areas of interest to children, provision of direct participation in career experiences, introduction of role models, and relating of careers to values of children.

The second component of the program was composed of a career decision-making course for parents. The course, which was designed to help parents facilitate the career development process among their children, allowed parents to explore careers in relation to their interests, aptitudes, abilities, values, and life experiences. Instruction included discussion, lectures, guest speakers, self-exploration exercises, administration of an interest inventory, a research project, and visits to a work site.

The third component was a course for teachers, counselors, paraprofessionals, teacher aides, school secretaries, and administrators that was designed to prepare school personnel to infuse curriculum with career development concepts. The activities contained in this course involved the provision of basic knowledge, understanding, and methods of teaching career education, assistance with the integration of career education into the existing school curriculum, and implementation of ideas, goals, and methods of career education in teachers' classrooms or school settings.

The final component of the program consisted of offering children who participated in the project a recreation component to complement the activities in the career clusters in which they engaged. To the degree possible, recreation activities were used to complement that which was occurring in the career clusters.

An extensive evaluation system found that children significantly increased their career awareness and knowledge. School personnel reported increased confidence in their ability to incorporate career education into their curricula, and community response was found to be overwhelmingly enthusiastic.

Career Guidance Strategies for Decision Making and Problem Solving

The examples just cited respond to elements of career development at a rather gross level and are basically similar to those activities recommended for the elementary school. To meet more specific goals, some differences in strategy or context are useful.

Wood (1990) has advocated the use of *group career counseling* to aid ninth graders in making career plans. In her view, it is useful to seek permission from teachers of classes in which all students are enrolled (such as English) to work with such classroom-sized groups for four days in sequence. She developed a unit that can be done in four sequential class periods. The content includes getting acquainted, learning about the services of the counseling office, discussion of career plans, completion of a career interest survey and feedback about the meaning of the results, researching at least one career using available materials in the counseling office and the media center, and planning a tentative high school schedule for the next three years. These activities are conducted within a group counseling context that allows students to raise personal issues about career-related concerns and experience how other ninth-graders are processing such concerns in their own lives. In follow-up to the four-day sequence, these activities provide the stimulus to arrange individual counseling sessions, interviews with parents, and further uses by students of the resources available. To implement such an approach, Wood addressed the essential importance of collaborating with teachers to inform them about the career group objectives, to arrange times convenient to them, and to provide some evaluative feedback about student participation and initiative using a point system that teachers can incorporate in their grading system to cover the students' involvement for four days of the particular marking period.

Motsch (1980) studied the efficacy of peer social modeling in assisting girls with career exploration. She assigned 180 ninth-grade girls to one of four treatment conditions or to a control group. She assigned an additional 36 girls randomly selected from another high school to a second control group. A videotape of a female counselor and a female high school student discussing different career information-seeking behaviors presented the modeled behaviors. The four treatment conditions and controls were: (1) videotape only, (2) videotape plus reinforcement, (3) videotape plus reinforcement plus stimulus materials, (4) stimulus materials plus reinforcement, (5) control group I, and (6) control group II. The findings were as follows:

> *Peer social modeling is related to increasing both the variety and frequency of information-seeking behaviors; more specifically, that a counseling group using modeling, positive reinforcement, and overt practice of the modeled behaviors with stimulus materials is more likely than the other treatment conditions investigated to provide an increase in the variety and frequency of information seeking behaviors among ninth grade girls. (pp. 238–239)*

Simulation as a Career Guidance Strategy

Johnson and Myrick (1971) have described the use of a simulation technique for middle school students called MOLD (Making Of Life Decisions). In this simulation, each student follows six basic steps:

1. He completes a personal profile sheet describing abilities and interests.
2. She becomes involved with small group procedures that assist her in self-appraisal.
3. He explores career fields and makes a tentative career choice based on his abilities and interests.
4. She plans on paper the next year of her life, making decisions about her education, job, home life, and leisure activities. The student chooses from alternatives actually available in the community, not fictional or hypothetical possibilities.
5. He receives feedback on his decisions, such as grades earned in each course and whether or not he got a job applied for. This feedback is derived from probability tables, which take into account such variables as ability, study time, and chance.
6. She uses the results and plans the following year. In this way, contingency plans and consequences of immediate decisions can be accounted for.

This simulation was used with a filmstrip on career and educational planning, a review of materials in the guidance center, and small-group discussion of reasons for personal choices, in which personal strengths were identified and reinforced.

Information Retrieval

Several projects have attempted to tie together exploration, simulation, and information retrieval with computer technology. Such computer-based systems will be discussed in Chapter 15. Here we will look at approaches to the use of information in the junior high school. In a larger sense, the examples cited throughout the chapters on the elementary school, the junior high school, and the senior high school are ways of delivering information, of responding to the characteristics of the consumers, and of giving students a context in which they can project themselves into the information and reality-test its personal meaning.

A growing method of providing self-information and career information to junior high school students is through the use of self-directed career planning instruments. These devices are particularly useful in schools in which resources are limited and needs exist to provide career guidance at a low counselor time investment. Jones (1983) evaluated two frequently used self-directed career planning tools—a self-guided occupational card sort known as the Occu-Sort (Jones, 1977, 1981) and the Self-Directed Search (Holland, 1970).

Jones studied the outcomes obtained by 578 eighth-grade and tenth-grade students from a school system in North Carolina who were randomly assigned to the use of the Occu-Sort, the Self-Directed Search, or neither. The evaluation focused on six types of outcomes important to career guidance: (1) proportion of nontraditional occupations (for the person's sex) suggested to the person by the instrument and subsequently being considered, (2) number of occupations suggested and later being considered, (3) understanding and recall of the three-letter occupational code found in the Holland approach, (4) stimulation toward seeking occupational and educational information, (5) student satisfaction with this vocational counseling experience, and (6) the reliability of the self-scored occupational code for the Occu-Sort. The findings were that students considered both instruments to be helpful. The Occu-Sort, in contrast to the Self-Directed Search, was found to be more effective in (1) encouraging students to consider nontraditional occupations, (2) suggesting potential occupations to students, and (3) communicating the meaning of the occupational code and its relation to Holland's theory (1973a). No differences were found between the Occu-Sort, the Self-Directed Search, and the no-treatment groups with respect to the number of occupations the students were considering after the experience or in other information-seeking behavior.

Barker and Patten (1989) studied the effectiveness of the Career Area Interest Checklist (CAIC) as compared to students' expressed interests after participating in a career guidance module. Based on a sample of 19 eighth-grade boys and 22 girls, statistically significant agreement was found between the order of career preference measured by CAIC work tasks and expressed student preference. They also found that junior high school students understand 144 work tasks used in the CAIC and that this tool can be useful in facilitating student awareness of career options that may make high school subject planning more focused and meaningful. Finally the preliminary evidence about the CAIC tends to validate student preferences about work tasks for which they express preferences or certain dislike and helps with clarification of work tasks about which they should engage in more exploration.

These findings and others affirm that the ingredients of career development discussed throughout this book are important to all students, not just a certain stratum. They also reemphasize that although information availability and help with sorting out one's self-implications are not the whole of career development, they are an important component of it. Finally, by implication, it is clear that the provision of information cannot be delayed until students are at the point of leaving school. Useful, meaningful data must be continuously accessible throughout the course of education. Computer-assisted career guidance systems and the Internet, discussed elsewhere in the book, are rapidly developing tools used to achieve such goals.

Career Guidance Strategies and Work

For many students, work is the best try-out experience. For some, organized work-study programs are ways of shortening the period of economic and psychological dependence under which so many youth chafe. If such work experience is also to facilitate career development, it should be more than casual, unsystematic ventures into whatever chance opportunity presents itself. If such goals are to be realized, education and the business-industry complex must come together in mutually creative exchanges to provide such opportunities systematically. One requirement would be that schools accept responsibility for helping youngsters find part-time or summer jobs in which they can use what they have learned. Equally important, guidance and counseling activities must be directed to helping students examine the work they are doing as they are doing it, if it is to help the career development of these students.

It is obvious that paid work has limited possibilities for fostering behavioral modification or career development in the junior high school in many parts of the United States because of federal, state, or local restrictions on age, the amount of time a student can commit to work, and the type of work he or she can do. As indicated earlier in this chapter, there are, junior high school students to whom none of these restrictions apply. A large proportion of youth start working at age 12 and a majority of youth work at ages 14 and 15 either in employee-based or freelance jobs. There are others for whom opportunities could be made available if job needs were communicated to educators or counselors by such community agents as the Chamber of Commerce, industrial personnel people, representatives of the National Alliance of Business, or the U.S. Employment Service. As discussed at some length in Chapter 9, it is also possible to use combinations of work shadowing, work visits, and work experience with junior high school students to introduce them to selected career development concepts (Herr & Watts, 1988).

Other Career Guidance Activities and Techniques in Junior High School

As is obvious, career guidance in the junior high school can be accomplished in many ways and related to many objectives. Teachers can achieve some career guidance objectives by making their subject matter more career-oriented. Teachers and counselors can collaborate in some program efforts. Counselors can achieve many career guidance objectives alone. Activities that take students into the community for exploratory purposes can be helpful. In addition to the approaches to career guidance that have already been described here, the following list of other possible activities or techniques that have been tried in career education or career guidance settings across the nation might suggest ways to meet the needs particular schools.

Curriculum Infusion

- Have students discuss the notion that "school is their work." Discuss the implications of this idea in relation to work habits and attitudes, skills required, supervision, and so on.
- Using census data, have students compare and contrast the composition of the U.S. labor market in 1940 and currently. Have them consider the percentages of workers employed in such areas as blue-collar versus white-collar families, or goods-producing versus service-producing industries. Discuss why shifts have occurred in these percentages.
- Discuss the rise in "knowledge workers" in the U.S. occupational structure. What does this term mean? How does it relate to a shift from a manufacturing to an information-based economy? To a global economy? To what one learns in school?
- Divide class into small groups and have them compete in naming the most occupations in goods-producing or service-producing occupations.
- Given a unit in consumer economics or similar topic, have students define in a two-page paper what job rewards mean to them. Consider such areas as fringe benefits, salary, vacations, shift work, lifestyle, supervision, and independent action.
- Given a list of activities (hobbies, sports, pets, clubs, and so on), have the student differentiate between those that require interpersonal skills and those that do not.
- After reading a biography of a famous person, have students identify risks the person took in implementing a career goal. Discuss.
- Have students write a theme describing a decision they made in the past that involved compromise.
- Teach students good study habits and relate these to good work habits.
- Develop "student days" in which students follow school and community officials in their daily job tasks. Have students report back to the class on what they learned about the various occupations and their responsibilities.
- Present students with a description of a hypothetical individual whose job was done away with through technological change. Have students work in groups to decide what that person might do to capitalize on existing skills and knowledge.
- Following group discussion on the effects of technology on the world of work, have students identify at least six occupations that existed twenty years ago and have now been combined with other occupations or have ceased to exist. Discuss why these results have occurred.
- Develop a bulletin board display illustrating the variety of tools and materials used by various occupations relating to subject areas taught in school.
- Given a situation of poor interpersonal relations between a subordinate and a supervisor, have the students role-play three ways to improve those relations.
- Following a class discussion on the effects of technology on society, have students name two areas (such as marine science, space exploration, ecology) that are most likely to create new occupations within the next ten years.
- Display posters in each subject matter area illustrating the contributions of workers in related occupations.
- Have students prepare bulletin board displays depicting marketable skills relating to academic subject areas.
- Have students look through job ads in local newspapers to identify as many marketable skills as possible. Have them relate identified skills to specific subject areas taught in school.
- Given their preferred occupation, have each student demonstrate in a role-playing situation examples of communication skills necessary for successful performance of the occupation.

• Examine current events in the news media with regard to present career, economic, social, and political climate and changes that will confront students when they plan for and enter the work world.

• Set up career cluster explorations in Technology Education classes that give pertinent hands-on experience in each cluster.

• Organize extracurricular career interest groups.

• Develop bulletin board displays illustrating the educational pathways to various careers (that is, four-year college, graduate and professional schools, two-year college, trade school, on-the-job training, apprenticeship programs, tech prep, on-line distance education).

• Select a consumer product and trace it back to its original raw material, showing the interdependency of various occupations necessary to produce the product.

Decision Making and Acquisition of Career Information

• Have students develop a career portfolio in which they include evidence of competencies attained, transcripts, projects completed, and their Individual Career Plan.

• Tape record a simulated interview between a counselor and a student engaged in the decision-making process or some aspect of it. Have students listen to the tape and discuss their view of what went on.

• Have students examine selected web sites on the Internet to identify jobs available across the nation, application procedures, and types of preparation required.

• Use a variety of simulated decision-making games and compare the steps they portray (such as Life Career Game, Consumer, Economic System).

• Given a curriculum decision that students will confront in the future, have them list the alternatives, advantages, and disadvantages of each and make a tentative decision. Consider the consequences likely to occur in terms of future educational and occupational possibilities.

• Have students list major decisions regarding their future that they must make:

a. Within two years (such as high school course selection)

b. Within five years (such as trade school, college, occupation)

c. Within ten years (such as where to live, work, marriage)

Have them consider at least three alternatives in each decision that will be available and discuss the implications of each.

• For a hypothetical situation in which an individual clearly made an inappropriate occupational selection, have students identify reasons why the occupation was inappropriate for the person in question.

• Using a tentative identification of a preferred occupation, have the student list chronologically the steps that need to be taken to prepare to enter the occupation.

• For the USOE career clusters, have students give at least two reasons why they would or would not consider occupations within each cluster.

• For a preferred career cluster, have students select four occupations within that cluster and gather information about them. Have them state the criteria by which they chose the four and on which they might rank them.

• Provide role models who not only have nontraditional careers, but also are raising children to help both female and male students understand ways in which career and lifestyle decisions can be integrated.

• Use any or all of the following systematically to reinforce the need and the way for girls to do career planning: role-plays, creative problem solving, values clarification, goal-setting activities, conflict resolution, assertiveness training, guided fantasy, and work exploration.

• Provide group sessions for parents to increase awareness of their attitudes about the career development of girls, the changing role of women, the issues their daughters face, and ways to help their daughters keep their options open.

• Through individual or group counseling, have students develop a set of personal criteria for use in exploring occupations.

• Using a list of ten qualities desired by individuals in fellow workers, have the students discuss at least one way in which each quality could improve individual chances for advancement in a selected career.

• Using a list of twenty common occupations, have students classify each in terms of its relationship to data, people, and things using the categories "highly related, related, not related."

• Have the students list examples of talents or other contributions they might make to a hypothetical talent show.

• Create a series of posters or displays illustrating women doing a variety of occupations previously thought of as masculine roles and men in such occupations as nursing, secretarial work, and so on.

• Use a "problem bucket" to which students anonymously contribute problems facing them. Discuss problems in small groups and explore possible solutions.

• Conduct job clinics relating to those jobs open to junior high school students, such as babysitting, lawn work, newspaper delivery, and so on.

• Play match-up games in which students are expected to choose the correct types of educational requirement for various occupations.

• Have the student develop a tentative outline of the course of study he or she plans to pursue in high school, including program choice, required courses, and electives.

• Have students list ten occupations in which socialization skills and interpersonal relationships are crucial (such as salesperson, teacher) and ten occupations in which these skills are less important (such as research scientist, chemist, veterinarian).

• Invite business personnel into the school to conduct mock job interviews with students and discuss the results with them.

• Using a list of six occupations commonly stereotyped as to sex roles, have the student look up each occupation in available resource materials and be able to give specific reasons why such stereotyping is wrong.

• Have students role-play a decision situation involving the need for compromise.

• Make posters illustrating various phases of the decision-making process.

• Have students solve a scrambled letters puzzle based on decision-making terminology.

• Have students identify the entry-level skills for five occupations within an occupational cluster of their choice. (Make use of career information, field trips, talks with workers in the field, and so on.) Have the student identify those skills he or she feels could now be performed and those in which additional training needs to be acquired.

• Have students construct an individual educational career plan that includes goals for the senior high school, post-secondary education, and the entry to work, and strengthen their use of a career portfolio.

Community Involvement

• After listening to a resource speaker on a career of his or her choice, have students list at least four new ideas concerning that career area that each had not previously considered.

• Encourage students to participate in a career camp during the summer that explores a variety of careers.

• Have students tape record an interview with a worker whose job has come into existence in the past ten years as a result of scientific technology. Discuss the implications for planning that the interviews suggest.

• After a field trip to a setting representative of a particular occupational cluster, have the student list tools or materials he or she observed workers using.

• After having interviewed a person who works in the student's general field of interest, have a career or group discussion on how this person's occupation is an integral part of his or her total lifestyle.

• Develop a directory of entry-level jobs in the community, including job descriptions, requirements, contact persons, and procedure for applying.

• Have students engage in volunteer community service work in hospitals, nursing homes, orphanages, and so on. Discuss their experiences in helping others in class and explore the potential occupations related to them.

• Invite local employment service counselors to talk with students about jobs available in the community.

• Develop a Youth Employment Service to bring students seeking part-time work together with employers having short-term or odd jobs.

• Develop performance contacts with students relative to community projects that would help them acquire career awareness.

• Given an opportunity to observe an experienced individual and a trainee in a specific career cluster, have the student compare at least five different levels of capability between the two individuals as they perform their work roles.

• Design a Human Resource Book that lists members of the community who are willing to share their knowledge and expertise with students. Identify these persons by address, phone number, occupational title, and area of expertise.

SUMMARY

In this chapter, we have examined the implications for career guidance and career counseling of youth occupied primarily with issues of exploration, planning, and identity formation. We have noted the effects on the development of career guidance programs that are associated with gender, differences in maturity, and early school leaving. Themes and practices recommended in Chapter 7 for use at the elementary school level have been longitudinally extended and reshaped to make them appropriate for the middle/junior high school. Examples of program content, activities, and techniques appropriate to youth are described and, when possible, relevant research findings are presented.

CHAPTER NINE

Career Development in the Senior High School

KEY CONCEPTS

- Students in senior high school vary in their career development and in their needs for career guidance and counseling.
- Career guidance in senior high school can be conceived of in terms of three emphases: stimulating career development, providing treatment, and aiding placement.
- Major goals of career development programs for senior high school students are specific planning of next steps in education and work; values clarification of life roles as a worker, a consumer, a leisurite, and a family member; and assuming responsibility for decision making and its consequences.
- Career guidance techniques in senior high school include structured classes, group and individual counseling, topical workshops, computer-assisted programs, self-directed activities, use of information systems, career exploration on the Internet, assessment, mentoring, the integration of work and education for reality-testing, exploration and behavioral modification, and job placement.
- Consistent with the setting, resources, and program design, the facilitation of some career development goals is best achieved by teachers, others by counselors, and still others through co-operative activity between school personnel and specialists in the community.
- The transition from school to employment consists of three phases: that which occurs in schools, in transition mechanisms, and in the induction to work by employers.

The major factor that senior high school students must deal with is the imminence of reality as defined by the rapidly approaching separation from senior high school and passage into the independence of young adulthood. Like other factors in decision making and intermediate choices, reality—defined as how the alternatives of postsecondary school life are considered by the individual—will have different implications for each individual.

As with any population, there is considerable variation in the precision of the plans for the future held by high school students. But, there are surveys that give a snapshot of what adolescents generally believe about their goals, school experiences, and thoughts about the world around them. For example, 1300 students, ages 14–18, completed a survey from the Horatio Alger Association in 1999 (Techniques, 1999) asking these students about what was important in achieving personal success: 99 percent of the respondents said work and career, 97 percent identified personal development and satisfaction, 95 percent said friendships, and 94 percent said immediate family. Other possible success factors generated far less consensus. When asked about their plans after high school, 58 percent reported that they planned to attend a four-year college or university; 16 percent a two-year college; 10 percent a vocational technical school; 29 percent, get a job; 8 percent, get married; 8 percent, join the armed forces; 2 percent, join a volunteer organization; 9 percent, travel; and 13 percent, undecided. In general, males and females had similar plans although more girls than boys intended to attend college, get married, or travel. More boys than girls reported plans to attend a vocational school or join the armed forces. More boys (15 percent) than girls (12 percent) were undecided about their plans after high school.

While such perspectives on factors in success and plans for the future seem conventional and logical, there are obviously many potential educational and career patterns embedded in such reported data. And, if extrapolated across the total national adolescent population, 13 percent undecided suggests a large target population for career guidance and career counseling. Against such a context, postsecondary school reality might be cast in any one of the following forms:

1. Choosing a postsecondary vocational or technical school in which to pursue some skilled specialty
2. Gaining access to a college and selecting a major field of study with its myriad implications for later career paths
3. Converting part-time work experience while in school into a full-time position in the labor market
4. Entering the labor market for the first time
5. Deliberating about military service, marriage, and combining work and continuing education
6. Participating in an apprenticeship or other school-to-work transition process

There will also be many students, however, for whom none of these possibilities seems viable or appealing; for them, the future represents threat or trauma. Some of these students see the future beyond high school as a confrontation with their indecisiveness about life and their place in it. Others find the burden of decision making untenable and try to escape or postpone facing such a commitment directly. Still others experience a generalized anxiety about the decisions they face. In many instances, adolescent boys and girls experience considerable stress in relation to life events related to employment (dealing with a new job, seeking a job, or changing a job). Adolescent stress also arises from inability to meet one's psychological needs and to resolve personal identity issues. In several national studies of adolescent transition from high school to employment or unemployment in Canada, Borgen and Amundson (2000) found:

> *Post high school transition periods is a time of personal and career related turmoil...psychological well being as indicated by measures of depression, self-esteem, and anxiety were correlated with a range of perceived problems. Most prominent were money and activity problems...general transition and unemployment problems, lack of job satisfaction and lack of support from family and friends.... The data suggest that the ways in which young people make sense of their situations, their ability to meet basic needs for financial security, their opportunities to engage in meaningful leisure and work activities and support from others are crucial in maintaining a positive sense of self. (p. 37)*

Among the many important recommendations of Borgen and Amundson is their concern that career counseling of adolescents broaden, rather than narrow their thinking. They state:

> *The studies that we have conducted indicate that many young people leave high school with one plan and a high level of expectation that the plan can be realized. They become discouraged if the plan does not work and seem to lack the tools to generate another one. We suggest that a part of career counseling now includes assisting young people to develop lateral thinking skills, the ability to visualize different futures for themselves, the ability to effectively assess options and make decisions within a context of uncertainty. (p. 39)*

In both sociological and psychological terms, many teenagers are apparently worried that for them the American dream is being jeopardized, and their visions of the future are restricted by the problems of money, future, the complexity of choices, and health.

Hamburg and Takaniski (1989) have indicated that recent historical events have drastically changed the experience of adolescence, in some ways making it more difficult than ever before. Among these events are the lengthening period of adolescence; the disjunction between biological and social development; confusion about adult roles and difficulty in foreseeing the future; the erosion of family and social support networks; and greater access to potentially life-threatening activities. These events have introduced a high degree of uncertainty into the lives of many adolescents and have potentially, or actually, affected their decision-making styles and career maturity.

As Mangum (1988) has observed, "the transition from adolescence into the adult world of work is inherently difficult in a society which persistently separates home and workplace and extends adolescence. There is a substantial minority, primarily from culturally and economically deprived backgrounds, who are permanently scarred by their unsuccessful experiences" (p. 1). Many youth have been cast into a marginal role in adolescence—one that is likely to be reflected in economic marginality in adulthood—because they have grown up in families with lower economic resources, or they have experienced parental divorce; a lack of significant adult role models; poor educational outcomes or the noncompletion of high school; or, possibly, involvement in alcohol and drug abuse, teenage pregnancy, or crime. A sizable proportion of these youth are from minority groups who have faced discrimination in education and the workplace and as a result have become alienated from the larger society or lack aspirations to have a meaningful job that will provide sufficient income to permit them to support a family. Indeed, among Hispanic and African American adolescent populations, the unemployment rates have continued to be two to three times that of the white adolescent population, especially in inner cities.

CAREER DEVELOPMENT AMONG SENIOR HIGH SCHOOL STUDENTS

Although little is known specifically about when adolescents state their occupational choices or the numbers of them who are essentially decided about such commitments, some rough estimates are available. Crites (1969) reviewed several pertinent studies and concluded that about 30 percent of students are undecided during the high school and college years. This is somewhat more than Fottler and Bain's finding (1980a) of 18 percent undecided among a sample of high school seniors in Alabama and less than Marr's longitudinal study (1965), which reported that 50 percent of the subjects did not make a choice until about age 21. Hollender's research (1974) has shown that decisiveness among senior high school students varies with their intellectual characteristics. Among male students, decidedness increases significantly from the lowest intellectual quartile to the highest. Girls showed a similar trend, although the percentage decided dropped in the top intellectual quartile, perhaps because of the conflicts bright girls continue to experience between nurturant roles and further educational achievement.

Depending upon one's definition of adolescent decisiveness, recent surveys continue to indicate that large numbers of high school students reflect uncertainty about their career plans and desires for more career guidance. Illustrative of such research studies is the work of Gray and Xiaoli (1999) in their benchmarking study of the class of 1998 in which they found that most students surveyed indicated that they wished they had more opportunities to explore careers. Further, among three academic levels, those who graduated from high school with the poorest academic credentials were the most likely to wish they had more career guidance. Similarly in a 1999 national Shell Poll of high school students, only 50 percent of the students indicated they felt confident about their choices, 40 percent said they had not received adequate career guidance, and 30 percent indicated that they had not received much help in selecting their high school courses.

The research of Super and Nevill (1984) has demonstrated that career maturity among high school students is not simply a function of sex or socioeconomic status. They have shown instead that work salience, the relative importance of work to the individual, is directly related to career maturity. Thus, if work and career have not yet become important to some high school students, it is not likely that much career development has taken place for them. Similarly, if career development is minimal, expressed preferences and scores on vocational interest inventories are not likely to have much permanent meaning. Without studies of large numbers of high school students across the United States, it is difficult to know the proportions of such students as stratified by their attributions of work salience or their career maturity, but it is clear that the population is quite diverse in these dimensions. To the degree that the facilitation of career planning, participation in work, and commitment to work are goals integral to the educational mission of the school, findings such as those of Super and Nevill affirm that "career education and counseling must in such cases aim first at arousal, at creating awareness of the place of work in life, its possible meanings, and how to make it real and meaningful" (p. 42).

Whichever of the numbers or trends regarding decisiveness in senior high school population one accepts, it is clear that career development needs among senior high school students are wide-ranging.

Many of them have little or no knowledge of career options available to them or what will be required of them in the workplace. In the final analysis, such data indicate that high schools vary widely in the status of their career planning services, including planning for postsecondary and collegiate education.

A persistent issue in the unevenness of the career services provided by secondary schools is the degree to which school counselors are familiar with changing needs for workplace skills and career competencies, knowledgeable about major analyses of workplace requirements such as the SCANS report and the National Career Development Guidelines discussed elsewhere in this book and in this chapter, and committed to providing students with the information, developmental programs in career guidance, and skills in career planning required by both employment-bound and college-bound students. Unfortunately, as the vital agents in insuring that such outcomes are achieved by high schools, surveys indicate that many school counselors are unfamiliar with key and timely resources in career guidance of youth, they view their roles in helping students obtain career planning skills as less important than other roles they play, or they focus their attention on college-bound rather than on employment-bound youth (Barker & Satcher, 2000; Bloch, 1996; Gray & Herr, 2000; Stanciak, 1995; Von Villas, 1995).

Need for Increased Availability of Career Guidance Services

The evidence cited about the unevenness of career guidance services in high schools has been echoed in a range of national reports over the past two decades arguing for more such services for youth in schools, for more school-community cooperation on behalf of such needs, and for the necessity of parental involvement in more systematic and comprehensive ways if the career guidance needs of diverse populations of students are to be met. Some examples follow.

The Business Advisory Committee of the Education Commission of the States (1985), in a national report dealing with the problem of alienated, disadvantaged, disconnected, and other at-risk youth recommends "new structures and procedures for effecting the transition from school to work or other productive pursuits.... Adolescents today need more and better guidance than ever before" (p. 26). The report discusses the need for coordinated programs including career counseling, financial assistance, summer jobs, cooperative education options, and role models, if such at-risk youth are to be reconnected to schooling and to work. Such perspectives imply the need for community involvement in the career guidance of youth and in the provision of opportunities by which they can be supported and encouraged to move forward with purpose and productivity.

The Research and Policy Committee of the Committee for Economic Development (1985), in a major report dealing with business and the public schools, strongly recommended that schools provide employability counseling and exploratory programs to assist in career choice, job search, and general employability. This report specifies the legitimate role for the business community in interacting with and supporting quality education in schools and in the community. The report talks about the range of the business community's involvement in schooling: for example, serving of business representatives on school boards; providing vocational education and, particularly, cooperative education; sponsoring of athletic and extracurricular activities; adopting schools; providing resource personnel for instructional or guidance purposes in schools; serving on guidance advisory groups; offering student internships in business and industry; providing mentoring of disadvantaged and minority students; providing project fundings for educational purposes; and offering school-to-work programs, donations of equipment, and teacher or student awards and recognitions (Research and Policy Committee, Committee for Economic Development, 1985).

The National Alliance of Business and the National Advisory Council on Vocational Education (1984), in a major analysis of the United States at work and particularly of relationships between education and the private sector, has argued for more school-to-work transition programs, including job placement assistance, career counseling, cooperative career education activities with business, and counseling about vocational-technical program alternatives to college degree programs. Many of the recommendations about the business community's interaction with the schools are essentially the same as those proposed in the report previously cited.

Also concerned with children at risk and counseling for employment, the 1988 report of the William T. Grant Foundation Commission on Work, Family, and Citizenship goes further than the others cited to describe needed community involvement with the guidance needs of children. The following excerpt is an example:

> *In the United States, the almost exclusive responsibility for youth's transition to work is lodged with parents and the schools. Many parents have networks and as-*

sociations that allow them to give their teenagers a hand in finding jobs. But particularly in poverty families, these informal but important connections are too often absent, leaving teenagers dependent on their own initiatives or on the schools. Yet our schools are largely isolated from the community and from the workplace. A host of blue ribbon panel recommendations calling for an end to the school's isolation from the larger community have been largely ignored. (p. 39)

Obviously, this is not a problem that can be solved by the schools alone. The Commission urges school authorities, business leaders, and community officials to join together in greatly expanded efforts to aid youth. The image of these foundering young people should not be seen as evidence that young people have failed, but rather that adults of the community have failed to give them a fair chance to get started. (p. 40)

The Commission urges new consideration by state policymakers, school and community leaders of a variety of out-of-school learning possibilities which use the schools as the nexus of community-based programs and resources. (p. 41)

The Commission report then goes on to identify examples of programs in which the community and parents can play major roles:

- Monitored work experience
  Cooperative education
  Internships
  Apprenticeship
  Preemployment training
  Youth-operated enterprises
- Community neighborhood services
  Individual voluntary service
  Youth-guided services
- Redirected vocational education incentives
  Guaranteed postsecondary and continuing education
  Guaranteed jobs
- Career information and counseling
  Career information centers
  Parents as career educators
  Improved counseling and career orientation
  Community mentors and community-based organizations
- School volunteers

Other national reports have given particular attention to the major void in the provision of counseling and other support services for many youth at the point of the school-to-work transition and at the point of entry into a specific job. The Commission on the Skills of the American Workforce (1990) stated the issue in the following manner: "the lack of any clear direct connection between education and employment opportunities for most young people is one of the most devastating aspects of the existing system" (p. 72). This point is echoed by the Educational Testing Service (1990) in its report *From School to Work.* As stated in the latter:

> *There are two difficult life-time transition points—into the work force for young people and out of the work force for older people. Given the rapid shifts in the American economy, currently the more difficult transitions are into the U.S. work force.... And the U.S. record in assisting these transactions is among the worst in the entire industrial world...school counselors are overburdened, and helping with job placement is low on their agendas. The U.S. Employment Service has virtually eliminated its school-based programs. Our society spends practically nothing to assist job success among those who do not go directly to college. On the whole, the answer to the question,'who links school and work?' is the young themselves largely left to their own devices. (p. 3)*

Although these perspectives do not exhaust the potential of either communities or parents to become more intimately involved with schools, they do illustrate ways to augment the schools' programs and processes, on the one hand, and, on the other, to create a sense of community responsibility for socializing youth to the behaviors, skills, and opportunities important to their future mobility.

These national perspectives reinforce the need for expanded conceptions and availability of career guidance services in the United States and, at least implicitly, contend that differences in career aspirations and developmental experiences require comprehensive approaches to career guidance and counseling.

These perspectives now appear in federal legislation designed to increase work-based learning and mechanisms by which to smooth the school-to-work transition.

Differences in Career Aspirations

Available data tend to confirm that within the subpopulations comprising senior high school students, there are substantial differences in career development and maturity needs for career guidance and career counseling. Many factors produce these differences: levels of parental support, styles and levels of parental attachment, work salience, gender and racial background, self-concept, and health and physical development.

Racial Background. Jaramillo, Zapata, and MacPherson (1982), in a study of 213 Mexican American college-bound high school students, found that there were subgroups within such a population related to gender and rural or city location. They found, in particular, that girls in the sample were more concerned than boys about the financial condition of the family and their own personal vocational and educational future. Dillard and Campbell (1981) compared the influence of 304 Puerto Rican (154), African American (154), and white (99) parents on the career behavior of their 194 adolescent children in grades nine to twelve. Represented were both intact and non-intact families with middle and lower socioeconomic characteristics. They found that these parents differentially affected their children's career development. For example, it was found that parental career *values* did not have much influence on their children's career aspirations in any of the three groups. The parental career *aspirations* for their children, however, were significantly related to the child's career aspirations in both African American and Puerto Rican families but not in the white families. Mothers in the African American group seemed to contribute more strongly to their children's career development than did fathers. In general, white parents' career values or aspirations are much weaker predictors of children's career development than are those of African American or Puerto Rican parents.

In related research on the career choice attitudes of rural African American, white, and Native American high school students, Lee (1984) found that parental influence has a greater impact on the career choice attitudes of African American and Native American students than on that of white students. Using a sample of 520 tenth-grade students in five public high schools in rural North Carolina, Lee also found that self-concept interacted with ethnicity to produce different groups of predictors of career attitude maturity for African American, white, and Native American students. It seemed clear that the cultural and ethnic differences in views about self among these groups had important implications for their career behavior. For example, the research suggested that in the case of Native American students, historic socioeconomic hardships and unique cultural traditions may "affect the development of self-perceptions and their influence on behavior and attitudes in ways that are different from the other two ethnic groups" (p. 192). Thus, this study suggests that more needs to be known about how parenting differs across the rural ethnic groups studied here and about how such effects have an impact on their self-concept development and career behaviors.

Parental Effects. Influences on high school students' current career expectations are complex. In examining the perceptions of 464 high school students (226 girls and 238 boys), Paa and McWhirter (2000) divided such factors into three major categories: background, personal, and environmental influences. For both boys and girls, ability, role models, and media were the top three background influences. Interestingly, ethnicity, gender, and amount of money their family has were the three least influential factors. Among the personal influences, the three most strongly perceived factors for boys and girls were interests, personality, and values.

In the environmental influences category, boys and girls differed in the ordering of the factors, but not in which were the three most important. Girls identified in order, mother, father, and female friends. Male teachers and counselors had the lowest perceived influences for girls. For the boys, the three strongest perceived influences were, in order, father, mother, and male friends. Counselors, female teachers, and female friends were perceived as least influential. In both boys' and girls' perceptions, same-sex role models were perceived as more influential than role models of the other sex: Fathers for boys; mothers for girls. But, in either case, it is clear that high school students view their parents as important influences in their career decisions.

Another factor related to parental effects on career expectations and efficacy is found in the literature on parental-child attachment. O'Brien, Friedman, Tipton, and Linn (2000) tested a model of the relations among attachment, separation, career self-efficacy, and career aspiration in women's lives overtime. Based upon a growing research literature that shows that a healthy or secure attachment to parents may facilitate the career development of women, relate positively to commitment to career choice and negatively to premature career selection, and can facilitate confidence and exploration in career development, this longitudinal study examined the hypothesis that attachment to parents would have a direct effect on career self-efficacy.

To do so, 409 female high school seniors were asked in a survey in 1991 to report their educational and career aspirations and the role attachment to and separation from their parents in their career development over time and in 1996, 207 of these women were again asked to provide such information. In addition, changes in relational and career development variables were assessed five years after the sample of young women graduated from high school. In sum, among many other findings, the results indicated at Time 1, when still in high school, attachment to mother had a significant direct effect on career self-efficacy and career self-efficacy directly influenced career aspiration. At Time 2, attachment was the only significant direct effect on career self-efficacy, and career self-efficacy again influenced career aspirations. The researchers caution that the path coefficients for attachment to mother and to father were relatively similar. Thus, in pragmatic terms, this study indicated that attachment to parents was directly related to career self-efficacy. Further, the findings suggested that at this point in their life, attachment to parents was more important than separation from them. Attachment to parents in high school and beyond may function as a protective factor, a safe base, from which young women can explore but return to as useful. The attachment of daughters to mothers in high school, because of the mothers' more direct involvement in their daughters' daily activities, may support the development of confidence and facilitate exploration and efficacy. Subsequently, daughters' attachment to fathers may lead to identity with them, and to observation of their strategies for pursuing career-related tasks, thus again resulting in increased career self-efficacy.

Other recent research has addressed the importance of attachment styles (e.g. secure, ambivalent, avoidant) and attachment security to late adolescent development. Examples of the findings include those of Vivona (2000) that demonstrate that insecurely attached late adolescents to parents reported greater depression, anxiety, and worry than their severely attached counterparts and for women, but not for men, insecure attachment was related to diminished college adjustment and lower intimacy development. The research of Kenny and Rice (1995) suggested that college students who experienced low attachment security also experienced diverse adjustment difficulties. Blustein, Walbridge, Friedlander, & Palladino, 1991) reported research that linked secure parental attachment and committing to career goals.

In essence, these research studies indicate that parental influences on late adolescent development start early in life and continue to impact on the lives of children throughout adolescence and subsequent development. Such findings accent the importance of the family environment and its impact on the decisions made by its members and the certainty and confidence with which such decisions occur.

One of the results of research on adolescents in the past decade is a renewed emphasis on the family as the context for adolescent development. It is contingent on counselors and others to help parents provide the kind of family context and specific assistance appropriate to adolescents at their developmental level. Because career choice is one of the primary developmental tasks of adolescence, it represents an important means for constructive parent-adolescent engagement. Conversely, because of the salience of career issues, they can exacerbate conflict between parents and adolescents (Young, 1994, p. 196).

The breadth of the areas in which parents can help adolescents with career development has been described in one study (Young, Friesen, & Dillabough, 1991) as framed by five constructs:

- Open communication between parents and adolescents
- In the development of responsibility
- The active involvement of parents in the lives of adolescents
- The encouragement of autonomy and specific direction and guidance that parents can provide

These constructs are not all used by a family or they may change, but they are useful for counselors to use in discussions with parents and with students about family influence on career development. Certainly at a minimum, counselors need to help parents consider what is in their area of control and influence: their intentional, planned, and goal-directed action as well as the likely sources of conflict about career issues in the parents or adolescents themselves and those that can exist between them (Young, 1994).

Studies of the effects of parents on their children's values, aspirations, and achievement show that such effects can be both direct and indirect. For example, children whose parents do not have much education or financial security are not likely to receive information about postsecondary opportunities or assistance in choosing curricular patterns that will give them the most challenging future options. As suggested in the previous chapter, many of these students take the easiest academic route they can and thereby prematurely foreclose many educational or occupational alternatives or, indeed, drop out of school before graduation. One national report (College Board Commission on Precollege Guidance and Counseling, 1986) indicates that children of lower-income families turn to the school for information and academic support that their families cannot provide. Unfortunately, in many schools in which low-income children predominate, there is insufficient counseling or career guidance available to meet their needs. Where it is available, however, the research shows that counselor and teacher influence on students' post—high school plans increases as socioeconomic level and parental educational level decreases (p. 11). Counselors do make a difference to these students.

Other research has examined the relationships among student employment status, family structure, socioeconomic position, and adolescent academic success. In one study of 4587 high school students in Washington State (Schill, McCartin, & Meyer, 1985), it was found that families do pass on employment advantage—or disadvantage—to their children, depending on the characteristics of the family structure. For example, students who had part-time employment while in high school were likely to be from intact, middle-income families rather than lower-income families, thus deriving more financial advantage and experience from adult contacts than did lower socioeconomic students. The latter were doubly disadvantaged in that they were less able to obtain part-time employment and less able to acquire the information and experience of those who did. Other findings were that employed students were likely to have higher GPAs and have a mother or father employed in a higher-status occupation. Although middle-income students are more likely to have a job than lower socioeconomic status students, they are apt to work fewer hours than the latter. Working mothers seem to have a positive effect on their offspring, providing a model (much like the father) for their employment experiences. The research also found a curvilinear relationship between hours worked and GPA, with those students working less than 20 hours a week having higher GPAs than students working more than 20 hours a week. These data suggest an intertwining of family variables and student adolescent employment experiences and, indeed, the effects of such experiences on subsequent employment.

Another interesting evidence of family effects on high school student career choice is found in the research of Noeth, Engen, and Noeth (1984). In this research, 1200 juniors in Washington State were randomly sampled from 21,060 who were college-bound and had taken the Washington Pre-College Test. These students completed a survey instrument designed to examine the factors that they believed influenced their educational and occupational plans by helping them make career decisions. Both boys and girls reported that interesting classes (93 percent) and students' families (91 percent) were most helpful in terms of assistance with career decisions in the expected college major. The next level of helpfulness was ascribed to grades (87 percent), friends (76 percent), Washington Pre-College Test scores (74 percent), and teachers (73 percent). The two factors seen as providing the least help were counselors (59 percent) and out-of-school activities (54 percent). Similar findings were reported for receiving help with the planned occupation.

The role of parents as primary determinants of children's career development has been identified in a number of studies (Birk & Blimline, 1984; Otto & Call, 1985). Parents also have a dominant role in their children's anticipation and preparation for college (College Board Commission on Precollege Guidance and Counseling, 1986). Parental influence has much to do with children's self-concepts, values, and personality as well as with the focus of their aspirations and achievement. Therefore, as part of programs of career development, parents must be empowered to be positive motivators of children's ambition, work habits, and commitment to study.

One approach to such empowerment comes from the work of Cochran and colleagues through the use of planning workbooks, activity self-exploration workbooks, and career grids combined into a Partners Program that parents used in helping their children's career planning (Cochran & Amundson, 1985). The research of Palmer and Cochran (1988) found that such approaches were effective in supporting parents as agents of career guidance for their children. Indeed, this research suggests that even though counselors can offer group career programs in interest testing, computer-assisted interactions, and other techniques, parents can be enabled through workshops tailored for parents to help their children sort out ideas, information, and values, particularly when provided a structured program they can follow.

Parents must have access to resources and training to play a positive role in meeting the career guidance needs of children. Among the useful possibilities are creating parent resource libraries; distributing to them lists of practical suggestions about ways they can help their children in study habits, exploration, and information seeking; and offering parent group meetings at convenient places and times. School counselors can conduct parent study groups and can help them to serve in liaison roles between the school and the community. Parents can be invited to and supported in roles as minicourse instructors or resource persons in the classrooms; teacher aides on field trips; members of advisory or planning committees; and technical advisors on particular work settings, colleges, or other postsecondary opportunities. Parents can be the major targets of information about college or career nights and can provide incentives for their children if they attend together. Student/parent handbooks on educational planning and financial aid can be prepared and reinforcements developed to have parents and children jointly examine such information.

Career Maturity in Special Populations

Plata (1981) compared the occupational aspirations of 40 normal and 40 emotionally disturbed male adolescents randomly selected from a midwestern public school (20 from a general studies program and 20 from vocational education) and from a special education program administered in a state institution for the mentally ill in which the students were residents (20) or part of an outpatient population (20). He found, using the Occupational Aspiration Scale, that the level of occupational aspiration for regular normals (students in general secondary school studies) was significantly higher than for either of the emotionally disturbed groups. The latter scores reflected that emotionally disabled adolescents do maintain their aspirations "at a low level or that their level of occupational aspiration vacillates" (p. 134). This finding is consistent with a series of earlier research studies. In addition, it was found by Plata that the level of occupational aspirations of normal vocational students did not differ significantly from either of the emotionally disturbed groups but was significantly lower than the scores of normal students enrolled in general academic secondary school studies. Thus, we find again that there are subgroups of secondary school students who differ in their occupational aspirations. Although emotional disturbance apparently depresses such aspiration, it does not explain the fact that the normal vocational students in the sample also had low occupational aspirations.

Karayanni (1981) compared the career maturity of emotionally maladjusted and emotionally well-adjusted high school students in two medium-sized schools in north-central Florida. Eighty-nine students were classified as emotionally maladjusted from their scores on the Minnesota Counseling Inventory (MCI), and 92 were classified as well-adjusted using the same procedure. Using the Attitude Scale of the CMI as the dependent variable, Karayanni found significant differences in career attitude maturity between well-adjusted and maladjusted students. The well-adjusted students had a significantly higher score on the CMI-Attitude Scale than did the emotionally maladjusted students. He interpreted this to mean that any disturbance in personality will affect an individual's vocational development. Although he did not find sex differences in career attitude maturity scores, when they were pooled without regard to level of adjustment, he did find significantly higher scores for white students than for African American students.

Perrone, Male, and Karshner (1979) have studied the career development concerns of talented students. Their findings include the following:

1. The talented are often told, "You can be anything you want," which somewhat negates and denies what and who they already are, placing them on a treadmill of continually becoming something beyond their immediate selves. This anything-is-possible attitude often makes it difficult for talented students to acknowledge their weaknesses,

and any evidence of personal limitations is ignored or rejected.

2. Talented persons may receive a great deal of reinforcement from others for their endeavors, making it difficult to sort out what they value from what others value for them. In attempting to set priorities they often adopt the value systems of powerful or influential models, which makes it hard to measure up.
3. Talented persons sometimes have a tendency to commit themselves to career choices prematurely, based on subject-matter fields in which they achieve considerable recognition and success. (p. 18)

In a follow-up study of 648 talented high school students in young adulthood, Post-Kammer and Perrone (1983) extended these findings about talented students and their career guidance needs. In particular, they found that approximately 30 percent of the respondents reported that on high school graduation they felt unprepared to make career decisions; about one-quarter of the sample indicated that in high school they did not know how their interests and abilities related to various career possibilities. By young adulthood, approximately one-quarter of the talented students did not believe they had lived up to their educational and occupational abilities. Although boys and girls did not differ in their perception of measuring up to educational abilities, girls were more self-critical about not living up to their occupational abilities.

As suggested in other studies, these findings indicated that for many gifted individuals, work is a form of self-expression; indeed, careers contribute significantly to their self-concept. Sometimes gifted students experience tension between careerism and intellectualism: between strong professional commitment based on the desire to become affluent and other career interests based more on a search for satisfying work (Pendaris, Howley, & Howley, 1990). They also often have problems learning that college planning is part of life career planning, rather than a finite event that ends abruptly (Berger, 1989).

In addition, while work is equally important to both boys and girls, talented girls value relationships and marriage more highly than do boys. Within work itself, relationships were also found to be more important for girls than for boys, suggesting that many talented girls continue to have attitudes consistent with sex-role stereotyping. Other research by Gassin, Kelly, and Feldhusen (1993) of 605 former and current gifted students in the Midwest, however, reported that girls were significantly more involved in career planning than boys at grades ten through twelve. Gifted and talented boys and girls experience needs for career guidance to:

1. Help with educational and career decision making.
2. Learn how their values can be used in career planning and career decision making.
3. Relate choice of college majors to their career implications.
4. Differentiate the career expectations they have for themselves as compared with expectations others hold for them.
5. Acquire ways to identify careers by which to satisfy their needs for challenge and continual skill development.

Leung, Conoley, and Scheel (1994) studied the career and educational aspirations of 194 (69 boys and 125 girls) high school juniors who participated in a one-day career development counseling program offered by the Laboratory of Gifted and Talented on the University of Nebraska-Lincoln campus. In this study, the student participants completed a demographic questionnaire, which provided background data about the student respondents and an indication of their postsecondary educational aspirations and the Occupations List, a checklist of 158 occupational titles to assess which occupations students had considered, at which of three time periods (0 to 8 years, 9 to 13 years, or 14 and older) they first considered specific occupations, and the prestige levels and gender tradition of the career aspirations identified. In addition, a follow-up analysis was conducted to determine whether participants rated their giftedness as being positive or negative to their career decision making.

Selected findings from this study indicated that gifted and talented students often explore occupations of higher prestige with increasing age, probably as a result of an increase in awareness about career options and the use of a prestige value system to assess these options. Further, there was no difference found between girls and boys in the prestige level of career aspirations. Boys were more likely than girls to consider occupations that are gender traditional and to restrict themselves to a narrow range of occupational gender type. Girls were less likely than boys to aspire to a doctoral or professional degree, but more likely than boys to aspire to a master's or bachelor's degree. The latter differences suggested that gifted girls were less determined than boys to fulfill their career aspirations through postgraduate education and training and that having the opportunity to pursue extended years of postgraduate education as would be inherent in a doctoral or professional degree might be perceived as noncompatible with the desire to have a career and a family. Such perceptions could create significant internal conflicts and confusion among gifted girls and underlie the finding that girls tended to view their giftedness as less helpful to career decision making than boys did.

The findings reported here led Leung, Conoley, and Scheel to recommend such perspectives as the following to counselors of gifted and talented students:

1. Counselors should recognize the internal and external pressures for gifted students to pursue high prestige occupations and encourage the students to free themselves of some unnecessary assumptions about prestige attainment, so that they can participate in a process of full exploration....
2. ...Thorough exploration of a wide range of occupational alternatives is particularly important for persons who possess multiple talents....
3. It is also important for counselors to recognize the internal sex-role conflicts that female students may experience as a result of being a gifted person and a woman. Students can be encouraged not to perceive them as conflicting roles. Counseling approaches to increase the self-efficacy of students in taking multiple roles would be desirable....
4. Gifted students may not be aware of the educational commitments needed for certain occupations....
5. Although prestige and gender type preferences are formed in the early years and are resistant to change, a great deal of vocational exploration happens after the first ten years of life, and interventions of various types to facilitate the career development of gifted students to modify their beliefs and attitudes about their career are still possible and necessary.
6. Counselors should recognize that although being gifted is often an asset for a student, it can also become a source of confusion especially for girls. Counseling can help the individual to explore and clarify the dynamics behind the confusion, so that educational and career decisions are made in accordance with the gifts and talents of the student. (p. 302)

The research of Dayton and Feldhusen (1989) among secondary schools in Indiana has made clear that it is important to recognize that gifted students are not found only in academic or college-preparatory curricula. There are also vocationally talented high school students. These latter students tend to manifest academic talent or high ability, vocational talent or high ability, high levels of motivation or persistence, study skills, and leadership. Among the difficulties these talented students had as enrollees in vocational education were difficulties in scheduling both academic and vocational classes; boredom and maintaining self-motivation; the lack of articulation between vocational and postsecondary programs; and dealing with parent, teacher, and counselor pressure to stay in the academic track even though as students they wanted to be involved in vocational education. Career guidance services for such students were seen as needing to deal with the unique pressures they face, to assist them in scheduling and clarifying options, and to provide career education in more depth than usual.

Gender Differences

As suggested elsewhere in this book, the question of gender differences between males and females is an important one. In her summary of the literature comparing women's and men's career transitions, Sterrett (1999) has identified research studies that suggest major differences in how mean and women express their career patterns. For example:

> *It has been found that women emphasize salary less and job satisfaction more than men do" (McGowan & Hart, 1992)...the competitive orientation of the career ladder may not be attractive to many women.... Sacrifices demanded by organizations of those on a fast-track career exact a toll on personal lives, sacrifices which many women may be unwilling to make (Cook 1993).... Women measure their career success based on how they* feel *about their careers rather than how their careers* look *to others.... Women's career development is more complex and tied to context (Powell & Mainiero, 1992). (Sterrett, pp. 249–250)*

It is not clear from the professional literature when such perspectives on gender differences in career development arise or whether they are being reflected in the thinking of current high school students. Obviously, such perspectives would be useful content for discussion in career guidance activities in groups or in classrooms.

So, too, would be gender differences in job change. Sterrett (1999) studied the magnitude of job changes that occurred in the careers of some 215 males and females from ages 19 to 65, as reported in a survey. Her basic finding was that women's job changes were significantly more radical than men's. Radical in this study means "Large magnitude career changes which occur when leaving one field and moving to a job quite different from the previous job" (p. 251). Men's job changes tended to be more likely to move in a more linear fashion from one job to a similar one and more dependent on organizational affiliations than did women. In this sense, it may be that women making job changes are more flexible than men and less organization dependent. Again, within the different opportunity structures men and women face, their differential career patterns reflect models of job change which are not the same and not fully reflected in career theories nor in the change literature. Nor do they seem to be reflected fully in the reported research on the career differences of high school boys and girls.

Although not a part of Sterrett's research, one of the potential explanatory systems for the radical changes in female job changes is Gottfredson's compromise theory (1996). Basically, this theory suggests that individuals limit their occupational aspirations to a zone of acceptable alternatives, by a process called "circumscription." They also engage in a process of "compromise" by which individuals exchange their aspirations for more realistic occupational choices from within the zone of acceptable alternatives. The compromise process tends to be influenced by the different aspects of the individual's self-concept as these are incorporated during different stages of development. For example, if compromise is necessary, the adolescent is likely to give up prestige in a job choice in order to maintain gender traditionality, which is a more basic aspect of one's career self-concept.

In testing such concepts, Armstrong and Crombie (2000) studied 502 adolescents (245 male, 247 female) in grade eight or grade nine in a Canadian city. In particular, they studied the anticipatory compromises in process among adolescents whose aspirations and expectations for occupation were the same, nondiscrepant, as compared with those that were discrepant, their aspirations for occupations were not what they expected to achieve. It was expected that the latter group of adolescents would compromise; the former group would not. Consistent with Gottfredson's compromise theory, discrepant adolescents changed their aspirations in the direction of their expectations over time. In doing so, they tended to decrease the socioeconomic level of their aspirations to the level of their expectations. While males and females were both found in similar proportions in discrepant and nondiscrepant groups, there were significant differences in the degree to which gender traditionality was apparent in male and female aspirations and expectations.

Dunne, Elliott, and Carlsen (1981) studied the occupational aspirations of 1900 tenth graders, eleventh graders, and twelfth graders in 26 rural high schools in five regions of the United States. They found that girls had both higher educational and occupational aspirations (when measured by the Duncan SEI Scale) than did boys. In addition, they found that although the young rural women tended to aspire to female-stereotyped jobs, they did not restrict themselves to so narrow a range of choice as has been found in many other studies. Beyond the female-stereotyped occupations, however, girls tended to consider neutrally perceived occupations (such as artist, draftsperson), not jobs stereotyped for the opposite sex (such as logger, plumber, construction worker). Girls in this sample did not seem to consider homemaking to be a career to which they aspired.

Aspirations by high school students toward particular types of occupations have been studied by Heilman (1979). She found that projections of more balanced sex ratios (30 to 50 percent) encouraged greater occupational interest among women, but a totally balanced sex ratio (50:50) tended to reduce their occupational interest. Heilman suggests that, for boys, changes in sex composition appear to alter the perception of social rewards to be derived from a career, whereas for girls they alter the perceived likelihood of success. In addition, the data suggested that gradual increments in the number of women in nontraditional occupations, for example, up to 30 percent, did not cause major changes in men's interests or images of the field while increasing women's likelihood of viewing these occupations as realistic possibilities.

Koski and Subich (1985) examined sex differences among high school students concerning prestige and sex stereotypes of their realistic and fantasized occupational choices. These findings suggested less balance in the consideration of traditional and nontraditional occupations among boys and girls than some of the other studies cited. Specifically, male students' realistic and fantasied occupations had few female workers. Female students chose occupations either with more women than men workers or equivalent numbers of both sexes. Girls' realistic choices were less prestigious and more heavily populated by female workers than were their fantasized choices. Overall, the boys' choices were primarily in the traditionally male, high-prestige occupations. Girls aspire to such jobs but expect to be employed in less prestigious occupations traditional for their sex.

Macke and Morgan (1978) studied the work orientation of some 1067 high school senior girls, both African American and white, in Louisville, Kentucky. It was found that such work orientations were related to mothers' work *behavior* rather than to work values or proscriptions against maternal employment. It was also found that with equal commitment to families, African American girls were 20 percent more likely than white girls to expect to work after having children because of economic circumstances.

In the aggregate, the studies reviewed here show that high school students tend to fall into groups whose career development is different and reflective of family influences, ethnicity, and gender. Thus, the responses of career guidance and counseling need to be tailored to accommodate such differences.

Work Values

Many theorists believe, as do the authors of this book, that the clarity and priority of one's values are central to an individual's decision-making. While abilities may define the types of work performance one can do well or poorly, and self-efficacy may determine how one interprets the quality of one's likely performance related to the requirements of a particular job or set of tasks, values have to do with whether the results of applying one's self-efficacy and abilities to a particular job will yield the outcomes one values. As viewed by Brown and Crace (1996), "Values are the major factor in motivation because they form the basis for attributing worth to situations and objects" (p. 212).

As generally conceived, values are more basic internalized standards by which people make judgments about whether or not to pursue particular actions, than are interests or attitudes. In some ways, attitudes can be seen as overt but not perfect representations of one's values; interests are more typically conceived to be preferences for activities rather than end states, the realm of values. Thus, an individual can hold a relatively small number of values (e.g., achievement, altruism, personal growth, prestige, making a large amount of money) but have many attitudes and many interests. According to Brown and Crace, "Making choices that coincide with values is essential to satisfaction" (p. 215).... Values orient individuals to those aspects of their environment that may provide desired outcomes. When individuals identify opportunities that relate to their values, they establish goals, develop strategies for goal attainment, and initiate action" (p. 216). Values are learned through a complex of interactions with others, from social institutions (family, school), and from one's cultural traditions, views about gender differences, socioeconomic status and other factors. Thus, different individuals and subgroups in any society are likely to hold different values. In some instances, one's values may be poorly formed or lack clarity but by the time senior high school students begin to make decisions about their postsecondary options, values, stated or unstated, are likely to be important.

Of particular importance in understanding senior high school students is the status of their work values. In essence, work values represent one of many decision schemes by which to give coherence and meaning to an occupational choice. As Cochran (1986) has suggested, "In trying to make a vocational decision, a decider is faced with varying possibilities of what values can be realized in work. In response to this situation, people must form some view or theory of what values can be realized together and what cannot" (p. 25). Cochran's research with senior high school students in Vancouver, British Columbia, suggests that the most important values for setting occupational preferences need to be harmonious in their relationship to each other. If a person's most important values are disharmonious or conflicting among themselves, the decision scheme is in jeopardy. Thus, for a given individual, it makes considerable difference how values are given priority. Such perspectives lead to the validity of considering work values and their clarification as a major function of career guidance for senior high school students.

In a cross-cultural study of work values by samples of female and male secondary students in five nations—Australia, Canada, Finland, Japan and a Spanish-speaking United States students sample—Harrington (1993) found considerable commonality among the top values of these students. In each of these samples, good salary, job security, and work with people were included in the top five values. Reflecting some cross-cultural differences, all but one of the samples (U.S. Spanish) included variety-diversion as among the top five work values; all but two of the samples (Finland and Japan) included high achievement as among the top values; one sample included independence as one of its top five (Finland); and secondary students in one nation (Japan) included creativity as among its top five. Work values selected by secondary students reflect both highly personal and frequently situation-specific or culturally defined decisions. Nevertheless, knowing about work values important to large segments of the youth population provides opportunities by which to help students elaborate or clarify these values, and to express those values that depart significantly from the norms of a particular group.

With respect to the consistency or inconsistency of work values among students from the junior high school through senior high school, other research indicates that they are affected by several factors that have implications for working with any student. For example, sex differences in work values have been reported in the studies cited here and in others. In addition, the social positions of parents and racial differences are also related to students' work values.

Post-Kammer (1987) studied the work values and career maturity of some 402 boys and 483 girls in ninth and eleventh grades of a suburban public high school in a large midwestern city. She reported that work values and career maturity were not highly correlated in her analyses, which suggests that they are essentially independent constructs. She also found that boys and girls in her sample differed in their work values and in their career maturity: girls valued achievement and variety to a greater extent and security to a lesser extent than did boys. Boys more highly valued management, economic returns, and independence, whereas girls more highly valued altruism and way of life. On career maturity scales, she found that girls scored higher on involvement and independence than did boys. Given the differences in scale scores between the girls and the boys, this study suggested that understanding the career maturity of girls may be more complex than that of understanding boys' career maturity. Finally, she found that values tend to change from extrinsic to intrinsic between ninth and eleventh grades. For example, eleventh graders score significantly higher than ninth graders on three intrinsic work values (achievement, altruism, and creativity) and one extrinsic work value (variety). The ninth graders scored higher than eleventh graders on one extrinsic value (associates). The remaining three intrinsic values and seven extrinsic values were not significantly different in score between the ninth graders and eleventh graders.

Although not confined to work values, Munson (1992) investigated the self-esteem, vocational identity, and career salience in the content of Super's theory of life-span development. The instruments used to measure the constructs of importance in the study included the Self-Esteem Inventory, the Vocational Identity Scale, and the Salience Inventory, which includes a value measure. The purpose of the study was to test the hypothesis that high and low self-esteem students significantly differ in vocational identity and career salience, with high self-esteem students scoring higher. A second hypothesis investigated was that male and female students do not significantly differ in vocational identity and salience in participation, commitment, and values expectations in school, community, or leisure roles, but they do significantly differ in commitment to work and home or family roles, with women scoring higher than men.

Of 251 high school students from the junior classes of four high schools in northeastern Ohio, students with high self-esteem scored significantly higher than did low self-esteem students on vocational identity, and on greater participation, commitment, and values expectation in school and home/family roles. Female students scored significantly higher than male students on participation in school-work and home or family; commitment to school, community, and home or family; and values expectations in home or family.

Munson's findings indicate that self-esteem, vocational identity, and career salience are important factors in career counseling interventions with adolescents. They also find that girls and boys differ in their views of salience, participation, and commitment to work and other roles. Further, the findings indicate that students with low self-esteem would benefit from interventions that focus directly on vocational identification, self-esteem, and career salience.

Relationships among Curricula, Work Values, Work Salience, and Career Maturity

A longitudinal study by Kapes and Strickler (1975) suggests somewhat less consistency in work values from ninth to twelfth grades than do the other studies reported. Particularly significant is their finding that different high school curricula appear to cause different changes in work values. For example, home economics students tend not to change their work values from ninth to twelfth grade, whereas college preparatory students change their work values much more during the same period. Thus, some curricula tend to reinforce a set of work values, whereas others tend to challenge such values. This research further clarifies the status of work values in senior high school. Rather than having totally different shifts in work values, students are more likely to have work values changing in intensity, with strong values growing stronger and weak values growing weaker.

Herr and Enderlein (1976) found similar relationships between high school curricula and career maturity, as did Kapes and Strickler (1975) with work values. Their research indicated that students in the academic program were more career mature in ninth grade than students in vocational education, general education, or business education. Although academic students were still the most career mature at twelfth grade, students in business education had almost equaled them. Students in the other two curricula remained significantly less career mature than either the academic or business education students. Apparently, curricular content interacts with student characteristics differently in stimulating both work values and career maturity.

In a subsequent longitudinal study of 1007 of the students earlier studied by Herr and Enderlein, Herr, Weitz, Good, and McCloskey (1981) examined the relationship of high school curricula and personal characteristics while in high school to postsecondary educational and occupational patterns when these persons were 24 to 27. Young adults from an academic curriculum background were found to be significantly more career mature in their career-related exploratory behavior at ages 24 to 27, using the adult form of the Career Development Inventory (now the Adult Career Concerns Inventory) as the criterion measure, than persons from vocational curricula. Apparently, postsecondary school educational or occupational experiences do not equalize the gap in career maturity observed between academic and vocational students during secondary school. Indeed, these data suggest that persons who have completed a vocational education curriculum in high school enter the career establishment with significantly fewer and less complete developmental exploratory experiences than do persons from academic curricula. These findings are undoubtedly confounded somewhat by differences in ability and socioeconomic background found among persons who enter the academic or the vocational curriculums in secondary schools. Nevertheless, career development knowledge and experiences for students in the secondary school apparently differ in major ways, and the resulting differences in career maturity persist into young adulthood.

What this longitudinal study did not find, as compared with the earlier study of Herr and Enderlein (1976), were sex differences in career maturity. They earlier found that girls were significantly more career mature than boys regardless of curriculum in high school. As measured by their concern about and completion of career development tasks, however, Herr, Weitz, Good, and McCloskey (1981) found no sex differences in career maturity by ages 24 to 27. Thus, it appears that following high school women do not capitalize on the advantage they experience in career attitude maturity during high school, either because of homemaking and childrearing experiences or because of institutional discrimination. An alternate hypothesis (Pedro, 1982), developed in a study of high school girls in a nonurban high school in the Midwest, is that one needs to understand whether girls plan to achieve directly or vicariously in career and job areas to understand the extent of involvement for planning in these areas. Thus, gender-specific and general career maturity variables need to be considered in understanding the career development of female high school students and their subsequent career behavior.

In attempting to identify specific predictors of postsecondary educational and occupational behavior, Herr and colleagues (1981) found that in addition to sex and curriculum, the best predictors of postsecondary educational level completed were high school GPA and father's occupation. Of present occupational status, in addition to sex and curriculum completed, the top three predictors were satisfaction with current occupational plans and progress toward them, high school GPA, and career maturity in high school as measured by the Attitude Scale of the Vocational Development Inventory (now the CMI). The top three predictors of current salary, in addition to sex and curriculum, were satisfaction with current occupational plans and progress toward them, career maturity in high school as measured by the Attitude Scale score of the Vocational Development Inventory, and certainty of occupation plans.

Koski and Subich (1985) investigated the curriculum background of males and females relative to their homemaking commitment and career commitment as well as the prestige and sex-stereotype ratings for fantasized and realistic career choices. In a sample of 93 (41 male, 52 female) vocational education seniors and 48 (27 female, 21 male) college preparatory seniors, the investigators found differences in the career plans and desires of students from different curriculum tracks. More specifically, they found that vocational education students aspire to less prestigious careers than do college preparatory students and that the gap between their fantasized choices and their realistic choices is less wide than that of college preparatory students. Such findings lead to the intriguing view that although the aspirations of vocational education students are substantially lower than those held by college preparatory students, they also may be considerably more realistic than those of college preparatory students, leading to the view that the latter group would be well served in career guidance by a major focus on reality testing while they engage in career exploration.

Jordaan and Heyde (1979) completed a comprehensive longitudinal analysis of the vocational maturity of high school boys. This study traces the vocational development of a group of boys from approximately age 15 to 18, or grades nine to twelve. They found that few twelfth graders and still fewer ninth graders have decided on an occupation or a specialty within an occupation. Vocational preferences from the ninth to the twelfth grade tended to be "unstable, uncertain and unrealistic," with twelfth-grade preferences having little similarity to those expressed in the ninth grade. Some two-thirds of the twelfth-graders and even more ninth-graders had no confidence in their goals. In twelfth grade, nearly half of the boys were considering goals that were not consistent with their socioeconomic background or their measured interests and abilities. Most boys in the twelfth grade, as in the ninth grade, knew little about the occupation they thought they might enter; their use of appropriate resources of information, their knowledge of the world of work, and their plans for achieving their goals were often seriously deficient. Only about half of the twelfth-grade boys knew what they would or should do to qualify for their prospective occupations, and few had done any contingency planning.

In theoretical terms, Jordaan and Heyde (1979) contend that the data they examined support the conclusion "that awareness of concern with present and future decisions, awareness of factors to consider in making decisions, occupational information, and planning are important aspects of vocational maturity in adolescence" (p. 195). These findings have also been found to be true of Canadian youth in research reported by Borgen and Young (1982). As suggested elsewhere, particularly in Chapters 4 and 6, such behaviors are also related to career behavior at age 25 in other studies by Super and colleagues. As such, they represent important organizing themes around which program goals and career guidance activities in senior high school can be planned.

Transition to Work

A variety of perspectives not yet discussed in this chapter address the place of work while in high school and after. These perspectives are also descriptive of the senior high school students.

As E. C. Donaldson's (1989) research has shown, there are different patterns of students in senior high school in the transition to work. This research among Canadian youth indicates that those who do not go on to college are affected by four influences, all external to the formal curriculum: part-time work, dropping out, employment experience, and gender. Within that context, Donaldson has classified students into seven patterns of transition behavior, as follows:

1. *Passing through*—These are transfer students who have limited contact with the school who require a few credits to complete high school.

2. *Ongoing problems*—This group had difficulties that were identified earlier and persist. These students, all boys, had known social problems such as experimentation with drugs, dysfunctional families, and learning disabilities, that contributed to psychological difficulties.
3. *Floundering*—These students appeared lost and aimless with regard to goals, but were not drowning in confusion. As a consequence, they generally seemed to be underachieving in most areas of life. There were more boys then girls and many dropouts in this category.
4. *Bottleneck problems*—These students had problems specific to a certain time period in school; as adults, they were apparently successful but were bitter about negative school experiences, such as confrontations with teachers.
5. *Apprenticeship*—Subsequent to leaving school, these boys enrolled in a formal program to learn a trade.
6. *Postsecondary education*—After a period of time in the workplace, approximately one year, these youths enrolled in college; there were more girls than boys.
7. *Successfully established*—These students settle into an adult lifestyle, with more than half of these students directly linking part-time work to full-time work during the transition.

Although there is no research that shows the same patterns of transition behavior for U.S. secondary school students, there is no doubt that there are similar subgroups of students in most U.S. high schools who vary in their career commitments, skills, and clarity of goals. Similarly, there are different patterns of behavior in their transition from school to work. Indeed, most youth do not abruptly leave high school and enter into a stable job with a firm that provides security and mobility. Rather, as has been suggested elsewhere in this book, "For many youths, the process of entry and adjustment to the labor market is lengthy and involves distinct periods. The behavior of the youths changes over time, moving from a period of casual attachment to an increasing commitment to work and to stable behavior" (Osterman, 1989, p. 255). Osterman has explained this transitional period in the engagement of work as a moratorium. Specifically, he states:

> *[In the first several years after leaving school, adolescents are frequently in what might be termed a moratorium period, a period in which adventure seeking, sex, and peer group activities are all more important than work. Some years later comes a settling down, a stage characterized by a very different set of attitudes about work. (p. 244)*
>
> *This moratorium stage tends to be reflected in the reality that most youth spend their initial years after school in the secondary labor market (e.g., the fast food industry). Firms in such categories do not invest resources in training youth nor are there career ladders available to provide incentives to youth to settle into the firm and identify with it as an occupational commitment for an extended period of time. Such firms, with little investment in training, benefits, or long-term commitments to these workers, can accept the unstable behavior of youths in ways that primary firms cannot or will not. These secondary jobs meet the requirements of young people in the moratorium period because they are typically casual and unskilled, with little responsibility, and few penalties attached to unstable behavior.*

As youth complete the moratorium period and begin to "settle down," they gravitate to the primary labor market—the firms that are large, stable, and likely to provide long-term jobs, security, and reasonable opportunities for promotion and advancement through well-defined internal career ladders. Because of the benefits and the expectation that those hired will remain with the firm for a long time, as well as the investments in training and job security, jobs in the primary labor market are rarely available to students directly out of high school. Employers in the primary labor market are interested in stability; some evidence of positive attitude and employment credibility as reflected in a period of work in the secondary labor market; and the individual's teachability, flexibility, and dependability (Mainquist & Eichorn, 1989).

In many ways, the moratorium notion of Osterman and the observed delay of many young people in entering the primary labor market are reflections of implicit or explicit constraints on their anticipation of and transition into the labor force. For some adolescents, there are issues of racism and prejudice; for others, sexual stereotype or discrimination against those with disabilities. For some adolescents, employers harbor notions of ageism, perceptions that somehow these young people are not ready at the conclusion of high school to assume the responsibilities or to manifest the personal and career maturity to take on ever more complex tasks or work roles.

Borman (1991), in her study of young workers, has contended, "the tendency to see the young as characterized by their weaknesses rather than by their strengths has been reflected in public policies and in attitudes of employers (and others) toward adolescents.... Thus, although youths value work and wish to become economically successful in terms of a middle class standard, employers' perspective toward this group remains negative.... As a result of this bias, youths who seek employment rather than postsecondary education after leaving high school suffer an extended floundering period in the labor market before beginning a real career.' They do so as a result of employers' actions, adults' attitudes and expectations for their behavior, and the viability of local labor conditions, but not as a result of the inherent characteristics of youth" (p. 26). As the research of Veum and Weiss (1993), among others, has shown, however:

> *"[I]ndividuals demonstrate a great deal of job mobility during their early years in the labor market. Brief and transitory periods of employment are common among young workers. Previous research indicates that the first 10 years of a young worker's career account for about two-thirds of all lifetime changes, and for nearly two-thirds of lifetime wage growth. During the first 10 years in the labor market, an individual works for an average of eight employers. Research also suggests that 1 of 20 male workers remains at his first job over a 10-year period. As workers age, employment patterns tend to stabilize and the probability of leaving or losing a job eventually declines.*
>
> *Young workers change jobs and employment status for a variety of reasons. Information about how to find a job and the nature of employment are difficult to acquire, particularly for young workers. Some individuals get a job offer and remain in that job so long as the wage paid exceeds alternative wage offers.*
>
> *Information about the quality of the match between a worker and a firm reveals itself over time. Workers who are well matched remain on the job, and those who are poorly matched are most likely to leave....*
>
> *Individuals may also move into and out of the labor market because of decisions relating to schooling, marital status, childbearing or other factors. In particular, decisions relating to education affect labor market experiences for young workers." (Veum & Weiss, 1993, pp. 11–12)*

In the U.S. literature describing the processes by which adolescents make the transition from school to work, it is almost an accepted truism that "typical high school graduates mill about in the labor market moving from one dead-end job to another until the age of 23 or 24" (Commission on the Skills of the American Workforce, 1990, p. 46). These adolescents are variously described as "floundering," "churning," in a period of "moratorium," from the point of high school graduation through the mid-20s, when they have only tentative commitment to work, they move into and out of the labor force, they hold numerous short-term and dead-end jobs, they are frequently unemployed, and they are, either in their perceptions or those of observers not moving toward some set of career goals. This period, then, particularly for employment-bound youth, is often seen as essentially unproductive, as not providing training or the elements of a productivity that lead in the mid-20s and 30s to quality jobs in the labor market.

Such views of employment-bound youth as those advanced here are not shared by all researchers or theorists. For example, some longitudinal studies do not suggest severe employment problems for high school graduates but rather, as a group, a smooth transition into the labor force (Meyer & Wise, 1982). Other findings (Klerman & Karoly, 1994) suggest that the adolescent school-to-work experience is not the same for all young men. Based on longitudinal analysis of the job patterns of the class of 1972, the experiences of school dropouts, high school graduates, persons with some college, and college graduates are different in the move to stable employment. Although young men typically hold a large number of jobs after leaving high school, the largest number of jobs is held by school dropouts, compared with other groups. "The median male high school dropout had held six jobs by age 24 and eight jobs by age 28" (p. 40). High school graduates held about one-half as many jobs by the same ages. It was further found that rather than stable employment being unavailable to young workers until the mid-20s, as commonly reported in the literature, many young workers are in stable employment (defined as holding one job for three years or more) by their early 20s. For example, five years after leaving high school, at approximate ages of 22 or 23 years of age, about one-third of high school graduates had already held a job that lasted three years. The median high school graduate had held a job for at least two years by the age of 23. Such data do not suggest that the average high school graduate who is employment bound "mills" around unproductively until the mid-20s. While such persons do not settle into a long-term job immediately on leaving high school (by 18 or 19), many do begin to settle into long-term job commitments by the early 20s. Implicit in such findings is the view that employment-bound youth are heterogeneous, not homogeneous, in the skills and attitudes they bring to the choice of and adjustment to work. In addition, they learn these skills and attitudes in many ways, formal and informal—in the home, the school, the workplace—with different results.

In two studies of work skills required by employers in Canada for disadvantaged and unprepared youth and adults, Wilgosh and Mueller (1993) examined the vocational habilitation and rehabilitation research perspectives on the needs for individuals with disabilities of having both work skills training and social skills training. In one study, 241 employees rated "safe work behavior and safety awareness," "attendance and punctuality," and "dependability, reliability and ability to work unsupervised" as most important to job survival for workers with or without disabilities. In combining the outcomes of the studies done with employers, the findings suggest that any attack on the low employment participation of disadvantaged, disabled or unprepared individuals must "focus on the number of critical job-related skills that the individual has at the point of entry into the workforce because skills directly related to quantity and quality of work performance are essential to job success. However, because the most common reasons for firing relate to failing in the moral quality of the employee's behavior on the job, it becomes important that employees also demonstrate qualities such as a responsible attitude, good work attendance, dependability on the job, and honesty" (p. 104).

These studies also showed that for this sample of employees, the average length of probation closely approximated three months, the time permitted employees to learn fully the duties and requirements of even very low-skill, entry-level occupations.

One informal mechanism through which youth learn about work is part-time work. Many youth engage in part-time work because of economic necessity or for other reasons: as a way of filling free time, as a method of providing some discretionary spending money, or as a way of being with friends or other family members. At its best, however, part-time employment has significant potential for providing bridges to full-time work by inducting youth into the adult or mature culture in which work occurs and by training them in the cognitive and psychomotor tasks that constitute work content. Such part-time employment or other formal work-related learning—career education, career guidance, vocational education, cooperative education, apprenticeship—can reinforce the insights inherent in the notion that work adjustment involves more than learning to cope with the technical demands of job-related tasks. Successful adjustment at work requires mastery of a range of social learning tasks, such as when to take a work break, how and when to give advice to a co-worker, how to respond to and accommodate authority in the workplace, and, perhaps more important, how to understand and manipulate the culture of the workplace to one's personal benefit (Borman, Izzo, Penn, & Reisman, 1984).

As reported in the previous two chapters, the percentage of students who work part-time while they are in middle or senior high school increases and the focus of the work they do changes from age 12 to 16 or 17 years of age. Indeed, as data gathered from the National Longitudinal Surveys of Youth in 1979 and 1997 demonstrate, some 80 percent of youths aged 16 and 17 worked at some time during the school term. More than half of those who averaged 20 or fewer hours of work per school week at ages 16 and 17 had at least some college education by age 30; less than half of those who did not work at all or who worked more than 20 hours a week at ages 16 and 17 had at least some college education. Further, youths aged 16 and 17 regardless of gender, race or ethnicity show a relationship of amount of work per week at ages 16 and 17 and the amount of subsequent work per week from 18 to 30. For example, for youths who, at 16 or 17 years of age, did not work at all during school weeks worked 64 percent of weeks from ages 18 to 30; those who worked less than 50 percent of school weeks worked an average of 74 percent of weeks from ages 18 to 30; those who worked more than 50 percent of school weeks at ages 16 and 17 worked an average of 82 to 84 percent of weeks from 18 to 30. (Rothstein, 2001). Thus, these national data indicate that how much one works during school weeks at ages 16 and 17 relate to the likelihood of attending college and having a degree by age 30 and to the consistency with which one works from 18 to 30. The research findings of Rothstein also suggests that working patterns in school are also likely to relate to a student's knowledge of workplace norms and responsibilities and the ease by which the individual makes the transition from school to work full time.

Research about the effects of part-time work on subsequent access to and adjustment in the workplace has frequently been equivocal, but there are findings that indicate that high school graduates who had jobs during high school that gave them the opportunity to exercise and improve their skills in dealing with people, things, or data are able to earn more pay per hour and spend less of their time looking for work. These findings further suggest that less unemployment and higher hourly earnings are obtained by new graduates who spend a larger number of hours per week in paid employment during their junior and senior years (for example, 16 compared with 10 hours per week) and who, in qualitative terms, had jobs during high school that give them more chances to develop and use skills (Stern & Nakata, 1989).

Before leaving this topic, it is useful once again to acknowledge that there are connections between a student's part-time employment in high school, the nature of that work, and the student's subsequent experience in the labor market.

Vondracek and Schulenberg (1986) have observed that the reality is that youth in the United States, as in other nations, learn about and are trained to carry out work tasks in both formal and informal ways. Informal mechanisms include experiences in the home, where transferable skills sometimes develop from the home chores for which youth are held accountable by parents (such as the care of younger siblings, food preparation, grounds or building maintenance and repair). Children also learn about work tasks vicariously as they hear parental conversations about such matters or observe family members engaged in different types of work. In addition to being a place for specific learning about work tasks, the home is a place in which images of work are portrayed and reinforced, work habits are developed, and networks of job-access opportunities, whether limited or wide-ranging, find their roots (Herr & Best, 1984). Obviously the transition to work is a complex process that deserves intense and comprehensive attention within career development programs. The problem is that the influences of home, part-time employment, and other informal or formal work-related learning mechanisms are unevenly distributed across student populations, and by the time they enter high school, the career development of many students is uneven, if not impaired.

IMPLICATIONS FOR THE PRACTICE OF CAREER DEVELOPMENT IN SENIOR HIGH SCHOOL

Students in senior high school arrive at the differing degrees of career maturity described in the previous sections by differing routes of continuity or discontinuity. Vondracek and Schulenberg (1986) describe the categories of influence on adolescent career development as (1) normative, age-graded influences, either biological or environmental, that might include the development of physical characteristics requisite to certain careers or early socialization to work experiences; (2) normative, history-graded influences that may also be biological or environmental in nature and may include the effects of historical events, such as depression, war, or famine; and (3) nonnormative, life-event influences such as the unexpected death of a family breadwinner, illness, or injury that can alter previously made career plans. The combination as well as the single effect of these categories of influence on individuals shape the differential profiles of career development in adolescence that are described throughout this chapter.

Just as the categories of influence on career development differ, so must the career guidance activities or interventions provided to adolescents (Niles & Herr, 1989). In our perspective, career guidance activities must have three emphases: stimulating career development, providing treatment, and aiding placement (the latter refers to student movement to the next educational level or to the immediate life of worker, consumer, and citizen). Conceptually, it is important to recognize that in terms of career development, some senior high school students will be no more mature than are elementary school students. Therefore, they will need to acquire, in a shorter time, the vocabulary, self-awareness and career awareness, and exploratory experience that might have been expected to occur earlier. Treatment will need to occur when, even after being provided information and other exploratory experiences, students are still unable to make a choice or a commitment to some plan of action (Crites, 1981).

Which of the three career guidance emphases is implemented must depend on where the individual student is in career development and what he or she needs most at a given time: reassurance, information, reality testing, emotional release, attitude clarification, or work exposure. Obviously, career guidance activities at senior high school level, as at other educational levels, must be based on individual needs, readiness, and motivations.

The principal emphases in career guidance activities for different individuals must be on the intensity of planning, readiness to participate in life as an independent person, goal-directedness of the individuals to be served, and acquisition of the competencies required to make an effective transition to employment or to postsecondary education and a positive adjustment to work. These objectives must be elaborated and cast in behavioral terms as recommended in the preceding chapters, particularly Chapter 6. The significant point here is that career guidance activities in senior high school must take each student from where he or she is in coping with developmental tasks integral to career development and lead that person to the creation and achievement of a set of specific preferences and plans to implement them. For many students, the senior high school years are the crucible in which they test their vague aspirations by developing specific strategies for converting these aspirations into reality. Career guidance, in its repertoire of emphases, represents the last opportunity for many students to rehearse different coping behaviors and alternative actions and plans in a protected context and to assess these against a backdrop of self-characteristics and value sets before their induction into the adult society.

Planning Considerations in Senior High School

Within the systematic stages of planning for career guidance outlined in Chapter 6, there are several concerns of particular importance in relating career development to senior high school students.

1. Because many students will complete their formal education with the senior high school and thereby terminate their opportunities for the systematic analysis and facilitation of their career development, efforts need to be undertaken to reach all students with career guidance opportunities and to help them develop and implement an individual career plan, or a career portfolio.

2. The major career development emphasis in senior high school needs to be on the specific and comprehensive planning of immediate, intermediate, and future educational and occupational choices after high school. For many reasons, however, not all senior high school students will be ready for such planning. Many students will need intensive self-awareness or career awareness and exploration opportunities, either because they did not have such experiences in the junior high school or because they were not ready to profit from them at that time.

3. Owing to the nature of senior high school students and the diversity of their goals, career guidance in senior high school should include counseling and developmental guidance experiences dealing with study habits, human relations at work, career and educational planning, job search techniques, and job interview skills.

4. Decisions must be made about how career guidance and placement will correspond or differ in the senior high school. Will placement be seen as a process spanning the total senior high school period or an event primarily dealt with in the twelfth grade? Will counselors take sole responsibility for educational and occupational placement or will they share these elements with other persons (such as vocational teachers or employment service counselors) in the school and the community?

5. The senior high school student is confronted with internal and external pressures to make decisions and to pursue specific types of outcomes. Career guidance or career counseling can help students deal effectively with these pressures.

6. The verbal and conceptual skills of high school students are more developed than those of junior high students, permitting career development to proceed along multiple and complex dimensions.

7. Because the major combinations of possibilities following high school are reasonably clear—college, other postsecondary education, work, nonwork, military, or governmental service (such as VISTA, Action)—career guidance should help senior high school students to consider the advantages and disadvantages of each.

Goals for Career Development in Senior High School. In contrast to goals for elementary and junior high school populations, those for senior high emphasize specific planning and awareness of life roles as a consumer and as one engaged in leisure time pursuits. Examples of program goals that might be adapted to a particular senior high school (National Occupational Information Coordinating Committee, 1989) include the following:

Self-Knowledge

1. Understanding the influence of a positive self-concept
2. Skills to interact positively with others
3. Understanding the impact of growth and development

Educational and Occupational Exploration

4. Understanding the relationship between educational achievement and career planning
5. Understanding the need for positive attitudes toward work and learning
6. Skills to locate, evaluate, and interpret career information
7. Skills to prepare to seek, obtain, maintain, and change jobs
8. Understanding how societal needs and functions influence the nature and structure of work

Career Planning

9. Skills to make decisions
10. Understanding the interrelationship of life roles
11. Understanding the continuous changes in male and female roles
12. Skills in career planning

Using the National Career Development Guidelines (NOICC, 1988) each of the 12 competencies just identified has indicators that represent emphases or goals to be facilitated by the career guidance program. For example, competency 9, skills to make decisions, is composed of the following indicators or elements:

- Demonstrate responsibility for making tentative educational and occupational choices
- Identify alternatives in given decision-making situations
- Describe personal strengths and weaknesses in relationship to postsecondary education and training requirements
- Identify appropriate choices during high school that will lead to marketable skills for entry-level employment or advanced training
- Identify and complete required steps toward transition from high school to entry into postsecondary education and training programs or work
- Identify steps to apply for and secure financial assistance for postsecondary education and training

Also, Competency 12, Skills in career planning, includes the following indicators:

- Describe career plans that reflect the importance of lifelong learning
- Demonstrate knowledge of postsecondary vocational and academic programs
- Demonstrate knowledge that changes may require retraining and upgrading of employees' skills
- Describe school and community resources to explore educational and occupational choices
- Describe the costs and benefits of self-employment
- Demonstrate occupational skills developed through volunteer experiences, part-time employment, or cooperative education programs
- Develop an individual career plan, updating information from earlier plans and including tentative decisions to be implemented after high school

Consistent with the setting and the program design, the facilitation of some of these goals might be best achieved by teachers, others by the counselor, and still others in cooperative activity among various specialists or community persons.

Sequencing Career Development Experiences in Senior High School. A persistent theme in the chapters on career interventions in the elementary and junior high schools has been the need for many of the objectives of career development to be met within the goals of particular curricula. Implied has been the need for students continuously to connect what they are doing educationally with consequences in terms of occupational and educational alternatives, the lifestyles they represent, and their general requirements. Mention has also been made of the importance of teacher attitudes in encouraging planfulness among students, an appreciation of the spectrum of occupational alternatives in which knowledge of various subject matter is useful, and in some cases necessary, and other elements of career maturity.

Some Examples of Programs. The examples of comprehensive sequential career guidance or career education activity at the senior high school level differ from those at the elementary or junior high school. Presumably, this is because the organizational structures of these three educational levels vary. In particular, the typical senior high school structure is built around the need for students to acquire the knowledge and skills inherent in a subject rather than adapting subject matter to specific students' needs.

In essence, career education and career guidance both rest on the need to infuse general education subject matter with a greater career orientation. At a fundamental level, this requires incorporating and adopting many of the themes and activities emphasized in Chapter 6 and supplementing them with simulation, group processes, or work-study opportunities. For example, a continuing career development theme in courses designed to prepare students for college will diminish the persistent assumption that college is an end in itself. College, too, is an intermediate occupational choice for the vast majority of students who enter. With such an emphasis, students can be helped to see college less as a way of deferring career thinking and more as one way to achieve particular career goals. As will be indicated later, many of the students for whom college immediately follows high school can also profit from direct work experience or from access to vocational education experiences in the school itself, to heighten the purpose with which they approach college.

Not all the students to whom career development strategies have relevance in academic education and career guidance will have college as their major intent or work after high school as their immediate goal. Hoyt mounted a major research project some years ago concerned with those whom he has described as "the specialty oriented" (Hoyt, 1965). He contrasted the specialty-oriented with the liberal arts—oriented student. The former also has postsecondary education aspirations but is inclined to trade, technical, or business school training rather than college. He speaks of the specialty-oriented as those whose prime educational motivation is to acquire an occupational skill or set of skills that could be used to enter the labor market.

Hoyt indicates that for the specialty-oriented student, career development practices should include increased use of information in the counseling process and counseling for specific decision making. He asserts, "I think far too many students leave the secondary school today with, at best, some general notions of what they may do but without the slightest idea of when or how they will be able to convert these general notions into realistic actions" (p. 235).

The reader will note that many of Hoyt's concerns about schooling's lack of commitment to teaching decision-making skills to students are similar to the concerns that initiated the career education movement in the United States in the early 1970s. These concerns about what experiences and skills student need to make an effective transition from school to work remain a national issue. In addressing this matter, Mangum (1988) has stated, "There are cultural norms, labor market realities and human development processes which compose the transition environment. No program to improve a transition can expect success which does not take into account these constraints. Employers control and dispense jobs and any successful program must ultimately help youth to meet employer expectations" (p. i). Mangum goes on to state that "irresponsibility is a far more serious barrier to successful youth access to the labor market than inexperience and lack of skill. No more than one-third of U.S. jobs require preentry training and most job skills are learned on the job. Thus, job-getting and job-keeping skills are more critical to youth attractiveness as employees than are job-doing skills" (p. 1). Mangum's observations are supported by Hoyt's (2001) recent report of National data indicating that about 43.4 percent of the job openings through 2006 will require only two to three weeks of short-term, on-the-job training.

The perspectives of Mangum and Hoyt as well as the analysis of the School-to-work Opportunities Act contained in this chapter and elsewhere, the employment transition problems in Chapter 2, and the examples of career development content recommended as part of the planning process for career guidance in Chapter 6 take different forms in senior high school programs. For example, Herr (1984) and Herr and Johnson (1989) have suggested that work context skills, career management skills, and decision-making skills comprise the major elements of general employability skills and may be used as the objectives for programs aimed at increasing employability.

Work Context Skills. Work context skills relate to the psychosocial aspects of the situation in which work activity is carried on. They include emphases on employer-employee relations, accepting constructive supervision, interpersonal skills, willingness to follow rules, adaptability, punctuality, pride in work, self-discipline, efficiency, dependability, and understanding of life in an organization.

Career Management Skills. These are skills by which one brings self-information and career information together into a plan of action. They include career planning, job search and access skills, ability to use exploratory resources and to reality test alternative choices, engaging in the constructive use of leisure, personal economics skills, self-knowledge, and knowledge of occupational and educational opportunities.

Decision-Making Skills. Skills in this category include systematic methods of processing information, predicting and weighing alternatives, clarifying values, examining risk-taking styles, and projecting action consequences.

The categories briefly noted represent the types of content that can be directed to facilitating the transition to work, that reflect the types of skills employers expect, and that facilitate the acquisition of general employability skills. Such skills have their own substance and integrity as elements of career development; they can be conceived as a specified set of outcomes; and planning is essential to foster them. They can incorporate many of the other examples of content important to young workers identified in other parts of this chapter and in other chapters.

Table 9.1 lists some of the major types of interventions that can be used in school or out of school to enhance the acquisition by high school, and often by junior high school, students of general employability skills.

The interventions identified in Table 9.1, although not exhaustive of all such possibilities, are representative of those used as program content in career guidance programs in senior high schools. Some examples follow.

One such comprehensive sequential approach to career guidance is that developed through in-depth planning in the Corning–Painted Post Area Schools (New York). Table 9.2 presents the program outcomes for which the guidance program became accountable. As can be seen, the guidance program is responsible for five goal areas, each with specific themes around which guidance programming takes place in each grade. Each of these themes is supported in related documents by the specific activities intended to achieve the program goals and the student competencies intended. The assumption is that each of the activities implemented by grade will be instrumental in achieving the goals in the left-hand column (as per the perspectives provided in Chapter 6). The overall matrix provides administrators and the public with information about what the guidance programs includes, how it changes over time, and the broad goals for which it is accountable.

Table 9.3 presents the activities of the guidance program in each of the goal areas by grade. The assumption is that each of the activities implemented by grade and by goal will be instrumental in achieving the goals in the left-hand column.

In many parts of the United States, states and large cities have created sequential programs of career guidance or programs that blend career guidance and career education. For example, in the St. Louis School District, such programs include classroom curriculum modules in self-awareness, career awareness, career orientation, and career preparation. There is also a major emphasis on providing experiential career education learning components that embrace collaboration between education and the business community (Katzman, 1989). In senior high school, the latter includes such joint activities as the following:

- *Career prep club,* in which business and community persons team teach with the classroom teacher. This 12-lesson program draws on businesspersons to present job-seeking and helping skills. Topics include career planning, how to find job openings, applications (college, armed services, and jobs), résumés, interviews, job attitudes, and how to advance on the job. Every student is responsible for completing a personal job/college portfolio.
- *Decision-making seminars,* in which ninth graders learn from government and business speakers about individual and group decision making and how knowledge of social studies is used in public and private sector jobs.
- *Shadowing,* in which a tenth grader, eleventh grader, or twelfth grader investigates his or her interests at a business site. Usually designed as a three-hour experience, shadowing provides students an opportunity to observe in an actual work environment what a job entails. These shadowing sites vary extensively in their focus and provide not only direct experience for the students en-

TABLE 9.1 Interventions for Developing Employability Skills

	IN SCHOOL	OUT OF SCHOOL
Work Context Skills	Role models Skill-centered curricula Enhancing self-concept Group counseling Exploring work values Interpersonal skills training Assessing/modifying self-efficacy	Role models Interview parents/relatives Use community resources Work visits Work participation Work shadowing Mentoring
Career Management Skills		
Career planning	Infusing coursework with career concepts Work study Career counseling Career libraries Career information and planning courses Countering sex-typing Career awareness programs Work simulation	Work visits Work study Work shadowing Mentoring Use family and community role models
Job search and access	Job search training Job-finding clubs	Job clubs Stress management Interview skills training Stress management
Decision-Making Skills	Distinguishing indecision and indecisiveness Testing for decision making Group guidance programs Decision-making programs Group counseling/exercises in problem-solving Values and needs clarification	Information gathering Career decision making for parents Family and community role models Reality testing

Source: From E. L. Herr & E. Johnson. (1989). General employability skills for youths and adults: Goals for guidance and counseling programs. *Guidance & Counseling, 4*(4), p. 20. Reprinted with permission.

gaged in shadowing at a particular site, but also content for classroom sharing and the vicarious learning about the workplace for other students.

- *Men and women of tomorrow plan today,* in which high school juniors are paired with professional role models in the community for a day in a conference setting outside of school. The adult role models and the students attend sessions together on self-esteem, goal setting, manhood and womanhood, and communication skills. The adult role model and the student spend the day together, developing a contract about goals the student hopes to achieve and designing a follow-up shadowing activity.
- *Preemployment skills work programs,* in which juniors and seniors have an opportunity to work as well as attend school. Designed as an after-school program, students work two hours a day, five days a week in the private sector and attend a career prep club class every two weeks. Funding is provided by the Job Training Partnership Act.*

*From Susan Katzman, A response to the challenges of the year 2000. *Career Development: Preparing for the 21st Century* by the Comprehensive Career Development Project for Secondary Schools in Tennessee. Copyright © 1989 University of Tennessee, Knoxville, Department of Technological & Adult Education. Reprinted by permission.

TABLE 9.2 Corning–Painted Post Area Schools Core Guidance Program by Outcomes

GOAL	GRADE 6	7	8	9	10	11	12
Knowledge of self	Values	Interests	Aptitudes	Aptitudes	Work values	Interests	Values Aptitudes Interests Achievements
Knowledge of work and education	Sex-role stereotyping	Local opportunity	Occupational and educational resources Occupational structure	Attitudes toward and rewards of work	Job-seeking survival skills Leisure Education work link	Education/work link	
Decision making		Decisions and values	Course selection Curriculum selection	Course selection	Course selection Decision-making skills	Course selection Post–high school planning	Post–high school planning
Remedial and consultation	Behavior change	→	→	→	→	→	→
Placement	Academic adjustment	Academic adjustment	Academic adjustment Course selection Curriculum selection	Academic adjustment Course selection	Academic adjustment Course selection	Academic adjustment Course selection	Academic adjustment Post-high school plans

TABLE 9.3 Corning–Painted Post Area Schools Core Guidance Program by Activities

	GRADE						
GOAL	**6**	**7**	**8**	**9**	**10**	**11**	**12**
Knowledge of self	"Bread and Butterflies" "Deciding" Discussion	SRA, "What I Like to Do" "Picture Inventory Exploration Survey" (P.I.E.S.) Discussion	Differential Aptitude Test (DAT) Discussion	Guidance information systems Continued interpretation of DAT and SAT	"Work Values Inventory" Value clarification exercises (e.g., values auction) Guidance information system "Harrington-O'Shea System" Continued interpretation of DAT and SAT	"Strong Interest Inventory" or "Career Assessment Inventory" Guidance information system "Armed Services Vocational Aptitude Battery" Continued interpretation of DAT and SAT	Senior interviews "CEEB" and "ACT" "ASVAB"
Knowledge of work and education	"Jobs and Gender" "Job Prejudice" Discussion		Speakers Field trips Career days Interviews Shadowing Lecture and discussion Want ads	Media center "Hands-on" Lecture and discussion Career days Guidance information systems Audiovisual presentations Reading assignments	Media center "Hands-on" Lecture and discussion Career days Guidance information systems Audiovisual presentations Reading assignments	Media center "Hands-on" Lecture and discussion Career days Guidance Information systems Audiovisual presentations Reading assignments	Media center "Hands-on" Lecture and discussion Career days Guidance information systems Audiovisual presentations Reading assignments

(continued)

TABLE 9.3 Continued

GOAL	GRADE 6	7	8	9	10	11	12
Decision-Making		"Deciding" Discussion	Course selection Curriculum selection	Course selection	Course selection "Harrington-O'Shea System" Guidance information system	Course selection Post–high School Planning "Career Motivation Process"	Post–high School Planning "Career Motivation Process" "Short Job Search"
Remedial	Identification →	→	→	→	→	→	→
	Counseling →	→	→	→	→	→	→
	Referral →	→	→	→	→	→	→
	Consultation (team conferences, individual conferences, in-service training, departmental meetings, articulation meetings, curriculum review, special needs, faculty meetings, staff development days, case conferences, parent conferences, parent-counselor advisory groups, parent group meetings, home visits, newsletters, industry visitations, career days, industry internships, periodic meetings with industry, agency consultations, media communications, college days, agency board participation, health and welfare association)						
Placement	School visitations Principal-counselor presentations Student handbooks Open houses Newsletters Team-parent conferences Individual conferences	Student handbooks Open houses Newsletters Temp-parent conferences Individual conferences	Student handbooks Open houses Newsletters Temp-parent conferences Individual conferences High school visit	Course selection Group and individual conferences Individualized Test interpretation and achievement review	→ → →	→ → → Post–high school plans	→ → Post–high school plans

In Newburg High School, Oregon, counselors take responsibility for enabling students in each grade from nine through twelve to attain specified career goals and a set of objectives that support the goal for each grade. (Oregon Occupation Information Committee, 1989) For example, the overarching career development goals for each of the four years include the following:

- *Ninth grade:* The student will make tentative career development plans.
- *Tenth grade:* The student will assess career development plans and develop job search techniques.
- *Eleventh grade:* The student will assess career development plans as they relate to academic and personal choices.
- *Twelfth grade:* The student will assess career development plans and prepare for appropriate post—high school plans.

To illustrate how objectives are identified to support the grade-level goals, all students have four objectives that underlie the twelfth-grade goal just identified:

1. Review and update the educational plan and develop post—high school direction
2. Update résumé to be reflective of current goals and experiences
3. Gain firsthand insight into one of the following post—high school opportunities: entry-level employment, military, college/technical school training
4. Investigate the role of employment and labor market conditions in the economy

To tie the objectives cited for twelfth-grade students to the activities designed to facilitate these objectives, seniors are expected to engage in the following activities: counselor conference; personal résumé preparation; attendance at a job fair, military interviews, or college fair; and completion of the employment and labor unit in economics classes. Other activities are used at other grade levels. For example, at the tenth-grade level, students engage in such activities as taking a standardized aptitude test, interest survey, and career profile; completing a job search unit in a personal finance class; obtaining a social security number and work permit; and finding job openings, filling out application forms, writing a résumé and cover letter, learning techniques for interviewing, and writing follow-up letters. Other individual and small group activities are used at the ninth-grade and eleventh-grade levels.

A specific example of a particular activity that might be included in a state, district, or city plan is what Brown (1980) has described as a life-planning workshop for high school students. The life-planning workshop is conducted in structured small groups that cover seven components in six to eight one-hour meetings. The components are as follows:

1. Why people behave as they do—emphasizes that behavior is goal-directed and explores the concept of accepting responsibility for one's own behavior
2. Winners and losers—emphasizes how losers can become winners by accepting responsibility, making good decisions, and planning ahead
3. Your fantasy life—explores the relationship between fantasy and planning
4. Your real life—outlines what students consider to be a set of realistic life expectations regarding education, career, close relationships, leisure, and community involvement. Compares fantasy and realistic expectations and uses a lifeline exercise to help students note where they are now and where key decisions are made throughout life
5. Setting life goals—deals with the decision-making process and planning using a force-field analysis approach that requires students to list forces that contribute to or retard goal attainment
6. Short-term life planning, high school graduation—helps students identify all requirements for high school graduates and the positive and negative forces relating to the attainment of that goal
7. Long-term life planning—takes students through both short-term and long-term planning in education, career, close relationships, leisure, and community development. Shows students that each of these areas is related to all others and is potentially a source of personal fulfillment

Because the field testing of such an approach has shown positive results, it could be used within curricula or as the substance of group counseling or special career guidance units.

A sequential two-week-long unit focused on helping high school students clarify their life-role preferences as part of their career development has been described and evaluated by Amatea, Clark, and Cross (1984) and by Amatea and Cross (1986). This unit is comprised of ten structured class sessions designed to be introduced by a counselor into a regular class. (The authors have used sociology, psychology, and family life classes in four schools for this purpose.) Each of the ten sessions has a theme and is devoted to activities intended to achieve specific unit objectives. Activities include didactic presentations on life roles; students planning a day in the future; structured interviews of parents; role-plays; case simulations of decision making; completing a Role Conflict Assessment Scale; discussions of perceived ideal qualities of sex roles; developing lists of characteristics of ideal mates; checklists depicting simulated work and family commitments; assessments of the lifestyles of different family structures with and without children and with both spouses working or not; development of individual time lines related to such roles as marital, occupational, parental, and self-development roles; and methods of managing or reconstructing role commitments to moderate stress.

The objectives of the unit were (1) to increase students' awarenesses of their own values and preferences regarding work, family, and marital life roles; (2) to help students examine the sources of such life-role preferences; (3) to increase students' awareness of the relative benefits and costs of a variety of life-style choices; and (4) to help students examine their own unique styles of choosing a set of life-role priorities and planning for a particular life-style. A variety of evaluation strategies were carried out to test the effects of the unit in the four schools and by gender. Results of Analyses of Covariance between treatment and control groups on the Attitude Scale of the CMI and two of the scales of the Life Role Expectations Inventory—career-role salience and marital-role salience—were somewhat mixed. Although there were posttest differences found on the CMI in favor of the experimental groups, there were no significant effects by treatment or by sex on the scales of the Life Role Expectations Inventory. In qualitative terms, students who participated in the units were quite enthusiastic and recommended that the unit be lengthened. Analyses of their evaluative comments suggested that they had been helped to become aware of long-range and lifestyle planning (rather than only discrete decisions), and the affirmation or clarification of existing values.

McWhirter, Rasheed, and Crothers (2000) described the implementation and evaluation of a nine-week career education class that met daily for 50 minutes. This class is interesting in several ways. Among them is that it is a graduation requirement in the district and part of the standard sophomore curriculum rather than an elective. The content of the course is the same across each high school in the district, instructional methods include hands on activities, lectures, small-group work, and guest speakers. The class content includes the assessment of interests, abilities and personality; learning how to locate vocational information, to develop and maintain a budget, to understand standard employer expectations, identify educational requirements associated with specific employer expectations. In addition, students learned how to explore specific employer expectations. In addition, students learned how to explore postsecondary career, educational, and training options, write résumés, interview for jobs, find and use career information, identify sources of funding for postsecondary education, and calculate grade point averages.

The authors examined the influence of the career education class on career decision-making self-efficacy, vocational skills self-efficacy, perceived educational barriers, outcome expectations, educational plans, and career expectations among 166 high school sophomores. The authors collected pretest, posttest, and follow-up data with a health education class as the control condition. The post-test and follow up findings indicated that the students in the class demonstrated increased decision-making self-efficacy, vocational skills self-efficacy, and short-term gains in outcome expectations but did not change their perceptions of educational barriers.

Another career development class was implemented and evaluated by Mackin and Hansen (1981). The population for the class was eleventh-grade and twelfth-grade students at an inner-city high school in Minneapolis. Students were administered the attitude scale and three of the Competency Subscales of the CMI as part of a pre/post design. The Career Development Curriculum designed by the senior author served as the independent or treatment condition provided over 11 weeks. The Career Development program was based on development tasks for high school students drawn from the Career Development Curriculum developed by Tennyson, Hansen, Klaurens, and Antholz (1975). The goals of the curriculum are (1) to increase self-awareness, (2) to increase career awareness, and (3) to increase decision-making and planning skills. Self-Awareness consists of four units—self-concept, interests, abilities, and values and needs. Activities include student completion of a self-esteem measure, an adjective list, an occupational family tree, the Strong-Campbell Interest Inventory, Holland's Self-Directed Search, standard achievement and aptitude assessments, selected readings, values auctions, and a paper dealing with self and society.

Career Awareness included two units: Career Development and the Future. Activities included constructing personal lifelines, life-career rainbows, guest speakers, field trips, and occupational fantasy trips. Guest speakers included persons who would provide role models counteracting prevailing stereotypes of sex-typed or racially typed roles.

Decision Making and Planning was devoted primarily to "teaching decision-making skills and helping students identify goals and plans for the attainment of these goals. Emphasis is on learning a process of decision making. Activities used include selected exercises from *Decisions and Outcomes*" (Gelatt, Varenhorst, Carey, & Miller, 1973), analysis of decision making styles, a force-field analysis of student plans, and a career plans paper.

Although the sample size was small ($N = 15$) and there was no control group, the results were quite positive. Students were found to have significantly increased their scores on the attitude scale, self-appraisal scale, and goal selection of the CMI. On class-evaluation scales, the students indicated that the class was helpful in the eight areas of intended effect: interests, values, skills, needs, occupational and school information, setting goals, making decisions, and making plans.

Hansen and Minor (1989) have described emphases that need to be included in the career development curriculum of students, particularly as it reflects the changing roles of young men and women. Recommended as major topical areas in such curricula are (1) career decision-making skills; (2) work and family issues in the United States and across cultures; (3) changing roles of men and women gender issues; (4) changes in the workplace and the job market; (5) changes in the family; (6) life-role planning; (7) economic independence and survival skills; (8) entrepreneurship and job creation; and (9) managing change, negotiation, and transitions. Hansen and Yost (1989) have also suggested a career planning model that incorporates many of the topics identified. Entitled *Integrative Life Planning* (ILP), the model is intended to provide knowledge and skills by which students can identify primary needs, roles, and goals and integrate them into one's definition of self, work, and family. Included in the ILP are exploration of "such potential conflict areas in family and work as the power of gender in career; family and work priorities; societal, organizational, family, and individual goals and values; developmental tasks and priorities at different life stages; and how roles, contexts and domains can be integrated in individuals, couples, families and the community" (Hansen & Yost, 1989, p. 142). The Integrative Life Planning Model has now been discussed and expanded in a book by Hansen entitled *Integrative Life Planning* (1997) in which she discusses six critical tasks in career development. They include: (1) finding work that needs doing in changing global contexts; (2) weaving our lives into a meaningful whole; (3) connecting family and work; (4) valuing pluralism and inclusivity; (5) exploring spirituality and life purposes; and (6) managing personal transitions and organizational change. These themes would provide excellent content for career education and career guidance programs.

An additional example of a sequential approach has been designed to create a team effort to support career planning for academically disadvantaged students in East Lyme High School, Connecticut (Matthay & Linder, 1982). The team included two special educators, two counselors, and two cooperative work experience coordinators. Fifty-one tenth-grade students constituted the population of students who were included because of lack of decision-making skills, lack of motivation toward finishing high school, and low academic test scores (significantly below grade level and below state and local norms in standardized reading and math tests).

Participants in the program's career awareness classes met for 45 minutes every day for one semester, participated in weekly individual counseling with the school counselors, and received tutoring from the special educators as needed. The classes consisted of action activities; individual assessments of interests; aptitudes, and exercises; values clarifications discussions; activities, maintenance of journals; career decision-making exercises; audiovisual presentations; speakers; field trips; interviews with workers; assigned readings; and individual and group counseling. The content of the program included self-awareness, career awareness, and specific career discovery.

Based on pre- and post-testing, open-ended feedback from students, and the observations of students by teachers and counselors, the results of the program are as follows:

1. Students became more familiar with regional career opportunities and trends and increased their job-search and decision-making skills.
2. Thirty-nine of the 51 students were found to have improved academic performance, improved class and school attendance, more positive self-images, more dedication to their schoolwork, greater drive toward choosing career goals, and increased initiative to make meaningful choices about future goals.
3. Thirty-eight of the participating students planned to enter the cooperative work experience program in either their junior or senior year. Eight others believed the program was helpful in assisting them to consider entering vocational education programs.
4. Twenty-four of the students indicated that the program provided them an impetus to complete their high school education.
5. Students reported improved understanding of the relationship of school courses to specific careers and an understanding of the background knowledge and skills essential for successful job performance.

The program reported by Matthay and Linder includes many of the elements suggested by Levinson (1985) as necessary to sequential programs for emotionally disturbed secondary school students. Levinson suggests that programs designed for emotionally disturbed children must be highly structured, and the counselor should be involved with others—special educators and vocational educators—to deliver a series of career-related elements, including the following paraphrased elements:

1. *Behavioral management system* of rules and behavioral contracts designed to reduce socially undesirable behavior
2. *Social skills training* comprised of instructional modules formulated to help students develop such skills as those of hygiene, cooperation, self-initiative, sensitivity and concern, responsibility, attentiveness, and emotional expression
3. *Employment education,* which includes instructional modules to strengthen basic academic competencies necessary for employment
4. *Work adjustment training* designed to assist students to acquire general employability skills: punctuality, industriousness, thoroughness, acceptance of criticism, pride in workmanship, and knowledge of safety rules
5. *Occupational and career self-awareness activities,* including role playing, field trips, and printed materials focused on helping students acquire knowledge of the world of work
6. *Stress identification, management, and reduction* designed to help students identify sources of stress in their lives and acquire relevant coping skills
7. *Decision-making skills,* including the elements necessary to process choices and develop a decision-making style
8. *Work experience activities* in which students are placed in actual work settings, the characteristics of which would differ depending on the students' vocational readiness and emotional control

In a strategy to facilitate the employment of handicapped students, Elksnin and Elksnin (1991) advocate that school counselors use job clubs. Because an important component of career development for handicapped students is counseling them to use effective job strategies, there is empirical evidence, according to Elksnin and Elksnin, that the job club approach results in higher rates of employment than other more traditional job search methods. When implementing a job club approach, for adult or handicapped students, several emphases are essential to the program:

- Defining job search skills in behavioral steps
- Regarding job seeking as a full-time job that requires the job seeker to plan a structured job-seeking schedule
- Obtaining job leads on a systematic basis from friends, relatives, and acquaintances
- Learning how to use the telephone as the primary contact for job leads after identifying leads from

various sources including yellow pages and classified want ads in newspapers
- Participating in a group of other job seekers for support and assistance
- Learning to emphasize personal characteristics in résumés and applications
- Learning to identify and emphasize work skills acquired through work and leisure experiences
- Receiving training and practice in traditional job-seeking skills, such as interviewing, résumé and letter writing, and completing of applications
- Monitoring job-seeking progress as the basis for adjusting the process if needed

Omizo and Omizo (1992) have contended that since students with disabilities have had more difficulty, substantially more in many instances, in making the school-to-work transition than have students without disabilities, they need effective career and vocational practices that are tailored to their unique needs and capabilities. To achieve that goal, however, the authors contend that more attention must be given to the acquisition and application of career-vocational assessment information to long-range educational and training planning and programming decisions. They argue the need for data on career and vocational interests, aptitudes, and work-related adaptive habits and behaviors to be combined with data generated as part of medical, psychological, educational, economic, and sociocultural assessments "to encourage the development of a career-vocational education-training program based on all aspects of a student's functioning." They further contend that such procedures must occur as a function of the school counselor serving as part of a multidisciplinary team responsible for bringing their specific skills and insights together to focus on the planning, programming, and implementation of programs and practice that reflect the school's commitments to the positive work and life experiences of its student population with disabilities.

A variation on the types of sequential career guidance programs described previously is that discussed as developmental career counseling for teenage parents by Kiselica and Murphy (1994). These authors make the important observation that although adolescent pregnancy and parenthood is considered to be one of the most pressing problems in the United States and that programs to serve teenagers who are pregnant or parents have proliferated during the past twenty years, relatively few of these programs offer or broker career-related services to their clients. It is within this context that Kiselica and Murphy argue that career and educational counseling with teenage parents should consist of two phases. During the prenatal phase, before the child is born, such counseling can be seen as crisis-oriented and focused on helping the pregnant teenager to deal with immediate decisions related to school and work. In the postnatal phase, however, longer-term educational and career planning should take place.

In the prenatal phase, Kiselica and Murphy contend that several questions typically guide career counseling. In paraphrased form, they include: Should the teenage parent drop out of school? Should they pursue a G.E.D. diploma? Are there alternative school programs (e.g., that provide infant care and a special curriculum) available, and should the teenager enroll? If they continue their education in an alternative or a regular program, is a work-study cooperative education program an appropriate opportunity? If infant care arrangements are not available in a school-based program, are other child-care arrangements available? If the student plans to drop out of school, do they need to be provided job-seeking and job-keeping skills? Can the student remain in school while working during evenings or on weekends? How many hours must the student work? Has the ability and willingness of their family and their partner's family to provide financial support been adequately examined by the teenage parent? Did the student previously plan on attending college or technical school, and if so, what immediate changes in these plans are necessary?

In the postnatal period, after the teenage parent likely made crisis-oriented educational career decisions, which probably represented a compromise between the teenage parent's preferred plans and the responsibilities of parenthood, there are longer-range plans to be considered. How can premature career foreclosure be prevented by the earlier crisis-oriented decisions made? How can the student/parent be helped to realize that career planning is a process, not an event, and that they still need to complete the exploration tasks of career development? What kinds of developmental career assessment of the individual's abilities, interests, values, commitment to work, and career maturity should be undertaken? What resources does this particular student/teenage parent have or need and what might be useful (e.g., Garner, 1989, *Work Wise: A Career Awareness Course for Teen Parents*)? How might such resources be supplemented by training on social skills, assertiveness, and decision making; field trips to work sites, or other such interventions?

Career counseling programs for teenage parents, similar to those for other adolescent populations, need to be seen as sequential, developmental, and comprehensive. They need to be concerned not only with school or with work choices, but also those choices that integrate other life roles (e.g., parenting).

A research base is growing which affirms that students exposed to a fully implemented guidance program, such as that proposed in the Missouri Comprehensive Guidance Program which includes emphases on career planning and exploration, knowledge of self and others, and educational and vocational development, were more likely to report that they had earned higher grades, their education was better preparing them for their future, students took more advanced mathematics and science courses, their school made more career and college information available to them, students had higher scores on college entrance examinations, and their school had a more positive climate (Lapan, Gysbers, & Sun, 1997; Nelson & Gardner, 1998). While this research includes guidance programs which go beyond career guidance, the latter is a central emphasis of the program and the content is delivered sequentially, in various formats, and across time.

Space does not permit the examination of such other excellent examples of sequential career guidance approaches as Careers in Literature and Life (Bienstock, 1981); the Career Search Program (Castricone, Finan, & Grumble, 1982); Operation Guidance, which is a comprehensive and systematic approach to career guidance developed by the Center for Vocational Education at Ohio State University (Campbell, Suzuki, & Gabria, 1972); or such state programs as the Missouri Comprehensive Guidance Program Model (Gysbers, Starr, & Magnuson (1998). The last system involves carefully designed modules to assist schools to perform context validation, state behavioral objectives, methods selection, and testing. Although other examples of sequential career guidance activities in senior high schools might be cited, those given suggest examples of the content and organization that are frequently found.

Career Guidance Strategies to Foster Decision Making

Efforts to promote career decision-making among senior high school students is an important emphasis, in part because of the types and extent of career indecision experienced by those students. There have been a number of attempts to capture such decision-making variance among adolescents. On balance, many of these studies have focused on the likelihood that career indecision takes different forms. For example, Fuqua, Blum, and Hartman (1988) using cluster analysis in their study of adolescents, found four groups that varied on a continuum of decidedness (decided-undecided) and anxiety. In the latter groups, adolescents could be described as confident, concerned, indifferent, and anxious. Rojewski (1994) studied a group of 189 students in the ninth grade of a rural school system in the southeastern United States. His primary purpose was to classify different types of career indecision experienced by these adolescents. Using the results of the Career Decision Scale and cluster analysis he identified three types of career indecision experienced by these adolescents. Type 1, some 39.7 percent of the sample, was labeled *Tentatively decided-crystallizing preferences.* Adolescents in this category were engaged in theoretically appropriate exploratory tasks. They had narrowed or crystallized the options they were considering to a few career fields, but they were still uncertain about making a formal choice. Type 2, 38.1 percent, was labeled *Transitional indecision.* According to Rojewski, these adolescents were "beginning to consider possible career alternatives and were engaged to some degree, in broad exploration. However, they reported high levels of indecision, possessed immature career competence, and were somewhat overwhelmed and concerned with the process of making a career choice" (p. 362). Type 3, 22.2 percent, labeled *Chronic indecision-impaired development,* were the most indecisive group of adolescents. These students indicated:

> *Both concern and discouragement at their inability to identify career interests and viable career options... this situation is exacerbated by a lack of information about personal interests and abilities and careers.... Difficulty in the decision-making process has caused these students to put off making a decision. (p. 361)*

Interestingly, in this study, gender, race, and disadvantaged socioeconomic status were nonsignificant as factors related to placement in one of the three career indecision categories. However, it is clear that students need help with the career indecision they experience and that school counselors need to implement methods by which to address the developmental difference in career indecision that students experience.

In most of the sequential approaches to career development in senior high school, helping students acquire decision-making skills is a major objective. In some cases, this goal is made explicit, and in other cases, it is assumed to be a by-product of the other career guidance activities implemented. Regardless of whether these are seen as part of a sequential program, many career intervention techniques have been used to promote decision-making behavior among senior high school students.

Many appropriate techniques are discussed in other parts of this text. Those discussed here relate directly to senior high school students. In one study, Krumboltz and Schroeder (1965) randomly assigned 54 eleventh-grade volunteers for educational and vocational counseling to three treatments: (1) reinforcement counseling (information-seeking responses reinforced), (2) model-reinforcement counseling (tape-recording of a male counselee played to each student before reinforcement counseling), and (3) a control group. The findings were: (1) that the experimental groups engaged in more information seeking outside the interview than did control-group members, (2) that reinforcement counseling produced significantly more information seeking outside the interview (such as reading resources, taking about opportunities) for girls but not boys as compared to control-group behaviors, (3) that model-reinforcement counseling produced significantly more information seeking outside the interview for boys than for girls as compared to controls, and (4) that the ratio of information seeking to other responses in the interview was positively correlated with external information seeking.

In a related study, Krumboltz and Thoresen (1964) randomly assigned 192 eleventh-grade pupils to individual and group counseling settings in which the following four procedures were used by counselors: (1) the model reinforcement of verbal information-seeking behavior, (2) presentations of a tape-recorded model interview followed by reinforcement counseling, (3) presentation of film or filmstrip plus discussion as a control procedure, and (4) inactive control. The findings were: (1) that the model-reinforcement and reinforcement counseling produced more external information seeking than control procedures; (2) with a male model, model-reinforcement counseling surpassed reinforcement counseling for boys but not girls; (3) group and individual settings were about equally effective on the average, but interactions were found to be affected by counselor variables, schools, set of subjects, and treatments.

Young (1979) compared the effectiveness of a value confrontation procedure with a procedure based on verbal operant conditioning in enhancing career development attitudes and increasing the frequency of information seeking in 90 rural adolescent boys. The subjects were identified as internally or externally controlled, according to their locus of control scores, and were then randomly assigned to one of the two experimental treatment groups or a control group. The specific purpose of the value confrontation was to create an awareness of dissatisfaction about one's career planning and to relate this to inconsistencies in one's belief system. For these students, the dissatisfaction about their career planning had already been reported on the Career Development Inventory—Secondary School Form. It was brought to their attention by the counselor. The counselor then related how "good" career planners and "poor" career planners ranked the focus values "logical" and "responsible" and the priority of the values "ambitious," "logical," and "responsible" over other values (p. 16). At four times during the procedure, students had the opportunity to examine their own hierarchy of values. The reinforcement counseling treatment was to make the subjects aware of the relative strength of their career planning orientation, resources for exploration, and information and decision making. After the interpretation of the CDI, the counselors verbally and nonverbally reinforced those statements of the subject that were evidence of vocationally mature responses. These were expressions of behavior or of intentions. Seven weeks after the treatments, it was found that the value confrontation procedure resulted in significantly greater frequency of information seeking for internally controlled subjects when compared to the reinforcement counseling and control procedures. No statistically significant differences on the career planning orientation criterion between the cognitive and behavioral treatment groups were evident.

Kraus and Hughey (1999) reported on the impact of a career intervention, essentially a short course taught by a female school counselor twice a week for four weeks to a randomly selected group of male (15) and female (15) juniors in an urban comprehensive high school in the Midwest. The course content was developed in relation to career choice competencies identified by Crites (1978). The competencies included accurate self-appraisal, gathering occupational information, goal selection, making future plans, and problem solving. The content of the course offered was derived from the Career Decision-Making Course developed by Savickas and Crites (Savickas, 1990a) designed to teach students the attitudes and competencies needed for career choice readiness.

The eight lessons used in the career intervention were:

Lesson One. Overview. Discussed career choice competencies and the importance of developing career decision-making skills and confidence in one's career decision-making skills.

Lesson Two. Self-Appraisal. An introduction to self-appraisal was provided and students completed the Self-Directed Search Form R (SDS; Holland, 1994).

Lesson Three. Practice Self-Appraisal. Students practiced self-appraisal and based on their SDS results, selected at least one occupation to research.

Lesson Four. Gathering Occupational Information. Students researched occupations.

Lesson Five. Goal Selection. Students practiced goal selection for eight hypothetical students and wrote personal career goal statements.

Lesson Six. Making Future Plans. Students engaged in two activities related to making future plans.

Lesson Seven. Problem-Solving. Used the concept of roadblocks or barriers to career goals to which problem-solving strategies can be applied. Possible roadblocks were identified and coping strategies were discussed. Students were taught a problem-solving model and a list of unrealistic problem-solving strategies.

Lesson Eight. Review. The career competencies were reviewed and students were encouraged to actively participate in the decision-making process.

The outcomes of the career intervention were assessed immediately following the intervention and four weeks later, using the Career Decision-making Self-efficacy Scale-short Form (CEMSES-SF; Betz, Klein, & Taylor, 1996) and the Career Decision Scale (CDS; Osipow, Carney, Winer, Yanico, & Koschier, 1976a,b) as the measures of the dependent variables: self-efficacy expectations with regard to career decision-making behaviors and career indecisions. Analyses of variance and t tests for related samples were used to analyze the data and to compare the outcome for the treatment and control groups.

Among the multiple research questions studied, no significant differences were found between treatment and control groups in either career decision-making self-efficacy or career indecision. There was, however, a significant treatment by gender interaction found for career decision-making self-efficacy. The males in the control group demonstrated higher levels of career decision-making self-efficacy than the females, supporting an earlier proposition of Hackett and Betz (1981) that because of differences in sex-role socialization, "career-related self-efficacy expectations are lower, weaker and less generalized among women than among men" (p. 330). A second important finding of this study was that females in the treatment group scored higher on career decision-making self-efficacy than females in the control group after the intervention. No significant difference was found for males. Thus, this career intervention appeared to be effective in enhancing the career decision-making self-efficacy for females. Indeed after this career intervention, the mean score of the female students in the treatment group was similar to that of the male students, suggesting that career guidance activities vary in their impact on students, depending upon their previous learning experiences and socialization.

Collectively the studies reported here, although not exhaustive, provide insight into the potential of reinforcement-behavioral counseling, modeling, imitative learning, and filmed and audiotaped presentations of specific stimulus materials to influence different components of decision-making and information-seeking behavior among high school students. Perhaps more important, they demonstrate that gender and other individual characteristics are related to the effects of these approaches. In other words, they emphasize the necessity of matching technique with individual characteristics and needs.

Approaches Involving Parents and Group Counseling

It is clear in the research literature that parents do influence, positively or negatively, their children's career development. Parental childrearing practices; their provision of a socioeconomic context from which resources, role models, and status, or their lack, can facilitate or constrain their children's career development; their intentional exposure of children to developmental and exploratory experiences that help them consider the career options available to them; parental respect for their children's autonomy in choice-making are each factors, among many others, that relate to their children's formation of a personal and career identity. But the role of parents in the career development of their children is complex. Often parents live vicariously through their children's career choices, particularly if they are viewed by others as prestigious and positive, and see such choices by their children as a reflection of their own worth and as factors in the construction of their personal meaning in life (Young, 1994).

Depending on the intensity of the parents' involvement with their children's career development, the boundaries they impose on autonomous decision-making, and the techniques of bribery, punishment or persuasion to influence their children's choices, parental roles in their children's career development can be positive or negative.

Bregman and Killen (1999) interviewed 72 tenth graders and college students, males and females, about their reasons for making career decisions and their perceptions of the role of parental influence. The results suggested that adolescents and young adults felt that parents had a legitimate role to play in their children's career development. Parental judgment was judged to be most important when the adolescents' decisions had negative moral consequences or focused on short-term goals (e.g., choosing what a friend chooses, making a choice of a career path to stay close to a girlfriend, seeking a hedonistic result—I want to take it easy, not work hard); however, adolescents' perceptions of parental influence rejected use of bribery or threat of punishment as appropriate methods of parental influence.

It is against such a context that efforts are made in many schools to involve parents in positive ways in career guidance activities. As such, these initiatives both use parents as important resources for their children and educate them about how they might play such roles most effectively.

Amatea and Cross (1980) described a career guidance program designed for ninth-grade through twelfth-grade students and their parents, entitled *Going Places.* The program includes six components that are presented through discussion, small-group activities, reading materials, skill rehearsal, and at-home tryout and specialization. The program consists of six two-hour sessions, one per week. Through the use of a behavioral contract, participants commit themselves to homework that applies skills learned in the group sessions. The unique aspect of the program is the combination of parents and their children in the same group systematically learning about personal and occupational data and other specific career-planning skills. The goals of this program are:

> *(a) to develop a supportive family environment to encourage career planning and decision-making; (b) to provide an overview of the important elements involved in career planning and decision-making; (c) to encourage the development of self-management skills in goal setting and decision-making as useful tools in career planning; (d) to develop self-exploration skills and compile a base of self-information; (e) to encourage the development of organizing principles for viewing the work world as a method for expanding job options and comparing self and occupational data; (f) to develop systematic information-getting skills useful in exploring occupational and training paths; and (g) to provide information on various occupational and training paths. (pp. 277–278)*

Evaluated by anecdotal data from 24 students and 24 parents who participated in three different programs, reactions to the content and the format of the program were found to be favorable. The authors, however, did suggest several caveats. For example, because the program is designed primarily for literate, motivated parents and students, its content and format will not suit all types of students, parents, and family groups. In addition, the program is not designed to deal with deep-seated conflicts between parents and children in which career is a central issue; thus, families need to be screened before inclusion in the group. Finally, to accommodate the needs of parents, such a program typically needs to be offered in the evening.

Although not limited to a group counseling approach, Kush and Cochran (1993) have described the Partners Program designed to assist parents to help their adolescent sons and daughters develop a greater sense of agency regarding a career. While many career counseling approaches, individual or group, emphasize solving an immediate career problem or learning the steps of career planning and decision making, Kush and Cochran's approach addresses several fundamental attitudes that underlie the willingness to choose and act on one's choices. Described in terms of the concept of agency, the theoretical assumptions are that a person who has a strong sense of agency is one who has the confidence and self-determination to decide, plan, act, and make things happen. In contrast, a person with a weak sense of agency is one to whom things happen, who permits others to decide for them, who experience their own abilities to plan and act as meaningless and impotent.

Using such constructs of personal agency as described previously, Kush and Cochran have designed the Partners Program to help parents to offer career guidance to their sons and daughters by using a self-exploration workbook, a career grid workbook, and a planning workbook to encourage self-awareness and career planning. Embedded in contents of the workbooks are materials designed to stimulate a sense of agency in the adolescent: for example, crystallizing meaningful motives as part of self-awareness exercises, translating motives into career goals, and inspiring confidence in the possibility of obtaining personal meaning in a career. The other dimension of the workbook is the intent that the exercises incorporated in them not be done by adolescents alone but in discussion with a significant other (an adolescent's father or mother) as a way of energizing the adolescent's support network while career planning ensues as well as reinforcing the personal conditions for a sense of agency, confidence, and self-determination regarding selection and preparation for a career.

In an effort to assess the effectiveness of the Partner's Program, Kush and Cochran used a pretest-posttest control group design as well as a series of structured interviews with selected students to assess further why they did or did not change as a result of the program. The research was conducted in 3 high schools randomly chosen from 15 in Vancouver, British Columbia. The 64 students in the experimental groups and the 25 students in the control groups were enrolled in grade twelve English classes. The researchers used scores on dependent measures related to a sense of agency (the Career Decision Scale, Career Self-Efficacy Scale, Career Salience Scale, the Ego Identity Scale and the Alienation Test) after five weeks in the program to assess the effectiveness of the program.

A MANOVA, with group treatment as a classification variable, was conducted on the six dependent measures; the analysis yielded a significant effect for groups over time, T2 (6.51) = 3.51, p. = 0.005, indicating that the experimental group made significant improvement relative to the control group. Further, analysis of the treatment effects by experimental and control groups showed that students in the experimental group became more certain and less indecisive, regarded career as more salient in their lives, and experienced a stronger sense of ego identity. The results of both the dependent variables measured and the structured interviews showed that students who completed the Partners Program showed an enhanced sense of career agency regarding career. The results also suggest the importance of giving fuller consideration to facilitating a sense of agency as a theoretical basis for career counseling.

Gray and Herr (2000) have identified five points that need to be stressed with parents regardless of the particular form of communication used—individual or group counseling, parent meetings, newsletters. They include:

- Point 1. The school's role is to help you make the best decision for your child, not to make the decision for you.
- Point 2. Focus on postsecondary success, not on college admissions.
- Point 3. Know the odds and know the costs.
- Point 4. If the goal is a better job, then do not confuse education with occupational skills.
- Point 5. There are other ways to win, consider all the postsecondary alternatives (pp. 129–131).

At the end of this chapter, other methods of facilitating decision making in senior high school students are listed. General helping strategies are also provided in Chapter 13 and a discussion of the use of career information in schools is provided in Chapter 14.

CAREER GUIDANCE AND CAREER AND TECHNICAL EDUCATION, WORK-BASED LEARNING, AND CAREER-RELEVANT SCHOOLS

One of the most fruitful efforts of the school counselor will be direct collaboration with vocational educators, now known at the federal government level and in their professional organization as career and technical educators, to reshape both the image and the substance of their disciplines. From a career development standpoint, the important thing to remember about career and technical education is that it has been seen for too long as useful to only a highly restricted sample of the total student population rather than to all or most students. In recent decades, the image of vocational education has been that of a second-class alternative for those with low verbal skills or for those with interests in working with their hands rather than their minds.

Such images and circumstances have been exacerbated by the reality that in the United States, vocational education is an elective course of study, not a required course of study for students. With the intense arguments for more specifically defined subject requirements in such academic areas as math and science, spawned by the 1983 report of the National Commission on Excellence in Education, entitled the *Nation at Risk,* vocational education programs in many states experienced reduced enrollments and were often downsized in the offerings they provided. Such shifts in educational offerings and emphases were potentially detrimental to many youth for whom immediate entry to employment after high school is their goal, rather than that of college or professional occupations. Many such youth were and are more interested in hands-on technical training, not abstract academic work that is unrelated to their interests. In the process, many students in such programs and many vocational educators became defensive about their alleged inferior status, moved further into an isolationist stance divorcing themselves from so-called academic education, and tied themselves to training experiences rigidly defined by time and content. This condition has occurred not necessarily because vocational educators want it that way but because factors such as legislative funding and union or apprenticeship regulations have, in some instances, forced such restrictions.

Regardless of the reasons for the situation, many students who desperately need what vocational education can offer, including many college-bound students, have been blocked from this access. Such a condition has added fuel to the arbitrary separation of students into supposedly homogeneous categories of college-bound and non-college-bound, with the educational experiences offered each group seen essentially as mutually exclusive.

The means of releasing more of the potential contribution of vocational education to career development and, indeed, to career guidance lie not in assigning or recruiting more students for a vocational education track but in making vocational (career and technical) education an equal partner with all other aspects of the educational process. All the relationships between "general or academic education" and career development that have been suggested throughout this book apply to career and technical education with equal force. They must be incorporated into a reshaping of the many thrusts of career and technical education in such a way that the lines, or at least the images, that presently separate it from academic education are made to blur or vanish.

It is clear that a resurgence in the importance of career and technical education in the United States has been underway for at least a decade. Legislation (such as the Carl D. Perkins Vocational and Applied Technology Education Act, reauthorized in 1998) and reports of relevant national research (such as the National Assessment of Vocational Education, 1990) have contended that a major priority is an integration of academic and vocational skills in the secondary schools of the United States. These trends reflect the changing requirements of the occupational structure and the importance of the direct connections between academic and career and technical education. But, as important, they reflect the reality of the challenges of the global economy and the awareness that nations in Europe and Africa have created programs that do integrate academic and vocational skills and that provide mechanisms by which to facilitate the school-to-work transition.

These comments about vocational/career and technical education are not intended to preclude the continuation of specific job training for some students but rather to convey the urgent need to broaden the present interrelationships and pathways within career and technical education and between it and other educational experiences. Indeed, it is important that even more specific vocational education programs be developed that truly respond to both the low and the high ends of the intellectual continuum—whether the preparation is for becoming a helper, a waiter, a lawnmower repairperson, an industrial landscape gardener, a heavy construction equipment operator, or a computer programmer. The need is to create more tactics not only for fitting youth to programs but also for fitting programs to youth. The existing lock-step in many states of rigid training durations and specified training experiences as the only route to career and technical education must be broken to exploit the enlarging opportunities in the occupational structure for individuals with a wide range of capability. If career guidance is to be fully effective, career and technical education courses must not only teach skills for specific occupations or skills across families of jobs, but also they must develop within students the elements of career development that will free them to discern the alternative ways to use these skills and to attain the personal competence to capitalize on these skills. Further, more avenues must be created for all students to move freely between academic and vocational education, with the criteria for such movement being individual need, readiness, interest, motivation, and a blend of academic and vocational experiences to meet these criteria. The intent of such an approach is to increase, not close, student options to combine work and further education.

As suggested earlier, it now appears that federal policy and a variety of legislative initiatives have begun to reestablish the importance of vocational education in U.S. society, in so doing these initiatives acknowledge many of the important aspects of vocational education (e.g., integration of academic and vocational instruction and skills, cooperative learning, work-based problem solving that requires the use of interdisciplinary knowledge, close supervision of student competency development, and certification of student skills) that in many cases could be incorporated into academic instruction and make its content more understandable and applicable to the life events, choice making, and the skills required in different combinations in the occupational structure. Placing the spotlight on career and technical education as both content and process has illustrated as well the important role that vocational education or, more specifically, the instructional context, content, and processes summarized by that term play in educational reform and in preparing students for the school-to-work transition.

There are a variety of reasons that could be cited to explain the "rediscovery" of the importance of career and technical education as the United States considers the importance of workforce development for the twenty-first century. Among them are concerns about high youth unemployment among some special needs populations, the need to reduce drop-out rates from secondary schools in many parts of the United States and the concern that as new forms of work organizations and new more technologically intensive industrial and business processes are being introduced into the workplaces of the United States, many current workers do not have the basic academic skills to learn how to use these new processes or the equipment that is being adopted or to engage in life-long learning that such wide-ranging organizational and technological change demands of workers at all levels of the labor force. Certainly an overarching impetus for the current focus on improving the vocational and technological education of secondary school students and others is the growing knowledge about how other nations are preparing their citizens for participation in workplaces that are engaged in the complex challenges of international economic competition. In short, as the precursors of the emerging global economy have become evident during the past decade, U.S. industrialists and educational policy makers have increasingly become sensitive to how other nations with whom we are now engaged in economic competition are preparing their work forces.

As suggested in earlier chapters, many of the nations of Europe and Asia have been aware, for much of the past quarter century, that the key factor in a nation's ability to compete in the growing global economy is the quality of that nation's work force as defined by the literacy, numeracy, flexibility, teachability, and commitment to life-long learning by which it is characterized. In such an economically competitive world climate, it is no longer adequate for a nation to concentrate its educational opportunities on the social or intellectual elite of a nation. Rather the need for workers at all levels of industry or business to deal with technological processes, problem solving, and knowledge work requires that schools, transition mechanisms to employment, and employers be engaged in clarifying the skills and knowledge that students need to possess when they enter the work force and in providing mechanisms (e.g., apprenticeships, career counseling, follow-up and support services) that facilitate the student's movement from school to employment. Employers must then provide systematic on-the-job training, mentoring, and supervision during the period of the new workers' induction to the job and the workplace and in their ensuing years as adult workers. These are elements of career development for young workers, particularly those not bound for college, that have been less systematically implemented in the United States than in some other nations.

These constructs and models by which to educate students to prepare for the movement directly from school to employment assumes that mechanisms exist to make that movement as smooth, deliberate, and effective as possible. Unfortunately, in the United States, the school-to-work transition has not been viewed as a process that begins in the early years of schooling and proceeds systematically through' a series of career development tasks and experiences in the secondary school years, with clear, supportive mechanisms during the period and processes of transition from school to employment and, ultimately, into the choice of and induction into a job. In contrast, in the United States, many high school graduates as well as dropouts have been literally cut adrift when they leave high school with no follow-up, no support of their job seeking, no clear purposes, and a lot of floundering as they try to enter the work force.

The Commission on the Skills of the American Workforce (1990) stated the problem of the transition from school-to-work as follows:

> *The degree to which various career development opportunities are present in a given nation depends in large measure upon the country's vision about the value of employment to the lives of individuals, their development and the society as a whole. These overarching issues are critical to understanding and improving connections between education and employment.... Clearly, there is a difference between U.S. policy makers and practitioners and many of their counterparts in Europe, with the latter who clearly view the targeted goal of education as preparation for employment versus the more diverse and more general goals for education held by Americans. (The Council of Chief State School Officers, 1991, p. 6). [Indeed, as observers have visited and examined the educational systems of Europe and contrasted them with those of the United States, they have noted that] Work as an integral part of life and well being is central to the education provided in these countries. The philosophy is reflected in the curriculum and the pedagogy of the school and of the workplace. Hence, career guidance is begun at an early age. Structured pathways to education and employment are multiple, both divergent and convergent. There is much adding to and subtracting from these approaches as needs and interests dictate. (p. 6)*

One of the major differences between American approaches to the preparation for work of its adolescents and those of most European nations is the comprehensive and systematic attention of the latter to the collective responsibility of the combined private and public sectors to prepare youth for employment because it is both in the national interest and a service to youth as they prepare to take over their economic and social responsibilities. In this context, "a great variety of resources from the public and private sectors is committed to preparing youth for responsible roles in the workplace, and, more broadly, for adulthood. Youth are given not just one chance, but many opportunities to succeed. Standards for success are reflective of the standards of the workplace and co-determined by employers, employees and educators. These standards, however, are never lowered; nor are shortcuts devised for students. As a result, few youth are left on the margins of society" (p. 6). In summarizing their analyses of the European systems of school and workplace collaboration in the preparation for work, the Council of Chief State School Officers identified four dimensions that seemed to be of particular significance:

Inclusiveness—availability and access to a broad segment of the population. For example, two-thirds of German youth are educated in the dual or vocational training system, and 15 percent of college graduates hold an apprenticeship certificate. Publicly supported training is not limited to entry-level jobs or to special populations of the countries.

Flexibility—ability to change curricula relatively quickly in time with changing job requirements and the needs to initiate new training and career-path options for individuals. The relationship of government, business, and unions provides the mechanisms required for rapid change in response to new labor and economic needs.

Competition among different types of institutions and the autonomy to provide the types and quality of programs required to improve their efficiency and attractiveness to students.

There is also great competition among the best and the brightest of students for training positions in high-status industries, firms, and occupations.

High standards of quality, skills, and expectations that apply to all students and result in high levels of knowledge in a broad spectrum of careers (e.g., mechanics that have knowledge of calculus). The apprenticeship certificate is the credential of a fully accomplished adult in society. It is the ticket to a wide range of middle-management positions in a variety of professions, crafts, and careers in small and large companies. (p. 7)

Aring (1993) has compared in some depth the German system of vocational education with that of the United States. As she indicates, all education is considered inherently vocational in Germany, and thus many of the stereotypes and dichotomies inherent in American education are not present in the same way in Germany. Because some 70 percent of German youth between 16 and 19 enter the dual system of youth apprenticeships, it is a formidable aspect of the preparation for technical productivity in that nation. It is clearly one element of a career ladder for persons who are employment-bound youth as we define them in this book and who often progress to further technical education after completing the dual apprenticeship system. By one estimate (Marshall & Tucker, 1992), one-third of the German university-trained engineers came through Germany's apprenticeship system and then attended the university, a path that would be virtually impossible for most U.S. engineers. Aring has identified what she defines as the most salient features of the German vocational education system. They include in a slightly abridged form:

1. The system is called *dual* because students learn in two interconnected settings—the workplace and the school—by means of an interrelated curriculum.
2. Students' education and training are provided in the context of a particular industrial sector.
3. Because students in the *dual* system have to meet high standards of education and skills, educators and employers are willing to give them far more responsibility and at a much earlier age than their counterparts in the United States.
4. Disadvantaged students are expected to meet the same requirements as everyone else. They are provided, however, with substantially more resources in the process.
5. Education and training are not test-oriented. Students are seen as workers who are expected to acquire whatever competencies are necessary to do the job right.
6. The *dual* system of education requires that labor, business, education, and government collaborate closely.
7. There appears to be no evidence of a "forgotten half," and there appears to be virtually no secondary labor market (for example, dead-end jobs in fast-food chains or mall stores) where adolescents spend significant amounts of time.
8. Education and training at the job site are not job specific or entirely company specific. Instead the emphasis is on socialization and on broad, industry-wide training, so that the young person will have maximum job opportunities and mobility within the companies that make up the industry.
9. Education and training paths are structured so that virtually all adolescents can pursue further education, enter an occupation with a good future, or change industries and retrain.
10. Students going through the *dual* system must meet stringent requirements set by industry and state examination boards. They must not spend a certain amount of time in an apprenticeship but must demonstrate their knowledge and skills during a two- or three-day examination period. Performance standards for the final examination are determined by a consortium that represents the particular industrial sector along with the labor union and the ministry of education. (p. 399)

In contrast to Aring's observations about the dual system of vocational and academic education in Germany, many observers have noted that in the United States: "We have the least well-articulated system of school-to-work transition in the industrialized world. Japanese students move directly into extensive company-based training programs, and European students often participate in closely interconnected schooling and apprenticeship training programs. In Austria, Sweden, the former West Germany, and Switzerland, it is virtually impossible to leave school without moving into some form of apprenticeship or other vocational training" (Berlin & Sum, 1988, p. 72).

Against the growing realization of the reality of such challenges from abroad and a crescendo of observations in national reports professing various forms of concern about the education of students for work and human resource development across the life-span, there are now several major indications that the career relevance of schooling, its preparation of students to engage in vocational and technical occupations, and the creation of new emphases on the school to employment transition will be given significantly increased attention in the education policies and practices of the immediate future. Within that context, career guidance and career counseling are being reaffirmed as critical elements of career and technical education and, indeed, of academic education. These observations rest on several major resources, although others could be cited.

The first is the Carl D. Perkins Vocational Education Act of 1984, which provided more than $1 billion in federal support to states to provide strengthened and improved vocational education to major segments of secondary school populations and to groups with problems of access to the occupational structure. Thus, the Perkins Act is concerned with providing vocational education that manifests its own form of excellence and that is a major instrument to facilitate educational and occupational equity for subpopulations who have been denied equal opportunity for training and jobs. The Perkins Act—in addition to funding new program models and delivery systems and updating the capability of vocational education to deal with advanced technologies in the workplace—has made a major commitment of funds to tailor vocational education to the special needs for sex equity, handicapped persons, disadvantaged persons, single parents and displaced homemakers, criminal offenders, and adults needing retraining. Throughout the Perkins legislation, career guidance is mentioned time and again as a major mechanism in addressing both excellence and equity issues. Since its introduction, the Perkins Act has been the major source of funding for the provision of career guidance programs for vocational students and for students not in vocational education.

Reauthorized by the U.S. Congress in 1990 and again in 1998, the Carl D. Perkins Vocational Education Act was revised and renamed the Carl D. Perkins Vocational and Applied Technology Education Act Amendments. Although some aspects of the 1984 version of the law changed, the Perkins Act continues support for career guidance programs for their major role in meeting the Act's purposes of providing equity in the choice of vocational education for underserved populations and excellence in the programs chosen as reflected in likely placement into emerging and rewarding occupations for those served by these programs.

A second document having major implications for a renewed national emphasis on vocational education is the 1984 Report of the National Commission on Secondary Vocational Education. After a year of deliberation, this 14 person Commission comprised of persons representing business and industry, economics, guidance and counseling, secondary and higher education published its report entitled *The Unfinished Agenda* (National Commission on Secondary Vocational Education, 1985). This report was partially a response to the report of the National Commission on Excellence in Education, *A Nation at Risk* (1983), which advocated significant upgrading of the high school graduation standards in the United States (particularly in science and mathematics) and in so doing either ignored vocational education or treated it negatively. *The Unfinished Agenda* was an attempt to correct the stereotyped image of vocational education and to propose a series of recommendations that would strengthen vocational education in American schools.

Although the report of the National Commission on Secondary Vocational Education includes too many recommendations to be dealt with effectively here, there are several emphases deserving particular note, for example, the purposes of vocational education. In many stereotypes, vocational education is seen as focusing only on training for entry-level occupations for students who do not have the capability or motivation to go on to college. In contrast, the National Commission contends that vocational education in the secondary school should be and generally is concerned with the development of the individual student in five areas: (1) personal skills and attitudes, (2) communications and computational skills and technological literacy, (3) employability skills, (4) broad and specific occupational skills and knowledge, and (5) foundations for career planning and lifelong learning (p. 3). In stating such purposes, several other perspectives are evident. First, vocational education and academic education are not competitors but complementary; in an occupational climate in which advanced technology is pervasive, effective training in vocational education must rest on a firm foundation in the basic academic skills. Second, vocational education is not a monolith. It is comprised of a diversity of content and curricula ranging from those of less academic rigor to those that are highly technical. Third, vocational education programs differ in specificity from courses designed to train students for entry into a specific occupation (such as auto mechanics) to those designed to prepare people to enter a cluster of occupations that tend to share common entry-level skills requirements (e.g., construction). Fourth, vocational education is not only concerned with teaching the technical aspects of job performance, but also with work habits, career planning, and job-access skills. These perspectives are now embedded in contemporary programs of career and technical education.

Of particular interest to the major focus of this book is the National Commission's concern for improved and strengthened career guidance both as integral to vocational (and career and technical) education and in broader terms of its availability for all students. As a rationale for its support of career guidance, the Commission contends:

> *Inadequate student knowledge subtly but formidably constrains student access to vocational education. Students and parents need to be accurately informed about what vocational education is, how it relates to their personal and career goals, and how it can be used to help them achieve their goals.... We need comprehensive career guidance programs that will provide this information and remove some of the subtle status distinctions involving vocational education. Comprehensive guidance means counseling that is available to all students, covering all subjects, leading to all occupations.... We cannot achieve this goal of comprehensive guidance when counselors must deal, on the average, with 400 or more students. Nor can this goal be achieved unless counselors and teachers cooperate in new approaches to facilitate the career development of students, and unless counselors expand their use of group techniques, computer-assisted career guidance, comprehensive career information systems, and other methods designed to provide assistance to all students. Counselors must serve as a resource to integrate career guidance concepts and occupational information in the classroom. In addition, the amount of shared information between vocational educators and school counselors should be increased to reinforce the likelihood that counselors will effectively advise students to consider vocational education as an option. (p. 10)*

A more current legislative initiative and potentially the one with the most impact on creating new models of collaboration between schools, transition mechanisms, and employers as well as reinforcing the importance of career guidance and counseling as the processes that connect and give continuity to the career planning and purpose of students is the School-to-Work Opportunities Act, passed by the U.S. Congress in 1994. The School-to-Work Opportunities Act provides for (1) a school-based learning component, (2) a work-based learning component, and (3) a connecting activities component. It introduces the term *career major* to mean "a coherent sequence of courses or field of study that prepares a student for a first job and that (A) integrates academic and occupational learning, integrates school-based and work-based learning, establishes linkages between secondary schools and post secondary education institutions; (B) prepares the student for employment in a broad occupational cluster or industry sector...(D) provides the students to the extent practicable, with strong experience in and understanding of all aspects of the industry the students are planning to enter...(F) may lead to further education and training, such as entry into a registered apprenticeship program, or may lead to admission to a 2- or 4-year college or university" (Section 4. Definitions). The Act also defines *career guidance and counseling* to mean programs: "(A) that pertain to the body of subject matter and related techniques and methods organized for the development in individuals of career awareness, career planning, career decision making, placement skills, and knowledge and understanding of local, state, and national occupational, education and labor market needs, trends and opportunities; (B) that assist individuals in making and implementing informed educational and occupational choices; and (C) that aid students to develop career options with attention to surmounting gender, race, ethnic, disability, language, or socioeconomic impediments to career options and encouraging careers in nontraditional employment" (Section 4, Definition).

While the School-to-Work Opportunities Act specifies the elements of the school-based learning component and the work-based learning component of a school-to-work opportunities program, for purposes of this chapter it could be argued that the connecting activities component is most directly relevant. That component (Section 104) indicates that the connecting activities shall include:

1. Matching students with the work-based learning opportunities of employers
2. Providing, with respect to each student, a school site mentor to act as a liaison among the student and the employer, school, teacher, school administrator, and parent of the student, and, if appropriate, other community partners
3. Providing technical assistance and services to employers, including small- and medium-sized businesses, and other parties in
   - A. Designing school-based learning components described in Section 102, work-based learning components described in Section 103, and counseling and case management services
   - B. Training teachers, workplace mentors, school site mentors, and counselors
4. Providing assistance to schools and employers to integrate school-based and work-based learning and integrate academic and occupational learning into the program
5. Encouraging the active participation of employers, in cooperation with local education officials, in the implementation of local activities described in Section 102, Section 103, or this section
6. A. Providing assistance to participants who have completed the program in finding an appropriate job, continuing their education, or entering into an additional training program
   - B. Linking the participants with other community services that may be necessary to ensure a successful transition from school to work
7. Collecting and analyzing information regarding postprogram outcomes of participants in the School-to-Work Opportunities program, to the extent practicable, based on socioeconomic status, race, gender, ethnicity, culture, and disability and based on whether the participants are students with limited-English proficiency, school dropouts, disadvantaged students, or academically talented students
8. Linking youth development activities under this Act with employer and industry strategies for upgrading the skills of their workers.

As the School-to-Work Opportunities Act has been implemented across the nation it has had a major impact on educational reform, on career-related curriculum development, on the forging of partnerships between business and schools. In one report of this impact, the following data, reported in an abridged manner here included: Schools using work-related curricula increased from 66 percent in 1996 to 81 percent in 1999; schools integrating vocational and academic curricula increased from 59 percent to 69 percent; those connecting work-based learning to integrated curricula increased from 51 percent to 64 percent. More than 2.5 million secondary school students received classes with a career-related curriculum in 1998, up from one million in 1997; between 1997 and 1999, job shadowing in schools increased from 55 percent to 71 percent, school-based enterprises increased from 40 percent to 51 percent, and student internships from 34 percent to 45 percent; some 246,000 employers are now involved in school to work activities and 150,000 are providing work-based learning opportunities (Cutshall, 2001).

President Clinton, under whose administration the School-to-Work Opportunities Act was formulated and approved, has given these efforts across the nation very high praise and these positive comments are reflected in Cutshall's summary of the related research. He said:

> *Research shows that school-to-work students take more challenging classes, earn higher grades and are more likely to graduate from high school and enroll in college.... School-to-Work helps students see the relevance of their studies for their futures, motivating them to attend classes and study hard and has created thousands of new partnerships between businesses and schools. (Cutshall, 2001, pp. 18–19)*

It might be noted here that school-to-work programs and work-based learning are not only for students who are employment-bound or for students majoring in career and technical education, they also have significant advantages for college-bound students as they consider potential academic majors in college and their subsequent career paths.

The findings of Cutshall (2001) have been reinforced by the research of Joyce and Newmark (2001).

Using the data provided by the *National Longitudinal Survey of Youth, 1997,* and the *1996 School Administrator's Survey,* Cutshall found that nationally 64.2 percent of schools with a twelfth grade offered at least one school-to-work program to their students. "The most prevalent *work-based* activity offered by schools was job shadowing, with nearly 29 percent of schools offering such programs. Job shadowing was followed by internship, mentoring, apprenticeship, and school sponsored enterprise programs.... In 1996, school-based activities were more commonly offered by schools then were work-based activities. Technical preparatory and cooperative education programs were the most common *school-based* activities and were offered by approximately 33 percent of schools. Career major programs were less prevalent, with 13.2 percent of schools offering them" (p. 42). "In 1996, a higher percentage of suburban schools offered school-to-work programs than did urban or rural schools. This was particularly true for apprenticeship, school-sponsored enterprise, cooperative education, and tech prep programs" (p. 42). "Findings show that, if anything, individuals who perceive themselves as more likely to complete college have greater participation in school-to-work programs" (p. 46).

Integrating Work Experience with Schooling

Obviously the traditional concepts of vocational education, the newer forms of work-based learning promoted by the School-to-Work Opportunities Act and other relevant federal policy and legislation, and such other possibilities as a greater freedom of movement between or integration of academic and vocational education are not mutually exclusive ways to provide career guidance and career development. At the senior high-school level, the integration of work experience with schooling can be a reality. The age and sex of the student are no longer the contingencies they were at the junior high school level. Blocks of time can be developed when students will actually report to jobs instead of school part of each day for two or three weeks or a term at a time.

Although the economic appeal is obvious, the training and exploratory value of work experience must be fitted to individual needs. Hence, if a particular student is interested in electronics, a program can be made available by which he or she can complete required high school work and simultaneously secure on-the-job training through part-time employment. With creative business-industry-education cooperation, programs can be mounted that provide training at work stations in the community in the late afternoon or morning hours, with the rest of the day devoted to academic education in the school. For some students, this can be pretechnical training; for others, a permanent job; and for still others, precollege exploration.

Probably the most common name for programs of work-study is *cooperative education.* Joyce and Neumark (2001) define cooperative education as: "A method of instruction whereby students alternate or parallel their academic and vocational studies with a job in a related field. May or may not include paid work experiences" (p. 50).

Cooperative education or work experience programs are essentially a process of behavioral change for students through experience. At one level, experience comes from immediately determining how what one learns in the classroom is applied at work. At another level, it comes from being adult-oriented at the workstation rather than adolescent-oriented. In this sense, students have the opportunity to experience work norms as lived by adults rather than speculate about such things with one's adolescent peers. Finally, cooperative education programs assist students to see themselves and the work done as a whole. Frequently, classroom study fragments employability traits, work habits, human relations, and communications into small increments for purposes of learning. In the real world, all of these elements are part of a complete and constantly unfolding fabric that requires individual judgment and discrimination if career maturity is to result.

Work experience programs also allow the student to test which career development tasks have already been incorporated into his or her behavioral repertoire and which still need honing. In this way, work experience programs provide goal direction to learning and to student planning. A work experience in these terms is not just experience for its own sake but is related to employability. It represents a prime medium for career education and for developing effective work behaviors that help students acquire a positive career identity. Cooperative education can be seen as a powerful tool in career guidance on the secondary school level.

It might be noted here that elements of cooperative education are similar to those described in the literature on mentoring. For those school systems unable to develop cooperative education programs, mentoring programs may be a useful alternative. Mentoring has been mentioned elsewhere in this book as a process of providing role models from the community for students who will profit from being able to observe firsthand the work context and activity of a mentor. Mentoring programs are evident in business, in community colleges, and in other educational contexts. Borman and Colson (1984) have described the use of mentoring as a career guidance technique for high school students in the West Nyack, New York, schools. In this program eighth-grade, eleventh-grade, and twelfth-grade students were assigned to professionals (mentors) to learn about career fields of interest in the community. Students explore some 25 career fields a year by spending after-school hours with their mentors for one semester: Students in twelfth grade spend 3 hours per week or a total of 60 hours with their mentors; eighth-grade students tend to spend 1 to 1½ hours per week. Although the specific process of evaluation is not described, Borman and Colson indicate that most students and mentors judge the program as excellent. Colson, Borman, and Nash (1978) earlier developed such a mentoring program for gifted high school seniors in College Station, Texas. At the beginning of the program, an eight-week guidance laboratory in career investigations involved students with selected college professors for two months before they went into the mentorship experience. This program included a three-phase working internship in which the high school participants were placed in the community in career areas of interest to each student.

Work Shadowing. Another formal learning process related to mentoring or work experience is job or *work shadowing.* Although the term is virtually unmentioned in American career development literature, it has achieved increasing attention in British research. According to Watts (1986), "work shadowing describes schemes in which an observer follows a worker around for a period of time, observing the various tasks in which he or she engages, and doing so within the context of his or her total role" (p. 1). Although observation is critical to British models of work shadowing, this element does not stand alone. Rather, three other elements can be usefully added to observation: "*integration* with the work-guide (the worker being shadowed)—i.e., asking questions about what he or she is doing; *participation* in the work-guide's work—i.e., carrying out tasks for him or her; and *contextualization*—i.e., observing or talking to other workers with whom the work-guide comes into working contact" (p. 40).

When one compares work shadowing to work experience and work visits, clear conceptual distinctions can be drawn among these processes. Herr and Watts (1988) have suggested that "in work shadowing, the *prime* element is observation of work roles. In work experience, the prime element is performance of job tasks. In work visits, the prime element is contextualization and observation of the range of work processes performed within the work-place" (p. 81). In particular, "the student engaged in work shadowing will learn about the *tasks* in which the worker engages, about the *processes* within the workplace in which he or she is involved, and—often particularly striking to the young visitor—about the *environment* of the workplace as a whole" (Watts, 1986, p. 41). Because work shadowing focuses on the work role(s) of a particular individual (work guide), it can provide insight into informal aspects of human relationships at work, including power relationships. Such insights are obviously valuable within the broad context of vocational education; but the potential learning from work shadowing can also make it a powerful career guidance mechanism.

Apprenticeship. Perhaps the major form of work-based learning now undergoing considerable attention in the United States is the revitalization and extension of the availability and use of apprenticeships. Although apprenticeships in the United States have typically begun after one completes high school and fully enters the adult work world, demonstration programs are appearing in many states that begin youth apprenticeship programs while students are still in high school. Such programs provide students incentives to stay in school and begin the time earlier when a student will move through the apprenticeship process toward becoming a full-time, certified, journeyman. Hamilton (1990) has proposed a comprehensive apprenticeship system that is integrated into the K–12 educational system. In contrast to most other existing apprenticeship proposals, Hamilton argues for a *school-based* apprenticeship, primarily for career exploration, and a *work-based* apprenticeship for students with clear goals and who have clear occupational choices. The latter would start at grade eleven and essentially merge with tech prep or 2+2 models. These are models in which the technical curricula of the last two years of high school, and of the two years of community college are coordinated and cast into an articulated, sequential set of courses.

In most youth apprenticeship programs now offered, high school students in these programs go to school part-time and serve as apprentices part-time. On high school graduation, they are expected to continue with their sponsor as full-time apprentices. Sometimes students entering apprenticeships from vocational schools or the military receive advanced standing but these are less systematic than youth apprenticeships are likely to be.

In describing the characteristics of the Pennsylvania Youth Apprenticeship Program (PYAP), Wolfe (1993) indicated that this model is a school-to-work program that links the classroom to the worksite experience based on the premise that all students can learn. It stresses skills learned on a one-to-one basis, using mechanisms and processes that make academics relevant. PYAP grew out of a study done by the Pennsylvania Department of Commerce and the National Tooling and Machining Association, which showed that the most serious obstacle to competitiveness in the industry was a lack of skilled workers. At the local level, the model is guided by local consortia of education, business, labor, and other community organizations. Model programs in the 1990s operated in six sites and included 79 firms sponsoring 100 students. Of the firms, 76 are manufacturers using metalworking skills, and three are hospitals that provide training and education in health-care occupations.

While there are some differences in the models used in each site, the basic elements include a program designed around a four-year curriculum—approximately two years of high school and two years of postsecondary education; This is the format commonly known as Tech Prep or 2+2. The assumption is that to be successful in a technical environment, students must have some postsecondary skills. At the end of two years in the program, the students receive a high school diploma and can choose to seek employment, continue the program for two more years and receive an associate degree at the completion of four years, receive an associate degree and go directly to a skilled job or a registered adult apprenticeship program, or continue in a four-year program.

Other program components include a paid wage for time spent on job training, which is negotiated at the local level; an integrated curriculum based on the needs of industries and one that provides academics that relate to the worksite; broad-based skills that include critical thinking and problem solving; coordination between the teachers in the school and the mentors at the job site; and outcome, performance-based assessments or portfolios for the students that serve as credentials that can be used to apply for jobs or to enter college.

In addition to youth apprenticeships, there are also traditional apprenticeships. An apprenticeship is a formal, contractual relationship between an employer and an employee (apprentice) during which the worker (apprentice) learns a trade. The training lasts a specified length of time and varies in time required, depending on the skills or learning expected by a particular occupation or trade. Apprenticeships usually last about four years, but they range from one to six years in length. An apprenticeship covers all aspects of the trade and includes both on-the-job training and related instruction, which generally takes place in a classroom. The teaching by experienced craftworkers and other skilled persons requires the study of trade manuals and educational materials.

During the period of an apprenticeship, apprentices work under experienced workers known as journey workers, a status obtained after successful completion of an apprenticeship. Apprentices are employees, whose pay usually starts at about one-half that of an experienced worker in the trade being pursued. The apprentice's wage increases periodically through the apprenticeship as does the learning and skill level attained and the increasing ability to work with less supervision as the apprenticeship ensues. The sponsor of an apprenticeship program plans, administers, and pays for the program. Sponsors can be employers, employer associations, and unions.

The National Apprenticeship Act of 1937 (The Fitzgerald Act) and its amendments is the principal federal legislation identifying the criteria by which apprenticeship programs will be developed and evaluated and how the Secretary of Labor will work with appropriate state labor agencies and with State Departments of Education. Apprenticeship programs are commonly registered with the federal government or a federally approved state apprenticeship agency. These programs must meet federally approved standards related to job duties, wages, related instruction and health and safety regulations.

Currently, the Bureau of Apprenticeship and Training of the U.S. Department of Labor oversees the provision of apprenticeship training as a major method of providing the skilled workers needed to compete in a global economy. Most state governments also have Apprenticeship Councils that register apprenticeship programs and apprentices. Apprenticeships are offered in over 800 occupations. In most states or local level apprenticeship programs, outreach counselors are available to provide information about admissions to programs, the prerequisites and tasks involved, and related topics. These persons counsel participants about preparing for interviews, how to get technical task training, and other issues.

Although much more could be said about work-based or field-based learning, the basic point is that, however defined, these processes help potential workers understand not only the specific skills or jobs tasks with which they are concerned, but also the broader picture of "working in context," understanding the characteristics of the organization, its norms, its expectations, its mission, and the tasks at hand. These broader skills and understanding have the potential to clarify the young worker's contribution to the whole, to understand how his or her input relates to the productivity of the firm, and to give substance to such notions as the importance of life-long learning.

In addition to the forms of work-based learning discussed previously, there are other approaches that could be thought of as elements of "career relevant schools." As such, they are not part of the domain of career and technical educators or school counselors alone but rather need to permeate school culture and procedures. These ingredients of career relevant schools, like those of work-based learning or school to work programs are ways of sharing responsibilities for career exploration and guidance among a number of adults, including teachers, employers, counselors, and adult mentors at the work place. Such alternatives would include (Herr, 1999):

- Making college and career options known to students beginning in the middle schools if not before. Helping them link what they are studying in academic areas to the occupational problems in which that subject matter is relevant or critical. Helping them to understand that they have options and the skills to address and master them.
- A career guidance system, K–12, that focuses on, among other goals, helping students develop individual career development plans, the acquisition of self-knowledge and of educational and occupational opportunities, and the ways to explore and choose among these.
- The infusion of career development concepts into academic subjects to help students understand how course work fits together and forms a body of knowledge and skills related to performance in work and other aspects of life.
- Provide students access to computer assisted career guidance systems (CAGS) and the Internet to help them explore, identify and try out the implications of potential career choices in a virtual environment. Depending upon which CAGS is used, students can assess their interests, aptitudes, and values; match such profiles to job requirements, occupations, and programs of study available; determine their location on a world or work map; and engage in various decision-making exercises and other forms of inquiry.
- Increasingly, Computer Assisted Career Guidance systems are being augmented by use of the Internet. The Internet offers career planning resources that school counselors can use to provide college-bound, employment-bound, and undecided students with a wide range of information and counselors help in customizing career planning programs. Barker and Satcher (2000) have identified several examples of web sites that can provide school counselors particularly useful information. These include:

> The National Career Development Association web site (http://www.ncda.org) where one can find "career development activities by age level and links to web sites where students can take interest and personality assessments, search, and much more." (p. 138)
>
> The American School Counselor Association (http://www.school counselor.org) provides information on the role of career planning in the schools. A Career & College page offers several dozen links to web sites on topics that include occupational information, career guidance, school to work, tech prep, and college scholarship information. (p. 138)

The International Career Development Library can be used to develop an Internet-based career guidance program (http://icdl.uncg.edu/).

America's Career Info Net (http://www.acinet.org) offers current career and workplace information including a "State Profiles" section that provides information on the largest, fastest-growing, and highest-paying occupations in each of the 50 states along with links to career information sites specific to each state. This site also contains a resource library and a Career Exploration and Navigation Tool that students can use to begin their own career planning programs. (p. 138)

- The promotion of schools-within-schools, career academies, and alternative preparatory academies. The scale of these can vary dramatically in urban, suburban, or rural areas. These are typically not seen as academic tracks per se but rather as opportunities to provide special programs available to students that promote student pride and participation as well as family and community involvement in schools. For example, career academies, in which students get work experience as well as coursework that draws on a particular occupation, such as communications, computers, or teaching, help provide the kind of real-world experiences students need to appreciate better the education they are receiving. The curriculum organization of career academies typically enables students to complete college preparatory work in addition to hands on, work related knowledge and skill. However, academies frequently target high achievers, average, as well as at-risk students. In a major sense, career academies combine the advantages of traditional high schools and those of vocational schools in one facility, and thereby allow students to have a college bound academic experience, if they wish, and to concentrate in a specialized area of study (e.g., agriculture, health, finance, media) including internships and mentoring opportunities. Thus, many students graduate with a high school diploma and with a certificate attesting to the competencies they have gained in their career specialty. Beginning with opening of the career academy in 1969 in Philadelphia, there are now approximately 1500 academies across the nation (Underdue, 2000). These schools-within-schools, which occur in a number of states including California and Pennsylvania, are part of a larger continuum of special programs that give students learning experiences outside, and in addition to, the traditional classroom structure (Massachusetts Institute of Technology, 1990). Such special programs are, to an increasing degree, representative of school-business partnerships. By investing in and partnering with schools and school districts, major companies such as Boeing or Intel have provided training in the skills they need from their future workers (*Futurist,* 2000, November–December, p. 3). Frequently, these partnerships include internships, mentoring, career guidance and placement in the partnering firm. In a larger sense, the various methods of creating new forms of "career pathways" through the secondary school is also a major form of educational reform.
- The development of clear expectations for student learning, including the use of competency-based or Outcomes-Based Education (OBE) approaches. In a study by the U.S. General Accounting Office of the strategies used to prepare employment-bound youth for employment in the United States and four competitor nations—England, Germany, Japan, and Sweden—several findings were particularly telling (Warnat, 1991):

1. The four competitor nations expected all students to do well in schools, especially in the early years. U.S. schools expect that many students will lag behind.
2. The competitor nations have established competency-based national training standards that are used to certify skill competency. U.S. practice is to certify program completion. While the former is beginning to grow in the United States, in association with the development of career portfolios and the needs for young workers with occupational skills, implementation of certifying skill competency still quite uneven across the United States.
3. All four foreign nations invest heavily in the education and training of employment-bound youth. The U.S. invests less than half as much for each employment-bound youth as it does for each college-bound youth.
4. To a much greater extent than in the United States, the schools and employment communities in the competitor countries guide students' transition from school-to-work, helping students

learn about job requirements and assisting them in finding employment.

• Requiring participation in community service programs for high school graduation. The 1993 National Service Initiative of the Clinton administration for high school and college students provided funds to increase such service experiences of youth. As this initiative has advanced around the nation, awareness has grown that community or national service can be a major career exploration mechanism as well as one in which career skills can be learned. Data from 1984 to 1997 shows dramatic growth in high school service-learning programs. The portion of U.S. schools offering curriculum-linked service learning grew from about 9 percent in 1984 to about 56 percent in 1997, from 81,000 high school students involved in service-learning in 1984 to three million in 1997 (Greenberg, 2000). There are many different emphases in these programs, although a common thread is sharing of expertise and hands-on learning through community service. While there are many definitions of service learning, a composite one is as follows: A service-learning program is one that meets actual community needs and includes a learning component, either through integration with the school curriculum or some other conscious knowledge-building endeavor, such as independent study, report-writing, a reflection or discussion (Greenburg, 2000, p. 19).

As such, service-learning tries to place work within a context that allows students to provide a service and also learn from the experience. A student volunteer who helps build a house might learn not only about the skills and planning required to build the house, but also the chemistry of paint and the economics of the community at the building site. Service-learning projects are not primarily job-training programs but often participating students do acquire specific job skills, enhanced interpersonal skills, and increased self-confidence.

It can be argued that service-learning projects are as wide-ranging as the service needs of communities. Thus, participating students may engage in projects to restore a mural from an earlier period in American history, tutor at-risk children, beautify and clean public parks, volunteer in day-care centers, assist in a free dental clinic, work with residents of nursing homes, participate in home building for poor families or community outreach initiatives to the poor or the elderly.

• Providing educational opportunities that acknowledge that not only technical skills but also multilinguality, leadership and social studies skills, and knowledge of cultural differences, national histories, and political and economic systems of nations with whom we trade will become increasingly important in international trade.

• Focusing on life skills. Secondary schools including middle schools, should provide training in *life skills,* such as formulating good work habits, interaction with public agencies, job hunting, appropriate areas and behavior for the workplace, how to work in a team, how to complete applications and follow instructions, and how to look for meaningful employment. Many of these skills can arise from helping adolescents understand that school is their work and that attitudes dealing with punctuality, accepting constructive supervision, honesty, and self-discipline are those valued as well by the workplace. Many of these skills and others can be gained through a variety of cooperative education and work-based learning opportunities, including the use of summer and academic year internships, apprenticeships, and cooperative work site training.

• Enlarging the availability of cooperative education (which now enrolls about 5 to 10 percent of all students in high school and college) that structures students' experience in paid jobs to promote learning to extend what is taught in the classroom. The "co-op" method gives students direct practice in learning at the workplace. Many career and technical education programs also operate their own school-based enterprises, which likewise provide opportunities for students to learn through the process of producing real goods and services for community agencies. These options make deliberate use of work as part of the learning experience and bridge school and work directly.

• Providing certificates that recognize the demonstrated skills of students meeting articulated requirements for such skills in technical training or other program offerings in high school. Such demonstrations of skills increase the use of career portfolios describing examples of students' skills and more precise discussion of their skill development experiences as well as greater clarity about their achievement of competency-based career development experiences and associated attitudes.

• Increasing Tech-Prep or 2+2 programs. As defined by the U.S. Congress in 1990, a tech-prep program means a combined secondary/postsecondary program that (a) leads to an associate degree or a two-year certificate; (b) provides technical preparation in at least one field of engineering technology, applied science, mechanical, industrial, or practical art of trade, or agriculture, health or business; (c) builds student competence in mathematics, science and communications (including through applied academics) through a sequential course of study; and (d) leads to placement in employment (Congressional Record, 101st Congress, 2nd Session, August 2, 1990). These programs increase the availability of more rigorous coursework tied to occupational skills and at the same time give more students the option to go on to post-secondary education. They help students see more clearly the connection between school and work, the importance of continual or lifelong learning, the integration of academics and vocational skills, and the need to bridge both work-oriented courses and those oriented toward further schooling. In their articulated structures, they expedite student movement from high school programs to related community college programs and beyond with emphases on efficiency and equity.

• Some tech prep programs are combined with youth apprenticeship programs and school to work initiatives (Roberts, 2000). They also focus on aligning and sequencing existing and emerging curricula in the secondary school and in the postsecondary institution with which the program is articulated (Bragg, 2000). A national evaluation of tech prep by the U.S. Office of Vocational and Adult Education identified four accomplishments of tech prep programs. They include according to Bragg (2000):

1. Better communication and cooperation among educators through professional development and collaborative curriculum development processes.
2. Greater use of problem solving, application of theory to practice and "real-world" contexts in academic classes.
3. More involvement by employers in school functions.
4. Heightened awareness about the need to strengthen math and science instruction for students who have traditionally been labeled 'vocational' students, particularly by encouraging them to enroll in more applied math and science classes. (p. 15)

• Modifying the school curriculum to combine academic and vocational courses. Such an approach to an integrated curriculum, which like tech-prep and several others of the recommendations here have strong emphases in the Carl D. Perkins Vocational and Applied Technology Education Act, gives students the benefit of occupational preparation and college preparation at the same time. It also potentially infuses academic courses with the task-oriented, problem-solving, and cooperative learning approach to learning that has been successful in vocational-technical education. These approaches incorporate the findings of research in the cognitive sciences, which suggest that abstract information is often best learned through authentic application in task or problem solving learning (U.S. Department of Education, 1991).

• Apprenticeship schemes need to be expanded in availability after high school in new ways that begin in the high schools to provide skill development opportunities in ways similar to what is available in several of our competitor nations. Currently, with the exception of youth apprenticeship schemes now available in some states, in the U.S., traditional apprenticeships enroll almost no students in high schools and fewer than 2 percent of high school graduates in contrast to Europe, where 30 percent to 60 percent of employment-bound students are likely to be in apprenticeships following high school.

• Every employment-bound youth should receive placement in a job and post-secondary school education, if desired, after high school just as college-bound youth now do.

Hoyt (1994), in his analysis of youth apprenticeships and other forms of work-based learning in the United States, has suggested that regardless of the particular form of work-based learning or education reform that is at issue, career development specialists, including school counselors, need to help students, adults, educators, and industrialists reframe the basic question that underlies career guidance or work-based learning programs. Hoyt contends that too many of our citizens seem to be asking the question, "What do I need to know and do in order to get by?" In both Germany and Japan, however, the basic question citizens are raising is "What do I need to know and do in order to excel?" (p. 222). He advocates more attention to the latter question, if the types of efforts described in this chapter are going to be successful in helping Americans develop the skills and attitudes to compete effectively in the international arena.

Career Guidance in Career and Technical Education and Work-Based Learning

Career guidance in career and technical or vocational education is typically seen as a *support* to the latter. Although there is a historical rhetoric as well as more recent legislative support for career guidance and vocational education as a partnership, that view does not always predominate in practice.

Support services can be defined in many ways. By tradition, aspects of education tend to be included that facilitate the central role of instruction but are not themselves primarily instructional. Guidance and counseling generally meet these criteria and can play important support roles before and after vocational education instruction. For example, career guidance can play a significant role in attracting, recruiting, or selecting students for vocational education options. Because of the many educational choices for youth, attracting appropriately motivated and talented students becomes a major concern to career and technical educators in any setting. Career guidance can convey the image and possibilities of vocational education to potential enrollees, parents, sending schools, and other sources of input to such programs.

The view of career guidance as a process of support to vocational education seems to be a reality in many instances. For example, Sproles (1988) studied 100 traditional and 100 nontraditional finishers of vocational education in West Virginia and the influences on their choice of and completion of vocational education. As summarized by Sproles:

> *This research suggests that many sources influence students' choices of programs in vocational education. Guidance counselors seem moderately helpful and supportive, but many influential individuals were perceived to be equally or more helpful to most of these vocational educational students. This implies that counselors need to be aware that they may be only one source of information in a network of many sources, and there are times when their roles complement or supplement advice from others. The counselor's main role is likely to be in presenting factual information about vocational programs and careers. Thus, the counselor must be well-informed about vocational education, and objective in presenting the vocational choices. This seems especially true when a nontraditional student is counseled. (p. 21)*

The school counselor as a supporter of career and technical education and its appropriate choice by students should not be confused with being a salesperson for this format education. Counselors must be able to apprise students of the utilitarian value of particular courses of study as these are related to skills and credentials of importance to college or work after high school (DiRusso & Lucarino, 1989). But such roles must be cast with consideration given to the readiness of students to make such choices, levels of work salience, and their levels of psychosocial or career development as antecedents to career decisions, not in terms of meeting enrollment quotas in various vocational education curricula or courses.

A second role for career guidance in vocational education is that of *assisting* in the selection of students for admission to various vocational education programs. Such a role involves individual assessment of aptitudes and preferences that, in turn, must be considered in relation to probabilities of success and satisfaction as these derive from *research* about differences in career and technical education curricula and the characteristics of those who are successful in them. When individual desires and the realities of course availability or probabilities of success come into conflict, school counselors can help potential enrollees consider the alternatives in as nonarbitrary a manner as possible. Whether or not such conflict exists, school counselors have a major role in ensuring that students are properly motivated and equipped to take advantage of the vocational education instruction chosen. Where such a condition does not occur, career guidance personnel need to assist students in choosing a different option in vocational education or to exit from it into another option that promises to meet their current needs.

A third role of career guidance in vocational education is directly related to instruction itself. As will be discussed in the following section on placement, career and technical education students need access to instruction in work-context skills and guidance or career-development skills as well as in specific technical and occupational skills. Because these skills are composed of attitudes, emotions, psychological factors, and cognitive and informational aspects, school counselors often become involved with their provision. Counselors may work with vocational teachers as collaborators or consultants as such learnings are infused into curricula. Or, in some instances, school counselors may take direct responsibility for providing such instruction. Through separate group courses, seminars, interactive computer-assisted instruction, gaming, role playing, and other techniques students can gain work-context and personal guidance learnings. As this occurs, career guidance as a support service tends to blur into career guidance as subject matter.

A fourth support service contribution to career and technical education is the role of career guidance in the placement of students. Conceived in traditional terms, placement of vocational education graduates into suitable employment or postsecondary education has been seen as an event, not a process. The assumption has been that, in the case of work, for instance, when a student is about to complete the vocational education program, he or she would be brought into direct contact with an employer(s) seeking a person with such training. The rationale for such an assumption is that the student is employable—possesses the appropriate attitudes, marketable skills, job search and interview behaviors—and needs assistance only to obtain a suitable employer. The role of career, or earlier, vocational guidance was conceived as that of matchmaker at the point when the student exited the vocational education system.

Increasingly, placement is being conceived as a process, not an event. As such, it is seen as a stream of career development and guidance learnings that are acquired concurrently with occupation-specific task learnings throughout the students' career and technical education experience, not just when the student is about to enter work full-time. In this sense, assisting vocational education students to focus on their learning and performance capabilities, gain decision-making capacity, formulate an awareness of their options, how to prepare for them and gain access to them, and acquire job search and job interview behavior are seen as preparing these persons not only for the school-to-work transition but also for placement as a natural extension of their career and technical education. Career guidance is seen as a central component of this process, not something abrupt and different from it.

In broader terms than vocational education, as other forms of work-based learning are becoming operational (e.g., youth apprenticeships, tech-prep programs), there are attempts to define the roles of school counselors in ways that would support making schooling more career relevant. Two examples of such role perspectives include that of Aubrey (1985) and Chew (1993). Aubrey, in advocating greater participation by counselors in the learning environment of students, whether employment bound or not, has suggested seven tasks that include the following in paraphrased form:

1. Monitoring and assessing the student's educational progress
2. Helping students plan for and complete a semester of service in either a community agency or other setting
3. Providing instructional units that focus on guidance activities, such as human relationships, communications, values development, and ethics
4. Constructing coursework in technology, futures thinking, and cultural awareness
5. Helping students acquire critical thinking and decision-making skills through problem-solving challenges related to the real world
6. Guiding students in the acquisition and use of information related to their first tentative career decisions
7. Assisting teachers in the recognition and accomplishment of specific developmental tasks that each student needs to master

Directed more specifically to such work-based learning paradigms as "tech prep," Chew (1993) has suggested the following specific roles for counselors.

1. Counselors and school districts should implement a comprehensive developmental guidance model for K–12 students emphasizing technical career opportunities within the career component.
2. Counselors should provide all students with interest and aptitude assessments (beginning no later than the eighth grade) to help them plan meaningful four-year educational goals.
3. Counselors can provide schoolwide activities that promote the awareness of technical career opportunities.
4. Counselors can provide students with information about community or technical college summer camp opportunities.
5. Counselors should give attention to women and minorities by providing them with information regarding technical careers.
6. Counselors should assist special needs students (e.g., learning-disabled, physically disabled,

teen parents, economically disadvantaged) in making transitions from secondary to postsecondary education.

7. Counselors must have access to appropriate materials and resources that explain the options of tech-prep and technical careers.
8. Counselors should help students develop a portfolio that summarizes their credentials, both educational and experiential.
9. Counselors should use career planners with students. (pp. 32–35)

Perspectives on Placement

Historically, career guidance, counseling, and placement have been considered mutually exclusive functions. Our contention is that although they are not synonymous, neither are they mutually exclusive or discrete.

There are obviously many ways to think about the placement of students in the workplace or other educational settings after they finish their secondary schooling. This is the essence of the recent focus on the school-to-work transition. As suggested in the previous section, many people treat placement as an event: an independent activity that can be seen differently from other dimensions of a career guidance program. Such a view can create problems where none need to exist because it assumes that placement is different or unable to be accommodated within guidance programs or by their personnel.

As suggested in our analysis of the importance of the emerging views and models of the school-to-work transition, there are growing expectations that career development activities in the school will be fused with placement activities, whether or not the school does the latter. If there is a difference between career guidance and placement, it lies largely in the fact that the first concept is heavily involved with facilitating self-awareness and career-awareness, exploration, and formulating and choosing preferences. Placement, although not excluding these concerns, is more oriented to creating processes by which choices can be converted into action through gaining entry into available jobs or educational opportunities consistent with such preferences. Thus, career guidance is concerned with anticipating and sorting among alternatives; placement is concerned with implementing choices and adjusting to them. These differences in emphasis, however, do not preclude both objectives or processes being included in a career/vocational guidance program.

Part of the way to handle such disparities is to think about placement as a process, not an event. In a systems approach, career guidance as a stimulus to career development is a process that leads to placement. In a real sense, effective placement of students into the labor market is the end result of their readiness for career planning, crystallizing a job or occupational preference, and acquiring job search and employability skills and other attitudes, knowledge, and skills pertinent to the career guidance process.

Viewing placement as a process does not preclude the fact that individuals come to placement in different conditions of readiness for decision making and for assuming the responsibility for implementing a choice. The assumption is that these conditions will depend on the students' exposure to elements of career development, career education, or career guidance in concert with reinforcement, encouragement, and modeling in their family background and academic or career and technical educational experiences from elementary school through senior high school. If such development has not occurred in the personal history of the student to be placed, the counselor alone or in cooperation with others needs to assist the student, within an abbreviated time frame, with the placement prerequisites the individual lacks. This obviously may include some type of assessment to find out where the student stands with regard to the *process of choice*—independence, planfulness, possession of occupational information, knowledge of the decision-making process, his or her attitude toward choice—and to help him or her think about the *content of choice*—which includes the placement alternatives available, their characteristics, and their likely consequences.

If placement is viewed as a transition process as well as a point in time, as part of the career guidance program, the school counselor can, among other things, help the student prepare psychologically for placement. This may require role playing interview situations, assistance in completing or recognizing the importance of employment applications, or making compromises because of the restricted provision of jobs available in the local setting. It will also involve support and follow-up while the individual is moving through the placement process. In some cases, the counselor must lend strength to individual students who encounter initial rebuffs in the job-seeking process until the student's self-confidence and self-esteem are reinforced.

To be effective in the placement process, it is obvious that the school counselor needs to have the time and the ability to communicate with persons outside the school who are active in placement—personnel or training people in business and industry, employment service counselors, rehabilitation counselors, and others. Such communication requires that the counselor be able to talk knowledgeably about the competence, goals, and characteristics of persons to be placed as well as to secure information about openings that is relevant, accurate, and localized. In this regard, knowledge of regional labor trends as well as knowledge of available local jobs is important to the counselor, as is knowledge of apprenticeship or training opportunities, career paths, and career ladders in local industry and transition mechanisms available.

Placement of persons with a disability poses a particular challenge to the counselor to know the competencies and aspirations of such individuals and the specific competencies required in different occupations. Unless the counselor persists in being as precise as possible in determining what a particular person with disabilities is capable of doing and what is actually required in jobs, it is easy to lapse into generalized stereotypes about what the person can or cannot do and what jobs require. As an example of the importance (for placement) of going beyond generalities and stereotypes, Gottfredson, Finucci, and Childs (1984) studied the adult careers of persons who had been diagnosed in adolescence as dyslexic. "Dyslexia is a specific type of reading disability, and the term is generally applied to people who fail to learn to read with facility despite normal intelligence, good health, and ample opportunity" (p. 356). The sample of 579 dyslexic men in this study were compared to 612 abled men of the same age, social class, and intellectual levels. In contrast to the abled populations, the dyslexic adults rarely become professionals—physicians, lawyers, or college teachers—probably because of the emphasis put on academic skills, reading, and higher degrees. Rather, the dyslexic sample tended to have high-level occupations, primarily in management or sales, in which skills other than reading (such as taking initiative, being responsible, being persuasive) are accented, and the importance of a higher degree is diminished. These data show that placement activities with special groups, particularly those with conditions that are remediable, require learning about the cognitive, social, and physical skills that are actually critical in different occupations, not simply assumed to be important. Such information provides a better sense of the field of opportunities available to such individuals with disabilities and ways to identify those skills that the student might strengthen to become more competitive.

Because not all students to be placed will be high school graduates, school counselors concerned with placement will need to know of jobs available for the school dropout as well. At the point of placing dropouts, the counselor needs to reject the temptation to admonish them about how much monetary difference exists between them and high school graduates or why this choice condemns them to a lifelong position of unskilled or semiskilled work. Therefore, rather than moralizing about the decision of the student, the appropriate course of action is to provide the dropout with help in obtaining employment, information about ways to continue the student's education, and the reassurance that opportunities exist for resuming a high school program.

A further question that needs attention is: What will we include in the *placement* domain? Do we mean by placement facilitating student entry into jobs or postsecondary educational opportunities? Or do we mean, in addition, student placement into cooperative education, part-time employment, tech-prep, volunteer placement, summer employment, and a range of exploratory opportunities? The position taken in this book is that placement assistance to all students, the college-bound and the employment-bound, requires that placement be seen as a multi-dimensional activity that can be seen as an important component of career guidance. As such, placement is concerned with assisting students to identify, prepare for, and obtain full-time or part-time jobs; help school drop-outs find jobs and keep their educational options open; coordinate school-to-work and work-based learning opportunities for employment-bound and college-bound students; and advise students of alternate educational opportunities as they work on a full-or part-time basis. Such goals need to evaluate how school counselors will work with others to implement placement, what priority placement has for the school, and what resources will be required.

The fact is that placement for students entering the labor market has seldom been seen as a major responsibility of the school. It is true that vocational educators in different curricula, business teachers, and some school counselors have engaged in placing students. But it is less true hat these activities have been performed with purpose under the rubric of career guidance or have been seen as a natural extension of this process.

Yet job placement, and now more specifically the school-to-work transition, like other educational outcomes, cannot occur effectively unless it is seen as important and planned effectively. A study conducted at the National Center for Research in Vocational Education (1982) examined the factors relating to the job placement of former secondary vocational education students. They found that a strong commitment to job placement is one of the most important factors affecting job placement. National Center researchers found that higher job placement exist in those schools in which administrators, counselors, and teachers possessed both a clear understanding of the importance of job placement and a consistent belief that the major purpose of vocational education is the placement of students in jobs related to their training. They further found that enthusiasm for the goal of job placement is also an important part of this process. McKinney, the project director, stated, "There has to be a philosophical position on the part of the school system that job-related training and effective job placement programs are two very important and two very interrelated processes" (p. 1).

The study suggested that several activities seem to facilitate higher job placement rates in all labor markets. These include the following:

- Maintaining regular contact with employers regarding the job placement of students
- Providing coordination for job placement activities through a centralized job placement service and including teachers in job placement activities
- Helping students acquire the basic education skills needed to obtain a job and to perform on the job
- Orienting the vocational education curriculum to the needs of the employers in the community

Such activities in expanded form are certainly congruent with the expectations and goals of the School-to-Work Opportunities Act.

CAREER GUIDANCE TECHNIQUES FOR SENIOR HIGH SCHOOL

Throughout this chapter, examples of career guidance techniques have been discussed with different student populations and for different purposes. Dykeman, Herr, Ingram, Wood, Charles, and Pehrsson (2001) undertook a national study to identify the underlying taxonomy of career development interventions that occur in American secondary schools. The 44 career interventions included in the study were classified into five categories using cluster analysis. In addition, the interventions that most statistically exemplified each taxonomic category are identified. Table 9.4 reports these data.

Curriculum Infusion

- After reading a biography, have students describe how a career decision made by the subject influenced areas of his or her life, such as career paths, choice of friends, family life, location of residence, and so on.
- Have students complete a sample job or college application, write a job résumé, and successfully role play a job or college interview.
- Have students engage in appropriate research and prepare a term paper discussing the concept of supply and demand as it relates to a changing labor market. Have students consider the implications for personal flexibility, multiple career choices through their working life, and personal responsibility for career management.
- Develop a short unit in each subject matter area on how technology has affected the occupations related to that subject area (for example, implications of technology for office clerical workers as part of business education program, and so on).
- Have students keep idea journals in which they record their occupational daydreams and ideas that occur on a daily basis. These can be used as the basis for directed career exploration using biographies, career briefs, or other resources. Have students engage in "one minute free writes" in which they write down all the words, phrases, or sentences that occur to them about a specific vocational subject or daydream. Compare the vocabulary words different students choose and then use for exploratory activities.
- Have students demonstrate in a written assignment the ways in which technology has multiplied the

TABLE 9.4 Career Interventions by Taxonomic Cluster and Exemplary Cluster Member

TAXON	TAXON MEMBERS	TAXON EXEMPLARY
Work-based Career Interventions	Cooperative Education	*
	Internship	
	Job Shadowing	
	Job Coaching	
	Job Placement	
	Mentorship Programs	
	Service Learning/Volunteer Programs	
	Work Based Learning Project	
	Work Study	
	Youth Apprenticeships*	
	Academic Planning Counseling	
Advising Interventions	Career Focused Parent/Student Conference	
	Career Peer Advising/Tutoring*	
	Career Map	
	Career Maturity Assessment	
	Career Counseling	
	Career Interests Assessment	
	Career Library/Career Resource Center	
	Career Cluster/Pathway/Major	
	Career Passport Skill Certificate	
	College Admissions Testing	
	Computer Assisted Career Guidance	
	Cooperative/Dual Enrollment	
	Information Interviewing	
	Job Hunting Preparation	
	Personal/Social Counseling	
	Portfolio/Individual Career Plan	
	Recruiting	
	Referral to External Training Programs	
	Referral to External Counseling/Assessment	
Introductory Career Interventions	Career Day/Career Fair*	*
	Career Field Trip	
	Career Aptitude Assessment	
	Community Members Teach in Classroom	
	Guidance Lessons on Persona/Social Development	
	Guidance Lessons on Career Development	
	Guidance Lessons on Academic Planning	
Curriculum-Based Career Interventions	Career Information Infused into Curriculum	*
	Career/Technical Education Course	
	Career Skills Infused into Curriculum	
	Career Academy/Career Magnet School	
	School-Based Enterprise	
	Student Clubs/Activities	
	Tech Prep/2 + 2 Curriculum*	

This taxonomy of career interventions is also an inventory of career guidance techniques used in various programs throughout the United States. As such it may provide additional ideas for adaptation in the local setting. Many of these activities could be directly integrated into various subject matter areas as part of a career education infusion strategy, a work-based intervention, or used in conjunction with individual counseling or group career guidance activities. The interventions listed will provide additional intervention possibilities.

number of jobs, and have them associate this fact with the necessity for interdependence among workers in a particular industrial setting (that is, steel plants, space industry, and such). Have them discuss the relatively few times in which workers jobs require them to work alone rather than as part of a team.

• Have students define in writing the specific steps they must go through to obtain some future educational or career goal. The steps should be listed in chronological order.

• In art class, have students design and prepare a brochure describing student skills, desires for part-time work, and related matters to be sent to the community.

• Using the ingredients of their career portfolio, have students prepare a résumé listing the various skills they possess.

• After reading a biography in which the "career pattern" of a famous individual is described, have students identify the decision points in that person's life, the occupational roles played, and the stages of preparation leading to each role. Have students use this information to prepare a written assignment describing the "career pattern" of the subject in question.

• At the beginning of any course, the teacher might help each student write a brief assignment as to the relationship of the course to some educational or occupational goal of the student. Students could also formulate a list of individual goals pertaining to the course, that is, skills, knowledge, or attitudes they hope to develop.

• Have students read about and discuss the concept of a global economy. What are its implications for acquiring specific types of technical skills as well as foreign language and other communication skills, knowledge of cultural differences, history and economics.

Group Guidance Processes

• Have students participate in career bingo and sign the card when descriptions occur of their personality traits or career goals. Have students discuss the meanings of the different careers and personality types represented.

• Have students consider the concept of future uncertainty and how to develop alternative career plans in case their preferred plan is not possible.

• Have students construct an occupational family tree, or career genogram, in which they research the occupations held by each of their grandparents, parents, and siblings. Have them examine gender-specific reasons for choices as appropriate. Apply specific questions to the tree: Which family member am I most like? Why? What do my family members want me to choose? Why?

• Develop life-planning workshops in which life roles and the coping skills required in them are analyzed and shared.

• Given a career-related problem (such as selection of a college, trade school, or technical school; comparison of two or more occupations; need for financial assistance), have students locate appropriate informational resources.

• From a series of case studies illustrating examples of people making career decisions, have the students identify those examples that represent poor planning, and indicate what steps could have been taken that were not.

• Have the students write a long-range career plan identifying the specific steps each must take to reach preferred future goals.

• Have students develop a tentative long-range individual career plan on entering high school. This should be in writing and kept on file. It should include short-term as well as long-term goals and steps to reach such goals. The plan should be periodically reviewed and evaluated in individual counseling sessions.

• Have each student develop in writing a plan of access to his or her next step after high school, either educational or occupational, listing possible alternatives, whom to contact, application dates, capital investment necessary, and self-characteristics to be included on applications or résumés.

• Have students differentiate between the major occupations that make up the occupational cluster of their choice in terms of (1) the amount and type of education needed for entrance and advancement; (2) the content, tools, settings, products, or services of these occupations; (3) their alure to society; (4) their probability of providing the type of lifestyle desired; and (5) their relationship to personal interests, abilities, and values. Discuss in group sessions.

• Have students use one of the current computer assisted career guidance systems and have them describe what they learned from the modules about making decisions.

• Have students list at least six factors they are seeking in a career (such as opportunity to travel, meeting new people, responsibility, opportunity for advancement, and so on). Discuss in group sessions.

• Given information concerning global and national labor force trends, have the students discuss ways these trends might affect their own career selections.

• Discuss the kinds of decisions people of varying age groups must make: 5-, 10-, 18-, 21-, 35-, 50-, and 65-year-old persons. Relate these to long-term planning concerns.

• Present students with a series of hypothetical situations describing an individual with a decision-making dilemma (e.g., an individual who wants to be a professional athlete but has not displayed sufficient ability). Have students discuss and consider what compromises exist.

• Devote a section of the school newspaper to profiling the skills and abilities of selected graduating seniors, to posting job openings, and to providing various job tips.

• Create a job-finding club for seniors to facilitate the learning of job-search and related procedures.

• Draw on past experiences in decision making, and have students discuss how a decision that was made was influenced by some external factor (family, friends, geography).

• Have students list the relative advantages and disadvantages of each of the career alternatives they are considering in terms of their relationship to their expressed lifestyle goals.

• Have students take specific steps to implement a career-based decision before leaving high school (such as apply to a job or post–high school training program, engage in a job or college interview).

• Using appropriate resources, have each student develop a list of entry-level skills needed for an occupational area of his or her choosing.

• Have students read the classified ads in a major Sunday newspaper and list the names of jobs about which they know nothing about required preparation or job performance.

• Have students engage in mock job interviews.

• Have each student list at least six courses or school experiences in which he or she has been successful and relate these successes to the attainment of marketable skills currently possessed.

• For an identified social problem, such as air pollution, rehabilitation of drug users, the development of new uses for materials, or creating by-products of fishery harvesting, have students create a lattice of occupations at different levels (professional to unskilled) that might contribute to resolving the problem.

• Have students read books or other materials that depict work as a means of self-expression and discuss what this means for choice.

• Have students identify important skills or competencies related to some educational or occupational goal. Have them compare their progress in attaining these with that of the previous year in terms of (1) little or no progress, (2) fair progress, (3) great progress.

• Have students list ten means of furthering their education beyond high school (such as college, trade school, apprenticeship, on-the-job training, military, peace corps, reading, and so on), and discuss the advantages and disadvantages of each.

• Have students differentiate between the major occupations that make up a preferred career cluster in terms of the amount and type of education needed for entrance.

• For an occupational area of his or her choice, have the student list in order the educational experiences (courses and training) needed to enter and advance in that occupation.

• Have students contrast and compare a recent interest inventory with one taken in junior high school.

• Have students do a genogram of the occupations of members in their family of origin as a way of defining parental and family influences across generations and potential role models in the family who were previously unknown.

• Have students identify major Internet web sites that provide information about jobs available in educational opportunities.

Community Involvement

• Invite outside resource persons to discuss their own career patterns and emphasize the planning in which they engaged, the information they used, and information they would like to have had but did not.

• Establish a placement service to provide (part-time, summer, or simulated) job experiences for students to try out job skills.

• Have resource persons from the local Bureau of Employment Security discuss such matters as local employment trends, unemployment rates, and related factors.

• Take field trips to local industries followed by a discussion of how new technologies or automation has affected each one.

• Cooperate with the local Job Service to establish a program designed to inform students of local job opportunities.

• Establish a rent-a-kid activity program to facilitate the development of and information about part-time jobs in the community.

• Interview employers about personal qualities they look for in employees. After they interview employers in management or supervisory positions regarding qualities necessary for career success, have students write a short paper relating job attitudes to job success.

• After an opportunity to observe and interview workers in job settings relating to an occupational cluster of his or her choosing, have the student list the materials, tools, and processes associated with the observed occupations.

• Have students do a "job analysis" of an occupation of their choosing.

• Have students participate in part-time work experiences in a job related to an occupational cluster of their choosing.

• Using a list of community agencies, businesses, and so on and a description of their functions, have students select one and work there for a week, demonstrating punctuality, regular attendance, and the ability to perform tasks under the direction of a supervisor. Success will be judged by the job supervisor.

• Send follow-up questionnaires to working graduates, requesting their assistance as contact persons for students wanting occupational information about the kind of work in which they are now employed or as job-lead resources for current students.

• Have students discuss their service-learning experiences and the meaning of these for their career planning.

SUMMARY

In this chapter, we have discussed career development in senior high school as it is conditioned by the imminence of various forms of reality with which students must cope. Continuing themes regarding a systematic approach to career development that were begun in elementary school finally converge at the senior high school level. Implications for intensity of planning and the fostering of goal-directedness in different individuals are considered as correlates of different forms of behavior following high school. The mutual contributions of career and technical education and academic education to career development are examined as recommendations are developed for greater meshing of these two elements of the educational process, particularly in view of federal policy and legislative initiatives that are emphasizing more comprehensive approaches to work-based learning and the school-to-work transition. In addition, career guidance and placement processes have been discussed. Finally, career guidance techniques appropriate to senior high school have been identified.

CHAPTER TEN

The Practice of Career Development in Higher Education

KEY CONCEPTS

- Research studies tend to show repeatedly that 50 percent or more of all college students have career-related problems.
- The college-going population in the United States is composed of subgroups who differ in age, reasons for going to college, and motivation for achievement or other goals. Career development programs must provide differential services to persons in such groups.
- Comprehensive career programs in higher education should provide a complete range of services, including career advising, career counseling, and career planning involving cooperative activities between academic departments and career specialists.
- Colleges and universities typically have used five major approaches to deliver career guidance: (1) courses, workshops, and seminars that offer structured group experiences in career planning, job-access skills, decision making, and related topics; (2) group counseling activities; (3) individual counseling; (4) placement programs; and (5) automated placement services.
- College placement activities tend to be seen increasingly as part of a process, not an event. Thus, many career interventions throughout the college experience are sequenced to bring the college student to a point of maturity and decision making that can culminate in effective placement.

As colleges and universities in the United States have evolved from a few highly selective institutions a century or so ago preparing their students to enter the ministry, law, medicine, and the classics to the more than 3500 institutions of higher education today, most of which have open admissions, the purposes of a college education continue to be debated. In oversimplified terms, the fundamental question is should a college education be directed to learning for its own sake or to learning to provide students preparation for work at professional, technical, and managerial levels? Within such questions are subsidiary issues: should a college education be accessible to only the intellectual or social elite of the nation or to any one who desires to attend college? Should only those who pass rigorous academic preparation be permitted to attend college or should anyone who wishes to attend have the right to do so and to fail? Should potential students have to "pass" academic screening procedures that identify and select only the best qualified students for admission and, subsequently, with the highest likelihood of graduation or should students be admitted who then have the opportunity to prove they can graduate by their performance in college courses rather than on pre-college admission examinations?

Nations answer these questions differently. Some continue to screen college applicants rigorously to select only the "best and brightest" of their potential students. In such cases, there is limited college capacity for student enrollment and, in fact, the number of students enrolled in colleges and universities in such nations includes only a small proportion of the applicants compared to those admitted to college in the United States. For example, by some estimates only 13 percent of high school graduates attend universities in Great Britain, 20 percent in Germany, and 28 percent in France (Hoyt, 1994). In the United States, the percentage of youth, depending upon the specific region of the nation, that attends college following high school exceeds 70 percent and in some high schools more than 90 percent. However, compared to a much higher graduation rate for those attending universities in other nations where opportunities are more limited and applicants more rigorously screened before admission, in the United States only 50 percent of students who enter colleges and universities graduate in six years, if ever (Gray & Herr, 2000).

It is not the purpose of this chapter to debate whether it is better to be restrictive in admissions to college and university, to select only those most rigorously prepared academically, or to permit a much larger segment of the population, with a much larger range of intellectual ability and academic preparation, to enter higher education and take their chances, sometimes very slim, of successfully completing their college degree. Rather, it is to suggest that given the large proportion of the youth population, and increasingly the adult population, in the United States who are attending higher education at any given time, the motives for doing so, the certainty with which goals are sought, and the assurance that one can succeed in higher education varies enormously. What does seem clear is that a very large proportion of the student bodies of most higher education institutions are enrolled to improve their career prospects, to be able to gain access to jobs which they consider prestigious or well-paying. This motivation for economic gain and improved career opportunities has probably occurred in some fashion since colleges and universities were first created (Herr, Rayman, & Garis, 1993). Indeed, the question of whether or not colleges and universities should provide career services in some form as a part of the provisions available to their students seems no longer at issue in most colleges and universities. As discussed in this chapter, demonstrated needs by a large number of students for help with their career development is not a curiosity, it is a constant across institutions. For example, in one study compiled by the American Council on Education (1999), that assessed the reasons college freshmen indicated were very important in deciding to go to college, the top two reasons were "to get a better job" and "to make more money." Of the five major reasons identified for choosing to go to college, 77 percent of the college freshmen women and men participating in the study indicated that they want to get a better job and 75 percent (79 percent men/72 percent women) indicated they chose to go to college "to make more money." For the other three reasons, 62 percent (56 percent men/67 percent women) of the students indicated that their reason to go to college was "to learn more about things that interest me"; 49 percent (43 percent men/55 percent women) cited as a reason, "to prepare for graduate school"; and 40 percent (37 percent men/41 percent women) indicated that "parents wanted me to go."

Given such data, that which seems most debatable is not whether career services should be offered, but what types of career services in what forms of organization are most likely to meet the needs of the diverse students groups making up the student body: the career confident, the indecisive, the academically competent, the academically marginal, the traditional age student, the returning adult student, alumni, international students, minority students, males, females, resident or commuter students, students in specific majors?

THE EVOLUTION OF CAREER SERVICES IN HIGHER EDUCATION

Over the past century or two, the assistance to students making career plans in higher education has moved from an informal process between a professor and his or her advisees to a more comprehensive and professional process. For much of the early history of higher education, there were no formal career services per se. Rather, individual faculty members advocated for their graduating students with persons of importance who might employ the professor's "prodigy" as a favor to or as a sign of respect for the professor. While this was primarily a male activity, "an old boy's network," there were also instances of female students being assisted in the same fashion. Chronologically, the professor's assistance to his (or her) student occurred close to the time of the student's graduation from the college or university. As such, this transition from student status in the university to employment was typically seen as a "placement event," a rite of passage, that occurred under the sponsorship, networking, and mentorship of one's principal professor.

As can be readily imagined, this very personal process of sponsorship by an individual professor frequently led to favoritism and to unevenness among students in placement. As the size of colleges and universities grew and the demographic characteristics of student bodies became more comprehensive, it became increasingly difficult to expect individual professors to serve as the "placement agents" alone.

Thus began the rudiments of the placement of students into the professions, or other positions for which they prepared in colleges and universities, by more formal and centralized processes. Early forerunners of such centralized placement offices have been attributed to the Oxford University Committee on Appointments in England in 1899 (Wrenn, 1951) and to Yale University in 1919 (Teal & Herrick, 1962). These prototypical organizations were on the leading edge of a rapidly emerging collection of employment offices and placement offices in colleges and universities that took on a number of important tasks: for example, matching students with employment opportunities during the academic year and the summer, working with alumni to identify employment opportunities and matching students to these opportunities (Lorick, 1987). Placement offices, as they emerged as part of the organizational structure of colleges and universities, tended to be linked to business, economics, and employment, not to counseling, psychology, emotions, and personal development. Thus, in many instances, counseling offices and placement offices had distinct perspectives and functions. Counseling offices were responsible for self and career explorations and career planning; the placement office focused on facilitating specific skills needed by students for the job search (e.g., interviewing and resume preparation). Influenced by the matching models of Frank Parsons (1909) and his successors, placement offices typically used student traits (individual abilities, preferences and interests, attitudes) and job factors (job requirements, performance expectations) as the content by which to match students and jobs. These activities tended to occur within the weeks or months immediately before the student graduated and were limited to skills and issues directly related to employment.

By the late 1950s and early 1960s, under the influence of theories of career development that went beyond the early paradigms of matching of student traits and job requirements, student placement began to be seen as a process, not an event. It was increasingly assumed that the "placement event" needed to be seen as the conclusion of a process of career development that includes growth in career knowledge, exploratory activities, the development of skills, and career planning. In such a perspective, the choice of an academic major in college was seen as an intermediate career decision, a choice that opened access to and prepared persons for some types of future positions and closed off opportunities to enter other positions. In essence, this view would contend that career development began before the student entered the college or university and the subsequent experiences in higher education refined, retarded, or clarified the career goals to which students were moving. A further assumption was that deliberate programs of intervention (e.g., courses on decision making, exposure to computer-assisted career guidance systems, individual career counseling, participation in specific workshops or modules designed to address job search, job interviewing or career planning topics) in a student's career development throughout each of the college years would increase the likelihood that the student would arrive at the point of placement prepared with the career planning skills, self-understanding, and knowledge of opportunities available to make a serious and focused commitment to a job search.

By the early 1990s (College Placement Council, 1991), the career-planning activities formerly located in college counseling centers and the job search activities located in placement offices tended to be increasingly combined into one organization, typically called the "career planning and placement center" or "career services." Such structural revisions gave reinforcement to the career development of college students as a holistic and developmental process, central to the goals of higher education, rather than a peripheral and limited mission.

As suggested previously, an extraordinary proportion of Americans are enrolled in either two-year or four-year higher educational institutions.* In 2000–2001, approximately 15.4 million students were enrolled in the 3885 public and private institutions in higher education. Of these, about 6.3 million were enrolled in four-year public institutions and 3.2 million in private four-year institutions. Another 5.7 million were in two-year public institutions; 0.2 million were enrolled in private two-year institutions. Approximately 13.3 million were undergraduates, 1.8 million were graduate students, and 0.3 million were pursuing professional degrees. The U.S. Department of Education predicts that the number of students in higher education will continue to rise through 2010.

*All of the data presented here are taken from the *Chronicle of Higher Education Almanac,* September 1, 2001.

Women constitute about 57.5 percent of enrollees; foreign students constitute 3.2 percent of enrollees. Total minority enrollment of freshmen in fall 1999 was approximately 19 percent. The proportion of graduate students was about 22 percent.

Of the nearly 500,000 foreign college students in the United States in 2001, there is a decided Asian presence. In fact, Asia contributes eight of the top ten countries of origin of foreign students in the United States. In order, the top ten are China, Japan, Republic of Korea, India, Taiwan, Canada, Thailand, Indonesia, Malaysia, and Mexico. These students tend overwhelmingly to major in the "hard sciences" or technical areas, which might account, at least in part, for the substantial rise in "career" degrees (computer and information sciences, business and management, health sciences, and engineering).

Of course, there is virtually a linear relationship between family income and college attendance. In the freshmen class of fall 1999, some 10.5 percent came from families with income under $20,000. In contrast, more than 58 percent of freshmen came from families with incomes over $50,000. Currently, approximately 37 percent of undergraduate students receive federal and or state financial aid.

Returning adult students are another special and growing population. Estimates are that there are six million adult college students each year (Hirschorn, 1988). Indeed, in fall 1998, 39 percent of undergraduate college enrollments were beyond age 24, the upper limit usually considered the age of traditional undergraduates. These returning adults spanned a large age range including 1.5 percent over 55 years of age. Spanard (1990) urges that colleges create programs and support services that assist adult learners by reducing the effects of institutional, individual, and psychosocial barriers. Institutional barriers include schedules, fee structures, and campus friendliness. Situational barriers encompass such variables as job commitments, home responsibilities, and lack of child care. Psychosocial barriers are attitudes, beliefs, values, past experiences as a student, and self-esteem.

As we have said previously, during the past two decades, there have been numerous studies conducted that have assessed the academic, career, and personal needs of students on campuses of various types. Several such studies have been reported in Chapter 1. These needs analyses have been unanimous in highlighting the fact that students in higher education frequently perceive career development issues as paramount over either academic or personal needs. These career needs typically range from exploration of job opportunities related to majors, to development of job-seeking skills, to general issues of career preparation and choice. Usually, such surveys reveal the desire of baccalaureate-level students to explore their career interests, values, and abilities; to obtain information; to talk to a counselor about career plans; and to learn how occupations can affect future lifestyle. Taken together, these studies make clear the importance of career guidance and counseling services in postsecondary institutions—technical, two-year, and four-year—for all types of students.

As an illustration, using Holland's *My Vocational Situation* with about 3600 undergraduates at a midwestern university, Mauer and Gysbers (1990) determined that the career concerns of entering freshmen fell into four basic clusters. Cluster 1 was termed *anxiety* (e.g., "I am confused about the whole problem of deciding on a career"); cluster 2 was termed *confidence* (e.g., "I am uncertain about which occupation I would enjoy"); cluster 3 was termed *self-assessment* (e.g., "I don't know what my major strengths and weaknesses are"); and cluster 4 was termed *occupational information* (e.g., "I don't know enough about what workers do in various occupations"). Each of these need categories could be used by career planning personnel to serve as foci for workshops or for individual counseling.

The fact that needs are strongly expressed by students, however, does not mean that there will be a high demand for interventions designed to meet those expressed needs. Barrow, Cox, Sepich, and Spivak (1989) conducted a study that found only modest relationship between the services students said that they needed and those that they actually used. Of the eleven highest ranked needs, only two—stress management and time management—drew heavy outreach workshop attendance. The other nine highly rated needs—career planning, understanding interests, setting reasonable expectations, communicating more effectively, finding written information regarding career and educational programs, making decisions and solving problems, enriching relationships, improving relationships with others, and getting energized to tackle goals—were not highly requested or attended. Even so, as subsequent sections of the chapter demonstrates, the processes that are being included in "Career Services" in colleges and universities are becoming more comprehensive and more tailored to the characteristics of the student population.

CHARACTERISTICS OF THE STUDENT POPULATION

Certain selected characteristics of the college-going population have a bearing on the provision of career services. Among these are types of students and outcomes of the collegiate experience.

A. W. Astin's (1993) classification of types of college students is as good as any other (with the caveat that all human typologies are fallible, overlapping, not mutually exclusive, and probably best used only for heuristic purposes). As a result of collecting data on approximately 2600 students and factor analyzing these data, he labeled the resulting seven types as: the scholar, the social activist, the artist, the hedonist, the leader, the status striver, and the uncommitted student. The scholar has a high degree of academic and intellectual self-esteem, high expectations for academic success in college, and aspirations for high-level academic degrees. The social activist participates in community action programs, helps those in difficulty, and influences such variables as social values and the political structure. The artist has a high self-rating on artistic ability and values, on creating artistic work, on writing original works, and on becoming accomplished in one of the performing arts. The hedonist, in blunt terms, is a type of student who drinks, smokes, stays up all night partying, and advocates the legalization of marijuana. The leader self-rates high on popularity with the opposite sex, popularity in general, social self-confidence, leadership ability, and public speaking ability. The status striver is committed to success in one's own business, having responsibility for the work of others, being well-off financially, obtaining recognition from colleagues, and becoming an authority in one's field. The uncommitted student has a tenuous connection to his or her institution, anticipating changes in career choice or major, dropping out, or transferring.

The point is that whatever the motivations and values of college students, each can benefit from career assistance. This transcendence of career helping across types is illustrated by the fact that in the ACE and UCLA Higher Education Institute survey of college freshmen in fall 1993, more than eight in ten students listed "to get a better job" as a very important reason for attending college—a response leading all other motivations for college attendance. In the same poll, only about 13 percent expected to change majors or to change their career choices. Clearly a large percentage of students are going to be surprised, given data on the frequency of major and career change.

Obviously, students undergo change during the collegiate experience. It has always been moot how much of this change is a direct result of the experience of higher education, how much the result of the influence of a particular college, or even how much a result of the specific subculture within a college. A massive research effort has examined approximately 2600 research studies conducted during the 1970s and 1980s (Pascarella & Terenzini, 1991). These studies centered on the impact or outcomes of college for students. Basically the authors determined that students do change during college, that the collegiate experience caused that change, that the specific college contributed, and that individual student characteristics moderate these changes. Further, these collegiate effects are long-term.

The work of Smart (1986), is an example of an effort to explore the impact of college on student outcomes in a longitudinal study involving 4626 students. He was interested in determining what vocational outcomes could be ascribed to the cognitive attributes of the college attended (e.g., how selective the college is), to the student's educational performance (academic integration within the institution and overall educational degree attainment), to affective attributes of the collegiate experience (such as social integration and college satisfaction), and to attendance at certain types of institutions (e.g., public versus private, large versus small). He determined that for *professional* career attainment, the major influencers are cognitive attributes of the college and students' educational performance and degree attainment, whereas for *nonprofessional* careers, affective attributes and attendance at private institutions were paramount as influencers. Thus, "the kind of undergraduate institutions that students attend and their performance and experiences in those institutions do influence the occupational attainment process. At the same time, social origins and precollege characteristics continue to exert a substantial influence on occupational status attainment, although in an indirect manner" (p. 93).

In the latter sense, college students do not enter colleges in a pure and unaffected condition. They are products of their previous history, their interactions with their family (Ferry, Fouad, & Smith, 2000) and their stage of psychosocial development. For example, students' views of the parental relationship are related to career decision-making. This finding occurs in many studies with different foci including that of Guerra and Braungart-Rieker (1999), whose study of university undergraduates found that those students who experience their mothers as having been more encouraging of independence in childhood experience less career indecision than those who found their mothers to be overprotective. To accent the importance of this point, Blustein (1994) and Blustein and Novmair (1996) have discussed the notion of an "embedded identity" in late adolescents and in other stages of life. The important point is that such a concept integrates one's contextual experiences and one's relational experiences, the internal and the external forces, that affect one's identity. In essence, the embedded identity speaks to the interaction of several important elements: one's internal experience of self-definition (e.g., the status of self-knowledge, etc.), the degree to which possible identity options have been considered, how one evaluates the emotional aspects of identity (e.g., self-esteem, self-efficacy) and the experiences within one's family (e.g., attachment to parents and siblings) and the sociocultural factors that are integrated into one's identity. One can extend these concepts of the elements of the "embedded identity" quite comprehensively but the point here is that each college student engaged in the process of career development brings to this process an "embedded identity" that is clearly formed, poorly formed, secure, tentative, born of conflict or born of assurance and these issues will likely affect how their career development will be pursued and types of career services individuals will require.

An extensive and insightful review of the emotional-social issues that surround the development of college students has led Schultheiss (2000) to conclude that it is necessary to integrate the college student client's psychological, emotional, and social concerns with career issues as a framework for career counseling and for other career services. In her view, late adolescents and young adults are involved in "multiple concurrent developmental challenges and transitions" (p. 43). As such, they are "simultaneously striving toward self-definition, purpose, and connectedness" (p. 43).

These issues are intertwined and emphasize, in her view, identity development as a core therapeutic issue and as an issue in career maturity, career decidedness, career goals and career planning. Identity is also a function of psychosocial development, including addressing the seven dimensions proposed by Chickering and Reisser (1993); developing competence, managing emotions, moving through autonomy toward interdependence, developing mature interpersonal relationships, establishing identity, developing purpose and developing integrity. Each of the seven dimensions is also related to progress in the individual's career development; embedded identity; and the quality of relationships, "the role of significant attachments or long-term enduring emotional bonds of substantial intensity" (p. 50), particularly with family relationships. As in the other areas she cites, Schultheiss has summarized the important connections between the quality of relationships in one's life, career development, and vocational functioning. Of particular moment is the level of attachment between late adolescents and their parents and their significant siblings and their risk-taking, exploration, career planning, and career self-efficacy.

Schultheiss supports the view that career counseling and personal counseling should be treated as an integrated whole. She places these interventions within a relational career counseling perspective that is focused on the interaction between problems in career development and emotional and interpersonal concerns. She advocates the use of a relational lens to facilitate healthy functioning in the several domains previously cited—identity development, psychosocial development, embedded identity, the quality of relationships—as well as a template by which to identify career services and interventions related to the unique characteristics and needs of college students, whether delivered in individual group or other formats.

Other parts of this chapter will address issues and needs that affect other groups of college students—minority, international, nontraditional. The point to be made here, however, is that college students, however described, bring an array of embedded identity issues, different levels of psychosocial development, and varying clarity of career goals. Such complexity of development, maturity, and purpose must be reflected in planning for career services.

As suggested in the previous paragraph, students in higher education are a heterogeneous group in terms of age and socioeconomic status, motivation for college attendance, and sophistication of career planning. Women and minorities are attending college in increasing numbers and present career concerns that require special attention. Diverse student cultures offer a framework within which to view and to understand the college population. Finally, the outcome of higher education suggests a payoff in terms of careers, although some of the reasons for that advantage may have relatively little to do with the collegiate experience itself.

PLANNING CONSIDERATIONS

The first planning consideration relating to the provision of career guidance and counseling in higher education involves *institutional commitment.* Two-year and four-year colleges and universities must recognize the legitimacy of the career helping function as a bona fide part of the total higher educational enterprise. Further, these institutions must provide the trained personnel and facilities necessary to effect the career guidance function.

There is evidence that most institutions of higher education have made this commitment. Skills identification, values clarification, and speakers on the content of particular fields and job search skills are activities common at many institutions. Credit-bearing career planning courses are offered at many schools. In general, the larger the institution, the more varied the career services.

Some go even further in expanding the old brokerage role beyond career planning and career counseling and advocate a complete amalgamation of counseling and placement on the college campus. As phrased by Chervenik, Nord, and Aldridge (1982):

> *Career planning and placement are a wedded pair, interlocked and interrelated. The emphasis that may be given to one or the other depends on the operation's constituency, location, and direct assistance from employer representatives. In short, the objective of career services is to help students to understand the career planning and placement process, so that throughout life they will be prepared to cope with the inevitable changing situation: a future with jobs and circumstances unknown at this time. (p. 51)*

Commitment of faculty, even with institutional commitment, remains a troublesome problem. There is still a sort of antivocationalism in many faculty who represent arts and sciences disciplines. No cure for this vexing condition has yet been discovered, but there is some evidence to suggest that faculty who are involved in in-service training for career guidance in higher education are more likely to infuse career concepts into their classrooms than are faculty who receive no special training (Ryan & Drummond, 1981).

A second planning consideration in higher education relates to the *immediacy* of students' career guidance needs. Procrastination, dilatory behaviors, and other delaying tactics in decision making become less attractive alternatives as the imminence of the real world intrudes into students' lives. The Scarlett O'Hara syndrome—"I'll think about it tomorrow"—produces an increasing sense of uneasiness; one's tomorrows become fewer as one approaches a choice of major field or a career. As the graduation rite of passage comes closer, most students receive intensified pressure from parents, relatives, friends, and others to specify career goals. A few short years ago, the student was being asked what he or she wanted to be "when you grow up." Now, grown up, the student can no longer have the luxury of responding with some vaguely conceived career goal. The problem is in the here and now, not in the long-range future.

Sometimes, this "here and now" emphasis causes colleges and universities to concentrate primarily on those students who are exiting the system—seniors or two-year college students who are terminal or transferees. This concentration in the later years of college is indeed unfortunate, as Keller, Piotrowski, and Rabold (1990) concluded in their study of student needs that because many undergraduates make career choices early in college, career orientation and planning courses should commence in the first year of study, and, before senior year, students should be exposed to job-seeking skills.

Third, in planning comprehensive career programs in higher education, institutions should offer a *complete range of services.* A comprehensive delivery system for higher educational career services provides occupational and educational information, individual vocational assessment, job-seeking skills (e.g., résumé and interview preparation), workshops and group counseling, individual counseling, major selection advisement, training in decision making, special programs for all types of minorities and women, computer-assisted interventions, and a variety of other activities that extend beyond a narrow placement function. The continuum from career advising to career planning to career counseling should be represented.

The primary planning considerations relating to the provision of career guidance and counseling in higher education, then, include institutional commitment, responsiveness to immediate needs, and comprehensive, articulated delivery of services.

Another way to view planning is in terms of evaluation standards. In this regard, 34 professional associations combined to contribute to the Council for the Advancement of Standards in Higher Education (CAS). This consortium of professional associations in higher education publish *The Book of Professional Standards for Higher Education* (Miller, 2001) a document that recommends criteria for evaluating all aspects of student services. One of the important functional components of the 28 considered is, of course, career services. In abbreviated form, these standards recommend the following:

Part 1. Mission. The primary mission of career services is to assist students and other designated clients through all phases of their career development.

The stated mission should include helping students and other designated clients:

- To develop self-knowledge related to career choice and work performance by identifying, assessing, and understanding their competencies, interests, values, and personal characteristics
- To obtain educational and occupational information to aid career and educational planning and to develop an understanding of the world of work
- To select personally suitable academic programs and experiential opportunities that enhance future educational and employment options
- To take personal responsibility for developing job-search competencies, future educational and employment plans, and career decisions.
- To gain experience through student activities, community service, student employment, research or creative projects, cooperative education, internships, and other opportunities
- To link with alumni, employers, professional organizations, and others who can provide opportunities to develop professional interests and competencies, integrate academic learning with work, and explore future career possibilities
- To prepare for finding suitable employment by developing job-search skills, effective candidate presentation skills, and an understanding of the fit between their competencies and both occupational and job requirements
- To seek desired employment opportunities or entry into appropriate educational, graduate, or professional programs (p. 67)

Because of the expertise and knowledge on career-related matters, career services should be involved in key administrative decisions related to student services, institutional development, curriculum planning, and external relations.

Part 2. Program. Career services must promote learning and development in students by encouraging outcomes such as: realistic self-appraisal, appropriate career choices, enhanced self-esteem, critical thinking, clarification of values, intellectual growth, ability to communicate effectively, leadership development, fitness and wellness, meaningful interpersonal relations, ability to work independently and collaboratively, social responsibility, spiritual awareness, satisfying and productive lifestyles, appreciation of aesthetic and cultural diversity, and achievement of personal goals. (p. 67)

The overall institutional career services program must be (a) intentional, (b) coherent, (c) based on theories and knowledge of learning and career and human development, (d) reflective of developmental and demographic profiles of the student population, and (e) responsive to needs of individuals in a higher education setting.

The program must be based on an educational philosophy of teaching career development—and related processes. The program must assist students and other designated clients to develop the skills necessary to compete in a rapidly changing, competency-based, global workplace.

Components of the career services program must be clearly defined and articulated. To effectively accomplish its purpose, the career services program must include:

- Career counseling
- Information and resources on careers and further education

- Opportunities for career exploration through experiential learning
- Job search services
- Services to employers
- Consultation and outcomes assessment

Career services must be delivered in a variety of formats in recognition of institutional settings, different learning styles, cultural differences, and special needs. (p. 68)

Program components of career services must be designed for and reflective of the career development needs and interests of students and other designated clients; current research, theories, and knowledge of career development and learning; contemporary career services practices and national standards of practice; economic trends, opportunities, and/or constraints; the varying needs and employment practices among small businesses, large corporations, government, and nonprofit organizations; and the priorities and resources of the institution.

Career services must work collaboratively with academic divisions, departments, individual faculty members, student services, and other relevant constituencies of the institution to enhance students' career development (p. 68).

Career Counseling

The institution must offer career counseling that assists students and other designated clients at any stage of their career development to:

- Understand the relationship between self-knowledge and career choice through assessment of interests, competencies, values, experience, personal characteristics, and desired lifestyles
- Obtain and research occupational, educational, and employment information
- Establish short-term and long-term career goals
- Explore a full range of career and work possibilities
- Make reasoned, informed career choices based on accurate self-knowledge and accurate information about the world of work

Career counseling should:

- Be available to students throughout their academic experience
- Encourage students to take advantage of timely involvement in self-assessment, career decision making and career planning activities
- Assist students to assess their skills, values, and interests by reflecting on past experiences
- Assist students to integrate self-knowledge into their career planning
- Recognize that students' career decision making is inextricably linked to additional psychosocial, personal, developmental and cultural issues and beliefs
- Encourage and facilitate students' exploration of career interests through field visits, student employment, cooperative education, internships, shadowing experiences, research or creative projects, and informational interviews with working professionals
- Be provided through a variety of formats, such as scheduled appointments, drop-in periods, group programs, career planning courses, outreach programs, and information technology

Career counseling should be offered through career services in order to link students career exploration and decision making process with access to employers and employment information (p. 68).

Information and Resources on Careers

Career services must help students and other designated clients to identify and access valid career information for their educational and career plans. The scope of information and resources available to clients should include:

- Self-assessment and career planning
- Occupational and job market information
- Options for further study (e.g., community college articulation; graduate and professional school information)
- Job search information
- Experiential learning, internship, and job listings
- Employer information (p. 68)

Career services must provide access to information and resources on the Internet (p. 69). Career information, resources, and means of delivery must be compatible with the size and nature of the student population, the career and geographic interests of the students and scope of academic programs (p. 69).

In addition to the standards for mission, program, career counseling, and career information cited, the CAS Standards also include perspectives on other important components of career services in higher education including such topics as opportunities for career exploration through experiential learning; job search services; services to employers; consultation and outcomes assessment; leadership; organization and management; human resources, financial resources; facilities, technology and equipment, legal responsibilities; equal opportunity, access and affirmative action; campus and community relations; diversity; ethics; assessment and evaluation.

The content of the CAS Standards for Career Services is an excellent resource for clarifying the comprehensiveness of possible emphases in career resources as well as for planning a particular program of career services within a specific institution.

A final planning consideration has to do with tailoring the comprehensive set of career services—career guidance, career counseling, other career interventions—to the needs of the various constituencies in a particular college or university. This may entail the use of needs assessments or other survey instruments to determine specific areas of concern that particular student groups may have. It may involve focus groups or discussions with selected representatives of the particular subpopulation to be served. It undoubtedly will involve a review of the professional literature as it discusses new career interventions found to be useful for specific career concerns. In essence, while majority and minority, traditional and nontraditional, male and female, international and domestic students are likely to share many of the same career concerns, there are also likely to be concerns that are unique to each of these groups. However, whether or not career concerns overlap across these constituent groups, it is important that career services be seen as credible, accessible, relevant and welcoming to each of these constituent groups. This, then, requires planning about the content and processes provided by career services as well as about the marketing and the image portrayed about such services.

Rayman (1999) has captured many of the planning considerations in career services in his ten imperatives for the next millenium that were first offered in 1993 and revised in 1999. These imperatives, minus the accompanying narrative, include:

We must:

1. Acknowledge the lifelong nature of career development and initiate programs and services that enable and encourage students to take responsibility for their own career destiny
2. Accept and embrace technology as our ally and shape its use to free staff time for those tasks that require human sensitivity
3. Continue to refine and strengthen our professional identity and that of career services within the academy
4. Acknowledge and accept that individual career counseling is at the core of our profession and endeavor to maintain and enhance the credibility of individual career counseling in the career development process
5. Forge cooperative relationships with faculty, advising professionals, other student affairs professionals, administrators, parents, and student groups to take advantage of the "multiplier effect" that such collaborative relationships can have in furthering our goal of enhanced student career development
6. Redouble our efforts to meet the changing career development needs of an increasingly diverse student body
7. Accept our position as the most obvious and continuing link between corporate America and the academy, but we also must maintain our focus on career development and not allow ourselves to be seduced into institutional fundraising at the expense of quality career services
8. Acknowledge and accept that on-campus recruiting as we have known it is a things of the past and develop alternative means of facilitating the transition from college to work
9. Resolve the ambiguities that exist about our role in delivering alumni career services and solicit from our alumni associations the resource support necessary to provide these services
10. Advocate more effectively for resources to maintain and increase our role in facilitating student career development within the academy, and we must become more efficient and innovative in our use of existing resources. (pp. 176–182)

GOALS FOR CAREER DEVELOPMENT IN HIGHER EDUCATION

Goals for career development in higher education should be such that all types of career concerns and needs are addressed. It is, therefore, unlikely that many students will require each of the outcomes that follow; however, almost all students in higher educational institutions could probably benefit from one or more. In a truly comprehensive career guidance program, provision will be made to achieve the following goals.

Assistance in the Selection of a Major Field of Study

A majority of freshmen will change their major field at least once during their collegiate experience. Indeed, this phenomenon is to be expected, for the first two years of study at most colleges and universities are so structured as to allow students to explore academic experiences. Each change of academic discipline entails a commensurate alteration in career planning to which career guidance should respond. Part of the concern is that a large number of students choose a major field of study at the last possible opportunity because they run out of time, not because they have systematically explored the major field options available to them. In this case, students may not understand that a major field of study is a proxy for a set of career options, opening some career options and closing others. Thus, the choice of a major field of study is a fateful one in regard to whether or not it provides an adequate "fit" with a student's interests and aspirations. If not, the likelihood is that the student will seek a better fit in another curriculum or remain undecided.

Although being "undecided" does not necessarily put students at risk of not persisting in their college education (Lewallen, 1993), it is clearly better for a student to be comfortably decided on a major than not to be. These findings do not gainsay the fact that students certainly benefit from assistance in choosing a major and that providing advisement to targeted groups in ways that meet their needs can indeed enhance retention rates (Steele, Kennedy, & Gordon, 1993). Such programs are a staple on most college campuses. E. G. Jones and Schultz (1992), for example, describe an academic advisement program for undecided students at Shippensburg (Pennsylvania) University that uses both faculty and administrators. In general, however, the faculty advisor system requires advice and direction from professionals in career development to be most effective.

Assistance in Self-Assessment and Self-Analysis

As we have repeatedly stated in this book, career planning presumes self-knowledge of several types. Reasonable career choices cannot be made by individuals who do not have a fairly clear notion of who they are, their strengths and weaknesses, what they value, their motivations, their psychological characteristics, and their interests. In short, students must be aided to discover both a personal and a vocational identity that can subsequently be related to the world of work.

Within this context of self assessment and self-analysis, Sampson, Peterson, Reardon, and Lenz (2000) talk about the concept of *readiness,* defined as the "*capability* of an individual to make appropriate career choices, taking into account the complexity of family, social, economic, and organizational factors that influence an individual's career development" (p. 156). Further, these authors suggest that "capability refers to the cognitive and affective capacity of an individual to engage in effective career problem solving" (p. 157). Sampson and colleagues identify four categories of persons who vary in their readiness (capability and complexity): they identify persons who have low readiness and low capability who need a high degree of support (individual case-managed services), persons of moderate readiness and low capability who need a moderate to low degree of support (Brief Staff-Assisted Services), persons with moderate readiness and high capability who need a moderate to low degree of support (Brief Staff-Assisted Services) and persons who have high readiness, low complexity, and high capability who need no particular support (self-help services).

As each of these levels of readiness are defined and applied by intake workers at a college career center, students with different levels of readiness are assigned to the magnitude of support they may need. For example, self-help services "involve self-guided use of self-assessment, information, and instructional resources in a library-like or Internet-based remote setting, where resources have been designed for independent use by individuals with a high readiness for occupational and employment decision making" (p. 163). Brief staff-assisted services involve counselor-guided use of assessment, information, and instructional resources" in a library-like, classroom, or group setting for clients with moderate readiness for occupational and employment decision making. Exampes of brief staff-assisted services include: (a) self-directed career decision making, (b) career courses with large group interaction, (c) short-term group counseling, and (d) workshops (p. 164). Individual case-managed services with students demonstrating low-readiness for occupational and employment decision making might be assigned to (a) individual counseling, (b) career courses with small group interaction, and (c) long-term group counseling.

Assistance in Understanding the World of Work

At the collegiate level, it is likely that most students will have a broad and basic understanding of the occupational structure. Many students, however, may need help in exploring specific segments of that structure in personally relevant terms (e.g., What work is related to a given major? What is the employment outlook in a specific occupational field? What are the diverse opportunities available within a single chosen field?). Other students may need to expand their parochial view of the world in order to make it more catholic. In a global economy, for example, international careers are becoming more commonplace, and individuals can be helped to understand this broadened view of the world of work (Behrens, 1994).

Assistance in Decision Making

Information, whether pertaining to the self or to some area external to the self (that is, career options), is of little use if it is not effectively processed. Such information must be translated into short-range and long-range career goals and then reality tested. A personal plan must be developed that, ideally, is consistent with the information that one has gathered.

Essentially adapting Gottfredson's (1986b) taxonomic framework for assessing career choice problems, Carson and Dawis (2000) have suggested five criteria by which to determine what types of assessments and, by extension, other career interventions might be helpful to particular students. These criteria tend to encompass several of the goals for career guidance/career services in higher education. They include:

- Can the student identify occupational alternatives?
- Are the students' abilities and skills, values, and interests appropriate for choosing academic majors and occupations?
- Is the student satisfied with the choices?
- Has the student unnecessarily restricted choices?
- Is the student realistic about the accessibility of chosen alternatives?

A more comprehensive approach to a conceptual framework for career services in higher education and to the implementation of content and processes to affect student decision making has been offered by Peterson, Sampson, and Reardon (1991). Using a cognitive approach as the conceptual framework for career services in higher education initially, they have subsequently applied these to other settings and to a variety of career problems. In particular, in a recent article (Sampson, Lenz, Reardon, & Peterson, 1999) have applied their cognitive information processing approach to employment problem solving and decision making. In an oversimplified manner, this approach includes several key concepts. One of them is *problem,* which is defined as a gap between an existing and a desired state of affairs. A second concept, *problem solving,* has to do with the acquisition by student clients of information and the learning of cognitive strategies by which they can remove or narrow the problem gap and make a reasonable choice. Third is the concept of *decision making,* which involves converting one's choice into a plan of action. Fourth is a description of the types of content required in employment problem solving and decision making; these domains are included in what is labeled the Pyramid of Information Processing Domains discussed below. A final concept describes the processes by which problem-solving and decision-making can be facilitated; this set of processes is called the CASVE cycle (the Communications, Analysis, Synthesis, Valuing, Execution Cycle).

As suggested above the Pyramid of Information Processing Domains describes what students or other clients need to know as they seek to solve problems and make decisions. The domains at the base of the pyramid include two areas of content (knowing about myself—self-knowledge—and knowing about my options—options knowledge). The middle of the pyramid is content related to knowing how I make decisions or decision-making skills. And, at the top of the pyramid is content having to do with thinking about my decision making (e.g., the CASVE cycle) or metacognitions (e.g., self-talk, self-awareness, and so on).

In addition to having the content to engage in problem-solving and decision-making, there is also the issue of the process related to such outcomes. The CASVE cycle includes the sequence of steps, what needs to be done, to solve problems and make choices. Essentially, the CASVE cycle is depicted as starting with the *communication* phase, which has to do with the individual realizing that there is a problem, a gap between what exists and what is desired, a need to make a choice. The *analysis* phase focuses on understanding myself and my options and relating this information of the mental model they have created of their problem. The *synthesis* phase is a time when clients both expand and narrow the options they are considering. In the *valuing* phase, clients weigh or evaluate the costs and the benefits of each of the options they are considering to themselves, to significant others, possibly to their cultural group or their community; the outcome is a tentative choice. In the final phase, *execution,* the client seeks to implement the tentative choice by creating and then committing to a plan of action.

The clarity, sequencing, and interaction of content and process is a very useful conceptual framework for thinking about how career services might be organized and be implemented as well as how the counselor might work directly with an individual client. One major outcome of such a process is effective placement in the world of work.

Assistance with Access to the World of Work

Placement, in a broad sense, is more than an attempt to dovetail students seeking employment with available jobs. It consists of an array of services designed to help students with access to the world of work. It ranges from the scheduling of students for on-campus recruitment interviews to the dissemination of placement folders to prospective employers; it also entails assistance in developing student skills in selling oneself: résumé preparation, preparing career portfolios, interviewing behaviors, job-searching procedures, and so forth.

Assistance in Meeting the Unique Needs of Various Subpopulations

Some identifiable segments of the college population present special concerns for the career counselor. Among these subpopulations are visible minorities (such as African Americans, disabled persons, Hispanics, Native Americans, certain Asians, older men and women, and so on) and less visible minorities (such as gay students). Campuses with relatively large proportions of distinct minorities may well wish to mount programs directed toward meeting the career guidance needs of such groups, insofar as these needs extend beyond "normal" boundaries (that is, coping personally and legally with discriminatory practices, locating specialized sources of assistance, and such). Another group that may require additional career aid is women. Chapter 5 deals with the unique career concerns of various minorities and women. Here we point out some examples of other types of collegiate groups that may need special attention.

As indicated earlier in this chapter, international students constitute a substantial number of students in American colleges and universities. These students present specific career concerns. For instance, they study in the United States for so many years that they frequently are not aware of current career opportunities in their own home countries. Counselors need to be sensitized to their culturally engendered modes of coping with complex decision making. They need periodic reviews of progress and evaluations of the training to be sure that there are links to opportunities in their home countries. Preparation for reverse culture shock is another problem. Lifestyle, equipment, and role expectations will all be different from what they experienced in the United States. Some will expect the college or university to offer assistance in job placement at home. Finally, international students are more likely than American students to prefer help from faculty and counselors rather than from friends for various problems (Leong & Sedlacek, 1986), thus making them receptive to professional interventions.

Another college subpopulation with some unique career concerns is the adult student. Returning or first-time adult entrants to the college classroom are increasing, and some argue that new and different career services are necessary for adults. Others, however, maintain that modification of existing services is sufficient. Older college students are more likely than younger students to be high achievers. Married women are more likely to achieve than unmarried women. It is argued that adults' problem-solving orientation to learning and a desire to apply new knowledge immediately contribute to this higher academic achievement. Life experience and motivational factors seem to make adults more ready for learning and more open to career counseling. Some colleges offer a separate reentry course for adults, especially women and provide them with a designated counselor and other specific resources to meet their common needs.

A third subpopulation requiring a special type of career attention is the liberal arts student. Especially in an age of vocationalism, liberal arts majors may require different services from their more career-oriented counterparts. Several of the specific techniques for career interventions with these students are described later in this chapter. Because their needs are unique, specific sources of jobs for liberal arts students have been compiled (Basta, 1991; Figler, 1989; Flores-Esteves, 1985; Phifer, 1987), and studies have concluded that liberal arts graduates do not face so terrible an employment prospect as many fear. Nonetheless, the problem of helping students to translate liberal arts education into employable skills is formidable and requires special effort. Some studies (Buescher, Johnston, Lucas, & Hughey, 1989) suggest that early intervention with liberal arts students is the key to helping them vocationally.

Yet another group that some believe should receive special attention in terms of career and personal counseling is the gifted college student. By definition, any student in college could be considered gifted, but Schroer and Dorn (1986) describe an intervention for 71 academically talented college students at Texas A&M University. Their program was a six-hour group effort in career counseling, using the Career Motivation Program (CMP), a series of ten structured activities exploring interests, values, strengths, and personality in a group-interactive context. "At the conclusion of the group experience, gifted men and women demonstrated significant positive change on Certainty of Career and Major, significantly less indecision, significantly less anxiety about choice, and significantly less difficulty in deciding about several attractive options" (p. 570). A similar program has been reported for gifted students at the Ohio State University (Gordon, 1983).

Kerr and Erb (1991) describe a value-based career counseling intervention with academically talented (multipotentialed) students. Each participant experienced a single-time group life-planning workshop, an assessment session, and an individual counseling session. In the workshop, value exercises were conducted. During the assessment session, students took the Vocational Preference Inventory (VPI), the Personality Research Form (PRF), and the Rokeach Values Inventory (RVI). The individual counseling was conducted within the limits of a structured interview schedule and emphasized social persuasion. Students emerged with a stronger sense of confidence in their vocational identity, and about half changed their major and career goal.

There are other examples of college student populations with particular needs. For example, college students with disabilities is a rapidly growing subpopulation in many institutions of higher education because accessibility to buildings, classrooms, and labs has become much better in the last decade or so and so has the comprehensiveness of support services. Even so, however, research studies indicate that in comparison with students without disabilities, students with disabilities experience additional and, in many cases, different career concerns. In one such study, Luzzo, Hitchings, Retish, and Shoemaker (1999) explored the career making self-efficacy and the career decision-making attributional style of college students with and without disabilities. In this study, students with disabilities reported significantly lower levels of career decision-making self-efficacy and a more pessimistic attributional style for career decision making than did their peer college students without disabilities. The authors of the study strongly urged college counselors to include self-efficacy enhancing interventions and workshops designed especially for college students with disabilities. They also encouraged college counselors to develop attributional training interventions designed to encourage students with disabilities to assume more responsibility for their career decisions and to engage more systematically in career exploration and planning activities to increase their chances of experiencing satisfaction, stability, and success.

Another example of a special population whose career concerns may need special perspectives is that of minority students. Gloria and Hird (1999) studied the differences in career decision-making self-efficacy, trait anxiety, and ethnic identity for 687 (589 whites, 98 racial and ethnic minorities) undergraduate students in a Rocky Mountain Region University. Based on student scores on the Multigroup Ethnic Identity Measure, State-Trait Anxiety Inventory, and the Career Decision-Making Self Efficacy Short Form, the investigators found several interesting results. First, they found that white students reported higher career decision-making self-efficacy and lower trait anxiety and ethnic identity than did their racial and ethnic counterparts. Declared students (those who had declared a major) compared to undeclared majors reported higher career decision-making self-efficacy and lower trait anxiety. Racial and ethnic minority students who had lower trait anxiety also reported higher ethnic identity and other group orientation.

The findings of this study, according to the investigators, suggested that university counseling centers and career placement services should address and integrate sociocultural contexts into their programming and interventions. They also recommend that career counselors should consider ethnic identity and other group orientation relative to career-related self-efficacy. The latter approaches would help students to operationalize sources of efficacy and better understand contextual issues. In such circumstance, racial and ethnic minority clients could be helped to identify racially similar and dissimilar role models in their chosen field of work. Such analyses would help racial and ethnic minority students to assess how ethnic identity influenced their role models' self-efficacies and career development as well as how their role models identified and negotiated work barriers. "White role models, in particular, can provide racial and ethnic minority clients with an other-group orientation and perspective, increasing clients' bicultural flexibility to…succeed in different work environments" (p. 171). In addition to these interventions, other useful interventions include helping racial/ethnic minority students to develop coping mechanisms, anxiety management, and establishing social support networks as they explore and implement their declarations of academic major and career field.

These are selective examples of specific collegiate subgroups that may require intensive effort by career counselors. The list of such groups could be expanded. Some colleges, for instance, pay special attention to the career needs of student athletes (Denson, 1994; Howard-Hamilton, Lawler, Talleyrand, & Smith, 1994; Sedlacek & Adams-Gaston, 1992). Others provide special career services for veterans, especially Vietnam and Gulf War veterans.

Such approaches take different names and have different content for specific subpopulations of college students and they are comprised of many different processes. They include such possibilities as:

Freshman seminars focusing on academic and career issues
Advisement of undeclared majors
Academic career advising
Orientation of students to career services
Computer-assisted career guidance
Occupational and educational information
Resume preparation
Assertiveness training
Preparations for job interviews
Individual assessments of abilities, interests, and values
Coordination of cooperative education experiences with employers for selected students
Self-help materials for career exploration
Group career counseling
Consultation with faculty about the career implications of their academic courses
Resource speakers (employers and others)
Decision-making training
Multimedia materials
Self-directed work stations to explore interests, abilities, values, and academic majors
Library of educational and career materials
Mini-career courses on selected topics
Modules on study skills
Special programs for women, international students, alumni, and persons with disabilities
Employability skills training
Curriculum infusion of career materials
Faculty in-service training in career development
Match students and employers for job interviews

Some data exist on which types of career interventions have tended to emerge or become increasingly prominent in University Career Planning and Placement Centers. One survey by the College Placement Council (1991) suggests how particular interventions have ebbed and flowed in the percentage a representative sample of colleges and universities have offered each of them. Table 10.1 presents these data.

SEQUENCING CAREER GUIDANCE EXPERIENCES

A primary thrust of this book is that career interventions at every life stage should proceed in an orderly, systematic, sequenced, integrated, and articulated fashion in accordance with the common and unique needs of the particular clientele.

Within such a context, the first requisite in sequencing career interventions or career services in higher education is that these activities either logically emanate from or fit into a theory of career development that can, ideally, provide the framework for a comprehensive program.

In general terms, one can think of the higher education experience as a series of developmental tasks that students need to cope with and master as they enter and proceed through the collegiate experience toward a culminating event, graduation and the transition to employment or advanced graduate education.

Figure 10.1 in an oversimplified manner depicts career services that facilitate a continuum of career development in the college or university setting. Such a continuum of career development begins in the family, the cultural tradition, the community and the school settings that the student experiences before choosing and being admitted to a specific institution. The student's career development explorations are then affected by the information and images conveyed as the institution of higher education markets itself and the achievements of its students, and as it conducts the recruitment and admission of students. Upon entrance to the institution the student will be either formally or informally exposed to a process of career development, with potential career emphases occurring at each year level (e.g., freshman, sophomore, and so on). These emphases will include intermediate steps like choice of an academic major, choice of a specific job or position, the development of job search skills as processes that will lead ultimately to graduation, placement, and induction into a job or profession.

Figure 10.1 suggests that career services constitutes a process that provides support to students in each of their college years as they develop a growing career identity and the skills necessary to prepare for, identify preferred options, and choose a career path.

TABLE 10.1 Services Offered through Career Planning and Placement Center

	PERCENT OF RESPONDENTS			
	1975	1981	1987	1991
Career counseling	89.0	96.0	94.1	94.2
Occupational and employer information library	92.0	91.0	93.6	93.7
Placement of graduates into full-time employment	96.0	95.0	96.8	93.4
Campus interviewing	96.0	95.0	96.5	91.6
Placement of students into summer and part-time employment	81.0	83.0	87.0	83.2
Placement of alumni	87.0	90.0	88.9	82.7
Credential service	79.0	81.0	76.4	71.9
Resume referral	—	64.0	74.2	71.6
Cooperative education, intern, experiential program	26.0	49.0	53.7	62.8
Resume booklets	—	62.0	56.3	56.3
Vocational testing	31.0	51.0	53.2	52.1
Computerized candidate database	—	—	—	48.2
Career planning or employment readiness course	—	30.0	32.1	31.6
Academic counseling	30.0	37.0	33.0	28.7
Dropout prevention and counseling	22.0	26.0	19.9	16.2

Source: Reprinted from the "1991 Career Planning and Placement Survey," *Spotlight* (July 1991), with permission of the National Association of Colleges and Employers, copyright holder.

FIGURE 10.1 A Continuum of Career Services Facilitating Career Development in the College or University

PRE-ADMISSION		FRESHMAN	SOPHOMORE	JUNIOR	SENIOR	OUTCOMES FOR TRANSITION
Students have tentative career aspirations knowledge of interests, and abilities from previous school experiences, family, expectations, cultural traditions, cultural traditions possibly part-time work, observations in the community, on tv, etc.	As colleges and universities market themselves, they create images of career opportunities and other career relevant information (e.g., the outcomes achieved by former students)	• Freshmen seminars on career opportunities in a particular department/college • Beginning the process of self-assessment and self-analysis • Beginning the development of a career portfolio of one's achievements, competencies and certifications • Listen to faculty-staff discussions of curriculum and career implications in different majors • Identify technical courses of particular interest • Engage in individual study of an occupation or job family of interest	• Deliberations and exploration about the choice or an academic major • Assistance in decision-making • Assistance in understanding the world of work • Participate in a credit-bearing or non-credit course on career planning • Use a computer-assisted career guidance program for career exploration • Participate in a variety of career center outreach workshops of career choice and planning • Use career library to explore jobs and requirement	• Engage in internships, cooperative education, etc. to explore alternatives • Explore particular jobs and employers on the world-wide web • Engage in job search skills training • Attend workshops on the use of the Internet to identify jobs and employers and to submit resumes and other electronic information to employers • Participate in resume writing workshops • Observe video-tapes in the career center on job interviewing	• Assistance with access to the world of work • Participate in career center matching of one's skills and interests with employer needs • Participate in career days on opportunities in one's specialty • Finalize one's career portfolio • Participate in on-campus recruitment by employers	→ Self-knowledge → Knowledge of options → Career transition skills, job search → Graduation → Graduate school → Placement → Induction into a job or profession
		Process	———	———	———	Event

In pursuing such goals, career services need to interact with academic advisement at department or college levels and with other units of the college or university to provide clarity about the specific contributions of career services to student development and to the university's mission. Career services administrators in their planning must also ask how specific services will be tailored to the differential needs of students entering the university as freshmen or transfer students, maturing as potential professionals in their sophomore and junior years, and preparing for the steps that will follow their graduation in their senior year. In essence, what process elements at the freshman through senior years are vital to the achievement of such outcomes as graduation, placement, and induction into a job or profession.

The point with all systematic programs is that each stage builds on a previous stage to ensure comprehensive interventions. Simultaneously a student may enter at any stage of self-perceived or counselor-perceived need. Finally, all segments of the career-helping community need to have clearly delineated responsibilities to minimize the possibility of fragmented services.

EXAMPLES OF PROGRAM CONTENT

There are many ways to classify career services for college students. Lowman and Carson (2000) suggest that such services can be classified on a continuum ranging from high to low levels of student need for assistance. Within that context, these authors classify career services into *remediation services* and *enhancement services*. The former include interventions that are focused on students who experience relatively high levels of career-related distress and whose problems are reasonably well defined. The latter services or interventions are intended to help students who have relatively less career related distress but who seek assistance to optimize their career development, including exploration of their strengths and weaknesses, their interests, values, and abilities as well as identifying appropriate careers and identifying their best career options. One might further suggest that remediation services are more likely to be delivered on a one to one basis while enhancement services are likely to be delivered by both individual and group processes.

Spokane (1991) classified career services using two axes or continua. One had to do with minimum to maximum client investment of time and commitment. The other was minimum to maximum counselor involvement. For example, *maximum* counselor involvement in a career intervention would be in individual counseling. But, *minimum* counselor investment would be in areas like client reading information in an occupational library or engaging in self-directed activities such as self-paced work stations, computer-assisted career interventions and related activities. The point is that not all of the career interventions provided by career services centers in universities require the same amount of counselor involvement. In some cases, a counselor can explain available self-directed activities or information sources and then encourage clients to use these sources of information. After they have done so, it is important for the counselor to debrief the client's use of such resources, determine what the client has learned and then help the client to use such information as a base for sorting out future options, choosing among them, and creating a plan of action.

Obviously, the degree to which a career services center can provide intervention—information, structured work stations, computer-assisted career guidance systems—that student clients can access and use on their own to explore their career concerns, the fewer counselor hours need to be devoted to such information gathering by students, and the more can be devoted to the types of interventions where counselor involvement is essential: for example, workshops, group counseling, or individual counseling.

Trying to identify and use career interventions that minimize counselor involvement is not to suggest that such interventions can replace counselors or eliminate counselor involvement. The issue is the intensity of counselor involvement necessary to insure that particular interventions effectively augment individual or group counseling or other interventions in which counselors are intensely involved. For example, Garis and Niles (1990) and Niles and Garis (1990) found that computer-plus-counseling is more effective than computer-assisted career guidance systems alone. Niles (1993) studied the most effective periods for counselor intervention when clients are using computer-assisted career-guidance systems. In particular, Niles studied the differences among three strategies: interventions that occurred before student clients used the computer assisted career guidance system (preintervention); interventions that occurred during the use by students of the computer system (enroute) and interventions that focused on planning after using the system (postintervention). His results indicated that different outcomes arose from different counselor intervention strategies. For example, the "enroute" intervention by counselors resulted in higher enjoyment by student clients in using the computer-assisted career guidance system, in part because they probably felt more supported and able to use the technical aspects of the system more effectively. The postintervention group, that received counseling after using the computer-assisted career guidance system, reported less career indecision than the control group that did not receive any career counseling services. In such cases, it may be better for counselors to intervene briefly prior to their use of computer-assisted career guidance systems during the use of such systems, and after the use of such systems. Even so, however, it is likely that the first two interventions (pre to and during use of the system) would require considerably less time than if the counselor tried to replicate all of the exploration and information provided by the student-computer interaction. The counseling following the student-client use of the computer system would likely personalize and clarify the information, rehearse the consequences of options explored, and the planning of next steps. One could make similar comments about counselor involvement in other types of self-directed or informational items.

In broad terms, colleges and universities have used five major approaches to deliver career services: (1) courses, workshops, and seminars that offer structured group experiences in career planning; (2) group counseling activities that are generally less structured and emphasize broader, more affective aspects of human and career development; (3) individual counseling opportunities that accentuate diverse theoretical orientations to career concerns; (4) placement programs that culminate the career planning and decision-making process; and (5) computerized placement services.

Courses, Workshops, and Seminars

An increasingly popular career services delivery mode is the structured group experience in the form of a course, workshop, or seminar. In a survey conducted by Collins (1998), it was found that four out of five career centers provided group-oriented career counseling interventions and workshops. Halasz and Kempton's (2000) survey of 40 career centers suggested that career courses could be divided into three categories: (a) career decision making, (b) career exploration, and (c) job-search skills and strategies.

In an extension of the notion of using courses, workshops, and seminars to facilitate student career development, as suggested previously, some institutions integrate these interventions with other aspects of education. For example, Columbia University has reported (http://www.columbia.edu/cu/ccs) that the Center for Career Education will teach career as one of the three mobilities (intellectual, social, and career) in the educational experience at Columbia that students bring to their lives after graduation, to their work, their communities and the world. This program views career mobility as a function of career maturity, which is a matter of continuously seeking the intersections and finding the connections among one's values, interests, needs, skills, passions, and sense of responsibility to the rest of the world that allow us to feel fulfilled. In this sense, career mobility is one side of a triangular prism; intellectual and social are the other two. The intent is to view the other two mobilities from the perspective of the third, and integrate the three into the students' lives.

Through an evolving career development curriculum informed by research, the Center for Career Education provides course content designed to help students learn about:

- The relationship between what they are doing at Columbia and life after graduation
- Career options and alternatives
- Self-assessment of values, skills, and interests
- Informational interviewing and networking with alumni and employers
- Internships and summer job opportunities to gain experience in fields of interest
- International internships and employment opportunities
- Opportunities for value and service oriented careers
- Entrepreneurship and enterprise leadership

- Courses and employment alternatives
- Career fairs and employment recruiting on-campus interviews
- Graduate and professional school opportunities
- Teaching and learning, gaining, and improving teaching, research, writing, presentation and survival skills
- Economic and industry outlook
- Job search and workplace skills
- Employment opportunities after graduation

Shippensburg University (Pennsylvania) also had made a strong and comprehensive commitment to using classrooms and group meetings to orient students to the programming conducted by the Career Education program and to the career planning resources available in that program. Among career education's primary thrusts are to provide new students with an orientation to available career resources and to offer interested individuals the opportunity to participate in career planning designed to assess their career related interests, abilities, values, and experiences; identify and consider career options; gather and process career information/issues; and formulate their career plan. In addition to the professional staff, the Career Education program at Shippensburg University includes student assistants who act as peer career advisors as they work with students in career day, development of career publications, assisting in identifying and using career information, contacting students about participation in career planning, assisting students in the use of the DISCOVER program, a computer-assisted career guidance program, and the alumni career corrections program. In conducting an annual evaluation of the career education program, 84 users responded to an invitation to evaluate the program: 70 percent of the 84 indicated that the information they received about available career resources was helpful or very helpful, 14 respondents said the information was helpful, no respondents reported that the information was not helpful, of the respondents, 76 indicated the resources used to assess their interests, abilities, values, and experiences were helpful or very helpful. When asked how helpful the Career Education staff was in assisting you with DISCOVER, reviewing your results, and providing you with suggestions and information regarding other Shippensburg University career resources, 83 of the 84 respondents indicated helpful or very helpful (personal communication, Mr. Douglas Nichols, October 22, 2001).

In addition to using classes and group meetings to provide career interventions, there are also specific courses worth noting. For example, at the University of Oklahoma (Johnson & Smouse, 1993), a career and life-planning course extended for two semesters and carried one hour of credit. It provided students with concepts of life-span career development, accomplished some matching of their personal characteristics with occupations, and developed career choice skills. Such instruments as the Strong Vocational Interest Inventory, 16 PF, Myers-Briggs Type Indicator, and FIRO-B (see Chapter 16) were administered and interpreted, along with a variety of other self-exploration activities. Results indicated gains in the treatment group but little differentiation in outcomes between these clients and those in a control group.

Another interesting course intervention was designed by Betz and Schifano (2000) to increase the self-efficacy of college women in Realistic activities (e.g., using tools, assembling, building, operating machinery). It can be argued that the lack of women's interest and confidence in Realistic activities is associated with their underrepresentation in traditionally male-dominated careers, particularly those in science and engineering. In this intervention, 54 college women (24 in the treatment group and 30 in the control group) were studied to determine if interventions based on self-efficacy theory would increase their confidence and interests in Realistic activities. Measurements of Realistic interest and confidence were gathered pre-and post-treatment. The intervention used in this program focused on building, repairing, and construction activities as measured by the Realistic typology of Holland's (1997) career theory and as facilitated by Bandura's (1977) four sources of information through which self-efficacy expectations are learned and modified: (1) performance accomplishment; (2) vicarious learning or modeling, (3) verbal persuasion; and (4) lower levels of emotional arousal, such as anxiety.

The seven hour intervention was comprised of three sessions. The first session included a one-hour lecture on architectural design, followed by a tour of two different construction sites, at which construction techniques were explained and the participants were able to ask questions and observe the various phases of construction.

The second session consisted of a 30 minute lesson on the classification and use of various hardware items (e.g., nuts, bolts, screws, nails, and so on). Participants were divided into four groups, were asked to sort the pile of hardware items onto a prelabeled grid, and then they used the hardware and related tools to assemble metal shelving units.

In the third session, the participants were provided with various hand tools (e.g., wire cutters/strippers, screwdrivers, wrenches), their design and purposes were explained, and the participants then used the tools to perform such tasks as rewiring a lamp, assembling drainage pipes, and building a combination shelf unit and pegged coat rack. The post-test measures were administered two weeks after the interventions for both the experimental and control groups, which had a neutral intervention discussing recent films. The results indicated that participants in the treatment group showed a statistically significant increase in Realistic confidence compared to participants in the control group.

In another structured, career-focused course, Zagora and Cramer (1994) used results on Holland's construct of vocational identity as a means of grouping students. Students who were undecided to a high degree or to a low degree were identified, and high vocational identity students and low vocational identity students were assigned to one of three treatment conditions or to a control group. The treatment groups participated in a six-hour workshop in career decision making (three two-hour sessions over a three-week period). All treatment groups focused on self-knowledge, knowledge of the world of work, and decision-making strategies. One group consisted of only students with high vocational identity scores, a second involved only those with low scores, and a third consisted of students with both high and low scores. A single trained and experienced counselor, blind to the intent of the experiment, facilitated all groups. It became clear that group composition does have a significant main effect on decidedness. Those who participated in homogeneous treatment groups (high or low identity) were significantly more decided at the end of the intervention than either the heterogeneous group or the control group. It appears, then, that involvement in a career workshop with others of similar vocational identity status, whether high or low, results in greater gains in decidedness. Those who were in the heterogeneous group were not significantly more decided than the controls. Clearly, counselors should consider an undecided student's vocational identity status in determining appropriate interventions and group students more or less homogeneously.

Orndorff and Herr (1996) examined the differences between declared and undeclared students relative to their knowledge of career options. For these purposes, declared students had essentially chosen a major and, in general, were treated by the university as decided students; undeclared students had not chosen a major and were treated as undecided. In general, most universities treat undecided or undeclared students more assertively than students who appear to be decided about an academic major or career path. Indeed, many decision-making courses are targeted to undeclared students rather than all students. This research study found that most declared as well as undeclared students have limited knowledge about available career options. Nevertheless, declared students were found to possess higher levels of certainty about their major and career and lower levels of career uncertainty compared with undeclared students. In addition, the results of this study suggested that declared students are more involved in clarifying their values, interests, and abilities and in engaging in career planning than are undeclared students. Qualitative results gained from interviews with declared and undeclared students in the sample suggest that both declared and undeclared students possess relatively low levels of involvement and activity in exploring occupations, although the quantitative results yield a significant difference in such involvement in favor of the declared sample.

Further, this study found that declared students have engaged more in knowing their values, interests, and abilities than undeclared students have, but they have not engaged in exploring occupations more than undeclared students. This may help explain why so many declared students change their major.

Syntheses of research and specific research studies have shown that a career class was successful in improving the career decidedness, comfort, and self clarity of college students (Johnson & Smouse, 1993). Earlier research by Davis and Horne (1986) indicates that career courses and small-group career counseling interventions were equally effective in advancing students' career decidedness and career maturity.

In an important investigation of combining levels of treatment to increase career certainty and client satisfaction and decrease career indecision, Jurgens (2000) studied the impact of a four-phase combined intervention and compared it to a two-phase intervention. The four-phase intervention included a decision-making workshop, lasting approximately two hours and including the administration of the Career Decision Scale, a group cohesion exercise, sharing information about an eight-step decision-making model and Holland's Hexagon and the Organization of Occupations, a tour of the career resource library with instructions on how to use the DISCOVER system, taking the Myers Briggs Type Indicator, a two-hour session on the DISCOVER computer system, a one-hour computer session in which the participants explored the results of the instruments they took and their relation to their career decision making, a two-hour professional forum in which the participants met with eight professionals in a roundtable format to discuss occupations and gather information on various careers.

Treatment 2 was a condensed version of the four phase intervention that comprised Treatment 1. It took place over a two-week rather than a four-week period. Treatment 2 focused on the first week (phase 1) on administration of the CDS and a two-hour session on the DISCOVER computer guidance system, with participants completing modules 3, 4, and 5. Phase 2 of Treatment 1 (week 2) consisted of a one-hour individual counseling session in which the participants explored the results of their Career Decision Scale scores and the DISCOVER computer printouts. The participants in Treatment 2 were also invited in the professional forum, as guests, not participants.

Following the completion of the two treatments, the participants were given the Career Decision Scale as a posttest and a program evaluation form. The results of the study demonstrated that both the four-phase and the two-phase treatment conditions were effective in increasing career certainty in participants, although the four-phase intervention was significantly better at achieving such a result. Both treatments were effective in decreasing levels of career indecision and they did not differ significantly in achieving this result. There were not significant differences in ratings of satisfaction between the two groups. These findings suggest that brief and cost-effective intervention, as found in the two-week treatment of Treatment 2, can be beneficial to the undecided. Longer and more complex treatments may be more beneficial to students although fiscal and personnel resources may not be sufficient to support the longer and more complex treatment.

The courses illustrated here are examples of those frequently found in higher education. Each course, seminar, and workshop, in its own way, seeks to bring a systematic order to the often chaotic process of career planning. For further information on such structured group experiences, see Garis and Niles (1990); Gordon and Grites (1984); Henley (1986); Jones, Gorman, and Schroeder (1989); Kivlighan (1990); Orndorff and Herr (1996); Quinn and Lewis (1989); Schrank (1982); and Sherry and Staley (1984).

Group Counseling

The distinction between group counseling and more structured group guidance activities is frequently subtle, and the boundaries between the two are often obfuscated. Traditionally, group counseling has involved less formal structure, more affect, and greater utilization of the resources of group members. Attempts at group counseling with a career focus in higher education, however, often combine both structure and relative nonstructure, as the following examples of group counseling efforts illustrate.

Pickering and Vacc (1984) reviewed 47 research articles in refereed journals between 1975 and 1981 that addressed the effectiveness of career development interventions for college students and reached several conclusions. Although their method of analysis is relatively crude when compared with more sophisticated meta-analytic procedures, there is little reason to believe that other statistical techniques or approaches would produce contrary results. Among their findings were the following:

- More than half of the studies were reports of short-term interventions, 79 percent of which reported positive gains.
- About one-quarter of the reported programs were self-help interventions, with 67 percent of these demonstrating improvement.
- About another one-quarter were long-term (such as career courses), and 93 percent reported success.

- A few studies compared methods; in all, 79 percent of the studies reported positive gains or differences between treatments.
- The most frequently used outcome variables were career maturity and decision-making skills.
- The most common personality variables investigated were anxiety, locus of control, and self-concept.
- A majority of the interventions used behavioral interview techniques; trait and factor was the next most popular orientation.

The general conclusion was that "short-term interventions, designed to facilitate career maturity and the development of decision-making skills through a behavioral orientation, have been most widely used, and their effectiveness has been supported. Ideally, a comprehensive program consisting of self-help, short-term, and long-term (course) interventions should be available to students for their career development needs" (p. 156).

Davis and Horne (1986) compared the effectiveness of small-group counseling and a career course on the career decidedness and maturity of students at a midwestern university. The course met three times per week (50 minutes) for a 16-week semester and contained 16 to 19 students per section. It combined lectures on educational and career topics, a text, testing, guest speakers, homework, and discussion. The small-group treatment met for 12 sessions of one hour each and consisted of 12 members per group. Each session was loosely structured and emphasized group interaction, discussion, feedback, and sharing. There was no reading, tests, or homework. Using the Career Decision Scale (CDS) and the Career Maturity Inventory (CMI) as outcome measures, Davis and Horne found that both types of groups were effective in decreasing undecidedness and increasing maturity and that there were no significant differences between the two treatments.

There have been many comparisons regarding the relative career helping effectiveness of structured group experiences versus more counseling-oriented groups. A study by Perovich and Mierzwa (1980) is typical of the design and results of this type of research. They compared Vocational Information Groups (VIG) to Self-Growth Groups (SGG) to Control Groups (CG). VIGs in eight work sessions considered eight specific content areas for which vocational information was provided in a group context that allowed group member interaction (such as career development, strategies for employment, decision-making skills, sex-role stereotypes). The SGGs were aimed at self-growth through greater self-understanding by means of encounter with other group members; FIRO-B techniques were used as a starting point; T group techniques were employed for the remainder of the eight work sessions. The control group received no treatment. With the VIG, college students achieved desirable gains in vocational maturity, planning awareness, and self-esteem, and there were no sex differences. With the SGG, vocational maturity increased but not self-esteem or planning awareness. Both types of groups achieved results significantly better than the control group. The conclusion is that a structured group experience is preferable in meeting the vocational needs of college students.

Robbins and Tucker (1986) provide an example of a more sophisticated investigation of the effects of workshops in that they attempt to account for differences in client attributes in relation to outcomes. In this case, they studied the relation of goal instability (a general instability or absence of orienting goals) to self-directed and interactional career counseling workshops at the University of Maryland. Outcome measures were career information seeking, career maturity, and satisfaction with the workshop. The self-directed intervention consisted of three two-hour sessions and emphasized self-directed and individualized problem solving (e.g., information gathering and self-reflection, various exercises, Holland's Self-Directed Search). The interactional intervention also was composed of three two-hour sessions, but the leaders emphasized group interaction and self-disclosure (which they themselves modeled). The results indicated that individuals with high goal instability did better on the criteria when they were in interactional rather than in self-directed workshop formats. Further, participants seemed to prefer consistently the interactional workshop. The researchers conclude that an "emphasis on leader modeling and participant self-disclosure can boost the effects of information-oriented interventions for high and low goal instability people alike" and "that matching personality types with treatment strategy increases the outcomes of career intervention workshops" (p. 422).

Career interventions in higher education are not a panacea. Although the success of such interventions has been documented (see also Chapter 14), there is research that indicates occasional failures. For instance, Polansky, Horan, and Hanish (1993) determined that simply teaching study skills to a group of at-risk university students increased their GPAs and retention rate more than providing career counseling or even combining career counseling and study skills.

Individual Counseling

Individual career counseling continues to be at the center of most programs of career guidance or career services in higher education. Part of the explanation for this phenomenon is that counselors are socialized to view individual counseling as their primary tool and the source from which much of their identity derives. An equally important explanation for the primacy often given to individual career counseling is that it is effective. Elsewhere in this book research by Oliver and Spokane (1988) and other researchers has been cited to show that of all career interventions individual counseling is much more costly than other approaches, but also the most efficient in terms of amount of gain per hour of effort. As reported earlier in this book, Oliver and Spokane's finding indicate that longer (at least ten sessions) and more comprehensive sessions, although they require more time from the client and the counselor, yield roughly twice the beneficial effects of brief interventions.

The effectiveness of individual career counseling continues to be documented in comparison with other career interventions (computer assisted career guidance programs, career classes, workshops). For example, Whiston, Sexton and Lasoff (1998) conducted a meta-analysis of career interventions and found that individual career counseling was the most effective method among the interventions studied and the most expedient method of producing positive career outcomes for student clients. Similar to the outcomes found in the Oliver and Spokane meta-analysis, Whiston et al. found that individual career counseling tended to yield large gains quickly, within an average of 2.5 hours.

Aside from the well documented utility of individual career counseling in relation to a variety of career outcomes, individual career counseling is also expensive. Thus, many career centers have sought other methods to promote career development of students in groups (workshops, classes, group counseling) or by the use of technology (computer-assisted career guidance systems) rather than relying only on individual counseling. These career interventions have also been found to be effective in many studies and in spreading counselor time across groups of students, these group or technology-based interventions tend to be less expensive. In many cases, directors of career centers have to ask whether they can afford to maximize the use of individual career counseling, to rely on other forms of less expensive career interventions, or to combine individual counseling with computer-based career systems or workshops, a tactic which he also found to be effective.

It is accurate to suggest that many college students come to career centers for information and assistance that does not require individual counseling. In one major eastern university career center the reasons clients sought intake counseling in one academic year were as follows:

Choice of major/career	24%
Occupational information	6%
Job search	16%
Resume preparation	30%
Cover letter preparation	8%
Placement interview request	10%
Internship/Summer job search	6%
Graduate/professional school admissions	3%

While many of these categories of career concern could be effectively dealt with by individual career counseling they do not need to be so addressed: many of these concerns can be addressed by group approaches, by technology, by paraprofessionals, or by academic advisors working in conjunction with the career development and placement service. In a sense, it is possible to allocate different types of career interventions to students depending upon their level of indecision/indecisiveness, their decision style, and their level of career maturity. Relatively little systematic research has been devoted to relating different types of career interventions to specific career concerns and to specific client type (dependent, independent, rational, inductive, and so forth). Thus, there are major needs in the field for a comprehensive career diagnostic system, for more effective use of assessment, and for the matching of treatment and client characteristics in an attribute-treatment interaction matrix (Whiston, 2000).

Within such contexts, although continuing to recognize the importance of human assessment as a requisite to career planning and decision making, most modern counselors are placing increased emphasis on the importance of value clarification and the recognition of total life patterns in the counseling process. The trait-and-factor orientation that so long has dominated individual career counseling is still prevalent, but it has been increasingly supplemented by a consideration of the total life goals, commitments, and values of the individual.

Cooper (1986) compared the effects of group and individual vocational counseling on career indecision and personal indecisiveness. Both group and individual counseling were judged to be successful in reducing career indecision and personal indecisiveness.

The foci for career counseling at the collegiate level are indeed broad. One example is that of early dual-career couples. Almost one in five college students is married. On the assumption that many of these couples may be experiencing marital difficulty as a result of enacting dual roles of student and spouse (for instance, diversity of goals, strong achievement needs of both individuals, demanding schedules, and multiple-role responsibilities), Houser, Konstam, and Ham (1990) investigated coping strategies that are related to marital adjustment. They found that unsuccessful techniques for couples were confrontive coping (aggressive efforts to alter the situation) and escape-avoidance (wishful thinking and trying to avoid situations that are stressful). For men, distancing also was not a useful coping strategy. The authors suggest that "counselors in college counseling centers can potentially increase their effectiveness by identifying the coping strategies used by married couples who seek counseling and facilitate the acquisition of knowledge of alternative coping patterns that lead to greater marital adjustment. Furthermore, counselors can use coping skills training to increase adaptive mutual coping strategies for couples" (p. 329).

Rotberg, Brown, and Ware (1987) studied community college students and tentatively concluded that career choice is "influenced by both career interest and career self-efficacy expectations, which are themselves modified by gender and sex role orientations" (p. 166). The question for counselors thus becomes not only what are a person's aptitudes and interests, but also how do people themselves view their ability to perform the tasks of various occupations. Thus, their self-efficacy may require change to become more consonant with reality, and this focus would represent a further reason for counseling.

In terms of techniques, philosophies, and orientations to individual counseling, the reader is referred to Chapter 14. In general, the principles that govern all individual counseling pertain to career counseling.

Often, it is the more esoteric aspects of individual career counseling that are the focus of investigators. For example, in an analog study, Millar (1992) probed whether notetaking by a counselor during a videotaped career counseling session would make any difference in terms of subjects' perceptions of the career counselor as expert, attractive, or trustworthy. Notetaking did not appear to affect these three dimensions, but subjects expressed greater willingness to see the counselor who refrained from notetaking. Elwood (1992) suggests a pyramid model in the career counseling of university students. She describes a career triangle in which the three legs are interests, abilities, and personality traits. The points of the pyramid are tendencies toward emotionality, intellectuality, and sexuality. Impinging on each of these dimensions are needs, roles, creativity, and so on.

Peer Counseling

The use of students in paraprofessional roles is common in college and university career centers. One survey conducted by the American College Personnel Association (ACPA) (McKenzie & Manoogian-O'Dell, 1988) found a decade ago that 163 career centers reported the use of a paraprofessional program, including peer counselors. This trend continues to grow.

The use of peer counselors, or perhaps more appropriately paraprofessionals, is both a pragmatic and a training issue. In pragmatic terms, the use of selected and trained students to do intake, offer educational services or assist in a career library is a less expensive way to manage resources than to use professionally trained counselors to do the same work. From a training perspective, most colleges and universities that offer masters or doctoral level programs in counseling or in college student personnel need practica, internship or other experiential settings in which students can be socialized to a professional service delivery environment or to an environment in which they can receive supervision as they hone their counseling skills. Serving as a paraprofessional, or peer counselor, can meet such objectives.

Different universities give their paraprofessional advisers or peer counselors a variety of responsibilities. The University of Texas at Austin use their "career assistants" to engage in the following types of functions (Herr, Rayman, & Garis, 1993):

- Critique resumes and cover letters
- Teach or co-teach workshops/classes
- Perform intake counseling
- Coordinate and host receptions and panels
- Host visiting employers
- Interact with employers or alumni to develop recruitment visits, summer jobs, and internships
- Interact with professionals or alumni to develop career consultants, internship sponsors
- Complete administrative/clerical tasks
- Design fliers and other marketing devices
- Lead library and facility tours
- Deliver outreach programs and services
- Develop educational materials

In fact, there are other titles that can be used for such persons that may fit their role more effectively. For example, the Career Center at Florida State University uses students as paraprofessionals and refers to them as career advisers (Peterson, Sampson, & Reardon, 1991). The rationale for using this title is to be clear that these persons are not professionally trained and certified counselors. The term *adviser* is often used across university student services agencies to identify persons with a variety of staff backgrounds. Obviously, whatever the title used for peer counselors, their responsibilities need to be clearly defined and supervised. They also need to be provided a systematic training program.

Ash and Mandelbaum (1982) have advocated the effective use of peers in career counseling to supplement understaffed programs. Such paraprofessionals, it is argued, have a natural rapport with their peers and can be trained to perform the more rudimentary tasks attendant to counseling. One interesting side effect of such research is that professional staff are often stimulated by the enthusiasm of the peer counselors.

Kenzler (1983) has pointed out that peer counselors, with training, can handle initial assessment interviews and provide general job-search assistance. In such matters, they can be very effective. For example, Pickering (1986) compared three methods of career planning for liberal arts majors: career counselors, peer tutors, and self-study. All treatments were accomplished by means of groups, and sessions met six times for 60 to 90 minutes, focusing on Figler's PATH, which contains 18 individual exercises. Criterion measures were Crites's CMI and an examination on PATH. No significant differences in treatment were discerned, and all groups gained. The investigator concluded that structured career planning using tutors was effective. It should be recalled, however, that no deeper counseling was considered.

Placement

As was discussed at the beginning of this chapter, placement originally had the narrow purpose of maintaining a liaison between the school and potential employers and providing part-time, temporary jobs.

These purposes still exist; however, they are increasingly embedded in the processes of career development and career planning embraced by many, if not most, career development and placement centers in higher education. What used to be almost purely employment counseling is now expanded to a much more comprehensive set of career guidance and career counseling initiatives. To be sure, the placement function within such expanded career services still represents repositories of both occupational information and employer information; are a vehicle for bringing together industrial, business, and educational recruiters with students and alumni job seekers; and are dispensers of student and alumni career dossiers to potential employers. Many of these activities are now facilitated by technology as a tool for teaching students job interview and related skills, for career exploration, and for matching student characteristics and abilities with specific employer needs. In addition to increased career planning with individual students, placement offices are keeping academic departments aware of changes in particular labor markets, offering orientation to college-to-employment transition programs, including internships and cooperative education, and providing other group experiences to produce students who are better equipped to understand their work, family, and community roles. In sum, then, placement is a much more complex aspect of career development than simply posting job openings and scheduling recruiters for student interviews.

The placement function in different institutions of higher education may be part of a major, centralized career services center or be decentralized as a placement office in individual colleges or departments. While a narrow definition of placement suggests that its emphasis is only on job search and identifying employers with whom to interview, a more contemporary view of placement would see it as integrated into a set of processes to assist student clients in the choice of and implementation of career plans. Such a view goes beyond on-campus recruiting of students by employers to include career exploration, placement counseling, assistance in graduate/professional school admissions, computer-based job search systems, networking services, employment listing services, employment-oriented career days, and use of the Internet to do research on prospective employers and to submit resumes and make other electronic contacts with employers. In a sense, all of these emphases surround or enable the heart of the placement function: the on-campus recruiting system. By developing and offering such a service that brings students and employers together in order to discuss employment opportunities, the career center amplifies its mission to assist students not only in career development but in the implementation of career plans. It also represents the bridge between the particular institution of higher education and the world of employment in its focus on assistance to students to make the transition between these two worlds effectively.

There are many ways by which the placement function can be tailored to specialized placement needs. For example, some college career centers target on-campus recruiting to specialized groups of students (e.g., liberal arts, communications, education, information technology, engineering) at a particular time in the academic year, have a career day focused on opportunities in these fields for students in these majors, as well as on-campus recruiting interviews for graduating students in these majors.

While the range of placement programs that can be implemented is quite comprehensive, they will vary from institution to institution according to the career center mission; staffing, fiscal and physical resources; and the characteristics of the community college, college or university in which they are located. Some examples of the range of placement-oriented activities in addition to on-campus recruiting by employers, that a particular career center or placement office might engage in include:

1. Participation in regional consortia, job fairs, or career programs
2. Maintaining job notices and vacancy listings filed by academic programs and perhaps the incorporation of this information into newsletters or Internet listserves available to students in particular career fields or alumni
3. Developing a job bank or networking program utilizing computer-based and electronic bulletin board applications
4. Offering a credential service for education majors and for students seeking admission to graduate professional school
5. Helping students in specialized academic programs to develop resume books or career portfolios
6. Developing a computer-based or web-based resume matching and referral system for alumni
7. Maintaining employment and organizational directories, subscriptions to employment listings in specialized fields, and job search self-help books in the career information center
8. Providing career outreach programs and credit courses to assist clients in the development of job search skills
9. Providing individual and group counseling to assist clients in the employment search or graduate/professional school application process (Herr, Rayman, & Garis, 1993; Ottke & Brogden, 1990)

These are a variety of ways by which to organize and implement these various placement activities. From a conceptual standpoint, research studies on placement have suggested that there are several important concepts involved. Werbel (2000), for example, has studied the linkages among the constructs of career exploration, job search intensity, and job search effectiveness. Thus, in this study, preceding the job search component of the placement process is career exploration which involves information gathering about oneself and employment opportunities. According to the professional literature, inherent in this process is a readiness or cognitive preparation to identify desirable and realistic job opportunities. The assumption is that the tasks performed in this process will lead subsequently to a more "efficient and effective" job search process (p. 379). In turn, job search intensity describes the degree of job search effort by a job seeker and involves activities that are likely to lead to job interviews and job offers. Several studies suggest that self-esteem, self-efficacy, and financial need affects job search behaviors in different samples.

Reporting on a sample of 129 students graduating from a large state university responding to a survey, Werbel examined hypotheses related to the impact of self-exploration and environmental exploration on job satisfaction and initial compensation as mediated by job search entity. The result suggested that self-exploration appeared to have little direct impact on job search behaviors but environmental exploration was associated with job search intensity. Environment exploration has to do with "gathering information about the environmental aspects of person-environment fit that will help to determine the job seeker's degree of interest in a given employment opportunity" (p. 382). Further, job search intensity was significantly associated with initial compensation but not with job satisfaction. Thus, of the five variables studied in this study, the three of significance include the importance of environmental exploration in that it increases job search intensity which in turn is the mediating variable for the impact of initial compensation. In this study, self exploration was not found to be significantly related to job search intensity, initial compensation, or job satisfaction, although as the author suggested, this finding may be sample specific to college students majoring in business, but not necessarily to other adult populations or, perhaps, students in other academic majors. From a career counseling perspective, this research suggests that a greater emphasis needs to be given to the gathering of information about work opportunities to guide the job search and to the development of job search skill development, self-efficacy training, and preparation for interviews.

A relevant study by Arp, Holmberg, and Littrell (1986) describes a six-session structured job-search support group for adult students at Iowa State University. In the first session, emphasis was placed on participants' developing an awareness of internal barriers to their job search and setting short-term goals to remove barriers. Session two was devoted to skill assessment. During session three, the focus was on conducting informational interviews, establishing networks, and using library resources on employment to encourage awareness of job opportunities. Session four emphasized successful ways of finding employment. The penultimate session concentrated on résumé writing. The final session dealt with employment interviews.

One of the problems to be overcome in the provision of career guidance and counseling in higher education is the potential destructiveness of "territorial imperative" thinking. As higher education has increasingly accepted its role in enhancing the career development of students, various campus bailiwicks of helpers have staked claim to the career assistance function—placement, counseling, and advisement offices; academic departments; and units directed at specific subpopulations in academe (such as minority programs). Where it occurs, this compartmentalization has the potential of producing a fragmented, piecemeal, hit-or-miss, redundant provision of services, or of resulting in a coordinated, comprehensive, integrated program. Care should clearly be taken to ensure the latter outcome.

Some colleges and universities have installed automated placement services. Although both the technology and the know-how for planning and effecting such systems have existed for some time, they have not widely been implemented until the 1990s. Such systems sometimes involve a fee for the student (usually \$30 to \$50). This fee covers some sort of software e.g. career navigator, that assists in résumé construction, access to a job vacancy hotline résumé referral to regional, national, and international employment networks (e.g., Educators On-line, kiNexus, ETSI's Human Resource Information Network, SPANUSA, and AHEAD's database for students with disabilities). Via telephone, students can dial in (24 hours a day) to hear full-time current vacancy listings and electronically transfer their résumés to an employer in whom they are interested. They can also schedule on-campus interviews and learn about part-time jobs, internships, and summer job vacancies. Multiple laser-printed copies of résumés are provided. Virtually all such automated placement services can now be replaced by systematic use of web-sites on the Internet which provide the same types of information and functions.

CAREER GUIDANCE TECHNIQUES

In addition to the techniques previously described in this chapter, the following procedures and ideas illustrate the types of activities that can be used in the career guidance and counseling of college students:

- Arrange seminars involving recruiters and faculty in various allied fields.
- Set up internship programs to provide field experiences in subject matter disciplines.
- Role-play job interviews and videotape them for student feedback.
- Have students interview individuals currently working in their field of interest.
- Videotape recruiters and amass a library of such tapes for student viewing on demand.
- Administer personality assessment instruments and provide group or individual interpretation (such as Eysenck Personality Inventory, Edwards Personal Preference Schedule, Omnibus Personality Inventory, and so on).
- Conduct a credit-bearing or credit-free course or seminar on general or specific aspects of career planning.
- Administer various interest inventories and provide group or individual interpretation (such as Strong Interest Inventory, Self-Directed Search, Kuder Form DD, and so on).
- Develop shadowing programs to enable students to experience real day-to-day work situations.
- Administer various career planning forms and discuss the results (such as Self-Directed Search, Career Key, Career Navigator, and Programmed Guide to Career Decision-Making).
- Teach the use of the *Dictionary of Occupational Titles* and the *Occupational Outlook Handbook.*
- Use local campus computer network news to publicize events.
- Administer and interpret various career development or career maturity inventories (such as Super's Career Development Inventory, Crites Career Maturity Inventory, and so on).
- Arrange faculty-staff panels to talk about curriculum and careers in their fields.
- Conduct values clarification exercises as they relate to career planning and decision making.
- Arrange student panels composed of various majors to talk about their studies and aspects of making a decision about a major.
- Devise illustrative case study materials for use as a stimulus in career group guidance.
- Have individuals in a group present themselves as career "cases" to the other group members.
- Use status rankings of occupations as a discussion vehicle.
- Use the residence halls, the student union, and other areas as outreach career guidance possibilities.
- Set up mobile career information units (such as vans) and circulate around the campus.
- Locate jukeboxes, tape machines, VCRs, computers, or other media in high traffic locations around the campus to disseminate curricular and career information.
- Establish career information libraries or resource centers in libraries, unions, residence halls, and so on.
- Use electronic bulletin boards on the Internet to disseminate career information.
- Use the campus radio or TV stations for a regularly scheduled career program.
- Have a regularly appearing career planning column in the student newspaper.
- Organize cooperative education programs for students in various courses.
- Integrate a career planning unit within an existing academic course (such as Speech, any introductory course).
- Establish a computer-based academic advisement or career guidance system.
- Engage in in-service, updating workshops with faculty advisors.
- Have students write vocationally relevant autobiographies.
- Use films, videotapes, and filmstrips to stimulate discussions about career issues
- Teach students to write a résumé and have them write their own résumé.
- Engage in decision-making simulation and gaming activities.
- Have students engage in individual study of an occupation or an occupational field.
- Have students take a job satisfaction inventory and discuss the results.
- Directly teach theories of career development or theories of career decision making.
- Study the occupational structure according to one or more classifications (such as industrial, census, Holland, cluster).

- Have students conduct a career-related project as part of an academic course requirement.
- Teach students about the use of selected websites on the Internet to identify employment opportunities and by which to contact employers, submitting applications and resumes.
- Help students develop career portfolios, that include examples of their competencies, achievements, and certifications for use in the employment interview.
- Have students read the first several chapters of the *Occupational Outlook Handbook* to identify employment trends in the various sectors of the economy, (e.g. health care, information technology, business, manufacturing) and use as a stimulus to career planning.

SUMMARY

In this chapter, we have considered characteristics of students in higher education as they relate to career planning and decision making. Interventions designed to assist students with career concerns have been discussed. Guidelines were offered relating to the effective and efficient delivery of career services. If students were exposed to the type of career-related interventions described in earlier chapters, the need for such intensive career assistance at the collegiate level would probably be lessened. Currently, however, the higher educational setting is replete with students who have career problems to which career helpers must responding in multiple initiatives across the years of the higher education experience.

CHAPTER ELEVEN

Career Development in the Workplace

KEY CONCEPTS

- Both remedial and developmental functions of career counseling and other career services are important in the workplace.
- Adjustment in the workplace affects life adjustment.
- Human resources management, employee assistance programs, and career development in organizations are descriptions of major activities that include career counseling in the workplace.
- Work organizations create career patterns for their employees that may differ in timing and in substance from setting to setting.
- Career counselors working in business and industry engage in some functions that are different from those of career counselors employed in schools or colleges and universities, requiring them to understand both individual career development and organizational development.
- An important component of career development in the workplace is the recognition and management of occupational stress.
- The skills required for success in many workplaces are changing, emphasizing the importance of worker's abilities to change, be flexible, engage in lifelong learning, work in teams, and manage their own career.

This chapter concentrates on the types of career development activities taking place in the diverse organizational structures that constitute the workplace—stores, factories, laboratories, offices, agencies, and other institutions—in which people implement their job and occupational choices, their relationships with others, and their pursuit of outcomes they hope to achieve from work. The principles pertaining to both remedial and developmental functions described in earlier chapters can be put to use in the workplace, although the career interventions are broadened somewhat to include a wider array of activities, such as those typically found in employee assistance programs, in public and private employment services, and provided on site in specific workplaces.

WORK ADJUSTMENT AND PERSONAL ADJUSTMENT

Throughout this book, we have emphasized the central place of work in life. Personal adjustment and work adjustment appear to exist in a symbiotic relationship. Underwood and Hardy (1985), for example, studied 923 nonprofessional, nonmanagerial workers to determine the relationship between personal and vocational adjustment. The relationship was significant, with poorly adjusted individuals being poorly adjusted workers and well-adjusted individuals being well-adjusted workers. They concluded that vocational adjustment appears to be a specific aspect of personal adjustment, although it would be possible to conclude that work adjustment affects life adjustment. We are all familiar with the worker who has a bad day on the job and comes home to exhibit the kick-the-dog syndrome—transferring to those in the immediate home environment the anger and the frustration of unhappiness at work. There does appear to be some evidence, however, that stressors on the job seem to create more strain in an individual than do stressors of home and family (O'Driscoll, Ilgen, & Hildreth, 1992).

Occupational Stress

Indeed, one could argue that in many ways the experiences by workers of occupational stress and its diverse implications for behavior are at the heart of the need for career services in the workplace. Certainly, the results of national conferences addressing the interactions of work, health, and stress (McGuire, 1999) suggest that the rapid and comprehensive transformation of the American workplace has created an environment in which the workforce is more at risk than ever for psychological, physical and behavioral health problems and for social and family disruptions. Many factors have been indicted as the causes of such problems: the increasing workload of men and women in the United States compared to those in most other nations—American workers are now working harder and longer than they have in the past two decades just to sustain their standard of living. Related to such issues is the growing concern by workers that they are experiencing what is now being called "time poverty" or "time famine." Essentially, the point is that work is becoming so consuming of time and energy in many workplaces that employees do not have time to have dinner with their family or engage in other family activities. Estimates are that one-quarter to one-third of workers have high job stress such that they are drained of energy and exhausted at the end of the workday.

As suggested in chapter two and elsewhere in this book, job stress, absences due to stress-related illnesses, the fact that psychological disorders are now considered one of the ten leading occupational diseases and injuries are each major concerns of government agencies (e.g., the National Institute of Occupational Safety and Health) and employers. Within this context, it is increasingly clear that even though American workers are working longer and harder, in the last ten years the number who fear job loss has doubled. Some research has shown these phenomena to be associated with rising disability claims, decreased productivity, and increased health care costs. They also are associated with increased international economic competition that has led to wage cutting, downsizing of the workforce to reduce labor costs and increase units of productivity. This so-called "lean production," includes continuous quality improvement, improved inventory systems, and elimination of waste and motion (Clay, 1999). The intent of lean production is to decrease the number of workers in a particular workplace, improve worker productivity, enhance product quality and increase profits but researchers have found that such purported benefits are also associated with higher stress levels and injury rates as workers struggle to keep up.

As suggested above, although unemployment or the lack of work creates stress, actual employment also causes problems in terms of the stressors provided within the work environment. Stress is clearly endemic in contemporary society. As such it has been studied widely in the workplace and in other settings. While there are many important theories of stress, among them are two particularly prominent: appraisal-based stress theories and Conservation of Resources (COR) theories. Lazarus and Folkman (1984) depicted stress as the primary outcome of personal appraisal, the individual's idiographic assessment of what they are experiencing and how they have learned to interpret such appraisals as a function of sociocultural processes.

Basic to the appraisal approach to stress is the assumption that conditions are presented to individuals either within work or outside of work, that cause them to call upon their resources to adapt to the conditions. When these conditions (stressors) are greater than a person's abilities to cope or when they cause individuals to use their coping resources to the maximum degree possible, stress may be induced. People may see possible harm, threat, or challenge in the environment and this perception starts a potential stress-strain chain. Strain does not result, however, unless the stressors are first filtered through people's psychological systems (Lazarus & Folkman, 1984); once strain occurs, it may be more or less debilitating depending on individual's differing capacities to cope. The sequence is as follows:

1. There is a perceived work stressor in the environment.
2. Individual workers make cognitive appraisals of the stressors and view them in a way that may make the worker unclear about how to respond because the effects of response are important.
3. People experience the level of stress differentially, both psychologically and behaviorally.
4. People bring into play coping behaviors or strategies.

When the situation is both uncertain and important, the stress chain is evoked. In other words, when the environment imposes demands that are out of balance with the person's capacity to respond, strain may result. It should be noted here that stress may originate within the individual as well as the environment as we impose demands on ourselves. The father of stress research, Hans Selye (1976), pointed out that there can be too much stress or too little stress, good stress and bad stress within environments. *Overstress* (hyperstress) is obviously a condition wherein presenting stressors exceed or overtax one's abilities to deal with them; *understress* (hypostress) is the obverse condition wherein the environment presents no stressors and therefore does not challenge the individual to use one's abilities fully. Therefore, one's capabilities may grossly exceed demands, or demands may greatly exceed capabilities. In either case, stress may result. *Good stress* (eustress) is stress that provides an acceptable degree of challenge, a facilitating sort of anxiety. *Bad stress* (distress) produces actions inimical to the physical and mental health of the individual.

The second theory, Conservation of Resources (COR), is based upon the tenet "that individuals strive to obtain, retain, protect and foster those things that they value" (Hobfoll, 2001, p. 341). They do so in a world that they see as innately threatening and requiring a constellation of their personal strengths, social attachments, and cultural belonging in order to survive. Hobfoll (1998), and his colleagues, termed the variety of entities that persons value: resources. They have identified some 74 such resources that tend to comprehensively cover and have validity in many Western contexts. Selected examples of such resources include such possibilities as personal transportation, time for adequate sleep, good marriage, feeling valuable to others, feeling that I am accomplishing my goals, personal health, sense of optimism, stable employment, providing children's essentials, feeling that I have control over my life, understanding from my employer/boss, feelings that my life has meaning/purpose, people I can learn from, money for advancement, or self-improvement. These examples suggest that resources that people hope to conserve in the face of change in the workplace and other stressors can be tangible or intangible, economic or psychological, social or goal-oriented. Within the Conservation of Resources concept, then, stress is seen as occurring when individuals' resources are threatened with loss, are actually lost, or when individuals fail to gain sufficient resources following significant resource investment (Hobfoll, 2001). For the most part, the resources involved are objectively determined or observable or the ranking of their importance is a product of culture. In any case, however, the Conservation of Resources view of stress, is that it is fit of resources to demands, or the lack thereof within a particular work environment that constitutes stress. A major principle here is that resource loss is disproportionately more salient than resource gain; given equal amounts of loss and gain, loss will have significantly greater impact. This tendency to overweight negative or threatening information may be innate or learned strongly and early and becomes essentially automatic responses below the levels of awareness.

The Conservation of Resources theory has been used to explain burnout, as well as stress in work settings. The former, burnout, is seen as the outcomes of a process by which persons experience a gradual increase of distress that is associated with reduced productivity, alienation from others, and emotional exhaustion (Maslach & Leiter, 1997). In this interpretation of burnout, it is assumed that a lack of resource gain (and perhaps minor, chronic losses) follow significant investment of resources (time, energy, lost opportunities, borrowing from family time) to support one's work.

Although other parts of this chapter will discuss a variety of ways career counselors or counselors in industry can help workers experiencing occupational stress, suffice it to say here that the major and relevant career interventions can include a variety of approaches. Some of the most frequently advocated approaches to problems of occupational stress in the workplace are counselors training managers to recognize and deal with emotional stress in themselves and in their workforce; consulting about the likely consequences of change in the workplace and ways to help workers anticipate and cope with change; and helping managers and workers develop self-esteem, confidence, social relationship skills. Counselors can also provide brief therapy, solution-focused therapy, psychoeducational groups, or critical incident stress debriefing to help workers experiencing stress. Counselors can also teach communication and problem-solving skills to help workers identify and evaluate their options.

The Interaction of Work and Individual Adjustment

To an increasing degree the central role that work plays in human development is being studied across many disciplines (e.g., sociology, industrial/organizational psychology, gender studies) and settings. It has become implicit in the observations of many researchers that, certainly in highly industrialized societies, work and other aspects of identity and human development cannot be dichotomized and fragmented; the work one does, one's feeling about such work and its ability to meet individual needs for economic, social, and psychological outcomes are interwoven with one's feelings about oneself and about other aspects of life.

As discussed in Chapter 2, work serves many purposes beyond that of providing an economic livelihood. It also provides a vehicle for affiliation and friendship with coworkers, for reinforcing feelings of being part of a team, of being needed, of making a contribution to others, of being seen as a competent person. In contrast, the lack of work, of meaningful employment opportunities, can create painful social and economic conditions for individuals who are underemployed or unemployed. These conditions can lead to crime and violence, to self-destructive behavior, to behavior and physiological problems that can characterize individuals in inner cities, towns which have lost major industries, and other settings (Wilson, 1996).

One of the findings that threads through many research studies is that the anxiety and psychological distress one experiences in one aspect of life will likely affect other domains of life as well. Unhappiness or a lack of success at work is likely to be manifested in tensions and stress with one's family members, friends, and with other life roles beyond the workplace.

One of the emerging lines of research inquiry in career development is the connection and overlap between work, interpersonal relationships, social support networks, and other relational issues (Blustein, 2001). Such research has begun to identify the important relationships between the choice of work and successful transition and adjustments to the workplace and the support of family members and peers as these processes ensue (Bynner, 1998; Neff, 1985; Shellenbarger, 1999; Way & Rossman, 1996). A different but related issue is that of feminist theorists who have studied the different work styles and aspirations of males and females in the workplace and concluded that women in the workplace emphasize relatedness, human connections, closeness, and support more than do men (Gilligan, 1982b; Popcorn & Merigold, 1996). Men and women think differently: men tend to be goal-driven; women tend to be process-driven. Men tend to be single-minded; women multi-minded. In essence, research studies demonstrate that there are perceptual and cognitive differences between men and women that lead to differences in processing information, sensory discrimination, spatial relationships and other phenomena (Popcorn & Marigold, 1996). As a result of these differences, women and men contribute different assets, skills, insights to workplaces that are now in various stages of transformation as they cope with the demands of the global economy, the pervasiveness of advanced technology, and the rapidity of change in products and processes to be competitive.

In an oversimplified manner the perspectives we have been reviewing suggest that different groups of employees experience the stresses and the strains in the workplace in different ways and they respond in multiple forms. Some exhibit emotional problems, problem drinking, mental health problems, absenteeism, excessive use of sick leave, or low productivity. Others view the stresses and strains as challenges to be addressed. They turn to the use of support groups, commitments to family roles, the balancing of work and family roles, community service, hobbies and leisure opportunities as ways to approach the work place and their other life roles in more holistic ways. Certainly, counselors in the workplaces or subcontracted by them can provide assistance to help workers sort out the factors involved in the stresses and strains of the workplace and create plans of action by which they can effectively address such situations.

Therefore, for most persons, work becomes a center of intense feelings and beliefs. Neff (1985) states that there are three primary life domains—work, love, and play. In Chapter 2, we presented Neff's speculations regarding five types of inadequate or maladjusted work personalities. To these we might add several others. For example, it might be argued that the so-called *workaholic* has concentrated on work to the exclusion of love and play in his or her life. The compulsivity of work consumes this person's life; work is taken home constantly, the person feels guilty if not working, works long hours, is uneasy with leisure, cannot relax, and is unable to engage happily in any activity except work (Spruell, 1987). In contemporary workplaces, where competitive pressures and management decisions have pushed American workers to work more hours per week and per year than is true of workers in most other nations (Shellengbarger, 1999), it is increasingly difficult to determine when work ceases to be merely high career salience and becomes pathological. When does career commitment become an obsession and a compulsion? When do overwork and workaholic behavior merge and become one? Naughton (1987) suggests that the true workaholic is a person who is high in both job involvement *and* compulsive behavior. Thus, workaholism as a characteristic of committed persons would be viewed as nonpathological, whereas workaholism as a compulsion would be viewed as maladaptive behavior.

This discussion emphasizes a recurrent theme in this book—the central place of work in the lives of most adults. Consequently, the workplace becomes an environment in which both positive and negative, healthy and unhealthy, good and bad outcomes are stimulated. There are those who believe that the workplace is the proper setting for facilitating positive outcomes and preventing negative outcomes. Based on a variety of motivations, the need for career interventions in the workplace are becoming more apparent.

The Rise in Interest in Career Services

Career services in organizations have increased markedly in the last several decades. However, this has not been a linear growth starting from no such counseling programs in work organizations to a gradually evolving number of such programs. Rather it appears that the current interest in implementing counseling in the workplace is a resurgence of such interest after several decades of relatively little advancement of counseling programs in the workplaces of the United States. Indeed, "personnel counseling" in the 1930s, 1940s, and 1950s was considered to be "the cutting edge of psychology applied to the workplace" (Highhouse, 1999).

During these three decades, counseling spread rapidly through the Western Electric plants, the Bell system, AC Spark Plug Division of General Motors, Metropolitan Life Insurance, and other large corporations. For example, in 1941, the Western Electric company employed 55 counselors to cover 21,000 workers. "In 1946, 30% of large corporations had professionally trained psychologists on staff and 50% thought it was a good idea" (Highhouse, 1999, p. 324). These counselors took a number of roles in the workplace. They frequently symbolized a "positive Hawthorne effect," a positive organizational concern that could defuse worker dissatisfactions and increase productivity. Other major functions for these counselors were to respond to recruitment, absenteeism, and turnover problems, particularly during the Second World War, and in many cases to ease the transition of women into the workplace. They sometimes tried to resolve work-related issues with employees, conducted regularly scheduled interviews with employees, served as therapists—listening to both personal and work-related problems, and, in general, focused on the work adjustment of employees.

Following this aggressive growth of "personnel counseling" for several decades of the twentieth century, there followed a period of almost complete inactivity in these programs until the resurgence of interest and implementation in the 1980s and 1990s. Why the reborn or increased interest in career services? It would be pleasant to report that corporate America is motivated by humanistic concerns to let employees become all they are capable of being. In some corporations that is the case, in others it is likely that different motives prevail. Regardless of the specific motivations, however, more companies are attempting to be more supportive of their workers and of the changing demographics of the workforce as they add career services, flexible work schedules, day care centers, parental leave policies, and other mechanisms to address the needs of dual career couples, working mothers, single parents and others.

In addition, a variety of pressures external to the workplace and a growing recognition that good career management is also "good business" have led to the enhanced emphasis on career planning and development as stimulated by programs of career services. Equal employment opportunity enforcement, union bargaining for career ladders, shortages of certain specialized employees, growth in theory about the benefits of effective person-job fit, and competitive pressures on organizations have combined to cause extant, narrowly defined programs to expand or to stimulate companies into establishing initial programs of career services.

In support of such goals, many research studies reported in this chapter and elsewhere can be seen as examples of efforts to examine person-organization fit and the effects of such fit on the adjustment, tenure, productivity, and mental health of workers. The concept of person-organization fit obviously indicates that there are two entities involved in the issues of fit: the characteristics of the person and the characteristics of the organization. Some studies are concerned with what characteristics of organization are attractive to what type of personalities (e.g., Lievens, Decaesteker, Coetsier, & Geirnaert, 2001); many studies are concerned with what personalities are attracted to what occupations (e.g., Furnham, 2001); some studies are concerned with how person-organization fit varies across cultures and particularly in relation to cultures which vary in their emphasis on individualism or collectivism (e.g., Parkes, Bochner, & Schneider, 2001).

Studies of person-organization fit range widely in the particular dynamic explored. With regard to choice per se they assume that persons have alternative courses of action to choose from. They further assume that individuals' choice behaviors are based on their comparisons of their characteristics of different environments. From a career planning viewpoint this is a tricky concept because it implies that the individual knows his or her characteristics, experiences, and values accurately and comprehensively and also of the organization about which choices are being made. Further implied is the expectation that the person choosing can be "objective" rather than "subjective" about the characteristics of the organization. Such expectations are difficult to achieve even with the guidance of a career counselor who can help the prospective employee gather and analyze person and organization information objectively. As suggested previously, the outcomes of such choice processes may yield high person-organization fit or low person-organization fit. The former outcome is likely to be positive; the latter is likely to lead to stress, anxiety, perhaps low productivity, absenteeism and other negative outcomes.

Part of the problem for career counselors with notions like person-organization fit is that information related to the latter has frequently been generalized, not specific, or the emphases in choice have been focused on the personal traits of the individual rather than the culture and values of the organization in which a job being sought is located. Since stress occurs when jobs do not meet employee expectations, Maslach (quoted in Rabasca, 1999) has recommended assessing six areas with potential employees in order to be as specific about degrees of fit as possible. With the intent of helping determine whether an available position meets an employee's expectations, the six areas to be assessed include:

- Workload
- Control over one's work
- Tangible and intrinsic rewards of work
- The relationship and sense of community among co-workers
- The perception of fairness in the workplace
- The role of personal and organizational values

Obviously, these possible counseling and informational emphases can be augmented by the counselor as the attempt is made to maximize the employee's fit with job and organizational options available. For example, if the counselor is involved with a person with disabilities, there may need to be questions examined about accommodations available (job design, equipment modifications) to assist the worker with specific disabilities to be successful in the workplace; if the potential worker is a woman, questions about the availability of support groups, flexibility in work schedules, child care provisions may be relevant; for a minority group member, issues related to the availability of mentors, the proportion of minority group members employed, the record of minority group members promoted to supervisory or managerial roles in the organization may be pertinent.

In one sense, the promotion of an ideal fit between workers' expectations and the characteristics of positions they choose is not likely to be a possibility for all workers. Not all workers have free choice in the positions available to them. For a variety of reasons, many workers have to compromise between what their job could be and what is available to them to choose. For example, temporary positions are growing more rapidly than standard, full-time jobs. As we discuss in the following paragraphs, in many cases this growth in temporary jobs is pushing people into fragmented positions that do not offer security, advancement, or opportunity to use their creativity (Rabasca, 1999, p. 28). Many such persons are underemployed in relation to their ability to use a full range of their skills or to work a full schedule. This is one of the major issues associated with the changing occupational structures in many nations of the world.

Changing Occupational Structures and Career Patterns. As corporations in many sectors of the economy are engaging in organizational transformation—downsizing the number of permanent employees, increasing the use of advanced technology to speed up their production and distribution processes, changing the skills required to do the work available, merging with other companies domestically or internationally—the ultimate impact is on the number and types of employees to be recruited and retained.

Handy (1994), a British scholar of management and organizational development, has suggested that the changing structure of the workforces in firms in Europe and North America can be conceived of as consisting of three concentric rings: in the center is the smallest ring and it includes the permanent workforce needed by employers to do the critical tasks required in a particular work organization. These permanent employees are likely to be provided relatively long-term security, excellent health benefits and income, continuing education, and other support systems.

A second ring compromises contingent workers, part-time workers whose skills are purchased for limited amounts of time to do a specific type of work (e.g., retail work during the winter holiday season; seasonal farm work or construction). Such contingent workers are unlikely to have either institutional identity or health and pension benefits. They frequently have several part-time jobs but no long-term institutional identity.

The third ring of workers consists of those who work for specialty firms that do outsourcing—provide services that employers traditionally had provided in-house with a permanent workforce but now find it less expensive to provide through subcontracts with firms that specialize in needed functions (e.g., security, food services, custodial, advertising, marketing, legal services). Such workers may also be temporary workers who are paid by the outsourcing firm and assigned to the particular contractor for a specific work role.

While each of these three groups of workers need career planning, the only one of the three groups likely to receive it from their employer is the permanent work group in the inside ring of Handy's three circles. The other two groups if they receive any career counseling or planning help are likely to get it from government agencies such as the U.S. Employment Service or the one-stop job centers available in specific areas of the nation.

As different groups of workers vary in their needs for help with career planning, one overarching issue seems to be preeminent: workplaces, in general, are no longer assuming responsibility for their workers' career development. While more corporations and workplaces are clarifying and acting on their responsibilities to inform workers about open vacancies, changing career ladders and opportunities for advancement within the firm, or educational or training opportunities to strengthen one's skills, these same corporations are expecting workers to assume responsibility for the management of their own careers. This means, among other things, that workers must know what skills they have and what they need to have as workplace expectations change; they need to know which of their skills are elastic, transportable to other jobs in which they are useful; they must be able to assume responsibility for gaining new competencies and skills demanded by changing workplace practice and procedures; and they must learn to be psychologically and personally flexible in order to effectively cope with the career transitions they will encounter through their working life. As suggested elsewhere in this book, these types of responsibility for one's own career development are elements of what other authors have defined as "protean careers" (Hall et al., 1996) or "new careers" (Arnold & Jackson, 1997) in which personal flexibility and the ability to anticipate and act on changing conditions in the workplace are the rule, not the exception, for a growing proportion of workers. Because of the rapidly changing workplace structures, contingent workers, pervasiveness of technological applications in the workplace, and the increase of knowledge workers, these observers and others are forecasting a continuing reduction in traditional organizational careers. In contrast to such traditional career patterns, where loyalty, identity, stability, subordination of individual desires to organizational control of workers and to institutional criteria of success, the protean career is defined differently. It is seen as a career that is driven more by the individual than by the organization. It calls "for frequent change and self-invention and... [is] propelled by the desire for psychological success rather than by externally determined measures of success" (p. xi). In addition:

> *The protean career encompasses any kind of flexible, idiosyncratic career course, with peaks and valleys, left turns, moves from one line of work to another, and so forth. Rather than focusing outward on some ideal generalized career "path," the protean career is unique to each person—a sort of career fingerprint. (p. 21)*

The protean concept provides a different way of thinking about the relationship between the organization and employee: "in the protean career, the person is figure and the organization is ground. Organizations provide a context, a medium in which individuals pursue their personal aspirations" (Hall & Mirvis, 1996, p. 21). To pursue a protean career, individuals will need to be highly adaptable and flexible, possess a depth and variety of skills desired by employers, and have varied work experience as well as a clear sense of self-identity, autonomy, and personal direction so that they are able to self-design much of their personal and career development. They will also need skills in self-assessment and identity exploration, and a commitment to learning how to learn and to continuous learning.

These notions of the individual requirements for a protean career reflect both the changing nature of work organizations and of technology. The argument is that because the life cycle of technologies and products is so shortened, personal mastery cycles related to these processes and products are also shortened. Therefore, "people's careers increasingly will become a succession of 'ministages' (or short-cycle learning stages) exploration-trial-mastery-exit as they move in and out of various product areas, technologies, functions, organizations, and other work environments" (Hall & Mirvis, 1996, p. 33). Further:

> *this protean form of career involves horizontal growth, expanding one's range of competencies and ways of connecting to work and other people, as opposed to the more traditional vertical growth of success (upward mobility). In the protean form of growth, the goal is learning, psychological success, and expansion of the identity. In the more traditional vertical form, the goal was advancement, success, and esteem in the eyes of others, and power (p. 35).*

To make such a protean career possible, the work environments that employ such individuals will need to offer opportunities to develop them and to care for them; the work environments will also need to provide meaningful and challenging work that is combined with fairness, good pay and benefits, support, and efforts to meet the needs of the whole person.

The types of work environments in which persons pursuing protean careers will flourish will likely provide career services different from those traditionally related to organizational careers.

In fact, there have been relatively few attempts to identify what is new about career counseling for protean or new careers. One such framework for career self-management has been offered by King (2001) in Great Britain. In this perspective, King argues that adults need to learn how to self-manage their careers throughout their working lives and that such self-management needs to be dynamic and recursive, taking into account important aspects of the client's immediate social context, and the political nature of decisions about careers. In particular, King argues that career self-management should consist of four steps. In paraphrased form, they are:

1. Charting the institutional landscape of the institution or institutions of which the person is a part, or which they are exploring as a possible choice. This step is "essentially a process of intelligence-gathering whereby people acquire understanding of two aspects: opportunity awareness...understanding of the world of work, the opportunities if offers, the demands those opportunities make, and the rewards and satisfactions they offer (p. 68).... Individual mobility within an organization depends not only on the opportunities available, but also on the information available to and criteria used by those who decide who is eligible for such opportunities. Thus people need to be aware of who the key decision makers are within their organization or institution, and who these individuals are connected to and influenced by." (p. 68)

2. Identify gatekeepers who are responsible for the decisions that affect one's career outcome. People need to identify the criteria used by gatekeepers to make decisions about hiring, promotion, work allocation, or whatever other outcomes are personally important. "Also important is this step in understanding the value of one's current human and social capital and the degree to which it fits with gatekeepers' criteria" (p. 69). In this step, individuals can come to better understanding of the human and social capital they need to achieve their career goals, and whether further effort is needed to acquire such capital.
3. Implementing career strategies. These can be divided into two broad types of strategies: influence and positioning strategies. "Positioning strategies are concerned with optimizing one's contacts, skills and experience in order to maximize one's chance of achieving career outcomes. Influence strategies are concerned with actively attempting to influence the decisions of gatekeepers who control those desired outcomes" (p. 70). Influence strategies include self-promotion, ingratiation, upward influence tactics. Positioning strategies include active network development, strategic investment in human capital, and job content innovation.
4. Evaluating outcomes include two judgments: whether the strategies used were deployed effectively, and whether the strategies used actually constituted an effective route to achieving the desired ends.

Counselors can help clients with each of the four steps, and particularly the last step. They can help clients to identify and evaluate the effectiveness of career strategies they have used in the past and consider their effectiveness, execution, and contingency or means-end relationships.

The procedures suggested by Hall and Associates (1996) or King (2001) may seem utopian, but variations of them are being implemented in several of the most progressive of America's corporations and government agencies (such as General Electric, AT&T, Aetna, Xerox, National Aeronautics and Space Administration, and Government Accounting Office), and other firms are now following their lead. The implementing corporations and agencies have provided assessment centers, career resource centers, and computer-assisted career guidance programs or directories listing all of the education and training opportunities available in the corporation or agency as well as information on, for example, career ladders and requirements for specific jobs and for mobility to supervisory roles. Frequently these companies and government organizations provide career specialists to assist employees with their questions concerning career change and career mobility, work adjustment, and other issues. Certainly such provisions are uneven. Not every employer understands or implements such perspectives, and in many situations workers continue to experience less than enlightened personnel procedures. Even in the most progressive organizations and corporations, changes in management, in supervision, and in views of workers require time, reconfiguration of resources, and new information and support system for workers and supervisors alike. It is in such environments that the roles of counselors, counseling psychologists, and specialists in employer assistance become increasingly important.

Leibowitz, Farren, and Kaye (1986), for example, contended that a major change is taking place as the focus shifts from career planning programs for individual employees to the broader area of career development within organizations (p. xiii). Such programs are vital, in the authors' judgment, in order to provide "an organized, formalized, planned effort to achieve a balance between the individual's career needs and the organization's workforce requirements" (p. 4). But such programs can also provide mechanisms to support changes in business organizations that are fluid and developing.

Whether in contemporary or futuristic terms, counselors in business and industry can anticipate involvement in a wide range of activities that fall under the rubric of career but tend to push the limits of such a term beyond its traditional meaning. These counselors are likely to be involved in such services as advisement and support for external training, alcohol/drug counseling, retirement planning, leading or initiating support groups for minorities and women in particular work specialties (e.g., in engineering), job separation or outplacement counseling, career exploration and examination of available career ladders, teaching of interviewing or advancement strategies, leading seminars on preparing for supervision or dealing with financial issues, family/marital counseling, working with training specialists to design specific training for groups of workers, coaching middle level managers about ways to facilitate the career development of those whom they supervise, career planning workshops, and development of formal mentorship programs.

As suggested here, work life is basically an arena in which various types of conflict are likely to occur at all occupational levels. The solution to many conflicts in the workplace is probably best applied in the setting in which they occur. Safety and health hazards and hazards stemming from threatening interactions on the job (such as police work) can be addressed in the setting from which they arise. Factors such as work overload, work underload, working conditions, changing causes of stress throughout an individual's work life, supervision problems, role ambiguity and conflict, and other problems of work may be addressed in-house, by employee assistance programs, or by counselors in independent practice.

We may conclude that there is increasing excitement about the prospects of career development programs within organizations. At the same time, such programs are typically neither comprehensive nor common, and several issues and problems require resolution.

A Lexicon of Workplace Terminology

Within large organizations, there are a number of terms that require definition, either because they are used differently from standard usage within the counseling profession or because they are unfamiliar to counselors.

Human resources management is an organizational aspect of institutions that includes such activities as training, education, appraisal, recruitment, selection, career development, succession planning, workforce planning, employee assistance programs, job enrichment, and organizational staffing (Vetter, 1985).

Human resources development has to do with how new employees are oriented to their jobs, to the cultures of the workplace, and to their contributions to the mission of the enterprise. In addition, it includes this type of employer-provided training for new entrants to the workplace or for older employees whose job responsibilities are changing. At issue in any particular work setting are the human resource development processes and systems provided, the mentoring and information available to employees, the incentives to engage in life-long learning or other mechanisms to improve their competencies (Gray & Herr, 1998). Bowen and Greiner (1986) suggest that the human resources function is viewed, at least in theory, as essential to successful management in a "high-tech," services-based, global economy. In practice, managers often complain that the human resources function does not provide needed assistance, uses esoteric techniques, is out-of-touch and paper-ridden, and is too costly. This description does not sound too different from the way administrators frequently describe school guidance or college student personnel functions. *Human resources management* and *human resources development* are umbrella terms and usually consist of organizational development, training, personnel, and career development.

It can be argued that these are each areas about which human resource management can provide leadership and coordination. However, for successful outcomes to occur, managers must view workers as persons who do not leave their family or personal problems at the door when they enter the factory or office nor do they leave their problems on the job when they go home. Workers must also be seen as persons whose productivity and purpose ebb and flow as they experience personal transitions such as divorce, loss, or parenthood. Thus, as workers are perceived in holistic terms and as corporate resources to be nurtured, not consumed and tossed away, then employee assistance programs, human resource development, human resources management and career development services become viable parts of corporate strategy.

Employee assistance programs (EAPs), according to Lewis and Lewis (1986), are concerned with the potential and real productivity losses involved with the mental and physical health of workers (for example, stress, alcoholism, chemical dependency, family conflicts, interpersonal difficulties, or financial pressures). EAPs began in response to employee alcohol problems. They have now expanded to deal with other forms of employee or family problems. Presumably, these programs reduce absenteeism and the incidence of accidents and increase productivity. The number of EAPs continues to grow.

Most studies of the effectiveness of EAPs originate with management and are conducted by those who provide the services. Few studies are conducted by third-party, independent evaluators. Most of these studies, not surprisingly, demonstrate that an EAP has value to the organization (few concentrate on value to the employee). Kurtz, Googins, and Howard (1984) argue that if adequate research and evaluations are to be accomplished, evaluators need to concentrate on single concerns (such as alcoholism, wellness, counseling) rather than all concerns at once because so many independent variables attenuate results. Furthermore, the criterion measure of success is nebulous. Does it mean percentage of employees using the service? Does it mean productivity increase? Does it mean service provided? In addition, it is difficult to know what part of changes to attribute to EAP interventions and what part to associate with other aspects in an individual's life. Thus, lack of sophisticated design in evaluations and nebulous outcome measures make most evaluations of EAPs suspect.

All of these weaknesses in demonstrating the effectiveness of EAPs notwithstanding, we regard the activities of EAPs as important and as appropriate for career counselors in the workplace—provided that they have the necessary preparation to confront the wide range of presenting problems. In all, they address the symbiotic nature of work, family, and self-roles and can be approached from both a preventive and a remedial orientation. The object of EAPs, then, is to provide people who are having problems on and off the job with a place to go when they are having difficulties in order that their work will be more effective.

Career development within organizations is a recent concept in terms of popularity, although it has existed to some degree for a long time. There has always been informal career counseling, provisions of occupational information, assessments of varying sophistication, training of supervisors for career coaching, engaging in outplacement and pre-retirement activities, and consulting in the upper-level management.

Lewis and Lewis (1986) view career development programs as focused within the organization's human resource management and development area to help workers make and implement career decisions. Derr (1986) views career development as a set of activities and resources that a company provides to help its employees to achieve their career objectives (career enhancement), coupled with the organization's own attempts to recruit, develop, and move its employees according to its own short-term and long-term human resource needs (career management).

Just as with EAPs, career development programs allegedly bring about better retention and communication and lead to workers who are more motivated, loyal, and productive; whose lives are enriched; and who achieve a host of other positive outcomes. Unfortunately, research studies to validate such outcomes are quite rare.

OVERVIEW OF CAREER DEVELOPMENT FUNCTIONS

Career-related functions performed within organizations vary from setting to setting. They also change according to who is performing the role of career helper—career development specialist, supervisor, consultant. One of the most comprehensive listings of career functions in industry is provided by Leibowitz and Schlossberg (1981) and is reproduced in Table 11.1. Their perspective is that of how a manager or supervisor can perform a career-helping role. There is a potential problem, of course, when the person who evaluates work performance is also the person who serves as the counselor. Although some people maintain that the task is not only possible, but also desirable (Meckel, 1981), there is clear potential for role conflict and employee suspicion in these dual relationships.

Ballantine (1993), as a result of his work in British police organizations, underscores the need for individual and organizational perspectives to be relatively consonant. The normative, nomothetic dimension of sociology and the idiographic, individual focus of psychology need to be reconciled in the delivery of career interventions within organizations. In their research, O'Reilly, Chatman, and Caldwell (1991) offer empirical evidence of Ballantine's observation, finding that the greater the fit between individual and organization, the higher the job satisfaction and the less the turnover.

On the level of the functions of a *career counselor* in industry (or the career development specialist as opposed to a supervisor or manager), the literature is less instructive. One article (Merman & McLaughlin, 1982) suggests 11 counselor activities to achieve a like number of desired outcomes. The work is presented in Table 11.2 in adapted form.

TABLE 11.1 Roles and Associated Questionnaire Items

COMMUNICATOR
- Holds formal and informal discussions with employees
- Listens to and understands an employee's real concern
- Clearly and effectively interacts with an employee
- Establishes environment for open interaction
- Structures uninterrupted time to meet with employees

COUNSELOR
- Helps employees identify career-related skills, interests, values
- Helps an employee identify a variety of career options
- Helps employee evaluate appropriateness of various options
- Helps employee design/plan strategy to achieve an agreed-on career goal

APPRAISER
- Identifies critical job elements
- Negotiates with employee a set of goals and objectives to evaluate performance
- Assesses employee performance related to goals and objectives
- Communicates performance evaluation and assessment to employee
- Designs a development plan around future job goals and objectives
- Reinforces effective job performance
- Reviews an established development plan on an ongoing basis

COACH
- Teaches specific job-related or technical skills
- Reinforces effective performance
- Suggests specific behaviors for improvement
- Clarifies and communicates goals and objectives of work group and organization

MENTOR
- Arranges for an employee to participate in a high-visibility activity either inside or outside the organization
- Serves as a role model in an employee's career development by demonstrating successful career behaviors
- Supports employee by communicating to others in and out of the organization employee's effectiveness

ADVISOR
- Communicates the informal and formal realities of progression in the organization
- Suggests appropriate training activities that could benefit employee
- Suggests appropriate strategies for career advancement

BROKER
- Assists in bringing employees together who might mutually help each other in their careers
- Assists in linking employees with appropriate educational or employment opportunities
- Helps employee identify obstacles to changing present situation
- Helps employee identify resources enabling a career development change

REFERRAL AGENT
- Identifies employees with problems (e.g., career, personal, health)
- Identifies resources appropriate to an employee experiencing a problem
- Bridges and supports employee with referral agents
- Follows up on effectiveness of suggested referral agents

ADVOCATE
- Works with employee in designing a plan for redress of a specific issue for higher levels of management
- Works with employee in planning alternative strategies if a redress to management is not successful
- Represents employee's concert to higher-level management for redress on specific issues

TABLE 11.2 Suggested Counselor Functions in Industry

ROLE	EMPLOYEE OR ORGANIZATION OUTCOME
1. Advisor or Information-giver	Acquiring needed information to make informed choices
2. Teacher/Facilitator	Developing of skills needed for present and/or future positions
3. Process consultant	Improving of self-concept through awareness of goals, values, strengths, and weaknesses
4. Strategic planner	Taking personal responsibility to manage one's own career and market self for internal or external career opportunities (e.g., motivation, assertiveness, marketing, career management, and job search)
5. Consultant to organization	Making organization responsive to employee needs for career development
6. Creator and Enabler	Taking responsibility for complete control of own career (e.g., providing situations for employees to learn in a nonthreatening atmosphere)
7. Facilitator/Teacher (see #2)	Becoming an active problem solver and understanding and developing process skills
8. Integrator	Developing trust that the organization understands his or her needs, including the effect of career changes on personal lifestyles
9. Consultant/Mediator	Coordinating personal needs and organizational mission
10. Facilitator/Philosopher/Futurist	Participating in helping the organization identify the effect of current issues, trends, and social values
11. Manager of a system/Conceptualizer	Organization develops an appropriate and evolving career management system using emerging technologies

As the organization and the mechanisms by which work is produced changes, the roles of career counselors, counseling psychologists and other career helpers also change. The examples of counselor function just identified continue to expand and to take on new applications.

There are many challenges in the contemporary workplace that affect workers and which bring the world of business and psychology closer together. Many of these challenges have been discussed earlier in this chapter and in various places throughout this book. One of these is the nature of career itself. Traditionally, the term career was often used to describe the processes and stages workers went through within one occupation or job through their working life. Now persons are unlikely to commit themselves to one firm or one job for a long period of time. Rather, they are likely to have many jobs and engage in multiple career paths and transitions as their career unfolds. In such cases, career management has shifted from the workplace to the individual worker, from paternalism and dependency to the worker's entrepreneurial management of his or her career, from stability to personal flexibility. As suggested earlier in the chapter, work organizations have transformed themselves, downsized, and changed their missions; they also have induced stress for workers in various forms: the need to do more with less; the rapidly changing and expanding use of technology which sometimes surpasses human capability to cope with its volume and comprehensive output; the need to work in teams and rely on others. To these challenges, one can add those of women and minorities, two-career couples, single parents, and other groups of workers for whom work and other life roles may sometimes be in conflict.

Each of these challenges in the workplace broadens the function that counselors can play within the workplace or as a subcontractor to employers. In many of these circumstances, change and associated emotional stress in workers are beyond the training that managers have and counselor functions include dealing with workers who are experiencing behavioral, emotional, and psychological reactions. In some cases, counselors' functions may include training managers to understand where worker stress comes from and how to alleviate it. Increasingly, counselors in business and industry are providing brief or solution-focused therapy and/or psychoeducational methods to workers experiencing role conflict, stress, and other problem behavior. They also frequently teach workers how to use communication and problem-solving skills in the workplace to address ineffective interpersonal relationships and other workplace problems.

Clearly, counselors as well as counseling psychologists have roles to play in such areas as:

- Educating first-line supervisors and managers to current perspectives on job satisfaction, work motivation, and work performance
- Providing information to workers about career paths, career ladders, and the avenues and requirements for mobility within the organization
- Classifying workers with respect to their technical skills and their psychological needs in an attempt to maximize person-job fit with regard to content, supervisory style, and related factors
- Conducting workshops and seminars for workers designed to increase their understanding of their educational opportunities, their employability skills, and their understanding of the organizational characteristics with which they interact
- Consulting with managers about job redesign and work enrichment schemes
- Providing support groups for workers in various types of transitions (e.g., new jobs, geographical relocations, overseas travel, shifting family structures)
- Providing individual counseling about work behavior and career development

It seems clear that while these perspectives in the role of career helpers of various kinds in work settings are useful markers, potential changes in the organization of work are spawning a much wider array of career planning and career management services for employers. In one large scale survey of career development services within Canadian work organizations, Bernes and Magnusson (1996) reported that the key goals for these services were to promote job satisfaction, enhance employee productivity, reduce employee turnover, and increase employee motivation. They found that the array of services available in the 30 organizations, with 1,000 to 18,000 employees, could be classified into three major emphases: career planning, career management, and life planning. As portrayed in Table 11.3, the listing of services provided under each of the three emphases was wide-ranging suggesting a myriad of services in which counselors in business and industry could be involved.

While none of the thirty organizations studied had most of the career development services listed in Table 11.3, the services provided suggest that in some organizations the career development services provided are primarily focused on the needs of the organizations, typically termed *career management services.* In some organizations, career services are primarily directed to individual needs as reflected in terms such as *career planning* or *life planning* or related terms (e.g., career development). In some organizations, there is an integration of career services that meet the needs of both individuals and organizations. In many situations, the provision of career services in work organizations are intended to negotiate the tension that exists between the individual workers needs, goals, and aspirations, on the one hand, and the organizations needs and requirements on the others. Sometimes this tension is reflected in distrust or adversarial relations between workers and managers, paternalism and authoritarian behavior toward workers by managers, benign neglect of the career needs of workers, or other manifestations of a lack of understanding of or support for the provision of a comprehensive approach to career services.

Both in contemporary and futuristic terms, counselors in business and industry can expect to be involved in a wide range of activities that fall under the rubric of career but which push the limits of that term beyond its traditional meaning. These counselors are likely to be involved in such services as advisement and support for external training, alcohol/drug counseling, retirement planning, leading or initiating support groups for minorities in particular work specialties where they are traditionally underrepresented (e.g., engineering), job separation or outplacement counseling, career exploration and examination of available career ladders and lattices by which internal mobility in a firm can be characterized, teaching of interviewing or advancement strategies, leading seminars on helping workers prepare to become supervisors or to deal with budgeting and family issues, the provision

TABLE 11.3 Career Planning, Career Management, and Life Planning Services Investigated by Bernes and Magnusson

CAREER PLANNING
Informal counseling by personnel staff
Career counseling by supervisors
Job performance and development planning
Career exploration groups
Psychological testing and assessment
Career support groups
Testing and feedback regarding aptitudes, interests, etc.
Referrals of external counselors and resources
Training of supervisors in career counseling
Career counseling by specialized staff counselors
Individual self-analysis and planning workbooks
Assessment centers for career development purposes
Career planning workshops
Informal mentorship programs
Formal mentorship program
Teaching of advancement strategies

CAREER MANAGEMENT
Performance appraisal: planning and review
Promotion and transfer procedures
Educational assistance programs
External training and development programs
Designed training programs
Management succession and replacement planning
Communication of equal employment opportunity and affirmative action plans and policies
Recruitment procedures
Personnel information system
Job description and job evaluation
Manpower forecasting
Skill inventories
Job rotational programs
Flexible working arrangements (work at home, 4-day work week, etc.)
Communication on training and development options
Communication on job requirements
Communication on career paths or ladders
Job posting and communication on job vacancies
New employee orientation programs
Job redesign

LIFE PLANNING
Personal financial planning
Family/marital counseling
Alcohol/drug counseling
Workshops and communications on retirement preparation
Interpersonal skills training
Time management
Stress management
Weight control
Nutrition
Fitness
First aid
Preventive health care
Safety
Smoking cessation
Formal employee assistance program

of family/mental health counseling, working with training specialists to design specific training for groups of workers, coaching middle-level managers about ways to facilitate the career development of those whom they supervise, career planning workshops, and development of formed mentorship programs. Obviously, counselors in business and industry will have comprehensive roles to play in some organizations and limited roles in others. Regardless, they will need to understand and use the language of work relevant to their firm and its various processes and table of organization. But such counselors will also need to understand the dynamics of adult career development as it pertains to different groups (e.g., professional, skilled support staff employees, contingent workers, temporarily assigned subcontracted (outsource) workers, males, females, persons with disabilities, immigrant workers). These counselors will need to know how to design and implement career programs for their firm's employees as defined by the firm's commitment to such services. These counselors will need to have the skills associated with the provision of individual and group counseling, consultation, training and the management of career services.

Counselors in business and industry will need to be able to use various combinations of career development tools. Adapted from the five original categories of such tools classified by Gutteridge (1986), the content within them continue to expand. These categories in paraphrased and expanded form, with selected examples, include:

1. *Self assessment tools* (e.g., career workbooks, self-directed interest or ability evaluation)
2. *Individual counseling* (e.g., by personnel staff, managers, professional career or employee assistance counselors, outplacement specialists)
3. *Internal labor market information/placement exchanges* (e.g., systems of job posting, information on career ladders/career paths/career lattices, exploration and planning, career resources center, computerized career information or guidance systems, company newsletter, Internet, Intranet)
4. *Organizational potential assessment* (e.g., assessment centers, replacement/succession planning, psychological testing, career or vocational testing, classifying workers with respect to their technical skills and their psychological needs in an attempt to maximize person-job fit with regard to job content, supervisory style, and related factors)
5. *Developmental programs* (e.g., job rotation, workshops on topics related to human resource development, supervisor training, seminars on the use of educational benefits, support groups for selected employees)
6. *Consultation* (e.g., educating first-line supervisors and managers to current perspectives on job satisfaction, work motivation and work performance; consulting with managers about job design and work enrichment schemes)
7. *Promoting wellness* (e.g., counseling or training about self-help and self-care, stress reduction and management, exercise and leisure)

Organizational Career Patterns

When a concept such as person-environment fit is considered in career counseling, the paradigm has many possible applications. In its simplest form, person-environment fit models make two basic assumptions: (1) that human behavior is a function of the person and the environment, and (2) that the person and the environment need to be compatible (Kristof, 1996). In similar fashion, a major tenet of Holland's theory of vocational choice (1997) is that of congruence which suggests an individual's vocational satisfaction, stability and achievement depends on congruence (fit) between the individual's personality and the environment in which the individual works. While each of these constructs is important, there are also emerging issues that extend these perspectives. For example, Schneider (1996) has argued that research in person-fit studies has focused on outcomes of behavior as correlates of personality and have given us relatively little insight into the behavior that intervenes between the personality and the outcome. The assumption is that persons with different personalities express different behaviors, not just one. However, little attention has been given to the fact that behavior, not personality, causes outcomes. Therefore, there is a need to demonstrate clearly the relative contribution of personality to behavior and the relative contribution of behavior to outcome. A further issue related to person-environment fit and congruence relates to the discussion in this chapter and elsewhere in the book about the organizational changes that are affecting the narrowness or breadth of jobs and their propensity to form and reform as organizational changes take place. One implication of this notion is that in the organizational careers that are unfolding, performance criteria for specific jobs become harder to identify and pin down, these ideas of simple personality-fit will become less useful as individuals may fit a larger range of environment in a variety of ways (Nicholson, 1996).

In essence, the career counselor and the worker are concerned about the workers' attributes (e.g., interest, skills, values, personality traits, behaviors, and self-identity) as well as the culture that particular work environments express or reinforce. Some workers thrive in some environments and not in others. A basic premise of Holland's theory is that persons of different personality types (e.g., Realistic, Investigative, Social, Artistic, Enterprising, and Conventional) seek environments in which other workers share their values, interest, etc., in essence have similar personality profiles as they do. In this sense, persons with realistic personality profiles seek environments that can be described as realistic and, as such, are occupied primarily by workers who share such predispositions. This concept of fit is used extensively as the basis for many career counseling interventions (Spokane, Meir, & Catalano, 2000).

One of the aspects of environments which has not received major attention in the counseling literature is that of organizational career patterns or stages. The types of career patterns that are possible for individuals in organizations seem to depend on the type of management espoused by the organizations and by the career stages which workplaces impose on its employees.

A specific model of career stages is provided by London and Stumpf (1982). Using Buehler's original categories as adapted by Super (described earlier in this book), they offer developmental requirements associated with mastery of each adult career stage:

Stage I: Exploration and Trial (for example, taking a job offer, experiencing training and job challenges, setting goals, getting feedback)

Stage II: Establishment and Advancement (for example, developing expertise, experiencing success or failure, reinforcing self-image, forming a career strategy, finding a mentor)

Stage III: Midcareer

A. *Growth* (for example, evaluating goals, fearing stagnation, adjusting career direction, needing change, working through midlife crises)

B. *Maintenance* (for example, realizing the value of job security, fearing the risk of change, expressing loyalty to the organization, having a feeling of pride in professional accomplishments, becoming a mentor)

C. *Decline* (for example, sensing failure, insecurity, and crisis, anticipating early retirement with few plans, disengaging from work and nonwork prematurely, developing physical or mental illness)

Stage IV: Disengagement (for example, psychologically preparing for retirement, finding new interests and sources of self-improvement, learning to accept a reduced role)

Another delineation of the normal course of careers in organizations is provided by Schein (1978). He divides the career life cycle into four stages: entry, socialization, midcareer, and late career.

Entry Stage Tasks

1. Making a preliminary occupational choice that determines the kind of education and training to pursue
2. Developing a viable "dream"—an image of the occupation or organization that can serve as the outlet for one's talents, values, and ambitions
3. Preparing oneself for the early career through "anticipatory socialization," to develop what one considers to be the attitudes and values necessary for succeeding in one's chosen occupation
4. Facing the realities of finding a first job

Socialization Stage Tasks

1. Accepting the reality of human organization (e.g., dealing with people, communicating)
2. Dealing with resistance to change
3. Learning how to work; coping with too much or too little organization and too much or too little job definition
4. Dealing with the boss and deciphering the reward system—learning how to get ahead
5. Locating one's place in the organization and developing an identity

Midcareer Stage Tasks

1. Finding career anchors (a "career anchor" is an occupational self-concept resulting from self-perceived talents and abilities, self-perceived motives and needs, and self-perceived attitudes and values—in short, the pattern of self-perceived talents, motives, and values to guide, constrain, stabilize, and integrate the person's career). Five career anchors have been identified; four others are hypothesized. (A tenth career anchor, *warrior,* has been identified among army personnel [Derr, 1980]. Warriors have a basic psychological need for high adventure and action).
   a. Technical/functional competence
   b. Managerial competence
   c. Security and stability
   d. Autonomy
   e. Creativity
   f. Basic identity
   g. Service to others
   h. Power, influence, and control
   i. Variety
2. Specializing versus generalizing

Late-Career Stage Tasks

1. Becoming a mentor
2. Achieving a proper balance of involvement in work, family, and self-development
3. Letting go and retiring

Another attempt at defining career stages within organizations is that of Thompson, Baker, and Smallwood (1986). They see four stages occurring, as outlined in Table 11.4.

Each of these attempts at defining the course of careers within organizations as well as other attempts to describe the work life cycle potentially provides a theoretical base for in-house career development programs.

These outlines of organizational careers also provide taxonomic structures suggesting where individual problems may arise (e.g., early in the organizational career while learning performance tasks or adapting to the organizational culture; in midcareer as change occurs in how work is done, in the rapid incorporation of technologies into the work place, in feelings of vulnerability or growing inability to learn new techniques). In some of these organizational career stages, original person-environment fit or congruence may deteriorate in the face of change or objective fit may still be present but subjective fit, the individual worker's perception of their competencies or the environments expectations may distort actuality and create a career problem for the individual (Edwards & Rothbard, 1999).

TABLE 11.4 Characteristics of Career Stages

STAGE I

Works under the supervision and direction of a more senior professional in the field
Work is never entirely his or her own, but assignments are given that are a portion of a larger project or activity being overseen by a senior professional
Lacks experience and status in organization
Is expected to accept supervision and direction willingly
Is expected to do more of the detailed and routine work on a project
Is expected to exercise "directed" creativity and initiative
Learns to perform well under pressure and accomplish a task within the time budgeted

STAGE II

Goes into depth in one problem or technical area
Assumes responsibility for a definable portion of the project, process, or clients
Works independently and produces significant results
Develops credibility and a reputation
Relies less on supervisor or mentor for answers, develops more of his or her own resources to solve problems
Increases in confidence and ability

STAGE III

Is involved enough in his or her own work to make significant technical contributions but begins working in more than one area
Greater breadth of technical skills and application of those skills
Stimulates others through ideas and information
Involved in developing people in one or more of the following ways:
Acts as an idea leader for a small group
Serves as a mentor to younger professionals
Assumes a formal supervisory position
Deals with the outside to benefit others in organizations—i.e., works out of relationships with client organizations, develops new business

STAGE IV

Provides direction for the organization by:
"Mapping" the organization's environment to highlight opportunities and dangers
Focusing activities in areas of "distinctive competence"
Managing the process by which decisions are made
Exercises formal and informal power to:
Initiate action and influence decisions
Obtain resources and approvals
Represents the organization:
To individuals and groups at different levels inside the organization
To individuals and institutions outside the organization
Sponsors promising individuals to test and prepare them for key roles in the organization

Source: Reprinted from "Improving professional development by applying four-stage career model" by Paul H. Thompson from *Organizational Dynamics,* Autumn 1986 (15), pp. 49–62.

SELECTED FUNCTIONS OF CAREER DEVELOPMENT SPECIALISTS

Table 11.3 has illustrated there are many forms of career intervention being provided across work organizations. There are also many work organizations that provide no career planning assistance, preferring to see that as the worker's responsibility or the domain of the public employment system. Certainly, it is true that many workplaces may not be ready to employ career counselors or counseling psychologists and, if they do, the nature of the work involved may be different from classic notions of career counseling. In this chapter, we have tried to illustrate the range of potential or actual counselor functions in work organizations. There are some possibilities that are discussed in the following sections.

Although there is clearly interest in career development in the workplace, one would do well to heed Dorn's (1986) caution that industry may not be ready to employ traditionally trained counselors and that the nature of the work may be different from classic notions of career counseling. Up to this point, the reader must surely have picked up on the fact that career development as used in the workplace is a substantially different term from the more historical usage employed in other parts of this book. Nevertheless, some possible functions are identifiable. A discussion of a number of functions selected from a larger possible universe follows.

Working with Plateaued Workers

A number of organizations have attempted to intervene in the career development of so-called plateaued workers—those who have little or no prospect of continued vertical growth in an organization. These are usually competent individuals who, largely because of the pyramidal structure of many organizations, will simply not be promoted. This situation can be a function of outsourcing specific corporate activities to other firms, corporate managers, changing workforce demographics, economic competitiveness, or a host of other factors. This situation can lead to productive plateaued workers or to unproductive plateaued workers. Hall (1985) has suggested a number of possibilities to counter and assuage what could be a dysfunctional way of coping by the plateaued worker: for example, moving the mature professional to a different kind of work that places a premium on experience and is more generalized than the specialized work currently performed. To achieve this end, organizations could create more project-type jobs, periodically rotate technical specialists, allow temporary moves as well as downward moves, provide internal consulting projects, facilitate job switches, lend employees to other departments within the organization, use job redesign and training, and allow for second career chances. Each of these possibilities can become a career problem for the employee involved.

Dual paths have been created by many companies to try to address the issue of plateauing. For example, technical employees are provided with compensation and advancement opportunities comparable to those of management, thus creating alternatives to plateauing. Stout, Slocum, and Cron's longitudinal three-year study (1988) of 122 plateaued and nonplateaued salespeople indicated that, as one might expect, plateaued workers developed less commitment to the organization, a greater inclination to leave the organization, and a lesser concern with specific career issues. Some workers, however, were self-plateaued for reasons of self-satisfaction with current status and a sense of security.

The problem of midcareer boredom and dead-end prospects is not new, of course. The maintenance stage of careers, as lengthy as it is, offers a petri dish in which can grow all sorts of inimical as well as beneficial organisms that affect the health of a worker's career development. At some point in their careers, a large number of workers become emotionally desensitized to their work. Morgan, Patton, and Baker (1985) offer a number of suggestions to assist the midlife employee. The first step in combating the midcareer blues and blahs is creating an awareness program to sensitize individuals to the possibility of the problem and to provide information and professional counseling to prevent the occurrence. In terms of remedial activity, an organization can provide continuing education and opportunities for retraining to change jobs or careers, allow voluntary reductions of pay and responsibilities, develop a mentoring program, offer more autonomy and independence, provide support groups, and give sabbaticals for selected employees.

As was discussed under "protean careers" or "new careers" earlier in this chapter and elsewhere in the book, plateauing, lateral moves, and downward moves are becoming much more common in today's work world as slower corporate growth and population demographics combine to have their effects. The task for career helpers in the workplace is to provide the necessary assistance to ensure that plateaued or demoted workers remain both productive employees and mentally healthy individuals.

Training and Education Programs

Another aspect of the role of the career development specialist in the workplace is that of providing education and training programs. These programs can range from training in supervisory and management skills, to technical and communication skills, to new employee orientation programs, to training in performance appraisal, leadership training, word processing, interpersonal skills, time management, hiring and selection, and stress management, among others. Training may be conducted both on-site and off-site, and it typically includes all of the standard pedagogical techniques (for example, lecture, discussion, demonstration, role-playing, simulation, and gaming). Depending upon how needs are assessed in a given workplace or corporation, training can focus on induction of new job entrants into their particular job tasks in the firm, remedial basic academic skills (e.g., reading, mathematics), retraining for totally new job functions, learning to use new equipment or processes, acquisition of management and supervisory skills, networking, lateral moves, career ladders, career planning, self-improvement, and knowledge management. While it is unlikely that counselors will be involved in all of these areas of training, training opportunities do not stand apart from career services in business or industry. Indeed, in such a context, workers frequently need career counseling to help them understand why they should engage in training, what training would be best for them, and how to cope with their anxieties about being able to succeed in training (Gray & Herr, 1998).

A large part of the training performed by a career development specialist will be working with managers to improve their coaching and counseling skills in the career intervention process. Managers are encouraged to guide and develop their employees and are provided with the necessary information and attending and responding skills to do so.

Another part of the training and education function is providing workers with information of various sorts. Most large organizations have some systematic way of informing employees about career-related matters, whether done through a career information center or by some other method. Included are such dissemination techniques as web sites on the Internet, brochures, computer-accessed data, workshops, videotape presentations, general reference libraries, and other methods that diffuse information about career opportunities within a company. This function might include gathering, storing, retrieving, and disseminating information about such career-relevant aspects as career paths, career-related benefits, on-site and off-site courses and programs, company philosophy about career development, job postings, family-related benefits, and job matching.

Mentoring

Mentoring is a term that has come into prominence in the corporate world. Like many such terms it has been an unnamed and perhaps underappreciated part of these environments, probably for centuries. Examples of mentoring behavior are common in corporate, governmental, or military workplaces. We hear about senior persons taking junior workers "under their wings," "showing them the ropes," "getting them access to the right people or to assignments that would further their careers." What has been random behavior in many work organizations is increasingly being institutionalized so that the benefits of mentoring can be spread more evenly among workers, regardless of gender or race, who can profit from this form of assistance in their career development.

Mentoring has come to be seen as an extremely important mechanism by which a senior person undertakes to provide information and emotional support for a junior person. The intent is to facilitate the successful induction of the junior person into the norms and expectations of the work expectations of work organization as well as to help them advance their careers. Viewed from such a perspective, mentoring is a developmental experience of considerable value to the effective and efficient movement of people into and through institutional pathways and organizational cultures. Thus, mentoring is not only important at a beginning point in one's career, mentoring is likely to be important as one progresses through a career and faces new decision or transition points.

Mentoring can be conceived in many ways. Certainly, at a minimum, mentoring is a *transfer of knowledge.* The mentor is in a position to provide information about role expectations and role boundaries in a particular work or social context that the mentee would be likely to acquire only through trial and error, and after unpleasant and trying experiences. Frequently, the norms, role boundaries, and social expectations of organizational culture are not codified or clearly marked out, but they exist and they mediate one's acceptance by others and one's performance. The mentor can provide a "road map" by which the mentee can avoid or surmount the "pot holes," the unspoken obstacles, the organizational politics, the barriers to success in organizational cultures.

The importance of mentoring is not confined to transferring knowledge. A mentor is likely to play multiple roles: sounding board, counselor, provider of feedback, broker of opportunities and assignments, cheerleader, reinforcer, role model, advocate, a one-person support system. A mentor must be flexible in playing these roles as the needs of the mentee for knowledge, for psychological support, and for other assistance co-exist and emerge.

One of the reasons for the recent enthusiasm about institutionalizing mentoring is that it is a powerful relationship that is not equally distributed among potential recipients. For example, as women and persons of color have entered workplaces, populated primarily by white males, their access to women mentors or mentors who are themselves persons of color has been limited. Therefore, while preferences for mentors may be otherwise, many white males have served effectively for years as mentors of women and persons of minority backgrounds. In such cases, mentors and mentees have had much to learn from each other.

It is important to acknowledge that mentoring is an intense relationship between two persons which does not always yield positive outcomes. In one interesting study surveying participants in executive development programs at Southeastern University who had themselves been mentored or protégés of mentors (Eby, McManus, Simon, & Russell, 2000), a taxonomy of negative mentoring experiences was developed. As a result of content analysis of the 168 negative mentoring experiences described by the participants in the study, five themes and their metathemes were developed by the researchers. These are adapted in Table 11.5.

This taxonomy of negative mentoring experiences is instructive as career counselors engage in consulting about or training mentors. On a more positive note, mentors engage in a range of activities to assist their protégés. By means of in-depth interviews, Kram (1984) studied managers in a northeast public utilities firm ($N = 18$ mentoring relationships) and a Fortune 500 manufacturing company ($N = 15$ peer relationships). She discovered that mentors appear to serve both a *career* function (aspects of the relationship that enhance career advancement) and a

TABLE 11.5 Negative Mentoring Themes and Metathemes

Poor Match within the Dyad
- Due to a difference between mentor and protégé related to:
  - Values
  - Work-style
  - Personality

Distancing Behavior
- By mentor to mentee related to:
  - Neglect
  - Self-Absorption
  - Intentional Exclusion

Manipulative Behavior
- Essentially related to the position power exerted by the mentor to the mentee:
  - Tyranny
  - Inappropriate delegation

Politicking
- Related to the mentor's negative evaluation of mentee to others and the usurping of mentee's ideas:
  - Sabotage
  - Credit-taking
  - Deception

Lack of Mentor Expertise
- Interpersonal Incompetency
- Technical Incompetency

General Dysfunctionality
- Bad Attitude
- Personal Problems

psychosocial function (aspects of the relationship that enhance one's sense of competence, identity, and effectiveness). Career functions included sponsorship, coaching, challenging assignments, exposure (visibility), and protection. Psychosocial functions included acceptance, confirmation, role modeling, friendship, and counseling. According to Kram, the mentor relationship is characterized by phases: initiation, cultivation, separation, and redefinition, and these phases are tied to one's career stage (early, middle, and late career). Cross-gender issues tend to heighten within the mentor relationship. Kram argues that mentorship can be of as much benefit to the mentor as to the protégé, that all mentor relationships are not positive, that mentor stages and functions may vary according to the setting, and that all people do not have mentor relationships open to them. In another work, Kram (1985) points out barriers to constructive mentoring, including opposition to potential mentors because they never received mentoring, potential mentors who experience career blocks that impede their desire to help junior colleagues, potential protégés who distrust the motives of senior managers, a lack of respect for the capabilities of senior colleagues, and lack of interpersonal skills to engage in mentoring.

Mentoring is not necessary for all individuals, but it is certainly a help whether it is of a formal or informal nature. Informal mentoring occurs when a senior member of an organization informally gets to know a junior member and selects him or her as a protégé. Formal mentorships happen when the match between mentor and protégé is made by random assignment or simply by a senior member examining the file of a junior member. Chao, Walz, and Gardner (1992) examined the effects of both types of mentoring (and of no mentoring) in terms of organizational socialization, job satisfaction, and salary. Informally mentored workers were found to be slightly more advantaged in terms of these outcome variables, and both types were significantly higher than nonmentored individuals.

Clauson (1985) surveyed 76 managers and asked them to rate the degree of influence the three most influential people in their lives had in 14 different aspects of life. In general, managers tended to emulate their mentors in intellectual sharpness, job skills (managing, doing), managing a career (organizational life), social skills, and emotional characteristics. He found that although mentorship was not essential to success in the sense of being a necessary and sufficient condition, it was surely helpful. In another study, Reich (1985) determined that mentors were perceived as most valuable for offering concrete help: early transfer to more challenging jobs, opening up new positions, assignment to special projects, and providing autonomy in difficult projects. Less concrete was the function of offering political assistance (for example, pressure applied to key people to obtain promotions, advisement on good positions and company politics). Seventy-two percent of Reich's respondents indicated that mentors contributed substantially to their career development. Investigating the personality of workers in high-tech service companies, Fagenson (1992) determined that the personality variables of power and achievement distinguished protégés from nonprotégés; those who had acknowledged mentors had significantly higher needs in these two constructs. The implication of this study and others is that personality variables may explain why some people are receptive to mentoring, whereas others are less enthusiastic.

In terms of cross-gender mentoring, Bowen (1985) compared same-sex mentoring (MM, FF) with cross-sex mentoring (MF, FM). Although there is clearly a potential for mischief and misperception in cross-gender mentoring, Bowen found that it was not the sex of the mentor as such that accounted for self-perceptions of career enhancement as a result of the relationship but rather the functions provided by the mentor. Envy, jealousy by significant others in one's life, snide remarks, and so on are all possible evocations as a result of cross-gender mentoring, but sex-related problems appear to be minimal. A second study investigating same-sex and cross-sex mentoring of women (Gaskill, 1991) concluded that female protégés benefited from both male and female mentors.

In their interview study of male and female faculty members, Stonewater, Eveslage, and Dingerson (1990) investigated perceptions of past career helping relationships. Two major themes emerged. In terms of mentor influences, men and women on the faculty expressed differences. The men more often reported a sense of direction and professionalism; women generally seemed less confident about themselves and indicated less planning in their careers. In terms of mentoring, almost all who indicated that they could not have accomplished what they did without the assistance of a helper were women. Secondly, the type of support reported by women was either emotional caring or a combination of personal and work-related support. Conversely, men were likely to report support in terms of work-related assistance. These results suggest that men and women need different types of mentoring.

Carden (1990), based on her review of the mentoring literature, suggests the following research needs in terms of mentor-protégé relationships (MPRs):

> *Future research on mentoring and adult career development must begin with clearer definitions, better control of extraneous variables, and inclusion of subjects from populations that have been largely ignored thus far (e.g., racial and ethnic minority group members, male tokens in traditionally female occupations or professions, blue-collar workers, physically handicapped individuals, and mid-life career changers). In addition, studies aimed at identifying the cognitive and affective processes underlying the influence of "isms" (racism, sexism, ageism, etc.) on the formation, development, and effectiveness of MPR's are needed. (p. 293)*

The message of all of these studies is clear—whether mentoring is a formal, organizational-sponsored, and organization-encouraged activity or the more prevalent informal activity, having a powerful mentor greatly facilitates upward career mobility. For the career counselor within an organization, tasks built around the mentoring function might include setting up and monitoring mentorship programs and working with mentors to assist them in helping their protégés.

Career Ladders

Career ladders or career path charts are detailed descriptions employed to demonstrate possible job movements, laterally and vertically, that are available within an organization. They depict graphically a sort of road map for negotiating an organizational hierarchy, and they present information useful for professional, technical, and managerial staff in identifying opportunities for mobility.

According to McRae (1985), there are three kinds of career paths:

1. *Historical* paths are the informal paths easily analyzed by examining biographical histories of those who currently hold the job in question. Historical paths tend to perpetuate past practice.
2. *Organizational* paths are those defined by management; such paths are reflected in business plans, needs, and organizational structures. Representing relationships outlined in job descriptions, they are usually consistent with the salary progressions followed in practice.
3. *Behavioral* paths represent the logical and possible sequences of positions that people could follow in light of an analysis of what they actually do. Behavioral paths are rational definitions of what is possible rather than what has been done in the past or what is desired by management. (p. 58)

As suggested by McRae, career ladders take many forms, often combining historical, organizational and behavioral factors as such descriptions are formulated in a particular firm or setting. Examples of career ladders include the standard steps in the promotion of faculty members in colleges and universities. They are likely to include from the beginning to the final steps of an academic career the following positions: instructor, assistant professor, associate professor, professor. It is also possible that a career lattice might show the steps when an associate professor or, more likely, a professor would move from the academic track to an administrative track (e.g., department head, dean).

In the military, growing responsibilities are reflected in increases in rank, which also constitute a career ladder. For example, in the army, from the entry point as a commissioned officer to the highest rank possible would be depicted as follows: second lieutenant, first lieutenant, captain, major, lieutenant colonel, colonel, brigadier general, major general, lieutenant general, and general. In industry, a career ladder within a particular department of a firm might happen as follows:

In the latter illustration, you have both a career ladder and a career lattice. The bottom ladder indicates the job where those interested in planning and estimating the cost of jobs or other projects would start (e.g., cost estimator). Above that job are the vertical positions to which one might be promoted as one gains skill and experience in this career path. But, this illustration also shows the points where one might move to an administrative career ladder as section

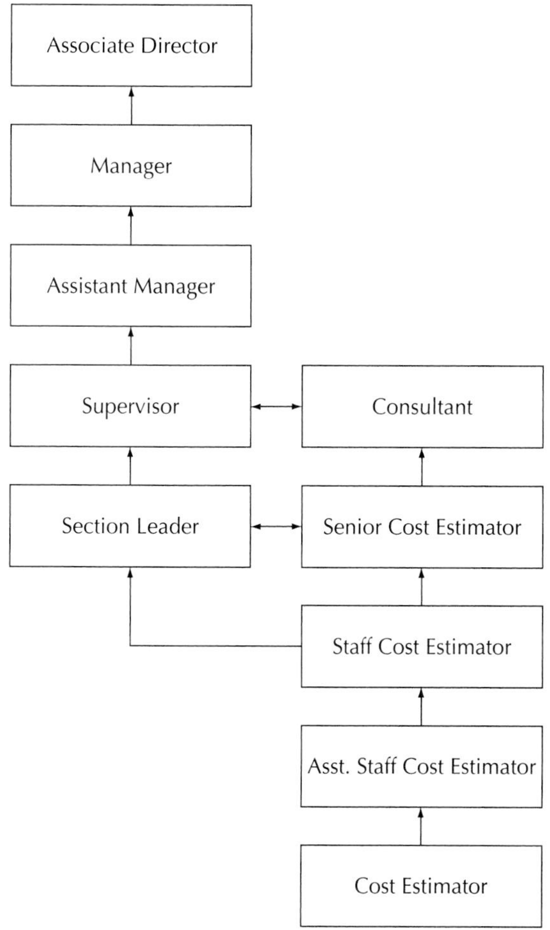

FIGURE 11.1 Career Ladder

leader or supervisor. These portrayals of horizontal moves from one to another career ladder are called career lattices. The larger and the more complex a firm or corporation is, the more career ladders and career lattices there are likely to be describing the structure, functions, and position available for the work force employed in that organization.

Within organizations, the career development specialist's role is to define and promulgate these career ladders or career path charts, trying to ensure that equal opportunity is available to all segments of the organization's workforce. In addition, career counselors are frequently involved in facilitating the provision or providing workshops designed to provide workers information about skills or other emphases related to mobility through the organization's specific career ladders or career paths.

Wellness Programs

One of the growing aspects of EAPs and other human resource management programs in business and industry is represented by wellness programs. As indicated earlier in this chapter, there is no reason why career counselors in the workplace should not get involved with typical EAP activities, provided that they have the training and skills to do so. Wellness programs are a case in point. Solomon (1985) indicates that wellness programs typically have several components: distribution of health information (ranging from chemical abuse to nutrition), workshops and seminars, fitness programs, and health screenings.

Myers, Sweeney, and Witmer (2000) have defined wellness as "a way of life oriented toward optimal health and well-being in which body, mind, and spirit are integrated by the individual to live life more fully within the human and natural community. Ideally, it is the optimum state of health and well-being that each individual is capable of achieving" (p. 252).

The model proposed by Myers and her colleagues indicates that five life tasks are central to healthy functioning: (1) spirituality, (2) self-direction, (3) work and leisure, (4) friendship, and (5) love. Each of these tasks has various components that are important ingredients of each of the tasks and represent the substance of workshops or career interventions that can focus on wellness. For example, the task of self-direction is comprised of twelve components: sense of worth, sense of control, realistic beliefs, emotional awareness and coping, problem solving and creativity, sense of humor, physical fitness, nutrition, self-care, stress management, gender identity and cultural identity.

Basic to such a model is research and theory that indicates that changes in one area of wellness affects other areas of life in both positive and negative directions. Another very important concept is that wellness, like many other aspects of life is a choice of lifestyles. Of particular significance here is that a variety of sources suggest that when rank ordered, at least seven of the ten major courses of death are directly related to lifestyle, personal behavior, and personal choices (U.S. Department of Health and Human Services, 2000). Costs of medical care to government, to employers, to individuals, related to individual choices that do not promote wellness, are in the billions of dollars. These high costs of illness and premature death, and the loss of productivity that ensues, can be largely offset through preventive measures frequently coordinated and/or taught by counselors in the workplace. (For a full explanation of the concepts of wellness and the preventive methods associated with this model, please refer to Myers, Sweeney, and Witmer, 2000.)

The most common foci of planned programs of wellness in business and industry have been stress management, weight control, nutrition, fitness, first-aid, preventive health care, safety, and smoking and the impact of personal decision-making on these behaviors. Obviously the underlying notion is that a sound mind in a sound body will lead to enhanced productivity.

Outplacement Counseling

A major stress inducer among workers is both the prospect and the actual act of an organization or a component of it ceasing to function. Numerous observations chronicle the dread and anxiety caused by a plant closing, as longtime workers, many of whom have limited skills, are put out of work. Sometimes companies provide outplacement counseling for such dislocated workers, although the extent of services and the target populations vary considerably.

Most companies who do support outplacement counseling use outside consultants exclusively. Fewer use both outside consultants and in-house staff; fewer still use exclusively in-house staff. Usually a high-level personnel or human resources manager effects whatever program is determined to be appropriate. Most programs concentrate on helping displaced workers to find new employment and on helping them to cope psychologically. Severance pay is almost always a part of the package. The primary technique used seems to be training in job-search skills (such as location of opportunities, résumé writing, interviewing, training opportunities, and so on). Eves (1986), for example, describes a program implemented during and after the process of a plant shutdown in which small-group sessions were held over a three-day period. These sessions focused on getting organized for the search, determining interests, analyzing experience and life history, preparing résumés and cover letters, targeting companies, interviewing, negotiating, and accepting an offer. Some organizations provide office space, telephone usage, secretarial assistance, and so on but usually limit such aid to executives. Less common is counseling assistance for families and referrals to community agencies. Lewis and Lewis (1986) see the basic activities involved in outplacement counseling as: (1) dealing with affect, (2) self-assessment, (3) goal setting, (4) strategy formulation, and (5) action or implementation.

One major development in work organizations, owing to downsizing and layoffs, discussed earlier in this chapter, is the increasing number of people who will never work within single companies where they can develop networks, negotiate the system, and feel a sense of attachment. Instead, companies have increased their use of temporary employment contracts, employee leasing, and outsourcing (Johnson, 1994). The obvious ramification of this development is the creation of a new workplace in which employment is viewed as a temporary assignment and work is transient, thus making it difficult for workers to establish social networks, form mentor-protégé relationships, and so on. One consequence of employment for a finite period of time and funded by "soft" monies is that many such workers feel a sense of being in a dead-end position. Johnson, Simpson, Williams, and Kotarba (1993) demonstrated that "temporary" workers who were upwardly aspiring and who sought additional credentials differed from those who did not in terms of mentor relationships, with active mentorship being more effective than passive mentorship.

Retirement Planning

In Chapter 12, we describe the career counselor's role in preretirement and retirement counseling, as this stage of life is the last in the work cycle. Some of this type of counseling is taking place within the workplace, although it can be more accurately termed planning rather than counseling. Federal legislation prohibits forced retirement in most types of work before age 70 (if at all), yet people seem to be retiring before that age, especially in industry. A minority of organizations has some form of organized assistance for employees in the retirement process, and most of these provide for an early retirement option. Information is provided to employees on such aspects of retirement as financial planning, tax information, company-provided postretirement benefits, group insurance conversion, company pension options, Medicare, estate planning, health care, legal considerations, housing, and the availability of volunteer work and occupational opportunities.

Often this information is imparted by outside experts who come into the workplace: Social Security staff, financial and legal experts, health care specialists, accountants, and so on. The major vehicles for information dissemination are lectures and seminars, written materials, group discussions, and referrals. Many organizations attempt to provide a mechanism so that retirees can continue some form of contact with the former employer (for example, through communications, benefits, part-time employment). There is evidence (Kamouri & Cavanaugh, 1986) that preretirement planning programs can be effective in sensitizing participants to the issues of planning for retirement, acquiring information about aspects of retirement, and participating in retirement roles. Therefore, it is a useful activity for career development specialists to coordinate or conduct.

Employee Assistance Programs

Whether staffed in-house or simply a referral service (the latter is more prevalent), EAPs attempt to prevent and remediate personal problems of workers to increase productivity, reduce absenteeism, enhance retention, and improve morale. If in-house, EAPs are usually located within personnel, human resource, or medical departments, and those organizations that do provide in-house services typically employ trained staffs, consisting of such personnel as counselors, nurses, doctors, psychologists, or social workers.

Even with in-house staffs, referral to outside agencies is a major function of EAPs. These referral sources include alcohol and drug rehabilitation facilities, mental health and social agencies, psychiatrists and psychologists, and self-help groups (such as Alcoholics Anonymous). In addition to referrals, EAPs provide an educative function in that they work with supervisors and managers to teach them how to recognize the need for assistance in those they supervise, and they work with employees to help them gauge whether they need help. The most common problems brought to EAPs are chemical dependency, marital difficulties, financial problems, on-the-job interpersonal difficulties, sexual harassment and discrimination (often handled by other than EAP), disruptive family relationships, and stress.

Only about 10 to 20 percent of today's workforce has the benefit of an EAP. The fact that an EAP is available does not, of course, mean that it will be used. In fact, there appear to be individual differences in the propensity of employees to use an EAP. To use it, they first need to know that it exists; it must be accessible; and they must perceive managerial support for the program. The ultimate mediating factor in whether or not they use it may well be the confidence that they have in the program (Milne, Blum, & Roman, 1994).

Some see the efforts of EAPs and career planning and development programs in industry as simply attempts by organizations to enhance the self-esteem of their employees to bring about greater productivity. Brockner (1988), for example, argues that everything from layoffs to negotiation behavior can be assuaged or enhanced by attention to employees' self-esteem. In a broad sense, he is probably correct, although our current understanding of the construct of self-esteem and the sophistication of its measurement are less than adequate. In general, supervisors seem to require employees to evidence some blatant and overt maladaptive behaviors before they refer them to EAPs. These behaviors typically include high absenteeism, irritability, decreased productivity, and apathy (Bayer & Gerstein, 1990).

Analyzing 91 EAPs in Ontario, Canada, Macdonald and Dooley (1990) concluded that current programs contain improved procedures to enhance the protection of confidentiality and to emphasize the voluntary aspects of referrals. Unions are becoming increasingly involved in EAPs. Nevertheless, issues persist. Although confidentiality protection has increased, for example, confidentiality typically does not guarantee anonymity. Also, awareness and education programs are less fully developed than is desirable; after-the-fact responses are much more prevalent.

Hosie, West, and Mackey (1993) surveyed EAP workers and determined that the primary mental health professionals employed were about equally divided between social workers and masters-level counselors. In terms of services offered, agencies engaged in the following top five activities: (1) training of managers and supervisors to use EAP services, (2) evaluation and referral (internal or external) of substance abusers, (3) case consultation for supervisors, (4) crisis intervention, and (5) assessment. There were, however, differences in the types of services offered by EAPs, depending on whether they were internal or external. Usage of EAPs does not appear to be restricted to any particular level within an organizational hierarchy. Gerstein, Gaber, Dainas, and Duffey (1993) determined that middle management tended to use the EAP most, but that both upper-level and lower-level staff members availed themselves of the service in equal measure.

THE CAREER COUNSELOR IN THE ORGANIZATION

A variety of observers have urged career counselors and counseling psychologists to intensify their role in organizations, especially in industry. Indeed, such a concept is not new; one can point to isolated instances of counseling by psychologists within industry as far back as the 1920s (Baker, 1944). Several contemporary writings about psychologists functioning as counselors within industry described in a sort of "how I spent my summer vacation" way the activities of academics on sabbatical leave who tried to link "town and gown" more closely by working within industry in their geographical area.

A somewhat less provincial approach is taken by Leonards (1981), who speaks more universally about the possibilities of corporate psychology. He believes that counseling psychologists are most appropriate for corporate clientele because of their emphasis on working with healthy personalities. Foci would include counseling resolution of midcareer issues, preretirement planning, and specific career development concerns. Further contributions to the corporate body would come from the counselor's assisting in organizational development, program evaluation, and general psychological consultation.

Osipow's ideas about applications in organizations for counseling psychologists are specific in their career-relatedness. He suggests, for example, 16 possibilities for useful contributions:

1. Helping employees and managers identify hazards in work
2. Training people to identify their work styles (especially those that might be deleterious to them) and teaching them to change them
3. The effects of repetitive work on people
4. The effects of transfers to new locations, especially if forced
5. Special stresses and strains in the two-career couple or family
6. Special stresses experienced by people employed in boundary spanning roles (for example, jobs that require employees to "split" allegiances)
7. Special stresses in people with high interpersonal demands in their jobs
8. Preparation for retirement
9. Dealing effectively with the process of job evaluation
10. Dealing with the special problems of entrepreneurs
11. Dealing with the problems of job loss
12. Dealing with the special problems of small-business people
13. Dealing with the special problems of professionals
14. Health care issues
15. Self-help and self-care
16. Family counseling

A unique perspective of when to use a psychologist in business has been provided by a businessman (McGrath, 1992). While similar in some ways to the other analyses presented here of what a counselor or counseling psychologist can contribute to business and industry, McGrath's comments relate to when a psychologist in business is particularly appropriate. He suggests the following presented in paraphrased form:

- Family business—In this view, the pressures of business often get entangled with the emotional ties of the family and create a complex and volatile situation, which a counseling psychologist can help untangle and identify.
- Leadership mentoring—Like other workers in today's rapidly changing economy, leaders also must change. Frequently, they understand the necessity for change and what is required but they cannot bring themselves to implement the change. Frequently, the leader in such a circumstance is experiencing a psychological barrier that a psychologist can help clarify and ameliorate.
- Dysfunctional teams—In some instances, very competent persons who work productively alone are unable to function as part of a team. Since teamwork is so much a part of contemporary business or industrial practice, the problems that affect dysfunctional teams or specific team members often require psychological interventions to improve these circumstances.

- Slow progress—It is not unusual for organizations to seek change, but they cannot seem to accelerate the process. Frequently, counseling psychologists as consultants can help managers clarify the barriers to more rapid success.
- Assessments—Whether or not a firm will find assessments useful and for what purposes frequently requires psychological consultation and, if implemented, planning and administration.
- A clear emotional problem that is beyond the scope of business coaching—These are the problem employees or the employees with problems for whom counseling in general and career counseling in particular deserve the attention of a counselor or counseling psychologist, either in-house or as part of an EAP or other psychologist subcontract.

Verlander (1985) argues that the effectiveness of a career management system (CMS) depends on how well it is integrated with all of the other human resource functions within an organization. Typical programs include management and supervisory training, career planning, career counseling, equal employment efforts, and career information systems. Almost all systems provide for performance appraisal and feedback. Lewis and Lewis (1986) advocate that counselors in the workplace develop a broad set of competencies to address these concerns, including skills in program development and management, counseling and assessment, resource utilization and networking, organizational consultation, education and training, and marketing and public relations. These competencies represent a formidable repertoire for any single discipline to master, and few, if any, formal preservice preparation programs address them in any complete sense.

Hall (1986), after reviewing the state of career development in organizations, arrived at seven conclusions:

1. No organization has the ability (in terms of either resources or information about the future) to manage an employee's career or to plan well-ordered career paths.
2. Therefore the employee must assume responsibility for his or her own career development (or at least 80 percent of it).
3. To be responsible for one's own career in today's turbulent organizational environments, the employee needs new *career competencies,* not just job skills. These career competencies might be called "metaskills" because they are skills in acquiring new skills. The most important metaskills are adaptability (routine busting), tolerance of ambiguity and uncertainty, and identity change.
4. It is in the best interests of the organization to help both the employee and his or her spouse assume the career responsibility and to develop their own career direction. (This makes it easier for the organization to pursue its own future directions.)
5. The organization should provide information and support to facilitate the person's assumption of career responsibility.
6. The organization should make possible wide degrees of freedom of movement for the individual. All directions of movement should be possible and valued by the culture: down, across, up, and out.
7. To provide an environment that is supportive of good career planning and career management, the organization needs a good strategic human resource management process. Career development activities are performed most effectively when they are one part of an integrated strategic human resource management system. This means that the organization must have clear business objectives and a clear set of human resource objectives and priorities growing out of those business objectives. (pp. 348–349)

Working within corporate structures can lead to all sorts of family stress that goes beyond typical workplace stressors and consequent strains. Relocation, for example, although not as traumatic as dislocation, can be problematic for families. Lawson and Angle (1994) report that in their study, employees' adjustment to relocation was considerably more difficult in terms of family effects than in terms of workplace effects. Thus, any relocation has an interactive effect on family adjustment. It is reasonable for companies to use trained counselors to assuage these effects.

Clearly the glass ceiling still exists. This inequity in salary and career progression between men and women is often ascribed to differences in family commitments, but Marsden, Kallenberg, and Cook (1993) found that although in the aggregate men exhibit somewhat higher organizational commitment than do women, the primary explanation for this disparity is not gender differences in family ties but rather that men are more likely than women to hold jobs with commitment-enhancing features (i.e., positive interpersonal climate, autonomous work opportunities). Davidson and Cooper (1992) give credence to this argument by pointing out that women managers rise much more quickly when they have been in line rather than staff positions. The career counselor within organizations can address these types of issues as well.

It may further be useful to address the micro-aspects of organizations as well as the macro-aspects. For example, some who study organizations suggest that it may be more productive to study the occupations within an organization (occupational subcultures) than to examine the total organizational milieu in which the occupations are pursued.

Each of these studies is representative of the current state of the career counselor or the counseling psychologist in industry. They offer tentative, exploratory proposals of how specialists can function to enhance career development in the organization. There are not, as yet, definitive answers to a number of questions. These questions are addressed later in this chapter.

Cairo (1985), acknowledging the absence of data, presents some tentative conclusions related to the design and implementation of career programs in organizations.

1. Program development should be preceded by a systematic, thorough assessment of the career development needs of the target population. This should include some effort to distinguish between employees who require help in obtaining the standard career development competencies and those with different, but equally important, career development needs.
2. To avoid the problems associated with employees' unrealistic expectations of career planning and development programs, information about career opportunities should be honest, accurate, and up-to-date. Whenever possible, this element of a program should include information about job requirements, career paths, training and development resources, and promotional possibilities.
3. Efforts to facilitate employees' appraisal of work-related skills must include the recognition that some important skills might be extremely difficult, perhaps even impossible, to acquire regardless of subsequent developmental activities. In such cases, employees might be encouraged to focus on finding positions that maximize strengths and minimize weaknesses rather than searching for suitable developmental activities.
4. Organizations that expect supervisors to take a central role in the career development of their subordinates should provide incentives and rewards for these efforts and ensure that supervisors possess or acquire the knowledge, skills, and attitudes required to be effective helpers.
5. Methods for helping employees monitor their career plans should be part of every program. This requires coordination among other career-related activities to provide employees with ongoing opportunities to review earlier goals and plans and modify them in light of any new information or circumstances.
6. Finally, there is a clear need for more and better program evaluations. Given the large number of existing career planning and development programs and the likelihood of continued growth in this area, it is important that we begin to examine carefully the effects of our efforts. (pp. 245–246)

Examples of Career Programs

As indicated by survey results, many organizations have formal, functioning career development programs. General Electric, AT&T, AirCal, Aetna, Xerox, the National Aeronautical and Space Administration, the U.S. Government Accounting Office, and the U.S. Postal Service, for example, all have formal materials and procedures to assist their employees with career development concerns. A brief description of several illustrative programs follows to give a flavor of the activity that is taking place.

One common strategy related to career development in organizations is the assessment center. There is little doubt that the assessment center is used more for personnel selection than for individual development, more for identifying potential managers than for diagnosing employee strengths and weaknesses. The concept began in World War II with selection of spies for the OSS and now concerns itself largely with selection for higher management and for management trainees. In a few situations, the assessment center is also used to select sales and technical personnel and other nonmanagement workers. Techniques used in assessment centers include in-basket exercises (an individual is provided with data relating to problems and must, within a specified time period, demonstrate effective decision making), related management games and simulations: leaderless group discussions; analysis and presentation of complex situations; role-playing exercises; essay writing; psychological aptitude and personality tests; and others. These techniques are designed to assess oral and written communication skills; leadership; ability to organize and plan; decision-making ability; tolerance for stress and behavioral flexibility; and energy, forcefulness, creativity, and risk taking among other traits.

It should be no surprise that computerized career interventions have been injected into the organizational career planning and development process. These range from simply computerizing an assessment device to more comprehensive systems. For example, Vale (1990) describes the use of the Minnesota Clerical Assessment Battery (MCAB) as an aid in personnel selection, while Forrer, Leibowitz, and Dickelman (1989) offer Career Point: A Computer-Based Career Development System for Organizations. Because this latter approach is increasing in use, we offer a description of its components. This system consists of twelve computer modules for use with an IBM PC (and compatibles). These modules include an introduction to the system, knowledge of the organization (made specific to the particular employer), several assessment modules (values, interests, and preferences; skills; goals), identifying job opportunities, planning for reaching goals, job search skills, and résumé writing. Incorporated in the system are such well-known career planning aids as the Work Environment Scales, the Myers-Briggs Type Indicator, the Career Leverage Scale, and the Self-Directed Search. Similar systems that combine extant instrumentation with the opportunity to customize the intervention to the particular organization are becoming increasingly common.

Many organizations have excellent in-house educational and occupational information materials. One is the Aetna Life and Casualty Company, which publishes several volumes for their employees in a *Develop Yourself* series. For example, *Develop Yourself: A Guide to Education and Training* is an almost 250-page catalog of all the education and training offered at Aetna. Each course is listed in terms of the purpose of the course, for whom it is designed, what its content is, how long it lasts, what the prerequisites are, how to get registered, and how much, if anything, the course will cost. This document puts to shame many college catalogs. A companion volume, *Develop Yourself: A Career Path Handbook,* is intended to provide Aetna's 36,000 employees with information about job possibilities within the company in fourteen job clusters and the career progression usually followed.

At Coca-Cola USA, the career development system has at its heart performance planning and review. These are followed by individual career development discussions in which employees can communicate career interests to their managers. Information from both the performance review and career discussion is used in department career development and succession planning reviews called People Days. The next step is finding a fit between available positions and people. This is done through a number of publications and job postings and through a two-day Career Strategies Workshop. Coca-Cola USA also offers an extensive in-house training program as well as 100 percent tuition reimbursement aid for outside courses.

These examples of program content indicate that many of the techniques developed outside of organizations are being put to use within the workplace. Also, however, specific techniques and materials are being developed to meet the unique needs of particular organizations.

There certainly are no extant rules for providing career assistance in the workplace. Developers are relatively unfettered in their attempts to implement a concept. That same freedom, however, leads to several questions.

Issues and Needed Research

Throughout the discussion in this chapter we have pointed to several unresolved issues and questions that lend themselves to researchable answers. To conclude our exploration of career counseling in the workplace, we summarize these concerns:

1. Can career counseling effectively occur within the workplace when there appears to be a basic conflict between the necessity for performance evaluation and the desirability of threat-free career development activity? Can both organizational and individual needs be met within the corporate body?

2. Who should provide career development services within industry? Supervisors? Career counseling specialists? Generic training and development personnel? Some new hybrid of human resource development specialist and career counselor?
3. What are the appropriate functions necessary to achieve which career development outcomes in organizations?
4. What methods and materials are best for what types of adult clients or concerns?
5. How do career identities develop? How are they shaped by work experiences?
6. How can we define success in career development? What criteria are appropriate? Are money earned, satisfaction, career maturity, and other outcome measures appropriate?
7. How can we best evaluate to demonstrate the effectiveness of career development programs in organizations? Can we successfully reconcile equal employment concerns and organizational needs?
8. What can be done to secure pervasive organizational support for career development programs?
9. Is there a "critical mass" of personnel and materials necessary to provide minimally acceptable career development services? Is there a minimum number of employees required before a program should be established?
10. Is it possible to apply generic career development systems in various organizations, or must systems be tailored to the unique needs and populations of each institution in the workplace?
11. What types of research are required to produce improved performance appraisal, a greater understanding of supervisor/supervisee relations, and so on?
12. What are the differential career development needs of diverse subpopulations within the organization (such as clerical, supervisory, managers, production, sales)?
13. How can many of the adult career concerns and special populations described in Chapters 5 and 12 best be addressed within the structure of workplace organizations?
14. How can temporary workers be accommodated with career development services?

SUMMARY

In this chapter, we have presented a discussion of a variety of topics related to career counseling and other career services in the workplace. This is a growing area of involvement for counselors and counseling psychologists as they assist managers and workers to deal with the implications of organizational change, the challenges of the global economy, and new expectations for management of their careers by individual workers. In broad terms, this chapter has addressed work adjustment and personal adjustment, occupational stress, person-organizational fit, perspectives on changing career patterns, workplace terminology, overview of career development functions, organizational career patterns, selected functions of career development-specialists, and research issues related to career services in the workplace.

CHAPTER TWELVE

Special Adult Career Concerns

KEY CONCEPTS

- Attention to the development of career theory focused on adults is recent in origin; until a relatively few years ago, most career theory was concerned primarily with the first two decades of life, not the last five.
- The adult population is heterogeneous and comprised of several differential subpopulations for which career problems and career interventions differ. Groups of particular interest in this chapter are: (1) midcareer changers, (2) women entering or reentering the labor force after a period of childrearing, (3) the older worker, and (4) preretirees and retirees.
- Planning models of career guidance or career counseling for adult populations are more recent than those developed for younger persons. Major principles underlying such program planning, however, should include specificity of planning as well as awareness that most adults have family obligations that affect their planning and that adults typically have immediacy, urgency, and concreteness to their concerns.
- Career counseling techniques useful with younger people are likely to be useful with adults. The career counselor of adults needs to understand principles of adult development and decision-making models as well as whether a particular person is primarily concerned with anticipation of or implementation of career issues.

Until fairly recently, anyone interested in career counseling might well have wondered if there is a career life after adolescence. Early work in career development and behavior focused on factors and processes leading to the initial choice of an occupation and rarely addressed adult career development. Furthermore, researchers and theorists generally were grounded in the specialties of child and adolescent psychology and ignored the portion of the career life span subsequent to exploration and initial choice.

Awakening to adult career behavior began with an interest in gerontology—the branch of knowledge dealing with aging and the aged. Thus, the last of the career life cycles was probably the first to be studied intensively with adults. Concerns about preretirement and retirement spawned a good deal of research. In fact, most postadolescent research since World War II had been related to old age, and the development of the middle-aged and older worker was still given little attention.

Developmental psychology, which is concerned with changes in behavior over periods of weeks, months, or years, has begun to investigate whether career changes with age extend beyond young adulthood. Specifically, developmental and vocational psychologists have been taking initial steps to determine whether career behaviors and other psychological characteristics are ontogenetic (age-related). Increasing attention, both in the popular press and in professional journals, has been given to the notion of adult life stages. Scholars such as Farrell and Rosenberg (1981); R. Gould (1972); D. J. Levinson (1986); D. J. Levinson, Darrow, Klein, M. H. Levinson, and McKee (1978); Raynor and Entin (1982); Vaillant (1977); and Wortley and Amatea (1982) and lay writers such as Gail Sheehy (1976, 1981) have turned the search for an explanation of the adult life cycle into a chic pursuit. Other observers suggest that these current models of adult life-span development have little or no relevance to practice and that different models are required (Courtenay, 1994).

This early research is tentative and is based on population samples that are both small and narrowly delimited. Yet it is a beginning. In relation to career behavior, this new and enthusiastic interest in adults is evidenced by the creation of various committees, commissions, institutes, and special interest groups within professional organizations, by a rapidly increasing number of articles relating to adult career behavior, and by new legislation. A recent "hot topic" related to career behavior in adulthood focuses on achieving balance in work-family life roles (Niles, Herr, & Hartung, 2001).

Indeed, the language applied to the career development and behavior of adults reflects these popular concerns. Terms such as *career menopause* or *career climacteric* are used with an assurance that is in direct contrast to what is actually known about the important changes that may occur in adult career behavior. In fact, we are only beginning to collect systematic data on adults, and there is some question about whether we possess any useful theory of general development in which to use these data. Of the human being's three score and ten years, relatively little attention has been focused on the last five decades of life. Using the work of Piaget and Erickson (or other behavioral scientists), we can build a reasonable model of development from infancy through adolescence; however, beginning with the young adult and through senescence, we are merely in the earlier stages of acquiring knowledge.

Certainly, as discussed in some depth in Chapter 4, there are those who in the past have addressed themselves to adult behavior in general and adult career behavior in particular. Not the least of these has been Buehler (1933), to whom Donald Super and others have acknowledged a great debt in the development of their own work. Buehler's attempts to evolve a comprehensive psychology of the entire course of life have provided a stimulus and a framework for many subsequent researchers. Among others, Tiedeman and O'Hara (1963) have also provided some valuable thoughts and data on adult career stages. We are beginning to receive the benefit of data from longitudinal studies such as the Career Pattern Study (Super, 1977, 1980; Super & Kidd, 1979), Career Development Study (Gribbons & Lohnes, 1982), and Project Talent (Abeles, Steel, & Wise, 1980; Flanagan, 1978), whose initial early adolescent subjects have now reached adulthood.

Newer adult instrumentation is also being developed. For example, Savickas, Passen, and Jarjoura (1988) compared two of an increasing number of adult career-related inventories: Super's Adult Career Concerns Inventory (ACCI) and Crites's Career Adjustment and Development Inventory (CADI). They determined that—for a group of salespeople at least—the two instruments actually measure different constructs. The CADI, in their judgment, measures vocational development, whereas the ACCI does not; instead it assesses concern with how requirements or opportunities for development, adaptation, or change in a career are being met. They consequently recommend that the instruments be used in tandem. Niles, Lewis, and Hartung (1997) converted the response options of the ACCI to a behavioral response format (i.e., *"I have not yet thought about it"* to *"I have already done this"*) and found that the behavioral version of the ACCI was a useful measure of career development task involvement for initial career explorers (i.e., traditional-aged college students). In a subsequent study using the ACCI to identify different ways in which adult career counseling clients use career exploratory behavior to cope with career development tasks, Niles, Anderson, and Goodnough (1998) found three clusters of career explorers. The first cluster was viewed as attempting to find ways to cope with current organizational demands—either to maintain, innovate, or advance in their current positions. The second cluster was viewed as using exploratory behavior to recycle into new occupations or to reenter to workforce after a period of unemployment. The third cluster of career explorers was exploring for the purpose of innovating. That is, they interested in acquiring new ideas and then using these new ideas either in the same organization, a new organization, in the same occupation, or in a new occupation. Niles and his colleagues contend that the results of this study help to operationalize Super's definition of career adaptability and highlight the importance of exploration regardless of one's career or life stage. Finally, these researchers suggest that the ACCI is a useful inventory for helping clients identify the focus of their exploratory needs and for determining the resources clients may need to sue to cope with their career concerns. Studies such as these help address Whiston's (1990) earlier caution in the use of the ACCI because of few validation studies, inadequate normative data, and lack of support for distinct stages. The cluster analysis results from the Niles, Anderson, and Goodnough

(1998) study also highlight the fact that adult career development is non-linear and adults recycle through career tasks and tend to have concern related to multiple tasks and stages simultaneously.

There is also increasing support for a *renewal* stage in the career development of adults. C. P. Williams and Savickas (1990) examined workers in the maintenance stage of their careers to test Super's notions about the developmental tasks necessary at this point in one's career development. They found that, in general, the tasks that these workers identified as important did correspond to Super's hypotheses, although some were suggested to occur sooner or later than Super surmised. These tasks included keeping up with new developments, struggling to hold on, shifting focus (developing new competencies, expanding, and so on), and preparing for retirement (decelerating). A fifth component—continuing education—was a task that was identified but that was not in Super's schema. Similarly, a sixth task—questioning future directions and goals—did not match Super's speculations. It is this last task that suggests a renewal component in the maintenance stage of career development. Clearly, this suggestion is supported by the results of the Niles, Anderson, and Goodnough (1998) study.

Thus, we do know something about adult behaviors and needs—at least enough to make an informed start at comprehensive delivery of career facilitating services, but there is much more to learn before the "science" of career facilitation with adults replaces the current "art." This chapter summarizes some of the existing knowledge, describes some of the delivery systems in use, and generally provides an introduction to the career counseling of adults.

FACTORS UNDERLYING COUNSELING ADULTS

Obviously the adult population is completely heterogeneous. It is not a population contained within a single institution, such as the school. The targets of career counseling, therefore, potentially include each person in the labor force and each adult seeking to enter the labor force. For our purposes here, however, some delineation is necessary. In Chapter 13, we will discuss several adult subpopulations: (1) unemployed, dislocated, and discouraged workers; (2) "burned-out" workers; (3) working mothers; (4) dual-career couples; (5) job seekers; and (6) dissatisfied workers. In this chapter, however, we will concentrate on the four adult subpopulations mentioned at the beginning of the chapter.

Characteristics of the Population

Career counseling of adults should be viewed within the context of changes in society, many of which have been discussed in Chapter 3. In general we may point to the following characteristics that significantly affect the career counseling of adults:

1. *Changing marital patterns.* The marriage rate remains lower than in times past, women are getting married later in life, and the divorce rate is substantial (for example, one out of every three married women 30 years old has been or will be divorced).

2. *Changing childbearing and childrearing patterns.* The birth rate has declined significantly from the past. Changes in the birth rate have caused increases and decreases in the number of workers in various age groups of the population; affecting both the opportunities open for workers and the types of goods and services in demand by society. Because of divorce and out-of-wedlock births, fewer than 70 percent of all children under 18 live with both of their natural parents.

3. *Changing occupational patterns.* The alteration of the occupational structure causes unemployment, underemployment, and frustration as well as opportunities. The information economy and the service economy require different workers from those needed in a goods-producing, industrial economy. The nature of work itself is in flux.

4. *Changing employment opportunities.* As corporations and organizations "downsize" their permanent work forces, they are increasing the number of part-time and temporary employees. Increasingly, workers work several part-time jobs to earn a sufficient income, have little likelihood of permanent institutional identity, and have inadequate health care benefits.

5. *Changing educational requirements for many occupations.* As a result of increases in the use of advanced technology throughout the occupational structure and the transfer of some industries to other nations, workers in virtually any context will be required to have greater technological competence than was the case when most industrial or business operations were done manually (Rifkin, 2000). That basic competences in reading, writing, and mathematics are necessary is a given in today's workplace.

All of these factors can have a profound effect on the kind and frequency of career counseling services required by the adult population.

Within this context of external changes, adults are also experiencing internal changes—mental, physical, and emotional—that are in symbiotic relationship with their work. The process of aging is indeed complex, stemming from endocrine changes; aspiration-achievement discrepancies; stagnation-versus-growth Ericksonian issues; the more apparent reality of death and dying; changes in relationships with spouse, children, and parents; role changes; and other factors. Each of these changes in life may affect attitudes toward and performance at work, just as the experience of work can affect attitudes toward and general behavior in one's nonwork life. By far the most common psychological difficulty of aging workers is depression (Yolles, Krinsky, Kieffer, & Carone, 1984).

The types of career problems with which adults may need to cope are numerous. One attempt at a taxonomy of these problems is that devised by R. E. Campbell and Cellini (1981). They categorize adult problems into four groups: (1) problems in career decision making, (2) problems in implementing career plans, (3) problems in organization/institutional performance, and (4) problems in organizational/institutional adaptation. The full taxonomy is presented in Chapter 2.

There are those who urge that as much attention must be given to educational opportunities across the life span as are now devoted to approximately the first quarter of one's lifetime. Harootyan and Feldman (1990), found, for example, that increasingly workers will be using lifelong education in a wide variety of ways, ranging from survival skills (for example, basic literacy and work-related learning) to exploring new roles (for instance, leisure, career shifts, and so forth). Some of this learning will be self-directed; some will involve technical support. Learning will occur in diverse locations, from shopping malls to websites to community centers. In short, lifelong learning is an activity expected to increase substantially from what exists now, and what is extant in stores, factories, laboratories, the military, and so on is already a huge enterprise.

Adult clients are indeed a diverse lot, and their need for holistic career counseling, that is counseling that addresses personal, family, leisure, and work concerns, will increase in the next decade. Given this complexity and heterogeneity, we turn now to discussions of planning considerations with adults and of career planning techniques with adults.

Planning Considerations

The framework of service delivery with adults is more problematic than it is with younger clients. Compared with programs and theory effected in educational institutions and with younger counselees, the field lacks historical perspective, empirically verified techniques, validated materials, and pertinent theory. Nevertheless, the career counseling of adults will probably be made more efficient and effective if attention is given to the following suggestions regarding planning.

1. Goals and objectives should be based on some model of the needs of adults at various stages of adult life and with diverse presenting problems. Although the body of knowledge pertaining to the needs of subpopulations of adults (as described in this book) is currently rather small, it is growing daily; there is enough useful material to begin. Particularly helpful to the counselor will be journals about which many counselors new to counseling adults may not be aware: *Industrial Gerontology, Journal of Gerontology, Monthly Labor Review, Industrial Sociology, Journal of Employment Counseling, Personnel Administration, Gerontologist,* and *Family Coordinator.*
2. The physical centrality of adult career counseling services, the hours of operation, and the publicizing of such services should be such that the populations to be served readily know what career counseling opportunities exist and that the facilities can be reached with minimum discomfort and maximum ease. Preretirement counseling located in places of employment; women's programs attached to continuing education programs of high schools, colleges, and universities; improved dissemination efforts by the U.S. Employment Service branches; on-line career services; and counseling with senior citizens in centers for the aged are all examples of attempts to expedite service delivery.

3. Middle-class adults who seek career counseling are typically highly motivated; however, they also participate in a complex web of life roles that can influence their sense of hope for being able to make career changes (e.g., an adult with children in high school may feel unable to make immediate career changes due to financial pressure associated with future college tuition expenses). Often, career decisions of adults will involve simultaneous demands on spouses, children, and the extended family People in earlier stages of career development frequently must establish readiness; the challenge for the counselor of adults is to capitalize on the readiness and motivation that the adult brings to career counseling. Understanding adult clients' readiness and their complex life structure involvements are essential starting points in career counseling with adults.
4. Adults generally have little tolerance for the abstract in career counseling. There is an immediacy, an urgency, and a concreteness to their concerns. They are, on the average, able to phrase their questions in self-referent terms that are concise and meaningful. They may expect career counselors to rely heavily on career assessments to help them resolve their career concerns, but they most value career counseling that is supportive, collaborative, and counseling-based.
5. The bases on which adults ought to make decisions are probably little different from those required by decision makers at an earlier stage of development. They should have a knowledge of self, a knowledge of the world of work, and decision-making skills. In some subpopulations of adults (such as midcareer shifters), these characteristics may be relatively well developed; in others (such as women seeking to enter the nonhousehold labor force for the first time at a relatively advanced age), these requirements may be as undeveloped as in the average adolescent. In all of these instances, career counselors pay attention to the degree to which career beliefs and self-beliefs may be facilitating or impeding career development.
6. The delivery of services should be systematic, although the progression may be accelerated because of the accrued experience of the clientele. In short, goals must be translated into activities, suitable materials for the conduct of these activities must be discovered or invented, and evaluation should occur to determine the extent to which goals have been achieved as a result of the activities provided.
7. Specificity, with flexibility, is a key in planning. Throughout most of the school years, relatively broad and broadening goals, such as career awareness, exploration, conceptualization, perceptualization, and generalization, are laudable ends in themselves. With some adults, it may be necessary to achieve these goals, but the counselor must go on from that point to help adults to narrow generated alternatives, to negotiate systems, to focus interests, to secure employment, or otherwise to deal in self-relevant specifics. Given the current nature of work, however, adults will need to become more comfortable with flexibility in their career plans. That is, career counselors will need to help their adult clients explore multiple ways in which specific goals can be implemented. Expansion is a primary goal for the young; specificity with flexibility is an aim with the adult.
8. A great many adults simply want information. Others may want counseling in addition to information. Thus, information dissemination becomes a highly important service for adults. Helping adult clients feel comfortable using various media (e.g., books, websites, information interviewing) in accessing career information is important.

S. S. Moore (1985) suggests six beliefs that might undergird the practice of counseling adults, no matter what specific theory of adult development a counselor espouses:

1. Adulthood is full of conflict and choice. Adults can expect to encounter change in their lives.
2. The work of psychological development does not end with the onset of maturity—personality development, character formation, and adaptation to and interaction with the external environment and the internal self all continue well beyond the age of 21.
3. As people grow older, they grow more and more different from one another—diversity increases with age.
4. Career development cannot be separated from the individual's physical, emotional, and cognitive

development. It is connected to all aspects of one's life—leisure, education, values, motivation, lifestyle, and self-concept.
5. Counselors can help adults negotiate change by helping them to identify and build on their natural strengths.
6. Counselors are caregivers, not caretakers. We are there to support, teach, and help individuals reach their own potential. We are not there to direct them into what we think is right for them or what we want for them. We believe that they are the architects of their own lives. (p. ix)

Career Counseling Techniques

Almost any career counseling technique used with younger populations can, of course, be used with adults. Basically the goals are the same: self-knowledge of various types, its relationship to the worlds of work and education or training, and effective decision-making skills, among others. Many of the techniques that the counselor will use in working with adults are implicit in the goal statements for each adult subpopulation and in the planning considerations just presented. Specifically, as counselors work with adults, they should remember the following unique considerations that should be added to their repertoire of career helping strategies and behaviors.

1. Especially with unskilled adults from lower occupational levels, *motivation* is a primary focus of career assistance. Readiness and motivation for work are frequently lacking in some adults, despite the axiom that people want to work. Counselors must seek to establish within some adults the desire to work.

2. Although much career counseling with adults can be developmental (in the sense of commonalities at given stages of life), a good deal of the focus of adult career counseling will be crisis-generated and crises-centered. Frequently, therefore, what have come to be termed *crisis intervention* techniques will be used. Crisis intervention provides quick, short-term relief in an emergency situation. The counselor deals with the immediate problem rather than with the underlying causes of the problem in providing the temporary relief.

3. Many adults will be searching for what has loosely been defined as *self-actualization.* Their expectations and perceptions that some future work will enable them to achieve self-actualization, however, often prove to be unrealistic. Counselors should work with adults within a framework of *reality.* This is not to say that adults ought to be discouraged from having their heads in the clouds; rather, they should be simultaneously aided to keep their feet on the ground.

4. The *dissemination of information,* a cognitive activity anathema to some counselors, is an important strategy in the career counseling of adults. Adults want answers to specific questions; counselors should provide those answers, or they should assist clients in finding answers for themselves.

5. *Testing* and the use of test results with certain adult subpopulations should be approached tentatively. Several researchers have pointed out that norms for adult populations are frequently nonexistent and that there is often not a demonstrated relationship between test score and job performance for a specified adult clientele. Certain types of test data, especially discriminant data that tell people how much they resemble certain groups, are often useful. However, testing should occur with a specific purpose in mind rather that simply for the sake of administering a test. Both objective and subjective assessments are useful. Clients should participate collaboratively with the counselor in determining whether a specific assessment may be useful in meeting a particular client need.

6. *Counseling techniques* that are generic to all forms of counseling (e.g., establishing rapport, reflective listening, providing support) are helpful in career counseling with adults as well. Being able to use these skills effectively with adults requires counselors to engage in self-examination to be sure that they are not consciously or unconsciously guilty of ageism (negative attitudes toward any age group).

MIDCAREER CHANGERS

It is difficult to discover exactly how many Americans change careers each year, partly because of differing definitions of exactly what constitutes a career change (a shift from one Holland or Roe category to another, from one occupational title to another, or from one job to another). We estimate that approximately 5 to 10 percent of Americans change occupations each year and that about one-half of these changers are over 30 years of age. It is safe to say that millions of other workers would like to change but do not or cannot.

Reasons for Change

The reasons that people voluntarily change jobs are many and varied. Sometimes interests, capacities, and values do not fit with the demands of an initial occupational choice. Expectation-reality gaps quickly become apparent upon one's entry into an occupation. Perhaps original occupational choice was determined more by the demands of a significant other (for example, a parent) than by the chooser's own expression of free will. Material needs or wants may have increased to the point where a current occupation fails to meet these enhanced living standards. Employer practices, work environments, the lack of variety in some occupations, too much or too little pressure, too many physical demands, no time for leisure activities, plateauing, boredom—all of these factors and many others may impel individuals to leave an originally chosen occupation, to *push* them out. Other factors may *pull* someone into a new occupation because the change seems attractive. Some changes are anticipated, whereas others are unforeseen. For example, unanticipated events such as illness, divorce, death of a spouse, and job dislocation cause individuals to change occupations.

Not too long ago, there was a prevalent notion that voluntary career shifters were "oddballs," individuals who because of some personality flaw or character disorder were deficient in adaptive skills, were professional malcontents, or were otherwise lacking in some way. In fact, most studies of career shifters versus career persisters indicate no differences in emotional adjustment; midcareer change does not necessarily constitute floundering or pathological behavior. In many instance, midcareer changers are responding adaptively to changes in themselves and in the world of work. Goodman and Savage (1999) use the metaphor of the "dental model" to describe how adults need ongoing career assistance throughout their working lives to receive "regular checkups, routine maintenance, and to navigate successfully in today's rapidly changing world" (p. 20). Thus, we believe that voluntary midcareer shifts are generally acts of a mentally healthy personality.

This general mentally healthy condition is not to say that shifters are without concerns and issues. Based on a longitudinal study of 647 clients who had been served by the University of Rochester Adult Career Counseling Center, Gladstein (1994) drew some conclusions about changing careers. Of these clients, 44.7 percent, already working, said that they wanted a career change. Despite their desire to move to new careers, however, the number of people who had changed five years after counseling was minimal. Clearly, changing careers is not easy. One apparent reason is that some clients had career problems that were enmeshed with personal difficulties because about 61 percent sought additional counseling or psychotherapy elsewhere. Gladstein advises that counselors therefore focus on multiple issues (e.g., family, social, role of significant others, couple career counseling) when working with midcareer shifters.

Anderson and Niles (2000) make similar recommendations to those offered by Gladstein (1994). Forty-three adult career counseling clients indicated that they found counselor acts that encouraged client self-exploration, were supportive, and provided relevant information were most helpful in the career counseling they received.

Developmentalists see midcareer changes as simply an alternative available in a predictable stage of adult life. D. J. Levinson and colleagues (1978), in their taxonomy of adult male development, suggest that midcareer shifts are most likely to occur during what they have termed the Becoming One's Own Man (BOOM) stage (about age 35 to 39). It is during this stage that men are evidently most prone to experience constraint and oppression in work and to seek resolution of these feelings. In their study of academics, Entrekin and Everett (1981) identified a similar stage that comes a bit later in life. The ages from 30 to 44 are described as a "settling in" period; 45 to 49 are seen as a span of years in which the individual reaches out and becomes restless, exhibiting more change needs; 50 to 54 are viewed as a settling down time; and after 55, the individual academic is thought to be finishing his career. Others have described a similar phenomenon that can occur anywhere from the late 30s to the early 50s as midolescence.

Others see midcareer change as a case of incongruity based on Holland's categories. Congruency in terms of Holland's theory has been found to be related to more stable careers in women and men (H. A. Rose & Elton, 1982) and to more career-mature individuals (Guthrie & Herman, 1982). Jepsen and Chouduri

(2001) used Holland codes to classify longitudinal data pertaining to midcareer occupational patterns. Specifically, Jepsen and Chouduri identified three groups of occupational patterns. The first group remained employed within the same Holland type category for the entire 25-year period of the study. There were two groups of midcareer changers. The first group consisted of individuals who switched occupational code categories during the first seven years following high school and then remained in that type of occupation for the rest of the 25-year period of the study. The final group was labeled as "advancing changers" because they started in an occupation and then "advanced" to an enterprising occupation sometime during the 25 years of the study. Interestingly, Jepsen and Chouduri found that occupational stability was negatively associated with overall career satisfaction and current job satisfaction.

Changing worker needs and interests are other reasons for career change. This thesis is supported in a study by Meir (1988) that suggests the lack of congruence between within-occupation interests and specialty in midcareer may be an impetus to career change. He contends that occupational choice satisfaction is more than a function of choice of correct occupational field in young adulthood; in the career maintenance stage, it is more a function of appropriate occupational specialty. Thus, it may be that original choice of occupation was reasonable, but later choice of specialty was inappropriate and could lead to career change.

Doering and Rhodes (1989) studied career change among teachers (defined as movement to an occupation that is not part of a teacher's traditional career progression). Using a semistructured, in-depth interview technique with 20 participants, they determined that the top five reasons that were cited for career change were push-out types of considerations: inadequate pay; lack of challenge, stimulation, or opportunity to grow; lack of advancement opportunities; dissatisfaction with classroom; and too demanding a workload. They also determined that the time between thinking about a change and deciding to change ranged from one month to six years, with a median of two years. Apparently the gestation period is usually quite long. The three major factors that facilitated a change were support of family, friends, and spouse; financial aid; and self-confidence. Interestingly, few of these career shifters availed themselves of career counseling opportunities.

It may be that the organizational, environmental, and personal variables that cause individuals to want to change careers vary from occupation to occupation. Using a sample of teachers, for example, Rhodes and Doering (1993) found that issues of career development (advancement, for instance), social status, and compensation all contributed to educators expressing an intent to change careers. Someone unhappy in an occupation in which each of these three variables is high would have other reasons for changing careers. Aryee, Chay, and Chew (1994) have suggested also that the career stage of an individual makes a difference. A person's *career* satisfaction is important in the stabilization stage, but it is his or her *organizational* commitment that is more important in the maintenance stage. Thus, *timing* may be important in the desire to make a career change. The particular set of needs, values, and career concerns of a given stage may cause a person to seek change, but at a later stage, the same set would not be bothersome.

Pursuing the concept of what resources facilitate or impede career shifts, Heppner, Multon, and Johnston (1994) have developed the *Career Transitions Inventory* (CTI), a 40-item multidimensional measure of the psychological resources that adults bring to a career transition. Five factors are investigated: (1) readiness (e.g., "Even though there are risks, I think there is a realistic hope of finding a better career choice"); (2) confidence (e.g., "I am not one of those people who was brought up to believe I could be anything I wanted to be"); (3) control (e.g., "If you think you are really calling the shots in your career transition, you are only fooling yourself"); (4) perceived support (e.g., "People whom I respect have said they think I can make this career transition successfully"); and (5) decision independence (e.g., "It is hard for me to juggle this career transition given the responsibilities I feel for people in my life"). Thus, the factors measure how people appraise the motivation for a career change, how effective they feel in completing the necessary tasks, how much they believe the choice is in their control, how much support and how much risk are involved, and how much the decision is autonomous or includes others.

In any case, whether midcareer changes are caused by frustration and anxiety; by growth, achievement, and expansion motives; by a recognition of one's individual differences; or by some other factor or a combination of factors, the midcareer shifter should be viewed, in general and barring evidence to the contrary, as a mentally healthy individual. Those in the process of midcareer change are usually at least in their late 20s and beyond. In a chronological sense, they are middle-aged, and with middle age comes many changes.

Those Who Change

Who goes through midlife career change? Every occupation is represented, but some are more visible than others. Classic cases of midlife career change can be found in the ranks of those who put in twenty years or so in the military or in municipal activities, such as fire and police protection, and then retire at a relatively young age, free to pursue a second career. In the 1970s, thousands of engineers and scientists became unemployed because of substantial cuts in space and defense spending; these workers in declining industries were often forced to seek unrelated types of employment, or to take lower-paying jobs in the same occupation. More recently, the field of education experienced cutbacks, causing teachers and other educational personnel to switch career paths. In the late 1980s, thousands of workers in the financial community lost their jobs. In the 1990s, large corporations downsized, causing many middle-aged individuals to make involuntary midcareer changes.

Whether voluntary or involuntary, it is clear that midlife career change is an increasingly visible phenomenon and that a significant proportion of workers will not fit the one life—one occupation mode.

Early research in career patterns gave little attention to the idea of *voluntary* career changes. Drawing on D. C. Miller and Form (1951), Super (1957) described four types of career patterns for men:

1. *The stable career pattern.* In this category are found most professional careers, many managers, some skilled workers, and to a lesser extent semiskilled and clerical workers. They are persons who have gone directly from school or college into a type of work that they have consistently followed: In other words, they have essentially skipped the trial work period.
2. *The conventional career pattern.* In this pattern, the sequence of jobs follows the typical progression from initial to trial to stable employment. This pattern is most typical of managerial, skilled, and clerical workers, but characterizes some professionals and domestic workers.
3. *The unstable career pattern.* Here the sequence is trial-stable-trial: The worker does not succeed in establishing himself permanently in what might have been a lifetime job or occupation but instead gives up his potential career in one field and goes off in a different direction in which he may or may not establish himself. This sequence is seen most often in semiskilled, clerical, and domestic workers.
4. *The multiple-trial career pattern.* This is the pattern of frequent change of employment, with no one type sufficiently prolonged or dominant to justify calling the person established in a career. This type of sequence is observed most often in domestic, clerical, and semiskilled workers, who not infrequently shift from one type of work to another and accumulate the most disconnected of work histories. (pp. 73–74)

Categories 3 and 4 pertain to midlife career shifters, but there is little cognizance of the voluntary or involuntary shifts of well-established workers within an occupation. As we have seen, such shifts by those who have indeed established themselves in an occupation are not at all rare.

More recently, Hall and associates (1996) have discussed the "protean career." They suggest:

> *People's careers increasingly will become a succession of "ministages" (or short cycle learning stages) of exploration-trial-mastery-exit, as they move into and out of various product areas, technologies, functions, organizations, and other work environments.... This protean form of career involves horizontal growth, expanding one's range of competencies and ways of connecting to work and other people, as opposed to the more traditional vertical growth of success.... In the protean form of growth, the goal is learning, psychological success, and expansion of the identity. In the more traditional form, the goal was advancement, success and esteem in the eyes of others, and power. (p. 35)*

Hall and Associates use of the term "protean" is apt. Adult career development in the future is likely to be ad hoc, spontaneous, unpredictable, and embedded in environmental and organizational flux. Flexibility on the part of the adult worker will not only be desired, it will be required. Put another way, "protean careers" will require "protean selves" (Herr, 2002).

McAuliffe's (1993) philosophical speculations about the way people extract meaning from experience and how they change (termed *constructive development*) suggest that individuals undergoing career transition redefine themselves. In the case of midcareer shifters, this transitioning requires counseling that treats the idea of career as a "quest, an unfolding that requires active participation by the meaning-making individual.... Career counselors from this perspective then...help them to identify their unarticulated fundamental values and needs, to explore the competing beliefs that leave those values unexpressed, and to translate the implications of this exploration into viable actions that are authentic responses to that data" (p. 27).

Midlife career changes are becoming increasingly common. Those in the midst of such voluntary or involuntary shifts require assistance in career planning. There is currently no pervasive delivery system for providing this aid, although isolated programs directed toward this end do exist.

Counseling Midcareer Shifters

In contrast to younger decision makers, midlife career shifters typically have accrued experience and developed judgment that enables them to approach the career decision-making process with maturity and knowledge. Even so, the career counselor working with this population should uncover certain common factors even within this group. Some of these factors are addressed in the following goals.

1. Help the individual to explore, specify, and evaluate the reasons for a career shift. Is the individual confused and anxious as a result of an involuntary career shift, secure and optimistic because of the prospects of a voluntary career shift, or some combination of both? Are stress factors with which an individual has difficulty coping in a current job likely to be present in an intended job? Does the individual appear distressed, depressed, or dysfunctional? How carefully has the individual planned? What are the individual's facilitating and constraining self-beliefs? These and other questions relate to the goal of shift clarification.

2. Assist the individual in acquiring all necessary information relevant to a career shift. Does the individual recognize the relationship between education or training and the proposed work shift? What steps are necessary to effect the change? Where and how does one get the necessary information?

3. Help the individual to envision the possible effects of a career shift. Will there be financial ramifications? Will family life be affected? Will lifestyle change appreciably? Will geographical relocation be required? What will be the immediate, intermediate, and long-range consequences? What resources (financial, emotional, and so on) does the individual have to manage these consequences?

4. Help the individual develop appropriate job-seeking or education-seeking behaviors. Can the person write an effective résumé? Does the individual have good skills as an interviewee? Has he or she narrowed down to manageable proportions the education or training universe? Does the person have adequate information? These concerns will be treated in detail in the next chapter.

5. Assist the individual in clarifying abilities, interests, values, and personal characteristics. Will the attributes of the person facilitate or impede the transition to a different career, occupation, or job? Does the person possess characteristics that would make his or her functioning unsatisfying in a particular job? Are there any physical, mental, or emotional problems to be considered?

6. Assist, if appropriate, in placing the individual in a job. Certain settings wherein counselors work with midcareer shifters will have placement as a goal (such as the Employment Service or outplacement counseling). Other agencies that do not perform a brokerage role may well consider performing this function if no alternative is readily available.

7. Gauge the extent of the individual's support network. Are social support and financial support adequate to meet the demands of the career change? What buffers exist to assuage the sometimes painful effects of a significant life change?

Because organizational responses are generally slow (see Chapter 11), it is likely that in the foreseeable future, midcareer shifters will be helped to rearrange their internal structures rather than the organizations within society acting to facilitate changes. In any case, we are now only beginning to understand the dynamics of midcareer shifts and to devise helpful interventions.

Although we have some rudimentary knowledge about midcareer shifters, the research in this area has been relatively sparse and has suffered from a number of methodological deficiencies. First, samples studied have been small and nonrepresentative. Subjects have typically been well-educated, white men with an overrepresentation of academics, both former and current. Second, subjects are often in school or in training for an occupation and have not actually effected a career change. Third, subjects vary considerably in terms of such variables as age and length of time in the first occupation. Fourth, definitions of *voluntary* and *career change* also vary. Fifth, relatively few comparison studies of changers versus nonchangers have been accomplished. Sixth, research designs are usually cross-sectional or retrospective; longitudinal studies would be less limiting. Finally, no standardized instruments of proven validity and reliability and with adequate normative data exist that are designed to operationalize the process of midcareer change. There is also no single overall theory of adult development in which to imbed midcareer research. It is little wonder, then, that research in this area is still in the exploratory stage and that researchers are trying simply to generate hypotheses rather than to test them.

WOMEN ENTERING OR REENTERING THE LABOR FORCE

In Chapter 5 we discussed some career considerations unique to women. A specific aspect of careers relating to adults is the case of women who enter or reenter the labor force after a period of childbearing and childrearing.

Career Patterns

Super (1957, pp. 77–78) has classified the career patterns of women as follows:

1. *The stable homemaking career pattern.* This category includes all women who marry while in or very shortly after leaving school or college, having expected to do so and having no significant work experience.

2. *The conventional career pattern.* In this pattern of working, followed by homemaking, the young woman leaving school or college goes to work for a period of several months or several years, in an occupation that is open to her without training beyond that which she obtained in her general education, in brief professional education substituted for general education, or in some relatively brief post–high school or post-collegiate education. Clerical work, teaching, nursing, occupational therapy, and secretarial work illustrate these types of occupations. They are generally viewed as stop gaps but may be thought of as life careers, with subsequent changes of aspirations. They are often valuable as an opportunity for developing independence and a sense of being a person in one's own right. Marrying after this relatively brief work experience, the young woman becomes a full-time homemaker.

3. *The stable working career pattern.* The sequence in this type of career pattern is one of entering the workforce on leaving school, college, or professional school and embarking on a career that becomes the woman's life's work. She may perceive it as a life career from the start: A small percentage of young women do have strong career (as contrasted with homemaking) motivation and interest [*Note:* This was in 1957]. Or she may at first view her working career as a preliminary to marriage or a working career to resume after a period of full-time homemaking.

4. *The double-track career pattern.* This is a pattern of the woman who goes to work after completing her education, marries, and continues with a double career of working and homemaking. She may take occasional time out for childbearing. The pattern is most common near the upper and lower ends of the occupational scale, among women physicians and scientists, and among women domestics, presumably because the challenge of the work, or the income it produces, is important to the woman in question. The double role is in neither case easy, for the married working woman usually has two jobs, one with and one without pay.

5. *The interrupted career pattern.* Here the sequence is one of working, homemaking, and working while or instead of homemaking. The young woman works for some time, then marries, and then, when her children are old enough for her to leave them, when financial needs—including those from being widowed or divorced—or interest in working becomes dominant, she returns to work.

6. *The unstable career pattern.* In women, this type of career pattern consists of working, homemaking, working again, returning to full-time homemaking, and so on. It results most often from irregular economic pressures that make extra earnings necessary despite homemaking preferences or needs from poor health necessitating giving up employment, or from a combination of these. This pattern is observed most often at the lower socioeconomic levels.

7. *The multiple-trial career pattern.* This pattern is the same in women as the similarly named pattern in men; it consists of a succession of unrelated jobs, with stability in none, resulting in the individual having no genuine life work.*

In this chapter, we are concerned with women in patterns 2, 4, 5, and 6. As we saw in Chapter 5, more women have entered and are entering the labor force; a significant proportion of those women are reentering the world of work and education after a substantial hiatus or are older women entering for the first time. These women feel considerable insecurity, stress, and a variety of emotions and uncertainties that call for professional career interventions.

More and more reentry or first-time entry women in their 30s and 40s are responding to social changes by moving in new directions: going to school, pursuing careers, or structuring family lives in innovative ways. When they do, however, they experience considerably more career indecision than do high school or college women. This finding adds further evidence to support the need for career interventions for reentry women. In addition, there are social and psychological barriers facing reentry women: job discrimination, lack of marketable skills, guilt feelings, and a low opinion of their own abilities.

Reasons for Returning to a Career

Reentry women is a term used to describe women reentering education or work after an absence ranging from a few to many years. Women return to careers for many reasons. Reentry women have reported vocational reasons as the primary motive for both educational and workforce reentry (Padula, 1994). Perhaps the most obvious reason for reentry, however, is financial. In an age of inflation, it is frequently necessary for both partners to work to maintain a standard of living gained when only the husband worked, let alone to increase a standard of living. In times of high unemployment, a wife may be the only marriage partner able to find work. Divorce and widowhood also may cause financial strain that necessitates reentry. In any case, financial necessity, however idiosyncratically defined, is a major work motivator for reentry women.

Padula (1994) reviewed literature related to reentry women. Padula noted that women chose to reenter education or work due to vocational factors, family variables, and the desire to increase their knowledge. Based on these findings, Padula recommend interventions for reentry women that include career planning classes, individual career counseling, classes in relationship and communication skills, group therapy, family therapy, and educational planning.

A related reason for women reentering work outside the home is fulfillment. Declining birth rates mean fewer years of childbearing and childrearing, and housekeeping duties are much easier, thus leaving women technologically unemployed in the sense of traditional motherhood. In many cases, such a condition leads to ennui, frustration, a deficient sense of personal worth and identity, and so on. There is some early research to suggest that for many women the empty-nest period is an acute crisis stage. With the termination of the family life cycle, when children have left the home and nurturing demands are no longer present, many women review their lives; find themselves fighting feelings of impotence, helplessness, and despair; and search for outlets to fill the void resulting from the empty nest. (At least that is the theory.)

Black and Hill (1984) discovered in their sample of 232 educated, married women in their 50s that these individuals appeared to be happy regardless of their employment status, age, socioeconomic status, educational level, husband's attitude toward his spouse, working life stressors, and menopausal symptoms. They conclude that for well-educated, middle-aged women, the empty nest is not an apparent problem. For women with other problems, however, the empty nest may touch off distress with which they have difficulty coping.

Confirming this reassessment of the presumed effects of the empty nest, Raup and Myers (1989)

**Source:* From Donald Super, *The Psychology of Careers.* New York: Harper Collins Publishers, 1957. Reprinted by permission.

concluded that the period represents a major life change or transition but that relatively few women experience negative effects because of the loss of an active parenting role. These are women who fail to invest in new life roles. What we do not know currently is how to identify at an earlier stage those who are potentially at risk in this normal phase of family development.

The historical period in which a woman lives is as important in determining her reentry into the labor force as are her personal circumstances. Moen, Downey, and Bolger (1990) looked at the decade of the 1970s and determined that better educated homemakers were more likely and older homemakers less likely to reenter the labor force. Martial dissolution also obviously affected a woman's decision to reenter. For each of these three variables, however, there were differences throughout the decade. In line with previously discussed research findings in this chapter, they discovered that the so-called empty-nest phase was not so strong a predictor of reentry as was the entry of the youngest child into a given phase of schooling (for example, elementary, middle, or high school). The differences in reentry rates throughout the decade were ascribed primarily to social changes during that time—changes in public perceptions of women's roles, the continued growth of the traditional female service sector, and new occupational opportunities for young adult as well as midlife women. Women with more education and those whose marriages had dissolved were most likely to take advantage of these opportunities.

Studying the influences that affect adult women's decisions to enroll in college, Mohney and Anderson (1988) concluded that for many such women, the decision was made in the context of what they perceived as other people's needs—children, spouses, and so on. Barriers to earlier enrollment included such variables as parenting demands, multiple roles (for instance, worker, mother, spouse), lack of spousal support, poor self-image (for example, not bright enough, shy), early marriage and pregnancy, lack of financial resources, and so on. Facilitating factors that enabled them later to enroll in college included their perceptions that their children were "old enough," adequate child care, discretionary time, social supports from friends and spouses, and adequate finances, among other influences. Spanard (1990) confirms the results of this study and identifies institutional, situational, and psychosocial barriers specifically related to adults' returning to higher education:

Institutional Barriers

1. Location (place)
2. Schedules (time)
3. Fee structures (cost)
4. Campus friendliness

Situational Barriers

1. Job commitments
2. Home responsibility
3. Lack of money
4. Lack of child care
5. Transportation problems

Psychosocial Barriers

1. Attitudes, beliefs, and values
2. Self-esteem
3. Opinions of others
4. Past experiences as a student (pp. 340–341)

An Australian study of 285 single and married mothers who were "mature age" returnees to education (Burns, Scott, & Cooney, 1993) indicates that on follow-up they were career committed, job satisfied, and in primarily traditional female occupations. Thus, although entry to the labor force may be delayed, once work begins, late entrants appear to be as effective and happy as earlier-entry workers.

We are now in an era when home-based work (especially white-collar work) is increasing because of technological advances in information processing (K. E. Christensen, 1988; Rifkin, 2000). This type of work may provide a bridge that permits many women to transition from no work to complete labor force participation.

The typical woman in the United States enters the labor force immediately after schooling and works for a few years before marrying and having a child. Few women permanently leave the labor force. Most return or never leave at all. Shortages of skilled workers in many professional, managerial, clerical, skilled craft, and service occupations offer women an excellent employment prospect. Nondiscrimination legislation helps to break down barriers to higher-level occupations and to traditionally male-dominated fields. New opportunities in expanding occupations are available. When these opportunities are combined with the trend toward more education for women and toward smaller families (thus muting the effects of fertility on work), the likely result is a modest increase in the labor force participation of women.

Counseling Reentry Women

Much of the counseling for reentry women depends on how long the women have been absent from paid employment and how large a hiatus exists between termination of formal education or training and entry into the labor force. For most women in late entry or in reentry situations, the following goals would seem to be appropriate.

1. Reinforce positive feelings about self-worth and ability to make a contribution in the work force outside the home. Many women lack specific saleable skills or possess obsolescent training; they irrationally translate these deficiencies into feelings of little personal worth. They should be aided to separate employability skills deficits from personal worth estimates. Many married women may have difficulty realizing an identity separate from their husbands after years of making their self-development subservient to family needs. They must be encouraged to assume a multirole existence after a period of essentially restricted roles.

2. Provide any information that may be lacking about basic career decision making: personal assets and limitations, values and attitudes, the world of work, resources, and so on. Despite social sophistication and a generally mature life orientation, women in this category may be vocationally illiterate and may require the most rudimentary types of career information.

3. Assist in exploring changes in lifestyle that may be occasioned by first-time entry or reentry into the labor force. What are the possible consequences of paid employment on marital relationships, continued childrearing, division of labor in the home, leisure activities, and so forth? Will paid labor result in actual economic benefit? In some cases, it will not.

4. Help clients to understand the implications of full-time versus part-time work. Not all women work full-time the year round.

5. Prepare women to deal with possible discrimination, both overt and covert. What possible discriminatory attitudes may be encountered among management? What possibilities exist for subtle or blatant sexual harassment by employers or by fellow workers? Do hiring, promotion, and retention practices present barriers because of sex or age? Do compensation differences exist that cannot otherwise be explained? What are intentional and unintentional sexist questions posed in an interview? How does one combat discrimination on a personal level?

6. Provide specialized experiences, if necessary, in such areas as consciousness raising and assertiveness training.

7. Explore entry-level jobs with extant education versus jobs attainable with additional education or training. Will any job do because of immediate economic necessity, or does she really want a vocation for the rest of her life, or is it some combination of both? Where and how does she obtain the additional education or training?

8. Provide a referral system for placement assistance, provide placement services if no alternative is available, and provide job-seeking and job-hunting skills.

9. Provide follow-up and continuing support. Once the individual has begun to work, there may be needs for assurance, enhancement of coping skills, and general support. Furthermore, the counselor may be able to secure feedback about the types of assistance that might have been provided in the prework situation but were overlooked or not given sufficient attention.

Many excellent programs have been devised to deal with issues of gender in the career development of women and reentry women in particular. These programs have produced some fine materials for use with this subpopulation (for example, EDC/WEEA Publishing Center, 55 Chapel Street, Newton, Massachusetts, 02160). In the best of all possible worlds, reentry women would be provided with mentors to help them negotiate both educational and work transitions (Bauer & Mott, 1990).

As for most other special populations, there are separate statements of principles for counseling and therapy of women. These principles begin where generic counseling competencies leave off and are largely directed toward eliminating sexism in counseling by urging the end of sexist language, banishing preconceived notions about goals for women, forbidding sexual relationships between counselor and client, recognizing unique women's issues and concerns, and remaining professionally alert to the burgeoning literature on women.

The so-called displaced homemaker is a special case of late entry or reentry. Displaced homemakers are usually women who have no income (because of death of a spouse, divorce, and so on), who usually have grown children, and who want to become employed and thus achieve economic independence. Although the number of displaced homemakers is estimated to be between 7 and 16 million, it is difficult to predict accurate numbers (Looby, 2002). Unfortunately, they typically lack job skills or work experience and thus have difficulty entering the labor market. This difficulty often translates into strained financial circumstances. Looby notes that the "most vulnerable of displaced homemakers are those between the ages of 45 and 65 years, who are without male partners and have to assume the financial responsibilities" (p. 205). Welborn and Moore (1985) aptly describe the condition of the displaced homemaker:

> *Often the displaced homemaker is in the position of not only actively needing and seeking employment, but also of being required to cope with a number of other issues, such as feeling out of control, feeling isolated from those segments of society in which she must now operate, feeling little sense of personal power, feeling a void where once she felt intimacy, and feeling a keen sense of disorientation as the emphasis on family is necessarily reduced as she prepares to go to work (p. 104).*

On the premise that reentry women require a different type of career assistance than do traditional students in higher education, Arp and associates (1986) have devised a support group approach for adult students. Over a six-week period, 90-minute sessions were used each week to help nine women and one man (ages 25 to 55) to set individual goals within a context of themes for each weekly session. The sessions addressed the following concerns: What is holding you back? What skills do you possess? Where do you fit in the job market? How do you uncover job openings? Does a résumé make a difference? What can you expect in an interview? Initial evaluations were generally positive.

There are many reports of successful programs designed for reentry women. One career-focused group intervention was provided in the YWCA for ten displaced homemakers over an eight-week period (McAllister & Ponterotto, 1992). The participants presented with a mean age of 44.5, with all but one divorced or separated. All were experiencing the need to find employment to support themselves and their households. Session 1 was "Self-exploration and identification of employment related needs and areas of difficulty"; Session 2, "Integration self-knowledge with career knowledge"; Session 3, "Identification of personal goals"; Session 4, "What kind of job do I want?"; Session 5, "Speaker day (role models)"; Session 6, "What do I know about specific jobs?"; Session 7, "What did I learn about myself from the *Quick Job Hunting Map?";* and Session 8, "My employment goals." About four weeks after the last session, there was a follow-up meeting. Overall, the evaluation was positive.

Drawing from the literature related to counseling displaced homemakers, Looby (2002) recommends that career counselors: refer displaced homemakers to relevant support groups and link displaced homemakers to relevant community support systems (e.g., the church) when appropriate, be familiar with government-sponsored training programs and sources for financial support for displaced homemakers, help displaced homemakers establish realistic career goals and cope with discrimination in hiring and at work, consider referrals to mental health and family counseling when appropriate. Clearly, this special population requires career assistance that involves multiple support systems to help displaced homemakers cope with the substantial challenges they face as they transition into the workforce.

THE OLDER WORKER

Generally speaking, the older or "mature" worker is considered to be over 45. Currently, one in five Americans is over 55; by 2010, one in every four will be. The ratio of Americans older than age 64 compared to Americans aged 20–64 will increase to almost 70 percent between 2000 and 2030 (Miller, 2002). Although age discrimination in employment hiring practices has been theoretically reduced by federal employment acts, there is little doubt that this category of worker faces considerable prejudice in terms of hiring or retention policies and that career problems are heightened for this age group. Older workers who become unemployed spend a longer time finding a new job than younger workers. The Work in America Institute (1980) has pointed out this problem and has recommended actions for employers to make policies age-neutral and responsive to the aging work force. These include the following:

- Review of nondiscriminatory hiring and separation practices to be certain that de facto systems are not operating despite apparent compliance with Equal Employment Opportunity
- Review of age distribution of employees within an organization to be sure that older workers are not overrepresented or underrepresented in any area.
- Examination of alternatives for older workers, such as part-time work, job sharing, work schedule variations, and flex time.

Discrimination against older workers is both morally reprehensible and economically counterproductive. M. L. Levine (1988) argues that age is a general characteristic, just as race or sex is, and is only peripherally related to productivity. Therefore, ageism has no reason for being. Active hostility to older workers in companies appears to be a relatively rare occurrence, but passive-aggressive policies and acts are somewhat more prevalent (for example, limited opportunities for promotion or lateral moves, early retirement incentives, and so on).

An increasing number of postretirement people are returning to the work force, thus swelling the ranks of older workers. In a study by Fontana and Frey (1990), most returnees chose to go back to work to have more contact with people, to earn money, or simply because they would rather work than stay at home. These workers believed that management held few negatively stereotypical views regarding older workers; in fact, they perceived managers as believing that older workers were more productive than younger workers. The 180 postretirement, over 55-years-of-age workers who returned expressed high job satisfaction. These results are consistent with recommendations of Cahill and Salomone (1987) that counseling should be provided for older workers for work life extension, whether individuals continue in a present career, change careers, or work part-time.

Certain firms welcome hiring employees over 55. These include Days Inn hotels, Travelers Corporation, the Riese Organization, and Tiffany & Company. Others do not, which is why the unemployment rate for those 55 and over in the United States has risen about 1.5 percentage points from 1987 through 1992 (3.3 to 4.8 percent), while the unemployment rate for all workers increased only 1.2 points (6.2 to 7.4 percent) during the same period. Perhaps this situation contributes, at least in part, to the fact that people over 60 are more likely to suffer from depression than any other age group.

Older workers are frequently plateaued workers; that is, they have reached the highest point to which they will progress in an organization. Tan and Salamone (1994) suggest that these individuals require a reassessment of career goals and refocused learning goals. They propose that counseling include "opportunity to deal with (a) loss of one's idealized career and personal goals, (b) anger concerning real or perceived negative circumstances or supervisory experiences, and (c) apprehension about the likelihood of future opportunities" (p. 300).

Miller (2002) suggests that career counselors need to be aware of the following trends when working with mature adult clients:

- The population of mature adults is increasing rapidly.
- Although it is possible to make generalizations about the mature adult group, there are also substantial within group differences.
- Many mature adult workers are struggling to comprehend the changes occurring in the nature of work and to understand the resulting workplace demands (e.g., the need for technological competence) resulting from these changes.
- The trend toward earlier retirement is reversing as older workers continue working beyond traditional retirement years.
- Increasingly, retirement is being viewed as a process rather than an event.
- Employers vary greatly with regard to their degree of support for older workers.

Miller recommends that career counselors use a theoretically eclectic approach in their work with older adults. Specifically, Miller incorporates developmental, transition, relational, cognitive-developmental, and narrative theories in her work with mature adult clients.

Brewington and Nassar-McMillan (2000) also recommend an eclectic approach in providing career counseling to older adults. They note that career counselors need to be aware of issues such as the psychological distress associated with job loss that older workers experience, the physical barriers older workers may encounter in their work, and older workers' vulnerability to experiencing skill obsolescence. To address these issues, Brewington and Nassar-McMillan recommend that career counselors draw upon the work of Erikson, Super, and Holland in constructing relevant career interventions.

Attitudinal and Development Factors

Although unemployment among older workers is generally low, when it does strike, it is likely to be for longer periods of time—the median duration is 18 weeks (Morrison, 1984)—and fraught with barriers that produce debasement, humiliation, and frustration. As age increases, occupational mobility decreases, thus cutting down the alternatives for the older worker. These workers experience considerable difficulty getting placed in a job. U.S. Employment Service data have consistently demonstrated over the years that older workers are a substantial proportion of their clientele (more than 30 percent) but that these workers are placed on a less than proportional basis (usually less than 20 percent). Because of their unique problems, the discipline of industrial gerontology has come into being to study the employment and retirement problems of middle-aged and older workers.

The labor force participation of workers over the age of 65 in the United States has actually declined in linear fashion since just before the turn of the century. In 1890, about 68 percent of all men over 65 were in the labor force; by 1930, that figure had dropped to 54 percent; and by 1970, only 25 percent of all men over 65 were still in the labor force (Graney & Cottam, 1981). In fact, the industries that employ the most people in the United States have provided few opportunities for older people's participation. It will be interesting to see how much the raised mandatory retirement age will affect these data and how much the data will be influenced by the declining youth population and the subsequent "graying" of traditional entry-level jobs (such as fast foods, retail sales, and so on).

Many of the problems of older workers are caused by the natural consequences of aging. Some jobs are difficult for those workers who are required to expend considerable physical energy or sustained exertion, to endure highly stressful work environments, or to work rapidly for prolonged time periods. The fact is that, in general, for older workers, intellectual functioning is not impaired. Whenever health has been preserved, verbal scores have remained relatively stable. There is, however, a persistent and progressive decline in performance on most speeded tasks. Hence, older workers are likely to remain stable in their cognitive abilities and to deteriorate in their psychomotor performance. Of course, when extreme old age is considered, the general trend in cognitive functioning is downhill. These conditions are perhaps responsible for the fact that the lowest retirement rates are found in white-collar and service occupations, and the highest rates exist in blue-collar and agricultural occupations.

In a comprehensive review of age-related differences in work attitudes and behavior, Rhodes (1983) reached some general conclusions with which we agree. She found that age is related to overall job satisfaction, satisfaction with work itself, job involvement, internal work motivation, and organizational commitment. Age appears to be negatively related to turnover intention. There also seems to be an increase with age in needs for security and affiliation and preferences for extrinsic job characteristics and having friendly co-workers and supervisors. In terms of career development, she states:

> *Recent studies based on life cycle and career stage models suggest that determinants of job satisfaction and job involvement change depending on one's career stage. Preliminary evidence suggests that task characteristics are more strongly related to job satisfaction and involvement in the trial or early career stage (after a learning period), personal characteristics achieve salience in the midcareer stage, and reward variables, although important throughout, become particularly important in the late career stage. (p. 356)*

The four out of ten American workers who are older face some formidable factors that work against their quickly finding new employment when they are displaced from jobs. Among these factors are (1) many employers' unfavorable attitudes toward older workers; (2) substitution of cheaper labor (such as illegal aliens or women) for older workers; and (3) changes in occupations, industry, and the geographical distribution of jobs that favor the hiring of younger workers who are more flexible and mobile.

This lack of flexibility of older workers is often referred to as the problem of obsolescence. Obsolescence is workers' lack of up-to-date knowledge and skills needed to perform effectively. In terms of employer bias, age does not seem to be a primary determiner of an employer's perception of personal work-related traits, but it does affect the hiring decision because of the potentially shortened work life. The same holds true for older women, who face greater unemployment difficulties than their young counterparts. Employer attitudes are also affected by fears that older workers have more accidents. This is not so; older workers are hurt less often than younger workers, but they are hurt more seriously when they do have an accident. Perhaps the negative association between age and accidents is caused by the fact that older workers who are less capable of meeting the physical aspects of jobs leave the more physically demanding and hazardous jobs.

Reducing the Negative Effect of Ageism

Several approaches have been advocated to reduce the negative effect of ageism in hiring, promotion, and retention. One suggestion has involved job redesign. Such a technique is frequently applied on an informal, personal basis in small enterprises, but it is now being advocated on a massive scale. Essentially, job redesign involves a determination of a job's physical demands and the minimum physical capacities necessary for its performance. Particularly noted are points of strain that might suggest job modification or reallocation to the benefit of the older worker. The attempt is to dovetail worker abilities and job requirements, taking into account both workers needs and production demands. Thus, removing pressures in the work environment can extend employment opportunities for older workers. Job reorganization might also entail allowing workers of greater experience to handle more complex tasks, while inexperienced workers tend to the simpler, more physical aspects of a job.

A related technique has involved the concept of functional age. The theory is that it is unfair and wasteful to judge workers based on chronological age; therefore, the idea is to rate a worker's functional ability on the job—to determine what the worker can do operationally. Two examples of the use of the functional age concept follow. R. A. Snyder, Williams, and Cashman (1984) advocate the use of functional age rather than chronological age as a predictor of reactions to performance feedback. An analog study by J. A. Lee and Clemons (1985) offers some interesting findings related to the kinds of decision-making input data that may be considered when an employer hires an older worker. According to the investigators, the chances of an older worker getting hired increase if the older worker does not have to compete with a younger worker and if the older worker is able to define performance functionally (that is, a behaviorally stated performance report), thus minimizing age stereotypes.

A third approach to accommodating older workers is retraining them to establish eligibility for jobs with specific training requirements. Getting older workers to be motivated for and to engage in retraining is, however, frequently difficult to accomplish. Perhaps some distinctions should be made between the younger older workers (45 to 54) and the older workers (55 to 70).

Counseling the Older Worker

As we have indicated previously, older workers are likely to experience employment difficulties that make them particularly vulnerable to trauma in the career domain. Therefore, many of the goals of career counseling with these clients involve reassurance and immediate assistance:

1. Provide support in building and maintaining positive attitudes toward one's worth and dignity. Is the individual confusing temporary rejection as a worker with rejection as a human being? Does the individual have a work history of rejection? Does the person express feelings of hopelessness, worthlessness, obsolescence, and despair? Is confidence shattered?
2. Explore possible retraining and other avenues for improving employment opportunities.
3. Provide any and all geographic information. Does the individual know where the best markets for employment are? Is mobility a problem?
4. Assess the actual reasons for employment difficulties. For example, is the person coming for assistance because of layoff, resignation, sickness, retirement, or firing?
5. Assist individuals in accurately gauging their present state of motivation, the expectations they hold for future employment, and their perceptions of themselves as workers.

6. Especially with managerial, professional, and technical occupations, help the individual to consider the relative importance of such factors as salary, use of abilities, status, amount of responsibility, security, opportunities for advancement, chance to make a contribution, and so on. Also important is the need to explore the possibilities and consequences of occupational downgrading and salary decrease.
7. Assist in developing job-seeking behaviors, if necessary.
8. Provide placement and follow-up services if no other opportunities exist in the area served; refer to appropriate agencies and institutions if placement services are available.

Rife and Belcher (1994) report a Job Club intervention designed to assist older workers in regaining employment. They found the Job Club method (e.g., half-day workshop on job search techniques and ongoing meetings two afternoons per week) was more successful than traditional job search assistance strategies in achieving reemployment. In fact, almost any type of group career intervention with middle-aged and older adults appears to be effective, whether leader-led or self-directed (Robbins, Chartrand, McFadden, & Lee, 1994).

One of the difficulties in building a research base to contribute to knowledge of older workers is that so many of the studies that have been accomplished are analog in nature and not drawn from actual work settings. Asking college students to engage in "as if" behaviors is a questionable practice in any analog research and may be especially problematic when the focus is the older workers. In addition, testing the physical characteristics, reaction times, and other physiological and psychological processes of older workers independent of the work they are performing is less helpful than assessing their functioning on the job.

PRERETIREMENT AND RETIREMENT

We sometimes forget that retirement and the time immediately preceding it are a part of one's career life; these times are as fraught with potentially anxiety-producing events as are any others. Most of that anxiety for those who have had a work life revolves around the possibility that the loss of work will cause serious problems of adjustment. In Chapter 2, we devoted attention to the purposes that work serves in maintaining an individual's psychological and social well-being.

If employment structures one's time, provides contacts outside the family, contributes to personal identity, enables one to remain active, and satisfies a variety of higher-order needs, the absence of work could have a deleterious effect on some individuals. If nothing is substituted in retirement to contribute to individual well-being, it is logical to assume that loss of work has the potential for inducing psychological malaise. For that reason, some people try to retire partially and ease into the stage, but this partial retirement is prevalent mainly among the self-employed. Many would like to stay in the job market, but discrimination, a lack of job opportunities, and other factors combine to force them to retire completely. Hence, despite the raising of the retirement age, early retirement among men has actually increased. Men, in general, plan to retire earlier than they actually do, however.

Some see loss of work as merely an informal nonceremonious rite of passage, a transition between the world of work and retirement. Even so, retirement for some comes as a great surprise. Several national surveys have indicated that more than 40 percent of individuals who state that they never expected to stop working are retired shortly thereafter. Many people do not plan for retirement at all (Kragie, Gerstein, & Lichtman, 1989). Some studies describe a *retirement syndrome,* characterized by anxiety and depression; other studies find that even people who were strongly committed to work do not demonstrate negative changes in retirement either immediately after the fact or 18 months later. The work-to-retirement transition may well stimulate anxiety of a type that has been termed *anxiety of the end* (Theriault, 1994).

As with most transitions in life, the presence of effective social support is helpful. Social support, however, will not guarantee satisfaction in retirement; it will, almost certainly help those most who have poorly formed personal goals, values, and commitment to retirement (Robbins, Lee, & Wan, 1994).

Much excellent retirement research emanates from a team of researchers at Duke University. Palamore, Burchett, Fillenbaum, George, & Wallman (1985) summarize the findings of seven significant longitudinal studies of retirement. Their analyses take into account the major ways in which retirement may be defined: a subjective assessment by the person; an objective retirement (that is, working less than full time and receiving a pension); or a significant reduction in the number of hours worked. Perhaps the major conclusion is that predictors of actual retirement and of successful retirement depend on the definition of retirement that is used. Predictors such as demographic variables, attitudes toward work and retirement, health, type of work, and so on seem to be differentially predictive, depending on which of the three definitions of retirement is adopted. A second enormously important finding of the Palamore et al. study is that contrary to popular folklore, the average retiree does not experience harmful effects in health. Of course, this may not be so in individual cases, but in terms of normative data, the conclusion of no decline in health as a result of retirement gainsays the conventional belief.

Another example of the potential healthful effects of retirement comes from a study by Howard, Rechnitzer, Cunningham, & Donner (1986). They found that people who were Type A (vigorous verbal and psychomotor mannerisms; sense of time urgency; easily aroused anger and hostility; and extremes of competitiveness, impatience, and achievement striving) decreased toward the more placid Type B behavior one year after retirement. Thus, the mental health of Type A people appears to improve with retirement.

Much of the conflict among findings may be an artifact of the samples used in the studies. We know that several individual differences seem related to successful retirement, and these dimensions may be more or less present in different samples. Among the dimensions that appear to be involved in a positive retirement transition are adequate income, voluntary rather than involuntary retirement, health, specificity of plans and staying active, and history of an orderly rather than a discontinuous career. To extend Super's career maturity idea, some people appear to be retirement-mature, whereas others seem to be retirement-immature. The notion that stress occurs when individuals are forced into a life stage before they are ready seems reasonable. Schultz, Morton, and Weckerle (1998) reported that participants in their study who perceived their retirement to be voluntary had higher life satisfaction scores and rated themselves as healthier both physically and mentally than those who perceived their retirement as involuntary. Quick and Moen (1998) found that men report greater retirement satisfaction than do women, although the differences are small. Reitzes, Mutran, and Fernandez (1998) found that unmarried workers, those more satisfied with their work, and having a working spouse were factors associated with a decreased likelihood of early retirement. Because of these individual differences in adjustment to, and timing of, retirement, studies that seek to place retirement among the hierarchy of stressful life events usually show it to be in the middle range.

Attitudes toward the Aged

Society's attitudes toward the aged have been less than benevolent (Offerman & Gowing, 1990). In many ways, we have rejected the older population. Some people apparently view age itself as an anathema and shun those who are old. About one-fifth of our current aged population is foreign born, and xenophobia (fear of foreigners) may well cause negative attitudes. Our old tend to have much less formal education than does the general population, and in a society that values educational attainments, the old are likely to experience prejudice because of this. Finally, as is well known, the old are usually poor; a great many who do not work are living on an annual income below that established by the U.S. Department of Labor as representing poverty level. Thus, age itself, discrimination toward the foreign born, lack of education, and poverty combine to evoke negative attitudes toward the aged in the United States. In a few years, as the aged population becomes more indigenous and their level of education (as well as their numbers) increases, these attitudes may soften. At the present time, however, they are real and destructive and give credence to Jonathan Swift's assertion: "Every man desires to live long, but no man would be old."

Adjustment to Retirement

Ultimately, adjustment to retirement is an individual matter. Some welcome retirement and embrace leisure and the relative lack of structure with guiltlessness and joy. Others fret and stew, experience trauma, and never adjust. It has been argued, for example, that "leisure is not quite leisure when you do not have to work." In other words, free time becomes a constant excess with which one must cope rather than a welcome temporary release from a basically time-structured life. Generally, retirement causes people to think about leisure more in terms of *pleasure* than in terms of *freedom*. Hence, retirement can be either a period of enrichment and opportunity to pursue avocational and leisure interests or a source of depression connected with the loss of a culturally dominant social role.

Much of the literature on retirement conceives that stage as a period of disengagement, a reversal of expansion, a period characterized by less involvement in social participation. Disengagement, however, is perhaps an erroneous concept. Those who adjust well to retirement are more likely to reengage society in a different way than they are to disengage society. To be sure, some retirees disengage, but others simply reorient the direction and intensity of their engagement.

Several studies attempt to categorize retirees according to adjustment in retirement or by activity level. The Americana Health Care Corporation's study, *Aging in America: Trials and Triumphs* (1980), divided its sample of 514 randomly selected older persons into three groups:

1. *Enjoyers* (27% of the sample) successfully cope with aging. Usually they are healthy, well-educated men who are financially secure.
2. *Survivors* (53%) are reasonably successful copers with age. They are largely men and women of average health, less than a high school education, and basically adequate financial resources.
3. *Casualties* (20%) are not very successful in coping. Usually they are female, without much education, in relatively poor health, and of low income.

Walker, Kimmel, and Price (1981) divided their sample of 1511 recent retirees from major corporations into four groups:

1. *The Rocking Chair Group* (44% of the sample) retired voluntarily at about 62 to 65; are generally healthy; and are reasonably content with their retirement associates, finances, and activities.
2. *The Reorganizer Group* (24%) retired voluntarily at 62 to 65, were generally better educated, more financially secure, and healthier. They looked forward to beginning a new pattern of activities and usually worked as volunteers.
3. *The Holding On Group* (about 19%) continued to work for pay. Some retired involuntarily and needed the income. Most had not thought about retiring or made plans for retirement. Availability of jobs for this group is absolutely necessary.
4. *The Dissatisfied Group* (13%) were working neither voluntarily nor for pay and had a hard time keeping busy. Income and health were relatively poor. They had little retirement satisfaction.

In short, these two surveys indicate that people of various educational levels, incomes, and activity focus can retire successfully by adopting different styles. They also suggest that teaching specific retirement lifestyles may be a useful preretirement counseling activity.

Despite folklore, studies have demonstrated repeatedly that retirement has little effect on physical health (Crowley, 1985). One large-scale study, however, has concluded that retirees report more psychological symptoms than workers, even when physical health factors are taken into account (Bosse, Aldwin, Levenson, & Ekerdt, 1987). This finding seems to hold for both early and late retirees. Of course, we are left with the question of whether retirement affects mental health or whether one's mental health affects the decision to retire. All we can say presently is that there appears to be a reciprocal effect between mental health and retirement.

Most people begin retirement with a higher level of enthusiasm and more satisfaction than they experience a year later (Ekerdt, Bosse, & Levkoff, 1985). Identifying those who are likely to experience trauma because of the loss of work in retirement is not an easy task. One study (Fretz, Klugl, & Ossana, 1989) suggests that the best predictors of preretirement anxiety and depression are low self-efficacy, feelings about being able to cope with retirement, and a low degree of planfulness, in addition to the usual health and financial concerns. This type of research is in its incipient stages, and much more needs to be accomplished before predictive psychological variables are forthcoming.

Counseling for Preretirement and Retirement

Retirement is indeed a time of appraisal and reappraisal. It is simultaneously a look backward and a look ahead. The goals that appear appropriate in working with this group are as follows:

1. Assist in planning. Provide information relating to health, finances, housing, appropriate agencies

for the elderly, and a variety of concerns relating to daily living.

2. Clarify affective reactions to retirement. Individuals vary in their reactions to retirement. The counselor should not assume any universal reaction: trauma, joy, anticipation, disengagement, and reengagement are equally likely responses. Forced versus voluntary retirement will probably evoke within the counselee two appreciably different sets of concern.
3. Make appropriate referrals to community agencies designed to deal with particular aspects of the aged.

In terms of suggestion 1, Blai (1982) has put together a compendium of resources for older people who desire to work. State employment service offices, agencies on aging, YWCAs and YMCAs, and Forty-Plus Clubs are all possibilities. In addition, various volunteer agency programs exist: Foster Grandparents Program (FGP), Retired Senior Volunteer Program (RSVP), Volunteers in Service to America (VISTA), Peace Corps, Senior Companion Program, Service Corps of Retired Executives (SCORE). Also the U.S. Department of Labor sponsors the Senior Community Service Employment Program (SCSEP), which employs economically disadvantaged older persons in part-time community service jobs.

Corporations have taken increasing action to provide their employees with preretirement programs, although the effect of these programs has not been carefully evaluated. Unfortunately, some of the careful evaluations we do have show few, if any, significant longitudinal differences between groups that have had a preretirement program and those that have not, although in the short run, there may be significant differences in favor of treatment groups. Nevertheless, their number is growing.

It is now estimated that about half of all large corporations offer preretirement programs (Feuer, 1985), although these programs obviously vary in terms of scope and depth. Some concentrate narrowly on Social Security benefits and financial benefits and options. Others are broader and add such foci as physical and mental health, leisure, and legal aspects. Still others are even more comprehensive, including additional emphases on factors such as employment, housing, community resources, interpersonal relations, and life planning.

Barriers to providing needed counseling with older adults in or near retirement include the fact that only 4 percent of older adults are serviced by mental health centers and few receive preretirement counseling. In addition, older adults may approach a counseling relationship with greater wariness. Also, assessment may be difficult with this population. Finally, there may not be many job or volunteer opportunities available for older adults (Jensen-Scott, 1993). Many firms *will* hire retirees (usually white collar) on an ad-hoc basis (i.e., they have no written policy) (Hirshhorn & Hoyer, 1994). This informality usually leads to employment of retirees on a part-time/full-year basis rather than a part-time/part-year basis.

Loesch (1980) suggests "life-flow leisure counseling" as an antidote to possible diminution of self-satisfaction and self-definition caused by loss of work in retirement. This system involves exploration of interests, values, satisfactions, and personal characteristics and subsequently integrating and synthesizing this information into leisure pursuits. Leisure counseling, in fact, is a part of virtually every prepackaged retirement planning program. For example, the National Council of Older Americans' eight-module program contains one on leisure and another on lifestyle.

Westcott (1983) has suggested a structured life-review technique in counseling elders who see no meaning in life or who have poor social relationships or who are having difficulty mentally recovering from an illness. The technique is advocated to encourage the elderly to reminisce and engage in a life review of specific events that may affect current adjustment, self-esteem, or intergenerational conflicts. There is no reason why the structured life-review technique could not be applied to retirees who are experiencing adjustment difficulties.

Although we pointed out in the previous section of this chapter that the workforce participation of workers over age 65 has declined in almost linear fashion throughout this century, there are those who persuasively argue that participation will increase in the future. Part-time reentry into the workforce after individuals have completed a career may require that they receive counseling. For example, retirees can be helped to understand their strengths, realize new conditions in the job market, and overcome potential discrimination in hiring.

Liptak (1990) offers a program for integrating leisure planning into preretirement programs. He presents a system of translating desires into specific goal statements for individuals—for example, "I want to utilize my leisure time better" is translated into "I will learn to manage my leisure time and structure my leisure activities more effectively," and "I want to attend more social functions" becomes "I will join groups and clubs associated with my leisure interests." Long-range, and medium-range, and short-range goals are thus effected. Several other examples of preretirement programs may be found in R. Morris and Bass (1988).

Genevay (2000) proposes that career counselors use the Shamrock Model to help individuals cope with retirement tasks. This model is based on the notion that ongoing self-renewal requires ongoing evaluation and action. Evaluation in Genevay's model involves engaging in life review to help past and current experiences inform future plans; prioritizing activities to increase the time spent in meaningful activities; and being systematic about self-evaluation and reflection (e.g., keeping a journal, engaging in periodic career counseling over planned time intervals). Action in Genevay's model involves engaging in grief work related to losses associated with work; creating new support systems; developing a specific plan of action for the future; and proactively planning strategies for coping with the physical and psychological effects of aging.

Although the research accomplished in the area of preretirement and retirement is much more advanced and sophisticated than that pertaining to most other types of adult career behavior, some unanswered questions persist. Atchley (1979, pp. 47–48) reports on a conference designed to assess research needs. Among the more interesting research questions are the following:

Physical and Mental Ability for Employment

1. How does functional capacity interact with occupation to influence the decision to retire or the timing of retirement? How do subjective and objective health factors compare as predictors of functional capacity for employment?
2. To what extent do various diseases such as heart disease, diabetes, or arthritis influence functional capacity for employment? Do these factors influence the decision to retire or the timing of retirement directly or do they operate through their effects on functional capacity for employment?
3. How do mental health factors such as anxiety or depression influence the decision to retire or the timing of retirement?
4. How does physical aging compare with health factors in predicting functional capacity for employment?
5. How do the following compare as factors influencing functional capacity for employment?
   a. Physical and mental aging
   b. Disability due to disease or accident
   c. Obsolete psychomotor skills
   d. Obsolete knowledge

   Does the relative importance of these various factors differ by occupation and how?

Economic and Noneconomic Rewards of Employment

1. To what extent does the fulfillment of individual occupational goals influence the decision to retire or the timing of retirement?
2. How are the meanings attached to the job related to the type of retirement, the decision to retire, or the timing of retirement?
3. Do people feel a need to replace job rewards (both economic and noneconomic) in retirement? If so, does this influence the decision to retire or the timing of the retirement?

Social-Psychological Characteristics

1. What are the determinants of attitude toward retirement?
2. What are the determinants of attitude toward the job?
3. How do attitudes toward the job influence attitudes toward retirement?
4. How do significant others influence attitude toward retirement?
5. How do attitudes toward retirement influence the decision to retire or the timing of retirement?
6. How does the perceived effect of retirement on prestige affect the decision to retire or the timing of retirement?

Personality Factors

1. How does a positive orientation toward planning (active manipulation of environment) influence the decision to retire or the timing of retirement?
2. All other things being equal, is the Type A person (i.e., hard-driving, competitive, pressed for

time) more or less likely to retire or retire early compared with the Type B person?

3. Do inner-directed people retire more frequently or retire sooner compared with other-directed people?

Information

1. What effects do retirement planning programs have on the decision to retire or the timing of retirement?
2. To what extent is the decision to retire the result of a "rational" process?

System Pressures to Retire

1. What effects do varying employer retirement policies, employer pressures toward retirement, and organizational characteristics have on the decision to retire and the timing of retirement?
2. How do employer policies, unemployment, job retrogression, peer pressures, employer pressure, and family pressures compare as influences on the decision to retire and on the timing of retirement?*

Over two decades after Atchley offered these research foci; definitive answers are yet to emerge. Yet retirement research is a lively center of attention for many scholars, and we are beginning to determine the factors that influence successful and unsuccessful retirement. Unfortunately, most retirement research has been conducted with men. Some studies strongly suggest that women retirees require separate examination (Dorfman & Moffett, 1987; Erdner & Guy, 1990; Riddick, 1985; Seccombe & Lee, 1986; Szinovacz, 1987). The great bulk of retirement research has also focused on whites and those with middle or upper social economic status. Cultural differences have been found that urge distinct research with people of color and the less affluent (R. C. Gibson, 1987; Richardson & Kilty, 1989).

**Source:* From R. C. Atchley, Issues in retirement research. *Gerontologist, 19*(1), 47–48, 1979. Reprinted by permission.

SUMMARY

In this chapter, we have outlined factors that contribute to an increasing need for adult career counseling. We have presented characteristics of four adult subpopulations: midcareer shifters, women entering or reentering the labor force after childrearing, older workers, and preretirees and retirees. We have suggested specific foci for the career counseling of these groups. We have further presented general guidelines for the career counseling of adults. In the following chapter, we will discuss several additional adult subpopulations for which the counselor requires specialized career knowledge and skills.

CHAPTER THIRTEEN

Helping Strategies in Career Guidance and Counseling

KEY CONCEPTS

- Because career choice is unique and relatively unrestrained in Western industrialized societies, individual decision making is fateful and deserving of assistance.
- Because so much of career counseling deals with intellective variables, concepts from the cognitive therapies are particularly useful.
- A fundamental element of career counseling is appraisal of personal attribute data, possible pathways for action, and personal outcomes preferred.
- Group processes have many potential uses in career guidance and career counseling.
- In career counseling, internal personal attributes and values must be balanced with external opportunities and barriers.
- Career indecision and undecidedness are complex multidimensional constructs.
- Individual career counseling is as systematic as more structured group interactions.
- Career coaching is a relatively recent career service that currently offers promise, but also presents challenges, for the career counseling profession.

Career guidance and counseling exist because of freedom of choice. Theoretically, individuals in free societies have an almost unlimited number of career and educational options from among which they can choose, free of political constraints. Because career choice is relatively unfettered for individuals, they must be given assistance in decision making. That assistance typically takes the form of helping individuals to discover those personal characteristics that make a career-related difference, aiding them to be aware of the array of educational and occupational alternatives from which they may choose, assisting them in processing the dimensions of these two worlds on both affective and cognitive levels, and supporting them as they implement their choices.

There are several purposes of guidance and counseling, depending on the particular type of problem. Gati, Krauz, and Osipow (1996) identified two broad categories of career difficulties. The first category relates to problems that occur prior to career decision making. These difficulties involve a lack of readiness due to a lack of motivation, indecisiveness, and/or dysfunctional career beliefs. The second category involves problems that occur during the decision-making process. The difficulties involve lack of information about the career decision making process, self, and/or occupations. Problems during the decision-making process can also arise due to unreliable information, internal conflicts, and/or external conflicts. Some counseling is directed at eliminating or improving dysfunctional or maladaptive behaviors. Other counseling emphasizes developmental and preventative aspects of helping in order to, in Shakespeare's words, "Meet the first beginnings (and) nip the budding mischief before it has time to ripen to maturity." Still other counseling is aimed at assisting in decision making (decision making and problem solving are often used as synonymous terms). These latter two purposes, development and decision making, are the goals of career guidance and counseling.

To accomplish these goals, two strategies are commonly employed: individual counseling and group methods. Each of these helping strategies will be discussed in terms of its relevancy for career development and decision making. We then conclude the chapter with a brief overview of career coaching.

INDIVIDUAL COUNSELING

Definition

There are hundreds of definitions of counseling, focusing on process, relationship variables, content, techniques, outcomes, counselor characteristics, and so on. We regard career counseling as (1) a largely verbal process in which (2) a counselor and counselee(s) are in dynamic interaction and in which (3) the counselor employs a repertoire of diverse behaviors (4) to help bring about self-understanding and action in the form of "good" decision making in the counselee, who has responsibility for his or her own actions.

Counseling requires some as yet undetermined threshold of verbal ability on the part of the counselees. One can help a person who is not yet verbally fluent but not typically through counseling. For example, some stereotypical behaviors of severe retardates (rocking, self-punishment, and such) can be eliminated by behaviorally manipulating the environment. Counseling, however, entails sensible verbalizations.

Being in dynamic interaction refers to the fact that both the counselor and the counselee(s) are constantly changing as individuals and that the relationship between them is in a continual state of flux. There is movement in the successful career counseling experience toward the development or resolution of factors affecting the decision-making process.

There is mutual participation in the counseling relationship. If the counselor assumes all responsibility for participation, the interview is nothing more than advice-giving. If the counselee is given all responsibility for participation, the interview becomes a soliloquy. Although some catharsis may result, little else of value emerges. These extreme examples of the structure-nonstructure or the directedness-nondirectedness continuum suggest that the counseling relationship is not a superordinate-subordinate one; the counselor and the counselee engage in collaborative activity in which they are equally responsible for participation. Because of individual differences in personality, types and levels of training, and experience, some counselors tend to be more active than others. Likewise, some counselees tend to be more verbally active in the relationship than others. But both counselor and counselee must interact in dynamic fashion if counseling is to affect the counselee's decision making.

In terms of this relationship, some conditions are thought to be facilitative and others are judged to be impeding. Briefly, this notion suggests that a counselor's effectiveness transcends any theory of counseling or the use of specific techniques. The crucial variables in success are assumed to be attitudes and sensitivity that create a "therapeutic" atmosphere. For example, Carkhuff (1983) maintains that the primary dimensions are the counselor's empathic understanding of the counselee, the respect shown for the counselee, the counselor's genuineness within the counseling session, and the concreteness or specificity with which problems are confronted. This suggestion was supported by Anderson and Niles (2000) in their study of 43 adult career counseling counselees. Post-counseling interviews revealed that counselees thought that the emotional support they received from their career counselors was significantly important to the success of their career counseling.

That counselees in career counseling find support to be useful in helping them move forward in their careers is not surprising. As Brammer (1993) noted, support "helps counter feelings of 'falling apart,' 'being at loose ends,' or 'pulled in many directions at once'" (pp. 105–106). Niles (1996) noted that career counselors can offer support to their counselees in three ways: (a) emotional support, (b) informational support, and (c) appraisal support. Offering emotional support to counselees requires career counselors to understand their counselees' multiple perspectives and subjective experiences. Emotionally supportive acts, therefore, are grounded in multicultural competencies (Niles & Harris-Bowlsbey, 2002). Informational support is useful in helping counselees understand the structure and potential content of career counseling. This is especially important given the common (mis)understanding that career counseling is not "personal" counseling. Reminding counselees that "few things are more personal than career choice" (Niles, p. 165) and that career concerns often overlap with other developmental issues gives counselees permission to discuss the full range of concerns they are experiencing related to their career development. Appraisal support provides clients with opportunities to acquire information that is useful in making accurate self-evaluations. Appraisal support can be provided through the application of both objective (i.e., standardized) and subjective (i.e., nonstandardized self-assessment activities). Supportive acts in career counseling helps counselees experience a sense of hope and control as they move forward to resolve their career concerns.

Other conditions might be equally facilitative: communicated competence, authoritativeness, confidence, self-disclosure, wisdom, noncondemnation of the counselee as a person, objectivity, ability to make accurate predictions, flexibility, high intelligence, absence of serious emotional disturbance, absence of communicated disruptive personal values, personal style, and so on. There is neither space nor intent to review exhaustively the counseling literature. The point is simply that there do seem to exist some conditions that facilitate career counseling. We may assume that their absence retards progress, or at least does not help the process or assist the counselee toward counseling relationship goals. For example, the counselees in the Anderson and Niles (2000) study mentioned above indicated that lack of support and inappropriate counselor activities (i.e., instances when career counselors addressed issues that were not salient for counselees) were the most often cited "not helpful" events in their career counseling.

The career counselor employs a repertoire of diverse behaviors. Each theory of counseling proposes its unique and sometimes not-so-unique set of procedures and techniques for dealing with the counselee. In Table 13.1, Herr (1995) has suggested how each of six major approaches to career counseling might potentially contribute to career counseling of employment-bound youth. Obviously such potential contributions have utility for other populations as well. We are convinced that there are few "truths" in counseling. Each counseling approach can lay claim to its share of successes—at least insofar as one can gauge successes from reports of clinical activity and can accept varied definitions of the term. Counselees, however, vary; each comes with need systems, backgrounds, psychological sets, and states of readiness that militate against undifferentiated treatment. Some counselees want information; some want help in thinking through a problem; some wish assistance in exploring feelings; some desire aid in ridding themselves of unwanted anxieties. Each counselee stimulus presents the counselor with an opportunity to make a differentiated, tailored response. Counselors frequently speak of inappropriate responses made by a counselee; however, the obverse is equally possible. The counselee who seeks information and finds himself or herself confronted by a counselor who clarifies, explores, diagnoses, reinforces, extinguishes, or engages in all sorts of behaviors except giving information has reason to wonder about the appropriateness of the counselor's response. All of these behaviors are appropriate as responses to various stimuli; their indiscriminant use, however, is likely to be counterproductive. Counseling procedures or behaviors ought to vary according to the needs of the counselee.

Certain types of counselor behaviors, are appropriate in certain situations and are inappropriate in others. For example, if one goal of career counseling is to promote counselee information-seeking behavior, evidence suggests that the behavioral technique of reinforcement is effective. There are specific career counseling concerns (such as valuing) that might be better approached by other procedures or techniques. It may help at specific times to clarify or reflect feelings. It may be useful at other times to summarize, restate, or interpret. There are occasions when a counselee is ready for confrontation, and that technique will be effective. On a more cognitive level, the counselor may want to point out alternatives directly or to provide information. At still other points, in the manner of some behavioral, rational-emotive, or transactional analysis counselors, homework assignments may be given. At times, the counselor might even want to persuade the counselee. These examples of counselor behaviors are by no means exhaustive; however, they do exemplify the diversity of approaches in a career helping individual relationship, and their diversity argues for their discriminative use.

Finally, career counseling should bring about self-understanding and action. Knowledge of self and its subsequent relationship to the worlds of work, education, or training are the aims of career counseling. Action suggests that the clearest criterion of counseling success is outcome, that is, decision-making behavior of an appropriate nature. The individual, not the counselor, selects from informed alternatives and acts on that choice. Career counseling is action-oriented in that it is ultimately concerned with affecting behaviors (decision making). It is helpful, therefore, just as with any other segment of a comprehensive career helping service, to approach individual counseling on a systematic basis: specifying goals in behavioral terms, evolving procedures to accomplish those behaviors, using whatever resources may be required,

TABLE 13.1 Examples of Potential Contributions of Six Approaches to Career Counseling for Employment-Bound Youth

APPROACH	MAJOR CONTRIBUTIONS IN CAREER COUNSELING
Trait and factor	• Matching of individual traits to the requirements of a particular job, occupation, or training opportunity • Helping employment-bound youth to examine the range of jobs or occupations for which their abilities, achievement, aptitudes, and interests would qualify them • Assisting employment-bound youth to understand the elasticity or transportability of their current knowledge or skills across jobs, occupations, and industries • Providing employment-bound youth a classification system of self-characteristics and language (e.g., interests, values, aptitudes, achievements, skills) and of jobs, occupations, and careers by which to facilitate identification of possible options to explore and information to secure • Facilitating individual assessment of the probabilities, the odds, of gaining access to and being successful in different jobs, occupations, or educational opportunities
Counselee-centered	• Providing a safe and accepting environment in which to explore career planning and work adjustment issues • Encouraging employment-bound youth to take control of their lives and to set goals for action that can be rehearsed and tried out in counseling • Helping employment-bound youth develop insights into their personal priorities, personal patterns of behavior, and barriers to their achievement of goals • Establishing a sense of hope that conditions which brought the counselee to the counselor can change in positive ways • Reinforcing that the counselor views the counselee as a person of value who has the ability to identify issues and barriers in his or her career life and ways to change them
Psychodynamic	• Providing a connection between past experiences and present behavior that is relevant to career choices or work adjustment • Assisting the counselee to understand unresolved conflicts in the family or in other past relationships that may be hindering current interactions with co-workers or supervisors • Facilitating the employment-bound youth's understanding of messages from and expectations of others that have been incorporated into the individual's negative view of self, sense of self-efficacy, or feelings about opportunities • Helping the individual to examine past educational, employment, or social experiences that may clarify needs or gratifications to be sought from work
Developmental	• Providing insight for employment-bound youth about developmental tasks that they may need to explore, complete, or anticipate in their career planning process • Helping counselees to clarify and integrate the role of work and its importance in comparison with other life roles: family, parenting, leisure, community service, and student • Assisting counselees to acquire awareness that work and occupation provide a focus for personality organization for most men and women, although for some persons this focus is peripheral, incidental, or even nonexistent • Facilitating clarification of the counselees' self-concept and ways to implement it in work • Assisting counselees to identify and act on their work values, resources, and self-concept in fashioning possible career patterns they wish to pursue • Facilitating counselee understanding of the process of change across time and the ways to anticipate and cope with such change

Developmental *(continued)*	• Helping counselees understand that success in coping with the demands of the environment and of the person at any given life-career stage depends on the readiness of the individual to cope with these demands. In particular, this means helping the individual to understand and acquire the elements of career maturity or career adaptability: planfulness or time perspective, exploratory skills, relevant information, decision-making skills, and a reality orientation • Providing counselees awareness of the important roles played by feedback and reality-testing in the developing of self-concepts and the translation of these into occupational self-concepts • Assisting counselees in understanding and acting on knowledge that work satisfactions and life satisfactions depend on the extent to which the individual finds adequate outlets for abilities, needs, values, interests, personality traits, and self concepts. They further depend on establishment in a type of work, or work situation, and a way of life in which one can play the kind of role that growth and exploratory experiences have led one to consider congenial and appropriate
Behavioral	• Helping to demystify employment-bound youth's concerns about or problems with career planning or work performance • Facilitating clarification of goals that counselees hope to achieve in counseling, in work, in social interaction and breaking them into increments that can be learned or relearned • Analyzing with counselees their environments to identify cues and reinforcers that are important in triggering and sustaining their behavior • Providing opportunities for social modeling, vicarious learning simulations, role playing, behavioral rehearsal and feedback so that counselees can be helped accurately to understand and learn desirable behaviors or skills important to their goals, improved work performance or adjustment, job choice and career planning • Assisting counselees specifically to identify behavioral deficits and create conditions or experiences that will provide reinforcement of appropriate learned responses important to goal attainment
Cognitive behavioral	• Helping employment-bound youth to modify inaccurate or maladaptive cognitive sets about self, others, and life events • Assisting counselees to understand the cognitive bases of their moods, anxieties, or depression and the direct connection between thoughts and feelings • Facilitating counselee analysis of their automatic thoughts and irrational beliefs about their abilities, worth, work opportunities, or performance • Providing employment-bound youth help in cognitive restructuring or reframing their concerns about career planning, the school-to-work transition, or work adjustment • Identifying with counselees' tendencies to over generalize or use cognitive distortions as they assess problems, issues, or barriers related to the choice of and implementation of work

Source: From E. L. Herr. (1995). *Counseling Employment Bound Youth*. Greensboro: University of North Carolina at Greensboro, ERIC Clearinghouse on Counseling and Student Services.

and evaluating to determine if behaviors have been achieved.

From the general areas of cognitive and behavioral psychology have emerged the so-called cognitive restructuring or reframing therapies, all of which lend themselves particularly well to career counseling. Attribution theory and self-efficacy theory suggest that people engage in perpetual internal monologues in which they make causal attributions about their behavior (and that of other people).

Hence, the emphasis is on cognitive processes. Such theorists as Beck (1993); Ellis (1993b); Meichenbaum (1993); and Trower, Casey, and Dryden (1988) have taken this idea and have developed cognitive therapies, the goal of which is basically to help people think straight.

This type of counseling is based on three premises: (1) Emotions and behavior are determined by the way we think; (2) emotional disorders and dysfunctional behaviors are the consequence of negative or unrealistic thinking; and (3) changing this type of thinking will bring about reduction or elimination of emotional disorders and dysfunctional behaviors. Consequently, counselors work to help their counselees identify maladaptive thinking. Nevo (1987) indicates 10 such irrational thoughts frequently encountered in career counseling:

1. There is only one vocation in the world that is right for me.
2. Until I find my perfect vocational choice, I will not be satisfied.
3. Someone else can discover the vocation suitable for me.
4. Intelligence tests will tell me how much I am worth.
5. I must be an expert or very successful in the field of my work.
6. I can do anything if I try hard, or, I can't do anything that doesn't fit my talents.
7. My vocation should satisfy the important people in my life.
8. Entering a vocation will solve all my problems.
9. I must sense intuitively that the vocation is right for me.
10. Choosing a vocation is a one-time act.

Stead, Watson, and Foxcroft (1993), using a sample of South African students, found that a relationship existed between irrational beliefs (e.g., "To be a worthwhile person, we should be thoroughly adequate, achieving, and competent in almost all ways") and certain aspects of career indecision. Richman (1993) also has demonstrated that cognitive barriers interfere with successful career development and that if a counselor helps counselees to modify their irrational beliefs, the likelihood of achieving career goals is increased.

Mitchell and Krumboltz (1987) studied the comparative effectiveness on enhancing career decision making in college students of a cognitive restructuring intervention versus a decision-making skills intervention and a no-treatment control. They found the cognitive restructuring intervention to be the most effective. This intervention consisted of five elements:

> *(a) didactic instruction about the role of maladaptive beliefs and generalizations in career indecision, (b) training in the monitoring of personal beliefs and their effect on behavior, (c) modeling by the counselor of the rational evaluation of beliefs and modification based on that evaluation, (d) feedback to the counselees on attempted modification of generalizations and beliefs, and (e) performance (homework assignments) designed to test new beliefs for their accuracy and usefulness. (p. 172)*

It is obvious that because so much of career counseling rests on a cognitive base, the cognitive therapies are highly usable. What people tell themselves about their abilities, appropriate aspiration levels, and so on are clearly the stuff of career counseling. Techniques such as conditioning, modeling, homework, behavioral rehearsal, and so on that are common in the cognitive therapies lend themselves to application in career counseling.

Krumboltz (1983) has offered an application of the cognitive therapies specifically to career counseling. Krumboltz notes that the "goal of career counseling is to facilitate the learning of skills, interests, beliefs, values, work habits, and personal qualities that enable each counselee to create a satisfying life within a constantly changing work environment" (Krumboltz & Henderson, 2002, p. 43). He emphasizes the use of learning theory to help counselees address certain faulty cognitions that cause trouble in career decision making (for example, "If I change, I have failed" or "I can do anything as long as I'm willing to work hard enough"). The result is that people fail to recognize that a remediable problem exists, or they fail to make the effort needed to make a decision or solve a problem, or they eliminate a potentially satisfying alternative for inappropriate reasons, or they choose a poor alternative for inappropriate reasons, or they suffer anguish and anxiety over a perceived inability to achieve goals. Krumboltz suggests a number of ways that individuals can be helped to achieve straight thinking, ranging from structured interviews to counselee self-monitoring to thinking aloud. Among the repertoire of counselor behaviors are such techniques as examining counselee assumptions and presuppositions of the expressed belief, looking for inconsistencies between words and behavior, testing simplistic answers for inadequacies, confronting attempts to develop an illogical consistency, identifying barriers to the goal, challenging the validity of key beliefs, and building a feeling of trust and cooperation.

Mitchell, Levin, and Krumboltz (1999) contend that to capitalize on chance events that occur daily in people's lives, career counselors need to integrate a model of planned happenstance into their career counseling. Planned happenstance helps counselees recognize and cope with unexpected events that influence their career development. The key skills to be developed in the planned happenstance model are: curiosity, persistence, flexibility, optimism, and risk taking. To sensitive counselees to happenstance in career development, career counselors can ask counselees to consider the following questions:

1. How have unplanned events influenced your career?
2. How did you enable each event to influence you?
3. How do you feel about unplanned events in your future? (Krumboltz & Henderson, 2002, p. 48)

By sensitizing counselees to the influence of unplanned events in career development, counselees can learn that "if I did it before, I can do it again" (Krumboltz & Henderson, p. 48). Such an attitude fosters the development of curiosity, persistence, flexibility, optimism, and risk taking with regard to incorporating planned happenstance into future career decision making.

To illustrate the heavy cognitive component of some types of career counseling, we cite a study by N. B. Taylor (1985) that investigated what career counselors in Australia actually do in interviews (10 counselors and 81 counselees). He discovered that the typical interview was primarily concerned with presenting, reviewing, and classifying information and then evaluating the information in terms of the counselee's interests, values, and abilities, and, subsequently, in terms of institutional barriers. Some time was also spent discussing and evaluating the counselee's vocationally relevant self. In this sample, tests were infrequently used, and there was rarely a concern with the counselee's general adjustment. The emotional climate of the interviews was basically neutral (that is, neither cold nor warm), and the stress was on the cognitive aspects of making a decision. Overall, it appears that the modal interview focused on specific vocational-educational concerns of the counselee by means of the counselor's providing information, rationally reviewing it with the counselee, and encouraging the counselee to evaluate alternatives. This mode is what has been called the "thinking man's" approach to sorting out alternative courses.

More affective approaches have also been employed successfully. For some counselees, under some circumstances, the technique of mental imagery in career counseling has proved effective (Skovholt, Morgan, & Negron-Cunningham, 1989). Encouraging counselees to go on guided mental imagery excursions allows them to visualize themselves in some imagined scene in the future. It formalizes what all of us do—daydream. It becomes a way of assessing one's vocational aspirations (for instance, inviting a counselee to imagine a typical day in the future, from start to finish). Such exercises usually begin with the application of relaxation techniques and then go on to provide the structure that permits the imagination to take hold. Because most career counseling is based on left-brained (logical) involvement and because the use of mental imagery calls for the application of right-brained (emotional) skills, the altered focus may be effectively used with some counselees at an appropriate level of readiness. The fact is that virtually all career counseling models are more or less systematic (see, for example, Olson, McWhirter, & Horan, 1989). It is probably fair to state that currently, whatever the theoretical orientation of career counselors, the preferred mode of delivery is systematic, more or less as delineated in this book. Each systematic approach has in common the notion that the goals of intervention should be specified in terms of the counselee's behavior; that a logical, differentiated series of techniques and strategies to achieve those goals should be effected; and that monitoring of progress and evaluation of results is important. No doubt the push for accountability in mental health services has spawned a great many more models of this type.

A Broad View of Career Counseling

Career counseling should not be viewed in a narrowly defined sense. It cannot be separated from various orientations to counseling that, in general, take into account an individual's total personality, culture, and environment. Super (1983) delineated a developmental model of career counseling that takes a comprehensive view of the process and contrasts markedly with the old matching model.

A broad perspective on career counseling has long been recognized by the Association for Counselor Education and Supervision (ACES) of the American Association for Counseling and Development. An ACES position paper (1976) recommends, "all students and adults should be provided with career guidance opportunities to ensure that they":

1. Understand that career development is a lifelong process based on an interwoven and sequential series of educational, occupational, leisure, and family choices
2. Examine their own interests, values, aptitudes, and aspirations in an effort to increase self-awareness and self-understanding
3. Develop a personally satisfying set of work values that leads them to believe that work, in some form, can be desirable to them
4. Recognize that the act of paid and unpaid work has dignity
5. Understand the role of leisure in career development
6. Understand the process of reasoned decision making and the ownership of those decisions in terms of their consequences
7. Recognize that educational and occupational decisions are interrelated with family, work, and leisure
8. Gather the kinds of data necessary to make well-informed career decisions
9. Become aware of and explore a wide variety of occupational alternatives
10. Explore possible rewards, satisfactions, life-styles, and negative aspects associated with various occupational options
11. Consider the probability of success and failure for various occupations
12. Understand the important role of interpersonal and basic employability skills in occupational success
13. Identify and use a wide variety of resources in the school and community to maximize career development potential
14. Know and understand the entrance, transition, and decision points in education and the problems of adjustment that might occur in relation to these points
15. Obtain chosen vocational skills and use available placement services to gain satisfactory entrance into employment in relation to occupational aspirations and beginning competencies
16. Know and understand the value of continuing education to upgrade or acquire additional occupational skills or leisure pursuits

As indicated earlier in this book, some consider career counseling "a great swindle," arguing that career choices defy logic and predictable order. The great majority of counselors take a more informed and balanced view. They acknowledge that counselees have limiting aspects (see Table 13.2), that counselors have their blind spots and limitations, and that the economy is difficult to predict; nevertheless, they point out that a broad view of career counseling, applied with skill, can do a great deal to mitigate malevolent and random influences on career development and choice and to help individuals to adapt to and cope with the buffetings of life.

The Counselor and the Counselee's Internal Frame of Reference

If career counseling is regarded in the broad sense of the term and if career development and choice are more than the results of haphazard external events, much of career counseling will be focused on the counselee's internal frame of reference. At the outset, the objectives of counseling include helping the counselee to cast in bold relief those factors that are an amalgamation of personal attributes, values, opportunities, and cultural factors (see Table 13.2). More than five decades ago, Super (1951) proposed a definition of career guidance that emphasized not solely the provision of occupational information at a particular time or a simple matching of person and job, but rather a "process of helping a person to develop and accept an integrated picture of himself and his role in the world of work, to test this concept against reality, and to convert it into a reality, with satisfaction to himself and to society" (p. 89). This definition blends those dimensions of counselees sometimes arbitrarily

TABLE 13.2 Examples of Self and Environmental Factors Influencing Career Choices

PERSONAL ATTRIBUTE FACTORS	VALUE STRUCTURE FACTORS	OPPORTUNITY FACTORS	CULTURAL FORCES FACTORS
Intellectual ability	General values	Rural-urban	Social class expectancies
Differential aptitudes	Work values	Accessibility of occupational opportunities	Family aspirations and experiences
Skills	Life goals	Accessibility of educational opportunities	Peer influence
Achievements	Career goals	Scope of occupational opportunities	Community attitudes and orientation toward education or work
Experiential history	Perceived prestige of occupations and curricula	Scope of educational opportunities	Teacher influence
Achievement motivation	Stereotyped attitudes toward occupations and curriculum	Requirements of occupations	Counselor influence
Responsibility	Psychological centrality of occupations or curricula in values	Requirements of curricula	General role model influences
Perseverance	People-data-things orientation	Availability of compensatory programs	Image of educational or occupational options within a culture
Punctuality	Attitude toward work	Exposure to interventions	High school climate and reward system
Warmth	Work ethic	Status of the economy	College climate and reward system
Risk-taking proclivities	Leisure		Primary referent groups influences
Openness	Change needs		
Rigidity	Order needs		
Ego strength	Nurturance needs		
Self-esteem	Succorance needs		
Decision-making ability	Power needs		
Vocational maturity	Security		
Sex	Altruism		
Race			
Age			
Physical strength			
Health			

separated into the personal and the vocational into a totality with interlocking relationships. Further, this process is seen as oriented to the self-concept, primarily focusing on self-understanding and self-acceptance. To these can be related the relevance of external factors that define the environmental options available to the individual.

This approach also stresses the importance of counseling's resting on a base of self-attitudes and value sets that the individual understands and accepts and uses to maximize his or her own freedom to choose the opportunities that seem to meet needs, desires, and inner urgings. In addition, a counseling relationship so defined means that the counselee and the counselor come to understand which personal characteristics are individual and unchangeable and which are modifiable. The counselee can then proceed from self-understanding to the matter of engaging in appropriate career-related behaviors.

Appraisal Information. To deal effectively with the latter dimension of the counseling process, the counselor will need to be an appraiser as well as an interpreter of data about the counselee. Essentially, three broad classes of information are important (Goldman, 1971). The order in which they are dealt with is in large measure a result of the individual counseling orientation.

The first set of appraisal information is concerned with personal attribute data—predictor variables. Given counselors may determine that they should begin counseling a given individual by presenting what they have learned about the counselee through information from tests of aptitude, achievement, interest, and personality; school grades; hobbies; work history; family background; and expressed attitudes. Frequently, counselors who start from this base treat each of these pieces of information as fixed and unmodifiable, as having immutable relationship to certain future outcomes that the individual should consider. Because of the overwhelming amount of information that can be collected about a given individual, much of it may be irrelevant to the counselee's questions. Or the counselee may accept the interpretation of the predictor variables as having a sophistication or expertness that permits him or her little room in which to maneuver. More important, counselees may play passive and dependent roles, awaiting with little personal investment or acceptance the expert's judgment about what they can and cannot do or what they should do or should not do. Recall that counseling is an activity of mutual participation. Such a counseling orientation, however, places the counselor in the role of expert and the counselee in a subordinate, dependent position, thereby making participation less than mutual.

A second set of appraisal data relates to certain pathways that counselees might follow. Should they take vocational education? Should they take a specific educational sequence? Should they attend a post—high school business or trade school? Should they return to school? Should they change jobs? Should they go into the armed forces? Should they enter college? Some counselors may choose immediately to compare the requirements for each of these avenues with the information available about predictor variables that describe the particular counselee. This approach, like starting immediately with predictor variables, is a trait-and-factor approach that, if treated superficially or mechanically, can be irrelevant to the real issues. For example, students who ask where they should go to college may really be asking whether they should go to college at all, or asking: Why are my parents so insistent on my attending college? Are there some other things I might do that can get me where I want to be? Instead of immediately turning to college catalogues and the predictor variables that describe the student, a counselor who senses the underlying questions may choose to help the student sort out what he or she would expect to gain as a result of pursuing one pathway rather than another.

A third piece of appraisal information with which the counselor might begin is the outcomes that are of consequence to the person at his or her present level of development. What kind of person are you? What do you see as your major strengths and limitations? As you think about the future, are you primarily interested in obtaining satisfaction from the work activity in which you are engaged or from the work situation? Do you feel the need for regularity and security, or do you desire variety and change? Do you like to work alone or with others? Are you principally concerned with income levels? Prestige? What possible choices have you already considered and why? What are your values? What influences are most important to you as you have shaped personal answers to these questions—parents, peers, generalized attitudes in the community, and so on?

Sampson, Peterson, Reardon, and Lenz (2000) recommend that career counselors follow a five-step model of "readiness assessment" in career counseling. The goal of readiness assessment is to help the counselee and counselor make informed collaborative choices about the career assistance the counselee is likely to find useful. The model begins with selecting a readiness construct (e.g., vocational maturity, career beliefs, career adaptability) that is congruent with the counselor's theoretical perspective of career development. Second, the counselor selects a readiness measure to assess the construct. The assessment results are then evaluated to determine the counselee's readiness for career decision making. At this point, the counselor and counselee work collaboratively to identify appropriate career interventions. Collaboration continues in the fourth step when the counselor and counselee establish goals for career counseling. In the final step of the model, the counselor monitors subsequent counselee behavior, cognitions, and emotions related to counselee use of assessment, information, and instructional resources, which serves to confirm or disconfirm the initial readiness hypothesis. The intent of the career readiness model is to increase the likelihood that the right career resources will be used with the appropriate level of support to meet the counselee's career needs.

A Counseling Cycle. From the beginning of the counseling relationship, this approach encourages the counselee to tune in to himself or herself and to organize those parts of self and self-concept that one thinks are of most significance. Super (1957) addresses this point in the following manner:

> *Since vocational development consists of implementing a self-concept, and since self-concepts often need modification before they can be implemented, it is important that the student, counselee, or patient put his self-concept into words early in the counseling process. He needs to do this for himself, to clarify his actual role and his role aspirations; he needs to do it for the counselor, so that the counselor may understand the nature of the vocational problem confronting him.*
>
> *This calls for the cyclical use of nondirective and directive methods. Schematically, vocational counseling can be described as involving the following cycle:*
>
> 1. *Nondirective problem exploration and self-concept portrayal*
> 2. *Directive topic setting, for further exploring*
> 3. *Nondirective reflection and clarification of feeling for self-acceptance and insight*
> 4. *Directive exploration of factual data from tests, occupational pamphlets, extracurricular experiences, grades, and so forth, for reality testing*
> 5. *Nondirective exploration and working through of attitudes and feelings aroused by reality testing*
> 6. *Nondirective consideration of possible actions, for help in decision making (p. 308)*

Such a frame of reference then gives the counselor and the counselee an opportunity to identify those predictor variables and those avenues that appear to be most relevant to the counselee. Further, having such a frame of reference from which to operate allows the counselor to help the counselee identify and clarify possible distortions between his or her self-perception and the behavior that the information suggests.

For example, people who overestimate their mechanical skills may not perform effectively as machinists. In other words, such individuals ascribe to themselves characteristics they actually do not possess. Following our previous line of thought, these counselees' personal characteristics and values do not seem to be congruent. Such a situation raises several questions for the counselor and the counselee. Is the degree to which one possesses mechanical skills modifiable? Are the elements of mechanical skills perceived by the counselee to be present but actually lacking a matter of spatial visualization, intelligence, manual dexterity, or experience? If the former types of variables are operative, the chances of becoming an effective machinist are minimal. If experience is the deficit, are there pathways in education or the community through which one can heighten skill proficiency? Another question is, of course, what prompts the person to want to be a machinist? Is it the work activity or the work situation? Is it because the person knows people who are machinists and is influenced by them, or is it because the person has been told that machinists are in great demand and thus gain good income and security? Is it because the person wants to remain in the community and the machining industry is a prominent one? If the person is concerned about something besides the work activity as a machinist, are there other skills or strengths on which to capitalize to gain the same outcomes that were perceived to result from becoming a machinist?

The second part of this concern is that choosing an occupation also includes choosing a lifestyle. In Western culture, one is largely labeled by one's occupational title. It must be realized that this, too, is an important ingredient of choice—deciding how much of self one desires to express in occupational commitment. How ego-involved is the counselee in work, in a choice of education or training, in school, in family? How committed is the individual? How committed can the individual become? A counselor and a counselee need to understand that a measured interest may indicate that one will direct effort to an area but does not say how much effort will be applied to get there. To cite an extreme analogy, a person may have an interest in going to Tahiti, and this interest may remain constant throughout life. But interest alone does not indicate that the individual will take steps or raise the finances to get to Tahiti. So it is with tentative occupational aspirations. Individuals will have to be helped to examine whether they have the dedicated involvement required by specific choice options. This, too, is a matter of values and characteristics of the self that may or may not be present or possible to acquire.

But the capacity for deep involvement relates also to the meaning one attaches to a particular lifestyle. How important is it to a particular counselee to be tagged a machinist? Is it important enough to delay certain personal gratifications through a lengthy apprenticeship? Is it important enough to labor over applied mathematics or physics? Is it important enough to accept the midnight shift rather than normal work hours? Is it important enough to gamble on attaining seniority as security against layoffs? Is it important enough to practice being punctual, reliable, and dependable? Is it important enough to try to be a machinist even if the odds are high against success? These are not necessarily the right questions, but they are all types of questions counselors and counselees must work through as personal attribute and value factors, as the self and the self-concept, are described and clarified. The process of doing so is the process of decision making.

Using Super's Thematic-Extrapolation Method, counselors help counselees construct life histories. These life histories are then examined for recurrent themes or "threads of continuity" which are used to "make sense of the past, explain the present, and draw a blueprint for the future" (Super, Savickas, & Super, 1996, p. 157). The developmental method is based on life patterns (e.g., What patterns are revealed in my life history? Which of these patterns and themes are important to incorporate in my future planning?). Jepsen (1994, p. 45) has noted that the developmental method contains three distinct steps:

1. Analyze past behavior and development for recurring themes and underlying trends.
2. Summarize each theme and trend, taking into account the other themes and trends.
3. Project the modified themes and trends into the future by extrapolation.

The thematic extrapolation method can be incorporated into career counseling by using Super's (1957, p. 308) cyclical model of nondirective and directive methods. This incorporation integrates "objective" trait-and-factor oriented approaches with more "subjective" approaches to career counseling. The former providing important information for career decision making, the latter helping to translate objective data into a more personalized career decision.

Integrating objective and subjective approaches to career counseling seems increasingly important. In Israel, Nevo (1990) assessed student reaction to career counseling they had received at the University of Haifa. Perhaps the most astonishing finding was that although counselees certainly perceived interest inventories, objective tests, and counseling to have helped them to understand themselves better, this self-understanding did not necessarily translate into making a career decision. They viewed "good" counseling as help in organizing their thinking and identifying their interests and abilities. Some were disappointed at the end either that they could make no career choice or that they had made a choice not entirely satisfactory to them.

This dichotomy between personal versus vocational outcomes in career counseling has been debated for many years. Although there are still those who try to separate the two domains, the fact is that they are symbiotic; in our judgment, no good career counseling can take place without personal investment and self-discovery. This is not to say that career counseling should have a predominately noncareer focus. Phillips, Friedlander, Kost, Specterman, and Robbins (1988), for example, studied career counseling outcome and determined that from the counselor's point of view, the more vocationally focused the sessions (and the greater the number of sessions), the greater the effect. Counselees' preferences were not so delimited; they seemed satisfied regardless of the non-vocational versus vocational emphasis. For example, Anderson and Niles (1995) investigated the content of 248 career counseling sessions with adults and found that a substantial number (36 percent) of the concerns counselees discussed in their career counseling were non-work concerns. These concerns related to family-of-origin, relationship, and ego dystonic emotional concerns. Thus, it would be difficult, if not impossible, to visualize career counseling without a degree of personal focus. Multon, Heppner, Gysbers, Zook, and Ellis-Kalton (2001) provide data to support the Anderson's and Niles's findings. Multon and her associates found that 60 percent of the 42 adult counselees they studied experienced psychological distress at the time they presented for career counseling. Niles and Anderson (1993) reported similar findings with men demonstrating significantly higher levels of psychological distress than women at the time they presented for career counseling. Clearly, and not surprisingly, people find career distress to be personally distressing.

Niles and Pate (1989) argue that all career counselors must have the basic skills of mental health counselors. A synthesis of the skills needed for both foci would require that in addition to the skill areas outlined in this text, career counselors would need to understand mental health areas such as psychopathology and the effects of psychotropic medications in the interaction between emotional disorders and career-related issues. Similarly, Corbishley and Yost (1989) propose that all but the simplest of career counseling mandates a psychological approach. Because career-related decisions have an impact on all other dimensions of a person's life, the psychological characteristics of counselees largely determine if they will hold reasonable expectations for career counseling, and the type of intervention used may well depend on the way that the counselee engages the world psychologically. Within the context of this type of psychological orientation, Yost and Corbishley (1987) suggest an eight-stage approach to career choice type of career counseling: initial assessment, self-understanding, making sense of self-understanding data, generating alternatives, obtaining occupational information, making the choice, making plans, and implementing plans. Although these stages do not seem different from the typical sequence approaches applied to career choice counseling described in this chapter, what sets them apart is the emphasis given to the counselee's psychological complexity. In any case, we reaffirm that in career choice counseling there is no such thing as a nonpsychological approach (however naively it is applied), and certainly in other non-first-choice lifestyle aspects of career counseling addressed in this book, psychological complexity is a given.

This notion of the unity of career and so-called personal counseling has been repeatedly reinforced in the professional literature. Rak and O'Dell (1994) have demonstrated how career and "traditional" counseling approaches are blended in good vocational interventions. Manuele-Adkins (1992) argues that career counselors would be remiss if they did not heed the affective, psychological issues of counselees with career problems, and Davidson and Gilbert (1993) offer the suggestion that *all* career counseling with adults is, in reality, the exploration of personal identity and meaning. Super (1993) proposes that there may indeed be two fields of counseling: "*situational,* which has subspecialties that focus on differing types of situations (career, family, and so on), and *personal* counseling, in which the focus is on individuals whose problems are based primarily in their own approach to and coping with situations, not on factors in the situations they encounter" (p. 135). He views these two types as not so much a dichotomy as they are a continuum, and the best counselors deal with them in combination. Finally, the amalgamation and commonalities of career and personal counseling are attested to by Krumboltz (1993), Betz and Corning (1993), and Gold and Scanlon (1993).

A number of career counseling approaches are constructed around a particular assessment instrument. For example, Hansen (1985) suggests a counseling sequence for use with the SVIB-SII (Strong Interest Inventory). She proposes a fourteen-step process. Clearly, such approaches are basically trait-and-factor oriented. Nevill and Super (1986) provide a further example of how particular assessment devices can be incorporated into a staged counseling intervention. They term their approach a Developmental Assessment Model for Career Counseling, and it assimilates instruments that they have developed to measure work salience, work values, and career maturity. More recently, Super and colleagues proposed a comprehensive wedding of appraisal data and counseling (Super, Osborne, et al., 1992). Called the Career-Development Assessment and Counseling model (C-DAC), it entails helping individuals understand life-stage and life-space development and the "normal" sequences and developmental tasks that people experience throughout their lives (see Chapter 4). Emphasized are the importance of life roles and changing values:

> *Finally, these developmental data can be applied to the results of interest inventories; aptitude batteries; and discussions of educational, occupational, and familial objectives, leading to the formulation of long-term plans and of strategies for immediate action to facilitate their attainment. Possible changes in interests, values, and careers, together with economic and industrial changes, are essential to consider in long-range planning (p. 79).*

Hartung and associates (1998) advocated the extension of the C-DAC model to include the formal appraisal of cultural identity in step one of the model and to consider cultural identity concerns throughout the C-DAC process. These authors noted that this extension of the C-DAC model should help counselors more clearly understand how cultural factors influence people's career development and vocational behavior.

Outcomes of Career Counseling

In other chapters of this text, we have reported research comparing the effectiveness of individual counseling with other helping modes in enhancing the career development and behaviors of counselees. Sometimes, individual counseling is found to be less effective in achieving desired career-related goals than are structured workshops, seminars, courses, and other intervention methods. Such findings may be specious because the counseling treatments are rarely as carefully and specifically defined as are the comparative intervention methods. In other words, the counseling treatment is frequently generic, broad, and unstructured, whereas the comparative treatment is goal-specific, narrowly delimited, and structured. Four reviews of career counseling outcome would appear to support this speculation. Holland, Magoon, and Spokane (1981) concluded the following:

> *The experimental evaluations of counselors, courses, career programs, card sorts, interest inventories, workshops, and related treatments imply that the beneficial effects are due to the common elements in these divergent treatments: (a) exposure to occupational information; (b) cognitive rehearsal of vocational aspirations; (c) acquisition of some cognitive structure for organizing information about self, occupations, and their relations; and (d) social support or reinforcement from counselors or workshop members. In addition, the strong tendency to find some positive effects for both diffuse interventions...and specific interventions...occurs because the average counselee knows so little about career decision making and career problems that a small amount of new information and support makes a difference.*
>
> *At the same time, the general failure to find different effects for different treatments demonstrates a large hole in our understanding of counselee-treatment interactions and indicates the need for more analytical and less shot-gun evaluation. (pp. 285–286)*

Fretz (1981) also concluded that most career interventions (individual counseling, group-oriented, or self-directed) appear to be beneficial and that there is no consistent body of data to suggest that any one mode of intervention is more effective than any other. Fretz attributed the lack of differential outcome to the failure of researchers explicitly to describe treatments, counselee characteristics, and outcomes; lack of random assignment of subjects to treatments; attempts to manipulate too many variables; use of a single outcome criterion rather than several; and not reporting intercorrelations among variables.

Spokane and Oliver (1983) reviewed career counseling outcome studies by calculating effect sizes (difference between the mean of a treated group and mean of a control group divided by the standard deviation of the control group on a given outcome measure). This procedure yields a finer delineation of differences between groups in a meta-analysis. Based on this more elegant statistical treatment of the data, the authors reached the following conclusions regarding differential effectiveness:

1. Counselees receiving any vocational intervention are better off, on the average, than 81 percent of the untreated controls.
2. Counselees receiving individual vocational interventions are better off, on the average, than 79 percent of untreated controls.
3. Counselees receiving group/class vocational interventions are better off, on the average, than more than 89 percent of untreated controls.
4. Counselees receiving a variety of alternative treatment (for example, computer-assisted, audiotaped, self-directing) are, on the average, better off than 59 percent of untreated controls.

After a more sophisticated analysis using a massive data set, Oliver and Spokane (1988) arrived at a somewhat different conclusion. First, increasing the number of hours or the number of sessions appears to enhance the chances for a favorable outcome. Second, individual treatments were judged to be the most effective (but the least cost-effective), whereas workshops and structured groups were somewhat less effective in the aggregate but also less expensive. Still, they were effective. Based on their findings, the investigators suggest that particular treatments be dictated by counselee preferences and that career counselors be wary of premature termination.

In one of the most comprehensive and insightful analyses of the diagnosis and treatment of vocational problems, Rounds and Tinsley (1984) argue that more attention must be paid to the behavior change *process* mediating intervention effectiveness. To do so requires the development of reliable vocational-problem diagnostic systems, and, within each of these systems, the mechanisms responsible for vocational behavior change must be specified theoretically and a relationship demonstrated between the change effects and the particular intervention. In short, we need to know what worked for whom and why.

An example of what Rounds and Tinsley advocate may be found in an article by Rosenberg and Smith (1985). Although they do not base their conclusions on research, Rosenberg and Smith do offer some fascinating speculation about the possible relationship between modal personality types and modes of career counseling that might be most effective. What are the career counseling interaction effects between interventions and counselee attributes? Specifically, do the various Holland types in college benefit from counseling approaches that dovetail with their type's characteristics? As an illustration, let us look to what Rosenberg and Smith say about social types along several dimensions (most sub-doctoral-level counselors are primarily or secondarily social types).

General approach: Social types obviously need career counseling that is verbal. They like to talk and prefer an environment that is friendly, open, and supportive. They will participate in group counseling far more than other types will.

Length and number of sessions: Social students prefer counseling to last several sessions, longer than other types prefer. They enjoy the counseling relationship and often may venture into areas of personal concern.

Self-knowledge: Several strategies are effective in helping social students discover their career-related needs, values, and interests. Counselors can ask them to describe what they like about people they idolize or about significant others. These admired traits can then be compared with the student's self-perceptions. Asking social types about classroom experiences—preferred teachers (or supervisors), classmates (or co-workers), atmosphere, working style, and tasks—frequently yields relevant information about personal needs and values. Good insights can also be gained by verbally investigating other social experiences such as past jobs, volunteer work, and participation in social clubs and other organizations. It is extremely important that social students have an opportunity to talk to counselors and other students before any real and lasting self-knowledge is acquired. Merely writing ideas on paper is not sufficient and will have a limited impact on these students.

Occupational information: Many methods are available to assist social types in gathering occupational information, but these students appear to benefit best from talking to people employed in occupations of interest. In addition to providing relevant career information, professionals in the field serve as a source of needed support. Only these personal visits can help answer questions such as "What do you really like about this career?" and "What is the personal atmosphere like?" Also, sustained visits of up to two weeks or internships can lead to solid career decisions.

Decision making and planning: Social types need to discuss their experiences and values with others before making an appropriate and enduring career decision. Counselors should provide a lot of support to these students. Social types are not skilled at planning and may need assistance in developing short-range and long-range goals. Providing names of other individuals who might help them plan, such as college advisors, is frequently worthwhile.

Follow-up: Social types appreciate periodic reassurance. Knowing that they can talk to a counselor when needed provides excellent support, but follow-up appointments do not need to be rigidly scheduled. A brief note or a phone call can be reassuring (p. 45).*

For each of the other Holland types—realistic, artistic, enterprising, conventional, and investigative—the authors have presented their impressionistic, experience-based prescriptions. What they have produced certainly has a good deal of face validity. The problem, however, is relatively easily researched, and it would seem to be a useful focus for more rigorous inquiry.

For example, Boyd and Cramer (1995) studied counselee-treatment interaction of Holland types in terms of their preferences for career counseling along such dimensions as time parameters, counselor and counselee roles, emphases in sessions, and so on. Some discrimination by type was found to occur. Similarly, Nelson and Roberge (1993) determined that psychological type, as measured by the Myers-Briggs Type Indicator (MBTI), generally correlated with preferences of college counselees for using certain types of career resources (e.g., career reading room, placement files, catalogs, and computerized systems). More such studies of counselee-treatment

*Source: Reprinted from the 1985 *Journal of Career Planning and Employment* with permission of the National Association of Colleges and Employers, copyright holder.

interaction are likely. Once counselors know with greater certainty what dynamics exist, they can move to more confident strategies for intervention.

Related to this type of speculation about differential counseling strategies based on counselee characteristics is the work of Kivligham and Shapiro (1987), who sought to determine if Holland types benefited differentially from a self-help approach. They found that personality type was indeed a predictor of counselee's benefit from and interest in a self-help treatment program, with those most likely to benefit and be interested being investigative and conventional types (and perhaps realistic, although the sample in this study included too few of this type to offer a conclusion).

In another example that conforms to the requirements of Rounds and Tinsley, Krumboltz, Kinnier, Rude, Scherba, and Hamel (1986) worked with a group of community college students who were classified as rational, intuitive, fatalistic, or dependent decision makers. All were exposed to a rational decision-making training intervention. Those who had been impulsive, dependent, or fatalistic in former curriculum choices and those who showed dependency in prior job choices seemed to gain most from the rational training curriculum. Obviously the major implication of this study is that there do indeed appear to be "different strokes for different folks" in terms of teaching a decision-making strategy.

To be sure, there are aspects of outcome research in career counseling that are at a rudimentary, even a primitive, stage. Both Feller (1992) and Spokane (1991) speak eloquently to the problems of such research that basically asks, "Did we do anyone any good?" The more sophisticated question that observers are now asking is: "Whom did we help, how, and why?"

All in all, the research on career counseling outcome is comforting and, taken as a whole, provides powerful documentation for the continued existence of legitimate career helping. It is, whatever the reasons, perhaps more persuasive than outcome research in any other subset of human intervention activity.

Decision Making

In Chapter 4, we presented a review of decision-making theories of career choice. Chapters relating to the provision of career guidance services from elementary school through adulthood each stress, to various degrees, the importance of decision-making skills. Decision making is a learned process crucial to career choice and behavior. Therefore, the nature of decision making and its relationship to helping strategies is discussed next.

The topic of decision making is complex indeed. It is clearly a multidimensional concept (Hartman, Fuqua, & Jenkins, 1986), and it can be no more than touched on in this book. Career decision making is a specific application of general theories and principles related to the way people make choices and exercise judgment. Consequently the broader field is one of the primary foci in all of psychology and has been approached from both cognitive and noncognitive perspectives (see, for example, Heesacker & Harris, 1993; Rachlin, 1989; Yates, 1990). Although the study of career decision-making processes is in only a rudimentary state, we can reach some conclusions that inform current, state-of-the-art practice.

Classifications. For purposes of explication, decision making can be classified in several ways. First, we may consider *institutional decisions* versus *individual decisions.* The former relate to judgments that affect organized groups of people; the latter pertain to choices that have largely personal consequences. The literature of management and administration is replete with discussions of institutional decision making, and the findings are summarized herein as they relate to effecting systematic service delivery within such institutions as schools, colleges, agencies, and others. Second, we may regard decision-making methodology in terms of *mathematical model decisions* versus *nonmathematical model decisions.* Mathematical decisions rely mainly on the rigid logic of the calculus of probability, whereas nonmathematical decisions are the result of a less formal symbolic logic. Statisticians tend to be skeptical of any decision theory that cannot be realized mathematically and experimentally; they assume complete information and rationality. Because human beings are sometimes not rational, and because they frequently make choices based on incomplete information, decision making is often more psychological than logical, and less rigorous methods are employed. These nonmathematical models of decision making are usually called *descriptive* models. Third, we may speak of *group decision making* versus *individual decision making.* Here we are concerned with the process of decision making. The literature of social psychology and group dynamics suggests that under certain types of conditions and for specified types of problems, groups consistently outperform individuals in decision making. Unfortunately, career choice is not one of those problems; it tends to be approached individually and, of course, it should be. Finally, we may regard *decisions under certainty* versus *decisions under risk*. In the former, an individual or institution will know with absolute certainty that a decision will be followed by a 100 percent probability of a given consequence. This state is often not as simple as it appears, for there may be many consequences possible, each a virtual certainty, and a choice must still be made. In the latter case, the degree of risk may range from a knowledge of different probabilities of occurrence to complete uncertainty.

When we speak of an individual and career-related choices, we refer to individual decisions that are basically nonmathematical in a formal sense (although probability data may be available), that are individually effected, and that, typically, are made under conditions of risk.

In terms of conditions of risk, we may think of four possibilities. *Certainty* is that condition described wherein choice *A* will surely lead to event *B*. *Objective probability* is a condition of risk wherein an individual becomes informed of the odds relating to the consequences emanating from the making of a given decision. Largely by the use of regression equations or less formal expectancy tables, individuals can be compared with others having similar characteristics and can be given relatively objective, actuarial probabilities of success or failure in some future event. *Subjective probability* is a risk condition in which individuals translate objective probabilities into personal or psychological terms. They may overestimate low probabilities or underestimate high ones, depending on their propensities for risk-taking and other factors. *Uncertainty* is a risk condition that exists when the consequences of a decision are not completely known or when the probabilities suggest that the outcome desired is not totally certain.

One of the aims of career counselors is to remove as much uncertainty as possible. The counselor accomplishes this condition by assisting the individual in grasping the objective probabilities (aptitudes, interests, work opportunities, education and training opportunities, and such) and in understanding how these objective data may be subjectively or psychologically processed (attitudes, values, aspirations, and so on). To do so requires a strategy for decision making.

Assumptions Underlying Intervention Strategies. Hence, the decision-making model that the counselor chooses to use may well depend on the particular stage of career development of the individual in relation to the immediacy of the career-related decision and the amount of information the individual is assumed to possess. Whatever model one chooses, however, there are certain basic assumptions that undergird all intervention strategies in assisting individuals to make decisions.

1. Many factors in decision making will be outside the control of the decider. These factors include such variables as the state of the economy and accessibility of education and training opportunities.

2. Individuals are rarely able to acquire and to process *all* relevant information in making some career-related decisions. They will tend to select out those data that they deem important or readily available, or that someone else thinks are important. Individuals typically realize their inability to acquire the entirety of information and to define the complete range of possible outcomes and so settle for a strategy of decision making that will lead to "good enough" decisions. Subsequently, that good enough decision may lead to a rationalization process in which decisions made based on bounded rationality are justified as the best decisions possible.

3. Decisions will generally be made ipsatively. That is, people usually have many objectives; to choose one is to lower the probability of attaining others. Choice optimizes the chances of a given outcome occurring and simultaneously suboptimizes the chances of conflicting outcomes. This condition suggests that short-range decisions that may seem good when they are made may be suboptimizing in the sense that they seriously affect the flexibility of a long-range plan.

4. The evaluation of a career-related decision is frequently more a matter of process than of outcome. If outcome is employed as the criterion of a good career decision, one must look to long-range favorable results. Counselors seldom have that luxury. As a result, process criteria are more frequently used. We tend to judge a career-related decision as "good" if it is logical and consistent when it is made or if it was the consequence of prescribed procedures and consonant with some specific model of decision making. It is possible for decisions that are judged "good" when they are made in terms of the process to be ultimately "bad" decisions in terms of outcome; conversely, it is possible, although unlikely, that "good" outcomes can result from "bad" process.

5. Individuals can be taught how to make career-related decisions. There are dozens of decision-making programs, each different yet each similar, that have reported at least short-range success. Some of these paradigms will be discussed later in this chapter. Further, it is likely that, once taught, a decision-making strategy and skills in decision making have transfer value.

6. Although we know that a great variety of factors influence individual career decision making, we do not presently have any definitive indication of which factors predominate for which individual under what conditions and of how these differential weightings evolve. We know relatively little about the correlates of decision making. There is some evidence to suggest that the following factors moderate decision-making abilities: values (M. Katz, 1980); previous exploratory behavior (Blustein, Pauling, DeMania, & Faye, 1994); propensity for risk (Slakter & Cramer, 1969); achievement motivation (Wish & Hasazi, 1973); coping style (O'Hare & Tamburri, 1986); prestige (N. B. Taylor & Pryor, 1985); neuroticism (Chartrand et al., 1993); and age (Guttmann, 1978). Among the factors that have been investigated and for which the relationship to decision making is conflicting or unclear are: sex (D. J. Milley & Bee, 1982; Slaney, 1980a; Foote, 1980); interests (Lowe, 1981); ego identity status (Blustein & Phillips, 1990); vocational maturity (Phillips & Strohmer, 1982); self-efficacy (Taylor & Popma, 1990; Luzzo, 1993b); anxiety (G. S. Brown & Strange, 1981); and self-esteem (Gordon, 1981).

In terms of the relationship between anxiety and career indecision, Fuqua, Seaworth, and Newman (1987) demonstrated that a substantial, unidimensional relationship exists. Fuqua, Newman, and Seaworth (1988) later determined that although there was indeed a substantial relationship, both state and trait anxiety differentially related to career indecision. They identified four factors in the Career Decision Scale (CDS) and found that measures of anxiety correlated differently with each. One factor (lack of information about self and careers) provided the strongest relationship. A second factor (uncertainty about appropriateness or degree of fit between self and career) and factor four (specific barriers to a previous choice) also correlated substantially with anxiety. The third factor (multiple interests), however, was unrelated to anxiety. Thus, anxiety may relate to certain aspects of indecision but not to other aspects. In a longitudinal study of college graduates, Arnold (1989) logically concluded that decidedness and well-being were significantly related (especially around graduation). Hence, there can be no doubt that undecided college students are more anxious than their counterparts who have made career decisions with which they are comfortable.

7. We do not have a clear notion of why deciding individuals emphasize one or another of these factors or others and how that situation develops. It is possible to construct a taxonomy that delineates the kinds of influences that impinge on career decision making. The interaction of these internal and external variables is paramount in the decision-making process. Personal attributes and characteristics, value structures, opportunity factors, and cultural forces, separately and in combination, are brought to bear in decisions (see Table 13.2). Their combination, weighting, and content vary from individual to individual.

This fact has led some researchers to propose a taxonomy of decision-making *styles*. Arroba (1977) proposed six styles of decision making:

> *Logical:* Situation appraised coldly and objectively, choice made based on what is best
> *No thought:* No objective consideration
> *Hesitant:* Postponement of final commitment to an alternative, inability to make a decision
> *Emotional:* Decision based on what the person subjectively wants or likes
> *Compliant:* Decision made in accordance with the perceived expectations of the situation or of others, passivity
> *Intuitive:* Decision based only on a personal feeling of rightness or inevitability (p. 151)

Janis and Mann (1977), who have produced some of the most significant work in decision making, have suggested four defective patterns of decision making:

> *Unconflicted adherence:* The individual simply denies any serious risks from current course of action.

Unconflicted change to new course of action: The individual simply denies any serious risks in making a decision or change.

Defense avoidance: The individual avoids anything that might stimulate choice anxiety or painful feelings and gives up looking for a solution.

Hypervigilance: The individual becomes extremely emotionally excited as the time constraints of decision making are made more pressing.

Harren (1979) proposed three vocational decision-making styles in undergraduate students: (1) *rational,* involving objective deliberation and self-appraisal; (2) *intuitive,* involving emotional self-awareness and fantasy; and (3) *dependent,* involving denial of responsibility. This classification system has been the focus of corroborative research by Rubinton (1980) and Daniels (1982), who suggest that rational decision makers do best with rational interventions; whereas intuitive decision makers do best with intuitive interventions. Harren's decision-making model for college students has also been supported in a study by R. G. Thomas and Bruning (1984) in which the investigators discovered that the effects of nonreduced cognitive dissonance concerning a vocational decision were regression to earlier stages of decision making and revocation of the commitment to the decision.

These attempts at describing decision-making styles differ in terms of the population from which they were derived (secondary school students, college students, adults), the time involved (one point in time or a span of time), and the methodological design. Each, however, offers some potentially fruitful areas for further investigation. It should be recalled that the term decision making is often used synonymously with problem solving.

D. J. Walsh (1987) attempted to synthesize the findings regarding individual variations within the vocational decision-making process. She concluded that decision-making approaches appeared to differ along six dimensions:

Internal/external orientation	Self versus others as a resource for the decision task
Factual/affective focus	Cognition versus emotion in the process
Systematic/haphazard approach	Within each step of the decision-making process
Vigilant/inattentive approach	Attention to planning, consequences, and so on
Amount of time spent	To complete phases of the process
Volume of data	High versus low

These categories, like most of those in the literature, are descriptive rather than prescriptive.

It is not uncommon that in the behavioral and social sciences certain techniques become popular and their use spurs new research findings or explains more fully some already extant knowledge. Meta-analytic techniques and multivariate techniques are two such examples. One of the most recently applied is cluster analysis, a kind of discriminant sorting of data into categories. Using this technique, Lucas and Epperson (1990) sought to determine subtypes of undecided students and to see if previously evolved rational category systems were consonant with those derived through cluster analysis. They confirmed that different forms of career indecision exist, that the cluster-derived categories were consistent with the logically-derived categories previously discovered by the investigators (Lucas & Epperson, 1988), and that each of the five types identified evidenced varying levels of anxiety. Further confirmation is provided by Lucas (1993).

Similarly, Larson, Heppner, Ham, and Dugan (1988) employed the cluster analysis technique to identify four distinct subtypes of undecideds: (1) planless avoiders, (2) informed indecisives (a small group), (3) confident but uninformed, and (4) uninformed. About 25 percent of the sample in this study of college sophomore students were planless avoiders, individuals who combined a lack of career planning activities with maladaptive coping behaviors and attitudes. These individuals reported poor problem-solving abilities, especially with respect to career-related concerns—a group with no information and no decision-making skills. The confident but uninformed group, also about one-quarter of the sample, evidenced a modest lack of career planning activities, assessed themselves as good problem solvers, but lacked information about the career planning process. The largest cluster (almost one-half of the sample) was the uninformed group. They self-appraised their problem solving as moderate and lacked career information. These were the individuals judged to be most receptive to career interventions.

Further confirmation of the existence of different types of undecided students comes from a study of high school students effected by Fuqua, Blum, and Hartman (1988). Again using the technique of cluster analysis, they identified four groups, generally distinguishable by level of problem and by the characteristic anxiety manifested by each group:

> *Group One (42%) seems to represent a career decided group, relatively free of excessive anxiety and relatively effective in terms of attribution and identity formation. Group Two (22%) appears to possess at least moderate career indecision, increased anxiety, less identity formation, and a fairly internalized locus of control. Groups Three (28%) and Four (8%) seem to suffer fairly serious career indecision, are more external in their attribution, and show poorer identity formation. Group Three has moderate levels of anxiety with Group Four alone showing excessive anxiety relative to their peers. (pp. 369–370)*

The four types of undecideds were confirmed by cluster analysis in a study of rural high school students (Rojewski, 1994). Four types of career undecideds were also observed in a study of banking managers and professionals (Callanan & Greenhaus, 1992).

Others have approached the search for subtypes of career indecision by means of the statistical technique of factor analysis, a precursor of cluster analysis that permits a bit more latitude in manipulating data. F. W. Vondracek, Hostetler, Schulenberg, and Shimizu (1990) investigated undecided adolescents and concluded once again that four subtypes existed in their sample, with each group having problems that ranged from minimal to severe.

It seems apparent, that there are different subtypes of undecided students that different studies have identified as having more or less the same characteristics, that these differences exist as early as high school and as late as college graduation (with a high probability of the differences extending both upward and downward), and that differential interventions are required based on counselee characteristics.

8. Each model of career decision making assumes motivation or tries to establish readiness on the part of the chooser to take responsibility for career decisions. Too frequently, career guidance is analogous to the Boy Scout who helped the "little old lady" across the street—when she did not want to go. The intentions are good, but the perceived needs of the person being assisted are ignored, or the individual is not helped to internalize the importance of the choices that must be made.

For instance, a study using careful analysis of a few subjects (Tinsley, Toakar, & Helwig, 1994) determined that counselees who have relatively positive expectations about career counseling are more involved during sessions than are counselees with relatively negative expectations.

9. The effects of information on decision making are highly intricate, as we shall see in Chapter 14. For example, whether a counselee is decided or undecided, giving positive information appears to enhance simplicity in terms of cognitive differentiation, whereas negative information seems to be associated with greater cognitive complexity (Cesari, Winer, & Piper, 1984).

Some Approaches. These commonalities, cut across all programs for teaching decision making. Some of the better known of the decision-making approaches were described in Chapter 4; others will be described next or are treated more fully to demonstrate how particular theoretical emphases get translated into practice.

Martin Katz of the Educational Testing Service has spent years developing a system with which to assist two-year college students in the career decision-making process (Katz, 1973, 1980). Katz works from the assumption that values are the major synthesizing force in decision making. "The basic choice is essentially a choice between arrays of values, or value systems" (1973, p. 116). Consequently, he has constructed the System of Interactive Guidance and Information (SIGI), a computer-based process designed to help students to examine their values, to explore options, to retrieve information that is related to their values, and to get relevant interpretations of the data. In effect, students are learning a strategy for relating information to values and are thus increasing their competence in decision making. Students may go through the system as often as they like, each time taking an active role in controlling inputs. It is, in fact, a humanistically conceived interactive system that attempts, by means of a detailed exposition of objectives, scope, and sequence, to help individuals to do the following:

- Understand the sequential nature of choices
- Gain a knowledge of options in the domain of human values
- Recognize that value systems can change
- Become aware of the full array of conditions of work and attitudes toward work
- Grasp the rewards and satisfactions characteristic of each specific option at each choice point so the individual can detect the fit of these characteristics to his own values as he perceives them at that time
- Become aware of the cost and consequences of each decision
- Know and understand the probabilities of entry and success in each option considered at any choice point
- Acquire information about ways and means of proceeding (1973, pp. 122–123)

Hence, the content of career decision making might well place a high emphasis on values and valuing. Further, Katz has demonstrated that an interactive, computer-based system can be used as an aid in teaching a decision-making strategy.

Janis and Mann (1977) propose five distinct stages of decision making: (1) appraising the challenge; (2) surveying alternatives; (3) weighing alternatives; (4) deliberating about commitment; and (5) adhering despite negative feedback. Within this system, a feedback loop permits reversions to earlier stages. The evaluation of a "good" decision is conducted in terms of seven specific criteria:

1. Thoroughly canvasses a wide range of alternative courses of action
2. Surveys the full range of objectives to be fulfilled and the values implicated by choice
3. Carefully weighs whatever he knows about the costs and risks of negative consequences as well as the positive consequences that could flow from each alternative
4. Intensively searches for new information relevant to further evaluation of the alternatives
5. Correctly assimilates and takes account of any new information or expert judgment to which he is exposed, even when the information or judgment does not support the course of action he initially prefers
6. Reexamines the positive and negative consequences of all known alternatives, including those originally regarded as unacceptable, before making a final choice
7. Makes detailed provisions for implementing or executing the chosen course of action, with special attention to contingency plans that might be required if various known risks were to materialize (p. 11)

Harren (1979) offers a model of decision making that includes stages of awareness, planning, commitment, and implementation. Within this context, self-esteem and identity are thought to be important. The tasks of decision making are to achieve autonomy, interpersonal maturity, and a sense of purpose. Harren describes the model in terms of four conditions: (1) *interpersonal evaluation* (positive and negative feedback); (2) *psychological states* (level of anxiety); (3) *tasks conditions* (specific career-relevant tasks, defined in terms of imminence, alternatives, and consequences); and (4) *context conditions* (interpersonal relationships defined in terms of mutuality, support, and probability). Pitz and Harren (1980) suggest that a "good" decision under these circumstances should be evaluated in terms of four behavioral criteria:

1. *Information-seeking:* What information has the person sought about alternatives being considered?
2. *Range of alternatives:* How many and what variety of choices has the person identified and considered?
3. *Knowledge of alternatives:* How much knowledge does the person have about the choices and how accurate is it?
4. *Rationality of choice:* How consistent is the person's behavior with the principles of expected utility theory?

Gati (1986, 1990) offers an example of a systematic model for choosing among successive alternatives to bring decisions down to an increasingly specific focus. He calls his model a Sequential Elimination Approach (SEM), and it essentially involves a continual ranking of alternatives, eliminating those that fail to receive higher assessments. Gati believes that it is the responsibility of the counselor to identify the counselee's type of decision problem (such as lack of occupational information, lack of self-information, inability to deal with uncertainty, and so on) and to determine the counselee's decision-making style. The SEM is one of several possible intervention modes. Gati suggests that the following sequence of stages might make sense:

1. Identify the counselee's problem.
2. Help the counselee define and structure the decision problem (for example, choosing a major).
3. Present the SEM as a framework for career decision making.
4. Help the counselee to identify the aspects that are important to him or her and relevant to the elimination process.
5. Help the counselee to clarify the relative importance of the aspects enumerated in Stage 4.
6. Help the counselee to identify the range of levels considered as acceptable or satisfying with respect to each of the more important aspects.
7. Help the counselee to organize the alternatives into meaningful clusters to reduce the complexity of the elimination process.
8. Provide feedback to the counselee regarding the available alternatives that remain after each additional aspect has been considered.
9. Help the counselee to check the relative insensitivity of the results to any particular judgment.
10. Help the counselee rank the alternatives that survive the elimination by identifying relations of dominance.
11. Help the counselee to outline the steps to be taken to actualize the preferred alternative(s).

Within the parameters of Gati's work, the idea of *compromise* becomes a key construct (Gati, 1993). He identifies three facets of compromise: (1) compromising between occupational alternatives (e.g., determining what occupational alternatives are closest to one's ideal image), (2) compromise in relative importance of aspects (e.g., deciding how much information of what type is appropriate for decision making) and; (3) compromise on within-aspect preferences (e.g., openness or readiness for change from a previously determined course). Gati contends that occupational choice rarely entails finding a single dominant occupation; rather, we compromise aspects of choice in our decision making.

Savickas (1990a) offered a career decision-making course to tenth graders and used didactic instruction based on the content of the Career Maturity Inventory (see Chapter 15) and the Holland typology (see Chapter 4). The course attempted to enhance the students' attitudes toward decision making and concepts about career choice by providing them with cognitive competencies that included self-appraisal skill for evaluating occupational capabilities, knowledge about the world of work, matching personal characteristics with occupational requirements, forming plans to enter an occupation, and developing coping skills to deal with any implementation problems. Designed for adolescents and young adults (grade seven through sophomore in college), the initial course evaluations were positive.

A shotgun approach to enhancing decision making may not be nearly so effective as tailoring interventions to the specific characteristics of counselees. For example, Mann, Beswick, Allouache, and Ivey (1989) conducted a decision-making workshop for counselees that was based on Janis and Mann's conflict theory and the five types of decision strategies described earlier in this chapter. Their 76 participants consisted of two basic groups: *problem counselees* (those who appraised themselves as poor in decision making and with specific problems) and *learners* (those who viewed themselves as competent decision makers but who wanted to improve their ability). These two groups proved to have different reactions to an intervention. The investigators concluded, "We believe that a general 'all-purpose' decision workshop program may succeed when participants are a homogeneous sample but could run into difficulties when participants have quite disparate competencies and reasons for attending" (p. 481).

Each of the preceding programs demands counselee involvement in the choice process. Other programs are more mechanistic, in the sense that the program has inherent in it the capacity to make the actual choice. J. L. Holland's *Self-Directed Search* (1994), for example, processes student input data in such a way that choices based on the data provided by the users are fed back to them for further exploration. In a sense, the system processes the data and makes the choices for the user rather than the user processing the data and making the choice. Even in this type of system, however, the user must subsequently choose from among the alternatives suggested by the mechanical processing.

A second example of a self-directed workshop is offered by Robbins, Chartrand, McFadden, and Lee (1994). They compared a leader-led career workshop to a self-directed intervention for middle-aged and older adults. In general, results were positive and comparable for each group. Although many self-help materials have been carefully tested and their effectiveness has been demonstrated, other such materials are "antiscientific and shoddy" (Ellis, 1993a, p. 335) and should be viewed by counselors with some skepticism.

Common to virtually all of these career decision-making programs and to others not specifically described here are several foci: (1) a knowledge of self, variously defined, but usually including aptitudes, interests, achievements, personality characteristics, attitudes, and values, with different emphases placed on each by different programs; (2) a knowledge of the world of work, variously described, but according to some generally accepted classification system (such as *DOT,* cluster, field and level, and others) and including work-related factors (such as rewards of work, requirements of work, and others); and (3) a decision-making strategy, variously conceived, but usually entailing a step-by-step, rational, logical, by-the-numbers procedure. Currently, no career decision-making system has been proven to be more effective than any other, although each lays claim to success. Comparative studies in this regard would prove interesting and useful.

These models of decision making differ on a variety of parameters. First, they vary in terms of being mathematical or descriptive. Second, they vary in terms of the decision-making variables that are considered most important (values, interests, self-concept, abilities, or motivation). Third, they differ in terms of the emphasis placed on environmental variables (economics, cultural factors, social conditions, and residence). Fourth, they diverge in their assessment of the amount and type of information necessary for good decision making. Fifth, they place differing accents on the probability factor. Sixth, they differ in their perception of the stages that decision makers experience. Finally, they differ in terms of evaluation (for example, outcome or process).

Bergland (1974), in a thoughtful review and synthesis of the career decision making literature that still is pertinent, has suggested that the basic strategy of decision making is problem solving. Consequently, he offers a series of stages that the decision making should be helped to negotiate:

1. Defining the problem
2. Generating alternatives
3. Gathering information
4. Developing information-seeking skills
5. Providing useful sources of information
6. Processing information
7. Making plans and selecting goals
8. Implementing and evaluating plan (p. 352)

All of these decision-making models for use in individual counseling are action-oriented. By whatever terminology they are called, they address choice in a staged, systematic manner. They are intended to assist individuals in filtering objective data through subjective systems of risk taking, emotionality, utility determination, and so on. Again, no single model has been determined to be superior to any other; yet each implies its own unique success. They suggest to counselors that virtually any model of assisting an individual in career decision making—extant or yet to be invented—can be successful if based on sound theoretical and research findings and if operationalized in logical, consistent ways.

Indecision and Indecisiveness. Before leaving the topic of decision making, it is necessary to point out the difference between undecidedness and indecisiveness and to describe several recent decision scales. Crites (1969) has defined *indecision* as "the inability of the individual to select, or commit himself to a particular course of action which will eventuate in his preparing for and entering a specific occupation" (p. 305). He specifies three possible cases for indecision: (1) the multipotential individual who is unable to designate one goal from among many choices; (2) the undecided individual who cannot make a choice from among available alternatives; and (3) the uninterested individual who is uncertain about a choice because of lack of an appropriate interest pattern. In contrast, *indecisiveness* emanates from general personal problems rather than from doubts related to a specific career choice, perhaps because of the pain involved in decision making. In indecision, there may be lack of information or knowledge of how to sort through alternatives; in indecisiveness, a generally dysfunctional personality orientation may cause such choice anxiety that an individual is rendered incapable of making a decision. Seldom are these distinctions made explicit when, for example, counselors speak of decided and undecided students.

Some theorists (Kinnier, Brigman, & Noble, 1990; Lopez & Andrews, 1987) view indecision as the result of interactional deficits within families. It is argued that a person's indecision might be the outcome of transactional "noise" between the person and the family—a failure in family transformation. Based on clinical intuitions, this idea argues that there is typically an overinvolvement of parents with their indecisive child over career and educational concerns, leading students to achieve inadequate psychological separation from their parents. As Lopez and Andrews suggest, empirical research would be useful to investigate the relationship between indecision or undecidedness and family history, structure, and communication patterns, among other variables. One of these variables might be enmeshment in family of origin.

Several decision scales are now being used, largely for experimental and research purposes. Osipow, Carney, Winer, Yanico, and Koschir (1976a, 1976b) are responsible for the Career Decision Scale (CDS), a 16-item instrument designed originally for college students. It yields scores for four types of indecision: (1) lack of structure (lack of confidence, choice anxiety, potential choice avoidance); (2) perceived external barriers (for example, financial or parental); (3) approach-approach (difficulty in deciding among alternatives); (4) personal conflict (difficulty choosing between occupations that reflect differing personal values) (Osipow, 1980). A study by Barak and Friedkes (1982) found that counselees who basically lacked structure received the greatest benefit from counseling; those in the personal conflict and perceived external barrier categories gained the least from counseling.

Another decision scale is the Vocational Decision-Making Difficulty Scale (VDMD) developed by Holland (Holland, Gottfredson, & Nafziger, 1975). Slaney, Palko-Nonemaker, and Alexander (1981) identified four factors of indecision measured by this scale: (1) lack of information, (2) lack of clarity of an individual's place in the world of work, (3) choice anxiety, and (4) questions about ability. Slaney (1980a) and Slaney, Palko-Nonemaker, and Alexander (1981) discovered significant differences between the VDMD and the CDS. Holland, Gottfredson, and Power (1980) categorized decision making difficulties as: (1) problems of vocational identification, (2) lack of information or training, (3) environmental or personal barriers, and (4) no problems. In an earlier study (Holland & Holland, 1977), a large majority of an undecided group were identified as simply delaying decisions until reality demanded action. Their indecision was not a matter of lack of information or immaturity. Holland and Holland believe that some students suffer, however, from an "indecisive disposition" resulting from a failure to acquire the necessary cultural participation, self-confidence, tolerance for ambiguity, concept of identity, and environmental and self-knowledge necessary for decision making. The point that indecision is not necessarily pathological is well taken and should temper the tendency of counselors to believe that decisions need to be made before they are necessary. After all, almost three out of every four college freshmen express some form of indecision, tentativeness, or uncertainty about selecting a major (Grite, 1981).

A third scale, the Vocational Decision Scale (VDS), has been developed by G. Jones and Chenery (1980). Three indecision subtypes were identified: (1) general self-uncertainty (indecisiveness, lack of self-confidence regarding decision-making ability and occupational ability, lack of clarity about oneself); (2) low choice/work salience (lack of relationship between interests or abilities and occupational field, low motivation); and (3) transitional self (scarcity of educational and/or occupational information, conflict with significant others).

Other scales are Harren's (1979) Assessment of Career Decision Making (ACDM), an instrument based on Tiedeman and O'Hara's stages of exploration, crystallization, choice, and clarification; Lunneborg's (1976) Career Decision-Making Questionnaire (CDMQ); and Appel, Haak, and Witzke's (1970) Career Decision Readiness Inventory (CDRI).

L. K. Mitchell and Krumboltz (1984a) point out that the problem with paper-and-pencil measures of career decision making is that they do not test behaviors; they measure only knowledge of decision-making skills. Consequently, experimental instruments focus on behavioral inventories and simulations. Yet, there is currently no persuasive evidence that these newer approaches offer any better data than the paper-and-pencil instruments. Mitchell and Krumboltz also catalog some research needs in the area of career decision making. These include the need for longitudinal as well as short-term outcome measures; the need for teaching counselees to recognize situations that require a decision-making strategy; the need for greater research involving varied populations and age groups; the need to investigate more thoroughly the personal cognitions affecting career decision making; and the need for better methodologies, such as causal path analysis (see, for example, B. Hartman, Fuqua, & Blum, 1985), multivariate research designs, and single-subject designs.

Finally, in addition to all those interventions previously mentioned that are designed to enhance career decision making, there is evidence that decision making can be improved through the use of behavioral interventions, group experiences, individual counseling (Kivligham, Hageseth, Tipton, & McGovern, 1981), self-administered instruments, simulations, contract counseling (Brooks & Haigler, 1984), matching workshop participants to differential treatments by specific deficits (Zagora & Cramer, 1994), and exploration (Carver & Smart, 1985).

GROUP PROCESSES

The second major strategy for implementing career guidance and counseling programs is the use of groups of one type or another. Many chapters of this book are liberally laced with examples of the use of group processes in such activities as disseminating information, using educational and career information, developing attitudes toward career planning and work, and learning decision making. Therefore, in this section, we present only a brief overview of the group strategy in career guidance.

Rationale

It should be evident that in any systematic approach a great many objectives of career guidance and counseling can be achieved through group methods. Traditionally, it has been maintained that group procedures provide *efficiency* and *effectiveness*. If, for example, the dissemination of information is a goal of career guidance at a specific point along the career development continuum, it is clearly more efficient to present the information once to a group than to present it individually to each member of the group. Also, if the goals of career guidance entail problem solving or if the immediate objective of career guidance is to treat dysfunctional behaviors that may be affecting career development, group methods are appropriate, for groups have been found to perform consistently better in certain types of problem-solving tasks and under certain conditions than do individuals attacking the same problem. In terms of correcting dysfunctional behaviors, it is reasoned that because these behaviors are typically learned in group situations, they are best unlearned or relearned or substitute behaviors learned in the same milieu.

Currently the majority of all employed persons work within the framework of corporate structures wherein the primary modus operandi is the group as a procedural vehicle. It would seem beneficial for individuals, especially youngsters, to become used to functioning in this manner as a part of their preoccupational experience. Some suggested themes by which such career-related learning might be facilitated in groups are presented in Chapters 7 through 12.

The use of group methods is further justified by the fact that various career guidance curricula and theories of career development suggest universal career needs. These are needs that are presumed to be required or felt by all individuals; therefore, common learnings of this sort may be facilitated in groups. The relevance of these learnings to an individual's unique situation may be recognized through both group and individual methods.

Characteristics of the Group

Counselors may work with collections of individuals or aggregates rather than with true groups. In a social psychology sense, a group is characterized by at least six criteria (J. C. Hansen & Cramer, 1971):

1. Members of the group are in *interaction* with one another; that is, there must be at least two-way communication.
2. Members of the group share a *common goal*. This goal may be set by the group itself, or it may be imposed by external forces.
3. The group members set *norms* that give direction and limits to their activity. Certain behaviors

come to be rewarded; others are punished in some way.

4. The members develop a set of *roles.* Certain functions are performed by group members.
5. The group members develop a network of *interpersonal* attraction (likes and dislikes for each other).
6. The group works toward the satisfaction of the *individual needs* of the group members. (p. 81)

Clearly, these characteristics will be present in varying degrees, depending on the type of group and the purpose of the group. The more in evidence they are, the more the likelihood that a group exists; the more these characteristics are lacking, the greater the chances that an aggregate or a simple collection of individuals exists. Large assembly programs in a school, for example, typically deal with aggregates. Usually, successful discussions, problem solving, and counseling work through groups. A collection of individuals can still have utility for counselors. The point is simply that a distinction should be made between groups, which offer great potential inner resources for career guidance and counseling, and aggregates, which are a convenience.

If the counselor works with true groups, there must be some understanding of at least the basic elements of the way in which groups function. As a group interacts, it becomes dynamic; members are constantly adjusting and changing in relation to each other and to themselves. As a group restructures and adjusts, tensions are reduced, conflicts eliminated, and problems solved. The study of the variables underlying group movement is called group dynamics. Understanding group dynamics leads to developing the techniques for effective group actions and decisions by using the forces that facilitate or inhibit group functioning. Such forces include the manner of interaction among the members, the amount of participation, the degree of group cohesiveness, the group values, the kind and quality of group leadership, and the internal structure of the group (degrees of permissiveness, competition, and communication).

Uses of Groups

The uses to which groups can be put in career guidance and counseling are limited only by the imagination and energy of the counselor. The following section presents some suggestions that provide an idea of the array of possibilities. Purposes for groups in career guidance are offered first; these are followed by a general discussion of the type of focus in career guidance groups.

Purposes

1. *Information dissemination:* Information about the world of work is required in career decision making. Certain elements of that information are pertinent only for given individuals; others are needed by all people. Information regarding the occupational structure, post-high school or post-college educational and training opportunities, and courses of study at various educational levels, to cite a few examples, are needed by every counselee and can be transmitted by means of group procedures, which will, of course, require follow-up.

2. *Motivation:* Motivation refers to the concept of convincing individuals of the value of some aspect of career guidance, whether this aspect involves the need for career planning in a broad sense or the need to take aptitude tests, for instance, in a much narrower sense. Readiness, if lacking, and an orientation to planfulness must be established.

3. *Teaching:* The most obvious application of group techniques occurs in the teaching process. In fact, the primary strategy for career education, infusion (that is, teachers highlighting the career relevance of existing subject matter content in the classroom), relies on the teaching strategy. There is certainly a place for teaching in career guidance. Some argue that group guidance often fails because counselors deal with guidance concerns by means of teacher behaviors. In other words, the *process* of teaching is seen as inappropriate for the *content* of guidance. This charge is certainly true in terms of the more affective elements of guidance content, but, as we have repeatedly stressed throughout this book, much of career guidance begins with a cognitive base. Goals ranging from the development of a vocabulary of work in youngsters to imparting decision-making skills to adults are effectively accomplished by means of a teaching strategy. To deliver a career development curriculum, a counselor simply must use structured groups.

4. *Practice:* Role-playing, dramatization, gaming, and other simulation techniques allow individuals to rehearse or to practice career-related behaviors in groups. Whether the practice is as specific as role playing a job interview or filling out an employment application or is as broad as playing the Life Career Game, group situations permit the rehearsal of necessary career behaviors in a protected context.

5. *Attitude development:* Attitudes are learned predispositions to respond in characteristic ways to certain stimuli. Because they are learned, they can be unlearned. Because they are learned within the family and other groups, they are logically unlearned and relearned within the group structure. Hence, the clarification of career attitudes and values and the crystallization and development of attitudes toward oneself can be fostered within groups.

6. *Exploration:* Because many individuals, whether schoolaged or adult, are in the exploratory stage of career development, various group activities designed to enhance that exploration are beneficial. Ranging from field trips to career conferences to less structured activities, groups provide a vehicle for this exploration.

7. *Counseling:* Related somewhat to attitude development but more specific is group counseling. Some view group counseling as simply a remedial activity (for example, dealing with specific fears and anxieties, coping with intrapersonal difficulties, and so on). Others conceive of it as having a developmental focus (such as developing interpersonal and social skills, learning decision-making skills, and so on). In either case, group counseling, as opposed to group guidance, is seen as a means of assisting individuals within a therapeutically created climate of respect and acceptance to recognize and to use their more affective aspects to their benefit.

Type of Focus. Fundamentally, group guidance and counseling should provide an opportunity to test or to discover one's own characteristics as related to particular environmental options. The following questions reflect such an intent: Knowing what I know about myself, how would I probably behave or perform in a situation with identified characteristics? Knowing what I know about a given occupation, what characteristics of mine can I compare and contrast with those required by the occupation? Through role-playing, case studies, selected audiovisual devices, discussion, speakers, structured exercises, and so on, an atmosphere can be created that will encourage individuals to project themselves vicariously into a given choice situation and to analyze how they personally would feel in that situation. Of course, it is not possible to create all the situations from which one might be able to choose or to have complete information. Also, it is possible to present irrelevant information to a group or to fail to encourage individuals to consider the characteristics of their behavior and performance that are related to choice making.

Whether one deals with individual counseling or with group processes, the same questions are relevant. Both should support those experiences that reinforce for individuals the validity of the questions: Who am I? Am I able to be what I want to be? What is my life likely to be if I succeed in becoming what I choose to be?

Throughout the career guidance process, individually and in groups, the counselor not only must ensure that counselees have access to accurate, relevant information about their personal characteristics and create conditions that will help them understand the implications of this information, but also the counselor must ensure that counselees have accurate, relevant information about the options open to them. In the final analysis, people's self-perceptions or the self-labels that direct their behavior relate to persons, objects, and possibilities that lie outside the self. In other words, one's self-descriptions, whether they are such adjectives as bright–dull, capable–incapable, or leader–follower, have meaning only in comparing oneself with others and with the requirements of specific situations. Appropriate information, much of which can be gleaned through groups, is vital to making good decisions about oneself as well as about what opportunities exist and what they require as one tests his or her personal fit with these opportunities.

A word of caution: too often a group strategy is employed simply because someone feels that it is time to launch a group guidance venture. Nothing comes before; very little comes after. The group guidance experience becomes a moment in time for its own sake. Group guidance is not "its own excuse for being." In a systematic approach to career guidance, one first determines goals and states them in behavioral terms; one then decides what activities are necessary and appropriate for achieving these goals; finally, one evaluates to discover if these goals have been achieved. One or more of the possible activities might involve the use of groups. This approach is quite a different matter from deciding to use a group strategy and then finding a focus for it. Intent determines strategy, not vice versa.

Much of career guidance and counseling can be accomplished by means of a group-helping strategy of one sort or another. Leading groups requires special skills or counselors, whether the purpose of the group is information dissemination, motivation, teaching, practice, attitude development, exploration, counseling, or some other aim. The use of group techniques is appropriate as a helping strategy in assisting individuals to answer a variety of career-related questions; it is not appropriate as an end in itself.

Career Coaching. Career coaching is a recent practice that appears to be gaining in popularity in the United States. Currently, there are 10,000 career coaches in the United States. Most theorists would contend that career coaches seek to help their clients make better career choices, make accurate self-assessments, develop job search skills, and become productive employees. As adult workers experience less job security and take more responsibility for managing their own career development, many people seek career coaching to help them develop strategies for managing their careers more effectively. Typically, career coaching is more task, advice giving, and problem solving oriented than career counseling. Thus, career coaching is a more narrowly defined service than is career counseling. Career coaches can offer valuable assistance to workers seeking to improve their work satisfaction and success.

The benefits of career coaching, however, are counterbalanced by potential pitfalls. For example, there are no professional standards and ethical codes of practice for career coaches. Coaches often have no or little formal training to prepare them to work with their clients. As those career coaches who do not have counseling credentials help their clients engage in self-assessment activities they come perilously close to engaging in career counseling. This raises serious ethical issues that the career counseling profession must address. Some have urged professional associations, such as the National Career Development Association, to take a more active role in developing training standards and monitoring the practice of career coaching. At the time of this writing, the National Career Development Association is responding to these suggestions with the goal of developing standards of practice and a curriculum for training career coaches.

Coaches who are also professional career counselors can offer their clients a wide range of services to help them move forward in their career development. We advocate for the development of professional standards for the training of career coaches and the practice of career coaching. Clearly, many adults seeking to improve their job search skills, resolve workplace issues, and acquire occupational information can benefit from the advice of a professionally trained career coach.

SUMMARY

We have discussed two primary helping strategies in career guidance: individual counseling and group counseling and guidance. We also briefly discussed career coaching. In one way or another, each of these strategies is designed to facilitate career decision making. The internal personal attributes and values an individual brings to the career decision-making process must be balanced with the external realities of opportunities and cultural factors that constrain one's choices. Each helping strategy can be effected systematically in itself and within a systematic program of career guidance.

CHAPTER FOURTEEN

Information in Career Guidance and Counseling

KEY CONCEPTS

- Information pertinent to the particular choices to be made—occupational, educational, personal, and social—is the fuel that drives personal decision making.
- Information can be accurate, current, and relevant or not. A major task of career guidance or career counseling is to assist persons in identifying what information they need, determining where such information can be obtained, ensuring that the information acquired is accurate and current, and planning how such information can be used as a basis for action.
- The mere availability of information does not ensure that it will be used or used effectively.
- Information delivery systems have evolved from printed matter to more interactive and personalized approaches, such as those found in multimedia simulation and computer-aided career guidance systems.
- The internet has become a vital source of career information.
- The fostering of planfulness and effective career behavior involves not only helping counselees to acquire information, but also assisting them in applying the knowledge gained to personal characteristics—preferences, values, commitments, and capabilities.

Most people are conversant with few occupations. They are aware, sometimes only vaguely, of the nature of the occupations of their immediate families and perhaps those of a small group of family-connected individuals. Because of the mass media, they may also be acquainted with an additional small number of occupations, frequently stereotyped. During the process of socialization, people have learned that some types of occupations are desirable and that others are taboo, at least within their cultural spheres. In attempting to relate self-characteristics to various occupations, they typically have few alternatives through which to sort unless some type of direct intervention occurs. This intervention usually takes the form of exposure to occupational information, mediated by a career guidance practitioner.

In addition to their need for occupational information, individuals require educational and personal information if their career development is to be complete. Because educational decisions are intermediate choices within the total context of career decision making, individuals must possess and be able to use information about various curricular opportunities, post-high school and post-college educational and training possibilities, and the relationship between education and work. If students make decisions to attend college, they need to understand such factors as how collegiate environments differ, how the overt characteristics of institutions of higher education (such as size, selectivity, geographical location, curriculum, and others) affect individuals, how to go about the application process, how to investigate financial aid opportunities, how to determine what national tests are required, and how to cope with many other variables in the process of educational choice. If students or adults are specialty-oriented, they must have similarly important information about opportunities for training. Hence, whether counselees are adolescents in the process of exploration; college students in the process of delimiting choice; or adults involved in midcareer change, preretirement programs, or other career-related decision making, information about educational or occupational opportunities can help individuals accomplish the necessary tasks.

Both educational and occupational information have meaning only insofar as such data are evaluated within the framework of what individuals know about themselves. Self-information is crucial to individuals seeing the relevance of the educational or occupational data that they receive. Counselees need an accurate picture and acceptance of their strengths and weaknesses in both the cognitive and the noncognitive domains to realize fully the value of information regarding the worlds of work and education. They must be aware of their diverse aptitudes, interests, values, and attitudes toward learning and work. Only then can they truly evaluate the information they receive. In effect, one asks, "Knowing what I know about myself, how can I use this information?"

Salomone (1989) suggests that *occupational* information is different from *career* information; consequently, counselors should be careful about which term they use. In his judgment, *occupational* and *career* are both adjectives that describe a *type* of information. Because an occupation is different from a career (see Chapter 1), career information is a much broader term than is occupational information (that is, information solely about occupations).

The process of career development requires that information continually reinforce planfulness; the interaction of educational or training alternatives, occupational alternatives, and self-characteristics is mandatory if good career decision making is to occur. Suggestions for enhancing the interaction of these topics have been offered in Chapter 13. People have different needs for career information depending on their developmental stage in the career life cycle (Bloch, 1989), on their learning styles (Goodman & Savage, 1999; McCormack, 1989) on their nationality (Bikos & Furry, 1999) and, perhaps, on their gender (Wolleat, 1989).

This chapter suggests processes to achieve the goals for career guidance offered earlier in this book. It presents a range of delivery systems by which the concepts, knowledge, and attitudes integral to career development can be attuned to the needs and characteristics of the various consumer publics. It seeks to identify the range of possibilities available within the many facets of the educational enterprise and within the community for reinforcing vocationalization—for helping the individual develop a vocabulary of work, acquire necessary career knowledge, develop healthy career attitudes, learn adequate decision-making skills, and so forth. Specifically, we set forth in this chapter some principles for effectively using information and discuss the evaluation of information, types of delivery systems, and illustrations of some of the more promising systems. We include also a discussion of the work of the National Occupational Information Coordinating Committee (NOICC) and its state counterparts (SOICCs), even though NOICC has been terminated at the federal level. Its substantial legacy of concepts and materials continue to be vital resources at state and local levels. A sampling of some of the specific materials available is also presented. Because of space limitations, we will concentrate primarily on career information and downplay sources of educational and personal information. Each year, more than 10 million people utilize computers, books, videos, and other media to explore the worlds of work, training, and education.

PRINCIPLES FOR USING INFORMATION EFFECTIVELY

It is obvious that simple exposure to information is insufficient. The mere availability of information about occupations, educational and training opportunities, and the characteristics of an individual does not mean that the information will be used or, if used, that it will be employed effectively. To increase the probability that data will be efficiently used, one must consider aspects of motivation, the quality of the information, and how information is assimilated.

Motivation

Need is the sine qua non of effective information acquisition and processing. Readiness must be present, because almost all learning is a function of motivation. Motivation, in turn, is based on a person's attempt to satisfy a career-related need. In other words, no need, no action; no action, no career-related learning. Almost all learning theories place a premium on motivation, readiness, and the establishment of a learning set in the learner. Career guidance processes would do well to follow this example. To become motivated, individuals must be assisted to see how their needs are met by whatever information is delivered.

Acquiring information is a mandatory element of occupational exploration. Grotevant and Cooper (1986) conducted a study in which they demonstrated that the wider the career exploratory behaviors in which adolescents engaged, the more congruent their stated occupational choices with dimensions of ability, interests, and personality. M. S. Taylor (1985) has demonstrated some relationship between an individual's occupational knowledge (for example, education-training requirements, job conditions and characteristics, worker relationships, and job knowledge within specific area of study) and job offers for college undergraduates and graduates in management fields. Her study also suggests that occupational knowledge may enhance students' abilities to present themselves better to employers. The major source of students' occupational information seemed to be information provided by others (such as professors, people in a job, outside speakers). Thus, although the possession of good occupational information does not guarantee good decision making, it is unlikely that career decisions will be favorable without the incorporation of occupational information in the decision-making process. Further, having that information seems to have a payoff in terms of enhancing the likelihood of desired outcomes.

It should be noted that occasionally, research results suggest that adolescents especially may not utilize available information. One British study (Hodkinson, 1998), for example, argues that adolescents are not future-oriented enough to pragmatically utilize most occupational information. Changes of mind and career direction are thought to be so common as to make protracted future planning moot for adolescents. Other reasons for adolescents not using information effectively are suggested by a Canadian Study (Julien, 1999). Her survey of 400 adolescents indicated that 40 percent did not know where to go for help with their decision making and 38 percent thought that they needed to seek out too many sources for required information. Nevertheless, we believe that information is vital to good career decision making, and the preponderance of evidence support this view.

Motivation and the establishment of readiness pertain to all scholastic ability levels within an educational setting and to adults. Although there is some evidence that brighter students have more knowledge of high-level than low-level occupations, most research suggests that academic achievers are no more knowledgeable about occupations than are lower achievers and that the social status of the students is also not a factor in the accuracy of information. The gifted student, for example, has some unique needs in terms of occupational information. Chapman and Katz (1983) have observed that although gifted high school students receive a great deal of educational information, largely related to accessing higher education, they are exposed to little occupational information. Further, because they are multitalented, as they continue to explore information, it constantly opens up new possibilities, often leading to the frustration of choice anxiety. All of this has led Frederickson (1986) to state that:

> *Gifted persons may be able to acquire and retain more information than most other persons, but the use of this information in a career-planning process is still a complex task requiring emotional support and assistance from parents, counselors, and teachers. Gifted students need just as much help as average students, if not more, in career planning. (p. 566)*

Based on cognitive information processing (CIP) theory, Peterson, Sampson, and Reardon (1991; later expanded in 2000) view the effective use of career information in counseling as a learning event. They maintain that any learning event consists of three components: "(1) an objective; that is, the capability to be acquired; (2) an intervention to bring about the desired capability; and (3) an evaluation to ascertain whether the objective was obtained" (p. 197). Clearly, if the use of career information in counseling is a learning event (and we agree that it is), career counselors need to be cognizant of the psychology of learning and the learning principles derived from that psychology. This orientation is completely consistent with the cognitive/behavioral counseling approach outlined in Chapter 14.

They urge a CASVE (communication, analysis, synthesis, valuing, and execution) decision making process in which learning is the undergirding structure for decision making and information is required in each phase of the learning process. We have noted at several points in this book that career decision making is sometimes more psychological than logical, but in those decision-making situations with which the majority of individuals are confronted in career planning and choice, a learning paradigm and the attendant use of strategies for incorporating self, educational, and occupational information make a great deal of sense. The Peterson, Sampson, and Reardon volume devotes a great deal of space to an excellent discussion of the use of career information in the decision-making process. An example of the use of information in the CASVE cycle may be found in Table 14.1 (See also Reardon & Wright, 1999; Sampson, Lenz, Reardon, & Peterson, 1999; Sampson, Peterson, Lenz, & Reardon, 1992a; and Sampson, Peterson, Lenz, Reardon, & Saunders, 1996).

These findings point to the necessity of helping individuals learn to use information. This end can be accomplished only after a learning set has been established.

Readiness and motivation are requisite to the effective use of occupational information at any intervention point in one's life span. Readiness assumes that we can accurately measure an individual's occupational information needs. There are some instruments available to do so, all of which measure the frequency and variety of vocational information-seeking behavior (see, for example, various career maturity measures).

Evaluation of Information

A second factor in the effective use of information is the caliber of the data. Whatever the vehicle through which the information is transmitted—print, film, slide, CD ROM, computer interactive systems, the internet, simulation, and such—there is a need to evaluate it in terms of some criteria of "good" information.

One important criterion is the source of the information. Some material is produced for recruitment, and although many such presentations are acceptable, some, because of their overzealousness, are misleading. For example, few college-produced videos mention any negative aspects of the institution. Other materials are produced specifically for guidance purposes and thus can frequently be considered more accurate at face value, although there are always decisions made in relation to inclusion and exclusion in preparing information that affect its objectivity to some extent.

Other important considerations are the currency, validity, and applicability of the data. Currency refers to the up-to-date nature of the information. Newness does not guarantee accuracy, but it is likely that information will be more accurate if it is recent. Validity refers to the accuracy of information, insofar as the data may be affected by such factors as the zealous recruitment motive discussed earlier. Finally, applicability may be considered from two points of view: (1) Are the data presented in such a manner that they can be easily used? (2) Is the level at which the data are presented appropriate to the consumer?

TABLE 14.1 Career Information and the CASVE Cycle

PHASE OF THE CASVE CYCLE	EXAMPLE OF CAREER INFORMATION AND MEDIA
Communication (identifying a need)	A description of the personal and family issues that women typically face in returning to work (information) in a videotaped interview of currently employed women (medium)
Analysis (interrelating problem components)	Explanations of the basic education requirements for degree programs (information) in community college catalogues (medium)
Synthesis (creating likely alternatives)	A presentation of emerging nontraditional career options for women (information) at a seminar on career development for women (medium)
Valuing (prioritizing alternatives)	An exploration of how the roles of parent, spouse, citizen, leisurite, and homemaker would be affected by the assumption of the worker role (information) in an adult version of a computer-assisted career guidance system (medium)
Execution (forming means-ends strategies)	A description of a functional résumé emphasizing transferable skills, followed by the creation of a résumé (information) presented on a computer-assisted employability skills system (medium)

Source: From G. W. Peterson, J. P. Sampson, and R. C. Reardon, *Career development and services: A cognitive approach.* Pacific Grove, CA: Brooks/Cole Publishing Company, 1991. Reprinted with permission.

Periodically the National Career Development Association's Career Information Review Service (CIRS) presents reviews of career and occupational information materials in the *Career Development Quarterly* based on guidelines determined by the profession.

There are both general guidelines and content guidelines that cover the following areas:

General Guidelines

Accuracy of information—current and nonbiased
Format—clear, concise, and interesting
Vocabulary—appropriate to target group
Bias and stereotyping—gender-, race-, and religion-free information
Graphics—current and nonstereotyped
Dating and revisions—frequent revisions required
Credits—who and where

Content Guidelines

Duties and nature of the work—purpose, activities, skills, specializations, and so on
Work settings and conditions—physical activities and work environment
Personal qualifications—specific to a particular occupation
Social and psychological factors—satisfiers and limiters associated with an occupation; lifestyle implications
Preparation required—length and type, cost, difficulty of entry
Special requirements—physical, personal, licensing, and so on
Methods of entering—typical and alternate approaches
Earnings and other benefits—current ranges
Usual advancement possibilities—typical career ladders
Employment outlook—short and long range
Opportunities for experience and exploration—part-time, summer, volunteer, and so on
Related occupations—alternate possibilities
Sources of education and training—schools, agencies, and so on
Sources of additional information—where to go, whom to see

A number of efforts provide a meta-evaluation of various types of informational media. For example, Feller and Wise (1993) present an evaluation of 63 videotapes that address areas of self-knowledge, educational and occupational explanation, and career planning. Sampson and colleagues (1993) offer a periodically updated differential feature—cost effective analysis of over a dozen computer-assisted career guidance systems. Similar guides are available to assist the less sophisticated and/or time-challenged practitioner to utilize the best information possible related to his or her purposes.

There does appear to be considerable agreement among both scholars in the field of occupational information and users of occupational information regarding the criteria of what constitutes "good" information (Bloch & Kinnison, 1989).

Use of Information

How individuals use information in career-related decision making is, in many respects, a highly personalized matter. Usually, information is assimilated, processed, and accepted or rejected in complex, idiosyncratic ways. Just as the intake of information is individualized, so too is the output of information as it affects career-related decision making.

The field of cognitive science is one of today's "hottest" and most exciting occupational areas. How people process information has captured the attention of computer scientists, cognitive and educational psychologists, and others. Much of this interest is spurred by the desire to create artificial intelligence, but some of the interest is also stimulated simply by the desire to know how more effectively to teach people to engage in a variety of information processing tasks, ranging from learning the three Rs to using career information.

It is clear that people have different learning styles—ways in which they prefer to gather, organize, and process information. This fact obviously affects how they handle occupational and educational information and can indicate how best to present such information to them. Styles of occupational information seeking vary from client to client; therefore, it is logical to make individual recommendations for occupational information seeking rather than to suggest uniformity to a group of students or clients.

One principle that seems to have been fairly well established through research is that behavioral reinforcement techniques are highly effective in promoting career information-seeking behaviors. Whether used with individuals or with groups, if motivation is present or lacking, verbal reinforcement of information-seeking statements of counselees apparently produces more information-seeking behaviors than not reinforcing. In a sense, counselors are establishing and stimulating a readiness of the type previously discussed.

As previously noted, the role of information in career decision making has not been clearly established. It seems logical, in a gain-loss sense, that a person will seek information only if the perceived payoff is greater than the cost of the information. We do know that occupational information influences occupational perceptions and that the same information can produce varied perceptions based on the perceiver's age and occupational status. We know also that receiving occupational information tends to increase the simplicity with which one perceives occupations. Learning theorists call this phenomenon *cognitive complexity.*

What is more, the *type* of occupational information also affects cognitive complexity; that is, negative information is likely to produce a less simplified view of an occupation, whereas positive information decreases cognitive complexity. These studies suggest giving career decision makers both the positive and negative information about an occupation. Because most information now is either neutral or positive, these findings would argue for more description of negative features. Neimeyer (1988, 1989a, 1989b); Neimeyer, Brown, Metzler, Hagans, and Tanguy (1989); Neimeyer, Metzler, and Bowman (1988); Neimeyer, Nevill, Probert, and Fukuyama (1985); and Nevill, Neimeyer, Probert, and Fukuyama (1986) draw on personal construct theory to explain how people use occupational information in the process of career decision making. Whether processing information cognitively or intuitively, people, according to this theory, tend to set up bipolar constructs (for instance, high versus low salary). Individuals will have different sets of bipolar constructs that are important to them; therefore, career information needs to be tailored to the individual. Increasing occupational information per se has been found not to lead to an increase in vocational *differentiation* (the number of different judgments and more cognitively complex processes used by the individual). The explanation may lie in the concept of *integration* (how dimensions are organized into an interrelated system of perceptions). In general, the higher the differentiation *and* integration, the more effective the occupational decision making according to a variety of criteria (for instance, self-efficacy, career exploration, recall of information, conflict, and so on). Moore, Neimeyer, and Marmarosh (1992) have determined that new information given to clients that disconfirms their prior career expectations *increases* vocational differentiation, whereas confirming information *decreases* vocational differentiation. Further, men tend to have higher vocational differentiation than do women (Parr & Neimeyer, 1994).

Finally, it would appear that the level of occupational knowledge can affect even our most basic tools of the trade. There are two ways to assess vocational preferences: by expressing preferences for job titles (such as mechanic) or by expressing preferences for behavioral activities (such as fixing a motor). Some research suggests that those with low-level knowledge should be assessed by behavioral activity preferences; those with high-level knowledge should be assessed on the basis of occupational titles.

Individualizing information appears to be a key requirement for its effective use. This means that there are a variety of approaches for gathering information, and the effectiveness of these approaches will vary from individual to individual. As the counselor helps individuals to sort through, comprehend, assimilate, and find meaning in information, the effectiveness or lack of effectiveness of such data becomes apparent.

Personalization of career information should indeed be paramount in the counselor's mind. Discussing client information processing in career interventions, Rounds and Tracey (1990, p. 31) propose that the level of the client's information processing should determine the counselor's type of intervention. In general, the higher the level of processing, the more straightforward the intervention. Table 14.2 presents their paradigm.

Other methods of personalizing career information, may be found in Amundson and Penner (1998), who present a paradigm for utilizing parents in the process of their children's acquisition of career information; Hartung (1999), who suggests the potency of visual images in career information materials; and Rodriquez (1999b), who highlights the importance of specifically targeting ethnic minorities in occupational information.

TABLE 14.2 Types of Treatment and Interventions Recommended as a Function of Level of Information Processing

LEVEL OF INFORMATION PROCESSING	TREATMENT CHARACTERISTICS	SAMPLE INTERVENTION
Very high	*Little needed* Brief, information focused	Assessment (e.g., MIQ, SDS) Occupational information Computer-assisted guidance
High	*Weak supportive* Mentor Short-term information and decision focused	Assessment, brief counseling Occupational information Brief discussion either individual or group based Career workshops
Medium	*Insight* Longer term Broad focus	Analysis of coping/problem-solving skills Individual counseling Career course
Low	*Strong supportive* Active guide Longer term Remedial Narrow focus	Teach, instruct, guide Individual counseling

Source: From J. B. Rounds and T. J. Tracey, "Trait-and-factor to person-environment fit counseling: Theory and process" from *Career counseling: Contemporary topics in vocational psychology* by W. B. Walsh and S. H. Osipow (Eds.). Copyright © 1990 Lawrence Erlbaum Associates. Reprinted by permission.

As we have indicated, career information is not simply career facts or job data. Career information results when a user attaches personal meaning to information. We also want to be sure that information at early developmental levels broadens the client's range of options and stimulates exploration rather than narrows choice and hurries decisions, and that clients receive information about the psychosocial characteristics of work, such as the interpersonal factors and peculiar values identified with various types of work. It is appropriate at this point to survey the types of delivery systems currently available to evaluate their potential effectiveness.

TYPES OF DELIVERY SYSTEMS

Media can be both interactive (e.g., computer-assisted, workbooks) and noninteractive (e.g., print). Until the last quarter-century, virtually all occupational information was printed and was primarily descriptive. Beginning with the *Dictionary of Occupational Titles,* information became more complex and comprehensive, and the possibilities for alternate ways of transmitting it became more numerous. The problem before us is a basic and complicated one—the acquisition, storage, retrieval, and dissemination of information. The information or knowledge explosion is a well-known reality. Knowledge in some fields doubles itself every few years. The generation of new knowledge, in fact, as achieved by various research and development programs, is mainly responsible for the changing occupational structure as described in Chapter 3. New jobs and occupations come about because new products, services, and industries evolve from new knowledge; these new jobs, in turn, generate more new jobs and occupations.

Occupational half-lives are continually constricting. The occupational half-life is the amount of time it takes for one-half of the knowledge, training, and skills for an occupation to become obsolete. On average, it is four or five years and decreasing (for example, for technical occupations it is about 18 months). The assault of information and new knowledge forces us to grope with new methods for storing the information so that it can be retrieved with maximum efficiency and disseminated in the most effective manner. The response has been the development of multimedia, multilocation occupational and educational information systems. The various delivery systems are outlined in the following pages along with representative listings of some of the more common modes.

Printed Matter

The most common and traditional form for career, educational, and personal-social information is published material. These materials range from occupational briefs to the *Dictionary of Occupational Titles* and the *Occupational Outlook Handbook,* from biographies to popular magazines, from booklets, catalogues, and brochures to newspapers. There are diverse prepackaged or home-grown systems available. There are all sorts of ways to file printed information.

Unfortunately, experience with occupational and educational literature indicates that all these systems present dissemination problems. The data are easily stored and readily retrieved, but they appear to be insufficiently used. Perhaps the motivation of the individual is missing. Perhaps the effort of reading is too much. Perhaps the printed material is dry and uninspiring. Whatever the reason, it is clear that although students, for example, are generally aware of the types of printed information the school has stored and know that it can be retrieved, they do not generally make use of the information. Likewise, adults surely know that they can get information at their public library, but they do not frequently exercise that option. It is apparent that methods other than or in addition to traditional printed materials are necessary or that counselors must deal more effectively with motivational concerns if individuals are to use printed data more extensively.

Acquisition of Information

The acquisition of educational and occupational information is a continual and formidable process. It requires a constant monitoring of commercial catalogues, professional publications, and other sources. Counselors must try to keep current with newer materials. The best way to do so is to consult the *Career Development Quarterly,* which offers periodic reviews of current career literature. Media are graded outstanding, good, satisfactory, or unsatisfactory. There are several bibliographic sources that contain much useful information. Some of the more prominent compendia follow:

- *Career Index,* Moravia, New York: Chronicle Guidance Publications. An annual compilation of an annotated list of occupational and educational guidance materials available from about 700 public and private organizations.
- M. H. Saterstrom (Ed.). *Educators Guide to Free Guidance Materials,* Randolph, WI: Educators Progress Service, annual. Listing of almost 2500 free films, filmstrips and slides, tapes, scripts, and printed materials that are yours for the asking.
- *Counselor's Information Service,* Washington, DC: B'nai B'rith Career and Counseling Services. Published four times per year, this newsletter presents an annotated bibliography of current literature on educational and vocational guidance. Special sections on adult education and the aging and on handicapped and rehabilitation counseling.
- *The Instructor's Manual* for this volume contains a section on sources of educational and occupational information.

Table 14.3 lists several references to occupational filing systems and to printed volumes that are useful for various career guidance purposes. This table is preceded by a listing of magazines and journals devoted to career guidance, as well as a sampling of aids of particular interest to college students and adults.

The following magazines and journals are devoted wholly or in part to career guidance:

Career World—Curriculum Innovations, Highwood, IL. Published monthly during the school year.

American Education—U.S. Department of Health, Education, and Welfare/Office of Education. Published ten times per year.

Career Development Quarterly—(formerly *Vocational Guidance Quarterly*). National Career Development Association. Published four times per year.

Term (Technical Education Research Monitor)—Atlanta Information Services. School-to-work news, research, and opinion.

TABLE 14.3 A Sampling of Printed Matter

NAME	PUBLISHER	DESCRIPTION
Occupational Filing Systems		
Careerdex	Career Associates	1000+ card-file guide to sources of career information
Career Information Kit	Science Research Associates	600 pieces of current literature filed alphabetically by job families. Cross-referenced by Dewey Decimal System
Career Kits and Career Opportunity Boxes	Houghton Mifflin	5 boxes of job information (100–125 cards each) relating to English, social studies, math, foreign languages, and science
Mini-Briefs	Occupational Awareness	Data regarding 1800 occupations related to school subject matter areas
COPSystem Career Briefs Kit	EdiTS	Over 400 cards describing occupations and organized by cluster sets; tied to COPSystem interest inventory
Occu-File	Career Aids	346 briefs
Printed Volumes		
Concise Handbook of Occupations	Doubleday & Company	300+ jobs described
Dictionary of Occupational Titles	U.S. Department of Labor	Described in detail elsewhere in this volume; a primary resource
Guide for Occupational Exploration		
Printed Volumes		
Guide to careers through College Majors and Guide to Careers through Vocational Training	Educational and Industrial Testing Service	As the titles suggest
Handbook of Job Facts		300 major occupations
Occupational Outlook Handbook and Occupational Outlook Quarterly	U.S. Department of Labor	Trends and outlook in over 800 occupations and industries with a quarterly supplement; another primary resource
Vocational Biographies	Vocational Biographies	Almost 400 biographies
The College Handbook and the College Handbook Index of Majors	College Entrance Examination Board	Descriptions of over 2000 colleges and universities and indications of what majors are available where
Annual Survey of Colleges and various other publications		Data on higher education and high schools
Various international education publications		Data and suggestions—recruitment of foreign students
Various admission publications		Data for facilitating the high school to college transition
A Student's Guide to Success in the Real World	Technomic Publishing	Textbooks and handbooks for the school-to-work transition
Cooperative Apprenticeship		
Education and Training for Work		

(continued)

TABLE 14.3 Continued

NAME	PUBLISHER	DESCRIPTION
Printed Volumes		
Beginning Career Exploration System	American Guidance Service	Work texts to enhance self and career exploration
Various books and other printed materials related to all types of career-related issues	New Careers Center	A multitude of career-based publications
Occupational briefs and books	Chronicle Guidance Publications	A long-standing source of printed information
Books and other media related to choosing and negotiating a career	VGM Career books	From courses to career behavior
Various books on career choice and behavior	Courage-to-Change	Some common-sense approaches to feeling good about your work
Self-esteem rating posters	Bureau for At-Risk-Youth	Some educational, personal/social, and career eye-catchers
Various workloads and texts	JIST	Job search, employability, welfare-to-work, etc.
Various self-help books	Consulting Psychologists Press	Do-it-yourself career improvement
Profiles of American Colleges, Vols. I and II	Barron's	Over 1400 colleges and universities described
Guide to Two-Year Colleges, Vols. I and II	Barron's	Information on over 1200 community colleges
College Learning Anytime, Anywhere	Harcourt, Brace, Jovanovich	Alternatives to a traditional college education
Comparative Guide to American Colleges and Comparative Guide to Two-Year Colleges and Career Programs	Harper & Row	Descriptions as indicated in titles with special emphasis on admissions criteria
Peterson's Annual Guides to Graduate Study	Peterson's Guides	Graduate and professional programs described in general or by specialty area

Career Opportunities News—Garrett Park Press.

School-to-Work Report. Business Publishers.

Journal of Career Development—(formerly *Journal of Career Education*).

Monthly Labor Review—U.S. Department of Labor.

Work and Occupations (formerly *Sociology of Occupations*)—Sage Publications. Published four times per year.

Journal of Counseling Psychology—American Psychological Association. Published four times per year.

Journal of Vocational Behavior—Academic Press. Published four times per year.

Journal of Counseling and Development—ACA. Published 12 times per year.

American Vocational Journal—American Vocational Association. Published ten times per year.

Journal of Employment Counseling—National Employment Counselors Association. Published four times per year.

Journal of College Placement—College Placement Council. Published four times per year.

Measurement and Evaluation in Counseling and Development—Association for Measurement and Evaluation in Counseling and Development. Published four times per year.

Journal of Career Assessment. Published four times per year.

Occupational Outlook Quarterly—U.S. Department of Labor. Published four times per year.

Washington Counselletter—Chronicle Guidance Publications.

The following is a sampling of printed aids for college students and adults. The list is presented solely as a more or less random sampling of the scores of books in this genre. Inclusion is not necessarily an endorsement of any book.

Bolles, R. N. (2001). *What color is your parachute?* Berkeley, CA: Ten Speed Press.

Carr-Ruffino, N. (1997). *The promotable woman* (3rd ed.). Franklin Lakes, NJ: Career Press.

Fogler, M. (1999). *Jobbing: The adult liberation handbook.* (2nd ed.). Lexington, KY: Free Choice Press.

Edwards, P., & Edwards, S. (2001). *Changing directions without losing your way.* New York: Teacher/Putnam.

Garber, J. (2001). *I need a job: Now what?* New York: Silver Lining Books.

Graber, S. (2000). *The everything in line job search book.* Holbrook, MA: Adams Media Corp.

Hochheiser, R. M. (1998). *It's a job, not a jail.* New York: Fireside.

Krannich, R., & Krannich, C. R. (1998). *The best jobs for the 21st century* (3rd ed.). Manassas Park, VA: Impact Publications.

Love, N. (1998). *The pathfinder.* New York: Simon & Schuster.

Reis, R. A. (2001). *The everything list careers book.* Holbrook, MA: Adams Media Corp.

Tieger, P. D., & Barron-Tieger, B. (1995). *Do what you are.* Boston: Little, Brown.

Unger, H. G. (1998). *But what if I don't want to go to college?* New York: Checkmark Books.

Yate, M. (2001). *Knock dead resumes.* Holbrook, MA: Adams Media Corp.

Weedle, P. D. (2001). *Weedle's guide to employment web sites 2001.* New York: American Management Association.

Media Approaches

In addition to printed matter, various audio and visual means of disseminating information are used: bulletin boards (electronic and static) and exhibits; commercial, educational, and close-circuit television; slides; films; records; cassettes; filmstrips; microfilm; and microfiche. At the elementary school level, activities in this category might even include "show and tell" exercises.

The use of an audio or visual aid often encourages students to seek additional career counseling and is an effective way to disseminate occupational information. A multimedia approach is valuable, especially with low-motivation counselees and with adults.

Colleges and universities now produce their own recruiting videotapes, and students can call 900 numbers to receive, for a fee, a description of many colleges. Many high schools and colleges also tape the visits of campus and corporate recruiters so that students may view the tapes at their convenience.

Audio and visual approaches provide an interesting and sense-appealing method of transmitting information. The career education movement stimulated a remarkable number of multimedia approaches to occupational information. Table 14.4 represents a sampling of that prodigious output.

Interview Approaches

Educational or occupational information can be gathered by a variety of person-to-person and group interactions with individuals who represent various careers, occupations, jobs, and educational institutions or with individuals also learning about the world of work or educational opportunities. The career conference or career day is one such approach. Here adult individuals represent their vocations, and students are free to talk with or listen to as many as possible within a restricted amount of time. The dangers inherent in this procedure are many: superficial or selective coverage of an occupational area, overemphasis on function to the exclusion of self-factors, proselytizing in the most negative sense, circus atmosphere, and such. Students sometimes go to hear people who represent jobs and occupations in which they are already interested and about which they already know something; thus, no new possibilities are explored. An educational analogue of this activity is the college night. In some cases, a professional organization (such as an ACA branch) organizes and conducts a regional job and educational opportunities fair. This trade fair type of approach can be valuable to individuals if it is preceded by adequate preparation and followed by ample opportunity for feedback.

TABLE 14.4 Examples of Career Guidance Media

NAME	PUBLISHER	DESCRIPTION
One Stop Career Center Video Series	New Careers Center	Various videos on such topics as interviewing, career planning, etc.
Multiple Videos	National Center for School to Work Training	Planning for the future, career search, career exploration and discovery, for all developmental levels
Career Counseling Series	Insight Media	Issues varying from career exploration to unemployment to retirement
Job Search Videos	Jist	Ten videos on deciding what job is for you and how to get it
Entry-level Job Opportunities	Sunburst Communications	100 videos; also many other videos on career planning and career management
Disabilities in the Workplace	Films for the Humanities and Sciences	Unique workplace concerns of people with disabilities having careers
Re-inventing Themselves: Adapting to Career Change	Chronicle Guidance	100 videos filmed at work sites
Enter Here		
Careers for the 21st Century Video Library	Delphi Productions	More than 170 career opportunities; interviews with on-the-job models
CDM Career Video Careers on Video	American Guidance Service	Career exploration 100 school-to-career videos

In a similar but more in-depth approach, students interview workers in various jobs or personnel directors who are familiar with the requirements of a relatively wide range of jobs. Students are not limited to those occupations represented at a career conference; they can explore any occupation available in the community. Students may be given an interview guide to ensure that important aspects of the occupation are covered in the conference. Again, however, this approach assumes that the student has some prior interest in an occupation and seeks to broaden his or her knowledge of it.

A still more detailed and thorough approach is the job analysis. In this case, students supplement direct-interview data with information gathered from other sources, such as occupational literature. Although this technique offers a comprehensive and intensive view of a single occupation, it can be a tedious exercise that turns off students if their motivation, either intrinsic or extrinsic, is not relatively strong.

A final interview-type approach to occupational information is the job clinic. Although the career conference has long-range goals, the emphasis in the job clinic is on immediate goals, usually job placement. The job clinic brings together many individuals who have jobs to offer. Other individuals who need jobs come to the clinic and decide whether their attributes and interests match the available jobs. This type of activity is most common in employment agencies and college placement centers.

Simulation Approaches

There are many simulation or gaming techniques by which counselees can vicariously explore careers as well as educational opportunities. Simulation must be used properly—that is, not in isolation as an end itself but along with meaningful discussion, follow-up, and explanatory material. Simulation is valuable in that it brings down to manageable proportions a complicated aspect of life. Although there is some disagreement about the relative merits of simulation, most agree that career exploration through work simulation is effective and that it stimulates students to seek additional information.

The simplest form of simulation is role playing. For example, individuals may role play job interviews to become more relaxed and prepared when an actual employment interview comes. They may also dramatize potential conflicts in work situations (for example, supervisor-worker tensions) on the premise that such an exercise will serve as a preventive function when a similar situation is encountered in a real work situation.

Taking role playing a step further, groups of individuals can be exposed to an occupation by means of a role model. Role models may be present in the form of a person, a film, or literature. Role models tell what they do, but, more important, they relate the personal meaning of their work—satisfactions, frustrations, and so on. In short, they give a picture of the kinds of people they are and help the group try for a short time to be a member of the occupation they represent. For example, a psychologist might present the group with a case study on a client and invite the group to attempt a diagnosis and to prescribe treatment. After the role model has been presented, counselees are asked to engage in reflective thinking, to compare and contrast what they know about themselves with what they know about the role model and the role model's work. Thus, individuals vicariously explore the personal relevance of a particular occupation. This type of activity calls for the individual to use educational, occupational, and personal-social information in an integrated manner.

Another potentially valuable simulation technique is gaming. A number of games exist that attempt, through a form of play, to get individuals to experience vicariously some aspect of career decision making, exploration, on-the-job behavior, and so on. Among these games are:

Workplace Skills (Western Psychological Services). A game for developmentally disabled or socially disadvantaged students and adults who are first-time workforce entrants. Teaches what to expect in a work environment.

The Career Game. (Rick Trow Productions) Grades 9–12. Really a workbook with game features designed to provide students with a better understanding of their interests and so on.

The Real Game (NOICC). Spread over 20 classroom periods. Students adopt an occupation and determine a lifestyle. How to make all this against the reality of a budget and job loss.

Working Together (Jossey-Bass/Pfeiffer). Games to enhance positive work behaviors.

A variety of games for use with younger students may be ordered through Child's Work/Child's Play, P.O. Box 1586, King of Prussia, PA 19406.

Career clubs provide still another type of simulation activity. Future Teachers of America and Distributive Education Clubs are examples of this approach. In the former, youngsters with an interest in teaching as a career can hear speakers, go on field trips, and sometimes actually gain some experience in teaching. Prelaw, premedicine, and other professions-related clubs are also in operation. In Distributive Education Clubs, students gain real experience in setting up and running a business enterprise.

Another type of simulation experience—job sampling—is simultaneously an assessment procedure. For example, the Singer Vocational Evaluation System provides actual work sample tasks for a variety of trade and skilled occupations. While the counselee is heuristically exploring some of the occupational functions, the counselor is able to assess aptitudes, attitudes, and interests. This system is one example of numerous hands-on techniques for exploration. A related technique is that of "shadowing," whereby individuals are permitted to spend time on the job observing a worker who is engaged in an occupation in which they might have an interest. Cairns (1998) offers a number of suggestions for utilizing simulation techniques to enhance career education.

Field Trips

Field trips (to plants, laboratories, offices, educational institutions, and so on) are a common method of gaining occupational and educational information. The opportunity to see work performed in an actual job setting and to interview those who perform the jobs, or the opportunity to get the feel of an educational institution can be a valuable experience. Too often, however, field trips are accomplished only en masse with little or no thought given to the interests of students. It is likely that a field trip program individualized to the extent that arrangements can be made for a single student's visit will be a better program, at least in relation to the exploratory phase of career development. Group trips can be useful, especially for career awareness and for expanding the educational and career worlds of the culturally different, but they must be preceded by careful planning and followed up with feedback.

Follow-up or debriefing activities include discussions individually and in groups, regarding the values gained from the trip. Appropriate questions are: How does the information that I gained relate to me? and How does what I observed affect my decision making?

It is also possible to videotape field trips into local workplaces. Videotaping is a relatively inexpensive technique in institutions that already have the necessary hardware. It may be an acceptable alternative or supplement to actual field trips, which frequently entail insurance, transportation, and supervision problems.

Field trips as exploration can be accomplished on a group or on an individual basis. Given what we have reported earlier in this chapter about the benefits of individualizing exploratory experiences, the individual, tailor-made approach is useful.

By observing a career in situ, the client acquires necessary career information and is an active participant in the process.

Formal Curriculum Approach

Certain aspects of career development are perhaps best affected by means of structured and direct teaching-learning. The question is, which of these experiences can be learned within an existing curriculum structure and which require a career guidance curriculum separate from subject matter classes? The old career education strategy of infusion is consistent with developmental theory, and, as research has demonstrated, it has proved effective when adequately planned and implemented. The great advantage of infusion is that in addition to career learnings, it seems to be a potent force in increasing student achievement. The state of New York, for example, requires specified units of career-related instruction for all middle school students in what used to be required home economics classes. The effectiveness of *acceleration* in career guidance has been repeatedly demonstrated in cited studies. Especially at secondary education, higher education, and adult levels, the use of concentrated intensive workshops, seminars, and courses has been shown to achieve desired goals of career guidance.

We do not want to imply that infusion and separate career guidance courses are an either-or proposition. Both can be useful. Our impressions of the career education infusion methodology is that in the elementary grades through middle school, teachers have generally embraced the concept. At the senior high school and higher educational levels, teacher resistance has appeared to be more marked; consequently, infusion has been less successful. Infusion may well be the primary method in elementary and middle schools, and discrete, structured career guidance group experiences the primary delivery mode beyond the middle school level. In either case, a systematic, planned program is required.

Direct Experience

The axiom that the best way to learn something is to do it probably holds true for the acquisition of information. Direct work experience clearly allows an individual to learn a great deal about a specific job and about the experience of work. Work experience is, therefore, a valuable strategy in career guidance. Many schools offer work experience programs and many job training programs provide on-the-job training. In schools, distributive education students are freed from academic courses for a half-day to work in retail establishments. This cooperation provides on-the-job training and the benefit of experiential learning. Increasing numbers of collegiate institutions are offering work-study programs. Part-time and summer jobs also provide exploratory opportunities that make the individual more occupationally aware. Again, however, these opportunities increase in value as participants have a chance for feedback to reinforce or stimulate career learnings.

Industrial "shadow" experiences are another form of acquiring experience of a sort. These visits to industry to observe and to experience work in situ are valuable for both counselors and students. For several years, the General Electric Company sponsored shadow experiences for counselors to give them a more realistic view of the work world. Counselees can also shadow workers for anywhere from a day to a week. Industry-education councils are also doing a great deal to provide valuable first-hand observations and experience for counselors and for students.

Computers

Throughout this chapter, a recurrent theme has been that "traditional" methods of occupational information acquisition, storage, retrieval, and dissemination have not proved to be as effective as desired. There are many possible reasons for this relative failure. In some cases, programs have been spontaneously mounted with no thought of what came before or of what would come after; they have lacked adequate preparation and feedback opportunities. Whatever the reasons, we are not suggesting that counselors give up traditional approaches. They require little expenditure of money, no fantastic hardware, and no new educational system. It is equally clear, however, that a systematic approach to career guidance can use technology effectively.

Electronic data processing techniques were touted in the late 1960s and early 1970s as a potentially revolutionary mode for career guidance. Only now are they beginning to live up to the great promise. In the last ten years scores of projects have attempted to use computer technology in career guidance and the Internet has exploded. Some are merely information vehicles; others are more ambitious, attempting something closer to an interactive counseling approach. Although the promise has not yet been completely fulfilled, the great potential is still there. So, too, are the potential pitfalls and disadvantages, ranging from the failure to accommodate human factors to the vulnerability of confidentiality. For these reasons and others, counselors must mediate person-machine systems. Counselors can help to assuage problems of user anxiety that might impede effective use of a system: inadequately prepared users who are not at ease with the process of a system, inadequate follow-up after the counselee has accessed and experienced a system, out-of-date or inaccurate information in a system, and malfunctions or improper working of a system.

Unfortunately the use of technology is not accomplished without concomitant problems. The financial outlay necessary for even simple turnkey computer usage can range from minimal to expensive, depending on the extent of hardware, software, and personnel. In fact, Krumboltz (1985) argues that, in many cases, there may well be less expensive ways to accomplish the same purposes. He further suggests additional presuppositions underlying computer use in counseling that are caveats to effective service delivery: programs may violate what we know about career development; computer use may lead to a lack of depth in career exploration; computer interventions may not take a lifelong focus; and certain programs may take decision making out of the hands of the client.

The use of technology opens other concerns. Counseling technology forces individuals to come to grips with their personal values and goals, which might otherwise remain unexamined. The result is frequently conflict. But this is true for much of career guidance. Invasion of privacy, or lack of safeguards for confidentiality, also can be troublesome. Faddism, intemperate usage, and depersonalization are further possible outcomes of the technology. With reference to the Internet, a major problem is that sites can set themselves up as "career counseling" experts and, in fact, have no certification or licensing to perform such functions.

Counselors may be resistant to using computers because of a relatively unsophisticated mathematical orientation that makes counselors feel inadequate in relation to the computer's complexity, the computer's accuracy in contrast to the counselor's fallibility, the fear of a loss of autonomy, and the perceived deterministic character of the computer. Yet with judicious planning and utilization, technology can provide a strong weapon among many in the counselor's arsenal (Hardesty & Utesch, 1996; Imel, 1996).

Counselors can use computers in career guidance in at least four ways. In the first application, computers serve as data processing tools for counselors by storing counselee data and subsequently retrieving them in various ways. Second, computers are used as substitutes for some counselor functions that go beyond simple information processing. Here one may think in terms of reference systems that often permit the user and the computer to engage in a dialogue. Examples are the matching of students and colleges or the matching of workers and jobs (such as Employment Service job data banks). In a third application, the machine is viewed as a substitute counselor, at least for some counseling functions that involve systematic, consistent, and selective use of a limited number of simple skills. A fourth use of computers concerns phone-linked job placement systems in colleges, universities, and other settings, whereby students can electronically transmit résumés, make appointments, locate jobs, and so on. At home, users can plug in, log on, and find a job. A fifth utilization is the internet for all sorts of information and other purposes. Finally, school, college, and agency career counselors can establish and maintain their own web sites.

In general, computer-assisted interventions have proved successful in terms of assessment, diagnostic interviewing and history taking, and career guidance. They are less successful in terms of psychotherapy, with cognitive and behavioral interventions generally showing much more promise than psychodynamic interventions (Bloom, 1992).

By far the best work on computer-assisted career guidance systems has been affected at the Center for the Study of Technology in Counseling and Career Development at the Florida State University. Here Sampson, Reardon, and their colleagues and students have produced a large output of bibliographies, evaluation studies, surveys, and other publications. Sampson (1998), for example, has identified a number of ethical issues arising from career services offered via the Internet. These include the *quality* of resources and services, the availability of needed user support, the credentials of those providing resources and services, the lack of awareness of local conditions and events, confidentiality and user privacy, and equality of access to Internet-based career courses and services (i.e., the more affluent are likely to have more access).

Computer-Assisted Career Counseling. Computerized Systems are typically based on one or another of the occupational classifications as described in Chapter 3 and one or another of the career development theories as described in Chapter 4. The DISCOVER program, for example, incorporates Super's developmental stages and Tiedeman and O'Hara's decision-making model along with the data-people-things orientation of the DOT and the Holland categories and the World-of-Work Map.

Computer-Assisted Career Guidance Systems (CACGS) can be leased or purchased for delivery in agencies, schools, colleges, and so on. Usually, they will provide both information and a career planning system. Some lean more to one or the other of these purposes. All suggest that the most effective program would be a combination of CACG and the intervention of a counselor, although all imply that the exercise can also stand alone.

Studies that report on the effectiveness of the use of computers in career guidance are generally positive (Carson & Cartwright, 1997; Eveland, Conyne, & Blakney, 1998; Fukayama, Probert, Neimeyer, Nevill, & Metzler, 1988; Garis, 1982; Garis & Hess, 1989; Garis & Niles, 1990; Kivilighan, Johnson, Hogan, & Mauer, 1994; Luzzo & Pierce, 1996; Pinder & Fitzgerald, 1984; Roselle & Hummel, 1988; Sampson, 1996; Sampson et al., 1992a). These studies typically review the results of using one system rather than another; involving a counselor rather than no counselor; comparing attitudes of users before and after utilization of a computer intervention; and assessing client-treatment interaction (i.e., given certain client characteristics, what interventions appear to be most effective). Virtually all evaluations indicate the worth of every system by itself with increments of value increasing with the group or individual intervention of counselors.

One reason that so many computer effectiveness studies show positive results is that the validity of user ratings may be influenced by a novelty or halo effect. Another problem with the research thus far accomplished on computer-mediated career guidance effectiveness is that frequently the criterion measures used to indicate success or failure have little relationship to the stated objectives of the system. For example, career maturity is a frequent outcome measure, but the construct is so global that a single computer-mediated intervention could hardly be expected to achieve a significant increase. When and if it does, one is skeptical. Still another area for further research would be the effects of individualized prescriptions versus nondifferentiated group treatments. We also need more detailed descriptions of the individual characteristics of users and the moderating effects these may produce. Finally, we may require development of computer interventions with a guidance rather than a simple information focus to be used with adults in settings other than educational institutions. At the least, studies should be conducted to see if systems designed to be used in educational settings are equally effective in other environments. Nevertheless, these and other studies are instructive in that they point toward the effectiveness of computer-mediated techniques for the dissemination of occupational information. At the same time, they suggest that indiscriminate use of the computer may not be appropriate; some types of students benefit from computer-generated information more than do others. Finally, research into the use of computers in career guidance confirms once again that information acquisition is merely a first, albeit important, step in career planning. Individuals must be assisted through a variety of techniques to use data in a personally meaningful manner.

It would be difficult, indeed, to find a high school (and to a somewhat lesser extent, a middle school), college, or agency that does not have an operational computer-assisted career guidance system of the type listed in Table 14.5. How these systems are utilized and the extent of their use is unclear. One small-sample study (Owen and Weikel, 1999), for example, found that in the state of Kentucky only about 19 percent of counselors who responded to a survey of computer applications in the schools indicated that interactive vocational guidance was being utilized. Most counselors reported using the computer for word processing, grade/record keeping, and class scheduling. After these "big 3" applications, usage dropped off considerably for statistical analysis, educational programs, email, testing, Internet research, teaching, and the aforementioned interactive vocational guidance.

The National Career Development Association produces an evaluative guide. *Career Literature, Software, and Video Review Guidelines.* In addition, the Association of Computer-Based Systems for Career Information has promulgated guidelines for the use of computer-based career information and guidance systems (Caulum & Lambert, 1985). These are reproduced here in abbreviated form. The reader will note

TABLE 14.5 Examples of Computer-Assisted Career Guidance Systems (CACGS) and Software in Career Counseling

SYSTEM	PUBLISHER	DESCRIPTION
DISCOVER	ACT	Middle, high school, and college/adult versions; self and world of work knowledge, financial aid; decision making
System of Interactive Guidance and Information, Plus More (SIGI Plus)	ETS	Similar to DISCOVER but with a focus on values; grade 9 reading level
Guidance Information System (GIS)	Houghton-Mifflin	Skill identification and educational and occupational information
CHOICES	CSG CHOICES	Skills, interests, values, educational, and occupational information
Discovering Careers and Jobs	Gale Research MC	Career search vehicle tied in to DOT and OOH
One-on-One with the SAT	College Entrance Examination Board	Test preparation program
ExPan	College Entrance Examination Board	College, career, and scholarship searching software; connects to college websites; connects to Next Step College
Focus II	Career Dimensions	Students and adults in transition; Career and educational planning (interests abilities, values, etc.); customizing possible
Career Finder	Wintergreen Software	Matching of student traits and occupations
Career Information System	National/Career Information System	Civilian and military occupations; financial aid
Career Point	Conceptual Systems	Primarily for organizational career development
Career Scan/College Scan	Educational Media Corp.	Explores careers and colleges
C-LECT	Chronicle Guidance	Interests, financial aid, educational and occupational information, values
Career Assessment and Planning Program	JIST Works	Career assessment and planning, job search, career exploration

that most of these topics are covered in depth in this book.

Theory and Practice

1.1 Each user site should adopt, adapt, or otherwise define its theory of career development.

1.2 Each user site should define a plan to facilitate the career-development process which will meet the needs of its students or clients.

1.3 The goals of the computer-based system should be compatible with the theory to which the user subscribes.

1.4 The process and content of the computer-based system should fit into the career development plan of the user site.

Process

2.1 Each user site should develop program goals for integrating use of the computer-based system into existing programs to meet student or client needs.

2.1 Each user site should develop objectives to implement each of the goals.

2.3 Each user site should develop a variety of activities to implement each objective.

2.4 The management team should recognize the importance of career planning in the context of the entire program and should monitor and evaluate its program.

2.5 Any student or client should e oriented to the system before usage and should be given follow-up assistance after use.

User Needs

3.1 Agencies should identify client populations.

3.2 The career-planning needs of each client population should be determined.

3.3 The career-planning needs of students or clients should be met by the counseling program by using the computer-based system as an integral tool.

System Site Management

4.1 All students or clients should have an opportunity to use the system.

4.2 The organization should make a long-term commitment to providing the system's service by including in the annual budget adequate funds to handle staff, system fees, hardware, and necessary supplies.

4.3 Site management should be involved in the evaluation of the system.

4.4 Site management should be involved with promotional activities at the site and in the local community.

4.5 The system should be regularly updated, based on releases from the system operator.

4.6 Management should insure that site coordinators receive periodic training from the system operator and that all staff receive "in-house" training in the use of the system each year.

Physical Environment

5.1 The facilities should have ample and accessible space.

5.2 The availability of computer equipment is essential to the use made of computer-based systems.

Personnel

6.1 Staff who are regularly involved with using the system should have thorough knowledge of its operation, theoretical process, and practical interpretation (a "facilitation" level of knowledge).

6.2 Each site should have at least one site coordinator. This person must have a special knowledge of the system through training offered by the system operator and needs to maintain liaison contact with the system operator.

6.3 Staff members should develop a process for identifying (and communicating or interacting with) related activities sponsored by other organizations (Examples: Career Days, College Fairs, College Representative Visitations).

6.4 Staff members should conduct in-house training and educational seminars for people needing "orientation" and "awareness" levels of knowledge, and for the end users of the system.

6.5 Incidental staff users need an orientation" level of knowledge that can be obtained through annual updates.

6.6 Administrators, students, or clients, and others should have an "awareness" level of knowledge about the system that can be obtained through a yearly demonstration.

Evaluation

7.1 Objective measurement techniques should be used to provide quantitative data about use of the system. Such measurements may include number of users of various components of the system, number and types of users, percentage of target population reached, and time-of-day usage patterns.

7.2 Subjective indicators of usage should be obtained at lease every other year by surveys of end users and staff members.

7.3 Evaluation information should be reported to site facilitators, administrators, the system operator, and other interested parties.*

Many of the standard tests, inventories, and decision-making systems traditionally available in paper-and-pencil form are accessible in computerized versions. Hence, a body of literature has evolved that compares older delivery modes with the delivery medium of the computer. Virtually all of these studies conclude that all of these systems have face validity, scoring errors are minimized, and interpretations are enhanced. No potent harm appears to be associated with computer assessments using instruments having recognized validity, reliability, and norms. Costs are generally more than a paper-and-pencil mode of delivery but permit instant results and interpretations.

Counselors are becoming increasingly sophisticated in the use of computers in career interventions, but not all have necessary skills and knowledge in applying this technology. These skills extend to understanding terminology and recognizing what interventions are *not* enhanced by computer technology. They include having a general notion of what CACGS are available and why one or another would be most appropriate for their setting and being cognizant of how the counselor can work in symbiotic relationship to the client's use of the computer to maximize the experience.

The Internet

Shakespeare's Othello said it first: "Tis true; there's magic in the web of it." The growth of the Internet has been no less than phenomenal, and it has profoundly affected the way we search for jobs, acquire educationally and occupationally related information, and plan our careers. Nonexistent about a quarter-century ago and begun as a United States Department of Defense experiment, it now pervades our lives. There are extant (and growing) over one billion Web pages, over 3200 search engines, and over 150 million searches each day (with an average of 124 minutes per person spent at search engine sites each month (*New York Times,* June 29, 2000). The United States alone has approximately 80 million users of the web (with Japan a distant second). This figure translates to about 6 in 10 Americans who now have access to home computers.

At the same time, the Internet is an anarchy. There are few safeguards and regulations; consequently, there is great potential for mischief, and *caveat emptor* is the overriding stance that users should take. Recall that previously in this chapter three bywords for judging information were offered: currency, validity, and applicability. There is no guarantee that Web information is up-to-date, accurate, or appropriate to the developmental level of the user. In fact, since many sites on the Internet require fees, there is a potential for harm in that "scams" and less than good value can occur as charlatans ply their trade. Further, whenever one logs onto a site, the site gathers information about the user, and privacy could be imperiled.

Given some user sophistication, however, the Web excites with its almost limitless possibilities for enhancing people's career development and career-related behaviors. These possibilities presently consist of several computer-driven modes: career counseling via the Web; job search resources; career assessment sites; bulletin boards; and other applications.

Career Counseling via the Web. "Counseling" via the Web is a different type of intervention from the "counseling" taught in graduate schools. "Counseling" can range from someone on the Psychics Network to bona fide, well-trained practitioners. Hohenshil and Delorenzo (1999) and Hohenshil (2000) address many of the issues inherent in providing career counseling services via the Web. For example, the National Board of Certified Counselors has a Code of Ethics for Web Counseling (www.nbcc.org/ethics/wcstandards.htm).

An assessment experience is frequently a part of the electronic counseling process. Sampson (2000)

*Source: From D. Caulum and F. Lambert (Eds.), *Guidelines for the use of computer-based career information and guidance systems.* Eugene, OR: Association of Computer-Based Systems for Career Information Clearinghouse, 1985. Reprinted by permis-

discusses how the Internet can be utilized to enhance testing in counseling. Long-distance delivery of test selection, administration and scoring, and interpretation are now possible, raising all sorts of ethical issues ranging from client confidentiality to invalid information to neglecting follow-up needs of clients. Oliver and Zack (1999), for example, surveyed 24 no-costs career assessments on the Web and found them as a group to be less than satisfactory.

Some online counselors offer testimony regarding the effectiveness of the medium. Sherman (1994), for example, describes his experiences as an early practitioner of Internet counseling. He argues that his online clients have made "substantial progress in a wide variety of career-exploration and job-conflict issues" (p. 31). He maintains that standard counseling responses such as reflection, summarization, probing, and validation are equally as applicable and effective on the Web as they are vis-à-vis traditional counseling. Among the advantages he sees for on-line counseling are increased focus and clarity (the counselor works harder at achieving this aspect to compensate for a lack of time, gestures, humor, and physical signals); elimination of potentially prejudiced reactions (the computer is colorblind, for example); broadening perspectives (clientele is wide-ranging); and integration of online technology (referral links to other Websites and electronic submission of resumes, applications, and so on).

This type of point-and-click career counseling (indeed, some say therapy) is typically conducted via email or by interactive real-time exchanges, often by appointment. When the National Board for Certified Counselors (NBCC) issued its previously cited standards for counseling over the Internet, they were greeted in some quarters with skepticism. How, some asked, can there be ethical standards for an activity that NBCC does not even regard as appropriate? Why should there be ethical guidelines when there is no enforcement mechanism? These and other concerns about the profession's trying to regulate the newly coined description, WebCounseling, are certainly legitimate. It is interesting to note, however, that the ethical standards are essentially no different from those prevailing in the metastructure of the profession. The details may differ, such as the concept of encryption (scrambling information to make it unintelligible), but the paramount concern of confidentiality is still at the forefront, for instance, whether counseling is face to face or over the Web. Among the NBCC standards are the following:

1. Review pertinent legal and ethical codes for possible violations emanating from the practice of WebCounseling and supervision.
2. Inform WebClients of encryption methods being used to help insure the security of client/counselor/supervisor communications.
3. Inform clients if, how, and how long session data are being preserved.
4. In situations where it is difficult to verify the identity of WebCounselor or WebClient, take steps to address imposter concerns, such as by using code words, numbers, or graphics.
5. When parent/guardian consent is required to provide WebCounseling to minors, verify the identity of the consenting person.
6. Follow appropriate procedures regarding the release of information for sharing WebClient information with other electronic sources.
7. Carefully consider the extent of self-disclosure presented to the WebClient and provide rationale for WebCounselor's level of disclosure.
8. Provide links to websites of all appropriate certification bodies and licensure boards to facilitate consumer protection.
9. Contact NBCC/CEE or the WebClient's state or provincial licensing board to obtain the name of at least one Counselor-on-Call within the WebClient's geographical region.
10. Discuss with their WebClients procedures for contacting the WebCounselor when he or she is off-line.
11. Mention at their Website those presenting problems they believe to be inappropriate for WebCounseling.
12. Explain to clients the possibility of technical failure.
13. Explain to clients how to cope with potential misunderstandings arising from the lack of visual cues from WebCounselor or WebClient.*

Another document that provides guidelines is that produced by the National Career Development Association (1997). These guidelines address eight

*Source: From NBCC® Standards. Reprinted with permission of the National Board for Certified Counselors and Affiliates, Inc., 3 Terrace Way, Suite D, Greensboro, NC 27403-3660.

areas of focus: (1) qualifications of the developer or provider; (2) access and understanding of environment; (3) content of career counseling and planning services on the Internet; (4) appropriateness of client for receipt of services via the Internet; (5) appropriate support to the client; (6) clarity of contract with the client; (7) inclusion of linkages to other Websites; and (8) use of assessment.

Bulletin Boards. Electronic bulletin board systems (BBSs) are common and require the use of a telephone or a modem for a PC. A number is dialed and the caller is presented with a listing of job opportunities. Some of these bulletin boards are sponsored by private employers, governments at various levels, personnel organizations, or professional associations. Some have fees; some do not charge. The easiest way to secure a listing of BBSs in any local area is to send an email request to employ@execon.metronet.com. Examples of BBSs include OPM Fed Jobs (215-580-2216) in Philadelphia, PA; Jobs BBS (503-281-6808) in Portland, OR; and CareerLink (602-973-2002) in Phoenix, AZ.

School, College, and Agency Websites. Given the number of homes that are currently capable of accessing the Internet or library access (and with due regard for the "digital divide" that separates the more well-off from the less fortunate), it is astounding that many agencies and schools still do not have Websites. Every school counseling office, for example, should have its own Website to supplement or to take the place of newsletters, to announce daily and weekly activities relevant to career and educational planning, to offer assistance to students and parents in the process of decision-making, and to address a wide variety of other appropriate foci.

It is not difficult to set up a Website. In fact, there are Websites to help you set up a Website. No fantastic cost or extraordinary hardware and software are required. We are amazed at schools where individual teenagers in fairly substantial numbers have their own Websites, but the Guidance Program does not. For assistance in establishing a Website see, for example, www.netstudio.com.

Online Services. Gopher Sites. A gopher is a menu system for organizing Internet information that can be utilized in a person's job search. The largest gopher on the Internet is perhaps the Online Career Center (OCC) (www.occ.com). This site is sponsored by many employers, has thousands of job listings, and permits the user to file a résumé. Other gophers specialize in certain types of occupations, such as jobs in higher education or the health sciences. Most colleges have their own gophers, as do many large agencies. The top Websites for job hunters are:

AOL Workplace Channel
Monster.com
Careermosaic.com
Hotjobs.com
Careerpath.com
Headhunter.net
Careerbuilder.com
Jobs.com
Dice.com
Nationjob.com
Careermag.com
Careercity.com
Espan.com
Career.com

Most of these sites charge a fee to employers, but the cost is considerably less than a newspaper advertisement, for example. Some of these sites claim about four million resumes and about 400,000 listings. Some employers are now even conducting initial interviews via computer.

The United States Department of Labor has created the Occupational Information Network (O*NET) to replace the Dictionary of Occupational Titles. O*NET is a changing database for occupational information that includes information on the knowledge, skills, abilities, interests, preparation, contexts, and tasks involved in 1,122 O*NET occupations, many of which were not in existence when the DOT was last revised. Brief occupational profiles and crosswalks are provided, but users may also customize for their needs with add-on software. Mariani's (1999) comparison of features of the DOT and O*NET makes clear that the newer technology is superior.

Posting a résumé at any Internet site carries with the act some potential downside. For instance, once people post on a Website, they may not necessarily have control over who sees it. While some Websites offer privacy commands, it is possible at other sites that your current boss, for example, could come upon your résumé. Some Websites permit users to effect unlimited changes in their résumés; others charge a fee for every change. Some Websites never delete a résumé, and it is there forever even though obsolescent. Even worse, a rejection may also be viewable. Finally, even if the economy is in a full-employment mode, some people never get a response to their postings. In other words, posting is no guarantee that any employer will respond.

Virtual job fairs are offered online, sponsored by various college consortia or loose conglomerates of employers. For example, www.collegecentral.com/nyjobs and www.sunyjobfairs.org are virtual job fairs for any student enrolled in a State University of New York institution of higher education.

The U.S. government is obviously a major provider. One of the largest of the job-opening databases is America's Job Bank (www.ajb.dni.us). All of the state employment services can be accessed along with O*NET, previously described. Related labor market information is located at www.dbm.com/jobguide/trends.html.gov. *The Occupational Outlook Handbook* is available electronically via http://stats.bls.gov/ocohome.htm. Military and apprenticeship information are accessed at www.militarycareers.com/ and www.doleta.gov/individ/apparent.htm respectively. Other resources for counselors may be found at www.uncg.edu/edu/ericcass/libhome.htm. A good example of a college Internet system is provided by Robinson and collegues (2000).

One of the major applications of the Internet has been in aiding the process of college and financial aid searches and applications. College searching via the Web attracts the great majority of high-ability students who use it to take a virtual tour of an institution of higher education or to experience a virtual open house where a potential applicant can engage faculty, students, or admissions personnel in a live chat. Some college-search sites permit the searcher to enter criteria such as size, cost, sports, major, etc. and receive a list of schools to investigate (e.g., Collegeboard.org, www.campustours.com, CollegeEdge.com, CollegeNet.com, or CollegeView.com).

Interested applicants can, at many schools, schedule a visit or even apply on-line. In fact, some schools now insist on only electronic filing of applications (e.g., West Virginia Wesleyan, MIT). Online application Websites include: APPLY (www.review.com); COLLEGEQUEST (www.collegequest.com); COLLEGENET (www.collegenet.com); EMBARK.COM (www.embark.com); and XAP.COM (www.xap.com). Also www.nces.ed.gov/ipeds/cool and www.collegelink.com. In addition, just about every state and province now has its own system for online applications to state schools.

College exploration is also enhanced by videos, some from the colleges themselves and others from independent companies. Some can be viewed via the Internet. These videos may be regarded as a "first screening" to determine if an in-person visit would be appropriate. Among sites for videos are www.klassport.com and www.searchbyvideo.com. The National Association for College Admissions Counseling holds a virtual college fair on the Internet.

Preparing for college entrance examinations is also enhanced by the Web. Keeping in mind the research on the effects of preparation for SAT, ACT, GRE, and other gatekeeping examinations, the following Websites are useful: www.kaptest.com; www.princetonreview.com; www.achieva.com; and www.turbograd.com.

One downside of all this convenience in college exploration via the Internet is that when potential applicants supply an email address or other identifying data, they are subsequently inundated with SPAM—solicitations for and information about a variety of organizations, good, and services, ranging from the armed services to specific Internet sites. Unless one wants this type of intrusion, he or she ought to be careful about what information is given to whom. Another downside is that bogus degrees are plentiful on the Internet. One policing site of a sort (www.degree.net) includes almost 500 schools that offer nonlegitimate degrees over the Web. Of course, legitimate institutions now offer degrees via the Internet. Two management schools, for example, (Duke and Maryland) are offering Web-based degrees. MIT is in the process of putting on the Internet the syllabus, class notes, and other accoutrements for every course it offers, inviting users of all sorts to audit the courses.

Financial aid planning and searching is also facilitated by the Internet. Here, the admonition *caveat emptor* is especially pertinent, since someone will want to sell information that is wrongly claimed to be available at no other Website. Other underhanded come-ons are also in evidence. The college one attends will typically package almost all of the student aid available. The remaining small percentage (perhaps 5–10 percent) is where the Internet is useful (and potentially full of pitfalls). Legitimate Websites for acquiring financial aid information include: www.fastweb.com; www.scholaraid.com; www.collegeboard.org; www.collegenet.com; www.collegequest.com; www.finaid.org; www.srnexpress.com; www.estudentloan.com; and www.Ed.gov/offices/OSFAP/students/. To fill out an application for aid online, go to www.fafsa.ed.gov/.

LISTSERVs. A form of email. People of similar interests or with a similar focus provide information for other "subscribers" to the LISTSERV. For example, JOBPLACE is a LISTSERV where career counselors can discuss topics of interest. Almost all occupations have a LISTSERV; some are bigger than others. A LISTSERV is a form of networking, and the value of networking for those looking for work has been long established.

USENETs. As previously indicated, BBBs require a telephone. The Internet's bulletin boards are termed USENETs and are online. Listings on a USENET are not restricted (as on a gopher) and anyone can list something. In the career realm, USENETs focus on geographical areas, job categories, and the like. These Websites are typically accessed via one or another of the major search engines, such as Yahoo, Lycos, or AltaVista.

Career Centers

Career centers have become prevalent. The terms *career resource center, educational information center,* or *career information center* are most often used. The idea of a career resource center is to enhance the use of career-related information by gathering together in a single place within an educational institution, an agency, or a workplace all educational, occupational, and financial aid information. The center also provides individuals with professional assistance in using the information and allows a physical space for clients to meet with representatives of educational and training institutions, potential employers, and community resource people. The emphasis is on facilitating easy accessibility for users.

Such a center, devoted to the acquisition, storage, retrieval, and dissemination of career-related information, may be a separate entity within an institution, such as the education information centers (EICs) in higher education, or in the community for adults in such locations as shopping centers, libraries, and other easily accessed public places. They are to be found in residence halls, guidance and placement offices, and so on. Usually, they contain such components as microfilm and microfiche viewers, viewdecks, books, pamphlets, occupational files, reference and resource volumes, catalogues, brochures, computers, videotapes, and audiotapes—virtually every kind of information media discussed in this chapter—and convenient spaces for clients to use the information. If in an educational setting, they may also serve as a dissemination center for other units within the educational enterprise (for example, adult and continuing education). At the elementary school level, it is sometimes called a guidance learning center. Outreach, consultation, and instruction are further activities often associated with centers. What few evaluations exist suggest the popularity and effectiveness of these types of centers. "How to" help with regard to the rudiments of setting up and evaluating a career center is available (S. T. Brown & D. Brown, 1990; Zunker, 1986a).

Career centers require planning and continual effort. They may require hiring a paraprofessional or training student or lay volunteer assistants. In any case, if career centers facilitate the acquisition, storage, retrieval, dissemination, and effective use of educational and occupational information, they are well worth the energy expenditure.

A career resource center requires planning and the whole-hearted support of an institution's "stakeholders." Planning entails determining what physical facilities are necessary and what professional, paraprofessional, or volunteer staff will be required. Planners need to consider what educational, occupational, and relevant personal-social informational materials will be required and how to make them accessible and user-friendly. Public relations and user orientations are mandatory. Behrens and Gordon (1997) have written a helpful article on marketing the career center. Finally, there should be an ongoing evaluation of the use and effectiveness of the center.

At the very least, a career resource center should contain the following:

1. A commercially purchased or locally derived printed information collection and filing system (including military careers)

2. A videocassette recorder and monitor along with a collection of appropriate videotapes (commercial and local)
3. Several computers for using both a comprehensive computer-assisted career guidance system and more specific computer programs and for accessing the Internet (Sampson, 1999; Stevens & Lundberg, 1998; and Smith, 1997, offer many good suggestions for integrating Internet-based distance guidance with services provided in career centers, as do Offer and Watts, 1997, from a European perspective).
4. Meeting spaces and study stations
5. Catalogs and other training and educational resource materials appropriate to the particular educational level
6. An inventory of resources for clients and instructional materials to enhance their use
7. Sufficient staff to ensure effective utilization
8. Gaming and simulation materials
9. Where available, a state occupational information system
10. School-to-work transition materials (e.g., aids for job searches, résumé writing, interviewing)
11. Other multimedia (e.g., filmstrips, microfilms)
12. Part-time employment opportunities

The National Occupational Information Coordinating Committee (NOICC). Previous editions of this volume carried a lengthy description of the major American network (NOICC) to provide counselors and other career development facilitators the most current, valid, localized, integrated, and comprehensive career information available. Congress established NOICC in 1976, and NOICC provided basic grants to State Occupational Information Coordinating Committees (SOICCs) until June of 2000. At that time, NOICC's career guidance functions were transferred to America's Career Resource Network (ACRN), part of the U.S. Department of Education's Office of Vocational and Adult Education. As of this writing, the ACRN website was not operational.

SUMMARY

In this chapter, we have discussed career guidance information in terms of criteria for "good" information and for the effective use of information. Various possibilities for the storage, retrieval, and dissemination of information have been explored. Examples of the types of materials available have been offered, including printed matter, media approaches, interview approaches, simulation, field trips, formal curricula, direct experience, and computers (including CACCSs and the Internet). The underlying view in this chapter has been one of counselors helping individuals to integrate educational, occupational, and personal information in the decision-making process. The fostering of planfulness and career development involves not only helping counselees to acquire information, but also assisting them to apply the knowledge to their personal characteristics.

CHAPTER FIFTEEN

Assessment in Career Guidance and Counseling

KEY CONCEPTS

- Assessment devices in career guidance and counseling provide vehicles to identify talent and to assist persons with self-understanding.
- The use of tests is extensive both for purposes of career development and for employment.
- Four major uses of tests are prediction, discrimination, monitoring, and evaluation.
- Prediction usually involves the use of either clinical or statistical processes.
- Computer-assisted testing is increasing in career guidance and counseling.
- Assessment is concerned with the content of choices to be made as well as with the readiness for choice of individuals doing the choosing.
- No assessment for career guidance and counseling is useful unless it is meaningfully interpreted.

We have been told so often that we are living in an age of extraordinary complexity, specialization, and growth that we frequently fail to realize the implications. We take for granted the vast proliferation of knowledge, the social mobility and flux of social roles, and the substantial changes in occupational structure and opportunity that characterize our time. Yet this "progress" presents us with problems unparalleled in world history.

Two problems directly relevant to career guidance are the training and allocation of personnel to ensure maximum use of this most valuable of all resources. We need talent of diverse specializations; we require a means of identifying that talent. The chief method that has evolved is the standardized test.

In addition, we have come to accept the premise that assessment procedures help individuals to understand themselves not only in terms of their talents, but also in terms of their interests, values, and personality characteristics. The greater the self-understanding an individual has, it is assumed, the more likely that person is to make realistic, satisfying educational and career choices. Although self-understanding does not guarantee good decision making, good decisions probably are facilitated by a realistic picture of one's abilities, interests, and other pertinent characteristics. Again, assessment devices provide a vehicle that contributes to the self-understanding and accurate appraisal of counselees.

Testing by private employers is not typically extensive, although larger companies (more than 25,000 employees) tend to test more than smaller companies. In the public sector, merit systems cover the great majority of employees, and about three-fourths of the systems use tests of some sort. Millions of individuals take machine-scored interest inventories each year. For example, about one million Self-Directed Searches (SDS) are given each year with the Armed Services Vocational Aptitude Battery (ASVAB). Thus, the use of tests is substantial for both career exploration and employment purposes. Alternatives to testing, such as interviews, experience and educational factors, biodata instruments, and simulations, are less widely used. It behooves us to use tests carefully to realize their full potential as an aid in career decision-making, exploration, and employment selection.

In this chapter, we will consider four major uses of tests or assessment procedures. We will deal first with the *predictive* uses of tests, with standardized appraisal data that forecast success in educational and career behaviors. Second, we will discuss the use of tests and inventories for *discrimination,* that is, for permitting individuals to discover what occupational or educational groups they resemble. Together, predictive and discriminative uses of tests deal with information pertinent to the content of choices. Third, the *monitoring* function of assessment will be discussed. In a systematic approach to career guidance, it is important that those responsible for intervention be able to identify the career development stage of any individual or group; monitoring provides this information. In essence, monitoring deals with the process of choice or readiness for choice. Further, monitoring indicates whether career behaviors are serving an adaptive or a maladaptive function, as in the measurement of job satisfaction, for example. Finally, we will summarize the use of assessment in *evaluating* how well goals are being achieved with the interventions provided. Thus, the four purposes of assessment in career guidance are prediction, discrimination, monitoring, and evaluation. A sampling of appropriate instruments for each function will be offered and related issues discussed.

PREDICTION

When the effectiveness of a test is evaluated in personnel selection and career guidance, the concern is how well test performance predicts some future performance (such as success in training, success on the job, and so forth). The test is called a predictor; the variable being predicted, a criterion. The entire procedure is one of establishing the predictive validity of a test. The higher the predictive validity of a test (as summarized in a correlation coefficient), the more adequately we can forecast group achievement and, to a lesser extent, individual achievement.

Clinical versus Statistical Prediction

The actual process of making a prediction based on assessment data can take one of two forms or can combine elements of both. The first is the clinical or case study. Here the counselor operates as a clinician, and based on an individual's test data and other observations, the counselor formulates some hypothesis about the counselee's behavior. This approach is largely intuitive and is probably the prevalent modus operandi for most counselors.

The second form of prediction is actuarial or statistical. Here the counselee's test data are classified into a category representing his or her performance. The counselor then uses an actuarial table that provides statistical frequencies of behavior for other persons classified in the same way. The data are thus mechanically combined (for example, by means of a regression equation or expectancy table), and a probability figure results.

A continuing argument in career guidance focuses on the relative effectiveness of these two methods of making predictions from test data. Meehl's (1954) early work in this regard is instructive. He investigated 19 studies with unambiguous results that predicted success in some kind of training or schooling, recidivism, or recovery from a major psychosis. Ten of these studies failed to find a difference between the two methods; nine found differences in favor of the statistical method of prediction; none produced a difference in favor of the clinical approach. Meehl's pioneering work has been supported by later studies.

The message that emerges from these studies is clear. In career guidance, the making of clinical predictions should be approached with extreme tentativeness. Further, whenever it is possible to collect the necessary data to make statistical predictions, this method is preferred. Therefore, it is mandatory that we know with what our tests correlate and precisely what we are predicting. Both test makers and counselors share responsibility for providing predictive validity data.

Validity of Aptitude Tests for Career Guidance

It is safe to say that aptitude tests predict school performance and success in training better than they do performance in an occupation. This difference in favor of the training criterion is probably due to the narrower band of activity being predicted and to the fact that "success" in an occupation is difficult to assess. The use of typical tests of scholastic aptitude produces correlation coefficients between test performance and grade point average at the graduate school level ranging from 0.20 to 0.60 with a mean of 0.40 and at the baccalaureate level from 0.30 to 0.70 with a mean of 0.50. At the high school level, ability and grades are correlated at about 0.60. Personality factors add little to predictive accuracy when they are combined with intellective factors because they are largely discriminant variables rather than predictive variables.

The prediction of success in an occupation shows more modest results. One of the monumental and highly publicized studies in this regard was carried out by Thorndike and Hagen (1959). Their results represent a devastating condemnation of the validity of tests in predicting job performance. Approximately 10,000 men who had taken a 1½-day battery of tests during World War II as applicants for aircrew training were followed up 12 years later in civilian life. The tests yielded 20 separate scores in the areas of verbal, numerical, spatial, perceptual, and motor abilities. The sample was sorted into 120 occupational groups, with each subject rated in terms of "success in the occupation." Within each occupational grouping, success indicators were correlated with each of the 20 test scores.

There were group differences in mean scores in sensible directions (for example, accountants scored better on numbers tests than on any other tests and also scored better than writers, for instance, on the measure of numerical ability). There was wide variability, however, in the total group of 10,000 (as an example, some accountants had numerical scores as low as the lowest truck driver's score). In general, the 12,000 correlations clustered around zero with as many in the negative direction as in the positive direction. The conclusion reached was that tests given at about age 20 cannot predict occupational success 12 years later.

Thorndike and Hagen offer some possible explanations for their findings. The most valid of these is probably the proposition that beyond survival in an occupation, "success" is a meaningless concept. Because of the institutionalization of rewards in many occupations (civil service, unions, and so on), in which pay scales, hours, and outputs are set by schedules or agreements, it is virtually impossible to secure a differential measure of success in an occupation. Yet, even granting this fact, the results of the research are most discouraging and point, at best, to the need for short-range rather than long-range career counseling.

A brighter picture of the validity of occupational aptitude tests is offered by Ghiselli (1966, 1973). He reviewed all the studies conducted before 1965 on the accuracy of tests in predicting training success and proficiency in occupations. For all occupations, the average of the validity coefficients is 0.30 for training criteria and 0.19 for proficiency criteria. This difference on the order of 0.10 in favor of training criteria holds for just about all occupational groups. Thus, predicting success in training for a job is more accurate than predicting success in the job itself.

Ghiselli's findings are confirmed in a follow-up of subjects in the well-known Project TALENT study. Eleven years after their high school graduation, Project TALENT participants were contacted to determine whether their occupational attainment was related to ability, interest, gender, and family socioeconomic status measures collected when they were in grade 10 (Austin & Hanisch, 1990). The results indicated that these types of data were indeed predictive of occupational categories over a protracted period of time, although the investigators suggest that the use of interest data for prediction purposes should be lessened from its current heavy use. This caveat regarding the predictive uses of interest inventories is echoed by Holland, Gottfredson, and Baker (1990), who determined that an expressed preference or aspiration is even more predictive of occupation choice than is a formal interest inventory.

Savickas (1993) thoughtfully explores the idea of validity criteria for career development measures as opposed to aptitude tests. Within the context of Super's notion of career development tasks, Savickas argues that coping responses enacted to deal with vocational development tasks should be the major criterion. Coping responses include such variables as exploration, decision making, planning, and implementing plans. Further, the focus should be on short-term not long-term criteria (see discussion of *10,000 Careers*). The argument persists regarding whether tests decline in validity over time. Researchers such as Hulin, Henry, and Noon (1990) argue that the greater the time between the administration of the predictor and the criterion data, the lower the correlation coefficient. Other researchers (Barrett, Alexander, & Doverspike, 1992) suggest that the issue of time-lagged validities for personnel selection is not at all clear.

Until relatively recently, it had been thought that although certain types of tests have significantly higher predictive power for training than for proficiency criteria, others do not. It seems that tests of intellectual, spatial, and mechanical abilities are more effective in predicting trainability than in predicting job proficiency. Tests of perceptual accuracy and motor abilities predict trainability and job proficiency equally well.

Thus, the efficiency of aptitude tests in forecasting occupational success and trainability is moderate. For any given job, tests of one kind seem to give better predictions than others. The predictive power of a test must be determined for a specific job. When this is done, the maximal power of tests to predict success in training jumps to 0.47 and success on the job itself to approximately 0.35.

Newer research, however, casts doubt on the situation-specific superiority of tests in prediction (F. L. Schmidt & Hunter, 1981). According to this research, standard aptitude tests (verbal, quantitative, mechanical, spatial, inductive and deductive reasoning, and so on) are valid predictors of performance on the job and in training *for all jobs and in all settings.* It is argued that differences such as those reported by Ghiselli are due to statistical artifacts and, therefore, that validities are generalizable. In other words, it is claimed that all tests are valid at substantial levels for all jobs. Further, it is claimed that, based on large sample research, job performance is about as predictable as training (Pearlman, Schmidt, & Hunter, 1980).

Jensen (1984) agrees that the so-called *g* factor has predictive validity for job performance for practically all jobs but argues that the value of *g* increases with job complexity. He reexamined available General Aptitude Test Battery (GATB) data and found the *g* factor about equally predictable for most jobs. Hence, he supported validity generalization in agreeing that most of the variation in validity coefficients across different studies, different jobs, and different situations is attributable to a number of statistical artifacts. Another voice is thus raised against the situational specificity of employment tests. Like Jensen, Thorndike (1985) reanalyzed extant data for the Differential Aptitude Tests (DATs), Army Classification Battery, and GATB. He concluded that 85 or 90 percent of predictable variance was accounted for by a single cognitive ability factor, *g*. The only exception appeared to be that the psychomotor tests seem to be a nearly independent domain from the cognitive domain.

Given these findings, it is somewhat surprising that *g* does not receive more attention in career development intervention research. Crites and Taber (2002) recommend that when there is sufficient time available, the Wechsler Adult Intelligence Scales III (WAIS III; Wechsler, 1997) yields a good estimate of level of occupational attainment. Crites and Taber also suggest that the Wonderlic Personnel Test (Wonderlic, 1989) serves as a possible test of *g* and is particularly useful in employee selection.

What these personnel selection studies analyses appear to indicate is that validity generalizes across situations within broad occupational clusters and that cognitive ability tests produce as high validity as any specific test. A challenge to these conclusions, however, comes from Schmitt, Gooding, Noe, and Kirsch (1984) who conducted a meta-analysis of published studies from 1964 through 1982 and determined that sample size differences accounted for nowhere near the variance in validities reported by Hunter and Schmidt and that, contrary to the *g* hypothesis, "work samples, assessment centers, and supervisor/peer evaluations yield validities which are superior to those of general mental ability and special aptitude tests which are closest to those labeled ability measures" (p. 420). Some differences in findings may be due to the use of published versus unpublished validity studies by investigators. Furthermore, L. R. James, Demaree, and Mulaik (1986) point out some of the methodological shortcomings in the analyses performed in validity generalization studies that may tend to overestimate the contributions of a *g* factor and minimize the contributions of situational specificity. Prediger (1989) also challenges the superiority of *g* in the prediction of job performance. More recently, Prediger (1994a) noted that "I expect any day now that some test publisher will use *g* (or IQ) to tell counselees whether they will be successful machinists, lawyers, school counselors.... One need not imagine the impact on racial/ethnic minorities" (p. 231).

In terms of the job-specific test versus the commercially available test debate, Hattrup, Schmitt, and Landis (1992) present the results of research that argues for the interchangeability of tests—neither is more valid than the other. The only clear advantage of a job-specific test is that user acceptance may be greater; otherwise, testers do not gain much from developing job-specific assessments.

The validity generalization procedure, in use for some time, may neglect certain crucial information. For instance, one proposal is that situational moderators (e.g., different individuals wanting to work in different types of environments) be factored into determinations (James, Demaree, Mulaik, & Ladd, 1992). Other researchers argue against the use of situationally specific moderators (Schmidt et al., 1993).

It is important to emphasize that in this book we are primarily concerned with the use of tests to help individuals enhance their self-appraisal knowledge and to make decisions based on that information along with a host of other data. We are only peripherally concerned with the use of tests in employment selection. Nevertheless, we have included a brief discussion of aspects of employment testing because the issue of "fairness" in employment testing remains a social concern (see, for example, Gottfredson & Sharf, 1988). Many individuals are convinced that tests have an adverse impact on the employment prospects of racial/ethnic minorities. Some argue that this potential brings about quota systems (L. S. Gottfredson, 1990) and sleight-of-hand, performance-based score adjustments, whereas others maintain that racial differences are real and cannot be addressed simply by using these techniques to bring about equality.

The controversy over race-norming persists. This employment practice adjusts job test scores according to separate racial or ethnic percentiles, and the applicants are then compared only to those of their own race. The Carter administration began to use race-norming with the General Aptitiude Test Battery (GATB). Later, use of the GATB was suspended altogether, on the grounds that using the GATB resulted in *adverse impact,* meaning minorities would not get hired as often based on a cognitive ability test. Quotas and lower cutoff scores are acceptable alternatives consonant with the Civil Rights Act of 1991, but subgroup norming is not. Gottfredson (1994) offers an excellent summary of the contentious nature of the practice.

The pendulum seems to swing historically between validity generalization and situational specificity, and it may be that newer statistical methodologies or better tests and criterion measures will cause additional swings in the future. Further, political considerations and implications are obvious. In any case, using tests for employment selection is quite a different matter from using them to help individuals in vocational self-exploration. Although aptitude tests clearly ought to correlate with criteria of vocational relevance, we can, using existing tests, help individuals to learn more about their possible differential abilities, no matter how much they are influenced by a *g* factor, to encourage differential exploration.

We have been speaking only of the predictive power of single tests. Combinations of tests yield greater validity. The evident conclusion is that tests can hold enough predictive power to be of practical value in the selection of personnel and of some value in counseling, depending on how they are used.

Appraisal and Career Guidance: Disillusionment

Several individuals have made derogatory and skeptical observations about the effectiveness of appraisal in career guidance. Career assessment procedures and their subsequent use have been termed "test 'em and tell 'em" activities and have been referred to as "three sessions and a cloud of dust." These are not the carpings of the ill-informed. In fact, some of the leading scholars in the field have expressed doubt about the usefulness of human assessment in enhancing career development and career choice (Bradley, 1994; Goldman, 1994b). These criticisms basically revolve around the fact that tests are still being used in the "square-peg, square-hole" trait-and-factor tradition and, usually, for purposes of informing immediate career choices rather than of enhancing general career development. Authorities generally agree, however, that if tests are not used in a mechanistic ritual, they can indeed be valuable for individuals (Prediger, 1994b). Zytowski (1994) aptly points out that there appears to have been a significant change (not a divorce) in the relationship between testing and counseling. There is much less emphasis on the older psychometric model of using regression analysis to predict success in different occupations; it has been replaced by the discriminant model previously described.

Healy (1990) has identified four obstacles to the effective use of appraisal data in career counseling: "(1) casting clients as subordinates rather than collaborators; (2) discounting self-assessment by favoring counselor assessments; (3) de-emphasizing the influence of contexts in clients' development; and (4) focusing on a single choice rather than on strengthening client decision making and knowledge for follow-through" (p. 214). Consequently, he urges that clients be encouraged to develop self-assessment skills and to focus more on implementing their choice rather than simply looking for a fitting choice.

So long as appraisal data are used in career interventions in combination with everything else we know about an individual and so long as the client is helped to sort through the personal relevance and meaning of the data, vocational assessment is useful. The data are not useful if used in isolation, if they represent incomplete or partial information, if they are not personalized, or if they have no pertinence to career choice and decision making.

Computer-Assisted Testing

As we observed in Chapter 15, computer applications in testing have become common and extend from administration through scoring to interpretation. Computer-based test administration and interpretation, like every other tool available to a counselor, can be both a boon and a bane. On the positive side, they can be cost-effective and, in the case of microcomputers, provide test information virtually instantaneously. In general, clients seem to enjoy the experience and to achieve as much self-knowledge as when paper-and-pencil tests are used. Further, no violence seems to be visited on the psychometric properties of accepted testing instruments that are computerized (that is, validity, reliability, and so on). The negatives of computer-based testing are more involved with the idiosyncratic aspects of a particular instrument, interpretive program, or hardware configuration than with the idea itself. Group administration is obviously difficult, if not impossible, because of the prohibitive cost of multiple stations; some programs are not user-friendly; some instruments are so new and rushed to market so quickly that they provide inadequate validity and normative data; and erroneous or overly generalized interpretations are possible. Further, there is as yet little research to determine individual differences in person-machine interactions. A final limitation is perhaps the most ominous: counselors may believe that because the machine is producing an impressive-looking report, they need not have an in-depth knowledge of the test, its underlying constructs, its psychometric strengths and weaknesses, appropriate interpretations, and the need to integrate the results with everything else of relevant importance in the career development of the client.

Most studies comparing algorithm-derived computer test interpretations to those of clinicians show little difference in results (see, for example, Gati & Blumberg, 1991). Consequently, they can be relied on for a *primary* interpretation. A skilled counselor can then enhance that interpretation in counseling. Counselors, in fact, exert enormous influence in test interpretation sessions. Because most clients are compliant in session, the counselor's leading of clients through questions and assessments represents a social influence (Reed, Patton, & Gold, 1993). Sampson and colleagues (1992a) provide a listing of the assessment components of various computer-assisted career guidance systems.

As yet, few if any automated testing systems can match the comprehensiveness of the interpretation of a truly skilled clinician who has other data available to him or her. The MMPI is a case in point. In a frequently cited study, Eyde and Kowal (1984) ran the profile of a young man through three computerized interpretation systems and through a blind review by a skilled clinician. In addition, they conducted a clinical interview with the client. Results indicated that although all three computer programs described aspects of the client's difficulties, none identified several other potentially significant problems. Hence, reliance on computer interpretations by counselors who do not possess sophisticated training in assessment can lead to simpleminded and possibly harmful practices. Most computer interpretation programs, however, probably function more efficiently, accurately, and reliably than average and below-average clinicians.

The important precept, again as always, would appear to be not to use computer-based testing in isolation, but to be sure it is integrated with all other aspects of a comprehensive, systematic, articulated counseling program. The prescription approach described in Chapter 15 with regard to the use of computer-based information systems would seem to be equally appropriate with computer-based testing.

Meier and Geiger (1986) point out two other important concerns in the use of computer-assisted testing: counselor preparation and ethical concerns. In terms of preparation, many counselors received their preservice education and training before the computer revolution. Their knowledge of computers has been gained largely through in-service preparation, formal or informal; consequently, it may be less complete than desirable. Newer counselors do not necessarily receive specialized training, although it is certainly becoming more common. In terms of ethics, we have the standard case of our hardware technology moving faster than our social and legislative technologies. Niles and Harris-Bowlsbey (2002) provide a useful comparison of three sets of ethical guidelines for using the Internet in career counseling (pp. 222–

223). This comparison indicates that the major counselor-related organizations are seeking to address the multiple ethical issues arising from the use of computer-based and Internet interventions in general as well as career counseling.

Pyle (2000) has noted that to use computer-assisted testing effectively, career counselors need competencies that include knowledge of computer-assisted software, the ability to diagnose the client's needs, the ability to motivate clients to invest their time in taking computer-based assessments, the ability to help clients make use of the data generated by the assessment, and the ability to help the client translate assessment data into an action plan. Obviously, these competencies apply to the use of any assessment instrument in career counseling. The first competencies, having good content knowledge of valid and reliable computer-assisted assessments, can be challenging. Unfortunately, psychometric data (i.e., reliability and validity evidence, normative data) are not always available for online measures. In some case, this is because no such data are available. In these instances, career counselors must proceed with extreme caution. In almost every situation in which these data are lacking, we recommend that counselors look elsewhere for career measures.

The profession is scampering to catch up to the proliferation of computer-assisted testing issues. For instance, the American Psychological Association (1986) has produced guidelines for computer-based tests and interpretations. This document outlines how computer usage in mental health fits into the general ethical principles provided by American Psychological Association (for example, *general principle*—"Psychologists shall limit their practice to their demonstrated areas of professional competence"; *specific computer application*—"Professionals will limit their use of computerized testing to techniques with which they are familiar and competent to use"). In addition, nine user responsibilities are offered (such as "Test performance should be monitored, and assistance to the test taker should be provided, as is needed and appropriate. If technically feasible, the proctor should be signaled automatically when irregularities occur.") Other sections detail the developers' responsibilities (such as "The validity of the computer version of a test should be established by those developing the test"). In addition to these guidelines, professional journals are increasingly and routinely reviewing software programs.

All in all, the potential advantages of computer-assisted testing seem clearly to outweigh the potential pitfalls. Abuses are certainly possible, however, and counselors should be alert both to their own deficits in knowledge and skill and to those of the providers as they both seek to serve the client's best interests.

Test Interpretation

Hansen, Rossberg, and Cramer (1994) have observed that assessment devices can benefit primarily the counselor or can have major meaning for the client. For example, the counselor's principal reason for administering instruments such as the MMPI, Rorschach, and Thematic Apperception Test is to aid him or her in understanding the internal dynamics of the client so that appropriate treatment interventions can be designed and implemented. Consequently the results are not interpreted to the client. Obversely, there are tests given mainly to enhance the client's knowledge, and these must be interpreted if they are to have any value. Such is the case with instruments designed to augment the client's career exploratory behaviors.

Given that all vocational assessments must be interpreted, what vocationally relevant instruments are most widely used? Surveys conducted over the years generally show a wide variety of assessment devices, but, in fact, the "big 3" lead the way (at least with counseling psychologists). These three most commonly used tests are the Strong Interest Inventory (SII), the Self-Directed Search (SDS), and the Kuder Occupational Interest Survey (KOIS). Counseling psychologists of every theoretical orientation (behavioral, cognitive, psychodynamic, humanistic, existential, and eclectic) employed these tests with equal emphasis (Watkins, Campbell, & Nieberding, 1993). Earlier surveys of a broader representation of counselors, not just counseling psychologists, indicated that over a span of two decades there was little change in the instruments used for vocational assessments. The most common instruments revealed by these surveys are (in addition to the SII, SDS, and KOIS): Career Development Inventory (CDI), Career Maturity Inventory (CMI), Harrington-O'Shea Career Decision Making System, Kuder General Interest Survey, Ohio Vocational Interest Survey, Armed Services Vocational Aptitude Battery (ASVAB), Differential Aptitude Tests (DAT), and Work Values Inventory.

Perhaps no other aspect of counselor functioning has received so little research attention as test interpretation. In fact, it is perhaps the most underresearched area in all of counseling. Although a plethora of articles appears in the professional literature in which scholars and clinicians offer suggestions for the most effective interpretation of test scores and how they might best be integrated with the entire guidance or counseling process (for example, Mehrens & Lehmann, 1985; H. E. A. Tinsley & Bradley, 1986), few articles report the results of empirical research; fewer still are recent; and yet fewer are able to stand up to close scrutiny regarding research design and methodology. It is ironic that one of the most continually debated areas of counselor functioning should be so ill-informed by research. One study in which researchers examined test-interpretation styles of career counselors indicated that clients receiving an "interactive" style of test interpretation considered their sessions to be deeper and their counselors to be more expert, trustworthy, and attractive than did clients who received a "delivered" interpretation (Hanson, Claiborn, & Kerr, 1997). In this study, an interactive interpretation involved clients in the test interpretation process by inviting them to note high or low scores, asking clients to provide behavioral descriptions of the constructs being discussed in the sessions, and inviting the client to summarize his or her own interpretation of the test results. In the delivered interpretation style the counselor was more in control of the test interpretation process and provided the client with the information that in the interactive style the client was asked to provide. Obviously, involving clients in the interpretation process provides a more meaningful career counseling experience for the client.

The effective use of tests in career guidance also depends on the extent to which counselees understand and accept the results of test performance. Because we are considering the use of test results in a programmatic, systematic approach to career guidance, in which everyone takes the same tests, our major concern is with group interpretation. Some research findings comparing various methods of group or individual interpretation are summarized as follows:

1. Whatever the method used, counselee attitudes toward the counselor or toward the value of the tests are much the same. Recall of test results, however, appears to be highest when the counselee has been dominant in an interpretation interview after a learning set for test interpretation has been established (J. Holmes, 1964).

2. Scholastic aptitude may be a significant variable in interpretation. Counselees with lower scholastic aptitude seem to recall scores more accurately with the use of audiovisual aids. In fact, graphic presentations may assist all clients (Strahan & Kelly, 1994). There is also some evidence to suggest that acceptance of test results is facilitated in individual sessions more than in group sessions (J. L. Walker, 1965).

3. Those who have the most accurate pictures of themselves before testing tend to learn most about themselves as a result of test interpretation, regardless of the interpretive technique used (Gustad & Tuma, 1957).

4. There is a good deal of evidence that counselors should be extremely careful about the manner in which they interpret test results for women (Tittle, 1973), visible minorities (Prediger, 1994a; Haverkamp, Collins, & Hansen, 1994), the disabled worker (Nester, 1993), and the older worker (Rimmer & Myers, 1982).

5. Mode of interpretation effectiveness studies are conflicting. Oliver (1977), for example, found individual interpretation superior to multiple interpretation or programmed interpretation. Sharf (1978) found no differences in effectiveness of interpretation when comparing a computer-based narrative report with standard profiles.

6. The client's previous vocationally related experience seems to have an effect on the interpretation of interest scores (Prediger & Swaney, 1986). People are more likely to have interest scores that correspond to their subsequent occupation when they have had experiences consonant with their predominant interests. Thus, when a client's major interests are without accompanying relevant experiences, test interpretation should be more cautious.

7. The type of language required in test interpretation should be related to the sophistication of the client. In the public eye, especially among younger individuals, concepts of intelligence and ability are distinguished from one another and mean different things (Nicholls, Patashnick, & Mettetal, 1986). In general, ability is thought of as more general than intelligence, thus having implications for the type of language required in test interpretation.

8. The test-taking disposition of the client is of considerable importance. Individuals' motivations can affect the validity of the test results in different ways, whether ability or personality measures are considered (Schmit & Ryan, 1992). Once again, these findings underscore the crucial variable of establishing client readiness for assessments.

9. Counselors should check to see if the group on which an instrument was normed is similar to the group being assessed, should modify administration procedures when testing individuals with disabilities, and should seek additional supporting information (Elmore, Ekstrom, & Diamond, 1993).

What these and other illustrative studies suggest is that no one method of test interpretation can be considered superior for all counselees. Given this finding, the following recommendations for test interpretation offered by Lister and McKenzie (1966) are still extremely helpful:

1. The counselee must experience a need for the test information. Therefore, the counselor's role in motivation is most important. Counselees must be assisted to see that a knowledge of test performance will be beneficial to them.

2. Counselees' questions must be translated into operational terms that are acceptable to them. This means that the interpretation must be made in terms of some criterion of importance to the counselee.

3. The information must be clearly communicated to the counselee. Lister and McKenzie argue that the evaluation of the effectiveness of test interpretation must be based on more than simple accurate recall of test information, that recall must be accompanied by significant behavior change. Some type of action must be taken. A counselee who understands and accepts test results given in the form of a probability statement would play the odds. The counselee's behavior would be consistent with the test results and with other data; that is, he or she would pursue alternatives with a reasonable prognosis of success and would avoid alternatives for which chances of success are minimal (pp. 62–63).

Goodyear (1990), based on his review of the literature in the area of test interpretation, suggests that the so-called "Barnum Effect" may be operative. The premise of this phenomenon is that test results do not have to be communicated accurately if they are communicated convincingly (for instance, subjects provided with fake interpretations accept them if they contain universal truths in the manner of psychics, graphology, astrology, and so on). Translated to the use of tests in counseling, the Barnum Effect would instruct counselors to provide interpretations that are positively rather than negatively worded. A related phenomenon has been labeled *confirmatory bias* (White, Brockett, & Overstreet, 1993). Individuals apparently indicate, more often than not, that they are being accurately described by a personality trait, for example, if what emerges is consistent with their self-perception—whether the trait is expressed in positive or negative terms.

Additional guidelines for interpretation are provided by Prediger (1994b) and N. J. Garfield and Prediger (1982), who discuss the testing competencies and responsibilities of vocational counselors. They suggest that counselors rate their own interpretation skills by using the following key:

1 = I do this routinely—as a regular practice.
2 = I have done this on occasion.
3 = I do not do this—but ought to consider doing this.
4 = Not applicable to the instrument(s) I am using.

Their list of interpretation responsibilities and competencies is as follows:

1. Study suggestions for interpretation provided by the test manual (or score report form) and determine which of them are supported by the psychometric data provided for the test.

2. Review, with the counselee, the purpose and nature of the test. Topics include the following:
- **a.** Why the test was given; what the test can and *cannot* do
- **b.** Who will receive the test results
- **c.** What the test results cover and how they will be used

3. Interpret test results in the context of the testing experience, the counselee's background, and other assessments (if any) of the same characteristics by doing the following:
- **a.** Encouraging a discussion of how the counselee felt about the testing experience, in general; his or her performance, in particular; and any difficulties or problems (such as nervousness, fatigue, or distractions) encountered

   b. Examining the possibility that the counselee's background (race, sex, handicap, age, and so on) may have influenced the test results
   c. Seeking additional information to explain any inconsistencies that become evident

4. Apply good counseling techniques to test interpretation by doing the following:
   a. Emphasizing "strengths" while objectively discussing "weaknesses"
   b. Allowing sufficient time for the counselee to assimilate information and respond
   c. Listening attentively to the counselee's responses (that is, attending to the counselee first and test results second)
   d. Checking the counselee's understanding of the test results from time to time; correcting misconceptions

5. Help the counselee begin (or continue) the career (educational and vocational) planning process by doing the following:
   a. Identifying, with the counselee, career options and steps for exploring each
   b. Providing assistance to the counselee through ongoing career guidance activities such as field trips, career conferences, filmstrips, library resources, and so on
   c. Monitoring and encouraging career planning efforts through progress reports, follow-through counseling sessions, and so forth.

There are all sorts of test interpretation suggestions that are based on one or another theoretical orientation or based on nontraditional types of assessments.

An alternative, among many, to paper-and-pencil evaluations is the use of behavioral assessment (Galassi & Perot, 1992). This technique utilizes observational methodologies to assess behaviors *in situ* (classrooms, hospitals, etc.). For certain types of vocational clients, in some situations, behavioral assessment is appropriate. Another alternative to traditional assessment is so-called person-centered assessment (Bozarth, 1991). Based on Rogerian principles, this approach advocates that since the client is a "self-authority," tests should be used sparingly, usually directed toward work-related concerns, and test interpretations would be such as to encourage integration into the client's frame of reference. Thus, the client must express a need for a test, and the test interpretation should be done to provide the client with an external referent in decision making.

Types of Aptitude Tests

Assessment in the cognitive domain is usually achieved by administering a standardized battery of tests or individual tests measuring common aptitudes for which adequate criterion data are available. An aptitude may be defined as readiness for learning. An aptitude test is therefore one that predicts success in some occupation or training course. At present, the number of aptitudes for which counselors and psychologists have determined even minimally adequate validity data is limited. At best, it includes scholastic aptitude (verbal, numerical, and performance), perceptual speed and accuracy (clerical), manual dexterities, mechanical reasoning, spatial visualization, aesthetic judgment, artistic ability, and musical talent. Of these, the last three are highly specialized and have limited application. Thus, we are left with five basic aptitudes.

Various individual tests are capable of assessing aptitudes in each of these areas. For purposes of career guidance testing, however, the selection of individual tests poses problems. The main obstacle is that they have been standardized on different populations, and therefore norms are not consistent from test to test. Also, some individual tests fail to provide specific educational or occupational norms that would be useful in career guidance. Finally, choosing individual tests to assess multiple potentialities can typically run into large costs and present clerical problems in scoring.

Because of these deficiencies, psychologists have developed the test battery. Here a number of tests are employed together to predict various criteria. Individuals have several aptitudes, or patterns of strengths and weaknesses, that contribute to their total potential. The battery yields a multiscore summary of these differential patterns. Because all the tests in a battery are standardized on the same group, norms take on added meaning. It is becoming increasingly difficult to find an aptitude measure that does not have an accompanying interest inventory and, frequently, other career planning materials. Several of the most widely used instruments of this sort are briefly described here.

Ability Explorer. Thomas F. Harrington and Joan C. Harrington. Level 1 is for students in grades six to eight and Level 2 is for students in grades nine to twelve and adults (1996).

Shows ability self-ratings and past activity and course performance for 14 life and workplace abilities:

Artistic
Clerical
Interpersonal
Language
Leadership
Manual
Musical/Dramatic
Numerical
Mathematical
Organization
Persuasive
Scientific
Social Spatial
Technical/Mechanical

Total test administration time is 50–55 minutes. Ability self-ratings are represented in graphical format from highest to lowest according to percentile rank for the norm group. Can be machine or hand scored. An Internet version is also available (http://www.abilityexplorer.com/demo/). For review see Borman (2002).

Ball Aptitude Battery (BAB). The Ball Foundation. Level 1A (ninth- and tenth-grade high school students) and Level 2 (eleventh- and twelfth-grade high school students) (1998).

Twelve tests:

Analytical Reasoning
Associative Memory
Auditory Memory Span
Clerical
Idea Generation
Inductive Reasoning
Numerical Computation
Numerical Reasoning
Paper Folding
Vocabulary
Word Association
Writing Speed

Total administration time is 2 hours and 10 minutes. Machine scoring only. Group summaries are available. Scores are expressed in percentile ranks, raw scores, and verbal labels (high, moderate, low). For review, see Thompson and Patrick (2002).

The Differential Aptitude Tests (DAT). Fifth Edition, Form C (1991). G. K. Bennett, H. G. Seashore, & A. G. Wesman. Grades seven to twelve (one level for seven to nine; another for ten to twelve; either level may be used with adults). Psychological Corporation. Requires approximately 2½ hours working time.

Eight tests yielding nine scores:

Verbal reasoning
Numerical reasoning
Abstract reasoning
Perceptual speed and accuracy
Mechanical reasoning
Space relations
Spelling
Language usage
Scholastic ability (verbal plus numerical)

Either hand or machine scored. Percentiles, stanines, and scaled scores separate for males and females (new norms). Career Interest Inventory also available. Both aptitude and interest data related to educational and occupational plans. Computerized Adaptive Edition available.

For personnel selection and classification in business, industry, government, and vocational education, the Differential Aptitude Tests for Personnel and Career Assessment are available.

For a review, see Willson and Stone (1994).

The General Aptitude Test Battery (GATB). Forms A and B (1982); Forms C and D (1983). United States Employment Service. Requires 2½ hours for administration.

Twelve tests measuring nine factors:

Intelligence (G)
Verbal aptitude (V)
Numerical aptitude (N)
Spatial aptitude (S)
Form perception (P)
Clerical perception (Q)
Motor coordination (K)
Finger dexterity(F)
Manual dexterity(M)

Standard scores (Mean 100; standard deviation 20).

Cut-off scores for various occupational groups and job families according to DOT within group scoring. Can be administered by those in non-USOE agencies if counselors take a short training course. Now related to USES interest inventory. Currently "on-hold" for use in personnel selection. For review, see Bolton (1994).

Armed Services Vocational Aptitude Battery (ASVAB). U.S. Department of Defense. High school level (juniors and seniors preferred). ASVAB 19 (1992).

Nine tests:

Coding speed
Word knowledge
Arithmetic reasoning
Tool knowledge
Space perception
Mechanical comprehension
Shop information
Automotive information
Electronics information

Yields three Academic Scales:

Academic ability
Verbal
Mathematics

And four occupational scales:

Mechanical and crafts
Business and clerical
Electronics and electrical
Health, social, and technological

Scores expressed in percentiles based on national norms. Basically a recruitment device, but can yield valuable information at no cost. Scores related to military and civilian occupations via the *U.S. Army Career and Education Guide.* Student interactive workbook at no cost and SDS at no cost. For review, see Jensen (1988). Excellent interpretive materials. Not just for students contemplating military careers.

ACT Career Planning Program (CPP). Grades eight–adult. (ACT) Manual 1994.

Components of CPP:

1. Interest scales (UNIACT)
   Social service
   Business contact
   Business detail
   Technical
   Science
   Creative arts
2. Experience scales
   Career-related activities and experiences
3. Ability scales
   Mechanical reasoning
   Space relations
   Clerical skills
   Numerical skills
   Reading skills
   Language usage

Various other informal assessment components. About 2½ hours required for total program administration. Short form, VIESA, substitutes self-ratings for aptitude measures. Abilities and interests reported in stanines and percentiles.

Components of CPP 12–13:

1. Interest scales
   Social service
   Business contact
   Business detail
   Trades, technical
   Science
   Arts
   Health
2. Ability scales
   Space relations
   Reading skills
   Clerical skills
   Numerical computation, math usage
   Language usage
   Mechanical reasoning
   Nonverbal reasoning

Related to ACT Occupational Classification System and World-of-Work map for Job Families. Student decision-making aids. For a review, see Anderson (1994).

Occupational Aptitude Survey and Interest Schedule—2 (OASIS—2) (1991). PRO:ED. R. M. Parker. High school students. An aptitude survey based on the GATB consisting of six measures and requiring about 35 minutes. Aptitudes measured are general ability, verbal aptitude, numerical aptitude, spatial aptitude, perceptual aptitude, and manual dexterity. Machine-scored or hand-scored. Results keyed to the DOT. Interest schedule measures USES 13 categories. For a review, see Borman (1994).

Career Survey. (1988; Manual 1992). J. W. Wick, J. K. Smith, D. L. Beggs, & J. T. Mouw. American. Grades seven to twelve and adult. Approximately 1¼ hours.

Yields two ability scores: verbal and nonverbal, accompanied by 12 interest scales. Grade-level percentile scores (also estimated ACT composite, SAT composite, and GATB-G score). Both same sex and combined sex norms. Machine-scored or hand-scored. Computer option available. For a review, see Domino (1994).

Other Aptitude Measures

- Adult Basic Learning Examination—2nd ed. (ABLE)
  Psychological Corporation
  For adult populations
- APTICOM
  Vocational Research Institute
  For disadvantaged and special needs students and adults
- Career Assessment Program (ABCD/IBCD)
  Educational Technologies
  Aptitudes related to 66 occupational families, grade eight–adult
- Employee Aptitude Survey (EAS)
  Psychological Services
  For adults in organizations (personnel selection and career guidance)
- Graflex Vocational Evaluation System
  Singer Education and Training Products
  Work sample tests used in work evaluation centers
- Tests of Adult Basic Education (TABE)
  CTB McGraw-Hill
  For age 16+; achievement in math, reading, and language
- TOWER (Testing, Orientation, and Work Evaluation in Rehabilitation)
  Institute for the Crippled and Disabled
  Work sample tests for rehabilitation purposes
- Work Keys Assessments
  ACT
  Seven assessments (more being developed for school-to-work transition or reentry)
- World of Work Inventory (WOWI)
  World of Work
  For high school to adult; concentration on person-job fit

DISCRIMINANT ANALYSIS

It is generally conceded that at least two types of measurement are required for career guidance, where choice is the purpose: assessment of various capacities or aptitudes and assessment of interests. Each of these should be surveyed at various stages of an individual's development. The results should be communicated to the counselee in two ways: first, in terms of the groups in which the counselee may succeed, and second, in terms of the groups that the counselee most resembles with regard to interests, values, personality, and such. The "most like" description is achieved by means of a statistical technique called discriminant analysis. The former "goodness" probability statement emerges as a result of the regression analysis procedure discussed earlier. Hence, it is desirable to assess personal traits from both the cognitive (aptitudes) and the noncognitive domains (interests) and to report results both in terms of the groups an individual is most like (discriminant analysis) and in terms of that individual's probability of success in given groups (regression analysis).

Interests and abilities are obviously not the same. Although there is some association, research suggests that they are sufficiently different constructs and, therefore, that they should be separately measured (Betsworth & Fouad, 1997; Swanson, 1993). Consequently an integrated assessment usually entails the regression analysis of abilities and the discriminant analysis of interests. To these two domains, Lowman (1993) would add assessment of personality characteristics. In terms of the group an individual most resembles, for example, Laing, Lamb, and Prediger (1982) in a large-scale study have affirmed the use of basic interest scales in suggesting college majors to explore. Interest measurement is the most common application of discriminant analysis in career guidance. Although it is possible to use interest inventories for prediction, we do not view prediction as their primary value.

Interests

We may assess an individual's interest in three ways. We may look to *expressed* interests—what an individual expresses an interest in. Second, we may observe *manifest* interests—what an individual actually does as an indication of what one's interests are. Third, we may examine *inventoried* interests—determining the pattern of an individual's interests from his or her responses to lists of occupations or activities.

This last technique is by far the most common means of assessing interests. Basically, two types of inventories have emerged. One is the so-called empirically keyed or criterion-keyed inventory, which results in interest scores related to specific occupations. The other is the ipsatively determined, or nonempirically keyed inventory, which yields score profiles in areas rather than in specific occupations and in relation to each other area rather than absolutely.

The interpretation of interest inventories is no more informed by definitive research than is the interpretation of other tests as discussed earlier in this chapter.

In a survey of 637 counseling psychologists, Watkins, Campbell, and Nieberding (1994) reported that the most frequently used measures used in vocational assessment by their study participants were the Strong Interest Inventory, the Self-Directed Search, and the Kuder Occupational Interest Survey, respectively. Clearly, counseling psychologists engaging in career counseling rely heavily on interest measures to conduct their work. The major use of interest inventories is the stimulus they provide individuals to explore careers. Much of the legitimacy of this usage is taken "on faith." A study by Randahl, Hansen, and Haverkamp (1993), however, provides documentation that the use of the Strong Interest Inventory (SII) with college students resulted in significantly more instrumental career exploration behaviors at a one-year follow-up than were evident in a contrast group. Day and Rounds (1997) investigated the structure of the SII scales and recommended that career counselors focus on the basic interest scales in interpreting inventory results to clients. They contend that the basic interest scales of the SII provide a better representation of the model of general occupations types articulated by Holland than do the other SII scales (e.g., the occupational scales). Studies such as the Day and Rounds study provide useful information to career counselors using interest inventories with their clients. When interest inventories such as the SII are adequately interpreted they provide useful catalysts to career exploration.

At the same time, however, college students who take the Strong Interest Inventory do *not* typically recall their scores a year after administration and interpretation (Hansen, Kozberg, & Goranson, 1994). Although there is some selective memory of results on certain scales, the overall rate of recollection is small. Something more than a brief interpretation may be required. For example, multiple interpretation sessions might enhance understanding and recall, as would placing the results within a context of what the clients already know about themselves.

That interests begin to be formed early in life is an indisputable given. What is fascinating, however, is the relative ease with which the development of these interests can be manipulated. In Israel, preschool children's preferences for game activities were altered simply by modifying their thinking about their ability to perform the activity, their expected success in the activity, and their likely satisfaction after doing the activity. These modified cognitions, in line with self-efficacy theory, provided support for the hypothesis that interests can be modified by a cognitive intervention at an early age. The implications are clear in terms of early-on enhancement of a youngster's perceptions of his or her ability, expected success, and anticipated satisfaction. Further confirmatory evidence of the relationship between self-efficacy and interests may be found in Lenox and Subich (1994), Tracey (1997), and Donnay and Borgen (1999).

Some researchers advocate a so-called integrative approach to test interpretation (Lange & Coffman, 1981). In this method, the counselor begins with the unique needs of the individual, compares these needs to those expressed by people in various occupations, and helps the individual to integrate this knowledge with an overview of the world of work. Several researchers urge the adoption of a systematic approach to the use and interpretation of tests—that is, specification of objectives, activities to achieve them, and careful evaluation of results. Obviously, we are in favor of such an approach.

Occasionally, studies have been carried out to try to determine if vocational preferences (as measured by interest inventories) are related to personality characteristics (as measured by personality inventories). The results have been inconsistent through the years. One study (Costa, McCrae, & Holland, 1984) compared scores on the Self-Directed Search (SDS) with scores on the NEO (Neuroticism-Extraversion-Openness) Inventory for 361 men and women aged 21 through 89. This study did, in fact, find strong relationships between personality dispositions and vocational interests, but the relationship may be simply a function of the two instruments used. Some relationships were in expected directions (such as extroversion with enterprising occupations). Others were intriguing (such as openness to new experience with investigative, artistic, and social occupations).

Gottfredson, Jones, and Holland (1993) investigated the relationship between Holland's six modal personality types (VPI) and five robust factors of personality (NEO Personality Inventory). They concluded that social and enterprising personality types were positively correlated with extraversion; investigative and artistic types were related to openness; and conventional types were correlated with conscientiousness. Nevertheless, the personality factor—personality type correlations were judged to be too low to suggest that one form of assessment could be substituted for the other.

Card sorts are another assessment device sometimes used in career counseling. More recent emphases on post-modern approaches to career counseling (e.g., Cochran, 1997) encourage the use of card sorts in career assessment. Card sorts are basically interest measurements or forced-choice devices that require the client to place cards, each, for example, containing an occupation or an activity, into a number of piles (the number varying with the particular card sort). These piles or categories might include such stimuli as: would not choose (or do), might choose (or do), and uncertain. The usual procedure is to take one pile and further refine it by forcing choice, until a rank-ordered, smaller number of options remain. Hartung (1999a) advocates for greater use of card sorts because they can be useful in avoiding certain pitfalls such as inattention to cultural identity issues and the potential for sex bias.

The most well-known of these systems are the Occu-Sort (L. K. Jones, 1980a, 1980b) and Holland's Vocational Card Sort (VCS). This type of self-report mode is perhaps good for clients who are tactilely oriented and who might have difficulty with a more conventional instrument. In another example, Wellington (1986) reports on a card sort system for therapists of working women. This sort presents working women with 24 cards, each of which describes an issue, usually one related to interrole conflict. Clients sort them into one of three piles: apply to you directly, does not apply, doubtful. The chosen cards then serve as a basis for discussion. Comparing a card sort (VCS) with the Strong-Campbell version of the Strong (SCII), Croteau and Slaney (1994) determined that career decision-making self-efficacy was not affected differentially by the two interventions—both were equally effective and evoked positive reactions, although in different ways.

One of the more interesting brouhahas in the use of appraisal data in career counseling (and counseling in general) concerns the Myers-Briggs Type Indicator (MBTI) (Myers & McCaulley, 1985). The MBTI was developed by a mother-daughter team who had no training in psychology but who were intrigued with Jung and his theory of psychological types. The instrument has been refined over half a century, and it elicits four preferences: (1) interests that represent *extraversion* (the world of actions, objects, and persons) or *Introversion* (the inner world of concepts and ideas); (2) perception on the basis of *sensing* (the immediate, real, practical facts of experience and life) or *intuition* (the possibilities, relationships, and meanings of experiences); (3) judgment or decision making on the basis of *thinking* (objectively, impersonally considering causes of events and where decision making may lead) or *feeling* (subjectively and personally weighing values of choices and how they matter to others); and (4) preferences for living based on *judgment* (in a planned, decisive, and orderly way aiming to regulate and control events) or *perception* (in a spontaneous, flexible way, aiming to understand life and adapt to it). These four preferences may be combined into 16 types and described based on the first letter of the descriptor (for instance, ISTJ means introversion, sensing, thinking, and judgment as the preferred interests, perceptions, decision making, and living modes of the individual). These four-letter code types are then all described in basically positive terms, leading some to maintain that the MBTI represents an example of the Barnum Effect previously discussed.

Advocates of the MBTI are a zealous group who have been known to put their four-letter code on personalized license plates. There is a journal devoted solely to the MBTI and Jungian types. Those who believed in the MBTI are almost religious in their fervor and are convinced of its usefulness and accuracy. Because presumably compatible occupations are suggested for each of the types, some practitioners use the MBTI in career counseling. One can find debates in the professional literature arguing the use of the MBTI (Carlson, 1989; Healy, 1989). For reviews, see Willis & Ham, (1988), DeVito (1985), and Thompson and Ackerman (1994). There is a huge literature regarding the MBTI (almost 200 articles from 1991 to 1994). A comprehensive analysis of *many* studies using the MBTI (Pittenger, 1993) concluded the instrument contained dubious validity.

Dillon and Weissman (1987) found many relationships between Holland and Jungian personality typologies when they administered both the MBTI and SCII to a group of college students. The best we can say at the present time is that there are extant instruments (described in this chapter) that offer measures of preferences, learning styles, and ways of viewing the world that have accumulated a great deal more validity data than has the MBTI. We would suggest that until further convincing data are available, counselors use the MBTI *only* in conjunction with other appraisal data and never as the sole self-information source.

The MBTI is one of a number of instruments designed to measure what might be termed a *response style* or a *learning style.* How crucial the measurement of such constructs is to career exploration and decision making is moot at this point in time. For example, would a measurement of interpersonal style or functioning be useful? Van Denburg, Schmidt, and Kiesler (1992) argue that interpersonal assessment is helpful because the client's pattern of transactions with others (adaptive and maladaptive) has a bearing on career. Measuring constructs such as control (dominance-submission) and affiliation (friendliness-hostility), for instance, may permit us more effectively to work with certain types of vocational clients. Pincus and Wiggins (1992) offer a similar, expanded assessment of interpersonal functioning.

Is an interest inventory in itself sufficient to meet the needs of clients, or is additional counseling required? Pinkney (1987), for example, maintains that clients frequently oversimplify the role of assessment in career planning and assume that a test will tell them what to do. The bottom line would seem to be that the administration and interpretation of an interest inventory in isolation—no matter how well done—is not likely to be sufficient to meet the career planning needs of most clients.

Finally, readers should be aware that there is an Association for Interest Measurement (949 Peregrine Drive, Palatine, IL 60067) that offers a great deal of information about the construction and use of instruments involving interests.

Interest Inventories

Several of the most commonly used interest inventories are briefly described here:

Ohio Vocational Interest Inventory (OVIS) (2nd ed.). (1981) A. G. D'Costa, D. W. Winefordner, J. G. Odgers, and P. B. Koons, Jr., Psychological Corporation, and others. Approximately 1½ hours. Grades seven to thirteen.

Twenty-three interest scales and a scale clarity score:

Agriculture and life sciences
Basic services
Clerical
Communications
Crafts and precise operations
Customer services
Education and social work
Engineering and physical sciences
Health sciences
Legal services
Machine operation
Management
Manual work
Marketing
Medical services
Music
Numerical
Performing arts
Quality control
Regulations enforcement
Skilled personal services
Sports and recreation
Visual arts

Scores expressed in percentiles.

Based on cubistic model (people, data, things) of DOT.

Includes a *Student Information Questionnaire* (six questions and one open-ended for a school to ask more questions of a locally pertinent nature).

Provides a *Student Report Folder* and a *Guide to Career Exploration* to link interests to the world of work. Machine-scored or hand-scored. For a review, see Campbell (1994).

Vocational Interests, Experience, and Skill Assessment (VIESA). Houghton Mifflin. Grades eight to twelve. Approximately 45 minutes.

Yields six job clusters (comparable to Holland's typology) and 25 job families that include 650 occupations. Self-scored. Related to *Career Planning Program* described elsewhere in this chapter (i.e., the unisex form of the UNIACT). Not a great deal of validity data yet accumulated regarding this instrument. For a review, see Mehrens (1988).

Strong Interest Inventory (SII) (formerly Strong-Campbell). E. K. Strong, Jo-Ida Hansen, and D. P. Campbell (1994). Stanford University Press, Consulting Psychologists Press. Grade eleven–adult. Approximately 30–45 minutes. 1985 Revised Norms. Yields 6 General Occupational Theme Scales (à la Holland) with 20 items in each scale.

These are related to 22 basic interest scales:

- Realistic theme
  - Agriculture
  - Nature
  - Adventure
  - Military activities
  - Mechanical activities
- Investigative theme
  - Science
  - Mathematics
  - Medical science
- Artistic theme
  - Music/dramatics
  - Art
  - Writing
- Social theme
  - Teaching
  - Social service
  - Athletics
  - Domestic arts
  - Religious activities
- Enterprising theme
  - Public speaking
  - Law/politics
  - Merchandising
  - Sales
  - Business management
- Conventional theme
  - Office practices

Also yields scores on 207 occupational scales, primarily professional level, although 17 vocational/technical occupations have been added. Related to *Pathfinder* career decision-making system using interactive video.

Academic comfort and introversion-extroversion scales (now Learning Environment and Work Style Scales). Newer additional Personal Styles Scales also include Leadership Style Scale and Risk Taking/Adventure Scale.

Broday and Braswell (1990) confirm that those who score higher on the artistic and investigative scales of the Strong tend to have higher academic comfort (AC) scores and that the AC scores of undergraduates are lower than those of graduate students. Microcomputer version available.

The computer-based version of the SCII may have even better test-retest reliability than the paper-and-pencil version (Vansickle, Kimmel, & Kapes, 1989). Bonynge (1992) suggests caution in interpreting scores of individuals who place no significance on work. For a review, see Westbrook and Norton (1994) as well as Vacc and Newsome (2002).

Occupational Preference Survey (COPS). R. R. Knapp and others (1995). Educational and Industrial Testing Service. Grades nine to twelve. Approximately 40 minutes. Yields scores in eight major groups according to two levels each (professional and skilled) à la Roe:

- Science
- Technology
- Business
- Linguistic
- Aesthetic
- Service
- Outdoor
- Clerical

Scores expressed in percentiles for males and females. Machine-scored or hand-scored. Computer version available.

Kane (1989) offers a review of the COPS instrument in positive terms as a stimulus to career exploration, although he is less enthusiastic about its use in decision making involving immediate occupational choice because of incomplete psychometric data. Bauernfeind (1988) offers a similar evaluation in his review of the COPS. Finally, Wickwire (2002) provides a review of the most recent version of COPS.

Career Key (CK). L. K. Jones. J. G. Ferguson. Produces a Holland code, listing of appropriate occupations, and references to the *Encyclopedia of Careers and Vocational Guidance.* Teaches the Holland theory. According to L. K. Jones (1990) and L. K. Jones, Gorman, and Schroeder (1989), the CK compares favorably with the SDS, at least in use with college students. L. K. Jones (1990, 1993) indicates validity and reliability for both high school and college students.

Internet version available at: http://www.careerkey.org/cgi/ck.pl

Career Assessment Inventory (CAI). C. B. Johannson (1984 and 1986). National Computer Systems. Grade eight to adult. Approximately 45 minutes. The Enhanced Version for careers requiring four years of college or less, or no postsecondary training. The Vocational Version for those entering careers immediately after high school or junior college.

Yields scores according to Holland's six types and 22 basic interests:

- Realistic
  - Mechanical/fixing
  - Electronics
  - Carpentry
  - Manual/skilled trades
  - Agriculture
  - Nature/outdoors
  - Animal service
- Investigative
  - Science
  - Numbers
- Artistic
  - Writing
  - Performing/entertaining
  - Arts/crafts
- Social
  - Social service
  - Teaching
  - Child care
  - Medical service
  - Religious activities
- Enterprising
  - Business
  - Sales
- Conventional
  - Office practices
  - Clerical/clerking
  - Food service

Also yields 91–111 specific occupational scores, two administrative indexes, and four nonoccupational scales. Microcomputer version available.

Similar format to the SII. For a review, see Vacc and Hinkle (1994).

Kuder Occupational Interest Survey (KOIS) (Form DD). CTB McGraw-Hill (1985). Grades ten to twelve and adult. About 30 minutes.

Yields 10 broad interest areas, 109 occupational scales, and 40 college major scales. Verification (V) score and eight experimental scales. Microcomputer version available.

Scores reported in terms of modified biserial correlations. Must be machine-scored. For a review, see Herr and Ashby (1994) and Kelly (2002).

Kuder General Interest Survey (KGIS). (Form E) CTB McGraw-Hill (1988). Grades six to twelve. Approximately 50 minutes.

Yields 10 interest scales plus verification (V) score and RIASEC code.

- Outdoor
- Mechanical
- Computational
- Scientific
- Persuasive
- Artistic
- Literary
- Musical
- Social service
- Clerical

Scores expressed in national percentiles. Can be hand-scored or machine-scored. Computer version available.

For a review, see Mehrens (1994). Zytowski (1992) provides a brief but excellent overview of the history of the Kuder Inventories. For a review, see Pope (2002).

Vocational Preference Inventory (VPI). J. L. Holland. Consulting Psychologists Press. Grade nine to adult. 1985 Revision. Approximately 30 minutes.

Yields six personality scales and five experimental scales:

- Realistic
- Investigative
- Social
- Conventional

Enterprising
Artistic
Self-control
Masculinity-femininity
Status
Infrequency
Acquiescence

Self-scored. Computer version available.

Whether this instrument is a personality measure is still moot (Gottfredson & Jones, 1993).

Vocational Interest Inventory, Revised (VII-R). P. W. Lunneborg (1981). Western Psychological Services. High school population. Intended for undecided students whose interests are not well differentiated. Approximately 20 minutes.

Forced choice format yields relative strength of interests in Roe's eight areas:

Service
Business Contact
Organization
Technical
Outdoor
Science
General cultural
Arts and entertainment

Machine-scored. Scores reported in terms of percentiles and T scores for each scale. Computer version available.

Controls for sex bias at item level and encourages exploration of nontraditional careers. For a review, see Krumboltz (1988b).

Jackson Vocational Interest Survey (JVIS). D. N. Jackson Sigman Assessment Systems (1999). Grade ten to adult. Approximately 45 minutes.

A Canadian-developed instrument that measures preferences in terms of vocational roles and vocational styles (activities and work environments).

Thirty-four basic interest scales arranged in 10 categories:

Arts
Science and mathematics
Practical, outdoor activities
Service activities
Medicine and health
Interpersonal and job-related work styles
Teaching and social welfare activities
Business, administrative, and related activities
Legal, professional, persuasive work roles
Literary, academic
Work styles related to job activities

Hand-scored or machine-scored. Computer version available. Males and females measured equally.

Ten general occupational themes (expressive, logical, inquiring, practical, assertive, socialized, helping, conventional, enterprising, and communicative). Academic orientation scale.

This inventory was carefully developed in terms of it psychometric qualities. For a review, see Jepsen (1994) and Shute (2002).

Geist Picture Interest Inventory. H. Geist. Western Psychological Services. Grade eight to adult. Some occupational norms. Intended for culture-limited and educationally deprived populations. Requires minimum language competency. Hand-scored.

Other nonverbal interest inventories are also available; for example, Reading-Free Vocational Interest Inventory-Revised (R-FVII-Revised) and the Picture Interest Exploration Survey (PIES).

JOB-O Career Interest Tests (Judgment of Occupational Behavior-Orientation). (1981) JIST.

Three versions: JOB-O Elementary for grades four to six; "classic" JOB-O for grades seven to ten; and JOB-O Advanced for grade ten through adult. 50 minutes. Hand-scored.

Interests related to 120 occupations and college majors. Nine scales: education, interest, inclusion, control, affection, physical activity, hands/tool/machinery, problem solving, and creating ideas.

Other Interest Inventories

- Campbell Interest and Skill Survey (CISS)
  NCS Assessments (1992)
  High school to adult (7 orientation scales, 29 basic scales, and 58 occupational scales)
- Career Directions Inventory (CDI)
  Sigma Assessment Systems (1986)
  High school to adult (7 general occupational themes, 15 basic interest scales)
- Career Occupational Preference System Interest Inventory (COPS)
  EdITS (1995)
  Grades seven to twelve (8 career clusters, 24 scales)

- Chronicle Career Quest (CCQ)
  Chronicle Guidance (2001)
  Grades seven to twelve (12 G. O. E. interest areas)
- College Major Interest Inventory (CMII)
  Consulting Psychologists Press (1990)
  High school seniors and college freshmen (65 academic major scales, 33 educational cluster scales, 12 personal characteristics scales, and others)
- Interest Determination, Exploration, and Assessment System (IDEAS)
  NCS Assessments (1996)
  Middle school to adults (16 broad interest categories, short version of CAI)

MONITORING

It is useful to have some assessment of the stage of career development or career maturity of an individual or group. In one sense, monitoring can be thought of as an evaluation of an individual's career progress. Depending on the instrument used, it can tell us about individual readiness for choice rather than the content of choice. It tells us where individuals are vocationally and where they have to go. In another sense, monitoring informs us of such work-related factors as work values, job satisfaction, and a wide variety of other measurable variables pertinent to work life.

The career-related needs of individuals determine the goals to be achieved in a systematic approach; monitoring permits a continued check on these needs. There are diverse types of measures, both extant and in-process, that relate to this function. In development, for example, there are scales to determine degree of career "undecidedness" (see Chapter 14). Instruments exist to assess everything from work environment preference to career education needs assessment to job satisfaction and satisfactoriness. We are unable to cover all possible instruments.

Innovative techniques have been advocated. For example, Neimeyer (1989a) has suggested the use of the repertory grid technique (specifically, the Role Construct Repertory Test, or reptest) in vocational counseling. These types of tests are based on an individual's reaction to bipolar dimensions of constructs important in the world of work (for instance, nonphysical activity—physical labor; requires college—no college required). The client rates a number of these bipolar dimensions that were evolved by the client or by the counselor. Thus a grid is created. Valence ratings for each occupation are then obtained. What emerges is a profile that provides information about the client's levels of differentiation, integration, and conflict (see Chapter 14). In its current form, the technique seems unwieldy in practice, although the theory appears reasonable. Better (that is, simpler) implementation would be desirable.

One aspect of human behavior that is rarely assessed in terms of providing vocational self-knowledge to clients prior to their entering an occupation (with the exception of the developmentally disabled population) is that of competence in personal and social relationships. Although effective interaction at work is frequently assessed after the fact, there is seldom any a priori attempt to measure these social and personal dimensions as an aid to initial career decision making. Thus, the assessment of competence in relational contexts would appear to be an unmet need in career assessment. An introduction to the general field may be found in Spitzberg and Cupach (1989).

In any case, in the following section, we will consider some of the more prominent monitoring instruments in four distinct areas: career maturity, work values and personality, career planning, and job satisfaction.

Career Maturity and Adaptability

As discussed at length in Chapter 4, career maturity is a construct that naturally emerges from developmentally oriented career theories. If people do indeed go through a systematic series of stages in career development, it ought to be possible to measure the rate and progress of that sequence and to compare where an individual is along that developmental line, both in terms of where one might reasonably be expected to be and in terms of where one's age peers are.

Depending on how far they depart from an expected norm, we may then classify them according to career maturity. Crites (1974a) has suggested that the measurement of career maturity has at least two types of utility: (1) a *research function* in that it enables us to "test" theoretical aspects of career development and (2) a *practical function* in that it diagnoses the rate and progress of the career development of an individual and consequently suggests intervention strategies to enhance that development. In the latter sense, career maturity measurement can be used as both a type of needs analysis and a criterion variable in the evaluation of the effectiveness of certain types of intervention strategies.

Generally, career maturity may be defined as the place reached on a continuum of career development from exploration to decline. Note that no current career maturity measure assesses any career-related maturational variables in the growth stage—that stage hypothesized to precede the exploratory stage. In broader terms, career maturity measures are an attempt to assess "the readiness of the individual to make decisions that are called for at a given decision point" (Super, 1974, p. 10).

A number of instruments designed to appraise career maturity from adolescence through adulthood have been devised. It should be noted that predicting the long-term effects of career maturity is much more difficult that proving the short-term effects (Seifert, 1994).

Career Maturity Measures

Career Development Inventory (CDI). D. E. Super, A. S. Thompson, R. H. Lindeman, J. P. Jordaan, and R. A. Myers (1981). Consulting Psychologists Press. About one hour to complete. School form and college and university form.

Eight scales assessing knowledge and attitudes about career choice:

Career planning (CP)—20 items
Career exploration (CE)—20 items
Decision-making (DM)—20 items
World-of-work information (WW)—20 items
Knowledge of preferred occupational group (PO)—40 items
Career development, attitudes (CDA)—(CP and CE combined)
Career orientation total (COT)—CP, CE, DM, and WW combined

Generally acceptable discriminant validity (Kuhlman-Harrison & Neely, 1980). For a review, see Pinkney and Bozik (1994).

Adult Career Concerns Inventory. D. E. Super and others (1988). Consulting Psychologists Press. Adult populations. 15–30 minutes. 12 substages to determine career planfulness in adults and their concerns with career development tasks at various life stages:

Exploration
1. Cystallization
2. Specification
3. Implementation
Establishment
4. Stabilization
5. Consolidation
6. Advancement
Maintenance
7. Holding
8. Updating
9. Innovating
Disengagement
10. Deceleration
11. Retirement planning
12. Retirement living

Subject rates self in relation to 61 concerns (for example, "using new methods and ideas on the job") on a 1–5 scale. Two separate scoring methods.

Supporting research from Smart and Peterson (1994). For a review, see Rounds (1994).

Career Maturity Inventory-Revised (CMI-R). (Formerly called the Vocational Development Inventory). John O. Crites and Mark Savickas (1995). Provides three scores: Attitude Scale (25 items), Competence Test (25 items), and Total Score. Normative data for grades five to twelve. Total test time approximately 45 minutes.

Attitude Test
Measures attitudes and feelings about making a career choice.

Competency Test
Measures knowledge about occupations and decisions involved in choosing a career.
No machine scoring is available. Scored by counselee in 5 minutes. For a review, see McDivitt (2002).

Westbrook (1974) examined career maturity inventories and evolved a composite outline of the career behaviors that the tests are attempting to assess. In abbreviated form, the outline is:

I. Cognitive domain (what the learner knows)
   A. Individual attributes
   B. Occupational information

C. Job selection
D. Course and curriculum selection
E. School and career planning
F. School and career problem solving

II. Psychomotor domain (what the learner says he or she has done)
A. Involvement in career planning activities
B. Involvement in wide range of worker activities
C. Involvement in activities related to preferred occupation(s)

III. Affective domain (attitudes, preferences, and perceptions of learner)
A. Attitudes
B. Preferences
C. Perceptions

Unfortunately, career maturity scores from different instruments still do not correlate highly with each other. They do seem to be affected by scholastic aptitude, but not by sex or race (Westbrook, Sanford, & Donnelly, 1990).

Another disquieting aspect is that when career maturity is used as an outcome measure in short-term and simpleminded career interventions, scores invariably increase. One would not think of being able to take someone who is generally determined to be "immature" in personality and to apply a two-session structured intervention, expecting to make the person "mature." Yet this is essentially what we have been doing in the area of career maturity. Clearly the construct's theoretical conceptions, operationalization, and measurement have to be developed further.

Work Values and Personality Instruments

A second type of monitoring instrument that is useful in both research and in career guidance is the work values measure. The values that one holds are clearly a determinant of career choice (Brown, 1996); therefore, an objective measure of the hierarchical structure of those values provides an individual with important input data for career decision making. Often these measures simply clarify what an individual already knows. Frequently, however, they open up hidden areas for exploration and consideration; they bring to the surface that which had remained dormant. Work values are sometimes confused with work interests. In fact, the two are distinctive domains, each measuring different variables. Work values appear to be related to job satisfaction (Rounds, Dawis, & Lofquist, 1987). A sampling of work values measures are described below. Newer research is assessing organizational work values, as opposed to individual work values (Judge & Bretz, 1992).

The Values Scale (VS). D. D. Nevill and D. E. Super (1989). Consulting Psychologists Press. Measures intrinsic and extrinsic life-career values. 30–45 minutes.

Twenty-one scales (106 items rated on a four-point scale).

Ability utilization
Achievement
Advancement
Aesthetics
Altruism
Authority
Autonomy
Creativity
Economic rewards
Lifestyle
Personal development
Physical activity
Prestige
Risk
Social interaction
Social relations
Variety
Working conditions
Cultural identity
Physical prowess
Economic security

Hand-scored or computer-scored. For a review, see Slaney and Suddarth (1994) and Schoenrade (2002).

L. V. Yates (1990) conducted research with the Values Scale that establishes some construct validity in that groups differ in their responses to the instrument according to age (for example, 18- to 25-year-olds place more emphasis on physical activity, advancement, and social interaction and less emphasis on autonomy and working conditions than 26- to 35-year-olds and 46- to 62-year-olds). In addition, the five occupational groups studied (by Holland code with artistic eliminated) differed in expected directions in their responses to the instrument.

Work Values Inventory (WVI). D. E. Super. Houghton Mifflin. Grade seven to adult. 15 minutes. Fifteen values relating to job success and satisfaction, combined into four factors: material, goodness of life, self-expression, and behavior control:

Intellectual stimulation
Job achievement
Way of life
Economic returns
Altruism
Creativity
Relationship with associates
Job security
Prestige
Management of others
Variety
Aesthetics
Independence
Supervisory relations
Physical surroundings

Factor analysis of the WVI suggests six second-order dimensions (rather than the structural four into which the 15 values were organized): stimulating work, interpersonal satisfaction, economic security, responsible autonomy, comfortable existence, and esthetic concerns.

Career Orientation Placement and Evaluation Survey (COPES). R. R. Knapp & L. F. Knapp (1995). Edits. Junior high school to community college. May be used separately or as part of the more comprehensive Career Occupational Preference System (COP-System).

Offers seven work-related value scales:

Investigative versus accepting
Practical versus carefree
Leadership versus supportive
Orderliness versus noncompulsive
Recognition versus privacy
Aesthetic versus realistic
Social versus self-concern
For a review, see Wickwire (2002).

Hall Occupational Orientation Inventory. Scholastic Testing Service. (1976)

Three levels: Grades three to seven; high school and college; handicapped adults. Based on Maslow's personality need theory and DOT.

Yields 22 scale scores:

Creativity, independence
Risk
Information, knowledge
Belongingness
Security
Aspiration
Esteem
Self-actualization
Personal satisfaction
Routine-dependence
Data orientation
Things orientation
People orientation
Location concern
Aptitude concern
Monetary concern
Physical abilities concern
Environment concern
Co-worker concern
Qualifications concern
Time concern
Defensiveness

Minnesota Importance Questionaire (MIQ). Vocational Psychology Research, University of Minnesota. Based on Theory of Work Adjustment (R. V. Dawis & L. H. Lofquist). Actually a measure of vocational needs rather than values. Most common form 1975 paired format with machine scoring. Fifth-grade reading level. 30–40 minutes. Twenty statements representing 20 needs (for example, authority: I could tell people what to do) are paired with each other for a forced choice, then each of the 20 is rated absolutely.

Yield is scores on the 20 needs:

Ability utilization
Achievement
Activity
Advancement
Authority
Company policies and practices
Compensation
Co-workers
Creativity
Independence
Moral values
Recognition
Responsibility
Security
Social service
Social status
Supervision–human relations

Supervision–technical
Variety
Working conditions

Occupational reinforcer patterns (ORPs) are descriptions of reinforcer systems of selected occupations (scores also on nine clusters of ORPs). Machine-scored only. For a review, see Brooke and Ciechalski (1994).

There are many other general values measures and many other work values instruments, but none have been more carefully devised and tested or have more direct applicability to careers than those we have listed. See, for example, Employment Readiness Scale, Study of Values, the Rokeach Value Survey, DF Opinion Survey, and so on.

Personality and Other Career Assessment Devices

Several other instruments have been devised to assess the knowledge or attitudes of individuals with regard to selected aspects of career development. These devices are intended to give both individuals and those responsible for career interventions a gauge of career-related awareness, knowledge, and attitudes. Some are criterion-referenced and others are norm-referenced. Some are based on psychological constructs; some are not. By and large, they are content measures. A sampling of some of these instruments follows.

It is possible to gain specific work-relevant information from extant instruments that are well-accepted measures of general personality. One example is the California Psychological Inventory (CPI) for which researchers (Gough, 1985) have developed a 40-item WO scale to measure work orientation in the sense of self-discipline, dedication to obligations, and adherence to rule (that is, to the so-called Protestant work ethic). We have previously described the Myers-Briggs Type Indicator. Examples of a few other instruments follow.

Edwards Personal Preference Schedule (EPPS). A. L. Edwards (1959). The Psychological Corporation. Age 18 to adult. Forty-five minutes.

Provides relative ranking of 15 "normal" personality variables and can be related to career choice considerations. Based on Murray's Need System:

Achievement
Deference
Order
Exhibition
Autonomy
Affiliation
Intraception
Succorance
Dominance
Abasement
Nurturance
Change
Endurance
Heterosexuality
Aggression

Hand-scored or machine-scored.

Sixteen PF Personal Factor Questionnaire. Cattell & Cattell (1993). Institute for Personality and Ability Testing. Age 16+. Test administration time is about 40 minutes.

Measures five global factors: Extraversion, Anxiety, Tough-Mindedness, Independence, Self-Control; and 16 Primary Factors: Warmth, Reasoning, Emotional Stability, Dominance, Liveliness, Rule-Consciousness, Social Boldness, Sensitivity, Vigilance, Abstractedness, Privateness, Apprehension, Openness to Change, Self-Reliance, Perfectionism, Tension. Composite scores for Creativity, Adjustment, and other scores are available.

Hand scoring only. For a review, see Rounds and McKenna (2002).

Other Career-Related Instruments

Occupational Stress Inventory (OSI). S. H. Osipow and A. R. Spokane. Psychological Assessment Resources (1998). Adults. 20–40 minutes.

Three questionnaires yielding 14 subscales:

1. Occupational roles questionnaire (ORQ)
   - **a.** Role overload
   - **b.** Role insufficiency
   - **c.** Role ambiguity
   - **d.** Role boundary
   - **e.** Responsibility
   - **f.** Physical environment
2. Personal Strain Questionnaire (PSQ)
   - **a.** Vocational strain
   - **b.** Psychological strain
   - **c.** Interpersonal strain
   - **d.** Physical strain

3. Personal Resources Questionnaire (PRQ)
   a. Recreation
   b. Self-care
   c. Social support
   d. Rational/cognitive coping

T-scores and percentiles for men and women. Machine-scored or hand-scored. For a review, see Powell (1994).

World of Work Inventory. J. W. Hudson and K. S. Hudson. World of Work, Inc. Grade eight to adult.

Three sections:

1. Career interest activities
2. Job satisfaction indicators
3. Vocational training potentials

Excellent interpretive manual.

Comprehensive Career Assessment Scales (CCAS). S. L. Jackson and P. M. Goulding. Learning Concepts. Three scales: grades three to seven; grades eight to twelve; teachers. Assesses familiarity with 75 occupations in the USOE clusters. Yields interest and familiarity profiles. Can be used for needs assessment, curriculum planning, or evaluation.

Self-Directed Search (SDS) Form E. J. L. Holland (1994). Consulting Psychologists Press. Self-administered and scored. Grade six to adult. 40 minutes.

Self-reports and estimates regarding:

1. Occupational daydreams
2. Preferences for activities
3. Competencies
4. Preferences for kinds of occupations
5. Abilities in various occupational areas

Yields summary codes according to Holland's scales and refers taker to *Jobs Finder.*

The Self-Directed Search has been combined with a Vocational Card Sort (VCS), an instructional booklet, and an action plan into the Vocational Exploration and Insight Kit (VEIK). In research on the VEIK, it is interesting to note that the VEIK failed to exceed the effect of its components (VCS and SDS) (Takai & Holland, 1979).

The Self-Directed Search is illustrative of self-administered, self-scored, and essentially self-interpreted instruments. Although the approach is promising and certainly has been and is being subjected to research to establish its validity and effectiveness, there are several caveats to be noted. First, the SDS (and, we may infer, similar instruments) may yield inaccurate results in a substantial number of cases simply because of self-scoring errors and despite efforts to simplify the instrument.

Holland has responded by producing Form E (for easy), which yields only a two-letter code, but there is no evidence to suggest that this instrument as well as other self-administered, self-scored, and self-interpreted devices is any less susceptible to error.

Second, the ability of individuals to estimate their own aptitudes is still an open issue. Some studies have suggested that counselees can accurately self-estimate aptitudes with which they have most familiarity (such as verbal and numerical). Prediger (1999) reviewed five studies that compared hit rates for test scores of abilities versus self-estimates. In each of the five studies, ability composites using self-estimates were more valid than test scores. Other studies, however, have suggested that a significant proportion of individuals cannot accurately self-estimate either familiar or unfamiliar (for example, mechanical reasoning, clerical speed and accuracy, and such) aptitudes (Anderson, Warner, & Spencer, 1984; Hodgson & Cramer, 1977; J. L. Swanson & Lease, 1990).

Third, there appears to be some disagreement regarding how much, if any, counselor assistance is or should be required in relation to interpreting the SDS. In view of these three factors and others, perhaps the best advice that can be offered to counselors is that they proceed cautiously, accumulate their own data for evaluation, and do their own interpretations. Yet the SDS is widely used. It is even recommended as a preferred assessment instrument for school psychologists who wish to include a vocational dimension in their psychoeducational assessments (E. M. Levinson, 1990).

For a review of the computer version of the Self-Directed Search (SDS: CV) see Urich (1990). N. J. Campbell's review (1988) is positive for *supervised* use. See also Daniels (1994) and Ciechalski (2002).

The Salience Inventory. D. D. Nevill and D. E. Super. Consulting Psychologists Press. Assesses relative importance of five major life roles: student, worker, homemaker, leisurite, and citizen. Evaluates client's orientation to life roles, readiness for career decisions, and exposure to work and occupations.

Research edition (see Super & Nevill, 1984). For a review, see J. I. C. Hansen (1994).

Career Decision-Making System (CDM-R). T. J. Harrington and A. J. O'Shea. American Guidance Service (2000). Junior high–adult. Either self-scored or computerized. Based on Holland's hexagonal theory of career development. Presumably systematic use of basic Holland-type data in decision making. Validity evidence from D. Brown, Ware, and S. T. Brown (1985). For a review see Vansickle (1994) and Campbell and Raiff (2002). One study determined that the computer-based CDM was more reliable than the paper-pencil form (Kapes & Vansickle, 1992). Validity data provided by Harrington, Feller, and O'Shea (1993).

My Vocational Situation. J. L. Holland, D. C. Daiger, & P. G. Power (1980). Consulting Psychologists Press. Grade, nine+. 10 minutes.

Attempts to identify possible causes of vocational difficulties from among three possibilities: lack of vocational identity, lack of information or training, or environmental or personal barriers.

Eighteen T–F statements and two multiple-part Y–N questions. Hand-scored only. For a review, see Westbrook (1988).

Vocational Identity Scale (VIS). J. L. Holland and others (1980).

A general measure (18 T–F items) of "psychological health" in that vocational variables are confounded by personal variables. General construct validity and good reliability (Holland, Johnston, & Asama, 1993).

Career Factors Inventory (CFI). Chartrand, Robbins, & Morrill (1997). Two information factors (need for career information and need for self-knowledge) and two personal-emotional factors (career choice anxiety and generalized indecisiveness). For a review, see Luzzo (2002).

Career Beliefs Inventory. (J. D. Krumboltz) Counseling Psychologists Press (1991). Identifies beliefs that prevent clients from achieving career goals. Twenty-five scales organized into five headings: (1) My Current Career Situation; (2) What Seems Necessary for My Happiness; (3) Factors That Influence My Decisions; (4) Changes I Am Willing to Make; and (5) Efforts I Am Willing to Initiate. For a review, see Wall (1994) and Hall and Rayman (2002). For descriptive and analytical articles, see Krumboltz (1994a), Fuqua and Newman (1994), and Watkins (1994).

Campbell Development Surveys (CDS). D. P. Campbell NCS; (1990–1992). A battery of surveys for use in educational and human resource settings. Five surveys: (1) Campbell Organizational Survey (COS); (2) Campbell Leadership Index (CLI); (3) Campbell Interest and Skill Survey (CISS); (4) Campbell-Hallam Team Development Survey (TDS); and (5) Campbell Community Survey (CCS). For a description, see D. P. Campbell (1993).

Career Thoughts Inventory (CTI). Sampson, Peterson, Lenz, Reardon, & Saunders; Psychological Assessment Resources (1996). A self-administered and objectively scored measure of negative career thinking designed to improve the quality of career decisions and the quality of career service delivery. Three scales: Decision-making Confusion, Commitment Anxiety, External Conflict, and a total score. The CTI is self-administered in 15 minutes and hand scored. For a review, see Feller and Daly (2002).

Job Satisfaction Measures

There are hundreds of measures of job satisfaction, worker attitudes, preference for work environments, and so on. A comprehensive annotation of these measures may be found in J. D. Cook and colleagues (1981). Discussions of job satisfaction are contained in Chapters 2 and 13. A sampling of some widely used instruments is presented here.

Job Satisfaction Blank. R. Hoppock. Venerable overall measure of job satisfaction, containing only four basic questions. Respondents check alternatives that best tell how they feel about their jobs.

Job Descriptive Index. P. C. Smith, L. M. Kendall, & C. L. Hulin. A heavily used instrument. Five subscales (type of work—18 items; promotion opportunities—9 items; supervision—18 items; pay—9 items; and co-workers—18 items). Each of the 72 items is an adjective or phrase and respondents indicate yes, uncertain, or no whether it describes the job aspect. Can also combine subscales for an overall score.

Michigan Organizational Assessment Questionnaire. C. Cammann, M. Fichman, D. Jenkins, & J. Klesh. Contains measures of overall job satisfaction (three-item scale); intrinsic and extrinsic rewards; social rewards satisfaction; work attitudes and perceptions; job involvement; internal work motivation; task, job, and role characteristics; supervision; and work group functioning.

Organizational Commitment Questionnaire. L. W. Porter & F. J. Smith. Fifteen items responded to on a seven-point scale. Organizational commitment is assumed to be more global and less transitory than job satisfaction. Measures how strongly an individual identifies with and is involved in a particular organization.

Job-Related Tension Scale. R. L. Kahn, D. M. Wolfe, R. P. Quinn, J. D. Snoek, & R. Rosenthal. Fifteen items responded to on a five-point scale. Respondents indicate how frequently they are bothered at work by each item (for example, "Feeling that you may not be liked and accepted by the people you work with").

Work Preference Questionnaire (WPQ). S. Fineman. Measures need for achievement in occupational settings. Twenty-four forced-choice items yield scores on 9 aspects of an achievement (for example, responsibility, risk-taking, competitiveness).

Role Ambiguity and Role Conflict Scales. J. Rizzo, R. J. House, & S. I. Lirtzman. Six-item scale measuring role ambiguity ("predictability of outcomes of one's behavior and the existence of environmental guidelines to provide knowledge that one is behaving appropriately") and eight-item scale measuring role conflict (incompatibility of demands).

Job Diagnostic Survey. J. R. Hackman & G. R. Oldham (1974). The most widely used instrument for assessing perceived job characteristics. Measures five core dimensions: skill variety, task identity, task significance, autonomy, and feedback.

Work Environment Scale. R. H. Moos. Measures perceptions of existing work environments. The 10 WES subscales assess three underlying domains or dimensions: the relationship dimension, the personal growth dimension, and the system maintenance and system change dimension. The relationship dimension is measured by the involvement, peer cohesion, and supervisor support subscales. These subscales assess the extent to which employees are concerned about and committed to their jobs; the extent to which employees are friendly to and supportive of one another, and the extent to which management is supportive of employees and encourages employees to be supportive of one another.

EVALUATION

Because a comprehensive discussion of evaluation in a systematic approach to career guidance was presented in Chapter 6, the following remarks are intended primarily as a summary. Built into any systematic approach is the process of evaluation. Evaluation is simply a series of activities designed to determine how well goals have been achieved. As such, evaluation implies valuing—saying what is desirable or good.

In a systematic approach, one looks for a relationship between career guidance processes (input) and counselee behavioral outcomes (output). To determine the strength of such a relationship, one must consider certain elements in the systematic model. These have been dealt with in earlier chapters; by way of review, selected aspects of the components of a systematic approach are presented:

1. *Needs.* The various developmental stages through which individuals pass determine their needs at various developmental levels and, in turn, determine the goals of career guidance.
2. *Goals and objectives.* Objectives and goals, which arise from counselee needs, are stated in both global and behaviorally specific terms.
3. *Process.* Process or treatment refers to specific activities carried out to achieve objectives. Treatments depend on and arise from the base built before their implementation and subsequently determine future process.
4. *Counselee variables.* Because certain career guidance processes depend on selected characteristics of the counselees who are exposed to those processes, it is frequently necessary in evaluation to conduct

cross-breaks—that is, to determine differential effects of process on counselees because of differences in sex, socioeconomic level, culture, ability, and so on.

5. *Situational variables.* It is equally likely that career guidance processes may have differential effects in different situations. What works in a vocational school may not work in a comprehensive high school; what works in a liberal arts college may not work in a more technically oriented institution; what is effective in a rural area may not be effective in an urban area, and so on.

6. *Outcome variables.* Outcome variables are defined by objectives that are behaviorally specific and must, in some cases, present immediate, intermediate, and long-range goals.

7. *Feedback.* This concept refers to the need for continuous evaluation. Just as one continually uses monitoring procedures to keep aware of counselees' career needs, the counselor employs continual evaluation to determine how closely goals are being achieved. If goals are not being achieved, then processes must be changed for future groups.

For a detailed description of evaluation techniques that even the counselor who is unsophisticated in research procedures can accomplish, see S. H. Cramer, Herr, Morris, and Frantz (1970).

The procedures for evaluation within a systematic approach to career guidance are as follows:

a. Formulate the broad goals of the career guidance program.
b. Classify these goals so that an economy of thought and action can be achieved. Decide what developmental stages require which guidance processes for implementation.
c. Define objectives in behavioral terms.
d. Suggest situations in which the desired objectives and behaviors might be observed.
e. Develop or select appraisal techniques such as standardized tests, monitoring instruments, questionnaires, and so on.
f. Gather and interpret performance data and compare these data with the stated behavioral objectives.

This system of evaluation is, in a sense, an absolute system because no comparisons are made between the career guidance program in a given institutional setting and the program in any other comparable setting. Those responsible for planning, implementing, and evaluating a systematic approach to career guidance may wish to make such comparisons to determine relative effectiveness.

SUMMARY

In this chapter, we have discussed the use of measurement and assessment procedures in four areas relating to career guidance: prediction, discrimination, monitoring, and evaluation. Selected aspects of each of these areas, with descriptions of a sampling of illustrative instruments, have been presented. Prediction and discrimination techniques provide data for individual decision making; monitoring and evaluation procedures enable counselors to plan more effectively in providing career guidance within a systematic framework. The use of any specific appraisal instrument, whether commercially standardized or locally developed, depends on the unique characteristics of a given population. Therefore, there is no such thing as *the* testing program in career guidance or *the* evaluation instruments. Institutions should be flexible and imaginative as they build their own appraisal programs.

An excellent resource for counselors who wish assistance in evaluating specific tests and inventories for use in career assessment is Kapes and Whitfield (2001). For a specific discussion of the use of career assessment with adults, see Crites and Taber (2002).

CHAPTER SIXTEEN

Research and Social Issues in Career Guidance and Counseling

KEY CONCEPTS

- Research studies have repeatedly demonstrated that career interventions do yield positive results and that their general utility is clear.
- Given the enormity of the possible questions that may be raised about the content and application of career interventions in different settings and with different populations, the quality and comprehensiveness of both the theory and research about career behavior and interventions in it are uneven.
- Because career behavior occurs within settings, life stages, and economic and political systems that are dynamic, new research questions are always forming.
- The fullest possible understanding of career development theory and of the effects of career interventions requires a wide range of theoretical paradigms (differential, structures, developmental, or lifespan constructivist), research techniques, and purposes: descriptive, correlational, case study, naturalistic, single subject, factorial, multivariate, subjective and qualitative, experimental, cross-sectional, ethnographic, longitudinal, and combinations of these.
- Although the typical statistical approaches to career behavior and treatment effects or interventions in career development have included discriminant analysis, analysis of variance, and correlational or regression approaches, additional and more sophisticated techniques are now emerging.

Research and speculation are abundant about the origins, structure, and persistence of career behavior and the forms of intervention that affect such behavior. Indeed, in the broadest sense, there is no longer a major question about the ability of career guidance or career counseling to improve or change career behavior. Meta-analyses and other research techniques have permitted researchers to summarize large numbers of studies and determine the collective effect of individual studies of a particular process on different forms of behavior. Such aggregate studies have shown that career education (Oliver & Spokane, 1988), career counseling (Holland, Magoon, & Spokane, 1981; Spokane and Oliver, 1983) and career guidance (Herr, 1986) do yield positive results and that the general efficacy of such interventions is no longer in question (Rounds & Tinsley, 1984; Whiston, Sexton, & Lasoff, 1998).

Against this context, the reader could appropriately ask, if the results of career education, career guidance, or career counseling are as positive as stated in the previous paragraph, why is this chapter needed? Is the chapter's content not redundant with what has been said throughout this book? These are important questions. Let us suggest first that the interpretation of the status of research in career education, career guidance, and career counseling was that "in its broadest sense" and in the aggregate the results are quite positive. Such a statement does not mean that every important question has been answered or that every study has yielded unequivocal results. Certainly the quality and the comprehensiveness of both the speculation and the research about career behavior and interventions in it are uneven and less than comprehensive. Such unevenness and deficits in coverage arise from the scope of the field and the enormity of the issues and questions across population characteristics (such as age, gender, minority group, ethnicity, religion), settings (such as schools, work sites, community agencies), historical or developmental time (such as cohort effects, social and economic conditions), or intervention form (such as individual counseling, group counseling, classes, self-directed instruction, computer-directed processes). The vastness of the field of inquiry about career behavior and the interventions in it also derive from the multiple disciplinary lenses that can be applied to the understanding of such phenomena.

Because the terms *career counseling, career education, career guidance,* and *career intervention* are each used to describe a large inventory of processes and techniques applied to career behavior, it is logical to suggest that relevant research and theory can be found in many academic disciplines and at many levels of quality and sophistication. This same observation can be made about any realm of human behavior, but it nevertheless suggests the difficulty of being encyclopedic in analyzing the research base of the field as fully as some readers would desire.

As generally positive findings about the effects of career guidance, counseling, or education on career behavior have accumulated, the research questions have become more conscious of both the structure of career behavior and its change over time. Because the content of career counseling (for example, type of work activities, environments and options, barriers or obstacles to freedom of opportunity, achievement images, systems of job information) is so dynamic and so intimately tied to changes in the occupational, political, social, and economic contexts of the nation, one could hardly expect that research on these matters would be static and totally encompassing. Individual behavior is a function of transactions with environmental expectations and opportunities intertwined with information about alternatives, perceptions of self-efficacy with regard to options available, preferences, personal values, abilities, and skills. As any of these ingredients changes, so does the system within which individual behavior is triggered. In a sense, theory and research are virtually always running to catch up with such circumstances.

Much of the theory and research on career development to the present has assumed that individual action has been the predominant factor in how careers are forged and where intervention in such career behavior should be aimed. This is, of course, a view in which the lens is primarily psychological. As we discussed in Chapter 4, however, this view tends to underestimate the degree to which environments create and reinforce work roles and career opportunities; the degree to which persons are chosen rather than do the choosing. The latter views are predominantly sociological, anthropological, organizational, and economic. The influence of such perspectives on how individual career behavior is stimulated and shaped has not yet been as fully integrated into the conceptual and empirical bases of career guidance or career counseling as is likely to emerge during the next decades (Bartol, 1981; Slaney & Russell, 1987).

The state of the conceptual and empirical bases of career guidance and career counseling is fundamental to the quality of services that practitioners offer in any setting. But these are not the only important issues to be raised. Also of concern are questions of social effects. As we have suggested, career guidance or career counseling does not occur in a political or social vacuum. Its content is largely derived from events in the larger society. Indeed, the types of questions that youths and adults bring to counselors are related to how they view current societal belief systems about personal choice, achievement, social interaction, self-initiative, marriage, prestige, occupational or educational status, role integration, and many other aspects of life. The resulting anxieties, deficits, or indecisiveness that persons experience as they compare themselves with what society's representatives (such as parents, employers, teachers, peers, spouses, the mass media) say they should believe or do constitutes much of the content with which counselors deal. Societal filters also permit or discourage persons asking certain questions about themselves or their opportunities. Different societies, deliberately or inadvertently, support the use of some guidance and counseling techniques as ethical or appropriate and restrict or prohibit the use of other forms of intervention. In either case, as discussed in Chapter 1, career guidance and counseling in all societies tend to be sociopolitical processes.

From such a perspective, the question of social effects can be succinctly stated in this way: Because one can change behavior in certain ways, should one do so? If so, to what ends? The answers to such questions are not necessarily empirical; they are more likely to be philosophical and value oriented.

Although we hope that we have made a case for career education, guidance, and counseling in the preceding chapters, we continue to acknowledge that many relevant research questions and social issues still need to be explored. Some are matters of substance; others, of methodology; still others, of philosophy. In this chapter, we briefly discuss some of the current views on these matters, identify some methodological issues, and inventory some research needs.

PERSPECTIVES ON CAREER DEVELOPMENT RESEARCH

Gelso (1979) has suggested that counseling has experienced a polarization of views on what constitutes an acceptable methodology and would continue to do so. He further suggests that it may well be the most prominent trend in the field and a healthy state of affairs "if it represents an expansion of what the field views as permissible bases for evidence, and if the strengths and limitations of each investigative style are recognized" (p. 9).

This chapter is not intended to be a research primer, but the maturing of theory development pertinent to career behavior and the understanding of the effects of career interventions of "treatments" are likely to require all the research tools now available; for example, descriptive, correlational, case study, naturalistic, single subject, multivariate, factorial, subjective and qualitative, experimental, cross-sectional, longitudinal, ethnographic, and a combination of these. It is unlikely that single studies, however large in scale, can answer all of the important research questions that lie before us. Rather, we are likely to continue to rely on the aggregate effects of several studies, each true to the assumptions and design precautions appropriate to the specific questions being studied. It is out of such multiple observations that theory is tested and refined and new theory developed.

It is often true that the research techniques available are significantly ahead of practice in the field or that there are more powerful ways to study certain questions than are used. The study of "treatment effects" is one example. Gelso (1979) appropriately notes the effects of Kiesler's work (1971) in using factorial designs to study both main effects of treatment and organismic or individual differences variables. In such designs, one can study two or more treatments in comparison to the outcomes associated with control groups as well as the effects of such treatments on different client populations defined by age, gender, experience, and so on, across time and as provided by counselors of different types. The study of interaction inherent in such factorial designs permits one to test several hypotheses simultaneously as one studies treatment effects against differences in client populations, counselor style, outcome measures, repeated observations, or other pertinent criteria. Factorial approaches typically involve analysis of variance or covariance or multivariate analysis of variance as the statistic of choice in addition to a post hoc significance test, although correlation or regression analysis is frequently the appropriate statistical approach.

As important as factorial designs are for comparative and experimental studies of *treatment effects* on different types of presenting problems, they are less useful for predicting patterns of longitudinal career development. For such purposes, it is more likely that some type of regression analysis (e.g., including path analysis or LISREL) or discriminant function procedure will be used.

In addition to the questions of whether one should use factorial designs, regression analyses, discriminant function, or other procedures, the past decade has seen increasing concern about the meaning of statistical significance versus practical significance of results, the effects of sample sizes on statistical/practical significance and on statistical power, the need to report the effect sizes (e.g., R2, eta2, omega2) that evaluate the proportion of variance explained in the analysis or that describe the magnitude of results that are independent of sample size and scale of measurement, and the need for the empirical replication or cross-validation of results. Recommendations about these matters are intended to increase the precision of what we know in counseling, in psychology, and in career development. Therefore, although specific treatments of these topics are beyond the scope of this chapter, they represent important issues in research design, in the interpretation of statistical significance, and in the accumulation of knowledge about career behaviors and interventions in it. Although many references could be cited that are relevant to such discussions, the following are particularly useful (Cohen, 1990; Heppner, Kivlighan, & Wampold, 1992; Thompson, 1993).

Search for Acceptable Methodology

The Issue of Careers. In 1969 (Super 1969a; 1969b), Super discussed the state of methodology bearing on career issues. He began with the premise that vocational psychology from the beginning of this century until shortly after 1950 was a *psychology of occupations.* Since that period, we have also seen the emergence of a *psychology of careers.* Methodological models in a psychology of occupations typically focus on the occupations as the subject and the persons in the occupations as the source of data about the occupation. According to Super (1969a), this model takes predictor data at an early stage of a career and uses regression methods to predict later success in one occupation or it uses discriminant analysis as a means of assessing the likelihood of being found—later—in each of several possible occupations. But such approaches tend to represent differential psychology, the study of individual differences, in a somewhat static sense. The psychology of careers requires more than differential diagnosis. It is more directly focused on the elements that underlie what Crites (1981) has called *dynamic diagnosis,* the concern with the cause of career behavior, not just its classification.

Spokane (1990) has addressed the issues defined earlier by Super's analysis of the research implications of a psychology of occupations versus a psychology of careers. Spokane suggests that "most research in vocational psychology can be described by reference to two fundamental methodological viewpoints that have clearly stated assumptions and a large evidential and historical base underpinning their tenets.... These paradigms are: (a) differential vocational psychology, and (b) developmental vocational psychology" (p. 25). Spokane then emphasizes in his discussion the characteristics of the differential tradition.

He contends that two methodological thrusts undergird the differential approach: actuarial and experimental. The actuarial approach contains studies "that involve the construction and validation of various interest, ability, style, and, occasionally, personality measures related to choosing and adjusting to work for normal individuals.... These actuarial emphases also include studies that employ ANOVA, ANOCOVA, MANCOVA, factor analysis, multidimensional scaling analysis, or other multivariate techniques in an effort to test a theory, where control over the independent variable rather than the construction of a new instrument is the principal focus of the study" (p. 25). The experimental thrust, according to Spokane, tests "the effects of a variety of career interventions and treatments ranging from a single 20-minute session of reinforcement for exploratory behavior to semester-long-evaluations of the effectiveness of curricular/class interventions" (p. 25). Although the purposes of his discussion were not to focus on the characteristics of the developmental approach, he does contrast the two approaches as follows: "I would include under the *differential* rubric any studies evaluating interventions that were based on inventories or tests whose purpose was to distinguish one group of respondents from another, just as I would include under the *developmental* rubric any studies evaluating the effects of a career intervention that was based on developmental assumptions" (p. 34).

Careers are by definition developmental. Indeed, career development is itself a rubric for the complex interactions between the affective, cognitive, and psychomotor characteristics of persons potentially mediated by their values, family history, school climate, community reward system, and many other possible variables that may or may not be affected by time. In a career model, we are interested in predicting the sequence of positions that a person will occupy in pursuing a career (Super, 1969a). To achieve this understanding of careers, however, we need to understand not only the positions people occupy during their working life, but also the interrelationship of factors that caused them to anticipate, plan, and implement one position rather than another at any given point in their life as well as the threads that link one choice to another or one position to the subsequent one. Our progress toward such goals has depended on the availability of statistical methods capable of handling the myriad of factors feeding into career development and on hardware (primarily computers) that allow a researcher to cope with sophisticated analyses of an enormous number of data points. Hardware problems are rapidly disappearing, but questions of statistical methodology continue to be formidable obstacles as we move forward with time series data.

Time series data, similar to any other research matter, must rest on a clear conceptualization of what one is attempting to study and of measurement strategies and instruments that capture the essence of the variables (constructs) of interest. Thus, because time series studies are frequently employed to study career development, it is first necessary to determine what is meant by development. The term *development* is not a singular term. It is a theoretical construct that has been defined in different ways by different theorists who have applied different sets of assumptions to the explanation of behavioral change: for example, mechanistic, organismic, developmental contextualism (Lerner, 1986).

Schulenberg (1986) has contended that most of the existing research on the changes over time (or the differences across groups) in work values and career interests has focused at the quantitative level—changes in the magnitude or frequency of a construct—rather than the qualitative level—change in the underlying meaning of a construct. Thus, if the meaning of a construct to males or females or different racial groups actually changes over time (comes to be seen as carrying a different definition or content), the utility of making purely quantitative comparisons becomes questionable. One proposed response to such quantitative/qualitative issues in time series data is the increased use of factor-analytic techniques to probe underlying meanings of constructs and their variance or invariance over time (Nesselroade & Baltes, 1984). As Schulenberg suggests, "for a developmentally meaningful construct, structural continuity across time or groups can be operationalized as the invariance of the factor loading patterns (i.e., factor invariances) while increased differentiations across time or groups can be represented by an increased number of factors and/or a decrease in the magnitude of the correlations among factors" (p. 20). Although not the only method of conceiving time series data, the work of Schulenberg, Nesselroade, and Baltes, and, more recently, of Vondracek, Lerner, and Schulenberg (1986) have introduced many of the research techniques traditionally used in developmental psychology to vocational psychology.

Without getting into the extended discussion warranted by their proposed methodological agenda for the study of vocational behavior and career development, it is useful to acknowledge that Vondracek, Lerner, and Schulenberg (1986) and Vondracek (1990) have outlined the essential elements of developmental or time series studies of careers. In so doing, they have examined three interacting components of such designs: developmental, relational, and contextual. They have advanced important notions in the study of careers that advocate the use in longitudinal designs of several birth cohorts to look at the interaction of individual lives and historical times and sequential designs to identify cohort effects, change-sensitive measures, multivariate measures, and multilevel research (psychological, biological, sociological, cultural, and historical).

Obviously, not all elements of career development require the same levels of sophistication or the same purpose as do time series questions. It is often necessary, for example, to conduct survey research by which the variables deserving systematic study in career development can be identified. Some questions that fall within this category are "What career behaviors develop as the individual matures? Are there group differences in the development of career behavior? What are the career behaviors essential to success in different work settings?"

Theoretical Research. Theoretical research has represented a stimulus to and an outcome of the survey and technique research cited. In the theoretical arena, hypothesis testing has attempted to evaluate the gross assumptions that career development is continuous and longitudinal, that it can be described as being composed of different developmental tasks at different life periods, that career development and personal development more broadly conceived are related, and that career development can be modified by certain forms of intervention or that specific variables are associated with the character of career development at some point in time. Much of this research is concerned with understanding the structure of career behavior as well as how it changes over time. Applied research, too, has been moving forward in testing various attempts to facilitate career development through the formal processes of schooling or other educative methods.

Chapter 4 and other chapters in this book have focused on research addressing the theoretical assumptions provided by the major researchers in the field (e.g., Betz, Gottfredson, Hackett, Holland, Krumboltz, Savickas, Spokane, Super, and others). Other important books and special journal issues have extended such analyses. For example, a special issue of the *Career Development Quarterly* (vol. 43, no. 1, September 1994) was devoted to the theoretical contributions of Donald E. Super (who passed away in June 1994). This journal issue addressed the research findings available and needed that bear on selected major constructs on career development as provided by Super: for example, work values, self-concept theory, readiness for career choices, career maturity and career adaptability, role salience and multiple roles, careers in cultural context, the thematic-extrapolation method in the prediction of career patterns, and instrumentation useful in measuring career development.

Other major treatments of the status of theoretical research across the range of career development include as examples:

Brown, D., Brooks, L., et al. (2002). *Career choice and development, Applying contemporary theories to practice* (5th ed.). San Francisco: Jossey-Bass Publishers.

Savickas, M. L., & Lent, R. W. (Eds.) (1994). *Convergence in career development theories. Implications for science and practice.* Palo Alto, CA: CPP Books.

Statistical Methods. To reiterate to some degree what has already been said about methodology, the statistical methods used in examining the major research questions in career theory have included the following:

1. *Discriminant analysis* is a way of examining predictive validity in regard to group membership particularly where the criterion variables are nominal or ordinal, rather than continuously measured traits, or where the predictor variables are multidimensional as found in personality profiles. This approach has been important to our understanding of the personality variables by which career or curriculum groups are separated in measurement space—how individuals with particular traits resemble groups of persons engaging in an occupation or curriculum, for example.

2. *Analysis of variance* (factorial approaches), although important as a part of discriminant analysis strategy and frequently the statistic of choice for testing the null hypothesis, has often been used as a descriptive or classification method rather than in an experimental form. As such it has helped in the identification of shifts in means or variance on some dependent variable over time but has not advanced our understanding of the dynamics underlying such shifts as much as we would hope.

3. *Correlational or regression analysis* has also been widely used to determine the predictive power of certain individual traits or trait sets to different classes of career-related criterion variables—academic decisions, vocational aspirations, and vocational adjustment. Indeed, the various correlational modes, parametric and nonparametric, have been highly valuable, particularly in identifying associations between variables requiring further study. Certainly, multiple regression and partial correlation have been exceedingly valuable in our understanding of the ranking or weights of predictive variables in relation to each other. In some instances, canonical correlations have been helpful in analyzing the stability of the dispersion of scores over time (Gribbons & Lohnes, 1969, p. 32), determining the full extent of the interrelatedness of two sets of scores, and indexing the amount of common variance shared by the functions of two sets of measurement.

Essentially the approaches that have just been identified are linear and represent an independent-variable predicting dependent-variable paradigm in which "the criterion variable is 'explained' by the pattern of its statistical dependency on a set of predictors.... Generally, the effort is to account for as much of the variance in the criterion as possible from the predictors' variance-covariance" (Gribbons & Lohnes, 1969, p. 185; 1982). Gribbons and Lohnes have attempted to move outside this perspective by using a stochastic model, in particular a Markov chain analysis, to examine the outcomes of a discrete measurement variable. Markov chains are probability models that can tell us how much of the variance in developmental outcomes can be explained by a theoretical model of the process itself without recourse to functional or statistical relations with outside variables (p. 186). Essentially the model observes the paths taken by the subjects through the states of the variable over temporally separated stages to see if there is a probability law inherent in the "process" (the tree structure) of possible paths through the states over the stages.

Treating Career Data. Path analysis, causal modeling, and structural equation modeling are among the best methods we now know to handle longitudinal data, not simply cross-sectional data at different points in time. More important, perhaps, is the fact that most of the statistical techniques we have used deal with direct effects, *Y* on *X*, rather than indirect effects among variables. Path analysis, however, facilitates the examination of the cumulative indirect effects of a variable on some other variable.

Causal modeling techniques (structural equation modeling and covariance structure analysis) incorporate the functions of path analysis and increase the power to study alternative models of structural equations hypothesized to represent certain relationships occurring over a period of time (Bentler, 1980). It is also possible to examine the effects of several measured variables on one latent variable (unobserved) and therefore to increase the number of hypotheses that can be considered in relationship to how underlying structures affect career outcomes across time, whether the question concerns the direct and indirect effects of latent variables on each other or the composition of latent variables themselves.

In addition to analysis of causal patterns among unobserved variables by multiple measures, "It permits testing of causal hypotheses and theory, examination of psychometric adequacy, and enhancement of the explanatory power of correlational data that characterize counseling psychology research" (Fassinger, 1987, p. 425).

Before leaving the treatment of career data, it is important to note other approaches that are relevant to but underused in examining the unfolding of career behavior. The first is P-technique factor analysis, which is a special case of single-subject research involving intense, repeated measurement of an individual (Nesselroade & Ford, 1985, 1987). Such a technique allows one to study in depth the consistency or the variability of individual interests, values, preferences, or other characteristics to test whether such characteristics are truly stable (as frequently projected after midadolescence) or whether they are labile and dynamic. The second is ethnographic methodology (Wehrly & Watson-Gegeo, 1985) as applied to cross-cultural approaches to career development or cross-cultural career counseling. A qualitative rather than quantitative approach, ethnography studies naturalistic interaction and behavior, ways of living, expectations for behavior, specific cultural patterns, and rules for interpreting shared meaning among members of particular groups. Such an approach applied to the career development of various minority groups would likely bridge the understandings of career behavior from quantitative findings reported for majority groups to the subjective differences in meaning systems of culturally different groups as related to work salience, orientation to time, information processing, and other cognitive or affective elements of significance to career behavior.

Methodologies useful to increasingly sophisticated study of career-related human behavior and the effects of interventions on this process are emerging rapidly. Even so, however, the complexity of the phenomena about which career guidance practitioners are concerned is vast enough to accommodate a wide range of research designs and statistical tools. In any case, there will continue to be an overarching need for what Goldman (1979) has called "disciplined creative search"; "ideas and theories which come from the imagination and vision of people who look at and listen to career development issues and behaviors, counseling, career guidance, social trends with openness and an urge to understand and conceptualize" (p. 44). Such creativity and vision yield the theory, ideas, and hypotheses that then lead to the methodological issues cited here as they relate to the testing of such ideas.

Qualitative Approaches to the Treatment of Career Data

One of the methodological issues that became prominent in the 1990s was the use of qualitative or alternative approaches in the study of career behavior. Most of the research techniques described thus far in this chapter, with the exception of ethnographic methodology discussed in the previous section, derive from a positivist, quantitative, empirical tradition. Growing concerns, however, that such linear, quantitative, and hypothetico-deductive approaches are failing to capture adequately the richness and complexity of the interaction of individual and contextual factors; human action, consciousness, and agency; and the multiprobabilistic dynamics of career development has led to an emerging attention to qualitative approaches (for example, Polkinghorne, 1984; Manicas & Secord, 1983). As Young and Borgen (1990) suggest, "The argument in favor of alternative (qualitative) methodologies does not negate the contribution that can be made to knowledge through the use of the hypothetico-deductive method" (p. xiv). Instead, it seems fair to contend that quantitative/qualitative, deductive/inductive, and traditional/alternative approaches are different ways of knowing, that is, different ways of capturing and classifying human experience in the realm of careers.

The perspectives of Young and Borgen (that, in methodological terms, there are different ways of knowing) are consistent with the view that there are also different questions emerging about career development and how it can best be studied. Savickas (1989a) has indicated:

> *[W]ithin the last five years career theorists and counselors have begun to explore how a new paradigm in developmental psychology, constructive-developmentalism,*

> *may inform their work.... The constructive-developmentalism perspective (Kegan, 1982) integrates constructivism (people constitute or construct reality) and developmentalism (people evolve through predictable eras) to conclude that what develops during the life cycle is the activity of meaning-making or making sense of self and situation. Products of this new perspective appeared in...publications on career theory and practice written by counselors who used constructs from hermeneutics (the practice of interpreting texts or narratives), family systems, or life-narrative psychology to look (beyond matching the content of self-concepts to occupations) to the processes of self-conceiving and meaning making. Although these authors used different constructs, they all seemed to (a) view people as self-organizing systems, (b) believe that behavior is purposive, (c) attend to meaning and how people construct it, and (d) emphasize that people use their experiences to reconstruct meaning and move toward more completeness.... To date, most publications on meaning-making in career development and counseling have not been based on quantitative research. (p. 102)*

In essence, such approaches have given renewed attention to qualitative or alternate methodologies.

There is a range of approaches that could be classified as qualitative or alternative approaches to the study of careers. For example, Bujold (1990) has described a biographical-hermeneutical approach based on a phenomenological perspective; Cochran (1990) uses narrative forms as one of his major paradigms for career research; Polkinghorne (1990) and Valach (1990) use action theory, a narrative attempt to describe the human capacity to choose freely from among alternatives in the context of other life choices and events. These approaches variously use autobiography, biography, life histories, psychobiography, life narratives, story or drama, ecological approaches, case studies, phenomenological approaches, self-confrontational interviews, and action analyses as career research methods.

Cochran (1990) in discussing the use of narratives in career research states:

> *[R]esearch on career development is not of the same order as research on intellectual or physical development. The topic of career is not so much concerned with parts as with how parts are related and brought to a point in living.... In contrast to the spatial emphasis of physical science, narrative emphasizes time as lived. Lived time relates to a human consciousness. (p. 71)*
>
> *In pursuing a career, we live meanings, and lived meanings make a career narratable, intelligible, and coherent. (p. 78)*
>
> *Case study is probably the preferred approach to narrative construction largely because as investigator can gather divergent sources of evidence and rich, compelling detail to support convergence into a narrative description. (p. 79)*
>
> *The great advantage of narrative research is that it offers the possibility of a greatly expanded scope for questions that are of direct significance to practice.... Having investigated many lives, one can investigate the plot of lives that are pervaded with meaning and those that are bereft of it.... One can examine common values, differences in decision making, the role of story telling to oneself, and so on. (p. 83)*
>
> *Hermeneutics, thick description, structural analysis, phenomenological reflection, and the like are powerful ways to enhance interpretation and they are certainly much more rigorous than the kind of interpretation found in most quantitative studies. (p. 82)*

Indications that qualitative research designs are emerging rapidly in rigor and in acceptance as important ways of knowing take several forms. One example is the publication in the October 1994 issue of the *Journal of Counseling Psychology* of a special section on qualitative research in counseling process and outcome. Although none of the studies reported deal directly with career issues, the processes used and the theoretical designs (e.g., grounded theory) are certainly applicable to the study of careers as ways of observing and capturing the richness and diversity of the lived experiences of individuals in choosing and acting out roles in difficult jobs and in different types of work environments. Analyses of the utility and implementation of qualitative designs are also appearing in and being endorsed by major books on research methods in counseling. For example, in discussing such qualitative designs as naturalistic-ethnographic and phenomenological research, Heppner, Kivligian, and Wampold (1992) discuss the use of grounded theory in qualitative research in the following terms: "The purpose of grounded theory is to systematically observe a phenomenon as a way of generating theory. This is opposed to theory verification, which is the goal of most quantitative research approaches" (p. 198). They go on to describe the five major steps in the conduct of a grounded theory investigation: (1) data collection, (2) categorization, (3) memory,

(4) movement toward parsimony, and (5) writing the theory.

Obviously the advocates for qualitative career research approaches have strong convictions about the importance of such approaches as methods to unearth how people interpret and make meaning from their career patterns. They believe that these approaches provide ways of knowing about career processes within individuals and across groups of individuals in ways that are not possible using traditional hypothetico-deductive designs. In addition, qualitative methods also add new vocabulary and affinities for theories of behavior that have not traditionally been used to examine career behavior. One of these theories, constructivist theory, will be discussed in the next section. Among the questions that researchers will need to address in the future are the following: Are qualitative career research methods most effectively used preceding traditional quantitative, empirical designs as a basis to identify and classify possible hypotheses to be tested? What are the most effective models by which to integrate traditional and alternate, quantitative and qualitative methodologies? Are qualitative approaches preferred methodologies for selected career questions?

Character of Career Development Theory

However important methodological issues are to understanding the state-of-the-art of research in career counseling and career guidance, they are not the only matters of concern. The character of career development theory itself is important.

Theoretical Base. Chapters 4 and 6, in particular, have described the conceptual streams of thought that make up the current theoretical base in career development. Much of this material is still speculative—however perceptive and logical—and untested. There are also other characteristics worthy of note.

Much career development theory has evolved from descriptive research with samples restricted in size and in composition. As a result, many relationships and hypotheses about career behavior, the influences on them, or the effect of attempts to intervene in them remain to be tested. Indeed, interpretations of existing findings are often made without the benefit of validation or replication across samples that diverge in characteristics from those on whom the original findings were obtained.

In addition to any other criticisms of samples from which career development theory or research has come (e.g., white, middle-class, males), many sample subjects have been students. In longitudinal samples, it makes sense to begin studying career development when individuals are in the early years of schooling and then watch their progression into and through adulthood. Secondary school and university student samples, however, have been the rule not only for longitudinal studies, but also for cross-sectional studies. Because most investigations of career development are conducted by persons in colleges and other educational settings, student samples are convenient, but they do not offer insight into the whole of career development, particularly its characteristics in childhood, adulthood, and in persons with minimal educational experience.

In the few longitudinal studies now being conducted, the original student samples are maturing and proceeding through adulthood, but little has been published about them other than in terms of adolescent exploration and the early stages of young adulthood. As a result, we know less about the predictive validity of various patterns of early career development in relationship to the linearity of career development, midcareer change, or occupational dislocation than we need if we are to make career interventions more effective for persons beyond adolescence (Niles & Herr, 1989). For example, we know comparatively little about the developmental progression of persons into retirement, although there is a growing demand for career guidance at this life stage. Thus, questions of when such career guidance should begin, what its emphases should be—use of leisure, volunteer possibilities, part-time work, economic planning—remain vague. Much the same could be said about the comprehensiveness of knowledge available about second careerists, midcareer dislocated, and other segments of the adult population, although recent findings about the relationships among unemployment, mental health, and stress-related diseases are yielding effective conceptual output.

Each of these observations is well known to researchers and theorists, and attempts to modify these voids, move away from restrictive samples, and improve the quality of theory and research in career development are proceeding apace. Indeed, there are many attempts now underway to create new approaches to theory, to consider the constructs on which existing theories converge, to develop ways by which existing theories can be extended, and to consider the changing conditions (e.g., the global economy, the global work force, contingency work force) that are challenging theorists to incorporate in their theories of work and behavior. Some examples of these trends in career development follow.

Constructivist Theory. It seems apparent, although no analysis of the issue has been made, that the rise of qualitative research methodologies as discussed earlier is linked loosely or firmly to a subtle but growing incorporation of constructivist thinking in counseling and in career theory. There is not one definition of constructivism, but the general thrust of such thinking is that human beings actively make meaning through their actions; they create their realities in the decisions that they make or avoid. Human beings then are not simply passive recipients of information, nor simply persons who share or receive one true reality. Rather, people are active organizers of their own experience-worlds. They are creators of a self or of personal constructs through organized patterns of meaning within a world of multiple realities. "Language in its function as communication, especially metaphor, narrative, and conversation is the means which humans use to construct realities and is central to the constructivist perspectives. It is because we all live out narratives in our lives and because we understand our own lives in terms of the narratives that we live out that the form of the narrative is appropriate for understanding the actions of others" (Peavy, 1994, p. 32). Peavy, a psychologist in Canada, has suggested that implications of the constructivist perspective for career counseling include:

1. *Reducing the conceptual gap between career and life.... Each person lives a life within which there are careers, within which there are jobs, and throughout all of which weaves the meaning of work (Ginzberg, 1972, 1984).... Career theory and counseling should recognize that "life career histories" are constructed by the individual out of an ongoing dialectic of circumstances and personal desires and abilities....*
2. *Placing meaning at the center of our conceptual space—meaning and personal constructs drive behavior (or "action," as we prefer to say), meaning-making and construing replace, at least in part, emphasis on information processing and behavior change....*
3. *Accentuating the role of "agency" for both clients and counselors....*
4. *Construing persons as self-organizing authors of their own lives—always within specific historical and cultural contexts....*
5. *Taking the epistemological stance that human realities, both personal and social, are "negotiated"—that is, constructed and reconstructed. From our perspective, counseling and inquiry are both processes of reconstruction and closely resemble each other. The "counselor" is also a "researcher" inquiring into the meaning structures of the other's life world.*
6. *Stressing two human universals...reflexivity (critical self-reflection)...and, the human ability to envision alternatives, that is, the ability to construe "other ways of being, of acting, of striving."*
7. *Overcoming reductionist concepts and practices in career counseling and the training of career counselors. For example, try to deemphasize the "matching" of client traits with job requirements; resist temptations to reduce the person of the client into "variables" through psychosometric procedures; refuse to involve images of "information-processing" and "machine/computer" as useful models in career theory and counseling and guard against procedures which train counselors to identify a client with that client's "file," thereby reducing chances for dialogue with the real client. (pp. 33–34)*

Clearly the notions advanced by Peavy are wide and different from an objectivist view that pervades much of U.S. career development theory and practice. Such a constructivist view raises questions about the validity of providing information to a counselee rather than stimulating the person's search for that which is relevant, the use of tests as representatives of an external reality by which an individual can be judged or understood, the client as a passive, impotent receiver of counseling rather than an active organizer of meaning. Beyond these challenges, there are also multiple research questions about the unique lived experiences of counselors in career counseling and in the construction of a career. Many of these research questions are yet to be formulated, but they are beginning to emerge as a separate theoretical stream of career behavior.

Convergence in Career Theory. Concerns about the fragmentation of current theories in psychology and, more specifically, in career development surface periodically. Indeed, several prominent career theorists have suggested that it is now necessary to assess the degree to which the major career theories have come to resemble each other and identify to what degree they have constructs that overlap. Osipow (1990) cited trait and factor, social learning, developmental, and work adjustment theories as being the most influential in shaping concepts of career choice and development and suggested that significant convergence had occurred in the central constructs of these theories. Super (1992), too, suggested the utility of viewing existing theories in the perspective of each others' constructs and complementarity. Hackett, Lent, and Greenhaus (1991) contended that there was a need to explore possibilities for theoretical integration in ways that would: "(a) bring together conceptually related constructs (e.g., self-concept, self-efficacy); (b) more fully explain outcomes that are common to a number of career theories (e.g., satisfaction, stability); (c) account for the relations among seemingly diverse constructs (e.g., interests, needs, ability, self-efficacy); and (d) identify the major variables crucial to an overarching theory of career development" (p. 28).

In 1993, Savickas and Lent initiated a conference to examine the possibilities of convergence across extant theories and subsequently published a book that described the outcomes achieved by the researchers and theorists involved in the convergence project (Savickas & Lent, 1994). Although there is much in the book for which space here does not permit analysis, several points seemed to be dominant. In general, participants tended not to believe that it was now possible to have fully converging theories. Rather the emphasis seemed to be on theory renovation and expansion. Within this context, Savickas (1994) suggested that "the ideas for refurbishing theories fall into two groups, namely issues that we have neglected and principles that we have forgotten" (p. 236).

It is useful to acknowledge that although much of the attention devoted to the current status of career development theory deals with ways to renovate and expand the constructs included within current theories, rather than trying to create one omnibus theory that incorporates the convergence of existing theories, there are also ongoing efforts to facilitate the identification of constructs that bridge theories and can serve as foci to unify rather than proliferate theories. One excellent example of such an initiative is that of Lent, Brown, and Hackett (1994) to create a unifying social cognitive theory of career and academic interest, choice, and performance. In doing so, they have integrated into their model constructs that often have been treated independently in the professional literature rather than as interactive. Included as foci of concern in their model are self-efficacy appraisals, outcome expectations, goals as symbolic representations of desired future outcomes, and self-evaluations based on internal standards for performance. These constructs and others are fashioned into models of three interlocking aspects of career development, including the formation and elaboration of career-relevant interests, selection of academic and career choice options, and performance and persistence in educational and occupational pursuits. In formulating these models and the constructs that are vital to their functioning, Lent, Brown, and Hackett have advanced twelve propositions that suggest the relationships among sociocognitive mechanisms, learning, values and aptitudes, race and ethnicity, sex and gender, and contextual influences. This type of theoretical construction holds the promise of providing a more comprehensive and cohesive understanding of that which is already known about the development of career behavior, choice, and work adjustment.

Changing Conditions of Work. As criticisms, inventories of neglected aspects, and expansions of current theories unfold, there continue to arise in the social, economic, and political dynamics of local, national, and international economies and occupational structures, new realities that confront career theory and practice. Many of these have been identified earlier in this book, but by way of inventorying existing trends likely to affect the modification of existing theory as well as the visions and processes by which career counselors reconstruct their roles vis-à-vis clients, Herr (1994a) has suggested the following:

- The globalization of the work force, its increased cross-national mobility, the problems of insufficient information, and loss of cultural identity as issues for counselors who will require enlarged paradigms and boundaries of the meaning and practice of career counseling to encompass such issues.
- A growing global labor surplus in response to which counselors have to change their orientations with many clients from the choice of jobs, or education, or career patterns to the choice of activities,

volunteer or otherwise, for those persons who may never be employed or reemployed.

• Organizational transformations in the workplace that are creating new models of personnel development, not just personnel management; eliminating much of middle-management and many white collar jobs; downsizing work forces to hold down permanent overhead costs and to incorporate newer forms of advanced technology to increase overall productivity-cost ratios. Such conditions are stimulating increased attention to human resource development, including incorporation of the skills of counseling psychologists who have expertise in vocational psychology and career counseling, while also changing the nature of career ladders, work cultures, and worker-management interaction.

• The rise of a contingent work force in the United States and around the world: temporary employees whose special skills are purchased for limited periods of time but who do not have long-term institutional identification as part of their career. This circumstance and those mentioned previously may herald the need for a new theory of work and its role in human identity, not just refinements in career theory and practice. Indeed, as companies in which people have historically built careers are downsizing or disappearing and a clear career path of advancing positions from initial employment through to retirement is becoming less available or obscured, some observers have questioned whether the concept of career as it has been portrayed over the past 40 years has a future or is now so fractured that the term needs to be reconceived (Savickas, 1994).

• The rising importance of the knowledge worker and of literacy, numeracy, communication, and computer literacy skills as prerequisites for employability and lifelong learning in many emerging occupations and in the primary labor market. While intellectual and academic skills have always been implicit aspects of career theory, the rising expectations for workers to have the educational skills, problem-solving skills, and higher-order thinking skills inherent in work as a learning activity will, in the future, make such skills an explicit part of career theory.

• The growing awareness of the linkages between positive career experiences and mental health, self-esteem, purposefulness, physical well-being, the ability to support and maintain a family, the perception that one has life options and can practice an internal locus of control. Many of these connections have been reinforced as researchers have probed the psychology of unemployment and its emotional, physiological, and behavioral results and the implications these hold for new paradigms that integrate personal and career counseling—that treat unemployment (and underemployment as well) not simply as an individual economic problem but as a major mental health issue deserving of comprehensive programs of service, including counseling.

• The appearance of new government policy and legislation addressing the problems of work-bound youth, those who also have been identified as the Forgotten Half, the non–college bound, the alienated, the disconnected, the at-risk, depending on which subset of this large population one addresses. In essence, these analyses have suggested that for perhaps 50 percent of adolescents, there are no transition services available between the time one leaves high school and one enters and successfully adjusts to employment. These young people are figuratively cut adrift psychologically as they try to convert their aspirations into actualities, however clear or vague they may be. It is likely that in the twenty-first century there will be major attention given to the interaction between the career-relevant processes of schooling, of transition, and of induction into work and the models of counseling necessary as the uniqueness and the connection between each of these three stages are further studied and their needs for differential treatment approaches made clearer.

• The implications for career theory and practice that comes from the demographic trends related to new entrants to the workforce between now and 2005 or beyond: primarily women, persons of color, and immigrants. The development of career counseling models for such persons related to their entrance, adjustment to, and mobility in work will stimulate far more attention to the impact of cultural diversity on career behavior and on multicultural interventions in that behavior.

The trends identified here are examples of how work opportunities, access requirements, and contexts are changing in the face of dramatic transformations of world wide economic and political systems. As such, they represent realities that career theories must incorporate and construct explanations by which to evaluate their impact on work and career behavior. They also represent the content for a research agenda designed to validate the theoretical constructions that evolve to guide understanding of amended forms of career development and the career interventions, individual and organizational, that are relevant.

In addition to the challenges to theorists and practitioners cited above, there are other challenges that will likely affect the conceptualization of emerging programs of career development speculation and research. One such challenge is found principally in life-span psychology.

Influence of Lifespan Psychology. Among other life-span psychologists, Vondracek and Lerner (1982); Vondracek, Lerner, and Schulenberg (1986); Vondracek (1990); and Vondracek and Fouad (1994) have been the most analytic in their view of the weaknesses of current views of career development as seen from the perspective of life-span psychology. They strongly suggest that many of the existing models of career development are personological and unidimensional rather than dynamic and interactional as would be useful. Citing the study of adolescents, in particular, they advocate the need for three key perspectives in the study of adolescent vocational role development: developmental, contextual, and relational. In a *developmental perspective,* "events prior to adolescence need to be considered as possible antecedents of vocational development; in turn, adolescent developments provide key antecedents of development in later life" (Vondracek & Lerner, 1982, p. 604). Longitudinal studies using Markov chains, path analysis, and causal modeling (mentioned in the previous section) would likely be of significant use in this area. A *contextual perspective* would emphasize the nature of the social (including political and economic), physical, and cultural milieu of adolescent vocational role development. "Thus the individual characteristics of the developing adolescent must be considered in relation to the particular features of the context within which the person is developing" (p. 604). A *relational perspective* would consider the goodness of fit between adolescent and contextual developments. It is further argued that although several important longitudinal studies of career development have been carried out (*The Career Pattern Study,* Super et al., 1957; *Project TALENT,* Flanagan, Shaycroft, Richards, & Claudy, 1971; the *Youth in Transition Study,* Bachman, Kahn, Mednick, Davidson, & Johnston, 1970; and the *Educational Development Study,* Herr et al., 1981), none of these has employed a historical (for example, sequential) design suitable for appraising age-cohort-related, and time-related variance. Vondracek (1990) and several of his graduate students are now engaged in a longitudinal study of adolescent career development that is intended to vary age, sex, and cohort membership to incorporate developmental-contextual perspectives and thereby rectify some of the shortcomings perceived by Vondracek and colleagues to be present in other longitudinal studies of vocational behavior.

As Vondracek and Lerner (1982) assert:

> *Although the current research literature on vocational development reflects a growing emphasis on a developmental perspective, there are still major shortcomings in the implementation of these orientations. These shortcomings involve problems or research design as well as problems of conceptualization—that is, a commitment to a life span developmental perspective cannot be best actualized in our view, through reliance on personological, organismic conceptions of vocational-role development. Instead, an appreciation of mutually adaptive interchanges between adolescents and their contexts must be attained. (p. 609)*

From such a perspective, Vondracek and Lerner (1982) then contend, "Traditional interventions in vocational development need to be broadened to incorporate interventions targeted to the individual, the family, the community, and its institutions, and family, social policy" (p. 612).

The challenge and observations posed by Vondracek and colleagues are certainly not confined to thinking about the career development of adolescents. Rather, such views are equally pertinent to understanding the career development of adults and particularly the effects of context and fit with context. To some degree this matter was discussed in Chapter 2 with regard to the meaning of work and person-job relationships. It was also dealt with in Chapter 4 as situational approaches to career development were described. The linking of career development theory, however, to the historical, political, and economic contexts that affect personological behavior and the effects of interventions on families and other institutions that reinforce or mediate individual behavior remain fertile fields for research designed to test, refine, and extend existing theories of career development.

Effects of Cultural Factors

As one might expect if the observations about a need for more attention to context are valid, less is known than is desirable about the effects of economic or cultural change on career behavior. Although most career development theorists have addressed the importance of situational variables to career development, they frequently have done so in abstract terms rather than researched the effects of such conditions on personal choice making and commitments. It is clear that the ethnicity, family history, home community, spirituality, and socioeconomic status of the person all affect career development. The questions are: How much, when, under what conditions, and for whom? We often continue to treat persons described by a group characteristic—racial, ethnic, religious, age, sex—as though they are part of a homogeneous group. We tend not to take into account the extent of variance that operates in any group and examine its implications for given individuals.

Cross-Cultural Information

The same point can be made about cultures beyond the boundaries of the United States. We know little about the socialization of career behavior in developing nations, or indeed, in many of the contemporary developed or postindustrial societies. In some instances this situation occurs because pertinent research has not been done in other societies in which we might be interested; in other cases the research is not developmentally focused; in still others, useful research findings exist but have not been assimilated into the American view of career development. For example, many excellent publications on career development, occupational classification systems, and career interventions have been developed by the Occupational and Career Analysis and Development Branch of the Canadian Employment and Immigration Commission in Ottawa. Similarly, excellent material is available from the Federal Employment Institute of West Germany, the National Institute for Careers Education and Counseling in Cambridge, England, and the National Institute for Vocational and Employment Research (now the Japan Institute for Labour Research) in Tokyo. Additional examples of guidance interventions or career development theory could be identified in other nations. The point is, however, that even when such material is available it is not typically known and used in the United States.

Obviously, one way of testing the effects of cultural and economic factors in career development is to study the fit of current American views of career development in societies with different economic characteristics, belief systems regarding work values, or political assumptions about individual choice and development. One major example of such an effort began in September 1976 to test the validity of Super's theoretical concepts with a British population. Based at the National Institute for Careers Education and Counseling in Cambridge, this research is a longitudinal effort to replicate many of the American findings from Super's research with samples of British youth and adults. One of the early outcomes of this project was *Career Development in Britain* (Watts, Super, & Kidd, 1981). Among its many useful aspects, the book addresses the current state of the art in careers theory in Britain and introduces to the American reader the powerful influence that sociological perspectives play in such careers theory. From such a frame of reference, American theories of career development are contrasted with those of the British, and several concepts new to most American readers (such as low autonomy—high autonomy) are provided as ways of analyzing career history. In addition to *Career Development in Britain,* the work at the National Institute of Careers Education and Counselling has become part of a 14-nation Work Importance Study initiated by Super (1984b).

There are issues being examined in Europe as well that have potential meaning for career development and career services in the United States. For example, under the sponsorship of the European Community, Watts in Great Britain and his colleagues in several European nations are studying the differences in the training, the processes, and the goals that describe persons engaged in vocational counseling in different European countries. Earlier comparative analyses by Watts, Dartois, and Plant (1988a) examined the comprehensiveness and focus of guidance services for adolescents and young adults, ages 14 to 25 in each of the nations making up the European Community. In addition, many international conferences have provided important insights into the effects of unemployment around the world and the types of career interventions that are possible and necessary (Herr, 1993) as well as international issues on human resource development and work force preparation for the twenty-first century (Herr, 1994b). These and other important cross-national studies provide insight into the political and economic contextual variables that shape the provision and purposes of career guidance and career counseling in specific nations and, indeed, internationally. More cross-cultural efforts to examine the effects of political, economic, and other social factors on career development need to become increasingly evident in the U.S. literature both to increase the understanding of such contextual factors and as a fertile arena for international cooperation.

Cross-cultural studies of career development are often seen as useful only in macro terms. The emphasis tends to be on comparisons among nations. At this level, frequent comparisons are made between the underdeveloped, developing, or developed nations, or between the nations of the Northern and the Southern Hemisphere or some other similar classification scheme. However useful such comparisons are across nations to study major cultural dimensions, it is also worth acknowledging the importance of such inquiry at a micro-national or subnational level (Herr, 1985a). Many nations, particularly the United States and increasingly the countries of Western Europe, are becoming pluralistic in the population groupings they contain. Therefore, within nations there are groups of persons who could be considered underdeveloped, developing, and developed. Undoubtedly the career development of each of these groups differs in ways that could be illuminated by applying paradigms similar to those useful in studies at national levels, and many of the cross-cultural constructs thought to be useful only to make national comparisons would also be helpful within multiethnic, multicultural populations.

Ultimately, as part of the analyses of the career development of different cultural groups, it will be necessary to identify those factors related to restricted socioeconomic status, barriers to jobs or selected occupations, and other variables that limit people's ability to cope with skill mastery, attitude development, or achievement motivation, and design experiences that can systematically overcome such deficits. To increase understanding of public policies influencing career development practices around the world, Heibert and Bezanson (2000) published papers from an international symposium sponsored by the Canadian Career Development Foundation. This edited volume provides an unique overview of how policy issues affect career practice in fourteen countries. Collectively, the papers provide a window through which policy makers, theorists, and practitioners can consider the degree to which our theories of career development are culture-bound or generally applicable and also whether our methods of intervening in career development are culture-bound; too focused on individual actions, and insufficiently attentive to interventions directed at families, communities, and social policy.

Changing Sex Roles. A related issue is that of changing sex roles. As a cultural phenomenon, the elimination of sex-role stereotyping—"masculine" versus "feminine" occupations—tends to be proceeding rapidly. Sundal-Hansen (1985) has suggested that a "new" psychology of men and women is emerging and that researchers are studying men's and women's lives in a more integrative manner. More research, however, needs to be directed to the career guidance processes most effective in facilitating this movement, when such interventions should occur, or how to most effectively help women or men reconsider their values in this area and consider nontraditional educational or occupational opportunities. That such work needs to and can be guided by theory has been well demonstrated by the recent work in self-efficacy and math anxiety as major constructs related to women's career development. Here again, it would be helpful to consider the experiences of other nations in dealing with such problems and how their career guidance responses might be adapted in the United States. Sundal-Hansen (1985) has suggested the following topics as relevant to sex-role issues across cultures:

1. Sex-role stereotyping and socialization
2. Individual goals versus family and societal goals
3. Literacy and education as options
4. Sexual division of labors
5. Men's changing role in family
6. Degree of commitment to equality
7. The rate of societal change (p. 215)

Importance of Economic Factors. Not only does career development research need to include greater attention to cultural factors and to sociological insights, it also needs greater attention to economic factors.

A greater attention to economic factors in career development will need to include increased research concern for the implications for career guidance or career counseling of different forms of employment or unemployment. These terms are frequently treated as though, for example, all unemployment were caused by the same factors and affects every person in the society equally. Depending on the definitions used, however, unemployment can be divided into at least four types: seasonal, frictional, cyclical, and structural. Each of these types of unemployment differs in its severity, its causes, and the groups most affected (Pierson, 1980). Determining which career guidance approaches are useful in reducing the severity or duration of these different forms of unemployment is an important research question that has rarely been asked. The question is likely to gain increased prominence in the next decade as the United States wrestles intensely with the wide-ranging effects of structural unemployment, the various transitions in job content and availability that accompany the widespread adoption of advanced technology in the workplace, the shifts from experience to knowledge as employability prerequisites, and the transformation from national economies and workforces to global economies and a global workforce.

A few of the research concerns related to structural unemployment and related occupational transformations might be the following:

1. Developing career information that identifies which occupations are likely to be most vulnerable to shifts in technology and which links the occupational possibilities in the emerging global economy and the regional transnational markets.

2. Assessing which worker skills are most elastic—able to be transferred across occupational boundaries with the least amount of retraining.

3. Creating models of choice that help persons understand the knowledge bases and skills inherent in new occupational configurations.

4. Examining changes in work organizations and their effects on dual-career families, length of work life, retirement, the availability of overtime or leisure time.

5. Investigating more fully the psychological and motivational implications of underemployment and the differential effects by gender.

6. Examining the effects on career identity and career motivation of persons for whom employment is primarily found in temporary or contingency workforces rather than stable, long-term employment.

7. Understanding more fully which persons function best under conditions of low or high autonomy in the workplace; identifying how differences in supervisory style or the psychological conditions of the workplace affect individual productivity.

8. Examining the direct relationships between education and work, training and retraining as work technologies rapidly change.

9. Studying how affective work competencies or industrial discipline change as a result of changes in the workplace occasioned by automation, computerization, and robotics.

10. Studying what happens to those persons in the workforce who are functionally illiterate, whose basic academic skills are inadequate to learning the skills necessary to new occupational technologies. Do we simply assume that under major occupation transitions some persons are destined to be unemployed and that one of the roles of career guidance is to assist such persons to prepare for unemployment just as one prepares for work?

11. Considering what advocacy roles career counselors have in assisting employers to recognize their employees as human capital resources to be developed and nurtured, just as they have historically emphasized the preventive maintenance of equipment; identifying what are the most effective models of career intervention in business and industry as shifts are made from personnel management to personnel development.

Such research areas are only the most superficial of possibilities as the implications of the changes in the occupational structure and the international economy for career guidance and counseling are studied in the years ahead. Ways will need to be found to increase the understanding of career counselors and other career guidance practitioners of the dynamics of employment and unemployment. Although career guidance is likely to facilitate "employability" in persons, help them to plan for work more knowledgeably and purposefully, and assist them in their adjustment to work, it cannot create jobs or employment for them; the latter is a function of many complex factors such as population demographics, international competition, and fiscal policies, which cannot be decisively influenced by career guidance. Therefore, to argue that career guidance or career counseling will "reduce unemployment" is to misunderstand the dynamics of unemployment and naively to overpromise what career interventions cannot deliver.

From the standpoint of social effects as well as research concerns, it is useful to note that uninformed understandings of the factors initiating and maintaining unemployment cause some counselors, like lay citizens, to assume that after receiving career guidance or training, if one is still unemployed, one must want to be. That might be a reasonable assumption if the nation were providing full employment or if it were not in the middle of a major structural transition in work technology, but it is not providing full employment and it is engaged in a major structural transition. Therefore, we sometimes inadvertently blame the victims of unemployment or underemployment for being victims and unintentionally intensify the feelings of frustration or helplessness they experience (Herr & Watts, 1981; Herr, 1993).

Another area of research concern still within the broad rubric of economic and cultural factors has to do with the characteristics of labor markets. Doering and Piore (1971) have described a dual labor market in the United States that has different "ports of entry" for workers depending on the industry involved; different levels of security, benefits, and training; and different possibilities for internal mobility. The primary and secondary labor markets, as they are known, require different job-search strategies, skills, and personal characteristics. The career ladders available, the commitments to and processes of on-the-job training and retraining, the sources of workers, and the hiring processes in the primary and secondary labor markets are each worthy of far more research attention than has been given to such matters to date. Without being aware of such distinctions in the labor force, career guidance practitioners and job seekers are likely to expend energies in efforts that are insufficiently tailored to the actual dynamics that occur in the various components of the structure. It is also likely that a person concentrating on seeking work in either the primary or secondary labor market underestimates the possibilities of self-employment (Gershuny & Pahl, 1979–1980). It seems likely that more work in the future than in the past will be subcontracted from large corporations to small entrepreneurs, sometimes to reduce the magnitude of permanent core employees and the overhead costs involved, in favor of using temporary contingency work forces; sometimes for economies of scale; and sometimes because small entrepreneurs offer specialized skills that can be purchased for specific purposes. Again, however, self-employment (or entrepreneurial behavior), its availability, and the specific skills required in both formal and informal labor markets have not typically been the subject of research in career theory. Until they are, the employment potential in such areas will be less systematically sought and prepared for than would otherwise be appropriate.

Given the likely effects of the global economy on work organizations and organizational change over the next decade, London and Stumpf (1986) have suggested research topics of particular importance within workplaces. Although these topics were suggested more than 15 years ago, it is interesting to note that they may be even more applicable today and the need for researchers to address these issues may be even more urgent. Specifically, London and Stumpf suggest that career researchers should examine:

> *[H]ow workers effectively adjust to periods of transition and stability at different career stages. Research also needs to investigate ways to help individuals search for suitable alternatives and make career changes without feeling "locked in" by financial obligations. (p. 43)*
>
> *Career research is needed to help define general competency areas that guide people in making career transitions. (p. 44)*
>
> *Career research should examine how career resilience develops and changes over time. (p. 45)*
>
> *Career research needs to take a developmental perspective by examining how people and organizations change and affect each other over time. People go through many critical stages during their careers—at which time they are particularly susceptible to influence and need to adjust to major role transitions. Research needs to identify these stages and transitions and help organizations evaluate their efforts to provide support for employees at critical times. (p. 46)*
>
> *Research is needed to examine how career identity is changing overtime.... The impact of new career management systems on career and organizational commitment needs to be addressed in light of such changes. Therefore, evaluation research is needed on such management systems as alternative work schedules, flextime, childcare options, preretirement planning, and career and life counseling. (p. 47)*

Although there are many other research questions that are affected by economic factors, those cited here exemplify topical emphases that should guide research about individual-organizational change in the next decade.

Awareness of Cost-Benefit Effects

One of the major research arenas of the future must be the cost-benefit effects of career counseling, career education, career guidance or other career interventions (Whiston & Brecheisen, 2002). Each of the research or evaluation studies that shows either positive or negative outcomes for such career services is important, in an empirical sense, for its value in testing some theoretical proposition or in evaluating the efficacy of a particular treatment in relation to some factor of age, gender, or population type.

The point of this section is, however, that research findings, particularly on the various career interventions, have meaning beyond the empirical (Kileen, White, & Watts, 1992). They are also important in cost-benefit terms: for example, private benefits that accrue directly to the individual as in greater job satisfaction and work productivity; external benefits that accrue to a third party, perhaps an employer, as in increased worker satisfactoriness or less absenteeism from work; social benefits that accrue to society as a whole as in reduced welfare payments or in increased contributions to taxes and charitable agencies. On the cost side are the expenditures for counselor salaries, facilities, staff training, materials purchased, employee released time from work and the money, energy, or time required to produce some form(s) of benefit. The central questions of cost-benefit analyses are: How much does it cost to have a career counseling, education, or guidance program? How much will it cost not to have such a career counseling, education, or guidance program? What are the cost-benefit ratios and the economic tradeoffs or payoffs of having or not having such career services? Under the pressures for accountability and the wise management of scarce resources, such questions will be essential to the future availability of career programs in many settings.

Cost-benefit analyses of career services are not easy, and they typically require a somewhat different mentality than ordinarily characterizes the practitioners of the field. For example, cost-benefit analyses require theorists, researchers, and practitioners to be willing to risk evaluating what they do, using as a criterion economic benefits that exceed economic costs. Within such a construct, if the economic benefits to individuals or to society exceed the cost of career guidance or career counseling one can argue that counselors are generators of resources, not simply consumers of them.

One might further argue that each of the positive effects of career counseling, education or guidance cited throughout this book makes a direct or indirect contribution to the gross national product by increasing educational and occupational attainment or productivity, by decreasing losses associated with absence or vandalism, or by precluding the need for more expensive treatment in the future. The logic of such a perspective seems unassailable, but the connections between the empirically derived findings about career counseling or guidance effects and the economic health of individuals or the society at large have not typically been made. Although there are useful examples of such efforts within industry (Alander & Campbell, 1975; Olbrisch, 1977; Reardon, 1976; Warren, 1978), and in health insurance plans (Cummings, 1977; Cummings, 1986; McGuire & Frisman, 1983), the systematic comparison of the economic benefit-cost ratios of career guidance to other systems of intervention is still in a primitive state. It has extraordinary promise, however.

Developing Measures of Career Development

Because much of our understanding of career development comes from observations of restricted samples, often not adequately representing women or minority persons, existing measures of career development can be considered susceptible to limited sensitivity in their observations of career behavior. When such instruments are applied to persons who might be different in their characteristics, they may miss, exclude, or overemphasize material relevant to the latter. Obviously, this criticism differs in its importance depending on whether the instrument is assessing values of unequivocal factual information or making judgments about the level of career maturity or aptitudes for education or a job. The last is most problematic, although each must be viewed with caution depending on the procedures followed in developing and validating the instrument.

No specific instruments are mentioned here because the concerns expressed are well known to test developers and they are working diligently to correct imbalances in samples represented in the validation procedures. Nevertheless, because of the unevenness of coverage in current theories of career development of women and minority groups, the construction of instruments to assess career behavior across all population types will be difficult.

Certainly a major concern in measurement has to do with the outcomes to be expected from career education, career counseling, or career guidance. Are each of these categories of intervention intended to affect the same behaviors or are they to serve different purposes? What are the outcomes expected for each or for all? Clearly, the outcomes expected to derive from career interventions are diverse and changing. Some are affective, others are cognitive, still others are behavioral. They frequently deal with a client's progress in decision making or the degree to which they experience indecision. They vary with regard to whether they assess knowledge of self-characteristics, occupational or educational options, career certainty, career beliefs, indecision, or the decision-making process. The foci of concern are often attitudes toward choice, independence in choice, or to adjustment. Sometimes the outcome measure focuses upon degree of anxiety, quality of job-search skills, achievement, persistence, work adjustment, academic performance, or other behavior. Sometimes measures obscure differences between groups of persons who approach career decisions as self selected or as chosen by others (Brisbin & Savickas, 1994). The complexity of assessment is compounded by both content and process issues related to predictive validity, diagnostic utility, and the matching of differential treatments to assessed outcomes. There is much to be done in such areas as theoretical concepts are translated into and evaluated as measurement dimensions.

Implicit in the development of career development measures are problems with the use of the language of careers. As has been suggested elsewhere (Herr, 1990):

> *Perhaps the primary issue in the study of career is, what do we mean by career? Is it different from occupation or job? When we speak of career, are we concerned with the lifelong behavioral processes and the influences upon them that lead to individual work values, choice-making styles, work salience, role integration, self and career identity, pre- and post-work involvement, and related phenomena? On the other hand, are we principally concerned with the subject of individual career development, which might be defined in organizational terms as the stages that one undergoes in different work settings from induction to consolidation to retirement? Do we really mean that we are concerned with who enters particular occupations and why, the individual differences in interests and abilities found in particular groupings, and the overlap in these characteristics across occupational groupings, or are we really concerned with job satisfaction and work adjustment? (p. 3)*

The point is that unless researchers are clear about what they perceive to be the boundaries of career versus occupation versus work choice or adjustment, it becomes difficult to know what the outcomes of research should be, how they should be addressed, or how research studies can be compared as to purpose and meaning. The language and constructs of career, then, need to be differentiated from the language of occupation, leisure, or general personal development in such a way that constructs and outcomes are clearly defined within such language systems.

The differential outcomes that career counseling or career guidance are intended to address require a variety of measurement forms. As work organizations change and the content of work undergoes modification, testing must also shift its emphases. As suggested in Chapter 2, the emerging concept of personal flexibility of workers to perform effectively within the change-filled environment of a global economy is likely to require new testing paradigms or processes to measure the ingredients of what individual nations or regional markets define as elements of personal flexibility. Among these emphases will likely be increased attention to testing in relation to the status of persons on various dimensions of the process of choice, in addition to testing about the content of choice. The "process of choice" is concerned with such behaviors as persons' independence from others in their choice-making orientation or commitment to choice, assessment of barriers to choice, possession of information about choice options, and knowledge of and ability in decision making. Thus, the historical reasons for testing in vocational guidance for purposes of classifying, identifying, and creaming talent has shifted increasingly from assessing individual differences in performance or the matching of traits and factors making up the content of individual choices—aptitudes, interests, job requirements—however important they continue to be, to assessments primarily concerned with such questions as how ready is the individual to choose, how planful, how knowledgeable about the choice process, how able is this person to define the choice problem immediately ahead, and to college pertinent information and weigh its personal value. Pursuing such understanding, psychometricians and researchers have directed their attention to identifying the important influences that mediate how one's career behavior unfolds: undecidedness and indecisiveness, work salience, different decision-making styles, perception, self-efficacy, the acquisition of academic and task approach skills, and the presence of irrational beliefs about work and personal capacity of career adaptability.

Historically, much of our routine testing has been concerned with content of choice issues, particularly the assessment of aptitudes, from which we can evaluate how competitive an individual can be in a particular job or career and the likely upper limits of their performance. In the future, however, as work organizations are likely to be less pyramidal or hierarchial in design, and less management driven, the assessment concerns of the global economy are likely to be less about how competitive the individual may be and more about the status of his or her skills in terms of *complementarity*. For example, how is this person likely to function in a group, as a facilitator of the performance of others in the workplace, as a leader of a problem-solving or participative decision-making group, as a conflict resolver? These are the skills of personal flexibility that are likely to be more and more prized in the work organizations that are emerging. Other assessments of growing importance to personal flexibility will be teachability, rigidity, and adaptability.

There are other changes in the need for assessments as well. One of them has to do with the quest for personal excellence. During the past decade, because of the rise in international competition and the increase in educational requirements stimulated by the pervasive adaptation of advanced technology, there has been much rhetoric in the U.S. about educational reform and the need for educational excellence. The pursuit of educational excellence is undoubtedly an appropriate national goal. Educational excellence, however, is shaped by and reciprocal with the willingness and the confidence of students or adults to pursue programs of action that challenge their abilities, provide access to earned opportunity, and rest on informed choice. Testing must increasingly be seen as primarily to inform, enlighten, and stimulate the person tested to individual commitment to personal excellence at whatever level of achievement one can accomplish.

The need to use testing as a form of empowerment, self-efficacy, and information, as a way of helping workers or clients develop theories about what is important and how to choose it, will likely change the testing process itself. As Healy (1990) has persuasively described:

> *If appraisals are to strengthen clients in their ongoing monitoring of their career...they need to improve clients self assessment skills. If appraisals intend to help clients create a career, rather than merely chart one leg of it, they need to assist clients in becoming aware of how influential their contexts are in shaping who they are, and they need to sensitize clients to how they can maneuver in their contexts to realize career ambitions.... Finally, leading the client through an expert's approach will strengthen a client in piloting a career only if the client clarifies how to incorporate aspects of the expert's process into his or her approach. (p. 22)*

Embedded in these shifting perspectives on what measurement outcomes need to address, the forms of measurement that might be required in the future, and the paradigms of how the purposes of testing need to be modified are psychometric and social issues that require multidisciplinary forms of inquiry. Such needs are fertile areas for research and for new conceptual models.

A major social issue that needs to be addressed intensively in research and practice are the implications of assessment for culturally different groups. As such research or practice proceeds, it should be cognizant of such important frames of reference as those advanced, for example, by Prediger (1993) in *Multicultural Assessment Standards: A Compilation for Counselors.*

Advances in Occupational Information in Relation to Career Decision Making

Considerable progress has been made during the last fifteen years in developing both affective and cognitive information about various forms of work that is sensitive to sexual stereotyping and responsive to the types of questions and conceptual ability pertinent to persons at various developmental levels. More, however, can be done.

Specifically, research needs to address such questions as, Do students or adults think in terms of careers or entry jobs, school subjects, and college majors or clusters of interests? How do such perspectives bear on achievement motivation, career motives, and occupational valuing as these bear upon planning or adjustment to work? How much information do persons need before they can make a commitment at a given choice point? What are the effects of the tentative goal-setting of preadolescent youth on later choice and how is available information related to such choice making? Are there differences among various population groups (defined by sex, race, ethnicity) in the types of occupational and career information preferred? Do variables such as learning style, intraversion-extraversion, and decision-making styles influence which type of information resource may be useful?

Another research issue concerning occupational or career information has to do with how to make it more localized. Most available information is national and, therefore, quite broad in its description of occupations and careers. Some research, however, has shown that local information, when it is available, is more important in decision making than is national information. Aside from Department of Labor regional labor surveys, the prototype computerized occupational information systems, job data bank information that is regionalized or localized in some areas in the country, or occasional community surveys taken by counselors, there is little local occupational or career information useful for decision making. How such information can be effectively secured and access given to the totality of persons in a community who can use it (e.g., students, clients, unemployed persons, career changers), what its characteristics are, and how valuable it is for different kinds of decisions are other important areas for research. Certainly, as users increasingly access on-line resources such as O-NET, it will become important to accumulate research evidence related to it use.

The Question of Work Values

A body of literature on worker alienation has emerged over the past several decades. Some speculate that its revelations about the tedium and limitations for personal fulfillment in work have turned many young people against a work ethic. Other speculation interspersed with some research suggests that young people want to work but primarily in occupations that are challenging, of service to humankind, and personally gratifying.

It is not now clear how or if such concepts have affected the thinking of most youth. For example, do vocational education and college preparatory students share similar perspectives on the meaning of work? Nor is it clear how youth view decision stress or the increasing burdens of psychological responsibility being portrayed by many writers as emerging social problems. Many research questions are pertinent to such emphases. Some examples follow.

Are youth experiencing indecisiveness as a general behavior pattern? Is it restricted to career choice? How widespread is indecisiveness among student populations of different socioeconomic or racial characteristics and at different educational levels? What characteristics and conditions differentiate those who are guided by security from those who are risk-takers in decision making? Are student values about work shifting dramatically? How? Are student values about education shifting? How? What forms of or emphases in career guidance, career counseling, or other career interventions do youth most value or desire? What career incentives do youth currently find most attractive (for example, contributions to others, service to society, high income, prestige) and what differences do these desires actually make at the point of choice? In a shifting employment picture, do youth find unemployment compensation, welfare, or other governmental subsidies attractive alternatives to work? Can youth or adults find personal significance outside of paid work if their physiological and security needs are met? Do the work values of youth and adults really differ or is this an intergenerational straw man?

Many of these questions might also be asked of various adult populations and the answers related to choices made. A fundamental question in either youth or adult populations is whether economic or psychological contingencies are really the more important at the point of choice for most persons in a highly industrialized society. A nagging concern among such questions is, What is the influence of the mass media in shaping personal aspirations and questions of psychological identity as compared with other mechanisms in the environment or the individual's intrinsic need structure?

The Question of Counselor Characteristics

Counselor role and function studies have a long and sometimes questionable history. Examples of recent position statements on counselor role in career guidance and in career education were cited in Chapter 1. For the most part, these position statements are based on speculation, not research about the most important functions of counselors in discharging their responsibilities in career guidance. Other research questions also remain.

What is the relationship of the counselor's socioeconomic background and work history to the knowledge of careers or occupations, to attitudes toward decision making and exploratory behavior, to the place of career counseling, education, or guidance within a repertoire of counselor priorities? Some data suggest that counseling psychologists in training (Heppner, O'Brien, Hinkelman, & Flores, 1996; Pinkney & Jacobs, 1985) and counselor educators who train such persons do not value the career aspects of their role as highly as those dealing with personal counseling, depression, and psychotherapy. Therefore, they have lost contact with the roots of their profession and have blurred their professional identity (for example, Fitzgerald & Osipow, 1986; Osipow, 1977). The questions are: How widespread among counselors and counseling psychologists is such a perspective? Do they really not value career work?

Beyond such questions, what are the effects of counselor preparation in nonschool settings (for example, industrial internships, different amounts or types of paid employment, intern experiences in community and government agencies) on subsequent counselor effectiveness in career guidance? What are the relationships between the counselor's effectiveness in career counseling or guidance and previous occupational experience? How do career counseling or guidance skills and emphases differ among counselors working in a vocational education setting, a comprehensive educational setting, and a community agency? What do counselors in different settings actually know about vocational education? How do counselors rate their competencies on the various career guidance skills recommended in the position statements cited in Chapter 1? What do counselors know about employment and unemployment? About skill elasticities across occupations and settings? About the primary and secondary labor markets? What types of retraining or preservice models are most effective in preparing career counselors for the needs of the future?

RESEARCH FOR THE FUTURE: SUMMARY REVIEWS OF RESEARCH NEEDS

In the *Annual Review of Psychology, Career Development Quarterly, Journal of Vocational Behavior,* and *Counseling Psychologist* as well as other pertinent journals, major summaries of the research literature and analyses of research needs in that literature are published. To conclude this chapter, selected highlights of reviews that go beyond what has been discussed earlier in this chapter will be summarized here.

Niles (1997) used NCDA's career counseling competencies as a framework for classifying the career literature from 1996. Using this framework revealed several gaps in the career development literature. For example, despite the dramatic increase in the number of online career services, Niles found little research investigating the efficacy of such interventions. Niles reminded the profession that it must take responsibility for addressing and monitoring this form of career service delivery. Niles also noted the need for greater attention to the career development of children, persons with disabilities, people who are gay, lesbian, or bisexual, racial/ethnic minorities, and elderly people.

Swanson and Parcover (1998) also reviewed the career development literature (1997) and noted their surprise as to the few articles that had been published in several areas. Specifically, they noted the need for more research evaluating career interventions, investigating supervision in career counseling, and the need for more research examining the career development of young persons and the elderly. Finally, Swanson and Parcover reinforced the usefulness of the notion of career "adaptability" as a perspective for understanding how individuals cope with the unpredictable nature of the world-of-work today.

Young and Chen (1999) were struck by the range and diversity of the career development and counseling literature published in 1998. Their study of the quality and diversity of the career literature led them to draw positive conclusions about the health and vitality of the career development field. They encouraged researchers to turn their attention to specific areas such as career timing, the use of career assessments in multicultural contexts, and the training of career counselors. The relational dimensions of career and the social and contextual dimensions of career processes were also areas they identified as being in need of greater attention by career researchers.

Arbona (2000) organized the literature according to publications that were related to career theories, new assessment instruments, and career interventions. She was pleased at the number of career articles that were grounded in career theory. Clearly, this bodes well for the continued evolution of theoretical perspectives. Arbona also noted that the increased attention to the career development of diverse populations was also encouraging. Topics such as acculturation, racial identity, and discrimination were prevalent in the 1999 literature. Consistent with the literature reviews mentioned previously, Arbona noted the need for more research in the areas of career counseling process and outcomes.

Given Arbona's observations regarding the need for greater attention to career counseling process and outcomes, Luzzo and MacGregor (2001) were pleasantly surprised to find a number of research articles published in 2000 that addressed career counseling practice. Luzzo and MacGregor also found a good number of articles that addressed the use of the Internet in career interventions, thereby, addressing a gap Niles (1997) had noted four years earlier. Finally, Luzzo and MacGregor noted the continued increase of publications addressing the career development needs of, and career interventions with, diverse populations.

Whiston and Brecheisen (2002) summarized 258 publications including one book, articles from 54 journals, and 12 book chapters published in 2001. They suggested that the literature published in 2001 provides a rich contribution to the extant career research. They noted a consistent theme within the research that career counseling is a multidimensional process that requires a holistic view of the client. The also noted the increased use of adolescent and adult research samples (as opposed to college student populations). Finally, the fact that career researchers are increasingly using diverse methodologies to examine important career development issues. The increased use of qualitative methodologies was noted in particular. On the other hand, Whiston and Brecheisen expressed concern over the continued lack of career intervention efficacy studies. The continued dearth of research related to children, individuals with disabilities, older adults, and persons who are gay, lesbian, or bisexual was also noted.

These literature reviews reflect a mixed bag of success within the career development literature. On the positive side, the increased use of technology in career services is resulting in increased numbers of research studies investigated their use (Luzzo & MacGregor, 2001). As the trend in the use of the Internet and computer-based interventions is likely to continue to grow, it is hoped that this area will continue to capture the interest of career development researchers. The fact that career researchers are increasingly addressing the career development of racially and ethnically diverse populations (Arbona, 2000) is also an important advance. Clearly, more research in this area is warranted, especially with regard to the use of career assessments. However, it is also clear that some groups are continuing to be ignored by career researchers.

Finally, five classic analyses of continuing research needs in career theory and practice are those suggested by Holland, Magoon, and Spokane (1981) in their comprehensive review of research and theory on career interventions; by Osipow in his master lecture for the American Psychological Association in 1986; by Gottfredson (1990) in his comprehensive analysis of where research on Holland's theory should go in the future and the status of research in career behavior more generally; by Fouad (1994) in her review of research in vocational choice, decision making, assessment, and intervention; and by Whiston, Sexton, and Lasoff (1998) in their replication of the Oliver and Spokane (1988) meta-analytic review. Among the suggestions of Holland, Magoon, and Spokane are the following:

- More rigorous evaluations of all forms of vocational interventions are still required. The analysis of how interventions work needs to be continued and reexamined in the context of instructional technology, decision making, and information processing.
- More analytical evaluations in which client goals are linked to treatments are needed to acquire a

comprehensive knowledge of client treatment interaction and related outcomes.

- More potent treatments should be developed by incorporating the influential characteristics of past treatments.
- The ordering effects of treatment chains should be investigated.
- The neglected but painfully relevant topics of job finding, placement strategies, and vocational adaptation require more attention.
- The classification research should be more completely exploited. (pp. 298–300)

Osipow (1986) suggested that there are several issues that should influence "the life span practice and research agenda for the near and middle-range future. Issues such as unemployment, underemployment, serial careers, the problems of part-time and temporary workers, disability and compensation, rehabilitation, labor force shifts, and working conditions have rarely been studied from a life-span perspective" (p. 164). In addition, however, he identified other topics that he also believed to be important and enduring concerns for research. They included, in adapted form, the following:

- The study of career stress and adjustment
- The effects of money and job security in career choices, adjustment, implementation, stress, and decision making
- Sexism and racism relative to assessment, equal worth of occupational activities, and discrimination and its effects in the workplace
- Midcareer change and multiple careers
- The impact of the family context on career decision making and adjustment
- Leisure and retirement

Osipow concludes his analysis of research issues with a fascinating observation that embodies wisdom about demographics, development, and research. He states, "Much of this anticipated research agenda is stimulated by the aging population. The baby boom has been a prime factor in determining the research agenda on career development since the 1950s. When the 'boomers' were young, education and career entry were major needs for assistance; as they have aged, a variety of other services have been emphasized. The professional and research agenda will continue to be defined by this population bulge as it goes through the life span" (p. 166).

Gottfredson (1990), as a function of identifying areas of future applications and research using Holland's Theory of Careers, suggested four areas for cultivation and several admonitions for better designs with regard to areas for cultivation. His suggestions follow, in adapted form:

- Self-efficacy expectations in career behavior—"We need to learn how self-efficacy expectations develop, how people come to see themselves as competent and potentially successful in different areas." (p. 2)
- Effects studies—Because counseling can be costly and difficult to provide to all who could benefit, the following research goals deserve renewed emphasis:
  a. We need a range of practical treatments for people who need different levels and types of treatment.
  b. We need more evidence about such basic items as the effects of providing different amounts and modes of information.
  c. We need *experimental* tests of the implications of the [Holland] typology for the design of career interventions.
  d. We should begin to link intervention research with social learning theory and attempt to develop interventions with dependable positive effects on self-efficacy expectations.
  e. We need *experimental* tests of diagnostic ideas linking identity, barriers, and typological assessments to *levels* and *varieties* of assistance (p. 4).
- Better designs
  Use simple designs if they are appropriate.
  Conduct longitudinal research on the attention, selection, and retention or attrition of persons by environments.
  Conduct true experiments of the effects of vocational interventions. A few days spent resolving perceived obstacles to randomization is time better spent than time spent on nonexperimental research.
  Attend to the population studies and the distribution of types of other variables in the population.
  Replicate excellent existing studies where few replications are available. (p. 7)

Fouad (1994), in a review of research through 1993 on factors related to vocational choice and decision making and processes of assessment and intervention, provided a variety of important observations and recommendations that are summarized in abridged form here. For example, she states, "We now have abundant evidence that men and women differ, that whites differ from minority group members, and that minority group members differ from each other...but implicit in much of this research is a standard from which special populations deviate. That standard is based on research on white heterosexual males.... We must move to exploring reality for women as their own referent [not in comparison to white men] and do the same for minority group members and lesbians and gays. This must include within-group studies, but also include awareness of individual differences that are not due to ethnicity, gender, or sexual orientation" (p. 157).

Fouad identifies priority areas for research that include the following:

1. Factors that influence male choices of nontraditional careers....
2. Understanding how successful minority group members differ from those that society considers to be nonsuccessful, and how cultural values interact with societal expectations to shape career choices.... We may also need to broaden our definition of success. We must consider whether researchers who may have a "traditional" focus on achievement themselves, are imposing a definition of achievement and success on the individuals they study.
3. The role of sexual orientation in vocational choice...and examination of the ways in which heterosexual counselors can work effectively with homosexual clients.
4. A better operationalization of vocational identity is needed.... More examination is needed on the self, self-in-relation to others, and self-in-relation to environments.
5. How families influence vocational choice.... We have limited knowledge of how family processes and functioning affects adolescents' career development.
6. How information processing occurs in vocational decision making...little is known about how best to help clients process the information.... The relation between disconfirming information and self-efficacy expectations may be an interesting area of future research.
7. The role of self-efficacy expectations in influencing career choices throughout the developmental process.... It may be important to study self-efficacy in early years, when expectations may be more modifiable.
8. The process of career counseling. What works with which career counseling clients?
9. The effectiveness of treatment interventions.... Researchers need to know what practitioners find effective, and they need to help inform practitioners of effective treatments." (pp. 160–161)

Whiston, Sexton, and Lasoff (1998) examined 268 treatment-control contrasts from 47 studies that involved a total of 4,660 participants. The average overall effect sizes they found were similar to those found previously. Individual career counseling was the most effective and efficient treatment strategy and computer-based career interventions were the most cost-effective. Whiston and her colleagues noted several implications from their meta-analysis. First, they observed a lack of sophistication related to the systematic diagnosis of research participants. Hence, they called for the development of standardized procedures for diagnosis in the career area. Whiston and her colleagues also noted that career intervention research is behind other areas of outcome research with regard to treatment integrity, thereby making it difficult to draw conclusions from research findings. They noted that more research is needed in which researchers systematically investigate which clients benefit from groups, which benefit from career planning classes, and which benefit from individual career counseling. They also called upon researchers, when possible, to report findings separately for ethnic groups in order to provide information concerning the effectiveness of different career interventions with distinct groups. Interestingly, Whiston and associates noted that unlike career research with women, no study since 1983 has examined career interventions with men exclusively. Thus, there may now be the need for researchers to understand more fully the effectiveness of specific career interventions with men. Finally, Whiston and her colleagues pointed to the need for researchers to more selective and discriminating in their selection of outcome measures

Although the sets of research priorities just summarized overlap in some areas, they nevertheless serve to establish the broad features of a map of needed research in career theory and practice. Whether a theorist, researcher, or practitioner, the serious reader will find much to contemplate and to stimulate action in the perspectives of the authors cited.

SUMMARY

In this chapter we have examined a broad spectrum of research issues and needs of relevance to the fuller understanding of both career behavior and potential interventions in such behavior. Research and statistical methods have been discussed in relation to how different statistical techniques are used to analyze particular types of questions. It has been suggested that quantitative and qualitative research methodologies are different ways of knowing. In particular, qualitative methods are emerging as ways of analyzing individual tendencies in "meaning making" and to capture the richness of individual careers. We have discussed the importance longitudinal career development studies of the challenges of life-span psychology and of such techniques as path analysis, causal modeling, and structural equation-modeling. We have also identified areas in which research questions in career practice as well as in career development theory are present and selected perspectives on such questions are provided. The range of such questions illustrates the complexity of career development processes and their dynamic quality. They also affirm that many of the major questions of concern to career theories and interventions are not empirical but rather matters of philosophy or values.

REFERENCES

AAUW Report. (1992). How schools shortchange girls. *AAUW Outlook, 86,* 1–8.

Abdel-Halim. A. A. (1981). Effects of role stress-job design-technology interact in employee work satisfaction. *Academy of Management Journal, 24*(2), 260–273.

Abeles, R. P., Steel, L., & Wise, L. L. (1980). Patterns and implications of life-course organization: Studies from Project TALENT. In P. B. Baltes & O. G. Brim, Jr. (Eds.), *Lifespan development and behavior* (pp. 308–339). New York: Academic Press.

Abrams, M. (1979). A new work sample battery for vocational assessment of the disadvantaged: VITAS. *Vocational Guidance Quarterly, 28*(1), 35–43.

ACES Position Paper. (1976). *Commission on counselor preparation for career development/career education.* Washington, DC: Association for Counselor Education and Supervision.

Ackerman, P. L., & Heggestad, E. D. (1997). Intelligence, personality, and interests: Evidence of overlapping traits. *Psychological Bulletin, 121,* 219–245.

ACT. (1985). *Interim psychometric handbook for the 3rd edition ACT Career Planning Program (levels 1 and 2).* Iowa City, IA: The American College Testing Program.

Adams, A. V., & Mangum, G. (1978). *The lingering crisis of youth unemployment.* Kalamazoo, MI: Upjohn Institute for Employer Research.

Adams, A. V., Mangum, G., & Lenninger, S. F. (1978). The nature of youth unemployment. In A. Adams & G. L. Mangum (Eds.), *The lingering crisis of youth unemployment* (pp. 1–13). Kalamazoo, MI: Upjohn Institute for Employment Research.

Adla, S. (1996). Personality and work behavior: Exploring the linkages. *Applied Psychology: An International Review, 45*(3), 207–224.

Adler, A. (1927). *The practice and theory of individual psychology.* New York: Harcourt.

Adler, A. (1935). The fundamental views of individual psychology. *International Journal of Individual Psychology, 1,* 5–8.

Adler, P. A., Kless, S. J., & Adler, P. (1992). Socialization to gender roles: Popularity among elementary school boys and girls. *Sociology of Education, 65,* 169–187.

Ainsworth, J., & Fifield, M. G. (1973, May). *Work simulation: An approach to vocational exploration* (Training paper). Logan, UT: Utah State University, Exceptional Child Center.

Alander, R., & Campbell, T. (1975). An evaluative study of an alcohol and drug recovery program: A case study of the Oldsmobile experience. *Human Resource Management, 14,* 14–18.

Allen, J. E., Jr. (1970, February). *Competence for all as the goal for secondary education.* Paper presented to the National Association of Secondary School Principals, Washington, DC.

Allen, L. R. (1980). Leisure and its relationship to work and career guidance. *Vocational Guidance Quarterly, 28*(3), 257–262.

Allen, R. E., & Kearny, T. J. (1980). The relative effectiveness of alternative job sources. *Journal of Vocational Behavior, 16,* 18–42.

Amatea, E., & Clark, J. (1984). A dual career workshop for college couples: Effects of an intervention program. *Journal of College Student Personnel, 25*(3), 271–272.

Amatea, E., Clark, J., & Cross, E. (1984). Life-styles: Evaluating a life role planning program for high school students. *Vocational Guidance Quarterly, 34,* 249–259.

Amatea, E., & Cross, E. G. (1986). Helping high school students clarify life role preferences: The life-styles unit. *The School Counselor, 33*(4), 306–313.

Amatea, E. S., & Cross, E. G. (1980). Going places: A career guidance program for high school students and their parents. *Vocational Guidance Quarterly, 28*(3), 274–282.

American Council on Education. (1999). *The American freshman national norms for fall 1998.* Washington, D.C.: Author.

American Institutes for Research (AIR). (1975). *Developing comprehensive career guidance programs.* Palo Alto, CA: Author.

American Personnel and Guidance Association. (1974, March). *Career guidance: Role and functions of counseling and guidance practitioners in career education* (Position paper). Washington, DC: Author.

American Psychiatric Association. (1981). *Diagnostic and statistical manual of mental disorders* (3rd ed.). Washington, DC: Author.

American Psychiatric Association. (1994) *Diagnostic and statistical manual of mental disorders* (4th ed.). Washington, DC: Author.

American Psychological Association. (1974). *Standards for educational and psychological tests.* Washington, DC: Author.

American Psychological Association. (1986). *Guidelines for computer-based tests and interpretations.* Washington, DC: Author.

American School Counselors Association. (1977a, August). *The unique role of the elementary school counselor* (Position paper adopted by ASCA Governing Board).

American School Counselors Association. (1977b, August). *The unique role of the middle/junior high school counselor* (Position paper adopted by ASCA Governing Board).

American School Counselors Association. (1985). The role of the school counselor in career guidance: Expectations and responsibilities. *The School Counselor, 32*(3), 164–168.

Americana Health Care Corporation. (1980). *Aging in America: Trials and triumphs.* New York: Research and Forecast, Inc.

Amundson, N. E. (1989). *Competence: Components and development.* Unpublished paper, University of British Columbia, Department of Counselling Psychology, Vancouver, Canada.

Amundson, N. E. (1998). *Active engagement: Enhancing the career counseling process.* Richmond, B. C., Canada: Ergon Communications.

Amundson, N. E., & Borgen, W. A. (1988). Factors that help and hinder in group employment counseling. *Journal of Employment Counseling, 25,* 104–114.

Amundson, N. E., Borgen, W. A., & Westwood, M. J. (1990). Group employment counseling in Canada. *Journal of Employment Counseling, 27,* 181–190.

Amundson, N. E., & Penner, K. (1998). Parent involved career exploration. *The Career Development Quarterly, 47,*135–144.

Anderson, C. D., Warner, J. L., & Spencer, C. C. (1984). Inflation bias in self-assessment examinations: Implications for valid employee selection. *Journal of Applied Psychology, 69*(4), 574–580.

Anderson, K. L. (1980). Educational goals of male and female adolescents: The effects of parental characteristics and attitudes. *Youth and Society, 12,* 173–188.

Anderson, S. B. (1994). ACT Career Planning Program (CCP). In J. T. Kapes, M. M. Mastie, & E. A. Whitfield (Eds.), *A counselor's guide to career assessment instruments* (pp. 50–56). Alexandria, VA: National Career Development Association.

Anderson, W. P., & Niles, S. G. (1995). Career and personal concerns expressed by career counseling clients. *The Career Development Quarterly, 45,* 240–245.

Anderson, W. P., Jr., & Niles, S. G. (2000). Important events in career counseling: Client and counselor descriptions. *The Career Quarterly, 48,* 251–263.

Angresano, J. (1980). Results of a survey of employer hiring practices. *Vocational Guidance Quarterly, 28*(4), 335–342.

Anh, N. T., & Healy, C. C. (1985). Factors affecting employment and job satisfaction of Vietnamese refugees. *Journal of Employment Counseling, 22,* 78–85.

Anthony, W. A. (1980). *The principles of psychiatric rehabilitation.* Baltimore: University Park Press.

Anthony, W. A. (1994). Characteristics of people with psychiatric disabilities that are predictive of entry into the rehabilitation process and successful employment. *Psychosocial Rehabilitation Journal, 17*(3), 3–13.

APA Office of Ethnic Minority Affairs. (1993). Guidelines for providers of psychological services to ethnic, linguistic, and culturally diverse populations. *American Psychologist, 48*(1), 45–48.

Apostal, R. A., & Holland, C. (1993). Commitment to and role changes in dual career families. *Journal of Career Development, 20*(2), 121–129.

Appel, V., Haak, R., & Witzke, D. (1970). Factors associated in the indecision about collegiate major and career choices. *Proceedings of the 78th Annual Convention of the American Psychological Association, 5,* 667–668.

Arbeiter, S., Aslanian, C. B., Schmerbeck, F. A., & Brickell, H. M. (1978). *40 million Americans in career transition: The need for information.* New York: College Entrance Examination Board.

Arbona, C. (1990). Career counseling research and Hispanics: A review of the literature. *The Counseling Psychologist, 18,* 300–323.

Arbona, C. (2000). Annual review: Practice and research in career counseling in development-1999. *The Career Development Quarterly, 49,* 98–134.

Arbona, C., & Novy, D. M. (1991). Career aspirations and expectations of Black, Mexican American, and White students. *Career Development Quarterly, 39,* 231–239.

Arbuckle, D. S. (1963). Occupational information in the elementary school. *Vocational Guidance Quarterly, 12,* 77–84.

Argeropoulos, J. (1981). *Burnout, stress management, and wellness.* Moravia, NY: Chronicle Guidance.

Aring, M. K. (1993). What the 'V' word is costing America's economy. *Phi Delta Kappan, 74*(5), 396–404.

Armstrong, P. I., & Crombie, G. (2000). Compromises in adolescents' occupational aspirations and expectations from grades 8 to 10. *Journal of Vocational Behavior, 56,* 82–98.

Arnold, J. (1989). Career decidedness and psychological well-being: A two-cohort longitudinal study of undergraduate students and recent graduates. *Journal of Occupational Psychology, 62,* 163–176.

Arnold, J., & Jackson, C. (1997). The new career: Issues and challenges. *British Journal of Guidance and Counseling, 25*(4), 427–434.

Arp, R. S., Holmberg, K. S., & Littrell, J. M. (1986). Launching adult students into the job market: A support group approach. *Journal of Counseling and Development, 65,* 166–167.

Arroba, T. (1977). Styles of decision-making and their use: An empirical study. *British Journal of Guidance and Counseling, 5*(2), 149–158.

Aryee, S., Chay, Y. W., & Chew, J. (1994). An investigation of the predictors and outcomes of career commitment in three career stages. *Journal of Vocational Behavior, 44,* 1–16.

Aryee, S., & Luk, V. (1996). Work and nonwork influences on the career satisfaction of dual-earner couples. *Journal of Vocational Behavior, 49,* 38–52.

Ash, K. S., & Mandelbaum, D. (1982). Using peer counselors in career development. *Journal of College Placement, 42*(3), 47–51.

Ashley, W. L., Cellini, J., Faddis, C., Pearsol, J., Wiant, A., & Wright, B. (1980). *Adaptation to work: An exploration of processes and outcomes.* Columbus, OH: National Center for Research in Vocational Education, Ohio State University.

Ashurst, P., & Hale, Z. (1989). *Understanding women in distress.* London: Tavistock/Routledge.

Aslanian, C. B., & Brickell, H. M. (1980). *Americans in transition: Life changes as reasons for adult learning.* New York: College Entrance Examination Board.

Association for Counselor Education and Supervision. (1976, April). *Position paper on counselor preparation for career development/career education.* Washington, DC: Author.

Astin, A. W. (1993). An empirical typology of college students. *Journal of College Student Development, 34,* 36–46.

Astin, H. S. (1984). The meaning of work in women's lives: A sociopsychological model of career choice and work behavior. *The Counseling Psychologists, 12*(4), 117–126.

Atchley, R. C. (1979). Issues in retirement research. *The Gerontologist, 19*(1), 44–54.

Atkins, C. P., & Kent, R. L. (1988). What do recruiters consider important during the employment interviews? *Journal of Employment Counseling, 25,* 98–103.

Atkinson, D. R., & Hackett, G. (1995). *Counseling diverse populations.* Madison, WI: Brown & Benchmark.

Atkinson, D. R., Morten, G., & Sue, D. W. (1983). *Counseling American minorities.* Dubuque, IA: William C. Brown.

Aubrey, R. (1985). A counseling perspective on recent educational reform reports. *The School Counselor, 32,* 91–99.

Aubry, T., Tefft, B., & Kingsbury, N. (1990). Behavioral and psychological consequences of unemployment in blue-collar couples. *Journal of Community Psychology, 18,* 99–111.

Austin, J. T., & Hanisch, K. A. (1990). Occupational attainment as a function of abilities and interests: A longitudinal analysis using Project TALENT data. *Journal of Applied Psychology, 75,* 77–86.

Austin, W. M. (1986). The occupational outlook in brief. *Occupational Outlook Quarterly, Spring,* 3–29.

Aycan, Z., Kanungo, R. N., Mendonca, M., Yu, K., Deller, J., Stahl, G., & Kurshid, A. (2000). Impact of culture on human resource management practices: A 10-country comparison. *Applied Psychology: An International Review, 49*(1), 192–221.

Axelrod, W. L., & Gavin, J. F. (1980). Stress and strain in blue-collar and white-collar management staff. *Journal of Vocational Behavior, 17,* 41–49.

Axelson, J. A. (1985). *Counseling and development in a multi-cultural society.* Pacific Grove, CA: Brooks/Cole Publishing Company.

Baca, P. M. (1980). Ex-P. O.: Exploring possible occupations. *The School Counselor, 28*(1), 54–58.

Bach, R. L. (1980). The new Cuban immigrants: Their background and prospects. *Monthly Labor Review, 103*(10), 39–46.

Bachman, J. G., Kahn, R. L., Mednick, M., Davidson, T. N., & Johnston, L. D. (1970). *Youth in transition* (Vol. 2). Ann Arbor: University of Michigan, Institute for Social Research.

Backman, M. E., Lynch, J. J., & Loeding, D. J. (1979). Sex and ethnic differences in vocational aptitude patterns. *Measurement and Evaluation in Guidance, 12*(1), 35–43.

Baeher, M., & Orban, J. A. (1989). The role of intellectual abilities and personality characteristics in determining success in higher-level positions. *Journal of Vocational Behavior, 38,* 270–287.

Bailey, B. A., & Nihlen, A. S. (1989). Elementary school children's perceptions of the world of work. *Elementary School Guidance & Counseling, 24*(2), 135–145.

Bailey, L. J., & Stadt, R. (1973). *Career education: New approaches to human development.* Bloomington, IL: McKnight.

Baker, H. (1944). *Employee counseling.* Princeton, NJ: Princeton University Press.

Ballantine, M. (1993). A new framework for the design of career interventions in organizations. *British Journal of Guidance and Counseling, 21*(3), 233–245.

Bamundo, P. J., & Kopelman, R. E. (1980). The moderating effects of occupation, age, and urbanization on the relationship between job satisfaction and life satisfaction. *Journal of Vocational Behavior, 17,* 106–123.

Bandura, A. (1977). Self-efficacy: Toward a unifying theory of behavioral change. *Psychological Review, 84,* 191–215.

Bandura, A. (1982a). The psychology of chance encounters and life paths. *American Psychologist, 37*(7), 747–755.

Bandura, A. (1982b). Self-efficacy mechanism in human agency. *American Psychologist, 37,* 122–147.

Bandura, A. (1986). *Social foundations of thought and action: A social cognitive theory.* Englewood Cliffs, NJ: Prentice-Hall.

Bandura, A., Adams, N. E., & Meyer, J. (1977). Cognitive processes mediating behavior change. *Journal of Personality and Social Psychology, 35,* 125–139.

Bank, I. M. (1969). Children explore careerland through vocational role models. *Vocational Guidance Quarterly, 17,* 284–289.

Barak, A., & Friedkes, R. (1982). The mediating effects of career indecision subtypes on career counseling effectiveness. *Journal of Vocational Behavior, 20,* 120–128.

Barak, A., & Rabbi Ben-Zion. (1982). Predicting persistence, stability, and achievement in college by major choice consistency: A test of Holland's consistency hypothesis. *Journal of Vocational Behavior, 20,* 235–243.

Barak, A., Shiloh, S., & Haushner, O. (1992). Modification of interests through cognitive restructuring: Test of a theoretical model in preschool children. *Journal of Counseling Psychology, 39*(4), 490–497.

Barker, J., & Satcher, J. (2000). School counselors' perceptions of required workplace skills and career development competencies. *Professional School Counseling, 4*(2), 134–139.

Barker, S. B., & Patten, G. L. (1989). Use of the Career Area Interest Checklist with junior high school students. *The School Counselor, 37,* 149–152.

Barner, R, (1994). The new career strategist. Career management for the year 2000 and beyond. *The Futurist, 28*(5), 8–14.

Barnett, R. (1971). Personality correlates of vocational planning. *Genetic Psychology Monographs, 83,* 309–356.

Baron, R. A. (1983). Sweet smell of success? The impact of pleasant artificial scents on evaluations of job applicants. *Journal of Applied Psychology, 68,* 709–713.

Barrett, G. V., Alexander, R. A., & Doverspike, D. (1992). The implications for personnel selection of apparent declines in predictive validities over time: A critique of Hulin, Henry, and Noon. *Personnel Psychology, 45,* 601–617.

Barrett, R. C., & Hyde, J. S. (2001). Women, men, work and family. *American Psychologist, 56*(10), 781–796.

Barrow, J., Cox, P., Sepich, R., & Spivak, R. (1989 January). Student needs assessment surveys: Do they predict student use of services? *Journal of College Student Development, 30,* 77–82.

Bartholomew, C. G., & Schnorr, D. L. (1994). Gender equity: Suggestions for broadening career options of female students. *The School Counselor, 41,* 245–255.

Bartol, K. M. (1981). Vocational behavior and career development, 1980: A review. *Journal of Vocational Behavior, 19,* 123–162.

Barton, P. E. (1991). The school-to-work transition. *Issues in Science and Technology, 7*(3), 50–54.

Baruch, G. K., & Barnett, R. C. (1986). Fathers' participation in family work and children's sex-role attitudes. *Child Development, 57,* 1210–1223.

Baruch, G. K., Biener, L., & Barnett, R. C. (1987). Women and gender in research on work and family stress. *American Psychologist, 42,* 130–136.

Basow, S. A., & Howe, K. G. (1979). Model influences on career choices of college students. *Vocational Guidance Quarterly, 27*(3), 239–243.

Bassi, L. J. (1996). Skills and the education level of U.S. workers. *Looking Ahead, 18*(1), 16–18.

Basta, N. (1991). *Major options: The student's guide to linking college majors and career opportunities during and after college.* New York: Harper Perennial.

Bauer, D., & Matt, D. (1990). Life themes and motivations of re-entry students. *Journal of Counseling and Development, 68,* 555–560.

Bauernfeind, R. H. (1988). Review of Career Occupational Preference System. In J. T. Kapes & M. M. Mastie (Eds.), *A counselor's guide to career assessment instruments* (pp. 81–85). Washington, DC: National Career Development Association.

Baydar, N., & Brooks-Gunn, J. (1991). Effects on maternal employment and child-care arrangements on preschoolers' cognitive and behavioral outcomes: Evidence from the children of the National Longitudinal Survey of Youth. *Developmental Psychology, 77*(6), 932–945.

Bayer, A. E. (1972). *The black college freshman: Characteristics and recent trends.* Washington, DC: American Council on Education.

Bayer, G. A., & Gerstein, L. H. (1990). EAP referrals and troubled employees: An analogue study of supervisors' decisions. *Journal of Vocational Behavior, 36,* 304–319.

Beane, A. L., & Zachmanoglou, M. A. (1979). Career education for the handicapped: A psychosocial impact. *Vocational Guidance Quarterly, 28*(1), 44–47.

Beautrais, A. L., Joyce, P. R., & Mulder, R. T. (1998). Unemployed and serious suicide attempts. *Psychological Medicine, 28*(1), 209–218.

Beck, A. (1993). Cognitive theory: Past, present, and future. *Journal of Consulting and Clinical Psychology, 61* (2), 194–198.

Beck, C. E. (1963). *Philosophical foundations of guidance.* Englewood Cliffs, NJ: Prentice-Hall.

Becker, B. E., & Krzystojiak, F. J. (1982). The influence of labor market discrimination on locus on control. *Journal of Vocational Behavior, 21,* 60–70.

Behrens, D. (1994). A different world: Preparing students for international careers. *Journal of College Student Development, 35,* 64–65.

Behrens, T., & Gordon, D. E. (1997). New direction in marketing the career center to students. *Journal of Career Planning and Employment, 57(2),* 35–39.

Bell, A. P., Super, D. E., & Dunn, L. B. (1988). Understanding and implementing career theory: A case study approach. *Counseling and Human Development, 20*(8), 1–20.

Benn, R. K. (1986). Factors promoting secure attachment relationships between employed mothers and their sons. *Child Development, 57,* 1224–1231.

Bennett, S. K., & BigFoot-Sipes, D. S. (1991). American Indian and White college student preferences for counselor characteristics. *Journal of Counseling Psychology, 38*(4), 440–445.

Ben-Shakhar, G., Bar-Hillel, M., Bilu, Y., Ben-Abba, E., & Flug, A. (1986). Can graphology predict occupational success? Two empirical studies and some methodological ruminations. *Journal of Applied Psychology, 71,* 645–653.

Bentler, P. M. (1980). Multivariate analysis with latent variables: Causal modeling. In M. R. Rosenzweig & L. W. Porter (Eds.), *The annual view of psychology* (Vol. 31). Palo Alto, CA: Annual Reviews.

Berg, I., & Hughes, M. (1979). Economic circumstances and the entangling web of pathologies: An esquisse. In L. A. Ferman & J. P. Gordus (Eds.), *Mental health and the economy* (Chap. 2). Kalamazoo, MI: The W. E. Upjohn Institute for Employment Research.

Berger, S. (1989). *College planning for gifted students.* Reston, VA: The Council for Exceptional Children.

Bergeron, L. M., & Romano, J. L. (1994). The relationships among career decision-making, self-efficacy, educational indecision, vocational indecision, and gender. *Journal of College Student Personnel, 35,* 19–24.

Bergland, B. W. (1974). Career planning: The use of sequential evaluated experience. In E. L. Herr (Ed.), *Vocational guidance and human development* (pp. 350–380). Boston: Houghton Mifflin.

Bergland, B. W., & Krumboltz, J. D. (1969). An optimal guide level for career exploration. *Vocational Guidance Quarterly, 18,* 29–33.

Berk, S. F. (1985). *The gender factory: The apportionment of work in American households.* New York: Plenum.

Berlin, G., & Sum, A. (1988). *Toward a more perfect union: Basic skills, poor families and our economic future* (Occasional Paper Number 3). New York: Ford Foundation.

Bernard, J. (1981). The good provider role: Its rise and fall. *American Psychologist, 6*(1), 1–12.

Bernes, K., & Magnusson, K. (1996). A description of career development services within Canadian organizations. *Journal of Counseling and Development, 74*(6), 569–574.

Berry, E. (1979). Guidance and counseling in the elementary school: Its theoretical base. *Personnel and Guidance Journal, 57*(10), 513–520.

Bertaux, D. (1982). The life course approach as a challenge to the social sciences. In T. K. Haraven & K. J. Adams (Eds.), *Aging and life course transitions: An interdisciplinary perspective* (pp. 127–150). New York: Guilford Press.

Betsworth, D. G., & Fouad, N. A. (1997). Vocational interests: A look at the past 70 years and a glance at the future. *The Career Development Quarterly, 46,* 23–47.

Betz, N. E. (1992). Counseling uses of career self-efficacy theory. *Career Development Quarterly, 41,* 22–26.

Betz, N. E., & Corning, A. F. (1993). The inseparability of "career" and "personal" counseling. *The Career Development Quarterly, 42*(3), 137–148.

Betz, N. E., & Fitzgerald, L. F. (1987). *The career psychology of women.* Orlando, FL: Academic Press.

Betz, N. E., & Hackett, G. (1981). The relationship of career-related self-efficacy expectations to perceived career options in college women and men. *Journal of Counseling Psychology, 28,* 399–410.

Betz, N. E., & Hackett, G. (1983). The relationship of mathematics self-efficacy expectations to the selection of science-based college majors. *Journal of Vocational Behavior, 23,* 329–345.

Betz, N. E., & Hackett, G. (1986). Applications of self-efficacy theory to understanding career choice behavior. *Journal of Social and Clinical Psychology, 4,* 279–289.

Betz, N. E., Klein, K. L., & Taylor, K. M. (1996). Evaluation of a short form of the career decision-making self-efficacy scale. *Journal of Career Assessment, 4,* 47–57.

Betz, N. E., & Schifano, R. S. (2000). Evaluation of an intervention to increase realistic self-efficacy and interests in college women. *Journal of Vocational Behavior, 56,* 35–52.

Beutell, N. J., & Brenner, O. C. (1986). Sex differences in work values. *Journal of Vocational Behavior, 28,* 29–41.

Beyard-Tyler, K., & Haring, M. J. (1984). Navajo students respond to traditional occupations: Less information, less bias? *Journal of Counseling Psychology, 31*(2), 270–273.

Bhaerman, R. D. (1977). *Career education and basic academic achievement: A descriptive analysis of the research.* Washington, DC: U.S. Office of Education.

Bienstock, J. K. (1981). Reading and writing and the study of careers. *The College Board Review, 110,* 14–16.

Bigoness, W. J. (1978). Correlates of faculty attitudes toward collective bargaining. *Journal of Applied Psychology, 63*(2), 228–233.

Bikos, L. H., & Furry, T. S. (1999). The job search club for international students: An evaluation. *The Career Development Quarterly, 48,* 31–44.

Bikos, L. H., & O'Brien, K. M. (1993). *Upward Bound Career Exploration Program Manual.* Available from the second author, University of Kansas, 116 Bailey Hall, Lawrence, KS, 66045.

Bird, C. (1975). *The case against college.* New York: David McKay.

Bird, G. W., Bird, G. A., & Scruggs, M. (1984). Determinants of family task sharing: A study of husbands and wives. *Journal of Marriage and the Family, 46*(2), 345–355.

Birk, J. A., & Blimline, C. A. (1984). Parents as career development facilitators: An untapped resource for the counselor. *The School Counselor, 31*(4), 310–317.

Bizot, E. B., & Goldman, S. H. (1993). Prediction of satisfactoriness and satisfaction: An 8-year follow up. *Journal of Vocational Behavior, 43,* 19–29.

Bjorkquist, D. C. (1970). Technical education for the underemployment and unemployed. *Vocational Guidance Quarterly, 18,* 264–272.

Black, S. M., & Hill, C. E. (1984). The psychological well-being of women in their middle years. *Psychology of Women Quarterly, 8*(3), 282–292.

Blai, B. (1982). Programs for older persons: A compendium. *Journal of Employment Counseling,* 19(3), 98–105.

Bloch, D. P. (1989). From career information to career knowledge: Self, search, and synthesis. *Journal of Career Development, 16,* 119–128.

Bloch, D. P. (1996). Career development and workforce preparation: Educational policy versus school practice. *The Career Development Quarterly, 45,* 20–40.

Bloch, D. P., & Kinnison, J. F. (1989). Occupational and career information components: A validation study. *Journal of Studies in Technical Careers, 11,* 101–109.

Block, H. H. (1983). Differential premises arising from different socialization of the sexes: Some conjectures. *Child Development, 54,* 1335–1354.

Bloland, P. A., & Edwards, P. B. (1981). Work and leisure: A counseling synthesis. *Vocational Guidance Quarterly, 30*(2), 101–108.

Bloom, B. L. (1992). Computer-assisted psychological intervention: A review and commentary. *Clinical Psychology Review, 12,* 169–197.

Blustein, D. L. (1988). A canonical analysis of career choice crystallization and vocational maturity. *Journal of Counseling Psychology, 35*(3), 294–297.

Blustein, D. L. (1989). The role of goal instability and career self-efficacy in the career exploration process. *Journal of Vocational Behavior, 35*(2), 194–203.

Blustein, D. L. (1994). "Who am I?" The question of self and identity in career development. In M. L. Savickas & R. W. Lent (Eds.), *Convergence in career development theories. Implications for science and practice,* (pp. 139–154). Palo Alto, CA: CPP Books.

Blustein, D. L. (1997). A context-rich perspective of career exploration across the life-roles. *Career Development Quarterly, 45,* 260–274.

Blustein, D. L. (2001). The interface of work and relationships: Critical knowledge for 21st century psychology. *The Counseling Psychologist, 29*(2), 179–182.

Blustein, D. L., Ellis, M. V., & Devenis, L. E. (1989). The development and validation of a two-dimensional model of the commitment to career choice process. *Journal of Vocational Behavior, 35,* 342–378.

Blustein, D. L., & Novmair, D. A. (1996). Self and identity in career development: Implications for theory and practice. *Journal of Counseling and Development, 74,* 433–441.

Blustein, D. L., Pauling, M. L., Demania, M. E., & Faye, M. (1994). Relation between exploratory and choice factors and decisional progress. *Journal of Vocational Behavior 44,* 75–90.

Blustein, D. L., & Phillips, S. D. (1990). Relation between ego identity status and decision-making styles. *Journal of Counseling Psychology, 37,* 160–168.

Blustein, D. L., Walbridge, M. M., Friedlander, M. L., & Palladino, D. E. (1991). Contributions of psychological separation and parental attachment to the career development process. *Journal of Counseling Psychology, 38,* 39–50.

Bobo, M., Hildreth, B. L., & Duradoye, B. (1998). Changing patterns in career choices among African-American, Hispanic, and Anglo children. *Professional School Counseling, 1*(4), 37–42.

Boese, R. R., & Cunningham, J. W. (1976). Systematically derived dimensions of human work. *JSAS Catalog of Selected Documents in Psychology, 6,* 57. (Ms. No. 1270)

Bollendorf, M., Howrey, M., & Stephenson, G. (1990). Project Career REACH: Marketing strategies for effective guidance programs. *The School Counselor, 37*(3), 273–280.

Bolles, R. N. (1997). *Job hunting on the Internet.* Berkeley, CA: Ten Speed Press.

Bolton, B. (1994). USES General Aptitude Test Battery (GATB)/USES Interest Inventory (USES-II). In J. T. Kapes, M. M. Mastie, & E. A. Whitfield (Eds.), *A counselor's guide to career assessment instruments* (pp. 115–123). Alexandria, VA: National Career Development Association.

Bonett, R. M., & Stickel, S. A. (1992). A psychometric analysis of the Career Attitude Scale. *Measurement and Evaluation in Counseling and Development, 25,* 14–26.

Bonynge, E. R. (1992). No work and all play: An analysis of a response style on the Strong-Campbell Interest Inventory. *Journal of Counseling and Development, 69,* 275–276.

Boocock, S. S. (1967). The life career game. *Personnel and Guidance Journal, 45,* 328–334.

Boocock, S. S. (1968). *Instructor's manual for life career.* New York: Bobbs-Merrill.

Bordin, E. S. (1946). Diagnosis in counseling and psychotherapy. *Education and Psychological Measurement, 6,* 169–184.

Bordin, E. S. (1955). *Psychological counseling.* New York: Appleton-Century-Crofts.

Bordin, E. S. (1984). Psychodynamic model of career choice and satisfaction. In D. Brown & L. Brooks (Eds.), *Career choice and development: Applying contemporary theories to practice* (Chap. 5). San Francisco: Jossey-Bass.

Bordin, E. S. (1990). Psychodynamic models of career choice and satisfaction. In D. Brown & L. Brooks (Eds.), *Career choice and development. Applying contemporary theories to practice* (2nd ed., pp. 102–144). San Francisco: Jossey-Bass.

Bordin, E. S. (1994). Intrinsic motivation and the active self convergence from a psychodynamic perspective. In. M. L. Savickas & R. W. Lent (Eds.), *Convergence in career development theories: Implications for science and practice* (pp. 53–61). Palo Alto, CA: CPP Books.

Bordin, E. S., & Kopplin, D. A. (1973). Motivational conflict and vocational development. *Journal of Counseling Psychology, 20*(2), 154–161.

Bordin, E. S., Nachmann, B., & Segal, S. J. (1963). An articulated framework for vocational development. *Journal of Counseling Psychology, 10,* 107–116.

Borgen, F. H., Layton, W. L., Veenhuizen, D. L., & Johnson, D. J. (1985). Vocational behavior and career development, 1984: A review. *Journal of Vocational Behavior, 27,* 218–269.

Borgen, F. H., Weiss, D. J., Tinsley, H. F. A., Dawis, R. V., & Lofquist, L. H. (1972). *Occupational reinforcer patterns: I.* Minneapolis, MI: Vocational Psychology Research, Department of Psychology.

Borgen, W. A. (2000). Developing partnerships to meet clients' needs in changing government organizations: A consultative process. *Career Development Quarterly, 48,* 357–369.

Borgen, W. A., & Amundson, N. (1984). *The experience of unemployment. Implications for counseling the unemployed.* Scarborough, Ontario: Nelson Canada.

Borgen, W. A., & Amundson, N. E. (1985). Counseling immigrants for employment. In R. Samuda & A.

Wolfgang (Eds.), *Intercultural counseling: Global dimensions* (pp. 269–279). Toronto: C. J. Hografe.

Borgen, W. A., & Amundson, N. E. (2000). Youth unemployment and the transition from high school. *Educational and Vocational Guidance Bulletin, 64,* 32–43.

Borgen, W. A., & Young, R. H. (1982). Career perceptions of children and adolescents. *Journal of Vocational Behavior, 21,* 37–49.

Borman, C. (1994). Occupational Aptitude Survey and Interest Schedule–2 (OASIS–2). In J. T. Kapes, M. M. Mastie, & E. A. Whitfield (Eds.), *A counselor's guide to career assessment instruments* (pp. 104–110). Alexandria, VA: National Career Development Association.

Borman, C. (2002). Review of the Ability Explorer. In J. T. Kapes & E. A. Whitfield (Eds.). *A counselor's guide to career assessment instruments* (4th ed., pp. 76–81). Tulsa, OK: National Career Development Association.

Borman, G., & Colson, S. (1984). Mentoring—an effective career guidance technique. *Vocational Guidance Quarterly, 32*(3), 192–197.

Borman, K. M. (1991). *The first "real" job. A study of young workers.* Albany: The State University of New York Press.

Borman, K. M., Izzo, K. V., Penn, E. M., & Reisman, J. (1984). *The adolescent worker.* Columbus: Ohio State University, National Center for Research in Vocational Education.

Borow, H. (1961). Vocational development research: Some problems of logical and experimental form. *Personnel and Guidance Journal, 40,* 21–25.

Borow, H. (1970). Career development: A future for counseling. In W. Van Hoose & J. Pietrofesa (Eds.), *Counseling and guidance in the twentieth century* (pp. 30–46). Boston: Houghton Mifflin.

Borow, H. (1984). Occupational socialization: Acquiring a sense of work. In N. C. Gysbers (Ed.), *Designing careers, counseling to enhance education, work and leisure* (Chap. 6). San Francisco: Jossey-Bass.

Borow, H. (1989). Youth in transition to work: Lingering problems. *Guidance and counseling, 4*(4), 7–14.

Bosse, R., Aldwin, C. M., Levenson, M. R., & Ekerdt, D. J. (1987). Mental health differences among retirees and workers: Findings from the normative aging study. *Psychology and Aging, 2*(4), 383–389.

Boston, B. (1980). Second-order dimensions of the Work Values Inventory (WVI). *Journal of Vocational Behavior, 17,* 33–40.

Botterbusch, K. F. (1987). *Vocational assessment and evaluation systems: A comparison.* Menomonie, WI: Materials Development Center, Stout Vocational Rehabilitation Institute.

Bouchard, T. J., Jr., Arvey, R. D., Keller, L. M., & Segal, N. L. (1992). Genetic influences on job satisfaction: A reply to Cropanzano and James. *Journal of Applied Psychology, 77*(1), 89–93.

Bowen, D. D. (1985, February). Were men meant to mentor women? *Training and Development Journal,* 30–34.

Bowen, D. E., & Greiner, L. E. (1986, Summer). Moving from production to service in human resources management. *Organizational Dynamics,* 35–53.

Bowlby, J. A. (1958). The nature of the child's tie to his mother. *International Journal of Psychoanalysis, 39,* 350–373.

Bowman, S. L., & Tinsley, H. E. A. (1991). The development of vocational realism in Black American college students. *Career Development Quarterly, 39,* 240–250.

Boy, A. V., & Pine, G. J. (1963). *Client-centered counseling in the secondary school.* Boston: Houghton Mifflin.

Boyd, C., & Cramer, S. H. (1995). Relationship between Holland high-point code and client preferences for selected vocational counseling strategies. *Journal of Career Development, 21*(3), 213–221.

Bozarth, J. D. (1991). Person-centered assessment. *Journal of Counseling and Development, 69,* 458–461.

Bradley, R. W. (1994). Tests and counseling: How did we ever become partners? *Measurement and Evaluation in Counseling and Development, 26,* 224–226.

Bragg, D. (2000). Tech-prep, winning ideas, challenging practices. *Techniques, 75,* 14–17.

Bramel, D., & Friend, R. (1981). Hawthorne, the myth of the docile worker, and class bias in psychology. *The American Psychologist, 36*(8), 867–878.

Brammer, L. (1993). *The helping relationship: Process and skills* (5th ed.). Boston: Allyn and Bacon.

Brammer, L. M., & Shostrom, L. L. (1960). *Therapeutic psychology.* Englewood Cliffs, NJ: Prentice-Hall.

Brand, L. (1990). Occupational staffing patterns within industries through the year 2000. *Occupational Outlook Quarterly, 34*(3), 40–52.

Brass, D. J. (1981). Structural relationships, job characteristics, and worker satisfaction and performance. *Administrative Science Quarterly, 26*(3), 331–348.

Braude, L. (1975). *Work and workers: A sociological perspective.* New York: Praeger.

Brayfield, A. H., & Crites, J. O. (1964). Research on vocational guidance: Status and prospect. In H. Borow (Ed.), *Man in a world of work* (pp. 310–340). Boston: Houghton Mifflin.

Breeden, S. A. (1993). Job and occupational change as a function of occupational correspondence and job satisfaction. *Journal of Vocational Behavior, 43,* 30–45.

Bregman, G., & Killen, M. (1999). Adolescents' and young adults' reasoning about career choice and the role of parental influence. *Journal of Research on Adolescence, 9*(3), 253–275.

Brenner, M. H. (1973). *Mental illness and the economy.* Cambridge: Harvard University Press.

Brenner, M. H. (1979). Health and the national economy: Commentary and general principles. In L. A. Ferman & J. P. Gordus (Eds.), *Mental health and the economy.* Kalamazoo, MI: The W. E. Upjohn Institute for Employment Research.

Brenner, M. H. (1981). Importance of the economy to the nation's health. In L. Eisenberg & A. Kleinman (Eds.), *The relevance of social science for medicine* (pp. 371–396). Dordrecht, Holland: D. Reidel.

Brenner, M. H. (1987). Economic change, alcohol consumption and heart disease mortality in nine industrialized countries. *Social Science and Medicine, 25*(2), 119–132.

Brenner, M. H., & Swank, R. T. (1986). Homicide and economic change: Recent analysis of the Joint Economic Committee Report of 1984. *Journal of Quantitative Criminology, 2,* 81–103.

Brewer, J. M. (1942). *History of vocational guidance.* New York: Harper.

Brewington, J. O., & Nassar-McMillan, S. (2000). Older adults: Work-related issues and implications for counseling. *The Career Development Quarterly, 49,* 2–15.

Bridges, J. S. (1988). Sex differences in occupational performance expectations. *Psychology of Women Quarterly, 12,* 75–90.

Bridges, J. S. (1993). Pink or blue: Gender stereotypic perceptions of infants as conveyed by birth congratulations cards. *Psychology of Women Quarterly, 17,* 193–205.

Bridges, W. (1994, September) The end of the job. *Fortune, 130*(6), 62–74.

Brill, A. A. (1948). *Psychoanalytic psychiatry.* London: John Lehman.

Brim, O. G., & Kagan, J. (Eds.). (1980). *Constancy and change in human development.* Cambridge, MA: Harvard University Press.

Brisbin, L. A., & Savickas, M. L. (1994). Career indecision scales do not measure foreclosure. *Journal of Career Assessment, 2*(4), 352–363.

Brislin, R. (1993). *Understanding culture's influence on behavior.* Orlando, FL: Harcourt Brace & Company.

Brizzi, J. S. (1986). The socialization of women's vocational realism. *Vocational Guidance Quarterly, 34*(3), 151–159.

Brockner, J. (1988). *Self-esteem at work: Research, theory, and practice.* Lexington, MA: Lexington Books.

Broday, S. F., & Braswell, L. C. (1990). The relationship between academic comfort and other Strong Campbell Interest Inventory scales. *Journal of College Student Development, 31,* 454–459.

Brolin, D. E., & Gysbers, N. C. (1979). Career education for persons with handicaps. *Personnel and Guidance Journal, 58*(4), 258–262.

Brolin, D. E., & Gysbers, N. C. (1989). Career education for students with disabilities. *Journal of Counseling and development, 68,* 155–159.

Bronfenbrenner, U. (1979). *The ecology of human development.* Cambridge, MA: Harvard University Press.

Brooke, S. L., & Ciechalski, J. C. (1994). Minnesota Importance Questionnaire (MIQ). In J. T. Kapes, M. M. Mastie, & E. A. Whitfield (Eds.), *A counselors guide to career assessment instruments* (pp. 220–225). Alexandria, VA: National Career Development Association.

Brooks, L., & Betz, N. E. (1990). Utility of expectancy theory in predicting occupational choices in college students. *Journal of Counseling Psychology, 37*(1), 57–64.

Brooks, L., & Haigler, J. (1984). Contract career counseling: An option for some help seekers. *Vocational Guidance Quarterly, 33*(2), 178–182.

Brown, D. (1981). Emerging models of career development groups for persons at midlife. *Vocational Guidance Quarterly, 29*(4), 332–340.

Brown, D. (1984). Trait and factor theory. In D. Brown & L. Brooks (Eds.), *Career choice and development, applying contemporary theories to practice.* San Francisco: Jossey-Bass.

Brown, D. (1985). Career counseling: Before, after, or instead of personal counseling? *The Vocational Guidance Quarterly, 33*(3), 197–201.

Brown, D. (1996). Brown's value-based, holistic model of career and life-role choices and satisfaction. In D. Brown, L. Brooks, et al. (Eds.), *Career choices and development* (3rd ed., pp. 337–372). San Francisco: Jossey-Bass.

Brown, D., & Brooks, L. (1991). *Career counseling techniques,* Boston: Allyn and Bacon.

Brown, D., Brooks, L., et al. (1990). *Career choice and development, applying contemporary theories to practice* (2nd ed.) San Francisco: Jossey-Bass Publishers.

Brown, D., & Crace, R. K. (1996). Values in life role choices and outcomes: A conceptual model. *The Career Development Quarterly, 44,* 211–224.

Brown, D., Minor, C. W., & Jepsen, D. A. (1991). The opinions of minorities about preparing for work: Report of the Second NCDA National Survey. *Career Development Quarterly, 40,* 5–20.

Brown, D., Ware, W. B., & Brown, S. T. (1985). A predictive validation of the career decision-making system. *Measurement and Evaluation in Counseling and Development, 17*(2), 81–85.

Brown, D. A. (1980). Life-planning workshop for high school students. *The School Counselor, 29*(1), 77–83.

Brown, G. S., & Strange, C. (1981). The relationship of academic major and career choice status to anxiety among college freshmen. *Journal of Vocational Behavior, 19,* 328–334.

Brown, M. T. (1995). The career development of African Americans: Theoretical and empirical issues: In F. T. L. Leong (Eds.), *Career development and vocational behavior of racial and ethnic minorities.* (pp. 7–36)

Brown, S. D., & Lent, R. W. (1996). A social cognitive framework for career choice counseling. *The Career Development Quarterly, 44,* 354–366.

Brown, S. J. (1975). Career planning inventories: "Do-it-yourself" won't do. *Personnel and Guidance Journal, 53,* 512–517.

Brown, S. T., & Brown, D. (1990). *Designing and implementing a career information center.* Garrett Park, MD: Garrett Park Press.

Bruch, M. A., & Krieshok, T. S. (1981). Investigative versus realistic Holland types and adjustments in theoretical engineering majors. *Journal of Vocational Behavior, 18,* 162–173.

Buckley, M. R., Carraher, S. M., & Cote, J. A. (1992). Measurement issues concerning the use of inventories of job satisfaction. *Educational and Psychological Measurement, 52,* 529–543.

Buehler, C. (1933). *Der menschliche lebenslauf als psychologisches problem.* Leipzig: Hirzel.

Buescher, K. L., Johnston, J. A., Lucas, E. B., & Hughey, K. F. (1989). Early intervention with undecided college students. *Journal of College Student Development, 30,* 375–376.

Bujold, C. (1990). Biographical-hermeneutical approaches to the study of career development. In R. A. Young and W. E. Borgen (Eds.), *Methodological approaches to the study of careers* (pp. 57–70). New York: Praeger.

Bunda, R., & Mezzano, J. (1968). A study of the effects of a work-experience program on performance of potential dropouts. *The School Counselor, 15,* 272–274.

Burack, E. H. (1977). Why all of the confusion about career planning? *Human Resources Management,* 21–23.

Burke, R. J. (1986). Reemployment in a poorer job after a plant closing. *Psychological Reports, 58,* 559–570.

Burke, R. J. (1989). Toward a phase model of burnout. *Group and Organizational Studies, 14,* 23–32.

Burke, R. J. (1993). Toward an understanding of psychological burnout among police officers. *Journal of Social behavior and Personality, 8*(3), 425–438.

Burlew, A. K., & Johnson, J. L. (1992). Role conflict and career advancement among African American women in nontraditional professions. *Career Development Quarterly, 40,* 302–312.

Burlew, L. (1989). The Life-Long Leisure Graph: A tool for leisure counseling. *Journal of Career Development, 15*(3), 164–172.

Burley, K. (1994). Gender differences and similarities in coping responses to anticipated work-family conflict. *Psychological Reports, 74,* 115–123.

Burns, A., Scott, C., & Cooney, G. (1993). Career trajectories of single and married mothers who complete tertiary study as mature age students. *Education and Society, 11*(1), 39–50.

Burnett, F., & Burnett, S. (1988). *Working together: Entrepreneurial couples.* Berkeley: Ten Speed Press.

Burnstein, E. (1963). Fear of failure, achievement motivation, and aspiring to prestigeful occupations. *Journal of Abnormal and Social Psychology, 67,* 189–193.

Burr, P. L. (1980). Women: The emerging labor force. In C. S. Sheppard & D. C. Carroll (Eds.), *Working in the twenty-first century* (pp. 98–105). New York: Wiley.

Business Advisory Committee, Education Commission of the States. (1985). *Reconnecting youth.* Denver, CO: Author.

Bynner, J. M. (1998). Education and family components of identity in the transition from school to work. *International Journal of Behavioral Development, 22,* 29–50.

Byrne, B. M. (1993). The Maslach Burnout Inventory: Testing for factorial validity and invariance across elementary, intermediate, and secondary teachers. *Journal of Occupational and Organizational Psychology, 66,* 197–212.

Byrne, R. H. (1958). Proposed revisions of the Borden-Pepinsky Diagnostic Constructs. *Journal of Counseling Psychology, 5,* 184–187.

Cabral, A. C., & Salomone, P. R. (1990). Chance and careers: Normative versus contextual development. *Career Development Quarterly, 39,* 5–17.

Cahill, M., & Martland, S. (1995) Extending the reach: Distance delivery in career counseling. In B. Hiebert (Ed.), *Exemplary career development programs and practices, the best from Canada.* Greensboro: ERIC/

CASS, School of Education, University of North Carolina, Greensboro.

Cahill, M., & Salomone, P. R. (1987). Career counseling for work life extension: Integrating the older worker into the labor force. *The Career Development Quarterly, 35*(3), 188–196.

Cairns, K. (1998). *Using simulations to enhance career education.* Greensboro, NC: ERIC Clearinghouse on Counseling and Student Services.

Cairo, P. C. (1983a). Counseling in industry: A selected review of the literature. *Personnel Psychology, 36,* 1–18.

Cairo, P. C. (1983b). Evaluating the effects of computer-assisted counseling systems: A selective review. *The Counseling Psychologist, 11*(4), 55–59.

Cairo, P. C. (1985). Career planning and development in organizations. In Z. Leibowitz & D. Lea (Eds.), *Adult career development* (pp. 234–248). Washington, DC: National Career Development Association.

California State Department of Education. (1972). *Identification of major occupational groups and entry level jobs in civilian public service.* Sacramento, CA: Author.

Callanan, G. A., & Greenhaus, J. H. (1992). The career indecision of managers and professionals: An examination of multiple subtypes. *Journal of Vocational Behavior, 41,* 212–231.

Campbell, C. A., & Dahir, C. A. (1997). *The National Standards for School Counseling Programs.* Alexandria, VA: American School Counselor Association.

Campbell, D. P. (1993). A new integrated battery of psychological surveys. *Journal of Counseling and Development, 71,* 575–587.

Campbell, D. P., & Holland, J. L. (1972). A merger in vocational interest research: Applying Holland's theory to Strong's data. *Journal of Vocational Behavior, 2,* 353–376.

Campbell, N. J. (1988). Review of Self-Directed Search. In J. T. Kapes & M. M. Mastie (Eds.), *A counselor's guide to career assessment instruments* (pp. 116–120). Washington, DC: National Career Development Association.

Campbell, N. K., & Hackett, G. (1986). The effects of mathematics task performances in math self-efficacy and task interest. *Journal of Vocational Behavior, 28*(2), 149–162.

Campbell, N. K., & Hadley, G. B. (1992). Creating options: A career development program for minorities. *Journal of Counseling and Development, 70,* 645–647.

Campbell, R. E., & Cellini, J. V. (1981). A diagnostic taxonomy of adult career problems. *Journal of Vocational Behavior, 19*(2), 175–190.

Campbell, R. E., Connel, J. B., Boyle, K. K., & Bhaerman, R. (1983). *Enhancing career development. Recommendations for action.* Columbus. OH: The National Center of Research in Vocational Education, The Ohio State University.

Campbell, R. E., Suzuki, W. N., & Gabria, M. J., Jr. (1972). A procedural model for upgrading career guidance programs. *American Vocational Journal, 47*(1), 101–103.

Campbell, V. L. (1994). Ohio Vocational Interest Survey—2nd Edition (OVIS II). In J. T. Kapes, M. M. Mastie, & E. A. Whitfield (Eds.), *A counselor's guide to career assessment instruments* (pp. 200–205). Alexandria, VA: National Career Development Association.

Campbell, V. L., & Raiff, G. W. (2002). Review of the Career Decision-Making System. In J. T. Kapes & E. A. Whitfield (Eds.), *A counselor's guide to career assessment instruments.* (4th ed., pp. 230–234). Tulsa, Ok: National Career Development Association.

Capintero, H. (1994). Some historical notes on scientific psychology and its professional development. *Applied Psychology: An International Review, 43*(2): 131–150.

Caplan, N., Whitmore, J. K., & Choy, M. H. (1989). *The boat people and achievement in America: A study of family life, hard work, and cultural values.* Ann Arbor: University of Michigan Press.

Caplan, P. J., & Hall-McCorquodale, I. (1985a). Mother-blaming in major clinical journals. *American Journal of Orthopsychiatry, 55*(3), 345–353.

Caplan, P. J., & Hall-McCorquodale, I. (1985b). The scapegoating of mothers: A call for change. *American Journal of Orthopsychiatry, 55*(4), 610–613.

Caplow, T. (1976). *Principles of organization.* New York: Harcourt, Brace Jovanovich.

Cappeto, M. A. (1987). Career interest test results: A paradox. *Journal of College Placement,* 69–71.

Card, J. J., Steel, L., & Abeles, R. P. (1980). Sex differences in realization of individual potential for achievement. *Journal of Vocational Behavior, 17,* 1–21.

Carden, A. D. (1990). Mentoring and adult career development: The evolution of a theory. *The Counseling Psychologist, 18,* 275–299.

Carey, M. L. (1980). Evaluating the 1975 projections of occupational employment. *Monthly Labor Review, 103,* 10–12.

Carey, M. L. (1981a). Three paths to the future: Occupational projections, 1980–90. *Occupational Outlook Quarterly, 25*(4), 3–11.

Carkhuff, R. R. (1983), *The art of helping* (5th ed.). Amherst, MA: Human Resources Development Press.

Carlson, J. G. (1989). Affirmative: In support of researching the Myers-Briggs Type Indicator. *Journal of Counseling and Development, 67,* 484–486.

Carnevale, A. P., & Gainer, L. J. (1989). *The Learning Enterprise.* Washington, DC: U.S. Department of Labor, Employment and Training Administration/The American Society for Training and Development.

Carney, C. G., & Barak, A. (1976). A survey of student needs and student personnel services. *Journal of College Student Personnel, 17,* 280–284.

Carson, A. D. (1992). On occupationism. *The Counseling Psychologist, 20*(3), 490–508.

Carson, A. D., & Cartwright, G. F. (1997). Fifth generation computer-assisted career guidance systems. Chapter 2 in *Career Planning and Adult Development Journal,* Spring, 19–38.

Carson, A. D., & Dawis, R. V. (2000). Determining the appropriateness of career choice assessment (pp. 95–120). In D. A. Luzzo (Ed.), *Career counseling of college students.* Washington, DC: American Psychological Association.

Carsten, J. M., & Spector, P. E. (1987). Unemployment, job satisfaction, and employee turnover: A meta-analytic test of the Muchinsky model. *Journal of Applied Psychology, 72,* 374–381.

Carter, L., & Wilson, G. (1989). *Eighth Annual Status Report: Minorities in Higher Education.* Washington, DC: American Counselor Education.

Carter, R. T., Gushue, G. V., & Weitzman, L. M. (1994). White racial identity development and work values. *Journal of Vocational Behavior, 44,* 185–197.

Carter, R. T., & Swanson, J. L. (1990). The validity of the Strong Interest Inventory with black Americans: A review of the literature. *Journal of Vocational Behavior, 36,* 195–209.

Carver, D. S., & Smart, D. W. (1985). The effects of a career and self-exploration course for undecided freshmen. *Journal of College Student Personnel, 26*(1), 37–42.

Cassel, R. N., & Mehail, T. (1973). The Milwaukee computerized vocational guidance system (VOCGUID). *Vocational Guidance Quarterly, 21,* 206–213.

Caston, H. L., & Watson, A. L. (1990). Vocational assessment and rehabilitation outcomes. *Rehabilitation Counseling Bulletin, 34*(1), 61–66.

Castricone, A. M., Finan, W. W., & Grumble, S. K. (1982). Focus on career search: A program for high school students and their parents. *The School Counselor, 29*(5), 411–413.

Caulum, D., & Lambert, F. (Eds.). (1985). *Guidelines for the use of computer-based career information and guidance systems.* Eugene, OR: Association of Computer-Based Systems for Career Information Clearinghouse.

Cedoline, A. J. (1982). *Job burnout in public education: Symptoms, causes, and survival skills.* New York: Teachers College Press.

Cellarius, R., & Platt, J. (1972). Classification of crisis research studies by project areas. In R. Theobald (Ed.), *Futures conditional* (pp. 336–346). Indianapolis: Bobbs-Merrill.

Cesari, J. P. (1985). New women professionals in higher education: Counseling for intrapersonal mentoring. In D. Jones & S. S. Moore (Eds.), *Counseling adults: Life cycle perspectives.* Lawrence: University of Kansas.

Cesari, J. P., Winer, J. L., & Piper, K. R. (1984). Vocational decision status and the effect of four types of occupational information on cognitive complexity. *Journal of Vocational Behavior, 25,* 215–224.

Cesari, J. P., Winer J. L., Zychlinski, F., & Laird, I. O. (1982). Influence of occupational information giving on cognitive complexity in decided versus undecided students. *Journal of Vocational Behavior, 21,* 224–230.

Chang, D. (2002). The past, present, and future of career counseling in Taiwan. *The Career Development Quarterly, 50,* 218–225.

Chansky, N. M. (1965). Race, aptitude and vocational interests. *Personnel and Guidance Journal, 43,* 783–784.

Chao, G. T., Walz, P. M., & Gardner, P. D. (1992). Formal and informal mentorships: A comparison on mentoring functions and contrast with nonmentored counterparts. *Personnel Psychology, 45,* 619–636.

Chapman, W. (1983). *A context for career decision making* (Research report). Princeton, NJ: Educational Testing Service.

Chapman, W., & Katz, M. R. (1982a). *Career information system in secondary schools: Final report of study 2: Comparative effects of major types of resources.* Princeton, NJ: Educational Testing Service.

Chapman, W., & Katz, M. R. (1982b). *Summary of career information systems in secondary schools and assessment of alternative types.* Princeton, NJ: Educational Testing Service.

Chapman, W., & Katz, M. R. (1983). Career information systems in secondary schools. A survey and assessment. *Vocational Guidance Quarterly, 31,* 165–177.

Charner, I., & Schlossberg, N. K. (1986). Variations by theme: The life transitions of clerical workers. *Vocational Guidance Quarterly, 34*(4), 212–224.

Chartrand, J. M. (1991). The evolution of trait-and-factor career counseling: A Person X Environment fit approach. *Journal of Counseling and Development, 69,* 518–524.

Chartrand, J. M., Camp, C. C., & McFadden, K. L. (1992). Predicting academic adjustment and career indecision: A comparison of self-efficacy, interest congruence, and commitment. *Journal of College Student Development, 33,* 293–300.

Chartrand, J. M., Dohm, T. E., Dawis, R. V., & Lofquist, L. H. (1987). Estimating occupational prestige. *Journal of Vocational Behavior, 31,* 14–25.

Chartrand, J. M., Robbins, S. B., Morrill, W. H., & Boggs, K. (1990). Development and validation of the Career Factors Inventory. *Journal of Counseling Psychology, 37,* 491–501.

Chartrand, J. M., & Rose, M. L. (1996). Career interventions for at-risk populations: Incorporating social cognitive influences. *The Career Development Quarterly, 44,* 341–353.

Chartrand, J. M., Rose, M. L., Elliott, T. R., Marmarosh, C., & Caldwell, S. (1993). Peeling back the onion: Personality, problem-solving, and career decision-making style correlates of career indecision. *Journal of Career Assessment, 1* (1), 66–74.

Chassin, L., Zeiss, A., Cooper, K., & Reaven, J. (1985). Role perceptions, self-role congruence and marital satisfaction in dual-worker couples with preschool children. *Social Psychology Quarterly, 48*(4), 301–311,

Cheatham, H. E. (1990). Africentricity and career development of African Americans. *The Career Development Quarterly, 38,* 334–346.

Cheloa, R. S., & Farr, J. L. (1980). Absenteeism, job involvement, and job satisfaction in an organizational setting. *Journal of Applied Psychology, 65,* 467–473.

Chen, H., Marks, M. R., & Bersani, C. A. (1994). Unemployment classifications and subjective well-being. *The Sociological Review,* 42, 62–78.

Cherniss, C. (1980a). *Staff burnout: Job stress in the human services.* Beverly Hills, CA: Sage Publications.

Cherniss, C. (1980b). *Professional burnout in human service organizations.* New York: Praeger.

Chervenik, E., Nord, D., & Aldridge, M. (1982). Putting career planning and placement together. *Journal of College Placement, 42*(2), 48–51.

Chew, C. (1993). *Tech-prep and counseling: A resource guide.* Madison: Center on Education and Work, University of Wisconsin.

Chickering, A. W., & Reisser, L. (1993). *Education and identity* (2nd ed.). San Francisco, CA: Jossey-Bass.

Choate, P. (1982). *Retooling the American force: Toward a training strategy.* Washington, DC: Northeast-Midwest Institute.

Christensen, K. C. (1988). *The new era of home-based work: Directions and policies.* Boulder: Westview Press.

Christensen, K. C., Gelso, C. J., Williams, R. O., & Sedlacek, W. E. (1975). Variations in the administration of the self-directed search, scoring accuracy, and satisfaction with results. *Journal of Counseling Psychology, 22,* 12–16.

Christy, P. T., & Horowitz, K. J. (1979). An evaluation of BLS projections of 1975 production and employment. *Monthly Labor Review, 102,* 8–19.

Chung, Y. B. (1995). Career decision making of lesbian, gay, and bisexual individuals. *The Career Development Quarterly, 44,* 178–190.

Church, A. T., Teresa, J. S., Rosebrook, R., & Szendre, D. (1992). Self-efficacy for careers and occupational consideration in minority high school equivalency students. *Journal of Counseling Psychology, 39*(4), 498–508.

Chusid, H., & Cochran, L. (1989). Meaning of career change from the perspective of family roles and dramas. *Journal of Counseling Psychology, 36*(1), 34–41.

Chusmir, L. H. (1990). Men who make nontraditional career choices. *Journal of Counseling and Development, 69,* 11–16.

Ciechalski, J. C. (2002). Review of the Self-Directed Search. In J. T. Kapes & E. A. Whitfield (Eds.), *A counselor's guide to career assessment instruments.* (4th ed., pp. 282–287). Tulsa, OK: National Career Development Association.

Clark, A., Oswald, A., & Warr, P. (1996). Is job satisfaction u-shaped in age? *Journal of Occupational and Organizational Psychology, 69,* 57–81.

Clark, A. K. (1975). Career entry skills gap in the guidance chain. *Canadian Counselor, 9*(2), 126–131.

Clark, A. M., & Seals, J. M. (1975). Student perceptions of the social status of careers for college graduates. *Journal of College Student Personnel, 16*(4), 293–298.

Clarke, K. M., & Greenberg, L. S. (1986). Differential effects of the Gestalt two-chair intervention and problem-solving in resolving decisional conflict. *Journal of Counseling Psychology, 33,* 11–15.

Clarke, R., Gelatt, H. B., & Levine, L. (1965). A decision-making paradigm for local guidance research. *Personnel and Guidance Journal, 44,* 40–51.

Clauson, J. G. (1985). Is mentoring necessary? *Training and Development Journal, 39*(4), 36–39.

Clay, R. (1999). "Lean production" may also be a lean toward injuries. *APA Monitor, 30*(5), 26.

Cobas, J. A. (1986). Paths to self-employment among immigrants: An analysis of four interpretations. *Sociological Perspectives, 29*(1), 101–120.

Cochran, D., Hoffman, S., Strand, K., & Warren, P. (1977). Effects of client/computer interaction in career decision-making processes. *Journal of Counseling Psychology, 24,* 308–312.

Cochran, L. (1986). Harmonious values as a basis for occupational preference. *Journal of Vocational Behavior, 29,* 17–26.

Cochran, L. (1994). What is a career problem? *The Career Development Quarterly, 42,* 204–215.

Cochran, L. (1997). *Career counseling: A narrative approach.* Thousand Oaks, CA: Sage.

Cochran, L., & Amundson, N. (1985). *Activity self-exploration workbook.* Richmond, British Columbia, Canada: Buchanan.

Cochran, L. R. (1990). Narrative as a paradigm for career research. In K. A. Young & W. E. Borgen (Eds.), *Methodological approaches to the study of careers* (pp. 71–86). New York: Praeger.

Cohen, J. (1990). Things I have learned (so far). *American Psychologist, 45*(12), 1304–1312.

Cole, J. D., & Dodge, K. A. (1983). Continuities and changes in children's social status: A five-year longitudinal study. *Merrill Palmer Quarterly, 29,* 261–282.

Coleman, J. S. (1974). *Youth: Transition to adulthood.* Chicago: University of Chicago Press.

College Board Commission on Precollege Guidance and Counseling. (1986, January). *Keeping the options open, an overview.* New York: Author.

College Placement Council. (1991, July). 1991 Career planning & placement survey. Special report. *Spotlight, the council.* Bethlehem, PA.

College Placement Council Foundation/Rand Corporation. (1994). *Developing the global work force—Insights for colleges and corporations.* Bethlehem, PA: The College Placement Council.

Collins, M. (1998). Snapshot of the profession. *Journal of Career Planning and Employment, 41,* 32–36, 51–55.

Colson, C., Borman, C., & Nash, W. R. (1978). A unique learning opportunity for high school students. *Phi Delta Kappan, 59,* 542–543.

Coltrane, S., & Adams, M. (1997). Work-family imagery and gender stereotypes: Television and the reproduction of difference. *Journal of Vocational Behavior, 50,* 323–347.

Colwill, N., & Pollock, M. (1987). The mentor connection update. *Business Quarterly, 52,* 16–20.

Commission on Pre-College Guidance and Counseling. (1986). *Keeping the options open.* New York: The College Entrance Examination Board.

Commission on the Skills of the American Workforce. (1990). *America's choice: High skills or low wages.* Rochester, NY: National Center on Education and the Economy.

Commission on Workforce Quality and Labor Market Efficiency, U.S. Department of Labor. (1989). *Investing in people, a strategy to address America's workforce crisis.* Washington, DC: Author.

Committee on Definition, Division of Counseling Psychology, American Psychological Association. (1956). Counseling psychology as a speciality. *American Psychologist, 11,* 282–285.

Comparisons of competencies required for career counseling, career development facilitators, and career coaches. Unpublished paper. (2002). NCDA Professional Standards Committee. Tulsa, OK: National Career Development Association.

Conneran, J. M., & Hartman, B. W. (1993). The concurrent validity of the Self-Directed Search in identifying chronic career indecision among vocational education students. *Journal of Career Development, 19*(3), 197–208.

Conyers, L. M. (2002). Disability: An emerging topic in multicultural counseling. In J. Trusty, E. J. Looby, & D. S. Sandhu (Eds.), *Multicultural counseling: Context, theory and practice, and competence* (pp. 173–202). New York: Nova Science Publishers.

Cook, D. W. (1989). Systematic need assessment: A primer. *Journal of Counseling and Development, 67*(8), 462–464.

Cook, E. P. (1993). The gendered context of life: Implications for women's and men's career-life plans. *Career Development Quarterly, 35,* 76–88.

Cook, E. P., Heppner, M. J., & O'Brien, K. M. (2002). Career development of women of color and white women: Assumptions, conceptualization, and interventions from an ecological perspective. *The Career Development Quarterly, 50,* 291–305.

Cook, H. E. (1968). Vocational guidance materials: A survey for teachers. *American Vocational Journal, 13,* 25–28.

Cook, J. D., Hepworth, S. J., Wall, T., & Warr, P. B. (Eds.). (1981). *The experience of work.* New York: Academic Press.

Cook, T. D., Church, M. D., et al. (1996). The development of occupational aspirations and expectations among inner-city boys. *Child Development, 67*(6), 3368–3385.

Cook, W. J. (2001). *Strategic planning for America's schools.* Montgomery, AL: The Cambridge Group.

Cooker, P. G. (1973). Vocational values of children in grades four, five, and six. *Elementary School Guidance and Counseling, 8*(12), 112–118.

Cooper, C. L. (1986). Job distress: Recent research and the emerging role of the clinical occupational psychologist. *Bulletin of the British Psychological Society, 39,* 325–331.

Cooper, C. L., & Cartwright, S. (1994). Stress-management Interventions in the Workplace: Stress Counseling and Stress Audits. *British Journal of Guidance and Counseling, 22*(1), 65–73.

Cooper, S. E. (1986). The effects of group and individual vocational counseling on career indecision and personal indecisiveness. *Journal of College Student Personnel, 27*(1), 39–42.

Cooper, S. E., & Robinson, D. A. G. (1987). A comparison of career, home, and leisure values of males and females in engineering and the sciences. *Journal of College Student Personnel, 28,* 66–70.

Cooper, S. E., & Robinson, D. A. G. (1989). Childhood play activities of women and men entering engineering and science careers. *The School Counselor, 36*(4), 338–347.

Corbishley, M. A., & Yost, E. B. (1989). Psychological aspects of career counseling. *Journal of Career Development, 16,* 43–51.

Corrigan, P. W., Holmes, E. P., Luchins, D., Buican, B., Basit, A., & Parks, J. J. (1994). Staff burnout in a psychiatric hospital: A cross-lagged panel design. *Journal of Organizational Behavior, 15,* 65–74.

Costa, P. T. (1996). Work and personality: Use of the NEO-PI-R in industrial/organizational psychology. *Applied Psychology: An International Review, 45*(3), 225–241.

Costa, P. T., Jr., McCrae, R. R., & Holland, J. L. (1984). Personality and vocational interests in an adult sample. *Journal of Applied Psychology, 69*(3), 390–400.

Costello, T. W., & Zalkind, S. S. (Eds.). (1963). *Psychology in administration: A research orientation.* Englewood Cliffs, NJ: Prentice-Hall.

Council of Chief State School Officers. (1991). *European lessons from school and the workplace.* Washington, DC: The Author.

Courtenay, B. C. (1994). Are psychological models of adult development still important for the practice of adult education? *Adult Education Quarterly, 44*(3), 145–153.

Covey, S. R. (1989). *The seven habits of highly effective people. Restoring the character ethic.* New York: Simon & Schuster.

Craft, J. A., Doctors, S. I., Shkop, Y. M., & Benecki, T. J. (1979). Simulated management perceptions, hiring decisions, and age. *Aging and Work, 2*(2), 95–102.

Cramer, S. H., Herr, E. L., Morris, C. N., & Frantz, T. T. (1970). *Research and the school counselor.* Boston: Houghton Mifflin.

Cramer, S. H., & Keitel, M. (1984). Family effects of dislocation, unemployment, and discouragement. In S. H. Cramer (Ed.), *Perspectives on work and the family* (pp. 81–93). Rockville, MD: Aspen Systems.

Cramer, S. H., Keitel, M., & Rossberg, R. H. (1986). The family and employed mothers. *International Journal of Family Psychiatry, 7*(1), 17–34.

Cramer, S. H., Wise, P. S., & Colburn, E. D. (1977). An evaluation of a treatment to expand the career perceptions of high school girls. *The School Counselor, 25,* 125–129.

Creason, F., & Schilson, D. L. (1970). Occupational concerns of sixth-grade children. *Vocational Guidance Quarterly, 18,* 219–224.

Cremin, L. A. (1961). *The transformation of the school.* New York: Alfred Knopf.

Crites, J. O. (1961). A model for the measurement of vocational maturity. *Journal of Counseling Psychology, 8,* 255–259.

Crites, J. O. (1969). *Vocational psychology.* New York: McGraw-Hill.

Crites, J. O. (1973). *Career maturity inventory.* Monterey, CA: California Test Bureau/McGraw-Hill.

Crites, J. O. (1974a). Career development processes: A model for vocational maturity. In E. L. Herr (Ed.), *Vocational guidance and human development* (pp. 296–320). Boston: Houghton Mifflin.

Crites, J. O. (1974b). Methodological issues in the measurement of career maturity. *Measurement and Evaluation in Guidance, 6,* 200–209.

Crites, J. O. (1974c). Problems in the measurement of vocational maturity. *Journal of Vocational Behavior, 4,* 25–31.

Crites, J. O. (1974d). A reappraisal of vocational appraisal. *Vocational Guidance Quarterly, 22*(4), 272–279.

Crites, J. O. (1976). A comprehensive model of career development in early adulthood. *Journal of Vocational Behavior, 9,* 105–118.

Crites, J. O. (1978) *Career maturity inventory: Theory and research handbook* (2nd ed.). Monterey, CA: California Test Bureau/McGraw-Hill.

Crites, J. O. (1978). *Theory and research handbook for the career maturity inventory.* Monterey, CA: CTB/McGraw-Hill.

Crites, J. O. (1981). *Career counseling: Models, methods, and materials.* New York: McGraw-Hill.

Crites, J. O. (1986). Appraising adults' career capabilities: Ability, interest, and personality. In Z. Leibowitz & D. Lea (Eds.), *Adult career development: Concepts, issues, and practices* (pp. 63–83). Washington, DC: National Career Development Association.

Crites, J. O., & Savickas, M. L. (1996). Revision of the Career Maturity Inventory. *Journal of Career Assessment, 4*(2), 131–138.

Crites, J. O., & Taber, B. (2002). Appraising adults' career capabilities: Ability, interest, and personality. In S. Niles (Eds.), *Adult career development: Concepts, issues, and practices.* (pp. 120–138). Tulsa, OK: National Career Development Association.

Cronbach, L. J. (1979). The Armed Services Vocational Aptitude Battery—a test battery in transition. *Personnel and Guidance Journal, 57*(5), 232–237.

Cross, W. E., Jr. (1994). Nigrescence theory: Historical and explanatory notes. *Journal of Vocational Behavior, 44,* 119–123.

Croteau, J. M. (1996). Research and the work experiences of lesbian, gay, and bisexual people: An integrative review of methodology and findings. *Journals of Vocational Behavior, 48,* 195–209.

Croteau, J. M., & Slaney, R. B. (1994). Two methods of exploring interests: A comparison of outcomes. *The Career Development Quarterly, 43,* 252–261.

Croteau, J. M., & Thiel, M. J. (1993). Integrating sexual orientation in career counseling: Acting to end a form of the personal-career dichotomy. *Career Development Quarterly, 42,* 174–179.

Croteau, J. M., & von Destinon, M. (1994). A national survey of job search experiences of lesbian, gay, and bisexual student affairs professionals. *Journal of College Student Development, 35,* 40–45.

Crowley, J. E. (1985). Longitudinal effects of retirement on men's psychological and physical well-being. In H. S. Parnes, et al. (Eds.), *Retirement among American men* (pp. 147–173). Lexington, MA: Lexington Books.

Csikszentmihalyi, M. (1975). *Beyond boredom and anxiety.* San Francisco: Jossey-Bass.

Cummings, N. A. (1977). The anatomy of psychotherapy under national health insurance. *American Psychologist, 32*(9), 711–718.

Cummings, N. A. (1986). The dismantling of our health system. Strategies for the survival of psychological practice. *American Psychologist, 41*(4), 426–431.

Cummings, R., Maddux, C. D., & Casey, J. (2000). Individualized transition planning for students with learning disabilities. *The Career Development Quarterly, 49,* 60–72.

Cummings, S. (1980). White ethnics, racial prejudice, and labor market segmentation. *American Journal of Sociology. 86,* 938–950.

Curnow, T. C. (1989). Vocational development of persons with disability. *The Career Development Quarterly, 37,* 269–277.

Cutler, A., Ferry F., Kauk, R., & Robinett, R. (1995). *The Job-O enhanced professional manual.* Auburn, CA: CFKR Career Materials.

Cutshall, S. (2001). School to work. Has it worked? *Techniques, 76*(1), 18–21.

Cytrynbaum, S., Ginath, Y., Birdwell, J., & Brandt, C. (1979). Goal attainment scaling. *Evaluation Quarterly, 3,* 5–40.

D'Alonzo, C. A., & Fleming, A. J. (1973). Occupational psychiatry through the medical periscope. In R. L. Noland (Ed.). *Industrial mental health and employee counseling* (pp. 160–167). New York: Behavioral Publications.

Dalton, G., Thompson, P., & Price, R. (1977). Career stages: A model of professional careers in organizations. *Organization Dynamics, 6,* 19–42.

Dambrot, F. H., Watkins-Malek, M. A., Silling, S. M., Marshall, R. S., & Garver, J. (1985). Correlates of sex differences in attitudes toward and involvement with computers. *Journal of Vocational Behavior, 27*(1), 71–86.

Daniels, M. H. (1982). The heuristic value of Harren's career decision-making model for practitioners. *Journal of College Student Personnel, 23*(1), 18–24.

Daniels, M. H. (1985). Review of Social and Prevocational Information Battery. In J. V. Mitchell (Ed.), *The ninth mental measurements yearbook* (pp. 1408–1409). NJ: Gryphon Press.

Daniels, M. H. (1994). Self-Directed Search (SDS). In J. T. Kapes, M. M. Mastie, & E. A. Whitfield (Eds.), *A counselor's guide to career assessment instruments* (pp. 206–212). Alexandria, VA: National Career Development Association.

Danish, S. J. (1981). Life-span human development and intervention: A necessary link. *The Counseling Psychologist, 9*(2), 40–43.

Danish, S. J., Galambos, N. L., & Laquatra, I. (1983). Life development intervention: Skill training for personal competence. In R. D. Felman, L. A. Jason, J. Mortisuqur, & S. S. Farber (Eds.), *Preventive psychology: Theory, research, and practice* (pp. 49–66). Elmsford, NY: Pergammon Press.

Darr, J. T. (1981). The role of the employment counselor as presented in the *Journal of Employment Counseling. Journal of Employment Counseling, 18*(2), 87–96.

DaVanzo, J., & Rahman, M. O. (1993). American families: Trends and correlates. *Population Index, 59*(3), 20–32.

Davenport, T. O. (1999). *Human capital. What it is and why people invest it.* San Francisco, CA: Jossey-Bass Publishers, Inc.

Davidson, M. J., & Cooper, C. L. *(1992). Shattering the glass ceiling: The woman manager.* London: Paul Chapman Publishing Ltd.

Davidson, S. L., & Gilbert, L. A. (1993). Career counseling is a personal matter. *Career Development Quarterly, 42* (2), 149–153.

Davis, K. R., Giles, W. F., & Field, H. S. (1985). Recruiter assessments of job applicants' preferences: How accurate are they? *Vocational Guidance Quarterly, 33*(4), 315–323.

Davis, P. A., Hagen, N., & Strouf, J. (1962). Occupational choice of twelve-year-olds. *Personnel and Guidance Journal, 40,* 628–629.

Davis, R. C., & Horne, A. M. (1986). The effect of small group counseling and a career course on career decidedness and maturity. *Vocational Guidance Quarterly, 34,* 255–262.

Davis, S. J. (1990). The 1990–91 job outlook in brief. *Occupational Outlook Quarterly, 34*(1), 18–45.

Dawis, R. V. (1984). Job satisfaction: workers aspirations, attitudes, and behavior. In N. C. Gysbers (Ed.), *Designing careers, counseling to enhance education, work and leisure.* San Francisco: Jossey-Bass.

Dawis, R. V. (1994). The theory of work adjustment as convergent theory. In M. L. Savickas & R. W. Lent (Eds.). *Convergence in career development theories: Implications for science and practice* (pp. 33–44). Palo Alto, CA: CPP Books.

Dawis, R. V., Dohm, T. E., & Jackson, C. R. S. (1993). Describing work environments as reinforcer systems: Reinforcement schedules versus reinforcer classes. *Journal of Vocational Behavior, 43,* 5–18.

Dawis, R. V., Dohm, T. E., Lofquist, L. H., Chartrand, J. M., & Due, A. M. (1987). *Minneapolis Occupational Classification System III: A psychological taxonomy of work.* Minneapolis: Vocational Psychology Research, Department of Psychology, University of Minnesota.

Dawis, R. V., & Lofquist, L. H. (1978). A note on the dynamic of work adjustment. *Journal of Vocational Behavior, 12,* 76–79.

Dawis, R. V., & Lofquist, L. H. (1984). *A psychological theory of work adjustment: An individual-differences model and its applications.* Minneapolis, MN: University of Minnesota Press.

Dawis, R. V., Lofquist, L. H., Henly, G. A., & Rounds, J. B., Jr. (1979). *Minnesota Occupational Classification System II (MOCS II).* Minneapolis: Vocational Psychology Research Work Adjustment Project.

Day, S. X., & Rounds, J. (1997). "A little more than kin, and less than kind": Basic interests in vocational research and career counseling. *The Career Development Quarterly, 45*(3), 207–220.

Dayton, J. D., & Feldhusen, J. F. (1989). Characteristics and needs of vocational talented high school students. *The Career Development Quarterly, 37*(4), 355–364.

Dearman, N. B., & Plisko, V. W. (1981). *The condition of education* (1980 ed.). Washington, DC: National Center for Educational Statistics.

Deater-Deckard, K., & Scarr, S. (1996). Parenting stress among dual-earner mothers and fathers: Are there gender differences? *Journal of Family Psychology, 10*(1), 45–59.

Decker, P. J., & Borgen, F. H. (1993). Dimensions of work appraisal: Stress, strain, coping, job satisfaction, and negative affectivity. *Journal of Counseling Psychology, 40*(4), 470–478.

DeFrank, R. S., & Ivancevich, J. M. (1986). Job loss: An individual level review and model. *Journal of Vocational Behavior, 28,* 1–20.

DeFreitas, G. E. (1981). What is the occupational mobility of black immigrants? *Monthly Labor Review, 104,* 44–45.

Denson, E. L. (1994). Developing a freshman seminar for student-athletes. *Journal of College Student Development, 35,* 303–304.

Deren, S., & Randell, J. (1990). The vocational rehabilitation of substance abusers. *Journal of Applied Rehabilitation Counseling, 21*(2), 4–6.

Derr, C. B. (1980). More about career anchors. In C. B. Derr (Ed.), *Work, family, and the career* (pp. 166–187). New York: Praeger.

Derr, C. B. (1986). *Managing the new careerists.* San Francisco: Jossey-Bass.

DeVito, A. J. (1985). Review of Myers-Briggs Type Indicator. In J. V. Mitchell (Ed.), *The ninth mental measurements yearbook* (pp. 1030–1032). Lincoln: University of Nebraska.

Dew, M. A., Penkower, L., & Bromet, E. (1991). Effects of unemployment on mental health in the contemporary family. *Behavior Modification, 15*(4), 501–544.

Dewey, J. (1931). *Democracy and education.* New York: Macmillan.

Dewey, J. (1956). *School and society.* Chicago: University of Chicago Press. (Originally published, 1900).

Diamond, E. (Ed.). (1975). *Issues of sex bias and sex fairness in career interest measurement.* Washington, DC: National Institute of Education.

Diamant, L. (1993). *Homosexual issues in the workplace.* Washington, DC: Taylor & Francis.

Dillard, J. M. (1976). Socioeconomic background and the career maturity of black youths. *Vocational Guidance Quarterly, 25*(1), 65–70.

Dillard, J. M., & Campbell, N. J. (1981). Influences of Puerto Rican, black, and anglo parents' career behavior in their adolescent & children's career development. *Vocational Guidance Quarterly, 2,* 129–148.

Dillon, M., & Weissman, S. (1987). Relationship between personality types on the Strong-Campbell and Myers-Briggs instruments. *Measurement and Evaluation in Counseling and Development, 20,* 68–79.

DiPrete, T. A. (1981). Unemployment over the life cycle: Racial differences and the effect of changing economic conditions. *American Journal of Sociology, 87*(2), 286–307.

DiRusso, L., & Lucarino, V. (1989). Vocational education versus back to basics: A dilemma for counselors. *The School Counselor, 37*(2), 98–101.

District of Columbia Schools. (1976). *Career education in the inner city.* Interdisciplinary curriculum, grades 1–6. Washington, DC: Author.

Division 17. Education and Training Committee. (1982). Cross-cultural counseling competencies. *The Counseling Psychologist, 10*(2), 45–52.

Doane, C. J. (1971). *Vocational exploration group* (3rd ed.). *Leader Manual.* Tempe, AZ: Studies for Urban Man.

Doering, M. M., & Rhodes, S. R. (1989).Changing careers: A qualitative study. *The Career Development Quarterly, 37,* 316–333.

Doering, P. B., & Piore, M. J. (1971). *Internal labor markets and manpower analysis.* Lexington, MA: Lexington Books.

Dohrenwend, B. P. (1975). Sociocultural and social psychological factors in the genesis of mental disorders. *Journal of Health and Social Behavior, 16,* 365–392.

Domino, G. (1994). Career Survey. In J. T. Kapes, M. M. Mastie, & E. A. Whitfield (Eds.). *A counselor's guide to career assessment instruments* (pp. 86–89). Alexandria, VA: National Career Development Association.

Donaldson, E. L. (1989). *Links between education and employment. A case study of the transition from school-to-work.* Toronto, OISSE. Unpublished dissertation.

Donnay, D. A. C., & Borgan, F. H. (1996). Validity, structure, and content of the 1994 strong interest inventory. *Journal of Counseling Psychology, 43*(3), 275–291.

Donnay, D. A. C., & Borgan, F. H. (1999). The incremental validity of vocational self-efficacy: An examination of interest, self-efficacy, and occupation. *Journal of Counseling Psychology, 46*(4), 432–447.

Dore, R. (1987). *Taking Japan seriously: A Confucian perspective on leading economic issues.* Stanford, CA: Stanford University Press.

Dorfman, L. T., & Moffett, M. M. (1987). Retirement satisfaction in married and widowed rural women. *The Gerontologist, 27,* 215–221.

Dorn, F. J. (1986). Career development in business and industry. *Journal of Counseling and Development, 64,* 653–654.

Doty, M., & Betz, N. E. (1979). Comparison of the concurrent validity of Holland's theory for men and women in an enterprising occupation. *Journal of Vocational Behavior, 15,* 207–216.

Douce, L. A., & Hansen, J-I. C. (1990). Willingness to take risks and college women's career choice. *Journal of Vocational Behavior, 36,* 258–273.

Doyle, M. (2000). Managing careers in organizations. In A. Collin & R. Young (Eds.), *The future of career* (pp. 228–242). Cambridge, England: Cambridge University Press.

Draguns, J. (1985). Psychological disorders across cultures. In P. Pederson (Ed.), *Handbook of cross-cultural counseling and therapy* (pp. 55–62). Westport, CT: Greenwood Press.

Dreher, G. F. (1980). Individual needs as correlates of satisfaction and involvement with a modified Scanlon Plan company. *Journal of Vocational Behavior, 17,* 89–94.

Drier, H. N. (1971, June). *Implementing career development programs in high schools.* Paper presented at the Workshop on the Development of Guidelines for Planning Career Development Programs, K–12, Columbus, OH.

Droege, R. C. (1988). Review of Harrington-O'Shea Career Decision-Making System. In J. T. Kapes & M. M. Mastie (Eds.), *A counselor's guide to career assessment instruments* (pp. 86–90). Washington, DC: National Career Development Association.

Drucker, P. F. (1982). *The changing world of the executive.* New York: Truman Talley.

Drucker, P. F. (1986). *Innovation and entrepreneurship. Practice and principles.* New York: Perennial Library.

Drucker, P. F. (1989). *The new realities in government and politics/in economics and business/in society and the world view.* New York: Harper & Row.

Drucker, P. F. (1993). *Post-capitalist society.* New York: Harper Collins.

Drummond, R. J., McIntire, W. G., & Skaggs, C. T. (1978). The relationship of work values to occupational level in young adult workers. *Journal of Employment Counseling, 15*(3), 117–121.

Dudley, G. A., & Tiedeman, D. V. (1977). *Career development, exploration and commitment.* Muncie, IN: Accelerated Development.

Duffield, M. (1994). *Management development and unemployment.* Bristol: Institute of management.

Duke, B. (1986). *The Japanese School: Lessons for industrial America.* New York: Praeger.

Dumont, F., & Carson, A. (1995). Precursors of vocational psychology in ancient civilizations. *Journal of Counseling and Development,* 73(4), 371–378.

Dunlap, D. W. (1994). Gay survey raises new question. *The New York Times,* October 18, p. B8.

Dunne, F., Elliott, R., & Carlsen, W. S. (1981). Sex differences in the educational and occupational aspirations of rural youth. *Journal of Vocational Behavior, 18,* 56–66.

Dykeman, C. Herr, E. L., Ingram, M., Wood, C., Charles, S., & Pehrsson, D. (2001). *The taxonomy of career development interventions that occur in America's secondary schools.* A research report funded by the National Research Center for Career and Technical Education, the University of Minnesota.

Eby, L. T., McManus, S. E., Simon, S. A., & Russell, J. E. (2000). *Journal of Vocational Behavior, 57*(1), 1–21.

The Economist. (1993, July 24). Chronic joblessness. *328*(7821), 101.

The Economist. (1993, August 28). Getting Europe back to work. *328*(7826), 43–44.

The Economist. (2000, April 21). Internet economics. A thinker's guide. 355(8184), 64–66.

The Economist. (2002, March 2). Economic and financial indicators. 362 (8262), 98.

Edelwich, J., & Brodsky, A. (1980). *Burnout: Stages of disillusionment in the helping professions.* New York: Human Sciences Press.

Eder, R. W., & Ferris, G. R. (Eds.). (1989). *The employment interview: Theory, research, and practice.* Newbury Park, CA: Sage Publications.

Educational Testing Service. (1990). *From school to work.* Princeton, NJ: Author.

Edwards, J., & Rothbard, N. (1999). Work and family stress and well-being: An examination of person-environment fit in the work and family domains. *Organizational Behavior and Human Decision Processes, 77,* 85–129.

Edwards, P. B. (1980). *Leisure counseling techniques: Individual and group counseling step by step.* Los Angeles: Constructive Leisure.

Eggeman, D. F., Campbell, R. E., & Garbin, A. P. (1969, December). *Problems in the transition from school to work as perceived by youth opportunity center counselors.* Columbus, OH: Center for Vocational and Technical Education. Ohio State University.

Eisenberger, R., Cummings, J., Armeli, S., & Lynch, P. (1997). Perceived organizational support, discretionary treatment, and job satisfaction. *Journal of Applied Psychology, 82*(5), 812–820.

Ekerdt, D. J., Bosse, R., & Levkoff, S. (1985). An empirical test for phases of retirement: Findings from the normative aging study. *Journal of Gerontology, 40,* 95–101.

Elan, C. (1994). Application of Holland's theory of vocational personalities and work environments for medical student specialty selection. *Journal of Career Development, 21*(1), 37–48.

Elbaum, B. (June, 1989). Why apprenticeship persisted in Britain but not in the United States. *Journal of Economic History,* 337–349.

Elby, L. T., & Buch, K. (1995). Job loss as career growth: Responses to involuntary career transitions. *The Career Development Quarterly, 44,* 26–42.

Elizur, D. (1994). Gender and work values: A comparative analysis. *Journal of Social Psychology, 134*(2), 201–212.

Elizur, D., & Shye, S. (1990). Quality of work life and its relation to quality of life. *Applied Psychology: An International Review, 39*(3), 275–291.

Elkin, A. J., & Rosch, P. J. (1990). Promoting mental health at work. *Occupational Medicine, 5,* 739–754.

Elksnin, L. K., & Elksnin, N. (1991). The school counselor as job search facilitator: Increasing employment of handicapped students through job clubs. *The School Counselor, 38*(3), 215–220.

Ellermann, N. C., & Johnston, J. (1988). Perceived life roles and locus of control differences in women pursuing nontraditional and traditional academic majors. *Journal of College Student Development, 29,* 142–146.

Ellis, A. (1962). *Reason and emotion in psychotherapy,* Secaucus, NJ: Lyle Stuart.

Ellis, A. (1993a). The advantages and disadvantages of self-help therapy materials. *Professional Psychology: Research and Practice, 24*(3), 335–339.

Ellis, A. (1993b). Reflections on rational-emotive therapy. *Journal of Consulting and Clinical Psychology, 61*(2), 199–201.

Elmore, P. B., & Bradley, R. W. (1994). Armed Services Vocational Aptitude Battery (ASVAB) Career Exploration Program. In J. T. Kapes, M. M. Mastie, & E. A. Whitfield (Eds.), *A counselor's guide to career assessment instruments* (pp. 71–77). Alexandria, VA: National Career Development Association.

Elmore, P. B., Ekstrom, R., & Diamond, E. E. (1993). Counselors' test use practices: Indicators of the adequacy of measurement training. *Measurement and Evaluation in Counseling and Development, 26,* 116–124.

Elwood, J. A. (1992). The pyramid model: A useful tool in career counseling with university students. *Career Development Quarterly, 41,* 51–54.

Employment and Training Administration, U.S. Department of Labor. (1980). *Self-directed job search: An introduction.* Washington, DC: Author.

Enderlein, T. E. (1974). *Causal relationships of student characteristics related to satisfaction in post high school employment.* Unpublished doctoral dissertation, Pennsylvania State University.

Endicott, F. S. (1965; 1975). *The Endicott report.* Evanston, IL: Northwestern University.

England, G. W. (1990). The patterning of work meanings which are osterminous with outcome levels for individuals in Japan, Germany and the U.S.A. *Applied Psychology: An International Review, 39*(1), 29–45.

Entrekin, L. V., & Everett, J. E. (1981). Age and midcareer crisis: An empirical study of academics. *Journal of Vocational Behavior, 19*(1), 84–97.

Epperson, D., & Hammond, K. (1981). Use of interest inventories with Native Americans: A case for local norms. *Journal of Counseling Psychology, 28,* 213–220.

Erdner, R. A., & Guy, R. F. (1990). Career identification and women's attitudes toward retirement. *International Journal of Aging and Human Development, 30,* 129–139.

Erez, M., & Shneorson, Z. (1980). Personality types and motivational characteristics of academics versus professionals in industry in the same occupational disciplines. *Journal of Vocational Behavior, 17,* 95–105.

ERIC/CAPS. (1982). *Conducting a needs assessment. Highlights…An ERIC/CAPS Fact Sheet.* Ann Arbor, MI: Author.

Erikson, E. H. (1950). *Childhood and society,* New York: Norton.

Erikson, E. H. (1963). *Childhood and society* (2nd ed.). New York: Norton.

Erwin, T. D. (1982). The predictive validity of Holland's construct of consistency. *Journal of Vocational Behavior, 20,* 180–182.

Estroff, S. (1981). *Making it crazy.* Berkeley, CA: University of California Press.

Etaugh, C. (1974). Effects of maternal employment on children: A review of recent research. *Merrill-Palmer Quarterly of Behavior and Development, 29*(2), 71–98.

Etaugh, C. (1980). Effects of nonmaternal care on children: Research evidence and popular views. *American Psychologist, 35*(4), 309–319.

Etaugh, C. (1984). Effects of maternal employment on children: Implications for the family therapist. In S. H. Cramer (Ed.), *Perspectives on work and the family* (pp. 16–39). Rockville, MD: Aspen Systems.

European Commission. (1998). *European economy.* No. 65. Brussels, Belgium: Author.

Evanoski, P. O., & Tse, F. W. (1989). Career awareness program for Chinese and Korean American parents. *Journal of Counseling and Development, 67,* 472–474.

Evans, B. K., & Fischer, D. G. (1993). The nature of burnout: A study of the three-factor model of burnout in human service and non-human service samples. *Journal of Occupational and Organizational Psychology, 66,* 29–38.

Evans, K. M., & Herr, E. L. (1994). The influence of racial identity and the perception of discrimination on the career aspirations of African American men and women. *Journal of Vocational Behavior, 44,* 173–184.

Evans, R. N., & Herr, E. L. (1978). *Foundations of vocational education* (2nd ed.). Columbus, OH: Charles E. Merrill.

Eveland, A. P., Conyne, R. K., & Blakney, V. L. (1998). University students and career undecidedness: Effects of two computer-based career guidance interventions. *Computers in Human Behavior, 14*(4), 531–541.

Eves, J. H., Jr. (1986). When a plant shuts down: Easing the pain. *Personnel, 62*(2), 16–23.

Exum, H. A., & Lau, E. Y. (1988). Counseling style preference of Chinese college students. *Journal of Multicultural Counseling and Development, 16,* 84–92.

Eyde, L., & Kowal, D. (1984, August). *Ethical and professional concerns regarding computerized test interpretation services and users.* Paper presented at the American Psychological Association Convention.

Fagenson, E. A. (1992). Mentoring—who needs it? A comparison of proteges and nonproteges' needs for power, achievement, affiliation, and autonomy. *Journal of Vocational Behavior, 41,* 48–60.

Fallows, J. (1989). *More like us.* Boston: Houghton Mifflin.

Family Service America. (1984). *The state of families, 1984–85.* New York: Author.

Fanning, D. (1990), June 24). Weighing the fast track against family values. *The New York Times,* pp. D1.

Farber, B. A., & Heifetz, L. J. (1981). The satisfaction and stresses of psychotherapeutic work: A factor analytic study. *Professional Psychology, 12*(5), 621–630.

Farley, R. (1996). *The new American reality. Who are we, how we got here, where we are going.* New York: Russell Sage.

Farmer, H. S. (1976). What inhibits achievement and career motivation in women? *The Counseling Psychologist, 6,* 12–14.

Farmer, H. S. (1985). Model of career and achievement motivation for women and men. *Journal of Counseling Psychology, 6,* 12–14.

Farmer, H. S., & Associates. (Eds). (1997). *Diversity and women's career development. From adolescence to adulthood.* Thousand Oaks, CA: Sage Publications.

Farmer, H., Rotella, S., Anderson, C., & Wardrop, J. (1998). Gender differences in science, math and technology careers: Prestige level and Holland Interest Type. *Journal of Vocational Behavior, 53,* 73–96.

Farrell, M. P., & Rosenberg, S. D. (1981). *Men at midlife.* Boston: Auburn House.

Fassinger, R. E. (1987). Use of structural equation modeling in counseling psychology research. *Journal of Counseling Psychology, 34*(4), 425–436.

Fassinger, R. E. (1990). Causal models of career choice in two samples of college women. *Journal of Vocational Behavior, 36,* 225–248.

Fassinger, R. E. (1995). From invisibility to integration: Lesbian identity in the workplace. *The Career Development Quarterly, 44,* 148–167.

Faver, C. A. (1984). Women, achievement, and careers: Age variations in attitudes. *Psychology: A Quarterly Journal of Human Behavior, 21*(1), 45–49.

Feather, N. T., & Davenport, P. R. (1981). Unemployment and depressive affect: A motivational and attributional analysis. *Journal of Personality and Social Psychology, 41*(3), 422–436.

Feather, N. T., & O'Brien, G. E. (1986). A longitudinal study of the effects of employment and unemployment on school-leavers. *Journal of Occupational Psychology, 59,* 121–144.

Feck, V. (1971). *What vocational education teachers and counselors should know about urban disadvantaged youth.* (Center for Vocational Technical Education, Information Series, No 46). Washington, DC: U.S. Government Printing Office.

Feinberg, W. (1993). *Japan and the pursuit of a new American identity: Work and education in a multicultural age.* New York: Routledge.

Feingold, S. N., & Miller, N. R. (1983). *Emerging careers: New occupations for the year 2000 and beyond.* Garrett Park, MD: Garrett Park Press.

Feller, R. (1992). Career development: A baseline of career counseling outcomes research. In G. R. Walz & J. C. Bleuer (Eds.), *Counselor efficacy: Assessing and using counseling outcomes research* (pp. 5–22). Ann Arbor: ERIC Counseling and Personnel Services Clearinghouse.

Feller, R., & Daly, J. (2002). Review of the Career Thoughts Inventory. In J. T. Kapes & E. A. Whitfield (Eds.), *A counselor's guide to career assessment instruments.* (4th ed., pp. 344–348). Tulsa, OK: National Career Development Association.

Feller, R., & Wise, N. (1993). *Video usage in career development project.* Fort Collins, CO: Colorado State University.

Fergusson, D. M., Horwood, L. J., & Lynskey, M. T. (1997). The effects on unemployment on psychiatric illness during young adulthood. *Psychological Medicine, 27*(2), 371–381.

Fernandez, M. S. (1988). Issues in counseling Southeast Asian students. *Journal of Multicultural Counseling and Development, 16,* 157–166.

Ferree, M. M. (1984). Class, housework, and happiness: Women's work and life satisfaction. *Sex Roles, 11*(11/12), 1057–1074.

Ferrini, P., & Parker, L. S. (1978). *Career change, a handbook of exemplary programs in business and industrial firms, education institutions, government agencies, professional associations* (p. 64). Cambridge: Technical Education Research Centers.

Ferris, G. R., Youngblood, S. A., & Yates, V. L. (1985). Personality training, performance, and withdrawal: A test of the person-group fit hypothesis for organizational newcomers. *Journal of Vocational Behavior, 27*(3), 377–388.

Ferry, T. R., Fouad, N. A., & Smith, P. L. (2000). The role of family context in a social cognitive model for career-related choice behavior: A math and science perspective. *Journal of Vocational Behavior, 57,* 348–364.

Feuer, D. (1985). Retirement planning: A coming imperative. *Training,* 49–53.

Fielden, S. L., & Davidson, M. J. (1996). Sources of stress in unemployed female manager—an exporatory study. *International Review of Women and Leadership, 2*(2), 73–97.

Fielden, S. L., & Davidson, M. J. (2001). Stress and gender in unemployed female and male managers. *Applied Psychology: An International Review, 50*(2), 305–334.

Fifield, M., & Petersen, L. (1978). Job simulation: A model of vocational exploration. *Vocational Guidance Quarterly, 24,* 229–237.

Figler, H. (1989). *Liberal education and careers today.* Garrett Park, MD: Garrett Park Press.

Fine, M., & Asch, A. (1988). Disability beyond stigma: Social interactions, discrimination, and activism. *Journal of Social Issues, 44*(1), 3–21.

Finn, J. D. (1989). Withdrawing from school. *Review of Educational Research, 58*(2), 117–142.

Fiorentine, R. (1988). Increasing similarity in the values and life plans of male and female college students? Evidence and implications. *Sex Roles, 18* (3/4), 143–157.

Firth, J., & Shapiro, D. A. (1986). An evaluation of psychotherapy for job-related distress. *Journal of Occupational Psychology, 59,* 111–119.

Fiske, M. (1980). Changing hierarchies of commitment in adulthood. In N. J. Smelser & E. H. Erikson (Eds.),

Themes of work and love in adulthood (pp. 238–264). Cambridge, MA: Harvard University Press.

Fitz-enz, J. (1990). *Human value management. The value-adding human resource: Management strategy for the 1990s.* San Francisco: Jossey-Bass.

Fitzgerald, L. F., & Betz, N. E. (1983). Issues in the vocational psychology of women. In W. B. Walsh & S. H. Osipow (Eds.), *The handbook of vocational psychology* (pp. 83–159). Hillsdale, N.J.: Erlbaum.

Fitzgerald, L. F., & Betz, N. E. (1984). Astin's model in theory and practice: A technical and philosophical critique. *The Counseling Psychologist, 12*(4), 135–138.

Fitzgerald, L. F., & Cherpas, C. C. (1985). On the reciprocal relationship between gender and occupation: Rethinking the assumptions concerning masculine career development. *Journal of Vocational Behavior, 27,* 109–122.

Fitzgerald, L. F., & Harmon, L. W. (2001). Women's career development: A post-modern update. In F. T. L. Leong & A. Barak (Eds.), *Contemporary models in vocational psychology* (pp. 207–230). Mahwah, NJ: Erlbaum.

Fitzgerald, L. F., & Osipow, S. H. (1986). An occupational analysis of counseling psychology: How special is the specialty? *American Psychologist, 41*(5), 535–544.

Fitzpatrick, E. W. (1979). Evaluating a new retirement planning program: Results with hourly workers. *Aging and work, 2*(2), 87–94.

Fitzpatrick, J. L., & Silverman, T. (1989). Women's selection of careers in engineering: Do traditional-nontraditional differences still exist? *Journal of Vocational Behavior, 34*(3), 266–278.

Flake, M. H., Roach, A. J., Jr., & Stenning, W. F. (1975). Effects of short-term counseling on career maturity of tenth-grade students. *Journal of Vocational Behavior, 6,* 73–80.

Flanagan, J. C. (1978). *Perspectives on improving education: Project Talent's young adults look back.* New York: Praeger.

Flanagan, J. C., & Cooley, W. W. (1966). *Project Talent: One-year follow-up studies.* Pittsburgh: University of Pittsburgh Press.

Flanagan, J. C., Shaycroft, J. E., Richards, J., Jr., & Claudy, J. G. (1971). *Project Talent: Five years after high school.* Pittsburgh, PA: American Institute for Research.

Fleishman, E. A. (1968). Attitudes versus skill factors in work group productivity. *Personnel Psychology, 18,* 253–266.

Fleming, K. (1974). Reflections on manpower. *Vocational Guidance Quarterly, 22*(3), 224–229.

Flores, T. R., & Olsen, L. C. (1967). Stability and realism of occupational aspiration in eighth and twelfth-grade males. *Vocational Guidance Quarterly, 16,* 104–112.

Flores-Esteves, M. (1985). *Life after Shakespeare: Careers for liberal arts majors.* New York: Penguin Books.

Florida Department of Education. (1988). *Blueprint for career preparation.* Tallahassee, FL: Author.

Florida Department of Education. (1990). *Blueprint for career preparation, special edition.* Tallahassee, FL: Author

Flum, H., & Blustein, D. L. (2000). Reinvigorating the study of vocational exploration: A framework for research. *Journal of Vocational Behavior, 56,* 380–404.

Flynn, C., Vanderpool, N. M., & Brown, W. E. (1989). Reentry women's workshop: Program and evaluation. *Journal of College Student Development, 30* (July), 377–378.

Fontana, A., & Frey, J. H. (1990). Postretirement workers in the labor force. *Work and Occupations, 17*(3), 355–361.

Foote, B. (1980). Determined and undetermined students: How different are they? *Journal of College Student Personnel, 21*(1), 29–34.

Ford, D. Y., Harris, J. J., III, & Schuerger, M. (1993). Racial identity development among gifted Black students: Counseling issues and concerns. *Journal of Counseling and Development, 71,* 409–417.

Forey, W. F., Christensen, O. J., & England, J. T. (1994). Teacher burnout: A relationship with Holland and Adlerian typologies. *Individual Psychology, 50*(1), 3–17.

Forney, D. S., Wallace-Schutzman, F., & Wiggens, T. T. (1982). Burnout among career development professionals: Preliminary findings and implications. *Personnel and Guidance Journal, 60,* 435–439.

Forrer, S. E., Leibowitz, Z., & Dickelman, G. J. (1989). *Career Point: A computer based career development system for organizations.* Silver Springs, MD: Conceptual Systems, Inc.

Foss, C. J., & Slaney, R. B. (1986). Increasing nontraditional career choices in women: Relation of attitudes toward women and responses to a career intervention. *Journal of Vocational Behavior, 28,* 191–202.

Fottler, M. D., & Bain, T. (1980a). Managerial aspirations of high school seniors: A comparison of males and females. *Journal of Vocational Behavior, 16,* 83–95.

Fouad, N. A. (1994). Annual review 1991–1993: Vocational choice, decision-making, assessment, and intervention. *Journal of Vocational Behavior, 45,* 125–176.

Fouad, N. A., Hansen, J. C., & Arias-Galicia, F. (1986). Multiple discriminant analyses of cross-cultural similarity of vocational interests of lawyers and engineers. *Journal of Vocational Behavior, 28*(2), 85–96.

Fowler, E. M. (1990, February 20). Outplacement firms aiding the spouse. *The New York Times,* p. B40.

Frank, E. J. (1988). Business students' perceptions of women in management. *Sex Roles, 19* (1/2), 107–118.

Frederickson, R. H. (1986). Preparing gifted and talented students for the world of work. *Journal of Counseling and Development, 64,* 556–557.

Free, C. G., & Tiedeman, D. V. (1980). Counseling and comprehension of the economics of change. *Personnel and Guidance Journal, 58*(5), 358–367.

Freedy, J. R., & Hobfoll, S. E. (1994). Stress inoculation for reduction of burnout: A conservation of resources approach. *Anxiety, Stress, and Coping, 6,* 311–325.

Freeman, B. (1994). Importance of the National Career Development Guidelines to school counselors. *Career Development Quarterly, 42*(3), 224–228.

Frese, M., & Mohr, G. (1987). Prolonged unemployment and depression in older workers. *Social Science and Medicine, 25*(2), 173–178.

Fretz, B. R. (1981). Evaluating the effectiveness of career interventions. *Journal of Counseling Psychology, 28*(1), 77–90.

Fretz, B. R., Kluge, N. A., & Ossana, S. M. (1989). Intervention targets for reducing pre-retirement anxiety and depression. *Journal of Counseling Psychology, 36,* 301–307.

Fretz, B. R., & Leong, F. T. L. (1982a). Career development status as a predictor of career intervention outcomes. *Journal of Counseling Psychology, 29*(4), 388–393.

Fretz, B. R., & Leong, F. T. L. (1982b). Vocational behavior and career development, 1981: A review. *Journal of Vocational Behavior, 21*(2), 123–163.

Freudenberger, H. J. (1974). Staff burnout. *Journal of Social Issues, 30*(1), 159–165.

Fricko, M. A., & Beehr, T. A. (1992). A longitudinal investigation of interest congruence and gender concentration as predictors of job satisfaction. *Personnel Psychology, 45,* 99–117.

Friesen, J. (1986). The role of the family in vocational development. *International Journal for the Advancement of Counseling, 9*(1), 5–10.

Froelich, C. P. (1949). *Evaluating guidance procedures.* Washington, DC: U.S. Office of Education.

Frone, M. R., & Rice, R. W. (1987). Work-family conflict: The effect of job and family involvement. *Journal of Occupational Behavior, 8,* 45–53.

Fuchs, K. D. (1978). Intervention and life-span developmental psychology. *Human Development, 21,* 370–373.

Fukuyama, M. A., Probert, B. S., Neimeyer, G. J., Nevill, D., & Metzler, A. E. (1988). Effects of DISCOVER on career self-efficacy and decision-making of undergraduates. *The Career Development Quarterly, 37,* 56–62.

Fuqua, D. R., Blum, C. R., & Hartman, B. W. (1988). Empirical support for the differential diagnosis of career indecision. *Career Development Quarterly, 36,* 365–373.

Fuqua, D. R., & Newman, J. L. (1994). An evaluation of the Career Beliefs Inventory. *Journal of Counseling and Development, 72,* 429–433.

Fuqua, D. R., Newman, J. L., & Seaworth, T. B. (1990). Relation of state and trait anxiety to different components of career indecision. *Journal of Counseling Psychology, 35*(2), 154–158.

Fuqua, D. R., Seaworth, T. B., & Newman, J. L. (1987). The relationship of career indecision and anxiety: A multivariate examination. *Journal of Vocational Behavior, 30,* 175–186.

Fuqua, D. R., Seaworth, T. B., & Newman, J. L. (1988). Relation of state and trait anxiety to different components of career indecision. *Journal of Counseling Psychology, 35,* 154–158.

Furnham, A. (2001). Vocational (preference and P-O Fit: Reflections on Holland's theory of vocational choice. *Applied Psychology: An International Review, 50*(1), 5–29.

The Futurist. (2000, November–December). Outlook 2001. *34*(6), p. 3.

Gade, E., Fuqua, D., & Hurlburt, G. (1984). Use of the Self-Directed-Search with Native American high school students. *Journal of Counseling Psychology, 31,* 584–587.

Galassi, J. P., & Perot, A. R. (1992). What you should know about behavioral assessment. *Journal of Counseling and Development, 70,* 624–631.

Gallup, A. (1985). The Gallup Poll of teachers' attitudes toward the public schools, part 2. *Phi Delta Kappan, 66,* 323–330.

Gallup Organization, Inc. (1987). *Career development survey.* Conducted for National Career Development Association. Princeton, NJ: Author.

Garbin, A. P., Salomone, J. J., Jackson, D. P., & Ballweg, J. A. (1970). *Worker adjustment problems of youth in transition with high school to work.* Columbus, OH: Center for Vocational and Technical Education, Ohio State University.

Garden, A. M. (1989). Burnout: The effect of psychological type on research findings. *Journal of Occupational Psychology, 62,* 223–234.

Garden, A. M. (1991). Relationship between burnout and performance. *Psychological Reports, 68,* 963–977.

Gardner, J. (1999, December 20). World class workacholics. *U.S. News & World Report, 127*(24), 42–45, 45, 50, 52–53.

Gardner, J. M. (1995, April). Worker displacement: A decade of change. *Monthly Labor Review* 45–53.

Garfield, N. J., & Prediger, D. J. (1982). Testing competencies and responsibilities: A checklist for vocational counselors. In J. T. Kapes & M. M. Mastie (Eds.), *A counselor's guide to vocational guidance instruments* (pp. 21–28). Washington, DC: National Vocational Guidance Association.

Garis, J. W. (1982, August). *The integration of a computer-based system in a college counseling center: A comparison of the effects of DISCOVER and individual counseling upon career planning.* Unpublished doctoral dissertation, Pennsylvania State University.

Garis, J. W., & Hess, H. R. (1989). Career Navigator: Its use with college students beginning the job search process. *The Career Development Quarterly, 38,* 65–74.

Garis, J. W., & Niles, S. G. (1990). The separate and combined effects of SIGI or DISCOVER and a career planning course on undecided university students. *The Career Development Quarterly, 38,* 261–274.

Garland, H., & Smith, G. B. (1981). Occupational achievement motivation as a function of biological sex, sex-linked personality and occupational stereotypes. *Psychology of Women Quarterly, 5*(4), 568–585.

Garner, B. (1989). Work Wise: A career awareness course for teen parents. Cambridge, MA: Cambridge Community Services.

Garraty, S. A. (1978). *Unemployment in history, economic thought and public policy.* New York: Harper & Row.

Garson, B. (1988). *The electronic sweatshop.* New York: Simon & Schuster.

Gaskill, L. R. (1991). Same-sex and cross-sex mentoring of female proteges: A comparative analysis. *Career Development Quarterly, 40,* 48–63.

Gassin, E. A., Kelly, K. R., & Feldhousen, J. F. (1993). Sex development in the career development of gifted youth. *The School Counselor, 41*(2), 90–95.

Gati, I. (1986). Making career decisions—a sequential elimination approach. *Journal of Counseling Psychology, 33*(4), 408–417.

Gati, I. (1990). Why, when, and how to take into account the uncertainty involved in career decisions. *Journal of Counseling Psychology, 37,* 277–280.

Gati, I. (1993). Career compromises. *Journal of Counseling Psychology, 40*(4), 416–424.

Gati, I., & Asher, I. (2001). Prescreening, in-depth exploration, and choice: From decision theory to career counseling practice. *The Career Development Quarterly, 50,* 140–157.

Gati, I., & Blumberg, D. (1991). Computer versus counselor interpretation of interest inventories: The case of the Self-Directed Search. *Journal of Counseling Psychology, 38*(3), 350–366.

Gati, I., Fassa, N., Houminer, D. (1995). Applying decision theory to career counseling practice: The sequential elimination approach. *The Career Development Quarterly, 43,* 211–220.

Gati, I., Krausz, M., & Osipow, S. H. (1996). A taxonomy of difficulties in career decision making. *Journal of Counseling Psychology, 43*(4), 510–526.

Gati, I., & Saka, N. (2001). High school students' career-related decision-making difficulties. *Journal of Counseling & Development, 79,* 331–341.

Gati, I., Shenhav, M., & Givon, M. (1993). Processes involved in career preferences and compromises. *Journal of Counseling Psychology, 40*(1), 53–64.

Gati, I., & Tikotzki, Y. (1990). Strategies for collection and processing of occupational information in making career decisions. *Journal of Counseling Psychology, 36*(4), 430–439.

Gelatt, H. B. (1962) Decision-making. A conceptual frame of reference for counseling. *Journal of Counseling Psychology, 9,* 240–245.

Gelatt, H. B. (1989). Positive uncertainty: A new decision-making framework for counseling. *Journal of Counseling Psychology, 36*(2), 252–256.

Gelatt, H. B., Varenhorst, B., Carey, R., & Miller, G. P. (1973). *Decisions and outcomes.* New York: College Entrance Examination Board.

Gelso, C. J. (1979). Research in counseling: Methodological and professional issues. *The Counseling Psychologist, 8*(3), 7–36.

Gelso, C. J., Collins, A. M., Williams, R. O., & Sedlacek, W. E. (1973). The accuracy of self-administration and scoring on Holland's self-directed search. *Journal of Vocational Behavior, 3,* 375–382.

Genevay, B. (2000). There is life after work: Recreating oneself in later years. In N. Peterson & R. C. Gonzalez (Eds.), *Career counseling models for diverse populations: Hands-on applications by practitioners* (pp. 258–269). Belmont, CA: Wadsworth/Brooks Cole.

Gerhart, B. (1987). How important are dispositional factors as determinants of job satisfaction? Implications for job design and other personnel programs. *Journal of Applied Psychology, 72,* 366–373.

Gershuny, J. L., & Pahl, R. E. (1979–1980). Work outside employment: Some preliminary speculations. *New Universities Quarterly, 34*(1), 120–135.

Gerstein, L., Gaber, T., Dainas, C., & Duffey, K. (1993). Organizational hierarchy, employee status, and use of employee assistance programs. *Journal of Employment Counseling, 30,* 74–78.

Ghiselli, E. E. (1966). *The validity of occupational aptitude tests.* New York: Wiley.

Ghiselli, E. E. (1973). The validity of aptitude tests in personnel selection. *Personnel Psychology, 26,* 461–477.

Gianakos, I., & Subich, L. M. (1986). The relationship of gender and sex-role orientation to vocational undecidedness. *Journal of Vocational Behavior, 29,* 42–50.

Gianakos, I., & Subich, L. M. (1988). Student sex and sex role in relation to college major choice. *The Career Development Quarterly, 36,* 259–268.

Gibson, J. J. (1979). *The ecological approach to visual perception.* Boston: Houghton Mifflin.

Gibson, J. T., & Associates. (1991). Youth and culture: A seventeen nation study of perceived problems and coping strategies. *International Journal for the Advancement of Counselling, 14,* 203–216.

Gibson, R. C. (1987). Reconceptualizing retirement for Black Americans. *The Gerontologist, 27,* 691–698.

Gibson, R. L. (1962). Pupil opinions of high school guidance programs. *Personnel and Guidance Journal, 40,* 453–457.

Gibson, R. L. (1972). *Career development in the elementary school.* Columbus, OH: Charles Merrill.

Gibson, S. F., & Depoy, E. (2000). Multiculturalism and disability: A critical perspective. *Disability and Society, 15,* 207–218.

Gifford, R., Ng, C. F., & Wilkinson, M. (1985). Nonverbal cues in the employment interview: Links between applicant qualities and interviewer judgment. *Journal of Applied Psychology, 70*(4), 729–736.

Gilbert, H. G. (1966). *Children study American industry.* Dubuque, IA: William C. Brown.

Gilbert, L. A. (1985). *Men in dual-career families: Current realities and future prospects.* Hillsdale, NJ: Erlbaum.

Gilbert, L. A., Holahan, C. K., & Manning, L. (1981). Coping with conflict between professional and maternal roles. *Family Relations, 30*(3), 419–426.

Gilbert, L. A., & Rachlin, V. (1987). Mental health and psychological functioning of dual-career families. *The Counseling Psychologist, 15,* 7–49.

Giles, W. F., & Field, H. S. (1982). Accuracy of interviewers' perceptions of the importance of intrinsic and extrinsic job characteristics to male and female applicants. *Academy of Management Journal, 25*(1), 148–157.

Gill, A., & Lewis, S. M. (1996). *Help wanted. An inexperienced job seeker's complete guide to career success.* Prospect Heights, IL: Waveland Press.

Gill, S. J., & Fruehling, J. A. (1979). Needs assessment and the design of service delivery systems. *Journal of College Student Personnel, 20,* 322–328.

Gilligan, C. (1982a). *In a different voice.* Cambridge: Harvard University Press.

Gilligan, C. (1982b, June). Why should a woman be more like a man? *Psychology Today,* pp. 68–77.

Gilligan, C. (1983, May). *Challenging existing theories: Conclusions.* Paper presented at Eighth Annual Conference for Helpers of Adults, University of Maryland, College Park.

Gilmore, D. C., Beehr, T. A., & Love, K. G. (1986). Effects of applicant sex, applicant physical attractiveness, type of rater, and type of job on interview decisions. *Journal of Occupational Psychology, 59,* 103–109.

Ginzberg, E. (1972). Restatement of the theory of occupational choice. *Vocational Guidance Quarterly, 20*(3), 169–176.

Ginzberg, E. (1984). Career development. In D. Brown & L. Brooks (Eds.), *Career choice and development, applying contemporary theories to practice.* San Francisco, Jossey-Bass.

Ginzberg, E., Ginsburg, S. W., Axelrad, S., & Herma, J. (1951). *Occupational choice: An approach to a general theory.* New York: Columbia University Press.

Glaberson, W. (1990, October 4). One in 4 young black men are in custody, study says. *The New York Times,* p. B4.

Gladstein, G. A. (1994). *Changing careers.* Rochester, NY: University of Rochester Press.

Gladwin, T. (1967). Social competence and clinical practice. *Journal for the Study of Interpersonal Processes, 30,* 30–38.

Gloria, A. M., & Hird, J. S. (1999). Influences of ethnic and nonethnic values on the career decision-making self-efficacy of college students. *Career Development Quarterly, 48,* 157–174.

Gold, D., & Andres, D. (1978). Developmental comparisons between adolescent children with employed and nonemployed mothers. *Merrill-Palmer Quarterly, 24,* 243–254.

Gold, J. M., & Scanlon, C. R. (1993). Psychological distress and counseling duration of career and noncareer clients. *Career Development Quarterly, 42*(2), 186–191.

Gold, S. J. (1988). Refugees and small business: The case of Soviet Jews and Vietnamese. *Ethnic and Racial Studies, 11*(4), 411–438.

Goldberg, R. T. (1992). Toward a model of vocational development of people with disabilities. *Rehabilitation Counseling Bulletin, 35*(3), 161–173.

Goldman, L. (1961). *Using tests in counseling.* New York: Appleton-Century-Crofts.

Goldman, L. (1971). *Using tests in counseling* (2nd ed.). New York: Appleton-Century-Crofts.

Goldman, L. (1979). Research is more than technology. *The Counseling Psychologist, 8*(3), 41–44.

Goldman, L. (1994). The marriage between tests and counseling redux: Summary of the 1972 article. *Measurement and Evaluation in Counseling and Development, 26,* 214–216.

Goldman, L. (1994). The marriage is over…for most of us. *Measurement and Evaluation in Counseling and Development, 26,* 217–218.

Goleman, D. (1990, July 10). Homophobia: Scientists find clues to its roots. *The New York Times,* pp. C1, C11.

Goleman, D. (1995) *Emotional intelligence.* New York: Bantam Books.

Golembiewski, R. T. (1988). A note on Leiter's study: Highlighting two models of burnout. *Group and Organizational Studies, 13,* 129–134.

Golembiewski, R. T., & Munzenrider, R. F. (1988). *The phase model of burnout.* New York: Praeger.

Golembiewski, R. T., Munzenrider, R. F., Scherb, K., & Billingsley, W. (1992). Burnout and psychiatric "cases": Early evidences of an association. *Anxiety, Stress, and Coping, 5,* 69–78.

Gomez, M. J., & Fassinger, R. E. (1994). An initial model of Latina achievement: Acculturation, biculturalism, and achieving styles. *Journal of Counseling Psychology, 41*(3), 205–215.

Gonsalves, C. J. (1992). Psychological stages of the refugee process: A model for therapeutic interventions. *Professional Psychology: Research and Practice, 23*(5), 382–389.

Goodman, J., & Savage, N. (1999). Responding to a community's need: Oakland University's adult career counseling center. *The Career Development Quarterly,* 48, 19–30.

Goodman, P. S., & Friedman, A. (1971). An examination of Adams' theory of inequity. *Administrative Science Quarterly, 16,* 271–288.

Goodson, W. D. (1982). Status of career programs on colleges and university campuses. *Vocational Guidance Quarterly, 30*(3), 230–235.

Goodyear, R. K. (1990). Research on the effects of test interpretation: A review. *The Counseling Psychologist, 18,* 240–257.

Gordon, E. E. (2000). Help wanted: Creating tomorrow's work force. *The Futurist,* 34 (4), 48–67.

Gordon, M. (1974). *Higher education and the labor market.* New York: McGraw-Hill.

Gordon, R. A., & Arvey, R. D. (1986). Perceived and actual ages of workers. *Journal of Vocational Behavior, 28*(1), 21–28.

Gordon, V. N. (1981). The undecided student: A developmental perspective. *Personnel and Guidance Journal, 49*(7), 433–439.

Gordon, V. N. (1983). Meeting the career needs of undecided honor students. *Journal of College Student Personnel, 24,* 82–83.

Gordon, V. N., & Grites, T. J. (1984). Freshman seminar course: Helping students succeed. *Journal of College Student Personnel, 25*(4), 315–320.

Gottfredson, G. D. (1977). Career stability and redirection in adulthood. *Journal of Applied Psychology, 62*(4), 436–445.

Gottfredson, G. D. (1982). An assessment of a mobility-based occupational classification for placement and counseling. *Journal of Vocational Behavior, 21,* 71–98.

Gottfredson, G. D. (1990, August). *Applications and research using Holland's theory of careers: Where we would like to be and suggestions for getting there.* Paper prepared for a symposium, "Applications and Researching Using Holland's Theory of Careers: Some Evaluations," at the annual meeting of the American Psychological Association, Boston, MA.

Gottfredson, G. D., & Holland, J. L. (1990). A longitudinal test of the influence of congruence: Job satisfaction, competency utilization, and counterproductive behavior. *Journal of Counseling Psychology, 37*(4), 389–398.

Gottfredson, G. D., Holland, J. L., & Ogawa, D. K. (1982). *Dictionary of Holland occupational codes.* Palo Alto, CA: Consulting Psychologists Press.

Gottfredson, G. D., & Jones, E. M. (1993). Psychological meaning of profile elevation in the Vocational Preference Inventory. *Journal of Career Assessment, 1*(1), 35–49.

Gottfredson, G. D., Jones, E. M., & Holland, J. L. (1993). Personality and vocational interests: The relation of Holland's six interest dimensions to five robust dimensions of personality. *Journal of Counseling Psychology, 40*(4), 518–524.

Gottfredson, L. C. (1996). Gottfredson's theory of circumscription and compromise. In D. Brown & L. Brooks (Eds.), *Career choice and development* (3rd ed., pp. 179–232). San Francisco: Jossey-Bass.

Gottfredson, L. S. (1980). Construct validity of Holland's occupational typology in terms of prestige, census, Department of Labor, and other classification systems. *Journal of Applied Psychology, 65*(6), 697–714.

Gottfredson, L. S. (1981). Circumscription and compromise: A developmental theory of occupational aspirations. *Journal of Counseling Psychology, 28*(6), 545–579.

Gottfredson, L. S. (1982). Vocational research priorities. *The Counseling Psychologist, 10*(2), 69–84.

Gottfredson, L. S. (1986a). The g factor in employment. *Journal of Vocational Behavior, 29(3),* 293–296.

Gottfredson, L. S. (1986b). Occupational Aptitude Patterns (OAP) Map: Development and implications for a theory of job aptitude requirements. *Journal of Vocational Behavior, 29,* 254–291.

Gottfredson, L. S. (1986). Special groups and the beneficial use of vocational interest inventories. In W. B. Walsh & S. H. Osipow (Eds.), *Advances in vocational psychology. Vol. I. The assessment of interests.* (pp. 127–198). Hillsdale, NJ: Lawrence Erlbaum.

Gottfredson, L. S. (1988). Reconsidering fairness: A matter of social and ethical priorities. *Journal of Vocational Behavior, 33*(3), 293–319.

Gottfredson, L. S. (1990, December 6). When job-testing "fairness" is nothing but a quota. *The Wall Street Journal,* p. 23.

Gottfredson, L. S. (1994). The science and politics of race norming. *American Psychologist, 49*(11), 955–963.

Gottfredson, L. S., & Becker, H. J. (1981). A challenge to vocational psychology: How important are aspirations in determining male career development? *Journal of Vocational Behavior, 18,* 121.

Gottfredson, L. S., Finucci, J. M., & Childs, B. (1984). Explaining the adult careers of dyslexic boys: Variations in critical skills for high-level jobs. *Journal of Vocational Behavior, 24,* 355–373.

Gottfredson, L. S., & Sharf, J. C. (Eds.). (1988). Fairness in employment testing [Special issue]. *Journal of Vocational Behavior, 31,* 225–230.

Gough, H. G. (1985). A work orientation scale for the California psychological inventory. *Journal of Applied Psychology, 70*(3), 505–513.

Gould, R. (1978). *Transformations: Growth and change in adult life.* New York: Simon & Schuster.

Gould, R. (1972). The phases of adult life: A study of developmental psychology. *American Journal of Psychiatry, 1929*(11), 33–43.

Goulet, L. R., & Baltes, P. B. (Eds). (1970). *Life-span developmental psychology.* New York: Academic Press.

Graef, M. I., Wells, D. L., Hyland, A. M., & Muchinsky, P. M. (1985). Life history antecedents of vocational indecision. *Journal of Vocational Behavior, 27*(3), 276–297.

Graney, J. J., & Cottam, D. M. (1981). Labor force nonparticipation of older people: United States, 1890–1970. *The Gerontologist, 21*(2), 138–141.

Grant, C. A., & Sleeter, C. E. (1988). Race, class, and gender and abandoned dreams. *Teachers College Record, 90*(1), 19–40.

Graves, L. M., & Karren, R. J. (1992). Interviewer decision processes and effectiveness: An experimental policy-capturing investigation. *Personnel Psychology, 45,* 313–340.

Gray, D. O., & Braddy, B. A. (1988). Experimental social innovation and client-centered job-seeking programs. *American Journal of Community Psychology, 16,* 325–343.

Gray, K. C., & Herr, E. L. (1998). *Workforce education: The basics.* Boston: Allyn and Bacon.

Gray, K. C., & Herr, E. L. (2000). *Other ways to win. Creating alternatives for high school graduates* (2nd ed). Thousand Oaks, CA: Corwin Press.

Gray, K., & Xiaoli, S. (1999). *A benchmarking study of the class of 1998.* Unpublished research manuscript, Pennsylvania State University, University Park.

Green, K., Mariani, M., Crosby, O., Carpio, M., & Lacey, A. (2001–2002). Charting the projections [Special issue]. *Occupational Outlook Quarterly, 45*(4).

Greenberg, R. (2000). They learn from whom they serve. *Techniques, 75,* 18–21.

Greenhaus, J. H., Parasuraman, S., Granose, C. S., Rabinowitz, S., & Beutell, N. J. (1988). Sources of work-family conflict among two-career couples. *Journal of Vocational Behavior, 34*(2), 133–153.

Greenhaus, J. H., & Sklarew, N. D. (1981). Some sources and consequences of career exploration. *Journal of Vocational Behavior, 18,* 1–12.

Greenlee, S. P., Damarin, F. L., & Walsh, W. B. (1988). Congruence and differentiation among Black and White males in two non-college-degreed operations. *Journal of Vocational Behavior, 32*(3), 298–306.

Gregg, C. H., & Dobson, K. (1980). Occupational sex role stereotyping and occupational interests in children. *Elementary School Guidance and Counseling, 15*(1), 66–75.

Greller, M. (1990). Managing careers with a changing work force. *Journal of Organizational Change Management, 3*(2), 4–12

Gribbons, W. D., & Lohnes, P. R. (1968). *Emerging careers.* New York: Teachers College Press, Columbia University.

Gribbons, W. D., & Lohnes, P. R. (1969). *Career development from age 13 to 25.* (Final Report, Project No. 6–2151). Washington, DC: U.S. Department of Health, Education and Welfare.

Gribbons, W. D., & Lohnes, P. R. (1975). *Readiness for career planning* (revised). Buffalo: State University of New York at Buffalo, Department of Educational Psychology.

Gribbons, W. D., & Lohnes, P. R. (1982). *Careers in theory and experience: A twenty-year longitudinal study.* Albany: State University of New York Press.

Grieco, M. (1987). *Keeping it in the family: Social networks and employment chance.* London: Tavistock.

Griff, N. (1987). Meeting the career development needs of returning students. *Journal of College Student Personnel, 28,* 469–470.

Griffith, A. R. (1980). Justification for a black career development. *Counselor Education and Supervision, 19*(4), 301–310.

Grite, T. J. (1981). Being "undecided" might be the best decision they could make. *The School Counselor, 29*(1), 41–46.

Gross, E. (1975). Patterns of organizational and occupational socialization. *Vocational Guidance Quarterly, 24*(2), 140–149.

Grotevant, H. D., & Cooper, C. R. (1986). Exploration as a predictor of congruence in adolescents' career choices. *Journal of Vocational Behavior, 29,* 201–215.

Guerra, A. L., & Braungart-Rieker, J. M. (1999). Predicting career indecision in college students: The roles of identity formation and parental relationship factors. *The Career Development Quarterly, 47,* 255–266.

Guidance information system guide: Edition 12. (1981). Hanover, NH: TSC. Houghton-Mifflin.

Gunter, B. G., & Gunter, N. (1980). Leisure styles: A conceptual framework for modern leisure. *The Sociological Quarterly, 21,* 361–374.

Gustad, J. W., & Tuma, A. (1957). The effects of different methods of test introduction and interpretation on client learning in counseling. *Journal of Counseling Psychology, 4,* 313–317.

Gutek, B. A., & Winter, S. J. (1992). Consistency of job satisfaction across situations: Fact or framing artifact? *Journal of Vocational Behavior, 41,* 61–78.

Guthrie, W. R., & Herman, A. (1982). Vocational maturity and its relationship to Holland's theory of vocational choice. *Journal of Vocational Behavior, 21*(2), 196–205.

Gutteridge, T. G. (1986). Organizational career development systems: The state of the practice. In D. T. Hall & Assoc. (Eds.), *Career development in organizations.* San Francisco: Jossey-Bass.

Guttmann, D. (1978). Life events and decision making by older adults. *The Gerontologist, 18*(5), 462–467.

Gysbers, N. C. (1990). *Comprehensive guidance programs that work.* Ann Arbor: University of Michigan. ERIC/CAPS.

Gysbers, N. C., & Henderson, P. (1988). *Developing and managing your school guidance program.* Alexandria, VA: American Association for Counseling and Development.

Gysbers, N. C., Heppner, M. J., Johnston, J. A. (1998). *Career counseling. Process, issues, and techniques.* Boston: Allyn and Bacon.

Gysbers, N. C., & Moore, E. J. (1971). Career development in the schools. In G. F. Law (Ed.), *Contemporary concepts in vocational education.* Washington, DC: American Vocational Association.

Gysbers, N. C., & Moore, E. J. (1981). *Improving guidance programs.* Englewood Cliffs, NJ: Prentice-Hall.

Gysbers, N. C., & Moore, E. J. (1986). *Career counseling, skills and techniques for practitioners.* Englewood Cliffs, NJ: Prentice-Hall.

Gysbers, N. C., Starr, M. F., & Magnuson, C. S. (1998). *Missouri comprehensive guidance: A model for program development and implementation.* Jefferson City, MO: Missouri Department of Elementary and Secondary Education.

Haccoun, R. R., & Campbell, R. E. (1972). *Work entry problems of youth: A literature review.* Columbus: Ohio State University, Center for Vocational Technical Education.

Hackett, D. F. (1966). Industrial element for the elementary school. *School Shop, 25,* 58–62.

Hackett, G. (1985). The role of mathematics self-efficacy in the choice of math-related majors of college women and men: A path analysis. *Journal of Counseling Psychology, 32,* 47–56.

Hackett, G., & Betz, N. E. (1981). A self-efficacy approach to the career development of women. *Journal of Vocational Behavior, 18,* 326–339.

Hackett, G., & Byars, A. (1996). Social cognitive theory and the career development of African American women. *The Career Development Quarterly, 44,* 322–340.

Hackett, G., Esposito, D., & O'Halloran, M. S. (1989). The relationship of role model influences to the career salience and educational and career plans of college women. *Journal of Vocational Behavior, 35*(2), 164–180.

Hackett, G., Lent, R., & Greenhaus, J. (1991). Advances in vocational theory and research: A 20-year retrospective. *Journal of Vocational Behavior, 38,* 3–38.

Hackett, R. D. (1989). Work attitudes and employee absenteeism. A synthesis of the literature. *Journal of Occupational Psychology, 62,* 235–248.

Hackman, J. R., & Oldham, G. R. (1981). Work redesign: People and their work. In J. O'Toole, J. L. Scheiber, & L. C. Wood (Eds.), *Working, changes and choices* (pp. 173–182). New York: Human Sciences Press.

Hageman, M. B., & Gladding, S. T. (1983). The art of career exploration: occupational sex-role stereotyping among elementary school children. *Elementary School Guidance and Counseling, 17,* 280–287.

Hahn, W. A. (1980). The post-industrial boom in communications. In C. S. Sheppard & D. C. Carroll (Eds.), *Working in the twenty-first century* (pp. 30–38). New York: Wiley.

Halasz, T. J., & Kempton, C. B. (2000). Career planning workshops and courses. In D. A. Luzzo (Ed.), *Career counseling of college students. An empirical guide to strategies that work.* Washington, DC: American Psychological Association.

Hales, L. W., & Fenner, B. (1972). Work values of 5th, 8th, and 11th grade students. *Vocational Guidance Quarterly, 20*(3), 199–203.

Hales, L. W., & Fenner, B. (1973). Sex and social class differences in work values. *Elementary School Guidance and Counseling, 8*(1), 26–32.

Hall, C. S., & Lindzey, G. (1957). *Theories of personality.* New York: Wiley.

Hall, D. T. (1976). *Careers in organizations.* Pacific Palisades, CA: Goodyear.

Hall, D. T. (1985). Project work as an antidote to career plateauing in a declining engineering organization. *Human Resource Management, 24*(3), 271–292.

Hall, D. T. (Ed.). (1986). *Career development in organizations.* San Francisco: Jossey-Bass.

Hall, D. T. (1990). Career development theory in organizations. In D. Brown & L. Brooks (Eds.), *Career choice and development. Applying contemporary theories in practice* (2nd ed., pp. 422–454). San Francisco: Jossey-Bass Publishers.

Hall, D. T., & Mirvis, P. H. (1996). The new protean career: Psychological success and the path with a heart. In D. T. Hall & Associates (Eds.), *The career is dead—long live the career. A relational approach to careers* (pp. 15–45). San Francisco, CA: Jossey-Bass.

Hall, D. T., & Schneider, B. (1973). *Organizational climates and careers: The work lives of priests.* New York: Seminar Press.

Hall, M. E., & Rayman, J. R. (2002). Review of the Career Beliefs Inventory. In J. T. Kapes & E. A. Whitfield (Eds.), *A counselor's guide to career assessment instruments.* (4th ed., pp. 318–322). Tulsa, OK: National Career Development Association.

Hall, R. H. (1986). *Dimensions of work.* Newbury Park, CA: Sage Publications.

Hallett, M. B., & Gilbert, L. A. (1997). Variables differentiating university women considering role-sharing and conventional dual-career marriages. *Journal of Vocational Behavior, 50,* 308–322.

Halpern, A. S., Raffeld, P., Irvin, L. K., & Link, R. (1975). *Social and Prevocational Information Battery.* Monterey, CA: California Test Bureau/McGraw-Hill.

Hamburg, D. A., & Takaniski, R. (1989). Preparing for life. The critical transition of adolescence. *American Psychologist, 44*(5), 825–827.

Hamilton, L. S. (1990). *Apprenticeship for adulthood: Preparing youth for the future.* New York: The Free Press.

Hamilton, R. F., & Wright, J. D. (1976). *College educated blue collar workers.* American Sociological Association meeting, New York.

Hammer-Higgens, P., & Atwood, V. A. (1989). The management game: An educational intervention for counseling women with nontraditional career goals. *The Career Development Quarterly, 38,* 6–23.

Hamrin, R. D. (1981). The information economy. *The Futurist, 15*(4), 25–30.

Handel, L. (1973). Three tips on career guidance activities. *Elementary School Guidance and Counseling, 7*(4), 290–291.

Handy, C. (1994). *The age of paradox.* Cambridge, MA: Harvard Business School Press.

Handy, C. (1996). *Beyond certainty. The changing worlds of organizations.* Cambridge, MA: Harvard Business School Press.

Hanisch, K. A. (1992). The Job Descriptive Index revisited: Questions about the question mark. *Journal of Applied Psychology, 77*(3), 377–382.

Hanisch, K., & Hulin, C. L. (1990). Job attitudes and organizational withdrawal: An examination of retirement and other voluntary withdrawal behaviors. *Journal of Vocational Behavior, 37*(1), 60–78.

Hansen, D. A., & Johnson, V. (1989). Classroom lesson strategies and orientations toward work. In D. Stern & D. Eichorn (Eds.), *Adolescence and work: Influences of social structures, labor markets, and culture* (pp. 75–100). Hillsdale, NJ: Lawrence Erlbaum Associates.

Hansen, J. I. C. (1985). *Users guide for the SVIB-SII.* Palo Alto: Consulting Psychologists Press.

Hansen, J. I. C. (1987). Cross-cultural research on vocational interests. *Measurement and Evaluation in Counseling and Development, 20,* 65–71.

Hansen, J. I. C. (1994). The salience inventory. In J. T. Kapes, M. M. Mastie, & E. A Whitfield (Eds.), *A counselor's guide to career assessment instruments* (pp. 231–235). Alexandria, VA: National Career Development Association.

Hansen, J. C., & Cramer, S. H. (Eds.). (1971). *Group guidance and counseling in the schools.* New York: Appleton-Century-Crofts.

Hansen, J. C., Rossberg, R. H., & Cramer, S. H. (1994). *Counseling: Theory and process* (5th ed.). Boston: Allyn and Bacon.

Hansen, J. I., Kozberg, J. G., & Goranson, D. (1994). Accuracy of student recall of Strong Interest Inventory results 1 year after interpretation. *Measurement and Evaluation in Counseling and Development, 26,* 235–242.

Hansen, L. S. (1964–1965). The art of planmanship. *Chronicle guidance professional services.* Moravia, NY: Chronicle Guidance Publications.

Hansen, L. S. (1977). *An Examination of the concepts and definitions of career education.* Washington, DC: National Advisory Council for Career Education.

Hansen, L. S. (1981). New goals and strategies for vocational guidance and counseling. *International Journal for the Advancement of Counseling, 4*(1), 21–34.

Hansen, L. S. (1997). *Integrated life planning: Critical tasks for career development and changing life patterns.* San Francisco, CA: Jossey-Bass.

Hansen, L. S. (2002). Integrative life planning (ILP): A holistic theory for career counseling with adults. In S. Niles (Ed.), *Adult career development: Concepts, issues and practices* (pp. 57–75). Tulsa, OK: National Career Development Associationism.

Hansen, L. S., & Keierleber, D. L. (1978). Born free: A collaborative consultation model for career redevelopment and sex-role stereotyping. *Personnel and Guidance Journal, 56* (17), 395–399

Hansen, L. S., & Minor, C. W. (1989). *Work, family, and career development: Implications for persons, policies, and practices.* Washington, DC: National Career Development Association.

Hansen, L. S., & Tenneyson, W. W. (1975, May). A career management model for counselor involvement. *Personnel and Guidance Journal, 53*(9), 638–646.

Hansen, L. S., & Yost, M. (1989). Preparing youth for changing roles and tasks in society, work, and family. In R. Hanson (Ed.), *Career development: Preparing for the 21st century.* Knoxville: University of Tennessee, Department of Technological and Adult Education.

Hanson, W. E., Claiborn, C. D., Kerr, B. (1997). Differential effects of two test-interpretation styles in counseling: A field study. *Journal of Counseling Psychology, 44*(4), 400–405.

Hanson, W. E., Claiborn, C. D., & Kerr, B. (2001). Differential effects of two test-interpretation styles in counseling: A field study. In C. E. Hill (Ed.), *Helping skills: The empirical foundation* (pp. 401–412). Washington, DC: American Psychological Association.

Hardesty, G., & Utesch, W. E. (1996). *Counselors and computers: A survey of compatibility and use (online).* Abstract from: OVID File: ERIC Item: ED 376418.

Haring, M. J., & Beyard-Tyler, K. C. (1984). Counseling with women: The challenge of nontraditional careers. *The School Counselor, 31*(4), 301–309.

Haring-Hidore, M., & Beyard-Tyler, K. (1984). Counseling and research on nontraditional careers: A caveat. *Vocational Guidance Quarterly, 33*(2), 113–119.

Harlow, H. F. (1953). Mice, monkeys, men, and motives. *Psychological Review, 60,* 23–32.

Harmon, L. W. (1973). Sexual bias in interest measurement. *Measurement and Evaluation in Guidance, 5,* 496–501.

Harmon, L. W. (1989). Longitudinal changes in women's career aspirations: Developmental or historical? *Journal of Vocational Behavior, 35*(1), 46–63.

Harmon, L. W. (1994). Frustrations, daydreams, and realities of theoretical convergence. In M. L. Savickas & R. W. Lent (Eds.), *Convergence in career development theories. Implications for science and practice* (pp. 225–234). Palo Alto: CA: CPP Books.

Harmon, V., Barton, M., Carson, A. (1999, August). *Further examination of relations between abilities and interest codes.* Paper presented at the American Psychological Association Convention, Boston, MA.

Harootyan, R. A., & Feldman, N. S. (1990). Lifelong education, lifelong needs: Future roles in an aging society. *Educational Gerontology, 16,* 347–358.

Harpaz, I. (1985). Meaning of working profiles of various occupational groups. *Journal of Vocational Behavior, 26*(1), 25–40.

Harren, V. (1979). A model of career decision-making for college students. *Journal of Vocational Behavior, 14,* 119–133.

Harren, V. A., Kass, R. A., Tinsley, H., & Morehead, J. R. (1978). Influence of sex role attitudes and cognitive styles on career decision-making. *Journal of Counseling Psychology, 25*(5), 390–398.

Harrington, C. C. (1975). A psychological anthropologist's view of ethnicity and schooling. *IRCD Bulletin, 10*(4).

Harrington, T. F. (1993). A comparison of work-related values of adolescents from five countries. *International Journal for the Advancement of Counseling, 16*(2), 81–88.

Harrington, T. F., Feller, R., & O'Shea, A. J. (1993). Four methods to determine RIASEC codes for college majors and a comparison of hit rates. *Career Development Quarterly, 41*(4), 383–392.

Harris, J. S. (1968). The computerization of vocational information. *Vocational Guidance Quarterly, 17,* 20–21.

Harris, L. (1989). 2001: The world our students will enter. *College Board Review, 150.* (Winter), 20–24.

Harris, M. (1981). *America now: The anthropology of a changing culture.* New York: Simon & Schuster.

Harris, M. B., & Jones, L. (1981). Occu-Sort: A new career planning tool. *Journal of College Placement, 42*(1), 47–50.

Harris-Bowlsbey, J. Dikel, M. R., & Sampson, J. P., Jr. (1998). *The internet: A tool for career planning.* Columbus, OH: National Career Development Association.

Hart, D. H., Rayner, K., & Christensen, E. R. (1971). Planning, preparation and chance in occupational entry. *Journal of Vocational Behavior, 1,* 279–285.

Hartman, B. W., Fuqua, D. R., & Blum, C. R. (1985). A path-analytic model of career indecision. *Vocational Guidance Quarterly, 33*(3), 231–240.

Hartman, B. W., Fuqua, D. R., & Jenkins, S. J. (1986). The reliability/generalizability of the construct of career indecision. *Journal of Vocational Behavior, 28,* 142–148.

Hartman, E. (1993). A change of course. *Phi Delta Kappan, 74*(5), 405–406.

Hartman, S., Grigsby, D. W., Crino, M. D., & Chokar, J. S. (1986). The measurement of job satisfaction by action tendencies. *Educational and Psychological Measurement, 46,* 317–329.

Hartman, S. J., Griffeth, R. W., Miller, L., & Kinicki, A. J. (1988). The impact of occupation, performance, and sex on sex role stereotyping. *The Journal of Social Psychology, 128*(4), 451–463.

Hartung, P. J. (1999). Interest assessment using card sorts. In M. L. Savickas, & A. R. Spokane (Eds.), *Vocational interests: Their Meaning, measurement, and counseling use* (pp. 235–252). Palo Alto, CA: Davies-Black Publishing.

Hartung, P. J. (1999). Work illustrated: Attending to visual images in career information materials. *The Career Development Quarterly, 44,* 234–241.

Hartung, P. J., & Rogers, J. R. (2000). Work-family commitment and attitudes toward feminism in medical students. *The Career Development Quarterly, 48,* 264–275.

Hartung, P. J., Vandiver, B. J., Leong, F. T. L., Pope, M., Niles, S. G., & Farrow, B. (1998). Appraising cultural identity in career-development assessment and counseling. *The Career Development Quarterly, 46,* 276–293.

Hatt, P. K. (1962). Occupation and social stratification. In S. Nosow & W. H. Form (Eds.), *Man, work, and society* (pp. 238–249). New York: Basic Books.

Hattrup, K., Schmitt, N., & Landis, R. S. (1992). Equivalence of constructs measured by job specific and commercially available aptitude tests. *Journal of Applied Psychology, 77*(3), 298–308.

Haverkamp, B. E., Collins, R. C., & Hansen, J. I. (1994). Structure of interests of Asian-American college students. *Journal of Counseling Psychology, 41*(2), 256–264.

Havighurst, R. (1953). *Human development and education.* New York: Longmans Green.

Havighurst, R. J. (1964). Human development and education. In H. Borow (Ed.), *Man in a world at work* (Chapter 10). Boston: Houghton Mifflin.

Havighurst, R. J. (1965). Counseling adolescent girls in the 1960's. *Vocational Guidance Quarterly, 13,* 153–160.

Haviland, M. G., & Hansen, J-I. C. (1987). Criterion validity of the Strong-Campbell Interest Inventory for American Indian college students. *Measurement and Evaluation in Counseling and Development, 20,* 196–201.

Hawks, B. K., & Muha, D. (1991). Facilitating the career development of minorities: Doing it differently this time. *Career Development Quarterly, 39,* 251–260.

Hayes, D. G. (1982). Future shock and the counselor. In E. L. Herr & N. M. Pinson (Eds.), *Foundations for policy in guidance and counseling* (pp. 20–33). Washington, DC: American Personnel and Guidance Association.

Hayes, J., & Nutman, P. (1981). *Understanding the unemployed: The psychological effects of unemployment.* London: Tavistock.

Hayes, R. (1986). Gender nontraditional or sex atypical or gender dominant or…research: Are we measuring the same thing? *Journal of Vocational Behavior, 29,* 79–88.

Hayes, R. L. (1979). High school students' occupational interest as a function of project sex ratios in male-dominated occupations. *Journal of Applied Psychology, 84*(3), 275–279.

Hayghe, H. (1981). Husbands and wives as earners: An analysis of family data. *Monthly Labor Review.* U.S. Department of Labor, Bureau of Labor Statistics, *104*(2), 47.

Hazler, R. J., & Latto, L. D. (1987). Employers' opinions in the attitudes and skills of high school graduates. *Journal of Employment Counseling, 24*(3), 130–136.

Hazler, R. J., & Roberts, G. (1984). Decision making in vocational theory: Evolution and implications. *Personnel and Guidance Journal, 62*(7), 408–410.

Healy, C. C. (1973). Toward a replicable method of group career counseling. *Vocational Guidance Quarterly, 21,* 214–221.

Healy, C. C. (1974). Evaluation of a replicable group career counseling procedure. *Vocational Guidance Quarterly, 22,* 34–40.

Healy, C. C. (1989). Negative: The MBTI: Not ready for routine use in counseling. *Journal of Counseling and Development, 67,* 487–488.

Healy, C. C. (1990). Reforming career appraisals to meet the needs of clients in the 1990s. *The Counseling Psychologist, 18,* 214–226.

Healy, C. C. (1994). Career Maturity Inventory (CMI). In J. T. Kapes, M. M. Mastie, & E. A. Whitfield (Eds.), *A counselor's guide to career assessment instruments* (pp. 268–272). Alexandria, VA: National Career Development Association.

Healy, C. C., & Reilly, K. C. (1989). Career needs of community college students: Implications for services and theory. *Journal of College Student Development, 30* (6), 541–545

Heath, D. (1976). Adolescent and adult predictors of vocational adaptation. *Journal of Vocational Behavior, 9,* 1–19.

Heesacker, M., & Harris, J. E. (1993). Cognitive processes in counseling: A decisional tree integrating two theoretical approaches. *The Counseling Psychologist, 21*(4), 687–711.

Hegenauer, M., & Brown, S. (1990). A review of the Social and Prevocational Information Battery. *Journal of Counseling and Development, 68,* 338–340.

Heilman, M. E. (1979). High school students occupational interest as a function of projected sex ratios in male-dominated occupations. *Journal of Applied Psychology, 84*(3), 275–279.

Heimlich, J. E., & Van Tilburg, E. V. (1988). RE:FIT: Assessing career potential for dislocated farmers. *The Career Development Quarterly, 37,* 87–90.

Helgesen, S. (1996). Leading from the grass roots. In F. Hesselbein, M. Goldsmith, & R. Beckhard (Eds.). *The leader of the future. New visions, strategies, and practices for the new era* (pp. 19–24). San Francisco: Jossey-Bass.

Helman, C. (1985). Psyche, soma, and society: The social construction of psychosomatic disease. *Culture, Medicine and Psychiatry, 9,* 1–26.

Helms, J. E., & Piper, R. E. (1994). Implications of racial identity theory for vocational psychology. *Journal of Vocational Behavior, 44,* 124–138.

Helms, S. T. (1973). Practical applications of the Holland occupational classification in counseling. *Communique, 2,* 69–71.

Helmstadter, G. C. (1964). *Principles of psychological measurement.* New York: Appleton-Century-Crofts.

Helpingstine, S. R., Head, T. C., & Sorensen, P. F. (1981). Job characteristics, job satisfaction, motivation and satisfaction with growth: A study of industrial engineers. *Psychological Reports, 49,* 381–382.

Helwig, A (1998). Occupational aspirations of a longitudinal sample from second to sixth grade. *Journal of Career Development, 24*(4), 247–266.

Henderson, K. A. (1990). The meaning of leisure for women: An integrative review of the research. *Journal of Leisure Research, 22*(3), 228–243.

Henderson, K. A. (1994). Broadening an understanding of women, gender, and leisure. *Journal of Leisure Research, 26*(1), 1–7.

Henderson, P., & Gysbers, N. (1998). *Leading and managing your school guidance program staff.* Alexandria, VA: American Counseling Association.

Henley, B. (1986). The job interview: A workshop on self-esteem and dress for black students. *Journal of College Student Personnel, 27*(6), 564–566.

Hennig, M., & Jardin, A. (1977). *The managerial woman.* Garden City, NY: Anchor Press.

Henton, J. M., Russell, R., & Koval, J. E. (1983). Spousal preceptions of mid-life career change. *Personnel and Guidance Journal, 61*(5), 287–291.

Heppner, M. J., Multon, K. D., & Johnston, J. A. (1994). Assessing psychological resources during career change: Development of the Career Transitions Inventory. *Journal of Vocational Behavior, 44,* 55–74.

Heppner, M. J., O'Brien, K. M., Hinkelman, J. M., & Flores, L. Y. (1996). Training counseling psychologists in career development: Are we are own worst enemies? *The Counseling Psychologist, 24,* 105–125.

Heppner, P. P., & Krauskopf, C. J (1987). An information-processing approach to personal problem solving. *The Counseling Psychologist, 15,* 371–447.

Heppner, P. P., & Krieshok, T. S. (1983). An applied investigation of problem-solving appraisal, vocational identity and career service requests, utilization and subsequent evaluations. *Vocational Guidance Quarterly, 31*(4), 240–249.

Heppner, R. P., Kivlighan, D. M., Jr., & Wampold, B. E. (1992). *Research design in counseling.* Pacific Grove, CA: Brooks/Cole Publishing Company.

Hernandez, T. J., & Morales, N. E. (1999). Career, culture, and compromise: Career development experiences of Latinos working in higher education. *The Career Development Quarterly, 48,* 45–58.

Herold, D. M. (1990). Using technology to improve our management and labor market trends. *Journal of Organizational Change Management, 3*(2), 44–57.

Herr, E. L. (1969, March). *Unifying an entire system of education around a career development theme.* Paper presented at the National Conference of Exemplary Programs and Projects Section of the 1968 Amendments to the Vocational Education Act, Atlanta, GA.

Herr, E. L. (1972). *Review and synthesis of foundations for career education.* Columbus, OH: Center for Vocational and Technical Education, Ohio State University.

Herr, E. L. (1974). The decade in prospect: Some implications for vocational guidance. In E. L. Herr (Ed.), *Vocational guidance and human development* (Chap. 22). Boston: Houghton Mifflin.

Herr, E. L. (1976, April). *Does counseling work?* Speech presented to the Seventh International Roundtable for the Advancement of Counseling, University of Würzburg, Germany.

Herr, E. L. (1977a). The roots of career education. *College Board Review, 105,* 6–17, 32–33.

Herr, E. L. (1977b). *Career education: The state of research.* Columbus, OH: ERIC Clearinghouse for Career Education.

Herr, E. L. (1978a). Career development concepts and practices: Some international perspectives. *Counseling and Human Development, 11*(1), 1–11.

Herr, E. L. (1978b). *Research in career education: The state of the art.* Columbus, OH: ERIC Clearinghouse for Career Education.

Herr, E. L. (1979). The outcomes of career guidance. *Journal of Counseling Services, 3*(2), 6–15.

Herr, E. L. (1981). Policy in guidance and counseling: The U.S. experience. *Educational and Vocational Guidance, 37*(1), 67–83.

Herr, E. L. (1982c). Comprehensive career guidance: Future impact. *Vocational Guidance Quarterly, 30*(4), 367–376.

Herr, E. L. (1982d). The effects of guidance and counseling: Three domains. In E. L. Herr & N. M. Pinson (Eds.), *Foundations for policy in guidance and counseling.* Washington, DC: APGA Press.

Herr, E. L. (1982e, May). *Counselor education programs: Training for career development for exceptional people.* Paper presented at Johns Hopkins University, Baltimore.

Herr, E. L. (1984). Links among training, employability, and employment. In N. C. Gysbers (Ed.), *Designing careers. Counseling to enhance education, work, and leisure.* San Francisco: Jossey-Bass.

Herr, E. L. (1985a). International approaches to career counseling and guidance. In P. Pedersen (Ed.), *Handbook of cross-cultural counseling and therapy* (pp. 3–10). Westport, CT: Greenwood Press.

Herr, E. L. (1985b). The role of professional organizations in effecting the use of technology in career development. *Journal of Career Development 12*(2), 176–186.

Herr, E. L. (1986). *Why counseling?* (2nd ed.). Alexandria, VA: APGA Press.

Herr, E. L. (1989a). Career development and mental health. *Journal of Career Development, 16*(1), 5–18.

Herr, E. L. (1990, August). *Counseling for personal flexibility in a global economy.* Plenary paper presented at the XIVth World Congress, Counseling in a Global Economy, of the International Association for Educational and Vocational Guidance, Montreal, Canada.

Herr, E. L. (1991). *Guidance and counseling: A shared responsibility.* Alexandria, VA: National Association of College Admissions Counselors.

Herr, E. L. (October, 1993). *The crisis of unemployment.* Paper presented at the International Conference on Unemployment and Counseling. Eotuos Lander University, Budapest, Hungary.

Herr, E. L. (1994a). *Toward the convergence of career theory and practice: Mythology, issues, and possibilities.* Paper presented at the National Conference on the Convergence of Career Theory and Practice at the Ohio State University, May 5–6, 1994.

Herr, E. L. (1994b, July 20). *The role of schools, universities, and enterprises in human resource development of the work force for the 21st century.* Theme paper presented to the XVI International Conference on Human Resources, Guidance and Labour, Madrid, Spain.

Herr, E. L. (1995) *Counseling employment bound youth.* Greensboro, NC: ERIC/CAPS Publication.

Herr, E. L. (1997). Career counseling: A process in process. *British Journal of Guidance and Counselling, 25*(1), 81–93.

Herr, E. L. (1998). *Counseling in a dynamic society. Contexts and practices for the 21st century* (2nd ed.). Alexandria, VA: American Counseling Association.

Herr, E. L. (1999, January 20). *Career guidance and counseling in the 21st century: Continuity and change.* Paper presented at National Consultation on Career Development, Ottawa, Canada.

Herr, E. L. (1999). *Counseling in a dynamic society, contexts and practices for the 21st century.* Alexandria, VA: American Counseling Association.

Herr, E. L. (2001). Career development and its practice: A historical perspective. *The Career Development Quarterly, 49 (3),* 196–211.

Herr, E. L. (2002). Adult career development: Some perspectives on the future. In S. Niles (Ed.), *Adult career development: Concepts, issues, and practices* (pp. 389–398). Tulsa, Ok: National Career Development Association.

Herr, E. L., & Ashby, J. S. (1994). Kuder Occupational Interest Inventory, Form DD (KOIS). In J. T. Kapes, M. M. Mastie, & E. A. Whitfield (Eds.), *A counselor's guide to career assessment instruments* (pp. 194–199). Alexandria, VA: National Career Development Association.

Herr, E. L., & Best, P. (1984). Computer technology and counseling: The role of the profession. *Journal of Counseling and Development, 63*(4), 192–195.

Herr, E. L., & Cramer, S. H. (1968). *Guidance of the college bound: Problems, practices, and perspectives.* New York: Appleton-Century-Crofts.

Herr, E. L., & Cramer, S. H. (1972). *Vocational guidance and career development in the schools: Toward a systems approach.* Boston: Houghton Mifflin.

Herr, E. L., & Cramer, S. H. (1987). *Controversies in the mental health professions,* Muncie, IN: Accelerated Development Press.

Herr, E. L., & Cramer, S. H. (1996). *Career guidance and counseling through the life span. Systematic approaches* (5th ed.). New York: Harper Collins.

Herr, E. L., & Enderlein, T. (1976). Vocational maturity: The effects of school, grade, curriculum, and sex. *The Journal of Vocational Behavior, 8,* 227–238.

Herr, E. L., & Johnson, E. (1989). General employability skills for youths and adults: Goals for guidance and counseling programs. *Guidance & Counseling, 4*(4), 15–29.

Herr, E. L., & Lear, P. B. (1984). The family as an influence on career development. In S. H. Cramer (Ed.), *Perspectives on work and the family* (pp. 1–15). Rockville. MD: Aspen Systems.

Herr, E. L., & Niles, S. G. (1998). Career: Social action in behalf of purpose, productivity, and hope. In C. Lee & G. Waz (Eds.), *Social action: A mandate for counselors* (pp. 117–136). Alexandria, VA: American Counseling Association.

Herr, E. L., Rayman, J., & Garis, J. (1993). *Handbook for the college and university career center.* Westport, CT: Greenwood Press.

Herr, E. L., & Watts, A. G. (1981). The implications of youth unemployment for career education and for counseling. *Journal of Career Education, 7*(3), 184–202.

Herr, E. L., & Watts, A. G. (1988). Work shadowing and work-related learning. *The Career Development Quarterly 37*(1), 78–86.

Herr, E. L., Weitz, A., Good, R., & McCloskey, G. (1981). *Research on the effects of secondary school curricular and personal characteristics upon postsecondary educational and occupational patterns* (NIE-G-80–0027). University Park: The Pennsylvania State University.

Herring, C., & Wilson-Sadberry, K. R. (1993). Preference or necessity? Changing work roles of Black and White women, 1973–1990. *Journal of Marriage and the Family, 55,* 314–325.

Herring, R. D. (1990). Attacking career myths among Native Americans: Implications for counseling. *The School Counselor, 38,* 13–18.

Herring, R. D. (1996). Synergetic counseling and Native American Indian students. *Journal of Counseling & Development, 74,* 542–547.

Herring, R. D. (2002). Multicultural counseling for career development. In J. Trusty, E. J. Looby, & D. S. Sandhu (Eds.), *Multicultural counseling: Context, theory and practice, and competence* (pp. 219–246). New York: Nova Science Publishers.

Hershenson, D. B. (1968). Life-state vocational development system. *Journal of Counseling Psychology, 15,* 23–30.

Hershenson, D. B. (1974). Vocational guidance and the handicapped. In E. L. Herr (Ed.), *Vocational guidance and human development* (pp. 478–501). Boston: Houghton Mifflin.

Hershenson, D. B., & Roth, R. M. (1966). A decisional process model of vocational development. *Journal of Counseling Psychology, 13,* 368–370.

Hertz, R. (1986). *More equal than others: Women and men in dual-career marriages.* Berkeley: University of California Press.

Herzberg, F. (1968). One more time: How do you motivate employees? *Harvard Business Review, 46*(1), 53–62.

Herzberg, F., Mausner, B., & Snyderman, B. (1959). *The motivation to work.* New York: Wiley.

Hesketh, B., Elmslie, S., & Kaldor, W. (1990). Career compromise: An alternative account to Gottfredsson's theory. *Journal of Counseling Psychology, 37*(1), 49–56.

Hetherington, C., Hillerbrand, E., & Etringer, B. (1989). Career counseling with gay men: Issues and recommendations for research. *Journal of Counseling and Development, 67,* 452–454.

Hetherington, C., & Orzek, A. (1989). Career counseling and life planning with lesbian women. *Journal of Counseling and Development, 68,* 52–57.

Heyns, B., & Catsambis, S. (1986). Mother's employment and children's achievement: A critique. *Sociology of Education, 59,* 140–151.

Hiebert, B., & Bezanson, L. (2000). *Making waves: Career development and public policy.* Ottawa, Canada: Human Resources Development Canada/Canadian Career Development Foundation.

Higgins, N. C. (1986). Occupational stress and working women: The effectiveness of two stress reduction programs. *Journal of Vocational Behavior, 29,* 66–78.

Highhouse, S. (1999). The brief history of personnel counseling in industrial-organizational psychology. *Journal of Vocational Behavior, 55*(3), 318–336.

Hill, R. B., & Rojewski, J. W. (1999). Double jeopardy: Work ethic differences in youth at risk of school failure. *The Career Development Quarterly, 47*(3), 267–279.

Hiller, D. V., & Philliber, W. W. (1982). Predicting marital and career success among dual-worker couples. *Journal of Marriage and the Family, 44*(1), 53–62.

Hilton, T. J. (1962). Career decision-making. *Journal of Counseling Psychology, 9,* 291–298.

Hilton, M. (1991). Shared training: Learning from Germany. *Monthly Labor Review 114*(3): 33–37.

Hinkle, J. S. (1994). Practitioners and cross-cultural assessment: A practical guide to information and training. *Measurement and Evaluation in Counseling and Development, 27,* 103–114.

Hirschhorn, L. (1988). *The workplace within. Psychodynamics of organizational life.* Cambridge, MA: the MIT Press.

Hirschorn, M. W. (1988). Students over 25 found to make up 45 percent of campus enrollments. *The Chronicle of Higher Education, 34,* A35.

Hirshhorn, B. A., & Hoyer, D. T. (1994). Private sector hiring and use of retirees: The firm's perspective. *The Gerontologist, 34*(1), 50–58.

Hobfoll, S. (1998). *Stress, culture, and community: The psychology and philosophy of stress.* New York: Plenum.

Hobfoll, S. E. (2001). The influence of culture, community, and the nested self in the stress process: Advancing conservation of resource theory. *Applied Psychology: An International Review, 50*(3), 337–370.

Hock, E., Morgan, K., & Hock, M. D. (1985). Employment decisions made by mothers of infants. *Psychology of Women Quarterly, 9*(3), 383–402.

Hodgson, M., & Cramer, S. H. (1977). The relationship between selected self-estimated and measured abilities in adolescents. *Measurement and Evaluation in Guidance, 10*(2), 98–105.

Hodkinson, P. (1998). How young people make career decisions. *Education and Training, 40(6/7),* 301–306.

Hoffman, L. W. (1977). Changes in family role, socialization and sex differences. *American Psychologist, 32,* 644–657.

Hoffman, L. W. (1979). Maternal employment: 1979. *American Psychologist, 34*(10), 859–865.

Hoffman, L. W. (1986). Work, family and the child. In M. S. Pallak & R. Perloff (Eds.), *Psychology and work: Productivity, change, and employment* (pp. 169–220). Washington, DC: American Psychological Association.

Hoffman, L. W. (1989). Effects of maternal employment in the two-parent family. *American Psychologist, 44,* 283–292.

Hofstede, G. H. (1980). *Culture's consequences: International differences in work related values.* Beverly Hills, CA: Sage Publications.

Hogan, D. P., & Pazul, M. (1981). The career strategies of Black men. *Social Forces, 59*(4), 1217–1228.

Hohenshil, T. H. (2000). High tech counseling. *Journal of Counseling and Development, 78,* 365–368.

Hohenshil, T. H., & Delorenzo, D. (1999). Teaching career development via the internet. *Career Planning and Adult Development Journal, 19(2),* 56–60.

Holahan, C. K. (1981). Lifetime achievement patterns, retirement and life satisfaction of gifted aged women. *Journal of Gerontology, 36*(6), 741–749.

Holland, J. L. (1963). Explanation of a theory of vocational choice: Vocational images and choices. *Vocational Guidance Quarterly, 11,* 232–239.

Holland, J. L. (1966). *The psychology of vocational choice.* Waltham, MA: Blaisdell.

Holland, J. L. (1970). *Self-directed search.* Palo Alto: CA: Consulting Psychologists Press.

Holland, J. L. (1972). The present status of a theory of vocational choice. In J. M. Whitely & A. Resnikoff (Eds.), *Perspectives on vocational development* (Chap. 3). Washington, DC: APGA Press.

Holland, J. L. (1973a). *Making vocational choices: A theory of careers.* Englewood Cliffs, NJ: Prentice-Hall.

Holland, J. L. (1973b). *Sexism, personal development, and the self-directed search.* Unpublished manuscript. Center for Social Organization of Schools, Johns Hopkins University.

Holland, J. L. (1982). *Some implications of career theory for adult development and aging.* Paper presented at the American Psychological Association, Washington, DC.

Holland, J. L. (1984). *A theory of careers: Some new developments and revisions.* Paper presented at the American Psychological Association Convention, Toronto, Canada.

Holland, J. L. (1985). *Making vocational choices. A theory of vocational personalities and work environments* (2nd ed.). Englewood Cliffs, NJ: Prentice-Hall.

Holland, J. L. (1992). *Making vocational choices* (2nd ed.). Odessa, FL: Psychological Assessment-Responses.

Holland, J. L. (1994). Separate but unequal is better. In M. L. Savickas & R. W. Lent (Eds.), *Convergence in career development theories. Implications for science and practice* (pp. 45–51). Palo Alto, CA: CPP Books.

Holland, J. L. (1997). *Making vocational choices: A theory of vocational personalities and work environments.* (3rd ed.). Odessa, FL: Psychological Assessment Resource.

Holland, J. L., & Gottfredson, G. (1976). Using a typology of persons and environments to explain career: Some extensions and clarifications. *The Counseling Psychologist, 6*(3), 20–29.

Holland, J. L., & Gottfredson, G. D. (1990). *An annotated bibliography for Holland's theory of vocational personalities and work environments.* Baltimore: Johns Hopkins University.

Holland, J. L., Gottfredson, G. D., & Baker, H. G. (1990). Validity of vocational aspirations and interest inventories: Extended, replicated, and reinterpreted. *Journal of Counseling Psychology, 37,* 337–342.

Holland, J. L., Gottfredson, G., & Nafziger, D. (1975). Testing the validity of some theoretical signs of vocational decision-making ability. *Journal of Counseling Psychology, 22,* 411–422.

Holland, J. L., Gottfredson, G., & Power, P. (1980). Some diagnostic scales for research in decision-making and personality: Identity, information, and barriers. *Journal of Personality and Social Psychology, 39*(6), 1191–1200.

Holland, J. L., & Holland, J. E. (1977). Distributions of personalities within occupations and fields of study. *Vocational Guidance Quarterly, 25*(3), 226–231.

Holland, J. L., Johnston, J. A., & Asama, N. F. (1993). The Vocational Identity Scale: A diagnostic and treatment tool. *Journal of Career Assessment, 1*(1), 1–12.

Holland, J. L., Magoon, T. M., & Spokane, A. R. (1981). Counseling psychology: Career interventions, research, and theory. *Annual Review of Psychology, 32,* 279–300.

Holland, J. L., & Powell, A. B. (1994). *SDS career explorer.* Odessa, FL: Psychological Assessment Resources.

Holland, J. L., Viernstein, M. C., Kuo, H. M., Karweit, N. L., & Blum, S. D. (1970, November). A psychological classification of occupations (Report No. 90). Baltimore: Johns Hopkins University, Center for the Study of Social Organization of Schools.

Holland, M. (1981). Relationships between vocational development and self-concept in sixth grade students. *Journal of Vocational Behavior, 18,* 228–236.

Hollander, M. A., & Parker, H. J. (1969). Occupational stereotypes and needs. Their relationship to vocational choice. *Vocational Guidance Quarterly, 18,* 91–98.

Hollander, M. A., & Parker, H. J. (1972). Occupational stereotypes and self-descriptions: Their relationship to vocational choice. *Journal of Vocational Behavior, 2,* 57–65.

Hollender, J. W. (1972). Differential parental influence on vocational interest development in adolescent males. *Journal of Vocational Behavior, 2,* 67–76.

Hollender, J. W. (1974). Development of vocational decisions during adolescence. *Journal of Counseling Psychology, 18*(3), 244–248.

Holmes, J. (1964). The presentation of test information to college freshmen. *Journal of Counseling Psychology, 11,* 54–58.

Holmes, T. H., & David, E. M. (Eds.). (1989). *Life change, life events, and illness: Selected papers.* New York: Praeger.

Holmes, T. H., & Rahe, R. H. (1967). The social readjustment rating scale. *Journal of Psychosomatic Research, 11*(2), 213–218.

Holms, V. L., & Esses, L. M. (1988). Factors influencing Canadian high school girls' career motivation. *Psychology of Women Quarterly, 12,* 313–328.

Holzer, H. J. (1996). *What employers want. Job prospects for less-educated workers.* New York: Russell Sage Foundation.

Hopke, W. (1979). Work classification in ancient times. *Journal of Employment Counseling, 16*(1), 26–31.

Hoppock, R. (1935). *Job satisfaction.* New York: Harper.

Hoppock, R. (1950). Presidential address 1950. *Occupations, 28,* 497–499.

Hosford, R. E. (1970). Behavior counseling: A contemporary overview. *The Counseling Psychologist, 1,* 1–32.

Hosie, T. W., West, J. D., & Mackey, J. A. (1993). Employment and roles of counselors in employee assistance programs. *Journal of Counseling and Development, 71,* 355–359.

Hotchkiss, L., & Borow, H. (1984). Sociological perspective on career choice and attainment. In D. Brown & L. Brooks (Eds.), *Career choice and development: Applying contemporary theories to practice* (Chap. 6). San Francisco: Jossey-Bass.

Hotchkiss, L., & Borow, H. (1990). Sociological perspectives on work and career development. In D. Brown & L. Brooks (Eds.), *Career choice and development. Applying contemporary theories to practice* (pp. 262–307). San Francisco: Jossey-Bass.

Hotelling, K., & Forrest, L. (1985). Gilligan's theory of sex-role development: A perspective for counseling. *Journal of Counseling and Development, 64,* 183–186.

House, E. A. (1986). Sex role orientation and marital satisfaction in dual- and one-provider couples. *Sex Roles, 14*(5/6), 245–259.

House, J. S. (1974). Effects of occupational stress on physical health. In J. O'Toole (Ed.), *Work and the quality of life.* Cambridge, MA: MIT Press.

Houser, B. B., & Garvey, C. (1983). The impact of family, peers, and educational personnel upon career decision-making. *Journal of Vocational Behavior, 23,* 35–44.

Houser, R., Konstam, V., & Ham, M. A. (1990). Coping and marital satisfaction in dual career couples: Early stage dual career couples—wives as college students. *Journal of College Student Development, 31,* 325–329.

Howard, J. H., Richnitzer, P. A., Cunningham, D. A., & Donner, A. P. (1986). Change in Type A behavior a year after retirement. *The Gerontologist, 26*(6), 643–649.

Howard-Hamilton, M., Lawler, A. M., Talleyrand, C., & Smith, R. (1994). Image enhancement and career workshops for female athletes. *Journal of College Student Development, 35,* 66–68.

Hoyt, K. B. (1965). High school guidance and the specialty oriented student research program. *Vocational Guidance Quarterly, 13,* 229–236.

Hoyt, K. B. (1975). *Career education: Contributions to an evolving concept.* Salt Lake City, UT: Olympus.

Hoyt, K. B. (1978). Refining the concept of collaboration in career education. *Monographs on career education.* Washington, DC: U.S. Office of Education.

Hoyt, K. B. (1979). *A primer for career education.* Washington, DC: Office of Career Education.

Hoyt, K. B. (1980a). Contrasts between the guidance and the career education movements. In F. E. Burtnett (Ed.), *The school counselor's involvement in career education.* Falls Church, VA: American Personnel and Guidance Association.

Hoyt, K. B. (1982). Federal and state participation in career education: Past, present, and future. *Journal of Career Education, 9*(1), 5–15.

Hoyt, K. B. (1988). The changing workforce: A review of projections—1986 to 2000. *The Career Development Quarterly, 37,* 31–39.

Hoyt, K. (1994). A proposal for making transition from schooling to employment an important component of educational reform. In *High school to employment transition: Contemporary issues.* Ann Arbor, MI: Prakken Press.

Hoyt, K. B. (1994). Youth apprenticeship "American style" and career development. *The Career Development Quarterly, 42,* 216–223.

Hoyt, K. B. (2001). Helping high school students broaden their knowledge at postsecondary education options. *Professional School Counseling,5*(1), 6–12.

Hoyt, K. B., & Lester, J. N. (1995). *Learning to work: The NCDA Gallup Survey.* Alexandria, VA: National Career Development Association.

Huang, L., Pergamit, M., & Shkolnik, J. (2001). Youth initiation into the labor market. *Monthly Labor Review, 124*(8), 18–24.

Hudson Institute. (1987). *Workforce 2000: Work and workers for the 21st century.* Indianapolis, IN: Author.

Huffine, C. L., & Clausen, J. A. (1979). Madness and work: Short and long-term effects of mental illness on occupational careers. *Social Forces, 57*(4), 1049–1062.

Huffman, M. L., & Torres, L. (2001). Job Search methods: Consequences for gender-based earnings inequality. *Journal of Vocational Behavior, 58,* 127–141.

Hughes, C. M., Martinek, S. A., & Fitzgerald, L. F. (1985). Sex role attitudes and career choices: The role of children's self-esteem. *Elementary School Guidance and Counseling, 20,* 57–66.

Hughey, K. F., Gysbers, N. C., & Starr, M. (1993). Evaluating comprehensive school guidance programs: Assessing the perceptions of students, parents, and teachers. *The School Counselor, 41,* 31–35.

Hulbert, K. D., & Schuster, D. T. (1993). *Women's lives through time: Educated American women of the twentieth century.* San Francisco: Jossey-Bass.

Hulin, C. L., Henry, R. A., & Noon, S. L. (1990). Adding a dimension: Time as a factor in the generalizability of predictive relationships. *Psychological Bulletin, 107,* 328–340.

Hull, D. M., & Pedrotti, L. S. (1983). Meeting the high-tech challenge. *VOCED, 58* (31), 28–31.

Hulsart, R. (1983). *Employability skills study.* Denver: Department of Education.

Hunt, E. E. (1970). *Career development K—6: A background paper or initial suggestions.* Paper presented to the Program Development Committee of the Cobb Country Schools, GA.

Hunt, J. M. (1961). *Intelligence and experience.* New York: Ronald Press.

Hurk, W. M., & Kim, K. C. (1989). The "success" image of Asian Americans: Its validity and its practical and theoretical implications. *Ethnic and Racial Studies, 12*(4), 512–538.

Hurst, J. B., & Shepard, J. W. (1986). The dynamics of plant closings: An extended emotional rollercoaster ride. *Journal of Counseling and Development, 64,* 401–405.

Hutchinson, T., & Roe, A. (1968). Studies of occupational history: Part II. Attractiveness of occupational groups of the Roe system. *Journal of Counseling Psychology, 15,* 107–110.

Iaffaldano, M. T., & Muchinsky, P. M. (1985). Job satisfaction and job performance: A meta-analysis. *Psychological Bulletin, 97*(2), 251–273.

Ibrahim, F., & Herr, E. L. (1983). Attitude modification toward disability: Differential effects of two educational modes. *Rehabilitation Counseling Bulletin, 26*(8), 29–36.

Iglitzin, A. B. (1972). A child's-eye view of sex roles. *Today's Education, 61,* 23–25.

Imel, S. (1996). *Computer-based career information systems.* ERIC Digest (online serial). Available: Doc. No. ED39521696.

Inkson, K., & Arthur, M. B. (2002). Career development: Extending the "organizational careers" framework. In S. Niles (Ed.), *Adult career development: Concepts, issues, and practices* (pp. 286–306). Tulsa, OK: National Career Development Association.

Institute for the Crippled and Disabled. (1967). *TOWER: Testing, orientation, and work evaluation in rehabilitation.* New York: Institute for the Crippled and Disabled.

International Labour Organization. (1977a). *The ILO and the world of work.* Geneva, Switzerland: Author.

International Labour Organization. (1977b). Why it's hard to cut youth unemployment. *ILO Information, 5*(1).

International Labour Organization. (1994). *World labour report.* Geneva, Switzerland: Author.

International Labour Organization. (1999). *World labour report.* Geneva, Switzerland: Author.

Irvin, F. S. (1968). Personality characteristics and vocational identification. *Journal of Counseling Psychology, 15,* 329–333.

Isaacson, L. E. (1985). *Basics of career counseling.* Boston, MA: Allyn & Bacon.

Isaacson, L. E., & Brown, D. (2000). *Career information, career counseling, and career development.* Boston: Allyn and Bacon.

Izraeli, D. N. (1993). Work/family conflict among women and men managers in dual-career couples in Israel. *Journal of Social Behavior and Personality, 8*(3), 371–388.

Jackson, A. W., & Hornbeck, D. W. (1989). Educating young adolescents. Why we must restructure middle schools. *American Psychologist, 44*(5), 831–836.

Jackson, D. N., & Williams, D. R. (1975). Occupational classification in terms of interest patterns. *Journal of Vocational Behavior, 6,* 269–280.

Jackson, E. L. (1988). Leisure constraints: A survey of past research. *Leisure Sciences, 10,* 203–215.

Jackson, L. M. (1983). *Linear structural equation. Analysis of technical versus nontechnical career paths of engineers.* Unpublished doctoral dissertation, Pennsylvania State University.

Jacobs, R., & Solomon, T. (1977). Strategies for enhancing the prediction of job performance from job satisfaction. *Journal of Applied Psychology, 62,* 417–421.

Jacobson, N. S., & Addis, M. E. (1993). Research on couples and couple therapy: What do we know? Where are we going? *Journal of Consulting and Clinical Psychology, 61*(1), 85–93.

James, L. R., Demaree, R. G., & Mulaik, S. A. (1986). A note on validity generalization procedures. *Journal of Applied Psychology, 71*(3), 440–450.

James, L. R., Demaree, R. G., Mulaik, S. A., & Ladd, R. T. (1992). Validity generalization in the context of situational models. *Journal of Applied Psychology, 77*(1), 3–14.

Janis, I., & Mann, L. (1977). *Decision-making: A psychological analysis of conflict, choice, and commitment.* New York: The Free Press.

Janoff-Bulman, R., & Freise, I. (1983). A theoretical perspective for understanding reactions to victimization. *Journal of Social Issues, 39,* 1–17.

Jaramillo, P. T., Zapata, J. T., & MacPherson, R. (1982). Concerns of college-bound Mexican-American students. *The School Counselor, 29*(5), 375–380.

Jarrett, R. L. (1994). Living poor: Family life among single parent African American women. *Social Problems, 41*(1), 30–49.

Jencks, C. (1972). *Inequality.* New York: Harper & Row.

Jenkins, L. E. (1989). The Black family and academic achievement. In G. L. Berry & J. K. Asamen (Eds.), *Black students: Psychosocial issues and academic achievement.* Newbury Park: Sage Publications.

Jenkins, S. R. (1989). Longitudinal prediction of women's careers: Psychological, behavioral, and social-structural influences, *Journal of Vocational Behavior, 34*(2), 204–235.

Jensen, A. R. (1984). Test validity: *g* versus specifity doctrine. *Journal of Social Biological Structures, 7,* 93–118.

Jensen, A. R. (1988). Armed Services Vocational Aptitude Battery. In J. T. Kapes & M. M. Mastie (Eds.), *A counselor's guide to career assessment instruments* (pp. 58–62). Washington, DC: National Career Development Association.

Jensen-Scott, R. L. (1993). Counseling to promote retirement adjustment. *Career Development Quarterly, 41,* 257–267.

Jepsen, D. A. (1974). Vocational decision-making strategy-types. An exploratory study. *Vocational Guidance Quarterly, 23*(2), 17–23.

Jepsen, D. A. (1984a). The developmental perspective on vocational behavior: A review of theory and research. In S. D. Brown & R. W. Lent (Eds.), *Handbook of counseling psychology* (pp. 178–215). New York: Wiley.

Jepsen, D. A. (1984b). Relationship between career development theory and practice. In N. C. Gysbers (Ed.), *Designing careers, counseling to enhance education, work and leisure* (Chap. 5). San Francisco: Jossey-Bass.

Jepsen, D. A. (1985). Review of Kuder Occupational Interest Inventory, Form DD. *Measurement and Evaluation in Counseling and Development, 17*(4), 217–219.

Jepsen, D. A. (1989). Adolescent career decision processes as coping responses for the social environment. In R. Hanson (Ed.), *Career development: Preparing for the 21st century* (Chap. 6). Knoxville, TN: The University of Tennessee, Department of Technological and Adult Education.

Jepsen, D. A. (1994). Jackson Vocational Interest Survey (JVIS). In J. T. Kapes, M. M. Mastie, & E. A. Whitfield (Eds.), *A counselor's guide to career assessment instruments* (pp. 183–188). Alexandria, VA: National Career Development Association.

Jepsen, D. A. (1994). The thematic-extrapolation method: Incorporating career patterns into career counseling. *The Career Development Quarterly, 43,* 43–53.

Jepsen, D. A., & Choudhuri, E. (2001). Stability and change in 25-year occupational career patterns. *The Career Development Quarterly, 50,* 3–19.

Jepsen, D. A., Dustin, R., & Miars, R. (1982). The effects of problem-solving training on adolescents' career exploration and career decision making. *The Personnel and Guidance Journal, 61,* 149–153.

Jepsen, D. A., & Prediger, D. J. (1981). Dimensions of adolescent career development: A multi-instrument analysis. *Journal of Vocational Behavior, 19,* 350–368.

Jex, S. M., Cvetanovski, J., & Allen, S. J. (1994). Self-esteem as a moderator of the impact of unemployment. *Journal of Social Behavior and Personality, 9*(1), 69–80.

Joelson, L., & Wahlquist, L. (1987). The psychological meaning of job insecurity and job loss. *Social Science and Medicine, 25*(2), 179–192.

Johnson, C. D., & Johnson, S. K. (1982). Competency based training of career development specialists or "Let's Get off the Calf Path." *Vocational Guidance Quarterly, 32*(4), 327–335.

Johnson, D. C., & Smouse, A. D. (1993). Assessing a career planning course: A multidimensional approach. *Journal of College Student Development, 34,* 145–147.

Johnson, G. J. (1990). Underemployment, underpayment, and self-esteem among Black men. *The Journal of Black Psychology, 16*(2), 23–44.

Johnson, J., Simpson, J. C., Williams, M. L., & Kotarba, J. A. (1993). New careers model revisited: The importance of mentoring. *Journal of Employment Counseling, 30,* 55–66.

Johnson, K. (1994). Evolution of the workplace alters office relationships. *New York Times,* October 5, B1, B8.

Johnson, M., Jr., Busacker, W. E., & Bowman, F. Q., Jr. (1961). *Junior high school guidance.* New York: Harper & Brothers.

Johnson, M. J., Swartz, J. L., & Martin, W. E., Jr. (1995). Applications of psychological theories for career development with Native Americans. In F. T. L. Leong (Ed.). *Career development and vocational behavior of racial and ethnic minorities* (pp. 103–136). Mahwah, NJ: Erlbaum.

Johnson, N. (1980). A free enterprise elementary career education project. *The School Counselor, 27*(4), 315–317.

Johnson, R. G. (1970). Simulation techniques in career development. *American Vocational Journal, 45,* 30–32.

Johnson, R. H. (1978). Individual styles of decision-making: A theoretical model for counseling. *Personnel and Guidance Journal, 56,* 530–536.

Johnson, R. H., & Myrick, R. D. (1971). MOLD: A new approach to career decision making. *Vocational Guidance Quarterly, 21*(1), 48–53.

Johnson, R. W., & Hoese, J. (1988). Career planning concerns of SCII clients. *The Career Development Quarterly, 36,* 251–258.

Johnson, W., & Kottman, T. (1992). Developmental needs of middle school students: Implications for counselors. *Elementary School Guidance & Counseling, 27,* 3–14.

Joint Committee on Testing Practices. (1988). *Code of fair testing practices in education.* Washington, DC: American Psychological Association.

Joint Economic Committee, U.S. Congress. (1980, November). *Human resources and demographics: Characteristics of people and policy.* Washington, DC: Author.

Jolly, D. L., Grimm, J. W., & Wozniak, P. R. (1990). Patterns of sex desegregation in managerial and professional specialty fields, 1950–1980. *Work and Occupations, 17,* 30–54.

Jome, L. M., & Tokar, D. M. (1998). Dimensions of masculinity and major choice traditionality. *Journal of Vocational Behavior, 52,* 120–134.

Jones, A. J. (1930). *Principles of guidance.* New York: McGraw-Hill.

Jones, E. G., & Schultz, M. B. (1992). An academic advising program for uneducated students. *Journal of College Student Development, 33,* 181–182.

Jones, G., & Chenery, M. (1980). Multiple subtypes among vocationally undecided college students: A model and assessment instrument. *Journal of Counseling Psychology, 27,* 469–477.

Jones, G. B., Helliwell, C. B., & Ganschow, L. H. (1975). A planning model for career guidance: *Vocational Guidance Quarterly, 23*(3), 220–226.

Jones, L. K. (1977). *Occu-sort: A self-guided career exploration system.* Raleigh, NC: North Carolina State University, School of Education, Office of Publications.

Jones, L. K. (1979). Occu-sort: Development and evaluation of an occupational card sort system. *Vocational Guidance Quarterly, 28*(1), 56–62.

Jones, L. K. (1980a). Holland's typology and the new guide for occupational exploration. Bridging the gap. *Vocational Guidance Quarterly, 29*(1), 70–75.

Jones, L. K. (1980b). Issues in developing an occupational card sort. *Measurement and Evaluation in Guidance, 12*(4), 206–215.

Jones, L. K. (1981). *Occu-sort* (2nd ed.). Monterey, CA: Publishers Test Service, McGraw-Hill.

Jones, L. K. (1983). A comparison of two self-directed career guidance instruments: Occu-sort and Self-Directed Search. *The School Counselor, 30,* 204–211.

Jones, L. K. (1987). *The career key.* Chicago, IL: Ferguson.

Jones, L. K. (1990). The Career Key: An investigation of the reliability and validity of its scales and its helpfulness to college students. *Measurement and Evaluation in Counseling and Development, 23*(2), 67–76.

Jones, L. K. (1993). Two career guidance instruments: Their helpfulness to students and effect on students' career exploration. *The School Counselor, 40,* 191–200.

Jones, L. K., & De Vault, R. M. (1979). Evaluation of a self-guided career exploration system: The Occu-sort. *The School Counselor, 26*(5), 334–341.

Jones, L. K., Gorman, S., & Schroeder, C. G. (1989). A comparison between the SDS and the Career Key among career undecided college students. *The Career Development Quarterly, 37,* 334–344.

Jones, L. K., Sheffield, D., & Joyner, B. (2000). Comparing the effects of the Career Key with Self-Directed Search and Job-OE among eighth grade students. *Professional School Counseling, 3,* 238–247.

Jordaan, J. P., & Heyde, M. (1979). *Vocational maturity during the high school years.* New York: Teachers College Press.

Joyce, M., & Neumark, D. (2001). School-to-work programs: Information from two surveys. *Monthly Labor Review,* 124, 8, 38–50.

Judge, T. A., & Bretz, R. D., Jr. (1992). Effects of work values on job choice decisions. *Journal of Applied Psychology, 77*(3), 261–271.

Judge, T. A., Locke, E. A., Durham, C. C., & Kluger, A. N. (1998). Dispositional effects on job and life satisfaction the role of core evaluations. *Journal of Applied Psychology, 83*(1), 17–34.

Julien, H. E. (1999). Barriers to adolescents' information seeking for career decisionmaking. *Journal of the American Society for Information Science, 50(1),* 38–48.

Jung, C. G. (1916). *Collected papers on analytical psychology.* London: Harcourt

Jung, C. G. (1933). *Psychological types.* New York: Harcourt.

Jung, C. G. (1966). *Analytical psychology.* New York: Moffat, Yard.

Junge, D. A., Daniels, M. H., & Karmos, J. S. (1984). Personnel managers' perceptions of requisite basic skills. *Vocational Guidance Quarterly, 33*(2), 138–146.

Jurgens, J. (2000). The undecided student: Effects of combining levels of treatment parameters on career certainity, career indecision, and client satisfaction. *The Career Development Quarterly, 48*(3), 237–250.

Jurgensen, C. E. (1978). Job preferences (What makes a job good or bad?) *Journal of Applied Psychology, 63,* 267–276.

Kabanoff, B., & Daly, J. P. (2000). Values espoused by Australian and U.S. organizations. *Applied Psychology: An International Review, 49*(2), 284–314.

Kacmar, K. M., & Carlson, D. S. (1994). Using impression management in women's job search processes. *American Behavioral Scientist, 37*(5), 682–696.

Kagay, M. R. (1994). From coast to coast, from affluent to poor, poll shows anxiety over jobs. *The New York Times,* March 11, A14.

Kahnweiler, J. B., & Kahnweiler, W. M. (1980). A dual-career family workshop for college undergraduates. *Vocational Guidance Quarterly, 28*(3), 225–230.

Kalder, D. R., & Zytowski, D. G. (1969). A maximizing model of occupational decision-making. *Personnel and Guidance Journal 47,* 781–788.

Kalmijn, M. (1994). Mother's occupational status and children's schooling. *American Sociological Review, 59,* 257–275.

Kammer, P. P. (1985). Career and life-style expectations of rural eighth-grade students. *The School Counselor, 33*(1), 18–25.

Kamouri, A. L., & Cavanaugh, J. C. (1986). The impact of preretirement education programmes on worker's preretirement socialization. *Journal of Occupational Behavior, 7,* 245–256.

Kanchier, C., & Unruh, W. R. (1988). The career cycle meets the life cycle. *Career Development Quarterly, 37*(2), 127–137.

Kando, T. M., & Summers, W. C. (1971). The impact of work on leisure: Towards a paradigm and research strategy. *Pacific Sociological Review, 14,* 310–327.

Kane, S. T. (1989). A review of the COPS Interest Inventory. *Journal of Counseling and Development, 67,* 361–363.

Kantor, R. M. (1977a). *Men and women of the corporation.* New York: Basic Books.

Kantor, R. M. (1977b). *Work and family in the United States: A critical review and agenda for research and policy.* New York: Russell Sage.

Kapes, J. T., & Mastie, M. M. (1982). *A counselor's guide to vocational guidance instruments.* Falls Church, VA: National Vocational Guidance Association.

Kapes, J. T., & Mastie, M. M. (Eds.) (1988). *A counselor's guide to career assessment instruments* (2nd ed.). Alexandria, VA: The National Career Development Association.

Kapes, J. T., & Strickler, R. T. (1975). A longitudinal study of change in work values between ninth and twelfth grade as related to high school curriculums. *Journal of Vocational Behavior, 6*(1), 81–93.

Kapes, J. T., & Vansickle, T. R. (1992). Comparing paper-pencil and computer-based versions of the Harrington-O'Shea Career Decision-Making System. *Measurement and Evaluation in Counseling and Development, 25,* 5–13.

Kapes, J. T., & Whitfield, E. A. (Eds.). (2001). *A counselor's guide to career assessment instruments* (4th ed.). Tulsa, OK: National Career Development Association.

Kaplan, S. P. (1984). Rehabilitation counseling students' perception of obese male and female clients. *Rehabilitation Counseling Bulletin, 27*(3), 172–181.

Kaplon, A. J., & Gordon, M. S. (1967). A critique of war and peace: A simulation game. *Social Education, 31,* 383–387.

Karayanni, M. (1981). Career maturity of emotionally maladjusted high school students. *Vocational Guidance Quarterly, 29*(3), 213–220.

Karpicke, S. (1980). Perceived and real sex differences in college students' career planning. *Journal of Counseling Psychology, 27*(3), 240–245.

Karre, I. (1976). Self-concept and sex role stereotype: An empirical study with children. *Dissertation Abstracts International, 36,* 4850–4851.

Kassera, W., & Russo, T. (1987). Factor analysis of personality preferences and vocational interests. *Psychological Reports, 60,* 63–66.

Katz, M. (1958). *You: Today and tomorrow.* Princeton, NJ: Educational Testing Service.

Katz, M. (1963). *Decisions and values: A rationale for secondary school guidance.* New York: College Entrance Examination Board.

Katz, M. (1969). Can computers make guidance decisions for students? *College Board Review, 13,* 13–17.

Katz, M. (1973). The name and nature of vocational guidance. In H. Borow (Ed.), *Career guidance for a new age* (pp. 83–134). Boston: Houghton Mifflin.

Katz, M. (1980). SIGI: An interactive aid to career decision-making. *Journal of College Student Personnel, 21*(1), 34–40.

Katz, M. (1986). Career and family values for males and females. *College Student Journal, 20*(1), 66–76.

Katz, M. R. (1993). *Computer-assisted career decision-making: The guide in the machine.* Hillsdale, NJ: Erlbaum.

Katz, R. L. (1974). Skills of an effective administrator. *Harvard Business Review, 52,* 90–102.

Katzell, R. A. (1964). Personal values, job satisfaction, and job behavior. In H. Borow (Ed.), *Man in a world at work.* Boston: Houghton Mifflin.

Katzman, S. (1989). A response to the challenge of the year 2000. In R. Houson (Ed.), *Career development preparing for the 21st century* (Chap. 2). Knoxville: University of Tennessee, Department of Technological and Adult Education.

Kaufman, F. A., Harrel, G., Milam, C. P., Woolverton, N., & Miller, J. (1986). The nature, role, and influence of mentors in the lives of gifted adults. *Journal of Counseling and Development, 64,* 576–578.

Kaufman, R. L., & Spilerman, S. (1982). The age structure of occupations and jobs. *American Journal of Sociology, 87,* 827–851.

Kazanas, H. C. (1978). *Affective work competencies for vocational education.* Columbus, OH: National Center for Research in Vocational Education, Ohio State University.

Kegan, R. (1982). *The evolving self: Problems and process in human development.* Cambridge: Harvard University Press.

Kegan, R. (1994). *In over our heads. The mental demands of modern life.* Cambridge: Harvard University Press.

Keita, T. P., & Sauter, S. (1992). *Work and well-being: An agenda for the 1990s.* Washington, DC: American Psychological Association.

Keith, P. M. (1981). Sex-role attitudes, family plans, and career orientations: Implications for counseling. *Vocational Guidance Quarterly, 29*(3), 244–252.

Keith, P. M., Goudy, W. J., & Powers, E. A. (1981). Employment characteristics and psychological well-being of men in two-job families. *Psychological Reports, 49,* 975–978.

Keith, P. M., & Schafer, R. B. (1980). Depression in one and two job families. *Psychological Reports, 47*(2), 669–670.

Keller, J. W., Piotrowski, C., & Rabold, F. L. (1990). Determinants of career selection in undergraduates. *Journal of College Student Development, 31,* 276–277.

Kelly, G. A. (1955). *The psychology of personal constructs.* New York: Norton.

Kelly, J. R. (1981). Leisure interaction and the social dialectic. *Social Forces, 60*(2), 304–322.

Kelly, K. R. (2002). Review of the Kuder Occupational Interest Survey Form DD. In J. T. Kapes & E. A. Whitfield (Eds.), *A counselor's guide to career assessment instruments* (4th ed., pp. 269–275). Tulsa, OK: National Career Development Association.

Kenny, M. E., & Rice, K. G. (1995). Attachment to parents and adjustment in late adolescent college students: Current states, applications, and future considerations. *The Counseling Psychologist, 23,* 433–456.

Kenzler, B. (1983). A model for paraprofessionals in career planning. *Journal of College Placement, 44*(1), 54–61.

Kerr, B. A. (1982). The setting of career counseling. *Vocational Guidance Quarterly, 30*(3), 210–218.

Kerr, B., & Erb, C. (1991). Career counseling with academically talented students: Effects of a value-based intervention. *Journal of Counseling Psychology, 38*(3), 309–314.

Kessler, R. C., & Clary, P. D. (1978). Social class and psychological distress. *American Sociological Review, 45,* 463–478.

Kessler, R. C., & McRae, J. A. (1982). The effects of wives' employment on the mental health of married men and women. *American Sociological Review, 47,* 216–227.

Khan, S. B., Alvi, S. A., Shaukat, N., Hussain, M. A., & Baig, T. (1990). A study of the validity of Holland's theory in a nonwestern culture. *Journal of Vocational Behavior, 36,* 132–146.

Kidd, J. M. (1982). *Self and occupational concepts in occupational preferences and entry into work.* Unpublished doctoral dissertation. National Institute of Careers Education and Counseling, Cambridge.

Kieselbach, T., & Lunger, A. (1990). Psychosocial counseling for the unemployed within the framework of trade-union oriented work. *Journal of Employment Counseling, 27,* 191–207.

Kiesler, D. J. (1971). Experimental designs in psychotherapy research. In A. E. Bergin & S. J. Garfield (Eds.), *Handbook of psychotherapy and behavior change.* New York: Wiley.

Kileen, J. (1996). The learning and economic outcomes of guidance. In A. G. Watts, B. Law, J. Killen, J. M. Kidd, & R. Hawthorn (Eds.), *Rethinking careers education and guidance. Theory, policy, and practice* (pp. 72–94). London, England: Routledge.

Kileen, J., White, M., & Watts, A. G. (1992). *Economic value of career guidance.* London: Policy Studies Institute/National Institute for Careers Education and Counselling.

King, S. (1989a). Sex differences in a causal model of career maturity. *Journal of Counseling and Development, 68,* 208–215.

King, S. (1989b). Unemployment and mental health in French Canada: *Journal of Counseling and Development, 67,* 358–360.

King, S. (1992). The career development of young people with hearing impairments (pp. 217–237). In T. N. Kluwin, D. F. Moores, & R. Gaustad (Eds.), *Toward effective public school program for deaf students: Content, process, and outcomes.* New York: TC Press.

King, Z. (2001). Career self-management: Framework for employed adults. *British Journal of Guidance and Counselling, 29*(1), 65–78.

Kinicki, A. J., & Griffeth, R. W. (1985). The impact of sex-role stereotypes on performance ratings and causal attributions of performance. *Journal of Vocational Behavior, 27,* 155–170.

Kinicki, A. J., & Latack, J. C. (1990). Explication of the construct of coping in the involuntary job loss. *Journal of Vocational Behavior, 36,* 339–360.

Kinicki, M. F., & Kammer, P. P. (1985). The effects of a career guidance program on the career maturity and self-concept of delinquent youth. *Journal of Vocational Behavior, 26*(2), 117–125.

Kinnier, R. T., Brigman, S. L., & Noble, F. C. (1990). Career indecision and family enmeshment. *Journal of Counseling and Development, 68,* 309–312.

Kinnier, R. T., & Krumboltz, J. D. (1984). Procedures for successful career counseling. In N. C. Gysbers (Ed.), *Designing careers* (pp. 307–335). San Francisco: Jossey-Bass.

Kipnis, D. (1997). Ghosts, taxonomies, and social psychology. *American Psychologist, 52*(3), 205–211.

Kirschenbaum, A., & Weisberg, J. (1994). Job search, intentions, and turnover: The mismatched trilogy. *Journal of Vocational Behavior, 44,* 17–31.

Kiselica, M., & Murphy, D. K. (1994). Developmental career counseling with teenage parents. *Career Development Quarterly.*

Kivlighan, D. M. (1990). Career group therapy. *The Counseling Psychologist, 18,* 64–80.

Kivlighan, D. M., & Hageseth, J. A., Tipton, R. M., & McGovern, T. V. (1981). Effects of matching treatment approaches and personality types in group vocational counseling. *Journal of Counseling Psychology, 28*(4), 315–320.

Kivlighan, D. M., Jr., Johnson, B., & Fretz, B. (1987). Participant's perception of change mechanisms in career counseling groups: The role of emotional components in career problem solving. *Journal of Career Development, 14*(1), 35–44.

Kivlighan, D. M., Jr., Johnston, J. A., Hogan, R. S., & Mauer, E. (1994). Who benefits from computerized career counseling? *Journal of Counseling and Development, 72,* 289–292.

Kivlighan, D. M., Jr., & Shapiro, R. M. (1987). Holland type as a predictor of benefit from self-help counseling. *Journal of Counseling Psychology, 34,* 326–329.

Kjos, D. L. (1988). Job search activity parents of successful and unsuccessful job seekers. *Journal of Employment Counseling, 25,* 4–6.

Klein, K. L., & Weiner, Y. (1977). Interest congruency as a moderator of the relationship between job tenure and job satisfaction and mental health. *Journal of Vocational Behavior, 10,* 91–98.

Kleinman, A. (1988). *Rethinking psychiatry. From cultural category to personal experience.* New York: The Free Press.

Klerman, J. A., & Karoly, L. A. (1994). Young men and the transition to stable employment. *Monthly Labor Review, 117*(8), 31–48.

Knapp, D. L., & Bedord, J. H. (1967). *The parent's role in career development.* Washington, DC: National Vocational Guidance Association.

Knapp, R. R., & Knapp, L. (1977). Interest changes and the classification of occupations. San Diego: Edits.

Knapp, L., Knapp, R. R., Strand, L., & Michael, W. B. (1978). Comparative validity of the Career Ability Placement Survey (CAPS) and the General Aptitude Test Battery (GATB) for predicting high school course marks. *Educational and Psychological Measurement, 38,* 1053–1056.

Knapp, L., & Michael, W. B. (1990). Relationship of work values to corresponding academic success. *Educational and Psychological Measurement, 40,* 487–494.

Knefelkamp, L. L., & Slepitza, R. (1976). A cognitive developmental model of career development—an adaptation of the Perry scheme. *The Counseling Psychologist, 6*(3), 53–58.

Knouse, S. B., Rosenfeld, P., & Culbertson, A. L. (Eds.). (1992). *Hispanics in the workplace.* Newbury Park, CA: Sage.

Kohlan, R. G. (1968). Relationship between inventoried interests and inventoried needs. *Personnel and Guidance Journal, 46,* 592–598.

Kohn, M. L. (1977). *Class and conformity: A study in values* (2nd ed.). Chicago: University of Chicago Press.

Koop, C. E. (1992). Remarks for the opening of the APA/NIOSH Conference on Work and Well-Being: An Agenda for the 1990s. In G. P. Keita & S. L. Sauter (Eds.), *Work and Well-Being: An Agenda for the 1990s* (pp. 3–4). Washington, D.C.: American Psychological Association.

Koski, L. K., & Subich, L. M. (1985).Career and homemaking choices of college preparatory and vocational education students. *Vocational Guidance Quarterly, 34*(2), 116–123.

Kossek, E. E., & Ozeki, C. (1998). Work-family conflict, policies, and the job-life satisfaction relationship: A review and directions for organizational behavior-human resources research. *Journal of Applied Psychology, 83*(2), 139–149.

Kragie, E. R., Gernstein, M., & Lichtman, M. (1989). Do Americans plan for retirement? Some recent trends. *The Career Development Quarterly, 37,* 232–239.

Kram, K. E. (1984). *Mentoring at work: Developmental relationships in organizational life.* Glenview: IL: Scott, Foresman & Company.

Kram, K. E. (1985). Improving the mentoring process. *Training and Development Journal, 39*(4), 40–43.

Kramer, H. C., Berger, F., & Miller, G. (1974). Student concerns and sources of assistance. *Journal of College Student Personnel, 15*(5), 389–393.

Krasnow, B. S. (1968). Occupational information as a factor in the high school curriculum chosen by ninth-grade boys. *The School Counselor, 15,* 275–280.

Krau, E. (1981). Immigrants preparing for their second career: The behavioral strategies adopted. *Journal of Vocational Behavior, 18,* 289–303.

Krau, E. (1982). The vocational side of a new start in life: A career model of immigrants. *Journal of Vocational Behavior, 20,* 313–330.

Krau, E. (1984). Commitment to work in immigrants: Its functions and peculiarities. *Journal of Vocational Behavior, 24,* 329–339.

Kraus, L. J., & Hughey, K. E. (1999). The impact of an intervention on career decision-making self-efficacy and career indecision. *Professional School Counseling, 2,*(5), 384–390.

Krefting, L. A., & Berger, P. K. (1979). Masculinity-femininity perceptions of job requirements and their relationship to job-sex stereotypes. *Journal of Vocational Behavior, 15,* 164–174.

Kriedberg, B., Butcher, A. L., & White, K. M. (1978). Vocational role choice in second- and sixth-grade children. *Sex Roles, 4,* 145–181.

Krieshok, T. S., Hastings, S., Ebberwein, C., Wettersten, K., & Owen, A. (1999). Telling a good story: Using narratives in vocational rehabilitation with veterans. *The Career Development Quarterly, 47, 204–214.*

Krieshok, T. S., Arnold, J. J., Kuperman, B. D., & Schmitz, N. K. (1986). Articulation of career values: Comparison of three measures. *Journal of Counseling Psychology, 33*(4), 475–478.

Kristoff, A. L. (1996). Person-organization fit: An integrative review of its conceptualizations, measurement, and implications. *Personnel Psychology, 49,* 1–49.

Krumboltz, J. D. (1979). A social learning theory of career decision making. In A. M. Mitchell, G. G. Jame, & J. D. Krumboltz (Eds.), *Social learning and career decision making* (pp. 19–49). Cranston, RI: Carrole Press.

Krumboltz, J. D. (1983). *Private rules in career decision making.* Columbus, OH: The National Center for Research in Vocational Education.

Krumboltz, J. D. (1985). Presuppositions underlying computer use in career counseling. *Journal of Career Development, 12*(2), 165–170.

Krumboltz, J. D. (1988a). *Career Beliefs Inventory.* Palo Alto, CA: Consulting Psychologists Press.

Krumboltz, J. D. (1988b). Review of Vocational Interest Inventory. In J. T. Kapes & M. M. Mastie (Eds.), *A counselor's guide to career assessment instruments* (pp. 137–142). Washington, DC: National Career Development Association.

Krumboltz, J. D. (1991). Brilliant insights—platitudes that bear repeating. *The Counseling Psychologist, 19,* 298–315.

Krumboltz, J. D. (1993). Integrating career and personal counseling. *The Career Development Quarterly, 42*(2), 143–148.

Krumboltz, J. D. (1994). The career beliefs inventory. *Journal of Counseling and Development, 72,* 424–428.

Krumboltz, J. D. (1994b). Improving career development theory from a social learning perspective. In M. L. Savickas & R. W. Lent (Eds.), *Convergence in career development theories. Implications for science and practice* (pp. 9–31). Palo Alto, CA: CPP Books.

Krumboltz, J. D., & Baker, R. D. (1973). Behavioral counseling for vocational decisions. In H. Borow (Ed), *Career guidance for a new age* (pp. 235–284) Boston: Houghton Mifflin.

Krumboltz, J. D., & Henderson, S. J. (2002). A learning theory for career counselors. In S. Niles (Ed.), *Adult career development: Concepts, issues, and practices.* (pp. 39–56). Tulsa, OK: National Career Development Association.

Krumboltz, J. D., Kinnier, R. T., Rude, S. S., Scherba, D. S., & Hamel, D. A. (1986). Teaching a rational approach to decision making: Who benefits most? *Journal of Vocational Behavior, 29,* 1–6.

Krumboltz, J. D., & Menetee, A. (1980). Counseling psychology of the future. *The Counseling Psychologist, 8*(4), 46–48.

Krumboltz, J. D., Mitchell, A., & Gellat, H. G. (1975). Applications of social learning theory of career selection. *Focus on Guidance, 8*(3), 1–16.

Krumboltz, J. D., & Schroeder, W. W. (1965). Promoting career planning through reinforcement and models. *Personnel and Guidance Journal, 44,* 19–26.

Krumboltz, J. D., & Thoresen, C. E. (1964). The effect of behavioral counseling in groups and individual settings on information-seeking behavior. *Journal of Counseling Psychology, 11,* 324–333.

Krumboltz, J. D., Varenhorst, B., & Toresen, C. E. (1967). Non-verbal factors in effectiveness of models in counseling. *Journal of Counseling Psychology, 14,* 412–418.

Kryger, G. R., & Shikiar, T. (1978). Sexual discrimination in the use of letters of recommendation: A case of reverse discrimination. *Journal of Applied Psychology, 63*(3), 309–314.

Kübler-Ross, E. (1969). *On death and dying.* New York: Macmillan.

Kuhlman-Harrison, J., & Neely, M. A. (1980). Discriminant validity of career development inventory scales in grade 10 students. *Educational and Psychological Measurement, 40,* 475–478.

Kuhn, T. S. (1962). *The structure of scientific revolutions.* Chicago: University of Chicago Press.

Kurhila, A., & Onnismaa, J. (2000). Career development in Finland. In B. Hiebert & L. Bezanson (Eds.), *Making waves: Career development and public policy* (pp. 149–167). Ottawa, Canada: Human Resources

Development Canada/Canadian Career Development Foundation.

Kurolesky, W. P., Wright, D. E., & Juarez, R. Z. (1971). Status projections and ethnicity: A comparison of Mexican American, Negro, and Anglo youth. *Journal of Vocational Behavior, 1,* 137.

Kurpius, D., Burello, L., & Rozecki, T. (1990). Strategic planning in human service organizations. *Counseling and Human Development, 22*(9), 1–12.

Kurtz, N. R., Googins, B., & Howard, W. C. (1984). Measuring the success of occupational alcoholism programs. *Journal of Studies on Alcohol, 45,* 33–45.

Kurtz, R. R. (1974). Using a transactional analysis format in vocational group counseling. *Journal of College Students Personnel, 15,* 447–451.

Kush, K., & Cochran, L. (1993). Enhancing a sense of agency through career planning. *Journal of Counseling Psychology, 40*(4), 434–439.

Kutscher, R. E. (1989). Outlook 2000: Issues and implications. *Occupational Outlook Quarterly, 33*(3), 38–40.

Labich, K. (1993). The new unemployed. *Fortune, 127*(5), 40–43, 46, 48–49.

LaFitte, P. C., & Phillips, B. (1980). Assertive job hunting: A lesson in integration. *Journal of College Student Personnel, 21,* 92–93.

LaFramboise, T. D., Coleman, H. L. K., & Gerton, J. (1993). Psychological impact of biculturalism: Evidence and theory. *Psychological Bulletin, 114*(3), 395–412.

LaFramboise, T. D., Trimble, J. E., & Mohatt, G. V. (1990). Counseling intervention and American Indian tradition: An integrative approach. *The Counseling Psychologist, 18*(4), 628–654.

Laing, J., Lamb, R. R., & Prediger, D. J. (1982). An application of Strong's validity criteria to basic interest scales. *Journal of Vocational Behavior, 20,* 203–214.

Lamb, R. R., & Prediger, D. J. (1979). Criterion-related validity of sex-restrictive and unisex interest scales: A comparison. *Journal of Vocational Behavior, 15,* 231–246.

Landy, F. J. (1989). *Psychology of work behavior* (4th ed.). Pacific Grove, CA: Brooks/Cole.

Landy, F. J. (1992). Work design and stress. In G. P. Keita & S. L. Sauter (Eds.), *Work and well-being. An agenda for the 1990s* (pp. 119–158). Washington, DC: American Psychological Association.

Lange, S., & Coffman, J. S. (1981). Integrative test interpretation. A career counselor tool. *Vocational Guidance Quarterly, 30*(1), 73–77.

Langer, K. G. (1994). Depression and denial in psychotherapy of persons with disabilities. *American Journal of Psychotherapy, 48*(2), 181–194.

Lapan, R. T., Gysbers, N. C., Sun, Y. (1997). The impact of more fully implemented guidance programs on the school experiences of high school students: A statewide evaluation study. *Journal of Counseling and Development, 75,* 292–302.

Laramore, D., & Thompson, J. (1970). Career experiences appropriate to elementary school grades. *The School Counselor, 17,* 262–263.

Larson, J. H., Busby, D. M., Wilson, S., Medira, N., & Allgood, S. (1994). The multidimensional assessment of career decision problems: The Career Decision Diagnostic Assessment. *Journal of Counseling and Development, 72,* 323–328.

Larson, L. M., & Heppner, P. (1985). The relationship of problem-solving appraisal to career decision and indecision. *Journal of Vocational Behavior, 26,* 55–65.

Larson, L. M., Heppner, P. P., Ham, T., & Dugan, K. (1988). Investigating multiple subtypes of career indecision through cluster analysis. *Journal of Counseling Psychology, 35,* 439–446.

Lasker, H., Moore, J., & Simpson, E. L. (1980). *Adult development and approaches to learning.* Washington, DC: National Institute of Education.

Lassalle, A. D., & Spokane, A. R. (1987). Patterns of early labor force participation of American women. *The Career Development Quarterly, 36*(1), 55–65.

Lassiter, R. A. (1981, December). *Work evaluation and work adjustment for severely handicapped people. A counseling approach* (pp. 13–18). Paper presented at the International Roundtable for the Advancement of Counseling Consultation on Career Guidance and Higher Education. Cambridge, England.

Lattanzi, M. E. (1981). Coping with work-related losses. *Personnel and Guidance Journal, 59*(6), 350–351.

Laudeman, K. A., & Griffith, P. (1978). Holland's theory of vocational choice and postulated value dimensions. *Educational and Psychological Measurement, 38,* 1165–1175.

Lauver, P. J., & Jones, R. M. (1991). Factors associated with perceived career options in American Indian, White, and Hispanic rural high school students. *Journal of Counseling Psychology, 38*(2), 159–166.

LaVan, H., Mathys, N., & Drehmer, D. (1983). A look at the counseling practices of major U.S. corporations. *Personnel Administrator, 28*(6), 143–145.

Lawler, E. E. (1973). *Motivation in work organizations.* Monterey, CA: Brooks/Cole.

Lawler, E. E. (1982). Strategies for improving the quality of work life. *American Psychologist, 37*(5), 486–493.

Lawson, M. B., & Angle, H. L. (1994). When organizational relocation means family relocation: An emerging issue for strategic human resource management. *Human Resource Management, 33*(1), 33–54.

Lazarus, A. A. (1976). *Multimodal behavior therapy.* New York: Springer.

Lazarus, R. S., & Folkman, S. (1984). *Stress, appraisal and coping.* New York: Springer Publishing Company.

Leclair, S. W. (1982). The dignity of leisure. *The School Counselor, 29*(4), 289–296.

Lee, C. C. (1984). Predicting the career choice attitudes of rural black, white, and native american high school students. *Vocational Guidance Quarterly, 32*(3), 177–184.

Lee, C. L. (Ed.). (1995). *Counseling for diversity.* Boston: Allyn and Bacon.

Lee, J. A., & Clemons, T. (1985). Factors affecting employment decisions about older workers. *Journal of Applied Psychology, 70*(4), 785–788.

Lee, R. (1982). The moderating effect of sex on the prediction of job satisfaction in the public sector. *Journal of Employment Counseling, 19*(1), 34–44.

Lee, R. T., & Ashforth, B. E. (1993). A further examination of managerial burnout: Toward an integrated model. *Journal of Organizational Behavior, 14,* 3–20.

Lefkowitz, J., & Brigando, L. (1980). The redundancy of work alienation and job satisfaction: Some evidence of convergent and discriminant validity. *Journal of Vocational Behavior, 16,* 115–131.

Lefstein, L. M., & Lipsitz, J. (1986). *3:00 to 6:00 p.m.: Program for young adolescents.* Chapel Hill, NC: Center for Early Adolescence, University of North Carolina at Chapel Hill.

Legislative Provisions for the Improvement of Guidance Programs and Personnel Development (1979). *Various modules.* Columbus, OH: National Center for Research in Vocational Education.

Leibowitz, Z. B., Garren, C., & Kaye, B. L. (1986). *Designing career development systems.* San Francisco: Jossey-Bass.

Leibowitz, Z. B., & Schlossberg, N. K. (1981). Training managers for their role in a career development system. *Training and Development Journal, 35,* 72–79.

Leigh, J. P. (1987). The effects of unemployment on the probability of suffering a disability. *Work and Occupations, 14*(3), 347–367.

Leiter, M. P. (1988). Burnout as a function of communication patterns. *Group and Organizational Studies, 13,* 111–128.

Leiter, M. P. (1992). Burnout as a crisis in professional role structures: Management and conceptual issues. *Anxiety, Stress, and Coping, 5,* 79–93.

Leiter, M. P., & Meechan, K. A. (1986). Role structure and burnout in the field of human services. *The Journal of Applied Behavioral Science, 22*(1), 47–52.

Lemkau, J. P. (1984). Men in female-dominated occupations: Distinguishing personality and background features. *Journal of Vocational Behavior, 24,* 110–112.

Lenox, R. A., & Subich, L. M. (1994). The relationship between self-efficacy beliefs and inventoried vocational interests. *Career Development Quarterly, 42,* 302–313.

Lent, R. W., & Brown, S. D. (1996). Social cognitive approach to career development: An overview. *The Career Development Quarterly, 44,* 310–321.

Lent, R. W., Brown, S. D., & Hackett, G. (1994). Toward a unifying social cognitive theory of career and academic interest, choice, and performance. *Journal of Vocational Behavior, 45,* 79–122.

Lent, R. W., Brown, S. D., & Hackett, G. (1996). Career development from a social cognitive perspective. In D. Brown, L. Brooks, et al. (Eds.), *Career choice and development* (3rd ed., pp. 373–416). San Francisco: Jossey-Bass.

Lent, R. W., Brown, S. D., & Hackett, G. (2000). Contextual supports and barriers to career choice: A social cognitive analysis. *Journal of Counseling Psychology, 47,* 36–49.

Lent, R. W., & Hackett, G. (1987). Career self-efficacy: Empirical status and future directions. *Journal of Vocational Behavior, 30,* 347–382.

Lent, R. W., Hackett, G., & Brown, S. D. (1999). A social-cognitive view of school-to-work transition. *The Career Development Quarterly, 47,* 297–311.

Lent, R. W., Larkin, K. C., & Hasegawa, C. S. (1986). Effects of a "focused interest" career course approach for college students. *Vocational Guidance Quarterly, 34*(3), 151–159.

Lent, R. W., Lopez, F. G., & Bieschke, K. J. (1991). Mathematics self-efficacy: Sources and relation to science-based career choice. *Journal of Counseling Psychology, 38*(4), 424–430.

Leonard, G. E., & Brooks, L. P. (1980). Developmental career guidance for girls and young women. In E. Waters & J. Goodman (Eds.), *Resocializing sex roles: A guide for education.* Washington, DC: The National Vocational Guidance Association.

Leonards, J. T. (1981). Corporate psychology: An answer to occupational mental health. *Personnel and Guidance Journal, 30*(1), 47–51.

Leong, F. T. L. (1991). Career development attributes and occupational values of Asian American and White

American college students. *Career Development Quarterly, 39,* 221–230.

Leong, F. T. L. (1993). The career counseling process with racial-ethnic minorities: The case of Asian Americans. *Career Development Quarterly, 42*(1), 26–40.

Leong, F. T. L. (Ed.). (1995). *Career development and vocational behavior of racial and ethnic minorities.* Mahwah, NJ: Lawrence Erlbaum Associates.

Leong, F. T. L., & Chou, E. L. (1994). The role of ethnic identity and acculturation in the vocational behavior of Asian Americans: An integrative review. *Journal of Vocational Behavior, 44,* 155–172.

Leong, F. T. L., & Gim-Chung, R. H. (1995). Career assessment and intervention with Asian Americans. In F. T. L Leong (Ed.), *Career development and vocational behavior of racial and ethnic minorities* (pp. 193–226). Mahwah, NJ: Erlbaum.

Leong, F. T. L., & Hayes, T. J. (1990). Occupational stereotyping of Asian Americans. *Career Development Quarterly, 39,* 143–154.

Leong, F. T. L., & Pope, M. (Eds.). (2002). Challenges for career counseling in Asia: Introduction [Special section]. *The Career Development Quarterly, 50*(3), 209–210.

Leong, F. T. L., & Sedlacek, W. E. (1986). A comparison of international and U.S. students' preferences for help sources. *Journal of College Student Personnel, 27,* 426–430.

Leong, F. T. L., & Serafica, F. C. (1995). Career development of Asian Americans: A research area in need of a good theory. In F. T. L. Leong (Ed.). *Career development and vocational behavior of racial and ethnic minorities* (pp. 78–99). Mahwah, NJ: Erlbaum.

Lerner, R. M. (1986). *Concepts and theories of human development* (2nd ed.). New York: Random House.

Lester, J. N., & Frugoli, P. (1989). Career and occupational information: current needs, future directions. In D. Brown & C. A. Minor (Eds.), *Working in America: A status report on planning and problems* (pp. 60–81). Alexandria, VA: National Career Development Association.

Leung, S. A. (1993). Circumscription and compromise: A replication study with Asian Americans. *Journal of Counseling Psychology, 40*(2), 188–193.

Leung, S. A. (2002). Career counseling in Hong Kong: Meeting the social challenges. *The Career Development Quarterly, 50,* 237–245.

Leung, S. A., Conoley, C. W., & Scheel, M. J. (1994). The career and educational aspirations of gifted high school students: A retrospective study. *Journal of Counseling & Development, 72,* 298–303.

Leung, S. A., Ivey, D., & Suzuki, L. (1994). Factors affecting the career aspirations of Asian Americans. *Journal of Counseling and Development 72,* 404–410.

Leveson, I. (1980). Technology and society in the next thirty years: We have manageable choices. In C. S. Sheppart & D. C. Carroll (Eds.), *Working in the twenty-first century* (pp. 39–48). New York: Wiley.

Levey, J., & Levey, M. (1998). *Living in balance: A dynamic approach for creating harmony and wholeness in a chaotic world.* New York: MJF Books.

Levi, L. (1984). *Stress in industry.* Geneva, Switzerland: International Labor Office.

Levin, E. L. (1986). A support group for midlife students reentering college. *Journal of College Student Personnel, 27*(4), 371–372.

Levine, A. (1976). Educational and occupational choice: A synthesis of literature from sociology and psychology. *Journal of Consumer Research, 2,* 276–289.

Levine, M. L. (1988). *Age discrimination and the mandatory retirement controversy.* Baltimore: Johns Hopkins University Press.

Levine, S. V. (1979). The psychological and social effects of youth unemployment. *Children Today, 8*(6), 6–9, 40.

Levinson, D. J. (1977). The mid-life transition: A period in adult psychosocial development. *Psychiatry, 40,* 99–112.

Levinson, D. J. (1986). A conception of adult development, *American Psychologist, 41,* 3–13.

Levinson, D. J., Darrow, C. N., Klein, E. B., Levinson, M. H., & McKee, B. (1978). *The seasons of a man's life.* New York: Knopf.

Levinson, E. M. (1985). Vocational and career-oriented secondary school programs for the emotionally disturbed. *The School Counselor, 33*(2), 100–106.

Levinson, E. M. (1990). Vocational assessment involvement and use of the Self-Directed Search by school psychologists. *Psychology in the Schools, 27,* 217–228.

Levinson, E. M. (1998). *Transition: Facilitating the post-school adjustment of students with disabilities.* Boulder, CO: Westview Press.

Levitan, S. A. (1987). Beyond "trendy" forecasts: The next 10 years for work. *The Futurist, 21*(6), 28–33.

Levitan, S., Johnston, W., & Taggart, R. (1974). Manpower programs and black progress. *Manpower, 6*(6), 2–10.

Levy, D. A., Kaler, S. R., & Schall, M. (1988). An empirical investigation of role schemata: Occupations and personality characteristics. *Psychological Reports, 63,* 3–14.

Lewallen, W. (1993). The impact of being "undecided" on college student persistence. *Journal of College Student Development, 34,* 103–112.

Lewin-Epstein, N. (1989). Work characteristics and ill-health. Gender differences in Israel. *Work and occupations, 16*(1), 80–104.

Lewis, J. A., & Lewis, M. D. (1986). *Counseling programs for employees in the workplace.* Belmont, CA: Brooks/Cole.

Lewis, J. M., & Looney, J. G. (1988). *The long struggle: Well-functioning working-class Black families.* New York: Brunner/Mazel.

Ley, R. (1966). Labor turnover as a function of worker difference. *Journal of Applied Psychology, 50*(6), 497–500.

Li, L. (2000). The Hong Kong special administrative region, People's Republic of China. In B. Hiebert & L. Bezanson (Eds.), *Making waves: Career development and public policy.* (119–128). Ottawa, Canada: Human Resources Development Canada and the Canadian Career Development Foundation.

Lichter, D. (1988). Race, employment hardship and inequality in American non-metropolitan south. *American Sociological Review, 54,* 436–446.

Lichtman, R. C. (1978), Jobs and mental health in a social context. *Center Magazine,* 11(6), 1–17.

Liem, R., & Rayman, P. (1982). Health and social costs of unemployment. *American Psychologist, 37*(10), 1116–1123.

Lievens, F., Decaesteker, C., Coetsier, P., & Geirnaert, J. (2001). Organizational attractiveness for prospective applicants: A person-organization fit perspective. *Applied Psychology: An International Review, 50*(1), 30–51.

Lifton, R. J. (1993). *The protean self. Human resilience in an age of fragmentation.* New York: Basic Books.

Liontos, L. B. (1992). *At-risk families and schools: Becoming partners.* Eugene, OR: ERIC Clearinghouse on Educational Management.

Lipman-Blumen, J., & Leavitt, H. S. (1977). Vicarious and direct achievement patterns in adulthood. In N. K. Schlossberg & A. D. Entine (Eds.), *Counseling adults.* Monterey, CA: Brooks/Cole.

Lips, H. M. (1992). Gender- and science-related attitudes as predictors of college students' academic choices. *Journal of Vocational Behavior, 40,* 62–81.

Lipsett, L. (1962). Social factors in vocational development. *Personnel and Guidance Journal, 40,* 432–437.

Liptak, J. (1990). Preretirement counseling: Integrating the leisure planning component. *The Career Development Quarterly, 38,* 360–367.

Lister, J. L., & McKenzie, D. H. (1966). A framework for the improvement of test interpretation in counseling. *Personnel and Guidance Journal, 45,* 61–66.

Littleton, S. M., Arthur, M. B., & Rousseau, D. M. (2000). In A. Collin & R. Young (Eds.), *The future of careers* (pp 101–114). Cambridge, England: Cambridge University Press.

Lobodzinska, B. (1986). Post-war immigration in the United States and the state of Minnesota. *International Migration, 24*(2), 411–439.

LoCascio, R. (1967). Continuity and discontinuity in vocational development theory. *Personnel and Guidance Journal, 46,* 32–36.

Locksley, A. (1980). On the effects of wives' employment on marital adjustment and companionship. *Journal of Marriage and the Family, 42,* 337–346.

Lockwood, O., Smith, D. B., & Trezise, R. (1966). Four worlds: An approach to vocational guidance. *Personnel and Guidance Journal, 45,* 641–643.

Loesch, L. C. (1980). Life-flow leisure counseling for older persons. *Journal of Employment Counseling, 17*(1), 49–56.

Loevinger, J. (1976). *Ego development: Conceptions and theories.* San Francisco: Jossey-Bass.

Lofquist, L. H., & Dawis, R. (1969). *Adjustment to work, a psychological view of man's problems in a work-oriented society.* New York: Appleton-Century-Crofts.

Lofquist, L. H., & Dawis, R. V. (1975). *Counseling and use of the Minnesota Importance Questionnaire.* Minneapolis: University of Minnesota Vocational Psychology Work Adjustment Project.

Lokan, J., & Biggs, J. (1982). Student characteristics and motivational and process factors in relation to styles of career development. *Journal of Vocational Behavior, 21,* 1–16.

Lombana, J. H. (1985). Guidance accountability: A new look at an old problem. *The School Counselor, 32*(5), 340–346.

Lombard, J. W. (1973). *Career guidance and the Kuder interest inventories.* Chicago: Science Research Associates.

London, M., & More, E. M. (1987). *Career management and survival in the workplace.* San Francisco, CA: Jossey-Bass.

London, M., & Stumpf, S. A. (1982). *Managing careers.* Reading, MA: Addison-Wesley.

London, M., & Stumpf, S. A. (1986). Individual and organizational career development in changing times. In D. T. Hall & Associates (Eds.), *Career development in organizations* (pp. 21–49). San Francisco: Jossey-Bass.

Looby, E. J. (2002). Counseling displaced homemakers. In D. S. Sandhu (Ed.), *Counseling employees: A multifaceted approach* (pp. 203–219), Alexandria, VA: American Counseling Association.

Lopez, F. G. (1983). The victims of corporate failure: Some preliminary findings. *Personnel and Guidance Journal, 61,* 631–632.

Lopez, F. G. (1989). Current family dynamics, trait anxiety, and academic adjustment: Test of a family-based model of vocational identity. *Journal of Vocational Behavior, 35*(1), 76–87.

Lopez, F. G., & Andrews, S. (1987). Career indecision: A family systems perspective. *Journal of Counseling and Development, 65*(6), 304–307.

Lopez, F. G., & Lent, R. W. (1992). Sources of mathematics self-efficacy in high school students. *Career Development Quarterly, 41,* 3–12.

Lorick, B. A. (1987). Career planning and placement services. In J. L. Amprey, Jr. (Ed.), *Student development on the small campus* (pp. 92–126). Washington, DC: National Association of Personnel Workers.

Loscocco, K. A. (1990). Reactions to blue-collar work: A comparison of men and women. *Work and Occupations, 17*(2), 152–177.

Lowe, B. (1981). The relationship between vocational interest differentiation and career undecidedness. *Journal of Vocational Behavior, 19,* 346–349.

Lowenthal, M. F. (1977). Toward a sociopsychological theory of change in adulthood and old age. In J. E. Birren & K. W. Schaie (Eds.), *Handbook of the psychology of aging.* New York: Van Nostrand-Reinhold.

Lowenthal, M. F., & Pierce, R. (1975). The pretransitional stance. In M. F. Lowenthal, M. Thurnher, & D. Chiriboga (Eds.), *Four stages of life: A comparative study of men and women facing transitions* (pp. 201–222). San Francisco: Jossey-Bass.

Lowenthal, M. F., Thurnher, M., Chiroboga, D., et al. (1976). *Four stages of life.* San Francisco: Jossey-Bass.

Lowman, R. L. (1993). The inter-domain model of career assessment and counseling. *Journal of Counseling and Development, 71,* 549–554.

Lowman, R. L. (1993). *Counseling and psychotherapy of work dysfunctions.* Washington, DC: American Psychological Association.

Lowman, R. L., & Carson, A. D. (2000). Integrating assessment data into career counseling. In D. A. Luzzo (Ed.), *Career counseling of college students. An empirical guide to strategies that work.* Washington, D.C.: American Psychological Association.

Lozada, M. (1999). Career learning to the nines. *Techniques, 74*(7), 30–31.

Lucas, M. S. (1993). A validation of types of career indecision at a counseling center. *Journal of Counseling Psychology, 40*(4), 440–446.

Lucas, M. S., & Epperson, D. L. (1988). Personality types of vocationally undecided students. *Journal of College Student Development, 29,* 460–466.

Lucas, M. S., & Epperson, D. L. (1990). Types of vocational undecidedness: A relication and a refinement. *Journal of Counseling Psychology, 37,* 382–388.

Luchins, A. S. (1960). Influences of experiences with conflicting information and reactions to subsequent conflicting information. *Journal of Social Psychology, 5,* 367–385.

Lundberg, D. J., Osborne, W. L., & Miner, C. U. (1997). Career maturity and personality preferences of Mexican-American and Anglo-American adolescents. *Journal of Career Development, 23,* 203–213.

Lunneborg, C. E. (1982b). Systematic biases in brief self-ratings of vocational qualifications. *Journal of Vocational Behavior, 20,* 255–275.

Lunneborg, P. W. (1976). Vocational indecision in college graduates. *Journal of Counseling Psychology, 23*(4), 402–404.

Lunneborg, P. W. (1980). Reducing sex bias in interest measurement at the item level. *Journal of Vocational Behavior, 16,* 226–234.

Lunneborg, P. W. (1990). *Women changing work.* Westport, CT: Greenwood Press.

Lunneborg, P. W., & Lunneborg, C. E. (1985). Nontraditional and traditional female college graduates: What separates them from the men? *Journal of College Student Personnel, 26*(1), 33–36.

Luzzo, D. A. (1993a). Predicting the career maturity of undergraduates: A comparison of personal, educational, and psychological factors. *Journal of College Student Development, 34,* 271–275.

Luzzo, D. A. (1993b). Reliability and validity testing of the Career Decision Making Self-Efficacy Scale. *Measurement and Evaluation in Counseling and Development, 26,* 137–142.

Luzzo, D. A. (1993c). Value of career decision-making self-efficacy in predicting career decision-making attitudes and skills. *Journal of Counseling Psychology, 40*(2), 194–199.

Luzzo, D. A. (2002). Review of the Career Factors Inventory. In J. T. Kapes & E. A. Whitfield (Eds.), *A counselor's guide to career assessment instruments* (4th ed., pp. 332–335). Tulsa, OK: National Career Development Association.

Luzzo, D. A., Funk, D. P., & Strang, J. (1996). Attributional retraining increases career decision-making self-efficacy. *Career Development Quarterly, 44,* 378–386.

Luzzo, D. A., Hitchings, W. E., Retish, P., & Shoemaker, A. (1999). Evaluating differences in college students' career decision making as the basis of disability status. *The Career Development Quarterly, 48*(2), 142–151.

Luzzo, D. A., & MacGregor, M. W. (2001). Annual review: Practice and research in career counseling in development-2000. *The Career Development Quarterly, 50,* 98–139.

Luzzo, D. A., & Pierce, G. (1996). Effects of DISCOVER on the career maturity of middle school students. *The Career Development Quarterly, 45,* 170–172.

Lynch, R. K., & Maki, D. R. (1981). Searching for structure: A trait-factor approach to vocational rehabilitation. *Vocational Guidance Quarterly, 30*(1), 61–68.

Lynch, R. L. (1991). Teaching in the 21st century. *Vocational Journal, 66*(1), *29.*

Ma, X., & Wang, J. (2001). A confirmatory examination of Walberg's model of educational productivity in student career aspiration. *Educational Psychology, 21,* 443–453.

Maccoby, M. (1976). *The gamesman.* New York: Simon & Schuster.

Maccoby, M. (1980). Work and human development. *Professional Psychology, 11,* 509–519.

Maccoby, M., & Terzi, K. (1981). What happened to the work ethic? In J. O'Toole, J. L. Scheiber, & L. C. Wood (Eds.), *Working, changes and choices* (pp. 162–171). New York: Human Sciences Press.

Macdonald, S., & Dooley, S. (1990). Employee assistance programs: Emerging trends. *Canadian Journal of Community Mental Health, 9,* 97–105.

Macke, A. S., & Morgan, W. R. (1978). Maternal employment, race, and work orientation of high school girls. *Social Forces, 57*(1), 187–203.

Mackin, R. K., & Hansen, L. S. (1981). A theory-based career development course: A plant in the garden. *The School Counselor, 28*(5), 325–334.

MacMichael, D. C. (1974). Work ethics: Collision in the classroom. *Manpower, 6,* 15–20.

Maddox, G. L. (1972). Retirement as a social event in the United States. In B. L. Neugarten (Ed.), *Middle age and aging.* Chicago: University of Chicago Press.

Mager, R. F. (1997). *Preparing instructional objectives* (3rd ed.). Atlanta, GA: Center for Effective Performance.

Magnuson, C. S., & Starr, M. F. (2000). How early is too early to begin life career planning? The importance of the elementary school years. *Journal of Career Development, 27,* 89–101.

Mahone, C. H. (1960). Fear of failure and unrealistic vocational aspiration. *Journal of Abnormal and Social Psychology, 60,* 253–261.

Mainquist, J., & Eichorn, D. (1989). Competence in work settings. In D. Stern & D. Eichorn (Eds.), *Adolescence and work. Influences of social structure, labor markets, and culture* (pp. 327–361). Hillsdale, NJ: Lawrence Erlbaum Associates, Publishers.

Malcolm, S. M. (1990). Reclaiming our past. *The Journal of Negro Education, 59*(3), 246–259.

Malen, E. A., & Stroh, L. K. (1998). The influence of gender of job loss coping behavior among unemployed managers. *Journal of Employment Counseling, 35,* 26–39.

Mallinckrodt, B. (1990). Satisfaction with a new job after unemployment: Consequences of job loss for older professionals. *Journal of Counseling Psychology, 37*(2), 149–152.

Mallinckrodt, B., & Bennett, J. (1992). Social support and the impact of job loss in dislocated blue-collar workers. *Journal of Counseling Psychology, 39*(4), 482–489.

Mallinckrodt, B., & Fretz, B. R. (1988). Social support and the impact of job loss on older professionals. *Journal of Counseling Psychology, 36,* 181–186.

Mangum, G. L. (1988). *Youth transition from adolescence to the world of work.* Paper prepared for Youth and America's Future: The William T. Grant Foundation Commission on Work, Family, and Citizenship. Washington, DC: The William T. Grant Foundation Commission.

Manicas, P. T., & Secord, P. F. (1983). Implications for psychology of the new philosophy of science. *American Psychologist, 38,* 399–413.

Mann, L., Beswick, G., Allouache, P., & Ivey, M. (1989). Decision workshops for the improvement of decision making skills and confidence. *Journal of Counseling and Development, 67,* 478–481.

Manuele, C. A. (1984). Modifying vocational maturity in adults with delayed career development: A life skills approach. *Vocational Guidance Quarterly, 33*(2), 101–112.

Manuele-Adkins, C. (1992). Career counseling is personal counseling. *Career Development Quarterly, 40,* 313–323.

Manzi, P. A. (1986). Cognitive appraisal, stress, and coping in teenage employment. *Vocational Guidance Quarterly, 34*(3), 160–170.

Maples, M. F. (1981). Dual career marriages: Elements for potential success. *Personnel and Guidance Journal, 60*(1), 19–23.

Marcia, J. E. (1980). Identity in adolescence. In J. Adelson (Ed.), *Handbook of adolescent psychology,* (pp. 159–187). New York: Wiley.

Mariani, M. (1999). Replace with a database: O*NET replaces the Dictionary of Occupational Titles. *Occupational Outlook Quarterly, 43*(1), 3–9.

Marin, P. A., & Splete, H. (1991). A comparison of the effect of two computer-based counseling interventions on the career decidedness of adults. *Career Development Quarterly, 39,* 360–371.

Marland, S. P. (1972). Career education 300 days later. *American Vocational Journal, 47*(2), 14–17.

Marr, E. (1965). Some behaviors and attitudes relating to vocational choices. *Journal of Counseling Psychology,* 12, 404–408.

Marsden, P. V., Kallenberg, A. L., & Cook, C. R. (1993). Gender differences in organizational commitment: Influences of work positions and family roles. *Work and Occupations, 20*(3), 368–390.

Marshall, R., & Tucker, M. (November 9–15, 1992). The best imports from Japan and Germany. *Washington Post National Weekly Edition,* p. 24.

Martin, J. (1992). Your new global work force. *Fortune, 126*(13), 52–68.

Martin, W. E., Jr. (1991). Career development and American Indians living on reservations: Cross-cultural factors to consider. *Career Development Quarterly, 39,* 273–283.

Martin, W. E., Jr. (1995). Career development assessment and intervention strategies with American Indians. In F. T. L. Leong (Ed.), *Career development and vocational behavior of racial and ethnic minorities* (pp. 227–246). Mahwah, NJ: Erlbaum.

Martinez, A. C., Sedlacek, W. E., & Bachhuber, T. D. (1985). Male and female college graduates—7 months later. *Vocational Guidance Quarterly, 34*(2), 77–84.

Maslach, C. (1981). Burnout: A social psychological analysis. In J. W. Jones (Ed.), *The burnout syndrome: Current research, theory, interventions.* Park Ridge, IL: London House Press.

Maslach, C., & Jackson, J. E. (1981). The measurement of experienced burnout. *Journal of Occupational Behavior, 2,* 99–113.

Maslach, C., & Jackson, S. E. (1986). *Maslach burnout inventory manual* (2nd ed.). Palo Alto: Consulting Psychologists Press.

Maslach, C., & Leiter, M. P. (1997). *The truth about burnout: How organizations cause personal stress and what to do about it.* San Francisco: Jossey-Bass.

Maslow, A. H. (1954). *Motivation and personality,* New York: Harper & Row.

Mason, E. S. (1994). Work values: A gender comparison and implications for practice. *Psychological Reports, 74,* 415–418.

Massachusetts Institute of Technology. Quality Education for Minorities Project. (1990). *Education that works: An action plan for the education of minorities.* Cambridge, MA: Author.

Mathabe, N. R., & Temane, M. Q. (1993). The realities and imperatives of career counselling for a developing South Africa. *Journal of Career Development, 20,* 25–32.

Mathews, R. M., Damron, W. S., & Yuen, C. K. (1985). A seminar in job-finding skills. *Journal of Employment Counseling, 22*(4), 170–173.

Matsui, T., & Onglatco, M-L. (1992). Career self-efficacy as a moderator of the relation between occupational stress and strain. *Journal of Vocational Behavior, 41,* 79–88.

Matsumoto, D. (1996). *Culture and psychology.* Pacific Grove, CA: Brooks/Cole.

Matteson, M. T., Ivancevich, J. M., & Smith, S. V. (1984). Relation of Type A behavior to performance and satisfaction among sales personnel. *Journal of Vocational Behavior, 25*(2), 203–214.

Matthay, E. R., & Linder, R. (1982). A team effort in planning for the academically disadvantaged. *The School Counselor, 29*(3), 226–231.

Matthews, D. B. (1990). A comparison of burnout in selected occupational fields. *The Career Development Quarterly, 38,* 230–239.

Mau, W. (1995). Educational planning and academic achievement of middle school students: A racial and cultural comparison. *Journal of Counseling and Development, 73,* 518–526.

Mau, W. (2000). Cultural differences in career decision-making styles and self-efficacy. *Journal of Vocational Behavior, 57,* 365–378.

Mau, W., & Bikos, L. H. (2000). Educational and vocational aspirations of minority and female students: A longitudinal study. *Journal of Counseling & Development, 78,* 186–194.

Mauer, E. B., & Gysbers, N. C. (1990). Identifying career concerns of entering university freshmen using My Vocational Situation. *Career Development Quarterly, 39,* 155–165.

Maurer, J. G., Vrendenburgh, D. J., & Smith, R. L. (1981). An examination of the central life interest scale. *Academy of Management Journal, 24*(1), 174–182.

Maynard, P. E., & Hansen, J. C. (1970). Vocational maturity among inner city youths. *Journal of Counseling Psychology, 17,* 400–404.

Mazen, A. A., & Lemkau, J. P. (1990). Personality profiles of women in traditional and nontraditional occupations. *Journal of Vocational Behavior, 37,* 46–59.

McAllister, S., & Ponterotta, J. G. (1992). A group career program for displaced homemakers. *The Journal for Specialists in Group Work, 17*(1), 29–36.

McAuliffe, G. J. (1993). Constructive development and career transition: Implications for counseling. *Journal of Counseling & Development, 72,* 23–28.

McBride, A. B. (1990). Mental health effects of women's multiple roles. *American Psychologist, 45,* 381–384.

McClellan, D. C. (1965). Toward a theory of motive acquisition. *American Psychologist, 20,* 321–333.

McCormac, M. E. (1989). Information sources and resources. *Journal of Career Development, 16,* 129–138.

McCowan, C., & Mountain, E. (2000). Career development in Australia. In B. Hiebert & L. Bezanson (Eds.), *Making waves: Career development and public policy* (pp. 84–97). Ottawa, Canada: Human Resources Development Canada/Canadian Career Development Foundation.

McDaniels, J. W. (1963). Disability and vocational development. *Journal of Rehabilitation, 29*(4), 16–18.

McDaniels, C. (1968). Youth: Too young to choose. *Vocational Guidance Quarterly, 16,* 242–249.

McDaniels, C. (1978). The practice of career guidance and counseling. *INFORM, 7,* 1–2, 7–8.

McDaniels, C. (1984a). The work/leisure connection. *Vocational Guidance Quarterly, 33*(1), 35–44.

McDaniels, C. (1984b). Work and leisure in the career span. In *Designing careers, counseling to enhance education, work and leisure* (Chap. 21). San Francisco: Jossey-Bass.

McDaniels, C. (1989). *The changing workplace: Career counseling strategies for the 1990s and beyond.* San Francisco: Jossey-Bass.

McDivitt, P. J. (2002). Review of the Career Maturity Inventory. In J. T. Kapes & E. A. Whitfield (Eds.), *A counselor's guide to career assessment instruments.* (4th ed., pp. 337–342). Tulsa, OK: National Career Development Association.

McDowell, C. F. (1976). *Leisure counseling: Related lifestyle processed.* Eugene, OR: University of Oregon.

McFadden, D. J. (Ed.). (1993). *Transcultural counseling.* Alexandria, VA: American Counseling Association.

McFarland, W. P. (1993). A developmental approach to gay and lesbian youth. *Journal of Humanistic Education and Development, 32,* 17–29.

McGowan, B., & Law, B. (2000, January). *Exploring career-related learning in primary schools.* NICEC Briefing. Cambridge, England: National Institute of Careers Education and Counseling.

McGowen, K. R., & Hart, L. E. (1992). Exploring the contribution of ender identity to differences in career experience. *Psychological Reports, 70,* 723–733.

McGrath, G. E. (1992). When to use a psychologist in business. *The Pennsylvania Psychologist Quarterly, 52*(11), 17.

McGuire, P. A. (1999). Worker stress, health reaching critical point. *APA Monitor, 30*(5), 1, 27.

McGuire, T. J., & Frisman, K. (1983). Reimbursement policy and cost-effective mental health care. *American Psychologist 38*(8), 939–940.

McIntire, S. A., & Levine, E. L. (1984). An empirical investigation of self-esteem as a composite construct. *Journal of Vocational Behavior, 25*(2), 290–303.

McKay, W. R., & Miller, C. A. (1982). Relations of socioeconomic status and sex variables to the complexity of worker functions in the occupational choices of elementary school children. *Journal of Vocational Behavior, 20,* 31–39.

McKenzie, I. L., & Manoogian-O'Dell, M. (1988). Expanding the use of students in career services: Current programs and resources. *American College Personnel Association Media Publication, NO. 45*

McLean, A. A. (1973). Occupational mental health: Review of an emerging art. In R. L. Noland (Ed.), *Industrial mental health and counseling* (Chap. 7). New York: Behavioral Publications.

McLean, A. A. (1985). One hundred years of occupational mental health. In P. A. Carone, S. N. Keiffer, S. F. Yolles, & L. W. Kvinsky (Eds.), *History of mental health and industry, the last hundred years,* Vol. 10 (Chap. 2). Problems of Industrial Psychiatric Medicine Series. New York: Human Sciences Press.

McMahon, G. G. (1970). Technical education: A problem of definition. *American Vocational Journal, 44,* 22–23.

McNair, D., & Brown, D. (1983). Predicting the occupational aspirations, occupational expectations, and career maturity of black and white male and female 10th graders. *Vocational Guidance Quarterly, 31,*(1), 29–36.

McRae, K. B. (1985). Career-management planning: A boon to managers and employees. *Personnel, 62*(5), 56–60.

McWhirter, E. H. (1994). *Counseling for empowerment.* Alexandria, VA: American Counseling Association.

McWhirter, E. H. (1997). Perceived barriers to education and career: Ethnic and gender differences. *Journal of Vocational Behavior, 50,* 124–140.

McWhirter, E. H., Rasheeds, S., & Crothers, M. (2000). The effects of high school career education of social-cognitive variables. *The Journal of Counseling Psychology, 47*(3), 330–341.

McWhirter, J. J., McWhirter, S. T., McWhirter, A. M., & McWhirter, E. H. (1994). High and low-risk characteristics of youth: The five C's of competency. *Elementary School Guidance and Counseling, 28*(3), 188–196.

Meckel, N. T. (1981). The manager as career counselor. *Training and Development Journal, 35,* 65–69.

Mederer, H. J. (1993). Division of labor in two-earner homes: Task accomplishment versus household management as critical variables in perceptions about family work. *Journal of Marriage and the Family, 55,* 133–145.

Medvene, A. M. (1973). Early parent child interactions of educational, vocational, and emotional-social clients. *Journal of Counseling Psychology, 20,* 94–95.

Meehl, P. E. (1954). *Clinical versus statistical prediction.* Minneapolis: University of Minnesota Press.

Mehaffey, J. I., & Sandberg, S. K. (1992). Conducting social skills training groups with elementary school children. *The School Counselor, 40,* 61–67.

Mehrens, W. A. (1988). Review of vocational interest, experience, and skill assessment. In J. T. Kapes & M. M. Mastie (Eds.), *A counselor's guide to career assessment instruments* (pp. 132–136). Washington, DC: National Career Development Association.

Mehrens, W. A. (1994). Kuder General Interest Survey, Form E (KGIS). In J. T. Kapes, M. M. Mastie, & E. A. Whitfield (Eds.). *A counselor's guide to career assessment instruments* (pp. 189–193). Alexandria, VA: National Career Development Association.

Mehrens, W. A., & Lehmann, I. J. (1985). Interpreting test scores to clients: What scores should one use? *Journal of Counseling and Development, 63,* 317–320.

Meichenbaum, D. (1977). *Cognitive-behavior modification.* New York: Plenum.

Meichenbaum, D. (1985). *Stress inoculation training.* New York: Pergamon Press.

Meichenbaum, D. (1993). Changing conceptions of cognitive behavioral model: Retrospect and prospect. *Journal of Consulting and Clinical Psychology, 61*(2), 202–204.

Meier, S. T., & Geiger, S. M. (1986). Implications of computer-assisted testing and assessment for professional practice and training. *Measurement and Evaluation in Counseling and Development, 19*(1), 29–34.

Meinster, M. O., & Rose, K. C. (2001). Longitudinal influences of educational aspirations and romantic relationships on adolescent women's vocational interests. *Journal of Vocational Behavior, 58,* 313–327.

Meir, E. I. (1988). The need for congruence between within-occupation interests and specialty in mid-career. *The Career Development Quarterly, 37,* 63–69.

Meir, E. I. (1989). Integrative elaboration of the congruence theory. *Journal of Vocational Behavior, 35,* 219–230.

Melamed, S., & Meir, E. (1981). The relationship between interests—job incongruity and selection of avocational activity. *Journal of Vocational Behavior, 18,* 310–325.

Mencke, R. A., & Cochran, D. J. (1974). Impact of a counseling outreach workshop on vocational development. *Journal of Counseling Psychology, 21,* 185–190.

Mercado, P., & Atkinson, D. R. (1982). Effects of counselor sex, student sex, and student attractiveness in counselors' judgments. *Journal of Vocational Behavior, 20,* 304–312.

Merman, S. K., & McLaughlin, J. E. (1982, August). *Unleashing human potential: The role of the career counselor in industry.* Paper presented to the International Federation of Training and Development Organizations, Calgary, Alberta, Canada.

Meyer, R. H., & Wise, D. A. (1982). High school preparation and early labor force experience. In *The youth labor market problem: Its nature, causes, and consequences* (pp. 277–339). Chicago: University of Chicago Press.

Mihal, W. L., & Graumenz, J. L. (1984). An assessment of the accuracy of self-assessment for career decision-making. *Journal of Vocational Behavior 25*(2), 245–253.

Millar, J. D. (1992). Public enlightenment and mental health in the workplace. In G. P. Keita & S. L. Sauter (Eds.), *Work and well-being: An agenda for the 1990s.* Washington, DC: American Psychological Association.

Miller, A. J. (1972, April). *The emerging school based comprehensive education model.* Paper prepared to the National Conference on Career Education for Deans of Colleges of Education, Columbus, OH.

Miller, A. L., & Tiedeman, D. V. (1972). Decision making for the 70's: The cubing of the Tiedeman paradigm and its application in career education. *Focus on Guidance,* 5(1) 1–15.

Miller, A. L., & Tiedeman, D. V. (1977). Structuring responsibility in adolescents actualizing "I" power through curriculum. In G. D. Miller (Ed.), *Developmental theory and its application in guidance programs: Systematic efforts to promote personal growth* (pp. 123–166). Minneapolis, MN: Minnesota Department of Education.

Miller, A. W. (1968). Learning theory and vocational decisions. *Personnel and Guidance Journal, 47,* 18–23.

Miller, C. D., & Oetting, G. (1977). Barriers to employment and the disadvantaged. *Personnel and Guidance Journal, 56*(2), 89–93.

Miller, C. H. (1974). Career development theory in perspective. In E. L. Herr (Ed.), *Vocational guidance and human development.* Boston: Houghton Mifflin.

Miller, D. C., & Form, W. H. (1951). *Industrial sociology.* New York: Harper.

Miller, G. (1980). The interpretation of nonoccupational work in modern society: A preliminary discussion and typology. *Social Problems, 27*(4), 381–391.

Miller, J. (1980). Individual and occupational determinants of job satisfaction. *Sociology of Work and Occupations, 7*(3), 337–366.

Miller, J. V. (1982a). Lifelong career development for disadvantaged youth and adults. *Vocational Guidance Quarterly, 30*(4), 359–366.

Miller, J. V. (1982b), 1970's trends in assessing career counseling, guidance, and education. *Measurement and Evaluation in Guidance, 15*(2), 142–146.

Miller, J. V. (2002). Career counseling for mature workers. Adult career development: Some perspectives on the future. In S. Niles (Ed.), *Adult career development: Concepts, issues, and practices* (pp. 267–285). Tulsa, OK: National Career Development Association.

Miller, M. F. (1974). Relationship of vocational maturity to work values. *Journal of Vocational Behavior 5,* 367–371.

Miller, M. F. (1978). Childhood experience antecedents of career maturity attitudes. *Vocational Guidance Quarterly, 27*(2), 137–143.

Miller, M. J. (1989). Career counseling for the elementary school child: Grades K–5. *Journal of Employment Counseling, 26*(4), 169–177.

Miller, R. R. (1986). Reducing occupational circumscription. *Elementary School Guidance and Counseling, 20,* 250–253.

Miller, T. K. (Ed.). (2001). *The book of professional standards for higher education* (2nd rev. ed.). Washington, DC: Council for the Advancement of Standards in Higher Education.

Miller-Tiedeman, A. (1999). *Learning, practicing, and living the new careering.* Philadelphia: Accelerated Development.

Milley, D. J., & Bee, R. H. (1982). A conditional logic model of collegiate major selection. *Journal of Vocational Behavior, 20,* 81–92.

Milliken, R. L. (1962). Realistic occupational appraisal by high school seniors. *Personnel and Guidance Journal, 40,* 541–544.

Milne, A. M., Myers, D. E., Rosenthal, A. S., & Ginsburg, A. (1986). Single parents, working mothers, and the educational achievement of school children. *Sociology of Education, 59,* 125–139.

Milne, S. H., Blum, T. C., & Roman, P. M. (1994). Factors influencing employees' propensity to use an employee assistance program. *Personnel Psychology, 47,* 123–145.

Miner, C. U., & Sellers, S. M. (2002). Review of the Career Assessment Inventory. In J. T. Kapes & E. A. Whitfield (Eds.), *A counselor's guide to career assessment instruments.* (4th ed., pp. 204–209). Tulsa, OK: National Career Development Association.

Missouri Department of Education (1990). *Missouri Comprehensive Guidance Program.* Jefferson City: Author.

Mitchel, J. O. (1982). Careers at the agency level. *Managers Magazine, 53*(3), 28–35.

Mitchell, A. (1984). *The nine American lifestyles.* New York: Warner Books.

Mitchell, A. M. (1975). Emerging career guidance competencies. *Personnel and Guidance Journal, 53*(9), 700–705.

Mitchell, K. E., Levin, A. S., & Krumboltz, J. D. (1999). Planned happenstance: Constructing unexpected career opportunities. *Journal of Counseling and Development, 77,* 115–124.

Mitchell, L. K., & Krumboltz, J. D. (1984a). Research in human decision making: Implications for career decision making and counseling. In S. Brown & R. Lent (Eds.), *Handbook of counseling psychology* (pp. 238–280). New York: Wiley.

Mitchell, L. K., & Krumboltz, J. D. (1984b). Social learning approach to career decision making: Krumboltz's theory. In D. Brown & L. Brooks (Eds.), *Career choice and development* (Chap. 9). San Francisco: Jossey-Bass.

Mitchell, L. K., & Krumboltz, J. D. (1987). Cognitive restructuring and decision-making training on career indecision. *Journal of Counseling and Development, 66,* 171–174.

Mitchell, L. K., & Krumboltz, J. D. (1990). Social learning approach to career decision making: Krumboltz's Theory. In D. Brown and L. Brooks (Eds.), *Career choice and development. Applying contemporary theories to practice* (pp. 145–196) (2nd Ed.). San Francisco: Jossey-Bass.

Mitchell, L. K., & Krumboltz, J. D. (1996). Krumboltz's learning theory of career choice counseling. In D. Brown, L. Brooks, et al. (Eds.), *Career choice and de-*

velopment (3rd ed., pp. 233–276). San Francisco: Jossey-Bass.

Moch, M. K. (1980). Racial differences in job satisfaction: Testing four common explanations. *Journal of Applied Psychology, 65,* 299–306.

Moen, P. (1989). *Working parents: Transformation in gender roles and public policy in Sweden.* Madison: University of Wisconsin Press.

Moen, P., Downey, G., & Bolger, N. (1990). Labor-force re-entry among U.S. homemakers in midlife: A life-course analysis. *Gender and Society, 4*(2), 230–243.

Mohney, C., & Anderson, W. (1988). The effect of life events and relationships on adult women's decisions to enroll in college. *Journal of Counseling and Development, 66,* 271–279.

Moore, M. A., Neimeyer, G. J., & Marmarosh, C. (1992). Effects of informational valence and occupational favorability on vocational differentiation: A test of the disconfirmation hypothesis. *Journal of Counseling Psychology, 39*(3), 335–341.

Moore, S. S. (1985). Introduction. In D. Jones & S. S. Moore (Eds.), *Counseling adults: Life cycle perspectives* (pp. vii–xii). Lawrence: University of Kansas.

Morgan, C., Isaac, J. D., & Sansone, C. (2001). The role of interest in understanding the career choices of female and male college students. *Sex Roles, 44,* 295–320.

Morgan, M. A. (1980). *Managing career development.* New York: Van Nostrand, Reinhold.

Morgan, P. I., Patton, J., & Baker, H. K. (1985). The organization's role in managing midlife crisis. *Training and Development Journal, 39,* 56–59.

Morris, J. L. (1966). Propensity for risk taking as determinant of vocational choice. *Journal of Personality and Social Psychology, 3,* 328–335.

Morris, R., & Bass, S. A. (Eds.). (1988). *Retirement reconsidered: Economic and social roles for older people.* New York: Springer.

Morrison, A. M., & VonGlinow, M. A. (1990). Women and minorities in management. *American Psychologist, 45*(2), 200–208.

Morrison, M. H. (1984). The aging of the U.S. population: Human resource implications. *Aging and Work, 7*(1), 79–83

Morrow, P. C., & McElroy, J. C. (1984). The impact of physical attractiveness in evaluative contexts. *Basic and Applied Social Psychology, 5*(3), 171–182.

Morrow, P. C., Mullen, E. J., & McElroy, J. C. (1990). Vocational behavior 1989: The year in review. *Journal of Vocational Behavior, 37*(2), 121–195.

Morse, W. (1963). *Foreword to the vocational education act of 1963.* PL-88210. Washington, DC: U.S. Government Printing Office.

Mortimer, J. T., & Finch, M. D. (1986). The development of self-esteem in the early work career. *Work and Occupations, 13*(2), 217–239.

Moses, B. (1999). *The good news about careers. How you'll be working in the next decade.* San Francisco: Jossey-Bass.

Moskowitz, R., & Warwick, D. (1996). The job outlook in brief. *Occupational Outlook Quarterly, 40* (1), 2–41.

Moser, H. P., Dubin, W., & Shelsky, I. (1956). A proposed modification of the Roe occupational classification. *Journal of Counseling Psychology, 3,* 27–31.

Moses, J. L., & Byham, W. C. (Eds.). (1977). *Applying the assessment center method.* New York: Pergamon Press.

Motowidlo, S. J., Carter, G. W., Dunnette, M. D., Tippins, N., Werner, S., Burnett, J. R., & Vaughan, M. J. (1992). Studies of the structured behavioral interview. *Journal of Applied Psychology, 77*(5), 571–587.

Motsch, P. (1980). Peer social modeling: A tool for assisting girls with career exploration. *Vocational Guidance Quarterly, 28*(3), 231–240.

Mottaz, C., & Potts, G. (1986). An empirical evaluation of models of work satisfaction. *Social Science Research, 15,* 153–173.

Mowbray, C. T., Lanir, S., & Hulce, M. (Eds.). (1984). *Women and mental health: New directions for change.* New York: The Haworth Press.

Muchinsky, P. M. (1978). Age and job facet satisfaction. A conceptual reconsideration. *Aging and Work, 1,*(3), 175–179.

Mueller, C. F. (1981). Migration of the unemployed: A relocation assistance program. *Monthly Labor Review, 104*(4), 62–64.

Mueller, D. J. (1985). Review of the Career Orientation Placement and Evaluation Survey. *Measurement and Evaluation in Counseling and Development, 17*(3), 132–134.

Multon, K. D., Brown, S. D., & Lent, R. W. (1991). Relation of self-efficacy beliefs to academic outcomes: A meta-analytic investigation. *Journal of Counseling Psychology, 38*(1), 30–38.

Multon, K. D., Heppner, M. J., & Gysbers, N. C., Zook, C., & Ellis-Kalton, C. A. (2001). Client psychological distress: An important factor in career counseling. *The Career Development Quarterly, 49,* 324–335.

Munson, W. W. (1992). Self-esteem, vocational identity, and career salience in high school students. *The Career Development Quarterly, 40,* 361–368.

Murphy, G. S. (1947). *Personality: A biosocial approach to origins and structure.* New York: Harper & Brothers.

Murray, H. (1938). *Explorations in personality.* New York: Oxford University Press.

Murrow-Taylor, C., Foltz, B. M., Ellis, M. R., & Culbertson, K. (1999). A multicultural career fair for elementary school students. *Professional School Counseling, 2*(3), 241–243.

Myers, I. B., & McCaulley, M. H. (1985). *Manual: A guide to the development and use of the Myers-Briggs Type Indicator.* Palo Alto, CA: Consulting Psychologists Press.

Myers, J. E., Sweeney, T. J., & Witmer, J. M. (2000). The wheel of wellness. Counseling for wellness: A holistic model for treatment planning. *Journal of Counseling and Development, 78,* 251–266.

Nafziger, D. H., Holland, J. L., Helms, S. T., & McPartland, J. M. (1974). Applying an occupational classification to the work histories of young men and women. *Journal of Vocational Behavior, 5,* 331–345.

National Alliance of Business. (1984). *A nation at work: Education and the private sector.* Washington, DC: Author.

National Alliance of Business. (1986). *Employment policies: Looking to the year 2000.* Washington DC: Author.

National Association of Secondary School Principals. (1975). EBCF: A design for career education. *Curriculum Report, 4*(3), 1–11.

National Career Development Association. (1985). Consumer guidelines for selecting a career counselor. *Career Development, 1*(2), 1–2.

National Career Development Association. (1991, January 11). Position paper approved by the Board of Directors.

National Career Development Association. (1997). *Career counseling competencies.* Alexandria, VA.

National Career Development Association. (1997). *NCDA guidelines for the use of the internet for the provision of career information and planning services.* Washington, DC: Author.

National Center for Educational Statistics. (1980). *Condition of education. 1980.* Washington, DC: Author.

National Center for Educational Statistics. (1981). *Digest of educational statistics, 1981.* Washington, DC: Author.

National Center for Research in Vocational Education. (1982). Factors relating to the job placement of former secondary vocational education students. *CENTERGRAM, 17*(3), 1–2.

National Commission for Employment Policy. (1981). *The federal role in vocational education.* Washington, DC: Author.

National Commission on Excellence in Education. (1983). *A nation at risk: The imperative for educational reform.* Washington, DC: U.S. Government Printing Office.

National Commission on Secondary Education for Hispanics. (1985). *Make something happen. Hispanics and urban school reform,* 2 vols. Washington, DC: Author.

National Commission on Secondary Vocational Education. (1985). *The unfinished agenda. The role of vocational education in the high school.* Columbus: Ohio State University, The National Center for Research in Vocational Education.

National Occupational Information Coordinating Committee. (1988). *The National Career Counseling and Development Guidelines-Postsecondary Institutions.* Washington, DC: Author.

National Occupational Information Coordinating Committee. (1989). *The National Career Development Guidelines,* Local Handbook. Washington, DC: Author.

National Occupational Information Coordinating Committee. (1990, January 11). Almost two-thirds of Americans would seek more information about career options if they had it to do over again, new survey finds. Press Release. Washington, DC: Author.

National Opinion Research Center. (1947). Jobs and occupations: A popular evaluation. *Opinion News, 9,* 3–13.

National Science Foundation. (1989). *Science and engineering indicators—1989.* Washington, DC: Author.

National Student Aid Coalition. (1985). *Closing the information gap: Ways to improve student awareness of financial aid opportunities.* Washington, DC: Author.

National Vocational Guidance Association. (1971). *Guidelines for the preparation and evaluation of career information media: Films, filmstrips, and printed materials.* Washington, DC: American Personnel and Guidance Association.

National Vocational Guidance Association. (1980). Guidelines for the preparation and evaluation of career information literature. *Vocational Guidance Quarterly, 28*(4), 291–296.

National Vocational Guidance Association. (1982, September). *Vocational/career counseling competencies approved by the board of directors.* Falls Church, VA: Author.

National Vocational Guidance Association/American Vocational Association. (1973). *The position paper on career development.* Washington, DC: Author.

Naughton, T. J. (1987). A conceptual view of workaholism and implications for career counseling and research. *Career Development Quarterly, 35*(3), 180–187.

Nealer, J. K., & Papalia, A. S. (1982). *So you want to get a job. A manual for the job seeker and vocational counselor.* Moravia, NY: Chronicle Guidance.

Near, J. P. (1985). A discriminant analysis of plateaued versus non-plateaued managers. *Journal of Vocational Behavior, 26*(2), 177–188.

Near, J. P., Rice, R. W., & Hunt, R. G. (1980). The relationship between work and nonwork domains: A review of empirical research. *Academy of Management Review, 5,* 415–429.

Neff, J. A. (1985). Race and vulnerability to stress: An examination of differential vulnerability. *Journal of Personality and Social Psychology, 49,* 481–491.

Neff, W. S. (1977). *Work and human behavior* (2nd ed.). Chicago: Aldine.

Neff, W. S. (1985). *Work and human behavior* (3rd ed.). New York: Atherton.

Neimeyer, G. J. (1988). Cognitive interaction and differentiation in vocational behavior. *The Counseling Psychologist, 16,* 440–475.

Neimeyer, G. J. (1989a). Applications of repertory grid technique to vocational assessment. *Journal of Counseling and Development, 67,* 585–589.

Neimeyer, G. J. (1989b). Personal construct systems in vocational development and information processing. *Journal of Career Development, 16,* 83–96.

Neimeyer, G. J., Brown, M. T., Metzler, A. E., Hagans, C., & Tanguy, M. (1989). The impact of sex, sex-role orientation, and construct type on vocational differentiation, integration, and conflict. *Journal of Vocational Behavior, 34,* 236–251.

Neimeyer, G. J., Metzler, A. E., & Bowman, R. (1988). Effects of sex, career orientation, and occupational type on vocational integration, differentiation, and conflict. *Journal of Counseling Psychology, 35,* 139–143.

Neimeyer, G. J., Nevill, D. D., Probert, B., & Fukuyama, M. (1985). Cognitive structures in vocational development. *Journal of Vocational Behavior, 27,* 191–201.

Nelson, D. E., & Gardner, J. L. (1998). *An evaluation of the comprehensive guidance program in Utah public schools.* Salt Lake City, UT: The Utah State Office of Education.

Nelson, G. (1990). Women's life strains, social support, coping, and positive and negative affect: Cross-sectional and longitudinal tests of the two-factor theory of emotional well-being. *Journal of Community Psychology, 18,* 239–256.

Nelson, J. C. (1983). *Family treatment: An integrative approach.* Englewood Cliffs, NJ: Prentice-Hall.

Nelson, L. S., & Roberge, L. P. (1993). The relationship between psychological type and preference for career services: Implications for career development strategies. *College Student Journal, 27*(3), 313–321.

Nelson, R. C. (1963). Knowledge and interest concerning sixteen occupations among elementary and secondary students. *Educational and Psychological Measurement, 27,* 741–754.

Nelson, R. C. (1979). The CREST program: Helping children with their choices. *Elementary School Guidance and Counseling, 14*(4), 286–298.

Nesselroade, J. R., & Baltes, P. B. (1984). From traditional factor analysis to structural-causal modeling in developmental research. In V. Garris & A. Parducci (Eds.), *Perspectives in psychological experimentations: Toward the year 2000* (pp. 267–287). Hillsdale, NJ: Erlbaum.

Nesselroade, J. R., & Ford, D. H. (1985). P-technique comes of age: Multivariate, replicated, single-subject designs for studying older adults. *Research on Aging, 7,* 46–80.

Nesselroade, J. R., & Ford, D. H. (1987). Methodological considerations in modeling living systems. In M. E. Ford & D. H. Ford (Eds.), *Humans as self-constructing living systems: putting the framework to work* (pp. 47–79). Hillsdale, NJ: Erbaum.

Nester, M. A. (1993). Psychometric testing and reasonable accommodation for persons with disabilities. *Rehabilitation Psychology, 38*(2), 75–85.

Neugarten, B. L. (1982, August). *Successful aging.* Paper presented to the annual meeting of the American Psychological Association.

Neugarten, B. L., Moore, J. C., & Lowe, J. C. (1965). Age nouns, age constraints and adult socialization. *American Journal of Sociology, 70,* 710–717.

Neukrug, E. S., Barr, C. G., Hoffman, L. R., & Kaplan, L. S. (1993). Developmental counseling and guidance: A model for use in your school. *The School Counselor, 40,* 356–362.

Nevill, D. D., Neimeyer, G. J., Probert, B., & Fukuyama, M. (1986). Cognitive structures in vocational information processing and decision making. *Journal of Vocational Behavior, 28*(2), 110–112.

Nevill, D. D., & Schlecker, D. I. (1988). The relation of self-efficacy and assertiveness to willingness to engage in traditional/nontraditional career activities. *Psychology of Women Quarterly, 12,* 91–98.

Nevill, D. D., & Super, D. E. (1986). *The Values Scale: Theory, application, and research manual* (research ed.). Palo Alto: Consulting Psychologists Press.

Nevo, O. (1987). Irrational expectations in career counseling and their confronting arguments. *The Career Development Quarterly, 35,* 239–250.

Nevo, O. (1990). Career counseling from the counselee perspective: Analysis of feedback questionnaires. *The Career Development Quarterly, 38,* 314–324.

The New York Times. UN Fears Divisive Impact of the Internet. Final Edition. Section A, page 16, Column 4. June 29, 2000.

New York State Education Department, Division of Occupational Education Programs. (1986). *Home and Career Skills. Grades 7 and 8.* Albany, NY: Author.

Nicholls, J. G., Patashnick, M., & Mettetal, G. (1986). Conceptions of ability and intelligence. *Child Development, 57,* 636–645.

Nicholson, N. (1996). Towards a new agenda for work and personality: Traits, self-identity, "strong" interactionism, and change. *Applied Psychology: An International Review, 45*(3), 189–205.

Niemann, Y. F., & Dovidio, J. F. (1998). Relationship of solo status, academic rank, and perceived distinctiveness to job satisfaction of racial/ethnic minorities. *Journal of Applied Psychology, 83*(1), 55–71.

Nieva, V. G., & Gutek, B. A. (1981). *Women and work.* New York: Praeger.

Niles, S. G. (1996). Offering appraisal support within career counseling. *Journal of Employment Counseling, 33,* 163–173.

Niles, S. G. (1993). The timing of counselor contact in the use of computer information delivery. *Journal of Employment Counseling, 30*(2), 2–12.

Niles, S. G. (1997). Annual review: Practice and research in career counseling and development-1996. *The Career Development Quarterly, 46,* 115–141.

Niles, S. G. (Ed.). (2002). *Adult career development* (3rd ed.). Tulsa, OK: National Career Development Association.

Niles, S. G., & Anderson, W. P. (1993). Career development and adjustment: The relation between concerns and stress. *Journal of Employment Counseling, 30,* 79–87.

Niles, S. G., Anderson, W. P., Jr., & Cover, S. (2000). Comparing intake concerns and goals with career counseling concerns. *The Career Development Quarterly, 49,* 135–145.

Niles, S. G., Anderson, W. P., Jr., & Goodenough, G. (1998). Exploration to foster career development. *The Career Development Quarterly, 46,* 262–275.

Niles, S. G., Erford, B. T., Hunt, B., & Watts, R. H. (1997). Decision-making styles and career development of college students. *Journal of College Student Development, 38,* 479–488.

Niles, S. G., & Garis, J. W. (1990). The effects of a career planning course and a computer assisted career guidance program (SIGI PLUS) on undecided university students. *Journal of Career Development, 16,* 63–73.

Niles, S. G., & Goodenough, G. (1996). Life-role salience and values: A review of recent research. *The Career Development Quarterly, 45,* 65–86.

Niles, S. G., & Harris-Bowlsbey, J. (2002). *Career development interventions in the 21st century.* Upper Saddle River, NJ: Merrill Prentice Hall.

Niles, S. G., & Herr, E. L. (1989). Using secondary school behaviors to predict career behaviors in young adulthood: Does success breed success? *Career Development Quarterly, 37,* 345–354.

Niles, S. G., Herr, E. L., & Hartung, P. J. (2001). *Achieving life balance: Myths, realities, and developmental perspectives.* Columbus, OH: ERIC Clearinghouse on Adult Career, and Vocational Education.

Niles, S. G., Lewis, D. M., & Hartung, P. J. (1997). Using the adult career concerns inventory to measure task involvement. *The Career Development Quarterly, 46,* 87–97.

Niles, S. G., & Pate, P. H., Jr. (1989). Competency and training issues related to the integration of career counseling and mental health counseling. *Journal of Career Development, 16,* 63–71.

Niles, S. G., & Sowa, C. J. (1992). Mapping the nomological network of career self-efficacy. *Career Development Quarterly, 41,* 13–21.

Noble, B. P. (1994). Coming soon: Get a life 101? *The New York Times,* February 27, 41.

Noeth, R. J., Engen, H. B., & Noeth, P. E. (1984). Making career decisions: A self-report of factors that help high school students. *Vocational Guidance Quarterly, 32*(4), 240–248.

Nolan, R. L. (Ed.), (1973). *Industrial mental health and employment counseling.* New York: Behavioral Objectives.

Novaco, R. (1976). Treatment of chronic anger through cognitive and relaxation controls. *Journal of Consulting and Clinical Psychology, 44,* 681.

Novi, M. J., & Meinster, M. O. (2000). Achievement in a relational context: Preferences and influences in female adolescents. *The Career Development Quarterly, 49,* 73–84.

Nozik, S. (1986). *The relation of sex role self-concept and work values to traditionality of occupational choice among employed men.* Unpublished doctoral dissertation. State University of New York at Buffalo.

Oakland, J. A. (1969). Measurement of personality correlates of academic achievement in high school students. *Journal of Counseling Psychology, 16,* 452–457.

O'Brien, K. M., & Fassinger, R. E. (1993). A causal model of the career orientation and career choice of adolescent women. *Journal of Counseling Psychology, 40*(4), 456–469.

O'Brien, K., Friedman, S. M., Tipton, L. C., & Linn, S. G. (2000). Attachment, separation, and women's vocational development: A longitudinal analysis. *Journal of Counseling Psychology, 47*(3), 301–315.

O'Connell, L., Betz, N., & Kurth, S. (1989). Plans for balancing work and family life: Do women pursuing traditional and nontraditional occupations differ? *Sex Roles, 20,* 35–45.

O'Driscoll, M. P., Ilgen, D. R., & Hildreth, K. (1992). Time devoted to job and off-job activities, interrole conflict, and affective experiences. *Journal of Applied Psychology, 77*(3), 272–279.

Offer, M., & Watts, A. G. (1997). *The internet and careers work.* NICEC Briefing. Cambridge, UK: National Institute for Careers Education and Counseling.

Offerman, L. R., & Gowing, M. K. (1990). Organizations of the future: Changes and challenges. *American Psychologist, 45,* 95–108.

O'Hara, R. P. (1966). Vocational self-concepts and high school achievement. *Vocational Guidance Quarterly, 15,* 106–112.

O'Hare, M. M., & Tamburri, E. (1986). Coping as a moderator of the relationship between anxiety and career decision making. *Journal of Counseling Psychology, 33*(3), 255–264.

Oinonen, C. M. (1984). *Business and education survey: Employer and employee perceptions of school to work preparation.* Madison, WI: The Wisconsin Department of Public Instruction/The Parker Fund of the Janesville Foundation.

Okey, J. L., Snyder, L. M., Jr., & Hackett, G. (1993). The broadening horizons project: Development of a vocational guidance program for eighth grade students. *The School Counselor, 40,* 218–222.

Olbrisch, M. E. (1977). Psychotherapeutic intervention in physical health: Effectiveness and economic efficiency. *American Psychologist, 32*(9), 761–777.

Oldham, G. R., & Fried, Y. (1987). Employee reactions to workspace characteristics. *Journal of Applied Psychology, 72,* 75–80.

Olds, J., Schwartz, R. S., Eisen, S. V., Betcher, R. W., & Van Niel, A. (1993). Part-time employment and marital well-being: A hypothesis and pilot study. *Family Therapy, 20*(1), 1–16.

Oliver, L. (1975). The relationship of parental attitudes and parent identification to career and home-making orientation in college women. *Journal of Vocational Behavior, 7,* 1–12.

Oliver, L. (1977). Evaluating career counseling outcome for three modes of test interpretation. *Measurement and Evaluation in Guidance, 10*(3) 153–161.

Oliver, L. W., & Spokane, A. R. (1988). Career-intervention outcome: What contributes to client gain? *Journal of Counseling Psychology, 35,* 447–462.

Oliver, L. W., & Zack, J. S. (1999). Career assessment on the internet: An exploratory study. *Journal of Career Assessment, 7,* 323–356.

Olson, C., McWhirter, E., & Horan, J. J. (1989). A decision-making model applied to career counseling. *Journal of Career Development, 16,* 107–117.

Olson, G. T., & Matlock, S. G. (1994). Sixteen PF Personal Career Development Profile (PCDP). In J. T. Kapes, M. M. Mastie, & E. A. Whitfield (Eds.), *A counselor's guide to career assessment instruments* (pp. 300–305). Alexandria, VA: National Career Development Association.

Olson, L. (1997). *The school to work revolution. How employers and educators are joining forces to prepare tomorrow's skilled workforce.* Reading, MA: Addison-Wesley.

Omizo, S. A., & Omizo, M. M. (1992). Career and vocational assessment information with program planning and counseling for students with disabilities. *The School Counselor, 40,* 32–39.

O'Neil, J. O., Price, G. E., & Tracy, T. J. (1979). The stimulus value, treatment effects, and sex differences when completing the Self-Directed Search and Strong-Campbell Interest Inventory, *Journal of Counseling Psychology, 26,* 45–50.

O'Neil, R., & Greenberger, E. (1994). Patterns of commitment to work and parenting: Implications for role strain. *Journal of Marriage and the Family, 56,* 101–118.

Oomen, A., & de Vos, J. A. M. (2000). The Netherlands. In B. Hiebert & L. Bezanson (Eds.), *Making waves: Career development and public policy* (pp. 221–232). Ottawa, Canada: Human Resources Development Canada/Canadian Career Development Foundation.

Oppong, J. R., Ironside, R. G., & Kennedy, L. W. (1988). Perceived quality of life in a centre-periphery framework. *Social Indicators Research, 20,* 605–620.

Oregon Occupational Information Coordinating Committee, Oregon Career Information System. (1989). *Schoolwork, lifework. Integrating career information into high school career development programs.* Eugene, OR: Author.

O'Reilly, C. A., III, Chatman, J., & Caldwell, D. F. (1991). People and organizational culture: A profile comparison approach to assessing person-organization fit. *Academy of Management Journal, 34*(3), 487–516.

O'Reilly, P. A. (1973). *Predicting the stability of expressed occupational choices of secondary students.* Unpublished doctoral dissertation, Pennsylvania State University.

Orndorff, R. M., & Herr, E. L. (1996). A comparative study of declared and undeclared college students on career uncertainty and involvement in career development activities. *Journal of Counseling and Development, 74,* 632–639.

Ornstein, S., & Isabella, L. (1990). Age vs. stage models of career attitudes of women: A partial replication and extension. *Journal of Vocational Behavior, 36,* 1–19.

Orpen, C. (1994). The effects of self-esteem and personal control on the relationship between job insecurity and psychological well-being. *Social Behavior and Personality, 22*(1), 53–56.

Orzek, A. M. (1992). Career counseling for the gay and lesbian community. In S. H. Dworkin & F. J. Gutierrez (Eds.), *Counseling gay men and lesbians: Journey to the end of the rainbow* (pp. 23–24). Alexandria, VA: American Association for Counseling and Development.

Osborn, D. P. (1990). A reexamination of the organizational choice process. *Journal of Vocational Behavior, 36*(1), 45–60.

Osborne, W. L., Brown, S., Niles, S. G., & Miner, C. (1997). *Career development assessment and counseling: Donald Super's C-DAC Model.* Alexandria, VA: American Counseling Association.

Osipow, S. H. (1968). *Theories of career development,* New York: Appleton-Century-Crofts.

Osipow, S. H. (1977). Will the real counseling psychologist please stand up? *The Counseling Psychologist, 7*(2), 93–94.

Osipow, S. H. (1980). *Manual for the career decision scale.* Columbus, OH: Marathon Consulting and Press.

Osipow, S. H. (1982b). Research in career counseling: An analysis of issues and problems. *The Counseling Psychologist, 10*(4), 27–34.

Osipow, S. H. (1983). *Theories of career development* (3rd ed.). Englewood Cliffs, NJ: Prentice-Hall.

Osipow, S. H. (1986). Career issues through the life span. In M. S. Pallak & R. Perloff (Eds.), *Psychology and work: Productivity, change and employment* (pp. 137–168). Washington, DC: American Psychological Association.

Osipow, S. H. (1990). Convergence in theories of career choice and development: Review and Prospect. *Journal of Vocational Behavior, 36,* 122–131.

Osipow, S. H., Ashby, J. D., & Wall, H. W. (1966). Personality types and vocational choice: A test of Holland's theory. *Personnel and Guidance Journal, 45,* 37–42.

Osipow, S. H., Carney, C., & Barak, A. (1976). A scale of educational-vocational undecidedness: A typological approach. *Journal of Vocational Behavior, 9,* 233–243.

Osipow, S. H., Carney, C. G., Winer, J. L., Yanico, B. J., & Koschier, M. (1976). *Career decision scale.* Columbus, OH: Marathon Press.

Osipow, S. H., Carney, C. G., Winer, J. L., Yanico, B. J., & Koschier, M. (1976). *Career decision scale* (3rd rev.). Odessa, FL: Psychological Assessment Resources.

Osipow, S. H., Doty, R. E., & Spokane, A. R. (1985). Occupational stress, strain, and coping across the life span. *Journal of Vocational Behavior, 27*(1), 98–108.

Osipow, S. H., & Reed, R. (1985). Decision making style and career decision in college students. *Journal of Vocational Behavior, 27*(3), 368–373.

Osipow, S. H., Temple, R. D., & Rooney, R. A. (1993). The Short Form of the Task Specific Occupational Self-Efficacy Scale. *Journal of Career Assessment, 1*(1), 13–20.

Osterman, P. (1980). *Getting started: The youth labor market.* Cambridge, MA: MIT Press.

Osterman, P. (1989). The job market for adolescents. In D. Stern & D. Eichorn (Eds.), *Adolescence in work: Influences of social structure, labor markets, and culture* (pp. 235–258). Hillsdale, NJ: Lawrence Erlbaum Associates.

O'Toole, J. (1981). Work in America. In J. O'Toole, J. L. Schiber, & L. C. Wood (Eds.), *Working: Changes and choices* (pp. 12–17). New York: Human Sciences Press.

Ott, E. M. (1989). Effects of the male-female ratio at work. *Psychology of Women Quarterly, 13,* 41–57.

Ottke, M. B., & Brogden, S. Y. (1990). The marketplace of skills: A different twist to career fairs. *Journal of College Student Development, 31,* 376–377.

Otto, L. B. (1984). Bringing parents back in. *Journal of Career Education, 10*(4), 255–265.

Otto, L. B., & Call, V. R. A. (1985). Parental influence on young people's career development. *Journal of Career Development, 12*(1), 65–69.

Owen, D. W., Jr., & Weikel, W. J. (1999). Computer utilization by school counselors. *Professional School Counseling, 2*(3), 179–182.

Paa, H., & McWhirter, E. H. (2000). Perceived influences on high school students' current career expectations. *The Career Development Quarterly, 49,* 29–44.

Padula, M. A. (1994). Reentry women: A literature review with recommendations for counseling and research. *Journal of Counseling & Development, 73,* 10–16.

Palamore, E. B. (1969). Predicting longevity: A follow-up controlling for age. *Gerontologist, (9),* 247–250.

Palamore, E. B., Burchett, B. M., Fillenbaum, G. G., George, L. K., & Wallman, L. M. (1985). *Retirement: Causes and consequences.* New York: Springer.

Pallone, N. J. (1977). Counseling psychology: Toward an empirical definition. *The Counseling Psychologist, 7*(2), 29–32.

Palmer, S., & Cochran, L. (1988). Parents as agents of career development. *Journal of Counseling Psychology, 35,* 71–76.

Palmer, S., & Dryden, W. (1994). Stress management: Approaches and interventions. *British Journal of Guidance and Counselling, 22*(1), 5–12.

Papalia, A. S., & Kaminski, W. (1981). Counseling and counseling skills in the industrial environment. *Vocational Guidance Quarterly, 30*(1), 37–42.

Parasuraman, S., & Alutto, J. A. (1981). An examination of the organizational antecedents of stress work. *Academy of Management Journal, 24*(1) 48–67.

Pardine, P., Higgins, R., Szeglin, A., Beres, J., Kravitz, R., & Fotis, J. (1981). Job-stress worker-strain relationship moderated off-the-job experience. *Psychological Reports, 48,* 963–970.

Parham, T. A. (1989). Cycles of psychological nigrescence. *The Counseling Psychologist, 17*(2), 187–226.

Parham, T. A., & Austin, N. L. (1994). Career development and African Americans: A contextual reappraisal using the nigrescence construct. *Journal of Vocational Behavior, 44,* 139–154.

Parham, T. (1996). MCT theory and African-American populations. In D. W. Sue, A. E. Ivey, & P. B. Pedersen (Eds.), *A theory of multicultural counseling and therapy* (pp. 177–190). Pacific Grove, CA: Brooks/Cole.

Parker, D. A., Parker, E. S., Wolz, M. W., & Harford, T. C. (1980). Sex roles and alcohol consumption: A research note. *Journal of Health and Social Behavior, 21,* 43–48.

Parker, H. J. (1970). 29,000 seventh-graders have made occupational choices. *Vocational Guidance Quarterly, 18,* 219–224.

Parker, M., Peltier, S., & Wolleat, P. (1981). Understanding dual career couples. *Personnel and Guidance Journal, 60*(1), 14–18.

Parkes, C. M. (1971). Psycho-social *transitions:* A field for study. *Social Science and Medicine, 5* (2), 101–115.

Parkes, L. P., Bochner, S., & Schneider, S. K. (2001). Person-organization fit across cultures: An empirical investigation of individualism and collectivism. *Applied Psychology: An International Review, 50*(1), 81–108.

Parr, J., & Neimeyer, G. J. (1994). Effects of gender, construct type, occupational information, and career relevance on vocational differentiation. *Journal of Counseling Psychology, 41*(1), 27–33.

Parsons, F. (1909). *Choosing a vocation.* Boston: Houghton Mifflin.

Parsons, T., (1951). *The social system.* Glencoe, IL: The Free Press.

Partin, R. L., & Gargiolo, R. N. (1980). Burned out teachers have no class! Prescriptions for teacher burnout. *College Student Journal, 14*(4), 365–380.

Pascarella, E. T., & Terenzini, P. T. (1991). *How college affects students: Findings and insights from twenty years of research.* San Francisco: Jossey-Bass.

Pavlak, M. F., & Kammer, P. P. (1985). The effects of a career guidance program on the career maturity and self-concept of delinquent youth. *Journal of Vocational Behavior, 26*(1), 41–54.

Pazy, A. (1992). Sex-linked bias in promotion decisions. *Psychology of Women Quarterly, 16,* 209–228.

Peabody, D. (1985). *National characteristics.* New York: Cambridge University Press.

Peace, C. H. (1973). Pastoral counseling with the problem employee. In R. L. Noland (Ed.), *Industrial mental health and employee counseling* (Chap. 22). New York: Behavioral Publications.

Pearlin, L. I. (1982). Discontinuities in the study of aging. In T. K. Haraven & K. J. Adams (Eds.), *Aging and life course transitions: An interdisciplinary perspective* (pp. 55–74). New York: Guilford Press.

Pearlman, K. (1980). Job families: A review and discussion of their implications for personnel selection. *Psychological Bulletin, 87*(1), 1–28.

Pearlman, K., Schmidt, F. L., & Hunter, J. E. (1980). Validity generalization results for tests used to predict job proficiency and training success in clerical occupations. *Journal of Applied Psychology, 65,* 373–406.

Pearson, Q. M. (1998). Job satisfaction, leisure satisfaction, and psychological health. *The Career Development Quarterly, 46,* 416–426.

Peatling, J. H., & Tiedeman, D. V. (1977). *Career development. Designing self.* Muncie, IN: Accelerated Development.

Peavy, R. V. (1994). A constructivist perspective for counseling. *Education and Vocational Guidance Bulletin, 55,* 31.

Pedersen, P. (1988). *A handbook for developing multicultural awareness.* Washington, DC: American Association for Counseling and Development.

Pedersen, P. (1990). The constructs of complexity and balance in multicultural counseling theory and practice. *Journal of Counseling and Development, 68,* 550–554.

Pedersen, P. (1994). *A handbook for developing multicultural awareness* (2nd ed.). Alexandria, VA: American Counseling Association.

Pedro, J. D. (1982). Career maturity in high school females. *Vocational Guidance Quarterly, 30*(3), 243–251.

Pedro, J. D., Wolleat, P., & Fennema, E. (1980). Sex differences in the relationship of career interests and mathematics plans. *Vocational Guidance Quarterly, 29*(1), 25–34.

Peeks, B. (1993). Revolutions in counseling and education: A systems perspective in the schools. *Elementary School Guidance and Counseling, 27,* 245–251.

Pendaris, E. D., Howley, A., & Howley, C. (1990). *The abilities of gifted children.* Englewood Cliffs, NJ: Prentice Hall.

Penley, L. P., & Hawkins, B. L. (1980). Organizational communication, performance, and job satisfaction as a function of ethnicity and sex. *Journal of Vocational Behavior, 16,* 368–384.

Pennsylvania Department of Education. (1994). Program of Developmental Guidance and Counseling, Harrisburg, PA: The Author.

Peregoy, J. J., & Schliebner, C. T. (1990). Long-term unemployment: Effects and counseling interventions. *International Journal for the Advancement of Counselling, 13,* 193–204.

Perosa, S. L., & Perosa, L. M. (1983). The mid-career crisis: A description of the psychodynamics of transition and adaptation. *Vocational Guidance Quarterly, 32,*(2), 69–77.

Perovich, G. M., & Mierzwa, J. A. (1980). Group facilitation of vocational maturity and self-esteem in college students. *Journal of College Student Personnel, 21,* 206–211.

Perrone, P. A. (1964). Factors influencing high school seniors' occupational preference. *Personnel and Guidance Journal, 42,* 976–979.

Perrone, P. A., Male, R. A., & Karshner, W. W. (1979). Career development needs of talented students: A perspective for counselors. *The School Counselor, 27*(1), 16–23.

Perrone, K. M., Sedlacek, W. E., & Alexander, C. M. (2001). Gender and ethnic differences in career goal attainment. *The Career Development Quarterly, 50,* 168–178.

Perry, L. (1982). Special populations: The demands of diversity. In E. L. Herr & N. M. Pinson (Eds.), *Foundations for policy in guidance and counseling.* Washington, DC: American Personnel and Guidance Association.

Perry, W. G. (1968). *Forms of intellectual and ethical development in the college years: A scheme.* New York: Holt, Rinehart & Winston.

Perry, W. G. (1970). *Intellectual and ethical development in the college years.* New York: Holt, Rinehart & Winston.

Petersen, M. L. (1974, July). *Simulated instructional systems SIS utilizing simulated occupational units in a career education program.* Paper presented at the meeting of the Utah Vocational Association, Salt Lake City.

Peterson, G. W., Long, K. L., & Billops, A. (1999). The effect of three career interventions on educational choices of eighth grade students. *Professional School Counseling, 3*(1), 34–42.

Peterson, G. W., Lumsden, J. A., Sampson, J. P., Jr., Reardon, R. C., & Lenz, J. G. (2002). Using cognitive information processing in counseling with adults. In S. Niles (Ed.), *Adult career development* (3rd ed., pp. 98–117). Tulsa, OK: National Career Development Association.

Peterson, G. W., Sampson, J. P., & Reardon, R. C. (1991). *Career development and services: A cognitive approach.* Pacific Grove, CA: Brooks/Cole Publishing Company.

Peterson, G. W., Sampson, J. P., Reardon, R. C., & Lenz, J. G. (1996). A cognitive information processing approach. In D. Brown, L. Brooks, et al. (Eds.), *Career choice and development* (3rd ed., pp. 423–476). San Francisco: Jossey-Bass.

Peterson, G. W., Sampson, J. P., Reardon, R. C., & Lenz, J. G. (n.d.) *Career counseling and guidance interventions.* Tallahassee, FL: Florida State University.

Peterson, K. L. (1985). Work commitment of college females. *College Student Journal, 19*(2), 213–216.

Peterson, R. R. (1989). *Women, work, and divorce.* Albany: State University of New York Press.

Phelps, L. A., & Lutz, R. J. (1977). *Career exploration in preparation for the special needs learner.* Boston: Allyn and Bacon.

Phelps, R. E., & Constantine, M. G. (2001). Hitting the roof: The impact of the glass-ceiling effect on the career development of African Americans. In W. B. Walsh, R. P. Bingham, M. T. Brown, & C. M. Ward (Eds.), *Career counseling for African Americans* (pp. 161–176). Mahwah, NJ: Erlbaum.

Phifer, P. (1987). *College majors and careers: A resource guide for effective life planning.* Garrett Park, MD: Garrett Park Press.

Phillips, A. S., & Bedeian, A. G. (1989). PMS and the workplace. *Social Behavior and Personality, 17*(2), 165–174.

Phillips, J. S., Barrett, G. V., & Rush, M. C. (1978). Job structure and age satisfaction. *Aging and Work, 1*(2), 109–119.

Phillips, L., & Weiss, B. (1972). Career development for handicapped youth. *Elementary School Guidance and Counseling, 7*(2), 154–155.

Phillips, M. G. (1966). Learning materials and their implementation. *Review of Educational Research, 36*(3), 373–379.

Phillips, S. D., Cairo, P. C., Blustein, D. L., & Myers, R. A. (1988). Career development and vocational behavior, 1987: A review. *Journal of Vocational Behavior, 33*(3), 119–184.

Phillips, S. D., Friedlander, M. L., Kost, P. P., Specterman, R. V., & Robbins, E. S. (1988). Personal versus vocational focus in career counseling: A retrospective outcome study. *Journal of Counseling and Development, 67,* 287–292.

Phillips, S. D., Friedlander, M. L., Pazienza, N. J., & Kost, P. P. (1985). A factor analytic investigation of career decision-making styles. *Journal of Vocational Behavior, 26*(1), 106–115.

Phillips, S. D., & Imhoff, A. R. (1997). Women and career development: A decade of research. *Annual Review of Psychology, 48,* 31–59.

Phillips, S. D., Pazienza, N. J., & Walsh, D. J. (1984). Decision making styles and progress in occupational decision making. *Journal of Vocational Behavior, 25,* 96–105.

Phillips, S. D., & Strohmer, D. (1982). Decision-making style and vocational maturity. *Journal of Vocational Behavior, 20*(2), 215–222.

Phillips-Jones, L., Jones, G. B., & Drier, H. N. (1981). *Developing training competencies for career guidance personnel.* Falls Church, VA: National Vocational Guidance Association.

Phillips-Miller, D. L., Campbell, N. J., & Morrison, C. R. (2000). Work and family: Satisfaction, stress, and spousal support. *Journal of Employment Counseling, 37,* 16–31.

Pickering, J. W. (1986). A comparison of three methods of career planning for liberal arts majors. *The Career Development Quarterly, 35*(2), 102–112.

Pickering, J. W., & Vacc, N. A. (1984). Effectiveness of career development interventions for college students. *Vocational Guidance Quarterly, 32,* 149.

Pierce, K. (1993). Socialization of teenage girls through teen-magazine fiction: The making of a new woman or an old lady? *Sex Roles, 29,* 59–68.

Piero, J. M., Garcia-Montalvo, J., & Gracia, F. (2002). How do young people cope with a job flexibility?: Demographic and psychological antecedents of the resistance to accept a job with non-preferred flexibility features. *Applied Psychology: An International Review, 51*(1), 43–66.

Pierson, F. C. (1980). *The minimal level of unemployment and public policy.* Kalamazoo, MI: The W. E. Upjohn Institute for Employment and Research.

Pietrofesa, J. J., & Splete, H. (1975). *Career development: Theory and research.* New York: Grune & Stratton.

Pilot, M. (1980). Job outlook projections: Why do them? How are they made? How accurate are they? *Occupational Outlook Quarterly, 24,* 3–8.

Pincus, A. L., & Wiggins, J. S. (1992). An expanded perspective on interpersonal assessment. *Journal of Counseling and Development, 71,* 91–94.

Pinder, F. A., & Fitzgerald, P. (1984). The effectiveness of a computerized guidance system in promoting career decision-making. *Journal of Vocational Behavior, 24,* 123–131.

Pine, G. J. (1964–1965). Occupational and educational aspirations and delinquent behavior. *Vocational Guidance Quarterly, 13,* 107–111.

Pines, A., Aronson, E., & Kafry, D. (1981). *Burnout: From tedium to personal growth.* New York: The Free Press.

Pines, A., & Maslach, C. (1980). Combatting staff burnout in a day care center: A case study. *Child Care Quarterly, 9,* 5–16.

Pinkney, J. W. (1983). The Myers-Briggs Type Indicator as an alternative in career counseling. *Personnel and Guidance Journal, 62*(3), 173–177.

Pinkney, J. W. (1985). A card sort interpretive strategy for flat profiles in the Strong-Campbell Interest Inventory. *Vocational Guidance Quarterly, 33*(4), 331–339.

Pinkney, J. W. (1987). Problem solving by career assessment: Some issues clients need to consider. *Journal of Career Development, 14,* 45–51.

Pinkney, J. W., & Bozik, C. M. (1994). Career Development Inventory (CDI). In J. T. Kapes, M. M. Mastie, & E. A. Whitfield (Eds.), *A counselor's guide to career assessment instruments* (pp. 263–267). Alexandria, VA: National Career Development Association.

Pinkney, J. W., & Jacobs, D. (1985). New counselors and personal interest in the task of career counseling. *Journal of Counseling Psychology, 32*(3), 454–457.

Pinson, N. M. (1980). School counselors as interpreters for and of the community: New roles in career education.

In F. E. Burtnett (Ed.), *The school counselor's role in career education* (pp. 123–149). Falls Church, VA: APGA Press.

Piost, M. (1974). Effect of sex and career models on occupational preferences of adolescents. *Audiovisual Communication Review, 22,* 41–50.

Pirnot, K., & Dustin, R. (1986). A new look at value priorities for homemakers and career women. *Journal of Counseling and Development, 64,* 432–436.

Pittenger, D. J. (1993). The utility of the Myers-Briggs Type Indicator. *Review of Educational Research,* 63 (4), 467–488.

Pitz, G. F., & Harren, V. A. (1980). An analysis of career decision-making from the point of view of information-processing and decision theory. *Journal of Vocational Behavior, 6,* 95–99.

Plant, P. (1993). Computers in transitional center guidance in the European Community. *Journal of Career Development, 20*(1), 73–84.

Plant, P. (2000). Career development in Denmark. In B. Hiebert & L. Bezanson (Eds.), *Making waves: Career development and public policy* (pp. 129–148). Ottawa, Canada: Human Resources Development Canada/ Canadian Career Development Foundation.

Plata, M. (1975). Stability and change in the prestige rankings of occupations over 49 years. *Journal of Vocational Behavior, 6,* 95–99.

Plata, M. (1981). Occupational aspirations of normal and emotionally disturbed adolescents: A comparative study. *Vocational Guidance Quarterly, 30*(2), 130–138.

Pleck, J. H., Staines, G. L., & Lang, L. (1980). Conflicts between work and family life. *Monthly Labor Review, 10*(3), 29–31.

Polansky, J., Horan, J. J., & Hanish, C. (1993). Experimental construct validity of the outcomes of a study skills training and career counseling as treatments for retention of at-risk students. *Journal of Counseling and Development, 71,* 488–492.

Polkinghorne, D. E. (1984). Further extensions for methodological diversity for counseling psychology. *Journal of Counseling Psychology, 31,* 416–429.

Polkinghorne, D. E. (1990). Action theory approaches to career research. In R. A. Young & W. E. Borgen (Eds.), *Methodological approaches to the study of careers* (pp. 87–106). New York: Praeger.

Poloma, M. M., & Garland, T. N. (1971). The married professional woman: A study in the tolerance of domestication. *Journal of Marriage and the Family, 33*(3), 531–540.

Pond, S. B., III, & Geyer, P. D. (1987). Employee age as a moderator of the relation between perceived work alternatives and job satisfaction. *Journal of Applied Psychology, 72,* 552–557.

Popcorn, F., & Marigold, L. (1996). *Clicking: 16 trends to future fit your life, your work, and your business.* New York: Harper & Collins.

Pope, M. (1995). Gay and lesbian career development: Introduction to the special section. *The Career Development Quarterly, 44,* 146–147.

Pope, M. (2002). Review of the Kuder General Interest Survey Form E. In J. T. Kapes & E. A. Whitfield (Eds.), *A counselor's guide to career assessment instruments.* (4th ed. pp. 258–264). Tulsa, OK: National Career Development Association.

Pope, M. (2002). Counseling with individuals from the Lesbian and gay culture. In J. Trusty, J. Looby, & D. S. Sandhu (Eds.), *Multicultural counseling: Context, theory and practice, and competence* (pp. 203–218). New York: Nova.

Pope John Paul II. (1981, September #21), Laboreum exercens (on human work): Papal Encyclical. *The Catholic Register,* p. 7.

Porter, L. (1970). Adults have special counseling needs. *Adult Leadership, 19*(9), 275–277.

Portes, A., & Stepick, A. (1985). Unwelcome immigrants: Experiences of 1980 (Mariel) Cuban and Haitian refugees in South Florida. *American Sociological Review, 50,* 493–514.

Post-Kammer, P. (1987). Intrinsic and extrinsic work values and career maturity of 9th and 11th grade boys and girls. *Journal of Counseling and Development, 65*(8), 420–423.

Post-Kammer, P., & Perrone, P. (1983). Career perceptions of talented individuals: A follow-up study. *Vocational Guidance Quarterly, 31*(3), 203–211.

Post-Kammer, P., & Smith, P. L. (1985). Sex differences in career self-efficacy, consideration, and interest of eighth and ninth graders. *Journal of Counseling Psychology, 32*(4), 551–559.

Potter, B. A. (1980). *Beating job burnout.* San Francisco: Harbor Publishing.

Powell, G. N., & Mainero, L. A. (1992). Cross-currents in the river of time: Conceptualizing the complexities of women's careers. *Journal of Management, 18,* 215–237.

Powell, T. E. (1994), Occupational Stress Inventory (OSI). In J. T. Kapes, M. M. Mastie, & E. A. Whitfield (Eds.), *A counselor's guide to career assessment instruments* (pp. 288–293). Alexandria, VA: National Career Development Association.

Prager, K. J., & Freeman, A. (1979). Self-esteem, academic competence, educational aspiration and curriculum choice of urban community college students. *Journal of College Student Personnel, 20*(5), 392–397.

Pratzner, F. C., & Ashley, W. L. (1985). Occupational and adaptability and transferable skills: Preparing today's adults for tomorrow's careers. *Adults and the changing workplace.* Alexandria, VA: American Vocational Association.

Prause, J., & Dooley, D. (2001). Favorable employment status change and psychological depression: A two-year follow-up analyses of the national longitudinal survey of youth. *Applied Psychology: An International Review, 50*(2), 282–304.

Prediger, D. J. (1974). The role of assessment in career guidance: A reappraisal. *Impact, 3,* 3–4, 15–21.

Prediger, D. J. (1989). Ability differences across occupations: More than *g. Journal of Vocational Behavior, 34*(1), 1–27.

Prediger, D. (1993). *Multicultural assessment standards: A compilation for counselors.* Alexandria, VA: Association for Assessment in Counseling.

Prediger, D. J. (1994a). Multicultural assessment standards: A compilation for counselors. *Measurement and Evaluation in Counseling and Development, 27,* 68–73.

Prediger, D. J. (1994b). Tests and counseling: The marriage that prevailed. *Measurement and Evaluation in Counseling and Development, 26,* 227–234.

Prediger, D. J. (1996). Basic structure of work-relevant abilities. *Journal of Counseling Psychology, 46*(2), 173–184.

Prediger, D. J. (1998). Is interest profile level relevant to career counseling. *Journal of Counseling Psychology, 45*(2), 204–211.

Prediger, D. J. (1999). Basic structure of work-relevant abilities. *Journal of Counseling Psychology, 46*(2), 173–184.

Prediger, D. J., & Swaney, K. (1986). Role of counselee experiences in the interpretation of vocational interest scores. *Journal of Counseling and Development, 64,* 440–444.

Prediger, D. J., Swaney, K., & Wei-Cheng, M. (1993). Extending Holland's hexagon: Procedures, counseling applications, and research. *Journal of Counseling and Development, 71,* 422–428.

Prince, J. P. (1995). Influences on the career development of gay men. *The Career Development Quarterly, 44,* 168–177.

Pritchard, R. D. (1969). Equity theory: A review and critique. *Organizational Behavior and Human Performance, 4,* 176–211.

Pritchett, P. (1994). *The employee handbook of New York habits for a radically changing world: 13 ground rules for job success in the information age.* Dallas, TX: Pritchett & Associates, Inc.

Pryor, G. L., Hammond, B., & Hawkins, T. L. (1990). New tasks, new visions: Employment counseling in Australia. *Journal of Employment Counseling, 27,* 160–170.

Pryor, G. L., & Ward, R. T. (1985). Unemployment. What counselors can do about it. *Journal of Employment Counseling, 22*(1), 3–17.

Pyke, K. D. (1994). Women's employment as a gift or burden? Marital power across marriage, divorce, and remarriage. *Gender and Society, 8*(1), 73–91.

Pyle, K. R. (2000). A group approach to career decision making. In N. Peterson & R. C. Gonzalez (Eds.). *Career counseling models for diverse populations. Hands-on applications by practitioners* (pp. 121–136). Belmont, CA: Wadsworth/Brooks Cole.

Pyle, K. R. (2000). Career counseling in the information age. *Career Planning and Adult Development Journal, 16,* 7–29.

Quick, H. E., & Moen, P. (1998). Gender, employment and retirement quality: A life course approach to the differential experiences of men and women. *Journal of Occupational Health Psychology, 3.* 44–64.

Quinn, M. T., & Lewis, R. J. (1989). An attempt to measure a career-planning intervention in a traditional course. *Journal of College Student Development, 30,* 371–372.

Quinn, M. T., Lewis, R. J., & Fischer, K. L. (1992). A cross-correlation of the Myers-Briggs and Keirsey instruments. *Journal of College Student Development, 33,* 27–28.

Quinn, R. P., & Mandilovitch, M. S. B. (1980). Education and job satisfaction: 1962–1977. *Vocational Guidance Quarterly, 29*(2), 100–111.

Rabasca, L. (1999, May) Stress caused when jobs don't meet expectations. *APA Monitor, 30*(5), 28.

Rabinowitz, W., Falkenbach, K., Travers, J. R., Valentine, C. G., & Weener, P. (1983). Worker motivation: Unsolved problems or untapped resources? *California Management Review, 25*(2), 45–56.

Rachlin, H. (1989). *Judgment, decision, and choice: A cognitive/Behavioral synthesis.* New York: W. H. Freeman & Company.

Raelin, J. A. (1980). *Building a career. The effect of initial job experiences and related work attitudes on later employment.* Kalamazoo, MI: The W. E. Upjohn Institute for Employment Research.

Ragheb, M. B., & Griffith, C. A. (1982). The contribution of leisure participation and leisure satisfaction to life satisfaction of older persons. *Journal of Leisure Research, 14,* 295–306.

Rak, C. F., & O'Dell, F. L. (1994). Career treatment strategy model: A blend of career and traditional counseling approaches. *Journal of Career Development, 20*(3), 227–238.

Randahl, G. J., Hansen, J. I., & Haverkamp, B. E. (1993). Instrumental behaviors following test administration and interpretation: Exploration validity of the Strong Interest Inventory. *Journal of Counseling and Development, 71,* 435–439.

Rantze, K. R., & Feller, R. W. (1985). Counseling career-plateaued workers during times of social change. *Journal of Employment Counseling, 22*(1), 23–28.

Rapoport, R., & Rapoport, R. N. (1971). *Dual-career families.* Middlesex, England: Penguin Books.

Rapoport, R., & Rapoport, R. N. (1976). *Dual-career families re-examined.* London: Martin Robertson & Co.

Rappoport, C. (December 14, 1992). Europe looks ahead to hard choices. *Fortune, 126*(1), 144–151.

Rasmussen, K. G., Jr. (1984). Nonverbal behavior, verbal behavior, resume credentials, and selection interview outcomes. *Journal of Applied Psychology, 69*(4), 551–556.

Raths, L., Harmin, M., & Simon, S. (1966). *Values and teaching.* Columbus, OH: Charles E. Merrill.

Raup, J. L., & Myers, J. E. (1989). The empty-nest syndrome: Myth or reality? *Journal of Counseling and Development, 68,* 180–183.

Rawlins, M. E., Eberly, C. G., & Rawlins, L. D. (1991). Infusing counseling skills in test interpretation. *Counselor Education and Supervision, 31,* 109–120.

Rayman, J. R. (1999). Career services imperatives for the next millennium. *The Career Development Quarterly, 48*(2), 175–184.

Rayman, J. R., & Harris-Bowlsbey, J. A. (1977). DISCOVER: A model for a systematic career guidance program. *Vocational Guidance Quarterly, 26*(1), 4–12.

Raynor, J. O., & Entin, E. E. (1982). *Motivation, career striving, and aging.* New York: Hemisphere.

Reardon, R. C., Bonnell, R. O., & Huddleston, M. R. (1982). Self-directed career exploration. A comparison of choices and the self-directed search. *Journal of Vocational Behavior, 20,* 22–30.

Reardon, R. C., Lenz, J. G., Sampson, J. P., & Peterson, G. W. (2000). *Career development and planning: A comprehensive approach.* Belmont, CA: Brooks/Cole.

Reardon, R. C., & Loughead, T. (1988). A comparison of paper-and-pencil and computer versions of the Self-Directed Search. *Journal of Counseling and Development, 67,* 249–252.

Reardon, R. C., & Wright, L. K. (1999). The case of Mandy: Applying Holland's theory and cognitive information processing theory. *The Career Development Quarterly, 47,* 195–203.

Reardon, R. W. (1976). Help for the troubled worker in a small company. *Personnel, 53*(1), 50–54.

Reed, J. R., Patton, M. J., & Gold, P. B. (1993). Effects of turn-taking sequences in vocational test interpretation interviews. *Journal of Counseling Psychology, 40*(2), 144–155.

Reeves, D. J., & Booth, R. F. (1979). Expressed vs. inventoried interests as predictors of paramedical effectiveness. *Journal of Vocational Behavior, 15,* 155–163.

Reich, M. H. (1985). Executive views from both sides of mentoring. *Personnel, 62*(1), 42–46.

Reich, R. (1991). *The work of nations: Preparing ourselves for 21st century capitalism.* New York: Alfred Knopf.

Reitzes, D. C., Mutran, E. J., & Fernandez, M. E. (1998). The decision to retire: A career perspective. *Social Science Quarterly, 79,* 607–619.

Rentsch, J. R., & Steel, R. P. (1992). Construct and concurrent validation of the Andrews and Withey Job Satisfaction Questionnaire. *Educational and Psychological Measurement, 52,* 357–367.

Renwick, P. A., & Tosi, H. (1978). The effects of sex, marital status, and educational background on selection decisions. *Academy of Management Journal, 21,* 93–103.

Repetto, E. (1994). Programa de exokiracio¢n y pianificacio¢n de la carrera (EPCE). Madrid: Ca¢tedra de orientacio¢n Educativa. UNED.

Repetto, E. (2001). Following Super's heritage: Evaluation of a career development program in Spain. International Journal for Educational and Vocational Guidance 1: 107–120.

Research and Policy Committee, the Committee for Economic Development. (1985). *Investing in our children, business and public schools.* New York: The Committee.

Research Utilization Branch. (1986, September). *Youth in trouble: A vocational approach.* Research brief. Washington, DC: Division of Research Demonstration Grants, Social and Rehabilitation Services, Department of Health, Education, and Welfare.

Reubens, B. G. (1974). Vocational education. Performance and potential. *Manpower, 6*(7), 23–30.

Rexroat, C. (1992). Changes in the employment continuity of succeeding cohorts of young women. *Work and Occupations, 19*(1), 18–34.

Rhodes, S. R. (1983). Age-related differences in work attitudes and behavior: A review and conceptual analysis. *Psychological Bulletin, 93*(2), 328–367.

Rhodes, S. R., & Doering, M. M. (1993). Intention to change careers: Determinants and process. *Career Development Quarterly, 42,* 76–92.

Rice, J. K. (1981). Career education comes of age. *Journal of Career Education, 7*(3), 212–219.

Rice, R. W., Near, J. P., & Hunt, R. G. (1980). The job satisfaction/life satisfaction relationship: A review of empirical research. *Basic and applied social psychology, 1,* 37–64.

Rich, N. S. (1979). Occupational knowledge: To what extent is rural youth handicapped? *Vocational Guidance Quarterly, 27*(4), 320–325.

Richard, G. V., & Krieshok, T. S. (1989). Occupational stress, strain, and coping in a university faculty. *Journal of Vocational Behavior, 34*(1), 117–132.

Richardson, Bellows, Henry & Co., Inc. (1981). *Supervisory Profile Record.* Washington, DC: Author.

Richardson, M. S. (1993). Work in people's lives: A location for counseling psychologists. *Journal of Counseling Psychology, 40*(4), 425–433.

Richardson, V., & Kilty, K. M. (1989). Retirement financial planning among black professionals. *The Gerontologist, 29,* 32–37.

Richman, D. R. (1993). Cognitive career counseling: A rationale-emotive approach to career development. *Journal of Rational-Emotive and Cognitive-Behavior Therapy, 11*(2), 91–108.

Riddick, C. C. (1985). Life satisfaction for older female homemakers, retirees, and workers. *Research on Aging, 7,* 383–393.

Ridener, J. (1973). Careers of the month program. *Elementary School Guidance and Counseling, 7*(3), 235–236.

Ridley, C. R., Mendoza, D. W., & Kanitz, B. E. (1994). Multicultural training: Reexamination, operationalization, and integration. *The Counseling Psychologist, 22*(2), 227–289.

Ridley, C. R., Mendoza, D. W., Kanitz, B. E., Angermeier, L., & Zenk, R. (1994). Cultural sensitivity in multicultural counseling: A perceptual schema model. *Journal of Counseling Psychology, 41*(2), 125–136.

Riegle, D. W., Jr. (1982). Psychological and social effects of unemployment. *American Psychologist, 37*(1), 113–115.

Rife, J. C., & Belcher, J. R. (1993). Social support and job search intensity among older unemployed workers: Implications for employment counselors. *Journal of Employment Counseling, 30,* 98–107.

Rife, J. C., & Belcher, J. R. (1994). Assisting unemployed older workers to become reemployed: An experimental evaluation. *Research on Social Work Practice, 4*(1), 3–13.

Rifkin, J. (1995). *The end of work. The decline of the global labor force and the dawn of the post-market era.* New York: Tarcher/Putnam.

Rifkin, J. (2000). *The age of access: The new culture of hypercapitalism where all of life is a paid-for experience.* New York: Putnam.

Riley, P. J. (1981). The influence of gender on occupational aspirations of kindergarten children. *Journal of Vocational Behavior, 19,* 244–250.

Rimmer, S. M., & Myers, J. W. (1982). Testing and older persons: A new challenge for counselors. *Measurement and Evaluation in Guidance, 15*(3), 182–193.

Ringle, P. M., & Savickas, M. L. (1983). Administrative leadership. Planning and time perspective. *Journal of Higher Education, 54*(6), 649–661.

Ritook, M. (1993). Career development in Hungary at the beginning of the 90s. *Journal of Career Development, 20,* 33–40.

Robbins, S. B., Chartrand, J. M., McFadden, K. L., & Lee, R. M. (1994). Efficacy of leader-led and self-directed career workshops for middle-aged and older adults. *Journal of Counseling Psychology, 41*(1), 83–90.

Robbins, S. B., Lee, R. M., & Wan, T. T. H. (1994). Goal continuity as a mediator of early retirement adjustment: Testing a multidimensional model. Journal of Counseling Psychology, 41 (1), 18–26.

Robbins, S. B., & Tucker, K. R., Jr. (1986). Relation of goal instability to self-directed and interactional career counseling workshops. *Journal of Counseling Psychology, 33*(4), 418–424.

Roberts, K. (1968). The entry into employment: An approach toward a general theory. *Sociological Review, 16,* 165–184.

Roberts, K. (1977). *From school to work, a study of the youth employment service.* Newton Abbott, England: David & Charles.

Roberts, M. (2000). Open for business. *Techniques, 75,* 18–21.

Robinson, F. P. (1963). Modern approaches to counseling diagnosis. *Journal of Counseling Psychology, 10,* 325–333.

Robinson, G., Awana, P., Kehle, T. J., & Jenson, W. R. (1986). But what about smart girls? Adolescent self-esteem and sex role perceptions as a function of academic achievement. *Journal of Educational Psychology, 78*(3), 179–183.

Robinson, J. W., & Kaplan, B. J. (1985). Counseling psychology and psychophysiology: The neglected interface. *Canadian Counsellor, 19*(2), 82–97.

Robinson, N. K., Meyer, D., Prince, J. P., McLean, C., & Low, R. (2000). Mining the internet for career information: A model approach for college students. *Journal of Career Assessment, 8*(1), 37–54.

Roche, G. R. (1979). Much ado about mentors. *Harvard Business Review, 57*(1), 14–28.

Rochelle, C. C., & Spellman, C. (1987). *Dreams betrayed: Working in the technological age.* Lexington, MA: Heath.

Rockwell, T. (1987). The social construction of careers: Career development and career counseling viewed from a sociometric perspective. *Journal of Group Psychotherapy, Psychodrama and Sociometry,* Fall (1), 93–107.

Rodriguez, M., & Blocher, D. (1988). A comparison of two approaches to enhancing career maturity in Puerto Rican college women. *Journal of Counseling Psychology, 35,* 275–280.

Rodriguez, M. A. (1999). Preparing an effective occupational information brochure for ethnic minorities. *The Career Development Quarterly,* 178–184.

Roe, A. (1953). A psychological study of eminent psychologists and anthropologists and a comparison with biological and physical scientists. *Psychological Monographs, 67*(2), 1–55.

Roe, A. (1954). A new classification of occupations. *Journal of Counseling Psychology, 1,* 215–220.

Roe, A. (1956). *The psychology of occupations.* New York: Wiley.

Roe, A., & Lunneborg, P. W. (1984). Personality development and career choice. In D. Brown & L. Brooks (Eds.), *Career choice and development, applying contemporary theories to practice* (Chap. 3). San Francisco: Jossey-Bass.

Roe, A., & Lunneborg, P. W. (1990). Personality development and career choice. In D. Brown & L. Brooks (Eds.), *Career choice and development. Applying contemporary theories to practice* (pp. 68–101). San Francisco: Jossey-Bass.

Roe, A., & Siegelman, M. (1964). *The origin of interests.* Washington, DC: American Personnel and Guidance Association.

Roessler, R. T. (1987). Work, disability, and the future: Promoting employment for people with disabilities. *Journal of Counseling and Development, 66,* 188–190.

Rogers, C. R. (1942). *Counseling and psychotherapy.* Boston: Houghton Mifflin.

Rojewski, J. W. (1994). Career indecision types for rural adolescents from disadvantaged and nondisadvantaged backgrounds. *Journal of Counseling Psychology, 41*(3), 356–363.

Roland, R. L. (1973). *Introduction to industrial mental health and employee counseling.* New York: Behavioral Publications.

Romero, G. J., & Garza, R. T. (1986). Attributions for the occupational success/failure of ethnic minority and nonminority women. *Sex Roles, 14*(7/8), 445–452.

Ronen, S. (1979). A cross-national study of employees' work goals. *International Review of Applied Psychology, 28,* 1–12.

Rooney, R. A., & Osipow, S. H. (1992). Task specific occupational self-efficacy: The development and validation of a prototype scale. *Journal of Vocational Behavior, 40,* 14–32.

Rose, H. A., & Elton, C. F. (1973). Sex and occupational choice. *Journal of Counseling Psychology, 18*(5), 456–461.

Rose, H. A., & Elton, C. F. (1982). The relation of congruence, differentiation and consistency to interest and aptitude scores in women with stable and unstable vocational choices. *Journal of Vocational Behavior, 20*(2), 162–174.

Rose, R., Hurst, M., & Herd, A. (1979). Cardiovascular and endocrine responses to work and the risk of psychiatric symptoms in air traffic controllers. In J. Barrett (Ed.). *Stress and mental disorder.* New York: Raven Press.

Roselle, B. E., & Hummel, T. J. (1988). Intellectual development and interaction effectiveness with DISCOVER. *The Career Development Quarterly, 36,* 241–249.

Rosen, H., & Kuehlwein, K. T. (Eds.). (1996). *Constructing realities, meaning-making perspectives for psychotherapists.* San Francisco, CA: Jossey-Bass.

Rosen, S., Cochran, W., & Musser, L. M. (1990). Reactions to a match versus mismatch between an applicant's self-presentational style and work reputation. *Basic and Applied Social Psychology, 11,* 117–129.

Rosenbaum, J. E. (1979). Tournament mobility: Career patterns in a corporation. *Administrative Science Quarterly, 24,* 220–241.

Rosenberg, A. G., & Smith, S. S. (1985). Six strategies for career counseling. *Journal of College Placement, 45*(3), 42–46.

Rosengarten, W. (1936). *Choosing your life work* (3rd ed.). New York: McGraw-Hill.

Rosenthal, D. A., & Chapman, D. C. (1980). Sex-role stereotypes: Children's perceptions of occupational competence. *Psychological Reports, 44,* 135–139.

Rosenthal, D., & Chapman, D. (1982). The lady spaceman: Children's perceptions of sex-stereotyped occupations. *Sex Roles, 8,* 959–965.

Rosove, B. (1982). Employability assessment: Its importance and one method of doing it. *Journal of Employment Counseling, 19*(3), 113–123.

Rotberg, H. L., Brown, D., & Ware, W. B. (1987). Career self-efficacy expectations and perceived range of career options in community college students. *Journal of Counseling Psychology, 34*(2), 164–170.

Roth, P. L., & Campion, J. E. (1992). An analysis of the predictive power of the panel interview and pre-employment tests. *Journal of Occupational and Organizational Psychology, 65,* 51–60.

Rothstein, D. (2001). Youth employment in the United States. *Monthly Labor Review, 124*(8), 6–17.

Rothstein, D. S. (2001). Youth employment during school: Results from two longitudinal surveys. *Monthly Labor Review, 124*(8), 25–37.

Rothstein, H. R., Schmidt, F. L., Erwin, F. W., Owens, W. A., & Sparks, C. P. (1990). Biographical data in employment selection: Can validities be made generalizable? *Journal of Applied Psychology, 75,* 175–184.

Rounds, J. B., Jr. (1990). The comparative and combined utility of work value and interest data in career counseling with adults. *Journal of Vocational Behavior, 37,* 32–45.

Rounds, J. B., Jr. (1994). The Adult Career Concerns Inventory (ACCI). In J. T. Kapes, M. M. Mastie, & E. A. Whitfield (Eds.), *A counselor's guide to career assessment instruments* (pp. 242–247). Alexandria, VA: National Career Development Association.

Rounds, J. B., Jr., Davison, M. L., & Davis, R. V. (1979). The fit between Strong-Campbell Interest Inventory general occupational themes and Holland's hexagonal model. *Journal of Vocational Behavior, 15,* 303–315.

Rounds, J. B., Jr., Dawis, R. V., & Lofquist, L. H. (1987). Measurement of person-environment fit and prediction of satisfaction in the theory of work adjustment. *Journal of Vocational Behavior, 31,* 297–318.

Rounds, J. B., Jr., Henly, G. A., Dawis, R. V., & Lofquist, L. H. (1981). *Manual for the Minnesota Importance Questionnaire: A measure of needs and values.* Minneapolis: Vocational Psychology Research, University of Minnesota.

Rounds, J., & McKenna, M. C. (2002). Review of the Student Styles Questionnaire. In J. T. Kapes & E.. Whitfield (Eds.). *A counselor's guide to career assessment instruments.* (4th ed., pp. 378–383). Tulsa, OK: National Career Development Association.

Rounds, J. B., Jr., Shubsachs, A. P. W., Dawis, R. V., & Lofquist, L. H. (1978). A test of Holland's formulations. *Journal of Applied Psychology, 63*(5), 609–616.

Rounds, J. B., Jr., & Tinsley, H. E. A. (1984). Diagnosis and treatment of vocational problems. In S. Brown & R. Lent (Eds.), *Handbook of Counseling Psychology* (pp. 137–177). New York: Wiley.

Rounds, J. B., Jr., & Tracey, T. J. (1990). From trait-and-factor to person-environment fit counseling: Theory and process. In W. B. Walsh & S. H. Osipow (Eds.), *Career counseling: Contemporary topics in vocational psychology* (pp. 1–44). Hillsdale, NJ: Lawrence Elbaum Associations.

Rubinton, N. (1980). Instruction in career decision-making and decision-making styles. *Journal of Counseling Psychology, 27,* 581–588.

Rubinton, N. (1985). Career exploration for middle school youth. A university-school cooperative. *The Vocational Guidance Quarterly, 33*(3), 249–255.

Russo, N. F. (1990). Forging research priorities for women's mental health. *American Psychologist, 45,* 368–373.

Ryan, C. W., & Drummond, R. J. (1981). University based career education: A model for infusion. *Personnel and Guidance Journal, 60,* 89–92.

Ryan, N. F. (1985). The mentor's place in an adult's life cycle. In D. Jones & S. S. Moore (Eds.), *Counseling adults: Life cycle perspectives.* Lawrence: University of Kansas.

Ryan, T. (1974). A systems approach to career education. *Vocational Guidance Quarterly, 22,* 172.

Ryland, E. K., & Rosen, B. (1987). Personnel professionals' reactions to chronological and functional resume formats. *The Career Development Quarterly, 35,* 228–238.

Rynes, S., & Gerhart, B. (1990). Interviewer assessments of applicant "fit": An exploratory investigation. *Personnel Psychology, 43,* 13–35.

Ryscavage, P. M. (1979). BLS labor force projections: A review of methods and results. *Monthly Labor Review, 103,* 12–19.

Salazar-Clemena, R. (2002). Family ties and peso signs: Challenges for career counseling in the Philippines. *The Career Development Quarterly, 50,* 246–256.

Salomone, P. R. (1982). Difficult cases in career counseling: II. The indecisive client. *Personnel and Guidance Journal, 60,* 496–500.

Salomone, P. R. (1988). Career counseling: Steps and stages beyond Parsons. *The Career Development Quarterly, 36,* 218–221.

Salomone, P. R. (1989). Are "occupational" and "career" information synonymous *The Career Development Quarterly, 38,* 3–5.

Salomone, P. R., & Daughton, S. (1984). Assessing work environments for career counseling. *Vocational Guidance Quarterly, 33*(1), 45–54.

Salomone, P. R., & Sheehan, M. C. (1985). Vocational stability and congruence: An examination of Holland's proposition. *Vocational Guidance Quarterly, 34*(2), 91–98.

Salomone, P. R., & Slaney, R. B. (1978). The applicability of Holland's theory to nonprofessional workers. *Journal of Vocational Behavior, 13,* 63.

Salomone, P. R., & Slaney, R. B. (1981). The influence of chance and contingency factors on the vocational choice process of nonprofessional workers. *Journal of Vocational Behavior, 19,* 25–35.

Samby, G., & Healy, C. (1979). Developing a replicable career decision-making counseling procedure. *Journal of Counseling Psychology, 26,* 210–216.

Sampson, J. P. (1980). Using college alumni as resource persons for providing occupational information. *Journal of College Student Personnel, 21,* 172.

Sampson, J. P. (1984). Maximizing the effectiveness of computer applications in counseling and human development: The role of research and implementation strategies. *Journal of Counseling and Development, 63*(3), 187–191.

Sampson, J. P., Jr. (1996). *Effective computer assisted career guidance.* (Occasional paper #2) (2nd ed). Tallahassee: Florida State University, Center for the Study of Technology in Counseling and Career Development.

Sampson, J. P., Jr. (1998). Potential problems and ethical concerns. In J. Harris-Bowlsbey, M. R. Dikel, & J. P. Sampson, Jr. (Eds.), *The internet: A tool for career counseling* (chap. 3, pp. 31–38). Columbus, OH: National Career Development Association.

Sampson, J. P., Jr. (1999). Integrating internet-based distance guidance with services provided in career centers. *The Career Development Quarterly, 47,* 243–254.

Sampson, J. P., Jr. (2000). Using the internet to enhance testing in counseling. *Journal of Counseling and Development, 78,* 348–356.

Sampson, J. P., & Kolodinsky, R. W., & Greeno, B. P. (1997). Counseling on the information highway: Future possibilities and potential problems. *Journal of Counseling and Development, 75*(3), 203–212.

Sampson, J. P., Jr., Lenz, J. G., Reardon, R. C., & Peterson, G. W. (1999). A cognitive information processing approach to employment problem solving and decision making. *The Career Development Quarterly, 48,* 3–19.

Sampson, J. P., & Loesch, L. C. (1981). Relationship among work values and job knowledge. *Vocational Guidance Quarterly, 29*(3), 229–235.

Sampson, J. P., Peterson, G. W., Lenz, J. G., & Reardon, R. C. (1992a). A cognitive approach to career services: Translating concepts into practice. *The Career Development Quarterly, 41,* 67–74.

Sampson, J. P., Peterson, G. W., Lenz, J. G., Reardon, R. C., & Saunders, D. E. (1996). *The career thoughts inventory* (CTI). Odessa, FL: Psychological Assessment Resources, Inc.

Sampson, J. P., Jr., Peterson, G. W., Lenz, J. G., Reardon, R. C., & Saunders, D. E. (1996). Negative thinking and career choice: In R. Feller & G. Walz (Eds.), *Career transitions in turbulent times* (pp. 323–330). Greensboro, NC: ERIC Counseling and Student Services Clearinghouse.

Sampson, J. P., Peterson, G. W., & Reardon, R. C. (1989). Counselor intervention strategies for computer-assisted career guidance: An information-processing approach. *Journal of Career Development, 16,* 139–154.

Sampson, J. P., Peterson, G. W., Reardon, R. C., Lenz, J. G. (2000). Using readiness assessment ot improve career services: A cognitive information-processing approach. *The Career Development Quarterly, 49,* 146–174.

Sampson, J. P., Peterson, G. W., Reardon, R. C., Lenz, J., Shahnasarian, M., & Ryan-Jones, R. E. (1992b). The social influence for two computer-assisted career guidance systems: DISCOVER and SIGI. *Career Development Quarterly, 41,* 75–84.

Sampson, J. P., & Reardon, R. C. (Eds.). (1990). *Enhancing the design and use of computer-assisted career guidance systems.* Washington, DC: NCDA.

Sampson, J. P., Shahnasarian, M., & Reardon, R. C. (1987). Computer-assisted career guidance: A national perspective on the use of DISCOVER and SIGI. *Journal of Counseling and Development, 65,* 416–419.

Sampson, J. P., Reardon, R. C., Wilde, C. K., Norris, D. S., Peterson, G. W., Strausberger, S. J., Garis, J. W., Lenz, J. G., & Saunders, D. E. (1993). *A differential feature-cost analysis of fifteen computer-assisted career guidance systems* (4th ed.). Technical Report Number 10. Tallahassee, FL: Center for Study of Technology in Counseling and Career Development.

Sander, D., Westerberg, W., & Hedstrom, J. E. (1978). Career education through children's literature. *Elementary School Guidance and Counseling, 13*(2), 129–132.

Sanna, L. J., & Pusecker, P. A. (1994). Self-efficacy, valence of self-evaluation, and performance. *Personality and Social Psychology Bulletin, 20*(1), 82–92.

Sarason, S. B., Sarason, E., & Cowden, P. (1975). Aging and the nature of work. *American Psychologist, 30,* 584–592.

Sauter, S. L. (1992). Introduction to the NIOSH Proposed National Strategy. In *Work and well-being: An agenda for the 1990s* (pp. 11–16). Washington, D.C.: American Psychological Association.

Sauter, S. L., Murphy, L. R., & Hurrell, J. J., Jr. (1992). Prevention of work-related psychological disorders: A national strategy proposed by the National Institute for occupational safety and health. In *Work and Well-Being: An Agenda for the 1990s* (pp. 17–40). Washington, DC: American Psychological Association.

Savickas, M. L. (1989). Annual review. Practice and research in career counseling and development, 1988. *The Career Development Quarterly, 38,* 100–134.

Savickas, M. L. (1989). Career-style assessment and counseling. In T. Sweeney (Ed.), *Adlerian counseling: A practical approach for a new decade* (3rd ed.), (pp. 289–320). Muncie, IN: Accelerated Development.

Savickas, M. L. (1990a). The career decision-making course: Description and field test. *The Career Development Quarterly, 38,* 275–284.

Savickas, M. L. (1990b January). *Career interventions that create hope.* Paper presented at the National Conference of the National Career Development Association, Scottsdale, AZ.

Savickas, M. L. (1991). The meaning of work and love. *The Career Development Quarterly, 39*(41), 315–324.

Savickas, M. L. (1993). Predictive validity criteria for career development measures. *Journal of Career Assessment, 1*(1), 93–104.

Savickas, M. L. (1994). Convergence prompts theory renovation, research unification, and practice coherence. In M. Savickas & R. Lent (Ed.), *Convergence in career development theories. Implications for science and practice* (pp. 235–257). Palo Alto: CA: CPP Books.

Savickas, M. L. (1997). Career adaptability: An integrative concept for life-span, life-space theory. *The Career Development Quarterly, 45,* 247–259.

Savickas, M. L. (1998). Interpreting interest inventories: A case example. *The Career Development Quarterly, 46,* 307–310.

Savickas, M. (2000). Career development and public policy: The role of values, theory, and research. In B. Hiebert & L. Bezanson (Eds.), *In making waves: Career development and public policy* (pp. 52–68). Ottawa, Canada: Human Resources Development Canada/Canadian Career Development Foundation.

Savickas, M. L. (2001). A developmental perspective on vocational behavior: Career patterns, salience, and themes. *International Journal for Educational Guidance* 1: 49–57.

Savickas, M. L., & Lent, R. W. (Eds) (1994). *Convergence in career development, Implications for science and practice.* Palo Alto, CA: CPP Books.

Savickas, M. L., Passen, A. J., & Jarjoura, D. G. (1988). Career concern and coping as indicators of adult career development. *Journal of Vocational Behavior, 33,* 82–98.

Savickas, M. L., Stilling, S. M., & Schwartz, S. (1984). Time perspective in vocational maturity and career decision making. *Journal of Vocational Behavior, 25,* 258–269.

Savickas, M. L., & Walsh, W. B. (1996). *Handbook of career counseling theory and practice* (pp.13–36). Palo Alto, CA: Davies-Black Publishing.

Savicki, V., & Cooley, E. (1987). The relationship of work environment and client contact to burnout in mental health professionals. *Journal of Counseling and Development, 65,* 249–252.

Scanlan, T. J. (1980). Toward an occupational classification for self-employed men: An investigation of entrepreneurship from the perspective of Holland's theory of career development. *Journal of Vocational Behavior, 16,* 163–172.

Scarr, S., Phillips, D., & McCartney, K. (1989). Working mothers and their families. *American Psychologist, 44,* 1402–1409.

Schaef, A. W., & Fassel, D. (1988). *The addictive organization.* San Francisco: Harper & Row.

Schaffer, K. (1976). Evaluating job satisfaction and success for emotionally maladjusted men. *Journal of Vocational Behavior, 9,* 329–335.

Schein, E. G. (1999). *The corporate culture survival guide. Sense and nonsense about culture change.* San Francisco, CA: Jossey-Bass Publishers.

Schein, E. H. (1968). Organizational socialization and the process of management. *Industrial Management Review, 9,* 1–16.

Schein, E. H. (1971). The individual, the organization, and the career: A conceptual scheme. *Journal of Applied Behavioral Science, 7*(4), 415–416, 421–424.

Schein, E. H. (1978). *Career dynamics: Matching individual and organizational needs.* Reading, MA: Addison-Wesley.

Scheye, P. A., & Gilroy, F. D. (1994). College women's career self-efficacy and educational environments. *Career Development Quarterly, 42*(3), 244–256.

Schill, W. J., McCarten, R., & Meyer, K. (1985). Youth employment: Its relationship to academic and family variables. *Journal of Vocational Behavior, 26*(2), 155–163.

Schlichter, K. J., & Horan, J. J. (1981). Effects of stress inoculation on the anger and aggression management skills of institutionalized juvenile delinquents. *Cognitive Therapy and Research, 5*(4), 359–365.

Schliebner, C. T., & Peregoy, J. J. (1994). Unemployment effects on the family and the child: Interventions for counselors. *Journal of Counseling and Development, 72*(4), 368–372.

Schlossberg, N. K. (1978). Five propositions about adult development. *Journal of College Student Personnel, 19*(5), 418–423.

Schlossberg, N. K. (1981). A model for analyzing human adaptation to transition. *The Counseling Psychologist, 9*(2), 2–18.

Schlossberg, N. K. (1984). *Counseling adults in transition, linking practice with theory.* New York: Springer.

Schlossberg, N. K. (1986). Adult career development theories: Ways to illuminate the adult experience. In Z. Leibowitz & H. D. Lea (Eds.), *Adult career development, concepts, issues and practices* (Chap. 1). Alexandria, VA: National Career Development Association.

Schlossberg, N. K., & Leibowitz, Z. (1980). Organizational support systems as buffers to job loss. *Journal of Vocational Behavior, 17,* 204–217.

Schlosstein, S. (1989). *The end of the American century.* New York: Congdon & Weed, Inc.

Schmidt, F. L., & Hunter, J. E. (1981). Employment testing: Old theories and new research findings. *American Psychologist, 36,* 1128–1137.

Schmidt, F. L., Law, K., Hunter, J. E., Rothstein, H. R., Pearlman, K., & McDaniel, M. (1993). Refinements in validity generalization methods: Implications for the situational specificity hypothesis. *Journal of Applied Psychology, 78* (1), 3–12.

Schmidt, J. A. (1976). Self-concepts and career exploration. *Elementary School Guidance and Counseling, 11*(2), 145–153.

Schmit, M. J., Amel, E. L., & Ryan, A. M. (1993). Self-reported assertive job-seeking behaviors of minimally educated job hunters. *Personnel Psychology, 46,* 105–124.

Schmit, M. J., & Ryan, A. M. (1992). Test-taking dispositions: A missing link? *Journal of Applied Psychology, 77*(5), 629–637.

Schmitt, N., Gooding, R. Z., Noe, R. A., & Kirsch, M. (1984). Metanalysis of validity studies published between 1964 and 1982 and the investigation of study characteristics. *Personnel Psychology, 37,* 407–422.

Schmitt, N., & Mellon, P. M. (1980). Life and job satisfaction: Is the job central? *Journal of Vocational Behavior, 16,* 51–58.

Schmitt-Rodermund, E., Vondracek, F. W. (1999). Breadth of interests, exploration, and identity development in adolescence. *Journal of Vocational Behavior, 55,* 298–317.

Schneider, B. (1996). Whether guest personality at work? *Applied Psychology: An International Review, 45*(3), 289–296.

Schoen, R., & Cohen, L. E. (1980). Ethnic endogamy among Mexican-American grooms: A reanalysis of generational and occupational effects. *American Journal of Sociology, 86*(2), 359–366.

Schoenrade, P. (2002). Review of the Values Scale. In J. T. Kapes & E. A. Whitfield (Eds.), *A counselor's guide to career assessment instruments* (4th ed., pp. 299–302). Tulsa, OK: Naitonal Career Development Association.

Schontz, F. C. (1975). *The psychological aspects of physical illness and disability.* New York: Macmillan.

Schore, L. (1984). The Freemont experience: A counseling program for dislocated workers. *International Journal of Mental Health, 13,* 154–168.

Schrank, F. A. (1982). A faculty/counselor implemented career planning course. *Journal of College Student Personnel, 23,* 83–84.

Schroer, A. C. P., & Dorn, F. J. (1986). Enhancing the career and personal development of gifted college students. *Journal of Counseling and Development, 64,* 567–571.

Schulenberg, J. E. (1986). *The factor structure of work values and career interests: Continuity and discontinuity during adolescence.* Unpublished doctoral dissertation. Pennsylvania State University.

Schulenberg, J. E., Vondracek, F. W., & Crouter, A. C. (1984). The influence of the family on vocational development. *Journal of Marriage and the Family, 46,* 129–143.

Schultheiss, D. P. (2000). Emotional-social issues in the provision of career counseling. In D. A. Luzzo (Ed.). *Career counseling of college students. An empirical guide to strategies that work* (pp. 43–62). Washington, D. C: American Psychological Association.

Schultz, K. S., Morton, K. R., & Weckerle, J. R. (1998). The influence of push and pull factors on voluntary and involuntary early retirees' retirement decision and adjustment. *Journal of Vocational Behavior, 53,* 45–57.

Schumacher, E. F. (1981). Good work. In J. O'Toole, J. L. Scheiber & L. C. Wood (Eds.), *Working, changes, and choices* (pp. 25–32). New York: Human Sciences Press.

Schwab, R. L. (1981). The relationship of role conflict, role ambiguity, teacher background variables and perceived burnout among teachers (Doctoral dissertation. University of Connecticut, 1980). *Dissertation Abstracts International, 41*(9), 3823-A.

Schwalbe, M. L. (1988). Sources of self-esteem in work. What's important for whom? *Work and Occupations, 15*(1), 24–35.

Schwartz, F. N. (1989). Management women and the new facts of life. *Harvard Business Review,* Jan/Feb, 65–76.

Schwartz, R. H., Andiappan, P., & Nelson, M. (1986). Reconsidering the support for Holland's congruence-achievement hypothesis. *Journal of Counseling Psychology, 33*(4), 425–428.

Schwarzwald, J., & Shoham, M. (1981). A trilevel approach to motivation for retraining. *Journal of Vocational Behavior, 18,* 265–276.

Scott, J., & Hatalla, J. (1990). The influence of chance and contingency factors on career patterns of college-educated women. *The Career Development Quarterly, 39,* 18–30.

Search Institute. (1988). The risky business of growing up female. *Source, 4*(1), 1–4.

Sears, S. (1982). A definition of career guidance terms: A national vocational guidance association perspective. *Vocational Guidance Quarterly, 31*(2), 137–143.

Sears, S. J. (1993). The changing scope and practice of the secondary school counselor. *The School Counselor, 40,* 384–388.

Seccombe, K., & Lee, G. R. (1986). Gender differences in retirement satisfaction and its antecedents. *Research on Aging, 8,* 426–440.

Sedlacek, W. E., & Adams-Gaston, J. (1992). Predicting the academic success of student-athletes using SAT and noncognitive variables. *Journal of Counseling and Development, 70,* 724–727.

Segall, M. H., Dasen, V. R., Berry, J. W., & Poortinga, V. H. (1990). *Human behavior in global perspective: An introduction to cross-cultural psychology.* New York: Pergamon Press.

Seidman, S. A., & Sager, J. (1987). The teacher burnout scale. *Educational Research Quarterly, 11,* 26–33.

Seifert, K. H. (1994). Improving prediction of career adjustment with measures of career development. *Career Development Quarterly, 42,* 353–366.

Sekaran, U. (1982). In investigation of career salience for men and women in dual-career families. *Journal of Vocational Behavior,* 20, 111–119.

Sekaran, U. (1986a). *Dual-career families: Contemporary organizational and counseling issues.* San Francisco: Jossey-Bass.

Sekaran, U. (1986b). Self-esteem and sense of competence as moderators of the job satisfaction of professionals in dual-career families. *Journal of Occupational Behavior, 7,* 341–344.

Seligman, A. (1992). The state of corporate health care. *Personnel Management, 3,* 24–31.

Seligman, L., Weinstock, L., & Owings, N. (1988, February). The role of family dynamics in career development of 5-year-olds. *Elementary School Guidance and Counseling,* 222–230.

Seligman, L. L., Weinstock, L., & Owings, N. (1991). The career development of 10-year-olds. *Elementary School Guidance & Counseling, 25*(3), 172–181.

Selye, H. (1975). *Stress without distress.* New York: Signet.

Selye, H. (1976). *The stress of life.* New York: McGraw-Hill.

Selz, N., Jones, J. S., & Ashley, W. L. (1980). *Functional competencies for adapting to the world of work.* Columbus, OH: National Center for Research in Vocational Education, Ohio State University.

Senzaki, T. (1993). Career education in Japan: Its current status and condition. *Career Development Quarterly, 41,* 291–296.

Sepich, R. T. (1987). A review of the correlates and measurements of career indecision. *Journal of Career Development, 1*(1), 8–17.

Sexton, T. L. (2001). Evidence-based counseling intervention program: Practicing best practices. In D. C. Locke, J. E. Myers, & E. L. Herr (Eds.), *Handbook of counseling* (pp. 499–512). Thousand Oaks, CA: Sage.

Sexton, T. L., Whiston, J. C., Bleur, J. C., & Walz, G. R. (1997). *Integrating outcome research into counseling practice and training.* Alexandria, VA: American Counseling Association.

Shamir, B. (1986a). Self-esteem and the psychological impact of unemployment. *Social Psychology Quarterly, 49*(1), 61–72.

Shamir, B. (1986b). Protestant work ethic, work involvement, and the psychological impact of unemployment. *Journal of Occupational Behavior, 7,* 25–38.

Sharf, R. S. (1978). Evaluation of a computer-based narrative interpretation of a test battery. *Measurement and Evaluation in Guidance, 11*(1), 50–53.

Sharf, R. S. (1992). *Applying career development theory to counseling.* Pacific Grove, CA, Brooks/Cole.

Sheehy, G. (1976). *Passages: Predictable crises of adult life.* New York: Dutton.

Sheehy, G. (1981). *Pathfinders.* New York: Bantam.

Shellenbarger, S. (1999). *Work and family.* New York: Ballantine Books.

Shell Poll. (1999). Peter Hart Associates. *Teens talk about their school experience.* www.countonshell.com/shell.html.

Shelton, B. K. (1985). The social and psychological impact of unemployment. *Journal of Employment Counseling, 20*(1), 18–22.

Shepard, J. M., Kim, D. I., & Houghland, J. G. (1979). Effects of technology in industrialized and industrializing societies. *Sociology of Work and Occupations, 6*(4), 457–481.

Shepelak, N. J., Ogden, D., & Robin-Bennett, D. (1984). The influence of gender labels on the sex typing of imaginary occupations. *Sex Roles, 11,* 983–997.

Shepard, B., & Marshall, A. (2000). Career development and planning issues for rural adolescent girls. *Canadian Journal of Counselling, 34,* 155–171.

Sheppard, D. I. (1971). The measurement of vocational maturity in adults. *Journal of Vocational Behavior, 1,* 399–406.

Sherman, D. (1994). Career counseling in cyberspace. *Journal of Career Planning and Employment.* November, 29–63.

Sherry, P., & Staley, K. (1984). Career exploration groups: An outcome study. *Journal of College Student Personnel, 25*(2), 155–159.

Shertzer, B. (1981). *Career planning. Freedom to choose* (2nd ed.). Boston: Houghton Mifflin.

Shilling, S., & Brackbill, R. M. (1987). Occupational health and safety risks and potential health consequences perceived by U.S. workers. *Public Health Reports, 102,* 36–46.

Shirom, A. (1989). Burnout in work organizations. In C. L. Cooper & I. Roberston (Eds.), *International review of industrial and organizational psychology* (pp. 25–48). Chichester: Wiley.

Shore, L. M., & Martin, H. J. (1989). Job satisfaction and organizational commitment in relation to work performance and turnover intentions. *Human Relations, 42,* 625–638.

Shultz, J. T. (1979). The private sector: A new frontier? *Vocational Guidance Quarterly, 27*(3), 276–280.

Shute, R. E. (2002). Review of the Jackson Vocational Interest Survey. In J. T. Kapes & E. A. Whitfield (Eds.), *A counselor's guide to career assessment instruments* (4th ed., pp. 252–256). Tulsa, OK: National Career Development Association.

Siegel, C. L. F. (1973). Sex differences in the occupational choices of second graders. *Journal of Vocational Behavior, 3,* 15–19.

Siegfried, W. D., MacFarlane, I., Graham, D. G., Moore, N. A., & Young, P. L. (1981). A reexamination of sex differences in job preferences. *Journal of Vocational Behavior, 18,* 30–42.

Sievert, N. W. (1972). The role of self-concept in determining an adolescent's occupational choice. *Journal of Industrial Teacher Education, 9*(3), 47–53.

Sigman, A. (1992). The state of corporate health care. *Personnel Management, 3,* 24–31.

Silberman, H. F. (1994). Research review of school-to-employment experience. In A. J. Pautler, Jr. (Ed.), *High school to employment transition: Contemporary issues* (pp. 61–72). Ann Arbor, MI: Prakken Publications, Inc.

Silliker, S. A. (1993). The role of social contacts in the successful job search. *Journal of Employment Counseling, 30,* 25–34.

Silver, C., & Spilerman, S. (1990). Psychoanalytic perspectives on occupational choices and attainment. *Research in Social Stratification and Mobility, 9,* 181–214.

Silverstein, L. B. (1991). Transforming the debate about child care and maternal employment. *American Psychologist, 46*(1), 1025–1032.

Silverthorne, C. P. (1992). Work motivation in the United States, Russia, and the Republic of China (Taiwan): A comparison. *Journal of Applied Social Psychology, 22*(20), 1631–1639.

Simmons, D. (1962). Children's ranking of occupational prestige. *Personnel and Guidance Journal, 41,* 332–336.

Simpson, E. J. (1972). The classification of educational objectives in the psychomotor domain. *The psychomotor domain: A resource book for media specialists* (pp. 43–56). The National Special Media Institutes. Washington, DC: Gryphon House.

Skorikov, V., & Vondracek, F. (1993). Career development in the Commonwealth of Independent States. *Career Development Quarterly, 44,* 314–329.

Skovholt, T. M., Morgan, J. I., & Negron-Cunningham, H. (1989). Mental imagery in career counseling and life planning: A review of research and intervention methods. *Journal of Counseling and Development, 67,* 287–292.

Slakter, M. J., & Cramer, S. H. (1969). Risk-taking and vocational or curriculum choice. *Vocational Guidance Quarterly, 17*(2), 127–132.

Slaney, R. B., (1980a). Expressed vocational choice and vocational indecision. *Journal of Counseling Psychology, 27,* 122–129.

Slaney, R. B. (1980b). An investigation of racial differences in vocational values among college women. *Journal of Vocational Behavior, 16,* 197–207.

Slaney, R. B. (1988). The assessment of career decision making. In W. B. Walsh & S. H. Osipow (Eds.), *Career decision making* (pp. 33–76). Hillsdale: Erlbaum Associates.

Slaney, R. B., & Croteau, J. M. (1995). "Two methods of exploring interests: A comparison of outcomes": Response to Goldman. *The Career Development Quarterly, 43,* 387–389.

Slaney, R. B., & Lewis, E. T. (1986). Effects of career exploration on career undecided reentry women: An intervention and follow-up study. *Journal of Vocational Behavior, 28,* 97–109.

Slaney, R. B., Palko-Nonemaker, D., & Alexander, R. (1981). An investigation of two measures of indecision. *Journal of Vocational Behavior, 18,* 92–103.

Slaney, R. B., & Russell, J. E. A. (1987). Perspectives on vocational behavior, 1986: A review. *Journal of Vocational Behavior, 31,* 111–173.

Slaney, R. B., & Suddarth, B. H. (1994). The Values Scale (VS). In J. T. Kapes, M. M. Mastie, & E. A. Whitfield (Eds.), *A counselor's guide to career assessment instruments* (pp. 236–240). Alexandria, VA: National Career Development Association.

Slaughter, D. T., & Johnson, D. T. (Eds.). (1988). *Visible now: Blacks in private schools.* Westport, CT: Greenwood Press.

Slocum, W. L., & Bowles, R. T. (1968). Attractiveness of occupations to high school students. *Personnel and Guidance Journal, 46,* 754–761.

Slocum, J. W., & Cron, W. L. (1985). Job attitudes and performance during three career stages. *Journal of Vocational Behavior, 26*(2), 126–145.

Smart, J. C. (1986). College effects on occupational status attainment. *Research in Higher Education, 24*(1), 73–94.

Smart, J. C., Elton, C. F., & McLaughlin, G. W. (1986). Person-environment congruence and job satisfaction. *Journal of Vocational Behavior, 29,* 216–225.

Smart, J. F., & Smart, D. W. (1995). Acculturative stress: The experience of the Hispanic immigrant. *The Counseling Psychologist, 23*(1), 25–42.

Smart, R. M., & Peterson, C. C. (1994). Super's stages and the four-factor structure of the Adult Career Concerns Inventory in an Australian sample. *Measurement and Evaluation in Counseling and Development, 26,* 243–257.

Smith, A., & Chemers, M. M. (1981). Misperceptions of motivation of economically disadvantaged employees in work settings. *Journal of Employment Counseling, 18*(1), 24–33.

Smith, E. D. (1968). Innovative ideas in vocational guidance. *American Vocational Journal, 43,* 19–21.

Smith, E. D. (1977, September). Personal communication.

Smith, E. R. (Ed.). (1979a). *The subtle revolution.* Washington DC: The Urban Institute.

Smith, E. R. (1979b). *Women in the labor force in 1990.* Washington, DC: The Urban Institute.

Smith, E. R. (1980). Desiring and expecting to work among high school girls: Some determinants and consequences. *Journal of Vocational Behavior, 17*(2), 218–230.

Smith, H. L. (1986). Overeducation and underemployment: An agnostic review. *Sociology of Education, 59,* 85–99.

Smith, H. L., & Powell, B. (1990). Great expectations: Variations in income expectations among college seniors. *Sociology of Education, 63,* 194–207.

Smith, M. (1943). An empirical scale of prestige status occupations. *American Sociological Review, 8,* 185–192.

Smith, M. (1994). A theory of the validity of predictors in selection. *Journal of Occupational and Organizational Psychology, 67,* 13–31.

Smith, M. (1997). The benefits of integrating internet technologies into career services. *Australian Journal of Career Development, 6,* 11–13.

Sneegas, J. J. (1986). Components of life satisfaction in middle and later life adults: Perceived social competence, leisure participation and leisure satisfaction. *Journal of Leisure Research, 18*(4), 248–258.

Snyder, B. A., & Daly, T. P. (1993). Restructuring guidance and counseling programs. *The School Counselor, 41,* 36–43.

Snyder, J. F., Hill, C. E., & Derksen, T. P. (1974). Why some students do not use university counseling services. *Journal of Counseling Psychology, 19*(4), 263–268.

Snyder, R. A., Williams, R. R., & Cashman, J. F. (1984). Age, tenure, and work perceptions as predictors of reaction to performance feedback. *Journal of Psychology, 116,* 11–21.

Snyder, T., & Shafer, L. (1996). *Youth indicators 1996: Trends in the well-being of American youth* (1'NCES Publication No. 96–027). Washington, DC: U.S. Government Printing Office.

Solomon, B. A. (1985). Consensus on wellness programs. *Personnel, 62,* 67–72.

Sorensen, E. (1991). *Gender and racial pay gaps in the 1980's: Accounting for different trends.* Washington, DC: U.S. Department of Labor.

Sorokin, P. (1972). *Social mobility* (pp. 225, 238), New York: Harper.

Sorrentino, C. (November, 1992). Analyzing labor markets in Central and Eastern Europe. *Monthly Labor Review,* 43–46.

Sovilla, E. S. (1970). A plan for career planning. *Journal of College Placement, 21*(1), 50–58.

Spaeth, J. L. (1968). Occupation prestige expectations among male college graduates. *American Journal of Sociology, 73,* 548–558.

Spanard, J. M. A. (1990). Beyond intent: Reentering college to complete the degree. *Review of Educational Research, 60*(3), 309–344.

Spicuzza, F. J., & DeVoe, M. W. (1982). Burnout in the helping professions: Mutual aid as self-help. *Personnel and Guidance Journal, 61*(2), 95–99.

Spiker-Miller, S., Kees, N. (1995). Making career development a reality for dual-career couples. *Journal of Employment Counseling, 32,* 32–45.

Spitzberg, B. H., & Cupach, W. R. (1989). *Handbook of interpersonal competence research.* New York: Springer-Verlag.

Spitze, G. D., & Huker, J. (1980). Changing attitudes toward women's nonfamily roles: 1938–1978. *Sociology of Work and Occupations, 7*(3), 317–335.

Spokane, A. (1985). A review of research on person-environment congruence in Holland's theory of careers. *Journal of Vocational Behavior, 26,* 306–343.

Spokane, A. (1990). Supplementing differential research in vocational psychology using nontraditional methods. In R. A. Young & W. A. Borgen (Eds.), *Methodological approaches to the study of careers* (pp. 25–36). New York: Praeger.

Spokane, A. R. (1979). Validity of the Holland categories for college women and men. *Journal of College Student Personnel, 20*(4), 335–340.

Spokane, A. R. (1989). Are there psychological and mental health consequences of difficult career decisions? A reaction to Herr. *Journal of Career Counseling, 16,* 19–24.

Spokane, A. R. (1991). *Career intervention.* Englewood Cliffs, NJ: Prentice-Hall.

Spokane, A. R. (1991). *Evaluating career interventions.* Englewood Cliffs, NJ: Prentice Hall.

Spokane, A. R. (1998). Risk versus reluctance: Understanding an ambivalent entrepreneur. *The Career Development Quarterly, 46,* 370–375.

Spokane, A. R., Meir, E. I., & Catalano, M. (2000). Person-environment congruence and Holland's theory: A review and reconsideration. *Journal of Vocational Behavior, 57*(2), 137–187.

Spokane, A. R., & Oliver, L. W. (1983). The outcomes of vocational intervention. In S. H. Osipow & W. B. Walsh (Eds.), *Handbook of vocational psychology,* Vol. 2. Hillsdale, NJ: Erlbaum.

Spranger, E. (1928). *Types of men: The psychology and ethics of personality* (Paul J. W. Pigors, Trans.), Halle, Germany: Max Niemeyer Verlag.

Sproles, E. K. (1988). Research indicates new approaches for counseling vocational education students. *The School Counselor, 36*(1), 18–23.

Spruell, G. (1987). Work fever. *Training and Development Journal, 41,* 41–45.

Staley, N. K., & Mangiesi, J. N. (1984). Using books to enhance career awareness. *Elementary School Guidance and Counseling, 18,* 200–208.

Stanciak, L. A. (1995). Returning the high school counselor's role: A look at developmental guidance. *NASSP Bulletin, 79,* 60–63.

Standards and guidelines. (1985). Council for the Advancement of Standards for Student Services/Development Programs. Consortium of Professional Associations in Higher Education.

Stanfield, J. B. (1998). Couples coping with dual careers: A description of flexible and rigid coping styles. *The Social Science Journal, 35*(1), 53–64.

Staples, R. (1986). The political economy of black family life. *The Black Scholar, 17*(5), 2–11.

Stead, G. B., Watson, M. B., & Foxcroft, C. D. (1993). The relation between career indecision and irrational beliefs among university students. *Journal of Vocational Behavior, 42,* 155–169.

Steel, R. P., & Rentsch, J. R. (1997). The dispositional model of job attitudes revisited: Findings of a 10-year study. *Journal of Applied Psychology, 82*(6), 873–879.

Steele, G. E., Kennedy, G. J., & Gordon, V. N. (1993). The retention of major changers: A longitudinal study. *Journal of College Student Development, 34,* 58–62.

Steers, R. M., & Porter, L. W. (1975). *Motivation and work behavior.* New York: McGraw-Hill.

Stefflre, B. (1966). Vocational development: Ten propositions in search of a theory. *Personnel and Guidance Journal, 44,* 611–616.

Steil, J. M., & Hay, J. L. (1997). Social comparison in the workplace: A study of 60 dual-career couples. *Personality and Social Psychology Bulletin, 24*(4), 427–438.

Stein, J. A., Newcomb, M. D., & Bentler, P. M. (1990). The relative influence of vocational behavior and family involvement on self-esteem: Longitudinal analyses of young adult women and men. *Journal of Vocational Behavior, 36*(3), 320–338.

Steinberg, L., Dornbusch, S. M., & Brown, B. B. (1992). Ethnic differences in adolescent achievement. *American Psychologist, 47*(6), 723–729.

Steiner, D. D., & Truxill, D. M. (1989). An improved test of the disaggregation hypothesis of job and life satisfaction. *Journal of Occupational Psychology, 62,* 33–39.

Steinweg, D. A. (1990). Implications of current research for counseling the unemployed. *Journal of Employment Counseling, 27,* 37–40.

Stenberg, C. W. (1994). *America's future work force: A health and education policy issues handbook.* Westport, CT: Greenwood Press.

Stephens, W. R. (1970). *Social reform and the origins of vocational guidance.* Washington, DC: National Vocational Guidance Association.

Stern, D., McMillan, M., Hopkins, C., & Stone, J. R., III (1990). Work experience for students in high school and college. *Youth and Society, 21*(3), 355–389.

Stern, D., & Nakata, Y. (1989). Characteristics of high school students' paid jobs, and employment experience after graduation. In D. Stern & D. Eichorn (Eds.), *Adolescence and work: Influences of social structure, labor markets, and culture* (pp. 189–234). Hillsdale, NJ: Lawrence Erlbaum Associates, Publishers.

Sterrett, E. A. (1999). A comparison of women's and men's career transitions. *Journal of Career Development, 25*(4), 249–259.

Stevens, D. T., & Lundberg, D. J. (1998). The emergence of the internet: Enhancing career counseling education and services. *Journal of Career Development, 24,* 195–208.

Stevenson, W. (1978). The transition from school to work. In A. Adams & G. L. Mangum (Eds.), *The lingering crisis of youth unemployment* (pp. 65–90). Kalamazoo, MI: Upjohn Institute for Employment Research.

Steward, R. J. (1993). Two faces of academic success: Case studies of American Indians on a predominantly Anglo university campus. *Journal of College Student Development, 34,* 191–196.

Stewart, A. J., & Healy, M. M., Jr. (1989). Linking individual development and social changes. *American Psychologist, 44*(1), 30–42.

Stewart, E. A. (1999). A comparison of women's and men's career transitions. *Journal of Career Development, 25*(4), 249–259.

Stickel, S. A., & Bonett, R. M. (1991). Gender differences in career self-efficacy: Combining a career with home and family. *Journal of College Student Development, 32,* 297–301.

Stockton, N., Berry, J., Shepson, J., & Utz, P. (1980). Sex role and innovative major choice among college students. *Journal of Vocational Behavior, 16,* 360–367.

Stoeva, A. Z., Chiu, R. K., & Greenhaus, J. H. (2002). Negative affectivety, role stress, and work/family conflict. *Journal of Vocational Behavior, 60,* 1–16.

Stone, D. L., & Stone, E. F. (1987). Effects of missing application-blank information on personnel selection decisions: Do privacy protection strategies bias the outcome? *Journal of Applied Psychology, 72,* 452–456.

Stonewater, B. B., Eveslage, S. A., & Dingerson, M. R. (1990). Gender differences in career development relationships. *Career Development Quarterly, 39,* 72–85.

Storey, W. D. (Ed.). (1978). *A guide for career development inquiry.* Madison, WI: American Society for Training and Development.

Stout, S. K., Slocum, J. W., & Cron, W. L. (1988). Dynamics of the career plateauing process. *Journal of Vocational Behavior, 34,* 102–114.

Strahan, R. F., & Kelly, A. E. (1994). Showing clients what their profiles mean. *Journal of Counseling and Development, 72,* 329–331.

Stryker, L. E., & Scorzelli, J. F. (1977). Work, counseling, and ex-offenders. *Offender Rehabilitation, 1*(3), 263–266.

Study finds 60% of 11 million who lost jobs got new ones. (1986, February 7). *The New York Times,* pp. A1, A5.

Stumpf, S. A., Austin, E. J., & Hartman, K. (1984). The impact of career exploration and interview readiness on interview performance and outcomes. *Journal of Vocational Behavior, 24,* 221–235.

Stumpf, S. A., & Rabinowitz, S. (1981). Career stage as a moderator of performance relationships with facets of job satisfaction and role perceptions. *Journal of Vocational Behavior, 118,* 202–218.

Subich, L. M. (2001). Dynamic forces in the growth and change of vocational psychology. *Journal of Vocational Behavior, 59,* 235–242.

Subich, L. M., & Taylor, K. M. (1994). Emerging directions of social learning theory. In M. L. Savickas & R. W. Lent (Eds.), *Convergence in career development theories. Implications for science and practice* (pp. 167–175). Palo Alto, CA: CPP Books.

Suchet, M., & Barling, J. (1985). Employed mothers: Interrole conflict, spouse support, and marital functioning. *Journal of Occupational Behaviour, 7,* 167–178.

Sue, D. W. (1994). Asian American mental health and help-seeking behavior: Comment on Solberg et al. (1994), Tata & Long (1994), and Lin (1994). *Journal of Counseling Psychology, 41,* 292–295.

Sue, D., & Padilla, A. (1986). Ethnic minority issues in the United States: Challenges for the educational system. In *Beyond language: Social and cultural factors in schooling language minority students* (pp. 34–72). Los Angeles: California State Department of Education.

Sue, S. (1999). Science, ethnicity, and bias: Where have we gone wrong? *American Psychologist, 54,* 1070–1077.

Sue, S., & Abe, J. (1988). *Predictors of academic achievement among Asian American and white students* (Report No. 88–11). New York: College Entrance Examination Board.

Sue, S., & Okazaki, S. (1990). Asian-American educational achievements: A phenomenon in search of an explanation. *American Psychologist, 45,* (8), 913–920.

Sullivan, P. R. (1970). Counseling in the employment service or Sullivan's theories of employment counseling. *Journal of Employment Counseling, 7,* 127–128.

Sundal-Hansen, L. S. (1984). Interrelationship of gender and career. In N. C. Gysbers (Ed.), *Designing careers: Counseling to enhance education, work, and leisure.* San Francisco: Jossey-Bass.

Sundal-Hansen, L. S. (1985). Sex-role issues in counseling women and men. In P. Pedersen (Ed.), *Handbook of cross-cultural counseling and therapy* (pp. 213–222). Westport, CT: Greenwood Press.

Sundby, D. Y. (1980). The career goal: A psychological look at some divergent dual-career families. In C. B. Derr (Ed.), *Work, family, and the career: New frontiers in theory and research,* (pp 329–353). New York: Praeger.

Sundstrom, E., Burt, R. E., & Kamp, D. (1980). Privacy at work: Architectural correlates of job satisfaction and job performance. *Academy of Management Journal, 23,*(1), 101–117.

Super, D. E. (1951). Vocational adjustment: Implementing a self-concept. *Occupations, 30,* 88–92.

Super, D. E. (1953). A theory of vocational development. *American Psychologist, 8,* 185–190.

Super, D. E. (1954). Career patterns as a basis for vocational counseling. *Journal of Counseling Psychology, 1,* 12–20.

Super, D. E. (1957). *The psychology of careers.* New York: Harper & Row.

Super, D. E. (1962). The structure of work values in relation to status, achievement, interest, and adjustment. *Journal of Applied Psychology, 46,* 227–239.

Super, D. E. (1969a). Vocational development theory: Persons, positions, and processes. *The Counseling Psychologist, 1,* 2–9.

Super, D. E. (1969b). The natural history of a study of lives and of vocations. *Perspectives on Education, 2,* 13–22.

Super, D. E. (1974). The broader context of career development and vocational guidance: American trends in world perspective. In E. L. Herr (Ed.), *Vocational guidance and human development* (Chap. 3). Boston: Houghton Mifflin.

Super, D. E. (1976). *Career education and the meaning of work.* Monographs on career education. Washington, DC: The Office of Career Education, U.S. Office of Education.

Super, D. E. (1977). Vocational maturity in mid-career. *Vocational Guidance Quarterly, 25*(4), 294–302.

Super, D. E. (1980). A life-span, life space approach to career development. *Journal of Vocational Behavior, 16*(30), 282–298.

Super, D. E. (1981). Approaches to occupational choice and career development. In A. G. Watts, D. E. Super, & J. M. Kidd (Eds.), *Career development in Britain.* Cambridge, England: Hobsons Press.

Super, D. E. (1982). The relevance and importance of work: Models and measures for meaningful data. *The Counseling Psychologist, 10*(4), 95–104.

Super, D. E. (1983). Assessment in career guidance: Toward truly developmental counseling. *Personnel and Guidance Journal, 61*(9), 555–562.

Super, D. E. (1984a). Career and life development. In D. Brown & L. Brooks (Eds.), *Career choice and development: applying contemporary approaches to practice.* San Francisco: Jossey-Bass.

Super, D. E. (1984b). Perspectives on the meaning and value of work. In N. C. Gysbers (Ed.), *Designing careers: Counseling to enhance education, work, and leisure* (Chap. 1). San Francisco: Jossey-Bass.

Super, D. E. (1985a). Career counseling across cultures. In P. Pederson (Ed.), *Handbook of cross-cultural counseling and therapy* (pp. 11–20). Westport, CT: Greenwood Press.

Super, D. E. (1985b). *New dimensions in adult vocational and career counseling.* Occupational paper No. 106. Columbus, OH: The National Center for Research in Vocational Education.

Super, D. E. (1990). A life-span, life-space approach to career development. In D. Brown & L. Brook (Eds.), *Career choice and development: Applying contemporary theories to practice* (pp. 197–261). San Francisco: Jossey-Bass.

Super, D. E. (1992). Toward a comprehensive theory of career development. In D. Montross & C. Shinkman (Eds.), *Career development: Theory and practice* (pp. 35–64). Springfield, IL: Charles C. Thomas.

Super, D. E. (1993). The two faces of counseling: Or is it three? *The Career Development Quarterly, 42*(2), 132–136.

Super, D. E. (1994). A life span, life space perspective on convergence. In M. L. Savickas & R. W. Lent (Eds.), *Convergence in career development theories. Implications for science and practice* (pp. 63–74). Palo Alto: CA: CPP Books.

Super, D. E., & Associates. (1974). *Measuring vocational maturity for counseling and evaluation.* Washington, DC: National Vocational Guidance Association.

Super, D. E., & Backrach, P. (1957). *Scientific careers and vocational development theory.* New York: Teachers College Press.

Super, D. E., Bohn, M. J., Forrest, D. J., Jordaan, J. P., Lindeman, R. H., & Thompson, A. A. (1971). *Career development inventory.* New York: Teachers College, Columbia University.

Super, D. E., Crites, J. O., Hummel, R. C., Moser, H. P., Overstreet, P. L., & Warnath, C. F. (1957). *Vocational development: A framework for research.* New York: Teachers College, Columbia University.

Super, D. E., & Forrest, D. J. (1972). *Preliminary manual: Career development inventory.* New York: Columbia University Teachers College.

Super, D. E., & Hall, D. T. (1978). Career development: Exploration and planning. *Annual Review of Psychology, 29,* 333–372.

Super, D. E., & Kidd, J. M. (1979). Vocational maturity in adulthood: Toward turning a model into a measure. *Journal of Vocational Behavior, 14*(3), 255–270.

Super, D. E., & Knasel, E. G. (1981). Career development in adulthood: Some theoretical problems and a possible solution. *British Journal of Guidance and Counselling, 9,* 194–201.

Super, D. E., & Nevill, D. D. (1984). Work role salience as a determinant of career maturity in high school students. *Journal of Vocational Behavior, 25,* 30–44.

Super, D. E., Osborne, W. L., Walsh, D. J., Brown, S. D., & Niles, S. G. (1992). Developmental assessment and counseling: The C-DAC model. *Journal of Counseling and Development, 71,* 74–80.

Super, D. E., & Overstreet, P. L. (1960). *The vocational maturity of ninth-grade boys.* New York: Teachers College, Columbia University.

Super, D. E., Savickas, M. L., & Super, C. M. (1996). The life-span, life-space approach to careers. In D. Brown, L. Brooks, et al. (Eds.), *Career choices and development* (3rd ed., pp. 121–178). San Francisco: Jossey-Bass.

Super, D. E., Starishevsky, R., Matlin, N., & Jordaan, J. P. (1963). *Career development: Self-concept theory.* New York: College Entrance Examination Board.

Super, D. E., & Sverko, B. (Eds.). (1995). *Life roles, values, and careers. International findings of the work importance study.* San Francisco, CA: Jossey-Bass, Inc.

Super, D. E., Thompson, A., Lindeman, R., Myers, R., & Jordaan, J. (1986). *The Adult Career Concerns Inventory.* Palo Alto, CA: Consulting Psychologists Press.

Sussal, C. M. (1994). Empowering gays and lesbians in the workplace. *Journal of Gay and Lesbian Social Services, 1*(1), 89–103.

Sverke, M., & Hellgren, J. (2002). The nature of job insecurity: Understanding employment security on the brink of a new millennium. *Applied Psychology: An International Review, 51*(1), 23–42.

Sverko, B. (1989). Origin of individual differences in importance attached to work: A model and a contribution to its evaluation. *Journal of Vocational Behavior, 34*(1), 28–39.

Swanson, G. (1982). Vocational patterns in the United States. In H. F. Silverman (Ed.), *Education and work.* Eighty-first yearbook of the National Society for the Study of Education, Pt. 2. Chicago: University of Chicago Press.

Swanson, J. L. (1993). Integrated assessment of vocational interests and self-rated skills and abilities. *Journal of Career Assessment, 1*(1), 50–65.

Swanson, J. L., & Hansen, J-I. C. (1988). Stability of vocational interests over 4-year, 8-year, and 12-year intervals. *Journal of Vocational Behavior, 33,* 185–202.

Swanson, J. L., & Lease, S. H. (1990). Gender differences in self-ratings of abilities and skills. *The Career Development Quarterly, 38,* 347–359.

Swanson, J. L., & Parcover, J. A. (1998). Annual review: Practice and research in career counseling and development-1997. *The Career Development Quarterly, 47,* 98–134.

Swanson-Kauffman, K. M. (Ed.). (1987). *Women's work, families, and health.* New York: Hemisphere.

Swatko, M. K. (1981). What's in a title? Personality, job aspirations, and the nontraditional woman. *Journal of Vocational Behavior, 18,* 174–183.

Swisher, J. D. (2001). The costs, cost-effectiveness, and cost-benefit of school and community counseling services. In D.C. Locke, J. Myers, & E. L. Herr (Eds.), *The handbook of counseling* (pp. 669–680). Thousands Oaks, CA: Sage.

Szafran, R. F. (1992). Measuring occupational change over four decennial censuses, 1950–1980. *Work and Occupations, 19*(3), 293–326.

Szilagyi, A. D., & Holland, W. E. (1980). Changes in social density: Relationships with functional interaction and perceptions of job characteristics, role stress, and work satisfaction. *Journal of Applied Psychology, 65*(1), 28–33.

Szinovacz, M. (1987). Preferred retirement timing and retirement satisfaction in women. *International Journal of Aging and Human Development, 24,* 301–315.

Taber, T. D., Cooke, R. A., & Walsh, J. T. (1990). A joint business-community approach to improve problem solving by workers displaced in a plant shutdown. *Journal of Community Psychology, 18,* 19–33.

Takai, R., & Holland, J. L. (1979). Comparison of the Vocational Card Sort, the SDS, and the Vocational

Exploration and Insight Kit. *Vocational Guidance Quarterly, 27*(4), 312–318.

Tan, C. S., & Salomone, P. R. (1994). Understanding career plateauing: Implications for counseling. *The Career Development Quarterly,* 42, 291–301.

Tan, E. (2002). Career guidance in Singapore. *The Career Development Quarterly, 50,* 257–263.

Tang, M., & Cook, E. P. (2001). Understanding the career concerns of middle school girls. In P. O'Reilly & E. M. Penn (Eds.), *Educating young adolescent girls.* (pp. 213–229). Mahwah, NJ: Erlbaum.

Tatsuno, R. (2002). Career counseling in Japan: Today and in the future. *The Career Development Quarterly, 50,* 211–217.

Taylor, A. (1986). Why women managers are bailing out. *Fortune, 114* (4), 16–23.

Taylor, K. M., & Betz, N. E. (1983). Applications of self-efficacy theory to the understanding and treatment of career indecision. *Journal of Vocational Behavior, 22,* 63–81.

Taylor, K. M., & Popma, J. (1990). An examination of the relationships among career decision-making self-efficacy, career salience, locus of control, and vocational indecision. *Journal of Vocational Behavior, 37,* 17–31.

Taylor, M. S. (1985). The roles of occupational knowledge and vocational self-concept crystallization in students' school-to-work transition. *Journal of Counseling Psychology, 32*(4), 539–550.

Taylor, N. B. (1985). How do career counselors counsel? *British Journal of Guidance and Counseling, 13*(2), 166–177.

Taylor, N. B., & Pryor, R. G. L. (1985). Exploring the process of compromise in career decision making. *Journal of Vocational Behavior, 27,* 171–190.

Taylor, R. L. (1990). Black youth: The endangered generation. *Youth and Society, 22*(1), 4–11.

Teal, E., & Herrick, R. F. (Eds.). (1962). *The fundamentals of college placement.* Bethlehem, PA: The College Placemente Council.

Techniques. (1999). What students are saying. 74, 36–37.

Tennyson, W. W. (1967). The psychology of developing competent personnel. *American Vocational Journal, 42,* 27–29.

Tennyson, W. W., Hansen, L. S., Klaurens, M. K., & Antholz, M. B. (1975). *Educating for career development.* St. Paul, MN: Minnesota Department of Education (Revised 1980, National Vocational Guidance Association).

Terry, J. (1999). A community/school mentoring program for elementary students. *Professional School Counseling, 2*(3), 237–240.

Tett, R. P., & Meyer, J. P. (1993). Job satisfaction, organizational commitment, turnover intention, and turnover: Path analysis based on metaanalytic findings. *Personnel Psychology, 46,* 259–293.

Theriault, J. (1994). Retirement as a psychological transition: Process of adaptation to change. *International Journal of Aging and Human Development, 38*(2), 153–170.

Thoits, P. A. (1982). Life stress, social support, and psychological vulnerability: Epidemiological considerations. *Journal of Community Psychology, 10*(4), 341–362.

Thomas, H. (1990). A likelihood-based model for validity generalization. *Journal of Applied Psychology, 75,* 13–20.

Thomas, L.E. (1980). A typology of mid-life career changes. *Journal of Vocational Behavior, 16*(2), 173–182.

Thomas, R. G., & Bruning, C. R. (1984). Cognitive dissonance as a mechanism in vocational decision processes. *Journal of Vocational Behavior, 24,* 264–278.

Thomas, W. G. (1966). Placement's role in the university. *Journal of College Placement, 26*(4), 87–92.

Thomason, T. C. (1991). Counseling Native Americans: An introduction for non-Native American counselors. *Journal of Counseling and Development, 69,* 321–327.

Thompson, B., & Ackerman, C. M. (1994). Myers-Briggs Type Indicator (MBTI). In J. T. Kapes, M. M. Mastie, & E. A. Whitfield (Eds.), *A counselor's guide to career assessment instruments* (pp. 281–287). Alexandria, VA: National Career Development Association.

Thompson, B., Guest Editor. (1993, Summer). Statistical testing in contemporary practice: Some proposed alternatives with comments from journal editors. *The Journal of Experimental Education, 61*(4), Whole Issue.

Thompson, D. E., & Thompson, T. A. (1985). Task-based performance appraisal for blue-collar jobs: Evaluation of race and sex effects. *Journal of Applied Psychology, 70*(4), 747–753.

Thompson, J. M., & Blain, M. D. (1992). Presenting feedback on the Minnesota Importance Questionnaire and the Minnesota Satisfaction Questionnaire. *Career Development Quarterly, 41,* 62–66.

Thompson, J. W. (1980). Burnout in group home houseparents. *American Journal of Psychiatry, 137*(6), 710–714.

Thompson, P. H., Baker, R. Z., & Smallwood, N. (1986). Improving professional development by applying the four-stage career model. *Organizational Dynamics, 15,* 49–62.

Thoni, R. J., & Olsson, P. M. (1975). A systematic career development program in a liberal arts college. *Personnel and Guidance Journal, 53,* 672–675.

Thoresen, C. E., & Krumboltz, J. D. (1968). Similarity of social models and clients in behavioral counseling: Two experimental studies. *Journal of Counseling Psychology, 15,* 393–401.

Thoresen, C. E., Krumboltz, J. D., & Varenhorst, B. (1967). Sex of counselors and models: Effect on client career exploration. *Journal of Counseling Psychology, 14,* 503–508.

Thoresen, C. E., & Mehrens, W. A. (1967). Decision theory and vocational counseling: Important concepts and questions. *Personnel and Guidance Journal, 46,* 165–172.

Thorndike, R. L. (1985). The central role of general ability in prediction. *Multivariate Behavioral Research, 20,* 241–254.

Thorndike, R. L., & Hagen, E. (1959). *10,000 careers.* New York: Wiley.

Thurow, L. C. (1977). Technological unemployment and occupational education. In T. Powers (Ed.), *Education for careers: Policy issues in a time of change.* University Park: The Pennsylvania State University Press.

Tiedeman, D. V. (1961). Decision and vocational development: A paradigm and its implications. *Personnel and Guidance Journal, 40,* 15–20.

Tiedeman, D. V., & Miller-Tiedeman, A. (1977). An "i" power primer: Part one: Structure and its involvements of introduction. *Focus on Guidance, 9*(7), 1–16.

Tiedeman, D. V., & Miller-Tiedeman, A. (1984). Career decision making: An individualistic perspective. In D. Brown & L. Brooks (Eds.), *Career choice and development: applying contemporary theories to practice* (Chap. 10). San Francisco: Jossey-Bass.

Tiedeman, D. V., & O'Hara, R. P. (1963). *Career development: Choice and adjustment.* New York: College Entrance Examination Board.

Tillinghast, B. S., Jr. (1964). Choice orientations of guidance. *Vocational Guidance Quarterly, 13,* 18–20.

Tinsley, H. E. A. (1994). Construct your reality and show us its benefits: Comment on Richardson. *Journal of Counseling Psychology, 40*(4), 108–111.

Tinsley, H. E. A., & Bradley, R. W. (1986). Test interpretation. *Journal of Counseling and Development, 64,* 462–466.

Tinsley, H. E. A., & Heesacker, M. (1984). Vocational behavior and career development: A review. *Journal of Vocational Behavior, 25*(2), 139–190.

Tinsley, H. E. A., & Tinsley, D. J. (1982). An analysis of leisure counseling models. *The Counseling Psychologist, 9,* 45–53.

Tinsley, H. E. A., Tokar, D. M., & Helwig, S. E. (1994). Client expectations about counseling and involvement during career counseling. *Career Development Quarterly, 42*(4), 326–336.

Tittle, C. K. (1973). Sex bias in educational measurement: Fact or fiction? *Measurement and Evaluation in Guidance, 6,* 219–226.

Tittle, C. K. (1988). Validity, gender research, and studies of the effects of career development interventions. *Applied Psychology: An International Review, 37,* 121–131.

Toffler, A. (1970). *Future shock.* New York: Bantam Books.

Toffler, A. (1980). *The third wave.* New York: Morrow.

Toffler, A. (1990). *Powershift, knowledge, wealth, and violence at the edge of the 21st century.* New York: Bantam Books.

Tokar, D. M., & Fischer, A. R. (1998). More on RIASEC and the five-factor model of personality: Direct assessment of Prediger's (1982) and Hogan's (1983) dimensions. *Journal of Vocational Behavior, 52*(2), 246–259.

Tolbert, E. L. (1980). *Counseling for career development* (2nd ed.). Boston: Houghton Mifflin.

Tolson, J. (2000, May 19). A not-so-lonely crowd. *U.S. News & World Report, 128,* 19, 46–48.

Townshend, A., & Gurin, P. (1981). Re-examining the frustrated homemaker hypothesis: Role fit, personal satisfaction, and collective discontent. *Sociology of Work and Occupations, 8*(4), 464–488.

Tracey, T. J. G. (1997). The structure of interests and self-efficacy expectations: An expanded examination of the spherical model of interest. *Journal of Counseling Psychology, 44*(1), 32–43.

Trebilco, G. R. (1984). Career education and career maturity. *Journal of Vocational Behavior, 25,* 191–202.

Treiman, D. J. (1977). *Occupational prestige in comparative perspective.* New York: Academic Press.

Triandis, H. (1985). Some major dimensions of cultural variation in client populations. In P. Pedersen (Ed.), *Handbook of cross-cultural counseling and therapy* (pp. 21–28). Westport, CT: Greenwood Press.

Triandis, H. C., Feldman, J. M., Weldin, D. E., & Harvey, W. M. (1975). Ecosystem distrust in the hard-to-employ. *Journal of Applied Psychology, 60,* 44–56.

Trice, A. D., Hughes, M. A., Odom, C., Woods, K., & McClellan, N. C. (1995). The origins of children's career aspirations. I. V. testing hypotheses from four theories. *Career Development Quarterly, 43,* 307–322.

Troll, L. E., & Nowak, C. (1976). How old are you? The question of age bias in the counseling of adults. *The Counseling Psychologist, 6*(1), 41–44.

Troutt-Ervin, E. D., & Isberner, F. R. (1989). A job search course for technical students. *Journal of Studies in Technical Careers, XI,* 139–146.

Trower, P., Casey, A., & Dryden, W. (1988). *Cognitive-behavioral counseling in action.* Newbury Park, CA: Sage.

Trusty, J. (2002). African Americans' educational expectations: Longitudinal causal models for women and men. *Journal of Counseling and Development, 80,* 332–345.

Trusty, J. (2002). Couseling for career development with persons of color. In S. Niles (Ed.), *Adult career development: Concepts, issues, and practices.* (pp. 190–213). Tulsa, OK: National Career Development Association.

Trusty, J., & Harris, M. B. (1999). Lost talent: Predictors of the stability of educational expectations across adolescence. *Journal of Adolescent Research, 14,* 359–382.

Trusty, J., Ng, K., & Plata, M. (2000). Interaction effects of gender, SES, and race-ethnicity on postsecondary educational choices of U.S. students. *The Career Development Quarterly, 49,* 45–59.

Trusty, J., Ng, K., & Ray, D. (2000). Choice of Holland's social type college majors for U.S. racial/ethnic groups. *Journal of Career Development, 27*(1), 49–64.

Tschirgi, H. D., & Huegli, J. M. (1979). Monitoring the employment interview. *Journal of College Placement, 39*(2), 37–39.

Tung, R. L. (1980). Comparative analysis of the occupational stress profiles of male versus female administrators. *Journal of Vocational Behavior, 17,* 344–355.

Tyler, L. E. (1961). *The work of the counselor.* New York: Appleton-Century-Crofts.

Tyler, L. E. (Ed.). (1969). *Intelligence: Some recurring issues.* New York: Van Nostrand Reinhold.

Tziner, A., & Latham, G. P. (1989). The effect of appraisal instrument, feedback and goal-setting on worker satisfaction and commitment. *Journal of Organizational Behavior, 10,* 145–153.

Underdue, T. (2000). It's academic. *Techniques, 75,* 16–19.

Underwood, J. W., & Hardy, R. E. (1985). The relationship of vocational adjustment to personal adjustment. *Psychology: A Quarterly Journal of Human Behavior, 22*(2), 24–30.

Upper Arlington City School District. (1992, November). *Counseling Program. Grades Kindergarten-Twelve,* Upper Arlington, OH: Author.

Urich, M. (1990). Software review of the Self-Directed Search: Computer version. *Measurement and Evaluation in Counseling and Development, 23,* 92–94.

Uris, A. (1988). *88 mistakes interviewers make and how to avoid them.* New York: AMACOM.

U.S. Bureau of the Census. (1982, March). *Provisional estimates of social, economic, and housing characteristics* (pp. 25–35). 1980 Census of population and housing. Supplementary Report. Washington, DC: U.S. Department of Commerce.

U.S. Bureau of the Census. (1989). *Current population reports* (P-60, No. 162 & P-20, No. 431). Washington, DC: U.S. Bureau of Labor Statistics, Employment, and Earnings.

U.S. Bureau of the Census, Bureau of Labor Statistics. (1997). *Occupational outlook handbook, 1997–1998 Edition.* Washington, DC: U.S. Government Printing Office.

U.S. Bureau of the Census, Bureau of Labor Statistics. (2002). *Occupational outlook handbook, 2002–2003 Edition.* Washington, DC: U.S. Government Printing Office.

U.S. Congress. (1984). Carl D. Perkins Vocational Education Act, PL-254.

U.S. Congress. (1998). Carl D. Perkins Vocational Education and Applied Technology Act, PL 105-332.

U.S. Congress, Office of Technology Assessment. (1988). *Technology and the American economic transition: Choices for the future.* Washington, DC.: U.S. Government Printing Office.

U.S. Department of Education. National Center for Educational Statistics. (1989). *Digest of Educational Statistics, 1988.* Washington, DC: U.S. Government Printing Office.

U.S. Department of Education. (1991). *Combining school and work: Options in high school and two year colleges.* Washington, DC: Author.

U.S. Department of Education & U.S. Department of Labor. (1988). *The bottom line: Basic skills in the workplace.* Washington, DC: U.S. Department of Labor.

U.S. Department of Health, Education, and Welfare. (1973). Special Task Force. *Work in America.* Cambridge, MA: MIT Press.

U.S. Department of Health and Human Services. (2000). *Healthy people 2010: Understanding and improving health.* Washington, DC: Government Printing Office.

U.S. Department of Labor. (1974a). *Job satisfaction: Is there a trend?* (Manpower Research Monograph No. 30). Washington, DC: U.S. Government Printing Office.

U.S. Department of Labor. (1974b). *Manpower report of the president, 1974.* Washington, DC: U.S. Government Printing Office.

U.S. Department of Labor. (1974c). *The United States economy in 1985.* Washington, DC: U.S. Government Printing Office.

U.S. Department of Labor. (1979). *International comparisons of unemployment.* Washington, DC: U.S. Government Printing Office.

U.S. Department of Labor. (1980a). *Occupational outlook handbook, 1980–1981 edition.* Washington, DC: U.S. Government Printing Office.

U.S. Department of Labor. (1980b). *Self-directed job search: An introduction.* Washington, DC: Employment and Training Administration.

U.S. Department of Labor. (1981). *Monthly Labor Review, 104*(2), Washington, DC: Bureau of Labor Statistics.

U.S. Department of Labor, Bureau of Labor Statistics. (1986). *Employment projection for 1995: Data and methods* (Bulletin 2253). Washington, DC: U.S. Government Printing Office.

U.S. Department of Labor. (1989). *The Commission on Workforce Quality and Labor Market Efficiency.* Washington, DC: U.S. Government Printing Office.

U.S. Department of Labor. (1990, July 24). Proposed revised policy on use of validity generalization—General Aptitude Test Battery for selection and referral in employment and training programs: Notice and requests for comments. *Federal Register, 55*(142), 30162–30164.

U.S. Department of Labor, Bureau of Labor Statistics. (1990). *Occupational Outlook Handbook.* (1990–1991, ed.) Washington, DC: U.S. Department of Labor.

U.S. Department of Labor, Bureau of Labor Statistics. (1994). *Occupational Outlook Handbook, 1994–95 Edition.* Washington, DC: U.S. Government Printing Office.

U.S. Department of Labor, Bureau of Labor Statistics. (1997). *BLS releases new 1996–2006 employment projections.* (USDL 97–429). Washington, DC: U.S. Government Printing Office.

U.S. Department of Labor, Bureau of Labor Statistics. (2000). *Occupational Outlook Handbook,* 2000–01 Edition, Bulletin 2520. Washington, DC: U.S. Government Printing Office.

U.S. Department of Labor, Bureau of Labor Statistics. (2000). The 1998–2008 job outlook in brief [Special issue]. *Occupational Outlook Quarterly, 44*(1).

U.S. Department of Labor, Secretary's Commission on Achieving Necessary Skills. (1991, June). *What work requires of schools.* Washington, DC: U.S. Government Printing Office.

U.S. House of Representatives. (1984, October 19) P. L. 98-524, The Carl D. Perkins Vocational Education Act.

Vacc, N. A., & Hinkle, J. S. (1994). Career Assessment Inventory—enhanced version and vocational version (CAI-EV/CAI-VV). In J. T. Kapes, M. M. Mastie, & E. A. Whitfield (Eds.), *A counselor's guide to career assessment instruments* (4th ed., pp. 144–150). Alexandria, VA: National Career Development Association.

Vacc, N. A., & Newsome, D. W. (2002). Review of the Strong Interest Inventory. In J. T. Kapes & E. A. Whitfield (Eds.), *A counselor's guide to career assessment instruments* (4th ed., pp. 292–297). Tulsa, Ok: National Career Development Association.

Vacc, N. A., Wittmer, J., & De Vaney, S. B. (1988). *Experiencing and counseling multicultural and diverse populations.* Muncie, IN: Accelerated Development press.

Vaill, P. B. (1996). *Learning as a way of being. Strategies for survival in a world of permanent white water.* San Francisco, CA: Jossey-Bass.

Vaillant, G. E. (1977). *Adaptation to life.* Boston: Little, Brown.

Vaizey, J., & Clark, C. F. O. (1976). *Education: The state of the debate in America, Britain, and Canada.* London: Duckworth.

Valach, L. (1990). A theory of goal-directed action in career analysis. In R. A. Young & W. E. Borgen (Eds.), *Methodological approaches to the study of careers* (pp. 107–126). New York: Praeger.

Vale, C. D. (1990). The Minnesota Clerical Assessment Battery: An application of computerized testing to business. *Measurement and Evaluation in Counseling and Development, 23,* 11–18.

VanBuren, J. B., Kelly, K. R., & Hall, A. S. (1993). Modeling nontraditional career choices: Effects of gender and school location on response to a brief videotape. *Journal of Counseling and Development, 72,* 101–104.

Van Denburg, T. F., Schmidt, J. A., & Kiesler, D. J. (1992). Interpersonal assessment in counseling and psychotherapy. *Journal of Counseling and Development, 71,* 84–90.

Van der Embse, T. J., & Childs, J. M. (1979). Adults in transition: A profile of the older college student. *Journal of College Student Personnel, 20,* 475–479.

Vanderslice, V. J., Rice, R. W., & Julian, J. W. (1987). The effects of participation in decision-making on worker satisfaction and productivity: An organizational simulation. *Journal of Applied Social Psychology, 17,* 158–170.

Vansickle, T. R. (1994). Harrington-O'Shea Career Decision-Making System—Revised (CDM-R). In J. T. Kapes, M. M. Mastie, & E. A. Whitfield (Eds.), *A counselor's guide to career assessment instruments* (4th ed., pp. 172–177). Alexandria, VA: National Career Development Association.

Vansickle, T. R., Kimmel, C., & Kapes, J. T. (1989). Test re-test equivalency of the computer-based and paper-pencil versions of the Strong Campbell Interest Inventory. *Measurement and Evaluation in Counseling and Development, 22,* 88–93.

Van Vianen, A. E. M. (2001). Person-organization fit: The match between theory and methodology: Introduction to the special issue. *Applied Psychology: An International Review, 50*(1), 1–4.

Varenhorst, B. B. (1969). Learning the consequences of life's decisions. In J. D. Krumboltz & C. E. Thoresen (Eds.), *Behavioral counseling: Cases and techniques* (pp. 306–319). New York: Holt, Rinehart & Winston.

Vaughter, R. M., Sadh, D., & Vozzola, E. (1994). Sex similarities and differences in types of play in games and sports. *Psychology of Women Quarterly, 18,* 85–104.

Vecchio, R. P. (1980b). The test of moderator of the job satisfaction-job quality relationship: The case of religious affiliation. *Journal of Applied Psychology, 65*(2), 195–201.

Vecchio, R. P. (1980c). Worker alienation as a moderator of the job quality-job satisfaction relationship: The case of racial differences. *Academy of Management Journal, 23*(3), 479–486.

Veninga, R. L., & Spradley, J. P. (1981). *The work/stress connection: How to cope with job burnout.* Boston: Little, Brown.

Verlander, E. G. (1985). The system's the thing. *Training and Development Journal, 39*(4), 20–23.

Vertiz, V. C., & Fortune, J. C. (1984). An ethnographic study of cultural barriers to employment among Indochinese immigrant youth. *College Student Journal, 18* (3), 229–235.

Vetter, B. M. (1989). *Professional women and minorities: A manpower data resource service* (8th ed.). Washington, DC: Commission on Professionals in Science and Technology.

Vetter, E. W. (1985). Getting human resource planning on the dean's list. *Training and Development Journal, 39*(4), 16–18.

Veum, J. R., & Weiss, A. B. (1993). Education and the work histories of young adults. *Monthly Labor Review, 116*(4), 11–20.

Viinamaki, H., Niskanen, L., & Koskela, K. (1995). How do mental factors predict ability to cope with long-term unemployment? *Nordic Journal of Psychiatry, 49,* 183–189.

Vincenzi, H. (1977). Minimizing occupational stereotypes. *Vocational Guidance Quarterly, 25*(3), 265.

Vivona, J. M. (2000). Parental attachment styles of late adolescents: Qualities of attachment relationships and consequences for adjustment. *Journal of Counseling Psychology, 47*(3), 316–329.

Vondracek, F. W. (1990). A developmental-contextual approach to career development research. In R. A. Young & W. A. Borgen (Eds.), *Methodological approaches to the study of careers* (pp. 37–56). New York: Praeger.

Vondracek, F. W., & Fouad, N. A. (1994). Developmental contextualism. An integrative framework for theory and practice. In M. L. Savickas & R. W. Lent (Eds.), *Convergence for career development theories. Implications for science and practice* (pp. 207–214). Palo Alto, CA: CPP Books.

Vondracek, F. W., Hostetler, M., Schulenberg, J. E., & Shimizu, K. (1990). Dimensions of career indecision. *Journal of Counseling Psychology, 37,* 98–106.

Vondracek, F. W., & Lerner, R. M. (1982). Vocational role development in adolescence. In B. Wolman (Ed.), *Handbook of developmental psychology* (Chap. 33). Englewood Cliffs, NJ: Prentice-Hall.

Vondracek, F. W., Lerner, R. W., & Schulenberg, J. E. (1983). The concept of development in vocational theory and intervention. *The Journal of Vocational Behavior, 23,* 179–202.

Vondracek, F. W., Lerner, R. M., & Schulenberg, S. E. (1986). *Career development: A life-span developmental approach.* Hillsdale, NJ: Erlbaum.

Vondracek, F. W., & Porfeli, E. J. (2002). Life-span developmental perspectives on adult career development: Recent advances. In S. Niles (Ed.), *Adult career development: Concepts, issues, and practices* (pp. 20–38). Tulsa, OK: National Career Development Association.

Vondracek, F. W., & Schulenberg, J. E. (1986). Career development in adolescence: Some conceptual and intervention issues. *Vocational Guidance Quarterly, 34*(4), 247–254.

Vondracek, S. I., & Kirchner, E. P. (1974). Vocational development in early childhood: An examination of young children's expressions of vocational aspirations. *Journal of Vocational Behavior, 5,* 251–260.

Von Villas, B. A. (1995). The changing role of high school guidance: Career counseling and school-to-work. *NASSP Bulletin, 79,* 81.

Voydanoff, P. (1980). Perceived job characteristics and job satisfaction among men and women. *Psychology of Women Quarterly, 5*(2), 177–185.

Vroom, V. H. (1964). *Work and motivation.* New York: Wiley.

Wagner, C. G. (2002). The rise of the knowledge manager. The age of do nothing managers is over. *The Futurist, 36*(2), 14–15.

Wagner, J. A., & Gooding, R. Z. (1987). Shared influence and organizational behavior: A meta-analysis of situational variables expected to modulate participation-outcome relationships. *Academy of Management Journal, 30,* 524–541.

Wahl, K. H., & Blackhurst, A. (2000). Factors affecting the occupational and educational aspirations of children and adolescents. *Professional School Counseling, 3*(5), 367–374.

Walker, J. L. (1965). Four methods of interpreting test scores compared. *Personnel and Guidance Journal, 44,* 402–404.

Walker, J. W., Kimmel, D. C., & Price, K. F. (1981). Retirement style, and retirement satisfaction: Retirees aren't all alike. *International Journal of Aging and Human Development, 72,* 267–281.

Walker, L. S., & Walker, J. I. (1980). Trait anxiety in mothers: Differences associated with employment status, family size, and age of children. *Psychological Reports, 47*(1), 295–299.

Wall, J. E. (1994). Career Beliefs Inventory. In J. T. Kapes, M. M. Mastie, & E. A. Whitfield (Eds.), *A counselor's guide to career assessment instruments* (4th ed., pp. 253–257). Alexandra, VA: National Career Development Association.

Walls, R. T. (2000). Vocational cognition: Accuracy of 3rd, 6th, 9th, and 12th, grade students. *Journal of Vocational Behavior, 56,* 137–200.

Walls, R. T., & Gulkus, S. P. (1974). Reinforcers and vocational maturity in occupational aspiration, expectation, and goal deflection. *Journal of Vocational Behavior, 5,* 381–390.

Walsh, D. J. (1987). Individual variations within the vocational decision making process: A review and integration. *Journal of Career Development, 14,* 52–65.

Walsh, S., & Jackson, P. R. (1995). Partner support and gender: Contexts for coping with job loss. *Journal of Occupational and Organizational Psychology, 68,* 253–268.

Walsh, W. B., Bingham, R. P., Brown, M. T., & Ward, C. M. (2001). *Career counseling for African Americans.* Mahwah, NJ: Erlbaum.

Walsh, W. B., Bingham, R., Horton, J. A., & Spokane, A. (1979). Holland's theory and college degreed working black and white women. *Journal of Vocational Behavior, 15,* 217–223.

Walsh, W. B., & Chartrand, J. M. (1994). Emerging directions of person-environment fit. In M. C. Savickas & R. W. Lent (Eds.), *Convergence in career development theories. Implications for science and practice* (pp. 187–195). Palo Alto, CA: CPP Books.

Walsh, W. B., Craik, K., & Price, R. (1992). Person-environment psychology: A summary and commentary. In W. B. Walsh, K. Craik, & R. Price (Eds.), *Person-environment psychology: Models and perspectives* (pp. 243–269). Hillsdale, NJ: Erlbaum.

Walters, K. L., & Simoni, J. M. (1993). Lesbian and gay male group identity attitudes and self-esteem: Implications for counseling. *Journal of Counseling Psychology, 40*(1), 94–99.

Walter-Samli, J. H., & Samli, A. C. (1979). A model of career counseling for international students. *Vocational Guidance Quarterly, 28,* 48–55.

Walz, G. R., & Benjamin, L. (1984). A systems approach to career guidance. *The Vocational Guidance Quarterly, 33*(1), 26–34.

Wanberg, C. R. (1997). Antecedents and outcomes of coping behaviors among unemployed and reemployed individuals. *Journal of Applied Psychology, 85*(5), 731–744.

Wang, J., & Staver, J. R. (2001). Examining relationships between factors of science education and student career aspiration. *Journal of Educational Research, 94,* 312–320.

Washaw, L. S. (1990). *Stress, Anxiety and Depression in the Workplace: Report of the NYGBH/Gallup Survey.* New York: New York Business Group on Health.

Ward, C. M., & Walsh, W. B. (1981). Concurrent validity of Holland's theory for non-college degreed black women. *Journal of Vocational Behavior, 18,* 356–361.

Ware, M. E. (1980). Antecedents of educational/career preferences and choices. *Journal of Vocational Behavior, 16,* 312–319.

Warnat, W. L. (1991). Preparing a world-class work force. *VOCED, 66*(5), 26–29.

Warner, R. (1985). *Recovery from schizophrenia: Psychiatry and political economy.* New York: Routledge & Kegan Paul.

Warner, S. G., & Jepsen, D. L. (1979). Differential effects of conceptual level and group counseling format on adolescent career decision-making processes. *Journal of Counseling Psychology, 26*(6), 497–503.

Warren, J. M. (1978). Changing attitudes of supervisors. *Labor-Management Alcoholism Newsletter, 1,* 9.

Wasil, R. (1974). Job placement: Keynote of career development. *American Vocational Journal, 49,* 32.

Watanabe, A. (1980). *Developing a causal model for predicting college adjustment from pre-college characteristics.* Unpublished doctoral dissertation. Pennsylvania State University.

Watanabe, A., & Herr, E. L. (1993). Career development issues among Japanese work groups. *Journal of Career Development, 20*(1), 61–72.

Watanabe, A. M., Masaki, N., & Kamiichi, S. (1990). Employment counseling in Japan: Current and future. *Journal of Employment Counseling, 27,* 171–180.

Watanabe-Muraoka, A. M. (1999). *Guidelines for career development: Programs and services. The competency-based model for career development from elementary to college level.* Paper presented at the 1999 IAEVG Conferences, Wellington, New Zealand.

Watanabe-Muraoka, A. M., Senzaki, T. A. T., & Herr, E. L. (2001). Donald Super's contribution to career guidance and counseling in Japan. *International Journal for Educational and Vocational Guidance,* 1: 99–106.

Watkins, C. E., Jr. (1994). Thinking about "tests and assessments" and the Career Beliefs Inventory. *Journal of Counseling and Development, 72,* 421–423.

Watkins, C. E., Jr., Campbell, V. L., & Nieberding, R. (1993). What types of vocational tests do behavioral (and other) counseling psychologists use? *The Behavior Therapist,* April, 111–112.

Watkins, C. E., Jr., Campbell, V. L., & Nieberding, R. (1994). The practice of vocational assessment by counseling psychologists. *The Counseling Psychologist, 22*(1), 115–128.

Watkins, C. F., & Savickas, M. L. (1990). Psychodynamic career counseling. In W. B. Walsh & S. H. Osipow (Eds.), *Career counseling: Contemporary topics in vocational psychology* (pp. 79–116). Hillsdale, NJ: Erlbaum.

Watson, G. (1966). Resistance to change. In G. Watson (Ed.), *Concepts for social change.* Washington, DC: National Training Laboratories.

Watts, A. G. (1980). Educational and career guidance services for adults. *British Journal of Guidance and Counseling, 9*(1), 6–15.

Watts, A. G. (1986). *Work shadowing.* Report prepared for the School Curriculum Industry Partnership. York, England: Longman.

Watts, A. G. (2001). Donald Super's influence in the United Kingdom. *International Journal for Educational and Vocational Guidance* 1: 77–84.

Watts, A. G., Dartois, C., & Plant, P. (1988a). *Educational and vocational guidance services for the 14–25 age group in the European Community.* Sittard, Netherlands: Commission of the European Communities.

Watts, A. G., Dartois, C., & Plant, P. (1988b). *Educational and vocational guidance services.* Education Policy Series 2. Sittard, Netherlands: Presses Interuniversitaires Europeans Maastricht.

Watts, A. G., & Herr, E. L. (1976). Career(s) education in Britain and the U.S.A.: Contrasts and common problems. *British Journal of Guidance and Counseling, 4*(2), 129–142.

Watts, A. G., Super, D. E., & Kidd, J. M. (1981). *Career development in Britain.* Cambridge, England: Hobson's Press.

Way, W. L., & Rossman, M. M. (1996). Family contributions to adolescent readiness for school-to-work transition. *Journal of Vocational Education Research, 21*(2).

Weagraff, P. J. (1974). The cluster concept: Development of curricular materials for the public service occupations clusters. *Journal of Research and Development in Education, 7*(3), 45–54.

Weaver, C. N. (1978). Black-White correlates for job satisfaction. *Journal of Applied Psychology, 63,* 255–258.

Weaver, C. N. (1980). Job satisfaction in the United States in the 1970's. *Journal of Applied Psychology, 65,* 364–367.

Wechsler, D. (1997). *Wechsler Adult Intelligence Scale-Third Edition.* San Antonio, TX: The Psychological Corporation.

Weddle, P. D. (2001). *Weddle's job-seekers guide to employment web sites 2001.* New York: American Management Association.

Wegmann, R., Chapman, R., & Johnson, M. (1989). *Work in the new economy: Careers and job seeking in the 21st century.* Indianapolis, IN: JIST Works.

Wehrly, B., & Watson-Gegeo, K. (1985). Ethnographic methodologies as applied to the study of cross-cultural counseling. In P. Pedersen (Ed.), *Handbook of cross-cultural counseling and therapy* (pp. 65–71). Westport, CT: Greenwood Press.

Weinrach, S. G. (1979). Trait and factor counseling: Yesterday and today. In S. G. Weinrach (Ed.), *Career counseling: Theoretical and practical perspectives.* New York: McGraw-Hill.

Weinrach, S. G. (1984). Determinants of vocational choice: Holland's theory. In D. Brown & L. Brooks (Eds.), *Career choice and development, Applying contemporary theories to practice* (Chap. 4). San Francisco: Jossey-Bass.

Weinrach, S. G., & Srebalus, D. J. (1990). Holland's theory of careers. In D. Brown & L. Brooks (Eds.), *Career choice and development: Applying contemporary theories to practice* (2nd ed., pp. 37–67). San Francisco: Jossey-Bass.

Weissberg, M., Berenstein, M., Cote, A., Cravey, B., & Heath, K. (1982). An assessment of the personal, career, and academic needs of undergraduate students. *Journal of College Student Personnel, 23,* 415–422.

Weissman, S., & Krebs, D. O. (1976). A decision-making model for career exploration. *Personnel and Guidance Journal, 54*(10), 517–518.

Welborn, A., & Moore, S. S. (1985). Counseling displaced homemakers. In D. Jones & S. S. Moore (Eds.), *Counseling adults: Life cycle perspectives* (pp. 103–107). Lawrence, KS: University of Kansas.

Wellington, J. (1986). A card sort system for therapists of working women. *Journal of Counseling and Development, 64,* 648–649.

Werbel, J. D. (2000). Relationships among career exploration, job search intensity and job search effectiveness in graduating college students. *Journal of Vocational Behavior, 57,* 379–394.

Werts, C. E. (1968). Paternal influence on career choice. *Journal of Counseling Psychology, 15,* 48–52.

West, M. A., & Nicholson, N. (1989). The outcomes of job change. *Journal of Vocational Behavior, 34*(3), 335–349.

Westbrook, B. W. (1974). Content analysis of six career development tests. *Measurement and Evaluation in Guidance, 7*(3), 172–180.

Westbrook, B. W. (1979). *Career development needs of adults. How to improve career development programs.* Washington, DC: National Vocational Guidance Association and the Association for Measurement and Evaluation in Guidance.

Westbrook, B. W. (1988). Review of My Vocational Situation. In J. T. Kapes & M. M. Mastie (Eds.), *A counselor's guide to career assessment instruments* (pp. 186–189). Washington, DC: National Career Development Association.

Westbrook, B. W., & Norton, J. J. (1994). The Strong Interest Inventory (SII). In J. T. Kapes, M. M. Mastie, & E. A. Whitfield (Eds.), *A counselor's guide to career assessment instruments* (4th ed., pp. 213–218). Alexandria, VA: National Career Development Association.

Westbrook, B. W., & Parry-Hill, J. W., Jr. (1973a). *The construction and validation of a measure of vocational maturity.* Raleigh, NC: Center for Occupational Education, North Carolina State University. (ERIC document #ED 101–145).

Westbrook, B. W., & Parry-Hill, J. W., Jr. (1973b). The measurement of cognitive vocational maturity. *Journal of Vocational Behavior, 3,* 239–252.

Westbrook, B. W., Sanford, E. E., & Donnelly, M. H. (1990). The relationship between Career Maturity 'Test" scores and appropriateness of career choices. A replication. *Journal of Vocational Behavior, 36,* 20–32.

Westbrook, B. W., Sanford, E. E., Merwin, G., Fleenor, J., & Gilleland, K. (1988). Career maturity in grade 9: Can students who make appropriate career choices for others also make appropriate career choices for themselves? *Measurement and Evaluation in Counseling and Development, 21,* 64–71.

Westbrook, B. W., Sanford, E. E., O'Neal, P., Horne, D. F., Fleenor, J., & Garren, R. (1985). Predictive and construct validity of six experimental measures of career maturity. *Journal of Vocational Behavior, 27,* 338–355.

Westcott, N. A. (1983). Application of the structured life-review technique in counseling elders. *Personnel and Guidance Journal, 62*(3), 180–181.

Wheeler, C. L., & Carnes, E. F. (1968). Relationships among self-concepts, ideal self-concepts, and stereotypes of probable and ideal vocational choices. *Journal of Counseling Psychology, 15,* 530–535.

Wheeler, K. G. (1988). Review of Temperament and Values Inventory. In J. T. Kapes & M. M. Mastie (Eds.), *A counselor's guide to career assessment instruments* (pp. 243–247). Washington, DC: National Career Development Association.

Wheeler, K. G., & Mahoney, T. A. (1981). The expectancy model in the analysis of occupational preference and occupational choice. *Journal of Vocational Behavior, 19,* 113–122.

Whiston, S. C. (1990). Evaluation of the Adult Career Concerns Inventory. *Journal of Counseling and Development, 69,* 78–80.

Whiston, S. C. (1996). Accountability through action research: Research methods for practitioners. *Journal of Counseling and Development, 74,* 616–623.

Whiston, S. C. (2000). Individual career counseling. In D. A. Luzzo (Ed.), *Career counseling of college students. An empirical guide to strategies that work.* Washington, DC: American Psychological Association.

Whiston, S. C. (2001). Selecting career outcome assessments: An organizational scheme. *Journal of Career Assessment, 9*(3), 215–228.

Whiston, S. C., & Brecheisen, B. K. (in press). Annual review: Practice and research in career counseling and development-2001. *The Career Development Quarterly.*

Whiston, S. C., Sexton, T. L., & Lasoff, D. L. (1998). Career intervention outcome: A replication and extension of Oliver and Spokane (1988). *Journal of Counseling Psychology, 45(2),* 150–165.

White, L., & Brinkerhoff, D. B. (1981). The sexual division of labor: Evidence from childhood. *Social Forces, 60*(1), 170–181.

White, M. J., Brockett, D. R., & Overstreet, B. G. (1993). Confirmatory bias in evaluating personality test information: Am I really that kind of person? *Journal of Counseling Psychology, 40*(1), 120–126.

White, R. M. (1990). Technology and the independence of nations. In H. E. Sladovich (Ed.), *Engineering and human development* (pp. 5–11). Washington, DC: National Academy of Engineering.

Wickwire, P. N. (2002). Review of the Career Occupational Preference System. In J. T. Kapes & E. A. Whitfield (Eds.). *A counselor's guide to career assessment instruments* (4th ed., pp. 212–217). Tulsa, OK: National Career Development Association.

Wiener, Y., Vardi, Y., & Muczyk, J. (1981). Antecedents of employees' mental health—The role of career and work satisfaction. *Journal of Vocational Behavior, 19,* 50–60.

Wiersma, U. J. (1994). A taxonomy of behavioral strategies for coping with work-home role conflict. *Human Relations, 47*(2), 211–221.

Wiggins, J. D. (1984). Personality-environmental factors related to job satisfaction of school counselors. *Vocational Guidance Quarterly, 33*(2), 169–176.

Wiggins, J. D. (1985). Six steps toward counseling program accountability. *NASSP Bulletin, 69*(485), 28–31.

Wigington, J. H. (1982). Career maturity aspects of the Kuder Occupational Interest Survey. *Journal of Vocational Behavior, 20,* 175–179.

Wilcox-Matthew, L., & Minor, C. W. (1989). The dual career couple: Concerns, benefits, and counseling implications. *Journal of Counseling and Development, 68,* 194–198.

Wild, B. K., & Kerr, B. A. (1984). Training adolescent job-seekers in persuasion skills. *Vocational Guidance Quarterly, 33*(1), 63–69.

Wiley, M. O., & Magoon, T. M. (1982). Holland high point social types: Is consistency related to persistence and achievement? *Journal of Vocational Behavior, 20,* 14–21.

Wilgosh, L., & Mueller, H. H. (1993). Work skills for disadvantaged and unprepared youth and adults. *International Journal for the Advancement of Counselling, 16,* 99–105.

Wilbur, J. (1987). Does mentoring breed success? *Training and Development Journal, 41,* 38–41.

William T. Grant Foundation Commission on work, family and citizenship. (1988). *The forgotten half: Non-college youth in America. An interim report on the school-to-work transition.* Washington, DC: Author.

Williams, C. L. (1989); *Gender differences at work: Women and men in nontraditional occupations.* Berkeley: University of California Press.

Williams, C. L., & Berry, J. W. (1991). Primary prevention of acculturative stress among refugees. *American Psychologist, 46*(6), 632–641.

Williams, C. P., & Savickas, M. L. (1990). Developmental tasks of career maintenance. *Journal of Vocational Behavior, 36,* 166–175.

Williams, G. D., Lindsay, C. A., Burns, M. A., Wyckoff, J. H., & Wall, H. W. (1973). Urgency and types of adult counseling needs among continuing education students. *Journal of College Student Personnel, 14*(6), 501–506.

Williams, J., & Whitney, D. (1978). Vocational interests of minority disadvantaged students: Are they different? *National Association of Student Personnel Administrators Journal, 15*(4), 20–26.

Williamson, E. G. (1939). *How to counsel students.* New York: McGraw-Hill.

Willingham, W. W. (1988). *Testing handicapped people.* Boston: Allyn and Bacon.

Willis, C. G., & Ham, T. L. (1988). Review of the Myers-Briggs Type Indicator. In J. T. Kapes & M. M. Mastie (Eds.), *A counselor's guide to career assessment instruments.* Washington, DC: National Career Development Association.

Willson, V. L., & Stone, E. (1994). Differential Aptitude Tests (DAT) with Career Interest Inventory (CII). In J. T. Kapes, M. M. Mastie, & E. A. Whitfield (Eds.), *A counselor's guide to career assessment instruments* (pp. 90–98). Alexandria, VA: National Career Development Association.

Wilson, J., & Daniel, R. (1981). The effects of a career-options workshop on social and vocational stereotypes. *Vocational Guidance Quarterly, 30*(4), 341–349.

Wilson, S. M., Peterson, G. W., & Wilson, P. (1993). The process of educational and occupational attainment of adolescent females from low-income rural families. *Journal of Marriage and the Family, 55,* 158–175.

Wilson, P. J. (1986). *School counseling programs: A resource and planning guide.* Madison, WI: Department of Public Instruction.

Wilson, R. N. (1981). The courage to be leisured. *Social Forces, 60*(2), 282–302.

Wilson, W. J. (1996). *When work disappears: The world of the new urban poor.* New York: Random House.

Winefield, A. H., & Tiggemann, M. (1989). Unemployment duration and affective well-being in the young. *Journal of Occupational Psychology, 62,* 327–336.

Winefield, A. H., Tiggemann, M., & Winefield, H. R. (1992). Unemployment distress, reasons for job loss, and causal attributions for unemployment in young people. *Journal of Occupational and Organizational Psychology, 65,* 213–218.

Winkles, E. J., & Johnson, R. H. (1973). A model for developing a career decision-making program. *Canadian Counselor, 7*(2), 139–143.

Winter, J., & Schmidt, J. S. (1974). A replicable career program for junior high. *Vocational Guidance Quarterly, 23*(2), 177–180.

Wircenski, J. L., Fales, J. G., & Wircenski, S. L. (1978). Career guidance in the elementary school. *Elementary School Guidance and Counseling, 12*(3), 212–215.

Wisconsin Department of Public Instruction. (1986). *School counseling programs: A resource and planning guide.* Madison: Author.

Wise, P. S. (1985). School psychologists' rankings of stressful events. *The Journal of School Psychology, 23,* 31–41.

Wise, R., Charner, I., & Randour, M. A. (1978). A conceptual framework for career awareness in career decision-making. In J. Whitely & A. Resnikoff (Eds.), *Career counseling* (pp. 216–231). Monterey, CA: Brooks/ Cole.

Wish, P. A., & Hasazi, J. W. (1973). Motivational determinants of curricular choice in college males. *Journal of Counseling Psychology, 20,* 127–131.

Witner, G., & Stewart, L. H. (1972). Personality correlates of preference for risk among occupation oriented junior college students. *Vocational Guidance Quarterly, 20*(4), 259–265.

Wolfe, J. (May 27–28, 1993). *The Pennsylvania Youth Apprenticeship Program Model.* Paper presented at the Governor's Conference on Workforce Development. Lancaster, PA.

Wollack, S., Goodale, J. G., Wijting, J. P., & Smith, P. C. (1971). Development of the survey of work values. *Journals of Applied Psychology, 55,* 331–338.

Wolleat, P. L. (1989). Reconciling sex differences in information-processing and career outcomes. *Journal of Career Development, 16,* 97–106.

Wonderlic, E. F. (1989). *Wonderlic Personnel Test.* Northfield, IL: E. F. Wonderlic & Associates.

Wood, S. (1990). Initiating career plans with freshmen. *The School Counselor, 37,* 233–239.

Woodward, J. M. B., & Chen, I-C. (1994). Effect of "mood that day" on pharmacists' job and career satisfaction. *Psychological Reports, 74,* 393–394.

Woody, B. (1992). *Black women in the workplace: Impacts of structural change in the economy.* New York: Greenwood.

Wool, S. T. (1974). Queries, influences, and vocational interests of junior high school students. *Journal of Career Education, 2,* 55–62.

Work in America Institute. (1980). *The future of older workers in America.* Scarsdale, NY: The Institute.

Wortley, D. B., & Amatea, E. S. (1982). Mapping adult life changes: A conceptual framework for organizing adult development theory. *Personnel and Guidance Journal, 60*(8), 477–482.

Wrenn, C. G. (1951). *Student personnel work in college.* New York: Ronald.

Wrenn, C. G. (1964). Human values and work in American life. In H. Borow (Ed.), *Man in a world of work.* Boston: Houghton Mifflin.

Wright, D., & Gutkin, T. B. (1981). School psychologists' job satisfaction and discrepancies between actual and desired work functions. *Psychological Reports, 49,* 735–738.

Wright, G. N. (1980). *Total rehabilitation.* Boston: Little, Brown.

Wright, J. D., & Hamilton, R. F. (1979). Education and job attitudes among blue-collar workers. *Sociology of Work and Occupations, 6*(1), 59–83.

Wright, P. M., Lichtenfels, P. A., & Pursell, E. D. (1989). The structured interview: Additional studies and a metaanalysis. *Journal of Occupational Psychology, 62,* 191–199.

Wright, T. A., Bennett, K. K., & Dunn, T. (1999). Life and job satisfaction. *Psychological Reports, 84,* 1025–1028.

Yankelovich, D., & Leftowitz, B. (1982). Work and American expectations. *National Forum, 62*(2), 3–5.

Yates, B. T. (1996) *Analyzing costs, procedures, processes, and outcomes in human services.* Thousand Oaks, CA: SAGE Publications.

Yates, B. T. (1996). *Analyzing costs, procedures, and outcomes in human services.* Applied Social Research Methods Series, Volume 42. Thousand Oaks, CA: SAGE Publications.

Yates, J. F. (1990). *Judgment and decision making.* Englewood Cliffs, NJ: Prentice Hall.

Yates, L. V. (1990). A note about values assessment of occupational and career stage age groups. *Measurement and Evaluation in Counseling and Development, 23,* 39–42.

Yee, A. H., Fairchild, H. H., Weizmann, F., & Wyatt, G. E. (1993). Addressing psychology's problems with race. *American Psychologist, 48*(11), 1132–1140.

Yogev, S., & Brett, J. (1985). Patterns of work and family involvement among single- and dual-earner couples. *Journal of Applied Psychology, 70*(4), 754–768.

Yolles, S. F., Krinsky, L. W., Kieffer, S. N., & Carone, P. A. (Eds.). (1984). *The aging employee.* New York: Human Sciences Press.

Yoon, Y. H., & Waite, L. J. (1994). Converging employment patterns of Black, White, and Hispanic women: Return to work after first birth. *Journal of Marriage and the Family, 56,* 209–217.

York, D. C., & Tinsley, H. E. A. (1986). The relationship between cognitive styles and Holland's personality types. *Journal of College Student Personnel, 27*(6), 535–541.

Yost, E. B., & Corbishley, M. A. (1987). *Career counseling: A psychological approach.* San Francisco, Jossey-Bass.

Young, J. M. (1974). Community-oriented exploration program. *Elementary School Guidance and Counseling, 8*(3), 209–212.

Young, R. A. (1979). The effects of value confrontation and reinforcement counseling on the career planning attitudes and behavior of adolescent males. *Journal of Vocational Behavior, 15,* 1–11.

Young, R. A. (1988). Ordinary explanations and career theories. *Journal of Counseling and Development, 66,* 336–338.

Young, R. A. (1994). Helping adolescents with career development: The active role of parents. *Career Development Quarterly, 42*(3), 195–203.

Young, R. A., & Borgen, W. A. (Eds.). (1990). Introduction. *Methodological approaches to the study of careers.* New York: Praeger.

Young, R. A., & Chen, C. P. (1999). Annual review: Practice and researching career counseling and development-1998. *The Career Development Quarterly, 48*(2), 98–141.

Young, R. A., & Collin, A. (2000). Introduction: Framing the future of career. In A. Collin & R. Young (Eds.), *The future of career* (pp. 1–20). Cambridge, England: Cambridge University Press.

Young, R. A., Friesen, J. D., & Dillabough, R. (1991). Personal constructions of parental influence related to career development. *Canadian Journal of Counseling, 25,* 183–190.

Yount, K. R. (1986). A theory of productive activity: The relationships among self-concept, gender, sex role stereotypes, and work emergent traits. *Psychology of Women Quarterly, 10,* 63–88.

Zaccaria, J. S. (1969). *Approaches to guidance in contemporary education.* Scranton, PA: International Textbook.

Zagora, M. A., & Cramer, S. H. (1994). The effects of vocational identity status on outcomes of a career decision-making intervention for community college students. *Journal of College Student Development, 35,* 239–247.

Zakay, D., & Barak, A. (1984). Meaning and career decision-making. *Journal of Vocational Behavior, 24,* 1–14.

Zane, N. W. S., Sue, S., Hu, L., & Kwon, J. H. (1991). Asian-American assertion: A social learning analysis of cultural differences. *Journal of Counseling Psychology, 38*(1), 63–70.

Zaslow, M. J., & Pederson, F. A. (1981). Sex role conflicts and the experience of childbearing. *Professional Psychology, 12*(1), 47–55.

Zehring, J. W. (1976). Employing students as para-professional counselors. *Journal of College Placement, 36*(1), 43–47.

Zehring, J. W. (1979). Job sources for liberal arts graduates. *Journal of College Placement, 39*(2), 28–31.

Zhang, W., Hu, X., & Pope, M. (2002). The evolution of career guidance and counseling in the People's Republic of China. *The Career Development Quarterly, 50, 226–236.*

Ziller, R. C. (1957). Vocational choice and utility for risk. *Journal of Counseling Psychology, 4,* 61–64.

Zimmer, L. (1988). Tokenism and women in the workplace: The limits of gender-neutral theory. *Social Problems, 35,* 64–75.

Zuboff, S. (1988). *In the age of the smart machine: The future of work and power.* New York: Basic Books.

Zunker, V. G. (1986a). *Career counseling: Applied concepts of life planning.* Monterey, CA: Brooks/Cole.

Zunker, V. G. (1986b). *Using assessment results in career counseling.* Monterey CA: Brooks/Cole.

Zunker, V. G. (2002). *Career counseling: Applied concepts of life planning* (6th ed.). Pacific Grove, CA: Brooks/Cole.

Zytowski, D. G. (1992). Three generations: The continuing evolution of Frederic Kuder's Interest Inventories. *Journal of Counseling and Development, 71,* 245–248.

Zytowski, D. G. (1994). Tests and counseling: We are still married and living in discriminant analysis. *Measurement and Evaluation in Counseling and Development, 26,* 219–223.

AUTHOR INDEX

SUBJECT INDEX